TODD & CURTI'S

THE AMERICAN NATION

CONTENT REVIEWERS

Richard D. Brown
  University of Connecticut
  Early America

John Buenker
  University of Wisconsin, Parkside
  Progressive era

Joyce E. Chaplin
  Vanderbilt University
  Colonial America

Clifford Clark
  Carleton College
  Cultural and intellectual history

John Milton Cooper, Jr.
  University of Wisconsin, Madison
  *South; late 19th- and early
    20th-century U.S.*

Carlos E. Cortés
  University of California, Riverside
  Multiculturalism; Latin America

Edward Countryman
  Southern Methodist University
  American Revolution

Lynn Dumenil
  Occidental College
  Modern U.S.

Eric Foner
  Columbia University
  Civil War and Reconstruction

William Freehling
  State University of New York, Buffalo
  Antebellum America

Ellis Hawley
  University of Iowa
  20th-century U.S.

George Herring
  University of Kentucky
  U.S. foreign relations; Vietnam

Michael Holt
  University of Virginia
  19th-century U.S.

Mary Kelley
  Dartmouth College
  U. S. intellectual history

Robin Kelley
  University of Michigan
  African American history

Lawrence Frederick Kohl
  University of Alabama
  Antebellum America

Bruce Laurie
  University of Massachusetts, Amherst
  Labor history

Jean B. Lee
  University of Wisconsin, Madison
  Early America

John F. Marszalek
  Mississippi State University
  Civil War

William H. McNeill
  Emeritus, University of Chicago
  History

Reid Mitchell
  University of Maryland, Baltimore
    County
  Civil War

Gary Mukai
  Stanford Program on International and
    Cross-Cultural Education
  Asian American issues

Mary Neth
  Virginia Tech
  Social history; women's history

James Oakes
  Northwestern University
  19th-century U. S.

Mary Odem
  Emory University
  *Late 19th- and 20th-century U. S.;
    women's history*

David Oshinsky
  Rutgers University
  Modern U. S.

Colin Palmer
  University of North Carolina
  African diaspora

B. Marie Perinbam
  University of Maryland, College Park
  West African history

Carla Rahn Phillips
  University of Minnesota
  Early modern Europe

Morton Rothstein
  University of California, Davis
  Agricultural history; economic history

Neal Salisbury
  Smith College
  *Colonial America; American Indian
    history*

Linda K. Salvucci
  Trinity University
  Spanish American and Mexican history

Linda Schott
  University of Texas, San Antonio
  Women's history

John Selby
  College of William and Mary
  Colonial America

J.C.A. Stagg
  University of Virginia
  Early America; diplomatic history

Ronald Walters
  Johns Hopkins University
  *Early national U.S.; African
    American history*

Richard White
  University of Washington
  American West; American Indian history

William M. Wiecek
  Syracuse University
  Legal and constitutional history

Marilyn Young
  New York University
  U.S.–East Asian relations

CONTRIBUTORS

Alice Kessler-Harris
  Rutgers University
  Women and labor history

Paul Hutton
  University of New Mexico
  U.S. history; military history

Carol Karlsen
  University of Michigan
  *Early American social and cultural
    history; women's history*

Joseph Kett
  University of Virginia
  American cultural history

Edward Linenthal
  University of Wisconsin, Oshkosh
  *Religion and American culture;
    war and memory*

Richard Salvucci
  Trinity University
  Latin American economic history

Holly Shulman
  University of Maryland
  20th-century U. S.

Sterling Stuckey
  University of California, Riverside
  African American history

EDUCATIONAL REVIEWERS

Dean C. Brink
  Chair, History Department
  Roosevelt High School
  Seattle, Washington

Michele Forman
  Middlebury Union High School
  Middlebury, Vermont

Dr. Karen Hoppes
  Lakeridge High School
  Lake Oswego, Oregon

Dr. Frances J. Powell
  Montgomery College, Takoma Park
  Social Studies Curriculum Director,
    District of Columbia Public
    Schools (Ret.)

Susan Reeder
  Port St. Lucie High School
  Port St. Lucie, Florida

Steven Seto
  Muriel S. Snowden International School
  Boston, Massachusetts

Dr. D. William Tinkler
  Administrator, Taylor Road Middle
    School, Fulton County School System
  Alpharetta, Georgia

TODD & CURTI'S
THE
AMERICAN
NATION

PAUL BOYER

HOLT, RINEHART AND WINSTON
Harcourt Brace & Company
Austin • New York • Orlando • Chicago • Atlanta
San Francisco • Boston • Dallas • Toronto • London

About the Author
PAUL BOYER

*P*aul Boyer is Merle Curti Professor of History at the University of Wisconsin, Madison, and a senior member of the university's Institute for Research in the Humanities. Dr. Boyer has held visiting professorships at UCLA and Northwestern University and received Guggenheim and Rockefeller Foundation fellowships.

Awarded a Ph.D. from Harvard in 1966, Dr. Boyer is the author of numerous articles, essays, reviews, and books. *Salem Possessed: The Social Origins of Witchcraft,* which he co-authored with Stephen Nissenbaum, won the John H. Dunning prize of the American Historical Association.

Director
John Lawyer

Executive Editor
Sue Miller

Managing Editor
Greg Metz

Project Editors
Melissa Langley
Pat Longoria
Diana Holman Walker
David Holford

Editorial Staff
Bob Fullilove
Katharine Graydon
Marsia Reese
Valerie Larson,
  Department Secretary

Special Acknowledgment
Katie Vignery,
  Senior Editor, Language Arts

Editorial Permissions
Lee Noble

Design and Production
Pun Nio, *Senior Art Director*
Nora Dodson, *Designer*
Beth Prevelige, *Production Manager*
Joan Eberhardt, *Production Assistant*
Linda Moyer, *Production Coordinator*
Debra Saleny, *Photo Research Manager*
Mavournea Hay, HB School Division,
  Shelley Boyd, *Photo Research*
Carol Martin, *Electronic Publishing Manager*

PE and ATE Design and Production,
  The Quarasan Group, Inc.

Cover Photo: Ralph Brunke.
Cover: (front to back) Statue of Liberty, Historical Pictures/Stock Montage; Thurgood Marshall, AP/Wide World Photos; FDR inauguration ribbon and button, John Harold Collection, photographed by Lance Shriner; Native American, Courtesy of the Lilly Library, Indiana University, Bloomington, Indiana; Red Cross pin, John Harold Collection, photographed by Lance Shriner; Suffragettes, Culver Pictures; Asian Women, California Department of Parks and Recreation; Frame, Courtesy of Sue Cook; Plaid, Southwestern, and paisley material, Courtesy of Robert Allen Fabrics, Chicago; Pocket watch, Courtesy of Barry Brill; Truman holding newspaper, UPI/Bettmann Newsphotos; Cinco de Mayo, David Young-Wolff/PhotoEdit; I Like Ike pin, John Harold Collection, photographed by Lance Shriner; Ration card, Courtesy Diana Walker; Book and canteen, Courtesy of Antiques Limited, Chicago; Striped material, Courtesy of Manuel Canovas, Inc.
Front and Back End Page: Stock Montage.
Half Title Page and Title Page: Stock Montage.

Printed in the United States of America

ISBN 0-03-074512-8

4 5 6 7 8 9 032 97 96

TODD & CURTI'S
THE
AMERICAN
NATION

CONTENTS

Toltec carving of
Quetzalcoatl

Colonial Williamsburg Foundation

St. Paul's Church, Parish of Trinity Church, City of New York

UNIT 3

Growth and Change 1815–1860
AMERICAN ALMANAC 222

Choctaw Removal (1966), painted by Valjean Hessing

Valjean Hessing, Choctaw Removal (1966), Philbrook Museum of Art, Tulsa

Identification badge of a free black person

UNIT 4 *War and Reunification* 1845–1900

AMERICAN ALMANAC 334

Teacher with students (1866)

The Granger Collection, New York

Painting (1889) of the First Battle of Bull Run

UNIT 5

The Nation Transformed   1860–1910

AMERICAN ALMANAC   422

Building the transcontinental railroad

Navajos at the Carlisle Indian School

UNIT 6

A World Power   1897–1920

AMERICAN ALMANAC   508

Souvenirs from the
Bull Moose campaign

Red Cross unit

Puerto Rican public school

World War II
homecoming

Elizabeth Eckford at Little
Rock's Central High School

Vietnamese refugees arriving in Hong Kong

UNIT 9 *Modern Times* 1970–the Present

AMERICAN ALMANAC 896

Tiananmen Square

Mao and Nixon

Reference Section

Features

Charts and Maps

Themes in American History

*T*odd & Curti's *The American Nation* begins every chapter with a set of theme questions. These questions are drawn from seven broad themes central to American history: global relations, our Constitutional heritage, democratic values, technology and society, cultural diversity, geographic diversity, and economic development. They provide a context for the historical events in each chapter. This context will help you understand the connections between historical events and see how past events are relevant to today's social, political, and economic concerns.

As you begin each chapter, examine the theme questions and answer them based on your own experiences or prior knowledge. At the end of each chapter, you will be asked to answer another set of theme questions, this time using specific facts learned from studying the chapter. This process will help you develop critical thinking skills and encourage you to synthesize the information you have learned. In addition, by tracing the themes through the book, you will be able to see how each theme has developed over time.

■ GLOBAL RELATIONS

This theme asks you to explore the global context in which the United States exists. From its settlement by Asian immigrants tens of thousands of years ago to the first arrival of European, African, and later Asian immigrants to today, America has influenced and been influenced by other parts of the world. Your exploration of the Global Relations theme will help you understand how the relations the United States has maintained with other countries over time have affected our nation's political, social, and economic development. It also will help you appreciate the problems and possibilities of living in an interdependent world community.

■ CONSTITUTIONAL HERITAGE

The study of American history would not be complete without an exploration of the Constitution, the legal framework that structures our democratic government. The Constitutional Heritage theme questions ask you to think about the origin of the Constitution and the ways in which the Constitution has been interpreted and amended over time. You will explore how the laws and government institutions established in the 18th century have evolved through amendments, Supreme Court rulings, and congressional actions. Your examination of this theme will encourage you to understand the part individuals play in promoting the goals—such as justice and democratic rights—enshrined in the Constitution's preamble.

■ DEMOCRATIC VALUES

This theme concerns the continuing struggle to define and protect such democratic values as individual liberty, political representation, freedom of religion, and freedom of speech. The Democratic Values theme questions ask you to consider the impact of changing social, economic, and political conditions on these values. For example, in the years before the Civil War, enslavement of African Americans—a violation of the democratic value of individual liberty—was practiced in the South. Some slaveholders justified this practice by arguing that the democratic value of right to property should be the overriding concern. It took a bloody civil war to settle the issue. Conflicts over democratic values recur throughout American history, and this theme explores the attempts at resolution.

■ TECHNOLOGY AND SOCIETY

From computers in your homes and classrooms to communications satellites orbiting the earth, technology influences many aspects of society. The Technology and Society theme questions ask you to trace technological developments and explore their influence on the economy and our lives.

■ CULTURAL DIVERSITY

Different ethnic, racial, and religious groups have all contributed to the creation of America's rich and unique culture. The Cultural Diversity theme questions ask you to explore how the United States has dealt with diversity from the days of the first encounters between Native Americans and Spanish and English settlers to its status today as a haven for immigrants from all over the world.

■ GEOGRAPHIC DIVERSITY

The majestic old-growth forests of the Pacific Northwest, the rich coal deposits of the Appalachian and Rocky mountains, the oil fields of Texas and Alaska, and the tropical plantations on the volcanic islands of Hawaii have enriched the U.S. economy. The Geographic Diversity theme questions ask you to consider how the development of the nation's diverse natural resources has shaped U.S. society, politics, and the economy. The questions also explore how government and public awareness of the effects of natural resource development on the environment has changed over time.

■ ECONOMIC DEVELOPMENT

The United States has developed one of the world's strongest economies. The Economic Development theme explores the influence of the nation's economy on domestic politics and social life and on international relations. The theme questions ask you to explore the implications of such economic issues as trade, depression and expansion, poverty, taxation, government regulation, and the status of workers.

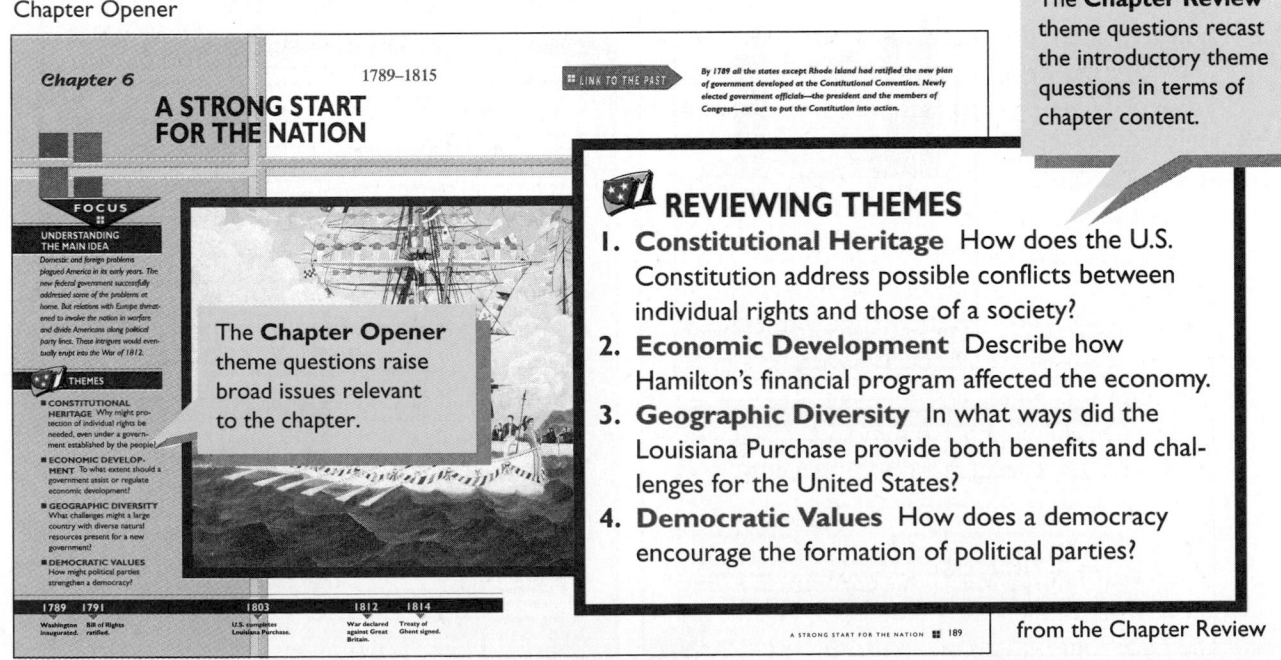

Chapter Opener

The **Chapter Review** theme questions recast the introductory theme questions in terms of chapter content.

The **Chapter Opener** theme questions raise broad issues relevant to the chapter.

REVIEWING THEMES

1. **Constitutional Heritage** How does the U.S. Constitution address possible conflicts between individual rights and those of a society?
2. **Economic Development** Describe how Hamilton's financial program affected the economy.
3. **Geographic Diversity** In what ways did the Louisiana Purchase provide both benefits and challenges for the United States?
4. **Democratic Values** How does a democracy encourage the formation of political parties?

from the Chapter Review

Critical Thinking and the Study of History

Throughout *Todd & Curti's The American Nation*, you are asked to think critically about the events and issues that have shaped U.S. history. Critical thinking is the reasoned judgment of information and ideas. People who think critically study information to determine its accuracy. They evaluate arguments and analyze conclusions before accepting them. Critical thinkers are able to recognize and define problems and develop strategies for resolving them.

The development of critical thinking skills is essential to effective citizenship. Such skills empower you to exercise your civic rights and responsibilities. For example, critical thinking skills equip you to judge the messages of candidates for office and to evaluate news reports.

Helping you develop critical thinking skills is an important goal of *Todd & Curti's The American Nation*. The following 14 critical thinking skills appear in the section reviews and chapter reviews. Additional skills strategies can be found in each unit's Strategies for Success and in the Skills Handbook, which begins on page 988.

Union mortar battery

the Americas. They encountered a land already settled by people with rich cultures.

3 **Recognizing Point of View** means identifying the factors that color the outlook of an individual or group. A person's point of view includes beliefs and attitudes that are shaped by factors such as age, gender, religion, race, and economic status. This thinking skill helps us examine why people see things as they do and reinforces the realization that people's views may change over time, or with a change in circumstances. When a point of view is highly personal or based on unreasoned judgment, it is considered *bias*.

1 **Using Historical Imagination** is mentally stepping into the past to consider an event or situation as people at the time would have considered it. In putting yourself in their place, you might note whether they lived *before* or *after* historical turning points. Ask yourself: Did these people live before or after major medical advances such as penicillin? before or after technological advances such as the automobile? before or after World War II? Keep in mind what the people of the time knew and did not know. For example, to grasp the experience of a soldier wounded in the Civil War, you need to understand that little was known then about the causes of disease and infection.

4 **Comparing and Contrasting** is examining events, situations, or points of view for their similarities and differences. *Comparing* focuses on both the similarities and the differences. *Contrasting* focuses on only the differences. For example, a comparison of early Irish and Chinese immigrants to the United States would point out that both groups were recruited to help build the transcontinental railroad and that both groups faced discrimination and experienced difficulties in finding well-paying jobs. In contrast, language and racial barriers generally proved more of a problem for Chinese immigrants. Other factors to compare and contrast could include reasons for immigrating to the United States.

2 **Gaining a Multicultural Perspective** means viewing historical events and situations in ways that are fair and sensitive to all cultural groups affected. A multicultural perspective broadens your understanding of American history while deepening your appreciation of the nation's diversity. For example, studying Native American cultures before the arrival of Columbus helps you understand that the Europeans did not "discover"

Toltec pillar

Railroad laborers

Struggle at Concord Bridge

example, you might study a map such as the one on this page. Analyzing the results state by state shows how Woodrow Wilson won a majority in the electoral college without winning a majority of the popular vote.

7 **Assessing Consequences** means studying an action, an event, or a trend to predict its long-term effects—and to judge the desirability of those effects. *Consequences* often are effects that are indirect and unintended. They may appear long after the event that led to them. An example of assessing consequences is the federal government's weighing of the positive and negative elements of a new drug or medical procedure before permitting its use. Consequences include side effects and other possible risks, as well as benefits.

5 **Identifying Cause and Effect** is part of interpreting the relationships between historical events. A *cause* is any action that leads to an event; the outcome of that action is an *effect*. To explain historical developments, historians may point out multiple causes and effects. For instance, the actions of the colonists as well as those of the British government brought about the American Revolution, which in turn had many far-reaching effects. (For a more detailed discussion of Identifying Cause and Effect, see page 989.)

6 **Analyzing** is the process of breaking something down into its parts and examining the relationships between them. Analysis enables you to better understand the whole. To analyze the outcome of the 1912 presidential election, for

Election of 1912

WILSON'S STRENGTH Wilson's strength was in the South. Although he won the electoral vote by a landslide, the only states outside the old Confederacy where he won at least half the popular vote were Kentucky, Maryland and Oklahoma.

? **LOCATION** Which state split its electoral vote?

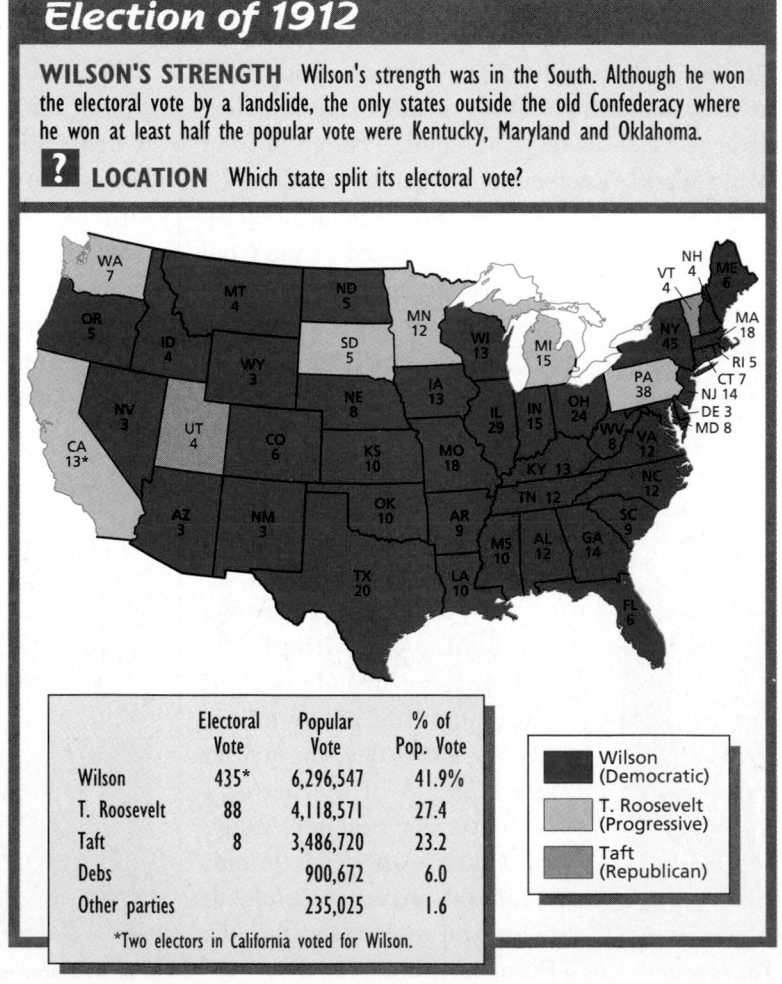

	Electoral Vote	Popular Vote	% of Pop. Vote
Wilson	435*	6,296,547	41.9%
T. Roosevelt	88	4,118,571	27.4
Taft	8	3,486,720	23.2
Debs		900,672	6.0
Other parties		235,025	1.6

*Two electors in California voted for Wilson.

- ■ Wilson (Democratic)
- ■ T. Roosevelt (Progressive)
- ■ Taft (Republican)

8 **Distinguishing Fact from Opinion** means separating the facts about something from what people say about it. A fact can be proved or observed; an opinion, on the other hand, is a personal belief or conclusion. We often hear facts and opinions mixed in everyday conversation—as well as in advertising, in political debate, and in historical sources. Although some opinions can be supported by facts, in an argument opinions do not carry as much weight as facts. (For a more detailed discussion of Distinguishing Fact from Opinion, see page 990.)

American buffalo

9 **Identifying Values** involves recognizing the core beliefs that a person or group holds. Values are more deeply held than opinions and are less likely to change. Values commonly concern matters of right and wrong and may be viewed as desirable in and of themselves. The values of freedom and justice, for example, motivated the struggle to abolish slavery, just as the value of equality has been a foundation of the civil rights and women's movements.

10 **Hypothesizing** is forming a possible explanation for an event, a situation, or a problem. A hypothesis is not a proven fact. Rather it is an "educated guess" based on available evidence and tested against new evidence. A historian, for instance, might hypothesize that the Civil War was primarily the result of a power struggle between the ruling classes of the North and the South over control of the United States' western frontier. The historian would then organize the evidence to support this hypothesis and challenge other explanations of the war's causes.

L. J. Cranstone's painting depicting a slave auction

Migrant Mother, photographed by Dorothea Lange during the Great Depression

You would then propose and evaluate possible solutions or courses of action, selecting the one you think best and giving the reasons for your choice.

13 **Evaluating** is assessing the significance or overall importance of something, such as the success of a reform movement or the legacy of a president. You should base your judgment on standards that others will understand and are likely to share. An evaluation of the early women's movement, for example, might assess the short- and long-term effects of the focus on women's suffrage.

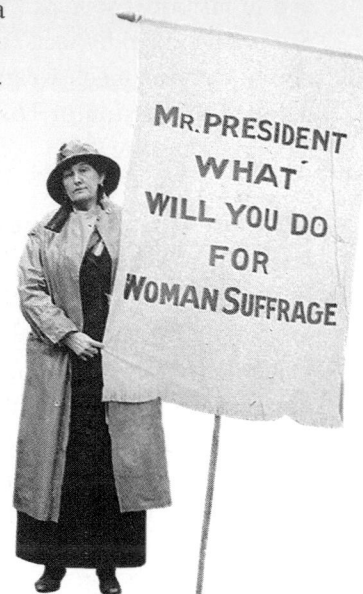

Woman suffragist

11 **Synthesizing** is combining information and ideas from several sources or points in time to gain a new understanding of a topic or event. Much of the narrative writing in *Todd & Curti's The American Nation* is a synthesis. It pulls together historical data from many sources into a chronological story of our nation. Synthesizing the history of the Great Depression, for example, might involve studying photographs and economic statistics from the 1930s, together with interviews of Americans who lived through the period.

12 **Problem Solving** is a process of reviewing a situation and making decisions and recommendations for improving or correcting it. Before beginning, however, the problem must be identified and stated. For instance, in considering a solution to the nation's drug-abuse crisis, you might state the problem in terms of the relationship of drug addiction to violent crime.

14 **Taking a Stand** is identifying an issue, deciding what you think about it, and persuasively expressing your position. Your stand should be based on specific information. In taking a stand, even on controversial or emotional issues, state your position clearly and give reasons to support it.

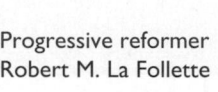

Progressive reformer Robert M. La Follette

PAUL BOYER

To the Reader of *Todd & Curti's The American Nation*

When I studied American history in high school, we used a textbook by a historian named David S. Muzzey. My teacher called him "Fuzzy Muzzey." Muzzey wrote in a lively style, but his history was limited. He focused mainly on politicians, military leaders, and other notables, most of them white males whose ancestors had come from the British Isles or northern Europe. Today's history is far richer in social texture, including not just elites but all Americans: men and women, Native Americans, and immigrants from Europe, Latin America, Africa, Asia, and all other parts of the world.

But my introduction to history did not come from a textbook. History begins in stories. I first learned history from grandparents who recalled their childhoods in Ohio in the 1870s and 1880s. My Grandfather Boyer once told me how he heard of the assassination of President James Garfield in 1881! My father remembered World War I. As a young man of German immigrant origins who held religious beliefs against war, he was forced to recite the Pledge of Allegiance by fellow workers who suspected him of disloyalty. My 99-year-old aunt recalls her grandfather, a 19th-century healer who treated the ill with herbs. This aunt also tells of a Native American ancestor in our family line. These are all strands of our American history, and they begin in family memories.

But why study history at all? History is to a nation what memory is to an individual. A person without memory is sad and tragic. A society that ignores its past and lives only in the present loses a vital element of what we call civilization. History can tell us how far we have come as a nation— and how far we have yet to go. Through history we can see the achievements, as well as the failures, of those who have gone before.

I hope this book will help spur for you a lifelong interest in the past. Its aim is not to provide all the answers, but to raise questions. History is not something fixed forever in concrete. There is no single version of "what really happened." Historians continually find new dimensions of the past to probe and explore. This is the appeal and sometimes the frustration of historical research.

But above all, history can be fascinating. The experiences of Americans of earlier generations were as gripping and vital for them as our lives are for us. History comes alive as we begin to grasp that vivid reality. When you move beyond the textbook to original documents, letters, diaries, and films and recordings, the past comes even more sharply alive.

This book brings the story of our national experience near to the present. The next chapter will be written by you and your generation. As you write that chapter, a knowledge of the past will provide guidance and perspective.

Sincerely,

Paul Boyer

Paul Boyer

American
ALMANAC

❖ Native American Life

In 1758 Mission San José de Aguayo in present-day Texas includes 84 houses; fields of corn, beans, and sugarcane; sugar mill; carpentry shop; chickens; 30 yoke of oxen; 1,500 cattle; 3,376 sheep; 80 mares; and several "swimming pools"; 281 Native Americans live there.

Native Americans use effective herbal remedies: roots of skunk cabbage for asthma; soaproot for dandruff; boiled wild mint for nausea; tiny cones of spruce trees for sore throats.

Boys of the Delaware group are initiated into manhood by spending several days fasting alone in the forest.

▲ Mission San José today in San Antonio

❖ The Early Economy

1500s Spaniards bring horses, cattle, barley, oats, rye, and sugarcane to North America; they take back potatoes, tomatoes, quinine, cocoa beans, tapioca, and tobacco.

1600s A Native American ceremonial pipe—decorated with beads, ribbons, horsehair, paint, and feathers—is worth a horse or several buffalo robes.

1655 A carpenter charges 600 lbs. of tobacco for building a house, while a doctor may charge 1,000–2,500 lbs. for seeing patients!

1700s Rice growers in South Carolina use methods brought by west-coast Africans, who also bring productive fishing methods.

Some Native American women use upper part of old tepee covers—made waterproof by the grease and smoke of cooking fires—to make raincapes.

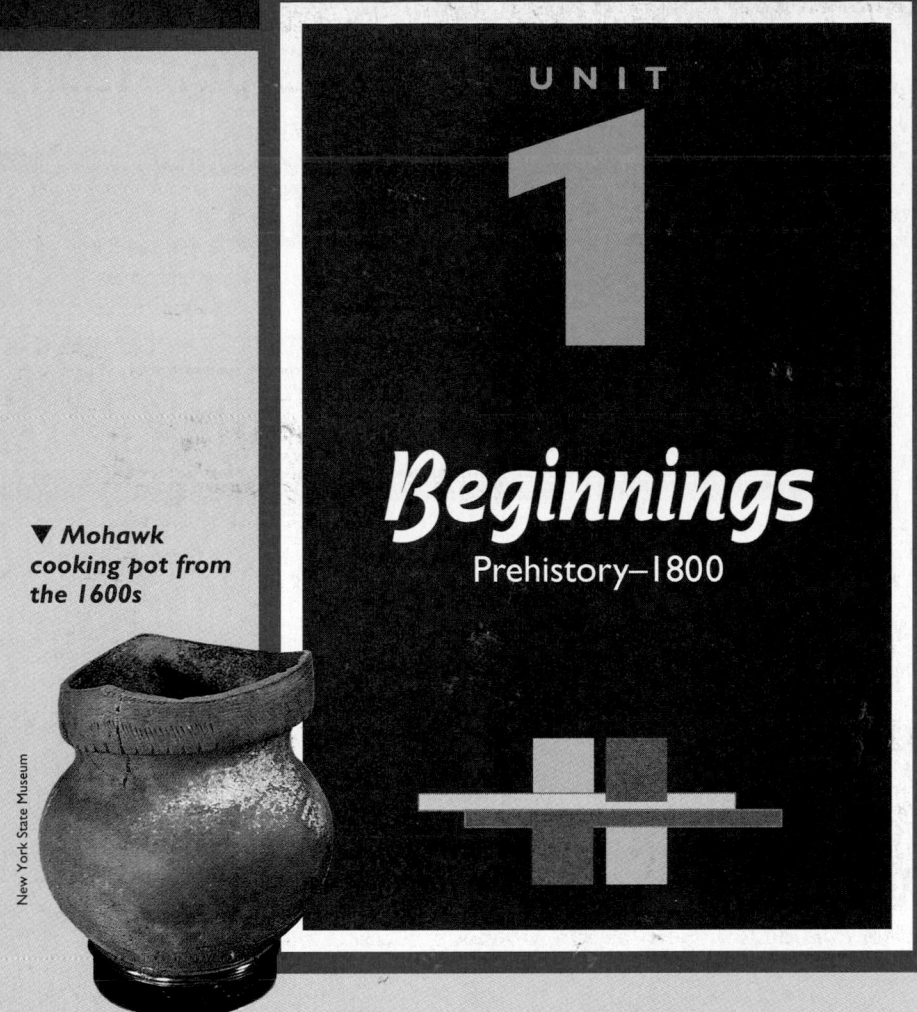

UNIT 1

Beginnings

Prehistory–1800

▼ *Mohawk cooking pot from the 1600s*

New York State Museum

❖ Colonial Life

1620 First public library in the English colonies opens in Virginia.

1638 Swedish settlers introduce log cabins in Delaware.

1656 Eavesdropping, scolding, bad grinding at a mill, and pulling hair are crimes in Massachusetts.

1675 Church doors in Massachusetts are locked to keep people from leaving during long sermons.

1700 Through contact with Native Americans, African slaves in South Carolina learn about the area and become guides for their slave-holders.

1700s English colonial recreation includes rabbit hunting, cockfighting, horse racing, and card playing.

❖ Food for Thought

1600s Native Americans teach English colonists to bake beans in clay pots—the dish known today as Boston baked beans.

1600s Africans bring many foods with them, including sesame seeds and okra.

1600s English colonists eat with knives and spoons; forks aren't used until the 1700s.

1621 Wampanoag chief Massasoit introduces Plymouth settlers to popcorn.

The Granger Collection, New York

▶ *Engraving entitled* **Employments for Gentlemen in New England** *by Theodore de Bry, 1618*

The Granger Collection, New York

THE WORLD BY 1500

FOCUS

UNDERSTANDING THE MAIN IDEA

For thousands of years great civilizations rose and fell throughout Europe, Asia, Africa, and the Americas. Some of these civilizations had little or no contact with one another. During the Middle Ages, however, people from diverse cultures increasingly came together to trade goods. By the 1400s the desire for an all-sea route to Asia inspired Europeans to explore beyond the frontiers of their known world.

THEMES

- **CULTURAL DIVERSITY** In what ways might a culture be affected by contact with other cultures?

- **ECONOMIC DEVELOPMENT** How might extensive contact with other societies both benefit and harm a society's economic development?

- **TECHNOLOGY AND SOCIETY** What impact might technological advances have on trade and exploration?

c.3500	c.1000 B.C.	A.D. 610	1096	1324	1498
Rise of farming in desert Southwest.	Kush founded.	Muhammad founds Islam.	Crusades begin.	Mansa Mūsā makes pilgrimage to Mecca.	Vasco da Gama sails to India.

World maps of the 1400s showed only three continents—Africa, Asia, and Europe. Many Europeans had some idea of the geography of Africa and Asia and had probably heard fabulous stories about the continents' riches. Likewise, many Africans and Asians knew of each other and of Europeans. Until the late 1400s, however, few knew that two other inhabited landmasses—the Americas—existed.

Incan ruins at Machu Picchu, Peru

This chapter may seem an odd way to begin an American history book. Why discuss the Ice Age hunters who crossed from Asia to North America tens of thousands of years ago? Why tell the story of their descendants, who wove a tapestry of Native American cultures over two continents? Why examine Europe, Asia, and Africa during the Middle Ages?

We start in prehistory, before the time of written records, because American history is more than a chronicle of wars, laws, politics, and economic changes. It is the story of a continent and its people and their rich cultures. That story begins with the Ice Age hunters—the first Americans—and their Native American descendants.

We focus on Europe, Asia, and Africa in the Middle Ages in order to understand what drove early explorers into the unknown. In 1492, Europe was at the dawn of a new age, ready to break free of its geographic isolation. As Europeans reached out beyond their borders, they met Asians and Africans engaged in trade. The desire to share in this trade launched Europeans on a remarkable journey of exploration that eventually brought them to the shores of the Americas.

National Maritime Museum Picture Library

World map published in 1486

PEOPLING THE AMERICAS

FOCUS

- When and how did the first people arrive in the Americas?
- How did the changing environment influence the first Americans?
- What were some of the effects of the Agricultural Revolution?
- What do the five themes of geography explore?

Long after Europe, Africa, and Asia were populated, the American continents remained empty of human life. From the frozen lands of the Arctic to the southernmost tip of South America, no human voice had ever echoed through the wilderness; no human foot had ever left a print in the soil. Sometime during the last Ice Age, however, men and women began crossing from Asia into North America. Over time, they spread throughout the Americas, adopting ways of life that were suitable to the environments they found.

Prehistoric rock carving of hunter, found in Michigan

THE FIRST AMERICANS

Most archaeologists—the scientists who study the remains of past cultures—agree that the first people who discovered the vast American wilderness came from Asia during the last Ice Age, when glaciers, or thick sheets of ice, covered much of northern Asia, North America, and Europe. The glaciers locked up so much of the world's water that the sea level dropped by several hundred feet. This drop in sea level exposed a wide land bridge—**Beringia**—between Siberia and what is now Alaska. The first Americans, whom archaeologists call **Paleo-Indians**, probably followed animal herds across Beringia to their new home in North America.

Archaeologists do not know exactly when—or in how many waves—these men and women came to North America. Estimates place the date for the first arrivals between 12,000 and 60,000 years ago. Nor do scientists know whether the migration ended when the glaciers began to melt around 10,000 years ago. Some archaeologists believe that when the land bridge disappeared beneath the rising waters of the Bering Strait, Asian immigrants paddled to America in skin boats or wooden dugouts or walked across the ice in winter.

Why is it not possible to talk with certainty about the Paleo-Indians? With no written records to guide them, archaeologists must rely on human and animal remains and on artifacts such as weapons, tools, pots, and jewelry for clues. The methods for analyzing these clues are not precise. Thus,

▼ **Beringia land bridge**

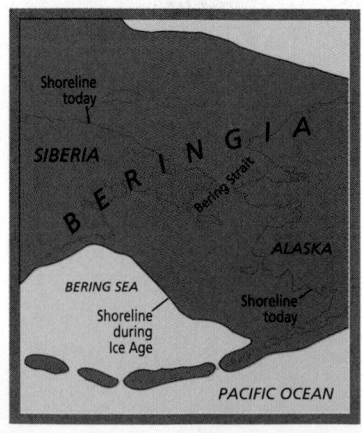

scholars can paint a broad picture of Paleo-Indian cultures, but details are often beyond their grasp.

■■ **Most scholars agree that during the last Ice Age, the first Americans crossed from Asia to North America by way of a land bridge called Beringia.**

LIFE IN A NEW LAND

Archaeologists have learned that the Paleo-Indians brought with them skills that were well suited to the **environment**, or physical surroundings, of their new homeland. They knew how to make fire and how to find food and shelter in a harsh environment.

The Paleo-Indians were **hunter-gatherers** who stalked whatever game their stone-tipped weapons could kill—bears, bison, and other mammals. The animals provided them with food as well as with furs and skins for clothing. In the few weeks of summer, when the vegetation of the tundra briefly flourished, the Paleo-Indians gathered roots, berries, and other edible plants. Like other hunter-gatherers, they lived as nomads, moving from place to place in search of food. They camped in caves or beneath rock overhangs on the vast treeless plains of the tundra.

The changing environment. Sometime between 10,000 and 5000 B.C., the climate of the Americas grew hotter and drier. This climatic change dramatically transformed the landscape, leaving the continents much as they must have appeared to the first European explorers (see map on page 6). Conifers—evergreen trees such as pine, fir, and spruce—and broadleaf trees—such as oak, hickory, and maple—eventually covered much of North America east of the Mississippi River. In what is today southern Florida, lush swamp vegetation thrived.

Much of the area between the Mississippi River and the Rocky Mountains became meadowland where tall prairie grasses and flowers grew, broken in places by cottonwood trees marking courses of rivers. Closer to the mountains, meadows gave way to the flat, treeless lands of the Great Plains. The Rockies, a snow-covered range with peaks rising more than 10,000 feet, marked the western edge of the Great Plains.

▼ **Fern fossil**

Coniferous and broadleaf forests spread over much of the land between the foothills of the Rockies westward to the Pacific coast. Giant fir trees, some soaring more than 150 feet above the ground, grew in the north. To the south, in present-day northern California, there were forests of redwoods, with some trees as large as 30 feet in diameter and as tall as a 30-story building.

Farther south, the coastal forests gave way to scrub forests of small trees and bushes. This landscape contrasted starkly with the bare desert of what is today the southwestern United States and northern Mexico. There, only cacti, sparse grasses, and small hardy plants could survive in the dry climate.

Tropical forests dominated the landscape of present-day southern Mexico and Central America as well as northern and eastern South America. Flat grasslands covered much of central South America, giving way in the far west to a vast stretch of scrub forest and desert. Cutting through this region were the majestic Andes Mountains, with peaks reaching 20,000 feet and foothills rising higher than the Appalachian Mountains of eastern North America.

Cultural adaptations. As the climate changed, groups of Paleo-Indians slowly moved south. In a migration that took many thousands of years, they spread throughout the Americas.

▲ **Fish fossils**

Americas Landscape Map

CLIMATE The type of vegetation that is found in a region depends largely on its climate.

❗ PLACE Which vegetation regions found in North America are not widely found in South America?

Dwarf shrubs, grasses, and lichens of the tundra are able to survive the severe winters and short growing season, which in some areas is only two weeks.

Mixed forests include both coniferous trees and broadleaf trees, which shed their leaves in winter. These forests support a wide variety of animal life.

Water-conserving cacti and thorny shrubs grow in the deserts of south-western North America.

The Amazon rain forest—the world's largest—supports a remarkable number of plant species.

A vast grassland in North America was home to huge herds of buffalo. Grasslands called *llanos*, which means "plains" in Spanish, also stretched across northern South America. To the south, Argentina's grasslands, called *pampas*, were originally covered with trees.

**Map labels:**

ARCTIC OCEAN
Bering Strait
Hudson Bay
NORTH AMERICA
ATLANTIC OCEAN
PACIFIC OCEAN
Gulf of Mexico
West Indies
CARIBBEAN SEA
CENTRAL AMERICA
Tropic of Cancer
Equator
Tropic of Capricorn
SOUTH AMERICA

Scale at equator:
0   500   1,000 Miles
0   500   1,000 Kilometers
Azimuthal Equal-Area Projection

Legend:
- Tropical forest
- Desert
- Scrub forest
- Grassland
- Coniferous forest
- Broadleaf forest
- Mixed forest
- Tundra
- Little or no vegetation

These men and women found lands rich in wildlife. Water from the melting glaciers had formed fast-flowing rivers and huge lakes teeming with fish. Musk-oxen, reindeer, mammoths, and giant bison roamed the vast lowland regions, while the hills and mountains abounded with saber-toothed tigers, mountain lions, and bears.

Many of the Paleo-Indians throughout North America and Central America hunted with spears armed with stone tips called Clovis points. Named after Clovis, New Mexico, where archaeologists first found them, these points were more effective against large game than earlier spear tips. Abundant wildlife and an effective method of hunting provided a plentiful and reliable supply of food for the Paleo-Indians.

Eventually the mammoths and other big game died out, perhaps hunted to extinction. Consequently, the Paleo-Indians had to develop new skills to help them adjust to the changing environment. The men and women of the eastern woodlands, for example, burned large areas of forest to make it easier to spot and track small game such as rabbit and deer. They also broadened their food-gathering activities to include trapping fish and birds and collecting a wider variety of plants.

■■ **The Paleo-Indians responded to the changing environment by adapting their hunting and gathering methods.**

◄ **The Imperial Mammoth was one of several species of elephants that inhabited Europe, Asia, and North America during the Ice Age.**

▼ **Paleo-Indians used spears armed with Clovis points to hunt large game. Clovis points ranged in size from approximately one and a half to five inches.**

4 inches = actual size

THE AGRICULTURAL REVOLUTION

The most revolutionary change made by Paleo-Indians, however, was the shift from hunting and gathering to the **domestication**, or adaptation and control, of plants and animals. This shift occurred worldwide as the big game died out, first in Africa, Asia, and Europe, and finally in the Americas.

Some historians speculate that the first people to move from gathering seeds to planting them in the ground were women. Because women did the bulk of gathering in hunter-gatherer societies, they were the most familiar with plants and the most likely to notice that the seeds that fell to the ground sprouted new plants.

Archaeologists continue to debate the dates for the spread of agriculture, but they generally believe that people in southwestern Asia had domesticated wheat and barley by 8000 B.C. and that those in southeastern Asia were growing rice by about 6000 B.C. No one knows exactly when the first Americans turned to farming, but archaeologists have found evidence that by 8000 B.C. communities in Mexico were growing maize (corn), and by 2000 B.C. people in the Andes region were growing potatoes. By 1500 B.C. farming was well established throughout much of Mexico, Central America, and the Andes region.

Farther to the north, the people of the desert Southwest began farming around 3500 B.C. Archaeologists believe that the desert people learned about farming techniques from their southern neighbors. The process of spreading cultural practices or beliefs from one group to another is called **cultural diffusion**.

Cultivating crops and domesticating animals transformed life and made it possible for human populations to increase. As people settled down to grow their own food, small villages formed. At

▲ The corn we eat today (left) evolved from smaller, earlier hybrids. The five cobs at the right were excavated from Bat Cave, Mexico, and date from as far back as 2000 B.C. to around A.D. 250.

first most people practiced **subsistence farming**—growing just enough crops for survival. Over time, though, many groups developed techniques—such as using animals to pull plows—that increased their food production. As a result, village populations rose.

As populations grew, villages gave way to cities. The first cities appeared in southwestern Asia about 3500 B.C. Over the next few thousand years, this "urban revolution" spread to other parts of Asia as well as to northern Africa, southern Europe, and the Americas.

With the rise of cities came a more elaborate division of labor. Some men farmed, while others became artisans, soldiers, laborers, merchants, scholars, physicians, priests, and government officials. Women took on such important tasks as spinning, weaving, baking, and raising children. As a result, the basic equality that characterized hunter-gatherer and simple farming societies gave way to the development of social classes. In most societies men became more powerful than women; and the small number of priests, government officials, and

▶ Paleo-Indians used stone slabs, or *metates,* to grind corn and wheat into grain.

successful merchants became more powerful than the masses of farmers, laborers, and artisans.

 The Agricultural Revolution led to the rise of cities, an elaborate division of labor, and the development of social classes.

HISTORY AND GEOGRAPHY

Many terms in this section may seem better suited to a geography book. But history and geography are closely linked. History describes the events that make up the human story from the earliest times to the present day. Geography, especially the branch called cultural geography, describes how physical environments influence human events and how human beings affect their surroundings. Therefore, to present the unfolding drama of people and events without placing them in their physical settings is to tell only part of the story. Geographers have developed a number of themes to help them organize information. Five common themes are location, place, human-environment interaction, movement, and region.

Location describes a site's position and can be expressed in two ways: absolute location and relative location. *Absolute location* describes the exact point on the earth that a site occupies. It is most often presented in terms of latitude and longitude. The absolute location of Chicago, for example, is 41°52′ north latitude and 87°37′ west longitude. *Relative location,* on the other hand, describes the position of a site in relation to other sites. Chicago's relative location might be given as the southwest shore of Lake Michigan or as about 355 miles south-southeast of Minneapolis.

Place refers to the physical features and human influences that define a site and make it different from other areas. Physical features include landscape, climate, and vegetation. Human influences include land use, architecture, and population size.

Human-environment interaction deals with all the ways in which people interact with their natural environments, like clearing forests, irrigating the land, and building cities. This theme is especially important to the study of history in that it shows how people shape and are shaped by their surroundings.

Movement describes the way people interact as they travel, communicate, and trade goods and services. Movement includes human migration as well as the exchange of goods and ideas.

To better study and understand the earth, geographers divide it into *regions*. Geographers might distinguish one region from another by comparing physical characteristics, such as landforms or climate, or by comparing cultural features like dominant languages or religions.

The geographic themes of location, place, human-environment interaction, movement, and region explore the interplay between people and their environment.

SECTION 1 REVIEW

IDENTIFY and explain the significance of the following: Paleo-Indians, environment, hunter-gatherers, domestication, cultural diffusion, subsistence farming.

LOCATE and explain the importance of the following: Beringia.

1. **MAIN IDEA** According to most scholars, when might the first people have arrived in the Americas? What route did they probably follow?

2. **MAIN IDEA** How did the Paleo-Indians respond to the changing environment?

3. **LINKING HISTORY AND GEOGRAPHY** What are the five themes of geography? How do they help explain historical events?

4. **WRITING TO EXPLAIN** Write a paragraph explaining how the Agricultural Revolution changed the structure of ancient societies.

5. **EVALUATING** How did the development of the Clovis point alter the culture of the Paleo-Indians?

NATIVE AMERICAN CULTURES

FOCUS

■ **What were the characteristics of the Aztec and Incan cultures?**

■ **Why was there so much variation among early North American cultures?**

■ **Why do some scholars believe that there was contact between the Americas and other cultures before the late 1400s?**

By 1200 B.C. the Native American societies that would one day intrigue European explorers were already forming. In Central America and South America, advanced farming societies created beautiful cities that were home to tens of thousands of people. Farther north, in what is now the southwestern United States, farmers built impressive cliff dwellings high above the desert floor. Over much of North America the abundance of wild animals and plants enabled large groups to support themselves through hunting, fishing, and gathering or by combining these activities with farming.

Toltec-carved figurine of plumed serpent Quetzalcoatl

VARIED CULTURES

Historians do not know how many people lived in the Americas before the arrival of Christopher Columbus in 1492. Population estimates for the late 1400s range from 8.4 million to 112.5 million. Historians do know, however, that the areas where the Agricultural Revolution had first taken hold— Mexico, Central America, and the Andes region— supported the largest populations. More than half the population of the Western Hemisphere may have lived in these regions.

Today it is common to refer to the early people of the Americas and their descendants as *Native Americans* or *American Indians*. They did not, however, consider themselves a single people. By the 1400s there were probably over 650 groups living in the Americas, each with a distinct culture and language.

THE CULTURES OF MESOAMERICA

Central America and the southern and central regions of Mexico—the area archaeologists call **Mesoamerica**, or Middle America—was home to some of the largest of the early cultures. It is estimated that at its height the region boasted a population of some 25 million who shared a common cultural heritage.

The Olmecs and the Mayas. The first great Mesoamerican culture was that of the Olmecs, who thrived on the fertile coastal lowlands along the Gulf of Mexico from about 1200 to 400 B.C. Historians call it the mother culture of Mesoamerica because it so strongly influenced later societies.

Like the Mesoamerican people who followed them, the Olmecs were farmers. They practiced

▲ The Olmecs carved jade figures and buried them underneath their ceremonial courts, perhaps as a means of removing power from the images.

slash-and-burn agriculture: toward the end of the dry season, the Olmecs cut down and burned sections of the jungle. Then, before the rainy season came, they planted corn, beans, and squash in the ash-enriched soil.

The Olmecs' reliance on farming influenced the culture they created. The Olmecs prayed to a rain god to protect their crops. They developed an accurate calendar to help farmers understand the seasons. Even the writing system they invented—a form of **glyph**, or picture, writing—probably served the needs of farmers and merchants who traded their goods (and spread Olmec culture) throughout Mesoamerica and beyond.

Olmec farms usually surrounded a large ceremonial center where priests, government officials, merchants, and craftsworkers lived. The ceremonial center was built around a sports arena and a raised courtyard on which stood a pyramid of packed earth. Olmec priests used the mound as a place of worship, and the arena probably was the site of a ritual ball game.

About 400 B.C., for reasons that are unclear to archaeologists, the Olmec civilization began to fade. However, the Olmec way of life was adopted by others in Mesoamerica, including the Mayas, who rose to prominence about A.D. 300. They flourished for more than 500 years, primarily in present-day Mexico and Guatemala.

The Mayas improved upon the Olmecs' accomplishments. Mayan astronomers developed a calendar that was more accurate than the one used in Europe. Mayan mathematicians devised a number system that included zero long before Europeans adopted the concept from the Arabs.

Mayan scholars developed a new form of glyph writing that included ideograms—characters that represented ideas—and phonograms—characters that represented words or syllables.

The Mayas also improved upon Olmec farming techniques. For example, they developed an intricate water-management system that ensured a steady supply of water even during the dry season. This allowed the Mayas to produce more food and support a larger population. In Guatemala the great ceremonial center Tikal (ti-KAHL)—with its six magnificent temple-pyramids and more than 3,000 other structures—is believed to have been home to some 100,000 people.

By about A.D. 900, however, the Mayas had abandoned Tikal and their other cities. Over time they merged with other cultures in the area. As with the Olmec, archaeologists are unsure why the Mayan civilization declined.

The Toltecs and the Aztecs. In the century before the Mayas' decline, invading groups from the north descended upon the Valley of Mexico. About A.D. 900, one of these groups, the Toltecs (TOHL-teks), came to dominate the area. Adopting the customs of the peoples they conquered, the Toltecs built a great city-state at Tula in central Mexico. Under the leadership of a warrior class, the Toltecs gradually extended their domain. During the 12th century, however, internal conflicts weakened the Toltec empire. As a result, it soon fell to invading groups from the north.

▼ This photograph shows part of the ruins of the ancient Toltec city of Tula in the present-day state of Hidalgo, Mexico. The inset shows one of the pillars atop the ruin.

▲ Aztecs created artwork with colorful figures and glyphs, such as this piece depicting the rain god Tlaloc.

The conquerors of the Toltecs fought among themselves until one group, the Aztecs, emerged victorious. Although they were a warrior society, the Aztecs, or Mexicas, as they called themselves, settled down and adopted the ways of the local people. They built their capital, Tenochtitlán (tay-nawch-tee-TLAHN)—the site of present-day Mexico City—on an island in Lake Texcoco (tay-SKOH-koh). Eventually Tenochtitlán grew into a magnificent city with hundreds of buildings, an elaborate system of canals, and an estimated population of 300,000.

Warfare continued to dominate Aztec life. Huge, well-trained Aztec armies conquered neighboring kingdoms. Over a period of two centuries, the Aztecs gained control of an empire of five million people. The Aztecs demanded tribute in gold, silver, and precious stones from those they conquered. They also took thousands of captives as sacrifices to their war god, Huitzilopochtli (wee-tsee-loh-POHCH-tlee).

Human sacrifice was central to the Aztec religion. The Aztecs believed that the world had been destroyed four times, each time by the death of a sun. To keep the present sun from dying, the Aztecs sacrificed captives to nourish it. By the time of the Spanish conquest in the early 1500s, thousands of prisoners had been sacrificed on Tenochtitlán's altars.

THE INCAS OF SOUTH AMERICA

As the cultures of Mesoamerica were developing, similar advances were taking place in South America. Farming cultures arose on the Pacific coastal plains, in the high valleys of the Andes, and along the upper Amazon. By the mid-1400s one group, the Incas, had gained control of the whole region.

The Incan state, based in the capital city of Cuzco (KOO-skoh), high in the Andes, was founded in the 11th century. Around 1440, the Incas began

a great campaign of expansion and conquest. Within 35 years the Incas controlled an immense realm that covered much of present-day Chile, Peru, Bolivia, and Ecuador. Until the arrival of the Spanish, it was the largest empire in the Americas—with an estimated six to nine million people who spoke more than 20 languages.

Unlike the Aztecs, the Incas did not force their subjects to pay tribute, but they did require their labor. With this labor they filled their armies and built palaces, temples, bridges, and the thousands of miles of roads that linked their empire.

Like many other advanced agricultural societies, Incan society was organized into strict social classes. The working class—the farmers, laborers, and artisans—made up the bulk of Incan society. Above them was the noble class—priests, teachers, military leaders, and government officials. At the top was the supreme ruler, the "Sapa Inca," who represented the Sun God.

Incan silver llama with gold trim

▪▪ The Incas of South America, like their contemporaries the Aztecs of Mesoamerica, were empire builders.

EARLY CULTURES OF NORTH AMERICA

The population of North America was too small and spread over too large an area to support societies of the size found in Mesoamerica and South America. Few groups north of Mesoamerica numbered more than a few thousand people. But because groups living in the same region made similar adaptations to the environment and often traded with one another, they generally shared many characteristics. For example, Native Americans in the southwestern region and Native Americans in the eastern half of the present-day United States developed distinct regional cultures.

Southwestern cultures. Native Americans who settled in the barren hills and deserts of the Southwest began to cultivate maize and other

Early Native American groups practiced a variety of burial customs and rituals to honor their dead. The Navajos, for example, buried treasured possessions with the deceased so that they would be content in their graves and not return to haunt the living. The Hurons placed their dead in mass graves lined with beaver robes and gifts. They believed that mingling their departed relatives' bones encouraged the living to exist in harmony.

Over the years many of these burial sites have been unearthed and even destroyed as bones and artifacts are removed from graves for research. This practice has led to a bitter conflict between Native American groups and the anthropologists and archaeologists doing the digging.

To these researchers, grave sites are windows into history that provide a glimpse of past cultures and clues to changes in peoples' ways of life over time. Researchers argue that studying skeletal remains

and the objects buried with them reveals much about Native American cultures that might otherwise remain unknown. For example, amulets (charms), prayer sticks, and figurines found buried with the corpses shed light on the religious life of early Native Americans. Other objects show the kinds of foods they ate and the utensils they made.

Researchers also argue that analyses of human skeletons can promote medical research. Bones—even those that are centuries old—provide a physical record tracing the development and spread of many diseases. They also show the effects of diet, pollution, and other factors on health. This

▲ **Bowl from a burial site in New Mexico**

information is useful in preventing and treating diseases today. "Indians living today," argues one anthropologist, "stand to benefit from our conclusions."

But to many Native Americans, the burial sites are sacred places not to be disturbed. They believe that destruction of the sites shows a disregard for Native American cultural traditions. As an attorney for a Native American group in New Mexico asks: "Why single out Indians? Why not dig up everybody's ancestors?"

There is a growing respect for the Native American point of view. Through recent lawsuits, some Native Americans have succeeded in obtaining the return of their ancestors' remains for reburial. They have also successfully applied political pressure to close museum exhibits displaying Indian relics. Native Americans have been assisted in their efforts by the Native American Grave Protection and Repatriation Act, which Congress passed in 1990. The act requires federally funded museums to provide Native American groups with a chance to retrieve selected items.

crops about 3500 B.C. Their farming methods, pottery styles, and social practices show very strong Mesoamerican influences.

One of these groups was the Anasazi (ahn-uh-SAHZ-ee). Between A.D. 800 and 1100 the Anasazi began to construct multistory rock and adobe dwellings—many nestled against cliffs and some containing as many as 800 rooms. Some of these rooms served as living quarters and others as ceremonial centers, or *kivas.* Spanish explorers

later called these huge buildings *pueblos* (villages). Each pueblo housed not only farmers but also weavers, potters, builders, and storytellers.

Archaeologists believe that a crisis of some kind caused the Anasazi to abandon their communities. By the mid-1400s they had ceased to exist as a distinct people. Researchers believe, however, that the Anasazi were probably the ancestors of the Pueblo Indians, whom the Spanish encountered in the 1500s.

▲ The Anasazi built their homes against cliffs to provide defense against enemies. These ruins are located in Mesa Verde National Park in Colorado.

Eastern cultures. The Adena and Hopewell cultures of the eastern woodlands and the Mississippian culture of the Southeast combined hunting and gathering with farming to support relatively large populations.

The Adenas and the Hopewells, who dominated the eastern region for about 1,700 years, are often called the Mound Builders because of the distinctive earthworks they created. Originating in the Ohio River Valley about 1000 B.C., the Adenas eventually occupied an area extending from present-day Kentucky to New York. About 300 B.C., however, the Hopewells began to push the Adenas out of the region. The Hopewell culture dominated the area until the more advanced Mississippian culture replaced it about A.D. 700.

Beginning in the lower Mississippi River Valley, the Mississippian culture spread out to occupy much of the Southeast and Midwest. Huge temple mounds, resembling Mesoamerican pyramids, dominated their villages. The largest Mississippian settlement was located at Cahokia (kuh-HOH-kee-uh), near present-day St. Louis. It extended six miles and contained 85 burial and temple mounds, the largest of which covered 16 acres and stood more than 100 feet high.

By A.D. 1200, Cahokia's population may have numbered about 40,000. Its rulers controlled a network of trade routes that stretched from the Great Lakes to the Gulf of Mexico and into Mesoamerica. Perhaps because of climate changes or crop failures, the Mississippians abandoned Cahokia during the 1200s, but their culture continued to flourish elsewhere for several centuries.

■■ There was great variety in North American cultures, in large part because of the effect the environment had on diet, housing, and social structure.

NORTH AMERICAN CULTURE AREAS

By the time of European contact, the Native American population of North America was divided into hundreds of different groups—none as large as the earlier mound-building societies. For the purposes of comparison, scholars often organize

▲ The Adenas and Hopewells built elaborate earthen mounds in the shape of animals as burial places for their dead. This aerial photograph shows the Great Serpent Mound, near present-day Hillsboro, Ohio.

Native American Culture Areas

CULTURAL DIVERSITY By 1500 Native Americans occupied every corner of the Americas. They thrived in vastly different geographic settings: frozen tundra, mountains, dry grasslands, deserts, lush woodlands, and tropical forests.

? HUMAN–ENVIRONMENT INTERACTION Scholars often group Native Americans into broad culture areas based on geographic location. They do this because they believe that environment influences a people's culture. Why might environment influence culture?

Robinson Projection

Legend

- Arctic
- Subarctic
- Northwest Coast
- Plateau
- Great Plains
- Northeast
- Great Basin
- California
- Southwest
- Southeast
- Mesoamerica
- Circum-Caribbean

Map labels (North America)

ASIA
ARCTIC OCEAN
PACIFIC OCEAN
UNINHABITED LAND
Arctic Circle
NORTH AMERICA
Hudson Bay
Great Lakes
ROCKY MOUNTAINS
Mississippi R.
Ohio River
Rio Grande
Gulf of Mexico
Yucatán Peninsula
CENTRAL AMERICA
ATLANTIC OCEAN
CARIBBEAN SEA
SOUTH AMERICA
Tropic of Cancer

INUIT, INGALIK, ALEUT, HAN, SASCHUTKENNE, TAGISH, DOGRIB, TLINGIT, SLAVE, BEAVER, CHIVEWYAN, HAIDA, HAISLA, CARRIER, SWAMPY CREE, NASKAPI, HEILTSUK, KWAKIUTL, SQUAMISH, SHUSWAP, PLAINS CREE, MONTAGNAIS, MAKAH, NOOKSACK, COAST SALISH, CHIMAKUM, CHINOOK, YAKIMA, KALISPEL, BLACKFOOT, MICMAC, KLICKITAT, COLUMBIA, SPOKANE, PLAINS OJIBWAY, SALTEAUX OJIBWAY, ALGONKIN, YAQUINA, MOLALA, WALLA WALLA, NEZ PERCE, CAYUSE, CROW, MANDAN, OTTAWA, HURON, ABNAKI, PENOBSCOT, UMPQUA, TOLOWA, NORTHERN PAIUTE, IROQUOIS, MOHAWK, ONEIDA, ONONDAGA, CAYUGA, SENECA, MOHEGAN, PEQUOT, HUPA, ACHOMAWI, BANNOCK, TETON SIOUX, CHEYENNE, SANTEE SIOUX, SAUK, FOX, POTAWATOMI, DELAWARE, WAMPANOAG, NARRAGANSET, YUKI, MAIDU, NORTHERN SHOSHONE, OMAHA, PAWNEE, IOWA, KICKAPOO, PEORIA, MIAMI, ILLINOIS, SUSQUEHANNOCK, WAPPO, WASHO, MONO, WESTERN SHOSHONE, UTE, ARAPAHO, MISSOURI, SHAWNEE, POWHATAN, MIWOK, COSTANO, ESSELEN, YOKUT, KAWAIISU, PAIUTE, MESA VERDE, KANSA, CAHOKIA, MONACAN, ENO, CHUMASH, KITANEMUK, HOPI, NAVAJO, APACHE, KIOWA, OSAGE, CHEROKEE, TUSCARORA, MOJAVE, ZUNI, PECOS, TUNICA, WACCAMAW, CHERAW, MARICOPA, YUMA, APACHE, COMANCHE, WICHITA, CHICKASAW, TUSKEGEE, CREEK, ALABAMA, HITCHITI, CUSABO, NAKIPA, PIMA, SUMA, JUMANO, TONKAWA, CHOCTAW, MOBILE, APALACHEE, COCHIMI, IGNACIENO, SERI, YAQUI, KARANKAWA, ATAKAPA, TIMUCUA, ZOE, TARAHUMARA, WAICURA, LAGUNERO, SEMINOLE, CALUSA, HUICHOL, TEUL, GUACHICHIL, GUACHICHIL, TAINO, ISLAND CARIB, CUNA

Inset map: Aztec, Maya, and Inca Empires

Tenochtitlán
Tikal
Copán
Valley of Mexico
ATLANTIC OCEAN
Equator
Amazon River
Machu Picchu
Cuzco
ANDES
SOUTH AMERICA
PACIFIC OCEAN

Legend:
- Aztec
- Maya
- Inca

0   1,000   2,000 Miles
0   1,000   2,000 Kilometers
Lambert Equal-Area Projection

Scale (main map)

0   500   1,000 Miles
0   500   1,000 Kilometers
Azimuthal Equal-Area Projection

these groups into broad cultural areas on the basis of geographical location and shared characteristics:

Northwest Coast: coastal dwellers; fishers; developed complex culture

Plateau: river dwellers; primarily fishers; relatively low population

Great Plains: grassland dwellers; nomadic buffalo hunters after introduction of the horse

Northeast: forest dwellers; primarily hunter-gatherers, but also farmers and fishers

Great Basin: desert basin dwellers; primarily gatherers due to barren surroundings; low population

California: desert, mountain, river, or coastal dwellers depending on location; primarily gatherers and fishers

Southwest: canyon, mountain, and desert dwellers; either farmers or nomadic hunters

Southeast: river-valley dwellers; primarily farmers, but also hunter-gatherers and fishers

COMMENTARY

Cultural Contacts

Did Native Americans develop their varied cultures in isolation, or were they influenced by contacts with the outside world? Most scholars agree that Asians probably continued to cross the Bering Strait into North America for thousands of years after the land bridge disappeared. They also accept that ships plying the Atlantic and Pacific oceans might have been blown by storms to the Americas. Most scholars also believe that about A.D. 1000, Vikings—Scandinavian people from Sweden, Norway, and Denmark—reached the North American coast at Vinland (most likely present-day Newfoundland, Canada) nearly 500 years before Columbus. But many assume that such contacts were rare and had little impact on Native American cultures.

Other scholars, however, insist that similarities between American artifacts and those of other world cultures suggest that significant transoceanic contacts did occur. For example, both Indian pottery found in the Pacific Northwest and that found in Ecuador bear striking resemblance to Japanese pottery dating from the same historical period. Furthermore, the designs of some Olmec sculptures and the likeness between Mesoamerican and Egyptian pyramids have led some to suggest that Africans may have voyaged to Mesoamerica in prehistoric times.

■■ **Native American artifacts have led some scholars to argue that there was early contact between the Americas and other world cultures.**

SECTION 2 REVIEW

IDENTIFY and explain the significance of the following: Mesoamerica, Olmecs, glyph, Mayas, Toltecs.

LOCATE and explain the importance of the following: Mexico, Guatemala, Tikal, Tenochtitlán, Peru, Cuzco, Cahokia.

1. **MAIN IDEA** How were the Aztec and Incan cultures similar?

2. **MAIN IDEA** Why was there great variety in early North American cultures?

3. **GEOGRAPHY: MOVEMENT** How do the Anasazi and Mound Builder societies provide evidence of the spread of Mesoamerican culture?

4. **WRITING TO DESCRIBE** You are an archaeologist investigating the possibility of prehistoric contact between the Americas and other continents. Write a brief report describing the types of evidence you might look for and how that evidence might be interpreted.

5. **SYNTHESIZING** What were the general traits of the early cultures of Mesoamerica, South America, eastern North America, and southwestern North America?

Section 3

EUROPE IN THE MIDDLE AGES

FOCUS

- What led to the rise and fall of feudalism?
- How did the Crusades affect European society?
- What was the Renaissance?
- What factors led to the rise of nations in Europe?

The fall of the Roman Empire in the fifth century A.D. led to cultural turmoil in Europe. During the Middle Ages (roughly A.D. 500–1500), Europe transformed itself from a warring group of small, isolated kingdoms operating under a strict class system to a continent of powerful trading nations.

14th-century Italian moneylenders and borrowers

THE EARLY MIDDLE AGES

By A.D. 500 the once-powerful Roman Empire lay in ruin in western Europe, victim of repeated attacks by nomadic tribes from northern Europe and Asia. In its place arose a multitude of small warring kingdoms. Within a few centuries most of the wonders of the Roman Empire—its laws, literature, and learning—disappeared. Its vast network of roads fell into disrepair. Cities shrank and trade slowed as lawlessness made travel dangerous. Fields went unplanted as peasants fled from the invaders.

Among the most feared of the attackers were the Vikings. These skilled seafarers sailed thousands of miles to raid and colonize. About A.D. 800 the Vikings moved into northern England and Ireland. By the early 900s many had settled in northern France—where they were called Normans—and others had ventured west to Iceland and Greenland.

The rise of feudalism. To combat the Vikings and other invaders, many European rulers enlisted the aid of nobles under a system known as **feudalism**. The nobles pledged their military assistance and their loyalty to the rulers in return for land and protection.

The land a noble received was called a **manor**. Each manor was a self-sufficient estate, which included a manor house, pastures, fields, and a village. Most of those who lived on the manor were **serfs**, men and women bound to the land by their labor. Serfs were required to work their lord's land in exchange for a share of the crops they grew and for protection from attack by outsiders.

▲ This scene from a medieval calendar shows serfs reaping grain in the fields.

The collapse of the Roman Empire and the continued threat of invasion led to the development of feudalism.

Feudal society operated under a rigid class system. At the top of society was the noble class. Noblemen spent their days managing their estates, hunting, or engaging in battle. Men held most of the power, although some women obtained positions of influence by inheriting land from male relatives. Most noblewomen married in their early teens and generally had large families. They spent their days directing the servants in such duties as cooking, cleaning, spinning, weaving, brewing, and caring for livestock.

Life for the serfs was more difficult than it was for nobles. Most spent their days in unending physical labor. Both men and women worked in the fields, and women had to perform the household tasks as well. Although the lords received the largest portion of the crops grown by the serfs, many also required their workers to pay them fees, such as marriage or inheritance taxes.

Some serfs were able to obtain their freedom, but most remained tied to the land. They were considered property—part of the estate—and their status was passed on to their children. Most serfs lived in small one-room cottages. Their diet consisted mainly of soup, bread, and ale, with some occasional meat. Life was difficult and short. Few serfs lived beyond age 40.

The role of the church. Most of the people living in feudal Europe had no sense of national identity and little awareness of the outside world. In fact, few people ever traveled more than 25 miles from their homes. Life centered around the manor and the church.

The Roman Catholic church, led by the pope, was the most important political and social force in medieval Europe. The village church was the center of social activity for the manor. All of the important events in a person's life took place there. Parish priests led the mass, conducted baptisms, weddings, and funerals, and performed acts of charity.

On a wider scale, the Roman Catholic church was the only institution in Europe that carried on the traditions of the Roman Empire. In monasteries and convents, the monks and the nuns worshiped, studied the scriptures, and preserved the writings of the ancient Greeks and Romans. The medieval church promoted art and culture, leaving a rich heritage of religious music, tapestries, illuminated manuscripts, and great cathedrals.

Most important, the Roman Catholic church, under the direction of the pope, played a leading role in guiding the politics of Europe. It often stepped in to settle disputes between warring Christian kingdoms, help negotiate political alliances, or suggest various courses of action.

Decline of feudalism. Beginning about 1100, a series of changes brought about a gradual end to feudal society. New farm equipment—such as heavy plows that could turn the

◀ In this 16th-century fresco by Sodoma, St. Benedict is shown supervising the completion of the abbey of Monteoliveto Maggiore Siena—one of the 12 monasteries he built in the 6th century.

rich, marshy soil of northern Europe and padded horse collars that allowed horses to pull heavier loads—increased the amount of land that could be farmed. Farm laborers could now produce enough food to sustain large armies and a growing number of townspeople as well.

As the military strength of the kingdoms grew, the Vikings and other invaders were less likely to attempt to take by force what they could get by trade. Soon trading towns and cities replaced manors as the focus of economic activity. As a result, many serfs moved from manors to towns, where they could either work for wages or farm rented plots on land surrounding the town.

■■ **Feudalism declined because of new farming technology, the rise of medieval towns, and the expansion of trade.**

ℐHE CRUSADES AND TRADE

The shift away from feudalism was further aided by the series of wars known as the **Crusades**. Between 1096 and the late 1200s, waves of Christian crusaders fought Muslims for control of the Holy Land, an area of Southwest Asia sacred to Jews, Christians, and Muslims. Various groups of Muslims—followers of Islam, the religion founded by the prophet Muhammad about A.D. 610—had held the Holy Land since the 600s. In 1071 the area fell to the Seljuk (SEL-jook) Turks, Muslims from Central Asia. Unlike earlier groups, the Turks prevented Christians from visiting the holy city of Jerusalem.

In the First Crusade in the 11th century, Christian invaders from Europe captured Jerusalem and established several kingdoms in the area. (The city was retaken by Muslims in the late

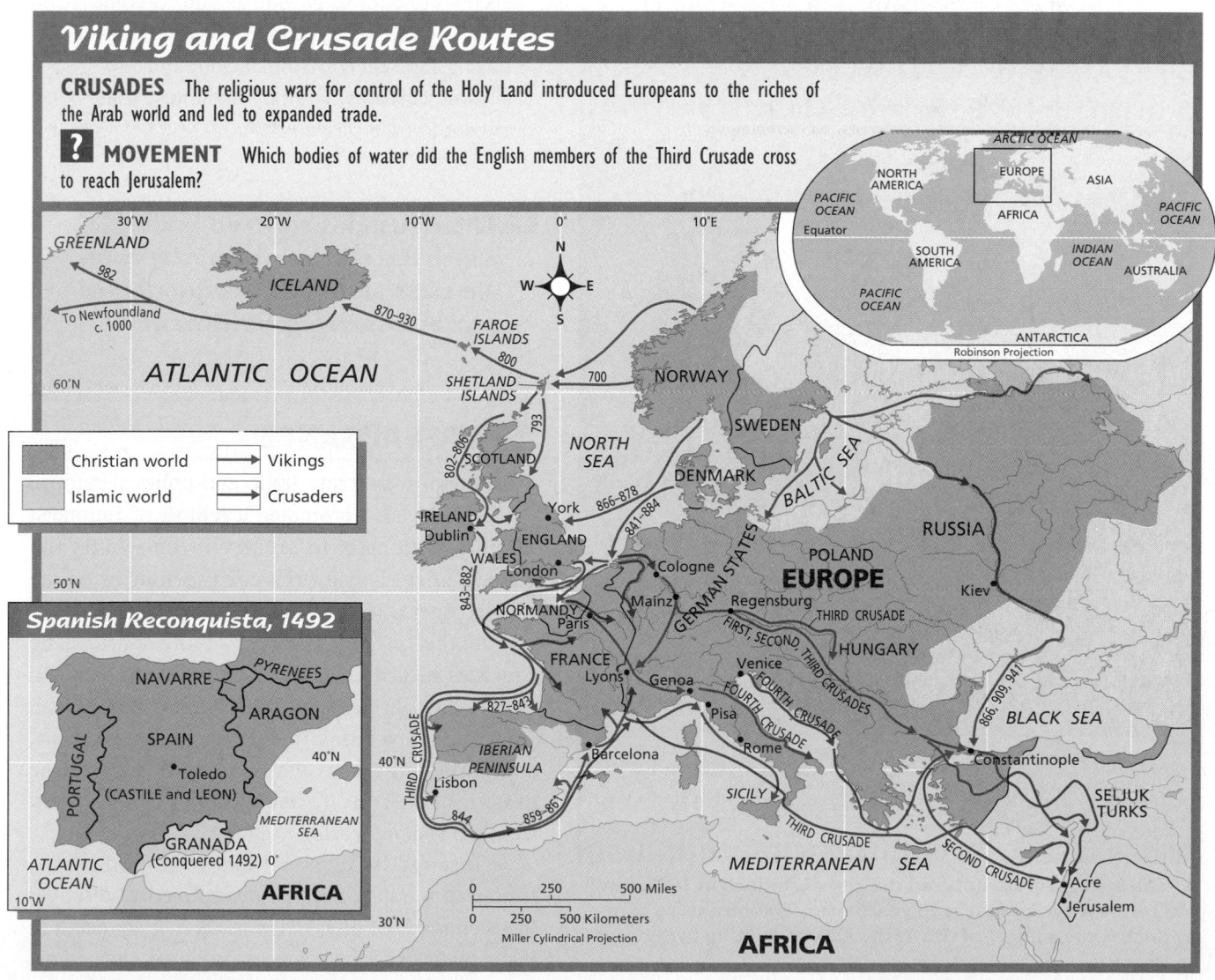

Viking and Crusade Routes

CRUSADES The religious wars for control of the Holy Land introduced Europeans to the riches of the Arab world and led to expanded trade.

❓ MOVEMENT Which bodies of water did the English members of the Third Crusade cross to reach Jerusalem?

Spanish Reconquista, 1492

1100s, however.) Though later Crusades were never as successful for the Europeans, the wars had important consequences for trade. Banks and merchants in the Italian city states of Venice, Genoa (JEN-uh-wuh), and Pisa funded the Crusades in return for trading privileges. Italian traders brought back from the Muslim lands rare spices, fine silks, and many other exotic goods. Europeans responded by demanding more.

The impact of trade helped change Europe's political and social order. The merchants who organized trading voyages and the bankers who financed these voyages formed a new social class—the **bourgeoisie** (boohzh-wah-ZEE), or middle class. They knew that political stability was needed for trade to flourish. Feudal nobles, who often fought with one another, could not provide this stability. However, central government under a strong king or queen could. Thus the bourgeoisie generally threw their support to the monarchs.

▲ The Seljuk Turks captured the city of Antioch in 1085, but it was retaken by Crusaders 13 years later. The recapture of Antioch is the subject of this 15th-century painting by Vincent de Beauvais.

The bourgeoisie's support came at a price, however: they demanded a greater degree of economic and political freedom for themselves and their cities. Kings and lords reluctantly granted towns self-government, and some even organized meetings attended by nobles and the leading people from each town. The delegates to these assemblies—the forerunners of modern parliaments—helped the monarchs decide on taxes and government policies.

The move toward greater political representation was under way even before the first European parliament was called, toward the close of the 13th century. In 1215, for instance, English nobles who were angered over new taxes forced King John to sign the **Magna Carta**, a charter limiting the power of the monarch. In addition to guaranteeing basic liberties for nobles, the charter protected trade:

66 All merchants shall have safe and secure conduct to go out of, and to come into, England . . . by land as by water, for buying and selling by the ancient and allowed customs, without any unjust tolls, except in time of war. 99

■■ **The Crusades spurred trade, which led to the rise of the middle class and the introduction of representative government.**

THE RENAISSANCE

In addition to spurring trade and political reform, the Crusades also promoted a rebirth of European learning and artistic creativity known as the **Renaissance**. During the early centuries of the Middle Ages, much of Europe had been closed off intellectually from the rest of the world. The Crusades helped end this isolation. Crusaders and traders brought back classical Greek and Roman works and new ideas in science, technology, art, and philosophy from the Byzantine Empire (the eastern half of the former Roman Empire) and from the Islamic world.

Inspired by classical and Islamic thinkers, European scholars became determined to discover the secrets of the physical world. Arab advances in mathematics and the sciences provided clues to the invention, in the 1450s, of a printing press that used moveable type made it possible to print a large number of books quickly—and thus to spread ideas far and wide.

Commerce also played a role in promoting the Renaissance. European cities, whose banks and treasuries were overflowing with profits from trade, tried to outdo one another by funding building projects and by supporting individual artists. Such Renaissance artists as Leonardo da Vinci and Michelangelo were supported by wealthy sponsors.

■■ Trade, a renewed thirst for knowledge, and the invention of the printing press helped spark the Renaissance—a rebirth of European art and learning.

▲ This 16th-century painting shows Muslim astronomers observing the sky from the tower of Galata in Constantinople (now Istanbul).

workings of nature, while Arab maps and geographic studies provided pictures of the world beyond Europe's borders. Practical inventions like the compass and the astrolabe (an instrument used to observe and calculate the positions of the planets and the stars) became important tools for world exploration.

The Renaissance began in Italy in the 14th century and soon spread to the rest of Europe. A major factor in this cultural diffusion was the work of a German printer, Johannes Gutenberg. His

𝒯HE RISE OF NATIONS

The other great transformation of the Middle Ages was the rise of nations. Feudal kingdoms, independent city-states, and church-controlled lands slowly gave way to national monarchies in most of western Europe. Most often these changes were accomplished through years of warfare, and at other times by marriage between royal families. By the 1400s national monarchies existed in Portugal, France, England, Spain, Denmark, Norway, Sweden, Poland, and Hungary.

Among the first to achieve national unity during this period were Portugal, France, and England. Portugal, which had won its independence from the Spanish kingdom of Castile (kas-TEEL) in the 12th century, was unified under King John I in the early 1400s. The various French provinces were unified under the rule of Louis XI by the time his reign ended in 1483. And England was unified under Henry VII in 1485 after 30 years of bloody fighting.

◀ The 12th-century Arab geographer Abū al-Idrīsī developed a map of the world that consisted of many different sections. One section displaying the "Seven Climatic Zones" is shown here.

▲ This detail from the *Fall of Granada* by Pradilla shows Ferdinand and Isabella receiving the surrender of the Kingdom of Granada from the Moors in 1492.

the ongoing battle to recapture Spanish lands from the Moors. The *Reconquista* ended in 1492, when Spain defeated the Moors in Granada.

Isabella and Ferdinand believed that the best way to truly unify their kingdoms—and to gain the approval of the pope—was to make Spain a completely Catholic nation by driving non-Christians from their lands. In March 1492 they ordered all Jews to convert to the Catholic faith or leave Spain.

The action did much to achieve the monarchs' goal of an all-Catholic Spain. But it carried a price for the country that was not immediately obvious. Among the nearly 150,000 departing Jews were some of the nation's leading scholars, bankers, merchants, and government officials. These people settled throughout Europe and the Muslim world, strengthening Spain's enemies. But in 1492 Spain's future looked bright as it joined other European nations in the search for new trade routes and the riches they would bring.

Spain faced a special problem, however. Four Christian kingdoms—Portugal, Castile, Navarre (nuh-VAHR), and Aragon—controlled most of the Iberian Peninsula. But the Moors—Muslims who were originally from North Africa—still held the kingdom of Granada in the southernmost part of the peninsula. The Moors, in fact, had controlled much of southwestern Europe during the Middle Ages.

The first step toward unification occurred when Isabella of Castile and Ferdinand II of Aragon married in 1469. They did not unite their kingdoms until 1479, but they did quickly join forces in the *Reconquista* (re-kawng-KEE-stah)—

■■ **Through royal marriages and warfare, monarchies built nations from feudal kingdoms, independent city-states, and church-controlled lands.**

SECTION 3 REVIEW

IDENTIFY and explain the significance of the following: feudalism, manor, serfs, Crusades, bourgeoisie, Magna Carta, Renaissance, Johannes Gutenberg, *Reconquista*.

LOCATE and explain the importance of the following: Jerusalem, Portugal, France, England, Iberian Peninsula.

1. **MAIN IDEA** What factors led to the rise of feudalism? What factors contributed to its decline?

2. **MAIN IDEA** In what ways did the Crusades change political and social life in Europe?

3. **MAIN IDEA** What caused the rise of nations in Europe?

4. **WRITING TO INFORM** In a short essay, explain what the Renaissance was and describe some of the technological advances that came to Europeans during the period.

5. **TAKING A STAND** Were the national monarchies that developed in the Middle Ages better for Europe than the old systems? Why or why not?

Section 4

ASIA AND AFRICA IN THE MIDDLE AGES

FOCUS

- How did Islamic religion and culture spread during the Middle Ages?
- How did China become open to world trade?
- What role did trade play in the development of African kingdoms?

As feudalism gave way to nation-states in Europe, large cultures flourished in Asia and Africa. When Europeans began to venture beyond their borders in search of trade, they encountered a commercial world dominated by merchants from these societies. As the different groups came together, they exchanged ideas and cultural practices as well as commercial goods. This exchange expanded the Europeans' knowledge of the world, stimulated their desire for more goods, and influenced the course of world events.

Bronze figurine of a flute player from Benin, West Africa

THE ISLAMIC WORLD

Trade between Asia and Africa had existed for centuries. Horses, cloth, and luxury goods from Asia were exchanged for ivory and gold—and slaves—from Africa. After 900, much of this trade was controlled by Muslim merchants.

Muhammad, the prophet of Islam, had commanded his followers to convert all nonbelievers—by force if necessary. Although Muslim armies did much to spread the faith, many people were drawn to Islam by merchants. Carrying the **Qur'an** (kuh-RAN)—the holy book of Islam—Muslim merchants tirelessly preached their religion wherever they went. The traders' devotion proved to be as potent a weapon as the sword in spreading Islamic faith and culture. By the late Middle Ages, vast areas of Asia, Africa, and Europe had become part of the Muslim empire.

■■ Muslim soldiers and merchants spread their religion and culture throughout Asia, Africa, and Europe during the Middle Ages.

The pursuit of knowledge flourished in the Islamic world during the Middle Ages. In the 10th and 11th centuries, two Muslim physicians, Rāzī (RAH-zee) and Ibn Sīnā (IB-uhn SEE-nah), compiled medical encyclopedias that quickly became the basis for teaching medicine in the educational centers of Baghdad. Muslim scholars excelled at mathematics and perfected algebra. Using knowledge gained from the mathematicians of India, they refined the Arabic numeral system and the concept of zero. Muslim geographers used travelers' observations and astronomical calculations to advance the art of cartography, or mapmaking. Through trade many of these advances found their way to cultures outside the Muslim world.

CHINA

Trade also played a role in spreading the culture of China to other parts of the world. For much of China's early history, the towering Himalayas (him-uh-LAY-uhz) of central Asia and the dry, barren Gobi (GOH-bee) Desert cut off the Chinese society from contact with other cultures. Because they were insulated from outside influences, the Chinese developed a distinctive culture, which was maintained through the moral code and philosophy of Confucianism. Confucius (551–479 B.C.) taught that people should strive to build a peaceful, well-ordered society.

In time, the Chinese developed a sense of cultural superiority, a belief that their country stood at the center of everything important. Their technological and cultural achievements lent support to this self-image. Among other things, the Chinese either invented or improved the compass, the water mill, the wheelbarrow, the horse harness, gunpowder, and paper. In addition, they made the world's first known printed book, the *Diamond Sutra,* in A.D. 868.

China's isolation ended in the 1200s, when invaders from Mongolia overran the country. The Mongol leader Kublai Khan (KOO-bluh KAHN)—the Great Khan—set up as his capital what is now the city of Beijing (Peking) in 1264. Under his rule China became the largest land empire in the world. It also opened up dramatically to the Western world. The Mongols protected the trade routes across Asia so that travelers were safe from raiding bands. As a result, trade flourished.

Among the Europeans to visit China between 1270 and 1300 was a young Italian, Marco Polo,

The Granger Collection, New York

an adventurer and merchant from Venice. Polo spent more than 20 years traveling through China and central Asia. In a chronicle about his travels, *Description of the World,* Polo wrote of the magnificent Mongol Empire, including the royal city now called Beijing:

> 66 This new city is a perfect square, with each side six miles long. The wall of the city has 12 gates, 3 on each side of the square. The whole city was laid out by line. The streets are so straight that if you stand above one of the gates, you can see the gate on the opposite side of the city. . . . Everything that is most rare and valuable in all the world finds its way here. This is especially true of India, which supplies precious gems, pearls, and spices. 99

■■ The Mongols under Kublai Khan protected Asian trade routes and opened China to world trade.

After Kublai Khan's death in 1294, the Mongols' power declined, and the Chinese regained control. The new leaders, wanting to return to the nation's ancient traditions, reintroduced Confucianism. To protect their culture from foreign influences, the Chinese once again sought to isolate their society from the world.

China did not withdraw from outside contact completely, however. Beginning in 1405, the nation launched a series of seven maritime expeditions. The expeditions—the largest and most far-reaching the world had ever seen—sailed to Vietnam, Indonesia, Ceylon (now Sri Lanka), India, the Arabian Peninsula, and numerous East African ports. The purpose of this vast undertaking was not to claim and conquer foreign territories, but to trade and to explore new lands. The Chinese also wanted to show the world their nation's wealth and achievements.

In 1433, however, China halted trade with the outside world. But China's withdrawal from trade did not reduce the West's desire for exotic Chinese goods. Dreams of trade with Asia still fueled European imaginations.

◀ **This detail from a Chinese scroll drawn during the Ming dynasty (1368–1644) shows the Chinese navy sailing against Japanese pirates.**

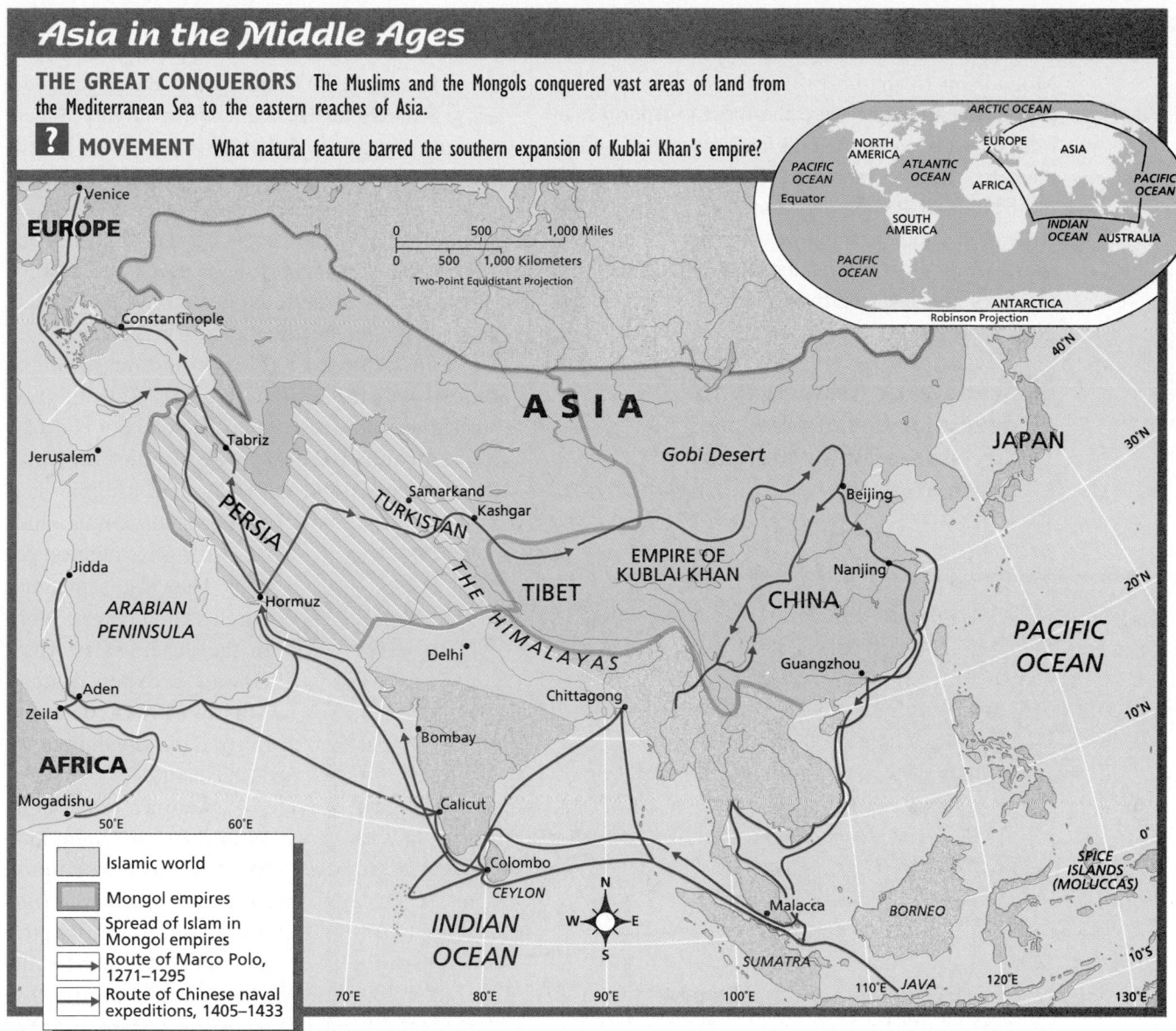

THE GREAT CONQUERORS The Muslims and the Mongols conquered vast areas of land from the Mediterranean Sea to the eastern reaches of Asia.

? **MOVEMENT** What natural feature barred the southern expansion of Kublai Khan's empire?

**Map labels:**

Venice
EUROPE
Constantinople
Jerusalem
Tabriz
PERSIA
Jidda
Samarkand
TURKISTAN
Kashgar
ASIA
Gobi Desert
JAPAN
ARABIAN PENINSULA
Hormuz
THE HIMALAYAS
TIBET
EMPIRE OF KUBLAI KHAN
Beijing
Nanjing
CHINA
Aden
Zeila
Delhi
Guangzhou
AFRICA
Mogadishu
Chittagong
Bombay
PACIFIC OCEAN
Calicut
Colombo
CEYLON
SPICE ISLANDS (MOLUCCAS)
Malacca
BORNEO
INDIAN OCEAN
SUMATRA
JAVA

ARCTIC OCEAN
NORTH AMERICA
EUROPE
ASIA
PACIFIC OCEAN
ATLANTIC OCEAN
AFRICA
PACIFIC OCEAN
Equator
SOUTH AMERICA
INDIAN OCEAN
AUSTRALIA
PACIFIC OCEAN
ANTARCTICA
Robinson Projection

0   500   1,000 Miles
0   500   1,000 Kilometers
Two-Point Equidistant Projection

Legend:
- Islamic world
- Mongol empires
- Spread of Islam in Mongol empires
- Route of Marco Polo, 1271–1295
- Route of Chinese naval expeditions, 1405–1433

THE AFRICAN TRADING KINGDOMS

Trade also was instrumental in the development of great kingdoms in East and West Africa. Early kingdoms—such as Kush (1000 B.C.–A.D. 350) and Axum (A.D. 50–600)—controlled highly developed trade networks and established the trading practices that later empires adopted. During the Middle Ages the city-states on the East African coast thrived on trade with Asia. In West Africa, kingdoms grew rich by trading in gold and salt.

East African city-states. During the 700s many of the people in what are today Somalia, Kenya, and Tanzania (tan-zuh-NEE-uh) moved to the coastal areas and became involved in trade between Africa and Asia. Most of the people specialized in mainland trade, or the bringing of goods from the interior to the coast. Other traders then shipped the goods to the Arabian Peninsula, where they would be traded to merchants from China. Many different goods were brought to the coast, but the most sought-after item was gold, which formed a large part of the trade.

Most of the traders who shipped goods to the Arabian Peninsula were Arabs who had come to East Africa after fleeing political and religious upheaval in their homelands. Over time the mix of newcomers and original inhabitants created a unique African culture. The people spoke **Swahili** (swah-HEE-lee), a form of Bantu that showed strong Arabic influences. (*Swahili* is an Arabic word meaning "of the coast.")

Over the years, trade between Africa and Asia expanded, and many East African trading villages grew into powerful and wealthy city-states. At first, northern city-states such as Mogadishu (mahg-uh-DISH-oo)—the present-day capital of Somalia—were the most prosperous. In time, however, commercial activity moved southward to Malindi, Mombasa (mahm-BAHS-uh), and the islands of Pemba and Zanzibar. By the 1200s Kilwa, on another island farther south, ranked as the leading East African port city. Meanwhile, many of the interior towns became rich on the gold trade.

■■ **Trade with Asia led to the development of wealthy city-states along the east coast of Africa.**

West African kingdoms. Trade also became an important activity early in the history of West Africa. In the western area of the Sudan—the vast grasslands to the south of the mighty Sahara—many important trade routes crisscrossed: traders with gold headed north from the Sudan as great caravans brought salt and other goods south from the Sahara. The people of the western Sudan oversaw the exchange of these goods and charged a tax on the transactions. Over time these trade centers grew into bustling trading kingdoms.

The earliest of these kingdoms—Ghana (GAHN-uh)—developed from a trading post founded around A.D. 300 at the southern end of a caravan route from Morocco (muh-RAHK-oh). North Africans and desert traders brought salt, copper, and various kinds of cloth to exchange for gold. They also sometimes purchased slaves to work in the desert salt mines. Ghana prospered until Muslims from the north overran the kingdom in the 11th century.

Another remarkable West African kingdom—Mali, which originated in the 7th century A.D.—rose to power shortly after the fall of Ghana. By the 1300s Mali controlled a huge empire that stretched from the upper Niger (NY-juhr) River westward to the Atlantic coast. Mali's best-known leader was Mansa Mūsā, who ruled from 1307 to 1332. A devout Muslim, he undertook a *hajj* (pilgrimage) to Mecca in 1324. Mansa Mūsā saw this journey to the holy city as an opportunity to display Mali's wealth. The ruler was accompanied by thousands of other pilgrims—among them 500 slaves, each of whom carried a four-pound gold bar.

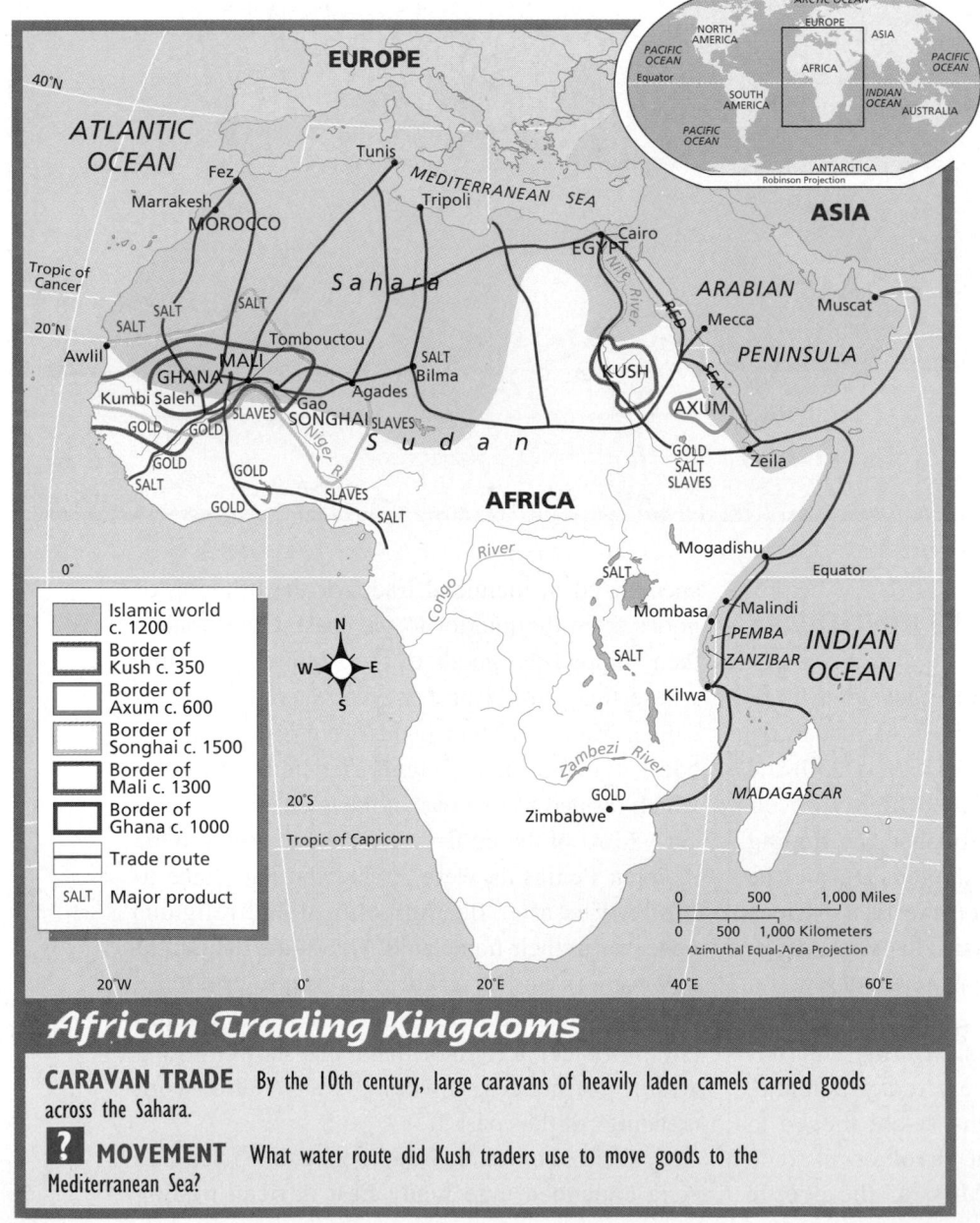

African Trading Kingdoms

CARAVAN TRADE By the 10th century, large caravans of heavily laden camels carried goods across the Sahara.

? **MOVEMENT** What water route did Kush traders use to move goods to the Mediterranean Sea?

Mansa Mūsā's trip was widely reported, and his fame spread far beyond the Muslim world. An atlas made for King Charles V of France showed a black man seated on a throne and clutching a huge gold nugget. Accompanying the picture was this inscription:

66 This black lord is called [Mansa Mūsā], lord of the negroes of Guinea [Mali]. The gold which is found in his country is so abundant that he is the richest and noblest lord in all the region. 99

After Mansa Mūsā died in 1332, Mali slowly lost its powerful position in the region.

In the mid-1300s, as Mali declined, the relatively weak state of Songhai (SAWNG-hy)—once under Mali's rule—won its independence. Songhai eventually became the dominant power in West Africa, growing rich on the trade in gold, ivory, and slaves. It also flourished as a center of Islamic learning. The city of Tombouctou (tohn-book-TOO) was home to three universities and 180 Islamic schools. The universities, which housed large collections of Greek, Roman, and Arabic manuscripts, taught religion, poetry, astronomy, and medicine. By the mid-1500s, education rivaled trade as Tombouctou's major activity.

▲ **Detail showing Mansa Mūsā from atlas of Charles V**

Despite the presence of large cities like Tombouctou, the majority of people in West Africa lived in small villages. They believed that many things in nature were sacred. They also placed great importance on family ties and on respect for their ancestors, which led to a strong sense of family loyalty and communal values. This whole world, however, would soon change with the arrival of the Europeans.

■■ **A succession of powerful kingdoms in West Africa controlled the major north-south trade routes.**

SECTION 4 REVIEW

IDENTIFY and explain the significance of the following: Muhammad, Qur'an, Confucius, *Diamond Sutra,* Kublai Khan, Marco Polo, Swahili, Mansa Mūsā, *hajj.*

LOCATE and explain the importance of the following: Beijing, Mogadishu, Sahara, Ghana, Mali, Tombouctou.

1. **MAIN IDEA** What role did trade play in spreading Islamic culture?

2. **MAIN IDEA** How did the Mongol invasion affect trade between China and the rest of the world?

3. **LINKING HISTORY AND GEOGRAPHY** How did the location of East and West African city-states prove important to their development?

4. **WRITING TO DESCRIBE** Imagine you are a member of Marco Polo's expedition. Write a journal entry that describes your impressions of the Mongol Empire.

5. **GAINING A MULTICULTURAL PERSPECTIVE** As a Chinese citizen in the year 1300, write a brief essay expressing your view on either expanding trade or returning to isolationism.

THE LURE OF TRADE AND EXPLORATION

FOCUS

- Why did Europeans seek a new route to the East?
- What were the origins of Portugal's involvement in the slave trade?
- How did Portugal gain control of East-West trade?

Europe was greatly enriched by the flow of ideas and technology from Africa and Asia. But Europeans were most interested in goods: grain and gold from Africa and perfumes, spices, and silks from Asia. By the early 1400s most of these items were readily available in Europe, but very costly. Goods coming from Asia and Africa were controlled by Muslim trading empires and Italian city-states. The newly emerging nation-states of Europe wanted to share in this wealth. To do so, however, they needed to find other routes to these distant markets. The seafaring nation of Portugal led the way in this great adventure.

Detail from woodcarving of Venice, 15th century

EAST–WEST TRADE

Wealthy Europeans wanted Syrian fabrics and Chinese silk to make fine clothes, and Persian rugs and Chinese glass and porcelain to decorate their homes. They also wanted cloves, cinnamon, and nutmeg from the Spice Islands of the Indies, ginger from China, and pepper from India to flavor and preserve their foods.

But trade routes overland from China or by sea from the Indies were long and dangerous. On the journey from the East, goods might change hands a dozen times, their prices marked up each time. Some of the profit went to the Muslim traders who controlled the Asian trade routes. Much more, however, went to the Italian merchants from Genoa and Venice who bought the goods from Muslim traders in North Africa or in Black Sea ports and shipped them across the Mediterranean Sea to be sold in Europe.

Hungry for trade goods and envious of Genoa and Venice's **monopoly**, or exclusive

◀ During the 13th century Genoa became the chief trading center in the Mediterranean region. This view of the city and its harbor was painted about 1481.

control, of East-West trade, other European merchants began looking for ways to get Asian goods more cheaply. An all-sea route to the East seemed the most promising answer.

■■ The control of trade by Muslim and Italian merchants made Asian goods very costly, causing Europeans to look for new routes to the East.

PORTUGAL LEADS THE WAY

Portugal, a small country with a long seafaring tradition, led the way in exploration. A strong desire to seize a share of the East-West trade drove the Portuguese of the early 1400s to seek a new route to Asia. Their country's geographic location, on the west coast of the Iberian Peninsula, determined the route the Portuguese

▲ These pictures from a 1492 book, *On the Nature of Created Things*, show two monsters that seafarers imagined could be found in mysterious lands across the Atlantic Ocean.

took—southward into the Atlantic Ocean and around Africa.

What knowledge of the world did the Portuguese possess as they set out on their voyages of exploration? Most Portuguese sea captains were aware of the works of Arab geographers and of books written by European travelers to the East. Much of the information contained in these

---

Trade Routes in the Middle Ages

COMPETITION FOR TRADE By the early 14th century Venice and Genoa competed for control of trade routes to Asia.

❓ MOVEMENT Why might Portugal have established trade routes around the Cape of Good Hope, instead of through the Mediterranean Sea?

(Map: Trade Routes in the Middle Ages)

Legend:
- Islamic world
- Christian world
- Italian trade routes
- Muslim trade routes
- Asian trade routes
- Portuguese explorations

Map labels include: Arctic Circle, 60°N, ATLANTIC OCEAN, ENGLAND, London, EUROPE, PORTUGAL, Lisbon, SPAIN, Sagres, AZORES, MADEIRA, 30°N, Marrakesh, SAHARA, Venice, Genoa, BLACK SEA, Constantinople, MEDITERRANEAN SEA, Tunis, Cairo, EGYPT, Jerusalem, Mecca, RED SEA, CASPIAN SEA, Baghdad, PERSIA, Samarkand, Gobi Desert, Beijing, ASIA, Delhi, CHINA, Guangzhou, JAPAN, Tropic of Cancer, PACIFIC OCEAN, CAPE VERDE ISLANDS, Tombouctou, Sierra Leone, Benin, AFRICA, Zeila, INDIA, Goa, Calicut, CEYLON, Equator, PHILIPPINES, SPICE ISLANDS (MOLUCCAS), Mombasa, Kongo, Zanzibar, DIAS 1487–1488, Mozambique, MADAGASCAR, INDIAN OCEAN, Tropic of Capricorn, SUMATRA, BORNEO, CELEBES, JAVA, AUSTRALIA, DA GAMA 1497–1499, 30°S, Cape of Good Hope, 30°W, 0°, 30°E, 60°E, 90°E, 120°E, 150°E

Scale: 0 1,000 2,000 Miles / 0 1,000 2,000 Kilometers, Miller Cylindrical Projection sources, however, was quite fanciful. For example, according to the popular 14th-century *Travels of Sir John Mandeville,* seafarers who survived the rough seas of the Atlantic might come upon lands inhabited by strange creatures:

> 66 In one, there is a race of great stature, like giants, foul and horrible to look at; they have one eye only, in the middle of their foreheads. . . . In another part, there are ugly folk without heads, who have eyes in each shoulder; their mouths are round, like a horseshoe, in the middle of their chest. . . . And there are in another place folk with flat faces, without noses or eyes. 99

BIO GRAPHY

Common sense, reason, and order were brought to the study of geography and exploration by Prince Henry of Portugal. Henry was born in 1394, the third son of King John I and Philippa of Lancaster. His burning desire was to find the African "gold kingdoms" he had heard of while fighting in Morocco. He also yearned to find an all-sea route to Asia.

In 1419 Prince Henry established a center for the study of navigation at Sagres (SAH-**greesh**), on the southwestern tip of Portugal. There, he brought together the country's best geographers, mapmakers, and ship designers. He

Prince Henry

oversaw all their work, encouraging them to experiment with new navigation methods, to draw more accurate maps, and to build ships capable of withstanding the stormy Atlantic. Henry put the results to practical use by sponsoring a number of voyages of exploration southward down the African coast.

By 1430 the Portuguese had explored and colonized the Madeira (muh-DIR-uh) Islands and the Azores off Africa's northwest coast. During the 1450s they reached the Cape Verde Islands off the Senegal coast. By 1462, two years after Henry died, Portuguese sailors had ventured as far as Sierra Leone, nearly around the great bulge of western Africa. Prince Henry never sailed on any of these voyages, but his immense contribution to Portugal's seafaring efforts earned him the nickname "the Navigator."

THE AFRICAN SLAVE TRADE

The first Portuguese to visit Africa's Atlantic coast were interested in trading for the spices that were in such great demand back home. They also sought gold, which they had heard frequently mentioned in tales about the continent. In time, however, another business—the trade in human slaves—came to dominate their dealings with Africa.

Slavery was not unknown to Africans, but its form was different from what it would eventually become under the Europeans. Many slaves in West African society were either criminals or captives taken in war. Their rights were restricted, but they did have some protection under the law. Most could marry, and their children did not become slaves. Moreover, slavery was usually temporary—individuals could obtain their freedom.

Portugal's role in the slave trade was relatively small in the late 1400s. But by the end of the following century, the slave trade had become a major economic activity. It eventually resulted in the **African diaspora** (dy-AS-pruh)—the forcible resettlement of millions of African people to the Americas from the 1500s through the 1800s. Estimates suggest that in the approximately 400 years the slave trade operated, some 10 million or more Africans were transported across the Atlantic as slaves. Countless more died as a result of capture or on the horrible voyage to the Americas.

■■ **Portuguese traders, first attracted to Africa's gold and other natural resources, soon became interested in the profitable slave trade.**

The slave trade devastated African society. Because of the enormous profits that the slave trade brought, villages began targeting their enemies for capture. The result was an increase in warfare among the various West African nations. Many people trapped in the slave trade were captives taken in war. The rest were usually those abducted by raiding parties and swiftly taken to slave traders on the coast.

It is hard to imagine the effect the slave trade had on those who experienced the capture of a

▲ The slave market at Yemen is the subject of this illustration from a 13th-century Arabic manuscript.

friend or family member. The experience would be devastating to anyone, but in a culture that placed such strong emphasis on family ties, it was especially painful. In 1444 Gomes Eanes de Zurara (GOH-mish A-nush duh zoo-RAH-ruh), the official reporter for the Portuguese king, described one of the miseries brought about by the traffic in human slaves:

 Mothers would clasp their infants in their arms, and throw themselves on the ground to cover them with their bodies, disregarding any injury to their own persons, so that they could prevent their children from being separated from them. 🙶🙶

A ROUTE TO THE INDIES

The profits from the African trade prompted further searches for new routes to Asia. During the mid-1480s, Portuguese sailors discovered the mouth of the Congo River and charted the southwest coast of Africa. In 1488 Bartolomeu Dias rounded Africa's southernmost tip, but he went no farther. His crew, fearing the great expanse of unknown ocean that lay ahead of them, forced the ship to turn back.

In 1497 a fleet of four ships outfitted by Dias and commanded by Vasco da Gama set out from Portugal to complete the African voyage. By early 1498 da Gama had rounded the Cape of Good Hope at Africa's southernmost tip and made his way to India. Over the next half century, the Portuguese established trading forts in West and East Africa, India, the Spice Islands (now the Moluccas of Indonesia), and southern China, thereby gaining control of East-West trade. Other powerful nation-states of Europe, envious of Portugal's success, soon began to sponsor voyages of their own.

■■ **Pioneering voyages of exploration around Africa and to Asia gave Portugal control of East-West trade.**

SECTION 5 REVIEW

IDENTIFY and explain the significance of the following: monopoly, Prince Henry, African diaspora, Gomes Eanes de Zurara, Bartolomeu Dias, Vasco da Gama.

LOCATE and explain the importance of the following: Spice Islands, Genoa, Venice, Sagres, Black Sea, Mediterranean Sea, Madeira Islands, Cape Verde Islands, Sierra Leone, Cape of Good Hope.

1. **MAIN IDEA** Why were most European nations unhappy with the trade system in the early 1400s? What was their solution?

2. **MAIN IDEA** Why were the voyages of Bartolomeu Dias and Vasco da Gama important to Portugal?

3. **GEOGRAPHY: LOCATION** Why did Portugal, rather than Italy, Spain, or England, lead the way in exploring the East?

4. **WRITING TO PERSUADE** Imagine that you are Gomes Eanes de Zurara. Write a report to the Portuguese king explaining how the slave trade began and why Portugal should abandon its involvement.

5. **EVALUATING** How did Prince Henry of Portugal improve the study of geography and exploration?

Rise of farming in desert Southwest.

Rise of Olmec culture.

Kush founded.

Rise of Hopewell culture.

Mayas rise to prominence.

Muhammad founds Islam.

| c.3500 | c.1200 | c.1000 | c.300 B.C. | c.A.D. 300 | 610 |

WRITING A SUMMARY

Using the essential points of the chapter as a guide, write a summary of the chapter.

REVIEWING CHRONOLOGY

Number your paper 1 to 5. Study the time line above, and list the following events in the order in which they happened by writing the first next to 1, the second next to 2, and so on. Then complete the activity below.

1. Rise of farming in the desert Southwest.
2. Prince Henry's navigation center established.
3. Vasco da Gama sails to India.
4. Muhammad founds Islam.
5. Crusades begin.

Linking History and Geography Pick five events on the time line and tell how each illustrates one of the five themes of geography.

IDENTIFYING PEOPLE AND IDEAS

Explain the historical significance of each of the following people or terms.

1. environment
2. cultural diffusion
3. pueblo
4. feudalism
5. Crusades
6. Qur'an
7. Confucius
8. Marco Polo
9. African diaspora
10. Vasco da Gama

UNDERSTANDING MAIN IDEAS

1. What effect did geography and the changing environment of the Americas have on Paleo-Indian culture?
2. What were the major economic, political, and social changes in Europe during the Middle Ages?
3. Describe the role of trade in one of the following: the spread of Islamic culture; relations between China and the West; the development of African kingdoms; or Portuguese exploration.

REVIEWING THEMES

1. **Cultural Diversity** What evidence suggests that cultural diffusion occurred between Native American cultures in Mesoamerica and in North America?
2. **Economic Development** How did the Crusades benefit European economies?
3. **Technology and Society** How did technological advances influence cultural development in medieval Europe?

THINKING CRITICALLY

1. **Evaluating** Why do historians consider the advent of farming in the Americas such an important event?
2. **Synthesizing** Describe daily life in feudal society, including the role of the Roman Catholic church.
3. **Analyzing** How did Muslims influence cultural diffusion between Africa, Asia, and Europe?

STRATEGY FOR SUCCESS

Review the Skills Handbook entry on Reviewing Map Basics on page 992. Then study the map below of Black Mesa in Arizona. A mesa is a flat-topped natural elevation, much like a plateau. The shaded area represents the site of an ancient Native American village. According to the map, approximately how far is Kayenta from Rough Rock? What features of the region might have encouraged Native Americans to settle there?

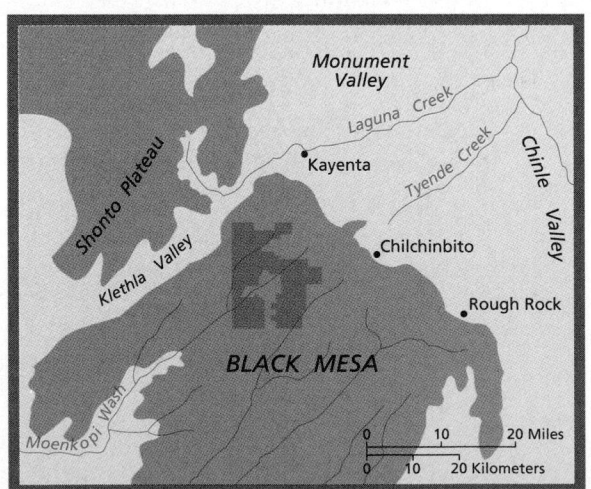

Rise of Mississippian culture.	Seljuk Turks conquer Holy Land.	Crusades begin.	Magna Carta signed.		Mongols rule China.	Mansa Mūsā makes pilgrimage to Mecca.		Prince Henry's navigation center established.	Rise of Incan civilization.	Bartolomeu Dias reaches Cape of Good Hope.	Reconquista ends.	Vasco da Gama sails to India.
c.700	1071	1096	1215	c.1250	1324	1419	c.1440	1488	1492	1498

WRITING ABOUT HISTORY

Writing to Create Research the ceremonies, social roles, or artistic expressions of one culture described in the chapter. Then write a poem or song celebrating the accomplishments of this culture.

USING PRIMARY SOURCES

Africa has a rich tradition of oral, or spoken, literature, such as the epic poem. One of the best-known African epic poems is *Sundiata,* the story of the 13th-century founder of the empire of Mali. The narrator is a *griot,* an oral historian named Mamoudou Kouyaté (KOO-yah-tai). Read the poem, then write a paragraph explaining the role of the griot in African culture.

Sundiata

I am a griot. It is I, Djeli Mamoudou Kouyaté, son of Bintou Kouyaté and Djeli Kedian Kouyaté, master of the art of eloquence [speaking]. Since time immemorial the Kouyates have been in the service of the Keita princes of Mali; we are vessels of speech, we are the repositories which harbour secrets many centuries old. . . . Without us the names of kings would vanish into oblivion, we are the memory of mankind; by the spoken word we bring to life the deeds and exploits of kings for younger generations. . . .

    I teach kings the history of their ancestors so that the lives of the ancients might serve them as an example, for the world is old, but the future springs from the past.

    My word is pure and free of all untruth; it is the word of my father; it is the word of my father's father. I will give you my father's words just as I received them; royal griots do not know what lying is. When a quarrel breaks out between tribes it is we who settle the difference, for we are the depositaries [people entrusted with something] of oaths which the ancestors swore.

    Listen to my word, you who want to know; by my mouth you will learn the history of Mali.

        —Translated by D. T. Niane

LINKING HISTORY AND GEOGRAPHY

Study the map on page 15. Locate the culture area in which your community is found. Then prepare a chart listing the Native American groups who lived in your area in 1500, the main features of each group, the major place characteristics of the area, and the influences of these groups that still exist locally—either through place-names, artifacts, or customs.

BUILDING YOUR PORTFOLIO

Complete the following projects independently or cooperatively.

1. TRADE Imagine you are a trader in the late 1400s. Prepare a map that shows trade routes between Europe, Africa, and Asia. Draw symbols on the map to indicate major items of trade.

2. CULTURAL EXCHANGES Imagine you are a museum researcher preparing an exhibit on cultural exchanges in the Americas. Select two groups that appear to have had cultural contact prior to 1500. Create a wall chart that illustrates the nature of the contact.

A MEETING OF CULTURES

*T*HE movement of people to North America took many paths over many thousands of years. The first settlers to come to North America were Asian hunters. They arrived more than 12,000 years ago by crossing the Beringia land bridge into present-day Alaska.

People from Europe and Africa only began arriving in North America in great numbers about 500 years ago. Like the immigrants from Asia centuries before, they brought ideas and customs from their homelands. Today, immigrants from around the globe continue to contribute to the rich cultural diversity that gives the United States its special character.

Mammoth fossils dating back some 25,000 years have been found in North America. Scientists believe the large creatures died out some 10,000 years ago.

Descendants of the Asian hunters moved into the interior of North America over ice-free routes along the eastern ridge of the Canadian Rocky Mountains. Once they reached the present-day United States, they spread to all corners.

Over the next several centuries, groups continued migrating south through Mexico and Central America to South America. Discoveries of grooved spear tips like this helped anthropologists trace the spread of these early peoples.

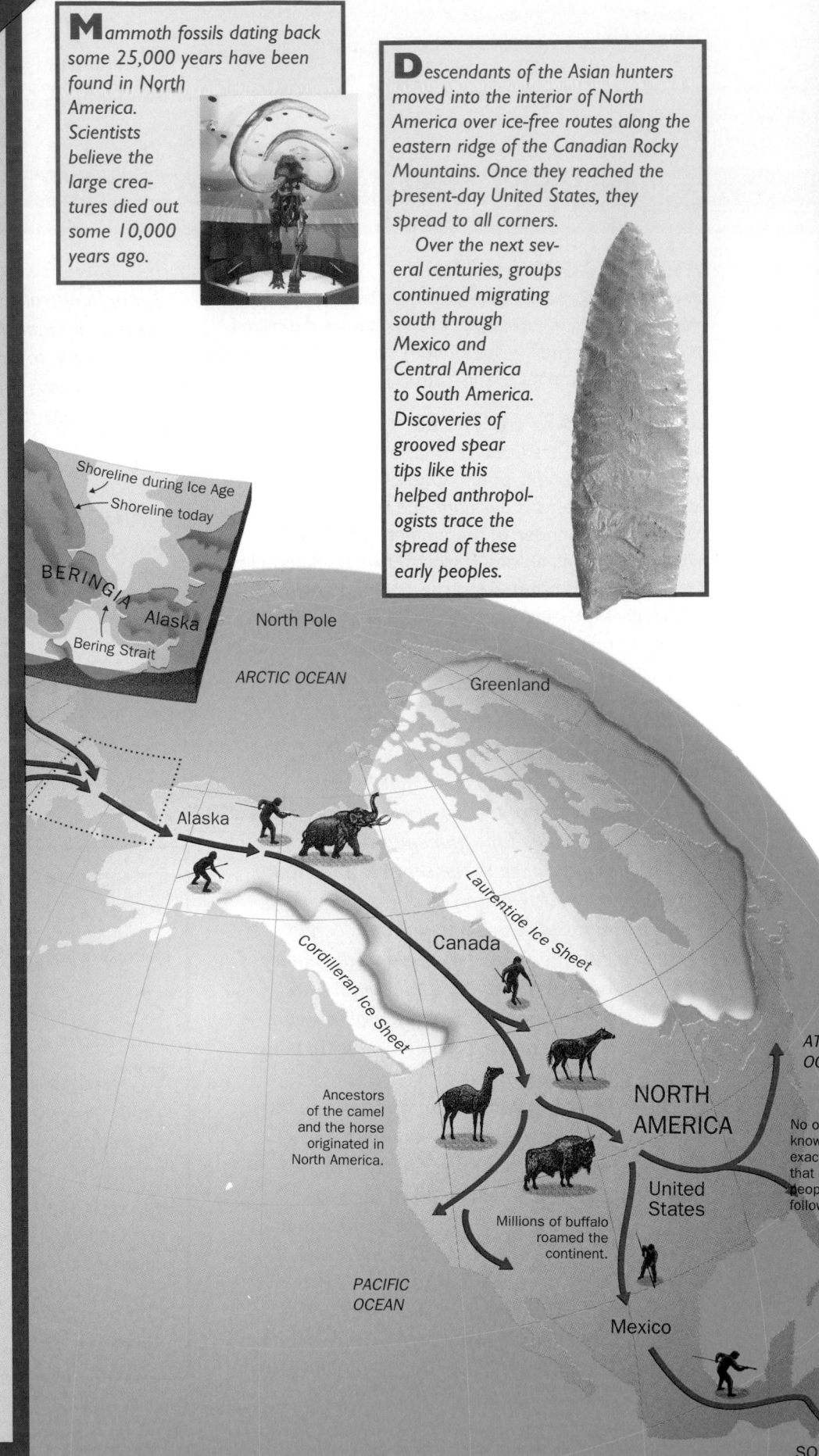

Shoreline during Ice Age
Shoreline today
BERINGIA
Alaska
Bering Strait

North Pole
ARCTIC OCEAN
Greenland

Alaska
Cordilleran Ice Sheet
Laurentide Ice Sheet
Canada

Ancestors of the camel and the horse originated in North America.

NORTH AMERICA

ATLA OCE

No one knows exact r that ea people followe

United States

Millions of buffalo roamed the continent.

PACIFIC OCEAN

Mexico

SOU AMERI

Equator

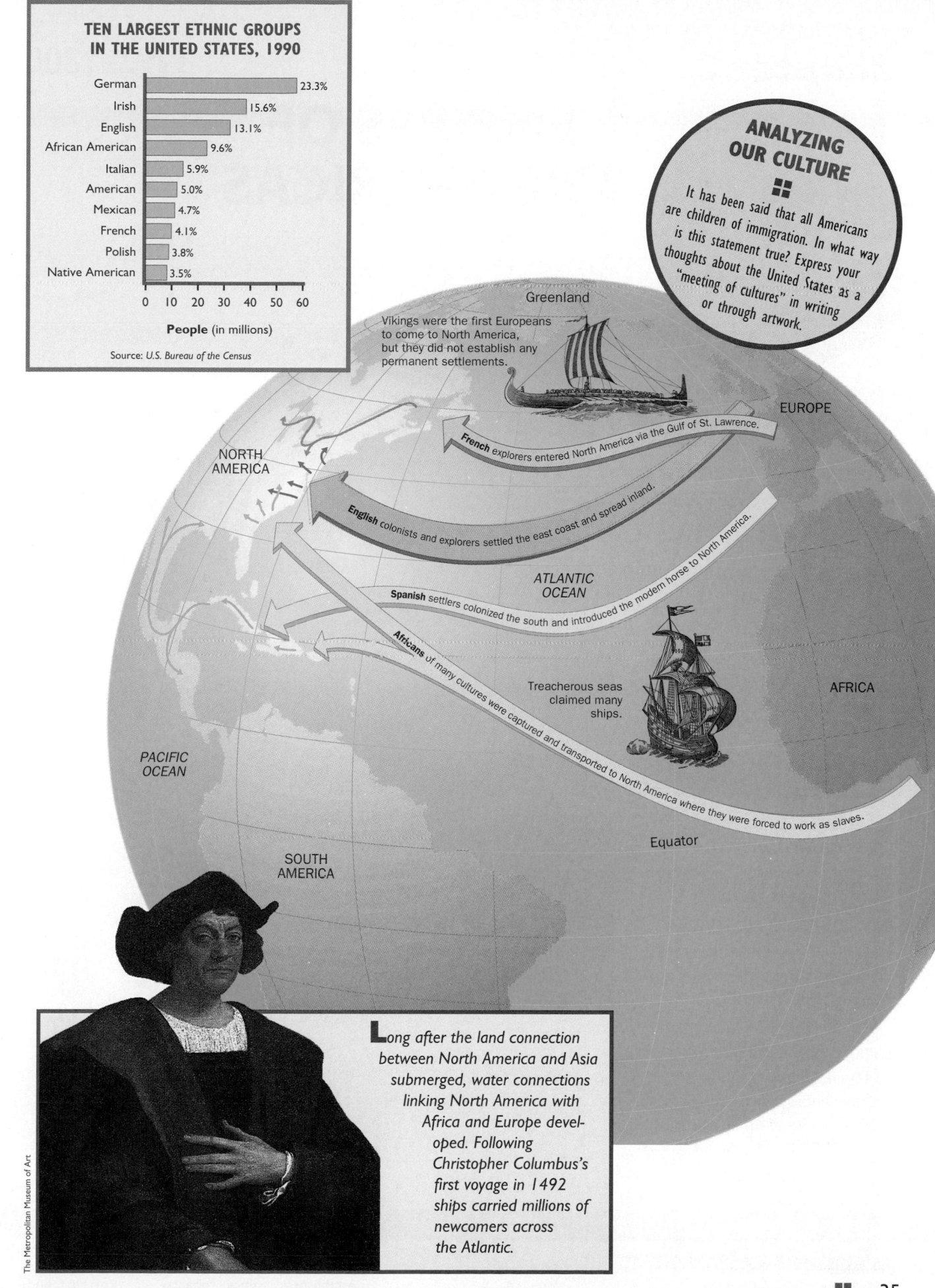

TEN LARGEST ETHNIC GROUPS IN THE UNITED STATES, 1990

Group	Percent
German	23.3%
Irish	15.6%
English	13.1%
African American	9.6%
Italian	5.9%
American	5.0%
Mexican	4.7%
French	4.1%
Polish	3.8%
Native American	3.5%

People (in millions)

0 10 20 30 40 50 60

Source: U.S. Bureau of the Census

ANALYZING OUR CULTURE

It has been said that all Americans are children of immigration. In what way is this statement true? Express your thoughts about the United States as a "meeting of cultures" in writing or through artwork.

Greenland

Vikings were the first Europeans to come to North America, but they did not establish any permanent settlements.

EUROPE

French explorers entered North America via the Gulf of St. Lawrence.

NORTH AMERICA

English colonists and explorers settled the east coast and spread inland.

ATLANTIC OCEAN

Spanish settlers colonized the south and introduced the modern horse to North America.

Africans of many cultures were captured and transported to North America where they were forced to work as slaves.

Treacherous seas claimed many ships.

AFRICA

PACIFIC OCEAN

Equator

SOUTH AMERICA

The Metropolitan Museum of Art

Long after the land connection between North America and Asia submerged, water connections linking North America with Africa and Europe developed. Following Christopher Columbus's first voyage in 1492 ships carried millions of newcomers across the Atlantic.

Chapter 2

1492–1800

EMPIRES OF THE AMERICAS

FOCUS

UNDERSTANDING THE MAIN IDEA

Christopher Columbus's landing in the Americas in 1492 marked a turning point in world history. The event forever altered the lives of people around the globe as the cultures of Europe, Africa, Asia, and the Americas came into contact with one another. Much of this encounter brought conflict; but it also united many separate societies into one connected world.

 THEMES

- **GLOBAL RELATIONS**
  What positive and negative effects might result from interactions between countries?

- **ECONOMIC DEVELOPMENT** How might devoting energy to overseas exploration and conquest help or hurt a nation's economy?

- **CULTURAL DIVERSITY**
  How do people's values and experiences affect their contacts with people of other cultures?

1492	1519	1565	1607	1612	1779
Columbus lands in the Americas.	Conquest of Aztecs begins.	St. Augustine founded.	Jamestown established.	Rolfe introduces tobacco in Jamestown.	Gaspar de Portolá founds San Diego.

In the 1400s, Europeans sought an eastward sea route to Asia to replace the long, dangerous, and expensive overland routes. Years of trading in the Mediterranean and the Atlantic had given many merchants valuable sailing experience. Moreover, scientific and technological advances had taken some of the guesswork out of navigation.

First contact between Columbus and Native Americans, 1492

Few dates in American history are as instantly recognizable as 1492. It was a year that shaped the destiny of continents. With Christopher Columbus's daring voyage, worlds apart became worlds in contact—and conflict.

On Friday, October 12, 1492, Columbus landed on an island in the Bahamas and "broke out the royal banner, and the captain's two flags with the green cross." These actions staked Spain's first claims in the Americas.

Columbus and his captains admired the beauty and abundance of this land: "Once ashore they saw very green trees and many ponds and fruits of various kinds." Columbus and the Europeans who followed him saw these lands as theirs for the taking. In their zeal to spread their cultures and enrich their treasuries, many Europeans imposed their ways of life on the original inhabitants of the Americas. Rich and varied Native American cultures were changed or destroyed as a result.

Still, Columbus's voyages and those of later explorers were remarkable feats. These first explorers and colonists carved out new lives for themselves, often in harsh environments. In the process, they created new American cultures and brought great riches to Europe.

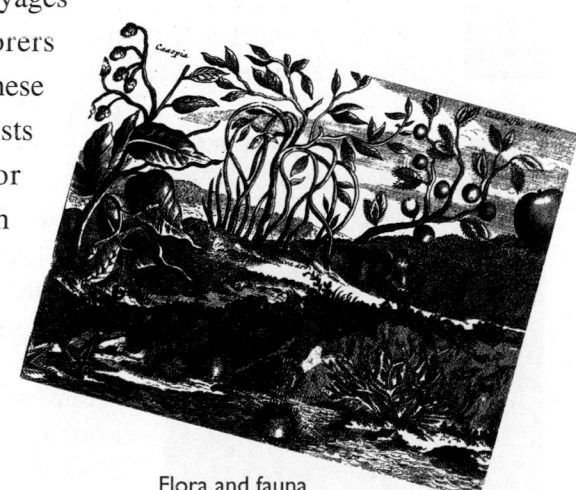

Flora and fauna of the Americas

FIRST CONTACT

FOCUS

- Why did Columbus sail west from Europe?
- What was the purpose of the *encomienda* system? How did it affect Native Americans?
- What reforms did Las Casas urge the Spanish Crown to undertake?
- What were some of the results of the Columbian exchange?

*B*y the 15th century, Europeans desired a cheaper, faster trade route to the East. Portugal took the lead, concentrating on finding a sea passage around the southernmost tip of Africa. But Spain, largely because of the boldness and imagination of one man—Christopher Columbus—looked westward. Columbus's landing introduced the Americas to the rest of the world, thus beginning a new era of trade, colonization, and cultural exchange.

The Granger Collection, New York

Portuguese astrolabe

CHRISTOPHER COLUMBUS

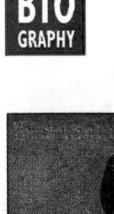
BIOGRAPHY

In 1492 a mariner named Christopher Columbus set sail from Spain on the first in a series of historic Atlantic crossings. He understood that the earth was round and concluded that if he sailed far enough west, he could establish a more direct trade route to Asia.

Columbus grew up in Genoa, a bustling port city on Italy's western coast. Fascinated by the sea, the adventurous youth sailed on Genoese trading vessels. He became an excellent navigator and learned to handle a caravel—a small, lightweight vessel most often used in sea trade. A former shipmate recalled Columbus's skill: "By a simple look at the night sky, he would know what route to follow or what weather to expect."

Eventually Columbus made his way to Lisbon, Portugal, the center of European knowledge about sea travel. While in Lisbon, he studied charts of contemporary geographers and astronomers and read ancient Greek and Roman texts, the Bible, and Marco Polo's exciting account of his travels in Asia. As a result of his studies, Columbus developed a theory about a westward route to Asia. He concluded that the western sea could not be very large and that the great trading cities of Asia lay about 2,400 miles west of Portugal.

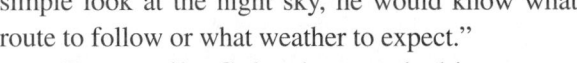
▉▉ Columbus believed that by sailing west from Europe, he could find a more direct route to Asia.

In the 1480s Columbus tried to persuade various European monarchs to sponsor a westward voyage across the Atlantic Ocean. He had little success. King John II of Portugal rejected the plan because he doubted Columbus's calculation of the

The Metropolitan Museum of Art

Christopher Columbus

distance to Asia. In fact, the actual distance to Asia proved to be about five times greater than Columbus had calculated.

Initially Columbus had no better luck with the Spanish monarchs, Ferdinand and Isabella. They devoted most of their energy and money to the *Reconquista,* the reconquest of Spain from the Moors. But Columbus persisted. He described to them the golden palaces and temples of Asia mentioned in Marco Polo's tales and tempted them with visions of the riches that could belong to Spain.

Columbus also vowed to take the Catholic faith to the peoples of foreign lands, a task for which he believed God had chosen him. This idea impressed the deeply religious Isabella. Nevertheless, it was only after the monarchs had defeated the Moors at Granada in January 1492 that they were willing to back an expedition. On April 17, 1492, the king and the queen authorized the necessary funding for Columbus's journey.

To reward Columbus for his future discoveries, Ferdinand and Isabella agreed that the mariner would be knighted, appointed admiral, and made **viceroy**, or governor, over all the lands he might discover. After his death these titles would be passed on to his descendants. In addition, he was to receive at least 10 percent of the riches he obtained on Spain's behalf.

THE FATEFUL FIRST VOYAGE

Columbus outfitted three vessels—the *Santa María,* the *Niña,* and the *Pinta*—and recruited an experienced crew of 90 sailors, most of whom were Spaniards. At dawn on August 3, 1492, Columbus and his crew departed from Palos, Spain. The small fleet first journeyed some 800 miles southwest to the Canary Islands, Spain's westernmost possession. Then in September the three vessels set out across the uncharted sea.

Imagine them one month later: Somewhere in the vast Atlantic, three small ships sail slowly westward. The men aboard have not sighted land since leaving the Canaries. The crew's patience is wearing thin, their hopes having risen like the waves with every sign of land—birds, green weeds, cloudbanks—only to be dashed. Many sailors demand that the ships turn back. Then, as the lookout on the lead ship scans the horizon in the early morning hours of October 12, he gives the long-awaited cry: *"Tierra!"* Land!

The October 12th entry in Columbus's *Journal,* his diary of the voyage, reads: "[At] daylight Friday . . . they reached an islet . . . which was called Guanahani [gwahn-uh-HAHN-ee]. . . . Soon they saw naked people, and the Admiral went ashore in his armed longboat." (The *Journal* survives only in a secondhand summary, which explains why Columbus is referred to as "the Admiral.")

The people of the Indies. Columbus and his men had struck land on a tiny coral island in the central Bahamas, about 400 miles southeast of present-day Florida. Columbus named it San Salvador (Holy Savior). Sure that he had reached Asia, the Admiral called the island dwellers "Indios," the Spanish word for inhabitants of the Indies.

The Native Americans Columbus encountered called themselves "Tainos" (TEE-nohs), the Arawak word for "good" or "noble." The Tainos were farmers who lived in settlements of some 100 to 300 people. Some groups traded salt, shells, and other goods peacefully with their neighbors. Other groups participated in raids against other islands. Taino war chiefs increased their power through successful raids.

On the larger islands of the Caribbean—such as present-day Cuba, Puerto Rico, Jamaica, and Hispaniola (his-puhn-YOH-luh)—lived groups with a more complex social and political organization. They built larger settlements with leaders living in a central area surrounded by the villagers' houses. They exported tobacco, salt, and handicrafts as far as the mainland.

The Spanish praised the Tainos' generosity. "They invite you to share anything that they possess, and show as much love as if their hearts went

▲ **This drawing by Gonzalo Fernández de Oviedo y Valdés shows the type of building in which Taino chiefs lived.**

with it," Columbus noted. He believed that they would make easy converts to the Catholic faith. But he also took the Tainos' generosity to mean that they "could all be subjugated [conquered] and compelled to do anything one wishes."

The search for gold. Because some of the Tainos wore gold ornaments, Columbus concluded that gold mines were close at hand. Over the next month Columbus and his men sailed from island to island—naming and claiming each for Spain—in search of gold. Then on Christmas Eve, 1492, the *Santa María* struck a coral reef off the island that Columbus had named Hispaniola—the site of present-day Haiti and the Dominican Republic. The crew was forced to abandon ship. Believing that the shipwreck was a sign from God, Columbus decided to establish the first Spanish colony here. He named the settlement La Navidad (The Nativity), in honor of the day of its founding.

Like the inhabitants of Guanahani, the Indians of Hispaniola were generous to the Spanish. Their chief, Guacanagarí (**gwah-KAHN-uh-gah-REE**), showered Columbus with gold nuggets and ornaments—even promising "a statue of pure gold" the size of Columbus himself. This impressive display convinced some of Columbus's men to remain in the settlement.

Columbus sailed back to Spain in January 1493, taking with him two dozen Taino captives and evidence of the riches of the Indies. Ferdinand and Isabella gave him a hero's welcome and speedily approved a second voyage.

The captive islanders were objects of both sympathy and curiosity. The queen ordered that the Indians on Hispaniola and elsewhere in the Americas be treated humanely and converted to the Roman Catholic faith. But she left open the possibility that anyone who resisted the authority of the Spanish Crown could be enslaved.

COLUMBUS THE COLONIZER

When Columbus returned to La Navidad 11 months later, he found the colony destroyed. All the Spaniards were dead or gone. Some probably had left to find gold elsewhere, but most either had fallen victim to illness or had died in disputes with one another or with the Tainos. Most likely, the colonists' excessive demands for gold and food had worn down the generosity of the Tainos, causing conflicts.

Columbus and some 1,500 male colonists—most of whom were craftsmen, builders, or farmers—built another settlement: Isabela. Columbus left the settlement under the care of his brother Bartolomé and spent the next three years sailing the Caribbean searching for gold. While Columbus was away, the pressure the colonists put on the Indians to provide food and gold led the Indians to revolt. Violent disputes over land and Indian labor also broke out between Bartolomé and the colonists. Columbus's failure to maintain order led to his eventual replacement as viceroy.

Before Columbus was replaced, he granted the colonists control over Indian labor. He thereby informally introduced to Hispaniola what would later become the *encomienda* (en-koh-mee-EN-duh) system. Under this system the colonists, or *encomenderos* (en-koh-muhn-DE-rohs), received the right to have a certain number of Indians work for them. The *encomenderos* used the Indians to mine gold, provide food, and build houses. The system required that the *encomenderos* instruct their charges in the Roman Catholic faith and permit them to grow food for themselves.

◀ **This scene, entitled "Baptism of the First Indians," is taken from a** *Conquista* **cloth.**

The First Voyage of Columbus

SAILING TO THE AMERICAS Christopher Columbus made four round-trip voyages to the Americas between 1492 and 1504.

? LOCATION On which voyage did Columbus visit Central America?

1 Aug. 3, 1492: First expedition sails from Palos, Spain

7 March 15, 1493: *Niña* and *Pinta* arrive at Palos

2 Aug. 12–Sept. 6, 1492: Layover in Canary Islands

Lands seen by Columbus and his crew

3 Oct. 12, 1492: Landfall on San Salvador

6 Jan. 16, 1493: *Niña* and *Pinta* set sail for Europe

4 Nov. 6, 1492: Existence of tobacco recorded

5 Dec. 25, 1492: *Santa Maria* grounded; La Navidad founded

Later Voyages

The Spanish Crown formally established the *encomienda* system in the Americas in 1503. In the monarchs' eyes Native Americans were not slaves—they were supposed to be paid a small allowance for their labor. But in practice the *encomienda* system amounted to enslavement for many Indians because they were seldom paid.

The *encomienda* also disrupted Indian economies and societies. Because of excessive Spanish demands for food and labor, Indians had little time to grow food for themselves. Widespread malnutrition resulted. The Spanish were thus able to take the most fertile pieces of land away from the Indians. The Spanish also disturbed Indian societies by weeding out Indian customs and religions.

■■ The *encomienda* system gave the Spanish control over Indian labor and disrupted Indian societies.

LAS CASAS AND SLAVERY

Some Spaniards protested the harsh treatment of Native Americans. One prominent critic, Bartolomé de Las Casas, had spent some years as

THE SLAVE TRADE

Nzinga Mbemba (en-ZING uhm-BEM-buh), **"Lord of the Congo,"** was a central-African ruler who hoped to increase contact and trade between the Congo states and the leading European powers. To aid this effort, he even adopted the Christian faith and assumed a new name: Dom Afonso. His dreams turned sour, however, as he watched Portuguese slave ships take more and more of his people by force to the Americas. In 1526 he urged King John III of Portugal to curb this practice:

> **"We** *cannot reckon how great the damage is, since the . . . [slave] merchants daily seize our subjects, sons of the land and sons of our noblemen and vassals and our relatives. . . . Thieves and men of evil conscience take them . . . and cause them to be sold: and so great, Sir, is their corruption . . . that our country is being utterly depopulated.* **"**

Afonso's pleas went unheeded, however. Spain and other European nations followed Portugal's lead. By 1600 several hundred thousand Africans were in bondage in the Americas.

---

an *encomendero* in Cuba. But after becoming a priest around 1512, he began to question the morality of the *encomienda* system. Eventually he gave up his *encomienda* and returned to Spain to plead the Indians' cause. In 1516 the Crown appointed him Protector of the Indians.

Las Casas described to European audiences how harshly the Spanish treated Native Americans and demanded an end to the *encomienda*. He urged Spanish colonists to live and work peacefully with Native Americans. He called for friars and priests to convert Indians to Catholicism gradually, through "love, gentleness, and kindness."

In the *Apologetic History of the Indies* (1566), Las Casas argued a radical idea for the time—that Indian humanity and wisdom equaled that of Europeans:

> **"** Not only have [the Indians] shown themselves to be very wise peoples and possessed of lively and marked understanding, . . . governing and providing for their nations . . . but they have equaled many diverse nations of the . . . past and present . . . and exceed by no small measure the wisest of all these. **"**

Las Casas argued for Indian rights at the same time that the Spanish king wanted to limit the growing independence of the colonists. To protect the Indians and to curb the colonists' power, the Spanish Crown enacted laws in 1542 restricting *encomiendas*.

◀ This illustration from an Aztec manuscript shows the devastating effects of smallpox on Native Americans. Smallpox, measles, and malaria were just a few diseases brought by Europeans that caused epidemics among Native American peoples.

The colonists refused to give up their control of Indian labor, however. The end of the *encomienda* would come not through the Crown's actions but through the catastrophic decline of the Native American population. The devastating effects of European diseases, overwork, and malnutrition reduced the Indian population in some areas by over 90 percent by the mid-16th century.

To replace the Indian laborers, the Spanish imported African slaves. By 1550 some 15,000 enslaved Africans had arrived in the Spanish colonies.

■■ **Las Casas urged the Spanish Crown to enact laws to end Spanish mistreatment of Native Americans.**

C O M M E N T A R Y

The Columbian Legacy

Historians offer different interpretations of Columbus's voyages to the Americas. Some have applauded him for enlarging geographic knowledge. Yet Columbus himself died without realizing he had encountered a continent. Columbus did not even get the honor of having the continent named after him. Another navigator, Amerigo Vespucci (ahm-ay-REE-goh vay-SPOOT-chee), received that honor. In 1507 the German mapmaker Martin Waldseemüller (VAHLT-zay-mool-uhr) credited Vespucci with the "discovery" of America and suggested the newly encountered continent be named America in his honor.

Other people have interpreted Columbus's voyages in a negative light. They blame him for introducing the encomienda system to the Americas and for the drastic reduction of the Native American population. But Columbus saw himself as a faithful Christian who had won new converts to Catholicism. Las Casas, the fierce Protector of the Indians, agreed.

With such conflicting interpretations of Columbus's significance, how can we judge his impact? Perhaps the best way to understand the legacy of Columbus's voyages is to see the enormous effect they had on the world. The transfer

THE COLUMBIAN EXCHANGE

THE AMERICAS

Plants
Corn, Potato, Tomato, Squash/Pumpkin, Peppers (Bell, Chili), Tobacco, Pineapple, Beans (Lima, Kidney, Navy, String), Cotton, Marigold, Wild Rice, Sunflower, Peanut, Pecan, Cashew, Cocoa Bean, Cassava/Tapioca

Animals
Turkey

Diseases
Syphilis

AFRICA, ASIA, & EUROPE

Plants
Wheat, Barley, Oats, Soybean, Peach, Pear, Sugar Cane, Rose, Onion, Okra, Coffee, Watermelon, Banana, Olive, Asian Rice, Lettuce

Animals
Horse, Cow, Hog, Sheep, Chicken

Diseases
Smallpox, Measles, Influenza, Diphtheria, Bubonic Plague, Whooping Cough, Malaria, Yellow Fever, Typhus, Cholera, Amoebic Dysentery

Sources: *Newsweek, Fall/Winter 1991; Columbus and the Age of Discovery*

TRANSFORMING THE WORLD Columbus's voyages initiated a global transformation involving the exchange of plants, animals, diseases, and people between Africa, Asia, and Europe and the Americas. This global transformation is called the Columbian exchange.

? **ASSESSING CONSEQUENCES** Research the origin of one of the plants, animals, or diseases on the chart and trace its impact on other countries.

of people, ideas, plants, animals, and diseases between the Americas, Europe, Asia, and Africa initiated by Columbus's journeys has come to be called the **Columbian exchange** (see chart on page 43).

The Columbian exchange transformed the world. As various cultures collided, they transformed each other. Precious metals and other resources taken from the Americas made many European nations wealthy and powerful. Exotic products from the Americas, such as corn, potatoes, and tomatoes, soon became staples for people everywhere.

Through settlement and the slave trade, the islands and continents formerly inhabited by only Native Americans were gradually peopled with Europeans, Africans, and Asians. But the Columbian exchange involved more than the transfer of crops and people. The introduction of European animals transformed the American landscape. Once cattle, sheep, and pigs arrived in the Americas, they multiplied rapidly in the abundant grazing lands.

The horse, introduced to the Americas by the Spanish by 1507, proved to be particularly suited to the Americas. At first, the horse terrified many Native Americans, but several groups used it to their advantage. The horse transformed the cultures of the Apaches and Comanches of North America. With the horse

these groups were able to give up their more difficult existence in the mountains and move onto the Great Plains. There, Native Americans hunted on horseback the plentiful buffalo, which became the cornerstone of their prosperous cultures.

The exchange also introduced deadly diseases—smallpox and measles from Europe and yellow fever and malaria from Africa. Because Native Americans lacked immunity, or resistance, to these diseases, many died. Historians have estimated that in some areas as much as 90 percent of the Native American population was wiped out. By 1600 practically all of the original inhabitants of the Caribbean were gone.

The tragic impacts of disease and military conquest on Native Americans and the introduction of slavery on Africans understandably overshadow many of the positive aspects of the Columbian exchange. But when determining the significance of Columbus's voyages, we must take into account the global transformation he initiated.

■■ The Columbian exchange resulted in the transfer of people, precious metals, crops, and animals between the Americas and Europe, Asia, and Africa.

SECTION 1 REVIEW

IDENTIFY and explain the significance of the following: Christopher Columbus, viceroy, Tainos, Guacanagarí, *encomienda*, Bartolomé de Las Casas, Columbian exchange.

LOCATE and explain the importance of the following: Bahamas, Hispaniola, La Navidad.

1. **MAIN IDEA** What did Columbus hope to find by sailing west from Europe?

2. **MAIN IDEA** How did the *encomienda* system benefit the Spanish settlers? What effect did it have on Native Americans?

3. **ASSESSING CONSEQUENCES** What reforms did Las Casas request on behalf of Native Americans? Why were the reforms of only limited success?

4. **WRITING TO EVALUATE** Write an essay examining the long-term effects of Columbus's voyages.

5. **USING HISTORICAL IMAGINATION** Imagine you are a Taino living on San Salvador. Draw a plan for a mural that portrays your interactions with the Spanish explorers.

Section 2

CONQUEST OF THE MAINLAND

F O C U S

- What were the Spanish explorers and the conquistadors seeking?
- What were the conquistadors' roles in building a Spanish empire in the Americas?
- How did Native Americans respond to the conquistadors?

*C*olumbus's claims fueled the rivalry between Spain and Portugal. To avoid open conflict, the two nations agreed to divide all non-Christian lands in the Western Hemisphere between themselves. Within decades Spanish adventurers had conquered the Aztecs of Mexico and the Incas of Peru and expanded Spain's colonial empire to include territory in North America.

Aztec soldier

EXPLORING THE AMERICAS

Portugal viewed Columbus's voyages as a threat to its control of the Atlantic. To settle the matter of boundaries, Spain and Portugal, both Catholic countries, agreed to divide control over any newly encountered lands. They signed the **Treaty of Tordesillas** (tawrd-uh-SEE-uhs) in 1494. This treaty drew an imaginary line of demarcation, or separation, around the world: territory explored west of the line would belong to Spain; east of the line, to Portugal.

Ferdinand Magellan, a Portuguese mariner sponsored by the Spanish Crown, explored the land west of the Line of Demarcation. Magellan set out in 1519 to find a westward route to Asia. After threading through the turbulent, narrow waterway at the southern tip of South America, Magellan sailed into the Pacific Ocean. In September 1522 the *Victoria*—the only ship remaining of Magellan's five-vessel fleet—sailed into the harbor near Cádiz (KAHD-iz), Spain. Captain Juan Sebastián de Elcano (el-KAHN-oh) and his 17 shipmates—the only survivors of the original 270-person expedition—thus became the first people to **circumnavigate**, or sail completely around, the world (see map below).

Other explorers focused on the lands of North America and South America, claiming them for Spain. In 1513 Vasco Núñez de Balboa (NOON-yays day bahl-BOH-uh) explored Panama and was probably the first European to glimpse the Pacific Ocean from the Americas. Juan Ponce de León (PAWN-say day lay-AWN) sought the mythical "Fountain of Youth" in Florida in 1513.

In the 1520s Pánfilo de Narváez (PAHM-fee-loh day nahr-BAH-ays) led an unsuccessful attempt to colonize North America's coastline along the Gulf of Mexico. A survivor of Narváez's

▲ **Magellan–Elcano Expedition**

expedition, Álvar Núñez Cabeza de Vaca (kah-BAY-sah day BAH-kah) explored much of present-day Texas, New Mexico, and Arizona. In 1539 another member of the expedition, Estevanico, an African, was the first non-Indian to visit the Pueblo Indians in present-day New Mexico. And in the 1540s Hernando de Soto explored southeastern North America and the Mississippi River, while Francisco Vásquez de Coronado marched through most of the present-day southwestern United States (see map on page 57).

ᴛHE SPANISH ENCOUNTER THE AZTECS

In the footsteps of the early explorers came the Spanish conquerors, known as **conquistadors** (kawng-KEES-tuh-dawrs). By the early 1500s Spanish soldiers had successfully expelled the Moors from Spain. These Spanish soldiers then set out to conquer the Americas and to gain riches for themselves. They also wanted to spread the Catholic religion throughout the world.

■■ **Spanish explorers and conquistadors sought wealth and glory and hoped to win new converts to Christianity.**

Among the most able and adventurous of the conquistadors was Hernán Cortés. A professional soldier in Spain, Cortés settled in Cuba as an *encomendero*. Intrigued by stories of gold on the Mexican mainland, Cortés gathered a force of

▲ In this mural, Hernán Cortés and Malintzin receive gifts from Aztec ambassadors.

some 600 Spaniards and African slaves and set sail in February 1519. On the Mexican coast he engaged Indians in battle. Cortés's army defeated the Indians, and through them he learned much about the wealthy Aztec Empire.

Among the Indians was a young Aztec woman, Malintzin (mah-LINT-suhn), called Doña Marina by the Spanish, who became Cortés's valuable interpreter and adviser. She described Aztec weaknesses to Cortés, explaining that many Indian groups hated the Aztecs. Most were being taxed heavily by the empire—forced to give up the best of their crops and handicrafts. Armed with this knowledge, Cortés set off to confront the Aztec ruler, Moctezuma II (MAWK-tay-SOO-mah).

BIO GRAPHY When Cortés set foot on the mainland, Moctezuma II had already ruled the Aztec Empire for 17 years. During his reign, he presided over the expansion of Aztec territory through military conquest and the vast extension of trade routes. Like his predecessors, he maintained strict control over Aztec subjects by requiring tribute.

Moctezuma learned of Cortés's arrival almost immediately. An Aztec scout had witnessed the Spanish defeat of the coastal Indians. He raced on foot to the capital city of Tenochtitlán to tell Moctezuma of the pale-skinned men who rode "deer" (horses) taller than a house. The scout

Moctezuma II

reported that these bearded strangers even had weapons (cannons) powerful enough to crack a hole in the side of a mountain!

The deeply religious ruler contemplated this amazing news. According to an ancient prophecy, a light-skinned god called Quetzalcoatl (ket-SAHL-kwaht-uhl) would one day return to rule over the Aztecs. Moctezuma feared that the prophecy was now coming true.

Moctezuma believed that the god's arrival would mean the end of his reign. Before Cortés had even arrived on the Mexican mainland, Moctezuma had been shaken by omens, such as the appearance of a brilliant comet, that he believed foretold the terrible destruction of his people. He sent gold and other gifts to Cortés to persuade him not to come to Tenochtitlán. Instead, the gifts made Cortés even more determined to conquer the Aztecs.

CORTÉS CONQUERS THE AZTECS

To defeat the Aztecs, Cortés knew he must increase the size of his army. With Malintzin's help, he recruited Indians who had been defeated by the Aztecs. As Cortés approached the Aztec capital, his army of Indian recruits grew to several thousand.

Moctezuma realized by this time that Cortés was not the god Quetzalcoatl. Hoping to save Tenochtitlán from destruction, however, the Aztec ruler welcomed Cortés as an honored guest. Cortés responded to this hospitable welcome by imprisoning Moctezuma. Cortés let Moctezuma retain his title—though not his power—as emperor of the Aztecs.

This fragile arrangement collapsed when Cortés temporarily left Tenochtitlán. In his absence his lieutenant, Pedro de Alvarado, ordered the killing of scores of men, women, and children attending an Aztec religious ceremony. The Aztecs saw Alvarado's actions as an unprovoked attack and fought back, forcing the Spanish to retreat to their quarters. When Cortés returned, he found things in chaos. In desperation he urged Moctezuma to try to calm his angry subjects. But the Aztecs no longer trusted their ruler. When Moctezuma attempted to intervene, he was killed—Spanish and Aztec sources dispute which side murdered the emperor.

With Moctezuma dead and the Aztecs in full revolt, the Spanish knew they had no choice but to leave the capital. They tried to escape during the middle of the night by crossing the main causeway over Lake Texcoco, but a woman drawing water sounded an alarm. Thousands of Aztecs attacked

▶ During *La Noche Triste*, the Aztecs forced the Spanish to retreat from Tenochtitlán across Lake Texcoco.

the Spanish. Though the Spanish managed to leave the city, heavy casualties resulted on both sides. While the Aztecs celebrated their victory, that night in 1520 is remembered in Spanish history as *La Noche Triste* (lah NOH-chay TREES-tay), the Night of Sorrow.

In the following months Cortés regrouped his forces and obtained reinforcements. In May 1521 he attacked Tenochtitlán. This time the whole Aztec population seemed determined to fight to the death. A four-month siege by the Spaniards, however, left the Aztecs worn out and starving. The Aztecs were also weakened by a smallpox epidemic that had swept through the city. On August 13 Cortés attacked, and the great city fell. Soon he controlled all of present-day central Mexico. An Aztec poet captured his people's sadness:

> 66 Broken spears lie in the roads;
> we have torn our hair in our grief.
> The houses are roofless now, and
>   their walls
> are red with blood. 99

After the conquest the Spanish leveled Aztec temples and other buildings, destroyed beautiful Aztec works of art, and melted down elaborate gold jewelry into bullion and shipped it to Spain. Over the ruins of Tenochtitlán, Cortés built Mexico City, the present-day capital of Mexico.

▶ This illustration by Felipe Guaman Poma de Ayala, a writer of Indian descent, satirizes the Spanish obsession with gold. When the Inca asks the Spaniard if he eats gold, the visitor replies, "Yes, we eat it."

▼ An assortment of Incan artifacts is shown here. Clockwise from right is a gold figurine, two drinking cups, and a shield with an image of the Incan corn god.

Cortés lived like a king within the conquered region. In 1522 the Spanish Crown appointed him viceroy. By the 1530s he was probably the wealthiest person in Spanish America. As for the Aztec people, they had fallen victim to the *encomienda* system.

PIZARRO CONQUERS THE INCAS

The Incan Empire, centered in the Andes Mountains of South America, became Spain's next target for conquest. In 1531 Francisco Pizarro (pee-SAHR-roh), a Spanish soldier and treasure hunter, led a small army to the very heart of the empire. Traveling cautiously along steep, narrow passes that snaked through rugged, snowcapped peaks, they reached the town of Cajamarca (kah-huh-MAHR-kuh) in present-day northern Peru.

Pizarro lured the Incan ruler, Atahuallpa (ah-tah-WAHL-pah), to his camp. A Spanish priest told Atahuallpa that the Incas must convert to Catholicism. Atahuallpa asked to see the book—the Bible—that "spoke" their god's words. According to an Incan account:

> 66 [Atahuallpa] took the book and began to leaf through its pages. And the Inca said, "Why does it not speak to me? This book tells me nothing!" And . . . [Atahuallpa] Inca threw the book from his hands. 99

The outraged Spaniards attacked the Indians and captured Atahuallpa.

To gain his freedom, Atahuallpa promised to fill his large prison quarters with gold and silver. Desperate to save their emperor-god, the Incas delivered a large ransom in gold and silver. Pizarro accepted the ransom but ordered Atahuallpa killed, not freed.

◀ Rumors of a gold-rich empire drew Francisco Pizarro to western South America, which he explored in the 1520s. Pizarro went to Spain in 1528 and convinced the Spanish king to authorize the conquest of the Incas.

The Mansell Collection

At the time of Pizarro's arrival in Cajamarca, the Incas were divided by an internal dispute. One group allied with Pizarro, and the other group retreated to a remote area of the Andes, where they held out against the Spanish for many years. But control of the vast South American empire finally passed into Spanish hands. Pizarro ruled until 1541, when he was murdered by one of his own men.

■■ **By conquering the Aztecs and the Incas, the conquistadors added vast territory and wealth to the Spanish American empire.**

▲ **This illustration, drawn sometime between 1540 and 1541, shows Native Americans from southern Mexico fleeing from the conquistadors.**

POSTCONQUEST INDIAN SOCIETY

To maintain control over the conquered Indians, the Spanish went to great lengths to wipe out Native American cultures. They tore down Indian temples, destroyed Indian art, and reorganized Indian settlements. Native American cultures were not completely destroyed, however; they live on in the people and customs of most modern Latin American nations.

Native Americans often took up arms against the Spanish to defend their lives, lands, and religions. Some fought the Spanish to the death. Others, worn down by superior Spanish weaponry or by the unbearable toll of disease, came to terms with a force they could not drive out. Some found ways to escape or make the best of Spanish rule.

For example, the Mayas in southern Mexico fled to the interior of the Yucatán (yoo-kuh-TAN) Peninsula. Others allied themselves with the Spanish and negotiated a place for themselves in the new social order.

Survival usually meant the mixing of Spanish and Native American peoples and cultures. For example, many Indians developed a new religion by mixing their rituals with Catholic rituals. Over time both Native Americans and Spaniards adopted elements of the other's language and customs. Eventually, there emerged a new culture that blended ingredients of Native American and Spanish ways of life.

■■ **The Spanish won official control over the Indians. Native Americans, however, developed ways to ensure their survival.**

SECTION 2 REVIEW

IDENTIFY and explain the significance of the following: Treaty of Tordesillas, Ferdinand Magellan, Juan Sebastián de Elcano, circumnavigate, Vasco Núñez de Balboa, Juan Ponce de León, Álvar Núñez Cabeza de Vaca, Estevanico, Hernando de Soto, Francisco Vásquez de Coronado, conquistadors, Hernán Cortés, Malintzin, Moctezuma II, Francisco Pizarro, Atahuallpa.

LOCATE and explain the importance of the following: Line of Demarcation.

1. **MAIN IDEA** Why did the Spanish explorers and conquistadors come to the Americas?

2. **MAIN IDEA** How did the conquistadors help Spain build an empire in the Americas?

3. **MAIN IDEA** What were some of the strategies Native Americans used to protect their ways of life?

4. **WRITING TO CREATE** Imagine you are an Aztec whose son or daughter has died fighting the Spanish. Write a poem describing why he or she fought.

5. **HYPOTHESIZING** Why do you think the Spaniards tore down Aztec temples? What impact do you think this had on Aztec religion?

THE SPANISH SETTLE THE AMERICAS

FOCUS

- **What was the extent of Spanish settlement in North America?**
- **How did missions and estates help establish Spanish rule in the Americas?**
- **What elements of their culture did Spanish colonists introduce to the Americas?**

Statue of the Virgin Mary, called *La Conquistadora*, taken to New Mexico in 1626

𝒯he explorations and conquests of Cortés, Pizarro, and others enabled Spain to claim vast portions of the Americas. For the next two centuries, the Spanish fanned out from Mexico City—the heart of their American empire—and from their island colonies in the Caribbean. Armed with the soldier's sword and the priest's cross, they set out to find riches and spread the Roman Catholic faith.

𝓕LORIDA

By the early 1500s the Spanish already had turned their attention to La Florida, the entire eastern seaboard from present-day Florida to Newfoundland. Because Spanish ships from the Caribbean often sailed up the Atlantic coast on

▲ **Settlers in St. Augustine tried to maintain Spanish culture and customs.**

their way back to Europe, Spain wanted to establish settlements to provide safe harbors.

One of the first attempts to establish a permanent settlement in Florida took place in 1526. Lucas Vázquez Ayllón (yl-YAWN) led some 500 colonists from Hispaniola to a site on the coast of present-day South Carolina. The expedition, which included families, missionaries, and African slaves, built San Miguel de Gualdape (gwahl-DAHP-ay), but the colony did not survive the first winter. Sick and too weak to farm or to catch fish, nearly two thirds of the settlers perished. The others straggled home in early 1527.

Farther south along the Florida coast, settlers again had trouble establishing a colony. Native American groups living in the area—such as the Timucuas (tim-uh-KOO-uhs), Calusas, and Apalachees—fought the Spanish to keep them from settling in the area. In 1565, however, an expedition led by Pedro Menéndez de Avilés (may-NAYN-days day ah-bee-LAYS) succeeded in planting a permanent settlement in Florida. This was St. Augustine, the oldest city established by Europeans in what is now the United States.

◄ The Pueblo Indians skillfully decorated pottery with beautiful symbols and designs.

Museum of Indian Arts and Culture, Santa Fe

NEW MEXICO AND ARIZONA

In 1609, some 1,500 miles west of St. Augustine, Pedro de Peralta (pay-RAHL-tah), the newly appointed governor of New Mexico, established its capital at Santa Fe. From this outpost the Spanish maintained a fragile hold on the northernmost borderland of New Spain for more than 200 years.

The Pueblo Indians and the Spanish struggled bitterly for control of this area, however. The Pueblos resented Spanish demands that they pay taxes and that they convert to Catholicism. In 1680 the Pueblos temporarily drove the Spanish out of Santa Fe. Under the leadership of Popé (poh-PAY), a Pueblo prophet, the Pueblos launched a series of attacks. By the time the **Pueblo Revolt** of 1680 was over, some 400 Spaniards lay dead, and some 2,000 settlers had fled south.

After the Spanish were driven out, according to Pueblo witnesses:

66 Popé . . . ordered . . . that they instantly break up and burn . . . everything pertaining to Christianity. . . . They were ordered likewise not to teach the Castilian [Spanish] language in any pueblo and to burn the seeds which the Spaniards sowed and to plant only maize and beans, which were the crops of their ancestors. 99

Popé hoped that by destroying all traces of Spanish culture, the Pueblos could reestablish their own customs and way of life. But the Pueblos regained control of their territory only temporarily. In the 1690s New Mexico's new governor, Diego de Vargas, reestablished Spanish rule. At the same time, the Spanish began moving into Arizona. Father Eusebio Kino (ay-oo-SAYB-yoh KEE-noh) built missions near present-day Nogales (noh-GAL-uhs) in 1687 and Tucson in 1700. He also explored the southern reaches of the Colorado River.

During the 1700s the fear of French and British expansion prompted the Spanish to speed up their colonization of Arizona and New Mexico. They established *presidios* (forts), missions, villages, towns, and large ranches across the region. The Spanish influence found today throughout the southwestern United States dates from this period.

TEXAS

Despite the early explorations of Cabeza de Vaca and others, Spanish settlement in present-day Texas proceeded slowly. The first permanent Spanish colony was founded at Ysleta (i-ZLAYT-uh) in 1681 by settlers driven from New Mexico by the Pueblo Revolt.

By 1690 France's colonizing activity in North America spurred Spain to strengthen its hold on Texas. The San Francisco de los Tejas mission was established near the Neches (NECH-uhz) River in 1690, and the San Antonio de Valero mission was built in 1718. A few other settlements emerged along the lower Rio Grande, but lack of mineral resources and constant raids by the Apaches and the Comanches slowed settlement.

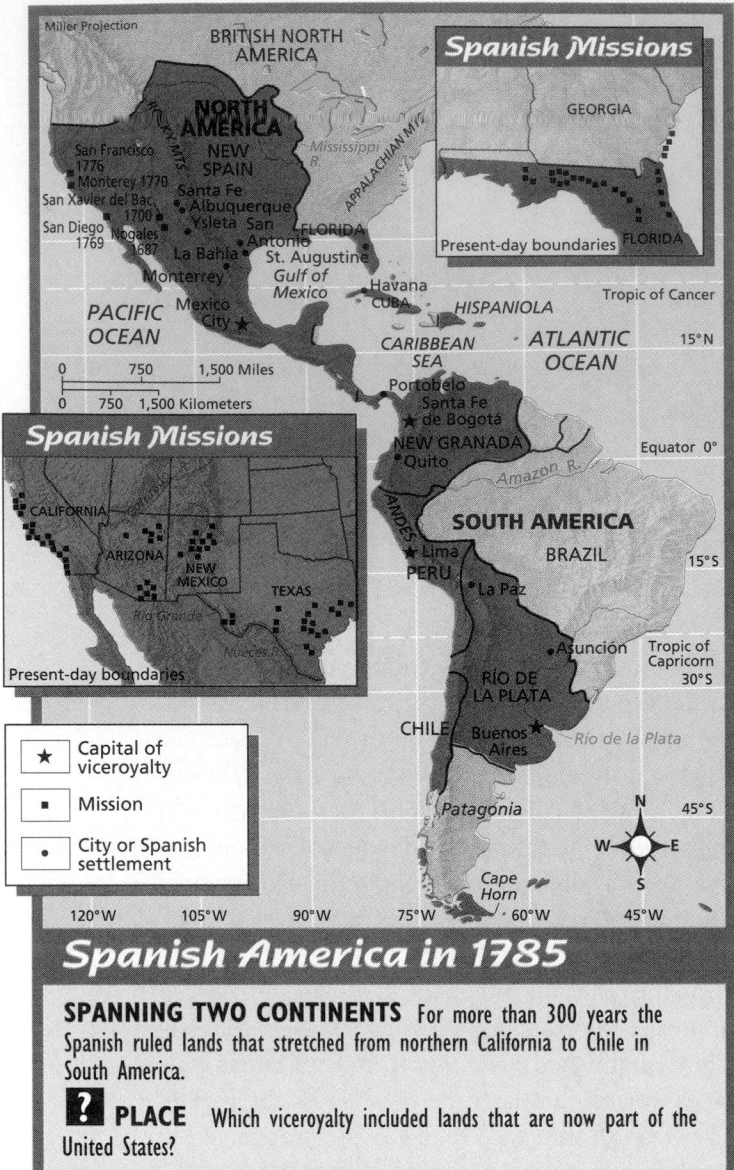

Spanish America in 1785

SPANNING TWO CONTINENTS For more than 300 years the Spanish ruled lands that stretched from northern California to Chile in South America.

❓ PLACE Which viceroyalty included lands that are now part of the United States?

CALIFORNIA

California was the last of Spain's northern territories to be colonized. Juan Rodríguez Cabrillo (kah-BREE-yoh) explored much of the California coastline for Spain as early as 1542. But not until the late 1700s did Spain, alarmed by Russian explorations in northern California, attempt to set up permanent settlements. In 1769 Gaspar de Portolá (pawr-toh-LAH) founded San Diego. Seven years later (as the British colonies on the eastern seaboard were declaring their independence) Juan Bautista de Anza (bow-TEE-stah day AHN-sah) founded San Francisco.

Friar Junípero Serra (hoo-NEE-pay-roh SER-rah), a scholarly Franciscan missionary, came to

California with de Portolá's expedition. Serra founded a mission at San Diego, and by the time of his death in 1784, he had founded eight more missions along the Pacific coast.

■■ **Beginning in the mid-1500s, Spain established settlements from coast to coast in what is now the continental United States.**

SPANISH AMERICA

By 1780 Spanish America was one of the largest colonial empires the world had ever known. Within its vast borders were lands of rich geographic diversity—from the coastal lowlands of Florida and the arid lands and mountains of northern Mexico to the rain forests of Panama and the Andean heights of Peru.

To oversee this huge and diverse empire, Spain organized it into viceroyalties. The first two viceroyalties established were New Spain and Peru. Each was governed by a viceroy, who acted as the king's representative and supervised lesser officials.

Colonial government worked better in theory than in practice, though. Orders issued by the Crown or the Catholic church in Spain had to be carried by messenger thousands of miles—first by ship and then by horseback or by foot—to the outposts of the empire. Government officials in Spanish America often became impatient with the delays and made their own decisions. Officials who ignored orders and laws were rarely penalized, however. Colonists, especially those in the remote corners of the empire, usually organized their own settlements and exercised some independence in local government.

Missions. The mission was one form of settlement established by the Spanish in the Americas. Historians have counted more than 150 Spanish missions founded in the present-day United States. At the center of each mission stood a simple church. Surrounding the church were living quarters and workshops where "mission Indians" worked at weaving, blacksmithing, and other crafts. In fields nearby, missionaries and Native Americans raised cattle and grew grain, grapes, and other crops.

The missionaries labored to win the Native Americans to Catholicism, to teach them Spanish ways, and to make them loyal Spanish subjects. But in their zeal they suppressed Indian culture and enforced a harsh labor system resembling the *encomienda*. Resentful of forced labor and harsh discipline, many Indians fled from the missions. Many others died from European diseases against which they had no immunity.

Haciendas and *ranchos*. Outside the missions the Spanish government divided the land into farming and ranching estates. Haciendas, some consisting of hundreds of thousands of acres, were the largest; smaller farms and ranches were called *ranchos*.

Peons, or landless laborers, most of whom were Indians, worked on the haciendas. In theory, hacienda owners paid the peons, who were free to come and go as they wished. In reality, however, many land owners kept the workers bound to the land by debts. Hacienda owners made the peons purchase daily necessities from the hacienda store, sometimes at inflated prices. Before they could seek employment elsewhere, workers had to pay off their debts—an impossible task for many. In addition, children often had to assume the debts of their deceased parents.

Most owners of *ranchos* lived on their land and worked alongside their laborers. The Spaniards who drove the cattle on haciendas and *ranchos* were excellent horsemen called *vaqueros* (vah-KER-ohs). Familiar words like *lasso, rodeo,* and *corral* originated with the *vaqueros,* whose life-style became a model for later North American cowboys.

▲ **A Mexican hacienda owner, his wife, an overseer, and a *vaquero* are shown in this watercolor from the early 1830s.**

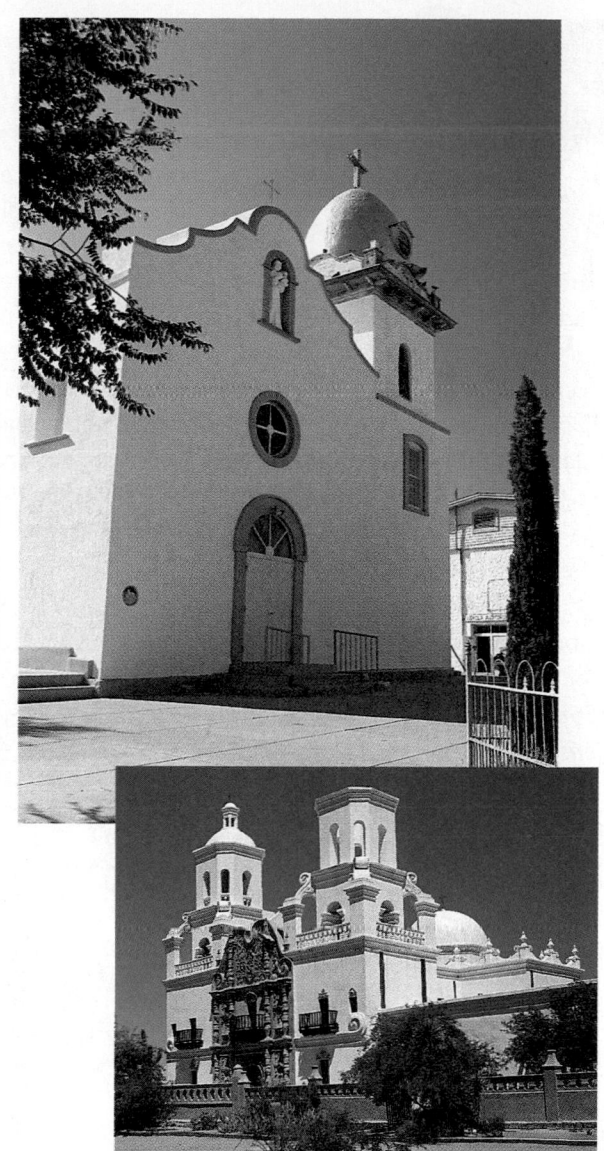

▲ **Ysleta Indian Mission (top) in Texas and San Xavier del Bac Mission (bottom) in Arizona are two examples of Spanish architecture.**

■ **Missions, haciendas, and *ranchos* established Spanish control over Indian labor and land.**

Colonial life. People living on haciendas, in missions, and in the bustling cities of Spanish America developed a unique social structure. *Peninsulares* (pay-nin-soo-LAHR-uhs), Spaniards born in Spain, and *criollos* (kree-OH-yohs), Spaniards born in the colonies, held the most privileged positions in the Americas. Most lived in huge houses with many servants and owned businesses and haciendas. Spaniards held high government positions and studied law, theology, or medicine.

In 1521 Hernán Cortés first laid eyes on Cuernavaca (kwer-nuh-VAHK-uh), an Indian town some 50 miles south of Mexico City. The lush orchards and fertile valleys surrounding the town so captivated Cortés that he secured five *encomiendas* in the area. These *encomienda* grants gave him control of the labor of tens of thousands of Indians. By the mid-1530s, Spaniards controlled 30 *encomiendas* in the region and close to 180,000 Indians.

As in most of Central America and South America, the *encomienda* Indians around Cuernavaca were forced to work long hours in the fields of Spanish estates and in the mines. Indian laborers built mills, churches, roads, and even a huge palace for Cortés. The Indians provided Cortés and the other *encomenderos* with gold and daily necessities like food and wood for fuel. They also wove textiles and grew crops such as sugar, wheat, and corn, which the *encomenderos* sold for a large profit.

Today, Hernán Cortés would scarcely recognize Cuernavaca. As the capital of the Mexican state of Morelos, it is home to some 230,000 people. Cortés's palace is now a tourist attraction. No longer surrounded by fields and orchards, its modern neighbor

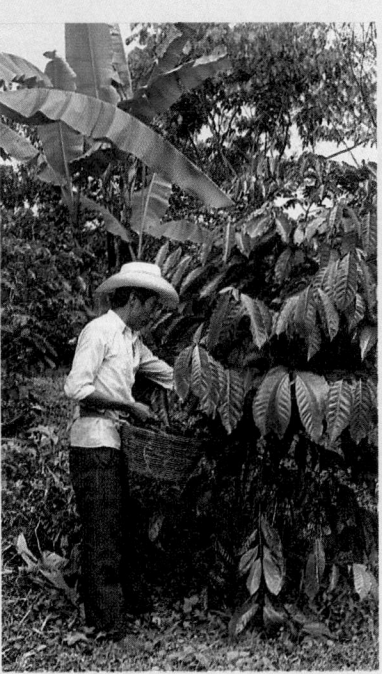

▲ **A Guatemalan plantation worker harvests coffee in southern Mexico.**

is, instead, a huge industrial complex. In fact, today in the entire state of Morelos, only about 30 percent of the population is involved in agriculture. Most of the old haciendas have been turned into hotels or spas for tourists.

Though many changes have come to Cuernavaca since 1521, remnants of the *encomienda* system endure. The Indians still lack control over major economic resources. Much of the agricultural land around the city remains divided into large estates owned mostly by wealthy families of European descent but worked mainly by Indians and *mestizos*. This situation persists despite both the Indian farmers' protests and the Mexican government's attempts at land reform. In industry as well, the descendants of the *encomienda* Indians toil in the new factories, the vast majority of which they neither own nor control. This is the social legacy of the *encomienda* system, not only in Cuernavaca but in much of the rest of former Spanish America.

Below the Spaniards were *mestizos* (me-STEE-zohs), men and women born of European-Indian unions. If they looked more Spanish than Indian or were related to important Spanish families, *mestizos* could aspire to the highest positions in Spanish American society. But most *mestizos* lived modestly as artisans, estate supervisors, traders, or shopkeepers. Roughly equal in status to *mestizos* were mulattoes (people of African-European ancestry).

At the bottom of the social structure were Indians, Africans, and *zambos* (people of Indian-African ancestry). These groups were legally prevented from holding public office and certain jobs. Most Indians were farmers or farm laborers, though some worked as tavern keepers, wagon drivers, or sailors. Most African slaves worked as hacienda supervisors or as artisans.

Women's roles were also determined by race or family background. Spanish women—who made up only 5 to 17 percent of migrants in the early 1500s—maintained a degree of economic independence because they could own property in their own names. Many also managed family businesses, either with their husbands or, if widowed, by themselves.

Many wealthy Spanish women were taught, at home or at convent schools, to read, write, sew, and cook. But the majority of Spanish American women could not read. They were also discouraged from pursuing higher education. Juana Inés de la Cruz, a noted Mexican poet in the late 17th century, described her efforts to receive an education:

The Granger Collection, New York

▲ This 18th–century painting shows a *mestizo* family in Mexico.

66 When I was six or seven and already knew how to read and write, . . . I discovered that in the City of Mexico there was a university . . . and as soon as I learned this I began to deluge [overwhelm] my mother with urgent and insistent pleas to change my manner of dress . . . so that I might study and take courses at the university. She refused . . . ; nevertheless, I found a way to read many different books my grandfather owned. 99

Cruz later entered a convent, a common practice for women who wanted to have the freedom for religious contemplation and study.

Indian, African, and Spanish-Indian women had even fewer opportunities to receive a formal education. Most women were taught useful skills at home such as cooking, pottery making, and weaving. This childhood training allowed them to own and run their own shops, produce clothes or textiles, sell food in markets, work as maids, or serve as midwives.

■■ Colonists brought Spanish government, architecture, and customs to the Americas.

SECTION 3 REVIEW

IDENTIFY and explain the significance of the following: Lucas Vázquez Ayllón, Pedro Menéndez de Avilés, Pedro de Peralta, Popé, Pueblo Revolt, Father Eusebio Kino, Juan Rodríguez Cabrillo, Friar Junípero Serra, peons, Juana Inés de la Cruz.

LOCATE and explain the importance of the following: St. Augustine, Santa Fe, Nogales, Ysleta, San Diego, San Francisco.

1. **MAIN IDEA** Where and when did Spanish colonists found settlements in North America?

2. **MAIN IDEA** How did the Spanish use missions and estates to administer their empire in the Americas?

3. **MAIN IDEA** What elements of Spanish culture were transplanted to Spanish America?

4. **WRITING TO INFORM** You are putting on a play about the residents of St. Augustine. Write a short script that presents the lives of *peninsulares, mestizos,* and *zambos.*

5. **IDENTIFYING CAUSE AND EFFECT** What Spanish actions led to the Pueblo Revolt?

THE ENGLISH IN NORTH AMERICA

FOCUS

- Why was the defeat of the Spanish Armada important?
- How did the English method of colonization differ from the Spanish method?
- How did the Jamestown colonists survive and prosper?
- How did the growth of Jamestown affect Native Americans' relationships with the settlers?

In the 1500s the Spanish began settling North America. At the same time, other European nations—especially England and France—began claiming large areas of the continent. However, since the French and the English were more concerned with events in Europe, it was nearly a century before these nations successfully colonized North America.

English pamphlet promoting colonization in 1609

EARLY CLAIMS

European contact with the Americas actually began well before Columbus. In the 11th century the Viking explorer Leif Eriksson sighted and temporarily settled parts of northeastern North America. Several Viking adventurers followed him. There are tales of earlier sightings and landings by Irish, Portuguese, African, and other sailors. But none established permanent colonies in the Americas.

Shortly after Columbus's first voyage, other mariners searched for a route to Asia. Another seafarer from Genoa, John Cabot, sailed along the coasts of what are now Newfoundland, Nova Scotia, and New England, first in 1497 and again in 1498. Cabot claimed these lands for England, which had backed his venture. In return he received a small payment and some trade privileges—little reward for the explorer who gave England its first claim in North America.

Geographic knowledge of the Americas slowly grew. Balboa's sighting of the Pacific Ocean and Magellan's voyage around the tip of South America sent explorers seeking a northern route—a **northwest passage**—to the Pacific and thus to Asia. Many European claims in North America resulted from failed attempts to find such a passage.

French claims to North America were based on the voyages of Giovanni da Verrazano (vayr-raht-SAHN-oh) and Jacques Cartier (kahr-TYAY). Verrazano, an Italian, failed in 1524 to find a

▲ **The Vikings are believed to have sighted the North American mainland as early as 986.**

European Exploration of North America

THE LURE OF RICHES European explorers sought both a northern trade route to the spices of Asia and cities of gold in North America.

? MOVEMENT Which European explorer first traveled down the St. Lawrence River? In which year was the Gulf of Mexico first explored?

Legend:
- English exploration
- French exploration
- Spanish exploration
- Dutch exploration
- English settlement
- French settlement
- Spanish settlement

westward route to Asia. But he did claim for France lands along the North American coast. Ten years later, Cartier explored the Gulf of St. Lawrence and the St. Lawrence River as far west as present-day Montreal. Cartier's attempts to start a settlement were unsuccessful, but his efforts strengthened French claims to what is now Canada.

The European powers thus made claims to North American territory early in the 1500s but did not establish permanent colonies. At that time most European countries were more concerned with trade with Asia than with organized efforts to settle the Americas.

Another reason for the delay in colonization efforts was the religious upheaval known as the **Protestant Reformation**. The Reformation began in Germany in 1517, when Martin Luther, a German monk, protested against corruption in the Roman Catholic church. Protests quickly spread to other European countries. As a result, a number of Protestant churches were established as alternatives to Catholicism.

This conflict between Protestants and Catholics became not only a religious struggle but also a territorial and political one. For a time the Reformation commanded Europe's attention.

France, for example, was too involved with a civil war (1562–1598) between Catholics and Protestants to follow up on its claims to Canada until the 1600s.

During the Reformation, Spain, the most powerful nation in Europe, clung to the Catholic faith. But other countries, such as England, officially became Protestant states. This division led to a drawn-out conflict between the two groups as each tried to achieve religious and political dominance in Europe.

ENGLAND CHALLENGES SPAIN

The earliest European challenges to Spain's American empire came in the late 1500s. European pirates—especially the English "sea dogs"—began attacking Spanish galleons as they left the Americas and seizing their cargoes of treasure.

One of the most successful sea dogs was Francis Drake. In 1577 Drake ventured from England with a fleet of swift, heavily armed vessels on a voyage of exploration and piracy. After sailing through the Strait of Magellan at the southern tip of South America, he turned north. Off the western coast of South America, Drake attacked Spanish ships carrying silver from the mines of Peru. With his vessels loaded with Spanish riches, he sailed along the Pacific coast of North America and slowly made his way home to England.

Queen Elizabeth I welcomed Drake as a hero, knighting him on the deck of his treasure-laden ship, the *Golden Hind*. The queen's action angered King Philip II of Spain, who viewed it as a defiant challenge to Spanish power.

King Philip decided to strike back. He assembled a massive force of some 130 ships and 30,000 men, known as the **Spanish Armada**, to invade England. In 1588 most of the Armada sailed to the port of Calais, France, just across the Strait of Dover from England. There they waited for additional troops.

The Spanish navy had a reputation in Europe for having large, well-armed ships. But England's sea captains skillfully used the speed of their smaller ships to great advantage. They loaded eight of their ships with gunpowder, set them afire, and propelled the burning ships toward the Armada. The heavy Spanish vessels could not get out of the way in time. Many caught fire or were blown up. The rest of the Armada was driven out to sea. As the Spanish ships attempted to escape, they were smashed by a furious storm. Only about half of the original fleet made it home to Spain.

The year 1588 was a turning point in history. The defeat of the Armada revealed Spanish military weaknesses. By the 17th century, Spanish economic weaknesses also became apparent. With tons of colonial silver flowing into its treasury, Spain seemed quite prosperous. But the prosperity was deceptive. The Spanish used most of the silver to buy goods from other countries. John Campbell, an English writer, explained:

> 66 [Spanish] galleons bring the silver into Spain, but . . . it runs out as fast as it comes in. . . . The silver . . . and very little of the goods or manufactures . . . belong to the subjects of the crown of Spain. It is evident, therefore, . . . that the greatest part of the returns from the West Indies belong to . . . [foreigners]. 99

The steady flow of silver caused **inflation**, or an increase in prices, throughout Europe. When the flow of silver slowed in the 17th century, Spain found itself with few resources to buy imported goods.

In order to launch the Armada, the Spanish government had taken out loans. These debts, and the weak Spanish economy, prevented Spain from launching new plans for further American colonization. The way was thus open for the English, the French, and the Dutch to begin colonization.

◀ **The faster English ships outmaneuvered the ships of the Spanish Armada.**

▪▪ The defeat of the Spanish Armada marked the start of England's power in the Americas.

ENGLAND'S FIRST ATTEMPTS AT COLONIZATION

Even before the defeat of the Spanish Armada, English adventurers had planned to colonize the lands claimed by Cabot and others. They were eager to develop commerce with the Americas as Spain had done.

Royal permission to start an English colony first went to a soldier, Sir Humphrey Gilbert. In 1583 he sailed to Newfoundland, but on the return journey he and his ship were lost in a storm. The following year Queen Elizabeth extended the permit to Gilbert's half-brother, Sir Walter Raleigh, who explored the Atlantic seaboard for a suitable site to colonize. He named the area that he chose Virginia, in honor of Elizabeth, the "Virgin Queen."

In 1585 Raleigh sent a small group of settlers to Virginia. They settled on Roanoke Island, off the coast of present-day North Carolina. After almost a year of hardship, the colonists returned to England. In 1587 Raleigh tried again, sending 117 people, including women and children, under the command of John White. After establishing a new Roanoke colony, White headed back to England for additional supplies.

Events in Europe—such as the attack on the Spanish Armada, which interrupted all English shipping—delayed White's return. When he finally reached Roanoke in 1590, all he found were the words CRO and CROATOAN carved into trees near the original settlement. "Croatoan" was the Native American name for an island off the coast. Searchers found no other trace of the colonists. The fate of the "Lost Colony" remains a mystery.

In 1606 the English again attempted to colonize Virginia. Unlike the Spanish government, which organized settlements in the Americas, the English government did not play a direct role in colonization. King James I issued the **Charter of 1606**, which licensed two merchant groups to orga-

▲ This map of Virginia was drawn by John Smith and appeared in his 1624 book, *General historie of Virginia*.

▲ This detail is from a supply list that was issued to all prospective colonists interested in settling in Virginia.

nize settlements in Virginia. The two groups, the Plymouth Company and the London Company, were **joint-stock companies**, which operated somewhat like corporations do today. Investors shared the cost of starting and maintaining the company; they also shared any profits or losses.

The Charter of 1606 gave the Plymouth and London companies the right to establish settlements in North America and "to dig, mine, and search for all manner of mines of gold, silver, and copper." No doubt everyone pictured the tantalizing treasures Spain had discovered in its American colonies. Like the Spanish before them, the English did not consider the land rights of Native Americans already living in the region they called Virginia.

■■ Great Britain, unlike Spain, played an indirect role in settling its American colonies.

THE EXPERIMENT AT JAMESTOWN

The first settlers—some 100 men provisioned by the London Company—reached Virginia in the spring of 1607. Sailing along Chesapeake Bay, they noted the "fair meddowes and goodly tall Trees, with Fresh-waters running through the woods." They chose a location near one of these rivers. In honor of their king, they named the settlement Jamestown.

The early years. Unfortunately, Jamestown rested on a low, wooded peninsula near a marsh infested with disease-carrying mosquitoes. Disease, exposure to the elements, or starvation—the settlers had arrived too late to plant a crop—killed many people the first year. After seven months only some 30 settlers were still alive. One survivor, George Percy, recalled:

> 66 Our men were destroyed with cruell diseases . . . but for the most part they died of meere famine. There were never Englishmen left in a forreigne Countrey in such miserie as wee were in this new dis-covered Virginia. 99

The colonists' situation was made worse by the decisions of the directors of the London Company. Hoping for quick returns on their invest-ment, the directors insisted that the settlers concen-trate on searching for gold. This demand proved foolhardy since there was no gold. Precious time that could have gone toward building better shel-ters and cultivating crops was therefore wasted.

The result was an appalling loss of lives. During the first three years, most of the Virginia settlers died. The death toll might have been higher had it not been for Captain John Smith. An adven-turous soldier, explorer, and mapmaker, Smith was elected president of the council of settlers in 1608. He called off the fruitless hunt for gold and imposed harsh discipline. He ordered wells dug, new shelters built, land cleared, and crops planted.

The help of the local Indians, whom the English called "Powhatans," pre-vented total disaster. The Powhatans, actually a large confederation of some 30 small tribes under the leadership of Wahunsonacock (wah-hoohn-SUH-nuh-kahk), were skilled in agriculture and fishing. The Powhatans gave the settlers food and taught them how to cultivate corn—a crop with which the English were not familiar.

George Percy described the relief brought by the Powhatans: "Bread, Corn, Fish, and Flesh in great plenty; which was the setting up

▲ **This Powhatan robe, made of tanned deerskin and decorated with shells, was possibly worn by Wahunsonacock.**

▲ **This portrait of Pocahontas at age 21 was painted shortly after her arrival in London in 1616.**

[reviving] of our feeble men: otherwise we had all perished." Pocahontas, the daughter of Wahunsonacock, also helped the English colonists. She delivered dried corn to them and established trade between the colonists and the Native Americans.

However, relations with the Powhatans were strained when Smith returned to England. Desperate for food in the harsh winter of 1609–10, the English raided local Native American villages—stealing food, burning down shelters, and killing many of the Indians. Wahunsonacock sought a truce, saying:

> 66 Why will you take by force what you may obtain by love? Why will you destroy us who supply you with food? What can you get by war? . . . We are unarmed, and willing to give you what you ask, if you come in a friendly manner. 99

Conflicts between colonists and Native Americans continued. In 1614 an uneasy truce was reached when Pocahontas married John Rolfe, an English colonist.

Tobacco and prosperity. But additional conflicts arose over the crop that would bring the colony economic prosperity—tobacco. The prof-itable cultivation of tobacco requires large amounts of land. The English settlers saw the abundant land around them as theirs for the tak-ing, since the Native Americans seemed to not fully use it. The Indians, however, wished to leave the lands uncultivated as hunting grounds.

When Jamestown was settled in 1607, the Caribbean islands produced all the tobacco imported to Europe. John Rolfe challenged this monopoly in 1612 by successfully adapting the desirable Caribbean tobacco to Virginia. Soon the colonists were shipping large quantities of it to England. The success of the crop allowed Virginia to grow and prosper.

The Granger Collection, New York

▲ Women were sent to Virginia and sold as wives to male settlers.

▪▪ Jamestown thrived with John Smith's leadership, the Powhatans' help, and profitable tobacco cultivation.

To provide laborers for tobacco cultivation, Jamestown's backers introduced headrights: 50 acres of land for anyone who paid for workers to come to Jamestown. They also set up a new arrangement for bringing settlers to Jamestown: indentured servitude. An **indentured servant** was bound for a period of years to the person who paid his or her way to America. At first, most of those who survived their term of service (far from a certainty in Jamestown) acquired land to work for themselves. Most historians believe that the first Africans to settle in the English colonies came as indentured servants.

Warfare with Native Americans. As Jamestown's population grew, the colonists' tobacco farms expanded onto Indian hunting grounds. Native Americans viewed the taking of their lands as an act of war.

In the spring of 1622, Indians attacked Jamestown's outlying farmhouses, killing some 350 settlers—including John Rolfe—and burning most of the buildings. The English struck back fiercely. They even concluded one "peace conference" by murdering some 200 Native Americans with poisoned wine. These actions brought an end to attempts at mutual understanding between the settlers and the Indians.

▪▪ Jamestown's prosperity attracted hundreds of new settlers. The colonists' demands for additional land brought them into violent conflict with Native Americans.

SECTION 4 REVIEW

IDENTIFY and explain the significance of the following: John Cabot, northwest passage, Giovanni da Verrazano, Jacques Cartier, Protestant Reformation, Francis Drake, Spanish Armada, inflation, Sir Walter Raleigh, Charter of 1606, Powhatans, Wahunsonacock, Pocahontas, indentured servant.

LOCATE and explain the importance of the following: St. Lawrence River, Roanoke, Jamestown.

1. **MAIN IDEA** What did the defeat of the Spanish Armada mean to Europe and to North America?

2. **MAIN IDEA** How did Native Americans first respond to the settlers at Jamestown? Why did relations worsen?

3. **GEOGRAPHY: RELATIONSHIPS** What impact did the cultivation of corn and tobacco have on Jamestown?

4. **WRITING TO PERSUADE** Imagine you are an investor in the London Company. Write a letter to a Spanish friend explaining how the English colonization process differs from the Spanish process. Be sure to describe how a joint-stock company works.

5. **EVALUATING** Do you think that John Smith was an effective leader? Provide examples from the text that support your position.

Columbus lands in the Americas.

Treaty of Tordesillas signed.

Conquest of Aztecs begins.

Magellan's crew completes circumnavigation of globe.

Verrazano establishes French claim in North America.

Conquest of Incas starts.

1492 1494   1519 1522 1524   1531

WRITING A SUMMARY

Using the essential points of the chapter as a guide, write a summary of the chapter.

REVIEWING CHRONOLOGY

Number your paper 1 to 5. Study the time line above, and list the following events in the order in which they happened by writing the first next to 1, the second next to 2, and so on. Then complete the activity below.

1. Jamestown established.
2. Conquest of Aztecs begins.
3. Pueblo Revolt drives Spanish from Santa Fe.
4. Treaty of Tordesillas signed.
5. Spanish Armada defeated.

Hypothesizing Select two events on the time line that affected Native Americans, and write a paragraph describing how Native Americans may have reacted to these events.

IDENTIFYING PEOPLE AND IDEAS

Explain the historical significance of each of the following people or terms.

1. Bartolomé de Las Casas
2. *La Noche Triste*
3. Hernán Cortés
4. Protestant Reformation
5. Francisco Pizarro
6. Charter of 1606
7. joint-stock company
8. John Smith
9. Wahunsonacock
10. indentured servant

UNDERSTANDING MAIN IDEAS

1. What instructions did Spain give Columbus and early settlers to guide them in their relationships with Native Americans? What changes did Spanish settiers introduce that affected Native Americans?
2. How were women's roles defined in Spanish America? What kinds of opportunities did Indian, African, and Spanish-Indian women have?
3. Why was Jamestown founded?

REVIEWING THEMES

1. **Global Relations** What were the positive and negative results of the Columbian exchange?

2. **Economic Development** How did the Spanish and English colonization of the Americas both benefit and hurt their economies?
3. **Cultural Diversity** How did differences in beliefs and values affect relations between Europeans and Native Americans?

THINKING CRITICALLY

1. **Evaluating** How successful was the Catholic church at protecting the Indians and improving their lives?
2. **Hypothesizing** Suppose the Spanish Armada had defeated the English in 1588. Do you think Spain would have continued to dominate the Americas?
3. **Analyzing** How did Native Americans respond to both Spanish and English colonization?

STRATEGY FOR SUCCESS

Review the Skills Handbook entry on Distinguishing Fact from Opinion on page 990. Read the excerpt below from a 17th-century Spanish judge's defense of Spanish treatment of Native Americans. Then identify which aspects of the argument are facts and which are opinions.

66 At each step they [critics] throw in our faces the fact that the Indians have been badly treated and that in many places they have completely disappeared. . . .

In many places the Indians gave cause for their mistreatment or for war to be made against them, either because of their bestial [brutal] and savage customs or because of the excesses and treason that they attempted or committed against our people. . . .

Moreover, it is not the Spaniards who have exterminated them, but their own vices and drunkenness or the earthquakes and repeated epidemics of smallpox and other diseases with which God in His mysterious wisdom has seen fit to reduce their numbers. 99

The Spanish Crown restricts the *encomienda*.	St. Augustine founded.	Spanish Armada defeated.	Jamestown established.	Santa Fe founded.	Rolfe introduces tobacco in Jamestown.	Pueblo Revolt drives Spanish from Santa Fe.	Cruz publishes her first book of poetry.	San Antonio de Valero mission founded.	Gaspar de Portolá founds San Diego.
1542	**1565**	**1588**	**1607**	**1609**	**1612**	**1680**	**1689**	**1718**	**1769**

WRITING ABOUT HISTORY

Writing to Evaluate Write an essay explaining why Columbus's first voyage was a turning point in history.

USING PRIMARY SOURCES

Read the following excerpt from Álvar Núñez Cabeza de Vaca's report to the Spanish king on his 8-year, 6,000-mile journey across North America. Then write a paragraph summarizing Cabeza de Vaca's experiences with Native Americans. What advice did he give the king about colonization?

 We hastened through a vast territory, which we found vacant, the inhabitants having fled to the mountains in fear of Christians. With heavy hearts we looked out over the lavishly watered, fertile, and beautiful land, now abandoned and burned and the people thin and weak. . . . Not having planted, they were reduced to eating roots and bark; and we shared their famine the whole way. . . . They . . . told us how [Christians] had come through razing [tearing down] the towns and carrying off half the men and all the women and boys; those who had escaped were wandering about as fugitives. We found the survivors too alarmed to stay anywhere very long, . . . preferring death to a repetition of their recent horror. While they seemed delighted with our company, we grew apprehensive that the Indians resisting farther on at the frontier would avenge themselves on us.

When we got there . . . they received us with the same awe and respect the others had—even more, which amazed us. Clearly, to bring all these people to Christianity and subjection to Your Imperial Majesty, they must be won by kindness, the only certain way. **99**

LINKING HISTORY AND GEOGRAPHY

Spain, Portugal, England, and France led the exploration of the Americas. Study the maps on pages 19 and 57, noting the locations of these countries in relation to the Americas. Then, in a brief essay, explain how geographic location helped these countries lead the way to the Americas.

British Museum

Spanish coin

BUILDING YOUR PORTFOLIO

Complete the following projects independently or cooperatively.

1. TRADE In Chapter 1 you portrayed a trader. Building on that material, expand your map to include trade routes between Europe, Africa, Asia, and the Americas during the 1500s. Include symbols to represent major items of trade.

2. SLAVERY Imagine you are a Spanish priest opposed to slavery in the Americas. Plan a mural that conveys your concerns about the *encomienda* system and about the introduction of African slavery to the Americas.

3. CULTURAL EXCHANGES In Chapter 1 you portrayed a museum researcher. Building on that material, expand your exhibit to include dramatic readings of first-person accounts of exchanges between Native Americans, Africans, and Spanish conquistadors, mission priests, or colonists.

THE ENGLISH COLONIES

FOCUS

UNDERSTANDING THE MAIN IDEA

The colonists who settled North America in the 1600s and 1700s came for many reasons. Many came for religious freedom, others for wealth; and some came because they had no choice. The communities they founded developed in different ways, giving rise to distinctive societies within England's North American colonies. In the process, colonists forever changed Native Americans' lives and cultures.

 THEMES

■ **CULTURAL DIVERSITY** How might the cultural backgrounds of settlers influence the development of a region?

■ **GEOGRAPHIC DIVERSITY** How might differences in environment and land use result in diverse ways of life?

■ **ECONOMIC DEVELOPMENT** Why might a nation find it useful to regulate trade with its colonies? What effect might this have on the colonies?

1620	1630	1651	1732	1754	1763
Mayflower lands.	**Massachusetts Bay Colony established.**	**Parliament begins passing Navigation Acts.**	**Georgia founded.**	**French and Indian War begins.**	**Treaty of Paris signed.**

In the early 1600s hard times in England limited opportunities for many people. So when the chance arose to go to North America, thousands of men and women sailed west. Some hoped to make their fortune in the Virginia tobacco fields. Others wished to establish a "New England" based on their religious beliefs.

A View of Bethlehem (1757) by Nicholas Garrison

In November 1620 a small ship sailing from England was blown off course into a harbor near what is now Provincetown, Massachusetts. It was the *Mayflower,* which had been bound for Virginia. The weary voyagers "fell upon their knees and blessed the God of Heaven, who had brought them over the vast and furious ocean," wrote William Bradford, a leader of the group.

The voyagers had indeed been over a "furious ocean." For more than two months, the *Mayflower* had been blown about by violent storms. The passengers were sick and weak, and they had landed far north of their destination at the wrong time of year. The "howling wilderness" terrified many of them, and the weather was cold and getting colder. While their shipmates huddled on board, some of the passengers searched for a place to settle. By mid-December they had found a site—Plymouth, named after the English port from which they had sailed. Who were these people? Why did they undertake such a voyage?

The Metropolitan Museum of Art

The Puritan

THE NEW ENGLAND COLONIES

FOCUS

- Why did the Pilgrims come to North America?
- What drove the Puritans to leave England for North America? What kind of society did they try to establish in America?
- Why were some colonists forced to leave Massachusetts Bay Colony?

Old Testament Psalms

𝒯he prospect of religious freedom drew many English men and women—as it would later draw others—to North America. But not everyone came for religious reasons. Poverty plagued 17th-century England and drove many people to look for a better life elsewhere. Still, religion was vitally important to most New England colonists. They organized their close-knit communities around shared religious beliefs, creating a distinct and prosperous way of life.

𝒯HE PILGRIMS

In 1620 the men and women aboard the *Mayflower* reached Cape Cod Bay, near what is now Provincetown, Massachusetts, and founded Plymouth Colony. Known as **Pilgrims**, they had left England because of religious conflict. They saw themselves as wanderers who, like the "pilgrims and exiles" of the Bible, traveled in search of a place to worship God in their own way.

Conflicts over religious doctrine had raged in England since 1534 when Henry VIII broke with the Roman Catholic church to form the Church of England (Anglican church). Henry's motives had been primarily personal—the pope had refused to grant him a divorce from his first wife. At heart still a Roman Catholic, he had created a church that remained largely Catholic in form. This deeply troubled the Pilgrims, who longed for a truly Protestant church.

The Pilgrims were **Separatists**, so called because they had broken with the Church of England. They were the most radical of the **Puritans**, English Protestants who wished to "purify" the Anglican church of all Catholic rituals and traditions. The Puritans objected, for example, to the clergy's elaborate robes, insisting that church leaders should be known for "their purity of mind, not their adornment of person."

Some Separatists, including the Pilgrims, left England for the more religiously tolerant Netherlands after James I threatened to "harry them out of the land, or else do worse." There, forced into

◀ **The *Mayflower* is shown covered with ice in this 19th-century painting by William Halsall.**

Pilgrim Society, Plymouth, Massachusetts

low-paid, unskilled work, they confronted what one Pilgrim called the "grimme & grisly face of povertie." Even more alarming, they faced the prospect of losing control of their children. The children were not only adopting Dutch ways but were also being led, as Pilgrim leader William Bradford saw it, by "evil examples into extravagant and dangerous courses, getting the reins off their necks and departing from their parents." Seeking "some place of better advantage and less danger," Bradford and others obtained permission to settle in Virginia.

■■ The Pilgrims came to North America for religious and economic reasons.

PLYMOUTH COLONY

The Pilgrims never reached Virginia. Their ship was blown off course, and they landed far north in Massachusetts' Cape Cod Bay. Rather than risk traveling farther, they decided to stay. Because Cape Cod Bay was outside the area controlled by the London Company, the *Mayflower*'s passengers had no legal government. In an effort to maintain order in the new settlement, Pilgrim leaders drew up an agreement and asked all the men to sign it. This document, the **Mayflower Compact**, established a self-governing colony based on the majority rule of male church members:

> 66 We, whose names are underwritten, . . . Having undertaken for the Glory of God, and Advancement of the Christian Faith, and the Honour of our King and Country, a Voyage to plant the first colony in the northern Parts of Virginia; Do by these Presents [this document], solemnly and mutually in the Presence of God and one another, covenant and combine ourselves together into a civil Body Politick, for our better Ordering and Preservation, and Furtherance of the Ends aforesaid; And by Virtue hereof do enact, constitute, and frame, such just and equal Laws, Ordinances, Acts, Constitutions, and Offices, from time to time, as shall be thought most meet and convenient for the general Good of the Colony; unto which we promise all due Submission and Obedience. 99

The Mayflower Compact was important because it helped set a precedent for local government based on written agreements and the consent of the governed.

Once the Compact was signed, the colonists elected Bradford as their governor and turned to

Joslyn Museum, Omaha, Nebraska

▶ *Europeans Encountering Indians* is the title of this painting by an unknown artist.

▶ These artifacts were used by the Pilgrims in the 17th century. Clockwise from top are a christening shirt and mitts worn by William Bradford, the wicker cradle used by Peregrine White, who was born aboard the *Mayflower,* and a pair of boys' leather shoes.

Peabody & Essex Museum, Salem, Massachusetts

Peabody & Essex Museum, Salem, Massachusetts

Pilgrim Society, Plymouth, Massachusetts

the challenge of surviving the winter. But the cold climate, disease, and hunger took their toll. The colony's record for March 24, 1621, notes: "In three months past dies halfe our company . . . Of a hundred persons, scarce fifty remain, the living scarce able to bury the dead."

The colony, like Jamestown, owed its survival to Native Americans. The settlers were particularly indebted to Squanto, a member of the Patuxet band of the Wampanoags (wahm-puh-NOH-ags). He taught them where to fish and how to plant corn. He also spoke English. Kidnapped in 1614, he had lived in Spain and England before returning home in 1619. The Pilgrims viewed Squanto, in Bradford's words, as "a special instrument sent of God for their good beyond their expectation." With Squanto's aid autumn brought a bountiful harvest. The Pilgrims then invited the Indians to a harvest feast—the first Thanksgiving.

THE PURITANS AND THE GREAT MIGRATION

In contrast to the Pilgrims, most Puritans remained in England and did not leave the Anglican church. These religious **dissenters** hoped to reform the church from within.

The Crown, however, opposed reform. James I feared that Puritan demands would lead to political upheaval. Religious dissent, he declared, "as well agreeth with a Monarchy as God and the Devill. Then Jack & Tom, & Will & Dick, shall meete and at their pleasure censure me, and my Councell, and all our proceedinges." King James's son Charles, who succeeded James in 1625, was even more determined than his father to stop dissent and suppress Protestant ministers and practices.

The English Puritans faced economic difficulties as well. England's population had dramatically increased, but employment had not. The growing profitability of wool production encouraged large landowners to turn from farming to raising sheep. They fenced their lands and drove off the tenant farmers, many of whom were Puritans. Then in the 1620s crop failures and an economic depression in the woolen industry hit Puritan farmers and weavers.

To escape both religious persecution and economic ruin, many Puritans decided to risk a move to the colonies. Beginning in 1630, in what is known as the **Great Migration**, some 60,000 people left England for the Americas. While most of them went to the West Indies, some 10,000 to 20,000 settled in Massachusetts.

Most Puritans, however, did not leave England. In 1642 the conflict between the Puritans and the Royalists, the supporters of King Charles I, erupted in civil war. Led by Oliver Cromwell, the Puritans won. During Cromwell's rule (1653–1658), Puritan emigration almost ceased.

■■ **The Puritans left England to escape religious conflict and economic problems.**

MASSACHUSETTS BAY COLONY

The year before the Puritan exodus began, a group of well-to-do Puritans secured a royal charter for the Massachusetts Bay Company, allowing them to establish a colony. In 1630 the company's fleet of 11 ships carried some 1,000 settlers to Massachusetts. These Puritans did not wish to cut all ties with England or the Anglican church. Inspired by a sense of mission, they hoped to provide other Christians with an example of a model community. While still aboard ship, John Winthrop, their governor, expressed their vision and warned against failure:

▲ John Winthrop

66 We must consider that we shall be as a city upon a hill. The eyes of all people are upon us. So that if we shall deal falsely with our God in this work we have undertaken, and so cause Him to withdraw His present help from us, we shall be made a story and a byword through the world. 99

Most colonists, wrote Winthrop, expected to find in their new home more of God's "wisdom, power, goodness and truth than formerly we have been acquainted with." Their expectations arose from their belief that they had a **covenant**, or contract, with God to build a society based on the

▲ This drawing shows a meetinghouse built at Plymouth in 1683. The building contained glass windows, a Gothic-style roof, and a bell.

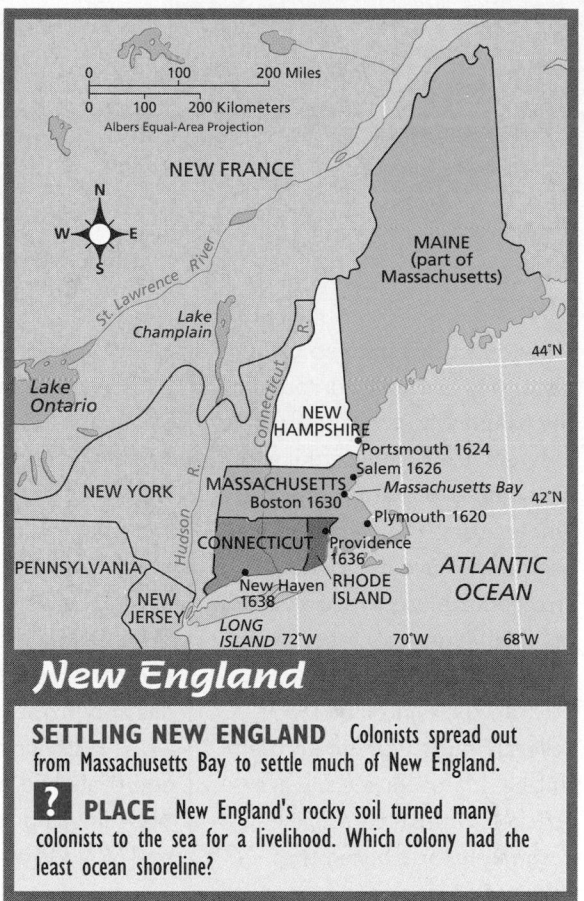

New England

SETTLING NEW ENGLAND Colonists spread out from Massachusetts Bay to settle much of New England.

❓ PLACE New England's rocky soil turned many colonists to the sea for a livelihood. Which colony had the least ocean shoreline?

Scriptures and a covenant with one another "to walk together in all His ways."

The Massachusetts Bay Company's charter allowed Winthrop and the other stockholders to govern the colony however they wished, so long as they did not violate English law. To fulfill their covenant with God, they established their colony as a Bible **commonwealth**, in which everyone, guided by English law and the Bible, was expected to work together for the common good. The stockholders granted voting rights to all **freemen**, that is, adult men who were church members and property owners. The freemen in each town then elected representatives to the **General Court**, or legislature, to make laws for the colony.

The Puritan commonwealth was based on cooperation between church and state. The colonists referred to this relationship as the **New England Way**. The meetinghouse, in which Puritans held both town meetings and church services, symbolized this unity. Its civil function was clearly visible: the outside walls of the plain, unpainted clapboard building served as a public notice board. Sermons delivered within on Sundays and on important occasions instructed the congregation in the New

The Salem Witchcraft Trials

Few questions have so baffled historians as those surrounding the Salem witchcraft trials. The answers are complicated, and no single explanation tells the whole story. But recent interpretations have profoundly changed the way we look at colonial America's most dramatic witch trials.

In the winter of 1692, several young women in Salem Village, Massachusetts, were stricken with seizures. The community attributed the seizures to demonic possession. Most people in Europe and America believed in the Devil's existence and ability to possess humans. They also believed that the Devil empowered human agents, called witches, to cause this possession.

Members of the village community pressed the possessed females to name those responsible for their afflictions. Once the young women began

identifying witches in their midst, hundreds of residents of Salem and other eastern Massachusetts towns came forward to testify that they too were victims of witchcraft. They claimed witches had used supernatural powers to kill their children, sicken their farm animals, and otherwise harm their families and property.

Witchcraft accusations and trials had taken place in New England many times prior to 1692. What made the Salem

trials so unusual was the number of people involved. In a matter of months, over 200 persons were named as witches. At least 59 were tried, 31 convicted, and 19 hanged. As in earlier times, older women were the main targets.

For a long time, many historians considered the Salem outbreak a bizarre and irrational event and argued that the young women were mentally disturbed. Other accusers, most of whom were adult men, were

▶ On August 5, 1692, a group of Salem girls accused George Jacobs (kneeling at right) of witchcraft. He was hanged two weeks later. T. H. Matteson painted this version of the trial in 1855.

England Way. First the minister explained the meaning of a Biblical text and then showed the congregation the way to apply the lesson in their spiritual and earthly lives. Such lessons were important because the Puritans believed that everyone in the community had to live a moral life; otherwise, the entire community would suffer God's wrath. When catastrophe struck, the faithful often blamed the occurrence on a member's sinfulness.

The Puritans also believed that God had already decided who would be saved. Just as God had entered a covenant with the saved, so New Englanders joined in a covenant with one another

to found churches and towns. The church granted full membership to those who convinced the congregation that they had undergone a "conversion experience." Those who did not were admitted to partial membership.

The New England Way depended on educated people who could understand the Scriptures. The General Court thus required parents to teach their children to read, and a law passed in 1647 required towns to maintain schools. The "Old Deluder Law," as it was known, was meant to foil the "chief project of that old deluder, Satan, to keep men from the knowledge of the Scriptures."

thought either to have been carried away with the hysteria of the moment or to have deliberately accused people they resented. The older women who were convicted and executed as witches were simply viewed as convenient targets.

Recent historians have challenged this view of the trials, emphasizing how the trials were rooted in the social and cultural climate of New England. The religious, economic, and family life of New England's settlers all fostered an environment in which witchcraft fears flourished and accusations were an accepted way of dealing with personal conflict and community tensions.

Ideas about witches, demons, and magical practices were a part of Puritan beliefs and popular folklore. New England ministers and their followers had brought these ideas with them from England. Rather than irrational responses, witchcraft accusations and trials were expressions of 17th-century religious thinking about the nature of society, the causes of misfortune, the existence of sin, and the rebelliousness of the human spirit.

The outbreak also had roots in decades of community conflict and economic tensions. Salem Village lay on the edge of Salem Town, a thriving port. Some village farmers had family and economic links to the town and shared in its growing prosperity. Other villagers, however, felt pinched as farmland grew scarce. These economic tensions produced deep divisions in the community. The witchcraft accusation, egged on by several of the village's less prosperous residents, provided an outlet for resentments and grievances. The way the community divided over the witchcraft scare paralleled the village's deeper factional divisions.

But why were most of the accused women? Historically, on the basis of the Bible and a vast body of witchcraft lore, witch belief had focused mainly on females. A more immediate answer, however, lies in the contradictory view of women held by Puritan men. On the one hand, men acknowledged women's value and held them in esteem as "helpmates." On the other hand, they feared women gaining economic and social independence. Such independence was seen as a challenge to men's power and a threat to the social order. Women who did not have brothers or sons were among the most feared. In New England, where property customarily passed from father to son, such women could and did become economically independent by inheriting property. Women without brothers and sons were the most likely targets of Salem's witchcraft trials.

With this better awareness of how witchcraft beliefs and accusations were deeply embedded in New England culture and society, the Salem outbreak appears less bizarre but no less fascinating. The story of Salem is still unfolding, however. Historians continue to reexamine the trials and reevaluate the surviving evidence, offering us new perspectives on what caused the tragic events of 1692.

■■ The Puritans hoped to build a model commonwealth in which the Bible guided all aspects of life.

NEW ENGLAND LIFE

By the time Massachusetts Bay Colony passed its school law, it had more than 20,000 inhabitants. The men who immigrated were primarily educated artisans or farmers—"godly men . . . endowed with grace and furnished with means," according to Deputy Governor Thomas Dudley. Three out of four had paid their own way to the colony.

In contrast to the Jamestown colonists, these men brought along their wives and children. Puritans considered orderly families to be essential to a stable society. Women were expected to defer to their fathers or husbands in most aspects of life. Single people had to live with a family, and children could be removed from "disorderly" ones. Town officials inspected families on a regular basis so that "disorders may be prevented, and ill weeds nipped before they take too great a head."

▲ These illustrations from the American edition of *The Book of Trades* show two colonial crafts: spinning (left) and coopering (right).

New England's environment encouraged the growth of large families. Food was plentiful, and the cold climate proved relatively hostile to some of the diseases that plagued Jamestown. As a result, some 80 percent of all children lived to adulthood. Colonist Mary Buell's tombstone shows just how large these families could be—it records that she died at age 90 leaving behind 336 living descendants.

Married in their early 20s, most women had at least six children, and families with nine or more were common. Such a large family led Sarah Ripley Stearns to lament that "the care of my Babes takes up so large a portion of my time and attention." Furthermore, because women bore children on into their 40s, a mother in New England could expect to be well into her 60s before her last child left home.

Following English custom, New England women usually did not work in the fields, although they often helped at harvesttime. Instead, they took on many other tasks required to run a farm. They made many of the things their families needed: soap, candles, yarn, clothes, butter, and cheese. Women might sell their occasional surplus in town to help support their families.

New Englanders with large families had relatively little need for indentured servants or slaves. Fathers and sons could supply all the labor needed to transform the "remote, rocky, barren, bushy, wild-woody wilderness," as Edward Johnson described it in 1653, into "a second England." However, because of long winters and the poor soil found in much of New England, farmers did not have a large surplus to market.

■■ New England was populated mostly by educated artisans and farmers who had immigrated with their families.

To pay for supplies and luxury items from England, some New Englanders turned to fishing, trade, and business. They distilled rum and built ships. They sold fish, grain, meat, naval stores (turpentine, pitch, and rosin), and lumber to England, Spain, Portugal, and the West Indies. New England merchants also prospered through trade with England's other American colonies. In time the merchants also earned substantial profits by selling their shipping services.

DISCONTENTED COLONISTS ESTABLISH NEW COLONIES

As Massachusetts Bay Colony prospered and grew, some colonists started new settlements. Thomas Hooker and his congregation left Massachusetts in part, they said, because its "towns were set so near to each other." To get more farmland, they moved southwest, establishing a colony in the Connecticut Valley. In 1639 Hooker's settlers adopted the **Fundamental Orders of Connecticut**, which some regard as the first written constitution in the colonies.

▶ Thomas Hooker was such a domineering figure that he was once described as a man who could put a king in his pocket. This picture shows Hooker and his congregation traveling through the wilderness.

Other colonists were forced to leave Massachusetts Bay Colony because they questioned Puritan ways. One such person was Roger Williams, a Puritan minister who, unlike most other Puritans, believed in strict separation of church and state. He also challenged the king's right to give Native American land to English colonists. These beliefs so angered Puritan leaders that they banished Williams. He purchased land from the Narragansets and in 1636 founded a settlement that became Providence, Rhode Island. An able politician, Williams secured a charter for the colony in 1644 that permitted its inhabitants complete religious freedom. Because of this tolerant attitude, the colony attracted those who, like Williams, held unpopular beliefs.

Another Puritan who found refuge in Rhode Island after refusing to conform to the New England Way was Anne Hutchinson. Born in England in 1591, Hutchinson came to Boston, the capital of Massachusetts Bay Colony, in 1634 with her family. "A woman of a ready wit and bold spirit," as Governor Winthrop acknowledged, she worked as a nurse and midwife and devoted herself to Bible study and teaching. At meetings in her home, she discussed the sermons of Boston's leading ministers. She attracted a following of women and wealthy merchants, many of whom resented the ministers' authority.

Increasingly, Hutchinson expressed ideas critical of the established clergy's teachings. In 1637 she was charged with weakening the authority of the church. The fact that she was a woman added to the people's displeasure. Her meetings, Governor Winthrop declared, were "not tolerable . . . in the sight of God nor fitting for your sex." The Puritans found especially dangerous Hutchinson's claim that she received her religious insights directly from God. To them this claim set the individual above the community and threatened the

Anne Hutchinson

authority of both the community and the church. Banished in 1638, she moved to Rhode Island and then to Long Island. When Hutchinson died in an Indian attack in 1643, Massachusetts ministers declared it the "just vengeance of God."

Hutchinson was not the only woman whose religious beliefs put her at odds with Puritan authorities. In 1643 Lady Deborah Moody and her followers left Massachusetts because of disagreements over religion. A few years later, she received permission to establish a self-governing colony on Long Island.

■■ **Massachusetts Bay Colony did not tolerate differences of opinion in religious matters and banished offending colonists.**

SECTION 1 REVIEW

IDENTIFY and explain the significance of the following: Pilgrims, Separatists, Puritans, Mayflower Compact, dissenters, Great Migration, covenant, commonwealth, freemen, General Court, New England Way, Fundamental Orders of Connecticut, Anne Hutchinson, Lady Deborah Moody.

LOCATE and explain the importance of the following: Plymouth, Massachusetts; Salem, Massachusetts; Connecticut; Rhode Island.

1. **MAIN IDEA** What conditions in England and Europe led the Pilgrims and the Puritans to settle in North America?

2. **MAIN IDEA** How did Massachusetts Bay Colony react to colonists who challenged Puritan ways?

3. **USING HISTORICAL IMAGINATION** Write an essay describing life in New England from the perspective of a woman colonist.

4. **WRITING TO PERSUADE** Imagine you are a Puritan dissenter who wishes to leave England to found a Bible commonwealth in North America. Write a pamphlet describing the type of society you hope to create.

5. **ANALYZING** Why was education important to the Puritan community?

SLAVERY AND THE SOUTHERN COLONIES

FOCUS

■ **What was life like for the Chesapeake colonists in the 17th century?**

■ **Why did planters turn to the use of slave labor?**

■ **What was the Middle Passage like for newly captured slaves?**

In the Chesapeake colonies of Virginia and Maryland, people developed a way of life different from that in the New England colonies. Most Chesapeake colonists lived on scattered farms and plantations, where they grew tobacco as a cash crop. The majority of them had come to the colonies as indentured servants, obligated to work for whoever purchased their contracts. However, by the end of the 17th century, more and more planters bought African slaves to work in the tobacco fields.

Slaves loading tobacco barrels at a Virginia wharf

THE CHESAPEAKE

Within 25 years of Jamestown's founding, Virginia was a thriving colony with a population of some 2,500. Tobacco fueled the economy, with production rising from some 50,000 pounds in 1618 to more than 1 million pounds in the 1630s. The promise of huge profits led more than one wealthy Englishman to dream of establishing a colony in the Chesapeake—the land surrounding Chesapeake Bay. The first to do so was Cecilius Calvert, the second Baron Baltimore.

In 1632 Charles I made Cecilius Calvert proprietor, or owner, of millions of acres on the upper Chesapeake Bay. The colony was named Maryland, after Charles's French wife, Henrietta Maria. As proprietor, Calvert was free to dispose of the land and to govern—within loose guidelines—as he wished.

Calvert wanted to create a haven for fellow Roman Catholics who faced persecution in Protestant England. But he also hoped to make money. Because there were not enough Catholic immigrants to make his venture profitable, he opened his colony to Protestants. Soon Protestants greatly outnumbered Roman Catholics. To protect the Catholic minority's legal rights, the Maryland Assembly passed the **Toleration Act** in 1649. The act guaranteed religious freedom to all Christians.

Population. Catholic and Protestant settlers in Maryland soon followed Virginia's lead and devoted much of their land to tobacco production. As a result, both colonies developed a distinct culture in response to life in the Chesapeake.

Most white colonists in the Chesapeake came as indentured servants. Many came because

◀ **Cecilius Calvert**

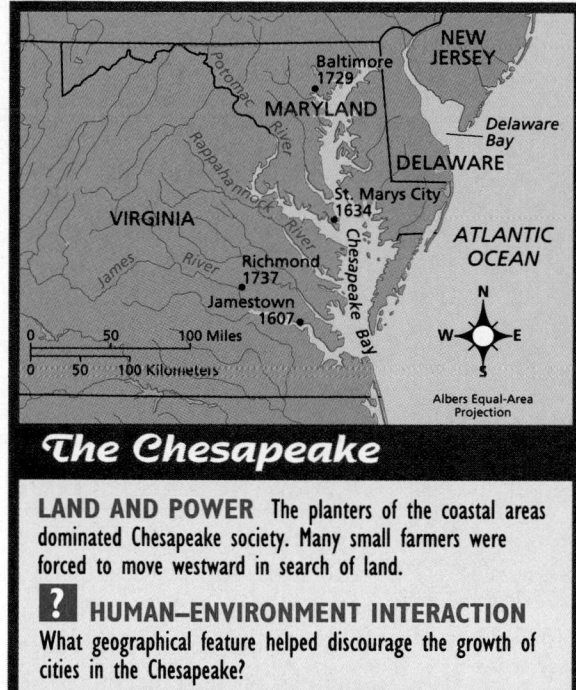

The Chesapeake

LAND AND POWER The planters of the coastal areas dominated Chesapeake society. Many small farmers were forced to move westward in search of land.

❓ HUMAN—ENVIRONMENT INTERACTION What geographical feature helped discourage the growth of cities in the Chesapeake?

they could not find work in England. But not all came willingly. In the 17th century some men, women, and even children were "spirited" and "snared"—kidnapped—from London streets to meet the demand for servants. A 1645 report to Parliament told of gangs who "in a most barbarous and wicked manner steal away many little children." Moreover, in the 1700s England sent an estimated 30,000 to 50,000 convicts to work as servants in the Chesapeake.

One indentured servant, John Harrower, described how some servants were bought and sold once they arrived in Virginia:

> ❝ Soul drivers. . . are men who make it their bussines to go on board all ships who have in either Servants or Convicts and buy sometimes the whole and sometimes a parcell of them, . . . and then they drive them through the Country like a parcell of Sheep untill they can sell them to advantage. ❞

Of the colonists who came as indentured servants, some 75 percent were men or boys between ages 15 and 24. Even as late as 1704, the Archives of Maryland show that there were more than three times as many white men as white women living in the colony. Because there were so few white women in these early years, many men never married.

High death rates also affected the population. Throughout the 1600s typhoid, malaria, and other diseases ravaged the colonists. Up to 55 percent of those born in the Chesapeake died before age 20. Life expectancy slowly improved around the turn of the century as the number of native-born colonists who had better immunity to the region's diseases increased.

The high death rates gave rise to family patterns that differed from those of New England. New England's low death rates meant that most people married only once. In the Chesapeake, however, one partner in most marriages died within seven or eight years of marrying. In most cases the surviving partner quickly remarried. Second and even third marriages were common. As a result, most families included stepparents, stepsiblings, half siblings, and possibly the orphans of deceased relatives or friends.

■■ In the 17th century, colonists in the Chesapeake suffered from high death rates, and white men greatly outnumbered white women.

A rural society. The vast majority of colonists in the Chesapeake lived on widely scattered farms and plantations. They produced tobacco for export and grew or made many of the things they needed. Away from the coast, poor settlers on small farms grew corn and vegetables, kept chickens and hogs, hunted, and trapped.

Most of the large plantations fronted one of the many navigable rivers that flowed into

◀ This ragged London oyster seller symbolized the class of people who indentured themselves as servants in order to start over in the colonies.

▲ *The Plantation* was painted by an unknown American artist about 1825. The roads leading down from the manor house to the river allowed for easy transportation of goods to or from ships docked at the wharf.

Chesapeake Bay. At first, English trading ships stopped at the planters' docks to collect the tobacco crops and to deliver goods previously ordered. Later, Scottish brokers set up stores and traded in tobacco.

The fact that planters did not need to bring their crops to a central market discouraged the growth of towns. As late as 1750 the only large town in the Chesapeake was Baltimore. Without towns to provide customers, the Chesapeake was slow to develop a substantial class of independent artisans and shopkeepers.

The slow growth of towns also hindered the development of schools. Education was left to individual families who either taught their children themselves or hired tutors. Wealthy families made sure their children—both boys and girls—were educated, but they did not support schooling for others. As a result, especially when compared with those in New England, literacy rates were low. They were very low for women: from the 1600s to the mid-1700s, less than 25 percent of Chesapeake women signing legal documents could write their names. In New England in the mid-1700s, the figure was about 50 percent.

In 1671 Governor William Berkeley, who had long governed Virginia and who had enriched himself in the process, proudly reported to the English government that Virginia had "no free schools nor printing, and I hope we shall not have these [for a] hundred years." Berkeley and many other wealthy planters agreed with English philosopher Francis Bacon that schooling made ordinary people—particularly women—"unfit" for their "station" in life.

■■ Most Chesapeake colonists lived on tobacco plantations or small farms.

*B*ACON'S REBELLION

A lack of schooling, however, did not stop colonists from challenging authority. Virginia was home to an increasing number of freed indentured servants. Around 1660, tobacco prices had tumbled, and with tobacco selling for so little, it was difficult for these people to earn enough money to buy land. Most were forced to rent land or to work as wage laborers for wealthy

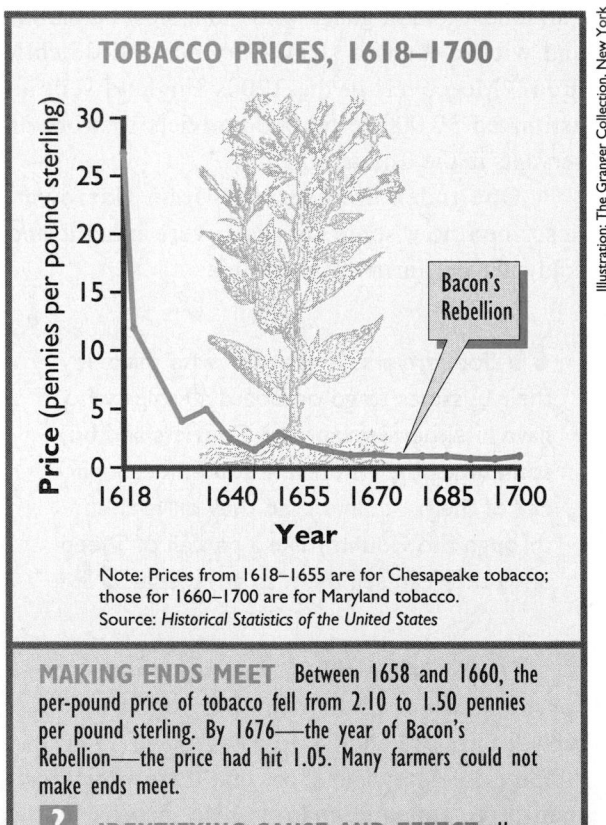

TOBACCO PRICES, 1618–1700

Price (pennies per pound sterling)

Bacon's Rebellion

Year

Note: Prices from 1618–1655 are for Chesapeake tobacco; those for 1660–1700 are for Maryland tobacco.
Source: *Historical Statistics of the United States*

MAKING ENDS MEET Between 1658 and 1660, the per-pound price of tobacco fell from 2.10 to 1.50 pennies per pound sterling. By 1676—the year of Bacon's Rebellion—the price had hit 1.05. Many farmers could not make ends meet.

? **IDENTIFYING CAUSE AND EFFECT** How might declining tobacco prices have influenced events leading to Bacon's Rebellion?

The Metropolitan Museum of Art

Illustration: The Granger Collection, New York

planters. Landless laborers and small landowners grew increasingly discontented. They were in debt, taxes were high, and as far as they could see, the colonial legislature was doing nothing to help them.

This discontent erupted in violence in Virginia in 1675. Many poor farmers and laborers, believing that access to land would solve their problems, wanted to settle the area in western Virginia guaranteed to the Powhatans in a 1646 treaty. The treaty did not stop settlers from moving onto Indian lands. When whites killed a group of friendly Susquehannocks (suhs-kwuh-HAN-uhks) and no compensation was made, the Susquehannocks attacked outlying plantations. The colonists then demanded war against all Native Americans in the Chesapeake.

The governor refused, but Nathaniel Bacon was willing. Described by his enemies as "ambitious and arrogant" with a "dangerous hidden pride of heart," this well-connected young planter raised an army of settlers in 1676 and randomly attacked Indians on the frontier. As one colonist later explained, "It matters not whether they be Friends or Foews Soe they be Indians." Bacon's followers, now joined by indentured servants and enslaved

▲ Shown here is an artist's depiction of a confrontation between Nathaniel Bacon and Governor William Berkeley.

Africans, looted wealthy plantations. The rebels also seized and burned Jamestown.

Bacon's Rebellion ended with Bacon's sudden death from one of the illnesses that plagued the Chesapeake. Charles II ordered Berkeley to return to England, and the large planters in the **House of Burgesses**—Virginia's assembly—quieted opposition by cutting taxes and opening Indian lands to colonists.

SLAVERY

While Bacon's Rebellion was short-lived, it had one far-reaching effect: it strengthened the move already under way among planters to switch from indentured to slave labor. More indentured servants ultimately meant more discontented freed servants. Slaves did not pose this problem. Slaves were also becoming more plentiful and—in the long run—cheaper than indentured servants. As employment opportunities improved in England, fewer people were willing to come to the Chesapeake under terms of indenture.

Surviving court records suggest that slavery as an institution developed gradually in the Chesapeake. The first Africans brought to the Chesapeake were treated as indentured servants. After completing their periods of indenture, they were free to work for themselves, and some became landowners. However, by the 1640s some, but not all, were slaves instead of servants.

■■ **Planters turned to slave labor in response to Bacon's Rebellion and to the declining number of indentured servants.**

The slave trade. During the early years of the slave trade, African traders sold criminals and war captives. As the demand for plantation workers increased, however, first in Spanish America and later in the Chesapeake, African raiders moved farther inland in search of slaves. Their constant attacks destroyed the countryside and emptied villages. In 1700 William Bosman, an agent for a Dutch slave-trading company, observed the effects of the slave trade on the once powerful city of Benin in West Africa. It had been "very thick and close-built," he wrote, "but now the Houses stand like poor men's corn, widely distant from each other."

In 1765 an Englishman, one of the few to accompany a slave-raiding expedition, described how raiders hid "under the bushes in the day when they came near a village," and at the right opportunity, seized "every one they could see." The raiders marched the captive men, women, and children hundreds of miles to the coast. There they were inspected, branded, and held in prisons until there were enough to fill a ship.

Once on the ships, the captives were packed in, one captain wrote, until "they had not so much room *as a man in his coffin.*" As a result, many died from suffocation, disease, or violence during the dread **Middle Passage**—the voyage across the Atlantic.

Some captives killed themselves rather than face further horrors. Another captain reported that they "often leap'd . . . into the sea, and kept under water till they were drowned."

■■ **Packed into ships for the Middle Passage, many African captives died from suffocation, disease, or brutality. Some committed suicide.**

BIO GRAPHY

Olaudah Equiano (oh-LOW-duh ek-wee-AHN-oh), who was kidnapped and sold into slavery in the mid-1700s, when he was 11 or 12, later described the ordeal of the Middle Passage in his autobiography. At first he was terrified that he and the other captives were "to be eaten by those white men with horrible looks, red faces, and long hair." He was eventually reassured that he would not be eaten, but new horrors confronted him when he was put below deck:

66 There I received such a salutation in my nostrils as I had never experienced in my life: so that with the loathsomeness of the stench, and crying together, I became so sick and low that I was not able to eat, nor had I the least desire to taste any thing. I now wished for the last friend, death, to relieve me; but soon, to my grief, two of the white men offered me eatables; and, on my refusing to eat, one of them held me fast by the hands . . . and tied my feet, while the other flogged me severely. 99

▶ **Olaudah Equiano**

Soon after Equiano arrived in the Americas, a Virginia planter purchased him and then sold him to a British naval officer, Michael Pascal, who renamed him Gustavus Vassa. Equiano served with Pascal in the Seven Years' War (see page 91). At the war's end he was again sold, this time to a West Indian merchant for whom he worked as a seaman. By 1766 Equiano had earned enough money to buy his freedom. He continued to work as a seaman and even accompanied an expedition to the Arctic.

In 1777 Equiano settled in England and devoted himself to the antislavery movement. He lectured widely on the evils of slavery. His popular autobiography, published in 1789, convinced many people of the need to stop the slave trade.

Early abolitionists. Equiano was not the only person to speak out against slavery. Other blacks and a few white colonists denounced the institution. Although **abolitionists**, those who wanted slavery abolished,

National Maritime Museum, London

▲ **This watercolor shows Africans below deck on the Spanish slave ship** *Albatross,* **bound for the West Indies. A British naval officer painted this grim scene from life in 1846.**

did not become a force in America until the early 1800s, a group of Quakers—members of a radical Protestant sect—took a public stand against slavery as early as 1688. In 1700 Puritan judge Samuel Sewall published an anti-slavery pamphlet, *The Selling of Joseph.* In it Sewall reminded his readers that "all Men, as they are the Sons of *Adam,* . . . have equal Right unto Liberty, and all other outward Comforts of Life."

By the mid-1700s most Quakers condemned slavery. John Woolman, a Quaker tailor, traveled throughout the colonies, urging Quakers to free their slaves. He urged those who were not slave-holders to refuse to use goods, such as sugar and dyed cloth, that were the products of slave labor.

AFRICAN POPULATION IN BRITISH NORTH AMERICA, 1650–1760

Source: *Historical Statistics of the United States*

GROWTH OF SLAVERY The colonial economy in the South depended on a steady supply of unskilled laborers. When the number of English indentured servants began to decline in the late 1600s, the colonists increased their reliance on African slaves.

? BUILDING GRAPH SKILLS By about how much did the African population of British North America increase from 1730 to 1760?

Slave codes. Despite such protests slavery was practiced in all the English colonies. As Africans became more numerous after 1660, they were—by law and by custom—treated as inferior to whites. In 1705 Virginia consolidated its various laws and customs into one "slave code." Other colonies did the same.

The slave codes were designed to prevent escape and discourage revolt. The codes forbade slaves to meet together, to leave the plantation, to learn to read or write, or to own weapons. The codes went so far as to declare that a master who killed a slave while "correcting" him or her could not be tried for murder!

Harsh rules did not prevent rebellion, however. Newly arrived Africans often ran away. There were also a few uprisings. The largest occurred in 1739 at Stono, South Carolina. Slaves killed some 30 whites before the militia quelled the uprising. The slaves who survived the rebellion were "put to the most cruel Death." Most slaves, however, resisted in other, less direct ways, such as by destroying property or working slowly.

SECTION 2 REVIEW

IDENTIFY and explain the significance of the following: Cecilius Calvert, Toleration Act, Nathaniel Bacon, Bacon's Rebellion, House of Burgesses, Middle Passage, Olaudah Equiano, abolitionists, Samuel Sewall, John Woolman.

LOCATE and explain the importance of the following: Chesapeake Bay; Baltimore, Maryland; Virginia.

1. **MAIN IDEA** Why did Chesapeake planters increasingly choose to rely on slave labor?

2. **MAIN IDEA** What were conditions like during the Middle Passage?

3. **WRITING TO DESCRIBE** Imagine you are one of the few white women living in the Chesapeake. Write a letter home to England, describing your life in the colonies.

4. **HYPOTHESIZING** How might the colonies in the Chesapeake have developed if they had had a more diversified economy?

THE COLONIES AFTER THE RESTORATION

FOCUS

- How did life in South Carolina differ from life in the other Restoration colonies?
- Why did England regulate colonial trade?
- What did the Glorious Revolution accomplish?
- Why did so many people respond to the Great Awakening?

The colonies established after the Restoration of the English monarchy in 1660 were, like Maryland, proprietary colonies. Eager to reap profits, some proprietors and land speculators recruited colonists from Europe as well as from the British Isles. The Crown, too, expected to benefit and made efforts to control colonial trade despite the colonists' opposition. At the same time, new intellectual and religious ideas transformed colonial life.

Detail from the 1670 painting
The Mason Children

THE CAROLINAS

After Cromwell's death and the Restoration of the monarchy, another wave of colonization began. The new king, Charles II, rewarded his supporters with grants of land. In 1663 he gave eight supporters a charter for a colony between Virginia and Spanish Florida. The colony was named Carolina in the king's honor. Later the colony was divided into North and South Carolina. The proprietors proved incompetent governors, and in the 1720s the Crown officially took over both colonies.

In North Carolina many settlers from the Chesapeake established small farms. The forests provided naval stores and furs and skins that the settlers could trade. In South Carolina the first colonists came primarily from Barbados. They and the few slaves they brought with them raised cattle, cut timber, and traded with Native Americans. Some settlers tried to grow rice but failed. However, slaves who came from Sierra Leone and other rice-growing regions of West Africa knew the proper cultivation techniques.

◀ This extract from *Colonial Office Papers* shows the earliest land grants, beginning in 1674, given to settlers in South Carolina. By 1765 more than 11,000 names appeared on this list.

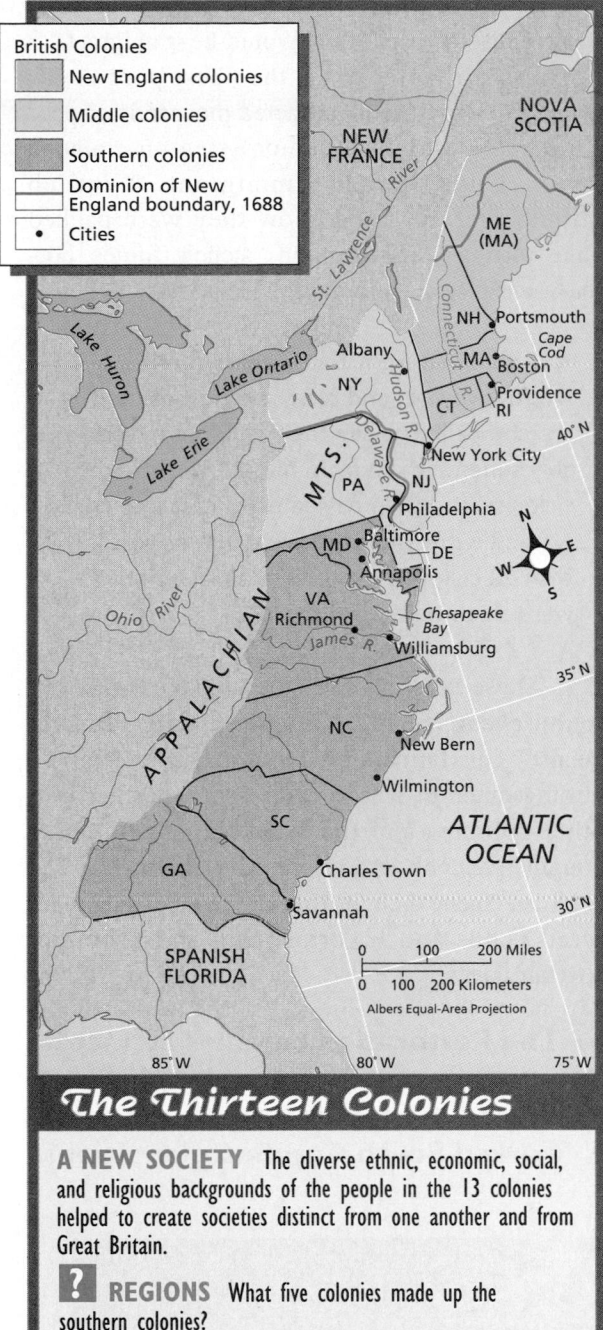

- New England colonies
- Middle colonies
- Southern colonies
- Dominion of New England boundary, 1688
- • Cities

NOVA SCOTIA

NEW FRANCE

St. Lawrence River

ME (MA)

NH Portsmouth

Cape Cod

Albany

NY

MA Boston

CT

Providence RI

Lake Huron

Lake Ontario

Lake Erie

Hudson R.

Connecticut R.

Delaware R.

New York City

PA

NJ

Philadelphia

MD Baltimore

DE

Annapolis

Ohio River

APPALACHIAN MTS.

VA

Richmond

James R.

Chesapeake Bay

Williamsburg

40° N

35° N

NC

New Bern

Wilmington

SC

Charles Town

GA

Savannah

ATLANTIC OCEAN

30° N

SPANISH FLORIDA

0   100   200 Miles

0   100   200 Kilometers

Albers Equal-Area Projection

85° W   80° W   75° W

The Thirteen Colonies

A NEW SOCIETY The diverse ethnic, economic, social, and religious backgrounds of the people in the 13 colonies helped to create societies distinct from one another and from Great Britain.

? REGIONS What five colonies made up the southern colonies?

Settlers used their slaves' knowledge and labor to transform the swampy coastal region into fabulously profitable rice plantations.

The Carolinas and the thriving port of Charles Town (Charleston) attracted Scots, Scotch-Irish, Germans, European Jews, West Indians, and in 1685, French Huguenots (Protestants) fleeing religious persecution. In South Carolina, however, the demand for plantation workers was so great that by 1720 African slaves made up about 70 percent of the population.

On the large rice plantations, the slaves had relatively little contact with whites. As a result,

▲ This late–18th-century painting by an unknown artist, entitled *The Old Plantation,* shows the merging of African and American cultures through slaves' musical instruments, dress, and dance.

they kept more African traditions than slaves in other areas kept. Even their language, Gullah, combined West African dialects and English.

Slaves on the rice plantations worked under the **task system**. Each day the slaves were assigned particular duties. Once they had completed them, the slaves could tend small plots and raise livestock. Some sold their hogs, chickens, and produce or worked for wages on their own time. A few slaves earned enough to buy their freedom. Slaveholders worried that their slaves—who now outnumbered them—were becoming too independent. Fearful of slave revolts, they urged passage of a harsh slave code.

NEW YORK AND NEW JERSEY

Besides rewarding his supporters, Charles II wanted to cripple Dutch trading interests. The Dutch West India Company, attracted by the profitable fur trade, had established a colony in North America. Its colony, New Netherland, extended inland along the Hudson River Valley and included the town of New Amsterdam, founded in 1626 on Manhattan Island. (The town was renamed New York in 1664.) Although successful at its trading activities, the Dutch West India Company had little luck attracting Dutch settlers. The company did attract others: primarily English, French Huguenots, Swedes, Jews, and free Africans. Colonists also purchased enslaved Africans. By 1750, blacks made up almost 20 percent of New York City's population.

Most settlers considered their governors inept. Consequently, they refused to defend the colony when an English fleet sailed into the harbor in 1664 and demanded that the Dutch hand over New Netherland. Without a shot being fired, the colony's governor, Peter Stuyvesant, a domineering old soldier with a wooden leg, surrendered to the English.

Charles II made his brother, James, the Duke of York, proprietor of New Netherland. James kept part of the colony—renamed New York—and gave the rest—New Jersey—to two friends.

PENNSYLVANIA AND DELAWARE

In 1681 Charles II repaid the £16,000 he owed Admiral Sir William Penn by making Penn's son William proprietor of a large tract of land near New York. Penn's holdings increased the following year when the Duke of York gave him Delaware.

Penn wanted to make his colony, which the king named Pennsylvania, a haven for his fellow Quakers. Persecuted by Anglicans and Puritans alike as "violators of order," the Quakers had no formal clergy, opposed warfare, and ignored class privileges.

Penn also wanted Pennsylvania to be a "Holy Experiment," where people of different nationalities and religious beliefs "could shape their own lives" and live peacefully together. He extended his policy to Native Americans, paying them for their lands and treating them fairly.

While Penn was a man with deep religious convictions, he was also a shrewd promoter who needed to raise cash. To recruit colonists, he published pamphlets in English, Dutch, and German that described his colony in glowing terms and promised prosperity to would-be immigrants.

Often referred to as the "best poor man's country," Pennsylvania attracted thousands of poor immigrants who made the crossing on cramped ships. One German immigrant, Gottlieb Mittelberger, described how they were packed "like herrings" and endured "stench, fumes, horror, . . . scurvy, . . . mouthrot." He added:

> 66 Children from 1 to 7 years rarely survive the voyage; and many a time parents are compelled to see their children miserably suffer and die from hunger, thirst and sickness, and then to see them cast into the water. I witnessed such misery in no less than 32 children in our ship, all of whom were thrown into the sea. 99

Those who survived the voyage, however, found cheap, fertile land and a mild climate. Pennsylvania farmers produced a surplus of grain, milling much of it into flour and exporting it to other colonies and the West Indies. Butchers bought livestock and exported salted meat. The colonists spent their profits on English manufactured goods and luxuries. Some also bought African slaves.

■■ The Restoration colonies attracted a diverse group of people. Most farmed their own lands, but slaves worked South Carolina plantations.

Winterthur Museum

▶ *The Peaceable Kingdom* was one of several paintings Edward Hicks made of animals living in harmony with nature. In this version, William Penn is shown in the background, meeting with other colonists.

GEORGIA

While Pennsylvania began as a "Holy Experiment," Georgia was a social experiment. This last British colony was established on the southern frontier of British North America in 1732, more than a century after Jamestown's founding. James Oglethorpe and a group of supporters planned the colony to give the English poor a fresh start. Parliament supported the project in the hope that it would "carry off the . . . poor that pester the streets of London." It also expected the colony to provide a buffer between South Carolina's prosperous plantations and Spanish Florida.

▲ This illustration from a 1733 book, showing Georgia in an idealized setting, was used to help promote colonization in that region.

As a social experiment the colony failed. Oglethorpe and his partners wanted to aid only the most "virtuous and industrious" poor. However, very few debtors qualified, and the colony attracted few other settlers because of its rigid rules.

Oglethorpe's rules included prohibitions against rum and slavery. The trustees wanted to prevent the "Sin of Drunkenness" and believed that slaveholders "would be less disposed to labor" for themselves. But the settlers complained that without slaves they could not compete with South Carolina planters. In 1750 the founders reluctantly gave in, but the colony still did not prosper. By 1760 Georgia's European population numbered only some 6,000.

TRADE

Above all else, the founding of the Restoration colonies was driven by the Crown's faith in the economic policy of **mercantilism**. Mercantilists held that a nation's power was a product of wealth, and a nation's wealth was measured by its stock of gold and silver. The best way for a nation to obtain wealth was to maintain a favorable **balance of trade**: to export more than it imported. But only nations that were relatively self-sufficient could maintain a favorable balance of trade. Thus the colonies were vitally important as a source of raw materials and as a ready market for goods from the homeland.

Mercantilist ideas had the support of the merchant class, which was well represented in England's Parliament. In 1651 Parliament began passing a series of mercantilist laws—the **Navigation Acts**—to promote the "wealth, safety, and strength of this kingdom." In part, these acts were designed to increase English merchants' profits by limiting direct trade between the English colonies and other European nations. The acts required European goods destined for the colonies to be routed through England. In addition, all colonial products had to be carried on ships built and owned by "his Majesty's subjects of England, Ireland, and the Plantations." The acts also listed, or "enumerated," colonial products that could be exported only to England or to other destinations within the empire. The list was added to over the years and eventually included tobacco, cotton, sugar, and naval stores.

▲ Tobacco was advertised for sale on trade cards, such as this one for Surby's Best Virginia.

Southern colonists, who produced most of the enumerated goods, resented the restrictions because they cut into profits. But the acts helped northern shipbuilders and merchants. As British subjects they could build and sail their own ships and provide shipping services. Because timber and naval stores were so much cheaper in America than in Europe, colonial shipbuilders thrived. By the early 1770s colonists had built about one third of all merchant ships flying the British flag.

■■ **England regulated colonial trade to achieve a favorable balance of trade and to benefit English merchants.**

JAMES II AND THE GLORIOUS REVOLUTION

The Lords of Trade, a committee established to oversee the colonies for the Crown, sent customs agents to the colonies to enforce the Navigation Acts. The colonists were often uncooperative. Massachusetts, for example, declared that it was exempt from English restrictions on trade. In response, the English government revoked the Massachusetts charter in 1684.

The following year James, Duke of York, became King James II. To increase royal authority over the colonies, the new king ordered the Lords of Trade to organize the northern colonies into the Dominion of New England. The committee placed the dominion under the control of Sir Edmund Andros in 1686. Andros quickly angered the colonists by imposing taxes without their consent and by abolishing the Massachusetts General Court.

James II was no more popular in England than Andros was in New England. James II's Catholicism rankled English Protestants, and his habit of ruling by decree angered Parliament. In 1688 the Protestant opposition staged a bloodless rebellion: the **Glorious Revolution**. They invited the king's Protestant daughter, Mary, and her Dutch husband, William, Prince of Orange, to take the throne. Unable to rally support, James II fled to France in 1688.

To prevent future abuses of power, Parliament enacted the Bill of Rights in 1689. The act listed the rights and liberties guaranteed to every citizen and to Parliament, including regular free elections and a prohibition against taxation without Parliament's consent.

Colonists used the Glorious Revolution to rid themselves of hated officials. Protestants in Maryland got rid of wealthy Catholic officials. Massachusetts colonists sent Andros back to England. The New York militia, under Jacob Leisler's leadership, ousted the

dominion's lieutenant governor. The new rulers, William and Mary, broke up the Dominion of New England and restored those representative assemblies that had been abolished. The Navigation Acts, however, largely remained in place.

■■ **The Glorious Revolution limited royal power and led to the passage of England's Bill of Rights.**

THE GREAT AWAKENING

The Glorious Revolution had another important effect. It established that royal power flowed from the consent of Parliament, not from the will of God. The idea that God did not directly intervene in human affairs was not confined to politics. Europe in the 18th century was experiencing the birth of a revolution in ideas called the **Enlightenment**. Enlightenment thinkers emphasized human reason and progress. Science and logic, they believed, provided the keys to understanding nature and improving society.

Enlightenment ideas found religious expression in Deism. Deists believed that God created the universe, set it in motion, and then let it run itself according to natural law. They placed more emphasis on leading a virtuous life than on piety or religious faith. In the colonies Deism appealed to many educated people, particularly merchants and wealthy planters.

Winterthur Museum

Religious revivals. Not everyone shared the Deists' belief in an orderly, predictable world. Changes in society that emphasized individual and material success rather than the common good of the community troubled many people, particularly those in rural areas. These people longed for religion that moved their hearts. They found it in a series of religious revivals—known as the **Great Awakening**—that swept through the British colonies in the mid-18th century.

▲ **This plate, depicting James II, appeared after the coronation of the new king.**

The minister often credited with launching New England's Great Awakening is Jonathan Edwards of Massachusetts. He believed that appealing to people's emotions—rather than to their minds—would open their hearts to God.

It was, however, the English revivalist George Whitefield who, beginning with his first trip to Georgia in 1738, spread the message of the Great Awakening throughout the colonies. During his several tours of the colonies, the minister inspired crowds of thousands. After hearing him, Nathan Cole, a farmer, wrote that Whitefield "looked as if he was Cloathed with Authority from the Great God," and "hearing him preach gave me a heart wound." One young woman, Fanny Lewis, wrote her father that at a Baltimore revival "there was such a gust of the power of God, that it appeared to me the very gates of hell would give way."

▲ **George Whitefield**

The Great Awakening's effects. Not everyone, however, was a New Light—a supporter of the Great Awakening. Those who opposed it—the Old Lights—objected to the New Lights' emotional, disorderly services. Such differences encouraged the growth of New Light Protestant churches, particularly the Baptists and the Methodists.

The New Light preachers also emphasized a personal relationship with God. They encouraged men, women, and even children to preach about their religious experiences. These emotional services appealed to many, especially to the poor and to the enslaved—whom the established churches often neglected.

Preaching to Virginia slaves, Presbyterian Cary Allen assured them that the "Savior died and shed his blood as much for you as for your master, or any of the white people." Christ has "opened the door of heaven . . . and invites you all to enter." Many blacks responded enthusiastically to Allen and other New Light preachers. The revivalists' emphasis on emotional religious experience more closely resembled African religious tradition than Puritan or Anglican Protestantism did.

The Great Awakening challenged established authority. The revivalist preachers appealed to ordinary people rather than to the educated upper class. And above all, they emphasized the equality of everyone—including women and slaves—before God.

■■ **The Great Awakening revivalists appealed to people's emotions and stressed everyone's equality before God.**

SECTION 3 REVIEW

IDENTIFY and explain the significance of the following: task system, William Penn, James Oglethorpe, mercantilism, balance of trade, Navigation Acts, Sir Edmund Andros, Glorious Revolution, Enlightenment, Great Awakening, Jonathan Edwards, George Whitefield.

LOCATE and explain the importance of the following: North Carolina, South Carolina, New York, Pennsylvania, Delaware, Georgia.

1. **MAIN IDEA** How did South Carolina's agricultural economy differ from the agricultural economies of the other Restoration colonies?

2. **MAIN IDEA** What effect did the Glorious Revolution have on England and the colonies?

3. **MAIN IDEA** Why did the Great Awakening revive people's interest in religion?

4. **WRITING TO INFORM** Imagine you are a customs agent sent to the colonies to enforce the Navigation Acts. Write a report to Parliament, outlining why England should regulate colonial trade.

5. **EVALUATING** What reasons did Charles II have for granting land in the Carolinas, New York, New Jersey, and Pennsylvania? Why was there renewed interest in founding colonies after the Restoration?

THE FRONTIER AND THE STRUGGLE FOR LAND

FOCUS

- What pressures in the colonies pushed settlers to the frontier?
- What was life on the frontier like?
- How did the fur trade and the conflicts over land affect Native American lives and cultures?
- What were the main causes and results of the French and Indian War?

Throughout the 18th century, English colonial cities grew rapidly. Philadelphia roughly doubled in size every 20 years, eventually becoming Great Britain's largest overseas port. But despite this growth British America remained overwhelmingly rural: about 95 percent of the some two million colonists lived on farms. Hungry for new land to farm, the colonists moved onto lands claimed by Native Americans and by the French.

Frontiersman's jacket, rifle, powder horn, satchel, and trap

GROWTH AFFECTS PROSPERITY

Throughout the colonial period New England's population roughly doubled every 25 years; the Middle Colonies—New York, New Jersey, Pennsylvania, and Delaware—grew even faster. As the population increased, social differences among community members became more obvious. A few families increasingly controlled the wealth. In 1693 the richest 10 percent of Philadelphia's taxpayers owned some 45 percent of taxable wealth; by 1772 their share had risen to some 70 percent.

In the major port cities of Boston, New York, and Philadelphia, wealthy merchant families imitated the homes, dress, and manners of the English upper class. Many other city dwellers, however, were less fortunate, though some "leather apron men"—butchers, carpenters, potters, smiths, and other artisans—prospered and moved up in society. Even in the 1700s cities experienced cycles of

▲ Colonial cities soon faced the problem of growing numbers of urban poor. This 1767 engraving commemorates the opening of new almshouses and workhouses in Philadelphia.

The Dietrich American Foundation, Philadelphia, Pennsylvania prosperity and hard times. Without good health, a fortunate marriage, or an ample inheritance, some people found hard work not to be enough to escape poverty. By the 1730s all major towns had poorhouses where the very poor lived at public expense.

Farms became smaller with each generation as the same amount of land was divided among ever more heirs. As more people competed for land within existing communities, it became expensive. Many of those who wanted to live near their families but were unable to afford land worked as farm laborers.

Instead of struggling to support themselves in the cities or in their communities, townspeople and farmers had another choice: they could leave for the frontier. And many colonists did, pushing north into New York's border areas and west into other newly opened areas such as the western portions of Massachusetts, Pennsylvania, Virginia, and North Carolina.

It was not easy, however, for people to leave their families, friends, and communities. One colonist who stayed behind expressed the widely held fear that the "desire after Land" would doom the pioneers' children to a life of "heathenish ignorance and barbarisme"—and all "so they might have Elbow-room enough in the world."

▪▪ Rapid population growth and economic problems encouraged many colonists to move to the frontier.

PIONEER LIFE

These were not idle fears. The frontier lacked schools and churches. Pioneers might live in crude shelters such as one "poor, dirty hovel, with hardly anything in it but children" that Virginia planter William Byrd observed in 1733. When they were able to build more-permanent housing, pioneers often built Swedish-style log cabins, which one traveler in 1679 praised as "quite tight and warm." They were, he wrote, made of "entire trees, split through the middle, or squared out of the rough, and placed in the form of a square."

Pioneers who prospered might lay wood floors in their cabins, cut windows in the walls, and nail clapboards over the logs. They might add

▲ A farm family at work in the fields is the subject of this 1760s woodcut from a Pennsylvania almanac.

sleeping lofts or small rooms. But others, who moved as frequently as the soil wore out, lavished little attention on their houses. In the frontier communities, Byrd observed, "a citizen . . . is counted extravagant if he has ambition enough to aspire to a brick chimney."

From childhood on, everyone had to work hard. Besides farming, the men and women had to do the work of butchers, carpenters, candle makers, soap makers, and other artisans. Those who could not, a frontier minister observed in 1711, would "have but a bad time of it; for help is not to be had at any rate."

In western Virginia and Pennsylvania—the backcountry—some pioneers grazed cattle in the woods. The settlers, reported a British seaman in 1755, "drive up their Herds on Horseback . . . for their Cattle are near as wild as Deer" and they "run as they please in the Great Woods, where there are no Inclosures to stop them." Pioneers also cleared and fenced some land and planted corn, wheat, and other crops among the stumps. Once backcountry farmers began to produce a marketable surplus, small market towns appeared.

Deep in the interior a few frontiersmen lived a roving existence. They adapted their clothing from Indian dress, wearing coarse linen hunting shirts and deerskin leggings and moccasins. They hunted for food and traded furs for supplies such as the powder and shot needed for their rifles.

▪▪ Frontier families grew their own food and made almost everything they needed.

THE FRENCH IN NORTH AMERICA

As frontiersmen and traders crossed the Appalachians into the Ohio Valley, they moved into territory claimed by several British colonies as well as by France. French claims to American land were based on the early voyages of Giovanni da Verrazano, who explored the coast of North America in 1524, and of Jacques Cartier, who explored the Gulf of St. Lawrence in 1534–1535. Samuel de Champlain's fur trading expeditions in 1603 and his founding of Quebec in 1608 strengthened these claims. Then in 1673 Jesuit missionary Jacques Marquette and fur trader Louis Jolliet (jahl-ee-ET) crossed the Great Lakes, made their way to the Mississippi River, and traveled down it as far as the Arkansas River. René-Robert de La Salle also explored the Mississippi, reaching the Gulf of Mexico in 1682. He claimed the Mississippi Valley for France, naming it Louisiana in honor of Louis XIV.

The founding of New Orleans in 1718 gave the French command of the Mississippi River. Control of the Mississippi, combined with their thriving colonies along the St. Lawrence River and their knowledge of a water route through the Great Lakes, put the French in a position to control the North American interior.

But New France—France's North American empire—never reached its potential strength. France claimed a huge area but settled very little of it. Most French colonists were single men in search of riches and adventure. The French *coureurs de bois* (kooh-ruhr duh BWAH), or runners of the woods, traded with Native Americans for furs. Many married Indian women.

CULTURES CLASH

The French colonial economy was tied to that of the Native Americans. Native Americans included French fur traders in their trade networks early in the 17th century. Native Americans desired European trade goods such as horses, firearms, and metal tools. To pay for those goods, they traded beaver pelts and other furs. "The beaver does everything perfectly well," one Indian explained. "It makes kettles, hatchets, swords, knifes, bread . . . in short, it makes everything."

The fur trade. The European clamor for furs, however, changed life for Native Americans, many of whom became dependent on the fur trade. For them, hunting became a commercial

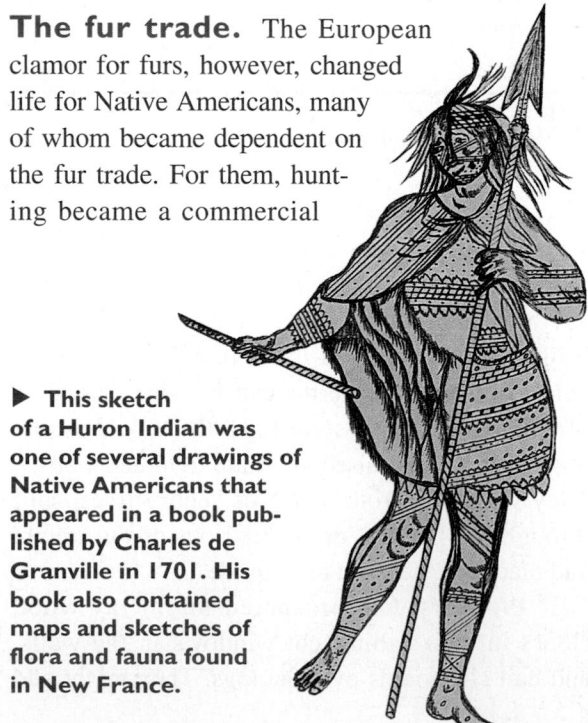

Map Legend
- British
- Spanish
- French
- Russian
- – – – Boundary of Iroquois League

NEWFOUNDLAND · Hudson Bay · **NEW FRANCE** · Disputed · NOVA SCOTIA · PACIFIC OCEAN · LOUISIANA · Mississippi · Ohio · THIRTEEN COLONIES · Rio Grande · Disputed · ATLANTIC OCEAN · Tropic of Cancer · NEW SPAIN · FLORIDA · Gulf of Mexico · West Indies · CARIBBEAN SEA · Equator

0   600   1,200 Miles
0   600   1,200 Kilometers
Azimuthal Equal-Area Projection

120° W   110° W   100° W   90° W   80° W   70° W   60° N   50° N   40° N   30° N   20° N   10° N

North America in 1754

OLD ENEMIES The rivalry in Europe between Great Britain and France carried over to North America.

❓ HUMAN–ENVIRONMENT INTERACTION Why do you think both France and Great Britain desired the lands of the Ohio Valley?

▶ This sketch of a Huron Indian was one of several drawings of Native Americans that appeared in a book published by Charles de Granville in 1701. His book also contained maps and sketches of flora and fauna found in New France.

Then and Now

Before European settlers arrived in North America, dense forests covered more than half of the some 7.2 million square miles of what are today the United States and Canada. The continent's abundant forests seemed endless.

Native Americans were the first to alter the forest landscape. Using fire, they cleared small patches of woodland to create space for their crops and to encourage the growth of the tender new vegetation that deer, elk, and other game preferred to eat. But Native Americans cleared no more of the wooded land than was necessary for their survival.

In the 1600s the newly arrived Europeans began clearing the forests at a rapid pace. In their eyes the wilderness was an enemy to be feared or conquered. Colonists cut the forests to make room for farms, towns, and roads. They used the wood for building. Wood was also the only fuel available to many settlers.

A logging truck

Soon logging was a major colonial industry, providing lumber for home and ship construction and yielding other needed products such as turpentine, charcoal, and paper. Even soap making relied on lye made from wood ash.

Large-scale logging began in the deep forests of Maine. Logs were floated downriver to sawmills in the harbors along the Atlantic seaboard. In a few decades all of Maine's old-growth (original) pine and spruce forests were gone, and the industry moved progressively westward and southward.

After some 300 years of deforestation (clearing of forests), only a fraction of old-growth forests in the United

States remains. Many claim that this destruction of the forests is having far-reaching environmental consequences. Clear-cutting (cutting down all trees in an area) wipes out the trees' root networks that hold soil in place and trap rainwater. The loss of forest cover can result in flooding and severe erosion, which strips away fertile topsoil. The disappearance of forests also means the loss of habitats for many wild animals, endangering or leading to the extinction of species. Deforestation even affects the air, because green plants add to the supply of oxygen in the atmosphere.

Many argue that what is needed now is more efficient management of the remaining forest lands. Old-growth forests need to be selectively logged, to leave enough of the ecological system in place to generate new growth. And new-growth forests need time to mature. The challenge is to find a balance between the demand for wood and paper products—and the jobs which that demand supports—and the need to conserve the vanishing forests.

---

enterprise, and they killed as many animals as they could. Some villages devoted so much time to trapping and preparing furs that they had to buy food that they had once produced for themselves.

The fur trade also disrupted relations among tribes. As they killed off the beaver and other fur-bearing animals in one area, Indian trappers moved their settlements to areas where the animals were still plentiful. Thus previously distant tribes came into contact and competition with each other. Firearms made the resulting conflicts particularly deadly.

■■ Some Native Americans became economically dependent on the fur trade, and competition for hunting territories caused conflict.

Conflicts over land. The European desire for land had even more-disastrous consequences for Native Americans than the European demand for furs had. Indian ways of using land did not fit European notions of landownership. Europeans thought that land that was not registered by deed, cleared, or built on was not owned. Since most Indian land appeared wild and unused, Europeans believed that it was there for the taking.

Native Americans viewed land differently. They recognized territorial boundaries, but not individual ownership. Individuals did have, however, the right to use land for growing crops and for hunting and gathering. The loss of the land had serious consequences because it meant losing sources of food. English agricultural practices further diminished these resources by destroying animal habitats. Miantonomo (my-an-tuh-NOH-moh), a Narraganset, observed as early as 1642:

66 Our plains were full of deer, as also our woods, and of turkies, and our coves full of fish and fowl. But these English having gotten our land, they with scythes cut down the grass, and with axes fell the trees; their cows and horses eat the grass, and their hogs spoil our clam banks, and we shall be starved. 99

War in New England. Less than 20 years after Plymouth Colony was founded, the Pequots and English were at war over land. The Pequot War, which began in 1636, ended in 1637 when the English burned a Pequot village, killing hundreds of people. A formal treaty was signed the following year. Friction between Native Americans and white settlers increased as

▲ Metacom

Massachusetts' growing population pushed onto Indian lands. War broke out again in 1675, when Metacom—whom the English named King Philip—led the Wampanoags and other Native Americans against the colonists.

Metacom's well-armed forces attacked New England settlements, destroying 12 towns. The Indian war effort collapsed, however, when Metacom was killed in battle. An estimated 3,000 Indians died in the fighting, and the Puritans sold most of the surviving Wampanoags as slaves in the West Indies and in Spain. Ten years later, a Frenchman observed that Native Americans in New England posed little threat: "The last Wars they had with the English . . . have reduced them to a small Number, and consequently they are incapable of defending themselves."

■■ Conflicts over land led to wars that nearly wiped out the Native Americans of New England.

THE IROQUOIS LEAGUE

In part, the New Englanders owed their victory over the Wampanoags to the Mohawks. At the urging of the

▲ The English burning of a Pequot village is the subject of this engraving.

governor of New York, the Mohawks had driven Metacom's forces out of New York, dealing them a crippling blow.

The Mohawks belonged to the powerful **Iroquois League**. The Senecas, Cayugas, Onondagas, Oneidas, and Mohawks of New York and Pennsylvania had formed the confederation in the 15th or 16th century. In 1722 the Tuscaroras, who had been forced out of North Carolina by settlers, joined them, and the confederation also became known as the Six Nations. Each nation kept control of its local affairs, but larger issues—such as going to war or signing treaties—required the agreement of the league's leaders.

Their combined military strength allowed the Iroquois League to dominate the fur trade, to extend their influence over Native Americans to the west, and to protect their independence. They often acted as middlemen, obtaining furs from other Native Americans and selling the furs to the English. The Iroquois maintained their independence by skillfully playing the English and the French against each other. They willingly became involved in colonial conflicts if they thought they could further their own interests—sometimes siding with the French, other times with the British.

THE FRENCH AND INDIAN WAR

France, Spain, and England were engaged in a worldwide struggle for empire. The fighting often spilled over into North America. Between 1689 and 1748, English colonists were dragged into three wars: King William's War (1689–1697), Queen Anne's War (1702–1713), and King George's War (1744–1748). As long as fighting threatened to break out in Europe, the prospect of more colonial warfare remained.

To plan for defense and to recruit the Iroquois as allies, representatives from seven colonies and the Iroquois League met in Albany, New York, June 19–July 10, 1754. At the Albany Congress the colonies' delegates adopted Benjamin Franklin's **Albany Plan of Union**, which called for a loose confederation to promote defense. The colonial assemblies, however, rejected the plan, fearing that it would raise taxes and give Great Britain too much power. The Iroquois, concluding that the English were too

King George's War ended in Europe in 1748, but less than 10 years later, Europeans were again at war. This time, Europe's future course hinged on events happening more than 3,000 miles away in sparsely settled North America. The French and Indian War, begun in 1754 on American soil but not formally declared until 1756, expanded into a worldwide battle between Great Britain and France. At stake was control of North America as well as other colonial empires throughout the world.

At the time, the French philosopher Voltaire remarked how these increasing global connections were shaping history: "Such was the complication of political interests that a cannon-shot fired in America could give the signal that set Europe in a blaze."

disunited to defeat the French, would not commit their support.

Competition for the Ohio Valley. King William's War, Queen Anne's War, and King George's War had all been sparked by fighting elsewhere in the world. However, the next major colonial conflict—the French and Indian War (1754–1763)—began in the colonies and spread to Europe in 1756 as the Seven Years' War. Unlike the previous conflicts, which were mainly fought on New England's northern frontier and at Spanish posts in Florida, the French and Indian War broke out in the west in the Ohio Valley.

Virginia **land speculators**, who bought land expecting a quick profit from its resale, had acquired a large land grant in the Ohio Valley in 1749. To protect their interests, the Virginians began building a fort at the junction of the Ohio, Allegheny (al-uh-GAY-nee), and Monongahela (muh-nahn-guh-HEE-luh) rivers—which became the site of Pittsburgh, Pennsylvania. The French, who considered the land theirs, drove the Virginians off, completed the fort, and named it

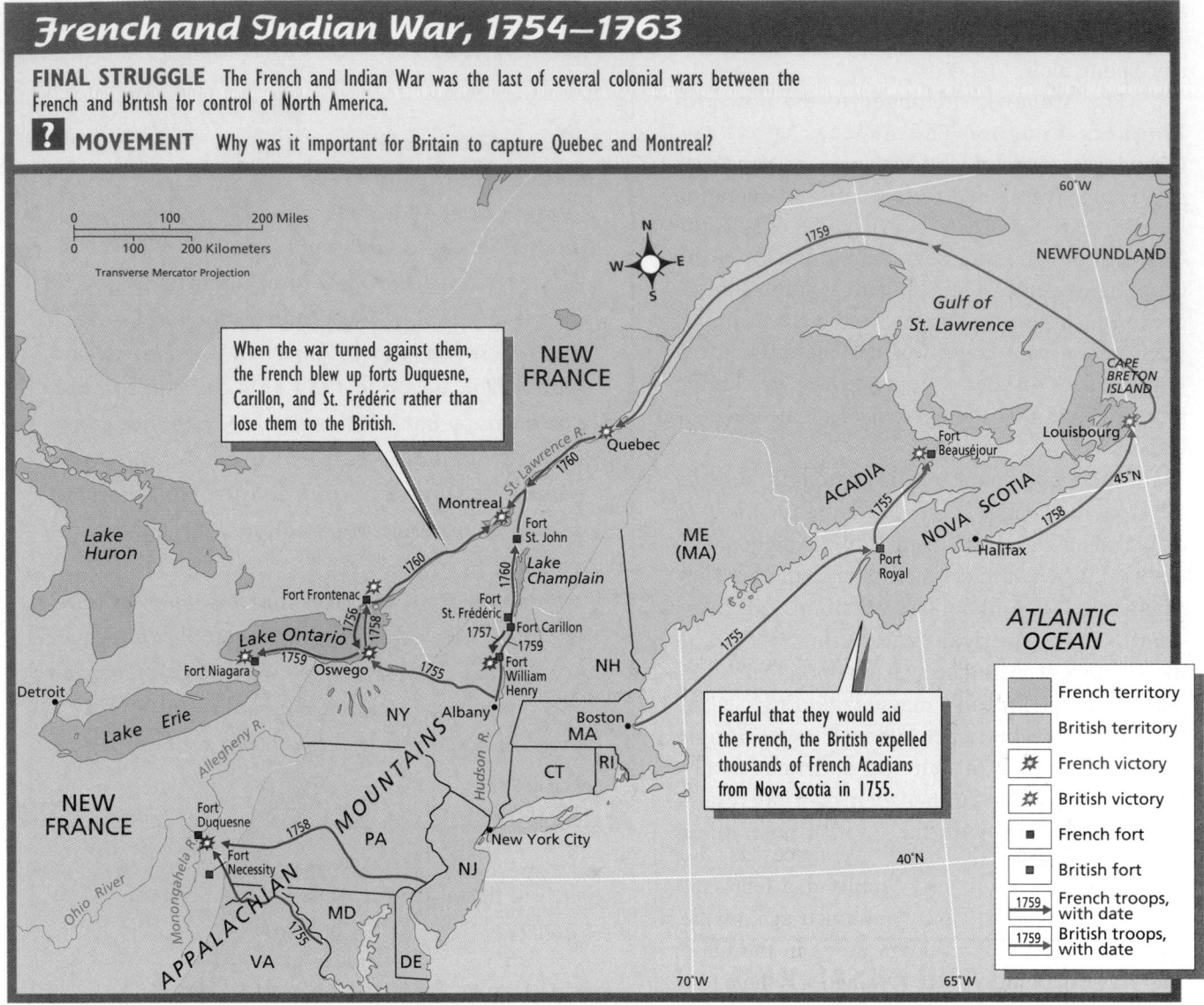

French and Indian War, 1754–1763

FINAL STRUGGLE The French and Indian War was the last of several colonial wars between the French and British for control of North America.

? MOVEMENT Why was it important for Britain to capture Quebec and Montreal?

When the war turned against them, the French blew up forts Duquesne, Carillon, and St. Frédéric rather than lose them to the British.

Fearful that they would aid the French, the British expelled thousands of French Acadians from Nova Scotia in 1755.

☐	French territory
☐	British territory
✸	French victory
✸	British victory
■	French fort
■	British fort
1759→	French troops, with date
1759→	British troops, with date

Fort Duquesne (doo-KAYN). Outraged, Lieutenant Governor Robert Dinwiddie of Virginia sent young George Washington and a company of militia to expel the French from the region. But the French held fast.

The British were unwilling to give up the area to the French, however. They sent General Edward Braddock, Washington, and a large force of British and colonial soldiers to take Fort Duquesne. Inexperienced in colonial warfare, the British forces panicked when they clashed with the French and their force of Delawares, Ottawas, Abnakis, and other Native Americans in July 1755. Washington described the British defeat in a letter to his mother:

> 66 The English soldiers . . . were struck with such a panic that they behaved with more cowardice than it is possible to conceive. . . . They broke and ran as sheep pursued by dogs. . . . I luckily escaped without a wound, though I had four bullets through my coat, and two horses shot under me. 99

In August 1757 the British lost Oswego and Fort William Henry to the French. The "lightly cloathed and armed" French and Indians succeeded, as one colonist reported, because they are "often on all Sides of us, . . . taking the Advantage of every Tree and Bush." The Delawares, whom the British had pushed out of eastern Pennsylvania, also launched attack after attack on the backcountry settlers.

British victories. Britain's fortunes improved when British cabinet minister William Pitt

◄ **George Washington experienced his first taste of military service during the French and Indian War.**

Washington/Curtis/Lee Collection, Washington and Lee University, Lexington, Virginia

assumed full control of Britain's war effort. He poured money and troops into the North American conflict. His efforts paid off. In July 1758 a British force under General Jeffrey Amherst captured Louisbourg on Cape Breton Island, which guarded the entrance to the Gulf of St. Lawrence. Louisbourg's fall meant that the British could prevent French supplies from reaching Canada. Then in August, the British captured Fort Frontenac on Lake Ontario. When the British marched on Fort Duquesne in November, the French blew up the fort rather than surrender it to the British.

After these British military successes, the Iroquois reassessed their neutrality and lent support to the British. As the tide turned against the French, they lost their Indian allies in the Ohio Valley. Abandoning their remaining forts there, the French withdrew to Canada.

The British followed, determined to take Quebec. But General James Wolfe could not entice the French commander, General Louis-Joseph de Montcalm, into battle—that is, not until the English discovered a path that led from the St. Lawrence River up the cliff to Quebec. Under cover of night the English army climbed up and assumed battle formation outside the city. The British emerged victorious from the ensuing battle although both Wolfe and Montcalm were fatally wounded. Quebec surrendered to the English in September 1759. Montreal fell in September of the following year, and with this defeat France lost the last of its Canadian holdings.

The spoils of war. The war in North America ended in 1761, but fighting continued for two more years in other parts of the world. In 1763 the Treaty of Paris ended all hostilities and awarded territories. The victorious British claimed Canada and all French holdings east of the Mississippi River except New Orleans. Spain, which had joined the French war effort in 1762, surrendered Florida to the British. In anticipation of this loss, Spain had received France's vast Louisiana territory west of the Mississippi in the 1762 Treaty of Fontainebleau.

■■ **Competition for the North American interior touched off the French and Indian War. The war cost France most of its North American holdings.**

SECTION 4 REVIEW

IDENTIFY and explain the significance of the following: Jacques Marquette, Louis Jolliet, René-Robert de La Salle, Metacom, Iroquois League, Albany Plan of Union, land speculators, William Pitt, James Wolfe, Louis-Joseph de Montcalm.

LOCATE and explain the importance of the following: Quebec, St. Lawrence River, Fort Duquesne, Oswego, Fort William Henry.

1. **MAIN IDEA** Why did some colonists choose to move to the frontier?

2. **MAIN IDEA** How did the Europeans' desire for furs and land affect Native Americans?

3. **LINKING HISTORY AND GEOGRAPHY** How did competition for land in North America cause conflicts between England and France? How did these conflicts end?

4. **WRITING TO CREATE** Imagine you are an author living on the frontier. Write a short fictional account of frontier life. Illustrate your story by including sketches of your surroundings.

5. **ANALYZING** Why did Native Americans become involved in conflicts between the French and the English?

Mayflower lands.

Massachusetts Bay Colony established.

Rhode Island receives royal charter.

Maryland passes Toleration Act.

Parliament begins passing Navigation Acts.

1620   1630   1644   1649   1651

WRITING A SUMMARY

Using the essential points of the chapter as a guide, write a summary of the chapter.

REVIEWING CHRONOLOGY

Number your paper 1 to 5. Study the time line above, and list the following events in the order in which they happened by writing the first next to 1, the second next to 2, and so on. Then complete the activity below.

1. Bacon's Rebellion erupts.
2. Rhode Island receives royal charter.
3. Treaty of Paris signed.
4. Glorious Revolution occurs.
5. Massachusetts Bay Colony established.

Analyzing What common goals did the founders of Massachusetts, Maryland, Rhode Island, and Pennsylvania share?

IDENTIFYING PEOPLE AND IDEAS

Explain the historical significance of each of the following people or terms.

1. Squanto
2. John Winthrop
3. Lady Deborah Moody
4. Toleration Act
5. Olaudah Equiano
6. Great Awakening
7. Glorious Revolution
8. George Whitefield
9. Albany Plan of Union
10. General James Wolfe

UNDERSTANDING MAIN IDEAS

1. How did mercantilism affect England's relations with the colonies?
2. In what ways did some colonists challenge established authority in the colonies?
3. Why did settlers continually start new settlements? How did Native Americans react to this expansion?

REVIEWING THEMES

1. **Cultural Diversity** How did the cultural backgrounds of the colonists affect the development of the colonies in which they settled?
2. **Geographic Diversity** What influence did environmental differences have on the development of colonies in New England and the Chesapeake?

3. **Economic Development** Why did England regulate colonial trade? What effect did this regulation have on the colonists?

THINKING CRITICALLY

1. **Evaluating** How effective was the English Crown in maintaining political authority in the colonies? Give reasons for your answer.
2. **Hypothesizing** Would Massachusetts Bay Colony's Bible commonwealth have worked in the Chesapeake? Why or why not?
3. **Comparing** How did women's lives compare in the New England and southern colonies?
4. **Identifying Cause and Effect** What were the causes and effects of Bacon's Rebellion?

STRATEGY FOR SUCCESS

Review the Skills Handbook entry on Identifying the Main Idea on page 988. Read the following excerpt from a 1705 study of Native American culture. Then identify the main idea of the selection.

> ❝ *They [Native Americans] have on several accounts reason to lament [regret] the arrival of the Europeans, by whose means they seem to have lost their felicity [happiness] as well as their innocence. The English have taken away [a] great part of their country and consequently made everything less plenty amongst them. They have introduced drunkenness and luxury amongst them, which have multiplied their wants and put them up to desiring a thousand things they never dreamt of before.* ❞

Glass necklace traded to Iroquois Indians

Bacon's Rebellion erupts.	**Pennsylvania founded. French claim Louisiana.**	**Glorious Revolution occurs.**	**Georgia founded.**	**Slave uprising occurs at Stono, South Carolina.**	**Albany Plan of Union adopted. French and Indian War begins.**	**Treaty of Paris signed.**
1675	1681	1688	1732	1739	1754	1763

WRITING ABOUT HISTORY

Writing to Evaluate Write an essay about the introduction of slavery into the English colonies. Be sure to include how changes in indentured servitude contributed to the introduction of slavery.

USING PRIMARY SOURCES

Colonists often resented the authority of English royal governors. Read the following excerpt from Nathaniel Bacon's "The Declaration of the People." Then write an essay evaluating whether or not Bacon's accusations against Governor William Berkeley were justified.

> **66** *FOR HAVING UPON specious [deceptive] pretenses of Public works raised unjust Taxes upon the Commonality for the advancement of private Favorites and other sinister ends. . . .*
>
> *For having abused and rendered Contemptible the Majesty of Justice, [by] advancing to places of judicature [law courts] scandalous and Ignorant favorites.*
>
> *For having wronged his Majesty's Prerogative and Interest by assuming the monopoly of the Beaver trade.*
>
> *By having in that unjust gaine Bartered and sold his Majesty's Country and the lives of his Loyal Subjects to the Barbarous Heathen [the Indians]. . . .*
>
> *For having . . . forged a Commission by we know not what hand, not only without but against the Consent of the People, for raising and effecting of Civil Wars and distractions. . . .*
>
> *Of these the aforesaid Articles we accuse Sir William Berkeley, as guilty of each and every one of the same, and as one, who has Traitorously attempted, violated and Injured his Majesty's Interest here.* **99**

LINKING HISTORY AND GEOGRAPHY

Study the map on page 92. How might the outcome of the French and Indian War have been different if France had established colonies along the Mississippi River and in the Ohio Valley?

 BUILDING YOUR PORTFOLIO

Complete the following projects independently or cooperatively.

1. TRADE In chapters 1 and 2 you prepared a map showing trade routes between Europe, Africa, Asia, and the Americas. Building on that material, revise your map to reflect French and English trade from North America during the 1600s. Add symbols to represent major trade items exchanged by French and English traders.

2. SLAVERY In Chapter 2 you planned a mural protesting slavery. Building on that material, now imagine you are a Quaker abolitionist. Prepare a newspaper advertisement or a handbill protesting the slave trade and outlining why slavery should be banned in North America.

Slaves in cargo hold

3. CULTURAL EXCHANGES In chapters 1 and 2 you researched cultural exchanges in the Americas. Building on that material, develop a series of drawings and captions that illustrate some of the ways in which contact between Native Americans, African slaves, and British and French colonists affected each culture.

American Letters

Native American Creation Myths

Native Americans, the first inhabitants of the Americas, developed a rich oral literature. In the following creation myths, the Iroquois of present-day New York explain the origin of the Iroquois League, the Jicarilla-Apaches of present-day Colorado and New Mexico account for the origin of fire, and the Abnakis of present-day Maine describe the mythic origins of corn.

▲ **Storyteller pottery figurine**

From *The Origin of the Iroquois League*

Iroquois

Long, long ago, in the great past, there were no people on the earth. All of it was covered by deep water. Birds, flying, filled the air, and many huge monsters possessed the waters.

One day the birds saw a beautiful woman falling from the sky. Immediately the huge ducks held a council. . . .

After some discussion, they decided to spread out their wings and thus break the force of her fall. . . . The beautiful woman reached them safely.

Then the monsters of the deep held a council, to decide how they could protect the beautiful being from the terror of the waters. . . . The monsters decided . . . that only Giant Tortoise was big enough to bear her weight. He volunteered, and she was gently placed upon his back. Giant Tortoise magically increased in size and soon became a large island.

After a time, the Celestial Woman gave birth to twin boys. One of them was the Spirit of Good. He made all the good things on the earth and caused the corn, the fruits, and the tobacco to grow.

The other twin was the Spirit of Evil. He created the weeds and also the worms and the bugs and all the other creatures that do evil to the good animals and birds.

All the time, Giant Tortoise continued to stretch himself. And so the world became larger and larger. . . .

After many, many years had passed by, the Sky-Holder . . . decided to create some people. He wanted them to surpass all others in beauty, strength, and bravery. So from the bosom of the island where they had been living on moles, the Sky-Holder brought forth six pairs of people.

The first pair were left near a great river, now called the Mohawk. So they are called the Mohawk Indians. The second pair were told to move their home beside a large stone. Their descendants have been called the Oneidas. Many of them lived on the south side of Oneida Lake and others in the valleys of Oneida Creek. A third pair were left on a high hill and have always been called the Onondagas.

The fourth pair became the parents of the Cayugas, and the fifth pair the parents of the Senecas. Both were placed in some part of what is now known as the State of New York. But the Tuscaroras were taken up the Roanoke River into what is now known as North Carolina. There the Sky-Holder made his home while he taught these people and their descendants many useful arts and crafts. ❖

From *Origin of Fire*

Jicarilla-Apache

Long, long ago, animals and trees talked with each other, but there was no fire at that time.

Fox was most clever and he tried to think of a way to create fire for the world. One day, he decided to visit the Geese, . . . whose cry he wished to learn how to imitate. They promised to teach him if he would fly with them. So they contrived [devised] a way to attach wings to Fox, but cautioned him never to open his eyes while flying.

Whenever the Geese arose in flight, Fox also flew along with them to practice their cry. On one such adventure, darkness descended suddenly as they flew over the village of the fireflies. . . . In midflight, the glare from the flickering fireflies caused Fox to forget and he opened his eyes—instantly his wings collapsed! His fall was uncontrollable. He landed within the walled area of the firefly village, where a fire constantly burned in the center.

Two kind fireflies came to see fallen Fox. . . .

Fox hoped to persuade the two fireflies to tell him where he could find a way over the wall to the outside. They led him to a cedar tree, which they explained would bend down upon command and catapult him over the wall if he so desired. . . .

Fox suggested to the fireflies, "Let's have a festival where we can dance and I will produce the music."

They all agreed that would be fun and helped to gather wood to build up a greater fire. Secretly, Fox tied a piece of cedar bark to his tail. Then he made a drum, probably the first one ever constructed, and beat it vigorously with a stick for the dancing fireflies. Gradually, he moved closer and closer to the fire.

Fox pretended to tire from beating the drum. He gave it to some fireflies who wanted to help make the music. Fox quickly thrust his tail into the fire, lighting the bark, and exclaimed, "It is too warm here for me, I must find a cooler place."

Straight to the cedar tree Fox ran, calling, "Bend down to me, my cedar tree, bend down!"

Down bent the cedar tree for Fox to catch hold, then up it carried him far over the wall. On and on he ran, with the fireflies in pursuit.

As Fox ran along, brush and wood on either side of his path were ignited from the sparks dropping from the burning bark tied to his tail.

Fox finally tired and gave the burning bark to Hawk, . . . who carried it to brown Crane. . . . He flew far southward, scattering fire sparks everywhere. This is how fire first spread over the earth. ❖

From *The Strange Origin of Corn*

Abnaki

A long time ago, when the Indians were first made, one man lived alone, far from any others. He did not know fire, and so he lived on roots, bark, and nuts. This man became very lonely for companionship. He grew tired of digging roots, lost his appetite, and for several days lay dreaming in the sunshine. When he awoke, he saw someone standing near and, at first, was very frightened.

But when he heard the stranger's voice, his heart was glad, and he looked up. He saw a beautiful woman with long *light* hair! . . . He sang to her about her loneliness, and begged her not to leave him.

At last she replied, "If you will do exactly what I tell you to do, I will also be with you."

He promised that he would try his very best. So she led him to a place where there was some very dry grass. "Now get two dry sticks," she told him, "and rub them together fast while you hold them in the grass."

Soon a spark flew out. The grass caught fire, and as swiftly as an arrow takes flight, the ground was burned over. Then the beautiful woman spoke again: "When the sun sets, take me by the hair and drag me over the burned ground."

"Oh, I don't want to do that!" the man exclaimed.

"You must do what I tell you to do," said she. "Wherever you drag me, something like grass will spring up, and you will see something like hair coming from between the leaves. Soon seeds will be ready for your use."

The man followed the beautiful woman's orders. And when the Indians see silk on the cornstalk, they know that the beautiful woman has not forgotten them. ❖

THINKING AND WRITING ABOUT LITERATURE

1. According to the Iroquois legend, how did animals and gods create the earth and people?
2. How does Fox outsmart the fireflies in the Jicarilla-Apache story about the origin of fire?
3. How does the Abnaki legend account for the existence of corn silk?

Strategies for Success

INTERPRETING THE VISUAL RECORD

Studying the visual record of a period or place can help you understand its history in ways the written word sometimes cannot. Paintings, photographs, and other types of images provide clues about an era's architecture and technology and can give the viewer a feel for the dress, work, and values of a people.

Visual artists often use their imagination and artistic freedom to add or omit details. Thus even the most realistic painting may not be an accurate record of history. In addition, artists sometimes depict a time period earlier than their own. They depend on others' accounts and may lack reliable enough information to portray the events accurately. Artists are also influenced by their own values and by social and artistic movements. Consequently, you must interpret what you view.

How to Interpret the Visual Record

1. **Determine the work's subject matter.** Note the people portrayed and any objects surrounding them. For clues about a work's theme, examine its title, if it has one.
2. **Examine the details.** Study the details and the background.
3. **Determine the artist's point of view.** Look for information in the picture that suggests the artist's purpose. Ask yourself: Is the subject depicted favorably or unfavorably?

Find out when the work was created and what contemporary influences may have shaped the artist's outlook.
4. **Use the information cautiously.** Compare what you know from other sources about the event, people, or period being portrayed.

Applying the Strategy

Study the untitled painting below of colonial Baltimore in the mid-1700s. Note the wide harbor, which made the site an appealing place to settle. The loading dock and British trading ship in the painting's center show that shipping was important to Baltimore from its founding. A striking feature of the painting is the sharp contrast between the orderly settlement and the thick woods beyond the back fence—the environment out of which the town was created. Few people are noticeably at work, but the many buildings that dot the landscape and the neat roads, fences, and rows of crops suggest how much work has gone into establishing the colony. This peaceful image of an enterprising new community was perhaps meant to attract additional colonists or to inspire others.

Practicing the Strategy

Study the images on pages 36–37 and 67 depicting European views of Native Americans during the colonial period. Then, on a separate sheet of paper, answer the following questions.

1. **(a)** How do the two illustrations differ in their presentation of Native Americans? How are they similar? **(b)** To what do you attribute the difference and similarities between the illustrations?
2. Based on what you have learned about Native Americans, evaluate the historical accuracy of each illustration.

▼ **Colonial Baltimore, 1752**

BUILDING YOUR PORTFOLIO

Outlined below are three projects. Independently or cooperatively, complete one and use the products to demonstrate your mastery of the historical concepts involved.

1 TRADE

Trade became truly worldwide from the time of the Crusades through the mid-1700s, bringing diverse cultures into contact with one another. Using the portfolio materials you designed in chapters 1, 2, and 3, write a proposal for a trade agreement to be presented at an upcoming international trade conference. Your trade proposal should take into account the interests of delegates from each participating nation.

2 SLAVERY

The *encomienda* system and the enslavement of Africans raised public debate in Europe and the Americas. Using the portfolio materials you designed in chapters 2 and 3, create a wall display that illustrates the nature and scope of this debate. Include in your display short biographies of Bartolomé de Las Casas, Benjamin Banneker, and other opponents of either or both systems.

3 CULTURAL EXCHANGES

Many different cultures exchanged technology, food, religion, and ideas in the Americas. Using the portfolio materials you designed in chapters 1, 2, and 3, prepare a brochure that explains the variety of cultural exchanges explored in your museum exhibit. Then present your brochure and exhibit to the class.

Video Review

In assigned groups, develop an outline for a video collage of the Americas from prehistory through 1763. Choose images that best illustrate the major topics of the period. Write a script to accompany the images. Assign narrators to different parts of the script, and present your video collage to the class.

Further Reading

Bakeless, John. *America As Seen by Its First Explorers: The Eyes of Discovery.* Dover (1989). Descriptions of North America taken from the firsthand accounts of early explorers.

Clendinnen, Inga. *Aztecs.* Cambridge University Press (1991). Explores life in the Aztec capital in the period immediately before the arrival of the first Spanish explorers and conquistadors.

Hawke, David F. *Everyday Life in Early America.* Harper & Row (1988). Portrait of life in early New England.

Hirschfelder, Arlene, and Paulette Molin. *The Encyclopedia of Native American Religions.* Facts On File (1992). Descriptions of Native American religious customs and leaders in encyclopedia form.

Josephy, Jr., Alvin M. *America in 1492: The World of the Indian Peoples before the Arrival of Columbus.* Random House (1991). Panorama of North and South American life from prehistoric times to the early 15th century.

Nash, Gary B. *Red, White, and Black: The Peoples of Early North America.* Prentice Hall (1992). Account of interaction between Native Americans, Africans, and whites during colonial times.

Weber, David J. *The Spanish Frontier in North America.* Yale University Press (1992). Overview of Spanish exploration and colonization in North America.

American ALMANAC

❖ The American People

Life expectancy in 1989 is more than twice that of 1789!

LIFE EXPECTANCY

Women
Men

Years

80
70
60
50
40
30
20
10
0

1789   1989

Source: Bureau of the Census

❖ Inventing America

1760s Ben Franklin invents bifocal lenses.

1767 Philadelphian David Rittenhouse builds first planetarium in America.

1769 Mansion in Maryland is built with only known indoor toilet in America.

1792 African American astronomer Benjamin Banneker publishes his almanac, which includes weather forecasts, times of eclipses, hours of sunrise and sunset, tide table for Chesapeake Bay, and phases of the moon.

1800 William Young of Philadelphia makes "left" and "right" shoes; before, shoes were interchangeable.

◄ Benjamin Banneker's almanac

❖ The Student Life

1765 Wealthy young southerners are typically taught reading, writing, arithmetic, geometry, trigonometry, Greek and Roman history, Latin, Greek, Hebrew, surveying, bookkeeping, and navigation.

1776 College of Philadelphia offers first college course in U.S. on Spanish grammar and literature.

1785 Integrated free school opens in St. Augustine, Spanish Florida; Spanish, Minorcan, African, Greek, and Italian boys attend.

1787 New York African Free School opens with 40 students; by 1820, 500 students are enrolled.

◄ Ben Franklin

▲ Ben Franklin's own eyeglasses

▶ New Orleans architecture showing Spanish influence

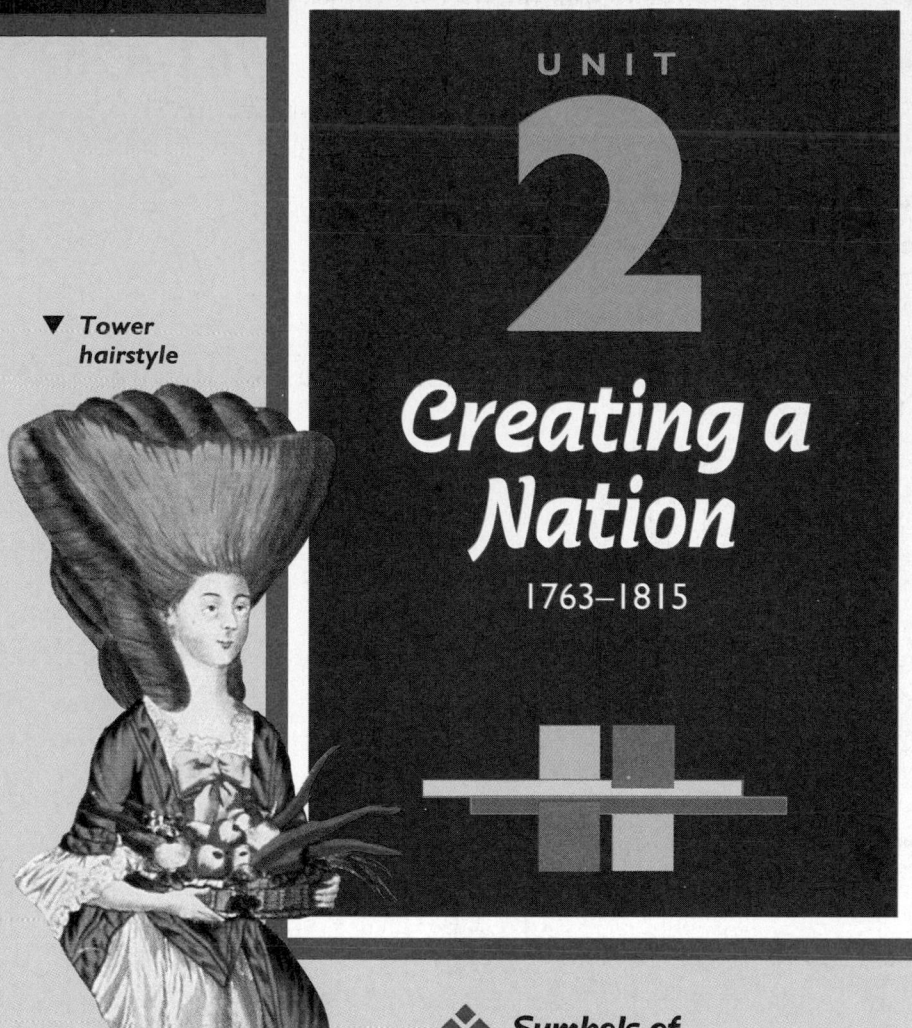

▼ Tower hairstyle

UNIT 2

Creating a Nation

1763–1815

❖ **At Your Leisure**

▲ Phillis Wheatley

1773 British readers rave over book of poetry by young Boston slave Phillis Wheatley, who couldn't find an American printer.

1801 Frontiersmen entertain themselves with wrestling, knife throwing, shooting, and logrolling contests.

1810 Newspapers in print number 359—up from only 37 in 1776.

1811 Rowing is a favorite sport—60,000 cheer as an American crew rows to beat British team off coast of New Jersey.

❖ **Symbols of a New Nation**

1776 E Pluribus Unum, "from many, one," is suggested as nation's motto by Ben Franklin, Thomas Jefferson, and John Adams.

1784 "The turkey is a much more respectable bird," says Ben Franklin, recommending it, not the bald eagle, as the national bird.

1812 Version of Uncle Sam legend starts with meat packer Sam Wilson in Troy, New York, who stamps containers of beef for U.S. Army with letters "U.S." for "Uncle Sam's beef." Soon anything having to do with federal government is called Uncle Sam's.

1814 Francis Scott Key writes words to "The Star Spangled Banner."

❖ **Town and Country**

Men who work outside wear inexpensive country boots—pieces of cloth wrapped around the calves and tied just below the knee and around the ankle.

By the early 1800s many New Orleans homes incorporate Spanish architecture—elaborate wrought-iron grillwork, balconies, and central patios with fountains.

Stylish women wear the tower hairstyle—piling their hair high over pads and decorating it with flowers, beads, ribbons, lace, even a yard-high ostrich feather!

Farmers and frontier men and women adopt Native American footwear—moccasins.

The Granger Collection, New York

Chapter 4

1763–1783

INDEPENDENCE!

▼ FOCUS

UNDERSTANDING THE MAIN IDEA

Colonial conflicts with the British eventually erupted into war. But the American Revolution was more than a war for independence. It established a new relationship between government and the governed and a new definition of human rights.

THEMES

- **ECONOMIC DEVELOPMENT** How might the economic interests of one country conflict with those of another?

- **DEMOCRATIC VALUES** In a democracy, when are individuals and groups justified in protesting taxes or specific laws? What kinds of actions are proper for people to take?

- **GLOBAL RELATIONS** Do powerful nations have any obligations toward less-powerful nations? If so, what kinds of obligations?

1763	1765	1770	1775	1776	1781	1783
▼	▼	▼	▼	▼	▼	▼
Pontiac's Rebellion crushed.	Stamp Act enacted.	Boston Massacre angers colonists.	Revolutionary War begins.	Declaration of Independence issued.	British surrender at Yorktown.	Treaty of Paris signed.

Through their victory in the French and Indian War, the British gained control of most of North America east of the Mississippi River. They now faced the tasks of governing, protecting, and financing their expanded empire.

Battle of Princeton

Ith the signing of the Treaty of Paris in 1763, Great Britain's future looked bright. Many people in Great Britain and elsewhere realized, however, that the British Empire faced new challenges. One of these observers, a French government official named Charles Gravier (grawv-yay) Comte de Vergennes (ver-ZHEN), believed that Great Britain's North American colonies would prove especially troublesome.

Mindful that France had lost its colonial claim in North America, Vergennes predicted a similar fate for Great Britain. "The American colonies stand no longer in need of England's protection," he said. "England," he continued, "will call on them to help contribute toward supporting the burden they have helped to bring on her, and they will answer by striking off all dependence."

Vergennes's prophecy would prove accurate. Thirteen years after his prediction, the British colonies along the Atlantic seaboard declared independence—and fought to win it.

Continental soldier

THE SEEDS OF UNREST

FOCUS

- Why did the Crown issue the Proclamation of 1763?
- Why did Parliament pass the Sugar Act and the Stamp Act?
- Why and how did the colonists protest British taxes?

Victory in the French and Indian War left Great Britain with a huge debt and more territory to govern and defend. British leaders expected the American colonists to help pay for administering this expanded empire. The colonists disagreed. With the French and Indian War over, the freedom many colonists sought to defend was their own. This attitude placed the colonies on a collision course with their protector.

Protests took many forms.

GOVERNING THE NEW TERRITORIES

The Treaty of Paris of 1763 forced the French to give up their North American empire. With the stroke of a pen, the British gained control of Spanish Florida, Canada, and the land between the Appalachian Mountains and the Mississippi River. It was rich land. Indian agent and trader George Croghan, who traveled through the western territory in 1765, noted in his diary that a "good hunter, without much fatigue to himself, could here daily supply one hundred men with meat." Croghan went on to describe the variety of the terrain:

> 66 We set out very early in the morning and marched through a high country, extremely well timbered, for three hours. . . . The remainder of this day we traveled through fine rich bottoms, overgrown with reeds, which make the best pasture in the world. 99

Such glowing reports drew pioneer farmers and speculators to the region. Ignoring Native American claims to the land, they demanded that the territory be opened for settlement. But British officials, fearing conflicts between pioneers and Native Americans, opposed this request.

Native American resistance. There was reason for concern. Following the war, the British had limited the amount of ammunition and rum available for trade with Native Americans. They had also abandoned the French practice of presenting annual gifts to the Indians. These changes angered many Native Americans who considered the trade goods

▲ **Settlers and traders to the Ohio Valley saw many colorful and unusual species of flora, such as this wild honeysuckle painted by naturalist artist Edwin Whitefield.**

and the presents fair payment for allowing colonists onto their lands. George Croghan warned that the Indians who "had great expectations of being very generally supplied by us" might wage war.

Native Americans' resentment grew as settlers poured into the western lands. Many Indian groups had already had their traditional ways of life disrupted by European trade. Now they were in danger of losing their lands as well. Alarmed, Neolin, known as the Delaware Prophet, traveled among western tribes, appealing for a return to ancient practices. He denounced the use of European goods and customs, urging his audiences to drive the settlers out. "They are my enemies," he said of the British. "They are your brothers' enemies."

Pontiac, an Ottawa chief, was inspired by Neolin's message. He called on the Delawares, Senecas, Shawnees, Wyandots, Ojibways, and other Indians to unite and "exterminate from our lands this nation which seeks only to destroy us." For most of 1763 war raged all along the frontier. Pontiac's forces killed some 2,000 settlers and destroyed many British forts.

Pontiac's Rebellion, however, ended when the Indians were unable to take Fort Detroit and Fort Pitt. For months they had besieged the forts. With winter approaching and ammunition in short supply, Pontiac's men began to doubt that victory was possible. Faced with disheartened warriors and no hope of French aid, Pontiac called off the siege.

The Proclamation of 1763. Pontiac's Rebellion and other Indian uprisings convinced British authorities that they could not effectively protect British settlers on the frontier. As a result, Great Britain issued the **Proclamation of 1763**, barring settlement west of the Appalachian Mountains. The law also required every fur trader to obtain royal permission before entering the territory.

The British hoped that separating settlers and Native Americans would end fighting on the frontier. But the proclamation was difficult to enforce. Land-hungry colonists resented the measure, and colonial governors, often land speculators themselves, did little to enforce it. Thus settlers continued to stream into the territory.

■■ **In the wake of Pontiac's Rebellion, the Crown issued the Proclamation of 1763 in hopes of bringing peace to the frontier.**

North America in 1763

GROWTH OF BRITISH NORTH AMERICA By the terms of the Treaty of Paris, Great Britain took control of millions of square miles of land in North America.

? **LINKING HISTORY AND GEOGRAPHY** Compare this map with the map on page 88. What new lands did Great Britain acquire between 1754 and 1763?

�峕INANCING THE EMPIRE

The royal proclamation was not the only British policy the colonists resented. They were also angered by Parliament's efforts to make them pay part of the costs of "protecting and securing" the frontier. Despite colonial protests, the government believed its position was justified. Thomas Whately stated the Crown's position in his pamphlet *Considerations on This Trade and Finances of the Kingdom*:

❝ We are not yet recovered from a War undertaken . . . for their Protection . . . and . . . no Time was ever so seasonable for claiming their Assistance. The Distribution is too unequal, of Benefits only to the colonies, and of all the Burthens [burdens] upon the Mother Country. ❞

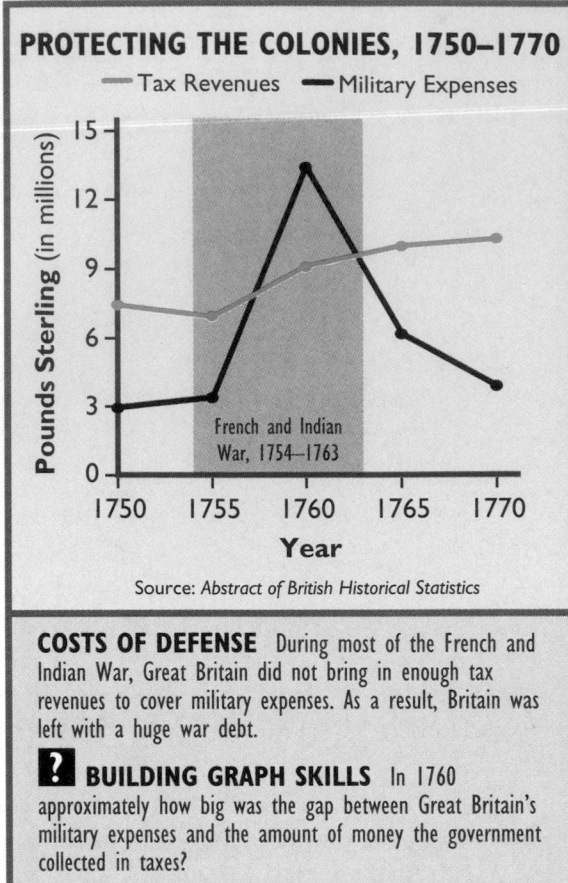

PROTECTING THE COLONIES, 1750–1770

— Tax Revenues — Military Expenses

Source: Abstract of British Historical Statistics

COSTS OF DEFENSE During most of the French and Indian War, Great Britain did not bring in enough tax revenues to cover military expenses. As a result, Britain was left with a huge war debt.

? BUILDING GRAPH SKILLS In 1760 approximately how big was the gap between Great Britain's military expenses and the amount of money the government collected in taxes?

The question of how to raise this needed revenue always came back to one solution—taxes. Thus as a first step to increase revenue, Parliament passed the **Sugar Act** of 1764, which set a **duty**, or import tax, on foreign sugar, molasses, and several other goods.

This was not the first time the British had imposed a duty on foreign molasses and sugar. In fact, the new law actually lowered the existing duty on molasses. It was, however, the first time officials seriously enforced such a law. Royal inspectors searched ships, warehouses, and homes for smuggled goods. The Crown's judges presided over courts without juries to hear smuggling cases.

For colonial merchants, shipowners, and rum distillers who profited from foreign trade and smuggling, the Sugar Act meant decreased business. They angrily protested the law.

Amid these protests, Parliament passed another revenue law, the **Stamp Act** of 1765. Far more sweeping than the Sugar Act, the Stamp Act levied a tax on printed matter of all kinds: newspapers, advertisements, playing cards, and legal documents. These materials had to be printed on stamped paper or have special stamps affixed to show the tax had been paid.

■■ The British government passed the Sugar Act and the Stamp Act in an effort to raise revenue in the colonies.

COLONIAL PROTESTS

British officials had expected the colonists to object to the Stamp Act, but they were not prepared for the level of outcry. In the past the colonists had accepted taxes levied by the colonial assemblies. In the colonists' eyes, however, this tax was different—it had been passed by Parliament, where the colonists had no direct representation.

Colonial assemblies met in protest. In May 1765 the Virginia House of Burgesses passed a series of resolutions condemning the act. The resolutions declared that

66 the taxation of the people by themselves, or by persons chosen by themselves to represent them, . . . is the only security against a burdensome taxation, and the distinguishing characteristick of British freedom. 99

British officials countered by claiming that the colonists had "virtual representation," since Parliament represented all British subjects. Many colonists rejected this argument and decided it was time to act.

The Granger Collection, New York

▶ **The Stamp Act required colonists to display tax stamps on all printed documents.**

A call to action. Colonial merchants signed **nonimportation agreements**, promising not to buy or import British goods. Workers and artisans who opposed the Stamp Act took to the streets in demonstrations. Though most of these protests were peaceful, some did turn violent. One of the most violent demonstrations occurred in Boston on a hot August night in 1765. A mob led by shoemaker Ebenezer MacIntosh wrecked a building belonging to stamp agent Andrew Oliver and then beheaded an effigy—a crude likeness—of Oliver. Within two weeks the mob struck again, destroying court records and wrecking the house of the chief customs officer. They then turned their anger on the elegant mansion of Oliver's brother-in-law Thomas Hutchinson—the lieutenant governor of the colony. Throughout the colonies terrified stamp agents resigned their posts—rendering the Stamp Act almost impossible to enforce.

British officials singled out MacIntosh as the mob's leader. But they also suspected that members of the Boston Sons of Liberty were involved. The **Sons of Liberty** were secret committees made up of politicians, lawyers, merchants, and artisans, formed to protest the Stamp Act. The Sons of Liberty generally relied on petitions, public meetings, and pamphlets to rally support, but they were not above employing violence.

Samuel Adams was one of the leaders of the Boston Sons of Liberty. Born in 1722, Adams graduated from Harvard College but failed in the family brewing business. He fared better at politics. After being elected to the Massachusetts House of Representatives in 1765, Adams made a career of politics. The Stamp Act crisis turned him into a key political activist.

Samuel Adams

A contemporary of Adams described him as a man who "eats little, drinks little, sleeps little, thinks much, and is most decisive and indefatigable [tireless] in the pursuit of his objects." A master of propaganda, Adams often worked behind the scenes, staging demonstrations and working to control the public's perception of events. He started a club to influence local politics and wrote often for the Boston *Gazette*. Adams was particularly popular among Boston's less-prosperous artisans and shopkeepers. They responded enthusiastically to his charges that the British were stealing money from the colonists' pockets:

> 66 We are told to be quiet when we see that very money which is torn from us by lawless force made use of still further to oppose us, to feed and pamper a set of infamous wretches [British officials and soldiers] who swarm like the locusts of Egypt. 99

REPEAL OF THE STAMP ACT

Led by Samuel Adams and others, the colonists made themselves heard in England. In October 1765, delegates from nine colonies gathered in New York City for the **Stamp Act Congress**. The delegates expressed the "warmest sentiments of

◀ Before the Stamp Act went into effect, the *Pennsylvania Journal and Weekly Advertiser* printed a skull and crossbones on its masthead in protest of the measure.

THE REPEAL.
OR THE FUNERAL OF MISS AME-STAMP.

◀ This 1766 British cartoon satirizes the repeal of the Stamp Act. As members of the British government carry the dead act in a coffin, background ships show that trade with America is already beginning.

affection and duty to His Majesty's Person and Government" and pledged "all due subordination" to Parliament. Yet they also sought repeal of the Stamp Act and denied Parliament's right to tax the colonies. The congress marked an important step toward more unified resistance.

British merchants who profited from colonial trade joined in the protest. The nonimportation agreements had hurt their businesses. Fearing financial ruin, and wanting to keep the colonies "firmly attached to their mother country," they pressured Parliament to repeal the Stamp Act. Thus people on both sides of the Atlantic rejoiced when Parliament repealed the act in March 1766.

■■ Colonists protested "taxation without representation" through petitions, nonimportation agreements, and demonstrations.

Busy celebrating the Stamp Act's demise, most colonists ignored the passage of the **Declaratory Act** of 1766. This bold declaration asserted the "full power and authority" of Parliament "to make laws . . . to bind the colonies and people of *America*." The issue of whether Parliament had the right to tax the colonists remained unresolved.

SECTION 1 REVIEW

IDENTIFY and explain the significance of the following: Pontiac's Rebellion, Proclamation of 1763, Sugar Act, duty, Stamp Act, nonimportation agreements, Sons of Liberty, Samuel Adams, Stamp Act Congress, Declaratory Act.

1. **MAIN IDEA** How did the Crown attempt to bring peace to the frontier following Pontiac's Rebellion?

2. **MAIN IDEA** What was the purpose of the Sugar Act and the Stamp Act? How did the colonists react to these measures?

3. **GAINING A MULTICULTURAL PERSPECTIVE** Imagine that you are a Native American living west of the Appalachian Mountains in the 1760s. Explain why you favor or oppose Neolin's message.

4. **WRITING TO EXPRESS A VIEWPOINT** You have just returned from the Stamp Act Congress. Write a letter to your colonial governor outlining the views of the congress's delegates.

5. **ANALYZING** Why did Parliament repeal the Stamp Act? Why did the repeal not solve the issue of taxation without representation?

Section 2

MOUNTING TENSIONS

FOCUS

- **What events led to the Boston Massacre?**
- **Why did the colonists stage the Boston Tea Party?**
- **Why did the British pass the Intolerable Acts?**

Although colonial protests helped repeal the Stamp Act, they did not end Parliament's efforts to raise revenue in the colonies. When Parliament tried a new approach that did not involve direct taxes, the arguments used against the Stamp Act were also applied to these new measures. These protests were unsuccessful, setting in motion events that pushed the colonies to the brink of war.

British troops occupy Boston in 1768.

THE TOWNSHEND ACTS

The colonists had objected to the Stamp Act because Parliament had imposed it. It was, they argued, just one more example of Great Britain's meddling in colonial affairs. But Charles Townshend, Great Britain's finance minister, like many other government officials, never grasped this point. Townshend believed that the colonists had opposed the stamp tax because it was collected within the colonies. They would, he reasoned, be willing to accept a tax that would be collected at colonial ports. Parliament agreed, passing the **Townshend Acts** in 1767. The Townshend Acts placed import duties on such common items as tea, lead, glass, and dyes for paint. British customs officials revived the use of special search warrants called **writs of assistance** to enforce the law. Unlike today's search warrants, which must state the exact articles sought and the specific

places to be searched, writs of assistance were general warrants. Armed with a writ, a customs officer could search any vessel, warehouse, or home on the mere suspicion that it contained smuggled goods.

The writs of assistance aroused powerful opposition, and many colonial courts refused to issue them. Although the colonists accepted Great Britain's right to regulate colonial trade, they strongly objected to duties intended strictly to raise money. The Crown, troubled by renewed protests, stationed additional soldiers in the colonies. The New York assembly responded by refusing to vote money to quarter, or house and supply, these troops as the **Quartering Act** of 1765 required. The British government promptly suspended the assembly.

But the real center of protest was Boston. In February 1768 the Massachusetts legislature drafted a letter attacking taxation without representation and sent it to the other colonial assemblies for endorsement. The British government responded by dissolving the Massachusetts assembly. This only served to fuel protests and a new round of nonimportation

▶ **Charles Townshend was responsible for passage of the Townshend Acts in 1767.**

The Granger Collection, New York

INDEPENDENCE! 109

agreements. A Massachusetts woman wrote that her friends would not touch "a Drop of Tea." Other women, rather than buy British cloth, held spinning parties to make their own. Angry demonstrators boarded and smashed British ships, attacked customs officials, and tarred and feathered anyone who informed on smugglers.

THE BOSTON MASSACRE

In 1768 General Thomas Gage dispatched British troops to Boston to quiet the protests and enforce the writs of assistance. But tensions exploded into one violent confrontation after another. On the evening of March 5, 1770, an angry crowd gathered outside a customs house. Some 50 or 60 colonists faced a small group of British soldiers. The crowd yelled insults and began throwing snowballs, rocks, oyster shells, and pieces of coal at the soldiers. Then, according to John Adams, "the motley mob of saucy boys, negroes, mulattoes, . . . and outlandish jacktars [sailors]" pressed so hard against the soldiers that there was no room to move. One soldier either slipped or was knocked down. His gun discharged, and the others opened fire on the crowd. Three colonists, including Crispus Attucks—a sailor and an escaped slave of African and Native American ancestry—lay dead. Two others died later.

News of the clash stunned the colonists. Lieutenant Governor Thomas Hutchinson claimed that "the people of Boston are run mad." Sam Adams and the Sons of Liberty promptly dubbed the incident the **Boston Massacre** and denounced British aggression. The victims received elaborate funerals and inspired poems and songs of patriotic resistance.

Months later the British soldiers were tried for murder. Josiah Quincy and John Adams—Sam's cousin—agreed to defend them. Neither man sympathized with the British, but both insisted on the soldiers' right to a fair trial. As John Adams later wrote:

> 66 Counsel ought to be the very last thing that an accused person should want [lack] in a free country; . . . and . . . persons whose lives were at stake ought to have the counsel they prefer. 99

In the end, two soldiers were convicted of a lesser charge. They were branded on their thumbs and released.

■■ **Mounting tensions between the colonists and the British soldiers stationed in Boston to enforce the Townshend Acts sparked the Boston Massacre.**

▲ Crispus Attucks

◀ Crispus Attucks, a sailor and runaway slave, was one of three men killed by British troops during the Boston Massacre.

CONTINUING UNREST

When Frederick, Lord North became Great Britain's prime minister in 1770, he hoped to pacify the rebellious colonies by a partial repeal of the Townshend Acts. Parliament consented and also allowed the Quartering Act to expire. But the British retained a small duty on tea. As the king explained, there must "always be one tax to keep up the right."

The repeal quieted the general unrest, but the calm was short-lived. In 1772 the Crown announced that it—not the colonial legislature—would pay the salaries of Massachusetts' governor and judges. The Crown reasoned that if these officials did not depend on the legislature for their pay, they might more readily ignore colonial demands.

Bostonians, led by Sam Adams, challenged this latest threat. They created a 21-member **Committee of Correspondence** charged with keeping the rest of the colony—and "the World"—informed about events. From 1772 to 1776, similar committees in Massachusetts and other colonies helped shape colonial opinion.

The Tea Act of 1773. Even the business of selling tea provoked a crisis. By 1773 the powerful British East India Company was almost bankrupt. To save the ailing company, Parliament passed the **Tea Act** of 1773. The law excused the company from paying certain duties and permitted it to bypass the wholesalers and sell tea directly to American agents. As a result the price of tea in the colonies was lower than ever before.

Most of the colonists, however, opposed the Tea Act and refused to buy the tea. What concerned many of them was the possible monopoly of the tea trade by the East India Company. American wholesalers and merchants feared that other British companies would secure similar privileges from Parliament and force them out of business.

The Sons of Liberty in Philadelphia and New York threatened anyone who imported tea. But the most famous protest against the Tea Act occurred in Massachusetts. On December 16, 1773, after the governor refused demands to send three shiploads of tea back to England, colonists held a mass meeting at Boston's Old South Church. Later that night, a well-organized group of colonists "dressed in an Indian manner" boarded the tea ships anchored in Boston Harbor and dumped 90,000 pounds of tea into the water. As one of the participants later remembered:

66 In about three hours from the time we went on board, we had thus broken and thrown overboard every tea chest to be found. . . . We were surrounded by British armed ships, but no attempt was made to resist us. 99

News of the **Boston Tea Party** drew widespread attention at home and abroad. Many colonists cheered the tea's destruction; others were shocked by such disregard for property rights.

■■ **Bostonians staged the Boston Tea Party to protest the Tea Act.**

The Intolerable Acts of 1774. British officials were furious. Parliament responded by passing the Coercive Acts, four laws designed to punish Boston and the rest of Massachusetts and to strengthen British control over all of the colonies. The colonists called the laws the **Intolerable Acts**.

THE POWER OF THE PURSE, 1763–1776

Value of British Imports (in millions)

Intolerable Acts—1774

British Troops sent to Boston—1768

Sugar Act—1764

Townshend Acts (except tea tax) repealed—1770

Year

Source: *Historical Statistics of the United States*

EFFECT OF PROTESTS Colonists reacted to British policies such as the Sugar and Stamp acts by refusing to import British goods. Parliament's repeal of the Townshend Acts resulted in a brief upsurge in imports. But soon British actions sparked new protests.

? BUILDING GRAPH SKILLS Between which two years did British imports experience the greatest drop?

Quebec Act of 1774

Quebec boundary, 1763
Quebec boundary, 1774
Western claims
The 13 Colonies
Colonial boundaries including western claims

COLONIAL LAND CLAIMS The Quebec Act extended Quebec's boundaries south to the Ohio River.

? LINKING HISTORY AND GEOGRAPHY Which colonies were most directly affected by Quebec's boundary change? Why?

meetings. The third act allowed royal officials charged with crimes related to their duties to be tried in England. Many colonists assumed the soldiers would be lightly punished or escape punishment entirely. The fourth law, a new Quartering Act, ordered local officials to provide food and housing, in private homes if necessary, for British soldiers stationed in the colonies.

▪▪ The British passed the Intolerable Acts to punish Massachusetts for the Boston Tea Party and to regain control over the colonies.

The Intolerable Acts deepened colonial hostility toward the Crown. Colonists everywhere responded with sympathy toward Massachusetts, while denouncing George III, the Parliament, and the threats to colonial liberty.

The **Quebec Act**, also passed in 1774, was not technically one of the Intolerable Acts, but it further inflamed colonial resentment. The law extended Quebec's boundaries south to the Ohio River, thus overriding the claims of Massachusetts, Connecticut, and Virginia to the western lands. It also granted full religious rights to French Roman Catholics, upsetting many Protestant colonists.

The movement toward colonial unity quickened after 1774. The colonists directed their anger no longer at specific British policies but at what they saw as a growing pattern of oppression. Among those who questioned loyalty to the Crown and Parliament, a new identity—not yet fully American, but no longer British—was emerging.

The first act closed the port of Boston until the colonists paid for the destroyed tea. The second act revoked the Massachusetts charter of 1691 and forbade Massachusetts colonists to hold town

---

SECTION 2 REVIEW

IDENTIFY and explain the significance of the following: Townshend Acts, writs of assistance, Quartering Act, Crispus Attucks, Committee of Correspondence, Tea Act, Intolerable Acts, Quebec Act.

1. **MAIN IDEA** Why were British troops stationed in Boston? How did their presence provoke the Boston Massacre?

2. **MAIN IDEA** How did the colonists react to the Tea Act of 1773?

3. **IDENTIFYING CAUSE AND EFFECT** Create a time line showing the events leading up to the passage of the Intolerable Acts.

4. **WRITING TO DESCRIBE** Imagine that you are a member of the Sons of Liberty. In a letter to the colonists outside Massachusetts, write an account of the Boston Massacre or the Boston Tea Party that will rally them to oppose Britain.

5. **ASSESSING CONSEQUENCES** How did the Intolerable Acts and the Quebec Act help unify the colonies?

Section 3

THE SHOT HEARD ROUND THE WORLD

FOCUS

■ How did the First Continental Congress respond to British actions?

■ What actions did the Second Continental Congress take?

In 1774, delegates from 12 colonies met in Philadelphia at the First Continental Congress to voice their opposition to British actions. The delegates demanded that the British government restore colonial rights. But Great Britain ignored the demands. Delegates called the Second Continental Congress in 1775 to plan their next move. As the crisis deepened, war seemed inevitable.

Struggle at
Concord Bridge

THE FIRST CONTINENTAL CONGRESS

Between September 5 and October 26, 1774, representatives from every colony except Georgia attended the **First Continental Congress** in Philadelphia to discuss their grievances. Some delegates to the Congress—which was a convention, not a lawmaking body—wanted the colonies to remain part of the British Empire; others favored independence.

The delegates' efforts to compromise between these two positions were reflected in the Congress's final resolution, the Declaration of Resolves. While expressing loyalty to the British Crown, the declaration outlined the colonists' rights as British subjects and asserted the peoples' right to the "free and exclusive power of legislation in their several provincial legislatures." To put teeth in their demands, the colonists also called for a ban of all trade with Great Britain. The delegates pledged to meet again in May 1775 if their demands were not met.

■■ Delegates to the First Continental Congress demanded that the Crown restore colonial rights and called on the colonists not to buy British goods.

For George III the Continental Congress was the last straw. In November 1774 he wrote to Lord North: "The New England Governments are in a

◀ George III, shown here at age 33, reigned as king of England for 60 years.

State of Rebellion, blows must decide whether they are to be subject to this Country or independent." Acting on the king's wishes, Parliament ordered General Thomas Gage to put down the rebellion.

LEXINGTON AND CONCORD

In an effort to reassert royal authority, Gage decided to seize rebel supplies stored at Concord, Massachusetts. On April 18, 1775, under cover of darkness, British troops left Boston and rowed across the Charles River. But they were expected. Colonists waited on the far shore, watching for signs of approaching troops. At first sight, Boston Patriots Paul Revere and William Dawes galloped off into the night shouting the fateful alarm: "The British are coming!" Patriots throughout the countryside hurriedly headed off to meet the British.

At dawn on April 19, Captain John Parker and 70 **minutemen**—members of the militia who promised to be ready at a minute's notice—waited on the Lexington village green. When the British patrol arrived, its commander shouted, "Lay down your arms, you damned rebels, and disperse!" The colonists began departing, still holding their guns. Suddenly someone—each side accused the other—fired "the shot heard round the world." A barrage

of British gunfire followed. When the smoke cleared, 8 colonists lay dead, 10 others wounded.

The British marched on to Concord and destroyed the Patriot supplies. Then the British started back toward Boston. From behind stone walls minutemen fired steadily at the retreating British, whose traditional marching formations made them easy targets. The Patriots made an impressive showing, suffering fewer than 100 casualties in the day's fighting. British casualties were 273. A humbled British officer wrote: "Whoever looks upon them [the Patriots] as an irregular mob will find himself much mistaken."

THE SECOND CONTINENTAL CONGRESS

With the news of Lexington and Concord on everyone's lips, the **Second Continental Congress** opened in Philadelphia on May 10. Although radicals such as Samuel Adams pushed for an immediate declaration of independence, conservatives led by John Dickinson of Pennsylvania urged restraint. By June, however, the delegates had agreed to establish the Continental Army.

The delegates unanimously chose George Washington of Virginia to command the Continental Army. Though not a fiery orator or a profound political thinker, Washington inspired confidence. His careful judgment, dignity, and imposing stature enhanced his reputation. After meeting him Abigail Adams wrote to her husband: "The gentleman and soldier look agreeably blended in him. Modesty marks every line and feature of his face."

George Washington

BIO GRAPHY Born February 22, 1732, George Washington first worked as a surveyor, later assuming control of the family's large Virginia plantation, Mount Vernon. Washington acquired military experience and a reputation for bravery while fighting for the British in the French and Indian War. He also served twice as a Virginia delegate to the Continental Congress. With his country now at war, Washington

Map: Lexington and Concord

Revere's route ········► Prescott's route

- -► Dawes's route ✸ Battle

Concord R.

✸ North Bridge
Concord
Lexington

0 — 5 Miles
0 — 5 Kilometers
Transverse Mercator Projection

BRITISH FORCES

Stopped by the British, only Prescott manages to reach Concord.

Charlestown

Cambridge

Charles River

Boston

Boston Harbor

N W E S

Lexington and Concord

FIRST BATTLES OF THE REVOLUTION In April 1775, on their way to seize rebel arms and ammunition at Concord, British forces clashed with colonial minutemen at Lexington. The American Revolution had begun.

? MOVEMENT As British troops began their march, Paul Revere and William Dawes rode off to alert the Patriots. They were later joined by Dr. Samuel Prescott. Why might Revere and Dawes have taken different routes?

Many leaders of the American Revolution found their inspiration in the Enlightenment, which stressed goodness and reason over faith. But for many colonists, the Protestant religious traditions of the Great Awakening—not Enlightenment ideals—shaped their views of the struggle for independence. Evangelicalism, with its emphasis on faith and individuality over absolute authority, seemed to echo the promise of the Revolution.

Revolutionary leaders were well aware of the power of religion to sway public opinion. Patrick Henry was among those who used the evangelical style in their political speeches. These leaders often spoke of the war as a moral struggle between good and evil.

While most colonial ministers tried to distance themselves from the political upheavals of the era, some pro-independence ministers preached the Revolution's message from their pulpits. Scores of Congregationalist ministers in New England, Presbyterian ministers in the middle colonies, and Baptist ministers in Virginia openly supported the Revolution. And although most Anglican ministers in New England and the middle colonies remained loyal to the British, about a third of the Anglican clergy in Maryland and Virginia threw their support behind the struggle for independence.

▲ The fiery style of the Great Awakening ministers and their message that good could triumph over evil hit a responsive chord in Revolutionary America.

In their sermons, pro-independence ministers reinforced the Revolution's political message of the moral struggle between good and evil. Thomas Craddock, a Maryland Anglican, warned his flock:

66 The life of every sincere Christian is a warfare against a great number of Enemies, some of them very potent, and others very politick. Virtue is a rich Prey rescued narrowly out of the Fire, the purchase of Labor and sweat of Care and Vigilance. We are too liable to loose it by our own Sloth and Treachery. 99

Some ministers were even more pointed in supporting the Revolution. Thomas Jefferson noted that one Anglican minister in Virginia urged his congregation "to support their Liberties . . . and in a room of God save the king he cried out

God Preserve all of the Just rights and Liberties of America."

The vast majority of Anglican ministers, however, did not share the southern clergy's zeal for the Revolution. Revolutionary leaders often used the tax-sponsored Anglican church as an example of the Crown's tyranny, thus the clergy feared that the Revolution might threaten the church's existence in America. Many German Reformed and Lutheran ministers in Pennsylvania and Scots-Irish Presbyterian ministers on the frontier also feared the consequences of the Revolution. As early as 1775, German Reformed ministers warned their congregations that they lived in dangerous times, "the like of which, so far as we know, has never been seen in America." Others agreed. No matter what the outcome, war was sure to divide communities and test the limits of religious authority.

◄ Martha Dandridge Custis, one of the richest women in America, married George Washington in 1759.

Washington/Custis/Lee Collection, Washington & Lee University

devoted himself and his fortune to the "glorious cause" of American independence.

After the fighting at Lexington and Concord, the Second Continental Congress moved beyond peaceful solutions and began active preparations for war.

𝒯HE BATTLE OF BOSTON

On June 17, 1775, the Patriot forces were again put to the test. Atop two hills overlooking Boston Harbor—Bunker Hill and Breed's Hill—New England militiamen dug in, awaiting an onslaught of British troops. To save ammunition, an American commander ordered his men: "Don't one of you fire until you see the whites of their eyes."

British troops commanded by General Sir William Howe advanced in three bold assaults. Corporal Amos Farnsworth of the Massachusetts militia later recalled the **Battle of Bunker Hill**:

66 We . . . sustained the enemy's attacks with great bravery. . . ; and after bearing, for about 2 hours, as severe and heavy a fire as perhaps ever was known, and many having fired away all their ammunition . . . we were overpowered by numbers and obliged to leave. 99

The British took both hills but suffered 1,054 casualties. Fewer than 450 Americans were killed or injured.

Even after the battle, conservatives worked to avoid a permanent break with Great Britain. They persuaded the Continental Congress to send a final plea to George III. This plea—the **Olive Branch Petition**—professed the colonists' loyalty to the king and asked for his help in ending the conflict.

■■ The Second Continental Congress established the Continental Army in June 1775. But the delegates held out the hope of peace with the Olive Branch Petition.

The king refused to accept the petition and ordered the Royal Navy to blockade all shipping to the colonies. He also sent Hessian (HESH-uhn) mercenaries—hired soldiers primarily from the German state Hesse—to help defeat the Americans.

Meanwhile, George Washington had plans of his own. In a surprise move on March 4, 1776, he positioned troops and cannon on Dorchester Heights overlooking Boston. From there, the Patriots could fire on British forces in the city. Washington hoped to force General Howe and his men to take the hill or flee Boston. General Howe chose to flee. On March 26, 1776, the British, joined by about one thousand colonists loyal to the Crown, sailed for Nova Scotia—leaving, said Washington, "in so much . . . confusion as ever troops did."

SECTION 3 REVIEW

IDENTIFY and explain the significance of the following: First Continental Congress, minutemen, Second Continental Congress, George Washington, Battle of Bunker Hill, Olive Branch Petition.

LOCATE and explain the importance of the following: Lexington, Concord.

1. **MAIN IDEA** What actions did the First Continental Congress take?

2. **MAIN IDEA** Why can it be said that the Second Continental Congress both prepared for war and hoped for peace?

3. **GEOGRAPHY: LOCATION** How did the Patriots attempt to use geography to their advantage at Bunker Hill and at Dorchester Heights?

4. **WRITING TO INFORM** Imagine that you are a reporter for the Boston *Gazette*. Write a short account of the Battle of Bunker Hill for your newspaper.

5. **HYPOTHESIZING** What arguments might the conservatives at the Second Continental Congress have used to convince the other delegates to send the Olive Branch Petition to George III?

INDEPENDENCE DECLARED

FOCUS

- How did the Declaration of Independence justify America's break with Great Britain?
- What roles did Loyalists, African Americans, Native Americans, and women play in the Revolutionary War?
- What problems did the colonial military have to overcome?

*F*ighting had begun. Yet most colonists insisted they were merely resisting unjust acts of Parliament, not waging war. Many hesitated to make a final break with Great Britain. After all, the British government maintained stability in the colonies and provided protection from France and Spain. But to others, the time was ripe for independence.

Carpenter's Hall in Philadelphia, site of Second Continental Congress

REASONS FOR INDEPENDENCE

Many colonists supported independence for two reasons. First, they believed that the British government had violated their rights as English subjects. Second, colonists had already died defending these rights.

▲ Thomas Paine

Thomas Paine's pamphlet *Common Sense*, published in January 1776, urged revolution. Paine wrote:

> 66 The period of debate is closed. Arms, as the last resource, must decide the contest. . . . Every thing that is right or reasonable pleads for separation. The blood of the slain, the weeping voice of nature cries, 'TIS TIME TO PART. 99

Common Sense sold some 120,000 copies in three months—the most any pamphlet had ever sold in the colonies. It helped transform a haphazard colonial rebellion into a focused crusade for independence.

◀ After declaring bankruptcy, Thomas Paine emigrated to America from Great Britain in 1774. He settled in Philadelphia, where he wrote for *Pennsylvania Magazine*.

THE DECLARATION OF INDEPENDENCE

On June 7, 1776, Richard Henry Lee of Virginia introduced a resolution in the Second Continental Congress declaring "that these United Colonies are, and of right ought to be, free and independent States . . . and that all political connection between them and the State of Great Britain is . . . totally dissolved." The resolution also called for planning a confederation, or loose pact, of the states and for securing foreign alliances.

Before voting on Lee's proposal, the Congress appointed a five-man committee to draft a formal **Declaration of Independence**. Thomas Jefferson, a Virginia lawyer and planter—and at 33 one of the youngest delegates—did most of the actual writing. On June 28 the committee presented the Declaration to the Congress.

Before turning their attention to the Declaration, the Congress debated—and quickly adopted—Lee's resolution for independence, officially declaring on July 2 the new United States of America to be independent of Great Britain. Two days later, on July 4, the Congress formally adopted the Declaration of Independence.

The Declaration's immediate purpose was to win public support for independence, both at home and abroad. To undermine loyalty to King George III, the Declaration detailed his misdeeds. It also outlined basic principles of representative government, listing these "self-evident" truths:

> 66 We hold these truths to be self-evident, that all men are created equal, that they are endowed by their Creator with certain unalienable Rights, that among these are Life, Liberty, and the pursuit of Happiness. 99

The document also proclaimed the right of people "to alter or abolish" a government that deprived them of life, liberty, or happiness. The men who signed the Declaration of Independence knew they were now traitors in the eyes of the Crown. The price for failing to win independence might well be imprisonment or even death.

■■ **The Declaration of Independence asserted the right of people to overthrow an unjust government.**

COMMENTARY

Independence for Whom?

Thomas Jefferson's words "all men are created equal" have, almost from the beginning, been a source of controversy. What exactly did he mean? Remember that 18th-century colonial America, like Europe, was full of social, political, and economic inequalities. The delegates to the Continental Congress, as citizens of their time, would not have viewed issues of justice as we do today. Besides, they were seeking to justify a political, not a social, revolution.

Nevertheless, the Declaration and the revolution it symbolized had social consequences. Many women organized boycotts and participated in street demonstrations. During the war women took over the work of their absent husbands, fathers, and brothers, or cared for troops. As a result, some women argued for a greater voice in politics.

"I desire you would remember the ladies," Abigail Adams appealed to her husband, John, a delegate to the Continental Congress. "Be more generous and favorable to them than your ancestors." John Adams did not agree. Like most men of his day, he believed that women's power came from their influence over the men in their lives.

► Mum Bett, a Massachusetts slave, believed that the words "all men are created equal" should apply to her. In 1781 she successfully sued for her freedom. Her lawyer's daughter, Susan Sedgwick, painted this portrait of her.

> *Whether the delegates intended the words men and mankind to include women is debatable. It is more certain that they did not intend the words to apply to slaves. This statement does not mean, however, that all of the delegates supported slavery. In Jefferson's original draft, he accused the king of violating the "sacred rights of life and liberty" of blacks "who never offended him, captivating and carrying them into slavery in another hemisphere." But some of the southern delegates objected, and the passage was stricken from the final document. Thus America's leaders for the first but not the last time sidestepped the explosive issue of slavery.*

REACTIONS TO INDEPENDENCE

News of independence inspired mixed reactions throughout the colonies. Patriots rejoiced wildly—ringing "liberty bells," singing and dancing around bonfires, celebrating at banquets. On July 13 Ezra Stiles noted in his diary that "the CONGRESS have tied a . . . knot, which the Parliament will find they can neither cut nor untie. The *thirteen united Colonies* now rise into an *Independent Republic* among the kingdoms, states and empires on earth."

Some Americans opposed or simply ignored the developments. Among those who refused to celebrate were the **Loyalists**, also known as Tories. Some Tories based their loyalty to Great Britain on the long-held belief that to resist the king was to rebel against God. "It is our duty not to disturb and destroy the peace of the community by becoming . . . rebellious subjects and resisting the ordinances of God," explained one Anglican minister. Other Loyalists, such as merchants and officials, stood to lose power and wealth if royal authority were undermined. Many more saw support for the king as they saw loyalty to family.

As support for independence mounted, Loyalists feared for their safety. To many a Patriot, a Loyalist was "a thing whose head is in England, and its body is in America, and its neck ought to be stretched [hanged]." More disquieting than the taunts were the threats of violence to the Loyalists, their families, and their property.

Many wealthy and influential Loyalists escaped to Canada, the British West Indies, or England. Loyalists who remained either tried to stay out of the conflict or openly aided the British forces.

■■ **During the war, Loyalists either left the colonies, hid out until the fighting ended, or supported the British.**

THE DECLARATION OF INDEPENDENCE

THROUGH OTHERS' EYES

*C*ommon Sense, with its call for American independence, made for shocking reading in Great Britain. But British reaction to the Declaration of Independence in 1776 was even stronger, for it was not just a call for independence but a statement of it signed by many prominent Americans. Both Parliament and the king knew that it seriously challenged British authority.

An outraged British press was first to respond. In a reply to the "DISUNITED STATES in AMERICA," the **Morning Post** accused Americans of scorning "the duty and allegiance which in honour and in necessity they owe" to Great Britain. The British government's response—an 80-page pamphlet, **The Rights of Great Britain Against the Claims of America**—soon followed, attacking the Declaration paragraph by paragraph. The British did not see an American people struggling for independence; instead, they saw ungrateful fellow subjects betraying their mother country, which had protected and helped them. The British government found the Americans' "pretended arguments justifying rebellion" so defiant and unfair that it saw no alternative but to crush the rebellion.

HISTORICAL
Document

The Declaration of Independence

Thomas Jefferson wrote the first draft of the Declaration in a little more than two weeks.

In the first paragraph, the signers are justifying why they are separating from Great Britain.

impel: force

endowed: provided

"Laws of Nature" and "Nature's God" refer to Isaac Newton's belief that certain patterns are constant and predictable. Natural or "unalienable" rights (the rights to life, liberty, and the pursuit of happiness) cannot be taken away. The signers supported John Locke's view that people created governments to protect their natural rights. A government, therefore, must have the consent of the governed. If a government abuses its powers, it is the right as well as the duty of the people to do away with that government.

usurpations: wrongful seizures of power

despotism: unlimited power

tyranny: oppressive power exerted by a government
candid: fair

In Congress, July 4, 1776 The unanimous Declaration of the thirteen united States of America,

When in the Course of human events, it becomes necessary for one people to dissolve the political bands which have connected them with another, and to assume among the powers of the earth, the separate and equal station to which the Laws of Nature and of Nature's God entitle them, a decent respect to the opinions of mankind requires that they should declare the causes which impel them to the separation.

We hold these truths to be self-evident, that all men are created equal, that they are endowed by their Creator with certain unalienable Rights, that among these are Life, Liberty, and the pursuit of Happiness.

That to secure these rights, Governments are instituted among Men, deriving their just powers from the consent of the governed,

That whenever any Form of Government becomes destructive of these ends, it is the Right of the People to alter or to abolish it, and to institute new Government, laying its foundation on such principles and organizing its powers in such form, as to them shall seem most likely to effect their Safety and Happiness. Prudence, indeed, will dictate that Governments long established should not be changed for light and transient causes; and accordingly all experience hath shown, that mankind are more disposed to suffer, while evils are sufferable, than to right themselves by abolishing the forms to which they are accustomed. But when a long train of abuses and usurpations, pursuing invariably the same Object evinces a design to reduce them under absolute Despotism, it is their right, it is their duty, to throw off such Government, and to provide new Guards for their future security.

Such has been the patient sufferance of these Colonies; and such is now the necessity which constrains them to alter their former Systems of Government. The history of the present King of Great Britain is a history of repeated injuries and usurpations, all having in direct object the establishment of an absolute Tyranny over these States. To prove this, let Facts be submitted to a candid world.

He has refused his Assent to Laws, the most wholesome and necessary for the public good.

He has forbidden his Governors to pass Laws of immediate and pressing importance, unless suspended in their operation till his Assent should be obtained; and when so suspended, he has utterly neglected to attend to them.

He has refused to pass other Laws for the accommodation of large districts of people, unless those people would relinquish the right of Representation in the Legislature, a right inestimable to them and formidable to tyrants only.

He has called together legislative bodies at places unusual, uncomfortable, and distant from the depository of their public Records, for the sole purpose of fatiguing them into compliance with his measures.

He has dissolved Representative Houses repeatedly, for opposing with manly firmness his invasions on the rights of the people.

He has refused for a long time, after such dissolutions, to cause others to be elected; whereby the Legislative powers, incapable of Annihilation, have returned to the People at large for their exercise; the State remaining in the meantime exposed to all the dangers of invasion from without, and convulsions within.

He has endeavored to prevent the population of these States; for that purpose obstructing the Laws for Naturalization of Foreigners; refusing to pass others to encourage their migrations hither, and raising the conditions of new Appropriations of Lands.

He has obstructed the Administration of Justice, by refusing his Assent to Laws for establishing Judiciary powers.

He has made Judges dependent on his Will alone, for the tenure of their offices, and the amount and payment of their salaries.

He has erected a multitude of New Offices, and sent hither swarms of Officers to harass our people, and eat out their substance.

Here the Declaration lists the charges that the colonists had against King George III. How does the language of the list appeal to people's emotions?

relinquish: release, yield

inestimable: priceless

formidable: causing dread

Why do you think the king had his legislatures in the colonies meet in places that were hard to reach?

annihilation: destruction

convulsions: violent disturbances

naturalization of foreigners: the process by which foreign-born persons become citizens

appropriations of land: setting aside land for settlement

tenure: term

a multitude of: many

◄ The Continental Congress is shown voting for independence in this painting by Robert Pine and Edward Savage.

The unanimous Declaration

What wrongful acts does the Declaration state have been committed by the king and the British Parliament?

The "neighboring Province" that is referred to here is Quebec.
arbitrary: not based on law
render: make

abdicated: given up

foreign mercenaries: soldiers hired to fight for a country not their own

perfidy: violation of trust

insurrections: rebellions

petitioned for redress: asked formally for a correction of wrongs

He has kept among us, in times of peace, Standing Armies without the Consent of our legislatures.

He has affected to render the Military independent of and superior to the Civil power.

He has combined with others to subject us to a jurisdiction foreign to our constitution, and unacknowledged by our laws; giving his Assent to their Acts of pretended Legislation:

For quartering large bodies of armed troops among us:

For protecting them, by a mock Trial, from punishment for any Murders which they should commit on the Inhabitants of these States:

For cutting off our Trade with all parts of the world:

For imposing Taxes on us without our Consent:

For depriving us in many cases, of the benefits of Trial by Jury:

For transporting us beyond Seas to be tried for pretended offences:

For abolishing the free System of English Laws in a neighboring Province, establishing therein an Arbitrary government, and enlarging its Boundaries so as to render it at once an example and fit instrument for introducing the same absolute rule into these Colonies:

For taking away our Charters, abolishing our most valuable Laws, and altering fundamentally the Forms of our Governments:

For suspending our own Legislatures, and declaring themselves invested with power to legislate for us in all cases whatsoever.

He has abdicated Government here, by declaring us out of his Protection and waging War against us.

He has plundered our seas, ravaged our Coasts, burnt our towns, and destroyed the Lives of our people.

He is at this time transporting large Armies of foreign Mercenaries to complete the works of death, desolation and tyranny, already begun with circumstances of Cruelty & perfidy scarcely paralleled in the most barbarous ages, and totally unworthy the Head of a civilized nation.

He has constrained our fellow Citizens taken Captive on the high Seas to bear Arms against their Country, to become the executioners of their friends and Brethren, or to fall themselves by their Hands.

He has excited domestic insurrections among us, and has endeavored to bring on the inhabitants of our frontiers, the merciless Indian Savages, whose known rule of warfare, is an undistinguished destruction of all ages, sexes and conditions.

In every stage of these Oppressions We have Petitioned for Redress in the most humble terms: Our repeated Petitions have been answered only by repeated injury. A Prince, whose character is thus marked by every act which may define a Tyrant, is unfit to be the ruler of a free people.

Nor have We been wanting in attentions to our British brethren. We have warned them from time to time of attempts by their legislature to extend an unwarrantable jurisdiction over us. We have reminded them of the circumstances of our emigration and settlement here. We have appealed to their native justice and magnanimity, and we have conjured them by the ties of our common kindred to disavow these usurpations, which would inevitably interrupt our connections and correspondence. They too have been deaf to the voice of justice and of consanguinity. We must, therefore, acquiesce in the necessity, which denounces our Separation, and hold them, as we hold the rest of mankind, Enemies in War, in Peace Friends.

We, therefore, the Representatives of the united States of America, in General Congress, Assembled, appealing to the Supreme Judge of the world for the rectitude of our intentions, do, in the Name, and by Authority of the good People of these Colonies, solemnly publish and declare, That these United Colonies are, and of Right ought to be Free and Independent States; that they are Absolved from all Allegiance to the British Crown, and that all political connection between them and the State of Great Britain, is and ought to be totally dissolved; and that as Free and Independent States, they have full Power to levy War, conclude Peace, contract Alliances, establish Commerce, and to do all other Acts and Things which Independent States may of right do.

And for the support of this Declaration, with a firm reliance on the protection of divine Providence, we mutually pledge to each other our Lives, our Fortunes and our sacred Honor.

unwarrantable jurisdiction: unjustified authority

magnanimity: generous spirit

conjured: called upon

consanguinity: common ancestry

acquiesce: consent to

rectitude: rightness

In this paragraph, the signers state their actual declaration of independence. What rights would the new United States of America now have as an independent nation?

Congress adopted the final draft of the Declaration of Independence on July 4, 1776. A formal copy, written on parchment paper, was signed on August 2, 1776.

John Hancock	Benjamin Harrison	Lewis Morris
Button Gwinnett	Thomas Nelson, Jr.	Richard Stockton
Lyman Hall	Francis Lightfoot Lee	John Witherspoon
George Walton	Carter Braxton	Francis Hopkinson
William Hooper	Robert Morris	John Hart
Joseph Hewes	Benjamin Rush	Abraham Clark
John Penn	Benjamin Franklin	Josiah Bartlett
Edward Rutledge	John Morton	William Whipple
Thomas Heyward, Jr.	George Clymer	Samuel Adams
Thomas Lynch, Jr.	James Smith	John Adams
Arthur Middleton	George Taylor	Robert Treat Paine
Samuel Chase	James Wilson	Elbridge Gerry
William Paca	George Ross	Stephen Hopkins
Thomas Stone	Caesar Rodney	William Ellery
Charles Carroll	George Read	Roger Sherman
of Carrollton	Thomas McKean	Samuel Huntington
George Wythe	William Floyd	William Williams
Richard Henry Lee	Philip Livingston	Oliver Wolcott
Thomas Jefferson	Francis Lewis	Matthew Thornton

FIGHTING THE WAR

To declare independence was one thing; to fight for it was another. The lack of a central government hindered the American war effort. The Second Continental Congress had no real authority. It could *ask* the states for supplies, troops, and funds, but it could not force the states to comply.

Supply shortages and disease. Without a strong government behind it, the Continental Army constantly faced supply shortages. Some colonial merchants charged high prices for shoddy goods. Farmers sold their produce to the highest bidder, whether American or British.

Because of these problems, Washington's troops suffered, enduring bitter winters at Morristown, New Jersey, in 1777 and at Valley Forge, Pennsylvania, in 1777–78. British soldiers meanwhile wintered in comfort in nearby cities.

Another problem the Continental Army faced was disease. Even though General Washington issued orders about cleanliness and hygiene, illness plagued the camps. Poorly prepared food spread germs, and camp toilets contaminated the water

supply. Dysentery caused by these unsanitary conditions killed thousands.

Building an army. Washington also faced troop shortages. He seldom had more than 16,000 Continentals available nationwide at any one time, although about 231,000 men served in the Continental Army over the course of the war. But quality, not quantity, was the general's main complaint. "What we need is a good army, not a large one," he once remarked. In his view the lack of quality stemmed from Congress's insistence on short-term enlistments:

> 66 Good God, gentlemen! Our cause is ruined if you engage men only for a year. You must not think of it. If we ever hope for success, we must have men enlisted for the whole term of the war. 99

Most men signed on for one year, some for just three months, so training of troops was especially difficult. By the time recruits gained the experience to be good soldiers, their enlistment was up. Despite his appeals, Washington fought the war with poorly trained, short-term troops.

There were other problems. Recruiting went well only after victories, and the soldier-farmers in the ranks often deserted at planting or harvesting time. Although state militias also fought, they, too, were poorly trained. But Patriot forces enjoyed two key advantages over the British: they often fought on familiar ground, and they were inspired by a revolutionary cause.

■■ **With no central government to enforce cooperation, the military faced supply and troop shortages; it also suffered from disease.**

African Americans in the war. Despite the shortage of troops, Washington initially ordered that no black soldiers—enslaved or free—could serve in the Continental Army.

▼ By the end of 1775, some 27,500 men were inspired by recruiting posters such as this one to enlist in the struggle for independence.

Some colonial leaders feared that slaves would revolt if given weapons; others believed that blacks would not make good soldiers. In late 1775, however, the British threatened to recruit African Americans, whether free or enslaved.

To counter this strategy, Washington ordered the Continental Army to enlist free blacks. Many served in fighting units alongside whites, but separate African American companies were also formed. Commanders of these all-black companies were usually white. At first, most white officers were reluctant to lead all-black groups. But the bravery of African American soldiers became so celebrated that many white officers changed their minds.

About 5,000 African American Patriots fought in the war. One Hessian noted that "no regiment is to be seen in which there are not Negroes in abundance." Numerous black soldiers, such as Salem Poor and Peter Salem, two of many African Americans who fought at Bunker Hill, received official recognition for their courage. Hundreds more served bravely but anonymously.

Native Americans in the war. Initially, both the British and the Patriots tried to keep Native Americans out of the war. Soon, however, the need for skilled fighters led each side to change its stand.

Both sides recruited members of the Iroquois League. In July 1777 the League held a council to discuss the war. The League split. Thayendanegea (thah-yuhn-dah-ne-GAY-uh), an important Mohawk chief known to whites as Joseph Brant, had received British assurances of Iroquois land rights. He was, therefore, staunchly pro-British. The Mohawks, Onondagas, Cayugas, and Senecas agreed to fight with the British under Brant; the Oneidas and Tuscaroras sided with the Patriots.

▪▪ African Americans and Native Americans fought on both sides in the war.

Women in the war. A few Patriot women fought in the war, while others undertook dangerous missions as spies or messengers. Although legends about women in the war abound, it seems certain that Margaret Corbin and Molly Pitcher took their wounded husbands' places. Young Deborah Sampson Gannett disguised herself as a man and became the "faithful and gallant soldier" Robert Shurtleff. She was said to be as "fleet as a gazelle, bounding through swamps . . . ahead of her companions." After she died in 1827, her husband was awarded a pension as the "widow" of a Revolutionary War veteran.

▲ Thayendanegea was given a captain's commission by the British during the Revolutionary War. He commanded Native American forces during the fateful Saratoga campaign.

◄ Women participated in the American Revolution in many ways. Nancy Hart is shown here defending her home from attack.

Many other women accompanied the troops and worked as laundresses, nurses, and cooks. But most Patriot women stayed behind. They supported the war effort by distributing medical supplies and by making uniforms. They also collected lead and helped in the manufacture of bullets. And with the men off to war, some women managed businesses and farms, helping to keep the colonial economy going.

Loyalist women were also caught up in the war. Many fled their homes or were exiled. Others spied for the British army, aided British prisoners, or hid British soldiers in their homes.

■■ **Patriot and Loyalist women assisted the war effort by aiding the troops, spying on the enemy, and even fighting in battles.**

SECTION 4 REVIEW

IDENTIFY and explain the significance of the following: Thomas Paine, Thomas Jefferson, Abigail Adams, Loyalists, Salem Poor, Peter Salem, Thayendanegea, Margaret Corbin, Molly Pitcher, Deborah Sampson Gannett.

1. **MAIN IDEA** What arguments did the Declaration of Independence offer in support of revolution?

2. **MAIN IDEA** What were the main problems that the Continental Army faced?

3. **GAINING A MULTICULTURAL PERSPECTIVE** How did African Americans, Native Americans, and Patriot and Loyalist women contribute to either the American or the British war effort?

4. **WRITING TO EXPLAIN** Imagine you are a Loyalist at the outbreak of the American Revolution. Write a letter to your local newspaper editor, explaining why you support the king rather than the colonial fight for independence.

5. **ANALYZING** Historians have pointed out that the Declaration of Independence was intended, in part, to convince the colonists to support the fight for independence. Provide several examples from the Declaration that support this view.

Section 5

AN AMERICAN VICTORY

FOCUS

- Why was the victory at Saratoga so important?
- How did the Americans defeat the British in the South?
- What were the main terms of the treaty that ended the war?
- What were some of the social and political effects of the American Revolution?

Counting on support from the colonists loyal to the Crown, confident British generals planned a quick end to the war. But British plans that looked good on paper failed on the battlefield. Key Patriot victories at Trenton and Saratoga fueled the momentum of the Revolution, attracting powerful European allies, such as France, to the American cause. When the war shifted to the South, combined American and French forces defeated the British. A favorable peace treaty capped the military victory.

The Granger Collection, New York

Raising the new American flag, 1783

THE WAR HEATS UP

With General William Howe's evacuation of Boston in March 1776, Washington knew the British would soon strike elsewhere. New York City, a Loyalist stronghold, seemed the most likely possibility. Anticipating that Howe would try to use the city as a base of operation, Washington brought his forces from Boston to guard it.

On July 2 Howe sailed into New York Harbor, landing his troops on Staten Island. The British won an easy victory at Brooklyn Heights in late August and continued to hit the Patriots hard. As the city fell to the British, Washington tried to regroup. Thomas Paine expressed the somber mood in his pamphlet *The American Crisis:*

      66 These are the times that try men's souls. The summer soldier and the sunshine patriot will, in this crisis, shrink from the service of their country; but he that stands it now deserves the love and thanks of man and woman. Tyranny, like hell, is not easily conquered. **99**

As winter neared, almost every "sunshine patriot" departed the ranks. To make matters worse, most regular-army enlistments were due to expire. Washington admitted in a letter to his brother that without new recruits "the game will be pretty near up."

▶ **General William Howe was commander in chief of the British forces from 1775 to 1778.**

THE BATTLE OF TRENTON

Thinking the war was almost won, General Howe prepared to celebrate Christmas in New York. As a precaution he stationed about 1,400 Hessians at Trenton, New Jersey, to keep a close eye on the Patriots nearby. But rather than build fortifications against a possible Patriot attack, the Hessian commander Colonel Rall boasted, "Let them come. We want no trenches. We will go at them with the bayonet."

And come the Americans did. Ignoring the customary winter halt in fighting, Washington and his troops boldly ferried across the ice-choked Delaware River on Christmas night. As Thomas Rodney, one of Washington's soldiers, vividly recalled:

> 66 It was as severe a night as ever I saw, and after two battalions were landed, the storm increased so much, and the river was so full of ice, that it was impossible to get the artillery over. 99

Although Washington's troops had, in Rodney's words, "then been on duty four nights and days . . . without six hours sleep in the whole time," they surprised the Hessian camp at daybreak. Henry Knox, one of Washington's officers, wrote his wife that in the **Battle of Trenton**, the "hurry, fright and confusion of the enemy was [not] unlike that which will be when the last trump [trumpet] shall sound." The Hessians surrendered as the "poor fellows . . . saw themselves completely surrounded."

Of the 1,400 Hessian soldiers, 106 were killed or wounded, and 918 were taken prisoner. The Americans suffered no casualties in the battle.

General Charles Cornwallis, the British field commander, prepared to counterattack. But the American troops slipped away by night, leaving their campfires burning to fool the British. Washington then struck inland, boldly ambushing British regiments at Princeton. British plans to end the war quickly were, as one London official wrote, "blasted by the unhappy affair at Trenton."

▲ A surprise Patriot attack the day after Christmas led to a complete defeat of the Hessian garrison at Trenton. It was only one of a few American victories during 1776–1777.

The Fight for Independence, 1776–1781

THE CHALLENGES OF TERRAIN The Revolutionary War was fought over a vast and varied landscape. Both sides faced the challenges of moving men and supplies across rivers and mountains and through dense forests and swamps.

❓ MOVEMENT George Rogers Clark moved his men and supplies from Fort Pitt to the western frontier by way of the Ohio River. Why do you think he chose this route? If he had taken a direct overland route from Fort Pitt to Kaskaskia, about how far would he have had to travel?

Powder horn, 1775

Legend — Battles:

- ✸ Brooklyn Heights August 1776
- ✸ Trenton December 1776
- ✸ Princeton January 1777
- ✸ Saratoga September–October 1777
- ✸ Vincennes February 1779
- ✸ Camden August 1780
- ✸ Kings Mountain October 1780
- ✸ Yorktown October 1781

Scale: 0 — 125 — 250 Miles / 0 — 125 — 250 Kilometers / Albers Equal-Area Projection

**Map labels:**
CANADA, QUEBEC, NOVA SCOTIA, Quebec, Montreal, ME (MA), Lake Superior, Lake Michigan, Lake Huron, Lake Ontario, Lake Erie, St. Lawrence River, Fort Ticonderoga, Saratoga, NY, Albany, NH, MA, Boston, Dorchester Heights, CT, RI, ATLANTIC OCEAN, HOWE, Hudson R., Delaware R., Fort Detroit, Morristown, New York, Brooklyn Heights, Staten Island, Princeton, Trenton, PA, Valley Forge, Philadelphia, NJ, DE, MD, BRITISH FLEET, Fort Pitt, CLARK, Ohio River, Vincennes, Cahokia, Kaskaskia, WASHINGTON & ROCHAMBEAU, VA, James R., Richmond, Yorktown, York R., Chesapeake Bay, DE GRASSE, SPANISH LOUISIANA, Mississippi River, Kings Mountain, CORNWALLIS, GREENE, NC, Camden, SC, Charleston, Wilmington, Savannah R., Savannah, GA, CLINTON & CORNWALLIS, Natchez, Baton Rouge, Mobile, Pensacola, New Orleans, BRITISH EAST AND WEST FLORIDA, Gulf of Mexico

Legend:
- → American forces
- → British forces
- ✸ American victories
- ✸ British victories
- ■ Forts
- - - - Proclamation Line of 1763

Bernardo de Gálvez, the Spanish governor of Louisiana, defeated the British at Baton Rouge and Natchez in August 1779, Mobile in March 1780, and Pensacola in May 1781.

Maj. Gen. Benedict Arnold heroically fought at Saratoga, but he later turned traitor.

Battle of Saratoga

Albers Equal-Area Projection

QUEBEC, Montreal, St. Lawrence R., Lake Champlain, BURGOYNE, Lake Ontario, Lake George, Fort Ticonderoga, Fort Edward, NH, Bennington, Saratoga, GATES, ARNOLD & MORGAN, NY, Albany, MA, Boston, CT, RI

Scale: 0 — 50 — 100 Miles / 0 — 50 — 100 Kilometers

90° W   80° W   30° N   40° N   70° W

▲ Kazimierz Pulaski

The Historic New Orleans Collection, Museum/Research Center

▲ Bernardo de Gálvez

▲ Tadeusz Kosciuszko

BRITISH DISASTER AT SARATOGA

The setbacks at Trenton and Princeton roused the British to greater effort. In control of Canada to the north and New York City to the south, the British set out to cut off New England from the other rebel colonies. General "Gentleman Johnny" Burgoyne devised the plan: three separate British forces would converge at Albany, New York. The plan seemed simple enough. What the British did not realize—or ignored—was that their lines of attack crossed lakes, swamps, hills, and forests teeming with Patriots.

Almost from the beginning Burgoyne's strategy failed. Two of the British forces—those under Lieutenant Colonel Barry St. Leger and General Howe—never arrived. General Burgoyne's troops left Canada in June and began moving southward. His long caravan of supplies and artillery moved at a crawl, hampered by blocked trails and bridges destroyed by American militiamen. In September Burgoyne and his men crossed the Hudson River, where they clashed with the Americans in the **Battle of Saratoga**. Outfoxed and outmanned, Burgoyne formally surrendered his troops on October 17, 1777.

EUROPEAN POWERS PROVIDE AID

Saratoga was a turning point for Americans. Encouraged by the victory, the French—who had been secretly aiding the Patriots—signed a formal alliance in February 1778. French aid provided Americans with gold, supplies, a fleet, and troops.

France also declared war on Great Britain. A year later Spain joined the war as an ally of France, followed in 1780 by the Netherlands. Bernardo de Gálvez, Spain's governor of Louisiana, aided the Patriots with needed supplies and defeated the British in several battles along the Gulf coast and the Mississippi River.

■■ The Americans' victory at Saratoga convinced France and other European powers to support the colonists.

New volunteers from Europe brought useful military skills. Even before the treaty, an impressive group of Europeans had aided the Patriots. From Minorca, off the coast of Spain, came George Farragut, who fought in both the army and the navy. From Prussia came Baron von Steuben, who took charge of organizing and drilling the Continental Army. From Poland came Kazimierz Pulaski (kah-ZEEM-yesh puh-LAS-kee), who trained the cavalry, and Tadeusz Kosciuszko (tah-DE-oosh kahs-ee-UHS-koh), an army engineer who planned Patriot fortifications. From France came the German-born officer Baron Johann de Kalb and 19-year-old Marquis de Lafayette (lahf-ee-ET), who became a valued member of Washington's staff.

For the Americans the alliance with France came just in time. During the severe winter of 1777–78, Washington's army was reduced to a sick and hungry handful of soldiers, some even lacking shoes. The glad news that powerful allies had joined them gave the Patriots new hope.

FIGHTING IN THE WEST AND SOUTH

Things were going better for the Patriots in the West. Lieutenant Colonel George Rogers Clark of Virginia, with a small group of frontier fighters and Native Americans, overran British posts at Kaskaskia (ka-SKAS-kee-uh), Cahokia (kuh-HOH-kee-uh), and Vincennes (vin-SENS) in 1778. The British recaptured Vincennes by year's end, only to lose it again to Clark in the **Battle of Vincennes** in February 1779. Clark's army went on to take control of the western lands.

Late in 1778 the British focused their attacks on the southern colonies, where they anticipated strong Tory support. Backed by their navy, the British occupied the seaport towns: Savannah, Georgia, fell in December 1778; Charleston, South Carolina, in May 1780. From Charleston, General Cornwallis attacked inland. After crushing the Americans in the **Battle of Camden** (South Carolina) in 1780, British forces marched toward North Carolina.

Cornwallis did not find the support he expected. Although companies of Loyalist militia terrorized the Carolina countryside, bands of Patriots retaliated in kind. Patriot hostility toward the Loyalists was never more apparent than at Kings Mountain, South Carolina, in October 1780. In that battle the victorious Patriots savagely killed the wounded who were trying to surrender.

It was a new Patriot commander, Nathanael Greene of Rhode Island, however, who stopped the British advances. Greene was a master of the tactics of **guerrilla warfare**—wearing down the enemy in hit-and-run skirmishes while avoiding direct battles. Even in defeat Greene bragged, "We fight, get beat, rise, and fight again." Using forest cover and the element of surprise, the Patriots made the most of their limited numbers and frustrated British hopes of winning in the South.

■■ **Americans used guerrilla warfare to defeat the British army and its Loyalist supporters in the South.**

VICTORY AT YORKTOWN

During the summer of 1781, Cornwallis moved his army into Yorktown, Virginia, located on the peninsula between the York and James rivers. There he had access to the British fleet and

▶ In 1779 Jones's ship, the *Bonhomme Richard*, engaged the British ship *Serapis* in battle. With his own warship about to sink, Jones lashed the two ships together and in desperate fighting won the victory.

▼ John Paul Jones was a commander in the Continental navy.

The Granger Collection, New York

The Granger Collection, New York

◀ John Trumbull painted a series of scenes from the Revolutionary War. Shown here is the surrender of Lord Cornwallis at Yorktown in October 1781.

Yale University Art Gallery, Trumbull Collection

supplies. A small Patriot army led by generals Lafayette, von Steuben, and Anthony Wayne kept close watch on the British but did not attack.

On August 14 a dispatch reached General Washington's New York headquarters: Admiral François de Grasse, the French naval commander in the West Indies, was moving his fleet north to block Chesapeake Bay. Meanwhile, Washington's army, along with a French force under Comte de Rochambeau (raw-shahn-boh), rushed south to Yorktown, completing the trap. Boxed in by the French fleet, the British faced vastly greater numbers of American and French troops.

After numerous attempts on land and sea failed to break the blockade, Cornwallis admitted defeat. On October 19, 1781, as their band played the old English folk tune "The World Turned Upside Down," the British surrendered their weapons. Cornwallis wrote to General Clinton to inform him of the disastrous outcome of the **Battle of Yorktown**: "I have the mortification [shame] to inform your Excellency that I have been forced to . . . surrender the troops under my command."

𝒯HE TREATY OF PARIS OF 1783

Although some fighting continued in the South and on the frontier, Cornwallis's surrender marked the end of the war. In the peace talks that followed, American negotiators Benjamin Franklin, John Adams, and John Jay won generous terms. The **Treaty of Paris**, signed on September 3, 1783, granted the United States (1) independence, (2) the land from the Atlantic coast westward to the Mississippi River and from the Great Lakes south to Florida, and (3) fishing rights in the Gulf of Saint Lawrence and off the coast of Newfoundland.

The treaty declared that Americans should pay debts owed to the British. The American negotiators also pledged that the Congress would "earnestly recommend" to the states that all property seized from Loyalists be returned. (The states chose to ignore this request.)

▪▪ The Treaty of Paris recognized American independence and greatly expanded the nation's boundaries.

Fortunately for the new nation, the American delegates negotiated with only Great Britain. If they had been forced to sit at a peace table with delegates from Spain and France as well, the Americans would have won their independence, but little else.

Spain wanted to confine the United States of America to the land east of the Appalachians. Having regained Florida in the negotiations ending the war, Spain hoped to expand northward to the Ohio Valley. However, George Rogers Clark's campaign in the West had established the new nation's presence within the region. His victories were important in shaping postwar America.

Consequences of the American Revolution

The American Revolution had important social and economic effects, both immediate and long-term. As a result of the war, many great fortunes were destroyed. Almost 100,000 Loyalists fled the colonies by war's end; few of these people ever returned. The British government provided lands in Canada as compensation, but many Tories, especially the wealthy, chose to start new lives in Great Britain.

Social implications. As you have read, the war for independence was not a fight for independence for everyone. American women continued to be excluded from political life. Many slaves fought for and gained their freedom, but slavery did not end.

Native Americans also failed to benefit. Many lost their lands and homes. The war destroyed the Iroquois League; the split in 1777 caused member groups to fight against each other as well as against whites. Sadly, few Native Americans were recognized by either side for their assistance.

Political implications. Few Americans at the end of the war dwelt on the Revolution's unfulfilled promise. To them, the overwhelming fact was independence from Great Britain. Inexperienced Patriot forces (aided by foreign allies) had defeated the world's greatest military power. They had won the fight for representative government. Their Revolution created and strengthened a new national unity.

Equally important, the Revolution began to change Americans' ideas about who had the right to rule. They no longer believed that only the well born should rule. This belief would eventually lead to the expansion of democratic rights to include all Americans, whatever their sex, race, or economic condition. This historic change in attitude is the Revolution's greatest legacy. Harrison Gray Otis, a Massachusetts politician, later wrote to a friend: "You and I did not imagine, when the . . . war with Britain was over, that revolution was just begun."

■■ **The Revolution achieved its goal—independence and self-government. But women, African Americans, and Native Americans did not share equally in the hard-won freedoms.**

SECTION 5 REVIEW

IDENTIFY and explain the significance of the following: William Howe, Battle of Trenton, "Gentleman Johnny" Burgoyne, Bernardo de Gálvez, Battle of Vincennes, Battle of Camden, guerrilla warfare, Battle of Yorktown.

LOCATE and explain the importance of the following: Kings Mountain, South Carolina.

1. **MAIN IDEA** How did the American victory at Saratoga affect the course of the war?

2. **MAIN IDEA** What tactics did the Americans use to defeat the British in the South?

3. **MAIN IDEA** What were the terms of the Treaty of Paris? Why might the terms have been less favorable to the United States if France and Spain had been included in the treaty negotiations?

4. **WRITING TO EVALUATE** Write an essay explaining the social and political significance of the American Revolution.

5. **ASSESSING CONSEQUENCES** British soldiers were well trained in traditional military procedures and tactics. How might this have been a disadvantage in the Revolutionary War?

Pontiac's Rebellion crushed. Proclamation of 1763 issued.

Stamp Act enacted. Stamp Act Congress meets.

Townshend Acts enacted.

Boston Massacre angers colonists. Townshend Acts repealed.

1763   1765   1770

WRITING A SUMMARY

Using the essential points of the chapter as a guide, write a summary of the chapter.

REVIEWING CHRONOLOGY

Number your paper 1 to 5. Study the time line above, and place the following events in the order in which they happened by writing the first next to 1, the second next to 2, and so on. Then complete the activity below.

1. Intolerable Acts passed.
2. Declaration of Independence issued.
3. Stamp Act enacted.
4. Pontiac's Rebellion crushed.
5. Boston Massacre angers colonists.

Identifying Cause and Effect Select two events on the time line, and in a paragraph, explain the cause-and-effect relationship between them.

IDENTIFYING PEOPLE AND IDEAS

Explain the historical significance of each of the following people or terms.

1. Proclamation of 1763
2. Pontiac
3. Stamp Act
4. Thomas Paine
5. writs of assistance
6. Crispus Attucks
7. George Washington
8. guerrilla warfare

UNDERSTANDING MAIN IDEAS

1. How and why did the British attitude toward the colonies change after 1763?
2. What were the main reasons the colonists protested British actions?
3. How did the colonists protest British policies?
4. Why did the Second Continental Congress issue the Declaration of Independence?
5. Why were the American victories at Trenton and Saratoga so important?

REVIEWING THEMES

1. **Economic Development** How did British attempts to raise revenues in the colonies conflict with colonial interests?

2. **Democratic Values** What role did democratic values play in colonial protests?
3. **Global Relations** How was the Revolutionary War affected by global relations?

THINKING CRITICALLY

1. **Evaluating** Some historians claim that wise leaders could have resolved the differences between Great Britain and the colonies before 1775. Do you agree? Explain.
2. **Hypothesizing** Explain how the war might have been different if the Loyalists had organized more effectively and in greater numbers.
3. **Analyzing** What theories of government were outlined in the Declaration of Independence?

WRITING ABOUT HISTORY

Using Historical Imagination Imagine that you are a Loyalist or a Patriot woman. Write a letter to a friend explaining why you chose the side you did and how you are attempting to help the war effort.

STRATEGY FOR SUCCESS

Review the Strategies for Success on Interpreting the Visual Record on page 98. Then study the 1774 picture below entitled *Bostonians Paying the Excise Man*. On a separate sheet of paper, explain the artist's point of view, using specific examples from the picture.

The Granger Collection, New York

Intolerable Acts passed. First Continental Congress meets.

Patriots stage Boston Tea Party.

British and Patriots clash at Lexington, Concord, and Bunker Hill. Second Continental Congress meets.

Declaration of Independence issued. Patriots win at Trenton.

British defeated at Saratoga.

British surrender at Yorktown.

Treaty of Paris signed.

1775   1780   1783

USING PRIMARY SOURCES

At first some Patriot leaders opposed enlisting African Americans in the fight for freedom. However, when soldiers were needed for the southern campaign, Washington's aide, Alexander Hamilton, suggested recruiting African Americans. Read the following excerpt from a letter by Hamilton, in which he outlines his plan. Then write a summary of the points outlined in the letter.

Head Quarters March 14th 79

Dear Sir:

Colonel Laurens, who will have the honor of delivering you this letter, is on the way to South Carolina on a project . . . to raise two[,] three[,] or four batalions of negroes . . . by contributions from owners in proportion to the number they possess. . . .

I have not the least doubt, that the negroes will make excellent soldiers, with proper management. . . .

I foresee that his project will have to combat much opposition from prejudice and self-interest. The contempt we have been taught to entertain for the blacks, makes us fancy many things that are founded neither in reason nor experience. . . .

An essential part of the plan is to give them their freedom with their muskets. This will secure their fidelity, animate their courage, and I believe will have a good influence upon those who remain, by opening a door to their emancipation [freedom]. . . .

Purple Heart

—Alexander Hamilton

LINKING HISTORY AND GEOGRAPHY

British forces fought the Revolutionary War in physical settings that were often unfamiliar to them. Study the map on page 129. Select one of the battles or campaigns included on the map and indicate how geography might have helped or hurt British efforts.

British soldier, 1778

BUILDING YOUR PORTFOLIO

Complete the following projects independently or cooperatively.

1. WAR Imagine you are a member of the Second Continental Congress assigned to oversee the American war effort. Create a poster aimed at recruiting Native Americans and free blacks for the Continental Army. Your poster should indicate reasons why both groups would benefit by joining the Patriot war effort.

2. DEMOCRATIC RIGHTS Imagine you are a reporter for a colonial newspaper. Select a specific tax, such as the stamp tax or sugar tax, and interview a British official responsible for collecting that tax and a colonist opposed to the tax. Your interview should include questions that examine Great Britain's point of view.

FROM CONFEDERATION TO FEDERAL UNION

FOCUS

UNDERSTANDING THE MAIN IDEA

During the war the colonies replaced their royal charters with republican constitutions. The Continental Congress then drafted the Articles of Confederation to guide the new nation. Soon after the Revolution, however, political problems led the Congress to call for revision of the Articles. In response, the Constitutional Convention drafted the Constitution of the United States of America.

THEMES

- **CONSTITUTIONAL HERITAGE** How does the organization of government affect the way power is distributed and exercised?

- **ECONOMIC DEVELOPMENT** How might a government's policies affect the economic well-being of groups or individuals within a society?

- **DEMOCRATIC VALUES** How can a nation ensure that every citizen has a voice in government?

1776	1777	1781	1786	1788
Congress urges states to draft new constitutions.	Articles of Confederation adopted.	States officially become "The United States of America."	Shays's Rebellion begins.	U.S. Constitution ratified.

Disagreements between the British government and its colonies in North America resulted in war. Recognizing the need for unity in their fight for independence, the colonies united under the leadership of the Continental Congress.

Scene at the Signing of the Constitution of the United States (1940) by Howard Chandler Christy

Within a few years of the American victory at Yorktown, influential Revolutionary leaders despaired for the future of the United States. In 1786 George Washington warned James Madison of an "impending storm" and sadly remarked: "No morn ever dawned more favorably than ours did; and no day was ever more clouded than the present." Madison wrote to James Monroe that if something was not done soon, "our case may become desperate."

These statesmen were alarmed by the quarreling among the states. Only five years after defeating the British, Americans were fighting one another!

What had happened? By the end of the war, the former colonies had united in a "firm league of friendship." But the league was not friendly in practice. Alexander Hamilton accurately described the league as "a number of petty states, with the appearance only of union, jarring, jealous and perverse, without any determined direction." This disunity was also apparent to Great Britain's foreign minister, who chose not to send any ambassador to the fragile American republic, remarking that it would be too expensive to send 13! The crisis of the 1780s put in jeopardy the future of the young nation that John Adams believed was "destined beyond a doubt to be the greatest power on earth . . . within the life of [a] man." If the newly independent states did not remain united, what would become of the Revolution's goals?

Great Seal of the Supreme Court

THE ARTICLES OF CONFEDERATION

FOCUS

- What issues did the new state constitutions address?
- Why were the Land Ordinances of 1785 and 1787 passed?
- What were the weaknesses of the Articles of Confederation? What problems did these weaknesses cause?
- What were the causes and consequences of Shays's Rebellion?

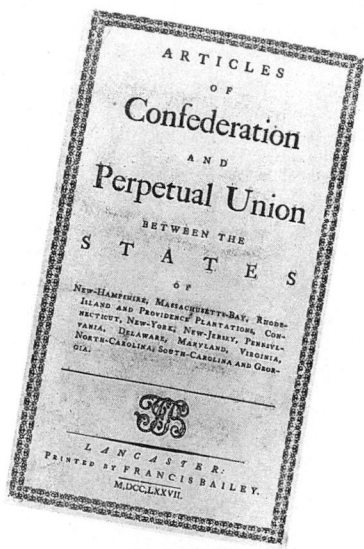

The American experiment in self-government began even before the Declaration of Independence. In May 1776 the Second Continental Congress urged the colonies to begin drafting new constitutions to replace their British royal charters. To unify the new state governments, the Congress adopted a plan for a national government in November 1777. This new form of self-government would face severe tests during the nation's first decade.

Articles of Confederation cover

THE STATE CONSTITUTIONS

The American Revolution brought an end to monarchical rule in America. The colonists' open rebellion forced royal governors from office. To fill this void, the Second Continental Congress advised the colonies "under the authority of the people" to form new governments. John Adams conveyed the optimism many felt:

66 You and I . . . have been sent into life at a time when the greatest lawgivers of antiquity would have wished to live. How few of the human race have ever enjoyed an opportunity of making . . . government . . . for themselves or their children! 99

Between 1776 and 1780 all of the states except Connecticut and Rhode Island drafted and ratified new constitutions. (Connecticut and Rhode Island revised their royal charters.) Despite differences in economy, geography, and population, the states adopted similar constitutions. All of the constitutions defined executive power and voting rights, and many states took steps to separate church and state. Many states also included a bill of rights that guaranteed freedom of speech, trial by jury, and the right to assemble.

The republican spirit. To form the new governments, the state legislatures relied on republican theory. A **republic** is a form

◀ Many American statesmen used the political theories of John Locke when framing state constitutions.

of government in which political leaders receive from the citizens their authority to make and enforce laws.

The ideas of self-government were not new to Americans. The Mayflower Compact of 1620 had incorporated these ideas. Americans were also familiar with the works of Enlightenment thinkers such as John Locke, the English philosopher who developed the theory of "natural rights." Locke believed that all people were born with the rights of life, liberty, and property and that the role of the government was to protect these rights.

American republicanism, however, went further than Locke's theory did in challenging older forms of political and social order. Americans took the radical step of rejecting monarchical government and began participating actively in politics. Americans had absorbed ideas of natural rights and self-government from reading popular newspapers and pamphlets and participating in revolutionary committees and public meetings. With this knowledge and experience, Americans were confident that they could govern their own communities.

Limits on executive power.

Many Americans had resented the powerful royal governors, who had often overturned laws the elected assemblies had passed. As a result, most of the new state constitutions limited the powers of governors. Nine states limited governors to one-year terms and denied them power to overturn laws. In other states the governors shared power with the legislatures. New York and Massachusetts had the most powerful governors. But in both states governors were elected rather than appointed.

Separation of church and state.

Besides curbing the powers of governors, many state constitutions reduced the influence the church had over government. Before the Revolution, several New England colonies had collected taxes to support the Congregational church. New York and some southern colonies used tax money to support the Anglican, or English, church. People had to pay the taxes even if they did not belong to the church.

Baptist and Presbyterian dissenters and liberal thinkers such as Thomas Jefferson opposed this close relationship between the government and one particular religion. Such a bond, they argued, often led to abuses of political power and to religious wars.

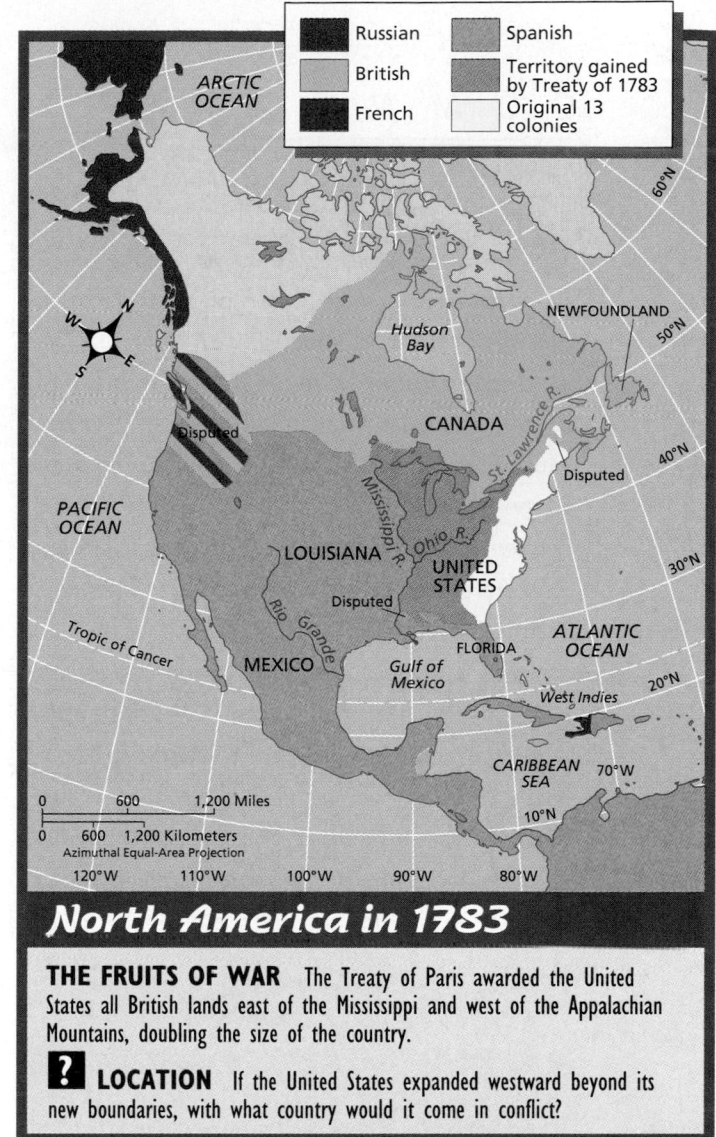

North America in 1783

THE FRUITS OF WAR The Treaty of Paris awarded the United States all British lands east of the Mississippi and west of the Appalachian Mountains, doubling the size of the country.

? LOCATION If the United States expanded westward beyond its new boundaries, with what country would it come in conflict?

In 1779 Thomas Jefferson drafted the **Virginia Statute for Religious Freedom.** The statute began "Whereas Almighty God has created the mind free; . . . legislators and rulers . . . have assumed dominion over the faith of others." It went on to argue that forcing a citizen to give money in support of "opinions which he disbelieves is sinful and tyrannical. . . . No man shall be compelled to . . . support any religious worship. . . . All men shall be free to profess . . . their opinion in matters of religion." Virginia adopted the statute in 1786. By 1833 all of the states had forbade the establishment of official state churches supported by tax dollars.

■■ **The state constitutions defined executive power and voting rights. Many also took steps to separate church and state.**

Women and Republicanism

The republican state constitutions, though much more democratic than the British royal charters, did not grant full citizenship to women. The state constitutions limited voting rights and office-holding to white male property owners. Most men, as well as many women, opposed women's participation in politics, believing that women should contribute to the republic by taking care of their homes and educating their children to be good citizens.

This teaching duty created both limitations and possibilities for women. Most people expected women to devote themselves exclusively to their families and their homes. But because women were responsible for their children's education, this responsibility provoked calls for expanding women's education. Judith

Sargent Murray, one of the first women playwrights in America, argued in 1790 that women and men had equal minds.

66 While we are pursuing the needle, or the superintendency [management] of the family, I repeat, that our minds are at full liberty for reflection; that imagination may exert itself in full vigor; and that if a just foundation [be] early laid, our ideas will then be worthy of rational beings. . . . Is it reasonable, that [women] . . . should at present . . . be allowed no other ideas, than those which are suggested by the mechanism of a pudding, or the sewing of the seams of a garment? 99

This debate led to the founding of several women's academies, or high schools. The opening of educational opportunities for women and the recognition of women's contributions laid the basis for an expanded role for women in public life in the next century.

How bleft the Maid whofe bofom no falfe glory enflaves,
Her days in fweet Peace, her nights in foft repose.

BE SURE. TO AVOID MANY TROUBLES,
KEEP WITHIN COMPASS AND YOU SHALL BE SURE. TO AVOID MANY TROUBLES, WHICH OTHERS INDURE. KEEP WITHIN COMPASS

KEEP WITHIN COMPASS

Virtuous Woman is a Crown to her Husband.

ENTER NOT INTO THE WAY OF THE WICKED AND GO NOT IN THE PATH OF EVIL MEN.

Winterthur Museum

▲ **This engraving advising women that their place was within the home reflected the attitudes of many men and women during the early republic.**

A PLAN FOR CONFEDERATION

The state constitutions established frameworks of government for the former colonies. But no such framework existed on the national level. The Continental Congress had been fulfilling the duties of a national government since 1774, but it lacked real authority. To secure national unity, the Congress knew that it had to create a plan for a central government.

Adoption of the Articles. The states were willing to join in a loose union but were reluctant to give up many powers to a national government. In 1776 a congressional committee began the difficult task of drafting a plan for national unity that the states would accept.

On July 12, 1776, the committee presented its plan—the **Articles of Confederation**—to the other congressional delegates. For 16 months the delegates debated this plan for a "Perpetual Union," finally adopting it on November 15, 1777.

The Articles created a confederation, or an alliance, of states while guaranteeing each state its "sovereignty, freedom, and independence." (A sovereign nation or state has supreme power over its own affairs.) All powers not "expressly delegated" to Congress were retained by the states.

The Articles authorized Congress to borrow and coin money, conduct foreign affairs, set policy toward Native Americans, and settle disputes between the states. In addition, Congress could ask the states to contribute money to the central government and to provide recruits for the military. The Articles allowed each state one vote in Congress.

The problem of land. For the plan to take effect, all 13 states had to ratify, or approve, it. One major issue blocked ratification: control of the land between the Appalachian Mountains and the Mississippi River. On the basis of their old royal charters, several states held vast tracts of western land. States without land claims wanted the other states to surrender their holdings to the new national government.

Part of the problem was money. Each state was expected to help pay the war debt. States with western lands had additional sources of revenue. States without surplus land faced the prospect of raising taxes—never a popular course of action.

▼ Surveyors used equipment such as a compass and a protractor when dividing land into tracts and sections. This set of equipment belonged to George Washington.

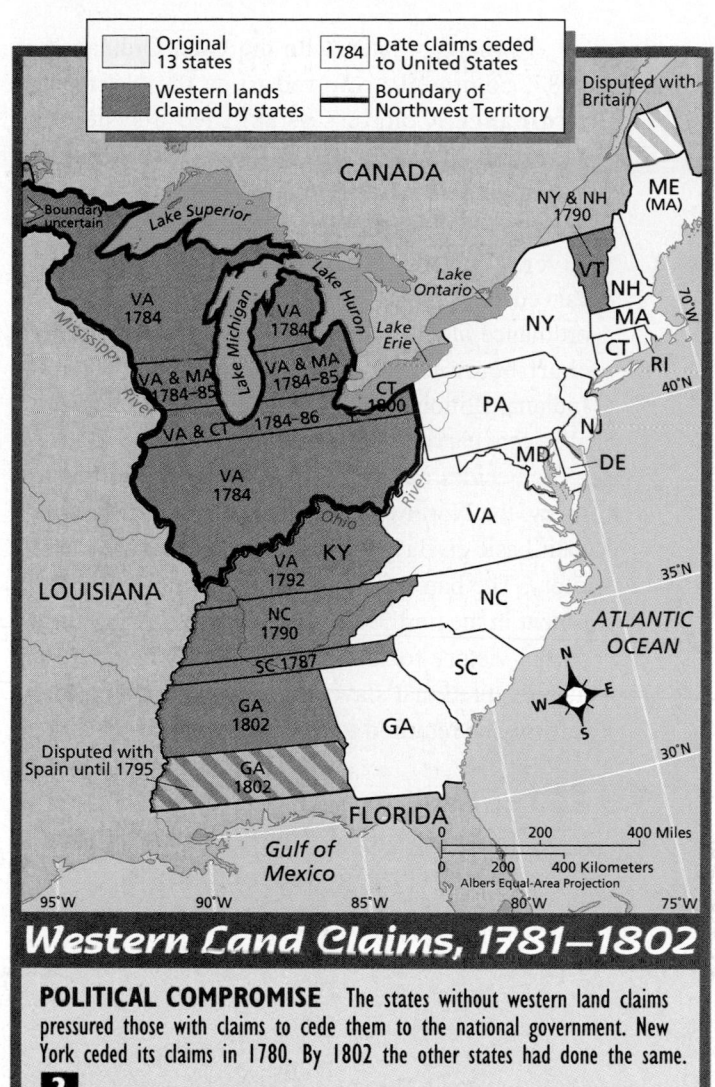

POLITICAL COMPROMISE The states without western land claims pressured those with claims to cede them to the national government. New York ceded its claims in 1780. By 1802 the other states had done the same.

? RELATIVE LOCATION New York continued to claim portions of Vermont until 1790—the year before Vermont entered the Union. What other state claimed part of Vermont?

Western Land Claims, 1781–1802

To promote national unity, New York and Virginia—the two states with the largest landholdings—yielded their land claims to Congress. Other states eventually followed suit. By 1781 all of the states had agreed to enter the Confederation. The states were now officially "The United States of America."

The Confederation knew, however, that the problem of western lands remained. To regulate the disposal of the land, Congress passed the **Land Ordinance of 1785**. The ordinance marked off the land into townships and divided each township into 640-acre sections. The ordinance permitted the cash sale of 640-acre tracts for not less than a dollar an acre and reserved one section of each township for the establishment of a school. This provision in the ordinance marked the first government aid given to public education.

Two years later, with the Land Ordinance of 1787, commonly referred to as the **Northwest Ordinance**, Congress established a system for governing the **Northwest Territory**. This area extended north of the Ohio River to the Great Lakes and west of Pennsylvania to the Mississippi River. Congress intended that states would be carved out of the Northwest Territory. Thus the ordinance also outlined the steps to statehood (see chart below). The present-day states of Ohio, Indiana, Illinois, Michigan, and Wisconsin eventually were carved out of the territory.

Besides ensuring eventual self-rule in the territory, the Northwest Ordinance guaranteed settlers their basic civil rights and banned slavery in the territory. The ban reflected a growing antislavery sentiment in the northern states. But the ban was only a partial victory for abolitionists, since the ordinance also required that slaves escaping to freedom in the territory be returned to their owners.

■■ **The Land Ordinances of 1785 and 1787 established rules for settling and governing western lands.**

WEAKNESSES IN THE CONFEDERATION

The land ordinances established a pattern of land settlement for the next 75 years and marked an important achievement for the Confederation. But Congress could point to few other noteworthy accomplishments.

On paper the Confederation government enjoyed broad powers, but in reality it was weak. Proposed changes to the Articles needed the consent of all 13 states. Major new legislation needed the approval of at least 9 states. Agreements were hard to reach because northern and southern delegates often had conflicting interests. The fragile bonds that had united the states during the war were weakening during peacetime.

The Confederation government also had financial problems. Congress desperately needed cash to pay the war debt. But it could only ask the states for funds; it could not tax the people directly. Some states hid behind their independent status to avoid paying their share of the debt.

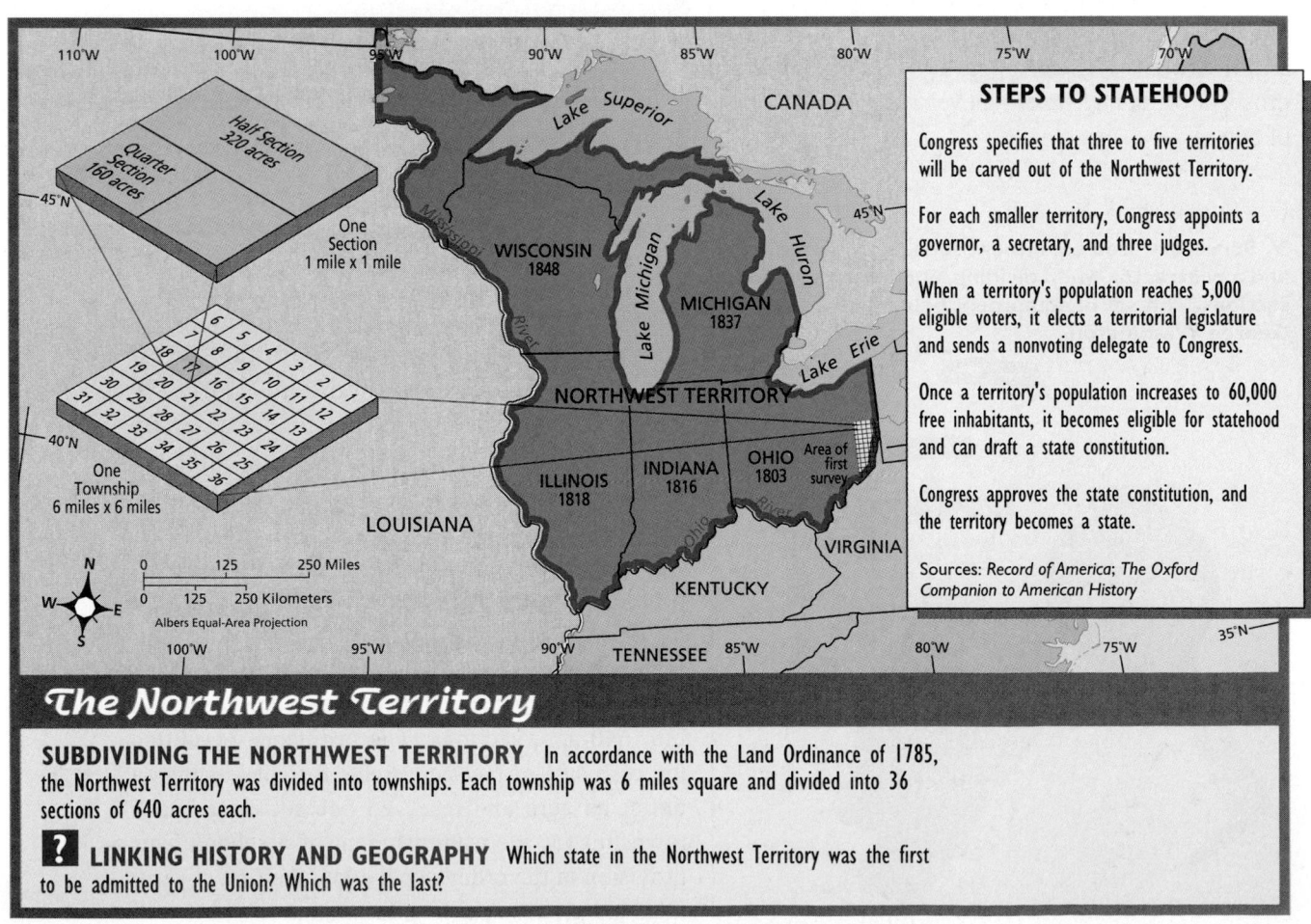

STEPS TO STATEHOOD

Congress specifies that three to five territories will be carved out of the Northwest Territory.

For each smaller territory, Congress appoints a governor, a secretary, and three judges.

When a territory's population reaches 5,000 eligible voters, it elects a territorial legislature and sends a nonvoting delegate to Congress.

Once a territory's population increases to 60,000 free inhabitants, it becomes eligible for statehood and can draft a state constitution.

Congress approves the state constitution, and the territory becomes a state.

Sources: *Record of America; The Oxford Companion to American History*

The Northwest Territory

SUBDIVIDING THE NORTHWEST TERRITORY In accordance with the Land Ordinance of 1785, the Northwest Territory was divided into townships. Each township was 6 miles square and divided into 36 sections of 640 acres each.

? LINKING HISTORY AND GEOGRAPHY Which state in the Northwest Territory was the first to be admitted to the Union? Which was the last?

Congress responded to the revenue shortage by printing paper money. The financial consequences were disastrous. These dollars, called "Continentals," were not backed by gold or silver, so merchants and lenders refused to accept them at face value. In 1779 it took about 38 Continentals to purchase a product worth a dollar in gold. By 1781 the price had skyrocketed to 100 Continentals! The widespread inflation frustrated many Americans. The popular expression "not worth a Continental" reflected Americans' anger over their nearly worthless currency.

The Confederation's economic worries multiplied. In 1786 the nation experienced a **depression**, a sharp drop in business activity accompanied by rising unemployment. The primary cause of the depression was the loss of British markets. Before the war American merchants had traded with Great Britain and other colonies within the British Empire. After the war Great Britain closed some of its colonial markets to American commerce.

To make matters worse, Great Britain and France were flooding the United States with inexpensive goods. Struggling American merchants and artisans could not match the prices and survive. Congress was powerless to help since the Articles did not give it the authority to draft international trade policies.

The young nation also faced challenges in international diplomacy. Great Britain refused to abandon its forts in North America on the grounds that Americans were not honoring the terms of the 1783 Treaty of Paris. Under the Articles the U.S. government could not force individuals or states to honor the treaty. As a result, few Americans paid their prewar debts to British merchants, even though the treaty required such payment. As one Virginian remarked, "If we are now to pay the debts due to British merchants, what have we been fighting for all this while?" The treaty also called for compensation to Loyalists for property seized during the war, but few states complied.

■■ The limitations on congressional power under the Articles caused serious economic and diplomatic problems.

SHAYS'S REBELLION

The weak Confederation also proved unable to help farmers, who had been particularly hard hit by the war and its aftermath. The depression and widespread inflation left farmers with fewer markets in which to sell their goods and little money to pay their debts. Instead of extending credit for equipment and other goods, merchants demanded hard money—gold or silver—which farmers seldom had in their possession.

In Massachusetts the merchant-controlled legislature passed a law that imposed a heavy tax on land. If a landowner did not pay the tax, the state would seize the property. Outraged farmers sent petitions to the legislature, complaining of "taxation without representation." Farmers asked the legislature to issue more paper money and to put a stop to the foreclosures. "Our property is torn from us," farmers complained, "our Gaols [jails] filled & still our Debts are not discharged."

When the Massachusetts legislature adjourned in July 1786 without addressing the tax or debt issues, farmers rebelled. Under the leadership of such men as Daniel Shays, a former Revolutionary War captain, angry farmers took up arms to defend their property rights and political representation. In what became known as **Shays's Rebellion**, mobs of farmers shut down debtor courts and stopped auctions of farm property.

The most serious threat to peace began in late 1786. On December 26, Shays and some 1,200 farmers set out for Springfield, Massachusetts, intent on seizing the federal arsenal. Worried that Shays's forces would overrun the militiamen guarding the arsenal, the governor quickly called for more than 4,000 additional recruits.

Shays and his men launched their attack in late January. However, when cannon fire killed four of the farmers, Shays's men fled. By the end of February the militia had crushed the rebellion.

Despite Shays's defeat, the rebellion helped the farmers. The Massachusetts legislature did away with direct taxes and passed debtor-relief legislation that prevented creditors from seizing household goods and tools.

The rebellion's most important legacy, though, was its effect on public opinion. The unrest frightened the wealthy and raised doubts about the government's ability to deal with civil unrest and to bring about national unity. As a result many people who had previously objected to a strong central government began calling for new powers for the Confederation.

▲ This 1884 painting by Howard Pyle shows Daniel Shays and his mob taking possession of a courthouse.

■■ **Farmers, angry over high taxes and heavy debts, launched Shays's Rebellion. The revolt led to calls for a stronger central government.**

SECTION 1 REVIEW

IDENTIFY and explain the significance of the following: republic, John Locke, Virginia Statute for Religious Freedom, Judith Sargent Murray, Articles of Confederation, Northwest Ordinance, depression, Daniel Shays.

LOCATE and explain the importance of the following: Northwest Territory.

1. **MAIN IDEA** How did the Land Ordinances of 1785 and 1787 help regulate the settlement of western territories?

2. **MAIN IDEA** What limits did the Articles of Confederation place on federal power? What were some of the consequences of these limits?

3. **IDENTIFYING CAUSE AND EFFECT** Why did farmers launch Shays's Rebellion? What was the rebellion's most important legacy?

4. **WRITING TO DESCRIBE** Write an essay describing what provisions the states wrote into their new constitutions.

5. **EVALUATING** What role did republicanism assign to women? How did this influence women's activities and opportunities?

DRAFTING AND RATIFYING THE CONSTITUTION

FOCUS

- Why did delegates to the Constitutional Convention agree to keep the proceedings secret?
- What major compromises are reflected in the Constitution?
- What kind of government did the Federalists want? Why did the Antifederalists oppose the Federalist position?

In February 1787, Congress requested that the 13 states name delegates to revise the Articles of Confederation. The delegates created a national document, the Constitution, which outlined a new structure of government. Its acceptance was not a foregone conclusion, and heated debates followed as the citizens of each state struggled over ratification.

Woodcut commemorating ratification of the Constitution, 1788

THE CALL TO PHILADELPHIA

Striking evidence of the disunity of the Confederation came in September 1786. A meeting held in Annapolis, Maryland, to work out a cooperative trade agreement failed because only five states sent delegates. This disappointment, followed soon after by Shays's Rebellion, made Congress consider the weaknesses of the Articles of Confederation. Congressional leaders issued a call for a **Constitutional Convention** to strengthen the government. The convention was to be held in Philadelphia beginning May 14, 1787.

The convention. By the appointed day only the delegates from Pennsylvania and Virginia had arrived. Others straggled in, delayed by muddy roads. By May 25 enough delegates were on hand to convene the proceedings.

The convention met in the Pennsylvania State House (now called Independence Hall), in the same room where the leaders of the American Revolution had signed the Declaration of Independence. The delegates agreed to keep the proceedings secret, believing that it would be easier to debate and resolve their differences behind closed doors. Despite the sweltering heat, even the windows were kept tightly closed.

▲ **Delegates to the Constitutional Convention walked to the City Tavern (extreme left) for meals or to discuss events of the day. This engraving was done by William Russell Birch and Thomas Birch between 1799 and 1800.**

THE AMERICAN EXPERIMENT

Anne Robert Jacques Turgot (toor-GOH), a retired French government official, was among the many Europeans watching America's experiment in democracy. In 1778 Turgot wrote his thoughts in a letter to Richard Price, a British philosopher and writer who championed the United States.

"*The fate of America is already decided,*" Turgot wrote. "*Behold her independent beyond recovery. But will she be free and happy?*" Turgot worried whether the 13 separate states would be able to work together. He also wondered whether people could be governed "*only by nature, reason and justice*" without falling prey to the greed and self-interest of individuals.

Despite his doubts Turgot wished the experiment well. Of the Americans he wrote, "*They are the hope of the world.*"

The delegates took seriously their vow of secrecy. When someone accidentally dropped some notes on the floor outside the meeting room, George Washington, the presiding officer, erupted in anger:

> 66 Gentlemen, I am sorry to find that some member of the body has been so neglectful to the secrets of the Convention as to drop in the State House a copy of their proceedings. . . . I know not whose paper it is, but here it is, let him who owns it take it. 99

Throwing the notes on the desk, Washington stalked from the room. Not surprisingly, none of the convention delegates made a move to claim the document.

The delegates. George Washington and the 54 other convention delegates were a remarkable collection of politicians. Most had helped to write their state constitutions. All had held public office, many as delegates to the Continental Congress. They were a young group: James Madison of Virginia was 36; Alexander Hamilton of New York, 32. The youngest delegate, Jonathan Dayton of New Jersey, was only 26. At 81, Benjamin Franklin was the elder statesman of the convention.

Several prominent Americans were absent from the convention, however. Thomas Jefferson and John Adams were in Europe on diplomatic missions. Patrick Henry refused to attend. Saying he "smelled a rat," Henry claimed that the delegates were plotting to undermine states' rights. He feared that "the tyranny of Philadelphia may be like the tyranny of George III."

Generally wealthy and well educated, most delegates represented the privileged ranks of society. Many were merchants, planters, and bankers; more than half were lawyers. Although the delegates were hardly "average" citizens, there was no public outcry against their appointment. Few Americans of the day questioned the assumption that the wealthy were best qualified to govern.

■■ **Convention delegates debated issues in secret because they believed it would make it easier to resolve differences.**

FEDERAL POWER VERSUS STATES' RIGHTS

Although charged by Congress to revise the Articles of Confederation, some delegates believed that the Articles should be replaced with a new plan of government. At issue were relations among the states and between the states and the central government.

On May 29, Governor Edmund Randolph of Virginia started a heated debate when he presented James Madison's **Virginia Plan**. Madison's proposal to restructure the government was a bold departure from the Articles. His plan shifted political power away from the states and toward the central government. The central government would coordinate the states' activities for the benefit of the entire nation. The plan expressed Madison's belief that the nation's survival depended on **federalism**, or the division of powers between a strong central government and the state governments.

▲ Governor Edmund Randolph of Virginia presented Madison's Virginia Plan to the Constitutional Convention.

BIO GRAPHY James Madison was born in 1751 to a prominent Virginia family of planters, lawyers, and judges. He was frail in childhood and prone to vague ailments affecting his "nerves." Ill health prompted Madison to concentrate on strengthening his mind rather than his body.

A contemporary described Madison as being "no bigger than half a piece of soap." He was so quiet and reserved that an acquaintance called him "a gloomy, stiff creature." Never-theless, Madison had a distinguished political career, helping draft Virginia's state consti-tution and ably serving as a member of the Continental Congress. Madison's leadership at the Constitutional Con-vention earned him the name "father of the Constitution."

James Madison

Madison's Virginia Plan gave Congress vast powers, including the rights to overturn state laws, tax the states, and "bring the force of the Union against any [state] . . . failing to fulfill its duty." Such a drastic move away from states' rights alarmed some delegates. Charles Pinckney of South Carolina feared that such a powerful federal government would "abolish the State Governments altogether."

The Virginia Plan called for a federal gov-ernment made up of three branches: executive, judicial, and legislative. Under this plan the legislature would be **bicameral**— made up of two houses. Voters would elect representatives to the lower house, who would then choose members of the upper house. State populations would determine the number of representatives in each house.

A dispute quickly arose over the num-ber of representatives each state could send to the legislature. States with large popula-tions, such as Virginia and Pennsylvania, natu-rally favored representation based on population. States with small populations insisted on an equal number of representatives for each state. Said a delegate from tiny Delaware: "We would sooner submit to a foreign power than . . . be thrown under the domination of the large states."

William Paterson of New Jersey offered an alternative to the Virginia Plan. Paterson's New Jersey Plan provided for a unicameral, or one-house, legislature in which each state would have one vote. Madison and others objected to Paterson's plan because they believed that it did not correct the weaknesses of the Articles.

COMPROMISE AT THE CONVENTION

Arguments raged over the Virginia and New Jersey plans. By the end of June the convention was in danger of collapsing.

To balance the interests of large and small states, Roger Sherman of Connecticut fashioned a compromise. He proposed a two-house legislature that would allow for both equal representation and representation based on population. This **Great Compromise** granted each state, regardless of size, an equal voice in the upper house. In the lower house, representation would be according to population. The delegates narrowly approved this proposal, ending what Madison later described as "the most serious and threatening excitement" of the convention.

The Three-Fifths Compromise. The del-egates resolved one dispute only to see another emerge. They now debated whether slaves should be counted as part of a state's population to determine representation. Delegates from the South insisted that slaves be included. Northern delegates strongly objected to this demand. Some deeply opposed slavery on moral grounds and argued that it violated the republican ideal of liberty. Others objected to including slaves for political reasons. Southern states would be able to increase their representation in the lower house if slaves were included in population counts.

In the end, northern and southern delegates accepted a compromise. The final agreement, known as the **Three-Fifths Compromise**, counted only three fifths of the slave population in determining total state population.

Compromises over commerce. The states also clashed over control of commerce. Northern delegates favored giving the national government the power to regulate all trade with foreign nations and among the states. Southern delegates opposed such broad powers.

The southern economy depended on exports of tobacco, rice, and cotton to Europe and to northern states. Southerners feared that if the national government imposed **tariffs**, or taxes, on exports, overseas buyers would have to pay more for southern agricultural products. If buyers refused to pay higher prices, sales would be hurt. Southern opposition finally forced another compromise.

Delegates agreed that Congress could levy tariffs on imports but not on exports.

Once again, however, problems arose. Planters now worried that Congress might use its power to tax imports to restrict or abolish the slave trade. Bowing to southern pressure, convention delegates voted to permit the slave trade until the end of 1807. They also gave slaveholders the right to pursue runaway slaves across state lines.

Some northern delegates agreed to the compromises because they feared the South would withdraw from the union if planters thought their property and rights were threatened. James Madison argued that great as the evils of the slave trade were, "dismemberment of the union would be worse." Others agreed to the compromise because they mistakenly believed that slavery was a dying institution. Little did they know that more than 70 years of bitter debate and a civil war lay ahead before Americans would see slavery end.

■■ **The Constitution included compromises over political representation, commerce, and slavery.**

Completing the Constitution. On July 26, 1787, five delegates began drafting the Constitution, which they presented to the full convention on August 6. Between August 6 and

▲ **This detail from an 18th-century map shows enslaved African Americans working on an indigo plantation in South Carolina. By 1775 some 35 percent of South Carolina's exports involved shipments of indigo.**

September 10, the delegates debated the draft, hammering out such specifics as the terms of office for the president and for the members of both houses. Another five-delegate committee then prepared the finished document.

On September 17, 1787, the committee presented to the other delegates the final version of the Constitution, neatly handwritten by Gouverneur Morris of Pennsylvania. Some of the 55 delegates had already left Philadelphia, but of those remaining, 39 signed it. With the convention over, the Constitution went to the states for ratification.

THE FEDERALISTS AND THE ANTIFEDERALISTS

To win ratification, the Constitution required the approval of 9 of the 13 states. Most convention delegates, however, hoped for unanimous approval as a show of national unity.

When local newspapers printed copies of the Constitution, many Americans were shocked by what they read. They expected a revision of the Articles; what they saw was a new framework of government. Citizens soon divided over the issue of ratification.

One group, who called themselves **Federalists**, favored ratification. Wealthy merchants, planters, and lawyers generally were Federalists. They advocated a strong national government that would assure a sound currency and protect property rights. Many Americans who were not wealthy also supported the Constitution, believing that a strong national government would provide stability and security against political unrest like Shays's Rebellion. Speaking before the Massachusetts ratifying convention, a farmer explained his reason for supporting the Constitution:

▲ This 1788 print by engraver Amos Doolittle shows George Washington encircled by the seals of the 13 states and the seal of the United States. The joined circles symbolize the unity of the states.

66 I have lived in a part of the country where I have learned the worth of good government by the lack of it. There was a black cloud of rebellion that rose in the east last winter and spread over the west. . . . Our distress was so great that we should have been glad to grab at anything that looked like a government. . . . Now when I saw this Constitution, I found it was a cure for these disorders. 99

▶ The Pennsylvania Packet, and Daily Advertiser was one of several newspapers that carried the full text of the Constitution on September 19, 1787. The preamble to the Constitution is shown here.

The Pennsylvania Packet, *and* Daily Advertiser.

[Price Four-Pence.]   WEDNESDAY, SEPTEMBER 19, 1787.   [No. 2690.]

WE, the People of the United States, in order to form a more perfect Union, establish Justice, insure domestic Tranquility, provide for the common Defence, promote the General Welfare, and secure the Blessings of Liberty to Ourselves and our Posterity, do ordain and establish this Constitution for the United States of America.

The other group, called **Antifederalists** by their opponents, feared a powerful national government. One Antifederalist described the Constitution as "a beast, dreadful and terrible" that "devours, breaks into pieces, and stamps [the states] with his feet."

The Antifederalists offered three objections to ratification. First, they argued that delegates to the Constitutional Convention had conspired under "a thick veil of secrecy" to create a new form of government. In doing so, the delegates had gone beyond what they had been charged to do. Second, the Antifederalists claimed that a strong national government would destroy states' rights. Third, they argued that the new system of government resembled a monarchy because of its concentration of power, and thus violated the principle of liberty that had guided the Revolution.

▮▮ The Federalists wanted a strong national government. The Antifederalists believed that such a government threatened the liberty of the states.

▼ *The Federalist* contained a collection of essays by Hamilton, Madison, and Jay in support of the Constitution. The book appeared in two volumes in 1788.

THE

FEDERALIST:

ADDRESSED TO THE

PEOPLE OF THE STATE OF
NEW-YORK.

NUMBER I.

Introduction.

AFTER an unequivocal experience of the inefficacy of the subsisting federal government, you are called upon to deliberate on a new constitution for the United States of America. The subject speaks its own importance; comprehending in its consequences, nothing less than the existence of the UNION, the safety and welfare of the parts of which it is composed, the fate of an empire, in many respects, the most interesting in the world. It has been frequently remarked, that it seems to have been reserved to the people of this country, by their conduct and example, to decide the important question, whether societies of men are really capable or not, of establishing good government from reflection and choice, or whether they are forever destined to depend, for their political constitutions, on accident and force. If there be any truth in the remark, the crisis, at which we are arrived, may with propriety be regarded as the æra in which

A   that

The Granger Collection, New York

The Antifederalists pointed to the election procedures outlined in the Constitution as proof that the new national government was undemocratic. Under the Constitution, voters did not elect the president and the vice president—**electors** would choose them. Moreover, voters would not necessarily choose the electors; state legislatures would select them, just as they chose U.S. senators. Voters would elect only members of the lower house of Congress, the House of Representatives. But even then, Antifederalists pointed out, the Senate had the power to take this authority away as well.

The anonymous "Cato" (believed by many to have been Governor George Clinton of New York) challenged citizens to consider the dangers of such a system:

❝ For what did you throw off the yoke of Britain and call yourselves independent? Was it from a disposition fond of change, or to procure new masters? . . . This new form of national government . . . will be dangerous to your liberty and happiness. ❞

The Federalists answered their critics in a series of 85 essays written by James Madison, Alexander Hamilton, and John Jay. Between the fall of 1787 and the spring of 1788, 77 of the essays appeared in newspapers throughout the states. The essays were later published in book form as *The Federalist*, also known as the *Federalist Papers*. The writers intended the essays to sway the ratification vote in New York, but they also influenced public opinion in other states. Today the essays are regarded as the most authoritative commentary on the Constitution.

𝒯HE RATIFICATION STRUGGLE

The question of federalism versus states' rights was at the heart of the ratification struggle. Another crucial issue was individual rights. Unlike most state constitutions, the U.S. Constitution did not contain a bill of rights. This omission outraged the Antifederalists, some of whom refused to sign the Constitution.

Ordinary citizens joined the debate over ratification. Amos Singletary, a Massachusetts farmer, argued that the Constitution would take away individual rights, just as Great Britain had done.

▲ On July 23, 1788, the people of New York City celebrated the adoption of the Constitution. The ship on wheels was pulled by 10 white horses and represented the new "ship of state."

66 We contended [fought] with Great Britain . . . because they claimed a right to tax us and bind us in all cases whatever. And does not this Constitution do the same? Does it not take away all we have—all our property? Does it not lay *all* taxes, duties, imposts [import fees], and excises? . . . These lawyers, and men of learning, and moneyed men . . . expect to be managers of this Constitution, and get all the power and all the money into their own hands, and then they will swallow up all us little folks. 99

The Federalists claimed that the state constitutions adequately protected the rights of American citizens. But several states, including Virginia and New York, agreed to ratify the Constitution only if a bill of rights was added. Although by June 21, 1788, enough states had ratified the Constitution for it to take effect, a union without these two large states had little chance of succeeding.

The debates were bitter in both states' ratifying conventions. In Virginia, Patrick Henry

eloquently argued against the Constitution, while James Madison and George Washington strongly urged the convention delegates to vote for ratification. New York Federalists, strongest in New York City, threatened to withdraw the city from the state if the state did not ratify the Constitution. In the end the Federalists won in both states, but only by very narrow margins.

The last state to ratify was Rhode Island, which had even refused to send delegates to the Constitutional Convention. After the Constitution had been drafted, the state legislature initially refused to call for a ratifying convention, prompting some towns to consider seceding. When the state—threatened with an economic boycott by Congress—finally did call a convention, the vote was so close that the governor had to break the tie.

The battle had been long, the final vote close, but with ratification most Americans embraced the Constitution. They had endured the Revolution and the turmoil of the Confederation years. They could now hope to launch constitutional government in the United States with solid prospects for success.

◄ This painting of Federal Hall, where the first Congress met under the Constitution, was completed in 1789.

which powers the states would retain. They decided to give the federal government authority in matters of concern to all the people. These **delegated powers**, which are outlined in the Constitution, include the rights to coin money, to regulate trade with foreign nations and among the states, and to raise and support an army and a navy.

All powers not specifically granted to the federal government or denied to the states are kept, or reserved, by the states. These **reserved powers** are guaranteed by the Tenth Amendment, adopted in 1791. Examples of the states' reserved powers include establishing local governments, overseeing schools, conducting elections, regulating businesses, and making marriage laws.

The powers that are held jointly by the federal government and the state government are called **concurrent powers**. Examples of concurrent powers include levying and collecting taxes, borrowing money, providing for the public welfare, and establishing courts to apply and enforce laws.

DELEGATED, RESERVED, AND CONCURRENT POWERS

Powers Delegated to National Government

Declare war

Maintain armed forces

Regulate interstate and foreign trade

Admit new states

Establish post offices

Set standard weights and measures

Coin money

Establish foreign policy

Make all laws necessary and proper for carrying out delegated powers

Powers Reserved to States

Establish and maintain schools

Establish local governments

Conduct elections

Create corporate laws

Regulate business within the state

Make marriage laws

Provide for public safety

Assume other powers not delegated to the national government or prohibited to the states

Powers Shared (Concurrent Powers)

Maintain law and order

Levy taxes

Borrow money

Charter banks

Establish courts

Provide for public welfare

FEDERALISM The division of power between a national government and the states is called *federalism*. The Constitution delegates certain powers to the national government, reserves other powers for the states, and allows some powers to be shared jointly.

? **EVALUATING** Why might the delegates to the Constitutional Convention have supported a division of powers?

▲ The state seals of Massachusetts, New York, and North Carolina are shown here. State legislatures use seals such as these on official public documents.

■■ **The Constitution identifies the powers of the federal government in order to define the scope of federal authority.**

National supremacy. The delegates to the Constitutional Convention recognized that the national government exercising its powers at the same time as the state governments could lead to problems. Which laws would have ultimate authority?

To help eliminate conflicts, the delegates added a clause to the Constitution, clearly stating that the federal constitution and all federal laws outrank state constitutions and state laws: "This Constitution, and the laws . . . and all treaties . . . of the United States, shall be the supreme law of the land." This clause, defined in Article VI of the Constitution, is called the **supremacy clause**.

SEPARATION OF POWERS

To prevent the federal government from abusing its powers, the framers separated the government into three branches: legislative, executive, and judicial. Each branch has specific powers the other branches cannot claim. The legislative branch makes laws, the executive branch sees that they are carried out, and the judicial branch interprets them and punishes lawbreakers. This **separation of powers** prevents any part of the federal government from becoming too powerful.

Checks and balances. The separation of powers is upheld by a system of **checks and balances** that gives each branch the means to restrain the powers of the other two. Congress, for example, has the responsibility to check presidential power. The Constitution's many checks on executive power reflect the framers' bitter experience with British royal governors. The most extreme restraint on presidential authority is the legal process of **impeachment**. The House of Representatives may impeach, or charge, a president who is thought to be guilty of "treason, bribery, or other high crimes and misdemeanors." The president would then be tried by the Senate and, if found guilty, removed from office.

There are other checks and balances between the legislative and the executive branches. The president has the power to make treaties, but a two-thirds vote of the Senate is necessary to ratify them. Similarly, the president can appoint ambassadors, federal judges, and other important officials, but only with the "advice and consent" of the Senate. Congress can also check the president through "the power of the purse"—because it has the authority to spend government monies, it can slow or stop a presidential action that requires funding.

The president, in turn, can curb the powers of Congress. The president can **veto**, or reject, laws passed by Congress. Although Congress possesses the power to **override**, or overrule, a presidential veto, the two-thirds majority necessary to do so is often difficult to obtain.

The president can also check congressional power through influence and pressure. The Constitution grants the president the authority to call Congress into special session to deal with a national crisis. The president can also adjourn Congress if its members cannot agree when to end

▲ **George Washington made numerous editorial changes on an early draft of the Constitution. The wording of Article III, Section 3, regarding trial by jury, is largely unchanged from his handwritten suggestions in the margin. The section that follows on impeachment, which he marked as "agreed," was later moved to Article I, Section 3 of the finished document.**

a session. In addition, the president can exert pressure on Congress by recommending measures "necessary and expedient" to maintaining effective government or by lobbying for specific legislation. The chief executive can also influence the thinking of Congress through annual State of the Union messages and through press conferences and public speeches.

The executive and legislative branches balance judicial power. The judicial selection process provides the most basic check. The Senate must approve all federal judges. Just as Congress has the power to impeach the president, it has the power to impeach judges for "high crimes and misdemeanors." In addition, Congress can propose constitutional amendments that overturn earlier court rulings. Similarly, the president can pardon or delay the punishment of persons convicted of federal crimes. But neither the president nor Congress can remove unpopular judges from the bench. Unless impeached and removed for "high crimes," federal judges may hold their offices for life.

Drawbacks of checks and balances. The framers built the system of checks and balances into the structure of government to keep any government branch from exercising too much power. The system, however, has always had its critics.

Some argue that checks and balances permit political disputes to hold up the workings of government. For example, a president who belongs to one political party and a Congress dominated by another party may not agree on necessary legislation. One branch may continually block the actions of the other. Nevertheless, the system has prevented what the framers of the Constitution feared most: unrestricted governmental power.

■■ **Separation of powers and checks and balances prevent any branch of government from becoming too strong.**

ƎLEXIBILITY AND CHANGE

The Constitution has remained effective for more than 200 years because it is a living document that can adapt to changes in our society. The Constitution works as well today for an industrialized nation of 50 states and some 250 million people as it did in 1790 for an agricultural nation of 13 states and fewer than 4 million people.

The continued effectiveness of the Constitution owes much to its flexibility. James Madison had urged his colleagues to consider "the changes which ages will produce." To allow for needed amendments, the framers specified a procedure by which the Constitution may be changed. The framers deliberately made the amendment process difficult, intending it to be used only when a change is critical (see page 164). Only 27 amendments have been added to the Constitution since 1789.

The Constitution's **elastic clause** has increased the document's flexibility. To the specific powers granted to Congress, this clause adds the power "to make all Laws which shall be necessary and proper for carrying into Execution the foregoing Powers." The elastic clause allows Congress to stretch its powers in ways not specifically outlined in the Constitution.

The Supreme Court's power of **judicial review**—the right to determine whether or not laws violate the Constitution—also ensures the Constitution's continued effectiveness. The framers did not write judicial review into the Constitution. Legal scholars, however, believe that the framers intended the Supreme Court to have such power. James Madison often argued that the Supreme Court could declare any law void if the justices found that the law violated the Constitution. But, Madison continued, the Court would still be compelled to uphold all laws "however unjust."

Alexander Hamilton anticipated problems that might arise from judicial review in *The Federalist* Number 78:

66 It can be of no weight to say that the courts . . . may substitute their own pleasure to the constitutional intentions of the

▲ The first two sessions of the Supreme Court were held in the Water Street Exchange, a building in New York City.

legislature. . . . The courts must declare the sense of the law; and if they should be disposed to exercise WILL instead of JUDGMENT, the consequence would be . . . the substitution of their pleasure to that of the legislative body. 99

Although judicial review has the potential for being abused, it remains one of the safeguards of individual rights in a changing society.

▪▪ The amendment process, the elastic clause, and judicial review allow the Constitution to adapt to changing conditions.

SECTION 3 REVIEW

IDENTIFY and explain the significance of the following: delegated powers, reserved powers, concurrent powers, supremacy clause, separation of powers, checks and balances, impeachment, veto, override, elastic clause, judicial review.

1. **MAIN IDEA** Why were the federal government's powers listed in the Constitution?

2. **MAIN IDEA** Why were checks and balances and the separation of powers written into the Constitution?

3. **MAIN IDEA** Why can the Constitution be considered a flexible, living document?

4. **WRITING TO EXPLAIN** Write an essay explaining how the executive, the legislative, and the judicial branches use the system of checks and balances.

5. **ASSESSING CONSEQUENCES** How might a system of checks and balances prevent government from being effective at times?

CHAPTER 5
Review

Congress urges states to draft new constitutions.

Articles of Confederation adopted.

Virginia Statute for Religious Freedom drafted.

Massachusetts state constitution ratified,

1776   1778   1780

WRITING A SUMMARY
Using the essential points of the chapter as a guide, write a summary of the chapter.

REVIEWING CHRONOLOGY
Number your paper 1 to 5. Study the time line above, and list the following events in the order in which they happened by writing the first event next to 1, the second next to 2, and so on. Then complete the activity below.

1. Virginia Statute for Religious Freedom drafted.
2. Congress passes Northwest Ordinance.
3. Congress passes Land Ordinance of 1785.
4. Articles of Confederation adopted.
5. U.S. Constitution ratified.

Identifying Cause and Effect Select two events on the time line, and in a paragraph, explain the cause-and-effect relationship between them.

IDENTIFYING PEOPLE AND IDEAS
Explain the historical significance of each of the following people or terms.

1. Virginia Plan
2. John Locke
3. Virginia Statute for Religious Freedom
4. Articles of Confederation
5. *The Federalist*
6. James Madison
7. checks and balances
8. Three-Fifths Compromise
9. Daniel Shays
10. supremacy clause

UNDERSTANDING MAIN IDEAS
1. Why did colonial leaders create a weak national government in the Articles of Confederation, and why did this cause problems for the new nation?
2. What were the main compromises reached during the Constitutional Convention?
3. What elements of the Constitution addressed concerns over governmental abuse of power?
4. How did the framers of the Constitution propose to solve economic problems caused by weaknesses in the Articles of Confederation?
5. What were the provisions of the ordinances to organize and govern the Northwest Territory?

REVIEWING THEMES
1. **Constitutional Heritage** How does the way the government was organized reflect concern about a powerful national government?
2. **Economic Development** How did the government's economic policies lead to Shays's Rebellion?
3. **Democratic Values** How might the framers of the Constitution have helped ensure that more citizens had a voice in government?

THINKING CRITICALLY
1. **Analyzing** What factors shaped the republican spirit?
2. **Hypothesizing** What might have happened if the framers of the Constitution had outlawed slavery?
3. **Evaluating** The proceedings at the Constitutional Convention were secret. Do you think such government activities should be open to the public? Explain your answer.
4. **Identifying Cause and Effect** How did colonial experiences influence the actions of the framers of the state constitutions?

STRATEGY FOR SUCCESS
Review the Skills Handbook entry on Building Vocabulary on page 991. Then define the following terms, and write a sentence using each word.

republic	*depression*
separation of powers	*judicial review*
federalism	*delegated powers*
reserved powers	*concurrent powers*
bicameral	*impeachment*
veto	*override*

WRITING ABOUT HISTORY
Writing to Persuade Imagine you are a business owner in New England who supports the Constitution. Write a letter to the editor of your local newspaper, explaining why you support the new plan of government over the Articles of Confederation.

States officially become "The United States of America."

Congress passes Land Ordinance of 1785.

Shays's Rebellion begins.

Congress passes Northwest Ordinance. Constitutional Convention meets.

U.S. Constitution ratified.

1782   1784   1786   1788

USING PRIMARY SOURCES

The following is an excerpt from a petition submitted to the Continental Congress in 1786 by elderly widow Rachel Wells. Like many patriots, Wells had bought loan certificates from the state of New Jersey during the Revolution. Wells appealed to the Congress to grant her payment on the certificates. Read the excerpt from her petition. What does she reveal about the contribution of ordinary citizens to the war and the government's responsibility to live up to the ideals of the Revolution?

> To the Honorable Congress,
>
> I, Rachel, do make this complaint, who am a Widow far advanced in years & Dearly have occasion [need] of the Interest for that Cash I Lent the States. . . . I Lent the State a considerable Sum of Moneys & had I justice done me it might be Sufficient to support me in the country where I am now, near Burdentown [New Jersey]. I lived here then . . . but Being . . . so Robbed by the Britains & others I went to Phila[delphia] to try to get a Living . . . & was There in the year 1783 when our assembly was pleased to pass a Law that No one should have any Interest that lived out of Jersey States. . . .
>
> Now, gentlemen, is this Liberty? . . . I have done as much to carry on the War as many that Sit now at the helm of government. . . . My dear Sister . . . wrote to me to be thankful that I had it in my Power to help on the War, which is well enough, but then this is to be Considered—that others get their Interest & why then a poor old widow be put of[f]? . . .
>
> If She did not fight She threw in all her might, which bought the Soldiers food & Clothing & Let Them have Blankets & Since that She has been obliged to Lay upon Straw & glad of that.

LINKING HISTORY AND GEOGRAPHY

Study the map, noting the numbers on it. The map shows the order in which the states ratified the Constitution. Number your paper 1 to 13. Identify each state on the map and write the correct name of each state next to the corresponding number on your paper, along with the date each state ratified the Constitution.

BUILDING YOUR PORTFOLIO

Complete the following projects independently or cooperatively.

1. **DEMOCRATIC RIGHTS** In Chapter 4 you served as a reporter interviewing people about taxes. Building on that material, now imagine you are one of Shays's rebels. Create a poster that communicates your position on taxes.

2. **THE CONSTITUTION** Imagine you are a woman interested in including women's rights in the new Constitution. Write a letter to the Constitutional Convention suggesting ways to represent women in the Constitution.

3. **POLITICS** Imagine you are attending a governors conference in 1790. Prepare a speech outlining the issues of concern to your region.

We the People

Article I.

Section 1. ...

Section 2. ...

Section 3. ...

Section 4. ...

Section 5. ...

Section 6. ...

Section 7. ...

Constitution Handbook

66 We the People of the United States, in Order to form
a more perfect Union, establish Justice, insure domestic
Tranquility, provide for the common defense, promote the
general Welfare, and secure the Blessings of Liberty to
ourselves and our Posterity, do ordain and establish this
Constitution for the United States of America. 99

—Preamble to the Constitution

The delegates who met in the spring of 1787 to revise the
Articles of Confederation included many of the ablest leaders of the
United States. Convinced that the Confederation was not strong
enough to bring order and prosperity to the nation, they abandoned all
thought of revising the Articles. Instead, they proceeded to draw up a
completely new Constitution. Patrick Henry called this action "a revolution as radical as that which separated us from Great Britain." Out
of their long political experience, their keen intelligence, and their
great learning, the framers of the Constitution fashioned a blueprint
for a truly united nation—the United States of America.

FOCUS

- **What do the first three Articles of the Constitution describe?**
- **How do the Articles attempt to protect people's civil liberties?**
- **What does the Bill of Rights protect?**

An observer once referred to the Constitution as "the most wonderful work ever struck off at a given time by the brain and purpose of man." Revised, modified, and amended, the Constitution has served the American people for more than 200 years, becoming a model for representative government throughout the world. The Constitution has successfully survived the years for two reasons. First, it lays down rules of procedure and guarantees of rights and liberties that must be observed even in times of crisis. Second, it is a "living" document, capable of being revised to meet changing times and circumstances.

U.S. Constitution commemorative stamps

TO FORM A MORE PERFECT UNION

The framers of the Constitution wished to establish a strong central government, one that could unite the country and help it meet the challenges of the future. At the same time, however, they feared a government that was too strong. The memories of the troubled years before the Revolution were still fresh. They knew that unchecked power in the hands of individuals, groups, or branches of government could lead to tyranny.

The framers response was to devise a system of government in which power is divided between, in the words of James Madison, "two distinct governments"—the states and the federal government—and then within each government. In *The Federalist* Number 51, Madison described the advantages of such a system:

66 In the compound republic of America, the power surrendered by the people is first divided between two distinct governments, and then the portion allotted to each subdivided among distinct and sepa-

rate departments. Hence a double security arises to the rights of the people. The different governments will control each other, at the same time that each will be controlled by itself. 99

The seven Articles that make up the first part of the Constitution provide the blueprint for this system. To help guard against tyranny and to keep any one part of the federal government from becoming too strong, the framers divided the government into three branches of government—the legislative branch (Congress), the executive branch (the president and vice president), and the judicial branch (the federal courts)—each with specific powers. As a further safeguard, the framers wrote a system of checks and balances into the Constitution (see Chapter 5). Articles I, II, and III outline the powers of each branch of government and the checks and balances.

■■ **Articles I, II, and III outline the rights and responsibilities of the legislative, executive, and judicial branches.**

AMENDING THE CONSTITUTION

Proposed by

CONGRESS
two-thirds vote
of each house

or

**NATIONAL
CONVENTION**
called by Congress
at the request of
two thirds of the
state legislatures

Ratified by

LEGISLATURES
of three fourths
of the states

or

CONVENTIONS
held in three
fourths of
the states

**Amendment
added to the
Constitution**

A LIVING DOCUMENT Anticipating the need for the Constitution to adapt to changing conditions, the framers specified an amendment process. But to avoid abuses, they deliberately made the process difficult.

? ANALYZING Why do you think the framers of the Constitution required that both the Congress and the states be involved in the amendment process?

Article IV outlines the relations between the states and between the states and the federal government. Among the issues addressed are each state's recognition of other states' public records and citizens' rights, the admission of new states, and the rights and responsibilities of the federal government in relation to the states.

Article V specifies the process by which the Constitution can be amended. The framers purposely made the process slow and difficult. They feared that if the process was too easy, the Constitution—the fundamental law of the land—would soon carry no more weight than the most minor law passed by Congress.

Article VI includes one provision that addressed the immediate concerns of the framers and two that have lasting significance. The short-term provision promises that the United States under the Constitution will honor all public debts entered into under the Confederation. The two long-term provisions declare the Constitution the supreme law of the land and prohibit religion being used as a qualification for holding public office.

Article VII is the framers' attempt to ensure ratification of the Constitution. The Constitutional Convention was summoned by the Congress to amend the Articles of Confederation. Under the Articles of Confederation, amendments had to be approved by all 13 states. Realizing that it would be difficult to get the approval of all the states— Rhode Island, for example, had not even sent delegates to Philadelphia—the framers specified that the Constitution would go into effect after ratifica-

tion by only 9 states, not 13. (This provision led opponents of the Constitution to claim that it had been adopted by revolutionary means.)

PROTECTING INDIVIDUAL LIBERTY

Opposition to a strong central government was in part a concern over states' rights. But it was also rooted in the desire to protect individual liberties. American colonists had always insisted on the protection of their **civil liberties**—their rights as individuals against the power of the government. The Articles of the Constitution contain many important guarantees of civil liberties. On a broad level, the separation of powers and the system of checks and balances help safeguard citizens against the abuse of government power. But the Articles also contain provisions that speak directly to an individual's right to due process of law. For example, Section 9 of Article I prohibits both *ex post facto* laws and bills of attainder.

An *ex post facto* **law** is a law passed "after the deed." Such a law sets a penalty for an act that was not illegal when it was committed. A **bill of attainder** is a law that punishes a person by fine, imprisonment, or seizure of property without a court trial. If Congress had the power to adopt bills of attainder, lawmakers could punish any American at will, and that person could do nothing to appeal the sentence. Instead, the Constitution provides that only the courts can impose punishment for unlawful acts, and then only by following the duly established law.

Section 9 of Article I also protects a citizen's right to the **writ of *habeas corpus*.** The writ of *habeas corpus* is a legal document that forces a jailer to release a person from prison unless the person has been formally charged with, or convicted of, a crime. The Constitution states that "the privilege of the writ of *habeas corpus* shall not be suspended, unless when in cases of rebellion or invasion the public safety may require it."

The Constitution also gives special protection to people accused of **treason**. The framers of the Constitution knew that the charge of treason was an old device used by tyrants to get rid of persons they did not like. Such rulers might bring the charge of treason against persons who merely criticized the government. To prevent such use of this charge, Section 3 of Article III carefully defines treason:

66 Treason against the United States shall consist only in levying War against them, or in adhering to their Enemies, giving them Aid and Comfort. No Person shall be convicted of Treason unless on the Testimony of two Witnesses to the same overt Act, or on Confession in open Court. 99

The Article also protects the innocent relatives of a person accused of treason. Only the convicted person can be punished. No penalty can be imposed on the person's family.

AMENDMENTS TO THE CONSTITUTION

Amendment	Year Enacted	Subject
1st	1791	Personal and political freedoms
2nd	1791	Right to keep weapons
3rd	1791	Quartering of troops
4th	1791	Search and seizure; search warrants
5th	1791	Rights of accused persons
6th	1791	Speedy trial
7th	1791	Jury trial
8th	1791	Bails, fines, punishments
9th	1791	Rights of the people
10th	1791	Powers of the states
11th	1798	Suits against states
12th	1804	Election of president and vice president
13th	1865	Abolition of slavery
14th	1868	Rights of citizens; privileges and immunities, due process, and equal protection
15th	1870	Extension of suffrage to black males
16th	1913	Income tax
17th	1913	Direct election of senators
18th	1919	Prohibition on liquor
19th	1920	Women's suffrage
20th	1933	Change in dates for presidential and congressional terms of office
21st	1933	Repeal of prohibition
22nd	1951	Two-term limit on presidential tenure
23rd	1961	Right to vote in presidential elections for residents of the District of Columbia
24th	1964	Poll tax banned in federal elections
25th	1967	Presidential disability and succession
26th	1971	Lowering of voting age to 18
27th	1992	Legislative salaries

THE AMENDMENT PROCESS The supreme law of the land has proven very durable. The Constitution has only been amended 27 times in over 200 years.

? **BUILDING CHART SKILLS** What is the longest interval between ratification of two consecutive amendments?

■■ **The Articles protect civil liberties by guaranteeing individuals due process of law.**

THE BILL OF RIGHTS

Despite the safeguards written into the Articles of the Constitution, some states at first refused to ratify the framework because it did not offer greater protection to the rights of individuals. They finally agreed to ratification after they had been promised that a bill of rights would be added to the Constitution by amendment when Congress was called into session following ratification.

In 1789 the first Congress of the United States wrote the ideals of the Declaration of Independence into the Bill of Rights, the first 10 amendments to the Constitution. The Bill of Rights protects individuals against any action by the federal government that may deprive them of life, liberty, or property without "due process of law."

Among the guarantees of liberty in the Bill of Rights, several are especially important. The First Amendment guarantees freedom of religion, speech, press, assembly, and petition. The Fourth Amendment forbids unreasonable searches and seizures of any person's home. The Fifth, Sixth, and Eighth amendments protect individuals from arbitrary arrest and punishment by the federal government.

■■ The Bill of Rights protects the rights of individuals against abuses of government power.

The Bill of Rights was ratified by the states in 1791. It has remained one of the best-known features of the Constitution. The American people have turned to it for support whenever their rights as individuals have seemed to be in danger. No document in American history, except, perhaps, the Declaration of Independence, has been cherished more deeply.

▼ Supreme Court justices (from left) Antonin Scalia, Ruth Bader Ginsburg, Anthony Kennedy, John Paul Stevens, Chief Justice William Rehnquist, Harry Blackmun, Sandra Day O'Connor, David Souter, and Clarence Thomas meet with President Clinton (center).

Contents of the Constitution

Bill of Rights

Civil War Amendments

The Constitution of the United States of America

Preamble
The short and dignified Preamble explains the goals of the new government under the Constitution.

PREAMBLE

We the People of the United States, in Order to form a more perfect Union, establish Justice, insure domestic Tranquility, provide for the common defense, promote the general Welfare, and secure the Blessings of Liberty to ourselves and our Posterity, do ordain and establish this Constitution for the United States of America.*

ARTICLE I

Section 1. All legislative Powers herein granted shall be vested in a Congress of the United States, which shall consist of a Senate and House of Representatives.

Section 2. The House of Representatives shall be composed of Members chosen every second Year by the People of the several States, and the Electors in each State shall have the Qualifications requisite for Electors of the most numerous Branch of the State Legislature.

No Person shall be a Representative who shall not have attained to the Age of twenty-five Years, and been seven Years a Citizen of the United States, and who shall not, when elected, be an inhabitant of that State in which he shall be chosen.

Representatives and direct Taxes shall be apportioned among the several States which may be included within this Union, according to their respective Numbers, which shall be determined by adding to the whole Number of free Persons, including those bound to Service for a Term of Years, and excluding Indians not taxed, three fifths of all other Persons. The actual Enumeration shall be made within three Years after the first Meeting of the Congress of the United States, and within every subsequent Term of ten Years, in such Manner as they shall by Law direct. The Number of Representatives shall not exceed one for every thirty Thousand, but each State shall have at Least one Representative; and until such enumeration shall be made, the State of New Hampshire shall be entitled to choose three; Massachusetts eight; Rhode Island and Providence Plantations one; Connecticut five; New York six; New Jersey four;

Legislative Branch
Article I explains how the legislative branch, called Congress, is organized. The chief purpose of the legislative branch is to make the laws. Congress is made up of the Senate and the House of Representatives. The decision to have two bodies of government solved a difficult problem during the Constitutional Convention. The large states wanted the membership of Congress to be based entirely on population. The small states wanted every state to have an equal vote. The solution to the problem of how the states were to be represented in Congress was known as the Great Compromise.

The number of members of the House is based on the population of the individual states. Each state has at least one representative. The current size of the House is 435 members, set by Congress in 1929. If each member of the House represented only 30,000 American people, as the Constitution states, the House would have more than 8,000 members.

* Parts of the Constitution that have been ruled through are no longer in force or no longer apply.

Pennsylvania eight; Delaware one; Maryland six; Virginia ten; North Carolina five; South Carolina five; and Georgia three.

When vacancies happen in the Representation from any State, the Executive Authority thereof shall issue Writs of Election to fill such Vacancies.

The House of Representatives shall choose their Speaker and other Officers; and shall have the sole Power of Impeachment.

Section 3. The Senate of the United States shall be composed of two Senators from each State, chosen by the Legislature thereof, for six Years; and each Senator shall have one Vote.

Immediately after they shall be assembled in Consequence of the first Election, they shall be divided as equally as may be into three Classes. The Seats of the Senators of the first Class shall be vacated at the Expiration of the second Year, of the second Class at the Expiration of the fourth Year, and of the third Class at the Expiration of the sixth Year, so that one third may be chosen every second Year; and if Vacancies happen by Resignation, or otherwise, during the Recess of the Legislature of any State, the Executive thereof may make temporary Appointments until the next Meeting of the Legislature, which shall then fill such Vacancies.

No Person shall be a Senator who shall not have attained to the Age of thirty Years, and been nine Years a Citizen of the United States, and who shall not, when elected, be an Inhabitant of that State for which he shall be chosen.

The Vice President of the United States shall be President of the Senate, but shall have no Vote, unless they be equally divided.

The Senate shall choose their other Officers, and also a President pro tempore, in the Absence of the Vice President, or when he shall exercise the Office of President of the United States.

The Senate shall have the sole Power to try all Impeachments. When sitting for that Purpose, they shall be on Oath or Affirmation. When the President of the United States is tried, the Chief Justice shall preside: And no Person shall be convicted without the Concurrence of two thirds of the Members present.

Judgment in Cases of Impeachment shall not extend further than to removal from Office, and disqualification to hold and enjoy any Office of honor, Trust or Profit under the United States: but the Party convicted shall nevertheless be liable and subject to Indictment, Trial, Judgment and Punishment, according to Law.

Section 4. The Times, Places and Manner of holding Elections for Senators and Representatives, shall be prescribed in each State by the Legislature thereof; but the Congress may at any time by Law make or alter such Regulations, except as to the Places of choosing Senators.

The Congress shall assemble at least once in every Year, and such Meeting shall be on the first Monday in December, unless they shall by Law appoint a different Day.

Every state has two senators. Senators serve a six-year term, but only one third of the senators reach the end of their terms every two years. In any election, at least two thirds of the senators stay in office. This system ensures that there are experienced senators in office at all times.

The only duty that the Constitution assigns to the vice president is to preside over meetings of the Senate. Modern presidents have given their vice presidents more and varied responsibility.

The House charges a government official of wrongdoing, and the Senate acts as a court to decide if the official is guilty.

Congress has decided that elections will be held on the Tuesday following the first Monday in November of even-numbered years. The Twentieth Amendment states that Congress shall meet in regular session on January 3 of each year. The president may call a special session of Congress whenever necessary.

Congress makes most of its own rules of conduct. The Senate and the House each have a code of ethics that members must follow. It is the task of each house of Congress to discipline its own members. Each house keeps a journal, and a publication called the *Congressional Record* records what happens in congressional sessions. The general public can learn how their representatives voted on bills by reading the *Congressional Record*.

The framers of the Constitution wanted to protect members of Congress from being arrested on false charges by political enemies who did not want them to attend important meetings. The framers also wanted to protect members of Congress from being taken to court for something they said in a speech or in a debate.

The power of taxing is the responsibility of the House of Representatives. Because members of the House are elected every two years, the framers felt that representatives would listen to the public and seek its approval before passing taxes.

Section 5. Each House shall be the Judge of the Elections, Returns and Qualifications of its own Members, and a Majority of each shall constitute a Quorum to do Business; but a smaller Number may adjourn from day to day, and may be authorized to compel the Attendance of absent Members, in such Manner, and under such Penalties as each House may provide.

Each House may determine the Rules of its Proceedings, punish its Members for disorderly Behavior, and, with the Concurrence of two thirds, expel a Member.

Each House shall keep a Journal of its Proceedings, and from time to time publish the same, excepting such Parts as may in their Judgment require Secrecy; and the Yeas and Nays of the Members of either House on any question shall, at the Desire of one fifth of those Present, be entered on the Journal.

Neither House, during the Session of Congress, shall, without the Consent of the other, adjourn for more than three days, nor to any other Place than that in which the two Houses shall be sitting.

Section 6. The Senators and Representatives shall receive a Compensation for their Services, to be ascertained by Law, and paid out of the Treasury of the United States. They shall in all Cases, except Treason, Felony and Breach of the Peace, be privileged from Arrest during their Attendance at the Session of their respective Houses, and in going to and returning from the same; and for any Speech or Debate in either House, they shall not be questioned in any other Place.

No Senator or Representative shall, during the Time for which he was elected, be appointed to any civil Office under the Authority of the United States, which shall have been created, or the Emoluments whereof shall have been increased during such time; and no Person holding any Office under the United States, shall be a Member of either House during his Continuance in Office.

Section 7. All Bills for raising Revenue shall originate in the House of Representatives; but the Senate may propose or concur with Amendments as on other Bills.

Every Bill which shall have passed the House of Representatives and the Senate, shall, before it become a Law, be presented to the President of the United States; If he approve he shall sign it, but if not he shall return it, with his Objections to that House in which it shall have originated, who shall enter the Objections at large on their Journal, and proceed to reconsider it. If after such Reconsideration two thirds of that House shall agree to pass the Bill, it shall be sent, together with the Objections, to the other House, by which it shall likewise be reconsidered, and if approved by two thirds of that House, it shall become a Law. But in all such Cases the Votes of both Houses shall be determined by Yeas and Nays, and the Names of the Persons voting for and against the Bill shall be entered on the

Journal of each House respectively. If any Bill shall not be returned by the President within ten Days (Sundays excepted) after it shall have been presented to him, the Same shall be a Law, in like Manner as if he had signed it, unless the Congress by their Adjournment prevent its Return, in which Case it shall not be a Law.

Every Order, Resolution, or Vote to which the Concurrence of the Senate and House of Representatives may be necessary (except on a question of Adjournment) shall be presented to the President of the United States; and before the Same shall take Effect, shall be approved by him, or being disapproved by him, shall be repassed by two thirds of the Senate and House of Representatives, according to the Rules and Limitations prescribed in the Case of a Bill.

Section 8. The Congress shall have Power To lay and collect Taxes, Duties, Imposts and Excises, to pay the Debts and provide for the common Defense and general Welfare of the United States; but all Duties, Imposts and Excises shall be uniform throughout the United States;

To borrow Money on the credit of the United States;

To regulate Commerce with foreign Nations, and among the several States, and with the Indian Tribes;

To establish an uniform Rule of Naturalization, and uniform Laws on the subject of Bankruptcies throughout the United States;

To coin Money, regulate the Value thereof, and of foreign Coin, and fix the Standard of Weights and Measures;

To provide for the Punishment of counterfeiting the Securities and current Coin of the United States;

To establish Post Offices and post Roads;

To promote the Progress of Science and useful Arts, by securing for limited Times to Authors and Inventors the exclusive Right to their respective Writings and Discoveries;

To constitute Tribunals inferior to the supreme Court;

To define and punish Piracies and Felonies committed on the high Seas, and Offenses against the Law of Nations;

To declare War, grant Letters of Marque and Reprisal, and make Rules concerning Captures on Land and Water;

To raise and support Armies, but no Appropriation of Money to that Use shall be for a longer Term than two Years;

To provide and maintain a Navy;

To make Rules for the Government and Regulation of the land and naval Forces;

To provide for calling forth the Militia to execute the Laws of the Union, suppress Insurrections and repel Invasions;

To provide for organizing, arming, and disciplining, the Militia, and for governing such Part of them as may be employed in the Service of the United States, reserving to the States respectively, the

The veto power of the president and the ability of Congress to override a presidential veto are two of the important checks and balances in the Constitution.

The framers of the Constitution wanted a national government that was strong enough to be effective. This section lists the powers given to Congress. The last sentence in Section 8 (see page 170) contains the famous "elastic clause," which can be stretched (like elastic) to fit many different circumstances. The clause was first disputed when Alexander Hamilton proposed a national bank. Thomas Jefferson said that the Constitution did not give Congress the power to establish a bank. Hamilton argued that the bank was "necessary and proper" in order to carry out other powers of Congress, such as borrowing money and regulating currency. This argument was tested in the court system in 1819 in the case of *McCulloch* v. *Maryland,* when Chief Justice Marshall ruled in favor of the federal government. Powers given to the government by the "elastic clause" are called implied powers.

Appointment of the Officers, and the Authority of training the Militia according to the discipline prescribed by Congress.

To exercise exclusive Legislation in all Cases whatsoever, over such District (not exceeding ten Miles square) as may, by Cession of particular States, and the Acceptance of Congress, become the Seat of the Government of the United States, and to exercise like Authority over all Places purchased by the Consent of the Legislature of the State in which the Same shall be, for the Erection of Forts, Magazines, Arsenals, dock-Yards, and other needful Buildings;— And

To make all Laws which shall be necessary and proper for carrying into Execution the foregoing Powers, and all other Powers vested by this Constitution in the Government of the United States, or in any Department or Officer thereof.

Section 9. ~~The Migration or Importation of such Persons as any of the States now existing shall think proper to admit, shall not be prohibited by the Congress prior to the Year one thousand eight hundred and eight, but a Tax or duty may be imposed on such Importation, not exceeding ten dollars for each Person.~~

The Privilege of the Writ of Habeas Corpus shall not be suspended, unless when in Cases of Rebellion or Invasion the public Safety may require it.

No Bill of Attainder or ex post facto Law shall be passed.

No Capitation, or other direct, Tax shall be laid, unless in Proportion to the Census or Enumeration herein before directed to be taken.

No Tax or Duty shall be laid on Articles exported from any State.

No Preference shall be given by any Regulation of Commerce or Revenue to the Ports of one State over those of another: nor shall Vessels bound to, or from, one State, be obliged to enter, clear, or pay Duties in another.

No Money shall be drawn from the Treasury, but in Consequence of Appropriations made by Law; and a regular Statement and Account of the Receipts and Expenditures of all public Money shall be published from time to time.

No Title of Nobility shall be granted by the United States: And no Person holding any Office of Profit or Trust under them, shall, without the Consent of the Congress, accept of any present, Emolument, Office, or Title, of any kind whatever, from any King, Prince, or foreign State.

Section 10. No State shall enter into any Treaty, Alliance, or Confederation; grant Letters of Marque and Reprisal; coin Money; emit Bills of Credit; make any Thing but gold and silver Coin a Tender in Payment of Debts; pass any Bill of Attainder, ex post facto Law, or law impairing the Obligation of Contracts, or grant any Title of Nobility.

If Congress has implied powers, then there also must be limits to its powers. Section 9 lists powers that are denied to the federal government. Several of the clauses protect the people of the United States from unjust treatment. For instance, Section 9 guarantees the writ of *habeas corpus* and prohibits bills of attainder and *ex post facto* laws (see page 163).

Section 10 lists the powers that are denied to the states. In our system of federalism, the state and federal governments have separate powers, share some powers, and are denied other powers. The states may not exercise any of the powers that belong to Congress.

No State shall, without the Consent of the Congress, lay any Imposts or Duties on Imports or Exports, except what may be absolutely necessary for executing its inspection Laws: and the net Produce of all Duties and Imposts, laid by any State on Imports or Exports, shall be for the Use of the Treasury of the United States; and all such Laws shall be subject to the Revision and Control of the Congress.

No State shall, without the Consent of Congress, lay any Duty of Tonnage, keep Troops, or Ships of War in time of Peace, enter into any Agreement or Compact with another State, or with a foreign Power, or engage in War, unless actually invaded, or in such imminent Danger as will not admit of delay.

ARTICLE II

Section 1. The executive Power shall be vested in a President of the United States of America. He shall hold his Office during the Term of four Years, and, together with the Vice President, chosen for the same Term, be elected, as follows.

Each State shall appoint, in such Manner as the Legislature thereof may direct, a Number of Electors, equal to the whole Number of Senators and Representatives to which the State may be entitled in the Congress: but no Senator or Representative, or Person holding an Office of Trust or Profit under the United States, shall be appointed an Elector.

The Electors shall meet in their respective States, and vote by Ballot for two Persons, of whom one at least shall not be an Inhabitant of the same State with themselves. And they shall make a List of all the Persons voted for, and of the Number of Votes for each; which List they shall sign and certify, and transmit sealed to the Seat of the Government of the United States, directed to the President of the Senate. The President of the Senate shall, in the Presence of the Senate and House of Representatives, open all the Certificates, and the Votes shall then be counted. The Person having the greatest Number of Votes shall be the President, if such Number be a Majority of the whole Number of Electors appointed; and if there be more than one who have such majority, and have an equal Number of Votes, then the House of Representatives shall immediately choose by Ballot one of them for President; and if no Person have a Majority, then from the five highest on the List the said House shall in like Manner choose the President. But in choosing the President, the Votes shall be taken by States, the Representation from each State having one Vote; A quorum for this Purpose shall consist of a Member or Members from two thirds of the States, and a Majority of all the States shall be necessary to a Choice. In every Case, after the Choice of the President, the Person having the greatest Number of Votes of the Electors shall be the Vice President. But if there should

Executive Branch
The president is the chief of the executive branch. It is the job of the president to enforce the laws. The framers wanted the president and vice president's term of office and manner of selection to be different from those of members of Congress. They decided on four-year terms, but they had a difficult time agreeing on how to select the president and vice president. The framers finally set up an electoral system, which varies greatly from our electoral process today. The Twelfth Amendment changed the process by requiring that separate ballots be cast for president and vice president. The rise of political parties has since changed the process even more.

In 1845 Congress set the first Tuesday after the first Monday in November of every fourth year as the general election date for selecting presidential electors.

The youngest elected president was John F. Kennedy; he was 43 years old when he was inaugurated. (Theodore Roosevelt was 42 when he assumed office after the assassination of McKinley.) The oldest elected president was Ronald Reagan; he was 69 years old when he was inaugurated.

Emolument means "salary, or payment." In 1969 Congress set the president's salary at $200,000 per year. The president also receives an expense account of $50,000 per year. The president must pay taxes on both.

The oath of office is administered to the president by the chief justice of the United States. Washington added "So help me, God." All succeeding presidents have followed this practice.

The framers wanted to make sure that an elected representative of the people controlled the nation's military. Today the president is in charge of the army, navy, air force, marines, and coast guard. Only Congress can decide, however, if the United States will declare war. This section also contains the basis for the formation of the president's cabinet. Every president, starting with George Washington, has appointed a cabinet.

Most of the president's appointments to office must be approved by the Senate.

~~remain two or more who have equal Votes, the Senate shall choose from them by Ballot the Vice President.~~

The Congress may determine the Time of choosing the Electors, and the Day on which they shall give their Votes; which Day shall be the same throughout the United States.

No Person except a natural born Citizen, ~~or a Citizen of the United States, at the time of the Adoption of this Constitution,~~ shall be eligible to the Office of President; neither shall any Person be eligible to that Office who shall not have attained to the Age of thirty-five Years, and been fourteen Years a Resident within the United States.

In Case of the Removal of the President from Office, or of his Death, Resignation, or Inability to discharge the Powers and Duties of the said Office, the Same shall devolve on the Vice President, and the Congress may by Law provide for the Case of Removal, Death, Resignation or Inability, both of the President and Vice President, declaring what Officer shall then act as President, and such Officer shall act accordingly, until the Disability be removed, or a President shall be elected.

The President shall, at stated Times, receive for his Services, a Compensation, which shall neither be increased nor diminished during the Period for which he shall have been elected, and he shall not receive within that Period any other Emolument from the United States, or any of them.

Before he enter on the Execution of his Office, he shall take the following Oath or Affirmation:—"I do solemnly swear (or affirm) that I will faithfully execute the Office of President of the United States, and will to the best of my Ability, preserve, protect and defend the Constitution of the United States."

Section 2. The President shall be Commander in Chief of the Army and Navy of the United States, and of the Militia of the several States, when called into the actual Service of the United States; he may require the Opinion, in writing, of the principal Officer in each of the executive Departments, upon any Subject relating to the Duties of their respective Offices, and he shall have Power to grant Reprieves and Pardons for Offenses against the United States, except in Cases of Impeachment.

He shall have Power, by and with the Advice and Consent of the Senate, to make Treaties, provided two thirds of the Senators present concur; and he shall nominate, and by and with the Advice and Consent of the Senate, shall appoint Ambassadors, other public Ministers and Consuls, Judges of the supreme Court, and all other Officers of the United States, whose Appointments are not herein otherwise provided for, and which shall be established by Law: but the Congress may by Law vest the Appointment of such inferior Officers, as they think proper, in the President alone, in the Courts of Law, or in the Heads of Departments.

The President shall have Power to fill up all Vacancies that may happen during the Recess of the Senate, by granting Commissions which shall expire at the End of their next Session.

Section 3. He shall from time to time give to the Congress Information of the State of the Union, and recommend to their Consideration such Measures as he shall judge necessary and expedient; he may, on extraordinary Occasions, convene both Houses, or either of them, and in Case of Disagreement between them, with Respect to the Time of Adjournment, he may adjourn them to such Time as he shall think proper; he shall receive Ambassadors and other public Ministers; he shall take Care that the Laws be faithfully executed, and shall Commission all the Officers of the United States.

Section 4. The President, Vice President and all civil Officers of the United States, shall be removed from Office on Impeachment for, and Conviction of, Treason, Bribery, or other high Crimes and Misdemeanors.

Every year the president presents to Congress a State of the Union message. In this message, the president explains the legislative plans for the coming year. This clause states that one of the president's duties is to enforce the laws.

ARTICLE III

Section 1. The judicial Power of the United States, shall be vested in one supreme Court, and in such inferior Courts as the Congress may from time to time ordain and establish. The Judges, both of the supreme and inferior Courts, shall hold their Offices during good Behavior, and shall, at stated Times, receive for their Services, a Compensation, which shall not be diminished during their Continuance in Office.

Section 2. The judicial Power shall extend to all Cases, in Law and Equity, arising under this Constitution, the Laws of the United States, and Treaties made, or which shall be made, under their Authority;—to all Cases affecting Ambassadors, other public Ministers and Consuls;—to all Cases of admiralty and maritime Jurisdiction;—to Controversies to which the United States shall be a Party;—to Controversies between two or more States;— between a State and Citizens of another State; —between Citizens of different States;—between Citizens of the same State claiming Lands under Grants of different States, and between a State, or the Citizens thereof, and foreign States, Citizens or Subjects.

In all Cases affecting Ambassadors, other public Ministers and Consuls, and those in which a State shall be Party, the supreme Court shall have original Jurisdiction. In all the other Cases before mentioned, the supreme Court shall have appellate Jurisdiction, both as to Law and fact, with such Exceptions, and under such Regulations as the Congress shall make.

The Trial of all Crimes, except in Cases of Impeachment, shall be by Jury; and such Trial shall be held in the State where the said Crimes shall have been committed; but when not committed within

Judicial Branch
The Articles of Confederation did not make any provisions for a federal court system. One of the first things that the framers of the Constitution agreed upon was to set up a national judiciary. With all the laws that Congress would be enacting, there would be a great need for a branch of government to interpret the laws. In the Judiciary Act of 1789, Congress provided for the establishment of lower courts, such as district courts, circuit courts of appeals, and various other federal courts. The judicial system provides a check on the legislative branch; it can declare a law unconstitutional.

Congress has the power to decide the punishment for treason, but it can punish only the guilty person. *Corruption of blood* means punishing the family of a person who has committed treason. It is expressly forbidden by the Constitution.

The States
States must honor the laws, records, and court decisions of other states. A person cannot escape a legal obligation by moving from one state to another.

Section 3 permits Congress to admit new states to the Union. When a group of people living in an area that is not part of an existing state wishes to form a new state, it asks Congress for permission to do so. The people then write a state constitution and offer it to Congress for approval. The state constitution must set up a representative form of government and must not in any way contradict the federal Constitution. If a majority of Congress approves of the state constitution, the state is admitted as a member of the United States of America.

any State, the Trial shall be at such Place or Places as the Congress may by Law have directed.

Section 3. Treason against the United States, shall consist only in levying War against them, or in adhering to their Enemies, giving them Aid and Comfort. No Person shall be convicted of Treason unless on the Testimony of two Witnesses to the same overt Act, or on Confession in open Court.

The Congress shall have Power to declare the Punishment of Treason, but no Attainder of Treason shall work Corruption of Blood, or Forfeiture except during the Life of the Person attainted.

ARTICLE IV

Section 1. Full Faith and Credit shall be given in each State to the public Acts, Records, and judicial Proceedings of every other State. And the Congress may by general Laws prescribe the Manner in which such Acts, Records and Proceedings shall be proved, and the Effect thereof.

Section 2. The Citizens of each State shall be entitled to all Privileges and Immunities of Citizens in the several States.

A Person charged in any State with Treason, Felony, or other Crime, who shall flee from Justice, and be found in another State, shall on Demand of the executive Authority of the State from which he fled, be delivered up, to be removed to the State having Jurisdiction of the Crime.

~~No Person held to Service of Labor in one State, under the Laws thereof, escaping into another, shall, in Consequence of any Law or Regulation therein, be discharged from such Service or Labor, but shall be delivered up on Claim of the Party to whom such Service or Labor may be due.~~

Section 3. New States may be admitted by the Congress into this Union; but no new State shall be formed or erected within the Jurisdiction of any other State; nor any State be formed by the Junction of two or more States, or Parts of States, without the Consent of the Legislatures of the States concerned as well as of the Congress.

The Congress shall have Power to dispose of and make all needful Rules and Regulations respecting the Territory or other Property belonging to the United States; and nothing in this Constitution shall be so construed as to Prejudice any Claims of the United States, or of any particular State.

Section 4. The United States shall guarantee to every State in this Union a Republican Form of Government, and shall protect each of them against Invasion; and on Application of the Legislature, or of the Executive (when the Legislature cannot be convened) against domestic Violence.

ARTICLE V

The Congress, whenever two thirds of both Houses shall deem it necessary, shall propose Amendments to this Constitution, or, on the Application of the Legislatures of two thirds of the several States, shall call a Convention for proposing Amendments, which, in either Case, shall be valid to all Intents and Purposes, as Part of this Constitution, when ratified by the Legislatures of three fourths of the several States, or by Conventions in three fourths thereof, as the one or the other Mode of Ratification may be proposed by the Congress; Provided that ~~no Amendment which may be made prior to the Year One thousand eight hundred and eight shall in any Manner affect the first and fourth Clauses in the Ninth Section of the first Article; and that~~ no State, without its Consent, shall be deprived of its equal Suffrage in the Senate.

ARTICLE VI

All Debts contracted and Engagements entered into, before the Adoption of this Constitution, shall be as valid against the United States under this Constitution, as under the Confederation.

This Constitution, and the Laws of the United States which shall be made in Pursuance thereof; and all Treaties made, or which shall be made, under the Authority of the United States, shall be the supreme Law of the Land; and the Judges in every State shall be bound thereby, any Thing in the Constitution or Laws of any State to the Contrary notwithstanding.

The Senators and Representatives before mentioned, and the Members of the several State Legislatures, and all executive and judicial Officers, both of the United States and of the several States, shall be bound by Oath or Affirmation, to support this Constitution; but no religious Test shall ever be required as a Qualification to any Office or public Trust under the United States.

ARTICLE VII

The Ratification of the Conventions of nine States, shall be sufficient for the Establishment of this Constitution between the States so ratifying the Same.

DONE in Convention by the Unanimous Consent of the States present the Seventeenth Day of September in the Year of our Lord one thousand seven hundred and Eighty seven and of the Independence of the United States of America the Twelfth. IN WITNESS whereof We have hereunto subscribed our Names.

George Washington—
President and deputy from Virginia

The Amendment Process
America's founders may not have realized just how enduring the Constitution would be, but they did make provisions for changing or adding to the Constitution. They did not want to make it easy to change the Constitution. There are two different ways in which changes can be proposed to the states and two different ways in which states can approve the changes and make them part of the Constitution (see the chart on page 163).

National Supremacy
One of the biggest problems facing the delegates to the Constitutional Convention was the question of what would happen if a state law and a national law conflicted. Which law would be followed? Who decided? The second clause of Article VI answers those questions. When a national and state law disagree, the national law overrides the state law. The Constitution is the supreme law of the land. This clause is often called the "supremacy clause."

Ratification
The Articles of Confederation called for all 13 states to approve any revision to the Articles. The Constitution required that the vote of 9 out of the 13 states would be needed to ratify the Constitution. The first state to ratify was Delaware, on December 7, 1787. The last state to ratify the Constitution was Rhode Island, which finally did so on May 29, 1790, almost two and a half years later.

New Hampshire
John Langdon
Nicholas Gilman

Massachusetts
Nathaniel Gorham
Rufus King

Connecticut
William Samuel Johnson
Roger Sherman

New York
Alexander Hamilton

New Jersey
William Livingston
David Brearley
William Paterson
Jonathan Dayton

Pennsylvania
Benjamin Franklin
Thomas Mifflin
Robert Morris
George Clymer
Thomas FitzSimons
Jared Ingersoll
James Wilson
Gouverneur Morris

Delaware
George Read
Gunning Bedford, Jr.
John Dickinson
Richard Bassett
Jacob Broom

Maryland
James McHenry
Daniel of St. Thomas Jenifer
Daniel Carroll

Virginia
John Blair
James Madison, Jr.

North Carolina
William Blount
Richard Dobbs Spaight
Hugh Williamson

South Carolina
John Rutledge
Charles Cotesworth Pinckney
Charles Pinckney
Pierce Buttler

Georgia
William Few
Abraham Baldwin

Attest: *William Jackson*, Secretary

Bill of Rights
One of the conditions set by several
states for ratifying the Constitution was
the inclusion of a Bill of Rights. Many
people feared that a stronger central
government might take away basic
rights of the people that had been guaranteed in state constitutions. If the
three words that begin the preamble,
We the people—were truly meant,
then the rights of the people needed to
be protected.

THE AMENDMENTS

ARTICLES in addition to, and Amendment of the Constitution
of the United States of America, proposed by Congress, and ratified
by the Legislatures of the several states, pursuant to the fifth Article
of the original Constitution.
*[The First through Tenth amendments, now known as the Bill of
Rights, were proposed on September 25, 1789, and declared in force
on December 15, 1791.]*

First Amendment

Congress shall make no law respecting an establishment of religion, or prohibiting the free exercise thereof; or abridging the freedom of speech, or of the press; or the right of the people peaceably to assemble, and to petition the Government for a redress of grievances.

The First Amendment protects freedom of speech and thought, and forbids Congress to make any law "respecting an establishment of religion" or restraining the freedom to practice religion as one chooses.

Second Amendment

A well regulated Militia, being necessary to the security of a free State, the right of the people to keep and bear Arms, shall not be infringed.

Third Amendment

No Soldier shall, in time of peace, be quartered in any house, without the consent of the Owner, nor in time of war, but in a manner to be prescribed by law.

Fourth Amendment

The right of the people to be secure in their persons, houses, papers, and effects, against unreasonable searches and seizures, shall not be violated, and no Warrants shall issue, but upon probable cause, supported by Oath or affirmation, and particularly describing the place to be searched, and the persons or things to be seized.

A police officer or sheriff may enter a person's home with a search warrant, which allows the law officer to look for evidence that could convict someone of committing a crime.

Fifth Amendment

No person shall be held to answer for a capital, or otherwise infamous crime, unless on a presentment or indictment of a Grand Jury, except in cases arising in the land or naval forces, or in the Militia, when in actual service in time of War or public danger; nor shall any person be subject for the same offense to be twice put in jeopardy of life or limb; nor shall be compelled in any criminal case to be a witness against himself, nor be deprived of life, liberty, or property, without due process of law; nor shall private property be taken for public use, without just compensation.

The Fifth, Sixth, and Seventh amendments describe the procedures that courts must follow when trying people accused of crimes. The Fifth Amendment guarantees that no one can be put on trial for a serious crime unless a grand jury agrees that the evidence justifies doing so. It also says that a person cannot be tried twice for the same crime.

Sixth Amendment

In all criminal prosecutions, the accused shall enjoy the right to a speedy and public trial, by an impartial jury of the State and district wherein the crime shall have been committed, which district shall have been previously ascertained by law, and to be informed of the nature and cause of the accusation; to be confronted with the witnesses against him; to have compulsory process for obtaining witnesses in his favor, and to have the Assistance of Counsel for his defense.

The Sixth Amendment makes several promises, including a prompt trial and a trial by a jury chosen from the state and district in which the crime was committed. The Sixth Amendment also states that an accused person must be told why he or she is being tried and promises that an accused person has the right to be defended by a lawyer.

Seventh Amendment

In Suits at common law, where the value in controversy shall exceed twenty dollars, the right of trial by jury shall be preserved,

The Seventh Amendment guarantees a trial by jury in cases that involve more than $20, but in modern times, usually much more money is at stake before a case is heard in federal court.

and no fact tried by a jury shall be otherwise reexamined in any Court of the United States, than according to the rules of the common law.

Eighth Amendment

Excessive bail shall not be required, nor excessive fines imposed, nor cruel and unusual punishments inflicted.

Ninth Amendment

The enumeration in the Constitution, of certain rights, shall not be construed to deny or disparage others retained by the people.

Tenth Amendment

The powers not delegated to the United States by the Constitution, nor prohibited by it to the States, are reserved to the States respectively, or to the people.

Eleventh Amendment

[Proposed March 4, 1794; declared ratified January 8, 1798]

The Judicial power of the United States shall not be construed to extend to any suit in law or equity, commenced or prosecuted against one of the United States by Citizens of another State, or by Citizens or Subjects of any Foreign State.

Twelfth Amendment

[Proposed December 9, 1803; declared ratified September 25, 1804]

The Electors shall meet in their respective states and vote by ballot for President and Vice President, one of whom, at least, shall not be an inhabitant of the same state with themselves; they shall name in their ballots the person voted for as President, and in distinct ballots the person voted for as Vice President, and they shall make distinct lists of all persons voted for as President, and of all persons voted for as Vice President, and of the number of votes for each, which lists they shall sign and certify, and transmit sealed to the seat of the government of the United States, directed to the President of the Senate;—The President of the Senate shall, in the presence of the Senate and House of Representatives, open all the certificates and the votes shall then be counted;—The person having the greatest number of votes for President, shall be the President, if such number be a majority of the whole number of Electors appointed; and if no person have such majority, then from the persons having the highest numbers not exceeding three on the list of those voted for as President, the House of Representatives shall choose immediately, by ballot, the President. But in choosing the President, the votes shall be taken by states, the representation from each state having one vote; a quorum for this purpose shall consist of a member or members from two thirds of the states, and a majority of all the states shall be necessary to a

The Ninth and Tenth amendments were added because not every right of the people or of the states could be listed in the Constitution.

The Twelfth Amendment changed the election procedure for president and vice president. This amendment became necessary because of the growth of political parties. Before this amendment, electors voted without distinguishing between president and vice president. Whoever received the most votes became president, and whoever received the next highest number of votes became vice president. A confusing election in 1800, which resulted in Thomas Jefferson's becoming president, caused this amendment to be proposed.

choice. ~~And if the House of Representatives shall not choose a President whenever the right of choice shall devolve upon them, before the fourth day of March next following, then the Vice President shall act as President, as in the case of the death or other constitutional disability of the President;~~ The person having the greatest number of votes as Vice President, shall be the Vice President, if such number be a majority of the whole number of Electors appointed, and if no person have a majority, then from the two highest numbers on the list, the Senate shall choose the Vice President; a quorum for the purpose shall consist of two thirds of the whole number of Senators, and a majority of the whole number shall be necessary to a choice. But no person constitutionally ineligible to the office of President shall be eligible to that of Vice President of the United States.

Thirteenth Amendment

[Proposed January 31, 1865; declared ratified December 18, 1865]

Section 1. Neither slavery nor involuntary servitude, except as a punishment for crime whereof the party shall have been duly convicted, shall exist within the United States, or any place subject to their jurisdiction.

Section 2. Congress shall have power to enforce this article by appropriate legislation.

Although some slaves had been freed during the Civil War, slavery was not abolished until the Thirteenth Amendment took effect.

Fourteenth Amendment

[Proposed June 13, 1866; declared ratified July 28, 1868]

Section 1. All persons born or naturalized in the United States and subject to the jurisdiction thereof, are citizens of the United States and of the State wherein they reside. No State shall make or enforce any law which shall abridge the privileges or immunities of citizens of the United States; nor shall any State deprive any person of life, liberty, or property, without due process of law; nor deny to any person within its jurisdiction the equal protection of the laws.

Section 2. Representatives shall be apportioned among the several States according to their respective numbers, counting the whole number of persons in each State, ~~excluding Indians not taxed.~~ But when the right to vote at any election for the choice of electors for President and Vice President of the United States, Representatives in Congress, the Executive and Judicial officers of a State, or the members of the Legislature thereof, is denied to any of the ~~male~~ inhabitants of such State, being ~~twenty-one years of age, and~~ citizens of the United States, or in any way abridged, except for participation in rebellion, or other crime, the basis of representation therein shall be reduced in the proportion which the number of such ~~male~~ citizens shall bear to the whole number of ~~male~~ citizens ~~twenty-one years of age~~ in such State.

Section 3. No person shall be a Senator or Representative in

In 1833 Chief Justice John Marshall ruled that the Bill of Rights limited the national government but not the state governments. This ruling meant that states were able to keep African Americans from becoming state citizens. If African Americans were not citizens, they were not protected by the Bill of Rights. The Fourteenth Amendment defines citizenship and prevents states from interfering in the rights of citizens of the United States.

Congress, or elector of President and Vice President, or hold any office, civil or military, under the United States, or under any State, who, having previously taken an oath, as a member of Congress, or as an officer of the United States, or as a member of any State legislature, or as an executive or judicial officer of any State, to support the Constitution of the United States, shall have engaged in insurrection or rebellion against the same, or given aid or comfort to the enemies thereof. But Congress may by a vote of two thirds of each House, remove such disability.

Section 4. The validity of the public debt of the United States, authorized by law, including debts incurred for payment of pensions and bounties for services in suppressing insurrection or rebellion, shall not be questioned. But neither the United States nor any State shall assume or pay any debt or obligation incurred in aid of insurrection or rebellion against the United States, ~~or any claim for the loss or emancipation of any slave;~~ but all such debts, obligations and claims shall be held illegal and void.

Section 5. The Congress shall have power to enforce, by appropriate legislation, the provisions of this article.

Fifteenth Amendment

The Fifteenth Amendment extended the right to vote to African American males.

[Proposed February 26, 1869; declared ratified March 30, 1870]

Section 1. The right of citizens of the United States to vote shall not be denied or abridged by the United States or by any State on account of race, color, or previous condition of servitude.

Section 2. The Congress shall have power to enforce this article by appropriate legislation.

Sixteenth Amendment

The Sixteenth Amendment made legal the income tax described in Article I.

[Proposed July 12, 1909; declared ratified February 25, 1913]

The Congress shall have power to lay and collect taxes on incomes, from whatever source derived, without apportionment among the several States, and without regard to any census or enumeration.

Seventeenth Amendment

The Seventeenth Amendment required that senators be elected directly by the people instead of by the state legislature.

[Proposed May 13, 1912; declared ratified May 31, 1913]

The Senate of the United States shall be composed of two Senators from each State, elected by the people thereof, for six years; and each Senator shall have one vote. The electors in each State shall have the qualifications requisite for electors of the most numerous branch of the State legislatures.

When vacancies happen in the representation of any State in the Senate, the executive authority of such State shall issue writs of election to fill such vacancies: *Provided,* That the legislature of any

State may empower the executive thereof to make temporary appointments until the people fill the vacancies by election as the legislature may direct.

~~This amendment shall not be so construed as to affect the election or term of any Senator chosen before it becomes valid as part of the Constitution.~~

Eighteenth Amendment

[Proposed December 18, 1917; declared ratified January 29, 1919; repealed by the Twenty-first Amendment December 5, 1933]

~~*Section 1.* After one year from the ratification of this article the manufacture, sale, or transportation of intoxicating liquors within, the importation thereof into, or the exportation thereof from the United States and all territory subject to the jurisdiction thereof for beverage purposes is hereby prohibited.~~

~~*Section 2.* The Congress and the several States shall have concurrent power to enforce this article by appropriate legislation.~~

~~*Section 3.* This article shall be inoperative unless it shall have been ratified as an amendment to the Constitution by the legislatures of the several States, as provided in the Constitution, within seven years from the date of the submission hereof to the States by the Congress.~~

Although many people felt that Prohibition was good for the health and welfare of the American people, the amendment was repealed 14 years later.

Nineteenth Amendment

[Proposed June 4, 1919; declared ratified August 26, 1920]

The right of citizens of the United States to vote shall not be denied or abridged by the United States or by any State on account of sex.

Congress shall have power to enforce this article by appropriate legislation.

Abigail Adams was disappointed that the Declaration of Independence and the Constitution did not specifically include women. It took almost 150 years and much campaigning by women's suffrage groups for women to finally achieve voting privileges.

Twentieth Amendment

[Proposed March 2, 1932; declared ratified February 6, 1933]

Section 1. The terms of the President and Vice President shall end at noon on the 20th day of January, and the terms of Senators and Representatives at noon on the 3rd day of January, of the years in which such terms would have ended if this article had not been ratified; and the terms of their successors shall then begin.

Section 2. The Congress shall assemble at least once in every year, and such meeting shall begin at noon on the 3rd day of January, unless they shall by law appoint a different day.

Section 3. If, at the time fixed for the beginning of the term of the President, the President elect shall have died, the Vice President elect shall become President. If a President shall not have been chosen before the time fixed for the beginning of his term, or if the President elect shall have failed to qualify, then the Vice President

In the original Constitution, a newly elected president and Congress did not take office until March 4, which was four months after the November election. The officials who were leaving office were called "lame ducks" because they had little influence during those four months. The Twentieth Amendment changed the date that the new president and Congress take office. Members of Congress now take office on January 3, and the president takes office on January 20.

elect shall act as President until a President shall have qualified; and the Congress may by law provide for the case wherein neither a President elect nor a Vice President elect shall have qualified, declaring who shall then act as President, or the manner in which one who is to act shall be selected, and such persons shall act accordingly until a President or Vice President shall have qualified.

Section 4. The Congress may by law provide for the case of the death of any of the persons from whom the House of Representatives may choose a President whenever the right of choice shall have devolved upon them, and for the case of the death of any of the persons from whom the Senate may choose a Vice President whenever the right of choice shall have devolved upon them.

Section 5. Sections 1 and 2 shall take effect on the 15th day of October following the ratification of this article.

Section 6. This article shall be inoperative unless it shall have been ratified as an amendment to the Constitution by the legislatures of three fourths of the several States within seven years from the date of its submission.

Twenty-first Amendment

[Proposed February 20, 1933; declared ratified December 5, 1933]

Section 1. The eighteenth article of amendment to the Constitution of the United States is hereby repealed.

Section 2. The transportation or importation into any State, Territory, or possession of the United States for delivery or use there-in of intoxicating liquors, in violation of the laws thereof, is hereby prohibited.

Section 3. This article shall be inoperative unless it shall have been ratified as an amendment to the Constitution by conventions in the several States, as provided in the Constitution, within seven years from the date of the submission hereof to the States by the Congress.

Twenty-second Amendment

[Proposed March 24, 1947; declared ratified March 1, 1951]

Section 1. No person shall be elected to the office of the President more than twice, and no person who has held the office of President, or acted as President, for more than two years of a term to which some other person was elected President shall be elected to the office of the President more than once. But this Article shall not apply to any person holding the office of President when this Article was proposed by the Congress, and shall not prevent any person who may be holding the office of President, or acting as President, during the term within which this Article becomes operative from holding the office of President or acting as President during the remainder of such term.

The Twenty-first Amendment is the only amendment that has been ratified by state conventions rather than by state legislatures.

From the time of President Washington's administration, it was a custom for presidents to serve no more than two terms of office. Franklin D. Roosevelt, however, was elected to four terms. The Twenty-second Amendment made into law the old custom of a two-term limit for each president, if reelected.

Section 2. ~~This Article shall be inoperative unless it shall have been ratified as an amendment to the Constitution by the legislatures of three fourths of the several States within seven years from the date of its submission to the States by the Congress.~~

Twenty-third Amendment

[Proposed June 16, 1960; declared ratified April 3, 1961]

Section 1. The District constituting the seat of Government of the United States shall appoint in such manner as the Congress may direct:

A number of electors of President and Vice President equal to the whole number of Senators and Representatives in Congress to which the District would be entitled if it were a State, but in no event more than the least populous State; they shall be in addition to those appointed by the States, but they shall be considered, for the purposes of the election of President and Vice President, to be electors appointed by a State; and they shall meet in the District and perform such duties as provided by the twelfth article of amendment.

Section 2. The Congress shall have power to enforce this article by appropriate legislation.

Until the Twenty-third Amendment, the people of Washington, D.C., could not vote in presidential elections.

Twenty-fourth Amendment

[Proposed August 27, 1962; declared ratified February 4, 1964]

Section 1. The right of citizens of the United States to vote in any primary or other election for President or Vice President, for electors for President or Vice President, or for Senator or Representative in Congress, shall not be denied or abridged by the United States or any State by reason of failure to pay any poll tax or other tax.

Section 2. The Congress shall have power to enforce this article by appropriate legislation.

Twenty-fifth Amendment

[Proposed July 6, 1965; declared ratified February 23, 1967]

Section 1. In case of removal of the President from office or of his death or resignation, the Vice President shall become President.

Section 2. Whenever there is a vacancy in the office of the Vice President, the President shall nominate a Vice President who shall take office upon confirmation by a majority vote of both Houses of Congress.

Section 3. Whenever the President transmits to the President pro tempore of the Senate and the Speaker of the House of Representatives his written declaration that he is unable to discharge the powers and duties of his office, and until he transmits to them a written declaration to the contrary, such powers and duties shall be discharged by the Vice President as Acting President.

The illness of President Eisenhower in the 1950s and the assassination of President Kennedy in 1963 were the events behind the Twenty-fifth Amendment. The Constitution did not provide a clear-cut method for a vice president to take over for a disabled president or for the death of a president. This amendment provides for filling the office of the vice president if a vacancy occurs, and it provides a way for the vice president to take over if the president is unable to perform the duties of that office.

HISTORICAL
Document

THE CONSTITUTION

Section 4. Whenever the Vice President and a majority of either the principal officers of the executive departments or of such other body as Congress may by law provide, transmit to the President pro tempore of the Senate and the Speaker of the House of Representatives their written declaration that the President is unable to discharge the powers and duties of his office, the Vice President shall immediately assume the powers and duties of the office as Acting President.

Thereafter, when the President transmits to the President pro tempore of the Senate and the Speaker of the House of Representatives his written declaration that no inability exists, he shall resume the powers and duties of his office unless the Vice President and a majority of either the principal officers of the executive department or of such other body as Congress may by law provide, transmit within four days to the President pro tempore of the Senate and the Speaker of the House of Representatives their written declaration that the President is unable to discharge the powers and duties of his office. Thereupon Congress shall decide the issue, assembling within forty-eight hours for that purpose if not in session. If the Congress, within twenty-one days after receipt of the latter written declaration, or, if Congress is not in session, within twenty-one days after Congress is required to assemble, determines by two-thirds vote of both Houses that the President is unable to discharge the powers and duties of his office, the Vice President shall continue to discharge the same as Acting President; otherwise, the President shall resume the powers and duties of his office.

Twenty-sixth Amendment
[Proposed March 23, 1971; declared ratified July 5, 1971]

Section 1. The right of citizens of the United States, who are eighteen years of age or older, to vote shall not be denied or abridged by the United States or by any State on account of age.

Section 2. The Congress shall have power to enforce this article by appropriate legislation.

Twenty-seventh Amendment
[Proposed September 25, 1789; declared ratified May 7, 1992]

No law, varying the compensation for the services of the Senators and Representatives, shall take effect, until an election of Representatives shall have intervened.

The Voting Act of 1970 tried to set the voting age at 18 years old. But the Supreme Court ruled that the act set the voting age for national elections only, not state or local elections. This ruling would make necessary several different ballots at elections. The Twenty-sixth Amendment gave 18-year-old citizens the right to vote in all elections.

REVIEW
The Constitution

REVIEWING CHRONOLOGY
Create an illustrated time line showing the dates of passage of the Bill of Rights and the remaining 17 amendments.

IDENTIFYING PEOPLE AND IDEAS
Explain the historical significance of each of the following people or terms.

1. Preamble
2. writ of *habeas corpus*
3. Bill of Rights
4. civil liberties
5. *ex post facto* law
6. bill of attainder
7. treason
8. James Madison

UNDERSTANDING MAIN IDEAS
1. According to Article II, what are the chief responsibilities of the president?
2. What is the purpose of the separation of powers in government?
3. How can the judicial branch check the power of the legislative branch? of the executive branch?
4. According to Article I, what are the chief responsibilities of the legislative branch?
5. What protections are listed in the Bill of Rights?
6. Why did the framers of the Constitution provide for an amendment process? Why did they make the process difficult?
7. Which amendment deals with women's suffrage? When was it ratified?
8. Which amendments are termed the Civil War Amendments? What does each cover?
9. How can the legislative branch check the power of the executive branch? of the judicial branch?
10. According to Article III, what are the chief responsibilities of the judicial branch?
11. What civil liberties are addressed in Section 9 of Article I? in Section 3 of Article III?
12. What six goals of government are listed in the Preamble?
13. According to the Constitution, what are the qualifications for becoming a representative? for becoming a senator? the president?
14. How can the executive branch check the power of the legislative branch? of the judicial branch?
15. Which two amendments deal with Prohibition? When was each ratified?
16. Which amendments deal with voting rights? When was each ratified?
17. Which part of the Constitution addresses possible conflicts between federal and state laws?
18. Which Article outlines the amendment process? According to the Article, how can the Constitution be amended?
19. What are some of the ways in which the Constitution protects the rights of the states?
20. Why did the framers of the Constitution include Article VII?

THINKING CRITICALLY
1. **Analyzing** In what ways does the Constitution reflect the reasons that Americans fought the Revolutionary War?
2. **Identifying Cause and Effect** Why were the framers of the Constitution especially interested in protecting civil liberties?
3. **Synthesizing** Using the information presented in Section 7 of Article I, create a diagram showing the steps involved in passing a bill.
4. **Comparing** Describe the connections between the Preamble to the Constitution and the theory of government that is described in the Declaration of Independence.
5. **Analyzing** How do the civil liberties guaranteed in the Constitution help to prevent abuses of power?
6. **Classifying** Classify the 27 amendments to the Constitution according to whether they protect rights, extend rights, or solve problems.

LINKING HISTORY AND GEOGRAPHY
Why was it important for the framers of the Constitution to include provisions for new states to enter the Union?

THE AMERICAN WEST

POPULAR views of the American West have changed greatly over time. As the United States expanded its borders from east to west, the area that most Americans once thought of as an uninviting wilderness became an exciting new land of opportunity. Yet many travelers, from Native American groups to Spanish missionaries and French soldiers, were drawn to the West long before citizens of the United States began to settle there. Today the West continues to be one of the most culturally and ethnically diverse regions of the nation, attracting visitors and new settlers from throughout the world.

The West, 1790

MAKAH
CHINOOK SPOKANE
KLIKITAT YAKIMA NEZ PERCÉ
CAYUSE WALLA WALLA
MODOC
BANNOCK
NORTHERN SHOSHONE
PAIUTE
WESTERN SHOSHONE
MIWOK
YOKUT
UTE
NAVAJO
YUMA
APACHE

ROCKY MTS.
CROW
CHEYENNE ARAPAHO
SPANISH TERRITORY
PAWNEE
KIOWA
COMANCHE

GREAT LAKES
SIOUX
SIOUX
SAUK FOX
Mississippi River
OSAGE
CHICKASAW
CHOCTAW
CREEK

THE TRANS- APPALACHIAN WEST
APPALACHIAN MTS.
VT NH MA CT
NY
IROQUOIS
PA
RI
NJ
DE
MD
VA
NC
CHEROKEE
SC
GA
SEMINOLE

0   200   400 Miles
0   200   400 Kilometers
Albers Equal-Area Projection

	American territory
	Spanish territory
	British territory
	Northwest Territory
■	Spanish settlements and missions
■	French forts and settlements
YAKIMA	Native American tribe

In 1790 most Americans considered the Trans-Appalachian West—the area between the Appalachian Mountains and the Mississippi River—to be "The West." Few dared move beyond the Mississippi River. Spain controlled most of the territory west of the Mississippi. With the exception of a few small Spanish and French settlements, this territory remained the free domain of Native Americans.

▲ As Americans moved west, they often adapted customs that closely resembled those of Native Americans. Just as some Native Americans built dwellings out of caves and soil, western settlers often lived in dugouts—homes dug out of the sides of hills or ravines—and sod homes built from bricks of soil.

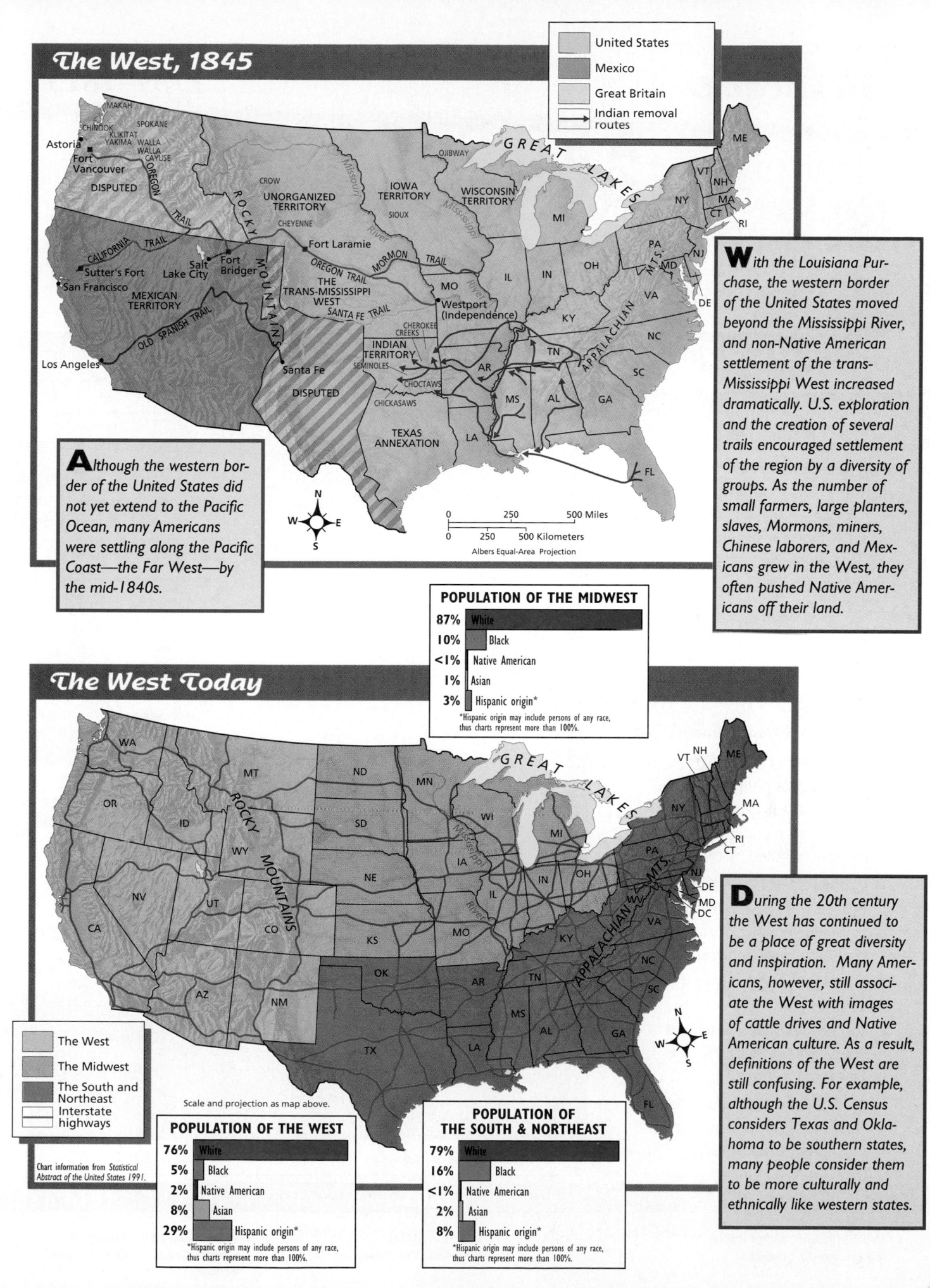

The West, 1845

MAKAH
CHINOOK
KLIKITAT
SPOKANE
YAKIMA WALLA
WALLA
CAYUSE

Astoria
Fort Vancouver

DISPUTED

OREGON TRAIL

CROW

UNORGANIZED TERRITORY

CHEYENNE

ROCKY MOUNTAINS

Sutter's Fort
Salt Lake City
Fort Bridger
San Francisco
CALIFORNIA TRAIL

MEXICAN TERRITORY

OLD SPANISH TRAIL

Los Angeles

Santa Fe

DISPUTED

Fort Laramie

OREGON TRAIL
MORMON TRAIL

THE TRANS-MISSISSIPPI WEST

SANTA FE TRAIL

Westport (Independence)

CHEROKEE
CREEKS

INDIAN TERRITORY

SEMINOLES

CHOCTAWS

CHICKASAWS

TEXAS ANNEXATION

OJIBWAY

IOWA TERRITORY

SIOUX

WISCONSIN TERRITORY

MI

GREAT LAKES

ME

VT
NH
NY
MA
CT
RI

PA
NJ
MD
DE

IL
IN
OH

MO

KY

VA

NC

TN

AR

APPALACHIAN MTS.

SC

MS
AL
GA

LA

FL

N
W E
S

Legend:
- United States
- Mexico
- Great Britain
- Indian removal routes

0   250   500 Miles
0   250   500 Kilometers
Albers Equal-Area Projection

Although the western border of the United States did not yet extend to the Pacific Ocean, many Americans were settling along the Pacific Coast—the Far West—by the mid-1840s.

With the Louisiana Purchase, the western border of the United States moved beyond the Mississippi River, and non-Native American settlement of the trans-Mississippi West increased dramatically. U.S. exploration and the creation of several trails encouraged settlement of the region by a diversity of groups. As the number of small farmers, large planters, slaves, Mormons, miners, Chinese laborers, and Mexicans grew in the West, they often pushed Native Americans off their land.

POPULATION OF THE MIDWEST

87% White
10% Black
<1% Native American
1% Asian
3% Hispanic origin*

*Hispanic origin may include persons of any race, thus charts represent more than 100%.

The West Today

WA
OR
MT
ID
WY
NV
UT
CA
AZ
NM
CO
ND
SD
NE
KS
OK
TX
MN
IA
MO
AR
LA
WI
IL
MI
IN
OH
KY
TN
MS
AL
GA
FL
PA
NY
WV
VA
NC
SC
VT
NH
ME
MA
RI
CT
NJ
DE
MD
DC

ROCKY MOUNTAINS
APPALACHIAN MTS.
GREAT LAKES
Mississippi River

N
W E
S

Scale and projection as map above.

Legend:
- The West
- The Midwest
- The South and Northeast
- Interstate highways

Chart information from *Statistical Abstract of the United States 1991*.

During the 20th century the West has continued to be a place of great diversity and inspiration. Many Americans, however, still associate the West with images of cattle drives and Native American culture. As a result, definitions of the West are still confusing. For example, although the U.S. Census considers Texas and Oklahoma to be southern states, many people consider them to be more culturally and ethnically like western states.

POPULATION OF THE WEST

76% White
5% Black
2% Native American
8% Asian
29% Hispanic origin*

*Hispanic origin may include persons of any race, thus charts represent more than 100%.

POPULATION OF THE SOUTH & NORTHEAST

79% White
16% Black
<1% Native American
2% Asian
8% Hispanic origin*

*Hispanic origin may include persons of any race, thus charts represent more than 100%.

Chapter 6

1789–1815

A STRONG START FOR THE NATION

FOCUS

UNDERSTANDING THE MAIN IDEA

Domestic and foreign problems plagued America in its early years. The new federal government successfully addressed some of the problems at home. But relations with Europe threatened to involve the nation in warfare and divide Americans along political party lines. These intrigues would eventually erupt into the War of 1812.

THEMES

- **CONSTITUTIONAL HERITAGE** Why might protection of individual rights be needed, even under a government established by the people?

- **ECONOMIC DEVELOPMENT** To what extent should a government assist or regulate economic development?

- **GEOGRAPHIC DIVERSITY** What challenges might a large country with diverse natural resources present for a new government?

- **DEMOCRATIC VALUES** How might political parties strengthen a democracy?

1789	1791	1803	1812	1814
Washington inaugurated.	Bill of Rights ratified.	U.S. completes Louisiana Purchase.	War declared against Great Britain.	Treaty of Ghent signed.

By 1789 all the states except Rhode Island had ratified the new plan of government developed at the Constitutional Convention. Newly elected government officials—the president and the members of Congress—set out to put the Constitution into action.

National Gallery of Art

Salute to George Washington in New York harbor

*I*t is April 30, 1789. In New York City, the nation's temporary capital, a crowd gathers on Wall Street to witness the inauguration of the first president of the United States. On the balcony of Federal Hall stands George Washington. The people fall silent while Washington takes the oath of office. As the last words echo in the air, the crowd bursts into wild cheers.

We do not know what Washington was thinking that day as he gazed on the sea of admiring faces. Perhaps he was weighing the new government's chances for success. Washington knew that America was not yet truly a nation. Most Americans still thought of themselves as members of individual states rather than as citizens of the United States.

If Washington's thoughts were on the nation's future, he was not alone in his concerns. John Adams, the new vice president, feared that the Republic might not last beyond his lifetime. Both men realized that the United States was, in Washington's words, an "experiment entrusted to the hands of the American people." Only time would tell how successful the experiment would be.

Between 1789 and 1815 the American people and their leaders laid the foundations for the "American experiment." They built new political, social, and economic institutions. They battled external threats to their way of life. In the process they built what Thomas Jefferson called "the empire of liberty." Yet as settlers pushed farther into the interior of the continent, they disrupted Native American societies that existed there.

Museum of the City of New York

Sampler celebrating Washington's inauguration

A FEDERAL GOVERNMENT IS ESTABLISHED

FOCUS

■ What steps did the First Congress take to establish the federal government?

■ How did Alexander Hamilton propose that Congress strengthen the nation's finances?

■ What controversies surrounded Hamilton's financial program?

Painting of American eagle

St. Paul's Chapel, Parish of Trinity Church, City of New York

𝓘n early 1789 newly elected federal officials gathered to organize the government. They relied on their experiences in colonial administration, the examples of historical and contemporary European governments, and the new federal Constitution. The Constitution provided only the outline of government. Congress and the president still had to fill in the details.

THE FIRST PRESIDENT

When Congress opened the ballots from the states on April 6, 1789, the unanimous choice for president was George Washington. The choice was not surprising. Washington's popularity had soared since the victory at Yorktown. Several states that had been unwilling to ratify the Constitution did so with the expectation that Washington would serve as the first president.

Yet, he was reluctant to accept this honor. Washington doubted his abilities and feared that people would think that

◄ "Hail, Columbia," composed for the inaugural, was performed as Washington crossed Trenton Bridge on his way to New York.

The Free Library of Philadelphia

he wanted to be a king. Leaving Mount Vernon for his inauguration, he said he felt like "a culprit who is going to the place of his execution." The muddy trip, though, was a triumph. Crowds cheered; towns celebrated.

But the festivities were soon over. President Washington and the other elected officials got down to work. They knew that each step they took set a **precedent**, or guide, for future leaders.

THE FIRST CONGRESS

Although Washington had the spotlight, the task of molding the new government belonged to the First Congress. The people's representatives faced a crowded agenda.

The first order of business was to add a protection of individual liberties to the Constitution—a promise that supporters of the Constitution had made during the struggle for ratification. From the 210 proposed amendments, 12 were recommended by Congress for adoption; of these, 10 were ratified

THE BILL OF RIGHTS

FIRST AMENDMENT guarantees freedom of religion, speech, and the press and the right to assemble peacefully and to petition the government.

SECOND AMENDMENT recognizes the necessity of state militias and thus the right to bear arms.

THIRD AMENDMENT prohibits quartering of troops without consent as regulated by law.

FOURTH AMENDMENT prohibits searches and seizures without warrants, which can be issued only upon probable cause.

FIFTH AMENDMENT requires a grand jury indictment before persons can be tried for serious criminal charges; prohibits persons from being tried twice for the same offense; prohibits forcing the accused to testify against themselves; guarantees that no one may be deprived of life, liberty, or property without due process of law.

SIXTH AMENDMENT guarantees the right to a speedy trial in criminal cases, the right to know all charges, the right to question and obtain witnesses, and the right to have counsel.

SEVENTH AMENDMENT guarantees a trial in most civil cases.

EIGHTH AMENDMENT prohibits excessive fines and bail; prohibits cruel and unusual punishment.

NINTH AMENDMENT protects individual rights not specifically mentioned in the Constitution.

TENTH AMENDMENT reserves for the states and the people those powers not delegated to the national government or prohibited by the Constitution.

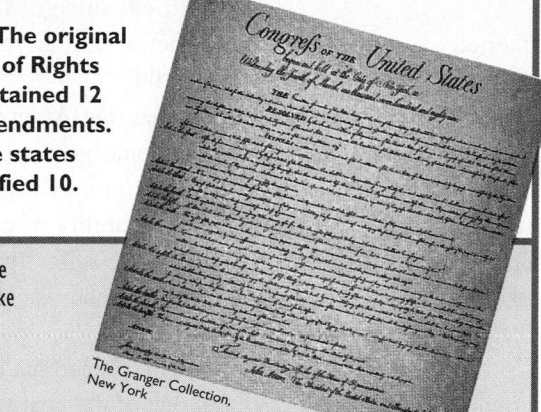

▶ **The original Bill of Rights contained 12 amendments. The states ratified 10.**

The Granger Collection, New York

PROTECTING LIBERTY Those who insisted that the Bill of Rights be added to the Constitution feared that a strong federal government might take away the basic rights of the people guaranteed by the state constitutions.

? **ANALYZING** How does the Bill of Rights help protect against the federal government gaining too much power over individuals?

---

by the states in 1791. They became known as the **Bill of Rights**.

Another task of Congress was the creation of a federal court system. By September, Congress had passed the **Judiciary Act** of 1789, which (1) established a federal district court in each state and three circuit courts of appeal; (2) provided for a chief justice and five associate justices of the Supreme Court to be nominated by the president and approved by the Senate; and (3) defined the federal courts' powers and the relationship between the federal courts and the state courts.

During its first session Congress also created three departments to assist the president: the State Department to handle foreign affairs, the War Department to manage military affairs, and the Treasury Department to oversee the nation's finances. The president appointed the heads, or secretaries, of these departments to serve as his advisers. Over time these advisers became known as the president's **cabinet**.

Washington's first cabinet included Thomas Jefferson as secretary of state, Henry Knox as secretary of war, and Alexander Hamilton as secretary of the treasury. The president also appointed an attorney general, Edmund Randolph, to advise him on legal matters.

■■ **The First Congress passed the Bill of Rights, set up the federal judiciary, and established three executive departments to assist the president.**

ℛESTORING THE NATION'S CREDIT

Next, Congress tackled the nation's finances, for the government had inherited serious financial problems. Not only did the Treasury lack funds to pay off war debts, it did not have enough money to run the country. Lawmakers turned to Secretary of the Treasury Alexander Hamilton for help. In doing so they set an important precedent: though Congress is responsible for passing laws, from its beginning it has sought guidance from the executive branch.

Alexander Hamilton

National Portrait Gallery

The slight, fair-haired Hamilton was one of the most brilliant, and controversial, of the nation's founders. He was born in the British West Indies in 1755, the son of a failed Scottish merchant. At an early age he went to work in a countinghouse, where his aptitude for transacting business became evident. In 1773 Hamilton went to New York City, where he attended King's College. He was ambitious in his pursuit of public praise and power. Through his writings, economic programs, and political intrigues, he exerted almost as great an influence on the young Republic as the early presidents did.

Alexander Hamilton believed that America's future depended on a strong national government controlled by the rich and well born. Although self-made, he had little faith in the ability of common people to govern. They were, he said, "turbulent and changing" and made decisions based on their immediate needs.

Hamilton's strong federalism shaped his economic plans. He believed that one of the best ways to strengthen the government, both financially and politically, was to establish economic policies that helped business and industry. If business people believed the federal government had their best interests at heart, they would support it.

The Scottish economist Adam Smith heavily influenced Hamilton's views. In his book *Wealth of Nations* (1776), Smith stated that industry and commerce—not farming—were the most important sources of wealth. Smith advocated **capitalism**—an economic system based on a free market and private ownership of property.

As a first step toward winning over the merchant class, Hamilton advised Congress to strengthen the nation's credit by paying off the **national debt**—the money that the federal government owed to its creditors. Hamilton knew that a nation that did not pay its debts would have trouble borrowing additional money. The total national debt was estimated to be a staggering $77 million.

▲ **The U.S. Mint began making coins in 1792. Shown here are some of the first pieces minted.**

Congress moved quickly to pay the $12 million owed to foreign nations, but Hamilton's proposal to pay the domestic debt met with strong resistance.

The Continental Congress had borrowed from individuals about $40 million during the war, mostly by selling **government bonds**—certificates issued by a government in exchange for loans of money. Each bond was the government's promise to repay the loan plus interest. But the government's credit had fallen so low that its bonds were almost worthless. Many original bondholders had panicked and sold their bonds to financial speculators at a fraction of their original value.

Hamilton's proposal to pay the bonds in full caused an uproar. His opponents rightly charged that speculators stood to make a fortune at the expense of ordinary citizens. In the end, however, Congress agreed with Hamilton that restoring the nation's credit depended on honoring these bonds.

Hamilton's next proposal—that the federal government take over about $21.5 million of the $25 million in state debts—met even stronger opposition. All the southern states except South Carolina had paid their debts and saw no reason why they should help pay the debts of other states.

Only a last-minute compromise saved the plan. In return for southern votes, Hamilton's supporters pledged that the national capital would be moved south to a site across the Potomac River from Virginia. Virginians believed this new location, later named Washington, D.C., would give them greater influence in the federal government.

HAMILTON'S BANK PROPOSAL

Establishing good credit was not the only solution to the nation's financial woes. The government also lacked the means to manage the nation's money supply. Thus, Hamilton asked Congress to create the Bank of the United States, a **national bank** consisting of a central bank with branches in major U.S. cities. Hamilton believed that such a national bank would provide (1) a safe place to deposit government funds; (2) a sound, uniform currency issued in the form of **bank notes**, or paper money; and (3) a source for loans to assist the government in times of emergency and to fuel commercial expansion.

■ **Hamilton proposed that Congress pay off the national debt, assume state debts, and organize a national bank to strengthen the nation's finances.**

Hamilton argued that the nation had much to gain from the creation of a national bank. Many Americans, particularly southern planters who were short of cash, did not share his enthusiasm. They feared that the bank would be controlled by wealthy northeastern merchants.

Thomas Jefferson raised a more serious charge: the bank was illegal! Nowhere in the Constitution was the federal government given the power to set up a bank. Jefferson believed that the government could do only what the Constitution specifically allows. This philosophy of constitutional interpretation is called **strict construction**.

Hamilton, on the other hand, supported the philosophy of constitutional interpretation called **loose construction**. That is, he believed that the government can do anything the Constitution does not specifically forbid. In support of this view, he pointed to the clause in the Constitution that grants Congress the right "to make all laws . . . necessary and proper" for running the country. The government's power to collect taxes and borrow money could only be exercised, he argued, with the aid of a national bank.

Jefferson replied that the "necessary and proper" clause was meant to limit—not stretch—the power of the federal government. In his eyes a national bank was not a *necessity*, and so Congress had no authority to establish one. The members of Congress debated the issue for months. In the end, President Washington sided with Hamilton, and Congress chartered the Bank of the United States in 1791. The charter granted the Bank the right to operate for 20 years, when it would again be subject to congressional approval.

*T*AX REBELLION ON THE FRONTIER

Hamilton's next task was to raise the money to pay off the national debt. Unlike today, the government did not have the power to collect an income tax. Instead it depended on various tariffs to raise money. Hamilton knew that the tariffs could not raise enough money to pay off the debt. He

therefore asked Congress to impose a tax on a few domestically produced items, most notably whiskey. The tax was to be paid by producers. When the measure passed, the cry "No taxation without representation" was again heard in the land—this time aimed at the U.S. government.

The new tax hit western farmers the hardest. Many turned corn, their most important crop, into whiskey, because it was easier to transport to the coast. News of the tax infuriated them. An anonymous poet noted the farmers' mood:

66 Some chaps whom freedom's spirit warms
Are threatening hard to take up arms,
And headstrong in rebellion rise

'Fore they'll submit to that excise:
Their liberty they will maintain,
They fought for't, and they'll
   fight again. **99**

In the hot summer of 1794, farmers in western Pennsylvania did rise in rebellion. When ordered to pay the tax, they attacked federal marshals, tarring and feathering some. A group of about 500 farmers burned the home of the head revenue agent, while others talked of starting a new country.

The **Whiskey Rebellion** challenged federal authority. Hamilton urged the president to take action. Calling out the militias from neighboring states, Washington assembled a force of some 13,000, almost as large as any he had commanded during the Revolutionary War. The "Whiskey Boys" quickly melted away into the backwoods rather than confront such an army.

In its response to the rebellion, the federal government had demonstrated the effectiveness of its power, even on the remote frontier. Yet this show of force cost the government support among western farmers who believed their interests were being ignored.

■■ **Hamilton's financial program led to charges of unfairness, constitutional controversies, and a tax rebellion.**

*E*VALUATING HAMILTON'S PROGRAMS

As secretary of the treasury, Hamilton aimed to create a strong government, a stable economy, and a favorable climate for business and industry. His financial programs largely succeeded. The tax brought in needed revenue. Reducing the national debt put the nation's credit on a firm footing. The national banking system provided the nation with a single currency.

But not everyone benefited equally from these measures. Hamilton's program favored the rich, as his opponents argued. His desire to win the loyalty of the commercial class often made him act against the interests of small farmers. Nevertheless, his federalist outlook enabled business to expand while laying the foundation for a new national prosperity.

The Granger Collection, New York

▲ **An excise officer is tarred and feathered by a mob in 1794.**

SECTION 1 REVIEW

IDENTIFY and explain the significance of the following: precedent, Bill of Rights, Judiciary Act of 1789, cabinet, Alexander Hamilton, capitalism, national debt, government bonds, national bank, bank notes, Whiskey Rebellion.

LOCATE and explain the importance of the following: Washington, D.C.

1. **MAIN IDEA** What actions did Congress take to establish the federal government?

2. **MAIN IDEA** How did Hamilton propose to solve the nation's financial problems?

3. **WRITING TO EXPRESS A VIEWPOINT** Imagine you are a newspaper editor in the 1790s. Select one controversy surrounding Hamilton's financial program. Write an editorial favoring or opposing that part of the plan.

4. **CONTRASTING** Define strict and loose construction, and explain how Jefferson and Hamilton used the philosophies in the debate over the national bank.

DEALING WITH A DANGEROUS WORLD

FOCUS

■ **How did conflicts in Europe affect Americans?**

■ **What was the significance of the Native American defeat at Fallen Timbers?**

■ **What did Jay's Treaty and Pinckney's Treaty accomplish?**

■ **How did the two-party system in American politics develop?**

Hamilton intended his financial program to enrich the American economy. In the 1790s, however, economic independence was not yet a reality. Americans still needed British money and technology to strengthen commerce and to develop manufacturing. France provided an important market for American agricultural products. Therefore, the political upheavals and wars that engulfed Europe between 1789 and 1815 had an important impact on the United States.

U.S. cannon, 1815

THE FRENCH REVOLUTION

The American Revolution influenced events across the Atlantic. On July 14, 1789, French revolutionaries—inspired in part by Enlightenment beliefs and by the American Declaration of Independence, which put those beliefs into practice—stormed the Bastille (ba-STEEL), the old royal prison in Paris. This attack was the start of the **French Revolution**.

The French revolutionaries proclaimed their goals in the ringing cry "Liberty, Equality, Fraternity," but soon the revolution turned into a bloodbath. During the period known as the Reign of Terror, thousands of men and women, including King Louis XVI and his queen, Marie Antoinette, were beheaded.

The French revolutionaries saw themselves as champions of the common people fighting against the nobility. European monarchs feared that

this revolutionary spirit would spread beyond France's borders. This fear was intensified when the new French Republic declared war on Great Britain, Spain, and the Netherlands in 1793.

▲ **The Bastille was stormed and destroyed by French revolutionaries on July 14, 1789.**

American seamen took to carrying proof-of-citizenship papers to guard against possible impressment by the British navy.

Americans' reactions to these events in Europe were mixed. From Paris, Thomas Jefferson wrote excitedly to his friend James Monroe, "All the old spirit of 1776 is rekindling." Many other Americans, however, did not share Jefferson's enthusiasm. Many found it shocking that liberty depended "on the right of cutting throats."

The European conflict disrupted American trade and threatened to draw the United States into war. Both France and Great Britain ignored the American declaration of neutrality and seized American vessels bound for enemy ports.

In addition, the **impressment**—or kidnapping—of U.S. sailors by the British aroused American hostility. Between 1790 and 1812, Great Britain, claiming to be capturing deserters from British naval vessels, impressed some 10,000 American sailors.

French actions also caused resentment. In early 1793 a French diplomat, Edmond Genet (zhuh-NE), arrived in America. Citizen Genet, as he was known, toured the nation, organizing "revolutionary clubs" and trying to persuade Americans to honor their 1778

▲ The arrival of fiery French diplomat Edmond Genet in 1793 caused many Americans to choose sides.

military alliance treaty with France. Years later, John Adams recalled the frightening passions that Genet excited:

66 Ten thousand people in the streets . . . threatened to drag Washington out of his house, and effect a revolution in the government, or compel it to declare war in favor of the French revolution and against England. 99

Washington, knowing that the United States was unprepared for war, refused to give in to pressure. On April 22 he issued a proclamation forbidding American support for any nation at war. Genet defied this neutrality policy by arming a ship in a U.S. port and sending it out to sea to attack British shipping. Washington demanded that France replace the French diplomat. Genet was quieted, but the divisions he created were not soon forgotten.

■■ Conflicts in Europe caused political tension in the United States, disrupted trade, and strained U.S. diplomatic relations.

TROUBLE ON THE FRONTIER

Washington managed to avoid foreign entanglements, but trouble brewed in the Northwest Territory. By the terms of the Treaty of Paris, which ended the Revolutionary War in 1783, the British granted the United States the Northwest Territory. But Native Americans considered the territory theirs and battled settlers to keep it. In response, President Washington sent federal troops against Native Americans.

To defend their homes, some 1,500 Miamis, Shawnees, Iroquois, Sauks (SAWKS), Fox, and Potawatomis (pahd-uh-WAHD-uh-mees) joined together in a loose confederation. Miami chief Michikinikwa (mi-chee-ken-EEK-wah), known as Little Turtle, led the group. He was a gifted strategist, and his leadership helped the confederation win several battles against American troops in 1790 and 1791.

The tide turned when President Washington sent some 3,000 well-trained and well-supplied soldiers under the command of Revolutionary War hero "Mad Anthony" Wayne to defeat the confederation.

▶ **Little Turtle led Native Americans in successful battles against American troops in the Northwest Territory during 1790–1791.**

Realizing that the Native Americans were outnumbered, Little Turtle advised his allies:

66 We have beaten the enemy twice under different commanders. We cannot expect the same good fortune to attend us always. The Americans are now led by a chief who never sleeps. Like the blacksnake, the day and the night are alike to him for during all the time he has been marching on our villages . . . we have not been able to surprise him. . . . It would be prudent to listen to his offers of peace. 99

The other chiefs in the confederation rejected his advice, so Little Turtle refused to remain in command. In the summer of 1794, the confederation clashed with Wayne's army in the **Battle of Fallen Timbers**. As Little Turtle had predicted, the fighting ended in defeat for the confederation. After the battle, Wayne's men burned Native American villages and crops.

The Battle of Fallen Timbers dealt a severe blow to Native American resistance in the territory. In 1795 over 1,000 chiefs, including Little Turtle, were forced to enter negotiations with the U.S. government. The result was the **Treaty of Greenville** (1795), which gave the United States title to Native American lands making up much of present-day Ohio and part of Indiana. In exchange Native Americans received $20,000 worth of goods and a formal acknowledgment of their claim to the lands they still held.

■■ **The Battle of Fallen Timbers weakened Native American resistance and led to the surrender of Indian lands.**

NEGOTIATING PEACE

Little Turtle's confederation had received weapons from British forts in the Northwest Territory. The existence of these British forts violated the 1783 Treaty of Paris. This situation further strained America's shaky relations with Great Britain. Hoping to avert a war that he believed the United States could not win, President Washington sent Chief Justice John Jay to Great Britain in 1794 to negotiate a settlement. Among the terms of the resulting treaty, known as **Jay's Treaty**, the British agreed to abandon their forts. In return the U.S. government agreed to pay debts owed to the British.

Great Britain, however, did not stop arming Native Americans, impressing American sailors, or seizing U.S. ships. These acts angered many Americans who thought Jay had sold out to the British. Mobs burned Jay in effigy, and the nation's political divisions deepened. Congress, nevertheless, ratified the treaty. Washington had realized his major goal—preventing war with Great Britain.

Jay's Treaty came just as Spain shifted alliances, joining France against Great Britain. Spain feared an American alliance with Britain could threaten Spanish territory in North America. Thus Spain moved quickly to settle its disputes with the United States. The result was **Pinckney's Treaty**, negotiated in 1795 by Thomas Pinckney of South Carolina. Pinckney's Treaty set the southern boundary of the United States near Florida at the 31st parallel.

Ohio Historical Society

▲ **General Anthony Wayne led the attack on Native Americans during the Battle of Fallen Timbers. The entire battle lasted about 40 minutes.**

◀ **Frontier farmers carried their goods on large flatboats down the Mississippi River to New Orleans.**

keenly aware that dangers threatened the young nation. In his farewell address he urged maintaining neutrality abroad and unity at home. "The great rule of conduct for us . . . is . . . to steer clear of permanent alliances with any portion of the foreign world."

Washington also warned of the dangers posed by political parties and regional interests:

❝ In contemplating the causes which may disturb our Union, it occurs as a matter of serious concern that . . . designing [plotting] men may endeavor to excite a belief that there is a real difference of local interests and views. . . . You cannot shield yourselves too much against the jealousies and heartburnings which spring from these misrepresentations. They tend to render alien to each other those who ought to be bound together by fraternal affection. ❞

Pinckney's Treaty also guaranteed American navigation rights on the Mississippi River. In an era dominated by water transportation, the Mississippi was the superhighway linking the American West to the rest of the nation and the world. Frontier farmers and merchants used the Mississippi and its westward-flowing tributaries, such as the Ohio River, to move their produce to New Orleans. From there goods were shipped to markets around the world. Pinckney's Treaty gave Americans the **right of deposit**—the right to temporarily unload goods at the port of New Orleans without paying a duty to Spain.

■■ **Jay's Treaty and Pinckney's Treaty prevented war and won important military and economic advantages for the United States.**

Dᴏᴍᴇꜱᴛɪᴄ Bᴀᴛᴛʟᴇꜱ

In 1796 President Washington announced that he would not seek a third term—setting an informal precedent for later presidents that was not broken until 1940. He had overseen the organization of the new government and had skillfully handled several crises in foreign affairs. Still, the president was

But Washington's warning was not heeded. By the mid-1790s heated debates over whether to side with Great Britain or France had already deepened political differences and aided in shaping the first American political parties. Washington also had underestimated the extent of regional and economic differences. In the mid-1790s **sectionalism**, or loyalty to a particular part of the country, helped to create two parties: the Federalists (the party of Hamilton and Adams) and the Democratic-Republicans (the party of Jefferson and Madison). As Americans sided with one party or the other, the two-party system that is still with us today took shape.

Merchants, manufacturers, lawyers, and church leaders from New England and the Atlantic seaboard—Americans whom Federalist John Adams called "the rich, the well-born, and the able"—tended to support the Federalist party. Federalists expected the rich to provide national

▶ The Republican party believed in an agricultural America full of orderly farms, such as the one shown here.

Abby Aldrich Rockefeller Folk Art Center

The Metropolitan Museum of Art

▶ The Federalist party drew its supporters from the ranks of wealthy men, such as cloth merchant Elijah Boardman.

leadership. As one leading Federalist said: "Those who own the country ought to govern it." Besides favoring a strong national government, Federalists wanted to promote the development of commerce, especially with Great Britain.

In contrast, the Democratic-Republican party (the name was soon shortened to Republican party) included planters, small farmers, and wage earners. The party (which has no historical connection to today's Republican party) was particularly strong on the frontier and in the South. Supporters favored agriculture over manufacturing and believed that farmers, who made up most of the population, deserved the most say in government.

But the party also found support in the North, especially in the middle states. Here, various groups who had little political power saw the Republican party as a means of challenging established leadership. These artisans, workers, and tradespeople were resentful of the rich and power-

ful Federalists. They sought, instead, the political equality promised them by the Revolution.

Both northern and southern Republicans were drawn together by common beliefs. Their main aim was to protect states' rights and individual liberties by limiting the federal government. They had a deep fear of a strong national government and the financial and political powers that could create such a system. Because they distrusted the aristocratic British, they tended to be pro-French.

■■ **The two-party political system arose from the rivalry between Federalists and Republicans and from the growing sectionalism of the nation.**

SECTION 2 REVIEW

IDENTIFY and explain the significance of the following: French Revolution, impressment, Edmond Genet, Little Turtle, "Mad Anthony" Wayne, Treaty of Greenville, right of deposit, sectionalism.

LOCATE and explain the importance of the following: New Orleans.

1. **MAIN IDEA** How did foreign events of the early 1790s affect Americans?

2. **MAIN IDEA** What did the United States gain through Jay's Treaty and Pinckney's Treaty?

3. **MAIN IDEA** How were Native Americans affected by the Battle of Fallen Timbers?

4. **WRITING TO INFORM** Write an advertisement that describes the Federalist party in 1796, telling why it came into existence and urging Americans to join the party. Then write a similar advertisement for the Republican party.

5. **ANALYZING** How did Washington's Farewell Address reflect the state of U.S. affairs at the time?

FEDERALISTS DOMINATE PARTY POLITICS

FOCUS

- Why did relations with France worsen in the 1790s?
- Why did Congress pass the Alien and Sedition Acts?
- According to the Kentucky and Virginia Resolutions, who should rule on matters of constitutionality?
- How did Chief Justice John Marshall influence the development of American law?

With the formation of political parties came problems for the American electoral system. The process for electing a president and vice president, which was outlined in the Constitution, proved flawed on two separate occasions. Furthermore, the rivalry between the Federalist and Republican parties had a major impact on both domestic politics and foreign affairs.

John Adams campaign button, 1796

THE ELECTION OF 1796

President Washington's decision not to seek reelection in 1796 set in motion the first real competition for the presidency. In that election Federalists John Adams and Thomas Pinckney faced off against Republicans Thomas Jefferson and Aaron Burr.

Envious of Adams, Alexander Hamilton schemed to keep his rival from winning. Acting from behind the scenes, he persuaded a few southern Federalist electors to vote only for Pinckney. According to the Constitution, whoever received the most votes became president; the runner-up became vice president. Hamilton's plot backfired, however, when northern Federalists discovered the plan and responded by not voting for Pinckney. When the votes were counted, Adams was president, and Jefferson—his Republican opponent—was vice president!

ON THE VERGE OF WAR

President Adams faced the same challenges as Washington. While maintaining America's status as an independent nation, Adams also had to protect America's access to world markets. In addition, he wanted to improve relations with France. The French viewed Jay's Treaty and the U.S. policy of neutrality as evidence of pro-British leanings. In response, the French navy had begun to seize American ships bound for British ports.

The XYZ affair. In 1797 President Adams sent three diplomats to Paris to negotiate a new treaty with France. Charles-Maurice de Talleyrand, France's foreign minister, spurned direct negotiations with the Americans. Instead, he sent three agents with his demands. Before talks could begin, the United States would have to (1) apologize publicly for anti-French remarks that Adams had made;

(2) grant France a multimillion-dollar loan; and (3) pay Talleyrand a bribe of $240,000. Diplomatic bribes were common in the 1700s, but the huge size of the bribe shocked the American diplomats, who refused to pay.

President Adams published the French demands—substituting *X*, *Y*, and *Z* for the names of Talleyrand's agents. Americans responded with fury against France, rallying around the slogan "Millions for defense, but not one cent for tribute." President Adams and Congress responded to the **XYZ affair** with a flurry of war preparations: creating the Navy Department, building warships, fortifying harbors, and strengthening the army. Congress also imposed taxes to pay for the military buildup. Although the United States had not declared war, U.S. warships began capturing French vessels.

Pro-British Federalists delighted in this growing anti-French sentiment. Here was a chance to smash revolutionary France and cement an economic and political alliance with Great Britain. Moreover, it was an opportunity to discredit the Republicans. Voters were dropping from the pro-French Republican party "like windfalls from an apple tree in September," wrote one happy Federalist.

War avoided. While many in his own party demanded military action, Adams was reluctant to go to war. He discounted the likelihood of a French attack, saying, "At present there is no more prospect of seeing a French army here than there is in Heaven."

▲ Many Americans were shocked and angered by the XYZ affair. France is symbolized as a multi-headed monster in this cartoon.

In 1799 Adams sent another peace mission to France. The timing was fortunate. Shortly before the delegation arrived in Paris, General Napoléon Bonaparte had overthrown the revolutionary government and made himself dictator of France. Napoléon recognized that French intrigue and hostility had pushed the United States closer to Great Britain.

Eager to forestall a stronger alliance between Great Britain and the United States, Napoléon worked out an agreement with the Americans. The terms required France to abandon the troublesome alliance treaty of 1778. In return the United States would drop claims against France for seized ships and cargo.

PRESIDENTIAL LIVES

JOHN ADAMS
1735–1826

in office
1797–1801

As the nation's second president, John Adams found that following in George Washington's footsteps was no easy task. Comparisons of the two men were inevitable: Adams's often irritating manner and fiery outbursts contrasted sharply with Washington's calm and stately disposition.

Yet John Adams possessed impressive credentials of his own. A brilliant lawyer and

John Adams

experienced diplomat, he had great self-discipline and a supreme confidence in his opinions and abilities. Adams was also a practical man. This practical nature helped him during his presidency. When Adams found his salary too small to keep the White House pantry fully stocked, he brought in meat, vegetables, and apple cider from his Massachusetts farm to keep down expenses.

Pleased with the settlement, President Adams later wrote, "I desire no other inscription over my gravestone than: 'Here lies John Adams, who took upon himself the responsibility of the peace with France in 1800.' "

THE ALIEN AND SEDITION ACTS

The crisis with France increased the bad blood between the Federalists and the Republicans. The Federalists viewed the pro-French Republicans as traitors. The Republicans, on the other hand, suspected the Federalists of using the crisis to retain power. Charges and countercharges finally gave way to action. In 1798 the Federalist majority in Congress passed the **Alien and Sedition Acts**, a series of laws aimed not only at protecting the country but also at weakening the Republicans.

The Alien Act and the Alien Enemies Act authorized the president to imprison or expel "all such aliens [foreigners] as he shall judge dangerous to the peace and safety of the United States." Enforcement proved unnecessary. The threat of imprisonment drove many French citizens from the country and quieted those who remained.

The Sedition Act targeted American citizens. **Sedition** is the stirring up of discontent or rebellion against a government. Under the Sedition Act anyone who wrote, said, or printed anything "false, scandalous, and malicious" about the government, the Congress, or the president "with intent to defame" could be fined and jailed.

▶ The Virginia State legislature passed the Virginia Resolutions on December 24, 1798.

The act was aimed at Republicans. Matthew Lyon, a Republican congressman, was jailed for four months and fined $1,000 for denouncing President Adams. Throughout the country, Republican newspaper editors and politicians were arrested for sedition; 25 were indicted and 10 convicted.

■■ Federalists passed the Alien and Sedition Acts to limit Republican power and to silence government critics.

KENTUCKY AND VIRGINIA RESOLUTIONS

Many Americans saw the Alien and Sedition Acts as attempts to curb the rights of individuals—foreigners and citizens alike. The Sedition Act interfered with freedom of the press and freedom of speech, two rights guaranteed by the First Amendment. Furious Republicans voiced their protests through the Kentucky Resolutions (written by Thomas Jefferson) and the Virginia Resolutions (written by James Madison), which were passed in 1798 and 1799 by those states' legislatures.

The **Kentucky and Virginia Resolutions** declared the Alien and Sedition Acts unconstitutional. In doing so, the resolutions raised an important question: Who should decide when a federal law or a government action violates the U.S. Constitution?—the states?—the Supreme Court? The Constitution did not say.

The resolutions came down on the side of the states. The states, they argued, had created the federal government as their agent, giving it specific powers defined by the Constitution. If the federal government exceeded those powers, it was the states' right—and duty—to declare the act unconstitutional and therefore void.

The Federalists disagreed. Firm believers

▲ When he was vice president of the United States, Aaron Burr fatally wounded Alexander Hamilton in a duel on July 11, 1804. The duel ended Burr's political career. The pistols shown here are dueling pistols of the period.

in a strong federal government, they argued that the Supreme Court should decide matters of constitutionality.

Because the Federalists controlled most state governments, the Kentucky and Virginia Resolutions failed to win wide support. But Jefferson and Madison had posed questions about the nature of the Union that would trouble Americans until the Civil War.

■■ The Kentucky and Virginia Resolutions argued that it was the states' right to decide whether a federal law or action was unconstitutional.

THE ELECTION OF 1800

By the election of 1800, the fortunes of the Federalist party were slipping. The election pitted Republicans Jefferson and Burr against Federalists Adams and Charles Pinckney (of South Carolina). Capitalizing on grievances against the Federalists, the Republicans swept to power, gaining control of Congress. However, neither the Republicans nor the Federalists had a formal ticket, as parties routinely do today. As a result, another electoral crisis arose: Jefferson and Burr received the same number of votes for president!

In the event of a tie, the Constitution clearly authorized the House of Representatives to decide who the president would be. Ordinarily, the House would have chosen Jefferson, the Republicans' preferred candidate. But some Federalists who hated Jefferson voted for Burr instead. Thirty-five attempts to select a president failed. With Inauguration Day just weeks away, the country was still without a president-elect.

This problem might have continued indefinitely had help not come from an unexpected source. Preferring Jefferson over the "unprincipled and dangerous" Burr, Alexander Hamilton persuaded several Federalists to vote for Jefferson. Thus, with the help of his former rival, Jefferson became the third president of the United States.

The hatred that Hamilton and Burr felt toward each other deepened over the years. In 1804 Hamilton publicly criticized Burr, who was then running for governor of New York. Burr's demand for an apology led to a duel in which Burr fatally wounded Hamilton.

To prevent future electoral crises, Congress proposed the **Twelfth Amendment** to the Constitution. Ratified in 1804, this amendment requires electors to vote for presidential and vice-presidential candidates on separate ballots.

THE FEDERALISTS AND THE JUDICIARY

Knowing their days in office were numbered, the Federalists feared that their programs would be abandoned. In the months between Election Day in November and Inauguration Day in March, the Federalist majority in Congress tightened its hold on the judicial branch to "protect" the country from Jeffersonian radicalism. They pushed through the Judiciary Act of 1801, which created a number of new circuit courts and federal judgeships. President Adams worked late into the night of his last day in office, signing the papers that appointed Federalists to these posts. These last-minute appointees were nicknamed "midnight judges."

Adams's most significant appointment, though not one of the midnight judgeships, was the selection of John Marshall of Virginia as chief justice of the Supreme Court. A firm Federalist with a brilliant legal mind and a shrewd grasp of politics, Marshall dominated the Supreme Court during the more than three decades he served (1801–1835). His more than 500 opinions influenced the political and economic structure of the new nation, molding a truly national union.

During his years on the bench, Marshall established many basic principles of American constitutional law. Among these was the principle of judicial review—the right of the Supreme Court to declare an act of Congress unconstitutional. The Court first exercised this right in the case of *Marbury v. Madison* (1803).

▲ **John Marshall was the fourth chief justice of the United States and a man of such integrity that he invariably won the support of his colleagues.**

For political reasons Secretary of State James Madison had refused to allow William Marbury, one of the "midnight judges," to take the bench. Marbury sued. When the case reached the Supreme Court, the Court sided with Marbury but said that it did not have the right to force the president to take action. Marshall declared unconstitutional the part of the Judiciary Act of 1789 that gave the Court that right. With this decision Marshall initiated the Supreme Court's most important role—that of final interpreter of the Constitution.

■■ **Chief Justice John Marshall shaped the development of American law through the principle of judicial review and through his many court decisions.**

SECTION 3 REVIEW

IDENTIFY and explain the significance of the following: Charles-Maurice de Talleyrand, XYZ affair, Napoléon Bonaparte, sedition, Twelfth Amendment.

1. **MAIN IDEA** What events in the 1790s strained relations with France and increased the risk of war?

2. **MAIN IDEA** What were the provisions of the Alien and Sedition Acts and why did Congress pass them?

3. **ANALYZING** How did Chief Justice John Marshall's decision in *Marbury v. Madison* influence the development of American law?

4. **WRITING TO EXPLAIN** Write a paragraph outlining the arguments presented in the Kentucky and Virginia Resolutions.

5. **ASSESSING CONSEQUENCES** What democratic values did the Sedition Act violate?

THE NATION EXPANDS

FOCUS

- **What policy changes did the Republican Congress make during President Jefferson's first term in office?**
- **Why did the United States purchase Louisiana from France?**
- **What did explorers of the Louisiana Territory accomplish?**
- **What were some of the positive and negative consequences of the Louisiana Purchase?**

*U*pon taking office, Jefferson pledged to preserve the government in its "constitutional vigor" and guard "the right of election by the people." His promise of moderation did not prevent Jefferson from taking action, though. During his two terms the United States expanded westward beyond the Mississippi River to take in the heartland of North America.

Sacagawea guides Lewis and Clark.

JEFFERSON TAKES OFFICE

Though Thomas Jefferson later heralded the Republican victory in the 1800 election as the "Revolution of 1800," the transition of power was peaceful. This was no small achievement in an era when many shifts of political power were accompanied by chaos or war. To fulfill his promise of moderation, Jefferson left untouched some Federalist programs, including the national bank and the debt payment plan, both of which he had once opposed. He also tried to maintain the neutral course set by Washington and Adams in foreign affairs.

But Jefferson had not abandoned his view that a federal government with too much power threatened individual freedoms and states' rights. Thus he urged the Republican-controlled Congress to overturn a number of Federalist programs. Congress responded by repealing the whiskey tax and the Judiciary Act of 1801, cutting military funding, and reducing the size of the army and the

navy. Jefferson saw trimming military spending as one way to achieve his campaign promise to pay off the national debt.

■■ **The Republican Congress repealed the whiskey tax and the Judiciary Act of 1801, cut military spending, and reduced the size of the army and the navy.**

THE LOUISIANA PURCHASE

In the election of 1800, the Republicans won every state that had a frontier on the **Trans-Appalachian West**, the area between the Appalachian Mountains and the Mississippi River. Unlike Federalists, who feared that westward expansion would weaken their power in Congress, Republicans favored expansion. Jefferson imagined "distant times, when our rapid multiplication will expand [the nation] . . . & cover the whole

◀ Americans pushed westward as new territories opened. This engraving shows a family crossing the Appalachians on their way to Pittsburgh.

northern if not southern continent." This view appealed to settlers. Because frontier farming practices were hard on the soil, settlers were always hungry for new, fertile land.

Fertile land was not enough, however. Western farmers also needed access to the Mississippi River and to the port of New Orleans to get their produce to market. Events in 1800 put that access in danger. Spain had held the Louisiana Territory since 1762. Now, in a secret treaty, the French ruler Napoléon regained Louisiana from Spain. The territory covered an enormous, though vaguely defined, area: roughly the northern and western reaches of the Mississippi River basin (see map on page 209).

Rumors of this transfer reached the U.S. government in 1801, alarming Jefferson and other Americans. French control of the mouth of the Mississippi River might severely limit American trade and block westward expansion. To remedy the situation, President Jefferson ordered Robert R. Livingston, the U.S. minister to France, to negotiate with France for a U.S. port at the mouth of the Mississippi or for access to New Orleans. Talks dragged on for almost two years.

In 1803 Jefferson sent James Monroe to Paris to assist Livingston with negotiations. Jefferson had instructed Monroe to offer Napoléon as much as $10 million for New Orleans and West Florida. No sooner had Monroe arrived, however, than Napoléon's representative asked how much the United States would pay for *all* of Louisiana. The astonished American diplomats quickly agreed to pay about $15 million for the entire area. Thus, for about four cents an acre, the United States com-

pleted the **Louisiana Purchase**, probably the largest land deal in history.

Although pleased with the purchase, Jefferson had reservations. He did not believe that the Constitution granted the government specific authority to buy territory from a foreign nation. Thus, he felt that a constitutional amendment might be necessary to permit the purchase. But he knew that ratifying an amendment would mean a delay, during which Napoléon might change his mind. So Jefferson advised his attorney general to "do what is necessary *in silence*" and pushed the purchase treaty through the Senate.

Why did France sell this valuable territory? The answer lay in Napoléon's failure to build an empire in the Western Hemisphere. To defend an empire in Louisiana, Napoléon needed a strong naval base in the West Indies. The most likely place was Saint Domingue (now Haiti) on the island of Hispaniola, yet the colony was no longer under French control. In 1791 the colony's slaves had revolted. Under the leadership of Toussaint L'Ouverture (TOO-san loo-vuhr-TOOHR)—a gifted

◀ This contemporary painting of Toussaint L'Ouverture is by African American artist Jacob Lawrence. It is one in his series of paintings dealing with the Haitian Revolt.

Jefferson's Image

Most of us today do not think of Thomas Jefferson as a controversial figure. But in his own day he inspired both admiration and ridicule. To some he was a champion of liberty. To others he was "Mad Tom," a frenzied supporter of the bloody French Revolution. Among his enemies he could count a president, John Adams; his own vice president, Aaron Burr; a secretary of the treasury, Alexander Hamilton; and a chief justice of the Supreme Court, John Marshall.

These conflicting images of Jefferson are not that surprising. Jefferson was a man of many contradictions. He was an aristocrat who championed the plain farmer and a slaveholder who wrote in the Declaration of Independence that "all men are created equal." He was opposed to a strong national government, yet he used the executive power of the presidency to double the size of the nation through the Louisiana Purchase.

The complexity of Jefferson's personality and his actions have allowed various groups—with vastly different aims—to use his name in support of their causes. In the 1830s those who demanded broader voting rights and other democratic reforms cast Jefferson as champion of the common people. In 1860–1861 the southern states that had seceded from the Union held Jefferson up as a believer in states' rights over federalism. In the late 1800s and early 1900s, Jefferson was a hero of social reformers fighting against big business and the negative effects of industrialization. During the Great Depression of the 1930s, Franklin Roosevelt argued that Jefferson's sympathy for the common people would have made him a supporter of Roosevelt's social-welfare policies.

A new image of Jefferson emerged during the struggle against dictatorships in World War II. Jefferson became the "Apostle of Freedom." To this end, the Jefferson Memorial in Washington, D.C., was dedicated in 1943, and his Virginia home, Monticello, became a historic site.

The enshrining of Jefferson coincided with a new interest in historical research—the examination of American society's shared values and beliefs. This new emphasis was evident in the 1948 publication of volume one of the first scholarly biography of Jefferson, Dumas Malone's *Jefferson and His Time*. Merrill Peterson's *The Jefferson Image in the American Mind* (1960) continued in the same vein.

The 1960s saw another new area of historical research emerge—social history. In the midst of the decade's social changes and conflicts, many historians turned their attention to examining the everyday lives of Americans—both famous and ordinary citizens.

From this emphasis on social history came Fawn Brodie's *Thomas Jefferson: An Intimate History* (1974). Brodie examined the rumors about a love affair between Jefferson and his slave Sally Hemings that first surfaced before the election of 1800. It is difficult to prove or disprove the story, but Brodie's revelations nonetheless caused a furor. That Brodie's allegations aroused such emotion reminds us how far Thomas Jefferson's image has come from the controversy that once enveloped the man and his views.

▲ **Jefferson designed Monticello in 1769.**

THROUGH OTHERS' EYES

Spain was unpleasantly surprised to discover in 1803 that France planned to sell the Louisiana Territory to the United States. Earlier, Spain had transferred the land to France on the condition that the French never part with it. Spain feared that if the United States acquired the territory, the young nation would threaten Spain's other colonies in North America, such as California and Mexico.

The Marques de Casa Irujo (eer-oo-hoh), Spain's minister to the United States, wrote a harsh letter to Secretary of State James Madison denying the United States' right to buy Louisiana: "The sale of that province to the United States is founded on the violation of a promise so absolute that it ought to be respected—a promise without which the king, my master, would not under any circumstances have let Louisiana go."

In a letter to his own government, Casa Irujo called the Louisiana Purchase "truly an evil" for the United States. He predicted the U.S. government would be unable to hold such a vast territory of diverse peoples together: "One does not need extraordinary wisdom to anticipate that the acquisition of Louisiana, far from consolidating the strength and vigor of this nation, will rather contribute to weaken it."

military strategist, former slave, and grandson of an African chief—blacks eventually took control of the whole colony.

In 1802 a French attempt to regain Saint Domingue ended in disaster. Although Napoléon's troops captured Toussaint (who later died in prison), his followers and the ravages of yellow fever combined to drive the French from the island. With no foothold in the West Indies from which to protect Louisiana, Napoléon decided to sell the territory—and gain $15 million to enlarge his war chest.

■■ **The United States purchased Louisiana from France in order to secure navigation rights on the Mississippi.**

EXPLORING THE LOUISIANA TERRITORY

Neither buyer nor seller knew the exact size or boundaries of the Louisiana Territory. President Jefferson assigned the task of mapping the new territory to two skilled frontiersmen, Meriwether Lewis and William Clark. The **Lewis and Clark expedition**, numbering about 45 men, left St. Louis in May 1804. In response to the president's instructions to record all observations "with great care and accuracy," Lewis and Clark kept detailed journals of their travels. Typical is the following entry from May 23, 1805:

66 The river has become more rapid, the country much the same as yesterday, except that there is rather more rocks on the face of the hills, and some small spruce pine appears among the pitch. The wild roses are very abundant and now in bloom; they differ from those of the United States only in having the leaves and the bush itself of a somewhat smaller size. We find the mosquitoes troublesome, notwithstanding the coolness of the morning. The buffalo is scarce to-day, but the elk, deer, and antelope, are very numerous. 99

Native Americans—particularly the Mandans and Shoshones (shuh-SHOHN-ees)—aided the expedition. After their first winter Lewis and Clark hired a French-Canadian fur trader and his Shoshone wife, Sacagawea (sak-uh-juh-WEE-uh), as guides and interpreters. Sacagawea proved invaluable to the expedition. She showed members of the expedition the best places to fish, to hunt game, and to forage for wild vegetables. As an interpreter, she helped the expedition obtain needed supplies at critical moments. For example, when the expedition reached the Rocky Mountains, Sacagawea helped Lewis and Clark purchase horses from the Shoshones. Without these horses the expedition could not have made the crossing through the high passes of the Rockies before snow blocked the way.

Relations with Native Americans were further enhanced by the presence of York, a slave. In his journal Clark observed that the Indians were "much astonished" by York, "who did not lose the opportunity of [displaying] his powers Strength etc." Apparently, they "never Saw a black man before."

The Lewis and Clark expedition traveled up the Missouri River, crossed the Rocky Mountains, and canoed down the Snake and Columbia rivers to the Pacific Ocean. After nearly two and a half years, the expedition returned—bringing with it plant and animal specimens, animal bones and pelts, and various soil and mineral samples.

Before Lewis and Clark had the chance to publish the chronicles of their expedition, the reports of another explorer, Zebulon Pike, appeared in print. Pike visited the upper Mississippi Valley in 1805 and went as far west as present-day Colorado before returning home via the Spanish town of Santa Fe. Pike's descriptions gave Americans their first glimpse of the lands beyond the Mississippi and helped spur expansion into Texas and the Southwest. His depiction of the Great Plains as a huge desert, however, led many to view that region as unsuitable for settlement.

■■ **Meriwether Lewis, William Clark, and Zebulon Pike mapped the Louisiana Territory and cataloged its valuable natural resources.**

𝒯HE IMPORTANCE OF THE LOUISIANA PURCHASE

The Louisiana Purchase added all or part of 13 future states to the nation. This increased size gave the United States a larger international stature. As Robert Livingston noted at the time of the purchase: "From this day the United States take their place among the powers of the first rank."

The purchase had important domestic consequences as well. In addition to removing the French threat from American soil, the purchase opened the interior of the continent to white settlement. As Americans devoted more energy to developing the

The Louisiana Purchase

EXPANDING WESTWARD The Louisiana Purchase added some 828,000 square miles of rich land to the United States, increasing its original size by about 140 percent.

? **MOVEMENT** What rivers did Lewis and Clark follow from St. Louis on their way to the Pacific Ocean?

Louisiana Purchase treaty cover with seals

Legend:
- States in 1804
- U.S. territories in 1804
- Louisiana Purchase
- ■ Fort
- → Lewis and Clark, 1804–1806
- → Pike, 1805–1807

THOMAS JEFFERSON
1743–1826

*in office
1801–1809*

Thomas Jefferson had a good-humored manner about him. He was a brilliant conversationalist who could talk just as easily about chemistry or horse racing as about politics or philosophy. He loved art, geography, and architecture and not only knew French, Italian, Spanish, Greek, and Latin but also studied some 40 Native American languages.

Though charming in person, Jefferson often hated his rivals and recorded in his diary the petty gossip he heard about them. Jefferson also struggled with a deep sense of loneliness. The death of his wife Martha Wayles Skelton and five of his six children caused him to mourn: "My evening prospects now hang on the thread of a single life."

frontier, they increasingly looked west, rather than east across the Atlantic. This shift promoted a greater sense of national identity. However, developments that followed the historic purchase were not as positive for Native Americans. When France transferred ownership of Louisiana to the United States, neither nation considered Native American claims to the land. Native American leader Sagoyewatha (suh-goh-ye-WAH-thah) (Red Jacket) lamented:

> 66 There was a time when our forefathers owned this great land. Their seats [homes] extended from the rising to the setting sun. . . . Our seats were once large and yours were small. You have now become a great people, and we have scarcely a place left to spread our blankets. 99

The purchase also had a negative effect on many African Americans. Historians John Hope Franklin and Alfred A. Moss, Jr., point out that the blacks of Saint Domingue, in throwing off slavery, helped make possible the purchase of Louisiana. Ironically, the purchase also made possible the extension of slavery by opening new lands to southern planters.

■■ **Although the Louisiana Purchase added to U.S. prestige and helped build national identity, it had negative consequences for Native Americans and African Americans.**

SECTION 4 REVIEW

IDENTIFY and explain the significance of the following: Robert Livingston, Louisiana Purchase, Toussaint L'Ouverture, Lewis and Clark expedition, Sacagawea, York, Zebulon Pike.

LOCATE and explain the importance of the following: Trans-Appalachian West, Haiti, Louisiana Territory.

1. **MAIN IDEA** What steps did the Republican Congress take against Federalist policies?

2. **MAIN IDEA** What did the United States hope to gain by purchasing Louisiana from France?

3. **ASSESSING CONSEQUENCES** What positive consequences did the Louisiana Purchase have for the United States? What negative impact did it have on Native Americans and African Americans?

4. **WRITING TO CREATE** Imagine you are a Native American living in the Louisiana Territory. Write an account that expresses your feelings about white exploration, conquest, and settlement of the territory.

5. **HYPOTHESIZING** Imagine you are President Jefferson. What reasons might you give for abandoning your strict constructionist stand in the case of the Louisiana Purchase?

Section 5

THE COMING OF THE WAR OF 1812

FOCUS

- What foreign actions in the early 1800s affected U.S. trade? How did the United States respond?
- What were the major causes of the War of 1812?
- What was the significance of the outcome of the War of 1812?

By 1800, U.S. trade was expanding worldwide. Thomas Jefferson hoped to protect America's freedom of the seas. As with earlier presidents, however, this goal remained out of reach. Events across the Atlantic pulled the nation into conflicts: first off the North African coast and then—because of Napoléon's attempted conquest of Europe—on the high seas and at home.

The *Chesapeake* and the *Leopard*, 1807

THE PERILS OF WORLD TRADE

Since 1783, U.S. merchants had been trading with the Barbary states of North Africa, including Morocco, Algiers (al-JIRZ), Tunis, and Tripoli. Barbary pirates demanded protection money from all ships that sailed there. This harassment of U.S. ships convinced many Americans of the need for a powerful navy.

That conviction grew stronger as Napoléon's war in Europe spilled over into the Atlantic Ocean. In 1807 Britain passed the **Orders in Council**, which forbade neutral vessels from trading with France, or even from entering ports under French control. Napoléon reacted by threatening to seize all foreign ships that cooperated with the British navy. America was again caught in the cross fire between France and Britain.

In the summer of 1807, events took an ugly turn. Britain, facing a manpower shortage in the Royal Navy, stepped up its long-standing practice of impressment. On June 22 the captain of the

British ship H.M.S. *Leopard* demanded the right to board the U.S. *Chesapeake* to search for 4 supposed British deserters. When permission was refused, the British opened fire, killing 3 U.S. seamen and wounding 18 others.

The *Chesapeake* incident outraged many Americans. President Jefferson shared this outrage but wanted to maintain U.S. neutrality. In an effort at "peaceable coercion," Jefferson urged Congress to pass the **Embargo Act** of 1807, which stopped shipments of food and other American products to all foreign ports.

Not surprisingly, New England merchants and western farmers angrily opposed this measure, as did many others who were thrown out of work because of it. John Lane Jones, an unemployed Boston laborer, complained directly to Jefferson:

❝ You infernal villain. How much longer are you going to keep this . . . Embargo on to starve us poor people. . . . You must . . . afford us some kind of relief. . . . I wish you could feel as bad as I do. ❞

A STRONG START FOR THE NATION ▪ 211

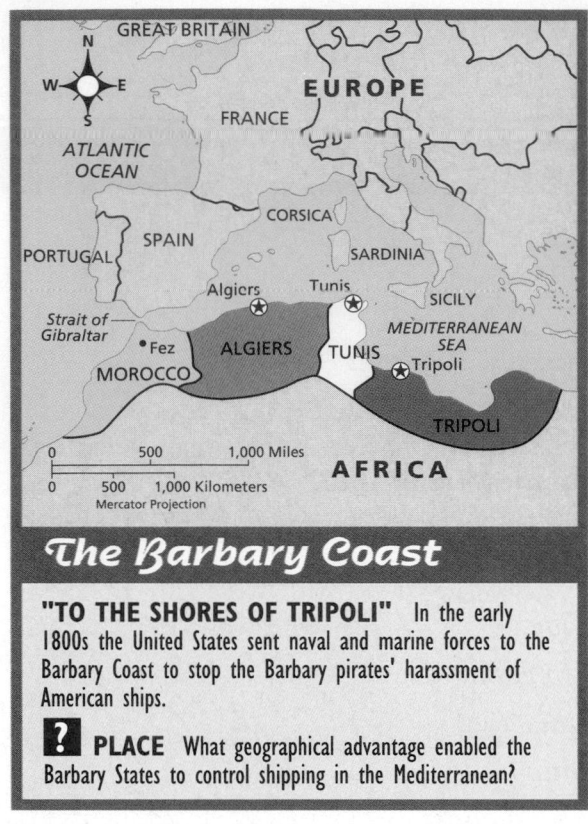

The Barbary Coast

"TO THE SHORES OF TRIPOLI" In the early 1800s the United States sent naval and marine forces to the Barbary Coast to stop the Barbary pirates' harassment of American ships.

? PLACE What geographical advantage enabled the Barbary States to control shipping in the Mediterranean?

James Madison, who succeeded Jefferson as president in 1809, at first kept the embargo in place. But public pressure became too great, and Congress repealed the embargo in March 1809. Congress then passed the **Non-Intercourse Act**, which only prohibited U.S. trade with Great Britain and France. The Non-Intercourse Act, like the embargo, did more harm to the American economy than to the economies of Great Britain and France. As the situation worsened, war with Britain or France, or both, seemed inevitable.

▪▪ In response to harassment of U.S. ships by foreign powers, the government strengthened the navy and set limits on foreign trade.

CONFRONTATION IN THE WEST

Problems abroad were compounded by events at home. Hunters, trappers, and farmers sought new lands in British Canada and Spanish Florida and also pushed westward into lands occupied by Native Americans.

Rapid westward expansion fueled tensions between settlers and Native Americans, who continued to look to Great Britain for assistance.

Westerners were particularly alarmed by the activities of the Shawnee leader Tecumseh (tuh-KUHM-suh).

BIO GRAPHY Settlers had a tireless and resourceful opponent in the tall, handsome Tecumseh (1768–1813). When his father was killed by whites, Tecumseh was adopted by the Shawnee chief Blackfish. As he grew older, Tecumseh became convinced that Native Americans' best hope for survival rested in a military alliance among the Indian nations.

Tecumseh

In the early 1800s Tecumseh set out to rally the Indian nations east of the Mississippi River. From the Great Lakes to the Gulf of Mexico, Tecumseh urged Native Americans not to sell land to the settlers: "Sell a country! Why not sell the air, the clouds, and the great sea? . . . Did not the Great Spirit make them all for the use of his children?"

As Tecumseh gained support, settlers pressured the government to take action. In the fall of 1811, while Tecumseh was in the South seeking support from the Creeks, Choctaws, and Cherokees, General William Henry Harrison decided to move against Tecumseh's stronghold on the Tippecanoe River in Indiana Territory. At dawn on November 7, the Indians struck the army camp first, ignoring Tecumseh's warning that the time was not yet right to fight. The **Battle of Tippecanoe** ended in defeat for Native Americans. When Tecumseh returned from the South in early 1812, he saw his dream of a united confederation shattered—replaced by isolated border wars between Native Americans and settlers.

CONGRESS DECLARES WAR

The British had supplied Tecumseh's forces with weapons. Thus, the clamor for war against Britain again arose in Congress. New congressmen, such as Henry Clay of Kentucky, John C. Calhoun of South Carolina, and Felix Grundy of Tennessee, exhibited such war fever that Congressman John Randolph of Virginia nicknamed them "War Hawks." They called for an attack on Canada in order to seize land and end the British–Native American alliance once and for all. Their cries, said Randolph, became "like the whip-poor-will, but one eternal monotonous tone—Canada! Canada! Canada!"

To reduce tensions, the British suspended the Orders in Council in June 1812. Before the news reached the United States, however, President Madison asked for a declaration of war. In his message to Congress on June 1, Madison cited repeated violations of neutral rights, continued impressment of American sailors, and British support of Native American uprisings on the frontier as reasons for the declaration. After some debate, the House voted on June 4 and the Senate on June 18 to support the declaration of war.

The vote was split almost exactly along sectional lines. The South and the West—suffering from an agricultural depression and Indian troubles that they blamed on Great Britain—overwhelmingly supported the declaration. The Middle Atlantic and the Northeast—fearing a British blockade of their coasts and the possible ruin of their shipping industry—almost unanimously opposed the declaration.

■■ **Frustration over violations of neutral rights, impressment of American sailors, and British support of Native American uprisings led to war.**

THE WAR OF 1812

The United States was ill prepared for war. The Republicans' reluctance to tax and their reduction of the military had left the American army weak and poorly equipped. Yet, despite Britain's great sea power, the American navy enjoyed the advantages of well-trained sailors and officers and a generally high morale.

Although the government made little effort to enlist blacks, African Americans—enslaved and free—took part in the war. Many fugitive slaves, hoping to win their freedom, fought for the Americans or the British. At least one tenth of the naval crews on the Great Lakes were made up of African Americans.

The war's first phase. American war strategy focused on the conquest of Canada by land and sea. With the British preoccupied by their struggle

PRESIDENTIAL LIVES

JAMES MADISON
1751–1836

in office
1809–1817

One of James Madison's former professors once remarked to Thomas Jefferson, "[I] never knew him [Madison] to do, or to say, an improper thing." Jefferson delighted in teasing his friend Madison with this story, for Madison was indeed regarded as a man of great virtue.

Madison was also shy and self-conscious, often feeling out of place in social settings. At his own inauguration party, he remarked to a friend, "I would much rather be in bed." But Madison's awkward manner vanished during a good dinner with close friends. He became relaxed and charming, entertaining his companions with stories and jokes and even poking fun at himself.

to stop Napoléon, Americans were confident of a quick victory. But repeated attempts to invade Canada failed.

The United States, however, did enjoy early successes at sea. In the first eight months of the war, U.S. frigates won many victories against British warships. Meanwhile, American pirates seriously disrupted British commerce by raiding British ships both in the Caribbean and around the British Isles.

The U.S. navy achieved even greater success on the Great Lakes. In 1813 a small ragtag naval force commanded by Captain Oliver Hazard Perry won control of Lake Erie, helping to secure America's northwestern border. After his victory Perry notified General Harrison: "We have met the enemy and they are ours."

Encouraged by these naval victories, General Harrison crossed into Canada. With some 4,500 troops, he defeated the British and their Native American allies at the **Battle of the Thames**. The British hold on the Northwest Territory was finally broken.

The war's second phase. Soon after ending its war against France early in 1814, Great Britain sent 14,000 reinforcements to Canada. British strategists planned a three-pronged attack. Britain would invade the United States from the north through Canada and from the south through New Orleans. They would also continue to raid points along the Atlantic coast to disrupt American commerce.

On the night of August 24, 1814, British forces struck Washington, D.C. Within a day they had captured the city, burning the executive mansion and other major public buildings before moving on. First Lady Dolley Madison escaped the mansion just minutes before the enemy crashed through the doors.

The next target for a coastal assault was the port city of Baltimore, on Chesapeake Bay. There, British vessels bombarded Fort McHenry, but the fort's brave stand—immortalized in Francis Scott Key's poem "The Star-Spangled Banner"—was a setback for the British.

Great Britain then assembled about 7,500 troops to strike at New Orleans. General Andrew Jackson, a ruthless Indian-fighter and commander of a frontier militia, led the American forces that included both whites and free African Americans. U.S. troops constructed a line of earthworks, or embankments of earth, fortified by cannons. When the invasion finally came on January 8, 1815, the well-protected U.S. sharpshooters and artillery easily won the **Battle of New Orleans**. Few Americans were killed, but British casualties topped 2,000.

Jackson had ignored the fear of many officers that it would be dangerous to arm African American troops. After the victory Jackson praised the African Americans: "I expected much from you, but you have surpassed my hopes."

The Treaty of Ghent. Tragically, the fighting at New Orleans came after peace negotiations had produced the **Treaty of Ghent** (GENT), signed on Christmas Eve, 1814. Reports of the Americans' New Orleans victory reached Washington, D.C., at the

CANADA (British)

① Detroit surrenders to British, Aug. 1812. Recaptured, Sept. 1813.

③ Perry's forces defeat the British on Lake Erie, Sept. 1813.

④ Jackson's forces defeat the Creeks at Horseshoe Bend, Mar. 1814.

⑤ British burn and occupy Washington, Aug. 1814.

⑥ British bombard Fort McHenry but fail to take Baltimore, Sept. 1814.

② U.S. warships enjoy victories against the British during the war's first year. But the British are still able to blockade the coast.

American forces
British forces
American victories
British victories

0   150   300 Miles
0   150   300 Kilometers
Albers Equal-Area Projection

The War of 1812

U.S. WAR STRATEGY The United States hoped to win the War of 1812 by invading Canada on three fronts: (1) along Lake Champlain toward Montreal; (2) across the Niagara frontier; and (3) from Detroit into upper Canada. Although U.S. forces achieved some successes at land and sea, the war ended without a victory for either side.

? MOVEMENT What route did Jackson and his troops follow to meet the British at New Orleans?

same time as news of the peace accord, leading many to assume that the victory had affected the treaty. General Jackson did nothing to correct this view and later used his fame as a war hero to win political power.

Neither side gained much by the Treaty of Ghent. By the terms of the treaty, prisoners of war were exchanged, and the territorial boundaries that existed before the war were restored. Nevertheless, the war was a turning point for the United States. It consolidated American control over the Northwest Territory through the defeat of Native Americans and the removal of their British allies. In addition, it resulted in a peace between the United States and Great Britain that marked the beginning of a long partnership.

■■ **The War of 1812 guaranteed U.S. control of the Northwest Territory while forging a new alliance between the United States and Great Britain.**

At the same time, however, the war further divided the nation along sectional lines. New England Federalists had bitterly opposed the war. So great was their discontent that they met in December 1814 at Hartford, Connecticut, to discuss seceding from the Union so that they could negotiate a separate peace with Great Britain. Moderates at the **Hartford Convention** voted down secession, suggesting instead that the Federalists push for a constitutional amendment that would limit the powers of Congress and the

▲ British troops were defeated as they attacked the line of earthworks built for the defense of New Orleans. Painted by H. Charles McBarron, Andrew Jackson is shown here mounted on a horse.

southern states. Delegates carried the proposal to Washington, D.C., but arrived just as the city learned of the peace treaty and Jackson's victory at New Orleans. Caught in the midst of the wild celebration, they slipped quietly out of town.

The Hartford Convention helped spell the end of the Federalist party. In the wake of the U.S. victory at New Orleans, the convention appeared treasonous. The party never recovered from the charge of disloyalty and collapsed a few years after the war.

SECTION 5 REVIEW

IDENTIFY and explain the significance of the following: Orders in Council, Tecumseh, William Henry Harrison, Battle of Tippecanoe, Battle of the Thames, Andrew Jackson, Battle of New Orleans, Treaty of Ghent, Hartford Convention.

LOCATE and explain the importance of the following: the Barbary states, Canada, Lake Erie.

1. **MAIN IDEA** What actions did the United States take to prevent continued harassment of U.S. ships on the seas?

2. **MAIN IDEA** Why did the United States declare war in 1812?

3. **MAIN IDEA** How was the outcome of the War of 1812 significant for the United States domestically and internationally?

4. **WRITING TO EXPRESS A VIEWPOINT** Write a letter to President Madison explaining why you oppose the Non-Intercourse Act just as you opposed the Embargo Act of 1807.

5. **ANALYZING** Why did Tecumseh try to create an Indian confederation? Why did the confederation fail to achieve its goals?

CHAPTER 6
Review

Washington inaugurated. French Revolution begins. Judiciary Act establishes federal courts.

Bill of Rights ratified.

Whiskey Rebellion erupts. Jay's Treaty signed.

Washington gives Farewell Address. Adams elected president.

Alien and Sedition Acts passed. Kentucky and Virginia Resolutions issued.

1789 1790   1795

WRITING A SUMMARY

Using the essential points of the chapter as a guide, write a summary of the chapter.

REVIEWING CHRONOLOGY

Number your paper 1 to 5. Study the time line above, and list the following events in the order in which they happened by writing the first next to 1, the second next to 2, and so on. Then complete the activity below.

1. Treaty of Ghent signed.
2. Bill of Rights ratified.
3. Washington gives Farewell Address.
4. Battle of Tippecanoe fought.
5. Alien and Sedition Acts passed.

Evaluating Select an event on the time line, and in a paragraph, state its significance in U.S. history.

IDENTIFYING PEOPLE AND IDEAS

Explain the historical significance of each of the following people or terms.

1. George Washington
2. precedent
3. Alexander Hamilton
4. right of deposit
5. John Marshall
6. Toussaint L'Ouverture
7. Sacagawea
8. Tecumseh

UNDERSTANDING MAIN IDEAS

1. What steps were taken by the First Congress to organize the federal government?
2. How did its close ties to France cause the United States problems in the 1790s?
3. What events pushed the United States toward war with Great Britain in the early 1800s?
4. Why can it be said that the Louisiana Purchase had negative effects for African Americans?

REVIEWING THEMES

1. **Constitutional Heritage** How does the U.S. Constitution address possible conflicts between individual rights and those of a society?
2. **Economic Development** Describe how Hamilton's financial program affected the economy.
3. **Geographic Diversity** In what ways did the Louisiana Purchase provide both benefits and challenges for the United States?
4. **Democratic Values** How does a democracy encourage the formation of political parties?

THINKING CRITICALLY

1. **Gaining a Multicultural Perspective** Why did Native Americans resist settlers moving west?
2. **Hypothesizing** What effect do you think a sedition act might have on today's press?
3. **Evaluating** Why do you think the Embargo and Non-Intercourse acts hurt the U.S. economy more than the economies of France and Britain?

STRATEGY FOR SUCCESS

Review the Skills Handbook entry on Reviewing Map Basics beginning on page 992. Then number your paper 1 to 13. Study the map below, noting the numbers on it. It illustrates the states, either in full or in part, that were formed from the Louisiana Purchase. Write the name of the state next to the corresponding number.

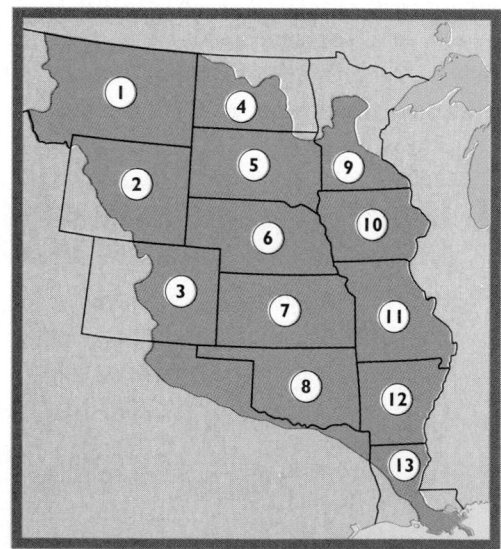

WRITING ABOUT HISTORY

Historical Imagination You are a newspaper editor in the early 1800s. Write an editorial about Tecumseh's confederation or the declaration of the War of 1812.

Jefferson elected president.

U.S. completes Louisiana Purchase.

Jefferson reelected president.

Tecumseh tries to unify Indians. Battle of Tippecanoe fought.

Madison elected president.

War declared against Great Britain.

Battle of New Orleans fought.

Treaty of Ghent signed.

1800   1805   1810   1815

USING PRIMARY SOURCES

In 1810–1811 Tecumseh traveled throughout Native American lands to seek support for his Indian Confederation. Read the following excerpts from his appeal to the Osages. Then state in your own words Tecumseh's reasons for forming a Native American confederation.

 Brothers—The white men are not friends to the Indians; at first, they only asked for land sufficient for a wigwam; now, nothing will satisfy them but the whole of our hunting grounds, from the rising to the setting sun.

Brothers—My people wish for peace; . . . but where the white people are, there is no peace. . . .

Brothers—if you do not unite with us, they will first destroy us, and then you will fall an easy prey to them. They have destroyed many nations of red men because they were not united . . . we must fight each other's battles. 99

LINKING HISTORY AND GEOGRAPHY

By the late 1700s, people were pouring into Trans-Appalachia. In *America and Americans*, John Steinbeck wrote about these migrants and their uses of the land. Read Steinbeck's comments, and in a brief essay, explain how he saw the effects of western migration on America's resources.

66 It is little wonder that they [the settlers] went land-mad, because there was so much of it. They cut and burned the forests to make room for crops; they abandoned their knowledge of kindness to the land in order to maintain its usefulness. When they had cropped [worn] out a piece they moved on, raping the country like invaders. The topsoil, held by roots and freshened by leaf-fall, was left helpless to the spring freshets [floods], stripped and eroded with the naked bones of clay and rock exposed. The destruction of the forests changed the rainfall, for the searching clouds could find no green and beckoning woods to draw them on and milk them. The merciless 19th century was like a hostile expedition for loot that seemed limitless. 99

Pioneer Mother *statue*

BUILDING YOUR PORTFOLIO

Complete the following projects independently or cooperatively.

1. **POLITICS** In Chapter 5 you attended a governors conference. Building on that experience, create a chart demonstrating ways in which the federal government is or is not meeting the political and economic interests of your region.

2. **THE CONSTITUTION** In Chapter 5 you focused on how women could be represented in the new Constitution. Building on that experience, imagine you are a member of a group that represents the rights of free blacks. Create a banner showing two rights you want Congress to include in the Bill of Rights.

3. **WAR** In Chapter 4 you served as a member of Congress overseeing the American war effort. Building on that experience, imagine you are a member of the War Department. Create a chart showing how you will coordinate supplies for the American army and navy during the War of 1812. Use icons to represent supplies.

American Letters

Revolutionary Literature

The Revolutionary era inspired many writers to take up the cause of liberty. Fiery orator and author Thomas Paine wrote pamphlets and songs urging the American colonists to fight for their freedom from Great Britain. During the war, women writers—among them dramatist and poet Mercy Otis Warren—encouraged American women to participate in the struggle. After the war, African American mathematician and almanac writer Benjamin Banneker argued that the liberty fought for in the Revolution should be applied to enslaved African Americans.

▲ **Mercy Otis Warren**

Liberty Tree

by Thomas Paine

In a chariot of light from the regions of day,
    The Goddess of Liberty came;
Ten thousand celestials[1] directed the way,
    And hither conducted the dame.
A fair budding branch from the gardens above,
    Where millions with millions agree,
She brought in her hand as a pledge of her love,
    And the plant she named *Liberty Tree.*

The celestial exotic struck deep in the ground,
    Like a native it flourish'd and bore;
The fame of its fruit drew the nations around,
    To seek out this peaceable shore.
Unmindful of names or distinctions they came,
    For freemen like brothers agree;
With one spirit endued,[2] they one friendship pursued,
    And their temple was *Liberty Tree.*

Beneath this fair tree, like the patriarchs of old,
    Their bread in contentment they ate,
Unvex'd with the troubles of silver and gold,
    The cares of the grand and the great.
With timber and tar they Old England supply'd,
    And supported her pow'r on the sea;
Her battles they fought, without getting a groat,[3]
    For the honor of *Liberty Tree.*

But hear, O ye swains,[4] 'tis a tale most profane,
    How all the tyrannical powers,
Kings, Commons and Lords, are uniting amain,[5]
    To cut down this guardian of ours;
From the east to the west blow the trumpet to arms,
    Thro' the land let the sound of it flee,
Let the far and the near all unite with a cheer,
    In defense of our *Liberty Tree.* ❖

---

1 angels
2 endowed
3 British coin made of silver, worth four pennies
4 country youths
5 with strength and speed

From To the Hon. J. Winthrop, Esq.[1]

by Mercy Otis Warren

    Lamira wish'd that freedom might succeed,
But to such terms what female ere[2] agreed?
To British marts forbidden to repair. . . .

    The good, the wise, the prudent, and the gay,
Mingle their tears, and sighs for sighs repay;
Deep anxious thought each gen'rous bosom fills,
How to avert the dread approaching ills;
Let us resolve on a small sacrifice,
And in the pride of Roman matrons rise;
Good as Cornelia,[3] or a Pompey's[4] wife,
We'll quit the useless vanities of life.

▲ **Liberty Displaying the Arts and Sciences,** *by Samuel Jennings*

Amidst loud discord, sadness, and dismay,
Hope spread her wing, and flit across the away:
Thanks to the sex, by heavenly hand design'd,
Either to bless, or ruin all mankind.

A sharp debate ensu'd on wrong and right,
A little warm, 'tis true, yet all unite,
At once to end the great politic strife,
And yield up all but real wants of life. ❖

---

1 Patriot who requested a poem urging women to boycott
   British goods
2 ever
3 Roman woman who, after the death of her husband, refused to
   remarry and was devoted to her sons and their education
4 Roman general

From *Letter to Thomas Jefferson*

by Benjamin Banneker

Maryland, Baltimore County
Near Ellicotts' Lower Mills, August 19th, 1791

Thomas Jefferson,
Secretary of State.

. . .

Sir, suffer me to recall to your
mind that time in which the arms
and tyranny of the British Crown
were exerted with every powerful effort in order to reduce you
to a State of Servitude, look back
I entreat you on the variety of

dangers to which you were exposed;
reflect on that time . . . and you cannot
but be led to a serious and grateful
sense of your miraculous and provi-
dential preservation; you cannot but
acknowledge that the present freedom
and tranquility which you enjoy you
have mercifully received and that it is
the peculiar blessing of Heaven.

This sir, was a time in which you
clearly saw into the injustice of a state
of slavery and in which you had just
apprehensions of the horrors of its
condition, it was now, sir, that your
abhorrence thereof was so excited,
that you publickly held forth this true
and valuable doctrine, which is worthy
to be recorded and remembered in all
succeeding ages. "We hold these truths
to be self-evident, that all men are created equal, and that they are endowed by their creator with certain unalienable rights, that among these
are life, liberty and the pursuit of happiness." . . .

But, sir, how pitiable is it to reflect that although
you were so fully convinced of the benevolence of
the Father of mankind and of his equal and impartial
distribution of those rights and privileges which he
had conferred upon them, that you should at the
same time counteract his mercies in detaining by
fraud and violence so numerous a part of my
brethren under groaning captivity and cruel oppression, that you should at the same time be found guilty
of that most criminal act which you professedly
detested in others with respect to yourselves.

Sir, I suppose that your knowledge of the situation
of my brethren is too extensive to need a recital
here; neither shall I presume to prescribe methods
by which they may be relieved, otherwise than by
recommending to you and all others to wean yourselves from those narrow prejudices which you have
imbibed with respect to them and as Job proposed to
his friends, "put your souls in their souls stead." ❖

THINKING AND WRITING ABOUT LITERATURE

1. In Thomas Paine's song, what does the "Liberty Tree" stand for?
2. In Mercy Otis Warren's poem, how does the author inspire
   women to support the revolutionary effort?
3. What is Benjamin Banneker trying to convince Thomas Jefferson
   to do? Summarize his argument.

Strategies for Success

RECOGNIZING FALLACIES IN REASONING

A fallacy is a mistaken idea; a fallacy in reasoning results in an unsound argument, or a mistaken, unsupported conclusion. Such fallacies in historical writing often produce statements that sound true but are not. Most reasoning errors occur either in determining cause and effect or in drawing conclusions. (You may want to review Identifying Cause and Effect beginning on page 989.) Following are some of the most common types of fallacies, with examples:

- **Single cause** is identifying only one cause for a major event while ignoring other causes.

    Example: *The ideas of the Enlightenment were the source of Americans' revolutionary zeal.*

History is complex. Events are seldom the result of a single cause. The Revolution was driven by social, political, and economic forces as well as ideas.

- **Coincidence as cause** means attributing the cause of one event to another that occurred earlier or at the same time—just because of the timing or *chronology* (the order) of the events.

    Example: *The U.S. victory at the Battle of New Orleans brought an end to the War of 1812.*

As you have read, the Treaty of Ghent, which ended the War of 1812, was negotiated *before* the Battle of New Orleans. But people learned of the battle and the treaty at the same time. Thus many people assumed that the battle led to the war's end.

- **Irrelevant evidence** means basing a conclusion on information that does not apply to it. Facts that support one conclusion may be useless regarding another.

    Example: *The Constitutional Convention was a success because Thomas Jefferson and John Adams were away in Europe and unable to participate.*

Evidence must be logically presented to support a conclusion. Jefferson's and Adams's absence from the Convention is a fact, and their participation would probably have been significant. But there is no logical or relevant relationship between the Convention's success and their being in Europe.

How to Recognize Fallacies in Reasoning

1. **Read the information carefully.** Find the main ideas and evaluate them.
2. **Determine the order of events.** Decide whether the order of events contributed to a cause-and-effect relationship. Remember that chronology is not always an indicator of cause and effect.
3. **Study the reasoning.** Ask yourself: Are the arguments logical? Have cause-and-effect connections been proven? Does the conclusion follow from the facts given?

Applying the Strategy

Review the account of the War of 1812 in Chapter 6, particularly the subsection "Congress Declares War," on pages 212–13. Then analyze the following statement for a fallacy in reasoning.

> The War of 1812 came to an end in 1814, as Federalist delegates from the antiwar meeting known as the Hartford Convention arrived in Washington, D.C., to demand action.

The statement contains a fallacy of "irrelevant evidence." Tired of the armed struggle, Great Britain and the United States reached a negotiated settlement while the secret Hartford meeting was in progress. The Federalists' opposition had no effect on the war's outcome.

Practicing the Strategy

Examine the following statements for fallacies in reasoning. Then, on a separate sheet of paper, list and explain any fallacies you have found.

1. Pontiac's rebellion ended because his forces failed to acquire military aid from the French.
2. The fact that the Bill of Rights was not added until after the Constitution was ratified shows that protection of individual liberties was not a part of the debate over the Constitution.
3. The U.S. offer of $15 million lured Napoléon Bonaparte of France into selling the territory of Louisiana.

BUILDING YOUR PORTFOLIO

Outlined below are four projects. Independently or cooperatively, complete one and use the products to demonstrate your mastery of the historical concepts involved.

1 WAR
The United States experienced many threats to its security between 1775 and 1815. Using the portfolio materials you designed in chapters 4 and 6, create an organizational chart that illustrates how the War Department will coordinate both the recruitment of troops and the provision of necessary supplies in the future.

2 DEMOCRATIC RIGHTS
The right to protest is one of many rights that colonists defended during the Revolution. Using the portfolio materials you designed in chapters 4 and 5, hold a debate between government officials and protesting citizens that focuses on the government's right to tax versus the citizens' right to oppose unfair taxes.

3 THE CONSTITUTION
The framers of the Constitution were determined to create a representative government. Using the portfolio materials you designed in chapters 5 and 6, write a petition to your state legislature asking members to modify the state constitution to include rights for women and free blacks.

4 POLITICS
Although George Washington hoped that the new nation would be spared from disunity, sectionalism encouraged the rise of political parties. Using the portfolio materials you designed in chapters 5 and 6, write a political party platform that addresses the concerns and interests of the states in your region. Your platform should outline the philosophy of the party, discuss specific issues affecting your region, and demonstrate how your party proposes to deal with those issues.

Video Review
In assigned groups, develop an outline for a video collage of America in the years between 1763 and 1815. Choose images that best illustrate the major topics of the period. Write a script to accompany the images. Assign narrators to different parts of the script, and present your video collage to the class.

Further Reading
Faber, Doris, and Harold Faber. *The Birth of a Nation.* Scribner (1989). Examination of the significant events from the organization of the U.S. federal government to the election of John Adams as president.

Hibbert, Christopher. *Redcoats & Rebels: The American Revolution through British Eyes.* Norton (1990). The War for Independence as seen through the eyes of the British.

Lavender, David S. *The Way to the Western Sea.* Doubleday (1990). Recreation of the key events surrounding Lewis and Clark's expedition.

Marrin, Albert. *1812: The War Nobody Won.* Atheneum (1985). Overview of the causes and major effects of the War of 1812.

Shorto, Russell. *Tecumseh and the Dream of an American Indian.* Silver Burdett Press (1989). Account of Tecumseh's struggle to forge an alliance among Native Americans.

Amelia Bloomer causes a sensation in 1050 by wearing pants beneath a short skirt—a fashion soon called "bloomers."

◆ The American People

POPULATION DENSITY

People per Square Mile

	1860	1990

Source: *Bureau of the Census*

◆ Hot off the Presses

1823 James Fenimore Cooper writes *The Pioneers*—considered by some to be the first truly American novel.

1827 *Freedom's Journal* is first African American newspaper.

1828 *Cherokee Phoenix* is first newspaper published in a Native American language—Cherokee.

1857 *Scientific American* magazine warns that the rise in literacy threatens whale population: more people read by light of whale oil lamps.

1865 Chilean writer and statesman Benjamín Vicuña Mackenna founds *La voz de America*—first periodical to promote unity of the Americas.

◀ **Benjamín Vicuña Mackenna**

◆ What Your Dollar Buys

1847 First national postage stamps are the 5¢ Franklin and 10¢ Washington; by 1851 a half-oz. letter costs 3¢ to send if prepaid, 5¢ if not.

1860 A shave at Tony Delight's barbershop in Chicago costs 6¢, a haircut 12¢, a shampoo 25¢.

1863 Baseball game admission is 10¢–25¢.

▼ **Championship game between Philadelphia Athletics and Brooklyn Atlantics**

◆ Fashion Plate

Shaving is a must for all men. In 1830 four men attack bearded Joseph Palmer in Massachusetts, wanting to shave him.

For an "hourglass figure," upper-class women wear their corsets so tight they can barely breathe; dresses are made from up to 20 yds. of fabric and weigh (with petticoats) up to 30 lbs.

In 1865 John Stetson makes the 10-gallon hat—a mispronunciation of the 10 "galloons" (decorative braids) worn on many Stetsons.

▼ **1850s baseball displayed in the Hall of Fame**

ECKFORD vs HARLEM 13–9 Oct. 12th 1858.

UNIT 3

Growth and Change

1815–1860

The Granger Collection, New York

◀ An "hourglass figure"

▼ 1857 sewing machine

The Granger Collection, New York

❖ American Science and Manufacturing

1834 African American Henry Blair receives patent for corn harvester.

1839 Telegraph inventor Samuel F. B. Morse produces first photographic portrait in America. In 1840 astronomer John Draper photographs the moon!

1846 Elias Howe patents the sewing machine.

1853 In New York, Native American chef George Crum makes first potato chips.

1854 First passenger elevator, invented by Elisha Otis, is installed in New York City.

1858 First dinosaur skeleton in America is excavated in New Jersey.

1858 Ezra Warner invents can opener; people no longer need a hammer and chisel to eat their beans.

❖ At Your Leisure

1818 Scots introduce golf to America.

1821 The African Company, first African American acting troupe, performs in New York.

1830s Fandango, a lively Spanish dance that can last several days, is popular in the California territory.

1836 About 30 circuses, one led by P. T. Barnum, travel the country.

1845 New York Knickerbockers become first baseball club.

1850s Gambling and horse racing are favorite pastimes—2,000 professional gamblers work the riverboats.

▲ Early 1800s circus poster

Chapter 7

1815–1845

NATIONALISM AND ECONOMIC GROWTH

FOCUS

UNDERSTANDING THE MAIN IDEA

The War of 1812 filled Americans with national pride and confidence in the future. The U.S. government began to assert a stronger foreign policy and to promote the growth of the domestic economy. A new spirit of democracy swept the nation, as symbolized by "the man of the people," Andrew Jackson.

THEMES

■ **ECONOMIC DEVELOP-MENT** What are some of the factors that might influence a region's economic development? Why might regions within a large country develop different economies?

■ **TECHNOLOGY AND SOCIETY** How might new technologies promote economic growth?

■ **DEMOCRATIC VALUES** How might economic change lead to greater political participa-tion by certain groups?

1816	1820	1825	1830	1841
James Monroe elected president.	Missouri Compromise passed.	Erie Canal completed.	Indian Removal Act passed.	John Tyler succeeds to presidency.

The War of 1812, although producing no clear-cut victory for the United States, proved that the country could stand up to a major European power. Americans began to believe that the United States could become a power in its own right, free from Europe's influence and control.

Verdict of the People (1855)
by George Caleb Bingham

The Boatmen's National Bank, St. Louis, Missouri

*I*n 1828 Fanny Wright, a world traveler, social reformer, and sometime U.S. resident, delivered a Fourth of July speech at New Harmony, Indiana. She praised the United States as the protector of "human liberty [and] the favored scene of human improvement." Soon, she predicted, "all mankind" would celebrate "the Jubilee of Independence."

The United States was far from granting liberty to all in 1828, as Native Americans and enslaved African Americans well knew. The nation also faced growing sectional differences. Yet most Americans of the time would have cheered Wright's speech. Americans during this period celebrated the Fourth of July with zest. One British visitor noted that American national pride "blazes out everywhere and on all occasions."

The new confidence that burst forth in this era took many forms. The United States built new roads and canals, developed new industries, launched a period of economic growth, secured its borders, and warned Europe to stay out of Latin America.

Fanny Wright

Section 1

THE RISE OF NATIONALISM

FOCUS

■ How did the War of 1812 help strengthen the U.S. economy? What weaknesses did the war reveal?

■ What did the American System attempt to accomplish?

■ How did U.S. foreign policy reflect a growing sense of nationalism?

The War of 1812 was a turning point for the United States. The young nation's stand against Great Britain gave Americans confidence and pride in their country. But the war also brought to light weaknesses in the nation's financial and transportation systems. Following the war, government leaders took steps to remedy these problems and to secure the nation's borders.

Flag of the United States, 1818

The Granger Collection, New York

NATIONALISM TAKES ROOT

The United States did not gain territory from the War of 1812. But confirmation of the young Republic's independence from Europe was vastly more important than any spoils of war. The war stirred a new sense of **nationalism**, or national pride and loyalty. The United States had successfully stood up to Great Britain! Americans for the first time began to believe—not just hope—that their new nation would survive and prosper. Baltimore newspaper editor Hezekiah Niles captured the growing economic vitality of the United States in an 1815 editorial in his *Niles' Weekly Register:*

66 *The republic, reposing [resting] on the laurels of a glorious war, gathers the rich harvest of an honorable peace.* Everywhere the sound of the axe is heard, opening the forest to the sun and claiming for agriculture the range of the buffalo. Our cities grow and towns rise up as by magic. . . . The busy hum of 10,000 wheels fills our seaports. . . . The *republic lives,* and in honor! 99

The war had given U.S. manufacturing a big boost. With the flow of European products all but stopped by embargoes and naval blockades, Americans had been forced to produce goods themselves. U.S. merchants used the opportunity to build new factories. The number of New England cotton mills, for example, jumped by 94 between 1805 and 1815.

But the war also revealed weaknesses in the nation's financial system. By mid-1814 the war had drained the U.S. Treasury. Without the Bank of the United States, which Congress had refused to recharter in 1811, the Treasury had to rely on state banks for loans. Instead of borrowing from one central bank, the government had to negotiate with scores of banks.

Securing loans was only part of the problem, however. Each bank printed its own notes, often in amounts far exceeding the **specie**—the gold or silver coin—that the bank held to back up the notes. As a result, banks often refused to accept one another's notes. Thus the government ran the risk of borrowing from one bank money that it could not deposit in another. New England banks, for instance, regularly refused to accept bank notes from the South or the West.

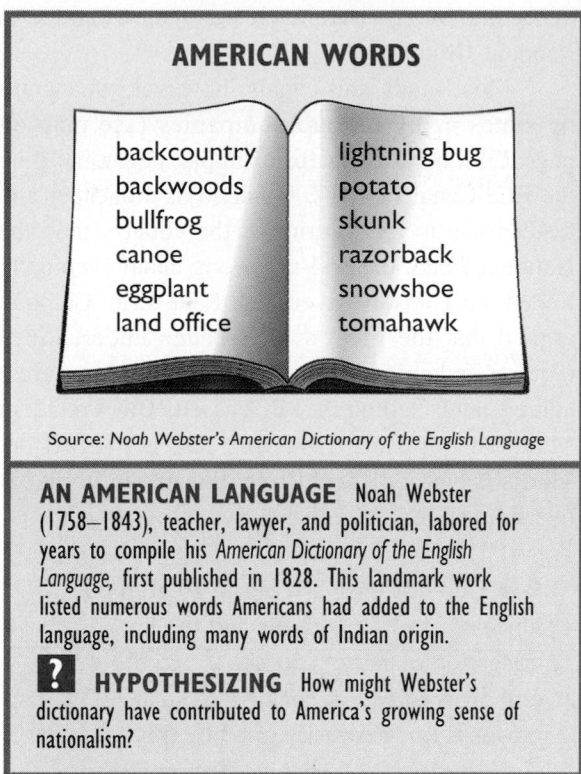

AMERICAN WORDS

backcountry	lightning bug
backwoods	potato
bullfrog	skunk
canoe	razorback
eggplant	snowshoe
land office	tomahawk

Source: *Noah Webster's American Dictionary of the English Language*

AN AMERICAN LANGUAGE Noah Webster (1758–1843), teacher, lawyer, and politician, labored for years to compile his *American Dictionary of the English Language*, first published in 1828. This landmark work listed numerous words Americans had added to the English language, including many words of Indian origin.

? **HYPOTHESIZING** How might Webster's dictionary have contributed to America's growing sense of nationalism?

■■ **The War of 1812 led to a boom in U.S. manufacturing but revealed weaknesses in the nation's financial and transportation systems.**

THE AMERICAN SYSTEM

While the War of 1812 convinced many older Republicans to support a stronger federal government, many younger party members had already been thinking in national terms. Chief among these "nationalists" was Congressman Henry Clay of Kentucky. After the war, Clay began to push for a program of federal support for economic development. Clay's program, which came to be called the **American System**, had three main features: (1) a national bank to provide sound currency and serve as the government's banker; (2) a protective tariff to encourage industrial development; and (3) a national transportation system to unite northern manufacturers, western farmers, and southern planters.

Banking and industry. By 1816 the public cry for a sound national currency was growing. Even Republican President Madison, who had opposed the First Bank of the United States, declared in his annual message to Congress that the establishment of a national bank warranted consideration.

Clay and other nationalists in Congress took this message as a sign that Republicans in Congress would no longer oppose the creation of a national bank. On January 8, South Carolina's John C. Calhoun introduced a bill to charter the Second Bank of the United States. President Madison signed the bill on April 10, 1816.

Clay's call for a protective tariff also met with approval. After the Treaty of Ghent was signed, British-made goods had again flooded American ports. New U.S. manufacturers, unable to sell their goods as cheaply as the much larger British firms, demanded protective measures. Congress responded by passing the **Tariff Act of 1816**, which put a 25 percent duty on most imported

Wartime also underscored the nation's transportation problems. With sea trade blocked by British ships, merchants had to transport goods over slow and costly land routes. Goods, although usually abundant and cheap where they were produced, became scarce and expensive in other areas. In 1813, for example, sugar that sold for $9 per 100 pounds in New Orleans cost $40 in New York.

By 1815 many Republicans—former opponents of a strong central government—were calling for national measures to promote manufacturing, strengthen the financial system, and improve transportation. The war won them over to the Federalist view that a strong America needed a balance among agriculture, manufacturing, and commerce. Even Jefferson had a change of heart. "To be independent for the comforts of life," he wrote a colleague, "we must fabricate [make] them ourselves. We must now place the manufacturer by the side of the agriculturist."

▶ **During this period, state banks issued their own currency. A five-dollar bank note from the Bank of Cincinnati is shown here.**

▲ *The Book Bindery,* a watercolor by an anonymous American artist, shows women workers.

factory goods. This made imported goods more expensive than similar U.S.–made goods.

The tariff had wide support among northern manufacturers and among westerners and some southerners who hoped to benefit from industrial development. However, New England importers and southern planters who relied on British trade opposed the tariff. Congressman John Randolph of Virginia saw the tariff as a conflict between southern planters who "bear the whole brunt of the war and taxation" and northern manufacturers who benefited from the tariff. Arguments like Randolph's arose repeatedly after 1816 as sectional economic interests began to override calls for national economic growth. Even Calhoun, among the tariff's strongest defenders, became a champion of southern interests by the 1820s.

Internal improvements. In 1817, though, Calhoun was still a nationalist. In February he introduced a bill to fund a national system of roads and canals. "Let us . . . bind the republic together with a perfect system of roads and canals," Calhoun told Congress. "Let us conquer space." Congress was receptive. The difficulty of transporting goods and troops during the war had convinced most people of the need for such **internal improvements**.

Some progress had already been made on a national transportation system. During Jefferson's presidency, Congress had authorized a paved highway from Cumberland, Maryland, across the mountains into the western territories. In 1811 construction of the National (or Cumberland) Road began. By 1819 it reached as far as present-day Wheeling, West Virginia. (It was later extended to Vandalia, Illinois.)

Most roads and canals, however, were built by states or by private companies (see map on page 233). New York, for example, began building the Erie Canal in 1817. Intended as a cheaper and faster route to the interior of the country than the National Road, the 363-mile-long canal eventually linked the Hudson River with Lake Erie. Calhoun argued that the great scale of such undertakings required federal aid. Enough members of Congress agreed, and Calhoun's bill passed. But President Madison opposed it. As his last act in office, Madison vetoed the bill on the grounds that it overstepped federal powers:

> ❝ I am not unaware of the great importance of roads and canals and the improved navigation of water courses . . . to the general prosperity. But seeing that such a power is not expressly given by the Constitution, . . . I have no option but to withhold my signature from it. ❞

■■ **The American System attempted to strengthen the economy with proposals for a national bank, a protective tariff, and a national transportation system.**

MONROE AND FOREIGN POLICY

In 1816 Congressional Republicans nominated Madison's secretary of state, James Monroe of Virginia, to run for president. Monroe easily defeated the Federalist candidate, Senator Rufus King of New York. The Federalist party had angered many Americans by its opposition to the War of 1812. The party was losing political power even in New England, long a Federalist stronghold.

The collapse of the Federalist party initiated a period of political harmony in the United States known as the Era of Good Feelings. President Monroe moved quickly to bring the same harmony to foreign relations.

Relations with Great Britain. After the War of 1812, the United States and Great Britain continued to sail warships on the Great Lakes.

Monroe, fearing further conflict, ordered Acting Secretary of State Richard Rush to negotiate a disarmament plan with British foreign minister Charles Bagot. In the resulting **Rush-Bagot Agreement** of 1817, each nation pledged to limit its military presence on the lakes to a few armed ships.

Next, Monroe moved to define the northern boundary of the Louisiana Purchase. In the **Convention of 1818** Great Britain and the United States set the U.S.–Canadian border at the 49th parallel west to the Rocky Mountains. Great Britain agreed to occupy **Oregon Country**—the disputed area of the Pacific Northwest—jointly with the United States for 10 years, with a boundary to be set later. The border agreement between the two North American neighbors was one of the most important outcomes of the War of 1812.

Relations with Spain. Settling border disputes with Spain proved much trickier. In 1812 the United States incorporated West Florida (a strip of land on the Gulf of Mexico in present-day

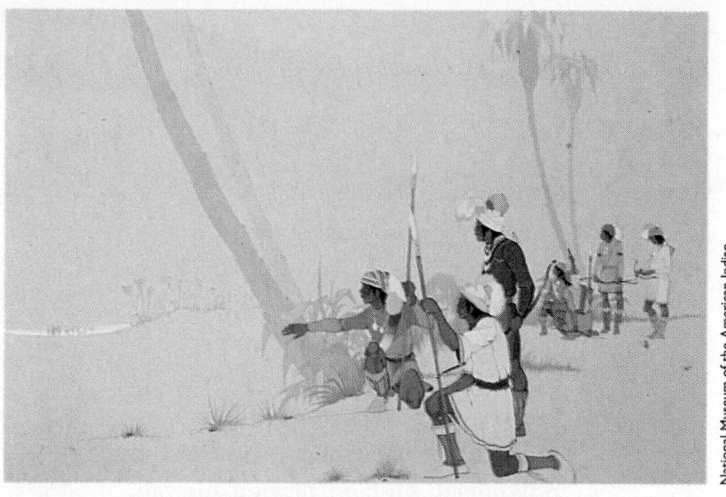

▲ *The Intruders* (1966) by Native American artist Jerome Tiger portrays the Florida home of the Seminoles.

Mississippi and Alabama) into the Mississippi Territory on the grounds that it was part of the Louisiana Purchase. Spain, preoccupied with war in Europe at the time, only protested.

Then in 1818 General Andrew Jackson went into East Florida (present-day Florida) to pursue a group of Seminoles who had been harboring runaway slaves and attacking U.S. border settlements.

U.S. Boundaries, 1820

SECURING U.S. BORDERS The Convention of 1818 and the Adams-Onís Treaty settled major U.S. boundary disputes with Great Britain and Spain.

? ABSOLUTE LOCATION About how many miles was the permanent boundary agreed upon by the Convention of 1818? What was its absolute location?

Albers Equal-Area Projection

Claimed by U.S., ceded to Great Britain in 1818

British Territory

49th Parallel

49° N

Disputed

PACIFIC OCEAN

Oregon Country

ROCKY MOUNTAINS

42nd Parallel

Lake of the Woods

0   225   450 Miles
0   225   450 Kilometers

Great Lakes

Michigan Territory

Mississippi R.

ME

VT NH

NY MA CT RI

42° N

40° N

The United States and Great Britain jointly occupied Oregon Country until 1846, long past the 10 years called for by the Convention of 1818.

Unorganized Territory

PA NJ

IL IN OH

MD DE

VA

Spanish Territory

Arkansas River
Red River

Missouri Territory

KY

Arkansas Territory

TN

NC

SC

ATLANTIC OCEAN

70° W

120° W

Sabine R.

LA

MS AL GA

By the terms of the Adams-Onís Treaty, Spain ceded East Florida to the United States and gave up all claims to West Florida.

Unorganized Territory

Gulf of Mexico

90° W   80° W

Convention of 1818
Adams-Onís Treaty of 1819
Louisiana Purchase
Florida Cession
British Cession of 1818

JAMES MONROE
1758–1831

**in office
1817–1825**

James Monroe was the last president to have fought in the Revolutionary War as well as the last of the "Founding Fathers" to occupy the White House. Indeed, Monroe looked very much the 18th-century statesman. He wore a powdered wig and draped his tall frame in the fashion of an earlier age: cutaway coat, waistcoat, knee britches, long stockings, and buckled shoes.

Monroe's generally quiet and modest manner matched his elegant appearance. In fact, his longtime friend Thomas Jefferson remarked that Monroe was "a man whose soul might be turned wrong side outward, without discovering a blemish to the world."

James Monroe

Jackson, unable to catch those responsible, instead claimed the territory for the United States. Secretary of State John Quincy Adams denied that President Monroe had authorized Jackson's actions. Nevertheless, Adams offered Spain a choice: either control the Seminoles or give Florida to the United States.

► Father Miguel Hidalgo was a priest in Dolores, Mexico. On September 16, 1810, Hidalgo called on the townspeople to revolt against the Spanish. His speech, known as the "Grito de Dolores," or "Cry of Dolores," launched the war for Mexican independence.

◄ Simon Bolívar, known as "the Liberator," was a South American revolutionary leader who helped fight for the independence of Colombia, Venezuela, and Peru. The new republic of Bolivia was named after him.

Spain decided to deal. In the **Adams-Onís Treaty** (1819), Spain transferred East Florida to the United States for $5 million. In return, the United States made a promise to drop its claim to Texas. The treaty also settled the southern and western boundaries of the Louisiana Purchase. The new border ran in a stair-step fashion to the Rocky Mountains and then along the 42nd parallel to the Pacific Ocean.

The Monroe Doctrine. In reality Spain had little option but to sell Florida. Most of Spain's colonies in Latin America were in rebellion. In 1808 Napoléon, the emperor of France, had seized the Spanish throne. Latin Americans, claiming both opposition to Napoléon and loyalty to the deposed Spanish king, organized independence movements. By 1819 these movements had spread throughout Spanish America.

Most Americans supported the rebellions, which were inspired in part by the American Revolution. Henry Clay hailed the "glorious spectacle of eighteen millions of people struggling to burst their chains and to be free." After formal negotiations with Spain over Florida were concluded, the United States moved to recognize the new republics.

American officials knew, however, that the independence of these new Latin American nations was far from secure. Thus, they were alarmed by reports that France was prepared to supply troops to help Spain retake its former colonies. In an October 1823 letter to former president Thomas Jefferson, President Monroe wrote:

"We would view an interference on the part of the European powers [into Latin America] as an attack on ourselves."

Adding to the unease was a dispute with Russia over territorial rights in the Pacific Northwest. In 1821 Russia had extended its land claims southward to the 51st parallel and had closed the surrounding coastal waters to foreign ships. In July 1823 Secretary of State John Quincy Adams warned the Russian foreign minister that the United States would not tolerate the establishment of *any* new European colonies on the American continents.

President Monroe reaffirmed this view in his annual message to Congress on December 2, 1823. In what came to be called the **Monroe Doctrine**, the president vowed that the United States would not interfere with any existing European colonies in Latin America. But he also warned Europe to keep its hands off the Latin American "governments who have declared their independence and maintained it." The United States, he said, would consider any European attempt to revive old colonies or establish new ones in the Western Hemisphere "as dangerous to our peace and safety." (See page 1004 for the Doctrine.)

 The United States expressed its nationalist spirit by securing its borders and declaring the Americas off-limits to European expansion.

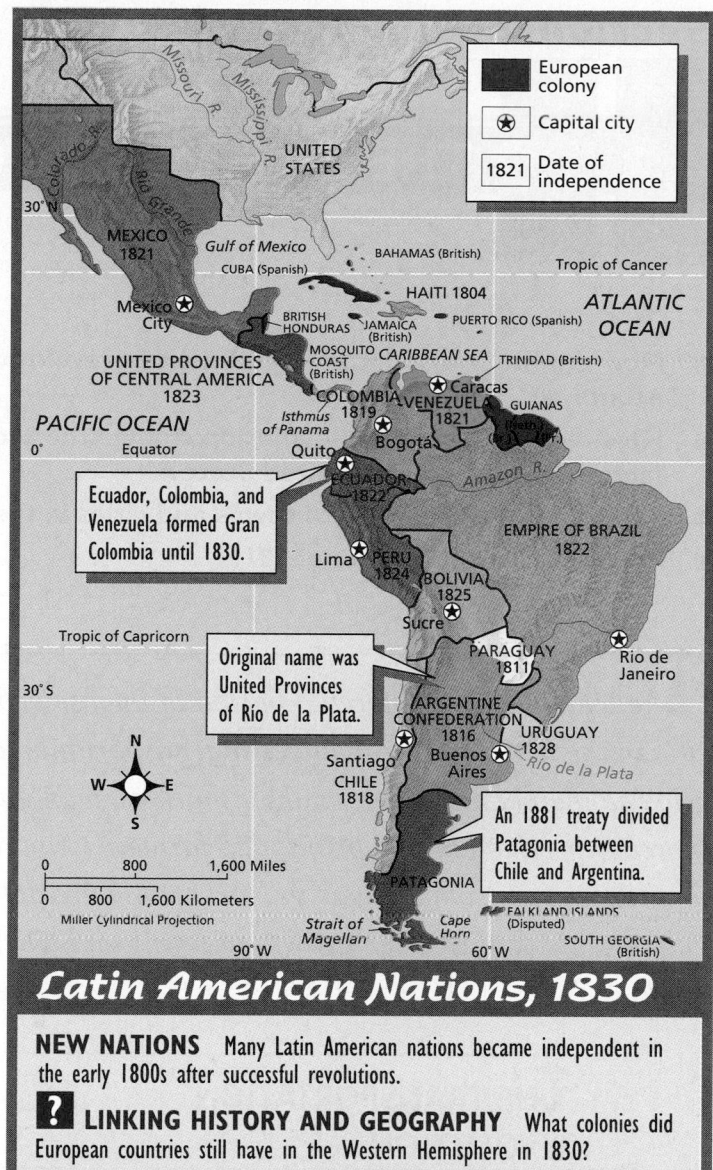

Ecuador, Colombia, and Venezuela formed Gran Colombia until 1830.

Original name was United Provinces of Río de la Plata.

An 1881 treaty divided Patagonia between Chile and Argentina.

Latin American Nations, 1830

NEW NATIONS   Many Latin American nations became independent in the early 1800s after successful revolutions.

❓ **LINKING HISTORY AND GEOGRAPHY**   What colonies did European countries still have in the Western Hemisphere in 1830?

SECTION 1 REVIEW

IDENTIFY and explain the significance of the following: nationalism, specie, Henry Clay, Tariff Act of 1816, internal improvements, James Monroe, Monroe Doctrine.

LOCATE and explain the importance of the following: National (Cumberland) Road, Erie Canal, Oregon Country, Latin America.

1. **MAIN IDEA**   Why was the War of 1812 good for the U.S. economy? What problems did it bring to light?

2. **MAIN IDEA**   What were the main features of the American System?

3. **GEOGRAPHY: LOCATION**   How did the Erie Canal help promote the nation's economic growth?

4. **WRITING TO PERSUADE**   Imagine that you are a newspaper editor in December 1823. Write an editorial describing and either supporting or opposing each of President Monroe's foreign policy actions.

5. **SYNTHESIZING**   Provide evidence for the view that the United States entered a period of growing nationalism after the War of 1812.

THE CHALLENGES OF GROWTH

FOCUS

- How did the transportation and market revolutions affect the U.S. economy?
- How did the Industrial Revolution change the process of manufacturing goods in the United States?
- What led to the growth of towns and cities in the mid-1800s?
- What sparked the Panic of 1819?

The United States entered a period of intense economic expansion in the mid-1800s. Advances in transportation and production allowed merchants to extend their markets, manufacturers to increase production and profit, and farmers to increase output and to transport their goods to market with greater ease. These changes also spurred the growth of towns and cities.

Leaving the Junction by Currier and Ives

THE TRANSPORTATION REVOLUTION

Before 1820 poor transportation made it difficult to sell manufactured goods and farm products between regions. Except for the National Road and a few other major routes connecting eastern cities,

▲ With the completion of Robert Fulton's *Clermont* in 1807, the era of commercial steamboat navigation began. This 1810 painting by Edward L. Henry shows the *Clermont* landing at Croton-on-Hudson, New York.

most roads between cities were little more than crude trails that turned to mud when it rained.

Middle Western farmers faced the most severe transportation problems. Flatboats could float farm products downriver but were useless in moving manufactured goods upriver. Most goods from the East were shipped to the interior of the country by wagon over mountain roads—a slow and costly process.

Canals offered one solution to the transportation problem, but they were expensive and time-consuming to build. By 1816 only about 100 miles of canals had been dug. Canal building soared, however, after New York State completed the Erie Canal in 1825. Impressed that the canal reduced the cost of moving goods between Buffalo and New York City by more than 90 percent, other states launched massive canal projects. By 1840, rivers and canals combined to provide a waterway that stretched from Illinois to the Atlantic.

Improvements in steamboat construction also aided transportation to the interior. The first steam-powered riverboat was launched in 1787, but only with the completion of Robert Fulton's *Clermont* in 1807 could steamboats carry heavy loads upstream. By 1817, steamboats were moving goods up and down the Mississippi River.

Another steam-powered invention, the locomotive, came into commercial use in the 1830s. Trains had one big advantage over steamboats—they could go anywhere tracks could be laid. But they also suffered from a serious drawback—early locomotives were plagued by mechanical troubles. Thus, few people were surprised when the *Tom Thumb*, America's first commercially successful steam locomotive, lost a race against a horse-drawn train in 1830. As an observer noted, all was going well until the locomotive's engine gave out:

66 At first the gray [horse] had the best of it, . . . the engine had to wait until the rotation of the wheels set the blower to work. The horse was perhaps a quarter of a mile ahead when the safety valve of the engine lifted and the thin blue vapor issuing from it showed an excess of steam. The blower whistled, . . . the pace increased, the passengers shouted, the engine gained on the horse, . . . the race was neck and neck, nose and nose—then the engine passed the horse, and a great hurrah hailed the victory. But it was not repeated; for just at this time, . . . the band which drove the pulley, which drove the blower, slipped from the drum, the safety valve ceased to scream, and the engine for want of breath began to wheeze and pant. 99

By 1840, engineers had solved most of the trains' early mechanical problems. Over the next decade companies spent more than $200 million laying nearly 9,000 miles of track. Railroads reached many isolated parts of the country and became symbols of industrialization and the growing interdependence of the national economy.

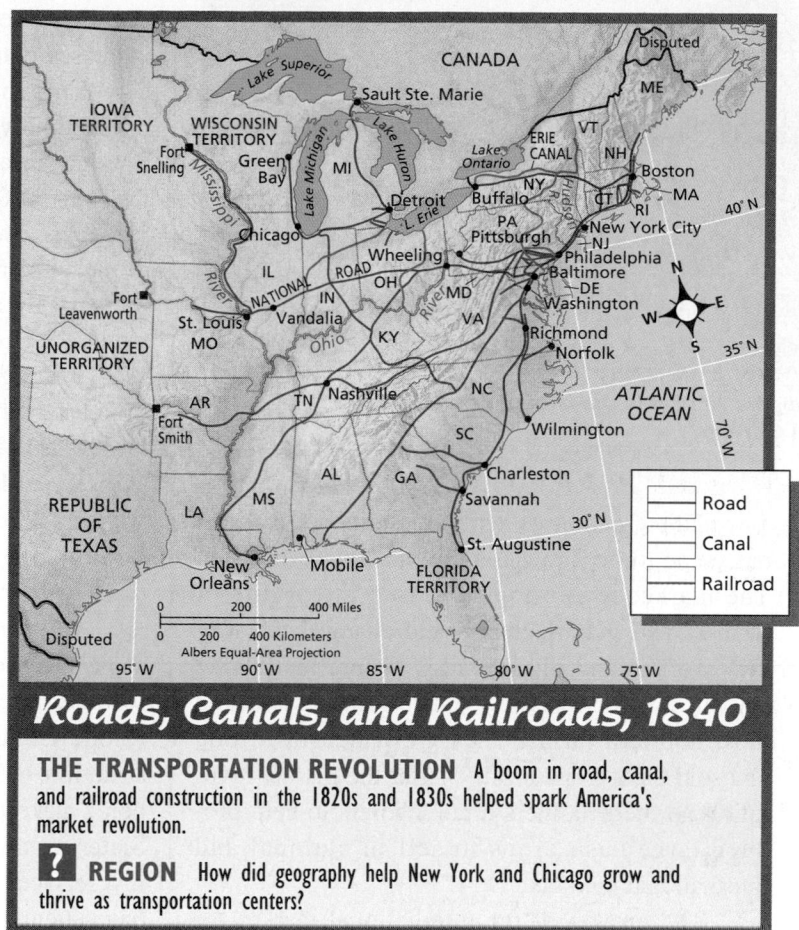

Roads, Canals, and Railroads, 1840

THE TRANSPORTATION REVOLUTION A boom in road, canal, and railroad construction in the 1820s and 1830s helped spark America's market revolution.

❓ **REGION** How did geography help New York and Chicago grow and thrive as transportation centers?

■■ The transportation revolution helped promote economic growth by making it easier to transport goods.

THE MARKET REVOLUTION

By making it easier and cheaper to move farm products, raw materials, and manufactured goods long distances, new transportation systems created national markets for the first time. Regions no longer had to be relatively self-sufficient; they could import some goods and concentrate on producing what was most profitable.

The Middle West, linked to eastern markets by the Erie Canal, specialized in wheat, corn, and hog production. Southern states west of the Appalachian Mountains focused on growing cotton, much of which was shipped to market down the Mississippi to the port of New Orleans. The Northeast, with abundant waterpower, concentrated on manufacturing such products as wool and cotton textiles and specialized machinery.

▲ *Preparing for Market* is the title of this 1856 print by Nathaniel Currier.

This creation of profitable national markets has come to be known as the **market revolution**. The market revolution increased the profits of farmers and manufacturers and changed the way they worked and did business. Before the market revolution, for instance, entire families worked most northern farms. They grew their own food and sold their crops locally. After the market revolution northern farmers hired laborers to help produce large cash crops to sell in national and international markets.

The growth of the international market for cotton increased the profits of southern plantation owners. Southern planters were able to meet the increased demand for cotton because of the **cotton gin**, invented by Eli Whitney in 1793. This machine made it easier to separate, or gin, the seeds from cotton fiber. A person operating a cotton gin could clean 50 times as much cotton in a day as a person working by hand.

■■ **The market revolution opened profitable national and international markets for each region's products.**

EARLY INDUSTRIALIZATION

The market revolution was tied to a change in manufacturing. Before the market revolution, importers and skilled artisans provided most manufactured goods. But as markets grew, artisans could no longer keep up with demand. To produce enough goods, manufacturers reorganized production. They hired more workers and divided tasks to speed up production.

They also began to invest in new machinery that increased output.

This shift from hand production to machine production was part of the **Industrial Revolution**. The Industrial Revolution began in Great Britain in the mid-1700s with the invention of new spinning machines. The machines, some so simple that children could run them, revolutionized the textile industry by allowing for **mass production**—the manufacture of large quantities of goods.

Fearing foreign competition, the British tried to keep their new technology a secret. They outlawed the sale of textile machines abroad and kept skilled textile workers from leaving the country. But some workers, posing as ordinary laborers or farmers, managed to slip out with the machine plans memorized to the last detail.

One such worker was Samuel Slater. Slater came to America in 1789 with hopes of making a fortune. He quickly convinced Moses Brown, a Rhode Island manufacturer, to finance the construction of an English-style spinning mill. "If I don't make as good yarn as they do in England," Slater promised Brown, "I will have nothing for my services, but will throw the whole of what I have attempted over the bridge."

Slater's gamble paid off. In 1790 his spinning machine, tended by 9 children, turned out its first yarn. By 1801 the mill employed more than 100 women and children. Brown and Slater soon had factories all over Rhode Island and Massachusetts.

Inventors also contributed to the rise of U.S. industry. Chief among them was Eli Whitney, who employed **interchangeable parts** in the manufacture of firearms. He reasoned that the various musket parts could be machine-produced in mass

▼ In 1770 James Hargreaves, an English weaver, patented the spinning jenny, which transformed the manufacture of textiles and helped start the Industrial Revolution.

quantities and used interchangeably in making individual weapons. This method would allow workers to assemble more guns in less time than it would take to make them by hand. In 1815 Seth Thomas applied the technique to the manufacture of wooden clocks. Soon workers in Thomas's factory were making some 500 clocks at a time.

New England merchant Francis Cabot Lowell introduced the next great improvement in American manufacturing. Workers in early textile mills made thread that was then delivered, or "put out," to nearby homes where women with hand looms wove it into cloth. To cut costs and increase output, Lowell had machines do everything—from spinning the thread to weaving the cloth—under one roof. This system of manufacturing came to be called the **factory system**. Lowell tested the system at his mill in Waltham, Massachusetts, and his partners later applied it in Lowell, Massachusetts, which was founded after Lowell's death (see map on page 253).

GROWTH IN URBAN POPULATION, 1800–1860

Source: *Historical Statistics of the United States*

GROWTH OF CITIES Spurred by rapid population growth and industrialization, urban areas grew dramatically between 1800 and 1860.

? **BUILDING GRAPH SKILLS** In which part of the country was urban growth most dramatic?

■■ **The Industrial Revolution shifted manufacturing from hand labor to machines, making possible the mass production of goods.**

URBAN GROWTH

Industrialization and the market revolution led to the growth of urban areas. In the 1800s, urban areas were defined as towns or cities with 8,000 or more people. America's urban population jumped from 3.3 percent to 16.1 percent of the nation's total population between 1790 and 1860. This growth was seen mostly in the Northeast and the Middle West, although the southern port cities of New Orleans and Baltimore also grew tremendously during this period.

In the Northeast, Philadelphia's population tripled to more than half a million between 1820 and 1860. New York City's growth was even more spectacular. Between 1820 and 1860 the city's population increased nearly tenfold, from 123,700 to 1,080,320. New York became a major commercial and manufacturing center because it had the nation's best harbor and access to the Hudson River, on which ships could travel some 150 miles inland.

Equally impressive was the birth of new industrial towns, especially along the larger eastern rivers, where rapids were plentiful to run water-powered machinery. For example, the mill town of Lowell, Massachusetts, on the Merrimack River, grew from 2,500 people to 21,000 between 1825 and 1840!

The Middle West also boasted booming urban centers. Growing rapidly during this period were such towns as Buffalo, New York; Pittsburgh, Pennsylvania; Cincinnati, Ohio; and Chicago, Illinois. Initially they grew because of their location near critical points in the transportation system—major roads, rivers, canals, or railroad lines. Soon they also became important business centers, providing goods and services to Middle Western farmers and preparing farm produce for shipment to the Northeast and the South. Among the fastest growing of these cities was Chicago. Between 1833 and 1860 the city's population skyrocketed from about 150 to 109,260.

■■ **In the mid-1800s the market revolution and industrialization led to rapid urban growth, most notably in the Northeast and the Middle West.**

THE PANIC OF 1819

By 1818, largely due to the growth of national markets, all sections of the country prospered. Increasing demand for cotton and farm products encouraged planters, farmers, and land speculators to buy up land, often at high prices. Northern manufacturers, eager for more business, built new mills and factories. To finance these enterprises, many manufacturers borrowed money from state banks, which tended to lend freely on the flimsiest security.

Late in 1818 the Second Bank of the United States attempted to bring state banks under control by ordering them to demand repayment of all loans. The Bank also required state banks to exchange their notes for gold and silver—something few banks could do. The result was the **Panic of 1819**: a chain reaction of bank failures, falling land prices, and foreclosures.

"The banking bubbles are breaking," Secretary of State John Quincy Adams wrote in his diary in May 1819. "The merchants are crumbling in ruin; the manufactures perishing, agriculture stagnating, and distress universal in every part of the country." The nation quickly sank into an economic depression that lasted several years.

■■ **The attempts of the Second Bank of the United States to curb state banks' lending policies helped trigger the Panic of 1819.**

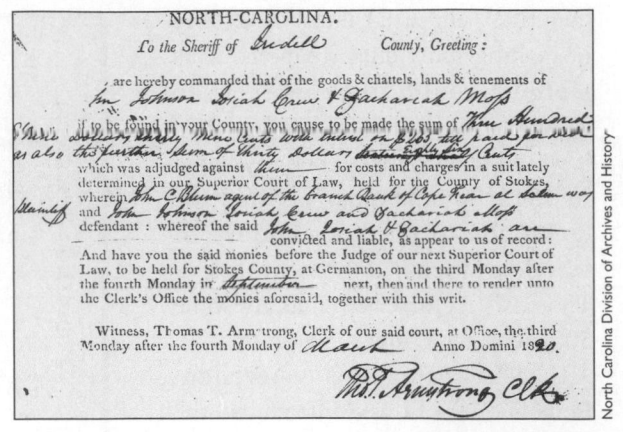

▲ Land foreclosure notices enabled the sheriff of a county to seize all property and goods to pay off debts. This notice was issued in North Carolina in 1820.

James Flint, a Scottish visitor to America, described the harsh effects of the depression on workers:

> ❝ I think that I have seen upward of 1,500 men in quest of work within eleven months past, and many of these declared that they had no money. . . . I have seen several men turned out of boardinghouses. . . . They had no other resource left but to lodge in the woods, without any covering except their clothes. ❞

For these homeless men—and many other Americans—the panic and depression ended the prosperity and optimism of the Era of Good Feelings.

SECTION 2 REVIEW

IDENTIFY and explain the significance of the following: market revolution, cotton gin, Eli Whitney, mass production, Samuel Slater, interchangeable parts, Francis Cabot Lowell, factory system.

LOCATE and explain the importance of the following: Buffalo, New York; Waltham, Massachusetts; Lowell, Massachusetts; Pittsburgh, Pennsylvania; Chicago, Illinois.

1. **MAIN IDEA** How was the U.S. economy helped by the transportation and market revolutions?

2. **MAIN IDEA** What effect did the Industrial Revolution have on the way goods were manufactured?

3. **IDENTIFYING CAUSE AND EFFECT** What factors contributed to the boom in urban growth during the mid-1800s?

4. **WRITING TO INFORM** Imagine that you are one of President Monroe's economic advisers. Write a short report for the president outlining the causes of the Panic of 1819.

5. **LINKING HISTORY AND GEOGRAPHY** Given the geography of the United States, why were railroads a particularly effective form of transportation in the mid-1800s?

THE RISE OF JACKSONIAN DEMOCRACY

FOCUS

- **What role did the Missouri Compromise play in the dispute over slavery?**
- **Why did the election of 1824 give rise to charges of a "corrupt bargain"?**
- **Why did Jackson favor the spoils system and rotation in office?**

*E*conomic matters had a strong effect on national politics. The transportation revolution encouraged westward expansion, which created political conflicts over governing the new western territories. As voting laws changed, politicians had to appeal to a wider range of economic interests. After the Panic of 1819 and the depression, voters wanted politicians who could handle economic problems.

Fabric made to celebrate Jackson's inauguration in 1829

THE MISSOURI COMPROMISE

The United States faced more than economic problems in 1819. The nation was also plagued by political conflict caused by westward expansion. In that year the Missouri Territory, which counted among its population some 10,000 enslaved African Americans, applied for statehood. Because the nation was equally divided between slave states and free states, Missouri's admission as a slave state would tip the congressional balance in favor of the South.

Congressman James Tallmadge of New York tried to amend the Missouri statehood bill to include the gradual elimination of slavery in Missouri. He argued that Congress had already exercised its power to ban slavery in the territories when it passed the Northwest Ordinance in 1787. Slaveholders, seeing this new proposal as an attempt to end slavery everywhere, reacted with alarm and anger. A Georgia congressman pointed a shaking finger at Tallmadge and cried: "You

have kindled a fire which all the waters of the ocean cannot put out, which seas of blood can only extinguish."

| Free state | Slave state |
| Free territory | Slave territory |

Missouri Compromise

EXTENSION OF SLAVERY The Missouri Compromise of 1820 permitted slavery in Missouri but outlawed it in other areas north of the Missouri Compromise Line.

? REGIONS How many free states were there following the compromise? How many slave states?

To end the bitter debate, Henry Clay of Kentucky led Congress in working out the **Missouri Compromise** in 1820. The agreement admitted Missouri as a slave state and Maine as a free state, thus maintaining the balance in Congress. Moreover, slavery was banned in the rest of the Louisiana Purchase north of latitude 36°30´—Missouri's southern boundary.

The Missouri Compromise calmed the sectional crisis, but many Americans still worried that the slavery issue would reemerge. Former president Thomas Jefferson later wrote:

66 This momentous question, like a fire-bell in the night, awakened and filled me with terror. I considered it at once as the [death] knell of the Union. It is hushed, indeed, for the moment. But . . . every new irritation will mark it deeper and deeper. 99

■■ **The Missouri Compromise resolved the crisis over Missouri statehood but left the larger issue of slavery unresolved.**

𝒯HE ELECTION OF 1824

Westward expansion also had an effect on the election of 1824. By the 1820s voting laws were becoming more democratic, particularly in the

▲ **Two campaign medallions from the 1824 election are shown here. One bears the likeness of Andrew Jackson, the other of John Quincy Adams.**

frontier states, where most white adult males could vote. This democratization of voting rights was accompanied by growing opposition to the nomination of presidential candidates by congressional caucus. Thus, in the 1824 election, state nominating conventions played a major role in deciding the list of candidates. The result was a crowded field of regional favorites.

Five candidates—all Republicans—ended up vying for the presidency: William Crawford of Georgia, John C. Calhoun of South Carolina, John Quincy Adams of Massachusetts, Andrew Jackson of Tennessee, and Henry Clay of Kentucky. Crawford, who portrayed himself as the "southern candidate," was the early favorite. But serious

PRESIDENTIAL LIVES
JOHN QUINCY ADAMS
1767–1848

in office 1825–1829

John Quincy Adams resembled his father, John Adams, in his brilliance and self-discipline. He also inherited his father's stern and reserved personality. One observer noted that Adams seemed "hard as a piece of granite and cold as a lump of ice." Adams's coldness contributed to his frustrating and largely unsuccessful presidency.

Adams's major achievements occurred outside

UNITED STATES POSTAGE
JOHN QUINCY ADAMS 1826-1829
6 CENTS 6

his White House years. He was a Harvard graduate, successful lawyer, minister to the Netherlands, U.S. senator, minister to Russia, and secretary of state to President Monroe—all before becoming president. After his presidency, Adams returned to public service. In 1830 Massachusetts voters elected him to the House of Representatives, where he criticized the expansion of slavery.

John Quincy Adams

illness marred his candidacy. Calhoun, although a favorite in the Deep South, failed to build a nation-wide following. He eventually withdrew to become the vice-presidential partner of both Adams and Jackson. Adams, an economic nationalist with antislavery views, had appeal primarily in the Northeast. Jackson, the popular military hero, represented the southern frontier. Clay, the architect of the Missouri Compromise and the American System, drew his support primarily from the Middle West.

Andrew Jackson received the most popular votes, but no candidate won a majority of the electoral votes. In such circumstances the Twelfth Amendment directs the House of Representatives to choose a president from the top three candidates. Having finished fourth, Clay was out of the running. But he was in a position to help determine the winner by recommending that his supporters back a particular candidate. Clay, who considered Jackson unqualified for the presidency, threw his support behind Adams. Adams became president. When Adams then named Clay his secretary of state, Jackson and his followers angrily accused the two men of making a "corrupt bargain." Adams and Clay denied any wrongdoing, but suspicions persisted.

■■ **When the House was forced to decide the outcome of the 1824 election, Clay threw his support behind Adams. When Adams won, Jackson charged that Adams and Clay had made a "corrupt bargain."**

President Adams supported a wide range of federal government projects, from canals and roads to a national university and a standardized system of weights and measures. Yet, owing largely to his desire to avoid "playing politics" and his unwillingness to compromise with Congress, he was unable to accomplish much during his term.

THE ELECTION OF 1828

Jackson, a sharp critic throughout Adams's presidency, resigned from the Senate in 1825 to campaign for the 1828 election. Opponents of the Adams administration rallied around the tall war hero from Tennessee.

BIO GRAPHY

Who was this man so eager to be president? Jackson was born in 1767 in a log cabin on the South Carolina frontier to Scotch-Irish immigrants. Orphaned at 14, he had little formal schooling and was a poor speller. Making his limitation a virtue, he later claimed to have no respect for anyone who knew only one way to spell a word!

After Jackson moved to the Tennessee frontier, one resident described him as a "roaring, rollicking, . . . horse-racing, card-playing, mischievous fellow." He became a successful lawyer, land speculator, and planter. In 1788 Jackson met Rachel Donelson Robards, who was then separated from her husband. Believing Rachel's divorce had been granted, the two were

Andrew Jackson

married in 1791. Her divorce, however, was not finalized until two years later, at which time the Jacksons amid much gossip quickly renewed their vows.

Jackson was the victor at the Battle of New Orleans in the War of 1812 and a ruthless Indian-fighter in campaigns against the Creeks and Seminoles. Soldiers called him "Old Hickory" because he seemed as tough as the strong hardwood. He entered national politics as congressman and then senator from Tennessee. Although a rich lawyer and planter, Jackson

◀ This portrait of Rachel Jackson was painted by Louisa Catherine Strobel. After his wife's death, Jackson wore this miniature wherever he went.

The Hermitage: Home of Andrew Jackson

stressed his military skills and frontier origins to portray himself as a "man of the people."

Jackson's image as a "common man" won the support of farmers, laborers, and frontier settlers. His supporters, having no official name at first, eventually became known as the Democratic party (the origin of today's party of the same name).

Then and Now   CAMPAIGNING

In many ways the presidential race of 1828 was the first modern election campaign. Unlike earlier candidates who relied mainly on party supporters to campaign for them, Andrew Jackson and John Quincy Adams actively pursued votes themselves. They used mass-produced trinkets such as buttons, metal tokens, bandannas, cups, and plates to sway public opinion. Jackson in particular appealed directly to the common voter for support and began campaigning three years before the election.

Today presidential candidates still focus on reaching out to the mass public. They blanket the country with bumper stickers, buttons, and posters. Today's officeseekers also appeal directly to voters, occasionally by touring the country in buses and trains, but more often by airing television

and radio commercials. And most candidates start running for office years before the election, just as Jackson did.

Jackson's 1828 campaign set another modern precedent by employing county and state campaign committees. These committees held parades, barbecues, and rallies to attract voters. Jackson also established a campaign organization of friends and advisers in Nashville to help him plot campaign strategies. His Washington-based correspondence committee was a forerunner of today's Democratic and Republican national committees. An organizational structure that was unusual in 1828 has become a political necessity in modern presidential races.

The 1828 race for president also signaled a profound change in the tone of presidential

▲ Bill Clinton and George Bush are shown debating in Missouri during the 1992 presidential campaign.

campaigns. The race has been called "spectacularly dirty," full of character assassinations and accusations. Indeed, Jackson's and Adams's campaigns focused as much on the candidates' personal qualities as on the issues. The same charge has been leveled against recent presidential campaigns. Although many years have passed since the 1828 election, Jackson and Adams might feel right at home in a modern presidential campaign.

Like many political campaigns today, the 1828 race focused more on personalities than on issues. Each side used personal attacks to win votes. Adams's purchase of a chess set and billiard table for the White House raised charges that he squandered money on "gambling devices." Supporters of Adams labeled Jackson an adulterer because of the circumstances of his marriage to Rachel Robards.

In the end Jackson swept the popular and electoral vote. "The virtuous portion of the people have well sustained me," Jackson rejoiced. "I am filled with gratitude."

Once in office, Jackson showed his appreciation by giving some of his supporters government jobs. This practice became known as the **spoils system**, from the expression "to the victor belong the spoils." Jackson also took steps to reform government bureaucracy by replacing all public servants he judged "unfaithful or incompetent." He believed that government workers who stayed in office too long often forgot that they were servants of the people. Thus he favored **rotation in office**—the periodic replacement of officeholders. Yet Jackson's changes fell far short of complete rotation. During his presidency he replaced only about one tenth to one third of the bureaucracy.

 Jackson backed the spoils system and rotation in office to reward his supporters and to reform government.

COMMENTARY

Jacksonian Democracy

Jackson's popularity reflected changes in American society caused by the market revolution. The old social order, led by the aristocracy, gradually gave way to a society based more on economic success than on birth. Jackson's image as a "self-made" man embodied this new sense of economic opportunity.

From today's perspective, changes in the Jackson era may seem small. Full political rights, including the right to vote, extended only to white males. Most African Americans lived under a brutal slave system; and women, Native Americans, and most free blacks could not vote.

Yet the changes of the early 1800s were significant. Voting rolls swelled as states dropped property requirements for voting and holding office. By 1828, voters, instead of state legislatures, chose presidential electors and most public officials in almost every state. Expanding voting rights paved the way for Jackson's reelection in 1832.

SECTION 3 REVIEW

IDENTIFY and explain the significance of the following: Missouri Compromise, John Quincy Adams, Andrew Jackson, spoils system, rotation in office.

LOCATE and explain the importance of the following: Missouri.

1. **MAIN IDEA** Why did Missouri's petition for statehood lead to a battle in Congress? How was the conflict resolved?

2. **MAIN IDEA** Why did Andrew Jackson charge that John Quincy Adams and Henry Clay had made a "corrupt bargain" in the election of 1824?

3. **IDENTIFYING CAUSE AND EFFECT** How did the election of 1828 signal a broadening of democratic rights?

4. **WRITING TO PERSUADE** Imagine that you are Andrew Jackson's press secretary. Write a defense of the president's support of the spoils system and rotation in office.

5. **GAINING A MULTICULTURAL PERSPECTIVE** Some historians argue that Jacksonian democracy was a limited expansion of democracy at best. What evidence might have led the historians to adopt this view?

Section 4

JACKSON'S POLICIES DEFINE AN ERA

FOCUS

- **Why did the U.S. government force eastern Indians to move westward? How did Native Americans resist removal?**
- **What sparked the nullification crisis?**
- **What factors contributed to the economic crisis of the late 1830s?**
- **How did the Whigs come to power in 1840?**

Andrew Jackson put his stamp on a decade, and his policies shaped the nation for years to come. He pushed for the removal of Native Americans from the East and fought to preserve the Union against sectional tensions. Jackson remained popular with the American people, but by the late 1830s severe economic problems had eroded his party's strength. In 1840 an opposition party, the Whigs, emerged to vie with Jacksonian Democrats for political power.

Statue of mourning Cherokee

A QUESTION OF LAND

Thomas Jefferson had hoped that eastern Indians would become farmers and blend into American society. But white settlers' hunger for land and Native American support for the British during the War of 1812 changed government attitudes. By 1824 many government officials were calling for the removal of all Native Americans to lands beyond the United States' borders.

This change in attitudes had a profound effect on many Native American groups, particularly the Creeks, Chickasaws, Choctaws, Cherokees, and Seminoles in the Southeast. Believing that their best hope for survival lay in adapting to white culture, many had given up hunting and had become farmers. The Cherokees, for example, had shifted to farming in the late 1700s. Over the next several decades, they built towns with thriving agricultural economies. They wrote a constitution modeled on that of the United States, created a judicial system, supported schools, and formed a militia.

BIO GRAPHY
The Cherokees were greatly assisted in their efforts by the work of one man—Sequoya (si-KWOY-uh), or Sikwayi. Sequoya was born in Tennessee sometime between 1760 and 1770 to a Cherokee woman. He variously used the names George Guess and George Gist, which has led some historians to suggest he was the son of Nathaniel Gist, an English explorer and friend of George Washington. Sequoya was a silversmith, blacksmith, and painter. In 1813 he fought against the Creeks as a member of a Cherokee regiment in the U.S. Army.

Although Sequoya neither spoke nor read English, he recognized the value of a written language. He saw how literacy benefited whites by enabling them to spread ideas, keep records, and communicate over long distances. He hoped that literacy

Sequoya
National Portrait Gallery

▶ The Cherokee primer shown here uses symbols based on the writing system created by Sequoya.

would do the same for the Cherokees. For 12 years he worked to create a writing system for the Cherokee language—a process he described as being like catching and taming a wild horse.

The system Sequoya developed contained 86 symbols based on the syllables of spoken Cherokee. Once the symbols were memorized, a person could read or write anything in Cherokee. By 1828 the Cherokees were publishing their own newspaper, the *Cherokee Phoenix*.

𝒥ACKSON'S INDIAN POLICY

Indian efforts to gain white acceptance made little difference. Native Americans in the Southeast occupied millions of acres of fertile land suitable for growing cotton. White farmers and land speculators pressured the government to open that land to white settlement. These farmers and speculators found a friend in Andrew Jackson. He viewed the continued presence of Native Americans in the East as a barrier to "the waves of population and civilization . . . rolling westward."

Jackson cloaked his calls for removal in humanitarian terms. He claimed that Native Americans would, for their own protection, be moved westward, where "their white brothers will not trouble them." In 1830 Congress passed the **Indian Removal Act**, providing for the relocation—by force, if necessary—of Indian nations living east of the Mississippi to Indian Territory in present-day Oklahoma. Indian Territory was part of the larger Indian Country the government had set aside for relocated tribes. Jackson promised eastern Indians the land for "as long as grass grows and water runs. . . . *It will be yours forever.*"

■■ **The U.S. government forced eastern Indians to move in order to open their lands to white settlement.**

Native American resistance. By the end of the decade, most Native Americans had been driven from the Southeast. Few, however, went willingly. They had little reason to believe Jackson's promise of a permanent homeland. Georgia and other southern states had already disregarded federal treaties and limited Indian rights within state boundaries. Georgia was even seizing Indian land and selling it to white settlers.

Fearing further betrayal, many Indians opposed removal. Some wrote appeals to Congress: "Our cause is your own," began one such letter. "It is the cause of liberty and of justice. It is based upon your own principles." Osceola, a Seminole leader, was more defiant:

❝ My Brothers! . . . the white man says I shall go, and he will send people to make me go; but I have a rifle, and I have some powder and some lead. I say, we must not leave our homes and lands. If any of our people want to go west we won't let them; and I tell them they are our enemies, and we will treat them so, for the great spirit will protect us. ❞

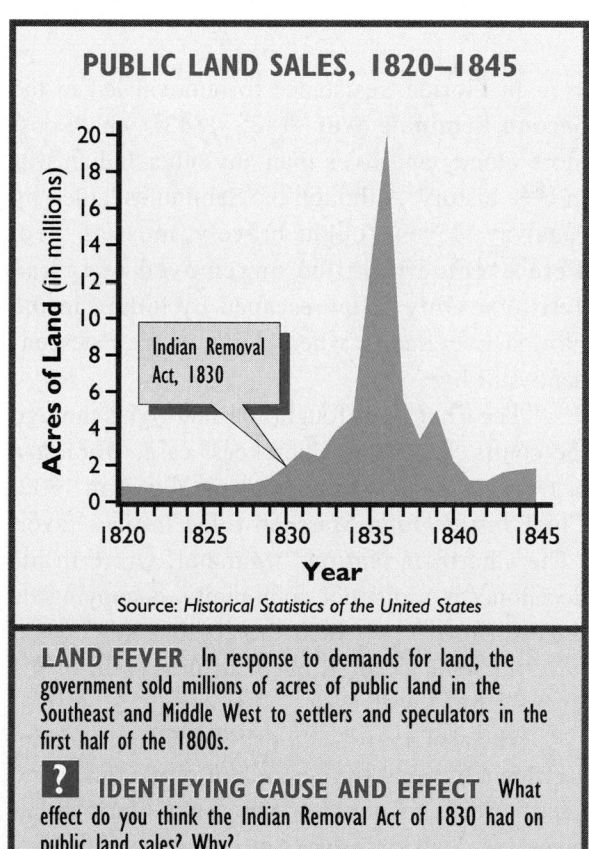

PUBLIC LAND SALES, 1820–1845

Indian Removal Act, 1830

Acres of Land (in millions)

Year

Source: *Historical Statistics of the United States*

LAND FEVER In response to demands for land, the government sold millions of acres of public land in the Southeast and Middle West to settlers and speculators in the first half of the 1800s.

❓ **IDENTIFYING CAUSE AND EFFECT** What effect do you think the Indian Removal Act of 1830 had on public land sales? Why?

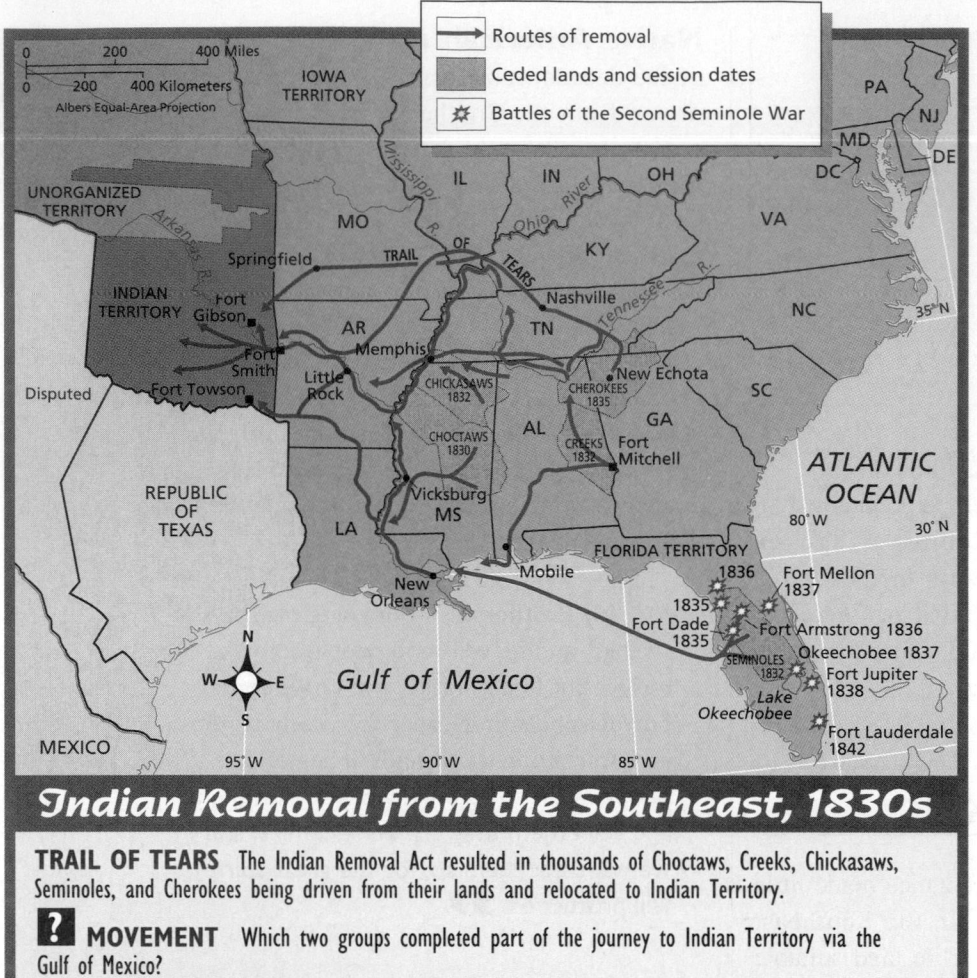

Indian Removal from the Southeast, 1830s

Legend:
- Routes of removal
- Ceded lands and cession dates
- ☀ Battles of the Second Seminole War

TRAIL OF TEARS The Indian Removal Act resulted in thousands of Choctaws, Creeks, Chickasaws, Seminoles, and Cherokees being driven from their lands and relocated to Indian Territory.

❓ MOVEMENT Which two groups completed part of the journey to Indian Territory via the Gulf of Mexico?

"now let him enforce it." The Cherokees, without federal protection, were unable to hold out. In 1835 they were forced to sign a treaty granting all their land to the United States in return for money and land in Indian Territory. They were ordered to move within three years.

■■ Many Native Americans resisted removal: the Seminoles went to war; the Cherokees appealed to the U.S. Supreme Court.

The Trail of Tears. By the 1838 deadline only a few of the some 18,000 Cherokees had moved west. Federal troops began forcing the remaining Cherokees to make the journey to Indian Territory. One U.S. soldier who witnessed the removal later recalled:

> ❝ I saw the helpless Cherokees arrested and dragged from their homes, and driven by bayonet into the stockades. And in the chill of a drizzling rain on an October morning I saw them loaded like cattle or sheep into wagons and started toward the west. ❞

An estimated 4,000 Cherokees died on the 800-mile journey that came to be known as the **Trail of Tears**. "Many fell by the wayside, too faint with hunger or too weak to keep up with the rest," remembered one of the survivors.

> ❝ A crude bed was quickly prepared for these sick and weary people. Only a bowl of water was left within their reach, thus they were left to suffer and die alone. The little children piteously cried day after day. . . . They were once happy children. ❞

In Florida, resistance to removal led to the **Second Seminole War** (1835–1842), which cost more money and lives than any other Indian war in U.S. history. Although the Seminoles, aided by runaway slaves, fought bravely, most of them were eventually killed or removed to Indian Territory. Only a few escaped by hiding in the Florida Everglades, where some of their descendants still live.

The Cherokees fought for their rights through the courts. When the Cherokees' case, ***Worcester v. Georgia***, reached the Supreme Court in 1832, Chief Justice John Marshall ruled in their favor. "The Cherokee Nation," Marshall wrote in his decision, "is a distinct community, occupying its own territory . . . which the citizens of Georgia have no right to enter, but with the assent of the Cherokees themselves."

The victory was short-lived. Georgia—with Jackson's blessing—ignored the Court's ruling and kept on seizing Cherokee land. "John Marshall has made his decision," Jackson was said to declare,

▲ In the early 1830s, under the provisions of the Indian Removal Act, the Choctaws were removed from Mississippi to Indian Territory. About one fourth of some 14,000 Choctaws died along the way. This painting of the journey, entitled *Choctaw Removal* (1966), was painted by Choctaw artist Valjean Hessing.

The Choctaws, Chickasaws, and Creeks also faced removal in the period from 1820 to 1840. During the Chickasaw removal, for example, the death rate was as high as that of the Cherokees during the Trail of Tears. Those who survived were left to rebuild their lives in the strange surroundings of Indian Territory.

𝒯HE NULLIFICATION CRISIS

Indian removal remains one of the Jacksonian era's most controversial legacies. Yet for many Americans at the time, the issue of states' rights seemed of more immediate concern. This issue, having troubled the Republic since its founding, was revived in the 1820s in debates over tariffs.

The doctrine of nullification. To protect U.S. manufacturers, Congress passed in 1828 a new tariff that doubled the rates set in 1816 for some items. Outraged southern planters charged Congress with promoting the interests of the industrial North at the expense of southern agriculture. The tariff would make British goods, on which southerners relied heavily, more expensive. Worse yet, Great Britain might fight back by buying less southern cotton. Thomas Cooper, president of South Carolina College in Columbia, warned that the South would soon have "to calculate the value of the Union, and ask of what use to us is this most unequal alliance."

By 1828 Vice President John C. Calhoun had abandoned his earlier nationalist views. He no longer believed that the national government represented the best interests of his native region, the South. Responding to this tariff, Calhoun wrote an anonymous essay outlining the South's position. The essay argued that the states, as creators of the federal union, had the right to nullify, or refuse to obey, any act of Congress they considered unconstitutional. This view became known as the **doctrine of nullification**.

South Carolina threatens secession. The tariff debate raged for the next two years. In 1830 Senator Robert Hayne of South Carolina, speaking for southern planters, argued for states' rights: "The very life of our system is the independence of the States." He called the 1828 tariff "unauthorized taxation" and warned that the South would resist.

Senator Daniel Webster of Massachusetts, widely recognized as an outstanding orator, rose to defend what he interpreted as an attack against the Northeast. Webster countered that only the Supreme Court had the power to decide whether acts of Congress were unconstitutional. In a moving speech to the Senate, Webster warned that if each state could decide which federal laws to obey, the result would be violence and needless bloodshed. Acceptance of the doctrine would shatter into "broken and dishonored fragments" the "once glorious Union." Webster closed his address with this memorable appeal: "Liberty and Union, now and forever, one and inseparable!"

■■ **Passage of a new tariff in 1828 sparked a bitter states' rights debate in Congress.**

Both sides eagerly awaited some indication of the president's stand on the issue. The answer was not long in coming. At a formal Washington dinner in April 1830, President Jackson rose from his chair and fixed his eyes on Vice President Calhoun. Then holding his glass in the air, he proposed a toast: "Our Union: it must be preserved!" After a moment of silence, Calhoun stood up. His hand trembling, he defiantly challenged: "The Union—next to our liberty, the most dear! May we always remember that it can only be preserved by respecting the rights of the states."

PRESIDENTIAL LIVES

ANDREW JACKSON
1767–1845

in office
1829–1837

As Andrew Jackson's presidency came to an end, well-wishers streamed into Washington, D.C., to say good-bye. "Old Hickory" received thousands of letters and many gifts as well: hats, pipes, canes, a wagon made of hickory, even a 1,400-pound cheese. On his last morning in office, Jackson rode with Martin Van Buren, the president-elect, to the inauguration. The crowds along the road did not cheer for Van Buren but removed their hats in respectful silence for Jackson instead. "For once," an observer noted, "the rising sun was eclipsed by the setting sun."

Jackson returned to the Hermitage, his plantation in Tennessee, where he remained an active, influential force in politics. Eager politicians sought his advice. Though he turned away most politicians, Jackson publicly supported his favorite candidates and causes.

Andrew Jackson

In 1832 Henry Clay attempted a compromise by pushing a slight tariff reduction through Congress. But it was too small a reduction to satisfy South Carolina. In November that state declared the 1828 and 1832 tariffs null and void. South Carolina threatened to secede if the federal government tried to collect tariffs within the state.

A furious Jackson privately warned that "if one drop of blood be shed there in defiance of the laws of the United States, I will hang the first man of them I can get my hands on to the first tree I can find." To calm tensions in South Carolina, Henry Clay convinced Congress to pass a compromise tariff in 1833 that lowered rates over a 10-year period.

At Calhoun's urging, South Carolina—with no support from other southern states—accepted the new tariff. The immediate crisis subsided, but sectional tensions continued to grow.

OPPOSING THE BANK

For all the passion around the issue of states' rights in the 1830s, the Second Bank of the United States may have caused even more excitement. Making the banking issue a personal crusade, Jackson attacked the Bank as a dangerous monopoly that benefited rich investors—many of whom were British—at the expense of the poor, the honest, and the industrious. Such a privileged group should not be allowed to control the nation's money, he

▲ This political cartoon satirizes the collapse of the Second Bank of the United States.

insisted. Americans who disliked the Bank's strict lending policies or simply feared concentrated power tended to agree.

The Bank became a campaign issue when Jackson sought reelection in 1832. Opposing Jackson was Henry Clay, nominee of the National Republicans (the party of John Quincy Adams). Clay, who supported the Bank, decided to force an election-year showdown over it. Though its charter was not due to expire until 1836, in the summer of 1832 Clay pushed a bill through Congress to recharter the Bank.

Jackson vetoed the measure, sparking a great controversy, just as Clay had hoped. Clay vigorously attacked the veto during the campaign. But voters sided with Jackson. He and his running mate, Martin Van Buren of New York, won by a large margin. Jackson then moved to shut down the Bank. The fight had become bitterly personal. "The Bank is trying to kill me, but I will kill it," he grimly vowed.

Jackson stopped depositing federal funds in the national bank. New deposits went to selected state banks chosen for their officers' loyalty to the Democratic party—**pet banks**, as Jackson's enemies called them.

The Bank, however, retained much of its existing federal deposits and still had financial influence. Nicholas Biddle, who had been president of the Bank since 1823, made one final effort to save the institution. He had the Bank tighten credit to force a financial crisis, in hope of convincing Jackson and the American public of the folly of attacking such a stabilizing institution. Instead, this exercise of power by Biddle reinforced Jackson's arguments that the Bank had dangerously concentrated powers that it could use against the public good.

THE PANIC OF 1837

Jackson had won his bank war. But by weakening federal control over the banking system, he also opened the door to financial crisis. Jackson's pet banks issued their own bank notes, often in amounts far exceeding what they could back up with gold or silver. Furthermore, the amount of money in circulation more than doubled between 1830 and 1837, as many banks eased their loan requirements.

Much of the money that was lent was used for land speculation. Speculators bought millions of acres of public land in the Middle West, hoping to make quick profits by reselling it to settlers at higher prices. But as land prices increased, so did the price of everything else. To curb this inflationary spiral and slow the feverish speculation, President Jackson issued the **Specie Circular** in July 1836. This executive order instructed the Treasury to accept only gold and silver (specie) as payment for public land. Because few people had specie, land sales plunged. Many people began demanding that their banks exchange bank notes for gold or silver. As in 1819, banks that could not do so failed. By June 1837, hundreds of banks had gone under.

Contributing to the panic was the economic crisis in Great Britain. Faced with financial

PRESIDENTIAL LIVES

MARTIN VAN BUREN
1782–1862

in office
1837–1841

Martin Van Buren loved stylish living. During his administration the White House was the scene of many galas. And it was common to see him about the streets of Washington riding in his olive green carriage pulled by fine horses in silver-mounted harnesses and attended by uniformed footmen. As a friend recalled, Van Buren was "as polished and captivating a person in the social circle as America has ever known."

Despite his aristocratic tastes, Van Buren was determined to appear friendly and approachable. Thus, he was grieved by his opponents' attacks on him: "Why the deuce is it that they have such an itching for abusing me? I try to be harmless, and positively good natured, and a most decided friend of peace."

problems at home, the British bought less southern cotton. British investors also pulled their money out of the United States, further decreasing the supply of specie. Factories closed; construction projects stood idle. Thousands of workers lost their jobs. In New York City alone, an estimated 50,000 workers were unemployed. In the cold winter of 1837–38, hungry people rioted in the streets of eastern cities. What had begun as a panic soon deepened into a depression that lasted until 1843.

■■ **The economic crisis of the late 1830s was caused by Jackson's monetary policies, easy credit, land speculation, and British economic problems.**

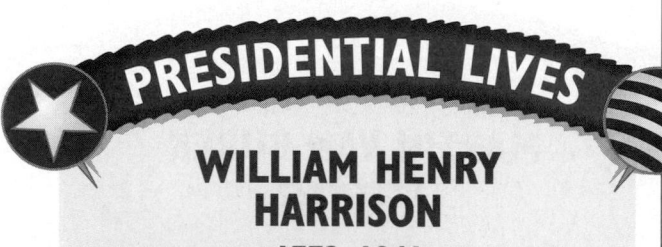

PRESIDENTIAL LIVES

WILLIAM HENRY HARRISON
1773–1841

in office 1841

William Henry Harrison was a military man and war hero with little political ambition or experience. But when the Whigs offered him the party's presidential nomination in 1840, he quickly embraced the idea. After Harrison's election, his predecessor, Van Buren, remarked that Harrison "is as tickled with the Presidency as a young woman is with a new bonnet."

His opponents were not so amused. They criticized his inexperience and accused him of drunkenness, bad language, and "loose living." But Harrison had little time to answer these charges; he died of pneumonia shortly after his inauguration.

THE RISE OF THE WHIGS

Jackson left office before the inflationary bubble burst. Martin Van Buren, Jackson's vice president and handpicked successor, who was elected president in 1836, suffered the consequences of mounting economic problems. Unwilling to take steps to help the economy, Van Buren fell prey to the new Whig party when he sought reelection in 1840.

Jackson's opponents had organized the Whig party in 1834, taking their name from the old Whig party in England that had opposed the power of the king. The Whigs initially attracted people united by their dislike of "King Andrew" Jackson's policies and use of federal power. Jackson's heavy-handed attacks on the national bank and his backing of Georgia against the U.S. Supreme Court, for example, led some Americans to distrust the growing power of Jackson's presidency. The Whigs did not defeat Van Buren in 1836, but their support grew over the next four years as the nation's economic problems deepened.

Rather than run Henry Clay—the acknowledged leader of the Whig party—the Whigs in 1840 ran General William Henry Harrison, like Jackson a war hero. Clay's nomination had been opposed by such influential Whigs as Calhoun and Webster. In addition, Clay's 1839 speech attacking some extreme abolitionists undermined his chances of winning votes in the North. Clay defended his remarks by saying, "I had rather be right than be president," but the Whigs wanted a candidate who could win. Harrison had the advantage of having few political (or sectional) enemies and thus received the party's nomination.

"My friends are not worth the powder and shot it would take to kill them," Clay bitterly said upon hearing the news of Harrison's nomination. "I am the most unfortunate man in the history of parties: always run by my friends when sure to be defeated, and now betrayed of a nomination when I, or any one, would be sure of election."

Clay's last assessment was probably right—the economic problems created during the Van Buren administration seemed to ensure the election of almost any Whig candidate. Although adopting no party platform, the Whigs targeted such economic issues as the Bank, the tariff, and especially the ongoing depression. The Whig campaign focused on presenting their candidate as a "man of the people." They portrayed Harrison, a rich landowner, as a poor, hardworking farmer who lived in a log cabin.

Whig rallies featured miniature log cabins and flowing barrels of hard cider, the favored drink of farmers and many workers. The Whigs' chant "Tippecanoe and Tyler too" referred to the general's 1811 battle against Indians at the Tippecanoe River and to his running mate, John Tyler of Virginia. Ridiculing Van Buren, they added: "Van, Van is a used up man!"

The Whigs' reliance on slogans during the campaign echoed the election of 1828 and set unfortunate precedents for U.S. politics. After 1840 the "packaging" of candidates—emphasizing their images as much as (or even more than) their ideas or abilities—became standard practice.

But the tactic worked. Harrison won an impressive 234 electoral votes to Van Buren's 60. Harrison, however, did not enjoy his triumph for long. The 68-year-old president died of pneumonia four weeks after his inauguration, making his the shortest presidential term in U.S. history. Vice President Tyler, a states'-rights southerner and strong opponent of Andrew Jackson, succeeded to the presidency and inherited the ongoing economic and sectional crises.

■■ **The Whigs came to power in 1840 by emphasizing economic issues—such as the Panic of 1837—and by relying on slogans and images.**

PRESIDENTIAL LIVES

JOHN TYLER
1790–1862

**in office
1841–1845**

John Tyler was a Virginia gentleman. A lover of music and literature, he played the violin and wrote poetry. The courtship leading up to Tyler's second marriage was so romantic that his bride's sister scolded: "You spend *so much* time in kissing, things of more importance are left undone."

In public, though, Tyler could be stubborn. When President Harrison died in 1841, he was the first president to die while in office. Many government leaders challenged then–Vice President Tyler's right to assume full presidential duties. But Tyler was determined not to be merely a "Vice President acting as President." His bold action set a precedent for the transfer of presidential power.

John Tyler

SECTION 4 REVIEW

IDENTIFY and explain the significance of the following: Sequoya, Indian Removal Act, Second Seminole War, *Worcester v. Georgia,* Trail of Tears, pet banks, Specie Circular, William Henry Harrison.

LOCATE and explain the importance of the following: Indian Territory.

1. **MAIN IDEA** What factors led the U.S. government to shift its policy toward Native Americans from one of coexistence to one of removal? How did Native Americans in the Southeast attempt to resist this policy shift?

2. **MAIN IDEA** How did the Whigs win the election of 1840?

3. **IDENTIFYING CAUSE AND EFFECT** Describe the relationship between the tariff of 1828, the doctrine of nullification, and South Carolina's threat to secede.

4. **WRITING TO EXPLAIN** Write a short essay explaining what led to the Panic of 1837 and the depression that followed.

5. **GAINING A MULTICULTURAL PERSPECTIVE** Imagine you are a Cherokee on the Trail of Tears. Write a poem or diary entry explaining your feelings at being forced to leave your home.

Monroe elected president. Second Bank of the United States chartered.

Adams-Onís Treaty signed. Financial panic begins.

Missouri Compromise passed.

Monroe Doctrine issued.

John Quincy Adams elected president.

Erie Canal completed.

1815   1820   1825

WRITING A SUMMARY

Using the essential points of the chapter as a guide, write a summary of the chapter.

REVIEWING CHRONOLOGY

Number your paper 1 to 5. Study the time line above, and list the following events in the order in which they happened by writing the first next to 1, the second next to 2, and so on. Then complete the activity below.

1. Jackson vetoes national bank recharter.
2. Cherokees begin Trail of Tears.
3. Missouri Compromise passed.
4. Tariff crisis resolved.
5. Monroe Doctrine issued.

Identifying Cause and Effect Select two events from the time line, and in a paragraph, explain the cause-and-effect relationship between them.

IDENTIFYING PEOPLE AND IDEAS

Explain the historical significance of each of the following people or terms.

1. American System
2. Martin Van Buren
3. Rush-Bagot Agreement
4. John Calhoun
5. Industrial Revolution
6. Sequoya
7. Indian Removal Act
8. doctrine of nullification

UNDERSTANDING MAIN IDEAS

1. How did the War of 1812 help prepare Americans for acceptance of Clay's American System?
2. How were the causes of the Panic of 1819 and the Panic of 1837 similar?
3. What roles did Samuel Slater, Eli Whitney, and Francis Cabot Lowell play in America's Industrial Revolution?
4. How did Native Americans in the Southeast resist their forced removal to Indian Territory?
5. How did westward expansion lead to passage of the Missouri Compromise?
6. Why did South Carolina not carry through on its threat to secede in the early 1830s?

REVIEWING THEMES

1. **Economic Development** How did the transportation and market revolutions lead to regional differences in economic development?
2. **Technology and Society** What were some of the ways in which 19th-century America was changed by the Industrial Revolution?
3. **Democratic Values** Why can it be said that the market revolution and industrialization aided the rise of Jacksonian democracy?

THINKING CRITICALLY

1. **Evaluating** What caused the upsurge of American nationalism after the War of 1812?
2. **Synthesizing** What did the Monroe Doctrine reveal about the way the United States viewed its role in the Western Hemisphere?
3. **Analyzing** Could industrialization and the transportation revolution have occurred without each other? Why or why not?
4. **Comparing** What did the crises over Missouri statehood and over tariffs have in common?

STRATEGY FOR SUCCESS

Following is an excerpt from the message President Jackson delivered to Congress in support of Indian removal. Review the Strategies for Success on Recognizing Fallacies in Reasoning on page 220. Then indicate what fallacy in reasoning is evident in Jackson's speech.

> ❝ Our children by thousands yearly leave the land of their birth to seek new homes in distant regions. . . . These remove . . . at their own expense, purchase the lands they occupy, and support themselves at their new homes from the moment of their arrival. Can it be cruel . . . when . . . the Indian is made discontented in his ancient home to purchase his lands, to give him a new and extensive territory, to pay the expense of his removal, and support him a year in his new abode? ❞

Tariff of 1828 passed.
Andrew Jackson
elected president.
Calhoun's doctrine of
nullification issued.

Jackson vetoes
national bank
recharter.

Specie Circular
issued. Van Buren
elected president.

William Henry
Harrison elected
president.

Indian Removal
Act passed.

Tariff crisis
resolved.

Cherokees begin
Trail of Tears.

John Tyler succeeds
to presidency.

1830   1835   1840   1845

WRITING ABOUT HISTORY

Using Historical Imagination Imagine that you are a reporter in 1828. Write a short article tracing Jackson's political career from the election of 1824 through the election of 1828.

USING PRIMARY SOURCES

When the U.S. government first began pressuring the Chickasaws to exchange their lands in the Southeast for lands in Indian Territory, the Chickasaw leaders offered the following reply. What reasons did the Chickasaws give for not wanting to move westward?

> 66 *We never had a thought of exchanging our land for any other, as we think that we would not find a country that would suit us as well as this we now occupy, it being the land of our forefathers, if we should exchange our lands for any other, fearing the consequences may be similar to transplanting an old tree, which would wither and die away, and we are fearful we would come to the same. . . .*
>
> *We have no lands to exchange for any other. We wish our father [the President] to extend his protection to us here, as he proposes to do on the west of the Mississippi, as we apprehend [fear] we would, in a few years, experience the same difficulties in any other section of the country that might be suitable to us west of the Mississippi.* 99

LINKING HISTORY AND GEOGRAPHY

Refer to the map on page 233, showing the major U.S. roads, canals, and railroads in 1840. In what parts of the country were most canals located?

Given the information on this map, why do you think the Erie Canal was so important?

The Granger Collection, New York

"Tom Thumb" locomotive racing a horse-drawn car, 1830

BUILDING YOUR PORTFOLIO

Complete the following projects independently or cooperatively.

1. THE ECONOMY Imagine you are a northern textile manufacturer. Create an illustrated chart for a new factory that shows what new technologies you will use to produce cloth from cotton and where you plan to build your factory for easy access to markets.

2. EXPANSION Imagine you are a reporter for the *Cherokee Phoenix*. Write a newspaper article in English that traces U.S. policy toward the Cherokee nation from 1789 to 1835. Include reasons for why these policies can be viewed as a product of U.S. expansionism.

3. INDIVIDUAL RIGHTS Imagine you are a western farmer supporting Andrew Jackson in the 1832 presidential election. Create a political poster that illustrates why Andrew Jackson is a "man of the people." The poster should draw on events from Jackson's first term in office.

EARLY INDUSTRIAL-IZATION

PATTERNS of early industrialization in the United States were largely influenced by geography. Early factories relied heavily on water power. Thus most industrial centers formed around the fall line of the eastern United States. As rivers descend from the uplands to the lowlands, they create waterfalls and rapids. A fall line is the imaginary line formed by connecting the waterfalls on numerous rivers. The fall line usually marks the farthest point that ships can travel inland. Thus many inland port cities, such as Philadelphia and Baltimore, can be found along the fall line. The multitude of waterfalls and streams in New England contributed to its becoming the leading region of early industrialization in America.

Legend:
• Industrial centers along Fall Line

0   100   200 Miles
0   100   200 Kilometers
Albers Equal-Area Projection

Graniteville became the first textile center in South Carolina. Today textiles represent the largest industry in that state, which houses some 430 mills.

SOUTH CAROLINA

Graniteville

Source: Eighth Census of the United States: Manufactures, 1860

U.S. MANUFACTURING CENTERS, 1860

New England 15%
Midwest 26%
South 15%
Other regions 8%
Middle Atlantic 38%

By 1860 the small region of New England had as many manufacturing establishments as the entire South. The industrial imbalance between the North and the South would have a major impact on the Civil War.

In the early 19th century canals created a revolution in transportation. In Ohio alone, some 1,000 miles of canals were constructed between 1825 and 1848. As railroads expanded, most canals fell into disrepair and eventually shut down, as did the Ohio system in 1909.

The boom in canal and railroad transportation had a tremendous impact on industry. Manufacturers could now ship materials and goods throughout the country. The three small states of Massachusetts, Connecticut, and Rhode Island already contained a multitude of waterways that helped power numerous industries, particularly textiles. By the mid-1800s these three states were covered by webs of railroad lines connecting their major industrial centers.

Chapter 8

1820–1860

SEPARATE SOCIETIES: NORTH AND SOUTH

FOCUS

UNDERSTANDING THE MAIN IDEA

The market revolution changed northern and southern societies. In the North, with its growing cities and factories, a new middle class and a new working class emerged. In the South, the dominance of cotton strengthened the slave-based social order.

THEMES

- **ECONOMIC DEVELOPMENT** How might economic changes affect society?

- **CULTURAL DIVERSITY** How might a people's culture be shaped by slavery?

- **TECHNOLOGY AND SOCIETY** What unexpected effects might a technological advance have on society?

1831	**1834**	**1844**	**1856**
Nat Turner leads slave uprising.	National Trades Union founded.	Lowell Female Labor Association organized.	American party nominates Millard Fillmore for president.

As early as the 1760s, the economies of the North and the South had begun to grow apart. Although farming was important in both regions, the North diversified its economy to include importing and selling manufactured goods.

Northern textile factory

In the early 19th century, new industries and growing cities changed how and where people worked. Before the market revolution, most people worked at home. People grew food and made cloth and other necessities for themselves. During the market revolution, however, people increasingly began to work outside the home—in factories, businesses, and on other people's farms. As a result, family members took on new roles.

Michel Chevalier (shuh-vahl-yay), a French visitor to America in the 1830s, noticed a new attitude among American men. The American man, he remarked, "is brought up with the idea that he will have some particular occupation, that he is to be a farmer, artisan, manufacturer, merchant, speculator, lawyer, physician . . . and that if he is active and intelligent he will make his fortune." In northern cities Chevalier noted that "men of business, instead of being scattered over the town, occupy a particular quarter, devoted exclusively to them, in which there is not a building used as a dwelling house and nothing but offices and warehouses to be seen."

Chevalier traveled to Virginia, where he observed a society in which the majority of the population—enslaved African Americans—had little choice of occupation. While Chevalier praised the flourishing tobacco and flour markets in Virginia, he also criticized southern slavery, noting that the slave "has no civil rights." Despite their lack of legal power, enslaved African Americans created a unique culture to resist and survive slavery.

Carrying cotton from southern fields

THE NORTH AND THE MIDDLE WEST

FOCUS

- Who made up the new middle class?
- How did northern workers react to the labor conditions they faced?
- What led to increased Irish and German immigration in this period?
- How did nativists react to Irish and German immigrants?

he market revolution profoundly affected the North and the Middle West. The growing economy brought better living conditions for many Americans. It also attracted many Irish and German immigrants in the first half of the 19th century. But economic growth did not always improve the lives of the working class. Northern factory owners often paid low wages and provided poor working conditions, causing northern workers to call for changes.

Detail of immigrants from Samuel Waugh's *The Bay and Harbor of New York,* 1847

Museum of the City of New York, gift of Mrs. Robert Littlejohn

NORTHERN SOCIETY

The market revolution created a wide gap between the rich and the poor. Prosperous merchants, bankers, manufacturers, and their families made up the wealthy upper class. These families lived in huge, lavish homes with running water, marble mantels, elegant furnishings, and the latest in household conveniences.

The poor, by contrast, crowded into small apartments, attics, or damp cellars with little furniture and few conveniences,

◄ Some rooms in middle-class homes were heated by modern downstairs heaters rather than by old-fashioned fireplaces.

including sewers. Poor neighborhoods were plagued by crime, soot, filth, and disease.

Between the wealthy and the poor arose a new social class—the **middle class**. Prosperous farmers, artisans, shopkeepers, ministers, lawyers, and their families made up the new middle class. Some free blacks, despite facing discrimination, shared in the economic prosperity of the growing middle class. Middle-class families lived in modest but comfortable homes with conveniences such as iron cookstoves, lamps, bathing stands and bowls, and rugs.

Middle-class families had the income to buy food, clothing, and other products made available by the market revolution. Thus, families no longer worked together at home to produce their food, clothing, and other necessities. Men were expected to work outside the home to bring in money to buy these items. Women were expected to work at home and care for the children, and children were expected to go to school. These new middle-class family roles became the ideal for most families, though not all could meet this economic and social arrangement.

■ The middle class consisted of prosperous farmers, artisans, ministers, lawyers, shopkeepers, and their families.

CHANGING WORKING CONDITIONS

The market revolution also changed how people worked. Workers still made most products, like shoes and barrels, by hand in small shops. In the early 19th century, however, workers began making more items in factories, which needed many employees. Early New England factory owners recruited whole families to work in textile mills. Such employment offers usually included housing. But the system of housing entire families became impractical when factories needed hundreds of employees.

Mill owners in Lowell, Massachusetts, overcame the problem by hiring young, single women. Most women had the necessary skills for textile mills, since they had made cloth at home. They were also cheaper to hire. Mill owners could pay single women less than men, since women were not seen as having to support their families.

These single women—known as **Lowell girls**—lived in closely supervised, company-owned boardinghouses. Mill owners organized cultural activities to provide "moral education" for the workers and required them to attend church. Housekeepers enforced curfews, banned alcohol, and reported on the Lowell girls' behavior. Despite such strict supervision, recruitment was easy in the early years. "The stage-coach and canal boat came every day, always filled with new recruits," wrote former Lowell girl Harriet Robinson.

Conditions changed by the 1830s, however. Owners—searching for larger profits—cut wages, sped up production, and increased working hours. Protests and attempts to form labor unions had little success, however, as more job seekers competed for factory positions. As a result of the Panic of 1837, which had cost many workers their jobs, there were many unemployed laborers willing to work for long hours and low wages. In New York City 50,000 people—a third of the working class—were unemployed.

Even in prosperous times workers barely got by. In New York City's garment-making district, entire families labored through the night, making barely enough money to survive. They lived mainly on bread and tea; even beans were too expensive and time-consuming to prepare. "It's awful," lamented a mother of four. "I must work, else we get nothing to eat and turned into the street besides. . . . Cooking? Oh, I cook nothing, for I haven't the time."

Children often worked as hard as their parents did. Child labor was common on farms, so manufacturers took it for granted in factory work. By 1832, two out of five New England factory workers were children. These children faced especially grim working conditions. Factory superintendents often forced children to run machines late into the night and kept them awake by splashing water in their faces.

LABOR FIGHTS BACK

As conditions worsened by the 1830s, workers organized more than 60 unions. Labor leaders held their first national convention in 1834 and founded the National Trades Union, which campaigned for a 10-hour workday. President Van Buren responded in 1840 with a 10-hour workday for selected groups of federal employees. Some states passed similar legislation, but working hours remained long in many occupations.

◀ This 1836 picture shows children employed in the weaving room of a New England textile mill.

Labor unions used many methods to press for reforms. A common tactic was the **strike**—the refusal to work until employers meet union demands. During the 1830s, workers led more than 100 strikes, mostly to protest low wages or to avoid wage reductions.

Women were very important in the early labor movement. After wages were cut in 1834, the Lowell girls went on strike, marching in the streets and shouting "Union is power." Reacting to the strike, Massachusetts legislators established a committee to investigate conditions in the textile mills. This was the first official investigation of labor conditions in the United States.

▲ This 1860 drawing accompanied an article in *Frank Leslie's Illustrated Newspaper* on a shoemakers' strike in Lynn, Massachusetts. According to the paper, 800 women led a strike procession through the city's streets on March 7, 1860.

Sarah G. Bagley, who went to work in the Lowell mills in 1836, was active in the labor movement. At first, she liked her job. In fact, in 1840 she wrote the article "Pleasures of Factory Life" for the *Lowell Offering,* a magazine published by women mill workers. But when mill owners sped up production without raising wages, Bagley urged coworkers to form a union. In 1844 she organized the Lowell Female Labor Reform Association. As its first president, Bagley denounced labor conditions and collected more than 2,000 signatures on a petition urging the Massachusetts legislature to limit the workday to 10 hours.

◄ Cover of the *Lowell Offering,* 1845

After leaving the mill in 1845, Bagley traveled across New England, organizing other mill workers. Later she became the first woman telegraph operator in Lowell. Although Bagley did not win her fight to limit working hours, her efforts pointed the way for future labor organizers.

While some early labor unions fought for better wages for white women, most unions excluded African American workers. Whites often refused to work with blacks, sometimes calling for laws barring African Americans from particular trades. Some African American workers, such as mechanics, coach drivers, and caulkers, eventually formed organizations to promote their interests.

■ **During the mid-1800s, northern factory workers campaigned for better labor conditions.**

GROWTH IN IMMIGRATION

The labor force grew considerably in the 1830s, as more than 500,000 newcomers—eager for work, land, and equality—poured into the country. By 1860 the total was nearly 4.3 million—about 14 percent of the U.S. population. This increase was aided in part by a transportation revolution in Europe. Railways made it cheaper to reach major ports, and steamships reduced the time and cost of ocean travel.

Irish immigrants. The largest group of immigrants—more than 1.9 million—came from Ireland. Poverty, hunger, and mistreatment by the British had driven them from their homeland. British Protestants had seized much of Ireland's farmland by the 1600s, forcing most of the country's mainly Roman Catholic population to rent land from Protestant landowners.

As Ireland's population nearly doubled from 1780 to 1840, the available land could no longer support the growing population. The situation worsened in the mid-1840s, when disease wiped out the potato crop—the major Irish food source—two years in a row. More than a million people (out of a population of some eight million) died from starvation or disease.

Most of those who could scrape together money for a steamship ticket left Ireland for the United States. Able to afford only the cheapest accommodations, these immigrants set off across the Atlantic Ocean, crammed together below deck in makeshift berths. Passenger Robert Smith described the conditions:

66 Hundreds of poor people, men, women and children of all ages, . . . huddled together without light, without air, . . . sick in body, dispirited in heart, . . . living without food or medicine, except as administered by the hand of casual charity. 99

Most Irish immigrants had been farmers, but few could afford farmland in the United States. Thus, the majority settled in crowded city slums, competing for the lowest-paying or most-dangerous jobs. Many laborers who helped build the nation's canals and railroads, mined coal, unloaded freight, and cleaned streets were Irishmen. Irishwomen cleaned the houses of the wealthy, washed and mended clothes, cared for children, and worked in factories. "You seldom see a gray-haired Irishman" became a common saying in the 19th century because the average life expectancy of Irish Americans was so short.

In addition to enduring such demanding work, the Irish often faced grim living conditions. Most lived in dark, poorly ventilated tenements. Whole families crowded into single rooms, cellars, or attics. Slum streets and yards, ankle-deep in garbage and sewage, spread diseases through Irish neighborhoods.

But Irish immigrants forged their own communities out of these conditions. They established hundreds of Catholic churches, making Roman Catholicism the nation's largest denomination by 1860. The Irish also actively participated in local politics. By the 1880s Irish Americans ran the local governments of Boston, Chicago, Buffalo, Milwaukee, New York City, Philadelphia, and San Francisco. In return for votes Irish politicians helped poor and working-class Irish by providing them with emergency food and money, city jobs, and legal aid.

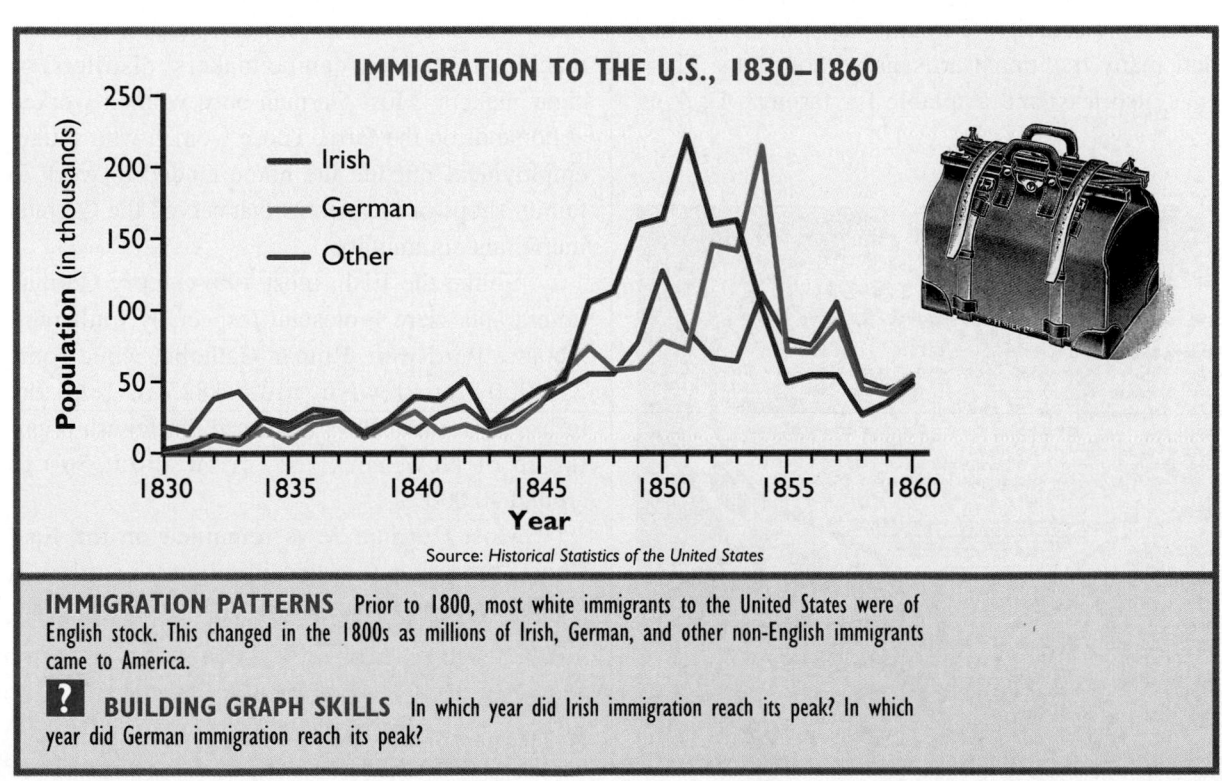

IMMIGRATION TO THE U.S., 1830–1860

Source: *Historical Statistics of the United States*

IMMIGRATION PATTERNS Prior to 1800, most white immigrants to the United States were of English stock. This changed in the 1800s as millions of Irish, German, and other non-English immigrants came to America.

? BUILDING GRAPH SKILLS In which year did Irish immigration reach its peak? In which year did German immigration reach its peak?

THROUGH OTHERS' EYES

Between 1820 and 1860 more than five million Europeans came to the United States in search of a better life. Although most arrived in the "promised land" with high hopes, many of them soon realized that their dreams would not come true. Skilled work was often hard to find, as competition for good jobs was stiff. One Scottish immigrant expressed both despair and disappointment in this new land:

> 66 *America is no place for lawyers, weavers, or shoemakers, for everyone is a pettifoger [corrupt lawyer], a weaver or a shoemaker. For masons there is little use, for slaters [stone roofers] none. The houses are chiefly built with wood, and the roofs are shingled. Watch and clockmakers may stay at home [in Europe], for the Americans are regulated by the sun. It is no place for printers, there are but few readers. . . . The houses being very simply furnished, cabinet-makers are consequently not much in request. . . . In short, to gain a decent livelihood, the tradesman and labourer, must be a 'Jack of all trades.'* 99

German immigrants. The second-largest group of immigrants in the mid-19th century was from the then-independent states that make up present-day Germany. From 1831 to 1860, more than 1.5 million Germans came to the United States. Some came for political reasons. A few thousand fled after the failed Revolution of 1848, which had tried to unify Germany. Others sought religious freedom. Most, however, came in search of economic opportunity. German industrialization had left many traditional artisans without jobs. There was also less land available for farmers. Lacking economic opportunity at home, both groups immigrated to the United States.

■■ **Irish and German immigrants left economic and social hardships in Europe to seek opportunities in the United States.**

Many German immigrants went into skilled occupations, becoming brewers, bakers, butchers, machinists, tailors, cabinetmakers, distillers, or cigar makers. Most German-born women worked at home or on the farm. Those women who sought employment outside the home tended to work in family shops or businesses that served the German immigrant community.

Unlike the Irish, most 19th-century German immigrants were Protestant (especially Lutheran). About a third were Roman Catholic, while some 250,000 were Jewish. From 1825 to 1860 the influx of German Jews increased the Jewish population of New York City from about 500 to around 40,000.

Most German Jews remained on the East Coast, but other German immigrants settled in small towns and rural areas in Wisconsin, Ohio,

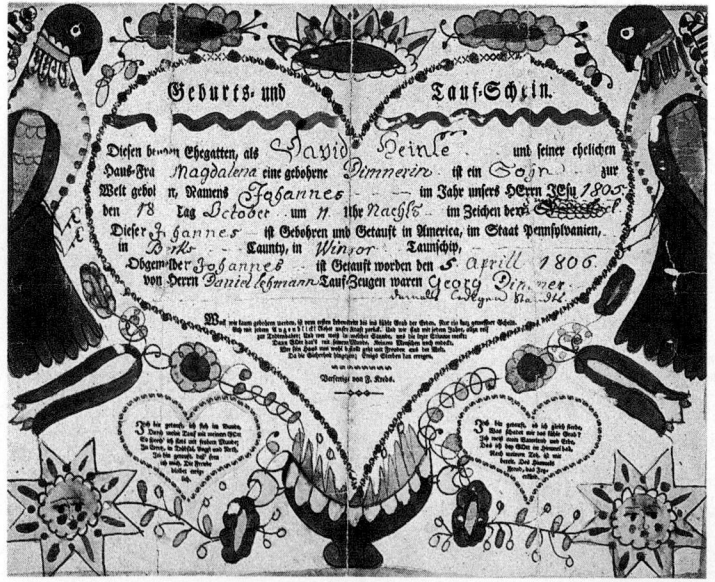

◄ This photograph shows a Pennsylvania-German birth certificate from the early 19th century.

Pennsylvania, Illinois, Missouri, and Texas. Those in larger cities usually lived in tightly knit German neighborhoods, complete with European-style beer gardens where families met to socialize. Many communities also published newspapers in German. In the mid-1850s, 56 German-language newspapers were published in the United States. And in some communities, public schools conducted classes in German rather than in English.

THE NATIVIST RESPONSE

Some native-born Americans were troubled by the new immigrants' customs. They disapproved of the beer gardens and the "clannishness" of the Germans. They feared the Roman Catholicism and the growing political power of the Irish. Such feeling gave rise to **nativism**—the policy of favoring native-born Americans over the foreign-born. Nativists viewed the immigrants, particularly the Irish, as politically corrupt and socially inferior. Were not, they asked, most of the people in jails Irish? Were not parts of Philadelphia, Boston, and New York controlled by Irish gangs with names like the "Dead Rabbits"?

From the 1830s through the 1850s, anti-Catholic riots hit eastern cities such as Boston, New York, and Philadelphia. Vandalism against Catholic institutions was so common that some insurance companies would not cover Catholic schools and churches. A Roman Catholic priest wrote in 1854 that he feared "to walk the streets after sunset":

66 Twice within the past month I have been stoned by young men. . . . The windows of the church have frequently been broken—the panels of the church door stove [smashed] in, and last week a large rock entered my chamber unceremoniously about 11 o'clock at night. 99

Some nativists urged limiting immigrants' rights to vote and to hold public office. Nativists wanted to limit Irish political power because they believed that the Pope directed decisions for Irish Catholics. In 1849 a secret society of nativists, the Order of the Star-Spangled Banner, emerged. Members swore to support only native-born Protestants for public office, to lobby for a 21-year waiting period for naturalization, and to fight the Roman Catholic church. The organization soon re-formed as the American party. When asked about their nativist activities, party members would answer "I know nothing." They were thus dubbed

The Granger Collection, New York

▲ This 1844 picture shows an anti-Catholic mob battling the state militia in Philadelphia.

the **Know-Nothings**, and their organization was called the Know-Nothing party.

The American party, with its slogan "Americans Shall Rule America," won numerous city and state elections. In the 1856 presidential election, the party ran former Whig Millard Fillmore, who had served as president from 1850 to 1853. Fillmore carried only Maryland, and the American party—though not the nativist backlash—soon faded away.

■■ **Nativists responded to increased German and Irish immigration with violence and demands for limits on immigrants' rights.**

THE MIDDLE WEST

Many immigrants, especially Germans, Swiss, Scandinavians, and Dutch, sought opportunity in the newly prosperous Middle West. Growing northeastern factories and cities needed more farm products, which middle western farmers began to supply. Some middle western areas developed lumbering or mining, but commercial farming dominated most of the region.

As the market revolution made many manufactured products less expensive, farm families began to purchase items they had previously made at home. For example, women stopped spinning and weaving cloth, which was cheaper to buy than to make. Most middle western communities eventually had enough settlers to attract merchants selling manufactured goods. Farm families could then buy household items and new mechanized farm machines, such as Cyrus McCormick's reaper, that increased crop yields.

Ruggles, Nourse, Mason & Co., Boston,

Manufacture, and Offer for Sale, the most Complete and Extensive assortment of

PLOWS

TO BE FOUND IN THE UNITED STATES.

Also, Hay, Straw and Corn Stalk Cutters, Corn Shellers, Fanning Mills, Corn and Cob Crushers, Burr Stone Portable Grinding Mills, Seed Sowers, Corn Planters, Horse Powers, Threshers, Carts, Cart Harness, Ox Yokes, Hand Corn Mills, Store, Steamboat and Wharf Trucks, Sugar Mills, &c. &c.

SEEDS.

▲ **This advertisement from a Boston company for farm equipment and seeds appeared in 1854.**

With reapers and other new devices, farm families could cultivate more land with less labor. As a result, they focused on growing wheat or corn or on raising livestock for the market.

Women also began making items to sell. Farm women had long made butter and cheese for their families. Now they began making such items for sale. In Ohio, women earned so much money making butter and cheese that some farms began to specialize in dairy production.

This work was handled by women who also performed other home and farm chores. An 1862 Department of Agriculture report noted that "on three farms out of four the wife works harder [and] endures more than any other [person] on the place." Many women took pride in their ability to contribute directly to the growing family income.

SECTION 1 REVIEW

IDENTIFY and explain the significance of the following: middle class, Lowell girls, strike, Sarah G. Bagley, nativism, Know-Nothings.

1. **MAIN IDEA** Identify some occupations that were considered part of the new middle class.

2. **MAIN IDEA** How did factory workers respond to unacceptable working conditions?

3. **MAIN IDEA** What kinds of restrictions did nativists try to impose on immigrants?

4. **WRITING TO DESCRIBE** Write an essay describing the life-style of middle-class families in the early 19th century. Include a discussion of male and female roles.

5. **CONTRASTING** How did life in America differ for Irish and German immigrants?

Section 2

THE COTTON KINGDOM

FOCUS

- **What factors led to the rise of the Cotton Kingdom?**
- **Why did manufacturing and cities develop more slowly in the South than in the Northeast?**
- **How did white southerners view the institution of slavery?**
- **What was the class structure of southern society?**

The market revolution helped tie the South's economy to agriculture. While tobacco, sugar, rice, corn, and hemp continued to be important cash crops in parts of the South, cotton came to dominate the Lower South and the expanding Southwest. As cotton succeeded tobacco as the most important crop, the plantation system and slavery tightened their grip on the South. This reliance on agriculture gave rise to a distinct southern social structure of planters, small farmers, poor whites, free blacks, and African American slaves.

Moving cotton bales at a warehouse

KING COTTON

When tobacco prices fell in the early 1800s, many Americans thought slavery and plantation agriculture would soon vanish. Before this could happen, however, new weaving machines that cut the cost and time of cloth making sent the demand for cotton skyrocketing. Armed with Eli Whitney's cotton gin, southern planters were ready to respond.

Cotton production in the South soared from around 731,000 bales harvested in 1830 to some 2,133,000 bales in 1850. By 1859 cotton production reached a peak of some 5,387,000 bales. From 1815 to 1860 cotton represented more than half of all American exports.

Periodic booms in the cotton export market drove planters to open new lands for cultivation. Cotton growers moved west from South Carolina and Georgia into the fertile lands of Alabama, Mississippi, Arkansas, Louisiana, and eastern Texas. By the 1850s the cotton belt stretched in a long crescent from central and western North Carolina to eastern Texas.

As cotton production expanded, the demand for slaves rose. The number of slaves grew from about 1.5 million in 1820 to some 4 million by 1860. Because of the abolition of the international slave trade in 1808, planters had to rely on natural increase, or births, for more slaves. The Upper South, with more slaves than the region needed, sold slaves to the cotton-producing states of the Lower South.

▉ Booming markets, the cotton gin, and newly cultivated lands created the southern Cotton Kingdom.

Extent of cotton growing by 1839
Extent of cotton growing by 1859

1793: At Mulberry Grove, Eli Whitney builds a cotton gin, a machine that removes seeds from cotton fibers.

The Cotton Kingdom

THE COTTON BOOM The market revolution coupled with the invention of the cotton gin caused a boom in cotton production by the mid-1800s.

? REGIONS Which two states began producing cotton after 1839?

SOUTHERN MANUFACTURING

Although cotton and other agricultural products formed the basis of the southern economy, manufacturing also played a role in economic growth, especially in the Upper South. Sawmills, ironworks, tobacco factories, textile mills, and brickyards, as well as rice, sugar, corn, and wheat mills dotted the region. The South also had one of the largest and best-equipped ironworks—the Tredegar Iron Works of Richmond, Virginia—which operated its rolling mills in the 1850s mainly by slave labor. The company manufactured steam engines for sugar mills, locomotives, cannons, railroad spikes and rails, and many other iron products.

Railroad construction and mining also added to the expanding southern economy. The Mississippi River and other inland waterways bustled with trade. Baltimore, Charleston, and Mobile were important ports. New Orleans grew to become the nation's most prosperous export center by 1840 and the fifth-largest U.S. city by 1860.

Industrialization and urbanization, however, developed more slowly in the South than in the North. The South in 1860 had 35 percent of the

nation's population but only 15 percent of the manufacturing centers. This occurred for several reasons. First, instead of investing in new factories, most southern investors continued to put their money in land and slaves. Second, planters used their influence to discourage states from passing taxes for internal improvements—improvements that might have promoted manufacturing. Third, there was a shortage of factory workers. The reliance on slave labor discouraged immigrants—the main source of cheap factory labor in the North—from coming South. Fourth, the market for manufactured goods was hurt by the fact that slaves and poor whites—the bulk of the rural population—had little or no purchasing power.

■■ **The South's continuing emphasis on plantation agriculture and slave labor slowed industrialization and urban growth.**

SOUTHERN ATTITUDES TOWARD SLAVERY

Though slave labor formed the foundation of the southern economy, some southerners criticized slavery. A few argued that an economy based on plantation agriculture and slavery was less profitable than one based on wage labor and industry. Others criticized slavery as incompatible with the American Revolution's spirit of liberty and freedom. People in the Upper South, who were less dependent on cotton, were among the most vocal critics of slavery.

Other criticisms came from southern reformers such as Jesse Burton Harrison of Virginia, who attacked the inhumanity of slavery. Fearing the upheaval that he was sure would result from

◀ Free black opponents of slavery used arguments from the Declaration of Independence to protest the enslavement of African Americans.

immediate abolition, Harrison called for a gradual end to slavery. He was not alone in his view. Most white southern abolitionists did not support immediate abolition or full equality for African Americans. Like many white abolitionists in the North, they did not believe that African Americans could fit into American society. To avoid the problem of having to accept freed blacks as citizens, many southern abolitionists joined northern abolitionists in suggesting that slaves be freed gradually and then sent to Africa. The idea of forcing freed slaves to leave the United States was especially strong among southerners who feared that free African Americans would encourage slave rebellions.

In 1817, prominent northerners and southerners founded the **American Colonization Society** for this purpose. The society's plan called for

◀ Free black opponents of slavery used arguments from the Declaration of Independence to protest the enslavement of African Americans.

slaveholders to free their slaves voluntarily. The society raised money to compensate slaveholders for the value of the freed slaves. Once freed, the former slaves were to be sent to Liberia—a nation the society carved out on the west coast of Africa. The impact of such efforts was limited, however. The number of slaves born in the United States in a week exceeded the number of blacks the American Colonization Society sent to Africa in a year.

One major obstacle for the colonization movement was the reluctance of African Americans to move from the United States to Africa. The idea of sending blacks "back" to Africa was a misconception. Most African Americans in the 19th-century United States had never been to Africa.

As northern attacks on slavery mounted in the 1800s, southern critics of slavery were drowned out by its supporters. Planters argued that slavery was the only way to ensure an adequate supply of field workers for southern cash crops. Slavery's defenders also insisted that planters who provided slaves with shelter, clothing, food, and care in sickness and old age were actually helping African Americans. Many masters saw themselves as kindly parents and their slaves as simple children. As

▶ In this 1832 engraving, freed slaves from the United States are shown arriving in Liberia under the sponsorship of the American Colonization Society. J. J. Roberts, the first president of Liberia, is also pictured.

The Granger Collection, New York

Thomas R. Dew, a professor at William and Mary College and noted defender of slavery, wrote:

66 We are well convinced that there is nothing but the mere relations of husband and wife, parent and child, brother and sister which produce a closer tie than the relation of master and servant. . . . The slaves of a good master are his warmest, most constant, and most devoted friends; they have been accustomed to look up to him as their supporter, director, and defender. 99

Another champion of slavery, southern lawyer and writer George Fitzhugh, contrasted the supposedly "secure" life of southern slaves with the sad plight of wage earners in northern and European factories and mines. Such workers, Fitzhugh argued, were at the mercy of employers who paid them little, fired them at will, and heartlessly abandoned them when they became too old or sick to work.

The Granger Collection, New York

▲ This 1850 cartoon compared slavery in America with the factory system in England.

Slavery mainly served the interests of the wealthiest planters. This troubled some nonslaveholding whites in the South. Most southern whites, however, supported slavery. Small farmers, even those who held no slaves, backed the institution because they hoped to become wealthy planters one day. Many poor whites supported slavery because it gave them a sense of superiority. As one white Missourian wrote in 1854:

66 With us, color, not money, marks the class: black is the badge of slavery; white the color of the freeman. . . . The white man, however poor, whatever be his occupation, feels himself a sovereign. 99

■■ Some southern whites opposed slavery for humanitarian or economic reasons, but most defended the institution.

SOUTHERN SOCIETY

The importance of land and slaves to the southern economy was reflected in the region's class structure. Only one in four southern whites owned slaves, but this small group dominated southern society and politics.

Planters. In 1860 less than 12 percent of the South's planter minority held 20 or more slaves; of these, less than 1 percent, or about 2,300, held 100 or more slaves. The 1860 census listed 14 slaveholders with as many as 500 slaves each; only one of these planters claimed control of 1,000 slaves.

The richest planters lived elegantly in beautiful tree-shaded mansions. Despite such trappings of wealth, planters often had little available cash. Much of their wealth went to brokers, mostly from the North or Great Britain, who bought their cotton and sold them household goods and farm equipment. Yet with good weather, high market prices, and skillful farm management, the cultivation of cotton or other cash crops could bring high profits.

The plantation owners' reputation for a life of ease often was more image than reality. The owners were usually quite busy managing the plantation: planning and supervising the work, assigning tasks to supervisors or slaves, keeping records of business transactions, writing to shipowners or bankers, and contracting with brokers.

Negroes.

George , age 30
Eggleston „ 27
Robert „ 25   Waggoner Henry Caspar
Joshua „ 28
Lovin „ 25
Alfred „ 26   Waggoner
BigBob „ 40
McGruder „ 34   Blacksmith Dead
BobHardy „ 22
Sam „ 20   Carpenter
Dudley „ 22
Luck „ 20

Eleanor S. Brockenbrough Library, The Museum of the Confederacy, Richmond, Virginia

▲ **Planters kept careful records of all business transactions on their plantations. A page from the 1854–56 record book of Jacob Thompson, listing the ages of his slaves, is shown here.**

The plantation mistress was not the lady of leisure depicted in myths of the Old South. In reality, she supervised the spinning, weaving, mending, housecleaning, and food preparation; cared for the sick; and often educated her children. In addition, the mistress was often expected to see to the needs of the slaves. "It is the slaves who own me," complained one mistress. "Morning, noon, and night, I'm obliged to look after them, to doctor them, and attend to them in every way."

The majority of planters, those owning less than 20 slaves, lived more modestly. Their homes were usually two-story, frame buildings with 8 to 10 rooms, deep porches, and comfortable but not luxurious furnishings.

Small farmers.

Below the planters on the social ladder were the hundreds of thousands of **yeoman farmers** who made up the majority of southern whites. Most of these small farmers lived on fertile lands but had no easy access to markets. They built simple two-room log cabins, raised cattle and pigs, and sold some crop (often grain) for cash. They grew their own food—usually in small patches around their homes. Most small farmers owned no slaves, but some managed to afford a few. The wealth and social status of small farmers, just as that of the planters, varied considerably.

Poor whites. The poorest whites, a small percentage of the South's population, farmed the least-productive soil—the pine barrens, sand hills, and marshes. They lived in rough cabins with few material comforts. Often these families survived by hunting, fishing, and raising a few pigs. Other white southerners looked down on the poorest whites and referred to them as "white trash," "crackers," or "clay eaters."

African Americans. In 1860, the African American population in southern states varied from about 10 percent in Missouri to nearly 59 percent in South Carolina. Although most southern blacks were enslaved, by 1860 about 260,000 free blacks lived in the South. Nearly half of all free blacks made their homes in the border states of the Upper South. In Baltimore, the number of free African Americans—some 25,000 by the late 1850s—far exceeded the city's slave population of some 2,000. And in the state as a whole, free blacks nearly outnumbered slaves. Things were much different in the Lower South. Less than 2

POPULATION IN THE SOUTH, 1860

Total Population: 47%, 1%, 2%, 16%, 34%

Slaveholding Households: 1%, 2%, 72%, 25%

Nonslaveholding whites | Slaveholding whites
Slaves | Free blacks | Others

Less than 10 slaves | 50–99 slaves
10–49 slaves | 100 or more slaves

Sources: *Historical Statistics of the United States; Slavery and the Southern Economy; The Black American Reference Book*

SLAVERY IN THE SOUTH Although slavery played an important part in the southern economy, only a small minority of southerners owned slaves.

? **BUILDING GRAPH SKILLS** Which group made up the largest section of the population in the South? What percent of all slaveholders owned 50 or more slaves?

◄ Some free blacks worked in skilled trades. This 1861 engraving shows a barber's shop in Richmond, Virginia.

◄ Free blacks were often required to wear identification badges such as this one when traveling through the South.

percent of the Lower South's black population was free.

Some free African Americans were skilled workers: mechanics, barbers, seamstresses, shoemakers, carpenters, or masons. Others found employment as cooks, waiters, laundresses, or domestic servants. Some free blacks had never been slaves, while others had worked extra hours to earn money to purchase their own freedom or were rewarded with freedom for years of dedicated service. William Ellison of South Carolina, for example, learned to repair cotton gins while a slave. After buying his own freedom, he purchased the freedom of his wife and children. A small minority of free blacks, including Ellison, became landowners and even masters of black slaves.

The social and economic status of free blacks in the South, however, was never really secure. White southerners restricted the freedom of all black people. After 1830, southern legislatures severely limited the movements of free blacks, requiring them to register with local authorities and to carry identification passes proving they were not runaway slaves. Free African Americans often had to post bonds—money or a pledge of property—as a guarantee of good behavior.

Free blacks in the South could not vote, hold public meetings, speak in public, bear weapons, or testify in court against whites. In many places free African Americans were forbidden to attend all-black churches unless a white person was present. Some states denied free blacks the right to go into business for themselves or to learn how to read and write. An editorial in a black newspaper put it simply: "Though we are not slaves, we are not free."

The South's nearly four million enslaved blacks lacked even the limited rights of free African Americans. The majority of these men and women—some 55 percent—lived in the Cotton Kingdom of the Lower South, where they tended the fields and houses of the planter class.

■■ **The southern class structure consisted of wealthy planters, small farmers, poor whites, free blacks, and slaves.**

SECTION 2 REVIEW

IDENTIFY and explain the significance of the following: Jesse Burton Harrison, American Colonization Society, Thomas R. Dew, yeoman farmers, William Ellison.

LOCATE and explain the importance of the following: cotton belt, Tredegar Iron Works.

1. **MAIN IDEA** What factors created the southern Cotton Kingdom? Why did industries and cities grow more slowly in the South than in the North?

2. **MAIN IDEA** Identify the five different social classes in the South.

3. **CONTRASTING** What reasons did some southerners give for opposing slavery? What reasons did other southerners give for supporting slavery?

4. **WRITING TO INFORM** Write an essay about the free African Americans in southern society. Who were they? What advantages and disadvantages did they face?

5. **RECOGNIZING BIAS** Defenders of slavery such as Thomas R. Dew and George Fitzhugh argued that slaves were better off than northern factory workers. What biases might have influenced their arguments?

Section 3

THE SLAVE SYSTEM

FOCUS

- **What was life like for slave laborers?**
- **How did slaveholders control slaves?**
- **How did African Americans resist slavery?**

The Granger Collection, New York

Advertisement for
a runaway slave

*S*lavery dominated southern society. Slaveholders and slave codes controlled the lives of enslaved African Americans, who nevertheless continued to hope and struggle for freedom. African Americans resisted slavery in many ways, from quiet sabotage to outright rebellion, and strengthened family and cultural life in efforts to survive the brutalities they suffered.

SLAVE LABOR

Most enslaved African Americans—more than 75 percent—lived and worked on southern plantations and farms. In the cities slaves worked as skilled seamstresses, shoemakers, weavers, and carpenters. Slave labor was also "hired out" to employers running coal mines, salt mines, ironworks, tobacco factories, sugar mills, or flour mills. Some slaves built canals, quarried rock, or drained swamps. Still others were dockworkers, loading and unloading ships in southern ports.

The life of slaves in the city was generally less grim than that of a field hand. Field hands worked from dawn to dusk and beyond, as many as 18–20 hours per day during the harvest. Ex-slave Peter Clifton wrote, "The rule on the place was: Wake up the slaves at daylight, begin work when they can see, and quit work when they can't see." Instead of working the fields, some slaves—especially women—served the plantation household as maids, cooks, or nannies. Others did sewing or laundry. Some male slaves worked as wheelwrights, coach drivers, gardeners, carpenters, or blacksmiths.

On small farms slaveholders usually supervised their slaves directly. On larger plantations **overseers**—who were usually planters' sons, other relatives, small farmers, or skilled workers—managed the slaves. To help supervise the slaves, overseers used **drivers**—assistants picked from among the slaves. Drivers occupied a difficult position between master and slave and were

◀ *Maid to the Douglas Family*, **painted by an unknown artist in 1840, shows a slave woman who worked in a plantation household.**

SEPARATE SOCIETIES: NORTH AND SOUTH ▪ 269

even expected to handle the hated whip. A driver might be praised by the master for a job well done but be despised by the slaves for driving them too hard.

On cotton and sugar plantations, slaves were organized into tight work crews with drivers as foremen. This system of **gang labor** allowed overseers to assign groups of slaves to do specialized jobs such as plowing, hoeing, or picking, depending on the season.

■■ Some slaves worked in manufacturing or skilled crafts, but 75 percent toiled in agriculture.

LIVING CONDITIONS

To make a profit using slave labor, planters had to make sure slaves were fed, clothed, and free from illness. Masters had reason to value their human property: at an average price in 1860 of $1,200 to $1,800 each, 50 young slaves represented an investment upward of $60,000. The death or serious injury of an able-bodied slave was a major financial blow.

Many enslaved African Americans did fall victim to illnesses. Infectious disease—common among whites as well—was made worse by slaves' living and working conditions. Pneumonia and dysentery were widespread. Malnutrition frequently led to dental and other health problems.

Slave quarters were cramped and sparsely furnished. An entire family might live in a small one-room log cabin with no more comforts than a fireplace. Gaps between the logs and the uncovered openings for doors and windows made for a cold cabin in the winter. In such homes, an observer noted, "the wind and rain will come in and the smoke will not go out."

Food was rationed on the plantation. Ben Horry, a former slave from South Carolina, explained that on Saturday every slave on the plantation lined up at the smokehouse to draw his or her share of meat, rice, grits, and meal. But these shares were seldom enough to feed slave families. To supplement their diet, slaves hunted and fished at night or on Sundays and grew greens or sweet potatoes in small gardens. House slaves sometimes received food from the planter's kitchen. Some slaves resorted to stealing food.

Slaves' clothing was simple, usually made of linsey-woolsey—a coarse woolen and linen or cotton material similar to burlap. Most slaves were given two outfits a year, one for summer and one for winter, though household slaves might receive hand-me-down clothing from the planter's family. On average, slaves got one pair of shoes a year and went barefoot when this pair wore out.

TREATMENT OF SLAVES

Some slaves fared better than others. Living conditions and treatment varied from plantation to plantation. Some planters used rewards instead of punishments to gain their slaves' obedience.

▶ *An Overseer Doing His Duty* is the title of this watercolor by Benjamin Henry Latrobe.

These planters promised money, gifts of extra food or clothing, easier tasks, dances, days off, or shorter working hours to dutiful slaves. Those who obeyed orders might be granted small favors, given a garden plot, or promoted from field work to easier and more-desirable tasks in the household. Domestic slaves were generally better fed and clothed than field slaves.

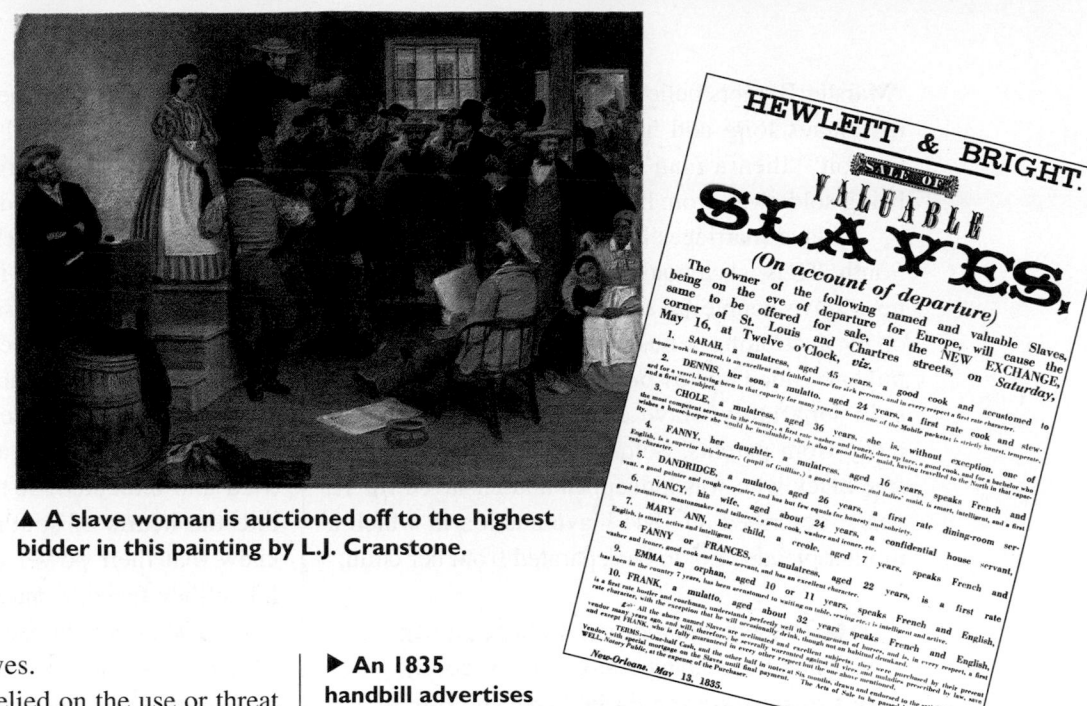

▲ A slave woman is auctioned off to the highest bidder in this painting by L.J. Cranstone.

▶ An 1835 handbill advertises slaves for sale at an upcoming auction in New Orleans.

Other slaveholders relied on the use or threat of violence to control their slaves. As a planter wrote in the *Southern Patriot,* "The fear of punishment is the principle to which we must and do appeal, to keep them in awe and order."

If slaves were late getting to the fields or did not work fast or hard enough, overseers could be particularly brutal. Prince Smith, a former slave on a South Carolina plantation, recalled the use of an especially harsh form of solitary confinement—the "sweat box":

66 [The box] was made the height of the person and no larger. Just large enough so the person didn't have to be squeezed in. The box is nailed, and in summer is put in the hot sun; in winter it is put in the coldest, dampest place. 99

Sometimes slaveholders and overseers disciplined slaves with extra work or reduced rations, but whipping was the most common form of punishment. William Wells Brown, a former slave and the author of the first published novel by an African American, wrote that the whip was used "very frequently and freely, and a small offence on the part of a slave furnished an occasion for its use."

Many recipients of the lash tried to resist the master's will as best they could—often by refusing to cry out. Frederick Douglass, an escaped slave who became a prominent abolitionist, remembered one slave woman who "was not subdued, for she continued to denounce the overseer, and to call him every vile name. He had bruised her flesh, but had left her invincible spirit undaunted [determined]."

Slaves who resisted authority or showed signs of independence were whipped. If such discipline failed, they were sometimes sold "down river"—away from family and community ties.

▲ One method of slave punishment involved placing a special brace around the head to restrict the person's movement. Wilson Chinn, a slave from Louisiana, is shown here in a restrictive brace. Notice also the brand across his forehead.

"Marster Biggers believe in whipping and working his slaves long and hard," wrote ex-slave Peter Clifton; "then a man was scared all the time of being sold away from his wife and chillun."

Slave marriages had no legal standing in the South. Thus, slaveholders would sometimes break up a slave couple by selling one but not the other or by auctioning a husband and wife to different buyers. Since slaves brought higher prices when sold separately, slave children were often sold away from parents. Solomon Northup, a northern free black who was kidnapped and enslaved for 12 years, described an 1841 slave auction in which a mother pleaded not to be separated from her child:

66 The afflicted mother . . . kept on begging and beseeching them, most piteously, not to separate the three. Over and over again she told them how she loved her boy. . . . But it was of no avail. . . . Then [the mother] ran to [her son] . . . told him to remember her—all the while her tears falling in the boy's face like rain. . . . It was a mournful scene indeed. I would have cried myself if I had dared. 99

Laws failed to protect enslaved African Americans from brutality. On the contrary, southern slave codes—which covered all aspects of slaves' lives—rendered slaves legally powerless. Slaves were forbidden to testify in court against whites, to own property, to possess firearms, to be out after curfew, or to leave their plantations without a pass. Any white person could stop any black person and demand to see proof of either free status or permission to be away from his or her master. White patrols roamed the rural South to enforce the laws and to apprehend any slaves trying to escape.

▪▪ Slaveholders used rewards, punishments, and laws to control slaves.

REBELLION AND RESISTANCE

Despite their lack of legal power, slaves used several strategies to improve their living and working conditions. From the quiet revenge of running away or working slowly to open rebellion, African Americans found ways to resist slavery.

Slave revolts. In the first half of the 19th century, there were several small uprisings involving slaves in the South. In 1800 a planned rebellion near Richmond involved hundreds of slaves led by Gabriel Prosser. Another plot surfaced in 1822 in Charleston. The plan, masterminded by African American Denmark Vesey, a prosperous carpenter and popular preacher, called for a massive slave uprising in Charleston and the surrounding areas.

The plan was discovered before it could be carried out, and Vesey and the other leaders were tried and executed. It nevertheless struck terror into the hearts of southern whites. Slaveholders knew that their power over slaves was based on force; they feared a massacre of the white population if slaves sought revenge. The sheer number of African Americans who might have joined the revolt—in 1820 the black majority in Charleston was near 57 percent—deepened whites' fears. Most of the accused slaves had been liked, respected, and trusted by their masters. Even three of the governor's own household servants had joined Vesey's revolt!

BIOGRAPHY White southerners' worst fears materialized in 1831, when Nat Turner led a violent slave uprising in Southampton County, Virginia. Nat Turner was born in 1800 to an African-born mother. Soon after, his father ran away to freedom. Turner was very bright, and he later claimed to have taught himself to read after his mother gave him a spelling book. Turner's grandmother, who took charge of his spiritual education, told him he was destined to grow up to be a great man. He prayed, fasted, and read the Bible to discover his life's purpose.

The deeply religious Turner believed that he had received his answer when he began seeing visions of white and black spirits battling in the heavens: God had chosen him to free the slaves. A solar eclipse in February 1831 was to him a sign that it was time for action.

Turner planned to start his rebellion on July 4, Independence Day, but illness forced a delay. On August 21 Turner and a small band of followers went into action. They killed Turner's master, the

The Granger Collection, New York

Nat Turner

master's family, and about 60 other whites in the area. The state militia and terrified local whites organized a hunt for Turner, killing at least 100 slaves during the two months that it took to track him down. After being captured at his hideout, a spot still called "Nat Turner's Cave," the fugitive was brought to trial. Asked why he refused to plead guilty, Turner replied, "Because I don't feel guilty." He was hanged on November 11, 1831.

Following these slave uprisings, some southern states passed stricter slave codes. These laws made it illegal to teach slaves to read and placed more restrictions on slaves' movements. Some whites took the law into their own hands, arresting, beating, and killing slaves at will. Recalled one slave woman:

66 The whites threatened to punish 'em dreadfully, if the least noise was heard. The patrols was low drunken Whites; and in Nat's time, if they heard one of the colored folks praying, or singing a hymn, they would . . . abuse 'em, and sometimes kill 'em. 99

Slave resistance. Open rebellion was rare. Slaves generally protested their bondage through individual actions. They might fake an illness, slow their work pace, or damage tools or other property in an effort to disrupt the plantation routine. In some cases, desperate slaves mutilated

themselves, cutting off toes or hands, hoping to avoid being sold or to escape harsh treatment and overwork. Others committed suicide.

The most tempting form of resistance was to run away, whether for only a few days or permanently. Chances of success were slim, and punishment if caught was brutal. Some aid came from the **Underground Railroad**, a network of white and black abolitionists who helped slaves escape to freedom in the North or in Canada. Escaping slaves slowly made their way out of the South, hidden in attics and haylofts by day and taken by

The Underground Railroad

	Counties with slave population 50% or more
	Counties with slave population 10%–49%
	Counties with slave population <10%
→	Escape route

ROAD TO FREEDOM It is estimated that the more than 3,000 members of the Underground Railroad helped from 50,000 to 75,000 enslaved African Americans escape to freedom.

? LOCATION Why do you think Cairo, Illinois, and Cincinnati, Ohio, were important stops on the Underground Railroad?

◀ Harriet Tubman used the Underground Railroad to free more than 300 slaves.

"conductors" to the next safe house at night. At first, most slaves were smuggled to safety at night and on foot. As more slaves made the attempt, covered wagons and carriages were used. Sometimes, runaway slaves were even smuggled by rail or boat, hidden inside crates. A song that inspired many slaves on their dangerous journeys expressed their hope for a new life in Canada:

> 66 Farewell, old master
> Don't come after me.
> I'm on my way to Canada
> Where colored men are
> free. 99

The conductors on the Underground Railroad helped thousands of slaves gain their freedom. Harriet Tubman, who escaped from a Maryland plantation in 1849, was the most famous and successful conductor. Risking her own freedom, Tubman returned to the South

▶ This colorful quilt, which was made about 1886 by an ex-slave named Harriet Powers, depicts Biblical themes.

19 times to lead more than 300 slaves to safety in the North.

■■ **Slave resistance took many forms, from work slowdowns and sabotage to escape and open rebellion.**

Despite the daring of the slaves and those people who aided them, many fugitives were captured and returned to their masters. But the stream of runaways never stopped.

SLAVE CULTURE

Although slaves' lives were controlled from sunup to sundown, their time was mostly their own when the workday ended. After dark and on Sundays and rare holidays, slaves devoted time to family and community, creating a unique African American culture. This culture blended to a remarkable degree the customs of the variety of African groups thrown together under slavery. At the center of this culture were family, religion, music, folktales, and humor.

Family and kinship bonds. Preserving family ties was a difficult challenge for enslaved African Americans. Slave marriages were not legally recognized, and slave families were always subject to being split up by the sale of individual members. In response to forced separations, slaves extended their family ties to include distant as well as close relatives. Nonrelated individuals also shared significantly in a family's life and were commonly known to children as aunts and uncles.

Many slaves made valiant efforts to stay in contact with family members despite being separated. One slave told how he ran away from his master to seek his mother on a distant plantation years after their forced parting:

> 66 I asked [my mother] if she knew me? she said, no. . . . I then asked her if she had any sons? she said, yes; but none so large as me. I then [described] . . . being sold into slavery, and how she grieved at my loss. . . . [Her] dire feelings on that occasion . . . rushed to her mind; she saw her own son before her, for whom she had so often wept; and, in an instant, we were clasped in each other's arms. 99

Religion and music. Religion played a vital role in the lives of enslaved African Americans. Most worship services were a rich blend of Christian elements and traditional African beliefs, music, and dance.

Embracing the Christian belief in salvation and a heavenly future helped some slaves endure the hardships they faced. Central to the slaves' religion was their belief that they were God's chosen people who, like the Hebrews in the land of the pharaohs, would eventually reach a "promised land" free from their oppressors. The slaves' promised land was not just an afterlife of freedom; it was also a world without slavery.

Unlike white ministers who preached obedience to masters, African American preachers spoke to what was close to the hearts of slaves. For example, in 1851 a black Baptist minister named Bentley preached a sermon on the occasion of President Millard Fillmore's visit to Savannah, Georgia. According to Bentley, when the president arrived in a "grand, beautiful carriage and drove to the best house in . . . town," blacks were kept from coming too close.

> 66 The great gentlemen and the rich folks went freely up the steps and in through the door and shook hands with him. Now, did Christ come in this way? Did He come only

to the rich? Did He shake hands only with them? No! Blessed be the Lord! He came to the poor! He came to us, and for our sakes, my brothers and sisters! 99

After Nat Turner's rebellion, many masters stopped allowing slaves to congregate, even for religious meetings. Slaveholders feared that the slaves would seize every opportunity to plot a rebellion. Enslaved African Americans continued to hold gatherings, but they took to hiding in the woods to avoid detection by white patrols. To quiet the noise during these secret meetings, the slaves devised methods of muffling sound, such as making enclosures of wet quilts. With the noise thus muted, one former slave explained, they "could shout and sing all they wanted to and the noise wouldn't go outside."

Of great importance to slave religion were the haunting songs called **spirituals**. Rich in Biblical lore, these "Sorrow Songs" were sung during work, relaxation, and worship. They were modeled in part on Christian hymns and in part on traditional African rituals and musical forms. Spirituals movingly expressed the slaves' deep longing for freedom. Favorites like "Go Down, Moses," "Blow Your Trumpet, Gabriel," and "Didn't My Lord Deliver Daniel?" tell of deliverance from bondage.

John Antrobus, *Plantation Burial*, (1860) oil on canvas, The Historic New Orleans Collection

▲ *Plantation Burial,* **painted by John Antrobus in 1860, records an African American funeral on a plantation in northern Louisiana.**

Then and Now

SHOUTS ACROSS THE OCEAN

▲ The influence of African musical forms is still evident in African American religious ceremonies. Shown here are members of the Bradford Singers, a noted gospel group.

When Africans were forcibly brought to North America as slaves, their culture and traditions crossed the ocean with them. Today, African influences are visible throughout American society. American dance and music, for example, have roots in the centuries-old dances and musical forms of Africa.

In much of Africa, religious and ceremonial dances are performed in a ring, with dancers slowly moving counterclockwise in a circle. Noting the subtle movements of a dancer, one observer remarked:

66 It takes time to appreciate the variety and detail in the different movements and the unceasing, wave-like ripple which runs down the muscles of the back and along the arms to the finger-tips. Every part of the body dances, not only the limbs. 99

The ring often symbolizes the life cycle—the circle of birth and death. Thus, it is an important part of many burial ceremonies, used to show respect for and a connection to one's ancestors.

The African ring dances were the source of the ring shout in American slave culture. Slaves sang, shouted, and clapped their hands as they moved counterclockwise in a circle. Barely lifting their feet from the ground, they rhythmically pounded the earth with their heels. As in Africa, the dancing and singing were forms of spiritual expression directed to ancestors.

Over time the ring shout and other African dances inspired new forms of dance in America. In the early 1900s jazz dance built on the rhythmic shuffling and pistonlike arm movements of the ring shout. But the influence of African dance was probably most widespread in the 1920s. The Charleston, which both blacks and whites danced, was wildly popular all over the country. Few people realized it was based on a religious dance in Africa.

With new forms of dance came new forms of music. Some slaves adapted songs with Christian lyrics to the ring shout. The result was the Negro spiritual, which remains an important part of many African American religious ceremonies. Several leading concert artists, such as Paul Robeson, Marian Anderson, and Leontyne Price, helped popularize spirituals.

The rhythms and emotional tones of the ring shout greatly influenced blues music as well. And the blues, in turn, shaped today's popular music. Rock musicians such as the Rolling Stones and Eric Clapton have drawn on the blues for inspiration.

Well-known performers, such as James Brown and Aretha Franklin, trained in the musical traditions of the black church, have also influenced a new generation of artists, among them Janet Jackson. In all these ways, African dance and music, like other features of African culture, have left strong and lasting imprints on American life.

—Dr. Sterling Stuckey

Folktales and humor. Slaves used folktales as an important means of passing on their culture. These folktales were based on African stories but related local situations, family histories, and personal experiences. Most of the tales concerned everyday human relationships, detailing the importance of friendship or a parent's love and caring. Children who misbehaved might be told the story of the chicks who disregarded their mother's warning cries and were eaten by a hawk. Moral tales warned of the pitfalls of excessive pride or stressed the ideals of cooperation and love.

Storytelling, especially the use of animal trickster tales, gave African Americans a way of talking about whites and slavery in a guarded form. In these humorous tales the attempt by the strong to trap the weak always fails. Instead, the weaker animal, such as Anansi the spider or Brer Rabbit, tricks the stronger animal and in the end gains wealth, success, and power.

Trickster tales allowed African Americans to reverse, at least in the mind, the harsh fact of the master-slave relationship. Laughter helped slaves deal with painful situations, allowing them to endure slavery, rather than be crushed by it. Wrote John Little, a former slave:

66 They say slaves are happy, because they laugh, and are merry. I myself and three or four others, have received two hundred lashes in the day, and had our feet in fetters [chains]; yet, at night, we would sing and dance, and make others laugh at the rattling of our chains. . . . We did it to keep down trouble, and to keep our hearts from being completely broken. 99

This ability to maintain hope in the face of overwhelming abuse was perhaps enslaved African Americans' most remarkable form of resistance.

■■ **Through family ties, religion, music, and folktales, African Americans endured slavery and created a unique culture.**

▲ Joel Chandler Harris popularized animal trickster tales in books such as *Uncle Remus and Brer Rabbit*. This collage contains original A.B. Frost illustrations for Harris's stories.

SECTION 3 REVIEW

IDENTIFY and explain the significance of the following: overseers, drivers, gang labor, Gabriel Prosser, Denmark Vesey, Nat Turner, Underground Railroad, Harriet Tubman, spirituals.

1. **MAIN IDEA** What kind of work did most slaves perform?

2. **MAIN IDEA** What strategies did African Americans use to resist slavery?

3. **IDENTIFYING CAUSE AND EFFECT** Why did many slaveholders use severe punishments such as whipping and the "sweat box" on slaves? How did the use of these methods affect the slave community?

4. **WRITING TO CREATE** Write a folktale that reflects the experiences of a slave living in the 1850s.

5. **USING HISTORICAL IMAGINATION** Imagine that you are Nat Turner facing trial for leading a slave rebellion in 1831. Prepare a speech to give to the jury explaining why you should not be found guilty.

CHAPTER 8
Review

Denmark Vesey
plots slave rebellion.

National Trades Union
founded. Lowell girls
go on strike.

Nat Turner leads
slave uprising.

| 1820 | 1825 | 1830 | 1835 |

WRITING A SUMMARY

Using the essential points of the chapter as a guide, write a summary of the chapter.

REVIEWING CHRONOLOGY

Number your paper 1 to 5. Study the time line above, and list the following events in the order in which they happened by writing the first event next to 1, the second next to 2, and so on. Then complete the activity below.

1. National Trades Union founded.
2. American party nominates Millard Fillmore for president.
3. Order of the Star-Spangled Banner formed.
4. Nat Turner leads slave uprising.
5. President Van Buren sets 10-hour workday for federal employees.

Writing to Create Create a poster that depicts any two events on the time line.

IDENTIFYING PEOPLE AND IDEAS

Explain the historical significance of each of the following people or terms.

1. strike
2. Sarah G. Bagley
3. nativism
4. Know-Nothings
5. Harriet Tubman
6. yeoman farmers
7. Thomas R. Dew
8. overseers
9. Nat Turner
10. spirituals

UNDERSTANDING MAIN IDEAS

1. What effects did increased immigration have on American society and politics?
2. How did the market revolution and industrialization change farming and farm life in the Middle West?
3. How did the slave economy influence the South's class structure?
4. Describe the working and living conditions of slaves on southern plantations. How did slaves respond to these conditions?

REVIEWING THEMES

1. **Economic Development** What are some of the ways in which the growth of manufacturing affected northern society?
2. **Cultural Diversity** How did slavery influence African American culture in the 1800s?
3. **Technology and Society** What effect did Eli Whitney's cotton gin have on the slave economy of the South?

THINKING CRITICALLY

1. **Evaluating** What factors led to the increase in immigration to the United States from 1820 to 1860?
2. **Analyzing** How did the lives of large planters differ from those of yeoman farmers?
3. **Hypothesizing** How might slavery have been affected if industrialization in the South had advanced as it did in the North?

STRATEGY FOR SUCCESS

Review the Skills Handbook entry on Studying Primary and Secondary Sources beginning on page 998. Then study the following verses from a slave spiritual. How do the words of the song relate to the life of a slave in southern society? What 19th-century people, places, and events might be represented by Moses, Israel, Egypt, and the Pharaoh and by the phrases "oppressed so hard" and "smite your first-born dead"?

> **❝** *Go down Moses,*
> *'Way down in Egypt land,*
> *Tell ole Pharaoh,*
> *To let my people go.*
> *When Israel was in Egypt land,*
> *Let my people go,*
> *Oppressed so hard they could not stand,*
> *Let my people go.*
> *Thus spoke the Lord, bold Moses said,*
> *Let my people go,*
> *If not I'll smite [strike] your first-born dead,*
> *Let my people go.* **❞**

President Van Buren
sets 10-hour workday
for federal employees.

Lowell Female
Labor Reform
Association
organized.

Order of the
Star-Spangled
Banner formed.

American party
nominates
Millard Fillmore
for president.

1840　　1845　　1850　　1855　　1860

WRITING ABOUT HISTORY

Writing to Describe You are a conductor on the Underground Railroad. Write a diary entry describing your most recent efforts to help a slave family escape to freedom.

USING PRIMARY SOURCES

Many of the Lowell girls were well-educated women who found that their daily work did not provide intellectual fulfillment. To fulfill this need they established the *Lowell Offering*, a literary magazine written and edited by female mill workers. Read the following excerpt from an article written by the magazine's editors in 1845. Then write a paragraph explaining how the editors believed the *Lowell Offering* was different from other magazines and why they thought others should support them.

66 *Our magazine is the only one which America has produced, of which no other country has produced the like. The* Offering *is . . . evidence, not only of the American "factory-girls," but of the intelligence of the mass of our country. And it is in the intelligence of the mass that the permanency of our republican institutions depends.*

And our last appeal is to those who should support us, if for no other reason but their interest in "the cultivation of humanity," and the maintenance of true democracy. There is little but this of which we, as a people, can be proud. Other nations can look upon the relics of a glory come and gone—upon their magnificent ruins. . . . We have other and better things. Let us look upon our "free suffrage," . . . our Common Schools, our Mechanics' Literary Associations, the Periodical of our Laboring Females; upon all that is indigenous [native] to our Republic, and say . . . these are our jewels. 99

LINKING HISTORY AND GEOGRAPHY

In the period from 1820 to 1860 some cotton planters, newly arrived immigrants, and established northern farmers moved westward. Write an essay explaining the reasons for such migrations.

Mississippi cotton plantation

 BUILDING YOUR PORTFOLIO

Complete the following projects independently or cooperatively.

1. **THE ECONOMY** In Chapter 7 you created a chart for a textile factory. Building on that material, imagine you are a southern plantation owner. Draw a map that illustrates how the transportation revolution will make it easier for you to transport your cotton to northern textile factories.

2. **IMMIGRATION** Imagine you are a newly arrived immigrant in New York City. Present an oral account of your trip to the United States, your passage through customs, and your current living and working conditions.

3. **INDIVIDUAL RIGHTS** In Chapter 7 you created a political poster. Building on that material, imagine you are a factory worker on strike. Create a speech to be given to your co-workers inspiring them to join you in protesting unfair treatment.

Chapter 9

WORKING FOR REFORM

FOCUS

UNDERSTANDING THE MAIN IDEA

Industrialization and the market revolution transformed American society. Not all of the changes were positive. The rapid growth of cities was accompanied by an increase in crime and poverty. Other changes, such as the mass departure of people for the West and the flood of new immigrants, threatened the familiar social order. Alarmed, Americans launched a variety of reform movements.

THEMES

■ DEMOCRATIC VALUES
What impact might citizens' reform groups have on public policies?

■ CULTURAL DIVERSITY
What changes in society might lead to a new interest in religion and to an interest in new forms of community?

1821	1829	1841	1848	1856
First public high school opens.	Walker's *Appeal* published.	Dorothea Dix begins crusade for mentally ill.	Seneca Falls Convention held.	Wilberforce University established.

During the early 1800s the United States changed with bewildering speed. Northeastern cities grew at spectacular rates as commerce quickened and new factories sprang up, attracting thousands of new residents from rural America and abroad. Boom times in the South helped tighten slavery's grip.

An antislavery meeting, 1841

One response to the rapid social change that transformed the United States in the early 1800s was an increase in religious activity. Religious revivalism swept the nation as huge crowds came together to listen to thunderous sermons, to sing hymns, and to seek God's help in reforming their lives. Many participants came away convinced of the possibility of attaining moral perfection, both for themselves and for society.

A few people formed new religions and established communities along new lines. "Americans of all ages, all conditions, and all dispositions," Alexis de Tocqueville (TAWK-veel) observed in 1831, "constantly form . . . associations of a thousand . . . kinds." The causes these associations worked for ranged from health and education reform to world peace. A variety of groups attacked slavery, and a growing movement for women's rights emerged.

Women's active participation in these reform movements brought criticism from those who insisted that women should restrict their reforming efforts to the family. But many women agreed with Sarah Grimké (GRIM-kee) that "the sphere which her Creator has assigned her" included speaking out against the sin of slavery as well as other evils.

Grimké's reform activities and those of countless other women and men— coupled with the advance of political democracy— inspired hope. Perhaps American democracy's larger vision—justice, equality, and opportunity for all—might be possible.

Tray depicting Reverend Lemuel Haynes preaching

RELIGIOUS ZEAL AND NEW COMMUNITIES

FOCUS

■ How did 19th-century Americans renew their enthusiasm for religion?

■ Why did Protestant church membership soar during the Second Great Awakening?

■ What were some common features of utopian communities?

After visiting the United States in 1831, Alexis de Tocqueville said he knew of "no country in the whole world in which the Christian religion retains a greater influence over the souls of men than in America." The America he observed was in the midst of a revival of religious faith. Revivalists established new religions, gave new life to old ones, and founded communities where they could live according to their religious values and philosophical beliefs.

Circuit rider preacher

THE SECOND GREAT AWAKENING

Americans responded by the thousands to waves of religious revivals that swept the country beginning in the 1790s. This renewal of religious faith was known as the **Second Great Awakening**, and it was every bit as intense as the Great Awakening of the mid-1700s. These revivals caught on because ministers expressed what many people were feeling: an optimistic belief in the individual's ability to improve his or her life. This optimism was fueled by both economic growth and the heralded, although still limited, expansion of democracy.

In the frontier areas of Kentucky, Ohio, Tennessee, and South Carolina, preachers traveled from town to town, promising that all sinners could find salvation. This promise, which contrasted sharply with the common belief that only a chosen few could be saved, broadened the appeal of formal religion. Frontier revivals were usually huge outdoor camp meetings that drew up to 10,000 people eager to accept God into their lives. In 1801 James Finley, later a Methodist preacher, captured the emotional intensity of one

◀ Religious revivals attracted people from throughout the frontier regions. This picture shows a group of Methodists traveling to a camp meeting.

of the earliest revivals, held at Cane Ridge, Kentucky:

> 66 The vast sea of human beings seemed to be agitated as if by a storm. I counted seven ministers, all preaching at one time. . . . Some of the people were singing, others praying, some crying for mercy. A peculiarly strange sensation came over me. . . . I felt as though I must fall to the ground. 99

Revivalist ministers also spread the word of God to urban audiences in the Northeast. Charles Grandison Finney—a powerful and persuasive preacher with piercing eyes and a low, solemn voice—delivered hundreds of sermons in the 1820s and 1830s. His sermons included calls for immediate conversion that stirred many to renounce their sins:

> 66 Let the truth take hold upon your conscience—throw down your rebellious weapons—give up your refuges of lies. . . . Another moment's delay, and it may be too late for ever. The Spirit of God may depart from you . . . and seal you over to all the horrors of eternal death. 99

Two African American women, Zilpha Elaw and Jarena Lee, separately traveled thousands of miles to preach sermons to both black and white worshipers. Lee said she was called to preach by a heavenly voice that told her, "Preach the Gospel; I will put words in your mouth, and will turn your enemies to become your friends." At first, Lee had reservations about her calling—especially since female Methodist ministers were unheard of at the time—but she followed her inspiration. "If a man may preach, because the Saviour died for him, why not the woman? seeing he

▲ Jarena Lee

▲ The Bethel African Methodist Episcopal Church in Philadelphia is shown here, along with its founder, Richard Allen.

died for her also," Lee questioned. "Is he not a whole Saviour, instead of a half one?"

■■ Americans rekindled their interest in religion through revivals, which captured the people's energy and optimism.

RELIGION FOR THE PEOPLE

The reawakening of religious enthusiasm sparked changes in Protestant congregations. By making salvation available to all, 19th-century churches encouraged new converts. As a result, membership soared in many Protestant **denominations**, or religious groups.

African American men and women joined Baptist and Methodist denominations in substantial numbers and formed their own churches as well. In 1794 the Reverend (later Bishop) Richard Allen founded in Philadelphia one of the first African American churches, the Bethel African Methodist Episcopal Church.

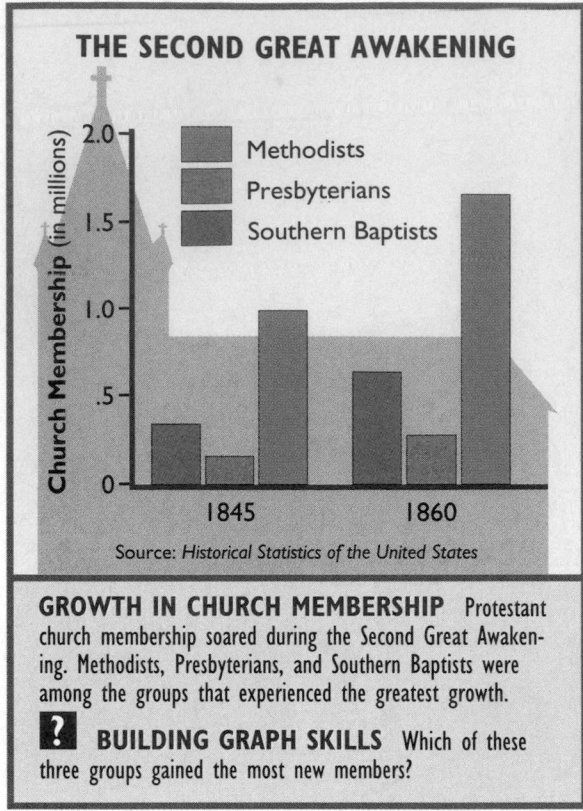

THE SECOND GREAT AWAKENING

Church Membership (in millions)

2.0

1.5

1.0

.5

0

Methodists
Presbyterians
Southern Baptists

1845   1860

Source: *Historical Statistics of the United States*

GROWTH IN CHURCH MEMBERSHIP Protestant church membership soared during the Second Great Awakening. Methodists, Presbyterians, and Southern Baptists were among the groups that experienced the greatest growth.

? **BUILDING GRAPH SKILLS** Which of these three groups gained the most new members?

Finney and other preachers in the industrializing Northeast attracted new members from the expanding middle class. Middle-class women, prosperous enough to hire servants to handle many household duties, generally had leisure time to devote to church activities. They led prayer groups, taught in and established Sunday schools, and supported missionary societies.

■■ Protestant churches attracted new converts by promising that salvation was available to all.

In the South, the spread of revivalism among enslaved African Americans met with a mixed reaction among slaveholders. Some slaveholders encouraged converting slaves to Christianity. Many others, however, believed that recognizing a slave's soul and humanity contradicted the notion that a slave was property. Although Protestants stressed reading the Bible, many southern states passed laws making it illegal to teach slaves to read. "Allow our slaves to read your writings [the Bible], stimulate them to cut our throats!" exclaimed South Carolina planter Jesse Hammond. "Can you believe us to be such unspeakable fools?"

UTOPIAN COMMUNITIES

The optimism that inspired revivalism also led men and women to found **utopias**—communities designed to create the perfect society. More than 90 utopias were established in the United States between 1800 and 1850. They were influenced by a wide range of religious beliefs and philosophies. But all utopias experimented with new ways of organizing family life, work, and property ownership. Their experiments with family organization ranged from the banning of sex and marriage to "free love" communities.

The Shakers. The Shakers, or United Society of Believers in Christ's Second Appearing, founded utopian communities in the eastern United States. Led by "Mother Ann" Lee, Shakers first arrived in America from England in 1774. Lee preached that God was both male and female.

Lee also claimed to be the messiah who would found a society free from sin. Shaker communities had separate but relatively equal roles for men and women, and community members jointly owned property. They also refrained from sex. Shakers saw no need to have children, since they believed that the millennium—a time in which some Christians think Christ will reign on earth—was at hand.

▲ **The Shakers were excellent woodworkers. This table is one example of their functional furniture designs.**

Shakerism declined after 1860 because it became difficult to recruit new members. Shakers are remembered for their useful inventions and their simple but beautiful furniture and music.

The Mormons. The most enduring utopian venture was undertaken by the Mormons, or members of the Church of Jesus Christ of Latter-day Saints. Joseph Smith, who founded the Mormon church, claimed that divine assistance had enabled him to discover and translate buried golden plates that contained religious revelations. Smith published his translation of these revelations as the

Book of Mormon and formed the first Mormon congregation in western New York in 1830.

Smith's religious teachings and call for group ownership of property and economic cooperation attracted many converts. They also attracted strong opposition. Non-Mormons were especially outraged by the Mormon practice of having more than one wife at a time. The Mormons encountered violence wherever they tried to establish a community. In 1844 a mob in Carthage, Illinois, killed Smith.

But the Mormons did not give up. Under the leadership of Brigham Young, thousands of Smith's followers crossed the Rockies and founded successful communities in the Great Salt Lake valley. Over the years, Mormons (who no longer practice group ownership of property or allow men to have multiple wives) have spread their religion throughout the world.

Brook Farm. Perhaps the most famous utopia, Brook Farm was founded in 1841 near Boston by Unitarian minister George Ripley. He was inspired by the philosophy of the **transcendentalists**, a small group of New England intellectuals led by writers Ralph Waldo Emerson, Henry David Thoreau, and Margaret Fuller and educator Bronson Alcott. Transcendentalists believed that people could attain perfection and could acquire knowledge about God, the self, and the universe.

To perfect themselves, the Brook Farm residents retreated from industrial society to live close to nature. They shared farm and household chores

▲ Ralph Waldo Emerson once described Brook Farm as "a perpetual picnic, a French Revolution in small, an age of reason in a patty [pie]-pan."

in order to have time for study and poetry readings. Dedicated to education, Brook Farm was a stimulating intellectual community. But the experiment ended in 1846 after a fire destroyed part of the farm.

■■ **Utopian communities experimented with new ways of organizing economic activities and family life.**

By 1850 the passion for cooperative living had faded. Rather than secluding themselves from society in utopian communities, some Americans began to translate the faith in human perfection into direct attempts to perfect society. They were encouraged by those revivalists who taught that salvation could be both demonstrated and gained by working to improve society.

SECTION 1 REVIEW

IDENTIFY and explain the significance of the following: Second Great Awakening, Charles Grandison Finney, Zilpha Elaw, Jarena Lee, denominations, Richard Allen, utopias, "Mother Ann" Lee, Joseph Smith, George Ripley, transcendentalists.

1. **MAIN IDEA** What effect did revivals have on religion in America?

2. **MAIN IDEA** How did Protestant churches attract new members during the Second Great Awakening? What effect did this have on church membership?

3. **COMPARING** What were some characteristics that the Shakers, Mormons, and residents of Brook Farm shared?

4. **WRITING TO PERSUADE** You are a Brook Farm resident. Write an advertisement for your local newspaper to recruit new members into your community.

5. **EVALUATING** Why can it be said that the Second Great Awakening had both positive and negative consequences for African Americans?

MOVEMENTS FOR SOCIAL REFORM

F O C U S

■ How and why did reformers work to improve prisons and other institutions?

■ What motivated the temperance reformers?

■ Why did reformers support free public education?

■ Why did reformers establish alternative schools for African Americans and women?

Men and women who joined the religious revivals of the Second Great Awakening firmly believed in the possibility of attaining individual perfection. Their optimism soon led them to believe they could perfect society as well. Troubled by the effects of rapid industrialization, people in the Northeast began to direct their religious zeal toward solving social problems. Their many concerns included better treatment of the mentally ill, prisoners, and the poor. They also tackled the problems of excessive drinking and an inadequate educational system.

Pupil working with slate and pencil

REFORMING INSTITUTIONS

In colonial days people cared for the mentally ill in their own homes. Criminals were punished but rarely confined for long periods of time. And townspeople helped the poor through informal charity. But by the early 19th century these solutions were no longer adequate. Cities had too many people in need of help, prisons were overcrowded, and too few family members could offer assistance to their kin.

Reformers responded by building new institutions and reforming existing ones for the mentally ill, criminals, and the poor. Reformers believed they could improve these people's lives by placing them in institutions that taught moral values and provided a stable environment free from the corrupting influences of city life. Middle-class women took the lead in many of these reform efforts.

Dorothea Dix and the mentally ill. One of these women was Dorothea Dix. A deeply religious teacher inspired by transcendentalist ideas, she led efforts to improve treatment for the mentally ill. Dix first became interested in the plight of the mentally ill in 1841 when she saw how they were treated in a Massachusetts prison. She was horrified to see that mentally ill women were kept in a damp dungeon with no attempts made to cure them. Dix learned that while a few mental hospitals had been established, the most common practice was to put the mentally ill in prisons and poorhouses without providing treatment.

Dorothea Dix

Outraged, Dix spent 18 months visiting jails and poorhouses throughout Massachusetts. She found that the mentally ill were kept "in *cages, closets, cellars, stalls, pens! Chained, naked, beaten with rods, and lashed* into obedience." In January 1843 Dix collected her observations into a detailed, factual report and plea for action and delivered it to Massachusetts legislators. Her report convinced them of the need to establish more institutions in which the mentally ill could be treated humanely. Dix emphasized the need to offer the mentally ill **rehabilitation**, or treatment to restore them to a useful and constructive place in society.

New ideas about mental illness—in tune with the optimistic spirit of reform—stressed that mental illness was a curable disease rather than a sin or moral defect, as had previously been taught. This changed point of view helped Dix carry her crusade to other states and even to other countries. She was responsible for the founding or enlarging of more than 30 mental hospitals in the United States, Canada, Europe, and Japan.

Prisons and poorhouses. Other reformers during this period worked to rehabilitate prisoners and the poor. Reformers persuaded lawmakers to provide money to build new prisons and poorhouses. New systems of prison organization placed prisoners in individual cells so that they would think about and repent their crimes. Prisons set up strict routines for inmates to teach them how to live disciplined lives. Reformers established institutions that housed only juvenile delinquents to separate them from hardened criminals. New

poorhouses taught work skills and discipline to help the poor become self-supporting.

■■ Reformers established mental institutions and reorganized and built prisons to offer rehabilitation to inmates.

▲ Prison reforms included teaching inmates special skills and jobs. This 1853 picture shows prisoners at **Sing Sing Prison** making hats.

THE CRUSADE AGAINST ALCOHOL

Other reformers attacked excessive drinking. Concerned people organized the **temperance movement** to persuade others to limit alcohol consumption. Reformers blamed nearly all social ills—including mental illness, poverty, and crime—on alcohol. A popular pro-temperance novel *Ten Nights in a Bar-Room and What I Saw There* (1854), which was later made into a play, echoed this sentiment. As a character observed, he "never knew a man to go to the almshouse that he hadn't rum to blame for his poverty."

The national temperance movement began in the 1820s. By the mid-1830s some 5,000 state and local organizations had sprung into being. Ministers won many converts to the temperance cause. In emotional sermons, they persuaded people to give up drinking completely in order to save their souls. According to a woman who attended an 1842 revival meeting in Maryland:

66 Upwards of 100 gallons of spirits were poured not down people's throats but on the sand and I believe there is now none in the place. Dean and Knotts [liquor sellers] have become members of the Temperance Society and are now earnestly seeking religion. 99

▼ The American Temperance Society was founded in 1826 with the aim of preaching the benefits of total abstinence from alcohol. Some temperance supporters, however, took more active roles by demolishing liquor stocks.

Businesspeople became enthusiastic supporters of the temperance movement, largely because they saw temperance as a way of creating a more disciplined work force. Temperance women linked abstaining from alcohol to preserving the family. African Americans, often excluded from white temperance organizations, formed their own temperance societies and spoke at rallies. African Americans tended to view temperance, like education, as a way to overcome prejudice and become accepted as political and social equals.

Many immigrants, on the other hand, viewed the temperance movement as an attack on their customs, which often differed from those of native-born Protestant Americans. Most German and Irish immigrants did not view alcohol consumption as a social evil. For them, German beer gardens and Irish pubs were places where people came together to socialize. Both institutions helped German and Irish immigrants preserve their cultures in the United States.

◀ As a step toward abstaining from alcohol, many families were encouraged to sign temperance pledges such as the one shown here.

■■ Reformers supported the temperance movement as a way to eliminate many social evils.

The temperance movement called for legal reforms to limit alcohol consumption. Some reformers went so far as to call for **prohibition**, or a ban on alcohol. In 1846 Maine became the first state to ban the sale of alcohol. A few other states followed, as did some communities. Many other states strictly licensed taverns and adopted heavy liquor taxes to help limit alcohol consumption. By the middle of the 19th century, the nationwide rate of alcohol consumption had declined substantially.

*R*EFORMING EDUCATION

In the 1840s and 1850s, reformers turned their attention to education. Most schools established before the 1840s were private, and most children could not afford to attend them. The few public elementary schools that existed—most of them in the Northeast—had little money for books, supplies, and teachers' salaries. The curriculum was basic: reading, writing, arithmetic, and a bit of history and geography. But the quality of teaching was often poor, attendance was irregular, and many students received only a few years of schooling.

The public school movement. Reformers worried that the existing schools were inadequate to meet the needs of a growing country and an expanding, if still limited, democracy. They argued that the nation needed public, tax-supported elementary schools to provide a free education for all students. Reformers insisted that schools were essential to educate citizens about democratic values, to unite an increasingly spread out and diverse population, and to create a literate and disciplined work force. The schools could achieve these goals, reformers hoped, by teaching a basic curriculum and instilling in students the middle-class values of hard work and respect for authority.

■■ Reformers supported free public schools to help children become good citizens and good workers.

Horace Mann's reform efforts in Massachusetts established the model for free public elementary education. In 1837, as Massachusetts's first secretary of education, Mann united local school districts into a state system, raised teachers' salaries, and increased spending on local schools. He also extended school terms, updated the curriculum, and established schools for training teachers. Mann's school reforms soon spread beyond Massachusetts as an increasing number of states set up state boards of education.

Historical Pictures Collection, Chicago

The Granger Collection, New York

▲ **This 1857 drawing shows a rural schoolmaster with his pupils. The lessons they are reading may have come from the *American Pictorial Primer*. Pages from this primer flank the drawing.**

Another educational reform during this period was the creation of the public high school. The nation's first, the English High School of Boston, opened in 1821. Free public high schools offered poor children a chance to pursue advanced courses that could prepare them for specialized careers in law or medicine.

Although these reforms provided a model for public education for all children, not all parents were pleased. Some farming and working-class families opposed public schooling because they depended on their children's labor. Also opposed were many Catholics who viewed public schools as a means of spreading Protestant beliefs.

Educational reform had little impact on the South. The antislavery movement made the South defensive about its "peculiar institution," and many southerners increasingly viewed all reform efforts with suspicion. As a result, the South lagged far behind the North in educational reform. Planters hired private tutors or established private schools for their own children, but they did not support public schools to educate all children.

African American education.

The public school movement also failed to benefit many African American children. By the 1850s only a few towns permitted black children to attend public schools. Some northern states maintained separate schools for African American children, but these institutions were generally underfunded.

Lewis Woodson, an African American educator, knew that this situation must be changed. He hailed education as a

66 jewel that will elevate, ennoble, and rescue the bodies of our long injured race from the shackles of bondage, and their minds from the trammels [restraints] of ignorance and vice. 99

This strong faith in education inspired free blacks to ensure an education for their children. African Americans successfully pressured a few public schools in the North to admit their children. They also set up private schools. John Melvin, an African American merchant, established Cleveland's first school for blacks and sponsored other such schools throughout Ohio in the 1830s.

Despite widespread opposition to educating African Americans, some colleges allowed free blacks to enroll. The first African American college graduate was probably Alexander Twilight, who received a degree from Vermont's Middlebury College in 1823. Within a few years other African Americans graduated from Amherst College in Massachusetts and Bowdoin College in Maine.

African Americans responded to their exclusion from most colleges by founding their own. Several colleges for black students were established in this period: Cheyney State College (1837), Avery College (1849), Lincoln University (1854), and Wilberforce University (1856).

Darius L. Donnell

Joseph S. Thompson

▲ Lincoln University in Pennsylvania is shown here, along with photographs of two early graduates.

Oberlin College was founded in Ohio in 1833 by ministers and abolitionists and soon became the nation's first integrated, coeducational college. In addition to its collegiate programs, Oberlin offered college preparatory courses for students who had not attended high school. By 1860, African American graduates of Oberlin, many of them fugitive slaves and the children of fugitive slaves, had gone on to become journalists, ministers, missionaries, and teachers.

Women and higher education. Women also challenged their lack of access to higher education. In 1841 the first three women to receive bachelor of arts degrees from a U.S. college graduated from Oberlin. In 1862 Mary Jane Patterson, also an Oberlin graduate, became the first African American woman to receive a college degree from a U.S. institution. These women's achievements were revolutionary because during this period women, as well as African American men, were widely considered unable to compete intellectually with white men.

Reformers realized that educational barriers prevented women from winning equal status to men. To help remedy this situation, several schools for women were established. Emma Willard founded the first women's high school, Troy Female Seminary, in New York in 1821. Two years later Catharine Beecher opened the Hartford Female Seminary, and in Alabama in 1831 the Huntsville Female Seminary opened. Mary Lyon, an accomplished teacher, founded the first women's college, Mount Holyoke Female Seminary, in 1836 in Massachusetts. The programs at Oberlin and Mount

▲ Mount Holyoke Female Seminary, in Massachusetts, became the model for institutions of higher education for women. A diploma is shown at left.

Holyoke allowed women to study, for the first time, subjects that society had thought only white men could master. Women graduates from these institutions launched careers as teachers, writers, journalists, doctors, and reformers.

■■ **Reformers established alternative schools to provide African Americans and women with educational opportunities denied them by public institutions.**

SECTION 2 REVIEW

IDENTIFY and explain the significance of the following: rehabilitation, temperance movement, prohibition, Horace Mann, John Melvin, Mary Jane Patterson, Mary Lyon.

1. **MAIN IDEA** How did reformers hope to rehabilitate prisoners?

2. **MAIN IDEA** Why did reformers believe that the nation needed free public education?

3. **MAIN IDEA** How did reformers attempt to provide educational opportunities for both African Americans and women?

4. **WRITING TO INFORM** You are a 19th-century business owner with a strict temperance policy for your employees. Write a letter to the president of another company informing him or her about the advantages and disadvantages of this policy.

5. **RECOGNIZING POINTS OF VIEW** How did Dorothea Dix view the mentally ill? How did this view influence her work?

THE CRUSADE FOR ABOLITION

FOCUS

- How did African Americans change the focus of antislavery efforts?
- What helped spark the call for immediate abolition?
- What obstacles did abolitionists face?

With the transportation, market, and industrial revolutions of the early 19th century, regional economic differences heightened the existing social and political tensions between the North and the South. The division between the systems of slave and free labor became more pronounced, leading to increased support for abolition among northerners. By the 1830s influential blacks and whites joined together in a vigorous, organized campaign to end slavery.

Coin bearing the seal of
an antislavery group

EARLY OPPONENTS OF SLAVERY

Most northern states had abolished slavery by the early 1800s. After working for abolition in their own states, many antislavery northerners wanted to end slavery across the country. To achieve this goal, many northerners supported the American Colonization Society's plan for ending slavery gradually.

Unlike many of the society's southern supporters, who saw colonization as a way to rid the South of free blacks, most northern advocates genuinely wanted to rid the country of slavery. Yet both groups shared the prejudice that all African Americans, both

▲ **Henry Highland Garnet**

enslaved and free, were inferior to whites and would never fit into U.S. society. In 1829 an American Colonization Society report described free blacks as "notoriously ignorant, degraded and miserable, . . . scarcely reached in their debasement by the heavenly light."

Northern free blacks strenuously objected to this unfair characterization. They opposed the American Colonization Society's plan to banish them from their country of birth. Henry Highland Garnet, a black abolitionist, declared:

66 America is my home, my country, and I have no other. . . . I mourn because the accursed shade of slavery rests upon it. I love my country's flag, and I hope that soon it will be cleansed of its stains, and be hailed by all nations as the emblem of freedom and independence. 99

To provide an alternative to the American Colonization Society, free blacks founded abolitionist societies. By 1826, African Americans

▲ Samuel Cornish (left) and John Russwurm (right) started the first African American newspaper, *Freedom's Journal,* in 1827. Cornish later served as editor of *The Colored American.*

had formed more than 143 antislavery societies. In 1827 Samuel Cornish and John Russwurm started the first African American newspaper, *Freedom's Journal,* to express African American opposition to slavery. Free blacks called on whites to join them in the fight to free "their brother[s] in chains."

These efforts helped mobilize public opinion against the American Colonization Society. By 1831 only some 1,400 African Americans had settled in Liberia, the West African republic founded by the society. The society had persuaded few slaveholders to free their slaves. And despite the discrimination that free blacks faced, few wanted to leave the United States.

■■ **Most free blacks objected to colonization efforts. They formed abolitionist societies as an alternative way to end slavery.**

*T*HE CALL TO ACTION

Although early black and white abolitionists had not shared common strategies, in the 1830s they began to join forces to call for an immediate end to slavery. The appearance of two important publications, David Walker's *Appeal* and William Lloyd Garrison's *Liberator,* marked the start of a bold,

energetic, and more organized attack on the institution of slavery.

In 1829 David Walker, a Boston businessman and free black, published the *Appeal to the Colored Citizens of the World,* in which he demanded immediate, universal abolition. Walker bid free blacks and slaves to take action—violent action if necessary—for freedom and equality. In a blistering attack he criticized slaveholders who used the Bible to justify slavery. He urged white Americans to condemn slavery and to recognize the rights and humanity of black Americans. Before he could put his words into practice, however, Walker died in 1830 under mysterious circumstances. Nevertheless, the publication of Walker's *Appeal* represented a new mood among abolitionists. Opponents of slavery, both black and white, were becoming impatient with their lack of progress in promoting abolition.

This impatience led William Lloyd Garrison, a New England journalist, to action. With the financial backing of wealthy African American and white abolitionists, Garrison launched the abolitionist newspaper the *Liberator* in 1831. In the first issue, Garrison expressed his determination to work for the immediate abolition of slavery:

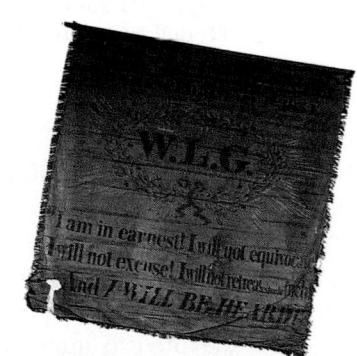

❝ I *will be* as harsh as truth and as uncompromising as justice. On this subject, I do not wish to think, or speak, or write, with moderation. . . . I am in earnest—I will not equivocate [evade the truth]—I will not excuse—I will not retreat a single inch—AND I WILL BE HEARD. ❞

▲ This colorful banner proudly displays William Lloyd Garrison's famous motto.

Garrison soon became one of the most articulate supporters of immediate abolition. He insisted that slavery was both a sin and a crime because it contradicted both the Bible and the Constitution. Garrison argued that the sin of slavery should be given up immediately in order to save the country. He fiercely attacked both slavery and racial prejudice and argued that blacks should enjoy equality with whites.

■■ **Demands for immediate abolition began with the publication of the *Appeal* and the *Liberator.***

▲ Abolitionists used antislavery songs to protest the evils of slavery. One notable example was "The Fugitive's Song," composed in honor of Frederick Douglass's escape from slavery.

THE AMERICAN ANTI-SLAVERY SOCIETY

In 1833, prominent black and white abolitionists formed the first national antislavery organization devoted to immediate abolition—the **American Anti-Slavery Society**. The society soon claimed more than 200 branches across the North and the Middle West. It papered the country with countless antislavery publications and organized petition drives to protest legislation supporting slavery. Most important, the society sponsored national lecture tours of abolitionists who hoped to convince Americans that slavery was morally wrong.

Frederick Douglass. Among the best at winning converts to the American Anti-Slavery Society was Frederick Douglass, a fugitive slave from Maryland. He was the first runaway to speak publicly against slavery. His moving speeches about his life as a slave who "suffered under the lash without the power of resisting" convinced many people to support abolition.

Douglass was also a powerful writer. His autobiography, *Narrative of the Life of Frederick Douglass* (1845), became a classic indictment of the slave system. In 1847 Douglass and a partner began an antislavery newspaper, the *North Star*, which was later renamed *Frederick Douglass's Paper*. Published in Rochester, New York, from 1847 to 1864, the paper won support for abolition. An editorial in the first edition urged those who had *"suffered the wrong"* to lead the abolitionist cause. "He who has *endured the cruel pangs of Slavery* is the man to *advocate Liberty*."

Frederick Douglass's wife, Anna Murray Douglass, was also an active abolitionist. Using their home in Rochester as a depot for the Underground Railroad, she helped runaway slaves flee to Canada and freedom.

BIO GRAPHY **Sojourner Truth.** Another ex-slave who worked tirelessly for the American Anti-Slavery Society was Sojourner Truth (c. 1797–1883). She was born Isabella Baumfree on the New York estate of a wealthy Dutch landowner. In 1827, the year before the mandatory freeing of slaves in New York, she managed to flee from her last master. After her escape she joined religious reformers who preached on the streets of New York City. Six feet tall, extremely thin, and speaking with a Dutch accent, she made a powerful impression.

Sojourner Truth

In 1843 Baumfree said she had a religious vision in which God instructed her to find a new mission and a new identity. Adopting the name Sojourner (visitor) Truth, she traveled through New England on foot, preaching the "truth"—abolition and women's rights.

RESISTANCE TO ABOLITION

By 1840, abolitionists had recruited some 200,000 northerners to their cause. Southern slaveholders, of course, felt threatened by the growing movement. But some northerners also opposed abolition. Garrison once remarked that he found "contempt more bitter, opposition more active, . . .

THE AMISTAD MUTINY

In 1839 the Spanish ship *Amistad* set sail from Havana, Cuba, bound for a plantation on the eastern end of the island. While at sea, Joseph Cinque and some 50 other enslaved Africans on board mutinied, killing the captain and part of the crew. The Africans tried to sail back to their homeland but were picked up by a U.S. warship. They were imprisoned and charged with piracy and murder.

Abolitionists, who saw the situation as an opportunity to rally support for their cause, arranged for the Africans' defense in court. Cinque told the court that he had been kidnapped in Africa and sold into slavery. The defense then successfully argued that because Spain had outlawed the international slave trade in 1820, the accused were not slaves but free men who had acted in self-defense.

American newspapers followed the trial closely, paying particular attention to the striking figure of Cinque. One newspaper described him as "possessing the true elements

▲ The mutiny aboard the *Amistad*, the return of the captives, and the subsequent trial are depicted here in a series of three paintings.

of heroism," and his dignified manner throughout the trial earned him the respect and sympathy of many.

In 1841 the U. S. Supreme Court, under Chief Justice Roger B. Taney, heard the case on appeal. Former president John Quincy Adams argued for the defense. Adams told the court that the Declaration of Independence guaranteed that "every man has a right to life and liberty." In summary, he said, "I ask nothing more in behalf of these unfortunate men than this Declaration." On March 9 the Supreme Court handed down its decision, which upheld the lower court.

Abolitionists rejoiced over the verdict, which freed the Africans. The decision, however, was more narrow than it seemed. Although the trial helped to focus national attention on the issue of slavery, the decision itself said nothing about the legality of slavery. Furthermore, the ruling implied that if the defendants *had* been slaves, they would not have been entitled to such a basic human right as self-defense. The *Amistad* case foreshadowed the later *Dred Scott* v. *Sandford* case, in which Chief Justice Taney ruled that slaves were indeed "property" and therefore had no fundamental rights.

and apathy more frozen" in New England than in the South. He exaggerated, but not by much.

As the antislavery movement gained momentum in the 1830s, mob violence increased. In 1835 Garrison was almost killed by a Boston mob. Elijah Lovejoy, an abolitionist editor in Alton, Illinois, was killed in 1837 as he tried to prevent a mob from destroying his printing press.

Why did some northerners oppose abolition with such fury? Much of the opposition was based on prejudice against African Americans. Many northern wage earners feared competing with free blacks for jobs. Many northern merchants feared abolition would disrupt cotton production, thus cutting into the profits they made from selling cotton on the world market. One merchant warned abolitionists: "We mean, sir, to put you Abolitionists down—by fair means if we can, by foul means if we must."

THE MOVEMENT SPLINTERS

Abolitionists also faced problems within their movement. William Lloyd Garrison's attacks on churches and the government for condoning slavery became more fierce and frequent. He also began to denounce the Constitution as an "agreement with hell," warning abolitionists to rely on moral appeals alone to end slavery. Garrison's stubborn refusal to use other tactics angered moderates, who supported change through the ballot box.

Just as troubling to many moderates was Garrison's call for equal rights for women. Many white male abolitionists viewed women as inferior to men and did not appreciate women's increased visibility and political activity within the movement.

Although excluded from formal membership in the American Anti-Slavery Society, women still assumed important roles in the movement. Maria W. Stewart, an African American journalist and teacher, won converts to abolition as early as 1832—the year before the formation of the American Anti-Slavery Society. She became the first American woman to speak publicly about abolition before mixed audiences. Other women organized female abolitionist societies, which sponsored petition drives and raised money.

▲ An abolitionist group is shown gathered on the porch of Lucy Stone's house. Lucy Stone was a well-known suffragist and abolitionist. Abby Kelley is seated in the middle of the top row.

When Garrison's supporters put a woman, Abby Kelley, on an important American Anti-Slavery Society committee in 1840, moderates formed their own organization. The split did not seriously damage the cause, however. The number of local abolitionist organizations continued to grow. By the late 1840s there were more than 2,000 local societies—most of them in New York, Ohio, Massachusetts, and Pennsylvania—that kept public attention focused on abolition.

Abolitionists faced violent opposition from some northerners and disputes within their own movement.

SECTION 3 REVIEW

IDENTIFY and explain the significance of the following: David Walker, William Lloyd Garrison, American Anti-Slavery Society, Frederick Douglass, Sojourner Truth, Maria W. Stewart.

1. **MAIN IDEA** Why did African Americans oppose colonization? What steps did they take to change the direction of the antislavery movement?

2. **MAIN IDEA** How did publications such as the *Appeal* and the *Liberator* affect the abolitionist movement?

3. **GAINING A MULTICULTURAL PERSPECTIVE** Why were the appeals of Frederick Douglass and Sojourner Truth so effective in persuading people to join the abolitionist movement?

4. **WRITING TO DESCRIBE** You are a woman abolitionist in 1840. Write an essay describing the obstacles you face and your experiences in the movement.

5. **ASSESSING CONSEQUENCES** Provide evidence to support the following statement: "African Americans hastened the end of slavery by taking an active role in the abolitionist movement."

Section 4

THE CAUSE OF WOMEN'S RIGHTS

FOCUS

■ What rights did the early women's rights activists demand?

■ What reforms did the women's rights activists achieve? What issues remained unresolved?

■ Why were middle-class women's rights groups unable to gain wide support among African American women and white working-class women?

Women played major roles in all reform movements. They ran organizations and mastered the skills of fund-raising, public speaking, and petitioning legislatures. But women still met opposition to their roles as reformers. Many women involved in reform movements realized that they needed secure economic and political rights to participate fully in society. As a result, women in the late 1840s expanded their work to include the struggle for their own rights.

Speaker for women's rights

ABOLITION AND WOMEN'S RIGHTS

The experiences of Sarah Grimké and Angelina Grimké, two early lecturers for the American Anti-Slavery Society, illustrate how supporting African Americans' rights led many women to work for their own rights. Daughters of a prominent Charleston, South Carolina, slaveholder, the Grimké sisters moved to the North in the 1820s and became abolition-ists. The sisters at first devoted their energies solely to the fight against slavery. But over time they came to

view abolition and women's rights as parts of the same struggle. Angelina Grimké argued:

66 The discussion of the rights of the slave has opened the way for the discussion of other rights, and the ultimate result will most certainly be the breaking of *every* yoke . . . an emancipation far more glorious than any the world has ever yet seen. 99

The Grimkés' efforts met sharp opposition. Cath-arine Beecher, an education reformer and advocate of women's traditional roles, criticized the

▶ Sarah Grimké

◀ Angelina Grimké

Grimkés and other women for participating in abolitionist petition campaigns. "Petitions to congress," Beecher argued, "seem, IN ALL CASES, to fall entirely without [outside] the sphere of female duty. Men are the proper persons to make appeals to the rulers whom they appoint."

A group of Congregationalist ministers from Massachusetts echoed such sentiments. In 1837 they denounced the Grimkés for speaking before mixed audiences. The ministers said women's influence should be "unobtrusive and private" through quiet prayers and through their work at home and in Sunday schools.

But the Grimkés refused to back down. "Men and women were CREATED EQUAL," Sarah Grimké wrote. "They are both moral and accountable beings, and whatever is *right* for man to do, is *right* for woman." Her sister agreed that "it is a woman's right to have a voice in all the laws and regulations by which she is to be *governed,* whether in Church or State." She added that society's "present arrangements" on these matters "are *a violation of human rights.*"

WOMEN DECLARE THEIR RIGHTS

The link between abolition and women's rights endured as the call for equal rights for women grew stronger in the 1840s. Two noted abolitionists who became leading active supporters of women's rights were Elizabeth Cady Stanton and Lucretia Mott.

Stanton and Mott were deeply troubled by women's status in American society. Denied the right to vote, women remained second-class citizens. They had far less access to education, especially higher education, than men. Social prejudices limited women to a few professions, and women received lower wages than men. Married women had few rights to own property (even inherited property) or to keep their own earnings. Women who divorced their husbands could not get custody of their children.

Stanton and Mott became painfully aware of these injustices in 1840 when they attended the World's Anti-Slavery Convention in London. Convention officials refused to allow women to speak. As a result, Stanton and Mott agreed that after the convention they would launch a movement to end the daily discrimination women faced. Their efforts led to the first U.S. women's

▼ Elizabeth Cady Stanton

▲ Lucretia Mott

rights convention, held in Seneca Falls, New York, in 1848.

More than 300 women and men attended the **Seneca Falls Convention**, which marked the birth of the organized women's rights movement in the United States. The convention adopted a Declaration of Sentiments modeled on the democratic ideals contained in the Declaration of Independence:

❝ We hold these truths to be self-evident: that all men and women are created equal; that they are endowed by their Creator with certain inalienable rights. . . .

Now, . . . because women do feel themselves aggrieved, oppressed, and fraudulently deprived of their most sacred rights, we insist that they have immediate admission to all the rights and privileges which belong to them as citizens of the United States. ❞

The Declaration of Sentiments also called for reforms to strengthen women's legal position.

These reforms included granting married women the rights to control property and earnings and to be awarded custody of their children in the event of a divorce. Most important, they included granting women the right to vote.

The Declaration of Sentiments publicly voiced the discontent many women felt. Emily Collins, a woman from a small town in western New York, expressed her reaction to the convention:

> 66 I revolted in spirit against the customs of society and the laws of the State that crushed my aspirations. . . . But not until that meeting at Seneca Falls in 1848 . . . gave this feeling of unrest form and voice, did I take action. 99

Collins went on to organize the women in her town to work for women's rights.

▪▪ Women's rights activists demanded the same rights white men enjoyed.

The most fiercely debated issue at the Seneca Falls Convention was **suffrage**, the right to vote. Stanton said attaining the right to vote was crucial to winning full equality because "the power to choose rulers and make laws, was the right by which all others could be secured." Opponents of women's suffrage said demanding the vote was too radical. Most people agreed with Catharine Beecher that women should not participate in political activities. Others believed that such an unpopular demand might jeopardize support from influential politicians.

▶ **"All men and women are created equal"**—the delegates at Seneca Falls adopted this Declaration of Sentiments, which contained resolutions patterned after the Declaration of Independence.

WOMEN'S RIGHTS ACTIVISM

Although the Seneca Falls reformers agreed to work for suffrage, early activists for women's rights devoted most of their energies to attaining other legal reforms called for in the Declaration of Sentiments. To achieve these goals, the activists organized a system of linked local organizations, held national women's rights conferences, and organized a series of state conventions across the North and the Middle West. At one such convention in Akron, Ohio, in 1851, Sojourner Truth gave a speech that convinced many men in attendance that women were their equals. She eloquently recounted her own experiences:

> 66 Look at my arm! I have ploughed and planted and gathered into barns . . . and ain't I a woman? I could work as much and eat as much as a man—when I could get it—and bear the lash as well! And ain't I a woman? I have born thirteen children, and seen most of 'em sold into slavery, and when I cried out with my mother's grief, none but Jesus heard me—and ain't I a woman? 99

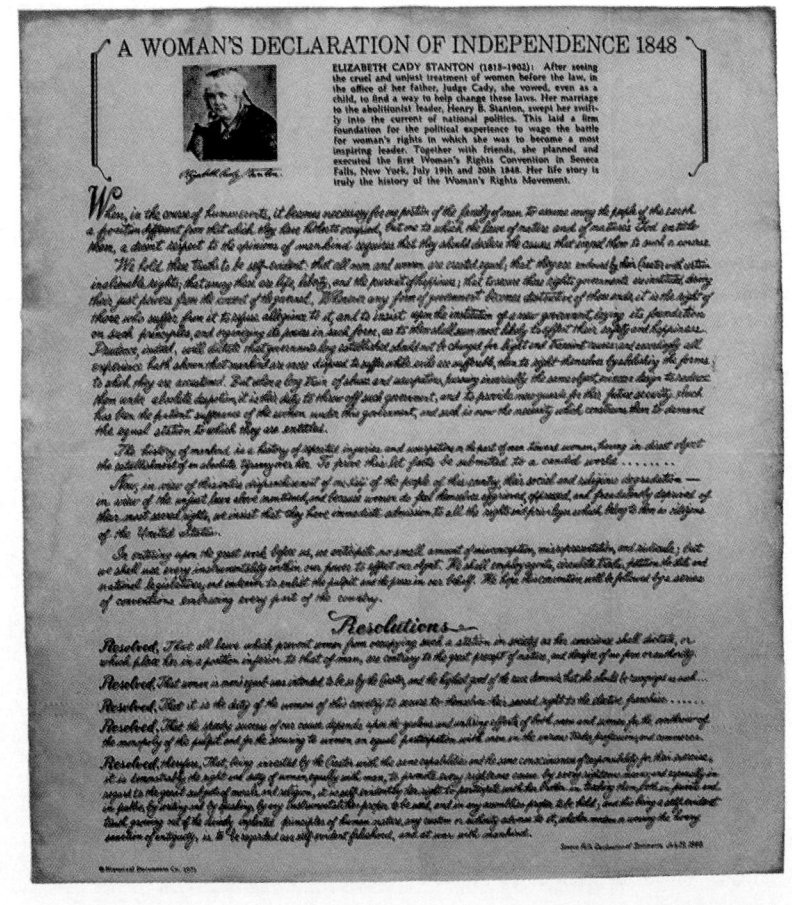

A WOMAN'S DECLARATION OF INDEPENDENCE 1848

▲ Susan B. Anthony participated in temperance and antislavery causes, as well as those of women's rights. In 1872 she was arrested for attempting to cast a vote in the Rochester city elections.

Another important women's rights leader was Susan B. Anthony. She was raised in a Quaker family that affirmed the equality of men and women. From her involvement in temperance and abolition, Anthony learned the limits society placed on women's roles in reform movements. In 1852 she was forbidden to speak at a temperance convention because she was a woman. This event convinced her that women could not be effective in reform movements unless they won political rights. At Elizabeth Cady Stanton's urging, Anthony dedicated the rest of her life to working for women's rights. She organized petition campaigns and meetings, gave speeches, and raised money for the cause.

Anthony, along with Stanton, Mott, and Truth, also argued for a variety of legal reforms that would benefit women. One of these reforms—women's right to own and control their property—had first been proposed by middle-class men. Some fathers had long supported this cause as a way of protecting what they saw as family property from untrustworthy sons-in-law.

In response to calls for reform, New York and other states revised their laws to permit married women to own property, file lawsuits, and retain their earnings. But political and legal equality on the national level, including the right to vote, would be slow in coming. Despite passionate demands for political rights in 1848 and the subsequent focus on suffrage, women did not gain a constitutional guarantee of voting rights until 1920. Nevertheless, the women's rights activists of the mid-1800s initiated the movement that continues today.

▉▉ Women's rights activists achieved some gains in legal rights on the state level but failed to win the right to vote.

▶ Male election judges refused to accept suffragist Victoria Woodhull's ballot when she attempted to vote. In 1872 Woodhull helped form the Equal Rights party and ran unsuccessfully for president with abolitionist Frederick Douglass as her running mate.

COMMENTARY

Who Participated in the Women's Rights Movement?

The grievances expressed at the Seneca Falls Convention were primarily white, middle-class, married women's concerns. The demands for married women's property rights, control of wages, and custody of children were meant to cement middle-class women's social status. These rights were not the main concerns of women with few resources, such as the majority of African American women and white working-class women.

Stanton, Mott, and other white women's rights activists showed a commitment to abolition and equal rights for African Americans. However, many local women's rights activists feared a shift in focus away from women's rights and toward abolitionism. Local and state organizations often discriminated against black women. When black abolitionist Sojourner Truth rose to speak at the Ohio convention, many people tried to keep her from speaking.

Although some African American women participated in women's rights groups, many more devoted their energies to building and aiding welfare and educational institutions in their own communities. They also participated in organizations devoted to abolition and equality for all African Americans. These black women believed that the best way to improve their status as women was to focus first on improving their status as African Americans.

Although Susan B. Anthony helped draft a code of fair wages for women in 1853, most women's rights activists ignored workplace issues. As a result, most white working-class women looked to other groups for support in their struggle for better wages and working conditions. For example, when women such as Sarah Bagley organized strikes (see Chapter 8), they allied themselves with white working-class men who shared their concerns.

It is therefore important to realize that the movement created at Seneca Falls failed to include all women. Most African American and white working-class women had concerns different from those of middle-class women and therefore did not participate in the mainstream movement. Instead, they either joined groups that shared their concerns or formed their own organizations and found a separate path to equality.

■■ Few middle-class women's rights groups addressed the needs and concerns of African American women and white working-class women.

SECTION 4 REVIEW

IDENTIFY and explain the significance of the following: Sarah Grimké, Angelina Grimké, Catharine Beecher, Elizabeth Cady Stanton, Lucretia Mott, Seneca Falls Convention, suffrage, Susan B. Anthony.

1. **MAIN IDEA** What was the goal of early women's rights activists?

2. **MAIN IDEA** How successful were women's rights activists in achieving reforms?

3. **MAIN IDEA** Why did African American women and white working-class women form their own organizations rather than join middle-class women's rights groups? What issues did these organizations tackle?

4. **WRITING TO CREATE** Write an inspirational song or poem that demonstrates the struggle for women's rights in the 1850s.

5. **ASSESSING CONSEQUENCES** How did the suffrage issue divide the women's rights movement?

First public
high school
opens.

African American Alexander
Twilight graduates from
Middlebury College.

Freedom's Journal
begins publication.

Walker's
Appeal
published.

Mormon church
founded.

Garrison's *Liberator*
begins publication.

American Anti-
Slavery Society
established.

1820   1825   1830   1835

WRITING A SUMMARY
Using the essential points of the chapter as a guide, write a summary of the chapter.

REVIEWING CHRONOLOGY
Number your paper 1 to 5. Study the time line above, and list the following events in the order in which they happened by writing the first next to 1, the second next to 2, and so on. Then complete the activity below.

1. Seneca Falls Convention held.
2. Wilberforce University founded.
3. Maine bans sale of alcohol.
4. Mormon church founded.
5. Garrison's *Liberator* begins publication.

Identifying Cause and Effect Select two events on the time line, and in a paragraph, explain the cause-and-effect relationship between them.

IDENTIFYING PEOPLE AND IDEAS
Explain the historical significance of each of the following people or terms.

1. Second Great Awakening
2. Frederick Douglass
3. temperance movement
4. Horace Mann
5. William Lloyd Garrison
6. utopias
7. Sojourner Truth
8. Lucretia Mott
9. suffrage
10. Susan B. Anthony

UNDERSTANDING MAIN IDEAS
1. Why did many southern states pass laws making it illegal to teach slaves to read?
2. Which kinds of reforms met significant opposition? Why?
3. What are some of the ways in which African Americans participated in the reform efforts of the 19th century?
4. Why were many women's rights reformers also abolitionists?
5. How did reformers work to improve the lives of poor Americans?

REVIEWING THEMES
1. **Democratic Values** In what ways were reformers successful in changing public policies that affected mental illness, prisons, schools, and women's rights?
2. **Cultural Diversity** What social factors contributed to the rise of revivalism and the spread of utopian communities in the 1800s?

THINKING CRITICALLY
1. **Synthesizing** Why did reformers tackle such a wide variety of causes during this period?
2. **Hypothesizing** What factors may have motivated reformers to persist in their efforts even under the threat of violence?
3. **Analyzing** How might the abolitionist movement have been different if William Lloyd Garrison had compromised with his opponents?

STRATEGY FOR SUCCESS
Review the Strategies for Success on Interpreting the Visual Record on page 98. Then study the painting of a camp revival meeting below. On a separate sheet of paper, describe the physical surroundings and suggest why the artist placed the meeting in an idealized setting.

The Granger Collection, New York

Abolitionist Elijah
Lovejoy killed.

Dorothea Dix
begins crusade for
mentally ill. Brook
Farm founded.

Maine
bans sale
of alcohol.

North Star begins
publication.

Wilberforce
University
founded.

African American
Mary Jane Patterson
graduates from
Oberlin.

Enslaved Africans
mutiny on Amistad.

Douglass's
autobiography
published.

Seneca Falls
Convention
held.

1840   1845   1850   1855   1860

WRITING ABOUT HISTORY

Writing to Express a Viewpoint You are a politician running for office in the 1850s. Write a short speech that explains your position on one of the following issues: prohibition, public education, abolition, or women's rights.

USING PRIMARY SOURCES

Fanny Wright was a reformer who scandalized many by her outspoken views. Read the following excerpt from her lecture entitled "Of Existing Evils and Their Remedy." Then write an essay explaining why Wright advocated reform as a necessary part of a democracy.

> 66 *Great reforms are not wrought in a day. . . . A free people may boast that all power is in their hands; but no effectual power can be in their hands until knowledge be in their minds.*
>
> *But how may knowledge be imparted to their minds? Such effective knowledge as shall render apparent to all the interests of all, and demonstrate the simple truths: that a nation to be strong, must be united; to be united, must be equal in condition; to be equal in condition, must be similar in habits and feeling; to be similar in habits and in feeling,* must be raised in national institutions, as the children of a common family and citizens of a common country. 99

LINKING HISTORY AND GEOGRAPHY

Study the map at the top of the next column. Each dot represents an organization associated with a reform movement. Note that reform organizations are concentrated in the Middle West and the Northeast—areas of intense urban growth. Why do you think reform movements were most active in urban areas?

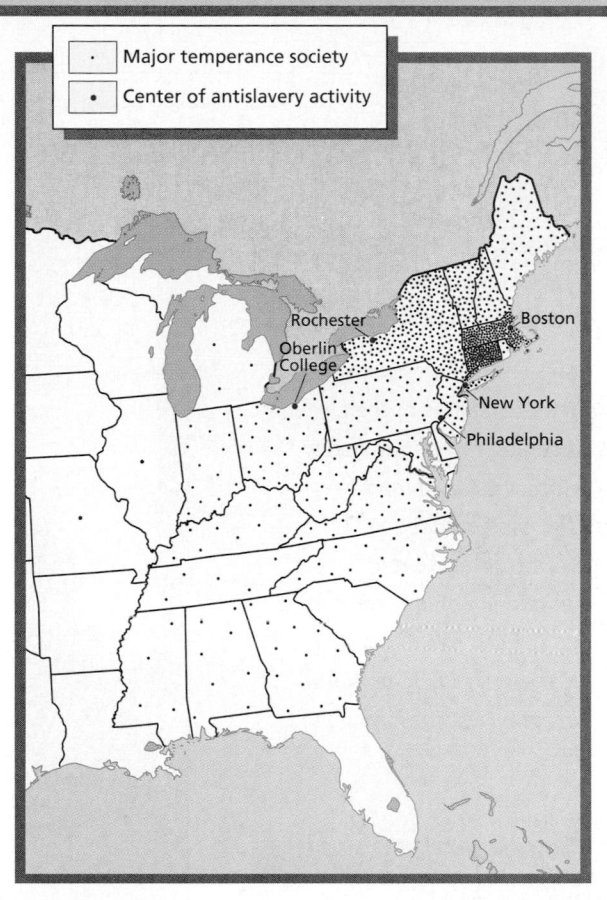

Major temperance society
Center of antislavery activity

Rochester
Oberlin
College
Boston
New York
Philadelphia

BUILDING YOUR PORTFOLIO

Complete the following projects independently or cooperatively.

1. INDIVIDUAL RIGHTS In chapters 7 and 8 you explored individual rights. Building on that experience, imagine you are a women's rights activist. Prepare a pamphlet calling for women's rights.

2. IMMIGRATION In Chapter 8 you were a newly arrived immigrant. Building on that experience, write an editorial casting temperance as an issue of immigrants' rights.

EXPANSION AND CONFLICT

FOCUS

UNDERSTANDING THE MAIN IDEA

In the early 1800s Americans moved beyond the boundaries of the United States and into present-day Texas, New Mexico, California, and Oregon. These migrations resulted in U.S. conflicts with Mexico and Great Britain and the expansion of U.S. territory to the Pacific Ocean. This expansion disrupted the ways of life of Native Americans and Mexicans living in these areas.

THEMES

■ **ECONOMIC DEVELOPMENT** How might individual economic choices affect a government's policies?

■ **CULTURAL DIVERSITY** Why might a nation of many cultures experience short-term conflict but emerge stronger in the long run?

■ **GLOBAL RELATIONS** Why might territorial expansion lead to international as well as domestic conflicts?

1836	1846	1848	1851
Texas declares independence.	U.S. Congress declares war on Mexico.	Gold discovered in California.	Treaty of Fort Laramie signed.

The 19th century was the principal era of U.S. expansion in North America. In 1803 the Louisiana Purchase added to the United States a vast portion of the continent west of the Mississippi River. Then in 1819 the nation acquired Florida from Spain.

Carl Nebel's 1851 print of U.S. troops entering Mexico City

In 1827 the Mexican government sent General Manuel Mier y Terán, a hero of the struggle for Mexican independence, to inspect Mexico's northeastern border. In a report written two years later he described the United States as hungry for more territory:

❝ The North Americans have conquered whatever territory adjoins them. In less than half a century, they have become masters of extensive colonies which formerly belonged to Spain and France, and of even more spacious territories from which have disappeared the former owners, the Indian tribes. ❞

He warned his superiors that people in the United States were already calling for the annexation of Texas. Mier y Terán predicted that soon U.S. settlers in Texas would begin to "incite uprisings in the territory." His words proved prophetic: in 1835, Texas settlers—both American and Mexican—rose up in revolt against the Mexican government.

Americans also moved to other territories in these years. After 1820 the search for trade and furs drew American settlers to the Mexican provinces of New Mexico and California and to Oregon Country, jointly occupied by Great Britain and the United States. These migrations caused conflicts as the United States sought to expand its boundaries to include the territories.

The Shelburne Museum, Shelburne, Vermont

Covered wagon moving westward

THE LURE OF THE WEST

FOCUS

- What argument did western expansionists use to win support for their views?
- Why did the Mexican government invite American settlers into Texas?
- What conflicts between the Texans and the Mexican government led to revolution?
- How did Texas independence affect Tejanos?

*B*efore 1820 few U.S. settlers ventured into the Spanish territories of Texas, California, and New Mexico. Even fewer, mainly trappers and traders, went to Oregon Country, the territory to which Great Britain and the United States shared a disputed claim. After 1820, however, U.S. settlers, driven by the search for economic opportunities and rich farmland, moved to the Far West in increasing numbers. U.S. expansionists urged them on.

Detail from *The Funeral of an Angel*

MANIFEST DESTINY

In 1845 the magazine editor John L. O'Sullivan coined the phrase **manifest destiny**, which expressed the popular belief that the United States was destined to extend its territory to the Pacific Ocean. O'Sullivan urged the United States to ignore other nations' claims to territory in North America.

66 Away, away with all these cobweb tissues of rights of discovery, exploration, settlement. . . . The American claim is by the right of our manifest destiny to overspread and to possess the whole of the continent which Providence [God] has given us for the development of the great experiment of liberty. 99

Many Americans supported manifest destiny. Northerners troubled by economic instability and urban crowding believed that expansion would lessen population pressures and would create new markets for U.S. products.

Southerners hungry for more land for cotton production also supported manifest destiny. To counter northern fears about the spread of slavery, they suggested that expansion would actually help end slavery in the Upper South by shifting the slave population westward. This argument appealed to northern whites who opposed slavery but did not want to see freed blacks settle in the North.

■■ U.S. expansionists argued that it was the nation's manifest destiny to claim all of North America.

Not all Americans supported manifest destiny, however. Some objected to expansion because the lands were already claimed by other nations. Others feared that expansion would produce a nation too large to govern. But for most Americans, particularly those facing the sometimes bitter realities of the market revolution, debates over manifest destiny were of little interest. Land and opportunity were their main concerns.

MEXICAN TEXAS

U.S. settlement of foreign territory was most clearly visible in the Mexican territory of Texas. By 1815 a few hundred Americans had already crossed the Sabine and Red rivers and settled in northeastern Texas.

This immigration increased after Mexico won its independence in 1821. After more than 10 years of fighting Spanish rule, Mexicans established the independent Republic of Mexico. Mexican authorities encouraged U.S. immigration to its northern territory to boost Texas's non-Indian population, which was about 4,000 in 1821. Officials hoped the non-Indian settlers would serve as a barrier between Mexico's northern settlements and Apache and Comanche raiders.

The tactic was a calculated risk. Mexican officials feared that the United States, which had twice tried to purchase Texas, would one day take the territory by force. The few thousand Tejanos (tay-HAH-nohs)—native Mexicans living in Texas—stood little chance of blocking an invasion. But if Mexico could recruit enough American settlers and turn them into loyal Mexican citizens—something it hoped to accomplish by making them landowners—the country might build a defensive force large enough to prevent a U.S. invasion. As a precaution, however, the Mexican government planned to recruit other foreign settlers to offset the American presence.

As an additional safeguard, Mexico did not open settlement to everyone. Instead, it gave generous land grants to *empresarios* (em-pruh-SAH-ree-ohs), businesspeople who agreed to recruit and take responsibility for new settlers. The *empresarios* attracted thousands of settlers to Texas. Though Mexico granted most *empresario* contracts to Americans, it gave some to Tejanos. Martín de León received a contract in 1824 to settle Mexican families in Texas. He founded Victoria, Texas, as the capital of his colony. Lorenzo de Zavala, a prominent Mexican politician, received a grant in eastern Texas in 1829, but transferred the contract the next year.

▪▪ Mexico promoted U.S. settlement in Texas to shield Mexico from Indian raids and a possible U.S. invasion.

Moses Austin, a Missouri businessman hoping to rebuild his fortunes after the Panic of 1819, was the first American granted an *empresario* contract. In 1821 the Spanish granted Austin permission to start a colony, but he died before he could recruit any settlers. His son, Stephen F. Austin, assumed the grant and went to Texas to select a site for his colony.

Recruitment proved easy, since Austin sold large lots for 12 cents an acre. (At the time, public land in the United States sold for $1.25 an acre.) Many of the settlers were cotton farmers who brought enslaved African Americans with them. By 1830 Austin and the other *empresarios* had relocated some 7,000 Americans to Texas.

▲ **Shown here are Mary and John Rabb, two of the first settlers to receive a land grant in Stephen F. Austin's colony.**

THE TEXAS REVOLUTION

By 1830, non-Mexicans outnumbered the Tejanos by about two to one. These new arrivals made little effort to learn Spanish or adapt to Mexican culture. In 1830, Mexico, fearing a rebellion in Texas as well as a U.S. invasion, closed the Texas border to further immigration from the United States and prohibited further importation of slaves to Texas. But these measures did little to slow immigration. By 1835 approximately 25,000 Americans, including some 3,000 slaves, lived in Texas. Many of these immigrants had entered illegally.

The recent immigrants deeply resented the 1830 measures. Slaveholders feared that Mexican authorities would soon crack down on the practice of slavery. The legislature had banned slavery in 1827, but Texans had negotiated a law to classify slaves as indentured servants. If the government overturned the law, the Texas cotton industry would collapse.

In 1834 the tense situation worsened when General Antonio López de Santa Anna seized control of the Mexican government. Santa Anna eliminated state representation by replacing elected representatives with his own appointees. The loss of state power angered the residents of many Mexican states, including Texans. Outraged American settlers and Tejanos rose up in revolt the next year. Isolated clashes quickly grew into a full-scale rebellion known as the **Texas Revolution**.

▪▪ Conflicts over immigration, slavery, and state power led to the Texas Revolution.

In December 1835, Texas rebels captured San Antonio. Other volunteers soon joined them. Santa Anna, leading several thousand Mexican troops, arrived at San Antonio in February 1836 to restore Mexican rule. From the Alamo, a stronghold built by Spanish missionaries, 187 Texas rebels fought off repeated attacks by Santa Anna's troops. On March 6, Mexican troops finally overran the fort, killing all 187 rebels (but sparing some 30 civilians). The Mexicans paid a heavy price for their victory, though—some 1,500 casualties. A few weeks later, Mexican troops defeated a Texas army near Goliad (GOH-lee-ad) and executed some 350 prisoners.

The Texans, who had declared their independence on March 2, were badly shaken by these defeats. On April 21, 1836, however, a Texas army under the command of Sam Houston surprised Santa Anna near the San Jacinto River. Shouting "Remember the Alamo!" and "Remember Goliad!" the Texans tore

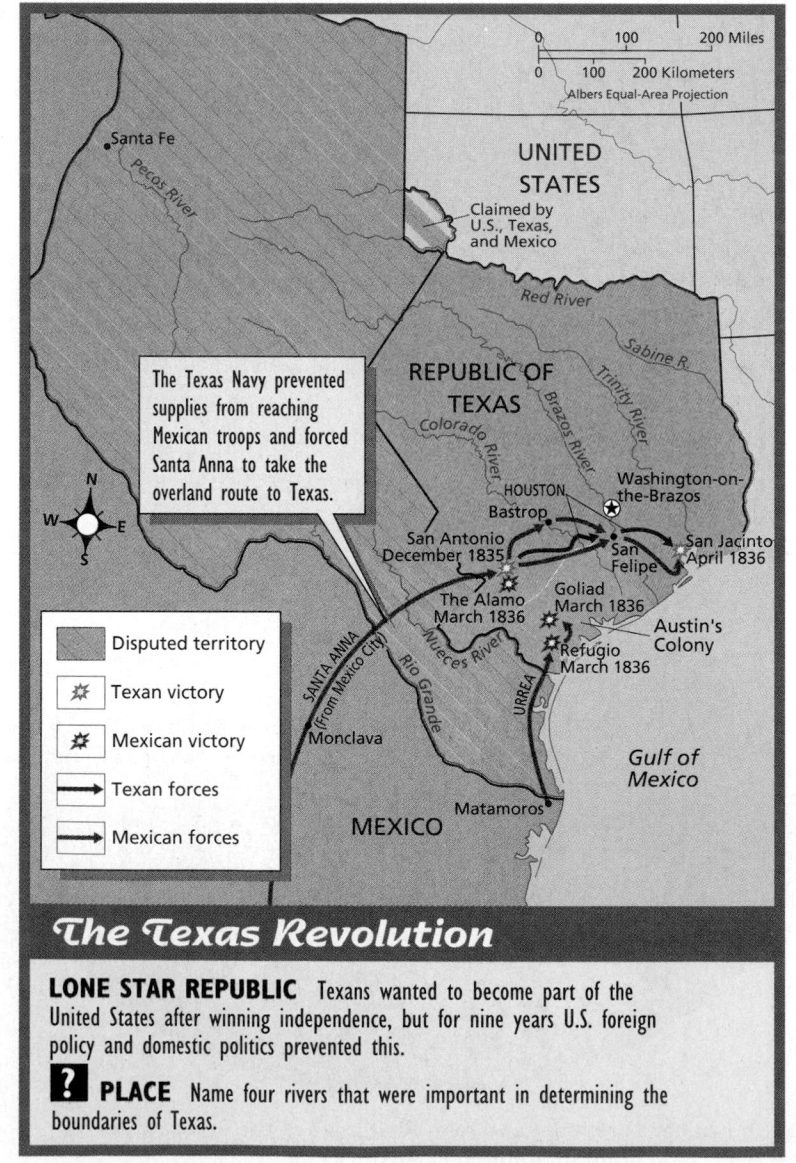

The Texas Navy prevented supplies from reaching Mexican troops and forced Santa Anna to take the overland route to Texas.

Disputed territory

☼ Texan victory

✹ Mexican victory

→ Texan forces

→ Mexican forces

The Texas Revolution

LONE STAR REPUBLIC Texans wanted to become part of the United States after winning independence, but for nine years U.S. foreign policy and domestic politics prevented this.

? **PLACE** Name four rivers that were important in determining the boundaries of Texas.

▲ In this painting by William H. Huddle, Santa Anna is shown surrendering to Sam Houston. Houston, who is lying on the blanket, was wounded in the ankle at the Battle of San Jacinto.

through Mexican lines, killing about 630 Mexican troops in less than 20 minutes and taking Santa Anna prisoner in the **Battle of San Jacinto**. With his troops already diminished and supplies low, Santa Anna agreed to remove his troops and grant Texas its independence. Texans set up the independent Republic of Texas, electing Sam Houston the first president and Lorenzo de Zavala the first vice president. The Mexican government refused to recognize the Republic.

LIFE IN THE REPUBLIC OF TEXAS

In 1837 Sam Houston petitioned the U.S. Congress for annexation. But northern opposition to admitting another slave state and a cautious foreign policy toward Mexico kept the U.S. Congress from granting the petition. From 1836 to 1845 Texas existed as an independent republic, known as the Lone Star Republic because its flag had a single star.

French and German immigration.
One of the Republic's first tasks was to bring more settlers to Texas. In 1842 the Texas congress awarded Henri Castro, a French banker of Portuguese descent, an *empresario* grant in central Texas. In September 1844 Castro brought his first 35 French colonists—many of them from the German-speaking region of Alsace—to found the town of Castroville just west of San Antonio. In the colony's first year, more than 2,000 settlers established farms with the seeds and supplies Castro provided.

The Texas government also allowed a German company to recruit settlers. In 1845 the company's agent, Prince Carl of Solms-Braunfels, and several German families founded New Braunfels in central Texas. From 1844 to 1847 the German company brought more than 7,000 German settlers to the land it called the "Paradise of North America."

Following a German tradition, most families in New Braunfels had a farm outside town and a small lot and house in town. Ferdinand Roemer, a German geologist and naturalist who traveled to Texas in the 1840s, described the new colony's houses:

66 The houses were of diverse architecture. . . . Some houses were of logs, some were of studding framework filled in with brick, some were frame while others were huts. . . . Several families were packed into one house, no matter how small it was. The interior of such a house, where men, women, and children were cooped up with their unpacked chests and boxes, often looked like the steerage of an immigrant ship. 99

▼ The first capitol of the new Republic of Texas, shown here in 1857, was located in Houston. The capital was later moved to Austin.

The families did not remain crowded for long, however, since most soon moved out of town and settled on their farms. Many families kept their homes in town, but used them only when they came into town for church or shopping.

German settlers spread their farming practices, language, and customs throughout the Hill Country of central Texas. German-language newspapers, church services, and social clubs helped them retain their language and customs for many generations.

Discrimination against Tejanos. The Tejanos did not fare as well as German settlers did in the Lone Star Republic. During the revolution, many Tejanos had fought and died alongside other Texans. After the revolution, however, a spirit of revenge against all Mexicans prevailed. Many Anglo Texans rushed to seize Tejano lands and property. Anglo Texans attacked some Tejanos and drove many others from the country.

Juan Nepomuceno Seguín (nay-poh-moo-SAY-noh se-GEEN), a member of a prominent San Antonio family and friend of Anglo settlers, was a tragic victim of prejudice. When the Texas Revolution began, Seguín joined the fight for independence and recruited Tejanos to face Santa Anna. After distinguishing himself in battle, he became a captain in the Texas cavalry.

Seguín escaped the slaughter at the Alamo only because he was sent through the Mexican lines in a desperate attempt to find help

Juan Seguín

for the besieged rebels. He then joined Houston's army and fought bravely in the Battle of San Jacinto. Seguín served as military commander of San Antonio after the war, bringing order to San Antonio and reassurance to the threatened Tejanos.

As a senator in the Texas congress and as the mayor of San Antonio, Seguín worked to improve conditions for Tejanos. "The American straggling adventurers," he later wrote of those early years, "were already beginning to work their dark intrigues against the native families, whose only crime was, that they owned large tracts of land and desirable property."

The pressure on Seguín gradually mounted. "At every hour of the day and night," he later recalled, "my countrymen ran to me for protection." In 1842 Anglo hatred and pressures forced Seguín to flee to Mexico. Seguín eventually returned to Texas for a time, but lived out his last years in Mexico, where he died in 1890.

■■ **After independence Tejanos faced increased discrimination and lost much of their land.**

SECTION 1 REVIEW

IDENTIFY and explain the significance of the following: manifest destiny, Tejanos, *empresarios,* Martín de León, Lorenzo de Zavala, Stephen F. Austin, Antonio López de Santa Anna, Texas Revolution, Sam Houston, Battle of San Jacinto, Henri Castro, Prince Carl of Solms-Braunfels, Juan Nepomuceno Seguín.

LOCATE and explain the importance of the following: San Antonio, Goliad.

1. **MAIN IDEA** How did western expansionists try to gain support for their views?

2. **MAIN IDEA** What did Mexico hope to accomplish by encouraging American settlement of Texas?

3. **IDENTIFYING CAUSE AND EFFECT** Describe the conditions faced by Tejanos after the Texas Revolution. What caused these conditions?

4. **WRITING TO INFORM** Imagine you are a newspaper reporter. Write a news story giving three causes of the Texas Revolution.

5. **GAINING A MULTICULTURAL PERSPECTIVE** How did Texas's *empresario* policy contribute to the state's cultural diversity?

Section 2

AMERICAN EXPANSIONISM

FOCUS

- **What issues and events led to the war between the United States and Mexico?**
- **What territories did the United States gain as a result of the war?**
- **What was the impact of the war on former Mexican citizens?**

Fueled by expansionist dreams, southerners and Democrats hoped to add Texas and the northern Mexican borderlands to the United States. By 1850 the United States did indeed expand to the Pacific Ocean— but only after a bloody war with Mexico and after intense political conflicts within the United States. This expansion disrupted the lives of former Mexican citizens living in the newly conquered regions.

1846 cartoon criticizing Polk's policies

TEXAS ANNEXATION

From 1836, when Texas won its independence, to 1845, the question of annexing Texas never died. Convinced of America's manifest destiny to expand westward, many citizens believed Texas should be added to the Union. The issue caused heated debate in Congress.

The debate over annexation. Supporters of Texas annexation argued that if Texas was not admitted to the Union, Great Britain might increase its influence there. Britain wanted an independent Texas as a source of cotton and as a market for British goods. Opponents of annexation, however, feared Texas's admission would increase the South's power in Congress by upsetting the balance between slave and free states.

The issue of western expansion dominated the 1844 presidential campaign, in which Whig party candidate Henry Clay of Kentucky opposed Democrat James K. Polk. A Tennessee politician, Polk called for annexation of Texas and Oregon. He became the dark horse choice of the Democrats

after they could not agree on a candidate at their convention. (A dark horse is a candidate who has not been considered a strong contender prior to the convention.)

Clay's Whig platform, on the other hand, made no mention of the Texas issue. Polk received 170 electoral votes to Clay's 105, but the popular vote was much closer. In fact, if Clay had won New York—which he lost by only 5,080 votes—he would have won the election by 7 electoral votes.

Polk's immediate call for Texas annexation pushed the United States closer to the brink of war with Mexico. Mexico had previously warned that it would consider U.S. annexation of Texas "equivalent to a declaration of war against the Mexican Republic." On March 28, 1845, in the wake of the

▶ **James and Sarah Polk were the first presidential couple to be photographed.**

James K. Polk Ancestral Home

congressional resolution annexing Texas, Mexico broke diplomatic relations with the United States.

Prelude to war. Polk fueled the Mexican government's anger by demanding that it recognize the Rio Grande as Mexico's northern border. The Rio Grande was about 100 miles south of the Nueces (nooh-AY-suhs) River, which Mexico recognized as the dividing line between Texas and Mexico. To back up the demand, Polk ordered troops under General Zachary Taylor to move into the disputed territory. As Polk was well aware, a U.S. military presence south of the Nueces River would almost certainly provoke an armed clash with Mexican troops.

After receiving information that Mexico was willing to resume diplomatic relations, Polk sent politician John Slidell to Mexico in late 1845 to establish the Rio Grande as the U.S.–Mexico boundary and to purchase the remaining Mexican territories in the Southwest. When Mexican citizens learned of Slidell's mission, they reacted angrily. Giving in to public outrage, the Mexican government refused to negotiate with Slidell. Polk immediately ordered General Taylor to move deeper into the disputed area. While publicly insisting that the troops were only defending American territory, Polk hoped that Mexico would commit an act that would justify war.

THE MEXICAN WAR

Months passed and Polk's impatience grew stronger. On May 9, 1846, he finally received the news he had been waiting for: Mexican troops had crossed the Rio Grande and had attacked a U.S. patrol. Polk sent his war message to Congress. "Mexico," he said, "has invaded our territory and shed American blood upon the American soil." On May 13 Congress declared war.

■■ **The U.S. annexation of Texas and its quest for more territory led to war with Mexico.**

Americans respond. Some Americans, particularly Whigs and northerners, criticized the **Mexican War**, calling it "Mr. Polk's war." Congressman Abraham Lincoln of Illinois, for example, introduced a series of "spot resolutions"

PRESIDENTIAL LIVES

JAMES K. POLK
1795–1849

**in office
1845–1849**

James K. Polk's contemporaries thought him unsociable—cold, formal, and closed-minded. Because of his wife's strict religious beliefs, Polk shunned the social life of Washington. Dancing was even banned in the White House. Besides, his work ethic left little time for recreation. "No President," Polk believed, "who performs his duty faithfully and conscientiously can have any leisure."

He usually rose at dawn, took a walk, and ate breakfast before most of Washington was awake. After a full day in his office, the president would return to his desk after dinner and work late into the night. Polk confided to his diary that the duties of the presidency sometimes bewildered him. After attending several elaborate diplomatic receptions, he wrote, "Such ceremonies seem very ridiculous to an American."

James K. Polk

in December 1847 challenging the president to show the exact spot where American blood had been spilled. If the site was indeed on American soil, he would support the war; if not, he said, the war was unjustified.

In addition, Polk's opponents charged that the war was aimed at acquiring more slave territory. The *Liberator* called the war one "of aggression, of invasion, of conquest." In Concord, Massachusetts, writer Henry David Thoreau went to jail rather than pay taxes to support the war. Abolitionist Frederick Douglass condemned the "disgraceful, cruel . . . war with our sister republic." In riveting public speeches, he demanded that Americans "leave off this horrid conflict, abandon their murderous plans, and forsake the way of blood."

Generally, however, Americans—especially southerners and westerners wanting Mexican lands—supported the war. Young men eager for adventure rushed to enlist.

The two sides clash. While Taylor pushed into northern Mexico, other U.S. forces seized New Mexico and California. In August 1846 an expedition led by Brigadier General Stephen Kearny (KAHR-nee) took Santa Fe and won control of New Mexico. Next, Kearny marched to California, where a group of U.S. settlers in northern California had recently revolted against Mexican rule. Declaring California an independent republic, the settlers raised a flag bearing the image of a grizzly bear, giving the uprising its name—the **Bear Flag Revolt.** Captain John C. Frémont, an American army officer and explorer who had led an expedition into California in 1845, helped organize the revolt after receiving a secret message from Polk.

U.S. marines under the command of Commodore John Sloat had already captured Monterey (the capital of the province) in July. Kearny's troops first faced armed resistance at San Pasqual (puh-SKWAWL) near San Diego. After several other battles, troops led by Kearny and Commodore Robert F. Stockton defeated Mexican troops in January 1847 at San Gabriel near Los Angeles, completing the U.S. conquest of California.

Soon thereafter, fierce fighting raged in northern Mexico near the hacienda of Buena Vista. In February 1847 Taylor's force of fewer than 5,000 men battled Santa Anna's force of some 15,000. Although the battle forced Santa Anna to withdraw, Taylor felt little joy at the victory. "The great loss on both sides," he wrote, "has deprived me of everything like pleasure."

A bold siege of Mexico City marked the war's final campaign. Led by General Winfield Scott, some 10,000 U.S. troops captured the fortified castle at Veracruz on the Gulf of Mexico in March 1847. Marching from the coast, General Scott daringly maneuvered into position to attack the very heart of the Mexican nation. He avoided large-scale battles, thereby preserving both supplies and soldiers for the siege.

Mexicans valiantly defended the long, mountainous road to the capital. One wounded U.S.

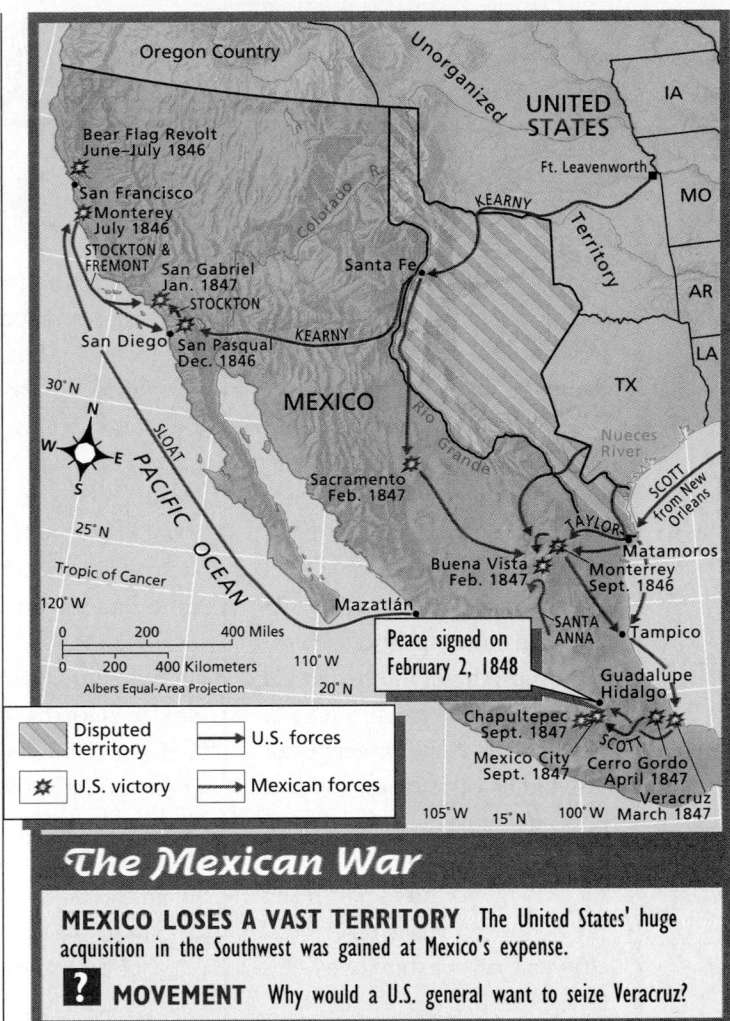

The Mexican War

MEXICO LOSES A VAST TERRITORY The United States' huge acquisition in the Southwest was gained at Mexico's expense.

? **MOVEMENT** Why would a U.S. general want to seize Veracruz?

soldier wrote: "Nobody ever told us how them [Mexicans] could fight. We thought they'd run like sheep; instead, they turned on us like bobcats." Despite the fierce resistance, U.S. troops reached Mexico City in September. They took over the National Palace, which President Santa Anna had already abandoned. In the hilltop garrison of Chapultepec (chuh-POOL-tuh-pek), young Mexican cadets fought hard to hold off U.S. soldiers. Despite their individual heroism, Mexico City's defenders fell as U.S. troops assaulted and captured the capital on September 14.

The Treaty of Guadalupe Hidalgo. By September 1847, U.S. forces held California and New Mexico; General Taylor's troops occupied much of northern Mexico; and General Scott's soldiers held Mexico City. In February 1848 the **Treaty of Guadalupe Hidalgo** (GWAHD-uhl-oop hi-DAL-goh) ended the war on terms dictated by the United States.

The Mexican War

Few Americans consider the Mexican War a major turning point in U.S. history. Even in Brownsville, Texas, the site of the battles of Resaca de la Palma and Palo Alto, no great monuments stand to mark the events.

In contrast, Mexicans view the war as a critical event in their history. Every year Mexicans make pilgrimages to a large monument in Mexico City that honors those who died in the fighting. Many streets bear the names of soldiers, and their portraits appear on Mexican currency.

Why do the Mexican and the American views differ? To answer that question, we need to look at the war through Mexican eyes. In early 1846 U.S. troops crossed into disputed territory on the border between Mexico and the United States. Mexico saw these troops as an invading force. The United States had been pushing its borders toward Mexican lands for decades. The Louisiana Purchase in 1803, the acquisition of Florida in 1819, the migration of settlers to Oregon Country, and the annexation of Texas in 1845 all convinced Mexico that Americans intended to occupy the entire continent. Mexico feared for its valuable California and New Mexico territories.

Thus, Mexico saw the United States as a land-hungry aggressor. Mexicans believed they had no choice but to defend their homeland against the "Colossus of the North." In addition, some Mexicans hoped to reconquer Texas, whose independence and annexation by the United States Mexico had not yet formally recognized. Although Mexico believed it had "right" on its side and fought bravely, its army could not withstand the U.S. attacks.

At the war's end the United States laid claim to Mexico's northern territories— about two fifths of all Mexican land—as the spoils of war. To Mexico the terms of the Treaty of Guadalupe Hidalgo were as unfair and unjustifiable as the U.S. attack had been. As one critic of the treaty, Mexican Congress member Manuel Cresencio Rejón, cried:

> 66 With all the right on our side, I cannot see by what justification [the United States] comes to us giving us as a condition for the reestablishment of the peace . . . , the renunciation [forfeit] of our northern frontier from sea to sea, and all for the measly sum of 18,250,000 pesos [15 million dollars]. 99

According to Rejón, the sum the United States offered for this land was less than one twentieth of its value.

The war and the terms of the treaty shattered Mexico. Its California and New Mexico territories were taken, and with

▲ Detail from the 1848 Treaty of Guadalupe Hidalgo

them some 80,000 Mexican citizens and the tremendous natural resources of the regions. Tragically for Mexico, gold, which could have boosted the Mexican economy, was discovered in California just nine days before the signing of the treaty.

For many years after the war, Mexico struggled to stabilize its government and develop its economy to prevent any further losses of territory to the United States. As a result, for most of the 19th century, Mexico focused on internal rather than external affairs. This inward-looking policy delayed Mexico's full entry into the world marketplace.

In the 20th century, as Mexico's government and economy have grown stronger, some political leaders have used the Mexican War to criticize U.S. expansionism and foreign policy. Many Mexicans have expressed resentment at the United States for becoming the most powerful country in the Americas at Mexico's expense. Thus, even today the Mexican War remains an important part of Mexican consciousness.

U.S. Boundaries, 1853

TERRITORIAL EXPANSION Many Americans supported westward expansion, believing that more territory would help ease social and economic problems.

? PLACE How many states were admitted to the Union between 1820 and 1853?

OREGON TREATY 1846
The treaty extended the 49th parallel boundary from the Rockies to Puget Sound, then through the channel around Vancouver Island to the Pacific.

WEBSTER-ASHBURTON TREATY OF 1842
The treaty with Britain settled the boundary between Maine and Canada. The treaty also adjusted the U.S.–Canadian border from Maine westward to the Lake of the Woods.

MEXICAN CESSION 1848
In the Treaty of Guadalupe Hidalgo, Mexico gave up much of its land in return for $15 million.

GADSDEN PURCHASE 1853
Pushed by southern transcontinental railroad builders, the United States paid Mexico $10 million for this land, which rounded out the boundaries of the continental United States.

Legend:
- Acquired by Oregon Treaty
- Mexican Cession
- Gadsden Purchase
- Texas Annexation
- 1845 Date admitted to the Union
- Acquired by Webster-Ashburton Treaty

By the terms of the Treaty of Guadalupe Hidalgo, Mexico gave up all claims to Texas and surrendered the vast territory known as the **Mexican Cession**: the present-day states of California, Nevada, and Utah, and parts of Arizona, Colorado, and New Mexico. In return, the United States agreed to pay Mexico $15 million and take over payment of the damages claimed by Americans against Mexico. The United States also agreed to grant full citizenship to Mexicans in the Mexican Cession and to respect their religious beliefs and property rights.

■■ **Mexico surrendered present-day California, Nevada, Utah, and parts of Arizona, Colorado, and New Mexico to the United States.**

In 1853 U.S. diplomat James Gadsden negotiated a deal with Mexico to purchase an additional strip of land south of the Gila (HEE-luh) River (in present-day southern Arizona and New Mexico) for $10 million. With the **Gadsden Purchase** the United States had acquired all of Mexico's territory north of the Rio Grande.

MEXICAN AMERICANS

With the Treaty of Guadalupe Hidalgo, two fifths of Mexico's territory and some 80,000 Spanish-speaking people became part of the United States. But many of these new citizens felt, as one Mexican American explained, like "foreigners in their own land."

▲ French artist Theodore Gentilz painted this scene of San Antonio, Texas, around 1848. The painting is entitled *Invitation to a Ball*.

For some Mexican American landowners with ties to Anglo Americans, adjustments were relatively easy. Despite the guarantees of the 1848 treaty, however, most Mexican Americans lost their lands. New American settlers challenged Spanish land titles, and Mexican Americans whose families had resided in New Mexico and California for generations fought costly legal battles to defend their claims. Many former landowners became peons or took low-paying jobs in the mines or on the railroads.

Many Americans looked down on the culture of the region, with its blend of Spanish, Mexican, and Indian ways. The resulting atmosphere of prejudice and discrimination helped spark Mexican American rebellions in the Southwest. Juan Nepomuceno Cortina, a Tejano rancher and politician, began one such rebellion in 1859. Cortina shot and wounded a Texas marshal who had been using excessive force to arrest a fellow Tejano. Cortina fled south across the Rio Grande to avoid imprisonment. There he found sympathetic supporters, whom he led in a raid across the border to avenge the murders of Mexicans by Anglos. Cortina explained:

66 There is no need to fear. Orderly people and honest citizens are inviolable [sacred] to us in their persons and interests. Our object . . . has been to chastise [punish] the villainy of our enemies. . . . These have connived with each other . . . to persecute and rob us, without any cause, and for no other crime on our part than that of being Mexican in origin. 99

Cortina continued his rebellion off and on into the 1870s. In response to such rebellions, Anglos in Texas and New Mexico intimidated Mexican American communities through harassment, beatings, and even murders. The bitter hatred raised by the Mexican War was slow to subside.

■■ **After the Mexican War, many Mexican Americans lost their lands and faced violence and discrimination.**

SECTION 2 REVIEW

IDENTIFY and explain the significance of the following: James K. Polk, Zachary Taylor, John Slidell, Mexican War, Stephen Kearny, Bear Flag Revolt, John C. Frémont, Winfield Scott, Treaty of Guadalupe Hidalgo, Gadsden Purchase, Juan Nepomuceno Cortina.

LOCATE and explain the importance of the following: Rio Grande, Nueces River, Monterey, Chapultepec, Mexican Cession, Gila River.

1. **MAIN IDEA** What events led to the Mexican War?

2. **MAIN IDEA** What problems confronted Mexican Americans after the Mexican War?

3. **GEOGRAPHY: LOCATION** What present-day states did the United States acquire as a result of the Treaty of Guadalupe Hidalgo and the Gadsden Purchase?

4. **WRITING TO CREATE** Imagine you are a Mexican cadet who fought in the siege of Chapultepec. Write a poem describing your efforts to defend the hilltop fort.

5. **HYPOTHESIZING** How might the terms of the Treaty of Guadalupe Hidalgo have been different if Stephen Kearny, John Sloat, and Robert Stockton had not contributed to the war effort?

Section 3

THE FAR WEST

FOCUS

- How did mountain men and Native Americans advance the fur trade and western settlement?
- What difficulties did U.S. settlers face on the Oregon Trail?
- How did Native Americans respond to the flood of white settlers?

In the early 1800s U.S. merchants carried on a lively trade with residents of New Mexico, California, and Oregon Country. These merchants and, later, fur trappers established trails that brought new settlers flooding into these regions in the 1840s. Missionaries and farmers moved into Oregon Country in the first half of the 19th century, disrupting Native American ways of life. U.S. settlement of Oregon Country also led to another international dispute, this time with Great Britain.

Fur trapper

THE PROMISE OF TRADE

U.S. merchants began trading in the Far West as early as 1790. Boston mariners sailed around South America and up the Pacific coast to trade with the coastal communities of California. People in these communities were eager to exchange furs, tallow (animal fat used in candles and soap), and cattle hides for U.S. manufactured goods. But American traders, not wanting to be arrested for violating the Spanish ban on foreign traders, seldom ventured far inland.

After Mexican independence in 1821, however, the new government encouraged trade with the neighboring United States. Many U.S. merchants looked to Mexico for new markets. One such merchant was William Becknell. In 1821 he loaded a wagon train with tools, clothing, and other goods and blazed a trail westward from Missouri to Santa Fe, New Mexico. There, he traded his merchandise for furs, livestock, and silver. Becknell's huge profits encouraged other merchants to cross the approximately 700-mile **Santa Fe Trail**. Within a decade U.S. merchants controlled much of the trade with the Mexican borderlands.

▶ **This print of Santa Fe is based on a drawing by Richard H. Kern. Before the opening of the Santa Fe Trail, New Mexicans relied on pack trains from the neighboring state of Chihuahua for most of their supplies.**

On the heels of the merchants came the fur trappers, or **mountain men**. Beaver pelts, which were used to make men's hats, were in great demand. Native Americans helped the mountain men extend the fur trade to new areas by negotiating with other Indian groups. Native Americans worked in the fur trade as trappers, guides, and interpreters. Native American women were vital to the functioning of the fur trade. They skinned and prepared the beaver pelts and provided food and special clothing for the trappers.

It was in the Rockies—along the Missouri River and its tributaries—that the fur trade proved most profitable. The Rocky Mountain fur trade was successful in part because of the **rendezvous system** worked out by William Ashley, a Missouri politician and owner of a fur-trading business. Ashley recognized that transporting furs out of the Rockies was expensive. Looking to cut costs, he convinced his trappers to remain in the mountains and gather once a year to sell their furs and purchase supplies. This system increased profits.

After each rendezvous the mountain men fanned out for hundreds of miles across the Rockies trapping beavers. In the process the restless and adventurous trappers explored every inch of the mountains and pioneered the trails that settlers later used to reach the Far West.

Mountain men Hugh Glass, Jim Bridger, and Kit Carson became American legends. African American mountain man James Beckwourth also won fame. Beckwourth spent his last years exploring and looking for gold. In 1850 he discovered a key mountain pass a few miles northwest of present-day Reno, Nevada. Today, the pass, mountain peak, valley, and nearby town bear Beckwourth's name.

■■ Mountain men and Native Americans trapped furs and blazed the trails that would take U.S. settlers to the Far West.

SETTLING OREGON COUNTRY

The fur trade also spread west of the Rockies to Oregon Country. In 1811, U.S. fur trappers founded the fur-trading post of Astoria near the mouth of the Columbia River on the Pacific coast. Although the fur trade proved disappointing, the venture paved the way for more U.S. settlers. U.S. newspapers publicized the trappers' route to Oregon Country in 1813. This route, known as the **Oregon Trail**, followed the Platte River across treeless plains to the towering Rockies, then descended into Oregon along the Snake and Columbia rivers.

Farmers and missionaries. The new route was of particular interest to farm families who wanted to settle in Oregon Country's Willamette Valley. The first U.S. settlers in the valley were American fur traders and their families who settled as farmers just south of present-day Salem, Oregon, in 1830.

Missionaries were also attracted to the region, not for farming but as a fertile ground for converting Native Americans to Christianity. In 1833 the *Christian Advocate and Journal,* a Methodist newspaper, published a letter supposedly from a Native American requesting missionaries to instruct the

Plumas County Museum

◀ James Beckwourth was known to exaggerate some of his daring deeds, but he did lead an interesting life. He served in two wars, lived among the Crow Indians, and established the trading post pictured here.

OREGON FEVER The presence of missionaries, fur traders and trappers, and settlers helped establish America's claim to the Oregon Country. In 1848 Oregon became a territory, from which Oregon and Washington territories were created in 1853.

? PLACE Look at the relief shown on the map. Did the Santa Fe Trail pass chiefly through flat or mountainous land?

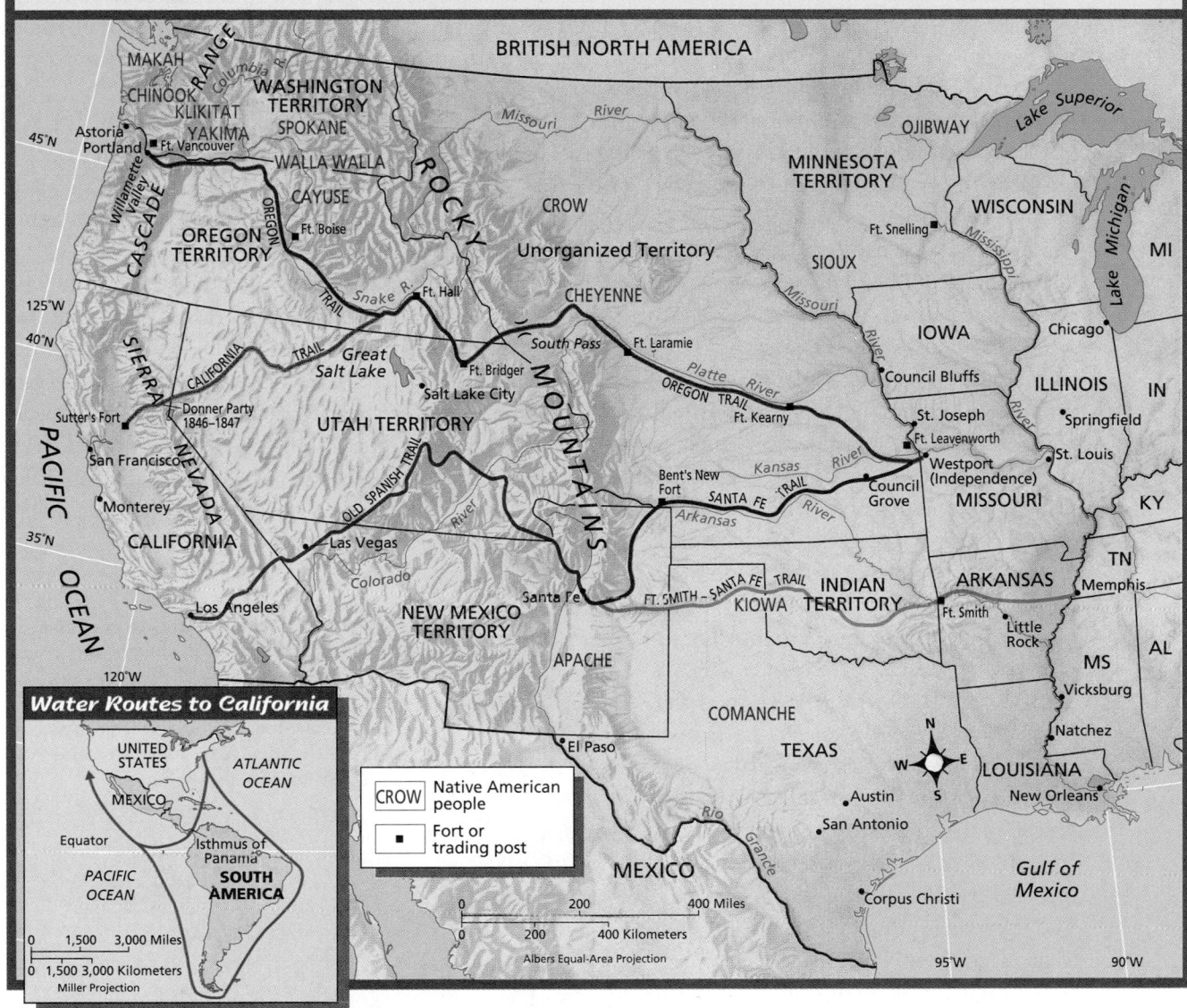

Indians of Oregon Country in the Christian faith. Historians suspect that the letter was a hoax, but Methodist response at the time was swift. Methodist missionary Jason Lee arrived in Oregon Country in 1834. Christian missionaries from other denominations soon followed.

Catholic missionaries from France established a church and boarding school for Indians near present-day Portland in 1840. In her journal Sister Mary Catherine Cabareaux described the language problem the missionaries faced when trying to teach Indians about Christianity:

66 The half Canadians were my portion. About twenty understood French, [which] I spoke simply to them. . . . Sister Mary Cornelia had the best portion, which consisted of about a dozen old Indian women who did not know a word of French, yet were requested to know their prayers in that language. Imagine, then, what a painful task for pupils as well as teachers! 99

Missionaries had little success, though, in converting the Indians to Christianity. Besides having a natural desire to retain their own beliefs and traditions, many Native Americans blamed the missionaries for spreading the diseases that severely reduced the Native American population. In addition, some blamed the missionaries for attracting waves of new settlers through their letters, speeches, and newspaper articles.

Political impact. As more U.S. settlers moved to Oregon Country, Oregon became an issue in the 1844 presidential campaign. Polk had already won southern support by calling for the annexation of Texas. To win northern support as well, Polk proclaimed America's right to all of Oregon Country. Using "Fifty-four forty or fight" as his slogan (meaning he favored setting the border with Canada at 54°40′ north latitude), Polk declared that it was the nation's manifest destiny to expand westward all the way to Oregon.

Once in office, Polk made good on his promise to acquire Oregon. Great Britain and the United States had quarreled for decades over the boundary of Oregon Country, which they had jointly occupied since 1818. Several times the United States had suggested a division of Oregon at the 49th parallel, but Britain had always refused. Now Polk astounded the British by claiming all of Oregon up to the southern border of present-day Alaska.

Polk was bluffing. He hoped the threat of war would persuade the British to accept the old American offer of a boundary at the 49th parallel. The two sides finally reached an agreement in June 1846 to extend the U.S. border to the 49th parallel (see map on page 315). The agreement allowed Britain to keep Vancouver Island. Polk, increasingly anxious about the growing tensions with Mexico, could afford to compromise over Oregon. And Britain concluded that the North American fur industry, which was in decline, was not worth fighting over.

𝒯HE OREGON TRAIL

Even before the boundary dispute had been settled, U.S. settlers flocked to Oregon Country. Between 1840 and 1848, thousands of settlers followed the overland trail to Oregon. Pioneer families organized themselves into large wagon trains to meet the challenges of the overland trail.

The difficult journey. The rugged journey required that the travelers pool their resources. The travelers helped one another repair broken equipment, shared information about the trail, and traded goods. Some of the larger traveling groups even wrote codes of law and elected officers for the journey. Traveling in large groups also helped the pioneers deal with such obstacles as ravines, deep mud, heavy snow, and rain-swollen rivers.

Even with cooperation, however, the trip could end in tragedy. Early snows left the Donner party snowbound in the Sierra Nevada in 1846. The survivors reached California only after resorting to cannibalism.

Even under the best circumstances, the journey was long, difficult, and extremely dangerous. A wagon train traveled slowly, even slower when it had to cross a river or stream. Since there were no bridges or ferries, a river was a major problem, sometimes taking days to cross and often exacting a toll in human and animal lives. Lucy Deady, who was 11 years old when her family

▼ Only 47 of the 87 members of the Donner party survived the snow-clogged passes of the Sierra Nevada. Before resorting to cannibalism, the group ate mice, twigs, and their own shoes. Two survivors, Margaret and James Reed, are shown here.

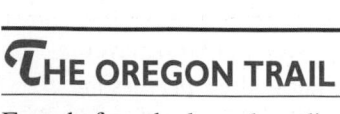

crossed the Oregon Trail in 1846, later described the hazards of the journey:

> 66 I remember how filled with terror I was when we experienced the violent thunderstorms. . . . Our oxen would try to stampede, our tents would be blown down, and everybody and everything would be soaked with the driving rains. . . . We had to cross a desert that took two days' and one night's travel. There was no water at all, so we filled every keg and dish with water so the cattle should have water as well as ourselves. 99

Pioneers often suffered from exhaustion and disease. To all the travelers, the trip to Oregon seemed to take forever. As historian David Lavender noted, it was a "remorseless, unending, weather-scoured, nerve-rasping plod on and on and on and on, foot by aching foot."

▪▪ Travelers on the Oregon Trail faced a long, difficult journey, with unpredictable weather and many natural obstacles.

Women played vital roles in this vast migration. They cared for children and cooked under difficult conditions. They also drove oxen and managed livestock. If their husbands fell ill or died, women had to take over entirely. The overland trek was especially difficult for pregnant women. Many women died in childbirth along the trail. Speaking of her sister, one woman wrote:

> 66 Her sufferings were so great that she does not remember anything for quite a space along there. It all seems like a jumble of jolting wagon, crying baby, dust, sagebrush and the never ceasing pain. 99

Native American assistance. Native Americans often helped migrants cross Indian lands. Native Americans acted as guides, carried messages between wagon trains, and sold wild game to the travelers. Settlers often complained that Native Americans drove hard bargains and charged stiff tolls for crossing their territories. One woman wrote, "The Indian is a financier of no

▲ **This painting by Alfred Jacob Miller shows Native Americans encamped at Fort Laramie.**

mean ability, and invariably [always] comes out A-1 in a bargain."

Although eastern newspapers played up reports of Indian massacres of hundreds of travelers, fewer than 400 pioneers lost their lives in Indian attacks between 1840 and 1860. Well-defended wagon trains were hard to attack, and Native Americans knew that most settlers were only crossing Indian lands to locate somewhere farther west.

Still, settlers feared the possibility of attack. Responding to such fears, the federal government held a conference with the Sioux, Cheyenne, and other Native Americans near what is now Laramie, Wyoming, in 1851. From this meeting came the **Treaty of Fort Laramie**. By the terms of the treaty, each Native American group accepted a defined territory, pledged not to attack settlers moving west, and allowed the U.S. government to build roads and forts in their territory. In return, the United States promised to make annual payments to the Indians and to honor the boundaries of each group's territory. For the most part, the treaty kept the peace until 1861, when the increasing presence of non-Indians touched off war.

CONFLICT IN OREGON

As the 1840s passed, the wagons' heavy wheels wore deep ruts in the roadway from Missouri to Oregon, and the trail became littered with household goods discarded to lighten the wagons. Once in Oregon Country, most migrants moved into the Willamette Valley to establish farms. Though

Oregon was not quite the paradise some had claimed it to be, the majority of farmers stayed and prospered.

A few African Americans were among the wave of new settlers coming to Oregon Country. Some had been brought west as slaves; others were free blacks or escaped slaves. White settlers in Oregon generally opposed slavery but did not necessarily accept blacks as equals. Concerned with competition from black labor, whites tried to discourage African Americans from settling in the region. New laws prevented free blacks from serving in the militia and from voting.

U.S. settlement of Oregon Country came at the expense of Native Americans and the region's rich natural resources. A variety of Native American groups lived in Oregon Country, including the Chinooks, Makahs, and Klickitats. These groups lived off ocean shellfish, river salmon, deer, elk, and wild vegetables and fruits.

By the 1840s, however, increasing contacts with settlers disrupted Native American life in Oregon Country. The contacts resulted in the spread of measles, smallpox, and other diseases against

▲ Missionary Narcissa Whitman was one of the first white women to travel along the Oregon Trail and across the Rocky Mountains.

which Native Americans had no immunity. In addition, non-Indians destroyed much of the wildlife the Indians depended upon for survival.

As settlers took more Indian lands, some Native American groups fought back. In the first of a series of Indian wars in Oregon Country, a group of Cayuses killed missionaries Marcus and Narcissa Whitman and 12 others near what is now Walla Walla, Washington. The resulting **Cayuse War**, which began in 1847, ended with the execution by U.S. officials of the five Cayuses judged responsible for the missionaries' murders. Later, in the early 1850s, the Yakimas (YAK-uh-maws), Walla Wallas, Spokanes, and others unsuccessfully fought to defend their lands. For many years Native Americans continued to fight settlers who trespassed on their territory.

■■ **U.S. settlement of Oregon Country disrupted the lives of Native American groups, some of whom fought to retain their lands.**

SECTION 3 REVIEW

IDENTIFY and explain the significance of the following: William Becknell, mountain men, rendezvous system, William Ashley, James Beckwourth, Jason Lee, Treaty of Fort Laramie, Cayuse War.

LOCATE and explain the importance of the following: Santa Fe Trail, Oregon Trail, 49th parallel, Willamette Valley.

1. **MAIN IDEA** What contributions did the mountain men and Native Americans make to the fur trade and western settlement?

2. **MAIN IDEA** What led Native Americans to armed resistance in Oregon Country?

3. **GEOGRAPHY: LOCATION** Why do you think the Oregon Trail was established beside rivers?

4. **WRITING TO EXPLAIN** Write a short guidebook warning travelers of some problems they might face on the Oregon Trail.

5. **ASSESSING CONSEQUENCES** What unintended consequences did the arrival of missionaries in Oregon Country bring for Native Americans?

Section 4

THE RUSH TO CALIFORNIA

FOCUS

- Who were the forty-niners, and how did most reach California?
- What was life like in the gold-mining camps?
- How did the gold rush change California society?

*E*ven as the Mexican War raged on, small groups of U.S. settlers made their way to California. But the Californios and Native Americans living in California in 1848 were soon to be swamped by a far greater migration of people from around the world. In cities across the United States, newspaper headlines shouted in their largest type a single electrifying word: "Gold!"

The Patron, or Ranchero of Old California by James Walker

EARLY SETTLEMENT

California, a land of rare beauty, vast distances, and unbelievable contrasts of climate and topography, has from its earliest days attracted diverse settlers. In 1769 more than 300,000 Native Americans lived in California. Spanish settlement began to increase in the 1790s. Since few Spanish women migrated to California in the late 18th century, many Spanish soldiers married Native American women and settled permanently in California. The Spanish government encouraged these unions by offering the Spanish soldiers land if they married Indian women. The first Spanish settlers and their descendants are known as Californios.

Spanish officials tried to bring more Spanish colonists to California by recruiting artisan families to teach mission Indians blacksmithing, carpentry, herding, cooking, and sewing. About 18 percent of these colonists and over half of the original settlers of Los Angeles were of African descent.

By the mid-1800s there were some 8,000 to 12,000 Californios dispersed throughout several settlements, among them San Diego, Los Angeles, Monterey, and Yerba Buena (yuhr-buh BWAY-nuh),

where San Francisco now stands. Also scattered over this immense territory were the haciendas—small communities in themselves.

In 1834 Mexico took land away from the Catholic missions and transferred the land to settlers. Mexican officials issued some 700 land grants after 1834, most along the California coast between San Diego and San Francisco. Some of the land was to be given to the mission Indians. Most of the land, however, went to Californios and Anglo settlers. As a result, many mission Indians either became peons or moved inland.

GOLD IN CALIFORNIA

As late as 1830 only about 500 Americans lived in California, most of them merchants. Among the earliest non-Spanish settlers in California was John Augustus Sutter, a Swiss adventurer who had acquired a huge Mexican land grant in 1839. Sutter's headquarters, an adobe fort and trading post near the Sacramento River, was a major stopping point on the California Trail, a trail that forked off southward from the Oregon Trail (see the map on page 319).

EXPANSION AND CONFLICT ■■ 323

▲ Forty-niners' tents cover San Francisco's Telegraph Hill in this gold-rush-era painting. Posters such as the one above encouraged immigrants to pool their resources and try their luck in the goldfields of California.

On January 24, 1848, one of Sutter's employees, James W. Marshall, detected flakes of heavy yellow metal at the bottom of a wooden canal used to divert water from the American River. Marshall later recalled, "I reached my hand down and picked it up; it made my heart thump, for I was certain it was gold." He was right, and word of the gold strike spread quickly.

Soon after the news reached San Francisco, a local newspaper complained:

66 The whole country from San Francisco to Los Angeles, and from the shore to the base of the Sierra Nevada, resounds with the sordid cry of *gold!* Gold!! GOLD!!! while the field is left half planted, the house half built, and everything neglected but the manufacture of shovels and pickaxes. 99

That was the newspaper's last issue. Left without staff, advertisers, or subscribers, the editor suspended publication and rushed to the goldfields himself.

News of the discovery reached the East Coast in September 1848. Dispatches told the exciting story of former laborers washing out $50 of gold a day with nothing but shovels and dishpans. Soon, President James Polk confirmed the accounts, and the great California gold rush was on.

By early 1849 hopeful gold seekers from as far away as Europe, Australia, and China sailed to North America to join the thousands of Americans, Mexicans, and South Americans trekking to the goldfields. Many of the U.S. **forty-niners**—so called because of the year, 1849—traveled to California through the mountain passes of the California Trail. The trail, which passed through the Salt Lake Valley, stretched almost 2,000 miles. By the end of May 1849, more than 40,000 people had set off from Independence, Missouri, on the dangerous trip to California. Other forty-niners sailed down the eastern seaboard and around the tip of South America or to Central America, where they crossed over by land to the Pacific Ocean and sailed north to San Francisco.

■■ By ship and covered wagon, forty-niners from all over the world rushed to California hoping to make their fortunes in gold.

Gold mining area
Leading gold mine
California Trail
Leading supply route

UTAH TERRITORY

CALIFORNIA

Lake Tahoe

January 24, 1848: James Marshall discovers gold while building a sawmill.

Sacramento   Sutter's Fort

SIERRA NEVADA

San Francisco

Stockton

In 1849 San Francisco grows from a village to a booming port of 25,000 people.

PACIFIC OCEAN

0   20   40 Miles
0   20   40 Kilometers
Albers Equal-Area Projection

The California Gold Rush

FORTY-NINERS The discovery of gold at Sutter's sawmill on the California Trail drew thousands of people from all over the world.

❓ **PLACE** Why did Sacramento and Stockton become important during the gold rush?

THE FORTY-NINERS

Most gold seekers were young, unmarried men—only 5 percent were women and children. The few women who went to California found a rough-and-tumble life far different from the one they left behind. Louisa Smith Clapp, who sailed to California with her husband in 1849, described the frantic atmosphere:

❝ The news spreads that wonderful "diggings" have been discovered . . . [men] rush vulture-like upon the scene and erect a round tent, where, in gambling, drinking, swearing and fighting, the *many* reproduce Pandemonium . . . while a *few* honestly and industriously commence digging for gold, and lo! as if a fairy's wand had been waved . . . , a full-grown mining town hath sprung into existence. ❞

The mining camps. These mining camps, with names like Skunk Gulch, Poker Flat, and Hangtown, were dirty, disorderly, uncomfortable, and dangerous. Law enforcement officers were scarce, but there was no shortage of thieves and gamblers ready to relieve miners of their money. A prospector could easily strike it rich one day and be broke a week later.

While some miners found riches beyond their wildest dreams—one man took out a whopping 52 pounds of gold from a single claim in just eight days—most found only disappointment. As the months went by, newcomers eager for fortunes passed disappointed forty-niners on the California Trail. Many of the latter probably felt as prospector William Swain did. After a summer of "hardship and exposure," Swain confided regretfully in a letter to his wife that "it is a fact that no energy or industry can secure certain success in the business of mining."

The gold rush added to the diversity of California society. Though nearly 80 percent of the forty-niners were Anglos or African Americans from the United States and about 8 percent were from Mexico, others came from around the world: almost 5 percent from South America and most of the rest from Europe, Australia, or China. This international mix of gold seekers helped swell California's non-Indian population from some 14,000 in 1848 to more than 200,000 in 1852.

■ **Many cultures mingled and clashed in the unruly mining camps during the California gold rush.**

▲ **Mining camps attracted groups of different ethnic and racial backgrounds. Miners at Auburn Ravine are shown here in 1852.**

THROUGH OTHERS' EYES

In April 1851 Belgian Jean-Nicolas Perlot arrived in Monterey, California, with 44 other men hired by a French gold-seeking company. Upon landing, the men discovered that during their six-month voyage from Europe the company had gone bankrupt. "There we were," Perlot wrote, "thrown on the shore like castaways, without money, without resources, in an unknown land whose language we did not understand."

The group looked for work in Hornitos, a mining camp near the Yosemite Valley. "All around . . . in the creeks, in the gulches, we saw nothing but people occupied in seeking this precious metal . . . ," reported Perlot. "I estimate that there could have been at Hornitos from 250 to 300 persons, all men in the prime of life: I saw no women there, nor children, nor old people. In business, they spoke English and Spanish; in the street, still covered with brush, we heard all possible tongues spoken."

When his prospects in California dried up, Perlot went to Oregon. There he started a business that would be more successful than his mining ventures. By relying on his skills as a gardener, he built a successful nursery and landscaping business and hired miners who had found the gold boom a bust.

Conflict in the mines. Because they reached the goldfields early, Californios made some of the first major gold strikes, or discoveries. By late in 1849, however, Anglo American miners outnumbered all other groups and increasingly drove Californios from their claims. They posted notices declaring that "foreigners" had no right to be there and must leave the mines. These Anglo American miners ignored the fact that the Californios were not foreigners: under the terms of the Treaty of Guadalupe Hidalgo, they were citizens of the United States. Many Californios who remained in the goldfields were beaten; some were killed.

The Chinese fared no better. Shortly after word of the gold rush reached China, men from Guangdong (GWAHNG-DOOHNG) Province headed for California, which they called Gam Saan (Gold Mountain). Prospective Chinese miners often borrowed money at high interest rates to buy passage to California. The majority were males who hoped to strike it rich quickly and return home. But Anglo prospectors—once they had arrived in force—often took advantage of the Chinese, using them as poorly paid laborers while keeping them from staking their own claims.

Many Chinese left the gold camps and returned to China. Others headed for rural areas throughout the Far West, where they became field workers or tenant farmers. Some settled in cities, where they worked as merchants, storekeepers, grocers, or unskilled laborers. By 1852 California's Chinese population numbered over 11,000.

African Americans—enslaved and free alike—also suffered at the hands of the white miners. In addition to racial prejudice, black miners had to deal with the strange but widely held notion that they possessed a mysterious power to detect gold. Fearing competition, white miners tried to drive African Americans from the goldfields.

▼ **Many Chinese abandoned mining camps and became laborers in areas throughout the Far West.**

Lawmakers showed similar prejudices. Urged by delegates from the mining districts, lawmakers seriously considered, but finally rejected, banning blacks from migrating to California. They did, however, agree to deny African Americans the rights to serve in the state militia and to vote.

In spite of these obstacles, some African Americans became independent miners, and a handful even struck it rich. By 1860 there were some 4,000 free blacks in California. Most settled in towns, where discrimination was usually less of a problem than in the mining camps.

■■ **Anglos soon took control of the goldfields, pushing Californios and other gold seekers from the mines.**

THE CALIFORNIA INDIANS

The gold rush increased pressure on the Native Americans of California, many of whom were already suffering hardships. Fur trappers had introduced malaria and other diseases, which physically weakened the Indians and contaminated many hunting grounds. By the early 1850s non-Indians outnumbered Indians nearly two to one.

Miners forced Native Americans off their gold-rich lands. Many were pressed into service in the mines. Volunteer militia companies and regular army units in California raided Indian villages, even attacking groups that did not take up arms.

In one incident, two miners returned to their camp to find the place ransacked and their five companions missing. The miners, assuming that Indians were responsible, organized a posse and raided several Indian villages, killing more than 130 people. When the miners gathered 7 Indians in front of a firing squad,

66 they [the Indians] broke and ran. . . . The word was given to fire, and two immediately fell. . . . The others who had fled to the hills were overtaken and stabbed with bowie knives. Of the two who plunged into the almost freezing waters . . . one was shot. . . . The other swam to the opposite shore, but was prevented from landing by two mounted men who threw stones at him until . . . he sank to rise no more. 99

Some Native Americans fought back. The Miwoks (MEE-wahks) and the Yokuts (YOH-kuhts) in the Sierra Nevada and the San Joaquin Valley, whose lands had been taken over by miners, began raids on Anglo property in 1850. The raids, which came to be known as the **Mariposa War**, lasted throughout 1851. In the early 1850s, attacks by Yumas and Mohaves (moh-HAHV-ees) of Arizona and California kept miners from crossing the Colorado River into Indian territory. The U.S. Army built Fort Yuma to end the raids, but was forced to abandon the fort for a year. Later army raids on Yuma villages weakened Indian resistance. By 1860 disease, starvation, and violence had reduced California's Native American population to about 35,000.

■■ **Once the majority population in California, Native Americans became a minority during the gold rush.**

SECTION 4 REVIEW

IDENTIFY and explain the significance of the following: Californios, John Sutter, James W. Marshall, forty-niners, Mariposa War.

LOCATE and explain the importance of the following: Sutter's Fort, American River.

1. **MAIN IDEA** What drew the forty-niners to California? From which areas did the forty-niners come?

2. **MAIN IDEA** How were the California Indians affected by the gold rush?

3. **GEOGRAPHY: MOVEMENT** What routes did the forty-niners use to get to California?

4. **WRITING TO CLASSIFY** Write an essay that characterizes the experiences of the following groups in the gold rush: Anglo Americans, Californios, Chinese, and African Americans.

5. **RECOGNIZING BIAS** Using the California gold rush as an example, explain why one social group might try to exclude another by stereotyping them as "foreigners."

CHAPTER 10
Review

Mexico wins independence from Spain. Moses Austin granted permission to start colony in Texas. William Becknell crosses Santa Fe Trail.

Mexico closes the Texas border.

General Antonio López de Santa Anna seizes control of Mexican government.

Missionaries arrive in Oregon Country.

1820   1825   1830   1835

WRITING A SUMMARY

Using the essential points of the chapter as a guide, write a summary of the chapter.

REVIEWING CHRONOLOGY

Number your paper 1 to 5. Study the time line above, and list the following events in the order in which they happened by writing the first next to 1, the second next to 2, and so on. Then complete the activity below.

1. Treaty of Guadalupe Hidalgo signed.
2. Missionaries arrive in Oregon Country.
3. Gadsden Purchase negotiated.
4. Juan Nepomuceno Cortina begins rebellion in Texas.
5. Texas declares independence.

Assessing Consequences What were the consequences of the Treaty of Guadalupe Hidalgo?

IDENTIFYING PEOPLE AND IDEAS

Explain the historical significance of each of the following people or terms.

1. *empresarios*
2. Texas Revolution
3. Oregon Trail
4. Gadsden Purchase
5. Mariposa War
6. William Becknell
7. rendezvous system
8. Juan Nepomuceno Seguín
9. Jason Lee
10. forty-niners

UNDERSTANDING MAIN IDEAS

1. What social changes did the Texas Revolution cause?
2. How did Americans' belief in manifest destiny lead to war with Mexico?
3. What were the main reasons non-Indian settlers journeyed to the Far West?
4. How did Native Americans in the Far West respond to U.S. settlers?

REVIEWING THEMES

1. **Economic Development** How did the U.S. government respond to farmers' and merchants' demands for land and trade in the Far West?

2. **Cultural Diversity** What were the positive and negative effects of the mingling of cultures in California during the gold rush?
3. **Global Relations** What international issues did Americans consider when debating the U.S. annexation of Texas?

THINKING CRITICALLY

1. **Hypothesizing** What policy changes might Santa Anna have made to increase Texans' loyalty to Mexico before the Texas Revolution?
2. **Evaluating** Why do you think Mexico did not launch a full-scale invasion to reconquer Texas after the Texas Revolution?
3. **Analyzing** How did women contribute to the survival of settlers on the Oregon Trail?

STRATEGY FOR SUCCESS

Review the Skills Handbook entry on Creating an Outline on page 999. Refer to the text discussion of the Far West on pages 317–322. Then study the outline below and supply the missing main ideas.

I. Lure of trade
  A. Santa Fe Trail
  B.
    1. Rendezvous system
    2.
II. Settling Oregon Country
  A. Early settlers
    1.
    2.
  B. Political impact
    1.
    2.
III. Oregon Trail
  A.
  B. Native American assistance
IV. Conflict in Oregon
  A. African American settlers
  B.
    1. Cayuse War
    2.

Battles of Alamo and San Jacinto fought. Texas declares independence.

Oregon boundary dispute settled. U.S. Congress declares war on Mexico.

Polk elected president.

Cayuse War begins.

Gold discovered in California. Treaty of Guadalupe Hidalgo signed.

Treaty of Fort Laramie signed.

Gadsden Purchase negotiated.

Juan Nepomuceno Cortina begins rebellion in Texas.

1840　　　1845　　　1850　　　1855　　　1860

WRITING ABOUT HISTORY

Writing to Persuade Imagine you are Juan Nepomuceno Seguín, mayor of San Antonio in 1842. Write a letter to Sam Houston, president of the Republic of Texas, persuading him to prevent Anglo Texans from taking land and property from Tejano families.

USING PRIMARY SOURCES

In *Mountain of Gold: The Story of the Chinese in America* (1967), Betty Lee Sung presents the following account of the leader of a Chinese miners' organization addressing a group of newly arrived Chinese forty-niners. What advice and support does the leader offer the new arrivals?

> 66 *When we set foot on these shores, . . . we were bewildered and lost. We did not know where to turn for shelter or food. Fortunately, there were enough of us so that some set to putting up these houses while others looked for food. . . .*
>
> *One valuable lesson we have learned and which you will soon appreciate is that we must stick together and help one another, even though we are not kin. That is why we have formed this organization. . . .*
>
> *You will always find food and shelter here among us. Any needed supplies can be purchased from the shops on [Chinese] street. No doubt you will want to send a letter home to let your families know of your safe arrival. Elder brother Leong is a learned man, and he will help you write your letters.*
>
> *When you have earned money from your diggings or from your wages, you will pay dues into the company fund. This fund helps us to maintain the company headquarters and helps us set up an orderly system to take care of our own.* 99

LINKING HISTORY AND GEOGRAPHY

Study the map on page 313. Then write a paragraph summarizing the general strategy of American forces in the Mexican War and the way the strategy was affected by geography.

American soldier, 1846

Mexican soldier, 1839

BUILDING YOUR PORTFOLIO

Complete the following projects independently or cooperatively.

I. EXPANSION In Chapter 7 you wrote an article about U.S. expansionist policies. Building on that material, now imagine you are a U.S. government representative in Texas. Interview a Tejano, a Mexican government official, and an Anglo settler to obtain their views about U.S. annexation of Texas.

2. IMMIGRATION In chapters 8 and 9 you portrayed an immigrant. Building on that material, now imagine you are a Chinese immigrant working in the goldfields. Write four diary entries that describe your reasons for coming to the United States, your life in a multicultural mining camp, and your hopes for the future.

American Letters

The Natural World

While American politicians argued over the creation of slave and free states in the early 19th century, writers had more philosophical concerns. Transcendentalist author Ralph Waldo Emerson and poet Emily Dickinson pondered the meaning of nature. A song from the Tewa (TAY-wuh) Indians and a Kiowa folktale recounted by Old Lady Horse offer a similar appreciation for the natural world.

▲ **Emily Dickinson**

From *Nature*

by Ralph Waldo Emerson

Crossing a bare common, in snow puddles, at twilight, under a clouded sky, without having in my thoughts any occurrence of special good fortune, I have enjoyed a perfect exhilaration. . . . In the woods is perpetual [everlasting] youth. Within these plantations of God, a decorum [orderliness] and sanctity [holiness] reign, a perennial festival is dressed, and the guest sees not how he should tire of them in a thousand years. In the woods, we return to reason and faith. There I feel that nothing can befall me in life—no disgrace, no calamity, (leaving me my eyes), which nature cannot repair. Standing on the bare ground—my head bathed in the blithe [free] air and uplifted into infinite space—all mean egotism vanishes. I become a transparent eyeball. I am nothing; I see all; the currents of the Universal Being circulate through me; I am part or parcel of God. The name of the nearest friend sounds then foreign and accidental: to be brothers, to be acquaintances, master or servant, is then a trifle and a disturbance. I am the lover of uncontained and immortal beauty. In the wilderness, I find something more dear and connate [essential] than in streets or villages. In the tranquil landscape, and especially in the distant line of the horizon, man beholds somewhat as beautiful as his own nature. ❖

▼ **Dover Plain, Dutchess County, New York (1848), by Asher Brown Durand**

Some Keep the Sabbath Going to Church

by Emily Dickinson

Some keep the Sabbath going to Church—
I keep it, staying at Home—
With a Bobolink[1] for a Chorister[2]—
And an Orchard, for a Dome—

Some keep the Sabbath in Surplice[3]—
I just wear my Wings—
And instead of tolling the Bell, for Church,
Our little Sexton[4]—sings.

God preaches, a noted Clergyman—
And the sermon is never long,

So instead of getting to Heaven, at last—
I'm going, all along. ❖

Song of the Sky Loom

Tewa

O our Mother the Earth, O our Father the Sky,
Your children are we, and with tired backs
We bring you the gifts you love.
Then weave for us a garment of brightness;
May the warp[1] be the white light of morning,
May the weft[2] be the red light of evening,
May the fringes be the falling rain,
May the border be the standing rainbow.
Thus weave for us a garment of brightness,
That we may walk fittingly where birds sing,
That we may walk fittingly where grass is green,
O our Mother the Earth, O our Father the Sky. ❖

1 the yarns stretched lengthwise on a loom
2 the yarns crossing the warp

Buffalo Folktale

by Old Lady Horse (Kiowa)

Everything the Kiowas had came from the buffalo. Their tipis were made of buffalo hides, so were their clothes and moccasins. They ate buffalo meat. Their containers were made of hide, or of bladders or stomachs. The buffalo were the life of the Kiowas.

Most of all, the buffalo was part of the Kiowa religion. A white buffalo calf must be sacrificed in the Sun Dance. The priests used parts of the buffalo to make their prayers when they healed people or when they sang to the powers above.

So, when the white men wanted to build railroads, or when they wanted to farm or raise cattle, the buffalo still protected the Kiowas. They tore up the railroad tracks and the gardens. They chased the cattle off the ranges. The buffalo loved their people as much as the Kiowas loved them.

There was war between the buffalo and the white men. The white men built forts in the Kiowa country, and the woolly-headed buffalo soldiers [the Ninth and Tenth Cavalries, made up of black troops] shot the buffalo as fast as they could, but the buffalo kept coming on, coming on, even into the post cemetery at Fort Sill. Soldiers were not enough to hold them back.

Then the white men hired hunters to do nothing but kill the buffalo. Up and down the plains those men ranged, shooting sometimes as many as a hundred buffalo a day. Behind them came the skinners with their wagons. They piled the hides and bones into the wagons until they were full, and then took their loads to the new railroad stations that were being built, to be shipped east to the market. Sometimes there would be a pile of bones as high as a man, stretching a mile along the railroad track.

The buffalo saw that their day was over. They could protect their people no longer. Sadly, the last remnant of the great herd gathered in council, and decided what they would do.

The Kiowas were camped on the north side of Mount Scott, those of them who were still free to camp. One young woman got up very early in the morning. The dawn mist was still rising from Medicine Creek, and as she looked across the water, peering through the haze, she saw the last buffalo herd appear like a spirit dream.

Straight to Mount Scott the leader of the herd walked. Behind him came the cows and their calves, and the few young males who had survived. As the woman watched, the face of the mountain opened.

Inside Mount Scott the world was green and fresh, as it had been when she was a small girl. The rivers ran clear, not red. The wild plums were in blossom, chasing the red buds up the inside slopes. Into this world of beauty the buffalo walked, never to be seen again. ❖

THINKING AND WRITING ABOUT LITERATURE

1. How does Ralph Waldo Emerson "become a transparent eyeball"? What relation to nature and God does he achieve in this state?

2. What metaphor does Emily Dickinson use to represent nature? Explain how this metaphor defines Dickinson's conception of the natural world.

3. In the Tewa song, what represents the natural world? How is this world created?

4. What does the buffalo represent for the Kiowas? How does the folktale account for the disappearance of the buffalo?

Strategies for Success

INTERPRETING EDITORIAL CARTOONS

Editorial cartoons are drawings that present points of view on the issues, ideas, people, and events of the day. They usually appear in the editorial sections of newspapers and newsmagazines. Although some express a positive outlook, many are critical of a person or policy.

To communicate their message, editorial cartoonists frequently use caricature and symbolism. A *caricature* is a drawing that exaggerates or distorts physical features. *Symbolism* is the use of one thing to stand for something else. For instance, cartoonists often use Uncle Sam to represent the United States, an elephant to symbolize the Republican party, and a donkey to stand for the Democrats.

Many editorial cartoons rely on labels to help identify symbols or other aspects of the picture. Most also include captions or "speech balloons," which may serve as a sort of punchline.

How to Interpret Editorial Cartoons

1. **Identify the caricatures.** Identify each figure and object. Note any distortions or exaggerations, and decide whether they cast the figure in a positive or negative light.
2. **Identify the symbols used.** Determine what each symbol stands for.
3. **Read the title and labels.** Read and determine the meaning of any title and labels.
4. **Consider the cartoonist's purpose.** Identify the points of view being expressed in the speech balloons or caption. Try to determine the cartoonist's message.

Applying the Strategy

Andrew Jackson was a popular subject for editorial cartoonists of his day. In the cartoon on this page, Jackson is shown wearing a crown and kingly robe, holding a scepter like a club and a "veto" as if it were a royal decree. Tattered papers labeled "Constitution of the United States," "Internal Improvements," and "U.S. Bank" and a book titled *Judiciary of the U. States* are strewn underfoot.

According to his critics, Jackson had abused his constitutional authority by his vetoes of bills that would have rechartered the national bank and provided for internal improvements. The cartoonist uses symbols of monarchy to accuse Jackson of acting more like a king than the president of a republic. This point is reinforced by the condition and position of the papers and by the title: "King Andrew the First."

Practicing the Strategy

Study the editorial cartoon on page 266 of your textbook. Then, on a separate sheet of paper, answer the following questions.

1. Who are the central figures in the cartoon? Are they portrayed realistically, or are they caricatures?
2. What symbols does the cartoon contain?
3. How do the labels and the title help make the cartoonist's point of view and message clear?
4. What is **(a)** the cartoonist's point of view and **(b)** the cartoon's message?

▼ **Cartoon satirizing Andrew Jackson**

KING ANDREW THE FIRST.

UNIT 3 Review

BUILDING YOUR PORTFOLIO

Outlined below are four projects. Independently or cooperatively, complete one and use the products to demonstrate your mastery of the historical concepts involved.

1 EXPANSION

The 19th century was the period of the greatest U.S. expansion in North America. Using the portfolio materials you designed in chapters 7 and 10, conduct a panel discussion about U.S. expansion that showcases the views of Anglo settlers, Native Americans, Tejanos, and government officials from both Mexico and the United States.

2 THE ECONOMY

The market and transportation revolutions brought significant economic changes to the North, the South, and the Middle West. Using the portfolio materials you designed in chapters 7 and 8, create a board game that shows the movement of cotton from a southern plantation to a northern factory and then to various markets. Games should illustrate the impact of transportation systems, new technologies, and economic policies on new markets.

3 IMMIGRATION

Poverty, hunger, and oppression drove many immigrants from their homelands to the United States in the 19th century. Using the portfolio materials you designed in chapters 8, 9, and 10, prepare a short one-scene play about an immigrant's experiences in the United States. Plays might describe life in an ethnic community, encounters with nativists, workers' strikes, or tenement housing conditions.

4 INDIVIDUAL RIGHTS

Rapid changes in U.S. society in the first half of the 1800s led to new social problems and threats to individual liberties. Using the portfolio materials you designed in chapters 7, 8 and 9, discuss the different ways political and social reforms were carried out by presenting your posters, speeches, and pamphlets to the class.

Videodisc Review

In assigned groups, develop an outline for a video collage of America between 1815 and 1860. Choose images that best illustrate the major topics of the period. Write a script to accompany the images. Assign narrators to different parts of the script, and present your video collage to the class.

Further Reading

Ehle, John. *Trail of Tears*. Doubleday (1988). History of the Cherokees' forced removal to Indian Territory.

Fisher, Leonard E. *The Oregon Trail*. Holiday House (1990). Firsthand accounts and photographs of life on the trail.

Holliday, J. S. *The World Rushed In. The California Gold Rush Experience*. S & S Trade (1981). Eyewitness accounts of the California Gold Rush.

Johannsen, Robert W. *To the Halls of the Montezumas*. Oxford (1985). The Mexican War examined through primary sources.

Luchetti, Cathy. *Under God's Spell: Frontier Evangelists 1772–1915*. Harcourt (1989). The lives and work of frontier evangelists told through primary sources.

Mellon, James, ed. *Bullwhip Days: The Slaves Remember*. Avon Books (1988). Interviews with ex-slaves conducted in the 1930s.

❖ The American People

POPULATION, 1860

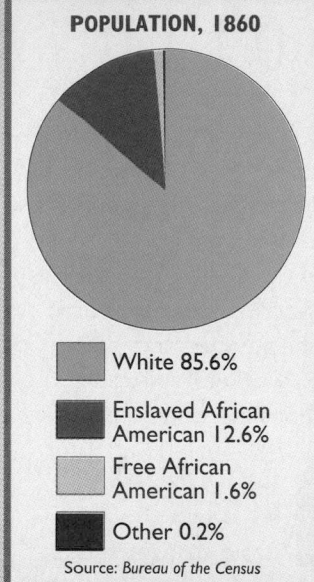

- ■ White 85.6%
- ■ Enslaved African American 12.6%
- ■ Free African American 1.6%
- ■ Other 0.2%

Source: *Bureau of the Census*

❖ Course of the War

1861 Native American cavalry regiment—Cherokee volunteers from Oklahoma—is commanded for Confederacy by Stand Watie, who in 1864 becomes only Native American brigadier general in the war. About 12,000 Native Americans fight for the South, about 3,500 for the North.

1862 First official Union African American regiment—1st South Carolina Colored Volunteers—forms.

❖ The Home Front

New York City Ladies' Military Blue Stocking Association knits 1,292 pairs of stockings in 3 months for Union soldiers; a Boston sewing group makes 1,000 shirts in a day.

A 93-year-old woman in Massachusetts knits stockings for soldiers just as she had, as a child, knitted for Revolutionary War troops.

A southern textbook contains this math problem: "If one Confederate soldier kills 90 Yankees, how many Yankees can 10 Confederate soldiers kill?"

▲ **Stand Watie**

1864 First successful attack by a submarine quickly turns to failure when Confederate sub *H.L. Hunley* becomes stuck in a hole it makes in Union ship *Housatonic*.

▲ *Advertisement for theater production of Uncle Tom's Cabin*

❖ Hot off the Presses

1852 *Uncle Tom's Cabin* by Harriet Beecher Stowe causes a sensation.

1853 *Clotel*, William Wells Brown's story of a slave born in Thomas Jefferson's household, is the first published novel by an African American.

1867 *Slave Songs of the United States*, first book of Negro spirituals, is published.

▲ **Confederate submarine H.L. Hunley**

UNIT
4

War and Reunification

1845–1900

▲ Soldier's love letter

❖ **A Soldier's Life**

Fresh fruits and vegetables are in short supply; one northern poster pleads, "Don't send your sweetheart a love-letter, send him an onion."

Soldiers spend an average of 50 days in camp to every day in battle.

Soldier's diet: hard bread, bacon, and coffee; when coffee is scarce, Confederate soldiers brew a hot drink from dried corn, sweet potatoes, peanuts, and rye.

▲ **Hiram R. Revels**

❖ **Changing Times**

1850 Female clerks are employed for first time in U.S. by Philadelphia storekeepers; female waiters go to work in 1853.

1869 Freedmen's Bureau oversees nearly 3,000 African American schools with more than 150,000 pupils. Literacy in African American population rises from 19% in 1870 to 55.5% in 1900.

1870 Hiram R. Revels becomes first African American senator.

1891 Dr. Dan Williams opens first interracial hospital in Chicago.

▼ **School for freed slaves**

SLAVERY'S EXPANSION

FOCUS

UNDERSTANDING THE MAIN IDEA

The U.S. acquisition of Mexican land in 1848 reopened the fierce debate over slavery in the West. Increasingly the issue divided the North and the South as northerners tried to limit the expansion of slavery and southerners refused to consider any alternative.

 THEMES

- **CONSTITUTIONAL HERITAGE** How might different groups use the Constitution to justify deeply held beliefs?

- **DEMOCRATIC VALUES** Majority rule is at the heart of the democratic system. Why is protection of the rights of those in the minority also essential to the system?

- **GEOGRAPHIC DIVERSITY** Why might people in different geographic regions have conflicting economic and political interests?

1845	1850	1854	1857	1861
Texas admitted to the Union.	**Compromise of 1850 enacted.**	**Republican party formed.**	*Dred Scott* **case decided.**	**Jefferson Davis elected president of Confederacy.**

The Northwest Ordinance of 1787 prohibited slavery in the Northwest Territory. By the early 1800s, however, several southern slave states had joined the Union. To maintain the balance between slave and free states, Congress passed the Missouri Compromise in 1820. But the compromise, which banned slavery in much of the Louisiana Territory, only postponed further conflicts.

Hauling the Whole Week's Pickings (1842), a detail from one of four pieces by William Henry Brown

*A*t midcentury the deepening conflicts between the North, the South, and the West involved many issues, including immigration, trade unionism, women's rights, and public-education reform. The main issue dividing Americans, however, was slavery. In 1850 Senator William H. Seward of New York warned of slavery's ever-lengthening shadow over the life of the nation:

66 We are now arrived at that stage of our national progress when [the] crisis [of slavery] can be foreseen—when we must foresee it. It is directly before us. Its shadow is upon us. It darkens the legislative halls, the temples of worship, and the home and the hearth. Every question, political, civil, or ecclesiastical [religious]—however foreign to the subject of slavery—brings up slavery. . . . We hear of nothing but slavery, and we can talk of nothing but slavery. 99

The issue of slavery indeed loomed large on the nation's political agenda. Slavery troubled many Americans, but their leaders could find no solution. Failed compromises, renewed strife, and increasingly urgent attempts to hold together a divided nation characterized this period of crisis on the brink of civil war.

Detail from photograph of slave leg irons

AN UNEASY BALANCE

FOCUS

■ Why did the admission of Texas and new territories create controversy in Congress? What solutions did Congress propose?

■ How did the slavery issue affect the presidential election of 1848?

■ Why did both proslavery and antislavery forces oppose passage of the Compromise of 1850?

With the Missouri Compromise in 1820, the North and the South resolved a serious clash over slavery. But many Americans realized that a showdown had merely been postponed. By the 1840s northern and southern members of Congress were in conflict over the admission of Texas and California to the Union. Arguments also erupted over the extension of slavery into the western lands acquired as a result of the Mexican War. As the conflict over slavery intensified, Congress found forging a compromise more difficult.

Zachary Taylor campaign pin, 1848

THE DEBATE REOPENS

The Missouri Compromise did not end the debate over the spread of slavery. Although Congress admitted Arkansas and Michigan to the Union

▲ **This painting by Donald M. Yena portrays the ceremony that took place on February 18, 1846, welcoming Texas into the Union.**

without dispute in 1836 and 1837, trouble arose when the Republic of Texas petitioned for annexation. Arkansas and Michigan had balanced each other: Arkansas allowed slavery, Michigan did not. The addition of Texas, which permitted slavery, would tip the balance of power in Congress toward the slaveholding states.

In 1845 Congress settled the dilemma on terms favorable to the South. Congress not only admitted Texas as a slave state but added that with the consent of the state's legislature, Texas could be divided into as many as five states. At the same time, Congress extended the Missouri Compromise line (36°30′ N) westward and barred slavery north of the line. (This affected only the northernmost tip of Texas.)

No sooner was the Texas question settled than the issue of slavery again confronted the nation, sparked this time by the prospect of victory in the Mexican War. Should slavery be allowed in any territory acquired from Mexico? Proslavery and antislavery forces in Congress quickly took sides.

To quiet the debate, President Polk and others suggested extending the Missouri Compromise line to the Pacific Ocean. Senator Lewis Cass of Michigan and Senator Stephen A. Douglas of Illinois offered another solution—rely on **popular sovereignty** to settle the issue: let the citizens of each new territory decide whether to permit slavery.

Neither proposal satisfied the hard-liners. Congressman David Wilmot of Pennsylvania introduced an amendment—the **Wilmot Proviso**—banning slavery in all lands acquired from Mexico. Senator John C. Calhoun of South Carolina responded by introducing a series of resolutions in support of slavery. The resolutions argued, in part, that a ban on slavery was unconstitutional since the Constitution protected slaveholders' rights to their property—including slaves—in all U.S. territories.

■■ **Admitting Texas and new territories reopened the debate in Congress over the expansion of slavery. Some favored compromise; others took a hard-line position.**

THE 1848 ELECTION

As the national election of 1848 approached, Congress still had not settled the issue. The Democrats chose Lewis Cass, who favored popular sovereignty, as their presidential nominee. The Whigs nominated a man whose political views, if indeed he had any, were unknown. Their choice—Mexican War hero General Zachary Taylor, "Old Rough and Ready"—had never even voted in a presidential election! The fact that Taylor held slaves, however, led both northerners and southerners to assume he was sympathetic to proslavery views.

Angered by the reluctance of each party to address the slavery issue, antislavery Whigs and Democrats formed the **Free-Soil party** in August 1848. The Free-Soilers demanded that Congress prohibit the expansion of slavery into the territories. Appealing to farmers, land reformers, and some industrial workers of the North and West, the Free-Soil platform also supported free western homesteads as well as federal funding for internal improvements. Proclaiming "Free Soil, Free Speech, Free Labor, and Free Men," the party nominated former president Martin Van Buren.

The Free-Soil party only received some 291,000 votes out of the nearly 2.9 million cast. But it won enough Democrats' votes in key northern states to enable the Whig candidate, Taylor, to win the election. Free-Soil candidates also won several seats in the House of Representatives. More important, the existence of the Free-Soil party showed that politicians could not continue to ignore the slavery question.

■■ **The Free-Soil party, formed by antislavery Democrats and Whigs, attracted enough votes in 1848 to cost the Democrats the presidency.**

THE SLAVERY ISSUE IN CONGRESS

When Congress assembled in December 1849, tempers ran so high that members in the House voted 63 times before electing their Speaker. Congress was particularly divided over issues involving California and New Mexico—the territories of the Mexican Cession, the fruits of America's victory in the Mexican War. California wished to enter the Union as a free state, something southern members of Congress hotly opposed. In addition, Texas was claiming that its boundary extended westward into an area the federal government considered part of the New Mexico Territory. Despite opposition from southern lawmakers, the antislavery members of Congress were intent on limiting the size of Texas and on barring slavery from the New Mexico Territory.

Arguments over other questions involving slavery also echoed through the halls of Congress. Southern congressmen resisted a plan to abolish the slave trade in the District of Columbia. They also continued to block passage of the Wilmot Proviso. Some of the proviso's southern opponents even demanded that Congress issue a statement affirming the right of settlers to hold slaves in the New Mexico Territory. In addition, proslavery forces called for a tougher fugitive slave law. In 1842 the Supreme Court had ruled that state officials did not have to assist federal officials in capturing runaway slaves. Southerners now wanted a law that forced state officials to help.

All these issues were politically explosive—both inside and outside the halls of Congress. The debates over slavery already had split two of the nation's largest religious groups. The Methodist and Baptist churches in the South broke from their northern counterparts, forming the separate denominations of the Methodist Episcopal Church, South (1844) and the Southern Baptist Convention (1845).

CLAY'S PROPOSALS

In January and February 1850, a weary Henry Clay again urged northern and southern senators to

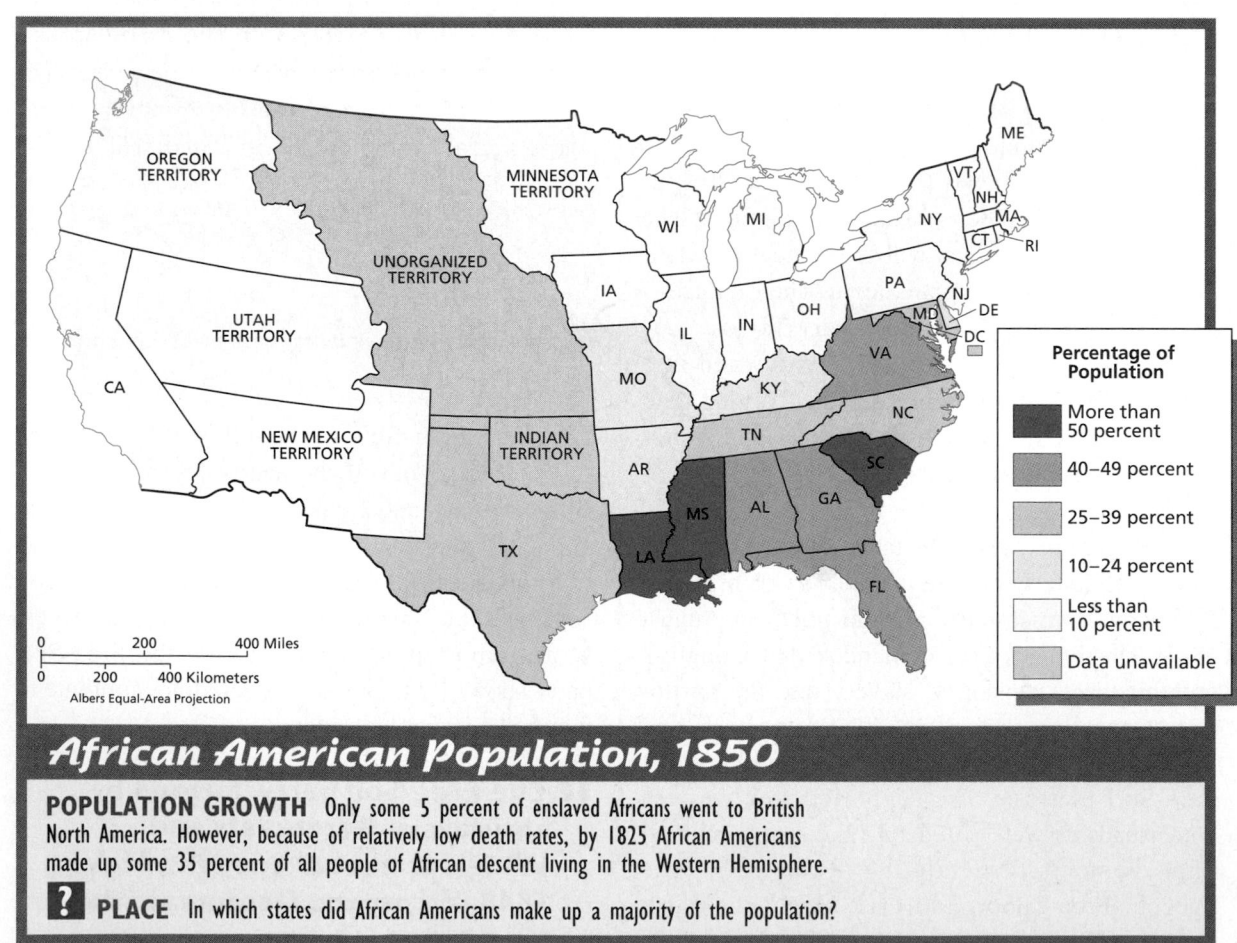

African American Population, 1850

Percentage of Population
- More than 50 percent
- 40–49 percent
- 25–39 percent
- 10–24 percent
- Less than 10 percent
- Data unavailable

POPULATION GROWTH Only some 5 percent of enslaved Africans went to British North America. However, because of relatively low death rates, by 1825 African Americans made up some 35 percent of all people of African descent living in the Western Hemisphere.

? PLACE In which states did African Americans make up a majority of the population?

compromise. "All society," he explained, "is formed upon the principle of mutual concession."

To satisfy northern antislavery interests, Clay proposed admitting California as a free state, abolishing the slave trade (though not slavery itself) in the District of Columbia, and paying Texas $10 million to abandon its claim to the eastern part of the New Mexico Territory. To persuade southerners to accept these terms, Clay further proposed that the New Mexico Territory be organized into two territories—New Mexico and Utah—on the basis of popular sovereignty. Further, he proposed that Congress pass a tougher fugitive slave law. This law would force state and local officials, and even private citizens, to aid federal officials in the capture and return of escaped slaves.

The Great Debate. For months Congress angrily debated Clay's proposals. The most bitter attack came from the South's elder statesman, John C. Calhoun. On March 4, 1850, visitors to the U.S. Capitol watched intently as Calhoun, near death, was half carried into the Senate chamber. Too ill to speak, he sat in silence as his speech was read. In it Calhoun warned that the time for compromise was past. The nation could avoid civil war only if the North allowed slavery to exist in the territories:

66 If something decisive is not now done . . . , the South will be forced to choose between abolition and secession. . . . The responsibility of saving the Union rests on the North, and not the South. 99

▶ John C. Calhoun defended slavery and worked to protect the rights of southern states against what he saw as the "tyranny of the majority."

Three days after Calhoun's speech, the veteran Whig leader Daniel Webster rose to support Clay's compromise measures. "I wish to speak today," Webster began, "not as a Massachusetts man, nor as a northern man, but as an American. . . . I speak today for the preservation of the Union." He argued that because the climate of the territories was unsuitable for growing cotton, slavery could not take root there. Therefore, legally barring slavery would anger southerners needlessly. Webster also endorsed Clay's proposal for a more enforceable fugitive slave law.

Many northern members of Congress, Whigs and Democrats alike, objected to Webster's speech and to Clay's compromise measures. While angrily denying that the Constitution protected slavery, they asserted that people were morally bound to "a higher law than the Constitution." They opposed stricter fugitive slave legislation and urged Congress to bar slavery from the territories. Many agreed with Senator Seward's opinion that on an issue like slavery, compromise was "radically wrong and essentially vicious."

The Granger Collection, New York

◀ Daniel Webster's controversial speech before the Senate in 1850 angered many northern lawmakers. This picture of the event was drawn in 1860.

PRESIDENTIAL LIVES

MILLARD FILLMORE
1800–1874

in office
1850–1853

UNITED STATES POSTAGE

MILLARD FILLMORE 1850–1853

13 CENTS 13

Millard Fillmore was born into a poor, hardworking family. As a child he was often without decent clothes or sufficient food. To ease their economic burden and provide Fillmore with a trade, his family apprenticed him at age 14 to a clothmaker.

Fillmore was almost an adult before he owned any books beyond a few primers. At age 17 he bought a dictionary to *Millard Fillmore* study while he worked. He placed the dictionary on a desk between the wooden milling machines. Each time he passed by, Fillmore looked up a word and fixed its meaning in his memory.

Fillmore's efforts paid off. With the help of his teacher—whom he later married—he, too, became a teacher, and then a lawyer, before entering politics.

■■ **Many northern abolitionists opposed Clay's compromise proposals on moral grounds; proslavery southerners rejected any compromise, insisting that slavery be allowed in the territories.**

The Compromise of 1850. Calhoun did not live to see the outcome of the Great Debate, nor did President Taylor, who died from a stomach ailment in July 1850. Taylor, who opposed Clay's compromise proposals, was succeeded by Vice President Millard Fillmore, who favored them. The 73-year-old Clay, however, was too exhausted to continue the fight. Senator Douglas, the Illinois Democrat, finally pushed the compromise measures through Congress. California was admitted to the Union as a free state on September 9, 1850. By September 20, the remaining measures had passed.

Many Americans hailed the **Compromise of 1850** as a triumph for national unity. Those who looked closely at voting records, however, saw that deep sectional divisions remained. More important, the basic issue—whether slavery would be allowed to expand—remained unresolved.

SECTION 1 REVIEW

IDENTIFY and explain the significance of the following: Stephen A. Douglas, popular sovereignty, Wilmot Proviso, Lewis Cass, Zachary Taylor, Free-Soil party, Daniel Webster, Compromise of 1850.

1. **MAIN IDEA** What reopened the controversy over the expansion of slavery? What proposals did Congress consider to settle the controversy?

2. **MAIN IDEA** What led to the formation of the Free-Soil party, and how did the party influence the outcome of the 1848 election?

3. **MAIN IDEA** Why did many northern abolitionists oppose passage of the Compromise of 1850? Why did proslavery southerners oppose the compromise?

4. **WRITING TO PERSUADE** Imagine you are a U.S. senator in 1850. Choose one of the measures that made up the Compromise of 1850, and write a speech in which you attempt to persuade other senators to vote either for or against it.

5. **EVALUATING** Why did John C. Calhoun believe that the responsibility for saving the Union belonged to the North and not the South?

COMPROMISE COMES TO AN END

FOCUS

- **How did the Fugitive Slave Act of 1850 affect northerners' views on slavery?**
- **Why did the Kansas-Nebraska Act reignite the debate over slavery? How did passage of the act affect Kansas?**
- **What led to the formation of the Republican party?**

The relative calm produced by the Compromise of 1850 was brief. Controversy over the fugitive slave issue continued in the North, and western settlement soon renewed the national debate over the expansion of slavery. On the frontier, fierce competition for control of the new territorial government of Kansas erupted in violent conflict. Chances for compromise seemed to be fading.

Fugitive slaves escaping from Maryland

THE ELECTION OF 1852

Although many people were dissatisfied with the Compromise of 1850, most Americans hoped that it had settled the slavery question. To tap into this optimistic mood, both major political parties adopted platforms supporting the compromise, vowing to avoid further debate over slavery.

At their 1852 convention the Democrats, after 49 ballots, united behind Franklin Pierce, a strong supporter of the Compromise of 1850. The likable Pierce persuaded many people on both sides of the slavery issue that he shared their views. Some Free-Soilers, convinced that Pierce could hold the South in check, returned to the Democratic party. Southerners in the meantime generally agreed that Pierce was "sound on all southern questions."

Having won the presidency in 1848 with General Taylor, the Whigs again turned to a Mexican War hero, General Winfield Scott. But many southern Whigs, angered at northern Whig

opposition to the **Fugitive Slave Act**, which was passed as part of the Compromise of 1850, refused to vote for Scott. Pierce won the election by a landslide.

In his Inaugural Address, the new president urged national harmony—even appointing a cabinet

▲ **Franklin Pierce was inaugurated as the 14th president of the United States on March 4, 1853.**

PRESIDENTIAL LIVES

FRANKLIN PIERCE
1804–1869

in office
1853–1857

Two months before his inauguration, Franklin Pierce and his wife witnessed a train crash in which their only child was killed. They never completely recovered from the loss.

Mrs. Pierce went into seclusion. She believed God had taken their son so that her husband would have no fatherly duties to distract him while in office. Pierce, however, interpreted the loss as punishment for his own sins and religious doubts. At his inauguration Pierce could not bring himself to swear on the Bible as was the custom. Instead, he simply raised his right hand and affirmed his loyalty to the Constitution.

Franklin Pierce

that included both southerners and northerners. But Pierce proved to be a weak leader, unable to control his diverse cabinet or to convince northerners that he was not caving in to southern pressure. Abolitionists labeled him a "northern man with southern principles."

THE FUGITIVE SLAVE ACT

The Compromise of 1850 began crumbling even before Pierce's election, largely because of the Fugitive Slave Act. The law, which made it a federal crime to assist runaway slaves and authorized the arrest of escaped slaves even in states where slavery was illegal, roused vigorous opposition in the North.

Harriet Beecher Stowe's powerful 1852 antislavery novel *Uncle Tom's Cabin* helped stir northern opposition to the law. The novel dramatized the plight of runaway slaves and showed how slavery degraded slave masters, broke up black families, and made a mockery of Christian morality. No previous antislavery publication approached the national impact of *Uncle Tom's Cabin,* which quickly sold over a million copies. The book convinced many northerners that the institution of slavery was morally wrong and should be abolished immediately.

Some northerners came face to face with the inhumanity of the Fugitive Slave Act. Caroline Seabury, a teacher from Massachusetts, confided to her diary the shock she felt the first time she witnessed a slave catcher at work:

> **66** We saw . . . a man on horseback riding at a quick pace, & by his side a tall negro coming steadily along. We wondered at the perfect uniformity of his steps—until, as they came nearer us, we saw one chain going from his wrists to the saddle, another was around his ankles—giving him just room enough to walk—following them were two large thick-headed fierce-looking dogs. **99**

◄ Anthony Burns

▲ Escaped slave Anthony Burns was returned to his owner under the provisions of the Fugitive Slave Act. Shown here is a Boston mob that tried unsuccessfully to rescue him in 1854. Outraged citizens rioted and then eventually paid $1,300 for Burns's freedom a year later.

As such scenes became more common, northerners reacted with horror. Abolitionist Frederick Douglass urged "forcible resistance." A former slave himself, Douglass protested that the Fugitive Slave Act made northerners "the mere *tools* and *body-guards* of the tyrants of Virginia and Carolina." People who had supported the Compromise of 1850 were shocked at the government's enforcement of the Fugitive Slave Act. Several northern states defiantly passed "personal liberty" laws, which prevented state officials from enforcing the Fugitive Slave Act and guaranteed captured runaway slaves legal assistance. Amos A. Lawrence, a northern Democrat, voiced a common sentiment: "We have submitted to slavery long enough, and must not stand it any longer. . . . I am done catching negroes for the South."

Some northerners took direct action. In New York and Massachusetts, angry mobs freed runaway slaves taken into custody and helped them on their way to freedom in Canada. One observer wrote, "We went to bed one night old fashioned conservative Compromise Union Whigs and waked up stark mad Abolitionists."

■■ **Enforcement of the Fugitive Slave Act strengthened antislavery sentiment in the North.**

▶ Posters such as this one from 1854 were circulated by antislavery forces to protest the Fugitive Slave Act.

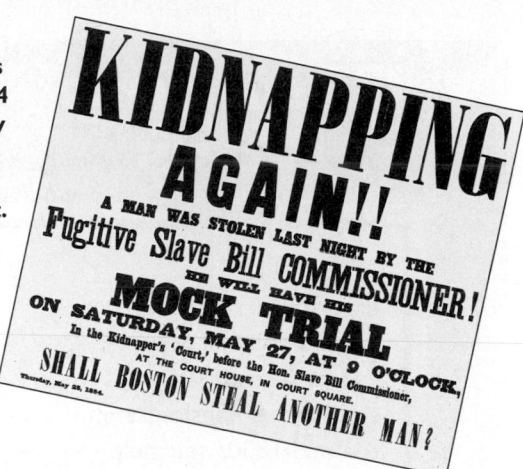

𝒯HE KANSAS–NEBRASKA ACT

Early in 1854, Senator Stephen Douglas inflamed passions further by reigniting the debate over the spread of slavery. An enthusiastic expansionist, Douglas supported settlement on the western prairies and the construction of a railroad to the West Coast. To benefit his constituents in Illinois, he wanted the railroad to run from Chicago to the Pacific Ocean.

Construction of the railroad required Congress to organize Kansas and Nebraska—the lands of the Louisiana Purchase west of Missouri and Iowa—into territories. This meant reopening the issue of slavery in the West. Hoping to quiet

Slave vs. Free Territory, 1850 and 1854

DEFUSING TENSIONS Passage of the Kansas-Nebraska Act convinced many northerners that the South was trying to extend slavery everywhere.

? **LOCATION** Compare the two maps. Which legislation allowed for the greater extension of slavery and why?

Compromise of 1850

Kansas-Nebraska Act, 1854

Free state
Free territory
Slave state
Slave territory
Popular sovereignty
Change from free territory to popular sovereignty

SOUTHERN EXPANSIONISTS AND THE FILIBUSTERS

Eager to increase the South's political power and to spread slavery, southern expansionists in the mid-1800s set their sights on conquering Mexico, Central America, and the West Indies. An 1848 New Orleans publication summed up the determined ambitions of these expansionists: "We have New Mexico and California. We *will* have old Mexico and Cuba!"

The expansionists were aided in their efforts by soldiers of fortune called "filibusters" (from a Spanish word meaning freebooters, or pirates). Recruited from the ranks of penniless immigrants, frontiersmen, and Mexican War veterans, the filibusters participated in numerous attempts to conquer Latin American lands between 1848 and 1860.

One of the first targets was Cuba in 1849. Southern

THE LAND OF LIBERTY.
RECOMMENDED TO THE CONSIDERATION OF "BROTHER JONATHAN."

▲ In 1847 the British magazine *Punch* published this satirical cartoon criticizing expansionist policies in the United States.

expansionists supported the efforts of Narciso López, a former Spanish general, to mount a revolution on the island. The attempt failed, but López tried two more times before being captured and executed in 1850.

Diplomatic efforts to obtain Cuba from Spain fared no better. Spain refused an offer of $100 million in 1848 and a second offer of $130 million in 1854. This greatly frustrated the Pierce administration, which had made acquiring Cuba a priority. At Pierce's urging, the U.S. ambassadors to Great Britain, France, and Spain met in Ostend, Belgium, in October 1854 to devise a plan for obtaining Cuba at any cost, even war. When their plan—the Ostend Manifesto—became

public, northerners were outraged. Pierce quickly withdrew his support.

Southern expansionists had no better luck acquiring lands in Mexico or Central America. In 1853 newspaper editor William Walker and a band of filibusters set sail from San Francisco for Lower California. After establishing an independent republic and declaring himself president, Walker "annexed" neighboring Sonora, Mexico. He was quickly chased out.

Undaunted, Walker joined in a Nicaraguan revolution two years later. Landing with only 58 men, in less than a year he had installed himself as dictator. One of his first official acts was to relegalize slavery, which had been abolished 30 years before. But his days in office were numbered. In April 1857, surrounded by the armies of four countries, he surrendered and was deported. Ever hopeful, he made three more attempts to invade Nicaragua, finally dying before a Honduran firing squad in 1860.

Walker's brief dictatorship in Central America was the closest any of the filibusters came to acquiring new territory for the United States. The dreams of expansionists for a new southern empire died with Walker.

▶ Narciso López

congressional debate, Douglas introduced the **Kansas-Nebraska Act**, which organized the lands on the basis of popular sovereignty.

By allowing the new states formed from the territories to "be received into the Union with or without slavery, as their constitution may prescribe at the time of their admission," the Kansas-Nebraska Act repealed the Missouri Compromise. Passage of the act in May 1854 renewed southern hopes of expanding slavery. Antislavery northerners were outraged. They called Douglas a traitor to the antislavery cause and accused him of caving in to southern pressure in an effort to gain support for a presidential bid. More and more, northerners viewed the South as intent on dominating the nation. The *New York Times* wrote that the Kansas-Nebraska Act was "part of this great scheme for extending and perpetuating the supremacy of the Slave Power."

■■ **The Kansas-Nebraska Act established popular sovereignty in the newly organized territories and overturned the Missouri Compromise.**

Not everyone opposed the Kansas-Nebraska Act on abolitionist grounds. Some critics had economic motives. These people argued that if slavery were allowed to spread to the territories, it would force out white workers. Why would employers choose to hire wage laborers when they could use slave labor? A western newspaper editor wrote:

> 66 I am opposed to slavery not because it is a misery to the downtrodden and oppressed, but that it blights and mildews the white man whose lot is toil, and whose capital is his labor. 99

Many people supported these arguments, increasing tension over the slavery issue.

"*B*LEEDING KANSAS"

The Kansas-Nebraska Act pitted antislavery and proslavery forces against one another for control of the new territories. To bolster the number of antislavery settlers, New Englanders formed the Emigrant Aid Company to help antislavery families move to Kansas. Proslavery forces countered by urging southerners to migrate to the new territories. "We are playing for a mighty stake," warned Senator David Atchinson of Missouri. "If we win, we carry slavery to the Pacific Ocean."

Proslavery forces took up the challenge in March 1855. As Kansas settlers prepared to elect

◀ Poster advertising land sales in Kansas, 1855

▶ This 1856 photograph shows a Free-State artillery battery in Topeka, Kansas, preparing to defend the territory from proslavery raiders.

▲ **A posse of proslavery men from Missouri are shown here on their way to plunder and burn Lawrence, Kansas, in 1856. Months of intense and bloody fighting followed the raid, giving rise to the phrase "Bleeding Kansas."**

their first territorial legislature, some 5,000 proslavery Missouri residents crossed into Kansas. Casting illegal votes, they helped elect a proslavery legislature, which antislavery settlers refused to accept as their legal government. The antislavery residents formed a Free State party and elected their own legislature. Kansas now had two territorial governments—one proslavery, the other antislavery!

With two rival governments in place, conflict was inevitable. Proslavery raiders from Missouri attacked antislavery Kansas settlers, and in May 1856 a proslavery mob of some 700 burned the town of Lawrence, Kansas. In revenge, a group led by abolitionist John Brown attacked a proslavery settlement along Pottawatomie (paht-uh-WAHT-uh-mee) Creek. They dragged five men from their beds and brutally murdered them. The **Pottawatomie Massacre** enraged southerners, shocked northerners, and sparked more violence in what newspapers began calling "Bleeding Kansas."

■■ **A bitter battle erupted between proslavery and antislavery factions for control of Kansas.**

Back in Washington the halls of Congress echoed the violence in Kansas. Among the most outspoken members of Congress was the abolitionist senator Charles Sumner. In his "Crime Against Kansas" speech, delivered on May 19–20, 1856,

Sumner declared the Kansas-Nebraska Act "a swindle":

❝ Slavery now stands erect, clanking its chains on the territory of Kansas, surrounded by a code of death, and trampling upon all cherished liberties. . . . It has been done for the sake of political power, in order to bring two new slaveholding senators upon this floor. ❞

In addition, Sumner ridiculed the proslavery senator Andrew Butler of South Carolina. Two days later Congressman Preston Brooks of South Carolina, a relative of Butler, savagely beat Sumner with a cane until it broke. The beating was so severe that it took Sumner years to recover from his injuries. Admiring voters in Brooks's district showered him with replacement canes. Whig leader David Davis wrote, however, that Brooks's shocking attack, coupled with the violence in Kansas, "made Abolitionists of those who never dreamed they were drifting into it."

THE REPUBLICAN PARTY

To carry their message to the nation, antislavery voters flocked to a new party growing in the North. In 1854 a group of antislavery Whigs and Democrats, together with some Free-Soilers, had organized a party firmly opposed to the expansion of slavery. At a convention in Jackson, Michigan, on July 6, 1854, the delegates revived the name of Thomas Jefferson's party, calling themselves Republicans.

The Republican party worked together with the Know-Nothings to defeat Democratic candidates in the election of 1854. By 1856, however, the slavery issue had split the Know-Nothing party. As a result, many antislavery Know-Nothings joined the Republican party, which was becoming a powerful force in national politics.

■■ **Antislavery Whigs and Democrats joined with Free-Soilers to form the Republican party to oppose any expansion of slavery.**

Running the popular western explorer John C. Frémont for president in 1856, the Republicans campaigned on the slogan "Free Soil, Free Speech, Free Men, Frémont, and Victory!" The Democrats abandoned Pierce, nominating James Buchanan of Pennsylvania. The Democratic platform praised the Kansas-Nebraska Act "as the only sound and safe solution of the slavery question" and portrayed the Republicans as a sectional party bent on destroying the Union. The remaining Whigs and the anti-immigrant, anti-Catholic Know-Nothings nominated former president Millard Fillmore.

The tactic of painting the Republicans as the party of sectionalism proved successful for Buchanan, who gathered 174 electoral votes to Frémont's 114 and Fillmore's 8. Buchanan won support in both slave and free states. Frémont, on the other hand, carried only free states, and Fillmore carried only Maryland.

Meanwhile, events in Kansas continued to boil. Early in 1857, elections were held to choose delegates for the upcoming constitutional

◄ This campaign poster appeared in 1856 in support of John C. Frémont's bid for the presidency.

convention. Suspecting that proslavery forces would rig the elections, the antislavery forces boycotted them. The constitutional convention, made up of exclusively proslavery delegates, met at Lecompton and drafted a constitution that protected the rights of slaveholders already living in Kansas. The **Lecompton Constitution** gave the voters of Kansas the right to decide only whether *more* slaves could enter the territory.

Senator Stephen Douglas attacked the Lecompton Constitution, arguing that the voters of Kansas should have the right to decide whether *any* slaves could enter their territory. This stand cost Douglas much support among southerners. Many thought that Douglas was siding with the Republicans in preventing another slave state from entering the Union. Despite the admission of Kansas as a free state in 1861, Douglas's principle of popular sovereignty had been severely discredited.

SECTION 2 REVIEW

IDENTIFY and explain the significance of the following: Franklin Pierce, Winfield Scott, Fugitive Slave Act, Harriet Beecher Stowe, Kansas-Nebraska Act, John Brown, Pottawatomie Massacre, Charles Sumner, John C. Frémont, James Buchanan, Lecompton Constitution.

LOCATE and explain the importance of the following: Nebraska Territory, Kansas Territory.

1. **MAIN IDEA** How did the Fugitive Slave Act affect public opinion in the North?

2. **MAIN IDEA** Why was the Kansas-Nebraska Act important? What happened after Congress passed the act?

3. **LINKING HISTORY AND GEOGRAPHY** Why did passage of the Kansas-Nebraska Act result in the repeal of the Missouri Compromise?

4. **WRITING TO CLASSIFY** Imagine you are a delegate to the new Republican party's convention in Jackson, Michigan. Write a letter to a newspaper editor, explaining why your party was formed and who it hopes to attract.

5. **HYPOTHESIZING** What actions might the federal government have taken to prevent bloodshed in Kansas?

ON THE BRINK OF WAR

FOCUS

- What effect did the Supreme Court's *Dred Scott* decision have on the national debate over slavery?
- How did the Lincoln-Douglas debates both help and hurt Stephen Douglas's political career?
- Why was John Brown's raid at Harpers Ferry important?
- Why did the results of the 1860 presidential election cause a crisis? How did the South justify its position?

From 1857 to 1861 the slavery issue pushed the United States further toward disunion. On March 6, 1857, two days after President James Buchanan took office, the Supreme Court issued the Dred Scott *decision, which intensified the slavery controversy. The following year Democrat Stephen Douglas and Republican Abraham Lincoln of Illinois debated the issue as they campaigned for the U.S. Senate. Douglas was elected, but two years later Lincoln defeated Douglas in the presidential election. Faced with a Republican president, the Deep South made good its threat to secede.*

Stephen Douglas campaign doll

THE DRED SCOTT DECISION

Dred Scott was the slave of John Emerson, an army surgeon from Missouri. Scott accompanied Emerson when he served on army posts in the free state of Illinois and the free territory of Wisconsin. Eventually the two men returned to Missouri. In 1846, after Emerson's death, Scott sued for his freedom, arguing that his residence in the free state of Illinois entitled him to it.

In 1857 the case reached the U.S. Supreme Court. Chief Justice Roger B. Taney, one of five southerners on the Court, wrote the majority opinion against Scott. Taney declared that Scott was not a citizen and therefore could not bring suit in U.S. courts. The nation's founders, Taney asserted,

had viewed blacks as "beings of an inferior order" having "no rights which the white man was bound to respect."

Taney also ruled that even if Scott had a legal right to bring suit, his claim to freedom had no merit. Taney based his decision on the view that the Missouri Compromise violated the Fifth Amendment to the Constitution, which forbids Congress to deny the right to property without "due process of law." Since slaves were legally classified as property, Congress had acted unconstitutionally in barring slavery from the territory north of 36°30′.

The ***Dred Scott* decision** outraged abolitionists and all who feared the extension of slavery. African American leader Robert Purvis, speaking at a protest rally held by northern blacks,

The *Dred Scott* decision struck a blow for slavery and fueled bitter sectional controversy. Chief Justice Roger Taney (left) and Dred Scott (right) are shown here with a detail from the Supreme Court's decision.

expressed the angry sentiments of the free black community:

> 66 This atrocious decision furnishes final confirmation of the already well-known fact that, under the Constitution and government of the United States, the colored people are nothing and can be nothing but an alien, disfranchised, and degraded class. 99

After the passage of the Kansas-Nebraska Act and the Supreme Court's ruling in the *Dred Scott* case, there seemed no way to keep slavery from spreading into the territories. The sectional struggle over slavery, declared Senator Seward of New York, had become an "irrepressible conflict."

■■ **The *Dred Scott* decision intensified the sectional conflict over slavery.**

LINCOLN WINS A NATIONAL REPUTATION

The 1858 U.S. Senate race in Illinois became the forum for debate over the *Dred Scott* decision and the slavery issue—as well as a rehearsal for the 1860 presidential campaign. If Senator Douglas could win reelection, he stood a good chance of winning the Democratic party's nomination for president.

Illinois Republicans chose Abraham Lincoln to oppose Douglas. Born in 1809 in a log cabin in Kentucky, Lincoln was truly a self-made man.

Although Lincoln had less than one year of formal education, he was intelligent and ambitious. During childhood he read the family Bible and walked miles to borrow books from neighbors.

In 1816 Lincoln and his family moved from Kentucky to the Indiana frontier. According to Lincoln, the move resulted in part because of the family's opposition to slavery and in part because of a disputed claim to their land.

Abraham Lincoln

When Lincoln was 21, his family moved to Illinois. The next year he left home and settled in New Salem, Illinois. He worked at various jobs, served in the frontier militia, and for a short time he and a partner owned a store. Although the business soon failed, Lincoln earned the respect of the townspeople and was appointed postmaster and deputy surveyor.

In 1834 he successfully ran for the Illinois legislature. A shrewd politician, Lincoln soon became the Whig floor leader. That same year he began studying law. Few law schools existed, and

▲ Robert Marshall Root's painting shows the fourth debate between Lincoln and Douglas, which took place in Charleston, Illinois. Douglas is seated to Lincoln's right.

Lincoln—like most other aspiring attorneys—learned law by reading textbooks at home. One lawyer who lent Lincoln books said of him:

66 He was the most uncouth looking young man I ever saw. He seemed to have but little to say; seemed to feel timid, with a tinge of sadness visible in the countenance, but when he did talk all this disappeared for the time and he demonstrated that he was both strong and acute. He surprised us more and more at every visit. 99

Shortly after he was admitted to the bar, Lincoln moved to Springfield, Illinois. There in 1839 he began courting Mary Todd—"the very creature of excitement," as one young lawyer described her—from a well-to-do Kentucky family. After an on-again, off-again courtship, the couple married on November 4, 1842.

A successful lawyer and persuasive politician, Lincoln was elected in 1846 to the U.S. House of Representatives. While a member of Congress, Lincoln opposed the Mexican War and the slave trade in the District of Columbia. After one term in the House, he returned to practicing law but remained active in Whig party affairs.

Conflict over slavery and the Kansas-Nebraska Act prompted Lincoln's return to public life in 1854, though not as a candidate for office. In October at the Illinois state fairgrounds in Springfield, Lincoln gave a speech attacking the act, which he said would raise slavery to a "sacred right." Later that month, he delivered the speech again in Peoria, Illinois.

THE LINCOLN-DOUGLAS DEBATES

For the next few years, Lincoln continued to speak out against the expansion of slavery, often in behalf of other candidates. He rose within the newly formed Republican party and was selected in 1858 as the party's candidate for the U.S. Senate seat that Douglas held. Lincoln used a quotation from the Bible as the foundation for his acceptance speech at the party's convention: "A house divided against itself cannot stand." The nation, he argued, could not remain divided into slave and free states for long:

66 I believe this government cannot endure permanently half slave and half free. I do not expect the Union to be dissolved; I do not expect the house to fall; but I do expect it will cease to be divided. 99

Seeking statewide exposure, Lincoln challenged Douglas to a series of seven debates between August and October 1858. Douglas accepted the challenge but acknowledged that Lincoln was "the best stump speaker in the West." Throngs of people turned out in seven Illinois towns to hear the two men debate the issues of the day.

On the platform the two men presented a startling contrast. Douglas—nicknamed the "Little Giant"—was well under 6 feet. When Lincoln, at nearly 6 1/2 feet, wore the high stovepipe hat then in fashion, he towered over Douglas. Journalists described Lincoln as lank and ungainly but were impressed by his "earnest truthfulness" and "kindly sympathy."

During the debates, Lincoln attacked the *Dred Scott* decision, which seemed to grant broad constitutional protection to slavery: "I do not believe it is a constitutional right to hold slaves in a territory of the United States. I believe the decision was improperly made." Lincoln, like the Republican party, viewed slavery as "a moral, social, and political wrong." Although he was willing to tolerate slavery in the South, he firmly opposed its expansion in the territories.

In the debate at Freeport, Illinois, Lincoln challenged Douglas to explain how popular sovereignty—the method the Kansas-Nebraska Act had used to settle the slavery issue in the new territories—was still workable in the wake of *Dred Scott*. Douglas replied that the people of a territory could still prohibit slavery simply by refusing to pass the local laws necessary to make a slave system work:

> 66 It matters not what way the Supreme Court may . . . decide. . . . The people have the lawful means to introduce [slavery] or exclude it as they please, for the reason that slavery cannot exist . . . unless it is supported by local police regulations. 99

This argument, which came to be called the **Freeport Doctrine**, helped Douglas narrowly defeat Lincoln in the U.S. Senate race. But in distancing himself from the *Dred Scott* decision, Douglas further damaged his standing with southern slaveholders. (His opposition to the Lecompton Constitution in Kansas had already enraged many southerners.) This proved to be a serious blow to Douglas's bid for the presidency in 1860.

■■ **The Lincoln-Douglas debates helped Douglas win the U.S. Senate race but hurt his chances of ever becoming president.**

JOHN BROWN'S RAID

The year after the Lincoln-Douglas debates, John Brown, leader of the Pottawatomie Massacre in 1856, again grabbed national attention. This time he set out to free slaves in Virginia. With money obtained from New England abolitionists, Brown armed a band of some 20 men, including 5 blacks. On October 16, 1859, this small force seized the federal arsenal at Harpers Ferry, in what is now West Virginia. Apparently Brown planned to give the guns to slaves living nearby and to establish an independent state in the southern Appalachian Mountains. He hoped to attract both runaway slaves and free African Americans to help him liberate slaves from their masters.

Brown and his followers easily took possession of the armory and rifleworks. However, no slaves came to their aid. On October 18, federal troops under the command of Colonel Robert E. Lee assaulted Brown's position, killing half of his men and capturing the rest.

Brown was convicted of "murder, criminal conspiracy, and treason against the Commonwealth of Virginia" and was hanged on December 2, 1859. Six of his followers were later executed. One of the condemned men, African American John

▲ **Thomas Hovenden painted *The Last Moments of John Brown* in 1884. This scene shows Brown being led to his place of execution on December 2, 1859.**

Reactions to John Brown's attack on Harpers Ferry were mixed, both in the United States and in Europe. William Edward Forster, who became a member of the British Parliament in 1861, sympathized with the abolitionist cause but was surprised by how much fear and conflict arose over Brown's small raid. The extent of the South's violent reaction only strengthened Forster's belief that the slave system would collapse. As Forster said:

> **"O**ne fact is quite evident, that whatever John Brown may have done toward freeing the slaves . . . he has exposed the utter weakness of the slave system—Virginia having been as much alarmed by an inroad [raid] of 22 abolitionists and colored men as England would have been by the landing of 22,000 French troops on the coast of Sussex. **"**

servitude. . . . I imagine that I hear you, and all of you, mother, father, sisters, and brothers, say—"No, there is not a cause for which we, with less sorrow, could see you die." **"**

Though many people questioned Brown's sanity, abolitionists saw Brown as a hero. Lydia Maria Child, a leading abolitionist writer, offered to help Brown while he was in prison. Henry David Thoreau hailed him as "an angel of light," while Ralph Waldo Emerson declared that Brown was "that new saint . . . [who] will make the gallows glorious like the cross."

In contrast, many southern whites, alarmed by the threat of slave revolts, viewed Brown as a bloodthirsty fanatic who got what he deserved. Southern secessionists, however, were actually pleased by the hysteria, believing that it helped their cause. In Congress, tension ran high. Senator James Hammond of South Carolina noted that "the only persons who do not have a revolver and a knife are those who have two revolvers."

■■ **Reactions to John Brown's raid on Harpers Ferry widened the rift between the North and the South.**

Copeland, wrote his parents to assure them that he faced death with no regrets:

> **"** Remember that if I must die I die in trying to liberate a few of my poor and oppressed people from my condition of

THE ELECTION OF 1860

Thus divided, the nation approached the presidential election of 1860. Southern moderates, most of whom had been Know-Nothings or Whigs, formed the Constitutional Union party. Nominating John

▲ The 1860 Republican convention nominated Abraham Lincoln of Illinois for president and Hannibal Hamlin of Maine for vice president.

The Lincoln Museum, Fort Wayne,

Bell of Tennessee for president, they ignored sectional differences and urged Americans to rally around the Constitution and save the Union.

The Democratic convention in Charleston, South Carolina, broke up without nominating a candidate. At a second convention in Baltimore, Stephen Douglas won the nomination he so desired. However, he no longer could count on the backing of southern Democrats, who held their own convention and nominated Senator John Breckinridge of Kentucky. Breckinridge, like many other southerners, interpreted the *Dred Scott* decision to mean that Congress would have to protect slavery in the territories.

The Republicans confidently gathered in Chicago for their nominating convention. Whigs and Know-Nothings, and even some northern Democrats, flocked to the Republican banner. Convinced that a moderate candidate from the

▲ **A Lincoln-Hamlin banner and Lincoln coins commemorate the 1860 presidential election.**

Midwest stood the best chance of winning, the convention delegates chose Abraham Lincoln.

The Republican party designed its platform to attract northern industrialists and wage earners as well as midwestern farmers. It opposed slavery in the territories and called for free homesteads for western settlers. It also included federal support for the construction of roads, canals, and a transcontinental railroad and for a tariff to protect industry. Moreover, the platform supported a liberal immigration policy—a measure favored by northern factory owners seeking cheap labor.

The election results mirrored the nation's sectional divisions. Breckinridge carried every state of the Deep South. Three states of the Upper South—Virginia, Kentucky, and Tennessee—went for Bell. Douglas, though second in the popular vote, won only Missouri and three of New Jersey's electoral votes. The remaining New Jersey votes went to Lincoln, along with those of the rest of the northern states, Oregon, and California. Although Lincoln received only about 40 percent of the popular vote, his electoral victory was a landslide: 180 electoral votes to 72 for Breckinridge, 39 for Bell, and 12 for Douglas.

Election of 1860

FRAGMENTED UNION Each section voted its interests, and the result was secession.

❓ REGION How does the map show you that the vote followed sectional lines?

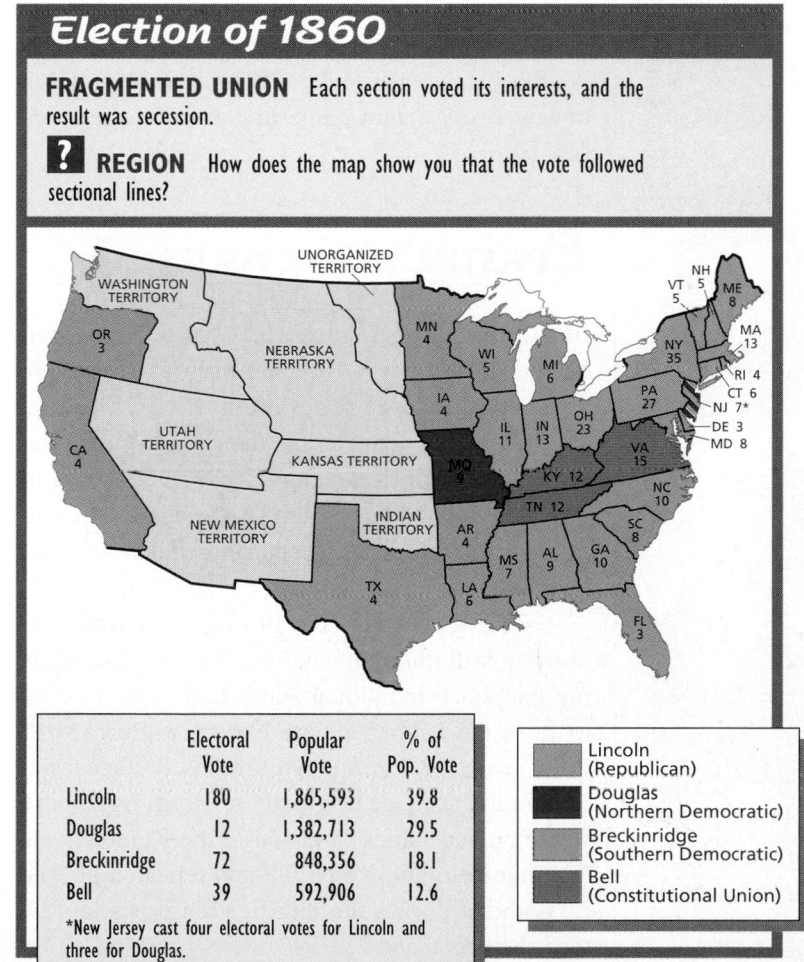

	Electoral Vote	Popular Vote	% of Pop. Vote
Lincoln	180	1,865,593	39.8
Douglas	12	1,382,713	29.5
Breckinridge	72	848,356	18.1
Bell	39	592,906	12.6

*New Jersey cast four electoral votes for Lincoln and three for Douglas.

Legend:
- Lincoln (Republican)
- Douglas (Northern Democratic)
- Breckinridge (Southern Democratic)
- Bell (Constitutional Union)

SECESSION!

The outcome of the election of 1860 mobilized the Deep South. That a president had been elected without winning a single southern state confirmed the South's deepening sense of political powerlessness. Within days of the election, the South Carolina legislature called a convention to consider secession. As onlookers cheered, the delegates unanimously voted for South Carolina to leave the Union. Mississippi, Florida, Alabama, Georgia, Louisiana, and Texas soon passed similar acts of secession.

■■ Many southern states decided to secede when Lincoln won the presidency.

Early in 1861, delegates from six of the seven seceding states met at Montgomery, Alabama, and drafted a constitution for the Confederate States of America. The Confederate Constitution resembled the Constitution of the United States, with two key exceptions: the Confederate Constitution guaranteed the right to own slaves, and it stressed that each state was "sovereign and independent." The convention chose Jefferson Davis as provisional president of the Confederacy. He won confirmation as president in an election held late in 1861. A Mississippi planter, Davis formerly served as a U.S. senator and as the secretary of war under Franklin Pierce.

Southern support for secession was far from unanimous. Many who supported slavery and were dismayed by Lincoln's election still could not bring themselves to secede. Even Alexander Stephens, who eventually became vice president of the Confederacy, made an impassioned speech against secession to the Georgia legislature:

> 66 In my judgement, the election of no man, constitutionally chosen to that high office, is sufficient cause for any state to separate from the Union. . . . Whatever fate is to befall this country, let it never be laid to the charge of the people of the South . . . that we were untrue to our national engagements. 99

As the secession movement gained momentum, however, dissenters came under increasing pressure to yield.

▲ **The December 22, 1860, edition of** *Harper's Weekly* **shows members of the South Carolina delegation who voted to secede from the Union.**

CONSTITUTIONAL ISSUES

In the months before he left office, President Buchanan tried to sit on the political fence. As southern states broke from the Union, he announced that no state had the right to secede but also agreed that the federal government had no power to hold a state in the Union against its will. Caught in a dilemma, Buchanan decided to let the incoming president deal with the problem.

The southern secessionists justified their position with the doctrine of states' rights, asserting that since individual states had come together to form the Union, a state had the right to withdraw from the Union. Arguments for secession refined the doctrine originally set forth by Thomas Jefferson and James Madison in the Kentucky and Virginia Resolutions in 1798 and repeated by John C. Calhoun during the nullification crisis in 1832 (see chapters 6 and 7).

all he hoped to offend no one and
raging con-
y. Though
slavery, he
the courts
g to remain
on the issue.
Hart Benton
was "never
high sense,
all] a man of

ed that restricting
ensure that the
voting bloc. Then
ss could not only
but also abolish it

aving comfortably
majority rule was a
blican government.
age to a special ses-
at the South had to
"When ballots have
ided," he said, "there
ack to bullets." Many
e.

VIEW

cision, Abraham Lincoln,

cott case? How did it affect the

the North and the South? What
South?

debates have both positive and

tor writing for a southern maga-
nts the South has used to justify

its actions

5. **SYNTHESIZING** What arguments did northern
unter the principle of secession?

Texas admitted to the Union.

Free-Soil party formed. Zachary Taylor elected president.

Compromise of 1850 enacted

1845 1847 1849

WRITING A SUMMARY

Using the essential points of the chapter as a guide, write a summary of the chapter.

REVIEWING CHRONOLOGY

Number your paper 1 to 5. Study the time line above, and list the following events in the order in which they happened by writing the first next to 1, the second next to 2, and so on. Then complete the activity below.

1. Lincoln-Douglas debates take place.
2. Kansas-Nebraska Act passed.
3. Compromise of 1850 enacted.
4. *Dred Scott* case decided.
5. Jefferson Davis elected president of Confederacy.

Synthesizing In a paragraph, provide evidence that neither the Compromise of 1850 nor the Kansas-Nebraska Act settled the issue of slavery in the new territories.

IDENTIFYING PEOPLE AND IDEAS

Explain the historical significance of each of the following people or terms.

1. Ostend Manifesto
2. popular sovereignty
3. Wilmot Proviso
4. Free-Soil party
5. Harriet Beecher Stowe
6. John C. Frémont
7. *Dred Scott* decision
8. Abraham Lincoln
9. Freeport Doctrine
10. John Brown

UNDERSTANDING MAIN IDEAS

1. Why did western expansion cause conflict? How did various members of Congress propose to deal with the issue?
2. How did the Compromise of 1850, the Kansas-Nebraska Act, and the *Dred Scott* decision intensify conflict over slavery?
3. Why did the Lincoln-Douglas debates receive national attention?
4. Why did the presidential election of 1860 lead to southern secession? What constitutional claims did southerners offer to justify secession? What arguments did northerners offer to counter these constitutional claims?

REVIEWING THEMES

1. **Constitutional Heritage** How did the South use constitutional arguments to try to protect its way of life?
2. **Democratic Values** How did Stephen Douglas try to use the principle of majority rule to end the debate over slavery in the territories? What other principle was in conflict?
3. **Geographic Diversity** How did geographic differences between the North and the South affect people's views on the expansion of slavery into the new territories?

THINKING CRITICALLY

1. **Hypothesizing** How might the history of the American political party system have been different if the Democrats or Whigs had taken a strong stand on the slavery issue?
2. **Evaluating** Do you think antislavery northerners were justified in disobeying the Fugitive Slave Act or supporting John Brown? Explain your answer.
3. **Problem Solving** As an aide to Senator Henry Clay in 1850, write a memorandum outlining two creative ways to settle the differences between the North and the South.

STRATEGY FOR SUCCESS

Review the Strategies for Success on Interpreting Editorial Cartoons on page 332. Then study the cartoon on the right, which appeared shortly after Lincoln was elected president. What is the cartoonist's message?

OLD ABE'S UNCOMFORTABLE POSITION
"Oh, it's all well enough to say that I must support the dignity of my high office by force—but it's darned uncomfortable sitting."

The Granger Collection, New York

1851	1853	1855	1857	1859	1861

Franklin Pierce elected president.

Kansas-Nebraska Act passed. Republican party formed.

Lawrence, Kansas, burns. Pottawatomie Massacre occurs. James Buchanan elected president.

Dred Scott case decided.

Lincoln-Douglas debates take place.

John Brown raids arsenal at Harpers Ferry.

Abraham Lincoln elected president. South Carolina secedes.

Jefferson Davis elected president of Confederacy.

WRITING ABOUT HISTORY

Writing to Explain Frederick Douglass explained his objections to slavery by saying: "I have held all my life, that the fundamental and everlasting objection to slavery, is not that it sinks a Negro to the condition of a brute, but that it sinks a *man* to that condition." Write a brief essay explaining what Douglass's statement means to you.

USING PRIMARY SOURCES

Shortly after James Buchanan was elected president in 1856, Governor James H. Adams of South Carolina expressed the fears of many southerners that the election had not put to rest the conflict over slavery. Read the following excerpt from his *Governor's Message* of November 24, 1856. Why does Adams believe that further conflict between the North and the South is inevitable?

> **66** *Slavery and Freesoilism can never be reconciled. Our enemies have been defeated—not vanquished. A majority of the free States have declared war against the South, upon a purely sectional issue, and in the remainder of them, formidable minorities fiercely contended for victory under the same banner. The triumph of this geographical party must dissolve the confederacy, unless we are prepared to sink down into a state of acknowledged inferiority. We will act wisely to employ the interval of repose afforded by the late election, in earnest preparation for the inevitable conflict. The Southern States have never demanded more than equality and security. They cannot submit to less, and remain in the Union, without dishonor and ultimate ruin.* **99**

Buchanan campaign button

LINKING HISTORY AND GEOGRAPHY

Daniel Webster said that geography would limit slavery because most of the West was unsuitable for growing cotton. Write a paragraph agreeing or disagreeing with him.

Cotton field

BUILDING YOUR PORTFOLIO

Complete the following projects independently or cooperatively.

1. SLAVERY Imagine you are the organizer of one of the Lincoln-Douglas debates. Create a poster announcing the debate, listing highlights of the opponents' careers and summarizing their differing views on extending slavery into western territories.

2. DEMOCRATIC RIGHTS Imagine you are a lawyer helping Dred Scott sue for his freedom. Conduct an interview with Scott. Your interview should include questions about the circumstances of Scott's case, his views on how his rights have been violated, and the reasons why he thinks he should be set free.

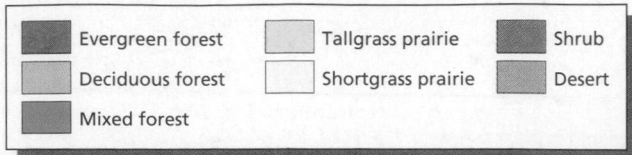

America's GEOGRAPHY

REGIONALISM

BY the middle of the 19th century, there were three distinct regions of the country, each with its own unique character and culture. Some people felt more loyalty to their regions than to the nation as a whole. This concept of *regionalism* was particularly evident in the South. Unlike sectionalism, regionalism focuses more on cultural than on political differences. Since regionalism primarily involves cultural identification, the regional identity of some states has shifted as the state's culture has changed. Many residents of Missouri, for instance, identified with the South before the Civil War. In the late 19th century, however, as transportation, trade, and industrialization increased in the state, its culture became closely identified with that of the Midwest.

The North Before the Civil War

POPULATION OF THE NORTH IN 1860

Other races <1%
Black 2%
White 97%
Rural 74%
Urban 26%

The smallest region—the North—was not only the center of industrialization in the United States, but was also the center of higher education. The North housed 63 percent of the country's colleges and universities in 1850.

The West Before the Civil War

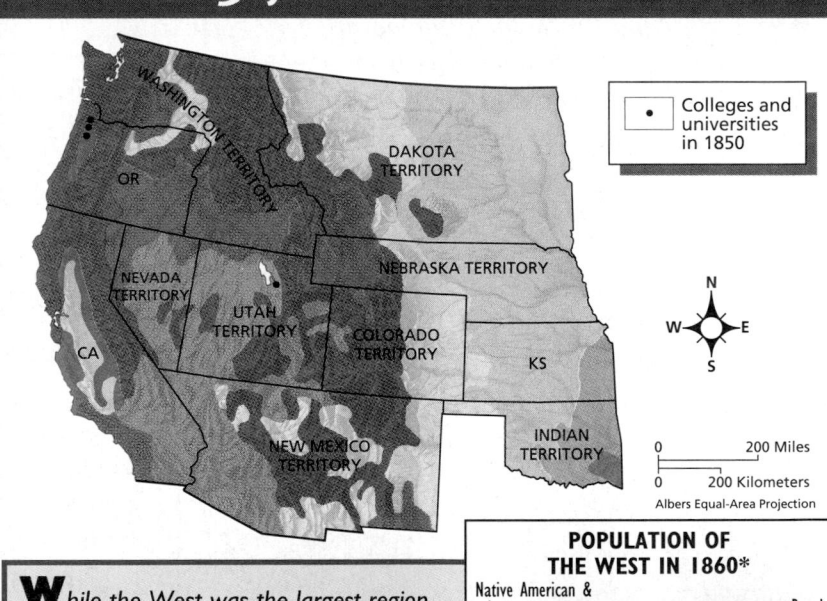

POPULATION OF THE WEST IN 1860*

Native American & other races 9%
Black <1%
White 91%
Rural 86%
Urban 14%
*Does not include Indian Territory.

While the West was the largest region of the country in 1850, it had the smallest population. Despite the large areas of land available for settlement, the West had a higher percentage of urban-dwellers than did the South as people flocked to cities such as San Francisco. Yet the first centers of education in the West were located on the frontier, not in the cities of California. As California attracted miners and other business-minded people, the Morman settlers of Utah and the followers of the Oregon Trail established the first western universities.

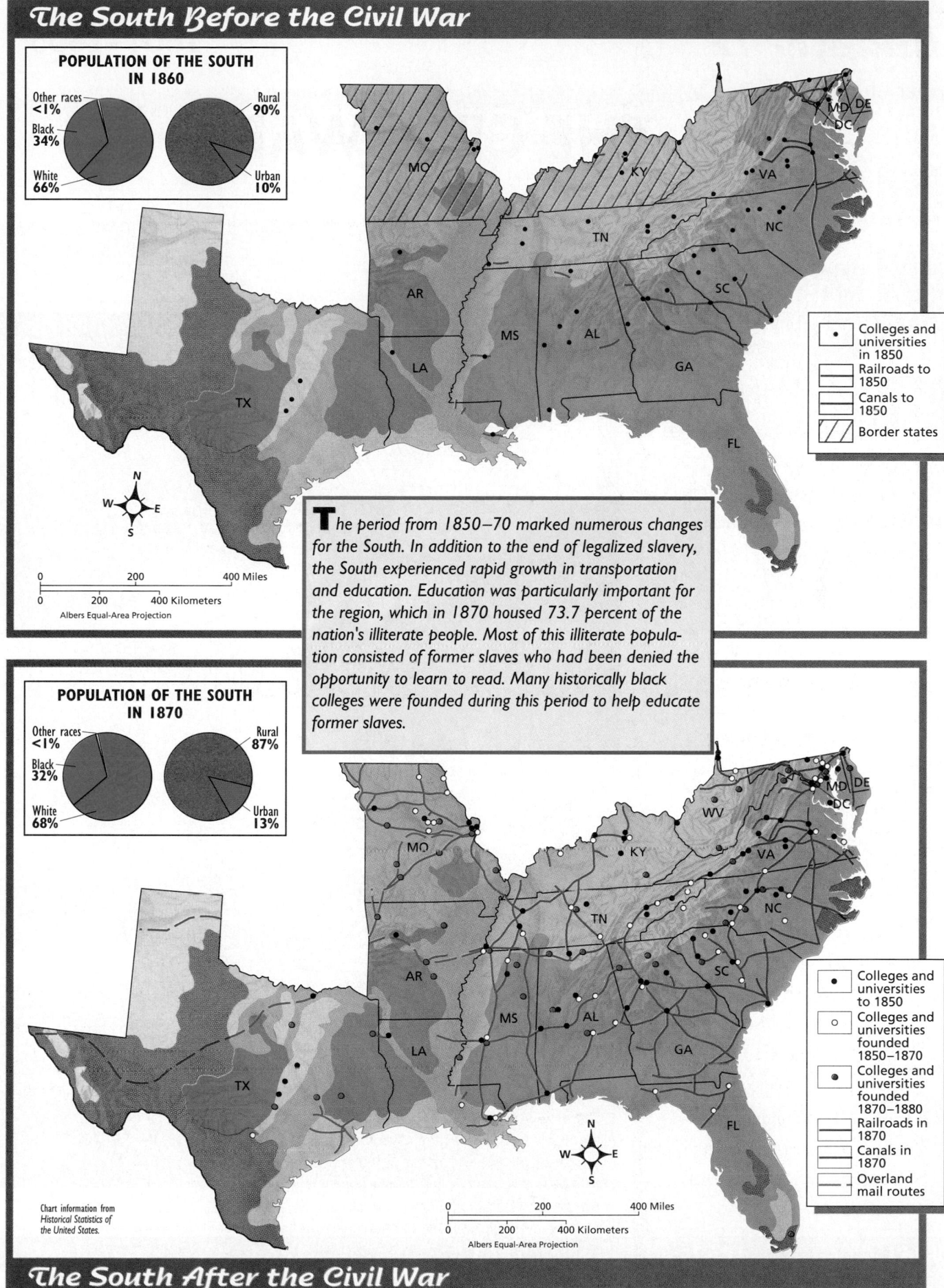

POPULATION OF THE SOUTH IN 1860

Other races <1%
Black 34%
White 66%
Rural 90%
Urban 10%

MO
KY
VA
MD DE
DC
TN
NC
AR
SC
MS
AL
LA
GA
TX
FL

Colleges and universities in 1850
Railroads to 1850
Canals to 1850
Border states

200   400 Miles
200   400 Kilometers
Albers Equal-Area Projection

The period from 1850–70 marked numerous changes for the South. In addition to the end of legalized slavery, the South experienced rapid growth in transportation and education. Education was particularly important for the region, which in 1870 housed 73.7 percent of the nation's illiterate people. Most of this illiterate population consisted of former slaves who had been denied the opportunity to learn to read. Many historically black colleges were founded during this period to help educate former slaves.

POPULATION OF THE SOUTH IN 1870

Other races <1%
Black 32%
White 68%
Rural 87%
Urban 13%

MO
WV
KY
VA
MD DE
DC
TN
NC
AR
SC
MS
AL
LA
GA
TX
FL

Chart information from *Historical Statistics of the United States.*

Colleges and universities to 1850
Colleges and universities founded 1850–1870
Colleges and universities founded 1870–1880
Railroads in 1870
Canals in 1870
Overland mail routes

200   400 Miles
200   400 Kilometers
Albers Equal-Area Projection

The South After the Civil War

THE CIVIL WAR

FOCUS

UNDERSTANDING THE MAIN IDEA

The Civil War dragged on far longer than anyone anticipated in 1861. The North was more populated and more heavily industrialized than the South, which was mostly agricultural. Consequently, the North was better prepared to fight a long war. Though the defensive strategy and superior military leadership of the South enabled it to win most of the early battles, the Confederacy was unable to overcome the staying power of the resourceful Union forces.

THEMES

■ **GEOGRAPHIC DIVERSITY** How might geography help or hinder a war effort?

■ **ECONOMIC DEVELOPMENT** What positive and negative effects might war have on a nation's economy?

1861	1862	1863	1864	1865
Fort Sumter falls.	Peninsula Campaign fails for North.	Emancipation Proclamation goes into effect.	Atlanta falls.	Lee surrenders at Appomattox.

The Battle of Chattanooga, 1863

The Granger Collection, New York

O n April 15, 1861, President Abraham Lincoln declared that the nation faced an armed revolt. Mary Ashton Livermore, who would soon join the war effort as a volunteer for the United States Sanitary Commission, recorded the reaction in Boston to the president's call to arms:

❝ Monday dawned, April 15. Who that saw that day will ever forget it! For now . . . there rang out the voice of Abraham Lincoln calling for seventy-five thousand volunteers for three months. They were for the protection of Washington and the property of the government. . . . This proclamation was like the first peal of a surcharged thunder-cloud, clearing the murky air. The . . . whole North arose as one man. . . .

Hastily formed companies marched to camps of rendezvous, the sunlight flashing from gun-barrel and bayonet. . . . Merchants and clerks rushed out from stores, bareheaded, saluting them as they passed. Windows were flung up; and women leaned out into the rain, waving flags and handkerchiefs. Horse-cars and omnibuses halted for the passage of the soldiers, and cheer upon cheer leaped forth from [their] thronged doors and windows. . . .

I had never seen anything like this before. I had never dreamed that New England . . . could be fired with so warlike a spirit. ❞

Union drum with federal eagle insignia

This "warlike spirit" pervaded the nation in early 1861. Amid the excitement, few Americans imagined the death and destruction that lay ahead.

THE UNION DISSOLVES!

FOCUS

- What were some of the effects of the fall of Fort Sumter?
- What military advantages did each side possess at the beginning of the war?
- How did the draft laws affect who fought the war?
- How did women contribute to the war effort?

When President Abraham Lincoln took office in 1861, the nation was on the brink of collapse. The situation came to a head with the fall of Fort Sumter to the Confederates in April 1861. As war became inevitable, both sides prepared for what they believed would be a short conflict.

The Spirit of '61 recruiting poster

LAST ATTEMPTS AT COMPROMISE

By Abraham Lincoln's inauguration on March 4, 1861, seven southern states had seceded from the Union: South Carolina, Mississippi, Florida, Alabama, Georgia, Louisiana, and Texas. But the debate over secession was far from settled in the border states of the Upper South. The slave states of Delaware, Missouri, Kentucky, and Maryland all had strong economic ties to the North.

To save the Union, Senator John J. Crittenden of Kentucky proposed the **Crittenden Compromise**. The plan called for the Missouri Compromise line to be drawn west through the remaining territories. North of the line, slavery would be illegal; south of the line, slavery could expand. Lincoln quickly rejected the plan. "No spread of slavery" was the principle that held the Republican party together. Many Republicans might have turned against Lincoln if he had allowed slavery to

▲ John J. Crittenden

expand. Lincoln was willing, however, to support another part of Crittenden's plan—that slavery be protected where it already existed.

Lincoln's gesture had little effect on the secessionists, who were caught up in the excitement of creating a new nation. "It is a revolution . . . of the most intense character," wrote one southern senator. "It can no more be checked by human effort, for the time, than a prairie fire by a gardener's watering pot."

The new president was determined to preserve the Union. In his inaugural address, Lincoln was firm but cordial when he reminded southerners that secession was unconstitutional: "No State upon its own mere motion can lawfully get out of the Union." As president, he was bound to enforce the Constitution in every state. Lincoln added:

66 There needs to be no bloodshed or violence; and there shall be none, unless it be forced upon the national authority. . . .

> In your hands, my dissatisfied fellow countrymen, and not in mine, is the momentous issue of civil war. The government will not assail you. You can have no conflict without being yourselves the aggressors. **99**

𝓣HE FALL OF FORT SUMTER

The "dissatisfied countrymen" had already demonstrated their intentions. Meeting little resistance, the Confederacy had taken over most federal forts, mints, and arsenals within its borders. However, one fort very important to the South—Fort Sumter—remained under federal control.

Fort Sumter was strategically located in the harbor of Charleston, South Carolina. The South needed the fort in order to control access to this major port city. By early March the fort's commander, Major Robert Anderson, had notified Washington that he was nearly out of supplies. Without reinforcements Sumter would soon fall to the Confederates.

The North did not want to lose the fort—it would be an admission that South Carolina was truly out of the Union. Yet Lincoln was hesitant to use force, fearing the reaction of the eight slave states that were still part of the Union. The leaders of several of these states had said that their states, too, would secede if Lincoln used force against the Confederacy.

To do nothing, however, would signify weakness. Thus, Lincoln decided to resupply Fort Sumter. If the Confederates fired on unarmed supply ships, they, not the Union, would be the aggressors.

On April 6 Lincoln sent a messenger to warn the South Carolina governor, F. W. Pickens, that supply ships were on their way. The messenger assured the governor that the ships were carrying only supplies, not troops or arms. Governor Pickens relayed the message to General P.G.T. Beauregard, local military commander of the Confederates. General Beauregard responded by ordering the federal troops to evacuate the fort. Major Anderson refused to obey the order.

At 4:30 A.M. on April 12 the Confederate forces opened fire on Fort Sumter. Abner Doubleday, Anderson's second-in-command, described the scene within the fort:

▲ **The firing on Fort Sumter on April 12, 1861, marked the beginning of four long, bloody years of war.**

> **66** Showers of balls . . . and shells . . . poured into the fort in one incessant stream, causing great flakes of masonry to fall in all directions. When the immense mortar shells, after sailing high in the air, came down in a vertical direction and buried themselves in the parade ground, their explosion shook the fort like an earthquake. **99**

For 34 hours the Confederates bombarded Sumter. Finally, with much of the fort ablaze and their ammunition running low, Anderson and his men formally surrendered on April 14. Surprisingly, no one on either side was killed or seriously wounded during the fighting.

On April 15 Lincoln publicly proclaimed the existence of a rebellion "too powerful to be suppressed by the ordinary course of judicial proceedings." He asked the governors of the loyal states to provide 75,000 militiamen to put down the uprising. The recruits were to serve for just three months.

▶ **This Union army recruitment poster was circulated in Philadelphia in 1862.**

TO ARMS!
RALLY FOR THE RIGHT!
Recruits Wanted
For THREE MONTHS SERVICE, IN
COMPANY A
GRAY RESERVES
CAPT. CHARLES S. SMITH.
ARMORY,
810 MARKET STREET,
UP STAIRS.

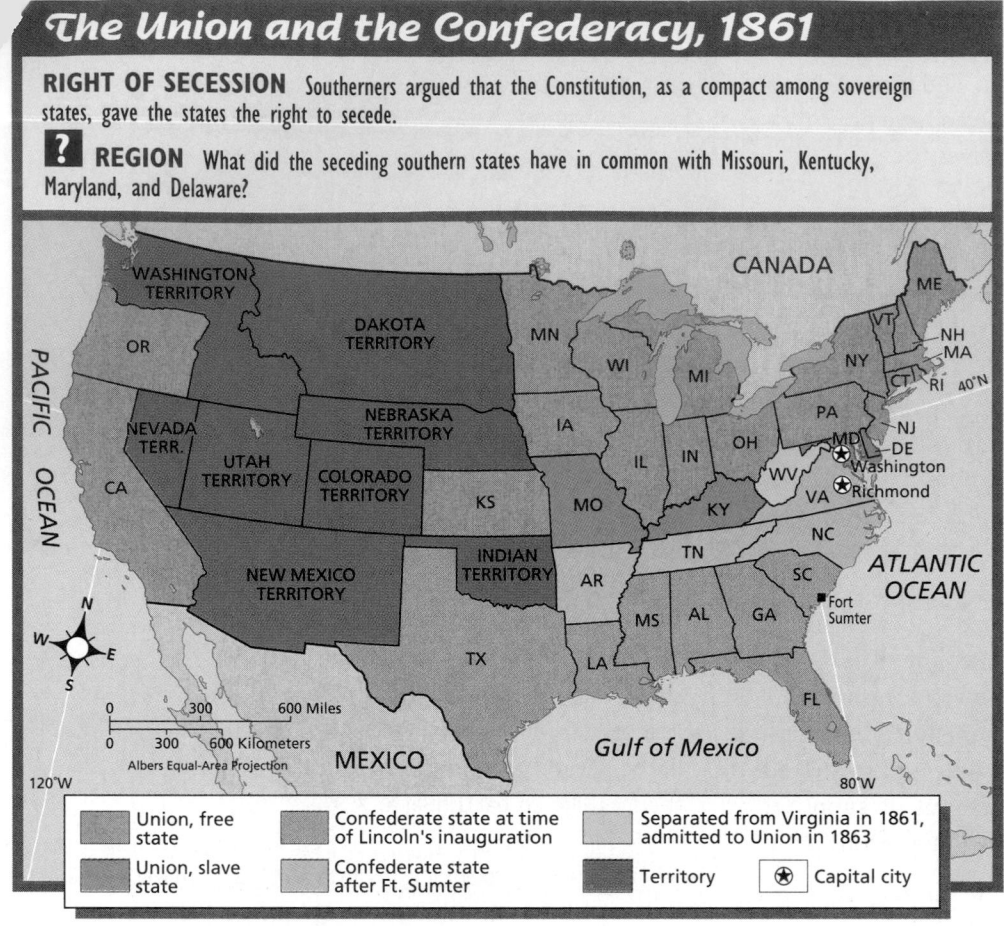

The Union and the Confederacy, 1861

RIGHT OF SECESSION Southerners argued that the Constitution, as a compact among sovereign states, gave the states the right to secede.

? **REGION** What did the seceding southern states have in common with Missouri, Kentucky, Maryland, and Delaware?

| Union, free state | Confederate state at time of Lincoln's inauguration | Separated from Virginia in 1861, admitted to Union in 1863 |
| Union, slave state | Confederate state after Ft. Sumter | Territory ⊛ Capital city |

CHOOSING SIDES

Lincoln's fear of losing more states to the Confederacy quickly became a reality. Four states—Virginia, Arkansas, Tennessee, and North Carolina—responded to the president's call for troops by seceding. Richmond, Virginia, became the Confederate capital.

Four other slave states—Delaware, Missouri, Kentucky, and Maryland—remained within the Union. Secession was never a serious threat in Delaware, where there were few slaves; Delaware sympathized much more with the North than with the South. Missouri, Kentucky, and Maryland, on the other hand, were sharply divided over the issue of secession. Though the governors of both Missouri and Kentucky supported secession, neither state voted to secede. Lincoln kept Maryland in the Union by quickly securing the state with federal troops. To lose Maryland would have meant to lose the Union capital, since the state surrounded Washington, D.C., on three sides.

The mountainous counties of northwestern Virginia remained loyal to the Union as well. The people there held few slaves and had long resented the rich planter elite of the lowlands. They set up their own state government, and in 1863 the state was admitted to the Union as West Virginia.

The people of the Upper South remained divided over the issue of secession. As a result, sections of several southern states raised Union regiments to fight fellow southerners. Some families were torn apart as members fought for different sides in the war. One of John Crittenden's sons became a Union general, and another became a Confederate general. Lincoln's wife, Mary Todd, a southerner by birth, had four brothers and three brothers-in-law fighting in the Confederate army.

▪▪ The fall of Fort Sumter brought on war, forcing the border states to choose sides.

COMPARING NORTH AND SOUTH

On the face of it, the war that loomed after the fall of Fort Sumter seemed a complete mismatch. The North—with more than 22 million people—had a huge advantage in population. The South's population was only slightly more than 9 million, of whom some 3.5 million were slaves. As a result, the South had a much smaller pool of available soldiers.

The North also enjoyed an economic advantage. When the war began, the North had over 85 percent of the nation's industries and almost all the known supplies of gold, iron, copper, and other metals. With such resources the North could produce war products and replace lost or damaged equipment faster than the Confederacy could. Southern wealth was largely in land and slaves.

In addition, most of the nation's railroad lines were located in the Northeast and the Midwest. Thus, the Union could move troops and supplies at will. Southern routes, on the other hand, were roundabout, with few connecting lines. Furthermore, because the North manufactured most of the nation's railway equipment, the Confederacy found it increasingly difficult during the war to replace broken or worn-out railway parts and equipment.

The North also held overwhelming superiority at sea. Most of the U.S. Navy remained loyal to the Union, including such southern naval officers as David Farragut and Percival Drayton. Lacking the expertise of such experienced naval men and with no ships or submarines, the South had to build its navy from scratch.

The South, however, did have two main advantages over the North. To win, the Confederacy had only to fight a defensive war, protecting its territory until the Union tired of the struggle. The Union, on the other hand, had to conquer an area almost as large as Western Europe. The South also had excellent military

RESOURCES OF THE NORTH AND SOUTH, 1861

	North	South
Total Population	22,000,000	9,000,000*
Bank Deposits	$189,000,000	$47,000,000
Railroad Mileage	20,000 miles	9,000 miles
Number of Factories	100,500	20,600

* Southern population includes 3,500,000 slaves.

Source: *American Heritage Picture History of the Civil War, Encyclopedia of American History*

NORTH vs. SOUTH At the beginning of the Civil War, the North's abundant resources gave it a military advantage over the South.

? EVALUATING Which resource do you think had the greatest influence on the outcome of the Civil War? Why?

leadership. In fact, most southern victories resulted from the battle strategies of skillful Confederate officers.

■■ **The North had numerical and economic advantages in the war, but the South had the advantage of fighting on its own soil with brilliant military leaders.**

THE CIVIL WAR

THROUGH OTHERS' EYES

The nations of Europe had their own aims and expectations with respect to the American Civil War. Judging that a divided United States would be less of a threat to Europe, France and England hoped the South would win. Sir Edward Bulwer-Lytton, a member of Parliament, remarked that a Confederate victory would "be attended with happy results to the safety of Europe." Believing that it was already too late to save the Union, Bulwer-Lytton noted that a united America "would have hung over Europe like a . . . thunder-cloud. No single kingdom in Europe could have been strong enough to maintain itself against a nation that had once consolidated the gigantic resources of a quarter of the globe."

Russia, on the other hand, supported the Union. Russia wanted to keep America united and strong—to help keep Great Britain and France in check and thereby maintain a balance of power in the world. Russian foreign minister Prince Gortchakov remarked to a U.S. diplomat: "We are very, very anxious . . . that any course should be pursued which will prevent the division. . . . One separation will be followed by another; you will break into fragments. You know the sentiments of Russia! We desire, above all things, the maintenance of the American Union as one indivisible nation."

Among the ablest of southern military leaders was Robert Edward Lee, who was born into a leading Virginia family in 1807. His father was Henry "Light-Horse Harry" Lee, a Revolutionary War hero. The young Robert excelled as a student at West Point. After graduating in 1829, he went on to serve first in the Army Corps of Engineers and then in the cavalry. In 1831 the young officer married Mary Custis, the great-granddaughter of Martha Washington.

Testing his military skills during the Mexican War, Lee served as a captain under General Winfield Scott and took part in the capture of Veracruz. Then in 1859, he led the federal troops that captured John Brown at Harpers Ferry.

Collection of the Corcoran Gallery of Art

Robert E. Lee

On Winfield Scott's recommendation, President Lincoln asked Lee to command the Union forces. Lee declined, resigning his commission. Although he opposed slavery and secession, he could not fight against Virginia. In a letter to his sister, he wrote:

❝ With all my devotion to the Union and the feeling of loyalty and duty of an American citizen, I have not been able to make up my mind to raise my hand against my relatives, my children, my home. I have therefore resigned my commission in the Army, and save in defense of my native State—with the sincere hope that my poor services may never be needed—I hope I may never be called on to draw my sword. ❞

Lee's wish would not be granted.

THE ARMIES

By the end of 1861, the Union had more than 527,000 soldiers, the Confederacy slightly more than 258,000. Most of these soldiers were between the ages of 18 and 29, with drummer boys as young as 9. All social classes fought, but a Confederate **conscription**, or draft, act in April 1862—the first draft law in American history— and a Union law in March 1863 put the major burden on poor farmers and working people. Wealthy men who were drafted could hire a substitute to serve for them or pay the government to be exempted from service.

In the South, anyone owning 20 or more slaves was exempt. This policy was a response to pressure from the planter class, who argued that some slaveholders had to remain at home to keep their slaves from running off. The exemption was also rooted in economics. The Confederacy needed

▶ Drummer boys not only provided music for daily calls and drills, but they also carried water, sold food to soldiers, and assisted in burying the dead.

▲ Confederate soldiers practice artillery-loading techniques near Charleston, South Carolina, in 1863.

food and cloth, but few southerners believed slaves would work without constant supervision.

The exemptions caused much resentment in both the North and the South. In the North, poor whites, many of them recent immigrants, rioted in protest. Draft riots did not break out in the South, but many whites openly criticized the draft, claiming it proved the conflict was a "rich man's war and a poor man's fight."

But resisting the war was not typical of either side. Estimates of how many men fought for the North vary because many men enlisted more than once. The U.S. government places the official wartime enlistment in the Union army at 2,672,341, with another 105,963 men enlisted in the navy or marines. Of the army's total, the government holds that some 180,000 enlistees were African Americans (of whom some 7,000 were noncommissioned officers and about 100 were commissioned officers) and that 3,530 were Native Americans.

Estimates of the number of Confederate enlistments stir even greater debate, but probably some 750,000 men enlisted in the Confederate army. Included in this number are some 5,500 Cherokees, Creeks, Chickasaws, and Choctaws, many of them slaveholders lured by the promise of an all-Indian state following the war. Mexican Americans from New Mexico and Texas fought on both sides during the war.

■■ **Both sides relied on volunteers and draftees to fight the war. Most soldiers were poor farmers and laborers.**

WOMEN AND THE WAR

Women in the North and in the South threw themselves into the war effort. Some women even dressed like men so that they could fight. Cuban-born Loreta Janeta Velázquez (vuh-LAHS-kuhs) disguised herself as a man and enlisted in the Confederate army. When she was found out for the third time and discharged, she became a spy for the South. A few other women also served as spies. Rose O'Neal Greenhow was imprisoned by the North for supplying information to the Confederacy. Elizabeth Bowser, a maid in Confederate president Jefferson Davis's home, and Harriet Tubman both supplied information to the Union from behind enemy lines.

▲ African American soldiers joined the Union cause in order to "assert their claim to freedom." Recruitment posters often were directed specifically to African Americans. The banner of the Third United States Colored Troops (bottom left) contains the slogan "Rather die Freeman than Live to be Slaves." (Image of soldier is detailed from the original photograph.)

Many more women served in medical roles. The first group of women to volunteer for medical duty were Catholic nuns, who transformed their convents into emergency hospitals throughout the North and South. Most of these neutral "nuns of the battlefield" were Irish or German immigrants. They treated all victims of the war, becoming the only group recognized by both Union and Confederate forces.

In the North, Elizabeth Blackwell, America's first professionally licensed female doctor, helped run the U.S. Sanitary Commission. The commission worked to battle the diseases and infections that killed twice as many soldiers as bullets alone. Approximately 3,000 women served in the Union army as nurses. Some, like Clara Barton, ministered to the wounded on the battlefield. After the war, Barton founded the American Red Cross, which today serves disaster victims and others in need of assistance all over the world.

De Paul Provincial House

◀ During the war, women, especially nuns, served in medical roles. Shown here are the Daughters of Charity from New York's Satterlee Hospital, along with doctors and soldiers.

◀ Elizabeth Blackwell

▶ Sally Tompkins

The Museum of the Confederacy, Richmond, Virginia

Women in the South also provided medical aid to soldiers. Sally Louisa Tompkins was among the Confederate women who founded small hospitals and clinics. She was eventually commissioned as a captain in the Confederate army so that her Richmond hospital could qualify as a military hospital. This made Tompkins the only recognized female officer in the Confederate services.

Nurses like Tompkins experienced the horrors of war firsthand. Kate Cumming, a Confederate nurse from Alabama, wrote in her diary of her experiences at a makeshift hospital:

66 The men are lying all over the house on their blankets, just as they were brought from the battlefield. . . . The foul air from this mass of human beings at first made me giddy and sick, but I soon got over it. We have to walk and, when we give the men anything, kneel in blood and water; but we think nothing of it at all. 99

Countless other women on both sides helped the war effort in less dramatic ways, such as by organizing soldiers' aid or hospital relief societies, raising money, or making bandages. In the North the American Freedman's Aid Commission provided hundreds of women schoolteachers to educate former slaves. Many women took over in offices and factories to replace men who were off fighting the war. Nearly 450 women worked in the Treasury Department as clerks—the government's first women office workers. Some 100,000 women worked in federal factories, sewing rooms, and military arsenals.

■■ A few women served as spies, but most aided the war by serving as nurses, doing volunteer work, and working in offices and factories.

SECTION 1 REVIEW

IDENTIFY and explain the significance of the following: Crittenden Compromise, Robert Anderson, Robert E. Lee, conscription, nuns of the battlefield, Elizabeth Blackwell, Sally Louisa Tompkins.

LOCATE and explain the importance of the following: Fort Sumter; Richmond, Virginia; West Virginia.

1. **MAIN IDEA** What were the immediate consequences of the fall of Fort Sumter for the Union and for the border states?

2. **MAIN IDEA** What were the North's military strengths at the beginning of the Civil War? What were the South's strengths?

3. **GEOGRAPHY: LOCATION** Refer to the map on page 366. Which states sided with the North and which states sided with the South during the Civil War?

4. **WRITING TO EXPLAIN** Write an essay on why the Civil War can be viewed as "a rich man's war and a poor man's fight."

5. **USING HISTORICAL IMAGINATION** Imagine that you are a woman in either the North or the South during the Civil War. Write a diary entry that describes the ways in which you might help the war effort.

Section 2

THE NORTH AND SOUTH FACE OFF

FOCUS

■ What were the consequences of the First Battle of Bull Run?

■ How did the military strategies of the North and the South differ?

■ What were some of the daily hardships faced by soldiers?

■ Why did some northerners oppose the war?

Like most people, Lincoln believed that the war would be short. In mid-July 1861 he sent General Irvin McDowell and some 35,000 barely trained troops "Forward to Richmond" (a popular Union newspaper slogan). Laughing and joking along the way, the troops were joined by sightseers and reporters. The onlookers hoped to view a quick Union victory. Instead, they witnessed a Union defeat. As both sides came to realize that victory would not come easily, they began to prepare for war more seriously.

Original pattern for the Confederate flag that flew over the CSS *Virginia*

THE FIRST BATTLE OF BULL RUN

Irvin McDowell's forces never reached Richmond, Virginia. On July 21, 1861, some 35,000 Confederates met McDowell's forces near Manassas (muh-NAS-uhs) Junction, a railroad crossing about 25 miles outside Washington. Under the command of General Joseph E. Johnston, the Confederates dug in on high ground behind a creek called Bull Run. The North called the fighting that followed the **First Battle of Bull Run**; the South called it the Battle of Manassas (see map on page 377).

At first the battle went in the Union's favor. The left flank of the Confederate line came close to cracking. Had it broken, the war might well have ended. But General Thomas "Stonewall" Jackson and his men stopped the Union assault. Jackson's troops raced toward the Union line, filling the air with a terrifying scream: "Woh—who—ey!

Who—ey!" The eerie sound, which came to be known as the rebel yell, struck fear in the hearts of the enemy. "There is nothing like it on this side of the infernal region," said one Union soldier. "The peculiar corkscrew sensation that it sends down your backbone under these circumstances can never be told. You have to feel it."

▲ This 1889 painting of the First Battle of Bull Run shows Confederate soldiers on horseback breaking through Union lines.

The Union soldiers fell back, slowly at first, then more rapidly, and headed for Washington. Union colonel Andrew Porter wrote of the retreat:

> 66 Soon the slopes . . . were swarming with our retreating and disorganized forces, while riderless horses and artillery teams ran furiously through the flying crowd. All further efforts were futile. The words, gestures, and threats of our officers were thrown away upon men who had lost all presence of mind, and only longed for absence of body. 99

If the Confederates had pursued the Union forces, they might have captured Washington. But the Confederates were as disorganized and exhausted in victory as the Union troops were in defeat.

The First Battle of Bull Run made everyone realize that the war would last longer than a few months. Each side began to train its forces for battle and to plan strategy. Jefferson Davis named Joseph Johnston to command the Army of Northern Virginia and chose Robert E. Lee as his personal military adviser. President Lincoln named George B. McClellan, known to be a gifted organizer, to head the Union forces.

The battle's most important consequences were probably psychological. The defeat shamed and shocked the North. Horace Greeley, the publisher of the New York *Tribune,* advised Lincoln: "If it is best for the country and for mankind that we make peace with the rebels, and on their own terms, do not shrink even from that." In Congress, however, there were many calls to step up the war effort.

In the South, newspaper editorials proclaimed the superiority of the Confederacy. In her diary Mary Boykin Chesnut, the wife of a Confederate officer, fretted over the consequences of such an attitude:

> 66 Trescot [a friend of the family] says this victory will be our ruin. It lulls us into a fool's paradise of conceit at our superior valor.
> And the shameful farce of [the North's] flight will wake every inch of their manhood. 99

Chesnut's friend was right. The Union army reacted to the defeat by becoming more determined. Many Confederates, on the other hand, were lulled into a false sense of security.

■ **The First Battle of Bull Run proved the war would not be short. Each side began to train its troops and to plan strategy.**

STRATEGIES OF WAR

From the beginning of the war, the North's primary goal was to restore the Union. To accomplish this goal, Lincoln and his military advisers adopted a three-part strategy: (1) capture Richmond, the Confederate capital; (2) gain control of the Mississippi River; and (3) institute a naval blockade of the South. The naval blockade was important because the South depended on foreign markets to sell its cotton and to buy supplies.

Much of the North's strategy depended on geography. The border of the Confederacy stretched from Virginia to Texas. The Appalachian Mountains divided most of the action in the Civil War into two arenas: the eastern theater and the western theater. The eastern theater lay east of the Appalachians, and the western theater lay between the mountains and the Mississippi River. Control of the Mississippi River would enable the North to penetrate deep into the South and keep the Confederacy from resupplying its western forces.

In contrast, southern war planners hoped to win by seizing Washington, D.C., and striking northward through the Shenandoah Valley into Maryland and Pennsylvania. This offensive move, they hoped, would shatter northern morale, disrupt Union communications, win European support, and bring the war to a speedy end.

A foreign ally—France or Great Britain—was central to a Confederate victory. Because the French and British economies depended heavily on cotton, the Confederacy was

◀ **Bales of cotton sit on Charleston's wharf, waiting for the end of the Union blockade.**

confident that one of the nations would respond to the naval blockade by coming to the South's aid.

Several factors worked against the South's strategy. For one thing, French and English mill owners had stockpiled cotton before the fall of Fort Sumter. Once the reserves ran out, the mill owners turned to Egypt and India for new supplies. Even more devastating to the South's hopes was the French emperor Napoleon III's preoccupation with events in Mexico. With Napoleon's blessing, Mexico's ruling elite made the Archduke of Austria, Maximilian, emperor. Napoleon sent French troops to Mexico to put down widespread opposition to Maximilian. Napoleon failed to aid the Confederacy in part because he did not want to fight two wars at once.

■■ **The North's strategy centered on dividing the South geographically, while the South planned to capture Washington, D.C., invade the North, and win European aid.**

ᵀHE MILITARY EXPERIENCE

While the high-level leaders were planning battle strategies, the officers under them had to train troops to fight the war. The young recruits in the Union and Confederate ranks were generally enthusiastic when they first joined up, but most were also unfamiliar with military life.

▼ **Confederate soldiers were often required to supply their own kitchen utensils. Some lacked regulation uniforms, such as these soldiers serving in Florida in 1861.**

Training and field officers had to contend with a lack of provisions. Food, clothing, and even rifles were often in short supply, especially for the Confederate army. At the beginning of the war, most troops wore their own clothes from home. Eventually each side adopted a distinguishing uniform—the Union blue and the Confederate gray—but many troops would lack good shoes and warm coats throughout the war.

The lack of provisions, coupled with unsanitary conditions in most field camps, led to a problem with disease. Thousands of soldiers died from illnesses such as typhoid, pneumonia, and influenza. Doctors and nurses could do little to help, since medical provisions were sorely lacking in most hospitals. Some soldiers had to endure surgery without pain-killing anesthetics. Many with seemingly minor injuries died from infected wounds. In fact, disease, infection, and malnutrition were responsible for more than 65 percent of troop deaths during the war.

▼ **In a moment of calm, Union soldiers try to relax in the field by reading or playing cards.**

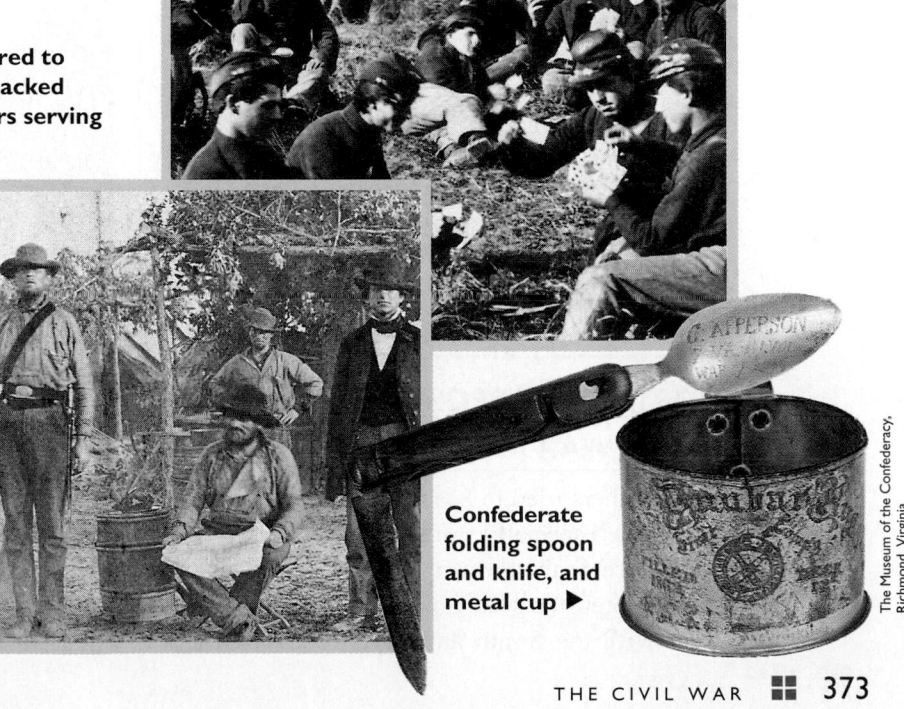

Confederate folding spoon and knife, and metal cup ▶

Abraham Lincoln suffered from periodic bouts of severe depression. Laughter was his cure for those times he found himself being morbid or superstitious. He used laughter "to whistle down sadness," as a friend put it.

Humor and homespun stories flowed from Lincoln. "The Lord prefers common-looking people," he said. "That is why he makes so many of them." "People who like this sort of thing will find this the sort of

thing they like" was his comment on a book. "I think you would have your joke if you were within a mile of hell," an annoyed congressman once told Lincoln. "Yes," the president replied, "that is about the distance to the Capitol."

Even in personal defeat Lincoln was able to use his famous wit. "I feel like the boy who stumped his toe," he said on losing the Senate race to Stephen A. Douglas. "I am too big to cry and too badly hurt to laugh."

Abraham Lincoln

Nowhere were conditions worse than in the filthy, overcrowded prisoner-of-war camps in the North and South. One nun who worked as a nurse during the war commented, "It is hard to be sick, but to be a sick prisoner of war is indeed a heavy cross." In some camps more than 25 percent of the prisoners died before the end of the war.

Under these difficult conditions, many of the soldiers suffered from extreme homesickness, loneliness, and boredom. Some of the soldiers reacted by deserting, but most coped by playing cards, attending prayer meetings, singing, writing letters home, or engaging in other recreational activities.

■■ **Troops faced many hardships, including disease, lack of provisions, and homesickness. Most coped through recreational activities.**

NORTHERN OPPOSITION TO THE WAR

As the soldiers tried to keep their spirits up, others back home, especially in the North, were voicing displeasure with the war. Not everyone in the North favored the war. Some northerners sympathized with the South and urged peace. Others

believed that the war was proving too costly in terms of money and human life.

When the Lincoln administration pushed through a draft law in 1863, violence broke out in New York City, a Democratic party stronghold.

▲ This wood engraving of anti-draft rioters destroying a house on Lexington Avenue in New York City was carried in *Leslie's Illustrated Newspaper*.

Democratic newspapers whipped their readers into a frenzy by claiming that the draft was designed to force white working-class men to fight for the freedom of African Americans who would then come north and steal their jobs. Men and women—many of them poor Irish immigrants—raged through African American neighborhoods, attacking people, looting, and burning buildings. By the time Union troops brought the rioting under control, more than 100 people were dead.

Northern Democrats who sympathized with the South were known as **Copperheads**. Few Copperheads actively interfered with the war effort. Most limited their antiwar activities to speeches and newspaper articles. One Democratic paper in Pennsylvania, for instance, published the poem "Abe's Visitor." In the poem, the devil and Lincoln converse:

> 66 How are you my Abe? Is the list
>   nearly filled
> Of the sick men and dying of
>   wounded and killed
> Of widows and tears, or orphans
>   unfed
> Of poor honest white men
>   struggling for bread?
> "Dear devil," quoth Abe, "I'm
>   doing my best
> To promote the interest of you and
>   the rest." 99

▲ The serpents in this 1863 cartoon represent the Copperheads, northern Democrats whose southern sympathies many northerners believed threatened the Union.

In an attempt to quiet the Copperheads, Lincoln suspended some civil liberties, including the ancient legal right of *habeas corpus*—a protection against unlawful imprisonment. At one time or another, thousands of Copperheads and other opponents of the war were arrested and held without trial. In some cases the arrests were justified, as with the draft riots. In many cases, however, people were arrested for peacefully stating their views.

▪▪ **Sympathy for the South, concern over costs, and fear of unemployment led some northerners to oppose the war.**

SECTION 2 REVIEW

IDENTIFY and explain the significance of the following: Irvin McDowell, Joseph E. Johnston, First Battle of Bull Run, Thomas "Stonewall" Jackson, Copperheads.

1. **MAIN IDEA** How did the result of the First Battle of Bull Run affect both the North and the South?

2. **MAIN IDEA** How did the North's strategy differ from the South's at the beginning of the Civil War?

3. **RECOGNIZING POINTS OF VIEW** What reasons did some northern Democrats and working-class whites have for opposing the war?

4. **WRITING TO DESCRIBE** Imagine you are a soldier in either the Union or Confederate army during the war. Write a letter to your mother and father that describes the daily living conditions in your camp.

5. **TAKING A STAND** Write a paragraph that explains why you either approve or disapprove of Lincoln's actions against the Copperheads.

EASTERN CAMPAIGNS AND THE WAR IN THE WEST

FOCUS

- How did the North and the South fare in the eastern campaigns?
- How did the battles of Antietam, Fredericksburg, Chancellorsville, and Gettysburg affect northern morale?
- How did the North achieve its goal of controlling the Mississippi River?

*D*uring 1862 and 1863 the Confederacy won many of the battles in the East. President Lincoln had no luck finding a general able to defeat Joseph E. Johnston, Robert E. Lee, and Stonewall Jackson. The Union's eastern forces had five different commanders in just one year. In the West, however, the Union forces led by Ulysses S. Grant achieved great success.

Union mortar battery

THE PENINSULA CAMPAIGN

Although the South won most of the early battles of the war, it was not because the northern army was poorly trained. In fact, the Union general George B. McClellan trained his men well, instilling in them both pride and discipline. But McClellan was overly cautious. He hesitated to commit his men to battle—much to the president's displeasure. (Lincoln once grew so frustrated with McClellan's delays that he threatened to send the general a letter asking if he could borrow the army if McClellan had no use for it.)

McClellan finally did move—in April 1862—launching a brilliant plan to take Richmond. Rather than marching directly on the city, McClellan transported more than 100,000 men, 300 cannons, and 25,000 animals by water to the peninsula between the York and James rivers. McClellan planned to hit Richmond from the southeast, where there were few fortifications. The strategy could have worked—McClellan's army vastly outnumbered the Confederate forces—but once again, McClellan hesitated.

◀ President Lincoln discusses war strategy with General McClellan in October 1862.

Union and Confederate soldiers met at Yorktown, Virginia, in the first week of April. Lincoln urged McClellan to attack, but the general refused, claiming that there were too many Confederate troops. Actually, he faced only some 13,000 Confederates, under the command of General John B. Magruder. McClellan wired Lincoln that he could only take Yorktown by siege. While McClellan waited, the Confederate general Johnston moved more troops into position.

Johnston and Magruder held on at Yorktown until the beginning of May. Just as McClellan was about to overrun the Confederate defenses, Johnston began a month-long retreat toward Richmond. McClellan soon followed. On May 31, 1862, the two sides clashed just east of Richmond at the **Battle of Seven Pines**. The South fared badly in this battle. Confederate colonel John B. Gordon wrote of the fight:

> 66 I was left alone on horseback, with my men dropping rapidly around me. . . . My field officers . . . were all dead. Every horse ridden into the fight, my own among them, was dead. Fully one half of my line officers and half my men were dead or wounded. 99

General Johnston was among the seriously wounded. Robert E. Lee assumed command of the Confederate forces and broke off fighting.

Even though the Confederates were badly weakened, McClellan again sat and waited. Lee did not. In a daring maneuver, Lee ordered a cavalry unit under the command of 29-year-old James E. B. (Jeb) Stuart to gather information on enemy positions. Armed with Stuart's information, the combined forces of Lee and Stonewall Jackson fell on the Union army in the **Seven Days' Campaign** (June 25–July 1). Union casualties numbered nearly 16,000. Although the number of Confederates killed or wounded was even higher—over 20,000—the battle was considered a victory for the South because McClellan retreated.

■■ **The Peninsula Campaign was a disappointment for the North since the ever-cautious McClellan retreated without taking Richmond.**

The War in the East, 1861–1863

MISSED OPPORTUNITIES General George B. McClellan's caution and delays meant that the Union failed to capture Richmond.

? LOCATION What two battles were fought on Union soil?

Confederates hoped to win the war by seizing Washington.

Union forces sought to capture Richmond.

President Lincoln, furious and frustrated, ordered McClellan back to Washington. General John Pope took command of the army in the field. In late August, while marching on Richmond, Pope and his men were defeated by Lee's forces at the **Second Battle of Bull Run**. Soon after Pope's defeat, McClellan once again found himself in command of the eastern forces.

ANTIETAM

Robert E. Lee took the offensive in September 1862. Confederate diplomats believed that Great Britain might yet provide support to the Confederacy if Lee could win a major victory on Union soil. On September 4, 1862, Lee began crossing the Potomac into Maryland with some

▲ Soldiers killed in the Battle of Antietam were photographed on September 17, 1862, as they were lined up for burial.

55,000 men. (Over the next few days Lee's forces dropped to around 50,000 as thousands of hungry, tired, and sick troops fell by the wayside.) Union forces lost track of the Confederate troops for four days, until two Union soldiers found a copy of Lee's battle plans wrapped around a pack of cigars.

Armed with this information, General McClellan and some 75,000 troops met Lee at Antietam (an-TEET-uhm) Creek. The **Battle of Antietam** raged all day, becoming one of the bloodiest battles of the war. The Confederates suffered more than 13,000 casualties; the Union more than 12,000.

Although Antietam was not a clear-cut Union victory, Lee's withdrawal to Virginia raised confidence in the North. A major Confederate offensive had failed, proving that General Lee, whom many had thought was unbeatable, could be beaten. Lee's defeat cost the South any hope of support from the European countries, which did not want to risk backing the losing side in the war.

Despite the Union army's good showing at Antietam, McClellan permanently lost his command. Lincoln fired the overcautious general for allowing the Confederates to escape into Virginia.

■■ **The Union victory at Antietam bolstered confidence in the North and dashed Confederate hopes of winning European support.**

FREDERICKSBURG AND CHANCELLORSVILLE

Lincoln's new commander, General Ambrose E. Burnside, did not want the job. He had little confidence in his abilities and knew the troops' loyalties were with McClellan. Nevertheless, he moved boldly—too boldly.

On December 11 and 12, 1862, General Burnside sent some 114,000 men across the Rappahannock (rap-uh-HAN-uhk) River near Fredericksburg, Virginia. General Lee and some 75,000 soldiers controlled the hills above the town. Reasoning that Lee would not expect a frontal attack, General Burnside ordered his men across an open plain toward the hills on the morning of December 13.

Lee took advantage of Burnside's positioning. From their high ground, the Confederates could easily pick off the Union soldiers as they crossed the open fields. As Lee's artillery commander told him, "A chicken could not live on that field when we open [fire] on it." The Union army suffered more than 12,000 casualties in the **Battle of Fredericksburg**, the Confederates some 5,000. One northerner bitterly referred to the battle as a "great slaughter pen." A Union soldier, William Lusk, wrote home:

66 Gone are the proud hopes, the high aspirations that swelled our bosoms a few days ago. . . . [The army] has strong limbs to march and meet the foe, stout arms to strike heavy blows, brave hearts to dare— but the brains, the brains! Have we no brains to use the arms and limbs and eager hearts with cunning? 99

The revolving door for Union generals whirled on. Lincoln transferred Burnside and gave command of the eastern forces to General Joseph ("Fighting Joe") Hooker. Although an effective general, Hooker was also opinionated. He once openly criticized President Lincoln, saying that the Union needed a dictator to win the war. Lincoln replied: "Only those generals who gain successes can set up dictators. What I now ask of you is military success, and I will risk the dictatorship."

Hooker offered a bold plan to crush Lee's forces. He proposed to divide his large army into three parts, cut off Lee's supply lines, and attack

▲ Stonewall Jackson's death in 1863 was a blow to the South. This photograph shows mourners at his grave in Virginia.

the Confederates from both flanks. The strategy seemed workable, especially since Hooker's forces outnumbered Lee's nearly 134,000 to 60,000.

By April 30, 1863, Hooker had his men positioned in a deep forest known as the Wilderness, near Chancellorsville, Virginia. But Lee once again stole the initiative from the Union army. In his most daring maneuver of the war to date, Lee divided his troops, sending Stonewall Jackson and some 30,000 men through the Wilderness to outflank Hooker. When Hooker discovered the troop movements, he assumed the Confederates were retreating. Instead, Lee and Jackson attacked the Union forces from two fronts. After several days of fighting, Hooker withdrew in defeat. Morale in the North plummeted. Once again, the South seemed unbeatable.

But the South had paid dearly for its victory at the **Battle of Chancellorsville**. Among the wounded was Stonewall Jackson. Riding back to Confederate lines after dark, Jackson was mistaken for a Union cavalryman and shot by his own men. His arm had to be amputated. Eight days later, Lee's most valued general died from pneumonia.

▪▪ Morale plummeted in the North after the Union defeats at Fredericksburg and Chancellorsville.

*G*ETTYSBURG

Following the victory at Chancellorsville, Lee decided to invade the North again. Not only would

this spare war-weary Virginia from further fighting, but it would allow Lee to resupply and feed his hungry troops as the Union had done in the South—by taking what was needed from the enemy.

In early June 1863 Lee crossed into Pennsylvania with some 75,000 troops. Lincoln urged General Hooker to attack the Confederates before they could consolidate their troops. Hooker, however, hesitated. Convinced that the government no longer had confidence in him, Hooker asked to be relieved of his command. He was replaced by General George Meade.

By the end of June the Confederates massed near the town of Gettysburg, Pennsylvania. When scouts reported that there was a supply of shoes in the town, the Confederates organized a raiding party. But the troops did not know that two Union brigades had positioned themselves on high ground northwest of Gettysburg. As the Confederate raiding party approached Gettysburg on July 1, it was met by Union fire.

On the first day of the **Battle of Gettysburg**, the Confederates pushed the Union line back to Cemetery Ridge. The Confederates held Seminary Ridge, a lower line of hills about a half mile away. But Lee knew that the fighting was not over as long as the North held the higher ground. On July 2, General Lee attacked the Union left, trying without success to capture a globe-shaped hill called Little Round Top. The next day he ordered some 15,000 men under the command of George Pickett to rush the Union center on Cemetery Ridge. Only half of the soldiers made it back.

The Granger Collection, New York

▲ The Battle of Gettysburg began when Confederates, looking for a rumored supply of shoes, clashed with a Union regiment.

The loss of life at Gettysburg was staggering. After three days of fighting, Union casualties numbered more than 23,000; Confederate casualties more than 20,000. Although the Union army emerged victorious, it once again failed to end the war while it had the opportunity. A disappointed President Lincoln lamented, "Our Army held the war in the hollow of their hand and they would not close it." Nevertheless, the battle marked a turning point in the war. The Union army had proved that the Confederacy could be beaten.

In November 1863 President Lincoln helped dedicate a cemetery at the Gettysburg battlefield. Lincoln spoke for only a few minutes, but his Gettysburg Address remains a classic statement of democratic ideals (see page 1008).

■■ **The Union victory at Gettysburg proved to the North that the South could be defeated.**

THE WAR IN THE WEST

From the start the war went far better for the Union army in the West. In February 1862 General Ulysses S. Grant of Illinois led an army into Tennessee and captured two important forts that guarded the Tennessee and Cumberland rivers—Fort Henry and Fort Donelson. Moving rapidly south on the Tennessee River, Grant paused at Shiloh Church near the Mississippi state line.

HISTORY in the Making

BY DR. EDWARD LINENTHAL

Remembering Gettysburg

I first visited Gettysburg during my junior year in high school. I remember standing on Cemetery Ridge, where Union troops turned back Major General George Pickett's charge. I closed my eyes to imagine the battle that raged there over a century ago and to picture President Lincoln as he stood in the nearby cemetery on November 19, 1863, to deliver the Gettysburg Address.

Lincoln said the living could not further *consecrate* Gettysburg—that is, make it sacred. Those who died there, he declared, had already "consecrated it, far above our poor power to add or detract." Yet Americans have treated Gettysburg as a special place by holding commemorations,

staging vivid reenactments of the battle, and preserving the field much as it looked in 1863. It became a national military park in 1895.

Today, Gettysburg is indeed a sacred site, a powerful place of remembrance where the course of history changed. But Americans do not always agree *why* Gettysburg should be remembered. What does the battle symbolize? What lessons can we learn from it, and how should we commemorate it?

Here is how some groups of Americans have answered these questions. After the war, veterans from both sides began taking part in patriotic ceremonies at Gettysburg. Especially popular were the 50th and 75th anniversaries. The climax of

these ceremonies was a meeting at the Angle, the site of Pickett's charge. As large crowds looked on, elderly veterans met and shook hands as a sign of the reborn Union. In these ceremonies Gettysburg symbolized courageous soldiers, both northern and southern.

Often neglected in these remembrances, however, was the issue at the heart of the war—slavery. In his Gettysburg Address, Lincoln had reminded the nation that the death of so many would gain meaning only if the country remained "dedicated . . . to the unfinished work which they who fought here have thus far so nobly advanced." Thus for some, Gettysburg symbolizes the movement to free the slaves

Grant knew that Confederate generals Albert Sidney Johnston and P.G.T. Beauregard were nearby in Corinth, Mississippi. He did not, however, expect them to attack. Thus, on April 6, 1862, Grant's soldiers were caught by surprise as thousands of Confederate soldiers rushed at them. By day's end the Confederate forces had pushed Grant's men back to the Tennessee River. The Confederate commanders went to bed confident that they could finish off Grant's army the next morning.

Early the next day, however, Grant launched an attack. The **Battle of Shiloh** raged all morning. By the middle of the afternoon, Grant's forces had subdued the Confederates, and Beauregard gave the order to retreat. Both sides paid dearly: more than 13,000 Union casualties and 10,000 Confederate casualties, including General Johnston.

To achieve a decisive victory in the West, however, the Union had to gain control of the Mississippi River. Toward this end, David Farragut, commander of a Union naval squadron, moved against New Orleans. In late April 1862, Union ships entered the mouth of the Mississippi and passed the two forts defending the city. Farragut and his forces took New Orleans by the end of April.

Despite these successes, Grant knew that gaining full control of the river meant taking Vicksburg, Mississippi. Vicksburg's high river bluffs gave Confederate artillery command of the

and an enduring commitment to racial justice.

More recently, ceremonies have posed new questions about the meaning of the battle and of war. A few days before the 125th anniversary in 1988, a crowd of some 130,000 spectators paid to watch more than 10,000 people—each carefully dressed to play the role of a Union or Confederate soldier—reenact parts of the battle. This commercialized event portrayed the battle as glamorous and exciting. Reenactors claimed to be honoring the courage of those who fought and stimulating interest in the past. Critics, on the other hand, argued that the battle should not be presented as sport or adventure, but only as a tragic event.

The official anniversary ceremony, whose theme was "Peace Eternal in a World United," presented a different commemoration of the battle. The event took place at the Eternal Light Peace Memorial, a large monument dedicated to reconciliation by Gettysburg veterans in 1938. The ceremony included a concert by an interracial choir, speeches by African American leaders, and an address by scientist Carl Sagan. Sagan told the audience that the nations of the world must heed the Gettysburg veterans' call for reconciliation "instead of the carnage and mass murder" of war.

These are some of the different, even conflicting, ways Americans commemorate Gettysburg and hold it sacred. Of course, Gettysburg is only one piece of our history. What other places have Americans consecrated and what do they symbolize? Think of places associated with the origins of the nation, of the monuments and memorials in Washington, D.C., of places sacred to Native Americans, of places where admired leaders were assassi-

▲ **Gettysburg National Cemetery in Pennsylvania stands today as a grim reminder of the tremendous losses of the Civil War.**

nated. As past generations have done, we continue to consecrate the places we consider crucial to the American identity and to debate their meaning.

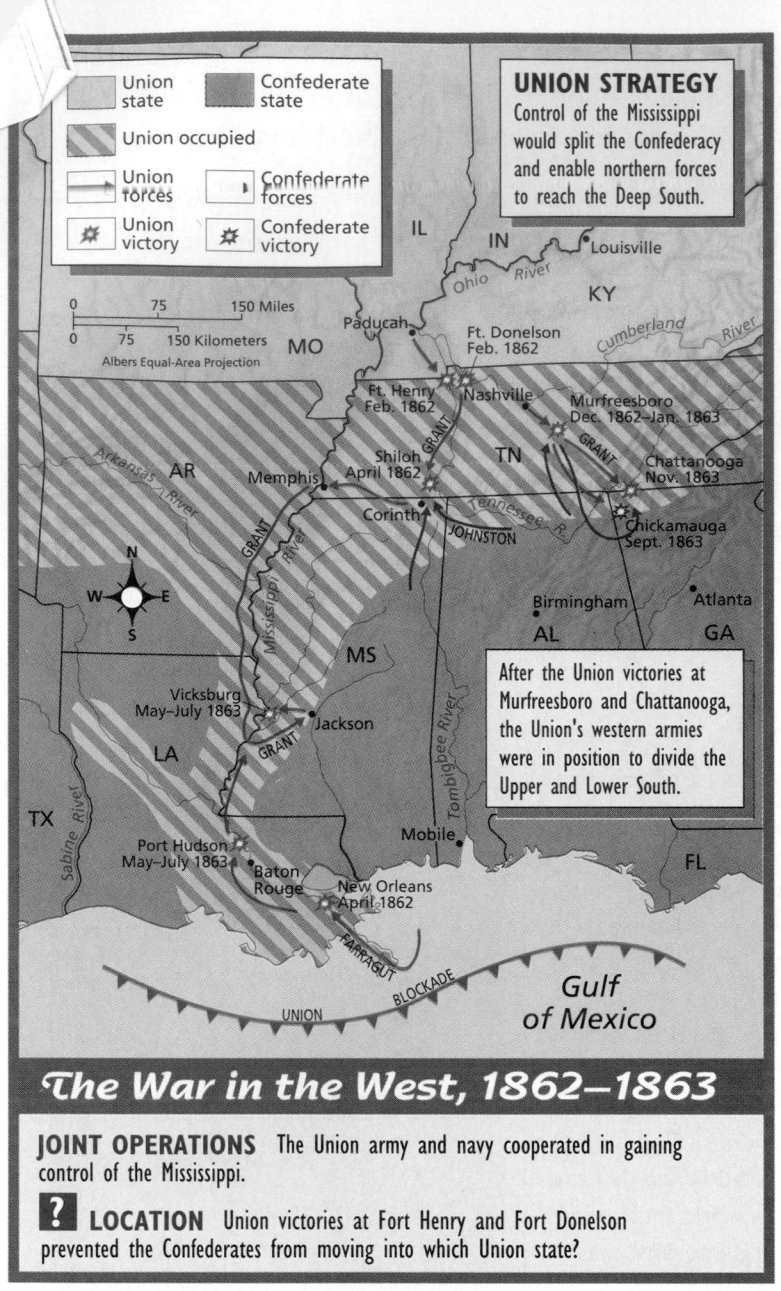

UNION STRATEGY
Control of the Mississippi would split the Confederacy and enable northern forces to reach the Deep South.

After the Union victories at Murfreesboro and Chattanooga, the Union's western armies were in position to divide the Upper and Lower South.

The War in the West, 1862–1863

JOINT OPERATIONS The Union army and navy cooperated in gaining control of the Mississippi.

? LOCATION Union victories at Fort Henry and Fort Donelson prevented the Confederates from moving into which Union state?

entire area. In May 1863 Grant hatched a risky but brilliant plan to take the city. Marching deep into enemy territory, he bottled up one Confederate force in Jackson, Mississippi, then raced west to trap the other enemy force inside Vicksburg.

For six weeks General Grant and his men laid siege to the town. Vicksburg's defenders devoured mules and rats to keep from starving. Finally, in late June the desperate Confederate soldiers sent a letter to their commander, urging him to surrender:

> 66 If you can't feed us, you had better surrender, horrible as the idea is, than suffer this noble army to disgrace themselves by desertion. 99

On July 3, 1863, General Grant and Confederate general John Pemberton met under an oak tree to discuss terms of surrender. The Confederates surrendered to Grant the next day. On July 8 the Confederate forces at Port Hudson, Louisiana, also fell. The Union now controlled the Mississippi River, thereby cutting off Arkansas, Louisiana, and Texas from the rest of the Confederacy.

■■ **The North achieved its goal of controlling the Mississippi River by capturing New Orleans and Vicksburg.**

SECTION 3 REVIEW

IDENTIFY and explain the significance of the following: George B. McClellan, John B. Magruder, Battle of Seven Pines, Jeb Stuart, Seven Days' Campaign, Second Battle of Bull Run, Ambrose E. Burnside, Joseph Hooker, David Farragut.

LOCATE and explain the importance of the following: Antietam, Fredericksburg, Chancellorsville, Gettysburg, Shiloh Church, Vicksburg.

1. **MAIN IDEA** Create a chart that lists each battle in the eastern campaign, along with its date and location. Include a brief description of each battle and identify the victor.

2. **MAIN IDEA** Why did the battles of Antietam and Gettysburg have positive effects on northern morale? Why did those of Fredericksburg and Chancellorsville have negative effects?

3. **GEOGRAPHY: PLACE** Why was Vicksburg essential to the North's strategy in the West?

4. **WRITING TO CLASSIFY** Create a time line that lists the events leading up to the North's successful control of the Mississippi River.

5. **ANALYZING** How did McClellan contribute to the North's difficulties in the eastern campaign?

Section 4

THE FINAL PHASE

FOCUS

- **How and why did the Union's war aims shift?**
- **Why did the Emancipation Proclamation apply only to slaves living in areas of rebellion against the United States?**
- **What strategies did Grant and Sherman employ to win the war?**
- **What were some of the consequences of the war?**

or the North, the Civil War began as a battle to save the Union. During the first year and a half of fighting, President Lincoln stated repeatedly that preserving the Union was his only goal. To retain the support of slaveholders loyal to the Union, he pledged not to interfere with the institution of slavery anywhere. Early on, however, abolitionists demanded that the North shift its war aims from saving the Union to ending slavery.

Defeated Confederates rolling up their flag

A SHIFT IN WAR AIMS

As the months of warfare dragged on, many northerners began to question whether saving the Union without ending slavery was worth the price. Was it just or sensible, they asked, to sacrifice so much without exacting a price from the secessionist slaveholders who had caused the terrible bloodshed? Slavery, they insisted, must be destroyed. "To fight against slaveholders, without fighting against slavery," charged Frederick Douglass, "is but a half-hearted business, and paralyzes the hands engaged in it."

After fierce debate, Republicans pushed two significant acts through Congress in July 1862. One authorized African Americans to serve in the military. The other freed slaves held by Confederate soldiers or by those who aided the Confederacy. Lincoln signed the acts, but Horace Greeley, the abolitionist editor of the New York *Tribune,* soon criticized Lincoln for not making slavery the central war issue. Lincoln replied by simply restating his war aim: "My paramount object in the struggle *is* to save the Union, and is *not* either to save or to destroy slavery."

Privately, however, the president had already concluded that slavery was too important to the southern war effort to be left alone. The Confederacy depended on slaves to raise food, haul supplies, build fortifications, and work in factories. Every slave at work released a white man to fight against the Union. Lincoln hoped that if slaves heard that the North was fighting to free them, they would desert their masters, thereby weakening the South's economy.

◀ **Members of the 2nd U.S. Colored Artillery are shown loading a cannon.**

THE CIVIL WAR ▪▪ 383

THE EMANCIPATION PROCLAMATION

Lincoln lacked the constitutional authority to abolish slavery. But as commander in chief he did have the authority to institute military measures. Thus, in July 1862 Lincoln informed his cabinet that he planned to issue a new military order: As of a certain date, all slaves living in areas still rebelling against the United States would be free. To quiet constitutional concerns, he assured his cabinet that this **Emancipation Proclamation** would apply only to states that belonged to the Confederacy, not to regions under Union control. Lincoln's assurance also quelled concerns about the status of slaves in the border states.

Secretary of State William H. Seward urged Lincoln to keep the Emancipation Proclamation secret until the Union won a major victory. To issue the proclamation when the war was going badly for the Union would look like an act of desperation. Lincoln agreed. The needed victory came at Antietam on September 17, 1862. On September 22 Lincoln issued a preliminary draft of the Emancipation Proclamation that would go into effect the first of the year.

■■ Because of constitutional issues the Emancipation Proclamation applied only to slaves living in areas of rebellion.

More than three years would pass before slavery was abolished everywhere in the United States. However, the institution of slavery was doomed when January 1, 1863, came and the Confederacy was still in rebellion. Lincoln's proclamation brought a decisive change in the war. The mere news of Union troops nearby inspired slaves to leave their masters to follow the Union army.

AFRICAN AMERICANS TAKE UP ARMS

Both the July 1862 act and the Emancipation Proclamation encouraged the enlistment of African American soldiers. The first official black regiments were organized in August 1862 in South Carolina. Frederick Douglass, who had been pressing for black troops since the beginning of the war, saw military service as an important step toward citizenship for African Americans:

> 66 Once let the black man get upon his person the brass letters, U.S.; let him get an eagle on his button, and a musket on his shoulder and bullets in his pocket, and there is no power on earth which can deny that he has earned the right to citizenship. 99

African American soldiers first saw serious action at Port Hudson, Louisiana, in 1863. Eight black regiments attacked a Confederate fortress seven times, suffering heavy losses. Their commander, General Nathaniel Banks, told the *New York Times*, "No troops could be more determined or more daring." By war's end nearly 180,000 African American men had served in the Union army. Some also served in the navy. The 166 all-black regiments fought in 449 engagements, including 39 major battles.

Although the Union army accepted African American volunteers, it did not offer them full

▼ Poster commemorating the Emancipation Proclamation

THE COURAGEOUS 54TH

On July 18, 1863, the men of the 54th Massachusetts Infantry sat in camp on Morris Island in South Carolina's Charleston Harbor. Three quarters of a mile away, guarding the harbor entrance, the sloping walls of Fort Wagner rose above the sands. More than 1,700 Confederate soldiers stood ready to defend the fort.

The Confederates held not only Fort Wagner but all the forts and batteries around Charleston, South Carolina. The Union campaign to seize control of Charleston's defenses had begun on July 10. Eight days later, despite a day of Union bombardment, Fort Wagner remained in Confederate hands. So Brigadier General Truman Seymour decided to send some 6,000 Union troops in a desperate frontal attack against the fort at dusk—with the 54th Regiment in the lead.

The 54th was no ordinary regiment. It was composed of some of the first African American soldiers recruited for the Union army. And this battle represented the first time that black troops had been assigned a key role. It was up to them to break through the Confederate line, and they would undoubtedly suffer great losses. These troops also faced a danger that white Union soldiers did not. Captured blacks were treated as outlaws—shot, hanged, or sold into slavery.

As night fell, the 54th's commanding officer, Colonel Robert Gould Shaw, gave the order "Forward!" and the troops advanced. The quiet evening exploded in a storm of gunfire. Confederate cannons all around opened fire, but somehow Colonel Shaw and his men clawed their way to the top of Fort Wagner's walls. There, they began fighting hand to hand

▲ Charles and Lewis Douglass, sons of Frederick Douglass, both served with the 54th Massachusetts, shown here charging Fort Wagner.

against the Confederate defenders inside. Shaw was killed, one of many casualties of the failed assault.

Union troops continued the siege until September 6, when Confederate forces, no longer able to hold out, finally evacuated the fort. Both armies had suffered staggering losses in the prolonged fight. Four survivors of the regiment received the Gillmore Medal for gallantry, and their courage won the 54th Regiment an honored place in U.S. military history.

equality. For much of the war, black soldiers earned less than half the pay of white soldiers. (Congress finally equalized the pay scale in June 1864, after much agitation by black soldiers and their commanding officers.) In addition, white officers commanded every black regiment. Only about 100 African Americans were commissioned as junior officers. In 1865 Martin Delany became the first African American promoted to the rank of major.

Yet the courage and dedication of African American soldiers impressed many. In 1863 Secretary of War Edwin M. Stanton noted:

66 Many persons believed, or pretended to believe, and confidently asserted, that freed slaves would not make good soldiers; that they would lack courage, and could not be subjected to military discipline. Facts have shown how groundless were these apprehensions. **99**

Stanton was right. Over 20 African American soldiers and sailors won the Congressional Medal of Honor. And more than 32,000 of their black comrades gave their lives for the Union cause.

▲ General Ulysses S. Grant and his staff were photographed at his headquarters at Cold Harbor in early June 1864. Lieutenant Colonel Ely S. Parker, a Seneca-Iroquois leader who was a close friend and military adviser to Grant, is standing next to the tree at the center of the picture.

Grant swung south yet again in order to attack Petersburg, Virginia, in mid-June. By capturing this railroad center, he hoped to cut off Richmond's supplies. But Lee held on. After three days even Grant was rattled. Since May 12 his army had suffered some 60,000 casualties. He called off the direct assault and settled down to besiege Petersburg. Grant was achieving his goal, however. Lee's army was dwindling, with no reserves available.

LINCOLN FINDS HIS GENERAL

Emancipation provided Lincoln with one key to Union success. The president found another key in General Ulysses S. Grant. This general understood that the North had advantages over the South in terms of soldiers and supplies. His strategy was to use these advantages against an enemy that was reeling from shortages. Grant told Lincoln that he would march on Richmond, take his losses, and press on. He was suggesting a **war of attrition**—to continue fighting until the South ran out of men, supplies, and will.

In May 1864 Grant, now commander of all Union forces, moved some 122,000 troops into the Wilderness near Chancellorsville, Virginia. For two days the northerners hurled themselves at some 66,000 Confederates, but the rebels held their ground. Grant's forces suffered nearly 18,000 casualties; the Confederates nearly 13,000.

Rather than rest, Grant pushed on, mile by bloody mile. "I propose to fight it out on this line if it takes all summer," he wrote. Grant swung his forces 10 miles to the south, forcing Lee to keep his weary men in the field. At Spotsylvania Court House, Virginia, Union and Confederate forces clashed several times between May 10 and May 19. As in previous battles, Union losses were heavy. Shocked by the number of casualties, a southern soldier remarked of Grant: "We have met a man this time, who either does not know when he is whipped, or who cares not if he loses his whole army."

■■ In 1864 General Grant began a war of attrition—wearing down the Confederates through constant attack.

SHERMAN'S MARCH TO THE SEA

Matching Grant in determination was the Union general William Tecumseh Sherman. Moody, ambitious, and brilliant, Sherman had performed ably at Vicksburg and other battles. Grant rewarded Sherman by making him commander of the Tennessee army.

While Grant was working his way toward Richmond, Sherman moved some 100,000 troops out of Tennessee toward Atlanta, Georgia, in early May. The Confederates fell back, and Sherman entered Atlanta on September 2, 1864.

▼ General Sherman, photographed outside of Atlanta on July 19, 1864, shortly before his army launched its attack against the city.

By capturing the city, General Sherman had cut the only Confederate railroad link across the Appalachians. Sherman ordered the evacuation of Atlanta and burned a significant portion of it. He defended his tactic:

66 If [southerners] raise a howl against my barbarity and cruelty, I will answer that war is war, and not popularity-seeking. If they want peace, they and their relatives must stop the war. 99

The fall of Atlanta gave a significant boost to Lincoln's reelection campaign. Up until then, it looked as if he might not even get his party's nomination. Many Republicans were upset that the war had dragged on for so long. Sherman's success, however, gave many hope that the conflict would soon be over. As a result, Lincoln won a substantial victory in the election of 1864 against Democrat General George McClellan.

After the burning of Atlanta, Sherman marched rapidly toward the port city of Savannah, Georgia. Cut off from their supply line, Sherman's

▲ Sherman's troops left a wake of destruction behind them, including torn-up railroad tracks and burned-out factories.

men stole what supplies they could and destroyed anything that might be useful to the Confederates. They uprooted crops, burned farmhouses, slaughtered livestock, and tore up railroad tracks, leaving nearly stripped a swath 60 miles wide and almost 300 miles long.

Although much of the destruction exceeded Sherman's orders, it was part of the general's tactic of fighting a **total war**. He believed that it was not enough to wage war against enemy troops. To win

The Final Campaigns, 1864–1865

GRANT'S CAMPAIGN Although he suffered defeat after defeat, Grant kept on the attack. When he failed to take Petersburg, Grant lay siege to the city for 9 months. Defeated at Five Forks, Lee abandoned Petersburg and Richmond on April 2. A week later Lee surrendered to Grant.

? MOVEMENT Sherman's army took 17 days to march from Savannah to Columbia. On average how many miles did his army need to cover each day?

Legend:
- Union state
- Union occupied
- Union forces
- Union victory
- Confederate state
- Union blockade
- Confederate forces
- Confederate victory

Sherman's Campaign

Union forces shatter the Confederacy's major western army.

Johnston fails to stop Sherman at Bentonville and accepts final surrender terms on April 26, 1865.

Lee surrenders to Grant on April 9, 1865.

IL, OH, PA, NJ, IN, WV, MD, DE, Washington, Culpeper, Richmond, Appomattox Courthouse, VA, KY, Durham, JOHNSTON, Nashville Dec. 1864, TN, Chattanooga, NC, Bentonville March 1865, Columbia Feb. 1865, SC, SHERMAN, Atlanta Sept. 1864, MS, AL, Charleston, BLOCKADE, ATLANTIC OCEAN, Savannah Dec. 1864, GA, FL, UNION BLOCKADE, Gulf of Mexico

0   100   200 Miles
0   100   200 Kilometers
Albers Equal-Area Projection

Grant's Campaign

APPALACHIAN MTS., WV, Shenandoah River, Washington DISTRICT OF COLUMBIA, MD, VA, Culpeper, Potomac R., Wilderness May 1864, Fredericksburg, Charlottesville, Spotsylvania May 1864, GRANT, Rappahannock River, James River, LEE, Richmond, Cold Harbor June 1864, York R., Appomattox Courthouse, LEE, GRANT, Five Forks April 1865, Petersburg June 1864, Chesapeake Bay

0   25   50 Miles
0   25   50 Kilometers
Albers Equal-Area Projection

the war, the Union had to strike at the enemy's economic resources. General Sherman was successful, but his actions left deep and bitter scars across the South.

On December 10, 1864, Sherman and his men reached Savannah, where they were resupplied by the Union navy. On December 22 Sherman sent President Lincoln a message: "I beg to present you, as a Christmas gift, the city of Savannah." In February 1865 Sherman and his troops turned north to link up with Grant and fight a final battle.

■■ General Sherman believed in fighting a total war—in defeating the enemy both militarily and economically.

STILLNESS AT APPOMATTOX

As Sherman's army moved northward through the Carolinas, Grant's troops hammered at the doors of Richmond. On April 2, 1865, with Grant close on his heels, Lee withdrew from Richmond. Within hours Union troops poured into the Confederate capital.

Lee now commanded an army only half the size of Grant's. Knowing his troops could not survive another summer like that of 1864, Lee tried to make a run to the west, hoping to join up with more troops. But Grant cut off Lee's escape. With his once-proud army reduced to 30,000 men, many without shoes, Lee asked for terms of surrender.

Grant and Lee met in a house in the tiny village of Appomattox Courthouse on April 9, 1865. Lee was in full dress uniform with a jewel-studded sword at his side. Grant wore a private's shirt, unbuttoned at the neck. For a time the two men talked about their Mexican War days. Then they turned to the business at hand. Aided by his military secretary—Lieutenant Colonel Ely Parker, a Seneca-Iroquois leader from New York—General Grant drafted the terms of surrender.

The terms were simple. Confederate officers could keep their sidearms, and all soldiers could keep their horses. "Let all the men who claim to own a horse or mule take the animals home with them to work their little farms," said Grant. "This will do much toward conciliating [uniting] our people," replied Lee.

As Lee rode off, Union troops started to cheer the Union victory, but Grant silenced them. "The war is over," he said; "the rebels are our countrymen again."

After the surrender, Lee returned to his men and quietly told them:

> **66** I have done for you all that it was in my power to do. You have done all your duty. Leave the result to God. Go to your homes and resume your occupations. Obey the laws and become as good citizens as you were soldiers. **99**

The weary Confederates were then fed and allowed to depart for home. On April 26, 1865, General Joseph Johnston surrendered to General Sherman under similar terms at Durham, North Carolina.

■■ Lee surrendered to Grant on April 9, 1865. Johnston surrendered to Sherman on April 26.

▲ Tom Lovell painted this version of Lee's surrender at Appomattox. As part of the terms of surrender, Grant ordered 25,000 food rations to be given to the starving Confederate troops.

THE CONSEQUENCES OF WAR

No other war on American soil has been as tragic as the Civil War in terms of human costs. Some 360,000 Union and 258,000 Confederate soldiers died during the struggle. More than a third of the young men who served during the war were killed, wounded, captured, or died of disease. More Americans were killed in the Civil War than in all other American wars combined.

Loss of life was not the war's only negative consequence, however. The war also devastated the southern economy. Southerners, including some four million enslaved African Americans who had gained their freedom as a result of the war, faced an uncertain future. Nearly all of the former slaves were without homes or jobs. Tens of thousands of white Confederate veterans were also homeless and jobless.

For the North, however, the war had many positive economic consequences. Agriculture and industry had expanded during the war to meet the needs of the military. The northern enterprises of steel, petroleum, food processing, manufacturing, and finance continued to expand after the war.

The war also finally resolved the long-debated issue of slavery. Never again would the United States government sanction the legalized enslavement of a group of people. In addition to ending slavery, the North's victory made the Republican party a dominant political force.

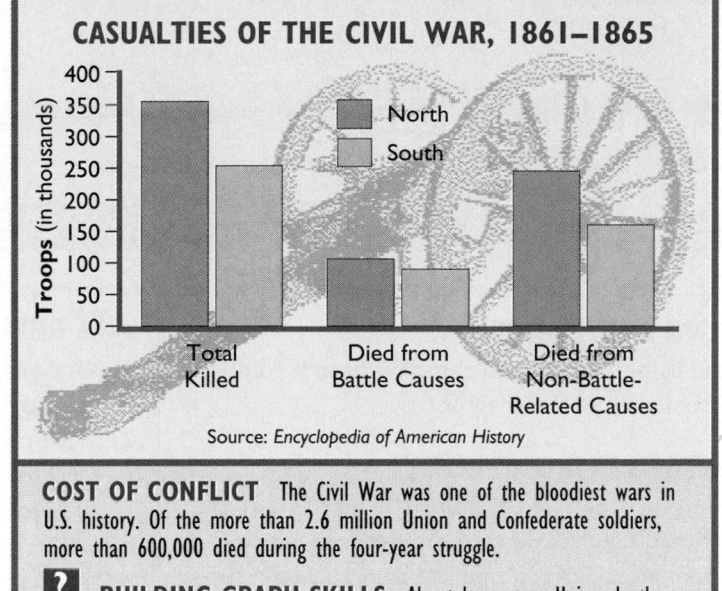

CASUALTIES OF THE CIVIL WAR, 1861–1865

Troops (in thousands)

North
South

Total Killed
Died from Battle Causes
Died from Non-Battle-Related Causes

Source: *Encyclopedia of American History*

COST OF CONFLICT The Civil War was one of the bloodiest wars in U.S. history. Of the more than 2.6 million Union and Confederate soldiers, more than 600,000 died during the four-year struggle.

? BUILDING GRAPH SKILLS About how many Union deaths resulted from non-battle-related causes? About how many Confederate deaths resulted from non-battle-related causes?

SECTION 4 REVIEW

IDENTIFY and explain the significance of the following: Emancipation Proclamation, 54th Massachusetts Infantry, Martin Delany, Ulysses S. Grant, war of attrition, William Tecumseh Sherman, total war.

LOCATE and explain the importance of the following: Spotsylvania Court House, Atlanta, Savannah, Appomattox Courthouse.

1. **MAIN IDEA** How and why did the North change its war aims during the Civil War?

2. **MAIN IDEA** Why were only those slaves living in areas of rebellion against the United States affected by the Emancipation Proclamation?

3. **ASSESSING CONSEQUENCES** How did the military strategies of Ulysses S. Grant and William Tecumseh Sherman finally bring an end to the war?

4. **WRITING TO EVALUATE** Summarize the consequences of the Civil War for the North and the South.

5. **ANALYZING** Imagine you are an African American who has just enlisted in a black regiment. Write a letter to President Lincoln that explains why you believe that your military service is an important step toward citizenship.

Lincoln inaugurated. Fort Sumter falls. Union and Confederate forces collide at First Battle of Bull Run.

1861

Peninsula Campaign fails for North. South defeated at Antietam. North defeated at Second Battle of Bull Run, Fredericksburg, and Chancellorsville.

1862

WRITING A SUMMARY

Using the essential points of the chapter as a guide, write a summary of the chapter.

REVIEWING CHRONOLOGY

Number your paper 1 to 5. Study the time line above, and list the following events in the order in which they happened by writing the first next to 1, the second next to 2, and so on. Then complete the activity below.

1. Atlanta falls.
2. South defeated at Antietam.
3. Lee surrenders at Appomattox.
4. Emancipation Proclamation goes into effect.
5. Lincoln inaugurated.

Hypothesizing How might northerners have received the Emancipation Proclamation if it had been issued before the Battle of Antietam, rather than after?

IDENTIFYING PEOPLE AND IDEAS

Explain the historical significance of each of the following people or terms:

1. Robert E. Lee
2. Elizabeth Blackwell
3. George B. McClellan
4. Thomas "Stonewall" Jackson
5. Copperheads
6. Martin Delany
7. Emancipation Proclamation
8. war of attrition
9. William T. Sherman
10. Ulysses S. Grant

UNDERSTANDING MAIN IDEAS

1. How did the political and military goals of the North change as the war progressed?
2. Why was the Mississippi River important to both sides during the war?
3. How did early Confederate victories affect northern attitudes toward the war?
4. What contributions did women make in the war? What contributions did African Americans make?
5. What were the effects of the Emancipation Proclamation?
6. Why did some people object to the military draft?

REVIEWING THEMES

1. **Geographical Diversity** What role did geography play in helping the North win the war?
2. **Economic Development** In what ways did the Civil War both help and hurt the economies of the North and the South?

THINKING CRITICALLY

1. **Hypothesizing** How might the outcome of the Civil War have been different if European powers had aided the South?
2. **Evaluating** How did fears of alienating the border states affect northern strategy during the war?
3. **Analyzing** How did the South, with fewer supplies and resources, prevent the North from ending the Civil War quickly?

STRATEGY FOR SUCCESS

Review the Strategies for Success on Interpreting the Visual Record on page 98, then study the picture below. It shows conditions at a Confederate camp at Corinth, Mississippi, in May 1862. Then, on a separate piece of paper, list clues that suggest the artist may have painted an idealized picture of actual camp life.

Valentine Museum

Emancipation Proclamation goes into effect. Draft riots in North. South defeated at Gettysburg. Vicksburg falls. Gettysburg Address delivered.

Grant named commander of Union forces. Troops clash at Spotsylvania and Petersburg. Atlanta falls. Sherman marches to the sea.

Lee surrenders at Appomattox. War ends.

1863   **1864**   **1865**

WRITING ABOUT HISTORY

Writing to Evaluate The wisdom of Sherman's total-war tactics has been debated by historians. Write an essay evaluating whether such tactics would be practical in every war.

USING PRIMARY SOURCES

Soldiers in the Civil War fought under difficult conditions. The South, in particular, suffered from shortages of food and supplies. Read the following excerpt from a letter written by a Confederate soldier describing conditions on a march from Yorktown to Richmond in 1862. Then write an essay expressing your feelings about the passage.

66 *I have never conceived of such trials as we have passed through. We were for days together without a morsel of food, excepting occasionally a meal of parched corn. . . . The army was kept on the march day & night and the roads were in some places waist deep in mud. . . . Many of the men became exhausted and some were actually stuck in the mud & had to be pulled out. . . .*

The men on the march ran through the gardens . . . devouring every particle of vegetables like the army worm leaving nothing at all standing. Whenever a cow or hog were found it was shot down & soon despatched. 99

The Museum of the Confederacy

Confederate soldier

LINKING HISTORY AND GEOGRAPHY

The Civil War was commanded by generals whose knowledge of the terrain was often hampered by inaccurate maps. Read the following excerpt from T. Harry Williams's *Lincoln and His Generals* (1952).

Then, in a paragraph, explain how unreliable information may have affected military campaigns in both the North and the South.

66 General Henry W. Halleck was running a campaign in the western theater in 1862 with maps he got from a book store. . . . Not until 1863 did the Army of the Potomac [the Union army] have an accurate map of northern Virginia, its theater of operations. . . . As late as 1864 there was not an office in Washington that could tell a general organizing a campaign what railroads were under military control . . . or how many men and supplies they could transport. 99

BUILDING YOUR PORTFOLIO

Complete the following projects independently or cooperatively.

1. **SLAVERY** In Chapter 11 you summarized Lincoln and Douglas's views on slavery. Building on that material, now imagine you are Frederick Douglass in 1862. Write a letter to President Lincoln urging him to take a strong stand against slavery by issuing the Emancipation Proclamation.

2. **SECTIONALISM** Imagine you are a member of a congressional committee attempting to formulate a compromise between the North and South to prevent a civil war. Create a chart that lists the political, economic, and social differences between the two sides that you think will be obstacles to an agreement and possible peaceful ways around these obstacles.

RECONSTRUCTION AND THE NEW SOUTH

FOCUS

UNDERSTANDING THE MAIN IDEA

After the Civil War, the nation struggled to restore the southern states to the Union and determine the status of the freed slaves. The Radical and Moderate Republicans, the freedpeople, and the planter aristocracy had conflicting goals for Reconstruction. Though the Union was restored, full and equal citizenship for African Americans was not achieved.

THEMES

- **CONSTITUTIONAL HERITAGE** Why is it necessary that a plan of government be adaptable? What might happen if a government cannot adapt to changes in society?

- **DEMOCRATIC VALUES** Why might a nation's definition of a democratic society change over time?

- **ECONOMIC DEVELOPMENT** How might a region's dependence on the sale of a single product limit the region's economic development?

1865	1867	1869	1877	1896
Thirteenth Amendment passed.	Reconstruction Acts passed.	Fifteenth Amendment passed.	Reconstruction ends.	Supreme Court issues ruling in *Plessy v. Ferguson*.

Ever since the nation's founding, slavery had caused political problems. Though many Americans agreed that slavery was incompatible with democratic ideals, the nation had to fight a civil war to end the "peculiar institution." The war, however, did not solve the problem of how to include emancipated slaves in free society.

The Granger Collection, New York

Freedmen's Bureau schoolroom, 1866

In 1864 abolitionist Frederick Douglass demanded that African American men be granted suffrage:

> 66 It is said that the colored man is ignorant, and therefore he should not vote. In saying this, you lay down a rule for the black man that you apply to no other class of your citizens. . . . If he knows enough to be hanged, he knows enough to vote. If he knows an honest man from a thief, he knows much more than some of our white voters. . . . All I ask, however, in regards to blacks, is that whatever rule you adopt, whether of intelligence or wealth, as the condition of voting, you should apply it equally to the black man. 99

Douglass's appeal struck at the heart of one of the most urgent questions facing the nation: What would be the fate of the some four million newly emancipated slaves? Before this question could be answered, however, the federal government would have to confront another issue: How should the Union be restored?

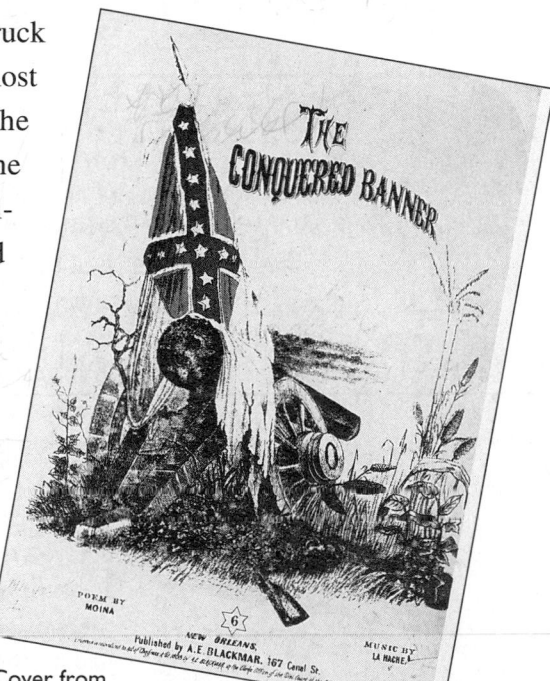

Cover from
The Conquered Banner song sheet

PRESIDENTIAL RECONSTRUCTION

FOCUS

- How did the Civil War affect southern life?
- How did Lincoln and Congress differ in their views on Reconstruction?
- What was Johnson's plan for Reconstruction?
- In what ways were the black codes like a continuation of slavery?

*A*mericans faced complex problems after the Civil War. Whites and blacks struggled to define the rights of freed African Americans. Politicians disagreed about how best to restore the Union. To heal the nation, President Abraham Lincoln offered generous peace terms to the former Confederate states. His successor, Andrew Johnson, was even more lenient toward the former rebels. Taking advantage of Johnson's lenience, southern legislatures restricted African Americans' rights.

Republican campaign poster, 1864

THE OLD SOUTH DESTROYED

As the war ended, most of the some four million emancipated slaves, or **freedpeople**, found themselves without money or homes. "It came so sudden on 'em," recalled freedman Parke Johnston:

❝ Just think of whole droves of people, that had always been kept so close, and hardly ever left the plantation before, turned loose all at once, with nothing in the world, but what they had on their backs. ❞

◀ This family record, showing a prosperous African American family, was marketed to former slaves after the war.

Despite the obstacles, however, most freedpeople looked eagerly to the future. Like freedman Henry Turner, they yearned to enjoy their "rights in common with other men." They hoped to form their own churches and schools and to legalize their marriages. Many freedpeople looked forward to choosing their own livelihood rather than working as servants or as field hands for others. With freedom anything seemed possible, even finding family members who had been sold away. Freedman Hawkins Wilson sent a letter to his sister—address unknown—believing that it would somehow find its way to her. "Dear Sister Jane," he wrote:

❝ Your little brother Hawkins is trying to find out where you are and where his poor old mother is—Let me know and I will come to see you—I shall never forget the bag of biscuits you made for me. . . . Please send me some of Julia's hair whom I left a baby in the cradle when I was torn away from you. ❞

▲ After the Civil War, many southern cities lay in ruins. This 1865 photograph shows the effects of war on a district in Richmond, Virginia.

Above all, African Americans hoped, like free black Garrison Frazier, "to have land, and turn it and till it by our own labor." Most wanted land to support themselves and to protect their independence; in fact, many believed that it was their due. "Our wives, our children, our husbands, has been sold over and over again to purchase the lands we now locates upon," argued freedman Bayley Wyat; "we have a divine right to the land."

General William T. Sherman had encouraged such hopes in January 1865, when he ordered part of South Carolina to be divided into 40-acre parcels and given to freedmen. Rumors persisted that the federal government would give each freedman "40 acres and a mule."

■■ **After the Civil War, African Americans were optimistic about new possibilities for shaping their own destinies.**

The planters still had land, but even they found their world "literally kicked to pieces." Mary Boykin Chesnut, a Confederate officer's wife, wrote about the despair she and many other white southerners felt:

National Portrait Gallery

▲ **Mary Boykin Chesnut**

❝ We are shut in here—turned with our faces to a dead wall. No mails. A letter is sometimes brought by a man on horseback, traveling through the wilderness made by Sherman. . . . We are cut off from the world—to eat out our own hearts. ❞

The Union army had laid waste to parts of the South—destroying railroad lines, blowing up bridges and wells, and stripping Confederate homes, barns, and gardens. Many cities, too, lay in ruins. A visitor to Columbia, South Carolina, described "a wilderness of crumbling walls, naked chimneys, and trees killed by flames."

Disease, the grim companion of hunger and bad sanitation, swept the South. Illness ravaged the cities, where families lived in makeshift shelters and thousands died in the year after the war.

■■ **At the war's end much of the South lay in ruins. Many southerners, both blacks and whites, suffered from poverty, hunger, and disease.**

PRESIDENT LINCOLN AND RECONSTRUCTION

President Lincoln had gone to war not to destroy the South but to preserve the Union. Even before the fighting ended, he had begun planning for **Reconstruction**—for rebuilding the former Confederate states and reuniting the nation.

To encourage southerners to abandon the Confederacy, Lincoln had issued the Proclamation of Amnesty and Reconstruction on December 8, 1863. The proclamation offered **amnesty**—a full pardon—to all southerners (except high-ranking Confederate leaders and a few others) who would swear allegiance to the

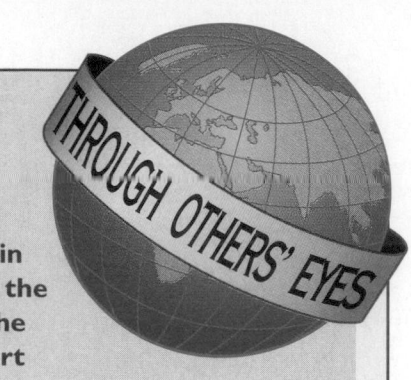

THE EMANCIPATION PROCLAMATION

In 1861, two years before President Lincoln issued the Emancipation Proclamation, Czar Alexander II of Russia promised more than 20 million Russian serfs freedom and land. Though the czar's own land policies eventually failed, in 1879 he criticized the Proclamation for having sidestepped the issue of land. The czar charged that the decree had freed the American slaves but had left them with no means to support themselves. Alexander boasted:

66 *I did more for the Russian serf in giving him land as well as personal liberty, than America did for the Negro slave set free by the Proclamation of President Lincoln. I am at a loss to understand how you Americans could have been so blind as to leave the Negro slave without tools to work out his salvation. . . . Without property of any kind he cannot educate himself and his children. I believe the time must come when many will question the manner of American emancipation of the Negro slaves in 1863.* 99

U.S. Constitution and accept federal laws on slavery. The proclamation also permitted a state to rejoin the Union when 10 percent of the state's residents who had voted in 1860 swore their loyalty to the United States.

Many members of Congress objected to the president's "10 Percent Plan." They did not trust the rebels to become loyal citizens or to protect the rights of former slaves. Furthermore, they believed Congress should help shape Reconstruction policy.

Congress laid out its own Reconstruction plan in the Wade-Davis Bill, passed in July 1864.

The bill called for the former Confederate states to abolish slavery and for a *majority* of each state's white males to take a loyalty oath. Lincoln vetoed the bill because he was not ready to "be inflexibly committed to any single plan of restoration." In his Second Inaugural Address, delivered on March 4, 1865, Lincoln made clear his underlying goal for Reconstruction:

66 With malice toward none, with charity for all, with firmness in the right as God gives us to see the right, let us strive on . . . to bind up the nation's wounds . . . to do all which may achieve and cherish a just and lasting peace. 99

■ Unlike Congress, Lincoln favored a flexible, lenient policy toward the former Confederates.

What course Reconstruction might have taken under Lincoln's direction will never be known. On April 14, 1865, just days after General Robert E. Lee's surrender, John Wilkes Booth, a half-crazed Confederate sympathizer, shot the president.

Lincoln's death was a tragic blow to the entire nation. Thousands of Americans stood beside the railroad tracks as the funeral train made its way from Washington to Lincoln's burial site in Illinois.

▲ Mathew Brady took this photograph of Abraham Lincoln delivering his Second Inaugural Address on March 4, 1865.

War Department, Washington, April 20, 1865.

$100,000 REWARD!
THE MURDERER
Of our late beloved President, Abraham Lincoln,
IS STILL AT LARGE.
$50,000 REWARD

▲ After Lincoln's assassination, the War Department offered a reward for the capture of John Wilkes Booth. The pistol Booth used to murder Lincoln is shown here.

PRESIDENT JOHNSON AND RECONSTRUCTION

At Lincoln's death Vice President Andrew Johnson became president. Johnson—a Democrat, a one-time slaveholder, and a former U.S. senator from Tennessee—had been chosen as Lincoln's running mate in 1864 because of his pro-Union sympathies. Republican leaders had hoped he would appeal to northern Democrats and southern Unionists.

Despite his support for the Union and experience as Tennessee's military governor during the war, Johnson was ill-suited to the challenges of Reconstruction and of defining African Americans' new rights. He suffered, one contemporary observed, from "almost unconquerable prejudices against the African race." Moreover, he lacked Lincoln's tact and political skill. The opinionated Johnson refused to compromise.

The president's weaknesses were not immediately apparent. At first Johnson denounced southern treason, even suggesting that Jefferson Davis and other high-ranking Confederates be hanged as traitors. This pleased many Republicans. "Johnson, we have faith in you. By the gods, there will be no trouble now in running this government," exclaimed Senator Ben Wade of Ohio.

In May 1865, however, in a startling about-face, Johnson issued a blanket pardon to all rebels except ex-Confederate officeholders and the richest planters. These he pardoned freely on an individual basis. Johnson's leniency extended to the rebel states as well. For readmission to the Union, he required only that they nullify their acts of secession, abolish slavery, and refuse to pay Confederate government debts. (The last provision was meant to hurt wealthy southerners who had financed the Confederacy.)

Johnson's plan allowed former Confederate leaders to take charge of Reconstruction. These men dominated the new legislatures—some still proudly wore their Confederate uniforms!—and benefited

PRESIDENTIAL LIVES

ANDREW JOHNSON
1808–1875

in office 1865–1869

Andrew Johnson was a self-made man. When Johnson was three, his father died. A few years later, his mother apprenticed him to a tailor. Johnson ran away from his master and eventually went to Tennessee. He never attended school, but he probably learned to read as an apprentice. Later his wife taught him to write and to do simple arithmetic.

Johnson did well as a tailor. He was able to buy property but never identified himself with the planter class. His loyalties were to farmers and artisans, and as a politician he saw himself as an outsider. "Andy Johnson," people in East Tennessee said, "never went back on his raisin'."

He continued to make all his own clothes until he went to Washington. Even after he became president, Johnson often dropped into tailor shops for a chat.

Andrew Johnson

▲ Newly freed slaves are shown here planting sweet potatoes on a plantation in Hilton Head, South Carolina.

from the president's support for "a white man's government." When they complained of the "painful humiliation" inflicted by the presence of black soldiers in the South, Johnson had the soldiers removed. When Mississippi refused to ratify the **Thirteenth Amendment**—which Congress had passed in January 1865 to abolish slavery—Johnson recognized the state's new government anyway.

■ **Johnson freely granted pardons and set lenient conditions for states' readmission to the Union.**

THE BLACK CODES

Johnson's actions encouraged former Confederates to adopt laws limiting the freedom of former slaves. These **black codes**, which African Americans denounced as "a disgrace to civilization," resembled prewar slave codes. Mississippi simply used its old code, substituting the word *freedman* for *slave*.

Under these laws African Americans could not hold meetings unless whites were present, travel without permits, or own guns. Blacks in New Orleans could not be on the streets after 10 o'clock at night, just one hour later than the previous slave curfew. The editor of the city's African American newspaper noted: "This additional hour is the fruit of our victories in the field. Four years of a bloody war have been fought to gain that one hour."

Above all, the codes reestablished white control over black labor. Without slaves to do the work, "our fields everywhere lie untilled," lamented a white Mississippian in April 1865. As a way to make former slaves return to field work, some local codes forbade blacks to live in towns unless they were servants. South Carolina and Mississippi required freedpeople to sign 12-month labor contracts. Those who refused could be arrested and have their labor for the year put up for auction. One black veteran demanded: "If you call this Freedom, what do you call Slavery?"

Northerners angrily denounced the black codes. The Chicago *Tribune* reprinted the Mississippi code and proclaimed:

66 The men of the North will convert the State of Mississippi into a frog pond before they will allow such laws to disgrace one foot of soil in which the bones of our soldiers sleep and over which the flag of freedom waves. 99

It would be up to Congress, however, to find a way to end the rule of the "white-washed rebels."

■ **The black codes limited the freedom of African Americans and tried to force former slaves back into plantation labor.**

SECTION 1 REVIEW

IDENTIFY and explain the significance of the following: freedpeople, Reconstruction, amnesty, John Wilkes Booth, Andrew Johnson, Thirteenth Amendment, black codes.

1. **MAIN IDEA**   How was southern life different after the Civil War?

2. **MAIN IDEA**   Under Johnson's Reconstruction plan, how could states gain readmission to the Union?

3. **CONTRASTING**   How did Congress's plan for Reconstruction differ from Lincoln's?

4. **WRITING TO DESCRIBE**   Imagine you are a newly emancipated slave. Write a letter to a relative in the North describing the effects of the black codes on your life.

5. **EVALUATING**   Why would "40 acres and a mule" be important to a freedman?

CONGRESSIONAL RECONSTRUCTION

FOCUS

- How did Moderate and Radical Republicans at first differ in their approaches to Reconstruction?
- Why did Moderate Republicans in Congress break with Johnson and join forces with the Radicals?
- How did the Fourteenth and Fifteenth amendments expand the civil rights of African Americans?

Cartoon mocking Johnson's veto of the Freedmen's Bureau Bill

*P*resident Johnson's support of the former Confederates and his failure to protect African Americans' rights angered even Moderate Republicans, who had hoped to cooperate with the president. As a result, the Moderates in Congress deserted him and joined forces with the Radicals. Together they took over Reconstruction.

*T*HE MODERATES VERSUS THE RADICALS

When Johnson took office in 1865, he did not face a united Congress. Even the Republicans were divided over the course Reconstruction should take. The Moderates, who made up the majority of the Republican party, viewed Reconstruction as a practical matter of restoring the southern states to the Union. Their main concern was keeping ex-Confederates out of government. They favored giving African Americans civil equality—which included the right to travel freely and to meet together—but not the vote.

Radical Republicans, on the other hand, insisted that African Americans be given the

▲ Thaddeus Stevens

right to vote. For them, the proper goal of Reconstruction was to create a new South where all men would enjoy equal rights. But for this goal to be reached, warned Thaddeus Stevens, the outspoken Radical from Pennsylvania, "the whole fabric of southern society *must* be changed."

Stevens believed that land reform could change southern society. He agreed with Senator Charles Sumner of Massachusetts, who insisted that "the great plantations . . . must be broken up, and the freedmen must have the pieces." According to Stevens, economic independence for the former slaves would ensure their freedom and destroy the political power of the "proud, bloated, and defiant rebels."

Despite the efforts of Stevens and Sumner, land reform—particularly government seizure of land—never won wide support. The *New York Times* accused land reformers of starting "a war on property . . . to succeed the war on Slavery." Even many Radicals believed that the ballot, civil equality, and free labor were enough to give African Americans a chance to succeed.

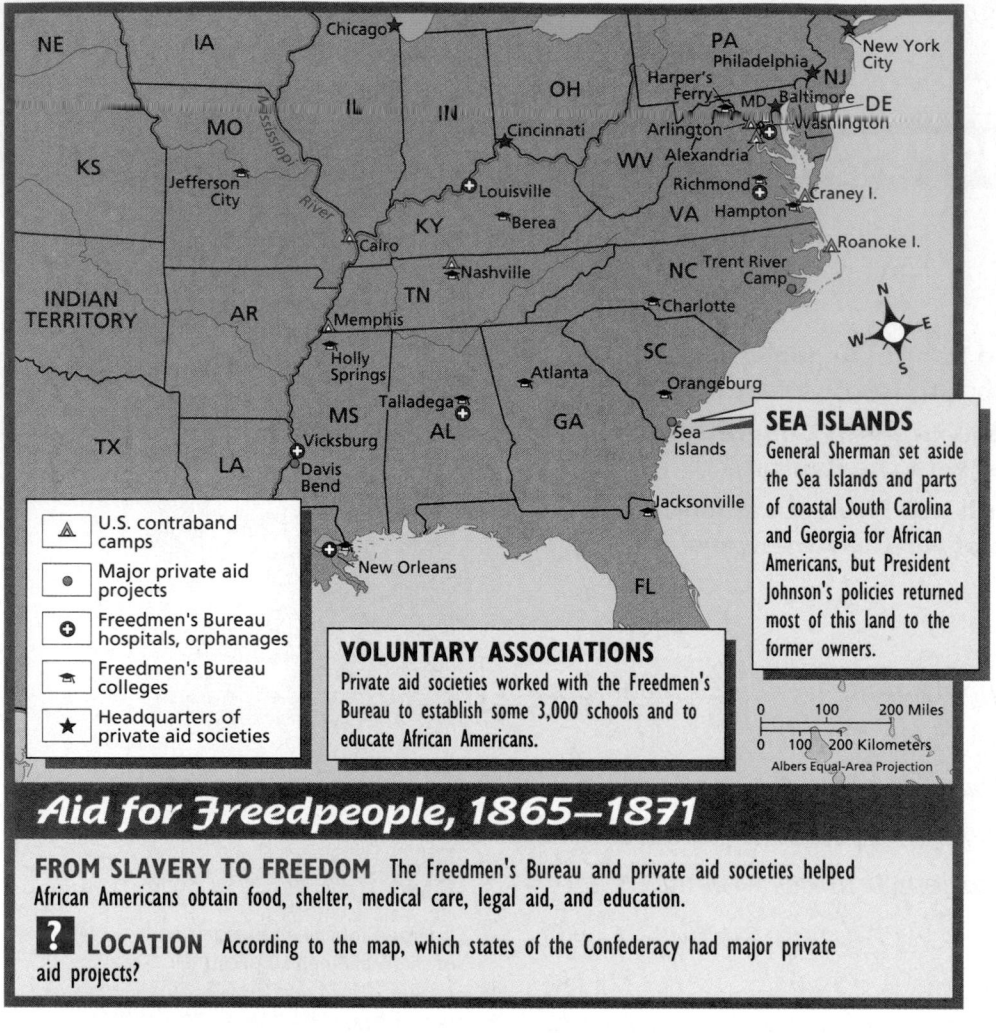

Aid for Freedpeople, 1865–1871

**Map labels:**
NE, IA, Chicago★, PA, Philadelphia, New York City, MO, IL, IN, OH, Harper's Ferry, NJ, MD, Baltimore, DE, KS, Cincinnati, Arlington, Washington, WV, Alexandria, Jefferson City, Louisville, Richmond, Craney I., KY, Berea, VA, Hampton, Cairo, Nashville, NC, Trent River Camp, Roanoke I., INDIAN TERRITORY, AR, TN, Charlotte, Memphis, Holly Springs, SC, Orangeburg, Atlanta, Talladega, Sea Islands, MS, GA, Vicksburg, AL, Davis Bend, TX, LA, Jacksonville, New Orleans, FL, Mississippi River

Legend:
- △ U.S. contraband camps
- ● Major private aid projects
- ✚ Freedmen's Bureau hospitals, orphanages
- 🎓 Freedmen's Bureau colleges
- ★ Headquarters of private aid societies

SEA ISLANDS
General Sherman set aside the Sea Islands and parts of coastal South Carolina and Georgia for African Americans, but President Johnson's policies returned most of this land to the former owners.

VOLUNTARY ASSOCIATIONS
Private aid societies worked with the Freedmen's Bureau to establish some 3,000 schools and to educate African Americans.

0   100   200 Miles
0   100   200 Kilometers
Albers Equal-Area Projection

FROM SLAVERY TO FREEDOM The Freedmen's Bureau and private aid societies helped African Americans obtain food, shelter, medical care, legal aid, and education.

❓ LOCATION According to the map, which states of the Confederacy had major private aid projects?

■■ **At first, Moderate and Radical Republicans were divided over land reform and African American suffrage.**

CONGRESS VERSUS JOHNSON

The split between the Moderates and the Radicals was not to last, however. In early 1866 Congress began hearings on conditions in the South. Witness after witness came before the Joint Committee on Reconstruction with stories of postwar violence. African Americans recounted stories of murder and of homes, schools, and churches reduced to "ashes and cinders." Southern Unionists told of death threats. These reports and others like them convinced the Moderates to join forces with the Radicals to protect the rights and safety of the ex-slaves. Work began on legislation to extend the life of the Freedmen's Bureau and to guarantee black civil rights.

The Freedmen's Bureau. Congress had set up the **Freedmen's Bureau** in March 1865 to aid the millions of southerners left homeless and hungry by the war. The bureau distributed food and clothing, served as an employment agency, set up hospitals, and operated schools. Not surprisingly, much of the bureau's efforts were directed toward easing the plight of ex-slaves.

Congress had intended for the bureau to remain in operation for one year. In light of the hearings, however, most members now favored legislation to extend the life of the agency. African Americans largely agreed, although they thought the Freedmen's Bureau too often encouraged blacks to remain on plantations and sign labor contracts. They acknowledged, however, that the bureau's very presence forced white southerners to recognize emancipation. One black told a government official that "if the Freedman Bureau was removed, a colored man would have better sense than to speak a word in behalf of the colored man's rights, for fear of his life."

In February 1866 Congress passed the Freedmen's Bureau Bill to extend the life of the agency. Much to Congress's surprise, Johnson promptly vetoed the bill.

The Civil Rights Act of 1866. Furious with the president, Congress quickly passed the **Civil Rights Act of 1866**. The act declared that everyone born in the United States was a citizen with full civil rights. (It did not guarantee voting rights, however.) The act was designed to overturn discriminatory laws and the Supreme Court's 1857 *Dred Scott* ruling that blacks were not citizens. "If the President vetoes the Civil Rights Bill," wrote one Ohio senator, "we shall be obliged to draw our swords."

▲ This 1866 poster mocks the effectiveness of the Civil Rights Act of 1866. As punishment for crimes, one freedman is being sold at auction while another is being whipped.

The Fourteenth Amendment did not guarantee African American voting rights. It did, however, reduce the number of representatives a state could send to Congress in proportion to the number of the state's male citizens denied the right to vote. Republicans hoped that southern states would give African Americans the right to vote rather than lose representation in Congress.

■■ **The Fourteenth Amendment provided for equal citizenship for African Americans and pressured states to grant them voting rights.**

Johnson did not heed the warning. He vetoed the bill, arguing that it would centralize power in the federal government. Johnson's veto message also underscored his racism; the president complained that the bill would "operate . . . against the white race."

Johnson's veto eroded his support in Congress and united Moderate and Radical Republicans against him. Congress overrode Johnson's veto of the Civil Rights Act. Then Congress returned to the matter of the Freedmen's Bureau, passed a new bill, and overrode yet another veto.

■■ **Postwar violence and Johnson's opposition to the Freedmen's Bureau Bill and the Civil Rights Act of 1866 united Moderate and Radical Republicans.**

The Fourteenth Amendment. Fearing that a future Democrat-controlled Congress might repeal the Civil Rights Act, congressional Republicans wrote its provisions into the **Fourteenth Amendment**, passed in June 1866. The amendment required states to extend equal citizenship to African Americans and all people "born or naturalized in the United States." It also denied states the right to deprive anyone of "life, liberty, or property without due process of law," and it promised all citizens the "equal protection of the laws." With its ratification in July 1868, the amendment created a national citizenship with rights—enjoyed equally by all—that were to be enforced by the federal government.

THE RADICALS COME TO POWER

Johnson tried to make the Fourteenth Amendment an issue in the 1866 congressional elections. He traveled throughout the Midwest, campaigning in support of candidates who opposed the amendment and calling the Radicals traitors.

Most voters were not receptive. Many were deeply troubled by the ongoing violence against blacks in the South. In Memphis in May 1866, white rioters killed 46 blacks and burned 12 schools and 4 churches. "If anything could reveal . . . the demoniac spirit of the southern whites toward the freedmen," one reporter noted, this violence would. On July 30 in New Orleans, more than 30 blacks and 3 white Radicals were killed in a riot. General Philip H. Sheridan, Johnson's military commander in Texas and Louisiana, called it "an absolute massacre."

▶ The August 1866 issue of *Harper's Weekly* included this illustration of the July riot in New Orleans.

Reconstruction in the South

MILITARY GOVERNMENT Republican opponents overrode President Johnson's veto and established military districts to enforce order and protect the rights of African Americans.

❓ **PLACE** Which state in the former Confederacy did not have a military government?

Map legend:
- Republican government defeated, 1869–1871
- Republican government defeated, 1872–1875
- Republican government defeated, 1876–1877
- 1870 Date Confederate state readmitted to Union
- Boundary of military district

Map labels: WI, MI, NY, CT, NF, IA, Lake Erie, PA, NJ, MD, DE, IL, IN, OH, WV, VA 1870, MILITARY DISTRICT 1, KS, MO, KY, TN 1866, NC 1868, MILITARY DISTRICT 2, NEW MEXICO TERRITORY, INDIAN TERRITORY, AR 1868, MILITARY DISTRICT 4, SC 1868, MS 1870, AL 1868, GA 1870, TX 1870, LA 1868, MILITARY DISTRICT 3, ATLANTIC OCEAN, MILITARY DISTRICT 5, FL 1868, MEXICO, Gulf of Mexico, 0 200 400 Miles, 0 200 400 Kilometers, Albers Equal-Area Projection

Such violence made Johnson's call for leniency toward the South seem absurd. Fearing they might lose the fruits of their Civil War victory, northerners overwhelmingly elected Republicans in 1866. Now firmly in command of Congress, the Republicans, with the Radicals at the helm, seized control of Reconstruction.

Over Johnson's angry vetoes, Republicans passed the **Reconstruction Acts** of 1867. These acts divided the former Confederacy (with the exception of already-reconstructed Tennessee) into five military districts. Union army troops were stationed in each district to enforce order. To gain readmission to the Union, states were required to ratify the Fourteenth Amendment and to submit to Congress new constitutions giving all men the vote.

CONGRESS IMPEACHES JOHNSON

The Radicals knew that the success of the congressional plan depended on enforcement. They were equally sure that Johnson would not cooperate. To protect its policies and Republican officeholders, Congress passed the Tenure of Office Act in 1867. It required Senate approval of a replacement before the president could remove an official earlier confirmed by the Senate.

▼ A ticket of admission to the U.S. Senate galleries was required for people wishing to attend the impeachment trial of President Johnson.

Believing the law unconstitutional, Johnson put it to the test. In February 1868 he ousted Secretary of War Edwin Stanton, an ally of the Radicals. The House responded by voting to impeach the president. The House charged Johnson with violating the Tenure of Office Act, making "scandalous" speeches, and exposing Congress to ridicule.

Some senators believed that Johnson, despite his flaws, had committed no impeachable offense. Senator Lyman Trumbull of Illinois, a Johnson critic, predicted: "No future President will be safe who happens to differ with a majority of the House and two-thirds of the Senate." Trumbull worried that an aggressive Congress undermined the checks and balances of the Constitution, and some other senators shared his fear. The Senate vote on May 16, 1868, fell one short of the two-thirds majority needed to convict. Johnson's power, however, was broken.

▲ **W.L. Sheppard sketched** *Electioneering in the South* **for** *Harper's Weekly* **in 1868 to illustrate African American interest in voting.**

THE FIFTEENTH AMENDMENT

The attempt to force Johnson from office cost the Radical Republicans some popular support. As the 1868 election neared, they sensed trouble. To retain voters, they nominated General Ulysses S. Grant for president. General Grant lacked political experience, but he had an important asset: he was a popular war hero.

Grant defeated his Democratic opponent, Governor Horatio Seymour of New York, in a very close race. As worried Republican leaders studied the election returns, they realized that new African American voters had given them their narrow win.

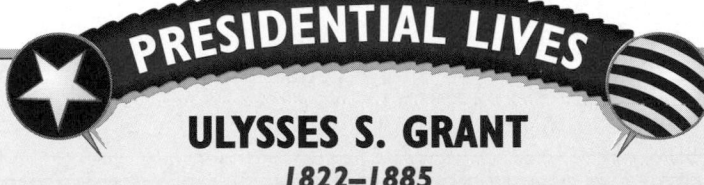

PRESIDENTIAL LIVES

ULYSSES S. GRANT
1822–1885

in office
1869–1877

Ulysses S. Grant graduated from the U.S. Military Academy at West Point in 1843 with no intentions of making a career of military service. "A military life had no charms for me, and I had not the faintest idea of staying in the army even if I should be graduated, which I did not expect."

After the Mexican War, Grant did pursue a military career on the western frontier. But missing his family, and amid rumors of his heavy drinking, he resigned from the army in 1854.

Failure seemed to dog him. He drifted through a series of jobs: peddling firewood, working in a customhouse, and collecting rents. He tried farming but failed. When the Civil War started in 1861, Grant was 39 years old and clerking at his family's leather goods store. He returned to the army and at last found success. The presidency followed in 1869.

▲ This poster was issued to celebrate passage of the Fifteenth Amendment.

The ratification of the Fifteenth Amendment in 1870 was a triumph for African Americans and Radical Republicans. "This wonderful, quiet, sudden transformation of four millions of human beings from . . . the auction-block to the ballot-box" was unprecedented, rejoiced abolitionist William Lloyd Garrison. But others criticized the amendment. Historian Henry Adams noted that it was most remarkable for what it did not do. It did not guarantee African Americans the right to hold office. Nor did it prevent states from limiting voting rights through discriminatory requirements, such as literacy tests.

Eager to protect their power in the North as well as in the South, the Republicans drew up the **Fifteenth Amendment**, which Congress passed in February 1869. It was short and to the point: "The right of citizens of the United States to vote shall not be denied or abridged by the United States or by any state on account of race, color, or previous condition of servitude."

▪▪ **The Fifteenth Amendment guarantees that the right to vote cannot be denied because of race.**

The Fifteenth Amendment also failed to extend the vote to women. Women's rights leaders, most of them former abolitionists, had split over the amendment. One group, arguing that "this hour belongs to the negro," had urged women to wait for the more controversial women's suffrage so as not to endanger passage of the amendment. Elizabeth Cady Stanton replied: "My question is this: Do you believe the African race is composed entirely of males?" Stanton and others had opposed ratification until all women were given the vote. The bitter debate over the amendment divided the women's suffrage movement for more than 20 years and alienated many African American women from the movement.

 SECTION 2 REVIEW

IDENTIFY and explain the significance of the following: Thaddeus Stevens, Freedmen's Bureau, Civil Rights Act of 1866, Fourteenth Amendment, Reconstruction Acts, Ulysses S. Grant, Fifteenth Amendment, Elizabeth Cady Stanton.

LOCATE and explain the importance of the following: Memphis, Tennessee.

1. **MAIN IDEA** What actions of President Johnson served to unite the Republican opposition?

2. **MAIN IDEA** What rights did the Fourteenth and Fifteenth amendments guarantee for blacks?

3. **CONTRASTING** How did the Moderate Republicans' attitudes toward Reconstruction differ from those of the Radical Republicans?

4. **WRITING TO PERSUADE** Imagine you are an African American woman working in support of the Fifteenth Amendment. Write a speech to deliver before Congress, urging the members not to include women's suffrage in the amendment. Be sure to give reasons for your position.

5. **ANALYZING** How did Andrew Johnson and Congress each use the Constitution's system of checks and balances to try to assert their plan for Reconstruction?

Section 3

RECONSTRUCTION IN THE SOUTH

FOCUS

- How did African Americans participate in rebuilding the South?
- How did the Ku Klux Klan try to influence Reconstruction?
- What factors contributed to the end of Radical Reconstruction?

*W*hile conflict over black suffrage continued, Congress imposed its Reconstruction plan. In 1867, under the provisions of the Reconstruction Acts, the southern states held conventions to draft new constitutions. Republicans dominated these conventions, and blacks as well as whites participated. Unwilling to accept African Americans as equals, many white southerners turned to violence. By Reconstruction's end in 1877, conservative whites once again firmly held power.

An African American addressing Congress

AFRICAN AMERICAN POLITICAL MOBILIZATION

With the passage of the Reconstruction Acts, African Americans saw a new era begin. The advent of Radical Reconstruction rekindled the former slaves' hopes for equal citizenship. Some southern blacks took dramatic actions—chasing overseers from plantations, or attempting to desegregate streetcars. But many registered to vote and turned to political activity to press for the equality promised by the Civil Rights Act and the Fourteenth Amendment. Even the churches found that "politics got in our midst" and overtook "our revival or religious work," one freedman minister recalled.

African Americans also joined political clubs, such as the Union League. Begun in the North as a patriotic club, the league brought the views of the Republican party to the freed slaves and to poor whites. It provided blacks in particular

with a place to develop their political skills. Literate members read newspapers aloud, and then everyone debated the issues of the day.

Most importantly, African Americans served as delegates to all the state constitutional conventions. In Louisiana and South Carolina, black delegates outnumbered whites; in other states they made up 10 to 40 percent of the delegates. Although many of the African American delegates were ex-slaves or southern blacks who were born free, northern blacks participated, too. Many African American communities in the North

▶ **Freedmen are shown registering to vote in Macon, Georgia, in this 1867 engraving.**

The Granger Collection, New York

▲ This 1872 print honored the first African Americans to serve in the U.S. Congress (left to right): Hiram R. Revels, Benjamin J. Turner, Robert C. DeLarge, Josiah T. Wells, Jefferson F. Long, Joseph H. Rainey, and Robert B. Elliott.

watched as their most talented teachers, lawyers, and other professionals went south to help with Reconstruction.

■■ Many African Americans participated in politics to protect their rights.

RECONSTRUCTION GOVERNMENTS

Most convention delegates were either northern Republicans or white southern Unionists. Many white southerners resented the arrival of northern Republicans—white or black—whom they called **carpetbaggers**. The newcomers, they jeered, were "needy adventurers" of "the lowest class" who could carry everything they owned in one carpetbag (a cheap suitcase). Some northerners had moved south after the war to advance their fortunes. Many, however, were simply eager to help the freedpeople.

Ex-Confederates heaped even greater scorn on southern whites who had backed the Union cause and now supported Reconstruction. Ex-Confederates viewed these whites—whom they dubbed **scalawags**, or scoundrels—as "southern renegades, betrayers of their race and country."

Groups favoring Reconstruction soon formed a Republican alliance. While they disagreed on such issues as land reform, as Republicans they saw themselves as the "party of progress, and civilization." They hoped to seize economic and political power from the planters and then rebuild the South and improve conditions for poor white farmers and freedpeople alike.

The Republican alliance created new state constitutions. The new state governments abolished property qualifications for jurors and for candidates for office and guaranteed white and African American men the right to vote. (Florida went further, extending political rights to the Seminoles.) Nine states expanded women's rights by permitting married women to own property separately from their husbands. Once Congress approved the new constitutions, state legislators raised taxes to pay for new road, bridge, and railroad construction and for increased services, such as free public education.

■■ Reconstruction legislatures, which included African Americans, made their state governments more democratic and increased services.

Many ex-Confederates ridiculed the new state constitutions and pointed out corrupt practices. Some southern legislators did use their offices to enrich themselves. But corruption was a nationwide problem, and the scandals involving Reconstruction governments paled in comparison with government scandals in the North (see Chapter 16).

▲ The Reconstruction policies of President Grant are satirized in this 1880 cartoon. The South is shown chained to two Union soldiers and weighed down by a chariot shaped like a giant carpetbag.

THE KU KLUX KLAN

The Reconstruction governments' reforms, the election of African Americans to office, and African Americans' growing political participation soon stirred a vicious white backlash. Angry white southerners formed secret terrorist groups to keep blacks from voting. The best known of these groups, the Ku Klux Klan, was founded in the mid-1860s by six ex-Confederates. The Klan quickly grew, attracting planters, lawyers and other professionals, and poor farmers and laborers.

The head of the Klan—"Grand Wizard" Nathan Bedford Forrest, a former slave-trader and Confederate general—bluntly warned Republicans that he intended "to kill the radicals." This was no idle threat. The Klan and similar groups, such as the Knights of the White Camelia, were determined to destroy the Republican party as well as to keep blacks from voting. In Yanceyville, North Carolina, Klansmen shot John W. Stephens, a white Republican state senator. The Klan also murdered Richard Burke, a black Alabama legislator.

The Klan, however, did not limit its attacks to politically active white and black Republicans. Klansmen beat and killed thousands of blacks whom they regarded as "uppity" or too successful. Sarah Song, an ex-slave from Louisiana, recalled the night Klansmen killed her husband:

> 66 I saw them kill my husband; . . . he was shot in the head while he was in bed sick. . . . There were between twenty and thirty men. . . . They came into the room. . . . Then one . . . put the pistol to his head and shot him three times. . . . Then one of them kicked him, and another shot him again when he was down. . . . He never spoke after he fell. 99

Seeking to intimidate African Americans and discourage them from challenging white rule, Klansmen sometimes refused to let relatives bury the victims of Klan terrorism. Former slave Millie Bates told of Klansmen who, after lynching freedman Dan Black, refused to "let his folks take him down. . . . He just stayed there, till he fell to pieces."

In addition, Klansmen frequently burned homes and schools and stole livestock and land in an effort to chase blacks and pro-Reconstruction whites from the South. The tactic often worked. After Klansmen destroyed his crop and murdered his neighbors, freedman Robert Fullerlove gave up the 400 acres he had "worked for and earned." "It isn't worthwhile for me to stay," he explained.

As the violence mounted, African Americans demanded that Congress act to "enable us to exercise the rights of citizens." Between 1870 and 1871 Congress responded by passing three **Enforcement Acts**—one dealt specifically with the Ku Klux Klan—in an effort to stop violence against African Americans. The Democrats called them the Force Acts and declared that they threatened individual freedom. The acts empowered the federal government to combat terrorism with military force and to prosecute guilty individuals. In Mississippi alone, the federal government charged some 700 Klansmen. But since most local whites resented federal intervention, convictions proved extremely difficult to win.

▲ These two members of the Ku Klux Klan, shown in their uniforms, were captured at Huntsville, Alabama, during an 1868 riot.

■■ The Ku Klux Klan used violence and fear tactics to keep African Americans and white Republicans from voting.

NORTHERN ATTITUDES TOWARD RECONSTRUCTION

For a time the federal government's intervention brought a dramatic decline in Klan violence. But as the attention of Republicans, and of northern voters in general, focused increasingly on economic issues and political corruption in the North, their interest in Reconstruction lessened. What remained of the Republicans' commitment to Reconstruction died with the Panic of 1873, which was a particularly severe economic downturn.

Faced with threats of strikes and the demands of hard-hit workers and farmers for relief, an Ohio Republican noted that "the overwhelming labor question has dwarfed all other questions." The partnership between northern businesspeople, who formed the heart of the Republican party, and the freedpeople had never been a stable one; now it dissolved altogether. Many northern Republicans held antilabor, probusiness views. "I suppose," said a former slave, "it is a fight between the poor people and the rich man now."

The party also abandoned its commitment to universal voting rights as thousands of immigrants joined the Democratic party. Some Republicans now claimed that universal suffrage "cheapened the ballot," and they called for restricting the voting rights of immigrants and the urban poor.

Concerned with their own problems and weary of Reconstruction, many northerners began to accept southern whites' racist propaganda that portrayed blacks as unfit for self-government. When Jacob Cox, former secretary of the interior, suggested that the South "be governed through the part of the community that embodies the intelligence and the capital"—by which he meant its former white rulers—many northern whites nodded in agreement.

■■ By the early 1870s conditions in the North undermined Republicans' commitment to Reconstruction.

𝒯HE SOUTHERN REDEEMERS

The discontent caused by the depression turned voters against the Republican-controlled Congress. In the 1874 congressional elections, Democrats gained dozens of seats in the House, giving them a 60-seat majority. In the South they had attracted white Republican voters by promises of lower taxes and by racist appeals to white supremacy.

When Congress reconvened, Republicans made one final effort to enforce Reconstruction. They pushed through the **Civil Rights Bill of 1875**, which prohibited discrimination by businesses serving the public, such as hotels and transportation facilities. Yet even white Republicans who supported the bill had begun to see Reconstruction as a political liability. They agreed with Congressman James Garfield that their recent defeats at the polls were due to "a general apathy among the people concerning . . . the negro."

Many southern white Democrats reached the same conclusion. Convinced that the federal government would not stop them, Mississippi

▲ This Thomas Nast engraving, entitled *To Thine Own Self Be True*, commemorates the passage of the Civil Rights Bill of 1875.

Democrats used terrorism to win the 1875 state elections. The next year, Democrats in Louisiana and South Carolina adopted the same strategy to "redeem," or win back, their states from the Republicans.

These "Redeemers," in contrast to the Klan, did not try to hide their identities or their actions. Senator Ben Tillman of South Carolina later admitted: "We took the government away. We stuffed ballot boxes. We shot them [blacks]." Whites armed with rifles—even cannons—kept black voters away from polling places. One black official remembered the period as "the most violent time that ever we have seen."

In 1876 the Redeemers turned their attention to the presidential election, which pitted Democrat Samuel J. Tilden of New York against Republican Rutherford B. Hayes of Ohio. Opponents of Reconstruction vowed to win the election even "if we have to wade in blood knee-deep." In the popular vote they were successful: Tilden beat Hayes by less than 250,000 votes. But the electoral vote was another story.

The election results in Florida, Louisiana, Oregon, and South Carolina were challenged. An electoral commission set up to rule on the validity of the returns gave Hayes the presidency by one electoral vote. Democrats in the House protested. To defuse the crisis, leading Republicans and southern Democrats struck a deal—the **Compromise of 1877**. The agreement's exact terms remain a matter of dispute. It is clear, however, that in return for the Democrats' acceptance of Hayes as president, the Republicans agreed not to use the military to enforce Reconstruction legislation.

Denied federal protection, the last of the Reconstruction governments fell. Once in power the Redeemers rewrote state constitutions and overturned many of the Reconstruction governments' reforms. They trimmed spending and cut services. Some states even closed public hospitals and did away with public education systems.

African Americans never accepted the Redeemer governments as legitimate. Charles Harris, a black former Alabama legislator, protested:

66 We are taxed without representation. . . . We obey laws; others make them. We support state educational institutions, whose doors are virtually closed against us. . . . From these and many other oppressions . . . our people long to be *free.* 99

COMMENTARY

Reconstruction Perspectives

In the late 19th century, many white southerners remembered Reconstruction as a time when they were bullied by Union soldiers, lorded over by former slaves, and exploited by carpetbaggers and scalawags. Similarly, many northerners came to believe that Radical Reconstruction was a mistake.

Such views were for many years reflected in American history textbooks and in popular culture. For example, both Thomas Dixon's 1905 novel The Clansman *and D.W. Griffith's 1915 film* Birth of a Nation, *which was based on Dixon's book, glorified the Klan and ridiculed Congress. Unfortunately, most white Americans accepted these views as fact, and such ideas only reinforced white southerners' opposition to African Americans' rights.*

Blacks preserved a different view of the period. They knew that their active participation had helped shape Radical Reconstruction. Francis L. Cardozo, who had been educated in Great Britain, ably served as South Carolina's treasurer from 1872 to 1876. Hiram R. Revels, who had recruited African Americans for the Union army and had taught school, represented Mississippi in the U.S. Senate. Blanche K. Bruce, a wealthy black planter from Mississippi, served as sheriff, tax collector, superintendent of education, and U.S. senator. "The Southern Reconstruction Governments," asserted John R. Lynch, a black who served as the speaker of Mississippi's House and as a representative to Congress, "were the best governments those States ever had."

These men and countless others left behind a positive social legacy. They created institutions—churches, schools, and strong family networks—that helped sustain black communities through the post-Reconstruction years. Later generations would draw upon these institutions in building the civil rights movement.

Reconstruction also left a legal legacy. Although practically ignored for almost a century, the Civil Rights Act of 1866 and the Fourteenth and Fifteenth amendments provided an important legal framework. They enabled later civil rights leaders to win back voting rights for African Americans and to end legal segregation.

SECTION 3 REVIEW

IDENTIFY and explain the significance of the following: carpetbaggers, scalawags, Enforcement Acts, Civil Rights Bill of 1875, Samuel J. Tilden, Rutherford B. Hayes, Compromise of 1877.

1. **MAIN IDEA** What role did African Americans play in Reconstruction?

2. **MAIN IDEA** How did actions of the Ku Klux Klan affect the progress of Reconstruction?

3. **ASSESSING CONSEQUENCES** How and why did northern Republicans' attitudes toward Reconstruction change during the 1870s?

4. **WRITING TO INFORM** In a paragraph, describe who the Redeemers were, and explain how they helped to bring about the end of Reconstruction.

5. **EVALUATING** Why might Reconstruction be seen as a short-term failure but long-term victory for African American civil rights?

THE NEW SOUTH

FOCUS

■ **What new labor arrangements appeared in the South after the emancipation of the slaves?**

■ **How did Reconstruction's end affect African Americans?**

■ **How did African Americans respond to segregation and to the loss of civil and political rights?**

During the 1880s white business leaders began to speak of the "New" South, urging that the region move away from its dependence on cotton toward a more varied economy. Inspired by this dream of a New South, southerners worked to build up the region's manufacturing enterprises. For years, however, many southerners remained in rural poverty. And for blacks in the South, racial discrimination made life harsher still.

▲ Grant Hamilton's *From Darkness to Light* (1895) shows a New South rising from the ashes of the Civil War.

TENANT FARMING AND SHARECROPPING

After the Civil War, some southern planters lost their lands because they could not pay their debts or their taxes. Most of their lands fell into the hands of other planters or northern investors. For instance, after 1870, northerners owned or financed about half of Louisiana's sugar plantations.

Whether planters were southerners or northerners, however, all faced a common problem: a shortage of labor. Few ex-slaves or whites wanted to work for the low wages planters were willing—or, in many cases, able—to pay. Some planters solved their labor problems by renting out their lands. Even more turned to **sharecropping**. Under this system a sharecropper, or cropper, agreed to work a parcel of land in return for a share of the crop, a cabin, seed, tools, and a mule.

Sharecropping appealed to planters for an obvious reason: they got their lands worked without having to pay cash. And, at least at first, the croppers—most of whom were ex-slaves—were also pleased. Sharecropping gave them places to live and lands to work without close supervision.

The system had a serious drawback, however. Croppers (and most farmers who rented land) had no income until harvesttime. To obtain needed supplies each year, they promised their crops to local merchants who sold them goods on credit.

▲ This 1903 photograph shows a sharecropping family in North Carolina.

Any debts they could not pay to the merchants after they sold their crops were added to their bills the following year. This arrangement was known as the **crop-lien system**. (A lien is a creditor's legal claim on the debtor's property.)

In effect, the system made it impossible for croppers—white or black—to work their way out of poverty. "Until he [the cropper] has paid the last dollar of his indebtedness, he is subject to . . . constant oversight and direction," economist Matthew Hammond noted at the time:

> 66 Every mouthful of food he purchases, every implement that he requires on the farm, . . . must all be bought of the merchant who holds the crop lien, and in such amounts as the latter is willing to allow. 99

And not all merchants were honest. They "didn't give no itemized statement. No, you just had to take their word," one sharecropper recalled. If the cropper argued, "there would be a shooting." In the judgment of former slave Thomas Hall, the system was "little better than slavery."

■■ Many southern landowners turned to sharecropping and the crop-lien system to keep cotton production up and wages down.

The crop-lien system kept the southern economy tied to one-crop agriculture. Merchants would only give credit to farmers who grew certain crops, most often cotton. As a result, cotton displaced other crops to such an extent that southerners had to import food and animal feed from the North.

ᖆNDUSTRIAL GROWTH

Some southerners, like newspaperman Henry W. Grady, the editor of the Atlanta *Constitution,* thought that one-crop agriculture kept the South in poverty and too economically dependent on the North. The New South, he argued, should manufacture its own goods.

Supporters of the New South joined with northern and British investors to finance factories and steel mills. Southerners themselves raised the capital to build textile mills and other enterprises. Southern railroads were rebuilt and integrated into northern rail systems.

Not everyone benefited equally from industrialization in the South, however. Factory owners and investors profited at the expense of poorly paid workers. White industrial workers earned wages that were some 40 percent below what their northern counterparts earned, and most African Americans could not find factory work at any wage. Many industrial workers were forced to buy goods on credit from the company store and to live in ramshackle company houses. Like sharecroppers, they soon found themselves locked in a cycle of debt.

▲ After the Civil War, the South began a slow course of industrialization. This photograph shows a worker at **White Oaks Mills,** a factory near **Greensboro, North Carolina.**

The day remembered as "Gun-Shoot" by the residents of the Sea Islands began on a cloudless fall morning in the early months of the Civil War. On November 7, 1861, distant cannon fire from the naval battle at Port Royal Harbor cracked the air over these marshy islands off South Carolina. Fearing a Union invasion, the white population abandoned their homes and hastily fled to the mainland.

This frantic exodus of the white residents suddenly and unofficially emancipated the thousands of slaves who worked the cotton plantations that dotted the islands. When news of the Sea Islands events reached northern newspapers, scores of idealistic teachers and missionaries sailed southward, intent on educating the former slaves.

One who answered the call was Charlotte Forten, the granddaughter of African American abolitionist James Forten. "Dear children! born in slavery, but free at last!" Forten

▲ **Penn School on St. Helena is shown here in a photograph taken about 1870.**

wrote in her journal soon after her arrival. "My heart goes out to you. I shall be glad to do all that I can to help you."

Many of the northerners, however, were not prepared for what they found on the islands. Because of their geographic isolation, the Sea Islanders retained many African traditions. For instance, they spoke Gullah, a combination of various African languages and English. (Gullah is still spoken by some African

Americans along the South Carolina and Georgia coasts.) Other African traditions among the Sea Islanders included manners of dress and the settling of community disputes by the advice of elders.

Despite the language barrier, the northerners found the former slaves ready and eager to learn. Two black schools were already operating on the islands. A black cabinetmaker who for years had taught secret

*T*URNING BACK THE CLOCK

For African Americans the New South was starting to look very much like the Old South. Tied to the land through sharecropping and excluded from most factory jobs, African Americans had few economic opportunities. Moreover, Democrats, now firmly in control of the southern state legislatures, stepped up their attempts to strip blacks of their rights.

In an effort to deprive African Americans of the right to vote, southern state legislatures insti-

tuted **poll taxes**—fixed taxes imposed on every voter—and **literacy tests**—tests supposedly intended to limit the vote to those who could read. Technically these measures did not violate the Fifteenth Amendment. However, since most black southerners were poor and had been denied an education, these laws accomplished their purpose. Even literate blacks could "fail" the test, since local white officials decided who passed. These rules, however, were often waived for poor or illiterate whites.

To further deprive African Americans of their rights, states passed laws designed to enforce night classes for slaves ran one school. The missionaries opened their first school—Penn School—on St. Helena in 1862. Charlotte Forten taught at the school during the day. At night she often tutored adults. The admiration she felt for the Sea Islanders was evident in her journal entries:

66 I never before saw children so eager to learn. . . . Coming to school is a constant delight and recreation to them. They come here as other children go to play. The older ones, during the summer, work in the fields from early morning until eleven or twelve o'clock, and then come into school, after their hard toil in the hot sun, as bright and anxious to learn as ever. 99

Historians have called what took place on the Sea Islands during the Civil War a "rehearsal for Reconstruction." As part of the Sea Islands "experiment," many of the area's plantations were unofficially divided among the former slaves. In 1865 General William T. Sherman made the land division official by issuing Special Field Order No. 15. This order reserved the Sea Islands and much of the coastal lands from Charleston, South Carolina, to the St. Johns River in Florida for African Americans.

To the bitter disappointment of the former slaves, the U.S. government failed to carry through on Sherman's plan during Reconstruction. As late as 1890, however, 60 percent of the Sea Islands property was still in the hands of African Americans—standing as a testament to what Reconstruction might have been.

◀ A schoolteacher is shown reading to two children in this 1866 photograph.

segregation, or separation, of the races. The first of these so-called Jim Crow laws, passed by Tennessee in 1881, required separate railway cars for blacks and whites. Florida adopted a similar law in 1887, and by the 1890s all southern states had legally segregated public transportation and schools. Segregation soon extended to parks, cemeteries, and other public places.

African Americans sued for equal treatment under the Civil Rights Act of 1875, but the Supreme Court refused to overturn the Jim Crow laws. In the *Civil Rights Cases* (1883), the Court

◀ An African American is expelled from a railroad car in Philadelphia after being told to sit in the car reserved for "colored people."

▲ Booker T. Washington

Confronted by segregation and denied basic political and civil rights, some African Americans left the South for the Midwest or moved to northern cities. Most, however, stayed in the South, where their ancestors had lived for generations. To improve their lives, African Americans formed mutual aid societies, started businesses, strengthened churches, and built schools. The African Methodist Episcopal (AME) church, the AME Zion church, and black Baptist churches grew rapidly.

The key question facing African American leaders after 1877 was how to fight discrimination. Two influential leaders, Booker T. Washington, a former slave who founded Alabama's Tuskegee Institute in 1881, and Ida Wells-Barnett, a teacher

ruled that the Fourteenth Amendment forbade only *states,* not individuals or businesses, from discriminating against blacks. The Supreme Court went further in upholding segregation in ***Plessy v. Ferguson*** (1896), ruling that "separate but equal" facilities did not violate the Fourteenth Amendment. Only Justice John Marshall Harlan disagreed. He declared that "our Constitution is color-blind, and neither knows nor tolerates classes among citizens."

■■ **After Reconstruction, African Americans were deprived of their rights and had few economic opportunities.**

▲ Tuskegee Institute was founded in 1881 to teach African Americans trades and professions. A dressmaking class for women and a printing class for men are shown here.

and journalist, offered different answers to the discrimination question.

Washington believed that African Americans should concentrate on economic advancement. To further blacks' economic independence—which he believed was the key to political and social equality—Washington urged blacks to seek practical training in trades and professions. He also discouraged them from protesting against discrimination, arguing that it merely increased whites' hostility. If economic and social progress was to be made, he claimed, blacks would need "the cooperation of the Southern whites" because "they control government and own the property."

He carried his message of peaceful coexistence to white audiences as well. In an 1895 speech known as the Atlanta Compromise, he told whites that while blacks and whites could live in separate social worlds, they needed to cooperate for economic progress: "In all things that are purely social we can be as separate as the fingers, yet one as the hand in all things essential to mutual progress." There were, he said, "no limits to the attainments of the Negro. . . . I want to see him enter the all-powerful business and commercial world."

Many African American leaders disagreed with Washington's position, arguing instead that blacks should protest unfair treatment. One such leader was Ida Wells-Barnett (born Ida Bell Wells). Born to a slave family in 1862, Ida Wells was educated in a Mississippi freedmen's school and became a teacher herself at age 14. In 1884 Wells moved to Tennessee, where she taught while attending Fisk University. She lost her teaching job, however,

Ida Wells-Barnett

The Granger Collection, New York

when she began protesting discrimination and segregated schools.

Ida Wells then turned to journalism, becoming part owner of the *Memphis Free Speech*. In 1892, after whites lynched three friends of hers, she vowed to put a stop to lynching. In a fiery editorial she charged "that neither character nor standing avails the Negro if he dares to protect himself against the white man or become his rival." Angry whites destroyed her newspaper office.

Wells urged African Americans to leave the South. She herself left Memphis for New York, where she continued her crusade against lynching. She conducted investigations, wrote exposés, lectured widely in the North and in Great Britain, and organized antilynching societies. After moving to Chicago and marrying lawyer Ferdinand Barnett in 1895, she published *A Red Record,* the first statistical study of lynching. Though lynchings decreased only slightly in the early 1900s, Wells's tireless efforts kept the public's attention focused on the issue.

▪▪ **African Americans built their own institutions, and they adopted several approaches to fighting discrimination.**

■ **SECTION 4 REVIEW**

IDENTIFY and explain the significance of the following: sharecropping, crop-lien system, poll taxes, literacy tests, segregation, Jim Crow laws, *Plessy* v. *Ferguson,* Booker T. Washington, Ida Wells-Barnett.

1. **MAIN IDEA** After slavery had been abolished, how did plantation owners deal with the shortage of labor?

2. **MAIN IDEA** In what ways did the New South resemble the Old South (before Reconstruction) for African Americans?

3. **MAIN IDEA** What actions did blacks take in response to their loss of rights?

4. **WRITING TO EVALUATE** Write an essay evaluating the consequences for a white sharecropper of leaving the land to seek work in a southern factory.

5. **SYNTHESIZING** How did changes in the post-Reconstruction New South harm some groups of people and benefit others?

Thirteenth Amendment passed.
Freedmen's Bureau established.

Lincoln issues
Proclamation
of Amnesty and
Reconstruction.

Civil Rights Act
passed. Fourteenth
Amendment passed.

Reconstruction
Acts passed.

Fifteenth Amendment
passed.

Reconstruction
ends.

| 1863 | 1865 | 1870 | 1875 |

WRITING A SUMMARY

Using the essential points of the chapter as a guide, write a summary of the chapter.

REVIEWING CHRONOLOGY

Number your paper 1 to 5. Study the time line above, and list the following events in the order in which they happened by writing the first next to 1, the second next to 2, and so on. Then complete the activity below.

1. Reconstruction Acts passed.
2. Freedmen's Bureau established.
3. Fifteenth Amendment passed.
4. Lincoln issues Proclamation of Amnesty and Reconstruction.
5. Reconstruction ends.

Assessing Consequences Choose the two events that you think had the most positive outcome for African Americans, and explain the reasons for your assessment.

IDENTIFYING PEOPLE AND IDEAS

Explain the historical significance of each of the following people or terms.

1. amnesty
2. Andrew Johnson
3. black codes
4. Thaddeus Stevens
5. Reconstruction Acts
6. carpetbaggers
7. Compromise of 1877
8. sharecropping
9. Jim Crow laws
10. Ida Wells-Barnett

UNDERSTANDING MAIN IDEAS

1. Describe conditions in the South after the Civil War, and explain how people tried to improve those conditions.
2. How did the Reconstruction plans of Lincoln, Johnson, and the Radical Republicans differ?
3. What political roles did African Americans play during Reconstruction, and how did some whites protest these new roles?
4. How did changes in the New South reverse the policies of the Reconstruction period?
5. How did conditions for southern farmers and laborers change from 1865 to 1900?

REVIEWING THEMES

1. **Constitutional Heritage** How did the Thirteenth, Fourteenth, and Fifteenth amendments attempt to adapt the U.S. Constitution to changing conditions after the Civil War?
2. **Democratic Values** How was democratic society in the U.S. expanded during Reconstruction? How did the expansion prepare for further changes in America's definition of democracy?
3. **Economic Development** In what ways did cotton continue to affect the New South?

THINKING CRITICALLY

1. **Hypothesizing** How might conditions in the New South have been different if African Americans had been given land after the war?
2. **Evaluating** Why did many southern whites react so strongly to gains made by African Americans during Reconstruction?
3. **Synthesizing** Compare and contrast the views of Booker T. Washington and Ida Wells-Barnett on the place of African Americans in society.

STRATEGY FOR SUCCESS

Review the Skills Handbook entry on Reading Charts and Graphs beginning on page 996. Then study the chart below. How did the value of cotton goods produced in the South change during this period? How did southern production compare with that of the New England and Middle Atlantic regions?

VALUE OF COTTON GOODS PRODUCED 1880–1900

(In millions of dollars)

Region	1880	1890	1900
New England	143	181	191
Middle Atlantic	29	40	48
Southern	16	41	95

Source: *The American South*

| 1880 | 1885 | 1890 | 1895 | 1900 |

First Jim Crow law passed in Tennessee.

Supreme Court issues ruling in *Civil Rights Cases.*

Ida Wells-Barnett publishes first statistical study of lynching.

Supreme Court issues ruling in *Plessy* v. *Ferguson.*

WRITING ABOUT HISTORY

Writing to Express a Viewpoint Imagine you are a planter in the postwar South. Write a letter to the editor of your local newspaper explaining how Reconstruction policies have affected your economic and social status and why you support the Compromise of 1877. Be sure to provide specific examples and reasons in your letter.

USING PRIMARY SOURCES

Read the following excerpt from a November 1865 letter that a group of African Americans from South Carolina wrote to the U.S. Congress. Then summarize the letter's main demands and explain the suggested basis for these demands.

66 *We would ask for no rights or privileges but such as rest upon the strong basis of justice. . . . We ask first, that the strong arm of law and order be placed alike over the entire people of this State; that life and property be secured, and the laborer free to sell his labor as the merchant his goods.*

We ask that a fair and impartial instruction be given to the pledges of the government to us concerning the land question.

We ask that the three great agents of civilized society—the school, the pulpit, the press—be as secure in South Carolina as in Massachusetts or Vermont.

South Carolina farmer and child

The Granger Collection, New York

We ask that equal suffrage be conferred upon us, in common with the white men of this State.

This we ask, because "all free governments derive their just powers from the consent of the governed"; and we are largely in the majority in this State, bearing for a long period the burden of onerous taxation, without a just representation. 99

LINKING HISTORY AND GEOGRAPHY

Review the map on page 402. Then explain what conclusions you can draw based on the dates of states' readmission to the Union and the defeat of Radical Republican governments.

BUILDING YOUR PORTFOLIO

Complete the following projects independently or cooperatively.

1. **SECTIONALISM** In Chapter 12 you served on a committee working on a compromise between the North and the South. Building on that experience, imagine you are a southern governor opposed to northern politicians' plans for the South during Reconstruction. Create an outline for a Reconstruction plan that would address the interests of planters, ex-soldiers, and African Americans in your state.

2. **DEMOCRATIC RIGHTS** In Chapter 11 you served as a lawyer helping Dred Scott win his freedom. Building on that experience, imagine you are working on the *Plessy* v. *Ferguson* case. Prepare a closing statement arguing that segregation, as practiced in "separate but equal" facilities for blacks and whites, violates the Fourteenth Amendment.

American Letters

The Pain of Slavery and Civil War

The tragedy of slavery and the Civil War echoed throughout the literature of the 19th century. The African American spiritual "Steal Away" and African American writer Paul Laurence Dunbar's poem capture the hardships of slave life. American poet Walt Whitman and African American poet Frances Ellen Harper explore some of the effects of the Civil War on the nation.

▲ **Walt Whitman**

Steal Away

African American spiritual

Steal away, steal away, steal away to Jesus,
Steal away, steal away home,
I ain't got long to stay here.

My Lord, He calls me,
He calls me by the thunder,
The trumpet sounds within-a my soul,
I ain't got long to stay here.

Steal away, steal away, steal away to Jesus,
Steal away, steal away home,
I ain't got long to stay here.

Green trees a-bending,
Po' sinner stands a-trembling
The trumpet sounds within-a my soul,
I ain't got long to stay here.

Steal away, steal away, steal away to Jesus,
Steal away, steal away home,
I ain't got long to stay here. ❖

Sympathy

by Paul Laurence Dunbar

I know what the caged bird feels, alas!
When the sun is bright on the upland slopes;
When the wind stirs soft through the springing grass
And the river flows like a stream of glass;
When the first bird sings and the first bud opes,
And the faint perfume from its chalice[1] steals—
I know what the caged bird feels!

I know why the caged bird beats his wing
Till its blood is red on the cruel bars;
For he must fly back to his perch and cling
When he fain[2] would be on the bough a-swing;
And a pain still throbs in the old, old scars
And they pulse again with a keener sting—
I know why he beats his wing!

I know why the caged bird sings, ah me,
When his wing is bruised and his bosom sore,—
When he beats his bars and would be free;
It is not a carol of joy or glee,
But a prayer that he sends from his heart's deep core,
But a plea, that upward to Heaven he flings—
I know why the caged bird sings! ❖

---

1 the cup-shaped inside of a flower
2 gladly

▼ **The Fisk University Jubilee Singers won fame for their concerts of spirituals in the late 1900s.**

Jubilee Singers, Courtesy of Fisk University

From *Beat! Beat! Drums!*

by Walt Whitman

Beat! beat! drums!—blow! bugles! blow!
Through the windows—through doors—burst like a
    ruthless force,
Into the solemn church, and scatter the congregation,
Into the school where the scholar is studying;
Leave not the bridegroom quiet—no happiness must
    he have now with his bride,
Nor the peaceful farmer any peace, ploughing his field
    or gathering his grain,
So fierce you whirr and pound you drums—so shrill
    you bugles blow. ❖

From *The Wound-Dresser*

by Walt Whitman

(Aroused and angry, I'd thought to beat the alarum,[1]
    and urge relentless war,
But soon my fingers failed me, my face drooped and I
    resigned myself,
To sit by the wounded and soothe them, or silently
    watch the dead.)
Years hence of these scenes, of these furious passions,
    these chances,
Of unsurpassed heroes, (was one side so brave? the
    other was equally brave.) ❖

---

1 call to arms

Learning to Read

by Frances Ellen Harper

Very soon the Yankee teachers
    Came down and set up school;
But, oh! how the Rebs did hate it,—
    It was agin' their rule.

Our masters always tried to hide
    Book learning from our eyes;
Knowledge didn't agree with
    slavery—
    'Twould make us all too wise.

But some of us would try to steal
    A little from the book,
And put the words together,
    And learn by hook or crook.

I remember Uncle Caldwell,
    Who took pot liquor[1] fat
And greased the pages of his book,
    And hid it in his hat.

And had his master ever seen
    The leaves upon his head,
He'd have thought them greasy papers,
    But nothing to be read.

And there was Mrs. Turner's Ben,
    Who heard the children spell,
And picked the words right up by heart,
    And learned to read 'em well.

Well, the Northern folks kept sending
    The Yankee teachers down;
And they stood right up and helped us,
    Though the Rebs did sneer and frown.

And I longed to read my Bible,
    For precious words it said;
But when I begun to learn it,
    Folks just shook their heads.

And said there is no use trying,
    Oh! Chloe, you're too late;
But I was rising sixty,
    I had no time to wait.

So I got a pair of glasses,
    And straight to work I went,
And never stopped till I could read
    The hymns and Testament.

Then I got a little cabin,
    A place to call my own—
And I felt as independent
    As the queen upon her throne. ❖

---

1 liquid left in a pot after cooking

THINKING AND WRITING ABOUT LITERATURE

1. African American spirituals sung by slaves often had hidden meanings. What do you think "steal away home" could have meant for slaves?
2. In Paul Lawrence Dunbar's poem, why does the "caged bird" sing?
3. What is the tone of the first Walt Whitman poem? In the second poem, how did Whitman's feelings about the war change?
4. In Frances Ellen Harper's poem, written during Reconstruction, what is the significance of reading for Chloe?

Strategies for Success

▶ Horace Greeley

COMPARING POINTS OF VIEW

We all bring to our experiences a point of view, a personal frame of reference from which we see or think about things. Besides such factors as age, sex, education, and family background, historical circumstances also shape our outlook. Comparing varied views and voices gives us historical insights. It helps us understand, for example, the roots of historical conflicts.

How to Compare Points of View

1. **Note the sources.** Find out about each author or speaker. Check whether each is an authority on the subject under discussion.
2. **Do research.** Find out all you can about the event, person, or situation.
3. **Compare and contrast the main ideas.** Note similarities and differences in the main ideas being expressed.
4. **Compare supporting details.** Consider whether the ideas are supported by relevant facts, by opinions, or by a combination of both. Evaluate the logic of the supporting arguments, and look for any bias.
5. **Evaluate the points of view.** Apply your critical thinking skills to appreciate why people have different points of view and to weigh the accuracy and reliability of each view.

Applying the Strategy

When the Civil War ended, Americans seriously disagreed over how the nation should proceed, especially how the South should be treated. Read and compare the following points of view.

“ These gentlemen of the South mean to win. They meant it in 1861 when they opened fire on Sumter. They meant it in 1865 when they sent a bullet through the brain of Abraham Lincoln. They mean it now. The moment we remove the iron hand from the Rebels' throats they will rise and attempt the mastery. ”
—*Horace Greeley, editorial in the* New York Tribune, *November 15, 1865*

“ The war being at an end, the Southern states having laid down their arms and the questions at issue between them and the Northern states having been decided, I believe it to be the duty of everyone to unite in the restoration of the country and the reestablishment of peace and harmony. ”
—*Gen. Robert E. Lee, letter, September 7, 1865*

◀ Abraham Lincoln

Greeley, a northerner, is pessimistic about the prospects for restoration. He fears that those he sarcastically calls "the gentlemen of the South" will rise again in rebellion. To support this view, he refers to the attack on Fort Sumter and the assassination of Lincoln. But these were the actions of only a few southerners. Greeley's worry seems exaggerated, but not totally unfounded. The war's massive destruction of the South made any new uprising unlikely; nevertheless, many ex-Confederates did regain power.

Lee's statement that the war's outcome has settled the issues that divided Americans is understandable for a military officer. Postwar struggles would prove, however, that this outlook was overly optimistic—and too simplistic as well. Many politicians and ordinary citizens, on both sides, did not share Lee's sense of duty; regional rivalries were not laid down so easily as guns.

Practicing the Strategy

Read the excerpt of President Lincoln's Second Inaugural Address on page 396, and compare it with the views quoted here. Then, on a separate sheet of paper, answer the following questions.

1. Whose point of view seems closer to Lincoln's—Greeley's or Lee's? Explain why.
2. Describe Lincoln's point of view.

BUILDING YOUR PORTFOLIO

Outlined below are three projects. Independently or cooperatively, complete one and use the products to demonstrate your mastery of the historical concepts involved.

1 SLAVERY
The Civil War ended the institution of slavery. It did not, however, end legal discrimination against African Americans. Using the portfolio materials you designed in chapters 11 and 12, hold a *New York Tribune* press conference with a representative from the Union League. Your questions at the conference should focus on the positive and negative consequences of the Civil War for African Americans.

2 SECTIONALISM
Differences between the North and the South created a rift that led to the Civil War and left deep scars that Reconstruction failed to erase. Using the portfolio materials you designed in chapters 12 and 13, hold a debate arguing whether Reconstruction served the political, economic, and social interests of the North more than the South.

3 DEMOCRATIC RIGHTS
The protection of the rights of different groups in society is at the heart of a democratic system. Using the portfolio materials you designed in chapters 11 and 13, prepare a one-scene courtroom play about the segregation of schools. Characters might include Ida Wells-Barnett, northern abolitionists, ex-slaves, and southern Redeemers.

Videodisc Review
In assigned groups, develop an outline for a video collage of America in the years between 1845 and 1900. Choose images that best illustrate the major topics of the period. Write a script to accompany the images. Assign narrators to different parts of the script, and present your video collage to the class.

Further Reading
Chesnut, Mary B. *A Diary from Dixie.* Ben Ames Williams, ed. Harvard University Press (1980). Firsthand account of everyday life in the Confederate South.

Emilio, Luis F. *A Brave Black Regiment.* Bantam Books (1992). Collection of documents written about the 54th Regiment of the Massachusetts Volunteer Infantry.

Foner, Eric. *A Short History of Reconstruction, 1863–1877.* HarperCollins (1990). Overview of the Reconstruction years.

Franklin, John Hope. *Reconstruction: After the Civil War.* University of Chicago Press (1961). An account of the Radicals' efforts to legislate the South during Reconstruction.

Meltzer, Milton, ed. *Voices from the Civil War.* HarperCollins (1989). Northern and southern views of the war and its effects from 1861–1865.

Nesbitt, Mark. *35 Days to Gettysburg.* Stackpole Books (1992). Events leading up to the Battle of Gettysburg as seen through the eyes of a Union soldier and a Confederate soldier.

Stampp, Kenneth M. *America in 1857: A Nation on the Brink.* Oxford (1990). Analysis of one key year in the movement toward Civil War.

Taylor, Susie K. *A Black Woman's Civil War Memoirs.* Patricia W. Romero, ed. Talman (1988). An African American woman's account of camp life with the 33rd U.S. Colored Troops.

American
ALMANAC

❖ At Your Leisure

1860s "Dime novels" about the West, like *Buffalo Bill, the King of the Border Men* and *Frontier Angel,* are popular.

▲ **Dime novels**

1870s Roller skating and ice skating are latest crazes.

1874 Tennis arrives from England. It's popular with women, who can play while wearing their fashionable long skirts.

1875 African American jockey Oliver Lewis wins first Kentucky Derby.

1880s Bicycling becomes popular for getting around—and for fun!

1896 First modern Olympic Games are held in Athens, Greece, with 12 events—U.S. and 12 other nations attend.

▲ **Immigrants at Ellis Island**

❖ The American People

Between 1861 and 1900 more than 14 million immigrants arrive on American shores!

The Granger Collection, New York

◀ **Cycling in the 1880s**

THE BUFFALO

Plains Indians used all these parts of the buffalo:

bones for arrowheads, knives	meat for food
hide for bedcovers, moccasins, snowshoes, tepee covers, clothing	ribs for sled runners
	rough side of tongue for hairbrushes
hooves for rattles	sinew for thread
horns for spoons, cups, ladles	tail for fly-swatting brushes

▲ Cowboy's spur

UNIT 5

The Nation Transformed

1860–1910

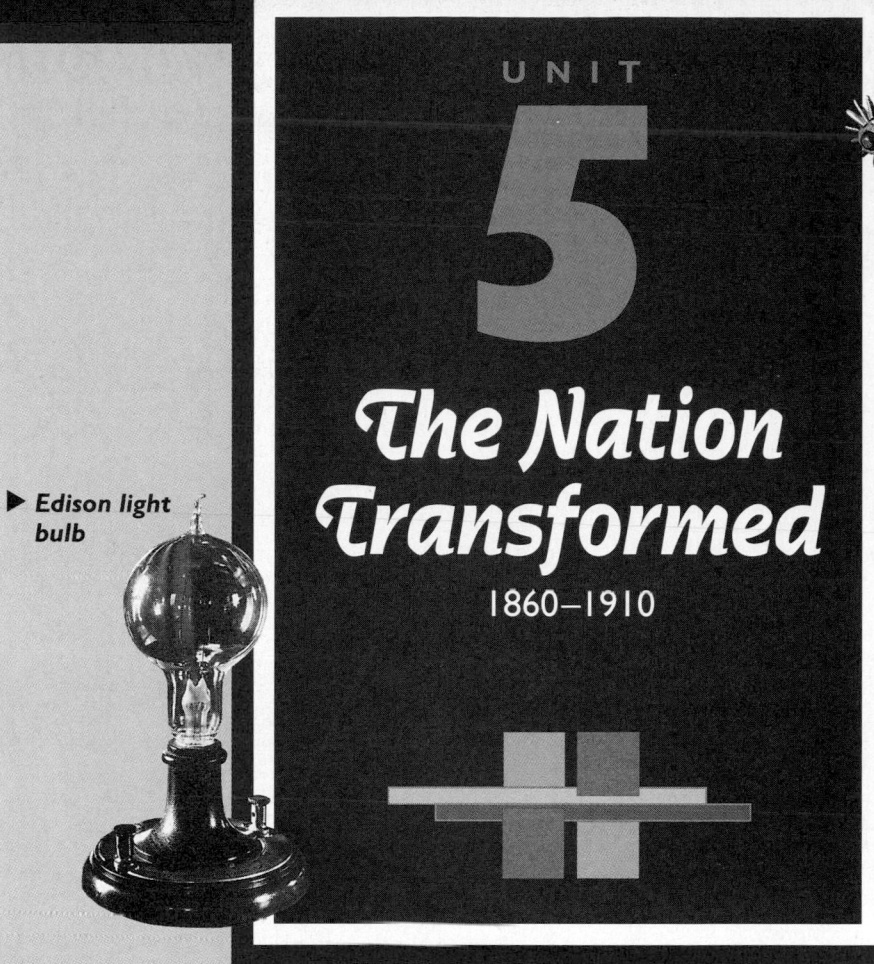

► Edison light bulb

❖ Inventing America

1868 Vicente Martínez Ybor opens cigar factory in Key West, Florida; his success leads many to do likewise.

1876 Alexander Graham Bell receives patent for the telephone.

1882 Thomas Edison lights up New York City with his electric lighting system; 85 paying customers are hooked up.

1883 African American Jan Matzeliger revolutionizes shoe industry with his invention: a machine that sews shoe uppers to soles.

1886 Josephine Cochrane patents the mechanical dishwasher.

1886 Dr. John Pemberton brews a new drink—Coca-Cola.

1888 African American Granville T. Woods's overhead conducting system for railways makes electric trolley cars an everyday city sight.

1894 First Hershey Bar is made (and eaten!).

► Jan Matzeliger

The Granger Collection, New York

"Coca-Cola" and the Contour Bottle design are registered trademarks of the Coca-Cola Company.

❖ The Changing West

1867 Between 1867 and 1881 more than 4 million cattle are driven north from Texas; roughly a third of the cowboys are African American, Mexican American, or Mexican.

1874 Barbed wire cuts across western prairies for first time; in 1880 over 80 million lbs. are made.

1874 More than 3.5 million buffalo are killed since 1872, mostly by white hunters and soldiers; the species is almost extinct.

1890 Non-Indian population triples from about 1 million in 1870 to more than 3 million; in some western states men still outnumber women by nearly two to one.

1890 More than 166,000 miles of railroad track cross the country—up from 30,626 miles in 1860.

1900 Native American population hits its lowest level—about 150,000.

THE WESTERN CROSSROADS

FOCUS

UNDERSTANDING THE MAIN IDEA

After the Civil War the regions of the West—the Great Plains, the Southwest, and the Far West—played important roles in U.S. economic growth. People moved to the West, encouraged by the U.S. government's offers of free land and the promise of profits from ranching, farming, lumbering, and mining. In many years of conflict and treaty negotiations, the U.S. government forced Native Americans to give up much of their lands.

THEMES

- **GEOGRAPHIC DIVERSITY** What strategies might people use to survive and prosper in arid or semiarid environments?

- **CULTURAL DIVERSITY** What problems might arise when one group attempts to force another group to give up its way of life?

- **ECONOMIC DEVELOPMENT** How might a government promote economic development in a new territory?

1862	1869	1876	1879	1896
The Homestead Act passed.	First transcontinental railroad completed.	Battle of Little Bighorn occurs.	Exodusters trek west.	Gold discovered in Yukon Territory.

The resolution of the Oregon boundary dispute in 1846 and the Treaty of Guadalupe Hidalgo in 1848 opened up millions of acres of western land for U.S. settlement. Native Americans faced increasing pressure on their lands and resources as non-Indian settlers moved to the Far West.

Miners at Auburn Ravine, California, 1852

*E*ver since the Spanish planted settlements in the present-day southwestern United States, the West has been a crossroads where Native American and Asian, African, and European cultures met and influenced each other. European horses and guns, for example, changed the culture of the Plains Indians, allowing them to hunt buffalo more successfully and to move permanently from the mountains to the Plains. The Comanches—possibly the most-skilled horse raisers of the Plains—used the guns and horses to raid settlements and to dominate other Indian groups on the southern Plains.

The Comanche way of life, however, required abundant land and buffalo. The Comanche freedom to roam the Plains was threatened after 1859, when the U.S. government stepped up its efforts to settle the Comanches on reservations in present-day Oklahoma. Ten Bears, a Comanche leader, argued against the government's plan:

❝ When I was in Washington the Great Father told me that all the Comanche land was ours, and that no one should hinder us in living on it. So, why do you ask us to leave the rivers, and the sun, and the wind, and live in houses? ❞

The federal government's reasons were overwhelmingly economic. As the U.S. government limited Native Americans to reservations, non-Indians rushed to the West to establish farms and ranches and to stake out mining claims. Soon the West began supplying the United States and the rest of the world with wheat, lumber, minerals, and cattle and sheep.

American Museum of Natural History

American buffalo

NATIVE AMERICAN RESISTANCE

F O C U S

■ Why did the U.S. government adopt the reservation policy?

■ Why did so much conflict erupt between Native Americans and the federal government in the late 1800s?

■ How did Sarah Winnemucca work to improve conditions for Native Americans?

■ How did the federal government attempt to "Americanize" Native Americans? How did the Navajos respond?

Sioux doll

Until the 1850s most American settlers who ventured to the West settled in California, Oregon, or Texas. By mid-century, however, settlers changed their destinations. With the U.S. government's encouragement and the military's protection, non-Indians began settling on the Great Plains and in other parts of the West. To make room for the settlers, the government forced Native Americans onto reservations, provoking nearly a half century of conflict.

INDIAN COUNTRY

By 1850 nearly all Native Americans—some 360,000—lived west of the Mississippi River. Indians from the old Northwest and the Southeast were confined to Indian Territory, in present-day Oklahoma. On the southern Plains, the Kiowas shared the land with the powerful Comanches. The Sioux, Blackfeet, and Crows dominated the northern Plains. In the Southwest the Apaches ranged throughout New Mexico, Arizona, and northern Mexico, while the Navajos and Hopis lived in farming or ranching communities.

In the Far West, disease and conflict associated with nearly a century of contact with Hispanic and other non-Indian settlers had reduced the Native American population, including the Paiutes (PY-oots), Pimas, Miwoks, and Maidus. In California alone the Native American population had dropped from an estimated 300,000 in 1769 to some 35,000 by 1860.

In the 1851 Treaty of Fort Laramie (see Chapter 10), the U.S. government promised Native Americans control of the Plains—the bulk of Indian Country. The government, however, soon went back on its promise. Hearing tales (both

Museum of the Great Plains

◀ Driven out of Montana by the Cheyennes and Sioux, the Kiowas settled on the southern Plains, in an area stretching from Kansas to Mexico.

exaggerated and accurate) about the mineral wealth and fertile land in the West, thousands of non-Indians streamed into the territory.

In a series of new treaties, the government forced Native Americans to give up their lands and move to reservations. The treaties promised permanent reservation land, money, and yearly supplies. The task of administering the reservations went to the **Bureau of Indian Affairs**, established in 1824 within the War Department. The bureau worked closely with the U.S. Army. The close ties between the army and the bureau sent a clear message: Native Americans who resisted confinement on reservations would be dealt with by force.

Even when Native Americans went quietly to reservations, the government rarely lived up to its side of the bargain. Corrupt bureau agents—most of whom were non-Indians—often sold to non-Indians the supplies intended for Native Americans. Furthermore, the government regularly reduced the size of reservations as settlers demanded more land. As Massachusetts newspaper editor Samuel Bowles noted in 1869, the government's actions sent Native Americans another clear message: "When the march of our empire demands this reservation of yours, we will assign you another; . . . so long as we choose, this is your home, your prison, your playground."

■■ **The U.S. government attempted to restrict Native Americans to reservations to make room for non-Indian settlers.**

𝒴EARS OF STRUGGLE

Angered by the government's double-dealings, several Plains peoples, including independent groups of Cheyennes, Arapahos, Comanches, and Sioux, fought back. To them a settled life without buffalo hunting was no life at all.

The Plains peoples faced strong opposition. Some 20,000 U.S. Army troops, many of them Civil War veterans, enforced Indian removal. Some 4,000 were African Americans, who served in four segregated units. Native Americans nicknamed African American soldiers "buffalo soldiers," after the sacred buffalo so important in Plains Indian culture. The army enlisted Indians as scouts or as soldiers by playing on rivalries among Native Americans. For example, many Pawnees, Crows, and Shoshones helped U.S. forces battle the Sioux.

Sand Creek. One of the earliest confrontations in the West between the military and Native Americans occurred in Colorado Territory. The territory's non-Indian population had been growing rapidly since the Colorado gold rush of 1858. Eager to open more land to U.S. settlers, John Evans, the territorial governor, pressured the Cheyennes and Arapahos to sell their hunting grounds and move to reservations.

In 1861 some Cheyenne and Arapaho leaders agreed to move their groups to a reservation south of the Arkansas River. Other leaders and their groups, however, refused to leave, and Evans feared a major Indian uprising. Throughout the summer of 1864, Cheyenne and Arapaho forces clashed with the local militia. By fall Black Kettle, a Cheyenne leader, had grown tired of fighting. He made his way to Fort Lyon to surrender.

When his group stopped to camp along Sand Creek, most of the men left to hunt. In their absence, some 700 troops under the command of Colonel John Chivington attacked the camp. Some 200 of Black Kettle's group, most of them women and children, were killed.

The slaughter horrified U.S. authorities. But Chivington was unrepentant. "Damn any man who sympathizes with Indians!" he exclaimed. "I have come to kill Indians, and believe it is right and honorable to use any means under God's heaven to kill Indians."

News of the **Sand Creek Massacre** swept across the Plains, prompting raids by the Arapahos and Cheyennes. The Sioux, engaged in a long-standing war against the U.S. Army, also

No Horse, *Women Honoring Warriors* (1875–1880), Collection of Heard Museum, Phoenix, Arizona

▲ Some time between 1875 and 1880, Cheyenne-Arapaho artist No Horse drew this scene, entitled *Women Honoring Warriors.*

FORT LARAMIE TREATIES
1851: Native Americans promised control of the Plains.
1868: Sioux agree to move to reservation in Black Hills.

1867 TREATY OF MEDICINE LODGE
Southern Plains Indians agree to move to Indian Territory.

Apache leader Geronimo surrenders at Skeleton Canyon in 1886.

- ■ Fort
- ✷ Battle
- △ Treaty site

→ Navajos' Long Walk, 1864
→ Route of Chief Joseph and Nez Percés, 1877
- Reservation in 1890

Indian Reservations and Battles, to 1890

AN UNEVEN STRUGGLE Fighting against overwhelming odds, Native Americans were forced to give up their lands and move to reservations.

? LOCATION When was the last major Indian battle fought? In what state?

Museum of New Mexico
Tomahawk

stepped up their efforts. But neither side emerged victorious. To end the fighting, U.S. authorities and the southern Plains leaders signed the **Treaty of Medicine Lodge** in 1867. By the terms of the treaty, southern Plains Indians agreed to give up much of their lands in exchange for reservations in Indian Territory. The following year, in a second Treaty of Fort Laramie, the Sioux agreed to move to a reservation in the Black Hills region of South Dakota and Wyoming.

The treaties did not end the fighting, however. As an editor of the *Army and Navy Journal* observed of U.S. treaty-making efforts: "One of our hands holds the rifle and the other the peace-pipe, and we blaze away with both instruments at the same time. The chief consequence is a great *smoke*—and there it ends."

Custer's last stand. The U.S. Army waged campaigns against the Sioux in 1875. Impatient to open up the Sioux's sacred Black Hills to gold prospectors, U.S. authorities ordered the Sioux to settle near the agencies, the local offices of the Bureau of Indian Affairs. Tatanka Iyotake, a Sioux medicine man called Sitting Bull by non-Indians, urged the hunters to defy the government order.

◀ Sitting Bull signed his name to this 1880s photograph shortly after it was taken.

Opposed to reservation life, Sitting Bull mocked reservation Indians: "You are fools," he argued, "to make yourselves slaves to a piece of fat bacon, some hard-tack [biscuits], and a little sugar and coffee." Many agreed, and by the spring of 1876, thousands of defiant Sioux and their Cheyenne allies were camped on Rosebud Creek in southern Montana.

Inspired by Sitting Bull's prophecy of a victorious battle against the U.S. Army, several hundred Native Americans rode off to engage the enemy. Although the **Battle of Rosebud** in June 1876 did not result in an outright victory for Native Americans, they gained confidence in their strong fighting force. They proceeded west to camp near a stream the Indians called Greasy Grass and the army called Little Bighorn River. There hundreds of Indians fleeing the agencies, where food was in short supply, joined them. By late June the camp contained almost 2,000 men prepared to fight.

This time the army decided to strike first. What the army did not anticipate was the size of the Indian fighting force. The Native Americans, outnumbering the army troops by three to one and led by Ta-sunko-witko (Crazy Horse), fought off two army attacks. On the morning of June 25, General George Armstrong Custer divided his force to strike the camp from three sides. Custer himself led a battalion of over 200 men. After the final attack, which lasted for less than an hour, Custer and every soldier in his battalion lay dead.

The **Battle of the Little Bighorn** gave the Native Americans only a momentary triumph, however. Over the next several months, the Indian forces broke into smaller groups to evade army troops. Group by group, they were forced to surrender and settle near the agencies. Sitting Bull fled to Canada but eventually returned and settled on Standing Rock Reservation, in Dakota Territory, where he continued to oppose non-Indian settlement of Sioux lands.

Wounded Knee. A tragic final chapter of the Plains Indian–U.S. Army wars unfolded on the plains of South Dakota. The seeds of this conflict were planted in 1889. Wovoka (woh-VOH-kuh), a Paiute holy man from Nevada, began the Ghost Dance religion, which combined Christian and Native American beliefs. Wovoka proclaimed that white settlers would vanish, the buffalo would return, and traditional Indian ways of life would revive if Native Americans performed the Ghost Dance. A young Sioux explained why Wovoka's message appealed to him:

> 66 The rumor got about: "The dead are to return. The buffalo are to return. The Dakota [Sioux] people will get back their own way of life. The white people will soon go away, and that will mean happier times for us once more!"
>
> That part about the dead returning . . . appealed to me. To think I should see my dear mother, grandmother, brothers and sisters again! 99

Wovoka preached peace. The Sioux living on reservations in the Dakotas, however, added a militant tone to the religion by donning "Ghost Shirts," whose special symbols, they believed, could stop bullets.

▼ While performing the Ghost Dance, dancers shuffled back and forth in a circle until one or more of them received spiritual visions and then collapsed in a trance. This photograph was taken in December 1890.

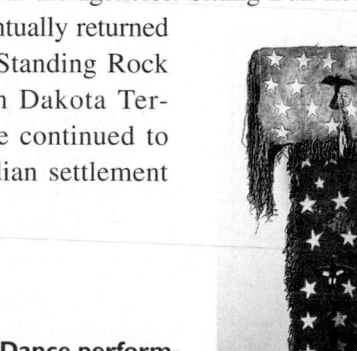

▶ Some Ghost Dance performers wore Ghost Shirts similar to this one. They believed that the symbols of stars, birds, and animals on the garment protected them from harm.

Field Museum of Natural History

Will the Real Custer Please Stand?

Picture a dashing young soldier of the 1870s sporting fringed buckskins, a scarlet scarf, and shoulder-length, flowing blond hair. This image of George Armstrong Custer survived for almost 75 years after his death in 1876. In the minds of many Americans, Custer symbolized the army's efforts to make the West safe for U.S. settlers.

Such was the popular view of Custer—but was it the truth? How did this heroic image arise and how has it changed? Journalists, poets, novelists, playwrights, painters, and filmmakers—rather than historians—have molded the public view of Custer. Artists first created the legend of America's most famously unfortunate soldier; decades later, artists again reshaped public

▶ **George Armstrong Custer posed for this photograph around 1870, when he was commander of the Seventh Cavalry.**

opinion of Custer—eventually destroying the legend and transforming a revered hero into a hated villain.

The real Custer was outgoing, strikingly handsome, and recklessly brave. But he was not an outstanding student: Custer graduated at the bottom of his 1861 West Point class. Upon graduation he saw immediate action in the Civil War. The young officer rose rapidly in the Union ranks through a series of field promotions, earning a brigadier general's star in 1863 at age 23. Newspapers dubbed him the "Boy General."

After the war Custer was returned to his regular rank of captain. But as the favorite officer of General

Philip Sheridan, he soon received an appointment as a lieutenant colonel in charge of the elite Seventh Cavalry. Custer's unit frequently battled the Cheyennes and Sioux on the Great Plains.

Custer's military exploits and news of his exploring expeditions into Montana's Yellowstone country in 1873 and the Dakota Territory's Black Hills in 1874 captivated the nation. Popular magazine articles and his memoir, *My Life on the Plains,* kept his name before the public. Thus the nation reeled in shock when word reached the East that Custer and every man of his detachment had been killed at the Battle of the Little Bighorn on June 25, 1876.

Though some Americans questioned Custer's motives at Little Bighorn, most held him up as a martyr. Poets, artists, and novelists promptly began to build the Custer myth. Just one day after hearing of the battle, Walt Whitman submitted his poem "A Death-Sonnet for Custer" to the *New York Tribune.* Poet Henry Wadsworth Longfellow also published his account of the battle. Both poems painted Custer in a heroic light. In addition, artists produced an endless supply of paintings of the gory battle, depicting Custer and his men as the victims of bloodthirsty Indians.

This image of Custer also appeared in the popular play *Custer's Last Charge,* which toured with Buffalo Bill's famous Wild West Show in the 1880s and 1890s. The play showed Custer fearlessly battling savage forces. He was also a favorite subject of early filmmakers. By 1941 close to 20 Custer movies had been made, all portraying Custer as a self-sacrificing defender of U.S. settlers.

Nevertheless, as early as the 1920s, Custer's image was beginning to change. From a symbol of heroic self-sacrifice in the winning of the West, he was gradually transformed into a symbol of white arrogance—a brutal conqueror of Native Americans. This change came about partly as a result of the reform movements of the early 1900s. As more people began looking at society—and its myths—with a critical eye, the treatment of Native Americans in general and the Custer legend in particular came under fire.

In the 1930s and 1940s, several novelists, such as Frederic Van de Water in *Glory-Hunter,* portrayed Custer as a vain, often brutal man. In the post–World War II era, a new wave of Custer movies re-created him as a ruthless leader of an army that slaughtered Native Americans. In such films

▲ **Kicking Bear painted this version of the Battle of the Little Bighorn. He included himself in the center of the picture, alongside Crazy Horse, Rain-in-the-Face, and Sitting Bull.**

as *Sitting Bull* (1954), *Chief Crazy Horse* (1955), *The Great Sioux Massacre* (1965), and *Little Big Man* (1970), courageous Indians defend their homelands against a cruel, glory-seeking, and even insane Custer.

Native American efforts to address their past treatment and present conditions influenced this new generation of Custer movies. Beginning in the late 1960s, such best-selling books as Vine Deloria's *Custer Died for Your Sins* (1969) and Dee Brown's *Bury My Heart at Wounded Knee* (1971) presented the Native American perspective of the Indian wars.

By the early 1970s public opinion had firmly shifted toward sympathy for the Native American view of the Battle of the Little Bighorn. In a 1971 *Life* magazine article, Alvin M. Josephy, Jr., labeled the Custer Battlefield National Monument in Montana "a sore from

America's past that has not healed." In response, Congress passed legislation in 1991 that stripped Custer's name from the national monument and authorized the construction of an Indian monument in its place. The once illustrious image of George Armstrong Custer was now thoroughly tarnished.

Early artists, writers, and filmmakers had created Custer's heroic image, "making history" in the process. Later generations of artists destroyed the myth and remade history. Twentieth-century social reformers and Native American civil rights groups forced society to take another, closer look both at Custer and at the plight of Native Americans. Artists and historians may again reinterpret and revise the Custer story, and this soldier's life and death will continue to provide Americans with lessons about their past, present, and future.

Government agents feared that the Ghost Dance would inspire Indian resistance. When the Ghost Dance religion spread to Standing Rock Reservation, the military ordered the arrest of Sitting Bull, who had joined the religion. When reservation police surrounded Sitting Bull's cabin on December 15, 1890, a skirmish broke out and Sitting Bull was killed. Frightened and angry, many Sioux joined the Ghost Shirt fighters farther west.

Government agents set out to arrest another Sioux leader, Big Foot. Although Big Foot had been a Ghost Shirt fighter, he decided to join Red Cloud, another Sioux leader, on Pine Ridge Reservation to end the fighting. Army troops caught up with Big Foot and some 350 members of his group. Waiting to be led to agency headquarters, the Sioux set up their tepees on Wounded Knee Creek.

The next morning—December 29—the army ordered the confiscation of Indian rifles. Mounted cavalry, reinforced by four Hotchkiss guns (which fired exploding shells), surrounded the camp. After the Indians surrendered only a few guns, the soldiers began to search the tepees. Tensions ran high. When someone fired a rifle—possibly during a scuffle, possibly as a signal—bursts of gunfire erupted between U.S. soldiers and Indians. The Hotchkiss guns ripped into the tepees, killing some 300 Sioux. About 30 U.S. soldiers were killed.

Though the **Wounded Knee Massacre** shocked many Americans, others grimly insisted that Custer had been "avenged." The battle marked the end of the Indian wars on the Great Plains.

CONFLICT IN THE FAR WEST

Native Americans west of the Great Plains also faced forced resettlement. In the Wallowa (wah-LOW-uh) River Valley of northeastern Oregon, the Nez Percés tried to avoid coming under government control. Although the Nez Percés had long maintained good relations with the U.S. government and white settlers, the government ordered the Nez Percés to move to an Idaho reservation in 1877. Chief Joseph, the Nez Percé leader, reluctantly agreed. Before his people could leave, however, a few Nez Percés killed some white settlers, whom they viewed as intruders. Joseph's group, fearing attack, fled.

Pursued by army troops for three months, the Nez Percés journeyed east and north through Idaho, Wyoming, and Montana, picking up additional

▲ **Before reaching the Canadian border, Chief Joseph surrendered to Colonel Nelson A. Miles on October 5, 1877. Shown here is** *Chief Joseph Rides to Surrender* **by Howard Terpning.**

followers along the way. The group eventually numbered from 700 to 800, including some 300 fighting men. The group's goal was to escape to Canada. But as winter approached, travel became harder. Chief Joseph surrendered only 30 miles from the Canadian border. An interpreter wept as he relayed the leader's surrender statement:

> ❝ I am tired of fighting. Our chiefs are killed. . . . It is cold and we have no blankets. The little children are freezing to death. . . . My heart is sick and sad. From where the sun now stands, I will fight no more forever. ❞

The Nez Percés, however, were not the last Native American group to surrender to the U.S. Army. The Apaches of the desert and canyon lands of New Mexico and Arizona mounted one of the longest campaigns against government control. The conflict began in the 1850s, when settlers began moving into Apache territory. Raids and attacks by both sides produced a climate of fear and hatred. In 1877 the U.S. government forced the seminomadic Apaches to settle on San Carlos Reservation, on the Gila River in Arizona.

Most Apaches complied, but life on the reservation proved harsh. In 1881, amid rumors of an Indian uprising, army troops moved into the territory. Fearing an attack, Geronimo, an Apache leader, fled the reservation with about 75 followers. Off and on for the next five years, Geronimo's group raided settlements and evaded capture. But on September 4, 1886, with his followers outnumbered, Geronimo gave up. "Once I moved about like the wind," he told his captors. "Now I surrender to you and that is all." His surrender marked the end of armed resistance to the reservation system.

■■ The U.S. Army and Native Americans clashed as the U.S. government took away Indian lands.

*V*OICES OF PROTEST

By the 1880s Native Americans had been forced to surrender more than 450 million acres to the U.S. government. Native Americans had been driven off their land and onto reservations by a number of pressures. The army had defeated many groups. In addition, U.S. settlers, whose presence increased as railroads snaked across the West, had moved onto Indian lands and killed off most of the buffalo herds. "Kill every buffalo you can," advised Colonel R. I. Dodge. "Every buffalo dead is an Indian gone." With the loss of the buffalo, Native Americans had little hope of maintaining an independent existence on the Plains.

Troubled by the treatment of Native Americans, a small but active group of reformers appealed to the government to craft a more humane Indian policy. Their cause won the support of Helen Hunt Jackson, whose influential

▲ Although the buffalo population once numbered in the millions, its ranks dwindled by the 1870s as hunters were paid from one dollar to three dollars for every hide sold. An 1883 study estimated that some 13 million buffalo had been slaughtered.

book *A Century of Dishonor* (1881) attacked the government for its years of broken promises and corrupt dealings with Native Americans.

Another reformer, Thoc-me-tony (Shell-Flower), a Paiute woman known as Sarah Winnemucca, publicized the plight of Native Americans. Born in Nevada around 1844, Winnemucca, who spoke English, Spanish, and several Indian languages, served for a number of years as an interpreter at U.S. forts. She also briefly taught school on the Paiute reservation in Oregon.

Although the Paiutes cooperated with the government, they often felt taken advantage of by Bureau of Indian Affairs agents. Winnemucca learned that the government had authorized two mills to be built on the Paiute reservation, but they were never constructed. She wondered:

66 The [mills] were never seen or heard of by my people, though the printed report . . . says twenty-five thousand dollars was appropriated to build them. Where did [the money] go? . . . Is it that the government is cheated by its own agents who make these reports? 99

Sarah Winnemucca

The Paiutes' forced removal to Yakima Reservation in Washington Territory in 1878 so outraged Winnemucca that she began lecturing on the Paiutes' behalf to non-Indian audiences. In 1880 she pleaded her cause—to allow the Paiutes to return to their lands—before President Rutherford B. Hayes. Hayes granted her request, but the bureau's agents did not carry out the president's order.

Three years later Winnemucca reached a wider audience with her book *Life Among the Piutes.* Though she died before age 50, Winnemucca helped awaken the nation to the injustices suffered by Native Americans.

■■ Sarah Winnemucca brought to the nation's attention the plight of Native Americans.

ASSIMILATING NATIVE AMERICANS

Many government officials and most reformers viewed **assimilation**, or the cultural absorption, of Native Americans into "white America" as the only long-term way to ensure Native American survival. The federal government urged Native Americans to become farmers and to move out of their dwellings and live in wooden houses. The government passed laws to force Native Americans to abandon their traditional appearance and to dress like "Americans." One law even ordered Indian men to cut off their long hair. Another outlawed Indian religious practices.

To speed assimilation, the government set up a system of Indian schools. Some Indian children attended reservation schools, while others were forced to leave their families to attend boarding schools. The Carlisle Indian School in Pennsylvania, which admitted its first class in 1879, typified the boarding school system. Students were forced to speak only English, wear "proper" clothes, and change their names to "American" ones. The school's founder summed up his aim: to "kill the Indian and save the man."

The government's most important assimilation strategy, however, was forcing Indians to give up tribal ownership of land in favor of private ownership. Private ownership, the government argued, lay at the heart of Americanization. Western settlers and developers wanted Native Americans to give up tribal ownership of land for another reason: if Native Americans could be forced onto small plots of land, settlers and developers could then buy up surplus reservation land.

The passage of the **Dawes General Allotment Act** in 1887 established private ownership of Indian land. The act required that Indian lands be surveyed and Indian families claim an allotment of 160 acres of reservation land for farming. The land that remained would be sold.

The Dawes Act proved to be a disaster for Native Americans. In less than 50 years, they lost two thirds of their land. Some of the land was sold to settlers and developers as surplus when allotments were made. In other cases, Native Americans sold or were cheated out of their allotments.

■■ **By outlawing Indian customs, establishing boarding schools, and enforcing private land ownership, the U.S. government attempted to assimilate Native Americans.**

THE NAVAJOS: A CASE STUDY

Despite the government's hopes, few Plains Indians became farmers. Even before passage of the Dawes Act, the government had tried to force the Navajos to give up their reliance on sheep raising and become settled farmers. This plan backfired.

To carry out the government's plan, the U.S. Army waged military campaigns against the Navajos in northwestern New Mexico and

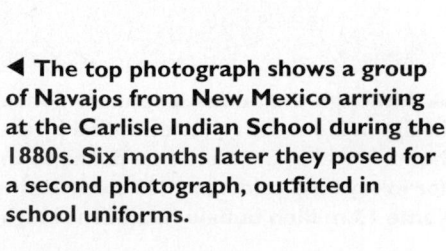

◀ The top photograph shows a group of Navajos from New Mexico arriving at the Carlisle Indian School during the 1880s. Six months later they posed for a second photograph, outfitted in school uniforms.

Museum of New Mexico

► The Navajos learned the art of weaving from the Pueblos and soon produced woolen blankets of exceptional quality. This photograph of a Navajo weaver outside her hogan, or home, was taken around 1890.

northeastern Arizona in 1863. Soldiers destroyed Navajo houses, sheep herds, and corn crops. Without food or shelter, many Navajos surrendered in early 1864. In what came to be known as the **Long Walk,** the Navajos were forced to travel on foot to Bosque Redondo, a reservation in eastern New Mexico. Soldiers stationed at nearby Fort Sumner prevented Navajos from leaving the reservation.

The U.S. government gave the Navajos seeds and farming tools, but the land proved unsuitable for farming. Living conditions at Bosque Redondo were harsh, and many Navajos died from malnutrition or disease. Realizing its plan was unworkable, the government signed a treaty with the Navajos granting them a reservation in New Mexico and Arizona in 1868. There the Navajos rebuilt their communities, concentrating on sheep raising, weaving, and silver-

smithing. By the 1880s their economy had prospered and their population had begun to increase.

■■ After great losses, the Navajos won their battle to maintain their communities.

Although the Navajos and other Native American groups overcame military defeat and resettlement, many groups did not. By 1890 warfare and forced assimilation had reduced the U.S. Indian population to fewer than 250,000. Native Americans were commonly referred to as "vanishing Americans." Despite suffering great hardships, though, Native Americans did not vanish.

SECTION 1 REVIEW

IDENTIFY and explain the significance of the following: Bureau of Indian Affairs, buffalo soldiers, Sand Creek Massacre, Treaty of Medicine Lodge, Sitting Bull, Battle of Rosebud, George Armstrong Custer, Battle of the Little Bighorn, Wovoka, Wounded Knee Massacre, Chief Joseph, Geronimo, Helen Hunt Jackson, Dawes General Allotment Act, Long Walk.

LOCATE and explain the importance of the following: San Carlos Reservation.

1. **MAIN IDEA** Why did the U.S. government attempt to resettle Native Americans on reservations? How did Native Americans respond to this attempt?

2. **MAIN IDEA** How did Sarah Winnemucca address the problems faced by the Paiutes?

3. **MAIN IDEA** What did the U.S. government do to try to assimilate Native Americans?

4. **WRITING TO EXPLAIN** Imagine you are a Sioux who took part in the Ghost Dance religion. Write an essay explaining the meaning of the Ghost Dance and Ghost Shirt.

5. **ANALYZING** Why were Navajo communities prosperous by the 1880s?

Who moved to the West? Migration westward after the Civil War differed from earlier migrations. The U.S. government now played a more active role in encouraging westward migration. The methods of transportation differed as well. Unlike earlier western settlers who traveled in large groups by covered wagon, these later migrants journeyed by themselves or with their families on the newly built railroads. The train rides to the West were quicker, safer, and more

Changing Ways THE TRANSCONTINENTAL RAILROAD

In the mid-1800s there was no easy way to get from the East Coast to the West Coast. Both the overland journey from New York to San Francisco and the boat trip around the tip of South America could last several months. To help open up the West to settlers, Congress passed the Pacific Railway Act in 1862. The act awarded contracts to build a transcontinental railroad to two companies: the Central Pacific Railroad and the Union Pacific Railroad.

The track had to be laid across some 1,500 miles of wilderness—over and through mountains and across steep ravines. The Central Pacific would lay track eastward from Sacramento, California, over the towering Sierra Nevada. The Union Pacific would work westward from Omaha, Nebraska, and cross the rugged Rockies.

To encourage the companies to take on the overwhelming job, the federal government gave them land. The project soon became a contest of which company would lay more track.

The railroad companies recruited thousands of workers for the backbreaking and often perilous work. Work crews competed against nature as well as each other as they blasted, shoveled, and pickaxed their way across the North American continent. During the frigid winters huge snowdrifts and avalanches blocked mountain passes. Some laborers died doing the dangerous blasting work. Railway gangs also faced attacks by Plains Indians, who attempted to prevent the invasion of their hunting grounds by "the wagons which make a noise."

Most of the Union Pacific's 10,000 workers were Irish immigrants. After the Civil War, veterans from both sides, many still wearing remnants of their

uniforms, also signed on. The Central Pacific's slightly larger work force consisted mostly of Chinese laborers. One observer called the sound of the crews' progress "a grand Anvil Chorus . . . playing across the plains and mountains, in triple time: three strokes to the spike; ten spikes to the rail; 400 rails to the mile." After seven years of exhausting labor, the railroad crews met at Promontory, Utah, on May 10, 1869.

Railroad officials, political dignitaries, infantry soldiers, and proud workers looked on as the last railroad tie—made of laurel wood, a symbol of victory in a contest of strength—was slipped into place. Leland Stanford, the president of the Central Pacific and former governor of California, then drove a golden spike to complete the railroad. The telegraph built alongside the tracks flashed the news from coast to coast that East and West were permanently linked.

◀ **Laborers from different ethnic backgrounds helped build the transcontinental railroad. This 1886 photograph shows members of a Northern Pacific Railroad crew.**

▲ Free black settlers moved west to escape persecution and violence in the South. The Shores family lived in Custer County, Nebraska, when this photograph was taken in the late 1880s.

1879. From 20,000 to 40,000 African Americans fled the South, where violence had broken out during elections in 1878. Seeking economic and political freedom, these black settlers, known as **Exodusters**, trekked west. With the help of established black settlers, the poor and ill-equipped Exodusters eventually settled some 20,000 acres.

European immigrants also flocked to the western United States. "America Fever" infected thousands of Norwegians, Swedes, and Danes. In 1882 alone more than 100,000 left their homes for the American West. In addition, many Irish who had helped build the railroads and a great number of Germans who had settled in the Mississippi Valley decided to move to the Plains. These Europeans were joined by Mennonites, Protestant pacifists who fled persecution in Russia. Their experience in farming wheat on the Russian steppes, or grasslands, was especially useful on the Great Plains.

Many of the Chinese immigrants who had come to California during the gold rush of 1849 had also turned to farming by 1880. In California alone some 3,200 Chinese raised crops in 1880. Throughout the West, many Chinese immigrants worked as farm laborers, sharecroppers, or produce

comfortable than the journeys on the Oregon Trail had been.

Economic motives, the search for racial tolerance, and the promise of a better life drew three main groups of people to the West: (1) white Americans from the East; (2) African Americans from the South; and (3) immigrants from Europe and Asia.

White newcomers came from more-settled areas of the United States. Because of the high cost of transporting supplies, it was mainly middle-class farmers and businesspeople who could afford to move to the West. New England farmers went west searching for more-fertile soil. Civil War veterans, especially those from the South, came to make a new start. The majority of white settlers, however, moved from states in the Mississippi Valley, which were rapidly filling up. A Nebraska settler explained simply: "I am well satisfied that I can do better here than I can in Illinois."

For African Americans, moving west had a special appeal. In the South, blacks faced violence and persecution after the withdrawal of federal troops at the end of Reconstruction. African American settlers who ventured onto the Plains in the 1870s sent letters to their friends and families, urging them to move west. Often these letters were read aloud in black churches.

Kansas, where John Brown had first fought against slavery, especially appealed to African American settlers. The biggest rush of black settlers occurred during the Kansas Fever Exodus of

▲ Shown here is a Chinese agricultural worker tending an irrigation ditch in a California orchard.

vendors. Some owned large farms. In 1870 a Chinese farmer in Sacramento County, California, earned $9,500 from farming—an enormous profit for the time.

:: Farmers moved onto the Great Plains for a variety of motives, but the main incentive was readily available land.

WESTERN ENVIRONMENTS

Although some 80 million acres of public land in the Great Plains were homesteaded between 1862 and 1900, the settlers did not immediately create a prosperous region. Though the land was free, supplies and transportation were expensive. In addition, the environments of the Southwest, the Far West, and the Great Plains posed problems for farmers. In the Southwest and the Far West, the new settlers had to learn irrigation techniques. To carve out farms from the Great Plains, the settlers relied on their resourcefulness, government support, innovative farming practices, and new technologies.

In parts of the Southwest, Hispanic and Native American farmers had developed effective irrigation systems that used canals, sloping fields, and dams to control water flow. They had also established farms that fanned out in thin strips from water sources so that all community residents had access to water. The new settlers had to adopt these methods to survive.

The Great Plains also had few water sources. In addition, trees that could provide fuel or building materials were scarce. The climate was also difficult: bitterly cold in the winter, blazing hot in the summer, and windy much of the time.

Plains farmers worked out clever solutions to some of these problems. To cope with the lack of wood, for instance, they built houses and barns of sod chunks cut from the heavy topsoil and stacked like bricks. A few scarce pieces of wood formed the roof, topped off with a layer of soil. Building with sod was difficult, however. Wrote a Kansas settler in 1877: "The sod is heavy and when you take 3 or 4 bricks on a litter or hand barrow, and carry it 50 to 150 feet, I tell you it is no easy work." Nor was it pleasant to live with the insects that dwelled in the sod.

The **U.S. Department of Agriculture**, created in 1862, helped farmers adapt to the Plains environment. Department experts sought out and publicized new varieties of wheat suitable for the Great Plains environment. (The cold winters of the northern Plains could not support traditional winter wheat.) These new wheat crops, along with the weeds introduced with the wheat seeds, soon replaced the grasses that had once covered the Great Plains.

Department of Agriculture agents also taught **dry farming** techniques, planting and harvesting

▼ Between 1830 and 1910 some 90 percent of all pioneers west of the Missouri River lived in sod houses. Shown here is the Scott family, photographed outside their Nebraska home in 1889.

▲ Bonanza farms applied the techniques of the factory system to agriculture. By 1890 there were some 300 farms in the Red River Valley that covered about 1,000 acres each. This photograph shows one such operation in the San Fernando Valley of California.

techniques that conserve moisture. For example, agents advised farmers to plow deep furrows to bring moisture to the surface and to break up the soil after a rainfall to prevent evaporation.

New technologies aided the Department of Agriculture's efforts to improve Plains farms. To tap water deep underground, farmers adapted drilling machinery developed by petroleum companies. Farmers also used new models of windmills—wind-powered water pumps designed to withstand the strong winds of the Plains.

New farm equipment also helped the Plains farmers. James Oliver's plow factory in South Bend, Indiana, produced thousands of plows with sharp, durable blades that could slice through the tough sod of the Plains. "Self-binding" harvesters not only cut wheat but also tied it into bundles. The combine—a sort of factory on wheels—cut wheat, separated the grain from the plant, and cleaned the grain all in one operation.

■■ Government support, innovative farming practices, and new technologies helped make farming on the Plains possible.

*L*ARGE–SCALE FARMING

Efficient new farm machinery and cheap, abundant land enabled some companies to create a new kind of large-scale operation, the **bonanza farm**. Most bonanza farms were owned by large companies and run like factories, with professional managers, laborers for different tasks, and machinery. Because these large farms required from 500 to 1,000 extra workers at planting and harvesting times, most owners divided their vast enterprises into smaller units, with a foreman in charge of each.

The first bonanza farms were established in the Red River Valley in Dakota Territory and Minnesota in the mid-1870s after the completion of the Northern Pacific Railroad. Investors also organized bonanza farms as far west as California.

In California's Central Valley one of the largest wheat farms covered more than 66,000 acres, stretching for 16 miles along the Sacramento River. Although California led the country in wheat production in the 1880s, by the 1890s most farmers there had turned to more-profitable fruit and vegetable crops. Refrigerated railcars allowed California farmers to ship these crops across the country.

The era of bonanza farming soon faded. When weather conditions were favorable, bonanza farms produced large profits because of lower production costs. Since bonanza-farm owners bought seed and equipment in bulk, suppliers often gave them special deals. But in times of severe drought or low wheat prices, bonanza-farm profits fell. Family farmers, who had fewer workers to pay and less money invested in equipment, could better handle boom-and-bust cycles. Thus by the 1890s

▲ Farmers settled in areas throughout the Great Plains. Shown here is the Ellefson family outside their home in Hendricks, Minnesota.

most bonanza farms had been broken up into smaller farms.

■■ **New farm machinery, cheap land, and high wheat prices allowed bonanza farms to flourish for a time in Dakota Territory, Minnesota, and California.**

𝔉ARM LIFE ON THE PLAINS

Farm families on the Plains faced many problems for which inventors, manufacturers, and agricultural experts had no ready answers. For example, sod houses, though well insulated, windproof, and fireproof, were also dank, dirty, and far from rainproof. One woman described her efforts to keep herself and her baby dry in their sod house during a spring rainstorm:

❝ The house leaked so badly that we rolled the bedding up and tied it with a rope, and put the oil cloth from the table over it to keep it dry. I put the baby on top of the roll and put the parasol over it to keep her dry. Soon the rain ran off the ribs of the parasol and soaked around the baby so I fixed a place for her in the cupboard shelf—the only dry place in the house. I walked around with a slicker, a man's hat and overshoes to keep dry. ❞

Moreover, winter on the Plains brought blizzards and bone-chilling cold. A Kansas settler wrote:

❝ The cold is a fierce north wind which will freeze man or beast. . . . [At night] my eyelids froze together so I picked off the ice, [and] the tops of the sheets and quilts . . . were frozen stiff with [our] breath. . . . We had not bedclothes enough to keep us warm and we piled on everything in the house. ❞

Summer on the Plains could be just as fierce. Settlers described droughts during which "the earth opened in great cracks several inches across and two feet deep," and "the leaves on the trees shriveled and dried up, and every living thing was seeking shelter from the hot rays of the sun." Summer also brought cloudbursts and tornadoes. In the 1870s farmers faced swarms of grasshoppers that devoured everything in their path. Farmers killed thousands of the greedy insects, but to little

◀ Plains women spent many long hours in the fields. Shown here is Ella Sly, who filed a homestead claim in Kansas in 1893.

effect. Moaned one homesteader: "Two new grasshoppers arrived to attend each dead one's funeral."

Even in good times, Plains farming demanded hard work from everyone in the family. Men did most of the heavy labor of building houses, fencing the land, and farming. Women, in addition to household and child-rearing tasks, often spent hours in the fields. Writing to her family in the East, one woman explained that she had been her husband's "sole help in getting up and stacking at least 25 tons of hay and oats." She might also have been responsible for tending farm animals, caring for a garden plot, and preserving fruits and vegetables.

Children had to do their share, too. They fetched water, tended gardens, and did such routine chores as churning butter. One farmer described how his two-year-old son, Baz, could "run all over, fetch up cows out of the stock fields, or oxen, carry in stove wood and climb in the corn crib and feed the hogs and go on errands down to his grandma's [house]."

 BIO GRAPHY Writer Hamlin Garland described the hardships of Plains farming. Garland's father had moved from Maine to Wisconsin, where Garland was born in 1860. To his father, as Garland put it, "change was alluring," and he moved his family to Iowa and later to Dakota Territory.

Hating the drudgery of farm work, young Garland moved east to Boston. He got a job as a teacher and educated himself by reading widely. But it was a trip back to the Plains in 1887 that determined his future. He now saw through an adult's eyes the land in which he had grown up. "Nature was as beautiful as ever," he wrote, but it could not "conceal the poverty of these people, . . . the gracelessness of these homes, and the . . . mechanical daily routine of these lives." Garland wrote about his experiences to a friend, who replied, "You're the first actual farmer in American fiction—now tell the truth about it."

Hamlin Garland

The Granger Collection, New York

Garland's collection of short stories, *Main-Travelled Roads,* published in 1891, stressed the difficulties of farm life on the Plains. The book's bitterness offended many readers, who imagined farmers as happy tillers of the soil. In later years, however, this book and other works of Garland's—especially his autobiography, *A Son of the Middle Border* (1917)—won admiration for their straightforward honesty.

Difficulties overwhelmed many western farmers, forcing some to abandon their farms. But thousands stayed, forming successful communities, with churches and schools, newspapers and clubs, and even theaters and concert halls. Though harvests might be poor one year, there was always hope for better luck the next year.

SECTION 2 REVIEW

IDENTIFY and explain the significance of the following: Homestead Act, Pacific Railway Act, Morrill Act, Exodusters, U.S. Department of Agriculture, dry farming, bonanza farm, Hamlin Garland.

LOCATE and explain the importance of the following: Central Pacific Railroad, Union Pacific Railroad.

1. **MAIN IDEA** Why did farmers move to the West in the late 19th century in such great numbers?

2. **MAIN IDEA** How were farmers able to adapt to the western environments?

3. **GEOGRAPHY: LOCATION** Where did bonanza farmers establish their operations? Why did these large-scale farms flourish and then fade?

4. **WRITING TO DESCRIBE** Imagine you are a member of an Exoduster family in Kansas in the late 1800s. Write a journal entry describing why you left the South and came to Kansas.

5. **EVALUATING** How might the development of the Great Plains have been different if the government and the railroads had not been involved?

THE CATTLE BOOM

FOCUS

- **What factors led to a cattle boom during the 1870s and 1880s?**
- **What was ranch life like for cowboys?**
- **What factors brought about the end of the cattle boom?**

Cattle ranchers were eager to use western lands that the government had originally reserved for Native Americans. Although Mexican settlers had been raising cattle since the 1600s, the boom era for cattle ranching arrived only after the Civil War, when railroads linked the West with growing eastern markets. The two-decade boom created cattle towns and new stresses on the Great Plains environment.

Female broncobuster

THE RISE OF THE CATTLE INDUSTRY

The earliest ranchers in the American West were Spaniards, who first imported cattle from Spain in the 1500s. By the 1850s English cattle brought to Texas by Americans interbred with Spanish cattle to produce a new breed—the **Texas longhorn**. Although their meat was tough and stringy, longhorns were hardy. They could travel long distances on little water and live year-round on grass. Equally important, longhorns were immune to a tick-born cattle disease called Texas fever.

Texas cattle ranching grew rapidly after the Civil War, spreading over the Great Plains as the buffalo vanished. As eastern cities grew, so did the demand for beef. In 1866 a steer that would bring about $4 in Texas could be sold for $40 or $50 in eastern markets.

A major problem was moving the cattle from Texas, where most of the earliest ranches were, to rail lines in Missouri and Kansas. To reach the railroads, cowboys herded as many as 3,000 cattle on **long drives**, overland treks that covered hundreds of miles and could take as long as two to four months. The long drives usually ended in Missouri. But Missouri farmers objected: unlike the longhorn, their cattle were not immune to Texas fever. Because of this opposition, later long drives avoided Missouri and headed for less-populated towns in Kansas. Over the years of the long drives, cowboys herded some four million cattle from Texas to Kansas.

On a typical long drive, a trail boss managed a crew of about 10 cowboys. The cook in the chuck wagon, which carried food and the cowboys' bedrolls, rode in front of the herd.

◄ **Trail bosses were responsible for the welfare of both cattle and cowboys during the many weeks it usually took to move a herd to a rail line.**

Railroads and Cattle Trails, 1870–1890

ROUTES TO THE WEST The railroads sped passengers and goods across the United States. Linked to western ranches by the cattle trails, the railroads made it possible for ranchers to ship cattle to eastern markets.

? LOCATION Which rail lines formed the first transcontinental route?

Rope and branding iron

On May 10, 1869, Leland Stanford drove the golden spike marking the completion of the first transcontinental railroad.

Legend:
- Cattle trail
- Transcontinental railroad
- Railroad

Managing the herd was a tough job, with the cowboys setting a brisk pace. Crossing rivers, where swift currents might drown hundreds of animals, posed one hazard. But the worst danger was a stampede. Almost any sound—a coyote's wail, a thunderclap, a sneeze—could panic the cattle.

■ **The cattle boom developed after the Civil War, when new railroads linked western ranges to growing eastern markets.**

CATTLE TOWNS

Every long drive ended at a **railhead**, a town located along a railroad. Here, brokers bought cattle and shipped them east. The railhead stops came to be known as cattle towns; the best known were the Kansas towns of Abilene, Ellsworth, and Dodge City. Farther north and west, long drives later ended in Cheyenne, Wyoming, and Ogallala, Nebraska.

At first a typical cattle town consisted of little more than a railroad depot, a stockyard, a hotel or boardinghouse, and a general store. But if the town attracted enough cattle business, it grew. Cattle towns bustled with activity from spring to fall, when the long drives took place. Cattle brokers, railroad men, and cowboys, who were paid at the end of the long drives, were eager to spend their money. Gambling halls, saloons, clothing stores, and barbershops were just as eager to take it. As the cattle towns prospered, they attracted more businesspeople, as well as doctors, lawyers, teachers, and their families.

In a cattle town's early years, the scarcity of labor provided many opportunities for both adults and children. Because of the high demand for lodging and food, many women took in boarders or opened restaurants. Some children worked as clerks or bookkeepers in the growing businesses.

Once families arrived, the cattle towns built schools and hired police forces to keep order. Reformers, many of them women, set out to civilize the rough cowboy towns by organizing poor-relief and temperance societies. Their calls for prohibition, however, met with little success as long as cattle town economies depended on gambling halls and saloons.

RANCH PROFITS

As the government converted more Indian territory into public lands, cattle ranching spread west into New Mexico and Colorado and north into Kansas, Nebraska, the Dakotas, Wyoming, and Montana. The government allowed cattle ranchers to use the public land as **open range**, or free grazing land. Access to free pasture land made cattle ranching profitable. The introduction of higher-grade cattle breeds from the East and from Europe led to even bigger profits.

Although many families established ranches, it was mainly large investment companies that took advantage of the government's offer of land. Financed by eastern and European investors, these companies created huge ranches. In 1883, for example, some 20 such companies invested $12 million in Wyoming alone.

Most ranches covered thousands of acres. Large ranches were essential because cattle on the semiarid Plains needed much grazing land to get enough feed. Ranches also needed access to water; streams, lakes, and rivers determined the size and location of ranches. "Wherever there is any water, there is a ranch," noted a Colorado cattleman.

▪▪ Cattle ranching was profitable because of high beef prices and access to free grazing land.

Sheep ranching, which was also introduced by the Spanish, was an important economic activity in the West. Native American groups, including the Pueblos and Navajos, raised sheep in New Mexico and Arizona. After the California gold rush began, sheep by the thousands were herded to California to feed the hungry miners.

Basque shepherds, originally from southwestern France and north-central Spain, immigrated from South America and ranged flocks of sheep in California. By 1900 there were some 10,000 Basques in the West.

RANCH LIFE

Both cattle and sheep ranches demanded intense effort from ranch families. Everyone had to work to make sure the ranch prospered. A Texas sheriff explained that ranch owners "got right out with the boys on the trail" and "did just as much work."

This description also applied to women, who played an integral role in daily ranch life. On most ranches, women did housework, cooked for all the hired cowboys, and helped out with fence-mending, herding, or other chores. Many women organized their own ranch-related businesses. Ella Bird, for example, accumulated her first herd of cattle by selling hand-sewn leather gloves and vests to cowboys in exchange for yearlings.

▼ **Women were responsible for a number of chores on a ranch, including branding cattle. The Becker sisters are shown on their ranch in Colorado's San Luis Valley in 1894.**

Because ranches were far apart, loneliness took its toll. Susan Newcomb, a Texas ranch wife, described the loneliness of ranch life:

    66 A man that is cowhunting with a lively crowd has no idea how long and lonesome the time passes with his wife at home. . . . A man can see his friends, hear the news and pass time . . . , while his wife is at home and sees and hears nothing until he returns from a long trip tired and worn out. **99**

Ranch children often took on adult responsibilities at a young age. In addition to doing chores around the house, some children, both boys and girls, broke horses and herded cattle. Many enjoyed the freedom, though. Ralla Banta, who spent her childhood on a Texas ranch, remembered, "When we returned home in the evening we enjoyed telling where we had been, to what creek, up what branch and what we had seen." Others hated the boredom. John Norton, a young cowboy, noted that he and his brother "leaped with joy" when the cattle they were herding were finally shipped for slaughter.

Ranch life centered on the roundup. Each spring and fall, ranchers, with the help of hired cowboys, drove their cattle from the open range to some central spot. Here cowboys from each ranch "cut out," or separated, the cattle, identified by each ranch's distinctive brand. The cattle would then be rounded up for the long drive to a railhead.

Later, books, movies, and radio and television programs romanticized the life of the cowboys. Actually, their life was difficult: they worked hard in all kinds of weather and made little money. The long drives also kept them away from their families for long periods. Most cowboys worked the range for only about seven years before they settled down in towns or on farms.

▶ **Ex-slave Nat Love, also known as Deadwood Dick, claimed to have carried the marks of 14 bullet wounds on his body, "any one of which would be sufficient to kill an ordinary man."**

▲ *Vaqueros of California Roping Horses in a Corral* is the title of this 1877 painting by James Walker.

Many of the white cowboys were Confederate veterans of the Civil War. About a third of the some 35,000 cowboys were African American, Mexican, or Mexican American. Some of the African American cowboys had been brought west as slaves before the Civil War. With their experience handling longhorns, they got jobs as ranch hands after emancipation. Other black cowboys moved west after the war. In an era when most African Americans faced harsh segregation, life for a black cowboy was relatively free of discrimination. He worked, bunked, and ate alongside fellow cowboys and received the same wages they did.

Long before the days of the cattle boom, Mexican *vaqueros* had developed many ranching practices. In the 1880s most Mexican and Mexican American cowboys worked on South and West Texas ranches. They were often sons of ranchers or farmers, and sometimes owned their own ranches. Although they were paid higher wages and treated better than those who handled menial ranch jobs, Mexican cowboys faced discrimination. Many Anglo ranchers considered them inferior to Anglo cowboys. Mexican cowboys were not allowed to supervise non-Mexicans, and they worked and lived separately from Anglo cowboys.

:: Ranch life was difficult for cowboys, who worked long hours outdoors in all kinds of weather.

THE END OF THE CATTLE BOOM

The cattle boom lasted only about 20 years. Several factors led to its early end. First, ranchers eager to make large profits filled the open range with too many cattle. This led to overgrazing, which damaged the grasslands. The vast herds also

▲ Barbed wire not only helped cattlemen protect their land, but also kept homesteaders away from valuable sources of water. This 1885 photograph shows a group of homesteaders cutting down wire fences.

following year, terrible blizzards struck the northern Plains. When cowboys could finally venture out of their bunkhouses, they found the remains of thousands of starved and frozen cattle. Ranchers suffered devastating losses, some losing as much as 90 percent of their herds.

▪▪ Boom times for cattle ranchers came to an end because of overgrazing, fencing of the open range, and bad weather.

By the 1890s the open-range cattle boom was over. Some of the big corporations went broke. With the end of the open range, ranchers had to buy their own range land. They also had to invest more in their operations. Learning from the blizzards of the mid-1880s, they began to raise hay to feed to their cattle during the harsh winters. Sheep ranching expanded, since sheep could survive on the weeds that replaced the native grasses. The long drives ended, and the cattle towns settled down. So did many of the cowboys. A popular song of the time ended with these words:

> 66 Good-by, old trail boss, I wish you
> no harm;
> I'm quittin' this business to go on
> the farm.
> I'll sell my old saddle and buy me
> a plow;
> And never, no, never will I rope
> another cow. 99

increased the supply of beef, driving down prices—and profits. Prices crashed in 1885, as supply far exceeded demand.

Second, open-range ranching declined after the invention of barbed wire. Joseph Glidden patented this cheap method of fencing in 1874. By the 1880s farmers and cattle ranchers had erected miles of spiky networks across the open range to control access to land and water. As overgrazing thinned the grass cover, cattle needed access to more pasture lands to survive. But fencing limited the amount of open land available.

Bad weather dealt the final blow. On the southern Plains a severe winter in 1885–86 and a drought in 1886 diminished many herds. The

SECTION 3 REVIEW

IDENTIFY and explain the significance of the following: Texas longhorn, long drives, railhead, open range, Basques, Joseph Glidden.

LOCATE and explain the importance of the following: Abilene, Kansas; Dodge City, Kansas; Cheyenne, Wyoming; Ogallala, Nebraska.

1. **MAIN IDEA** What factors allowed cattle ranching to be so profitable during the boom period?

2. **MAIN IDEA** What was cowboy life like?

3. **MAIN IDEA** What factors caused the decline of the cattle boom in the West in the late 19th century?

4. **WRITING TO INFORM** Imagine you grew up on a cattle ranch in the 1890s. Write a brief narrative about the joys and difficulties of ranch life.

5. **SYNTHESIZING** What contributions did the Spanish and Basques make to cattle and sheep ranching?

Section 4

A MINING BOOM

FOCUS

- **Where did important mining discoveries take place in the late 1800s?**
- **How did early mining camps differ from more-developed mining towns?**
- **Why did mining become big business?**

Ever since the forty-niners had flocked to California after the discovery of gold in the Sierra Nevada, miners from all over the world had been drawn to the American West. After the richest California diggings were claimed, hundreds of forty-niners moved eastward and northward into the Rockies and beyond. A few individuals prospered from new mineral discoveries. But large mining companies reaped the greatest profits.

Chinese miner in Alaska

WESTERN MINING

The first promising mining discoveries after the California gold rush were made in Colorado. Prospectors found gold near Pikes Peak late in 1858. By early 1859 thousands of people flocked to Colorado. Many of them, however, left in disappointment by midsummer.

Another center of frantic prospecting in 1859 was the Carson River Valley in present-day Nevada. In addition to gold, the area contained the famous **Comstock Lode**, one of the world's richest silver veins. Over 20 years its mines yielded more than $500 million worth of precious metals.

Some miners turned south into Arizona, where Hispanics had been mining silver since the mid-1700s. Hispanics introduced mining methods that had been developed in Mexico and South America. These included a mill for separating gold from quartz and the *patio* **process**—which used mercury to extract silver from the ore. The

newer arrivals used these methods to mine the Comstock Lode and in the region around Tucson. Others, trekking northward, made strikes in Idaho and Montana.

By the late 1850s others had pushed even farther north, into the Fraser River Valley of British Columbia. This movement into Canada had important consequences for Russia and the United States. Russia, which at the time owned Alaska, feared a territorial dispute with the United States. To avoid this, the Russians offered to sell Alaska to the Americans. U.S. Secretary of State William H. Seward negotiated the purchase of Alaska in 1867 for $7,200,000—about two cents an acre. Many Americans considered Alaska worthless, calling the purchase "Seward's Folly."

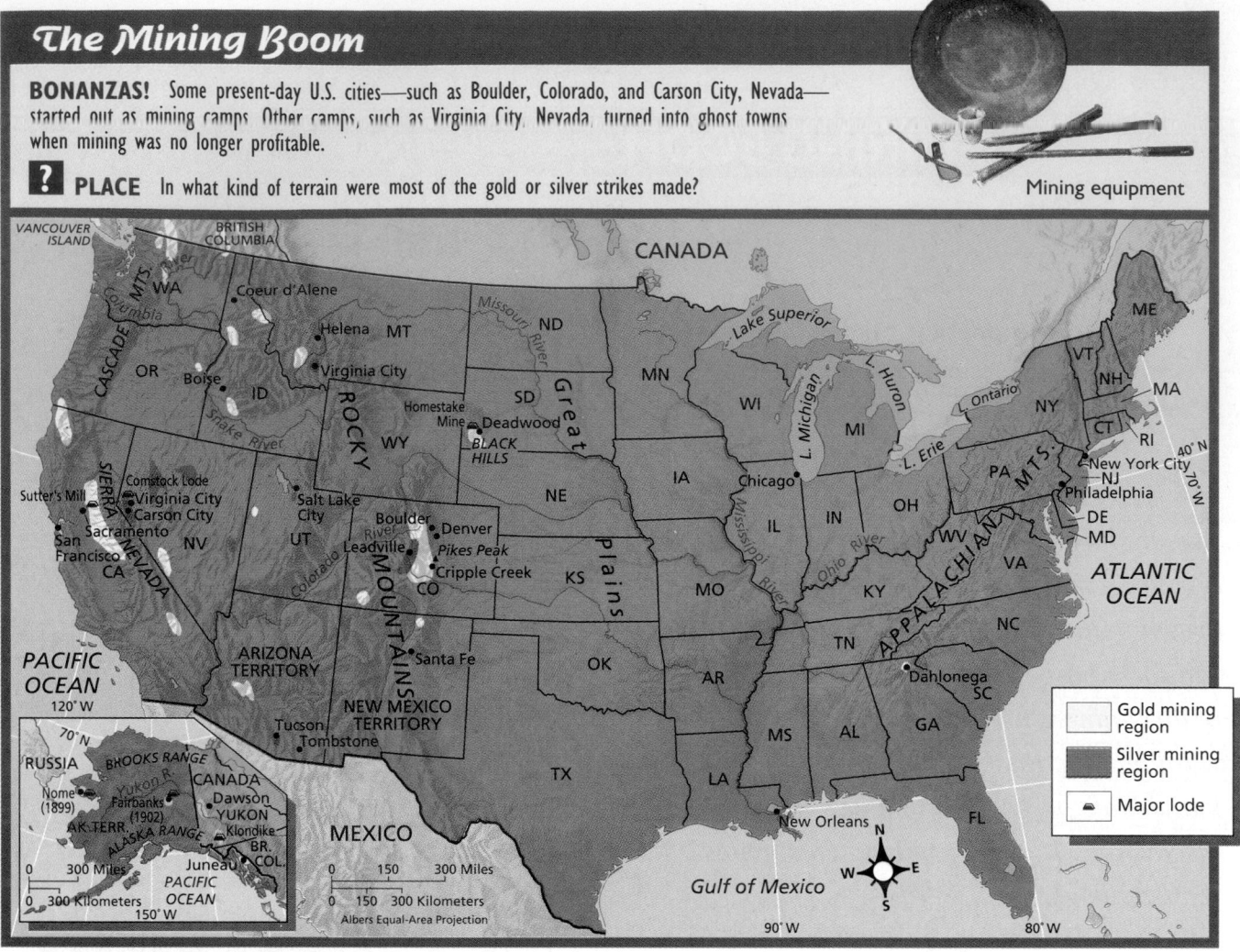

The Mining Boom

BONANZAS! Some present-day U.S. cities—such as Boulder, Colorado, and Carson City, Nevada—started out as mining camps. Other camps, such as Virginia City, Nevada, turned into ghost towns when mining was no longer profitable.

? **PLACE** In what kind of terrain were most of the gold or silver strikes made?

Mining equipment

Gold mining region
Silver mining region
Major lode

But Seward's confidence that Alaska "possesses treasures . . . equal to those of any other region of the continent" would prove correct. In 1896, prospectors discovered gold in the Klondike district of Canada's Yukon Territory, which bordered Alaska. This discovery launched the **Klondike Gold Rush**. By the summer of 1897, Yukon miners had extracted gold deposits worth more than a million dollars. From 1897 to 1899 almost 100,000 people traveled through Alaska to seek their fortunes in the Klondike. Gold discoveries in Alaska in 1898 and 1902 attracted settlers, who later established fish canneries, lumber companies, and coal and copper mining enterprises.

■■ **Mining booms attracted prospectors to present-day Colorado, Nevada, Arizona, Idaho, Montana, and Alaska.**

LIFE IN MINING COMMUNITIES

Mining camps grew up almost overnight wherever news of possible wealth brought prospectors together. Most mining communities started out inhabited almost entirely by men. Unlike ranching or farming, prospecting generally was not a family enterprise.

Mining camps drew a wide range of settlers. In the mining zones of southern California in the 1860s, Mexicans, Californios, Chileans, and Peruvians formed their own separate settlements. In other mining regions, the sometimes uneasy mixture of prospectors included U.S. citizens from all parts of the country, Irish and Chinese men who had come to work on the railroads, and miners from the Cornwall region of England. Some were drawn by the lure of quick wealth; others were fleeing difficult circumstances.

▲ The lure of gold and silver drew many families to the mining camps of the West. This photograph of an African American mining family in Colorado was taken in the late 19th century.

At first, life in the mining camps was crude and comforts were few. J. Ross Browne described the first shelters of Virginia City, Nevada:

66 Frame shanties, pitched together as if by accident; tents of canvas, of blankets, of brush, of potato sacks and old shirts, with empty whisky-barrels for chimneys; smoky hovels of mud and stone; coyote holes in the mountain side forcibly seized and held by men. 99

Moreover, the atmosphere in most camps was one of intense competition. Prospector William Parsons remembered

66 . . . a mad, furious race for wealth, in which men lost their identity almost, and toiled and wrestled, and lived a fierce, riotous, wearing, fearfully excited life; forgetting home and kindred; abandoning old, steady habits. 99

Competition sometimes led to violence in the mining camps. Conflicts arose between different ethnic groups. Miners in the Cripple Creek camp in Colorado forcibly excluded eastern and southern Europeans as well as Hispanics. In other camps, Cornish miners fought with Irish, German, and Chinese miners. Gamblers and con men swarmed in, and conflicts over claims set off brawls and gunfights. The mining town of Deadwood in South Dakota gained a reputation as an especially rough town. An outlaw's haven, Deadwood became the final resting place of lawman Wild Bill Hickok, shot dead as he played cards.

But stability eventually came to the mining camps as they grew into towns. Mining towns attracted a host of businesses eager to feed and clothe the miners. In fact, owners of saloons and stores were more apt to strike it rich than miners. Cooking, cleaning, and providing lodging were especially lucrative. One industrious woman "earnt . . . nine hundred dollars in nine weeks, clear of all expenses, by washing!" Elizabeth Collins, who later became known as the "cattle queen of Montana," was offered a job as cook for 18 men at a Montana mining camp. She later wrote: "Prompted by kindness and a desire to see these hardworking men as comfortable as possible—also craving for the $75 per month—I promptly accepted the offer."

The few children in the camps had unique roles. They hunted for gold dust and stray nuggets under sidewalks or panned and scavenged for gold dust after the miners were done for the day. Much more profitable, however, was selling fresh food to the miners, who quickly grew tired of eating canned food. One brother and sister made $800 one summer selling butter and bacon to the miners.

As more families moved into the camps, many camps turned into permanent communities. With prosperity came law and order and the establishment of schools, hospitals, churches, newspapers, and even debating societies and singing clubs. Denver and Boulder, Colorado; Carson City, Nevada; Boise, Idaho; and Helena, Montana all started out as mining camps.

■■ At first, mining camps were crude and often violent. With prosperity, however, came families, community life, and law and order.

▲ As settlement grew in the West, so did the need for schools. Blanche Lamont posed with members of her school at Hecla, Montana, in October 1893.

THE WILD WEST

Fantastic stories about the untamed western lands of the United States could be heard far from America's shores in the late 1800s. Fascination with outlaw gangs, shoot-outs, and man-eating wild animals lured many European travelers to America to see for themselves. But the "Wild West" rarely lived up to its reputation. Windham T. Dunraven, a British earl, wrote about what he did *not* find in the American West:

❝I *never have an adventure worth a cent; nobody ever scalps me; I don't get 'jumped' by highwaymen. It never occurs to a bear to hug me, and my very appearance inspires feelings of dismay or disgust in the breast of the puma or mountain lion. It is true that I have often been horribly frightened, but generally without any adequate cause.* **❞**

MINING AS BIG BUSINESS

Individual prospectors roaming the West with their pack horses and hand tools made the earliest mining discoveries, or strikes. But the day of the lone miner did not last long. Within a few years after a strike, most of the easily accessible mineral deposits were "worked out." To get at the hidden ore, miners had to use one of two methods: (1) **hydraulic mining**, which used water pressure to wash away mountains of gravel and expose the minerals underneath; or (2) **hard-rock mining**, which involved sinking deep shafts to get at ore locked in veins of quartz.

Both of these methods required considerable sums of money—far beyond the resources of individual prospectors. Thus mining became the province of large, well-financed companies. These companies relied on science rather than on instinct or luck. Corps of college-educated engineers helped locate the ore and instructed the companies on how best to extract the minerals in demand by eastern factories—zinc, lead, copper, and iron.

The federal government also helped develop mineral resources. It sent out several western expeditions in the 1860s. In 1879 the government organized the U.S. Geological Survey, which gathered and coordinated data about new mines.

■■ **As mineral deposits became harder and more expensive to locate and extract, big business dominated mining.**

Big mining companies also changed working conditions in the mines. The big companies used new machinery and hired armies of laborers to carry out the dirty, dangerous work. These laborers sank the shafts, built the tunnels, drilled, and processed the ore. Miners, no longer spurred on by the hope of sudden riches, grew dissatisfied with wages and working conditions.

In some communities miners formed unions. Dues paid to the unions often helped workers injured in the dangerous mines or assisted the families of miners killed on the job. Unions also negotiated with or fought against owners who tried to cut wages. Many also fought against the hiring of Chinese miners, who received lower wages. Union resistance to wage cuts proved most effective during boom times. In the early 1880s, union miners at the Comstock Lode successfully maintained their four-dollar-a-day salaries and eight-hour workdays.

▼ **New mining techniques removed ore quickly from the ground, but also eroded entire hillsides.**

When mining became big business, the land suffered. In their haste to extract ore, mining companies often ignored the environmental impact of their practices. Hydraulic mining leveled mountains and often left barren, eroded hills in its wake. Hydraulic mining dumped tons of earth and rocks into rivers, thus raising riverbeds and causing flooding. Flooding in some areas swept away towns and destroyed farmland. Hard-rock mining companies also destroyed forests to get wood for mine shafts.

COMMENTARY

Western Myths

The solitary miner, prospecting for gold on a remote mountain stream, is a well-known character in books, movies, and television programs. So is the cowboy who rides off alone into the sunset. Almost equally familiar is the farm or ranch family in its isolated home on the vast, empty plains. All these legendary western figures represent the American ideal of rugged individuals conquering barren and uninhabited land. But these images, while powerful, are inaccurate.

Most westerners, including cowboys on ranches and prospectors in mining camps, worked for or with others. The lands where ranchers or farmers grazed their cattle or sheep had already been settled for centuries by Native American or Hispanic farmers, ranchers, or hunters. Mining camps were crowded and noisy places, and most were established on or near lands inhabited by Hispanics or Native Americans. And the large companies, not the independent ranchers, farmers, or miners, generally made the biggest profits.

Furthermore, Americans who settled the West could not have survived without the help of the federal government. The U.S. Army opened by force Native American land for non-Indian settlement. The army also maintained forts to guard trails and protect settlements. The Department of the Interior, through its Bureau of Indian Affairs, resettled Native Americans and ran the reservations on which it placed them. The General Land Office disposed of public land at low rates, while Congress subsidized railroad development. The Department of Agriculture helped Plains farmers, and the Geological Survey aided mining interests.

Novels, songs, and traveling shows spread the myth of the "Wild West" as a region of outlaws, lone cowboys, and isolated pioneers. In reality, men and women lived and worked together in a West shaped as much by technology, big business, and the federal government.

SECTION 4 REVIEW

IDENTIFY and explain the significance of the following: Comstock Lode, *patio* process, William H. Seward, Klondike Gold Rush, hydraulic mining, hard-rock mining.

LOCATE and explain the importance of the following: Pikes Peak; Yukon Territory; Deadwood, South Dakota.

1. **MAIN IDEA** How did later mining camps differ from earlier mining camps?

2. **MAIN IDEA** Why did mining become the domain of large companies?

3. **GEOGRAPHY: LOCATION** Where did the most important mining discoveries take place in the late 19th century?

4. **WRITING TO EXPLAIN** Write an essay contrasting the myth of the rugged individual of the West with the lives of real westerners in the late 19th century.

5. **EVALUATING** How did western mining affect the environment?

Sand Creek Massacre occurs.

Treaty of Medicine Lodge signed. Seward negotiates purchase of Alaska.

The Homestead Act passed.

Second Treaty of Fort Laramie signed.

First transcontinental railroad completed

1860   1865   1870

WRITING A SUMMARY

Using the essential points of the chapter as a guide, write a summary of the chapter.

REVIEWING CHRONOLOGY

Number your paper 1 to 5. Study the time line above, and list the following events in the order in which they happened by writing the first next to 1, the second next to 2, and so on. Then complete the activity.

1. Beef prices crash.
2. Exodusters trek west.
3. First transcontinental railroad completed.
4. Battle of Little Bighorn occurs.
5. The Homestead Act passed.

Identifying Cause and Effect Select two events on the time line, and in a paragraph, explain the cause-and-effect relationship between them.

IDENTIFYING PEOPLE AND IDEAS

Explain the historical significance of each of the following people or terms.

1. Long Walk
2. Sitting Bull
3. Sarah Winnemucca
4. Pacific Railway Act
5. Exodusters
6. long drives
7. Basques
8. Comstock Lode
9. William H. Seward
10. hydraulic mining

UNDERSTANDING MAIN IDEAS

1. What caused settlers to travel to the West in the late 19th century?
2. How did farm life differ from life in the early mining camps?
3. In what areas were key mining sites and bonanza farms developed?
4. How had the businesses of cattle ranching and mining changed by the late 1890s?

REVIEWING THEMES

1. **Geographic Diversity** How did western farmers adapt to the weather and environment?
2. **Cultural Diversity** What problems arose from the federal government's attempt to assimilate Native Americans?

3. **Economic Development** How did the U.S. government promote western land development and settlement?

THINKING CRITICALLY

1. **Hypothesizing** How might Helen Hunt Jackson's *A Century of Dishonor* or Hamlin Garland's *Main-Travelled Roads* have shaped public opinion in the late 1800s?
2. **Evaluating** What positive and negative consequences resulted from development of the West?
3. **Synthesizing** How did different cultures influence one another in the West?

STRATEGY FOR SUCCESS

Review the Strategies for Success on Comparing Points of View on page 420. Then read the selections below. In the first selection, Priscilla Merriam Evans describes some of her responsibilities on a farm in Utah. In the second, author Hamlin Garland describes his mother's life. Compare and contrast their points of view.

66 We made our own cloth, which was mostly gray in color, for dresses. . . . With . . . Indigo . . . and other roots, I have colored beautiful fast colors. We were kept busy in those days carding, spinning, knitting, and doing all of our own sewing by hand. 99

66 All her toilsome, monotonous days rushed through my mind with a roar like a file of gray birds in the night . . . how tragically small her joys, and how black her sorrows, her toil, her tedium. 99

WRITING ABOUT HISTORY

Writing to Express a Viewpoint Imagine you are a prospector in a small mining camp. Write a speech expressing your views about the growth of big mining companies.

Joseph Glidden patents barbed wire. Gold discovered in Black Hills.

Battle of Little Bighorn occurs.

Exodusters trek west. U.S. Geological Survey organized.

Helen Hunt Jackson publishes *A Century of Dishonor.*

Beef prices crash.

Dawes General Allotment Act passed.

Wounded Knee Massacre occurs.

Hamlin Garland publishes *Main-Travelled Roads.*

Gold discovered in Yukon Territory.

1875   1880   1885   1890   1895

USING PRIMARY SOURCES

The following excerpt is from "Chief Joseph's Own Story," an 1879 account by the Nez Percé leader who had long been committed to peaceful relations with non-Indians. Based on the selection below, how did Chief Joseph's expectations differ from the reality of U.S. policies toward Native Americans?

> *We only ask an even chance to live as other men live. We asked to be recognized as men. We ask that the same law shall work alike on all men. . . .*
>
> *Let me be a free man—free to travel, free to stop, free to work, free to trade where I choose, free to choose my own teachers, free to follow the religion of my fathers, free to think and talk and act for myself—and I will obey every law, or submit to the penalty.*
>
> *Whenever the white man treats the Indian as they treat each other, then we shall have no more wars. We shall be all alike— brothers of one father and one mother, with one sky above us and one country around us, and one government for all. Then the Great Spirit Chief who rules above will smile upon this land, and send rain to wash out the bloody spots made by brothers' hands upon the face of the earth.*

Chief Joseph

LINKING HISTORY AND GEOGRAPHY

Review the map on page 445. What areas did railroad lines open to non-Indian settlers in this period, and how did the railroads foster development of these areas?

Railroad station, c.1870s

BUILDING YOUR PORTFOLIO

Complete the following projects independently or cooperatively.

1. **SOCIAL CONFLICT** Imagine you are a Sioux living on the Pine Ridge Reservation in South Dakota in 1895. Compose for your grandchildren an oral account that describes how conflict between the Sioux and farmers, ranchers, and miners has affected your life and the lives of other Sioux. Be sure to work in details of the conflict.

2. **TECHNOLOGY AND INDUSTRY** Imagine you are a land speculator who hopes to establish a small railhead in Nebraska. Prepare a plan for the town that shows the businesses and other public buildings—stockyard, rail station, church, school, and so on—you will include to attract residents.

THE TRANSFORMATION OF AMERICA

FOCUS

UNDERSTANDING THE MAIN IDEA

New technologies and new forms of business organization helped usher in a second industrial age in late–19th-century America. Millions of immigrants came to the United States in this period, lured by the prospect of work. By 1900 these developments had transformed the United States into an urban nation and an industrial power.

THEMES

■ **ECONOMIC DEVELOP-MENT** How might technological change affect a nation's economy?

■ **TECHNOLOGY AND SOCIETY** What role might technology play in social change?

■ **CULTURAL DIVERSITY** What challenges might an influx of people with different ways of life present to a community?

1867	1876	1879	1882	1889
Christopher Sholes invents typewriter.	**Alexander Graham Bell patents telephone.**	**Frank W. Woolworth founds first of his chain stores.**	**Congress passes Chinese Exclusion Act.**	**Jane Addams establishes Hull House.**

Industrialization and immigration helped fuel the growth of the United States in the first half of the 1800s. However, the United States remained primarily a rural nation whose people continued to depend on agriculture for a living.

Immigrants arriving from Germany

In the second half of the 1800s, the United States underwent another wave of industrialization. To many this process seemed almost a natural outcome of American life. "The American mechanizes as an old Greek sculptured, as the Venetian painted," the London *Times* noted in 1878. A debate quickly developed, however, over whether the negative side effects of industrialization—such as grinding poverty existing side-by-side with great wealth—were natural outcomes as well.

Critical of the new industrial order, economist Henry George condemned the growing contrast "between the House of Have and the House of Want." He argued that the poor should not have to suffer so that a few could be rich. Yale professor William Graham Sumner took the opposite view, claiming that the rich and the poor were just where nature intended and that any change would slow progress and harm society. Not all industrialists agreed with Sumner. Some proposed that they use part of their wealth to benefit all of society. But social reformer Frederic Howe argued that if industrialists really had the well-being of society at heart, they "would stop the twelve-hour day . . . increase wages and put an end to the cruel killing and maiming" of workers. Although this debate produced no solid answers about how to reconcile the existence of poverty in the midst of great wealth, it did lead to efforts to reform the worst abuses of the industrial order.

The Edison phonograph

INDUSTRY'S GOLDEN AGE

FOCUS

- What roles did steel, railroads, and innovations in communications and energy play in the new industrial order?
- How did businesses increase their profits in the late 19th century?
- How did the government attempt to regulate business?

From 1865 to 1910 the United States experienced a surge of industrial growth. These decades witnessed the beginnings of a "second industrial revolution." A "new industrial order" was created with the development of cheap steel, the completion of a nationwide rail network, the invention of the telephone and the typewriter, the introduction of new sources of energy, and the rise of big business.

First telephone, 1876

TECHNOLOGICAL INNOVATIONS

America's first industrial revolution was dependent on coal and steam. Coal-fed steam engines powered the factories, which produced the goods that generated economic growth. But it was steel—not steam—that spurred industrialization in the late 1800s. The heavy machinery used to mass-produce goods, the rails that enabled trains to move people and products, the bridges that spanned the rivers, and the tall buildings that dotted the cities all required steel.

Steel was not new. Until the mid–19th century, however, the process of converting iron ore into steel was expensive. In the 1850s Henry Bessemer in England and William Kelly in the United States independently developed a method of steel making that burned off the impurities in molten iron with a blast of hot air. The Bessemer process, as it came to be called, could produce more steel in a day than the older techniques could turn out in a week. American engineer Alexander Holley adapted and improved the Bessemer process. As a result, America's annual steel production grew from about 15 thousand tons in 1865 to over 28 million tons by 1910.

- **Steel provided the building blocks—the heavy machinery, rails, and beams—for industry's golden age.**

The Metropolitan Museum of Art

▲ *Forging the Shaft* by John Ferguson Weir depicts a scene from the West Point Foundry in Cold Spring, New York, during the 1870s.

Railroads. Steel had a tremendous impact on railroad expansion. Steel rails were better than iron rails, which splintered easily. At first, steel was much more costly than iron. As steel production soared, however, prices dropped dramatically. Steel that had sold for $100 a ton in 1873 sold for $12 by the late 1890s.

The availability of cheaper steel encouraged railroads to lay thousands of miles of new track. In 1869, when Leland Stanford had hammered in a golden spike to complete the country's first transcontinental railroad, the United States had less than 50,000 miles of railroad track. By the end of the century, total mileage had skyrocketed to some 200,000. Almost a half-dozen **trunk lines**, or major railroads, crossed the Great Plains to the Pacific coast. Feeder, or branch, lines connected the trunk lines to surrounding areas. This huge railroad grid joined every state and linked remote towns to urban centers.

At the same time, technological innovations helped improve rail transportation. Bigger, more efficient locomotives made it possible to pull larger loads at greater speeds. George Westinghouse's compressed air brake increased railroad safety by enabling the locomotive and all the cars to stop at the same time. Granville T. Woods, called by one newspaper "the greatest electrician in the world," improved Westinghouse's air brake and developed a telegraph system that let trains communicate with stations.

Changes in track design also improved rail service. Double sets of tracks

▲ Granville T. Woods

allowed traffic to roll in two directions at once. Equally important, the adoption in the 1880s of a standard gauge, or width between the rails, made rail transportation faster and cheaper. Passengers and freight no longer had to be transferred each time a train reached a different line.

The growth of railroads had far-reaching consequences. Railroads promoted western settlement by making travel affordable and easy. They also stimulated urban growth. Wherever the railroads went, new towns sprang up, and older towns grew into major cities.

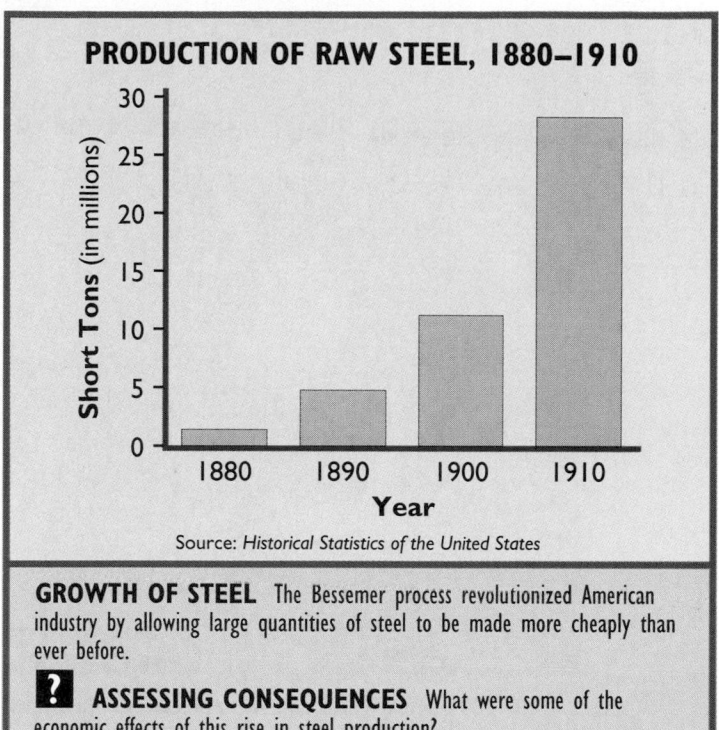

PRODUCTION OF RAW STEEL, 1880–1910

Short Tons (in millions) vs. Year

Source: *Historical Statistics of the United States*

GROWTH OF STEEL The Bessemer process revolutionized American industry by allowing large quantities of steel to be made more cheaply than ever before.

❓ ASSESSING CONSEQUENCES What were some of the economic effects of this rise in steel production?

The economic impact of the railroads was immeasurable. Not only were the railroad companies the country's major employers for much of the late 1800s, they also spurred the growth of other industries. The railroads' demands for rails, locomotives, and railcars poured money into the steel industry. Innovations like refrigerated freight cars helped develop the meat-packing industry. In addition, the network of railroad lines helped strengthen a national market. Now a Pennsylvania steel foundry could obtain iron ore from the Great Lakes region, or a Philadelphia furniture company could sell its products in small midwestern towns.

∷ Railroad expansion spurred the growth of other industries and strengthened national markets.

Communications. An equally remarkable transformation in communications accompanied the revolution in railroad transportation. The telegraph attracted little attention when Samuel F. B. Morse patented his version in 1837. In time, however, people saw its business potential. Using Morse's dot-and-dash code, a telegraph operator could send a business order to a distant location in minutes. By 1866 Western Union, the leading telegraph company, had over 2,000 telegraph offices.

▲ This 1892 photograph shows Alexander Graham Bell making the first long-distance call from New York to Chicago. Businesses across the country soon clamored for telephone service in their cities.

▲ In 1866 printer and newspaper editor Christopher Sholes developed a machine that numbered book pages. This machine was the forerunner of Sholes's first typewriter. Sholes is shown here with his typewriter.

The "talking telegraph," or telephone, which Alexander Graham Bell patented in 1876, had an even greater impact. When Bell demonstrated his gadget at the Philadelphia Centennial Exposition in June 1876, the judges pronounced it "perhaps the greatest marvel hitherto achieved by the electric telegraph." A reporter for the New York *Tribune* did not agree, asking "Of what use is such an invention?" But businesses quickly found the telephone indispensable. By the end of the 1800s, more than a million telephones had been installed in U.S. offices and homes. The telephones required operators, and many women rushed to fill these newly created jobs.

Another major achievement in communications was Christopher Sholes's development of the typewriter in 1867. After making a few improvements, Sholes sold the patent in 1873 to E. Remington & Sons. The typewriter improved communications by producing documents quickly and by making them easy to read. Carbon paper, also introduced during this period, allowed users of typewriters to produce multiple copies.

■■ The telegraph, telephone, and typewriter aided industrialization by speeding communication.

NEW SOURCES OF ENERGY

America's remarkable transportation and communications developments depended on abundant supplies of energy. In the late 1800s businesspeople and inventors began to tap into two new sources of power—oil and electricity.

The early oil industry. People in western Pennsylvania had known about oil for years. Medicine-show hucksters, seeing the chance to make a quick dollar, sold it as a miracle cure-all. But almost no one thought oil had any other uses. In the late 1850s, however, American chemist Benjamin Silliman, Jr., released a report noting that oil could be refined to make kerosene, which, when burned, produces light.

The growing demand for this inexpensive fuel prompted prospector Edwin L. Drake to drill for oil near Titusville, Pennsylvania, in 1859. At first, people questioned Drake's sanity. When the oil began to flow at a rate of some 20 barrels a day, however, other prospectors hurried to sink their own wells. By the 1880s, oil wells dotted Pennsylvania, Ohio, and West Virginia, producing more than 25 million barrels of oil in 1880 alone.

Harnessing electricity. As in the case of oil, people knew of electricity long before they put it to practical use. People considered it little more than a puzzling natural phenomenon. Then in the mid-1800s European and American scientists and engineers developed the dynamo, or electric generator. Driven by steam, water, or other energy source, the dynamo produced enough electrical power to run a factory. An American inventor, Thomas Alva Edison, realized that the dynamo could have wide-ranging applications.

BIO GRAPHY Born in a small Ohio town in 1847, Thomas Edison had only a few months of formal schooling. At age 12 he became a newsboy and later worked as a telegraph operator. An avid amateur scientist, Edison conducted experiments and read widely in his spare time.

The Granger Collection, New York

Thomas Edison

In 1868 Edison developed an electric vote recorder. The next year, he received his first patent, for an improved stock ticker, which telegraphed stock prices. Other inventions followed, and in 1876 he went into the "invention business" full-time, opening a workshop in Menlo Park, New Jersey, where he assembled a team of researchers. Excited, Edison sent a friend the following invitation:

66 Brand-new laboratory . . . at Menlo Park, Western Div., Globe, Planet Earth, Middlesex County, four miles from Rahway, the prettiest spot in New Jersey, on the Penna. Railway, on a High Hill. Will show you around, go strawberrying. 99

Edison promised that he and his fellow researchers would deliver "a minor invention every ten days and a big thing every six months or so." He was as good as his word. He invented the phonograph in 1877 and the light bulb in 1879. By the time he died in 1931, the "Wizard of Menlo Park" held 1,093 patents.

Lewis Latimer–who later worked for Edison–also contributed to light bulb design. He was also a skilled draftsman and an expert in patent law. Latimer testified in several court cases to support Edison's patents.

In 1882 Edison opened one of the world's first central electric power plants in New York City. But the plant could deliver electricity to homes and offices in only a very small area. George Westinghouse and Nikola Tesla solved this problem in the late 1880s by developing a transformer that could transmit a high-voltage current over long distances.

At the 1893 World's Columbian Exposition in Chicago, a Westinghouse-Tesla generator powered the twinkling lights outlining the major buildings. The electric lights enchanted visitors, who marveled at the "fairyland." To many it symbolized a transformation of American life. Indeed, by the end of the century, electric lights were replacing gaslights. And in many cities horse-drawn vehicles had given way to electric streetcars.

■■ **By the end of the 1800s, kerosene and electricity powered and illuminated American homes and factories.**

▲ Lewis Latimer is pictured at age 70 in this 1919 photograph. Shown at left is his patent drawing for a globe supporter for the electric lamp.

THE RISE OF BIG BUSINESS

Along with these technological developments emerged new ideas that revolutionized the business world. The late 1800s was the age of **laissez-faire capitalism**. (*Laissez faire* is French for "let it be.") The theory of laissez-faire capitalism calls for no government regulation of economic matters. Most business leaders believed that if businesses were freed from government regulation, the economy would prosper.

Another theory, **Social Darwinism**, reinforced the laissez-faire doctrine. Originally advanced by English social philosopher Herbert Spencer, Social Darwinism applied the biological principles of natural selection and evolution to society. Social Darwinists argued that society progressed through competition. The "fittest" people (or businesses or nations) should and would rise to positions of wealth and power, while the "unfit" would fail. Social Darwinists believed that any attempts to help the poor or less capable only slowed social progress: "Nature's cure for most social and political diseases," wrote American educator and philosopher Nicholas Murray Butler, "is better than man's."

Some clergy offered religious support for Social Darwinism by suggesting that great wealth was a sign of Christian virtue. Baptist minister Russell H. Conwell declared: "You ought to get rich, and it is your duty to get rich. . . . To make money honestly is to preach the gospel."

Bigger is better. Many people did get rich during this period, particularly industrialists. Industrialists were aided in their quest for wealth by new forms of business organization. At the close of the Civil War, most businesses were **proprietorships**—small enterprises owned by individuals or families—or **partnerships**—enterprises owned by two or more people. These forms of business organization were inadequate to manage giant new industries like railroads, steel, or oil. Nor could they raise the capital needed to finance such ventures. As a result, business leaders turned to another form of business organization—the corporation—which had existed in one form or another since colonial times.

In a **corporation** organizers raise capital by selling shares of **stock**, or certificates of ownership, in the company. **Stockholders**—those who buy the shares—receive a percentage of the corporation's profits in the form of **dividends**. But the stockholders play little or no part in the corporation's daily operations.

A corporation has several advantages over a proprietorship or a partnership. First, a corporation's organizers can raise enormous sums of money by selling stock to many people. Second, unlike proprietors and partners, stockholders enjoy **limited liability**—that is, they are not responsible for the corporation's debt. Third, a corporation is a stable organization because it is distinct from its owners. A corporation continues to exist no matter who owns the stock.

Corporations needed more than organizational stability to deal with the economic climate of the late 1800s. Because competition was fierce, prices and profits fluctuated wildly. Some corporations responded by forming trusts. In a **trust**, a group of companies turn control of their stock over to a board of directors. The directors then run the companies as a single enterprise. If a trust could gain exclusive control of an industry, it could form a **monopoly**.

Carnegie and steel. Andrew Carnegie, a Scot who immigrated to the United States in 1848, established some of the first monopolies. Carnegie entered the steel business in the early 1870s. He readily admitted that he understood little about making steel, but he did know how to run a business. He surrounded himself with skillful managers and drove them relentlessly. He fitted his

▲ At age 13, Andrew Carnegie began his first job winding thread on bobbins, or spools, for $1.20 a week. When he retired from the steel industry, he was worth nearly $500 million.

▲ In 1873 Andrew Carnegie built the largest steel mill in the country, the J. Edgar Thomson Steel Works, in Pittsburgh. This interior view of a steel mill was taken in 1900.

plants with the most modern machinery. But he was also not above using questionable tactics to beat out his competitors.

Carnegie's real success, however, lay in reducing production costs. Carnegie realized that by buying supplies in bulk and producing goods in large quantities he could lower production costs and increase profits. This principle is known as **economies of scale**. Carnegie also used **vertical integration** to control costs—that is, he acquired companies that provided materials and services upon which his enterprises depended. For example, Carnegie purchased iron mines and coal mines, which provided the raw materials for his steel mills, steamship lines, and railroads. An admirer explained the great advantage:

66 From the moment these crude stuffs were dug out of the earth until they flowed in a stream of liquid steel in the ladles, there was never a price, profit, or royalty paid to an outsider. 99

Because Carnegie controlled businesses at each stage of production, he could sell steel at a much lower price than his competitors.

In 1889 Carnegie organized all of his companies into the Carnegie Steel Company, which dominated the steel industry. When Carnegie sold his company to banking tycoon J. P. Morgan for nearly $500 million and retired in 1901, he became the world's richest man.

Rockefeller and oil. The business career of oil tycoon John D. Rockefeller—one of the founders of Standard Oil—followed a course similar to Carnegie's. Rockefeller got into the oil-refining business in its formative years, when many small companies were in fierce competition. Arguing that such competition was inefficient, Rockefeller set out to gain control of the industry.

Like Carnegie, Rockefeller used vertical integration to make his company more competitive, eventually acquiring oil fields, barrel factories, pipelines, railroad tanker cars, and oil-storage facilities. But his main method of expansion was **horizontal integration**—one company's ownership of other companies involved in the same business, in this case, oil refining. What companies Standard Oil could not buy, it tried to control through the establishment of the nation's first trust in the early 1880s.

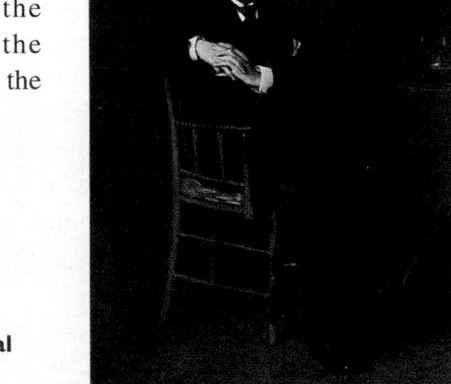

▶ Eastman Johnson completed this formal portrait of John D. Rockefeller in 1895.

To help drive his competitors out of business, Rockefeller made deals with suppliers and transporters to receive cheaper supplies and freight rates. George Rice, a small oil refiner driven out of business by Rockefeller's practices, complained to the U.S. Industrial Commission in 1899:

66 I have been driven from pillar to post, from one railway line to another, for twenty years, in the absolutely vain endeavor to get equal and just freight rates with the Standard Oil Trust, . . . but which I have been utterly unable to do. I have had to consequently shut down, with my business absolutely ruined. 99

Rice was not alone. Rockefeller forced most of his rivals to sell out. By 1899 the Standard Oil Company controlled some 90 percent of the country's petroleum refining capacity and had annual profits of some $45 million.

■■ Businesses used corporations, trusts, and vertical and horizontal integration to increase profits.

Government and business. Industrialists also had the government's support in making their enterprises more profitable. Although supporters of laissez-faire capitalism claimed to frown on government intervention in business activities, the government played a vital role in the rise of the new industrial order. For instance, by placing high tariffs on imports, the federal government allowed U.S. businesses to take command of the home market. In 1875, for example, Congress increased tariff rates to make imported steel 40 percent more expensive than domestic steel.

At the same time, however, the government took modest steps to regulate businesses. Perhaps the greatest push for government regulation of business came from the general public. As Carnegie Steel and Standard Oil grew in power, many Americans demanded that trusts be outlawed. Congress responded in 1890 by passing the **Sherman Antitrust Act**, which declared all monopolies and trusts in restraint of trade illegal. While its intentions appeared clear, the law failed to define what constituted a monopoly or trust. Thus the law proved difficult to enforce.

■■ The federal government adopted the Sherman Antitrust Act in an effort to eliminate monopolies.

Mass Marketing

Industrialists knew that cutting production costs and reducing competition were not the only ways to increase profits. They also developed new methods of marketing to sell their products.

Brand names and packaging played important roles in promoting goods. For example, the name Standard Oil conveyed the idea that the company's product set the industry standard. Other

▼ Colorful advertisements such as these for processed baby food and flour flooded newspapers and magazines by the end of the 19th century.

companies used brightly colored packages or distinctive logos to set their products apart.

Advertising, too, became an important promotional tool. Newspapers, magazines, and roadside billboards carried advertisements urging people to buy "The Purest" soap and telephones "warranted to work *one mile,* unaffected by changes in the weather."

New types of stores sold some of these highly promoted goods. The department store carried a wide variety of products—such as shoes, clothing, hardware, and appliances—under one roof. Pioneered by John Wanamaker in Philadelphia, Marshall Field in Chicago, and R. H. Macy in New York City, the department store bought products in bulk and, as a result, could offer low prices to consumers.

Department stores became the special domain of women, both as places to work and places to shop. Wanting to create a homelike and welcoming atmosphere in their stores (and also looking for ways to cut labor costs), department-store owners hired young, mainly middle-class women to work as clerks. In addition, department-store advertisements targeted women as the chief buyers of their products.

Like department stores, chain stores—stores with branches in many cities—bought goods in large quantities. They then passed on their savings to customers. Perhaps the most famous chain store was founded by Frank W. Woolworth in 1879. By 1900 Woolworth had a network of 59 stores.

▲ Mail-order catalogs brought the latest products and inventions into homes in even the most remote rural areas.

Department stores and chain stores were a part of the urban scene. Mail-order companies like Montgomery Ward and Sears, Roebuck, and Co. catered to the rural market. Customers selected goods from a catalog, then ordered, paid for, and received the merchandise by mail.

SECTION 1 REVIEW

IDENTIFY and explain the significance of the following: trunk lines, Granville T. Woods, Lewis Latimer, laissez-faire capitalism, proprietorships, partnerships, corporation, stock, stockholders, dividends, limited liability, trust, monopoly, economies of scale, vertical integration, horizontal integration.

1. **MAIN IDEA** How did steel, railroads, and innovations in communications contribute to American industry?

2. **MAIN IDEA** What organizational and selling methods did businesspeople use to increase their profits in the late 1800s?

3. **MAIN IDEA** Why did Congress pass the Sherman Antitrust Act in 1890? How did the act attempt to regulate business?

4. **WRITING TO INFORM** Write an essay describing the impact of the technological advances introduced by Thomas Edison.

5. **HYPOTHESIZING** How do you think the theory of Social Darwinism shaped the business practices of Andrew Carnegie and John D. Rockefeller?

THE NEW IMMIGRANTS

FOCUS

■ How did immigration change in the late 1800s?

■ What institutions helped new immigrants adapt to American life?

■ Why did some native-born Americans object to the new immigrants?

Immigration is one of the dynamic forces that has shaped the United States. Immigrants fleeing persecution or poverty or seeking a better life had founded the first colonies, and immigrants had continually added to the country's population. As the 19th century drew to a close, a wave of new immigrants came to America's shores in search of opportunity.

Handbill supporting immigration, 1909

The Strong Museum

THE LURE OF AMERICA

From 1800 to 1880 more than 10 million immigrants came to the United States. Often called the **old immigrants**, many of them were Protestants from northwestern Europe—Great Britain, Ireland, Germany, and the Scandinavian countries. Then, a new wave of immigrants swept over the United States. In less than two decades, between 1891 and 1910, some 12 million immigrants came to the United States. The increase was so great that by the early 1900s, about 60 percent of the people living in the nation's 12 largest cities either were foreign-born or had foreign-born parents.

About 70 percent of these **new immigrants** were from southern or eastern Europe. They were Italians, Greeks, Poles, Czechs, Slovaks, Hungarians, and Russians. In contrast to the old immigrants, most new immigrants were Catholic, Jewish, or Greek Orthodox. French Canadians, Armenians, Arabs, Chinese, and Japanese also arrived by the thousands.

■■ **Immigration soared in the late 1800s and early 1900s. Most new immigrants were southern or eastern Europeans.**

Like the old immigrants, many new immigrants came to the United States to escape poverty or persecution. Most of the Italian and Slavic immigrants were male and sought economic

◀ **This immigrant mother and her children arrived at Ellis Island, New York, around 1910.**

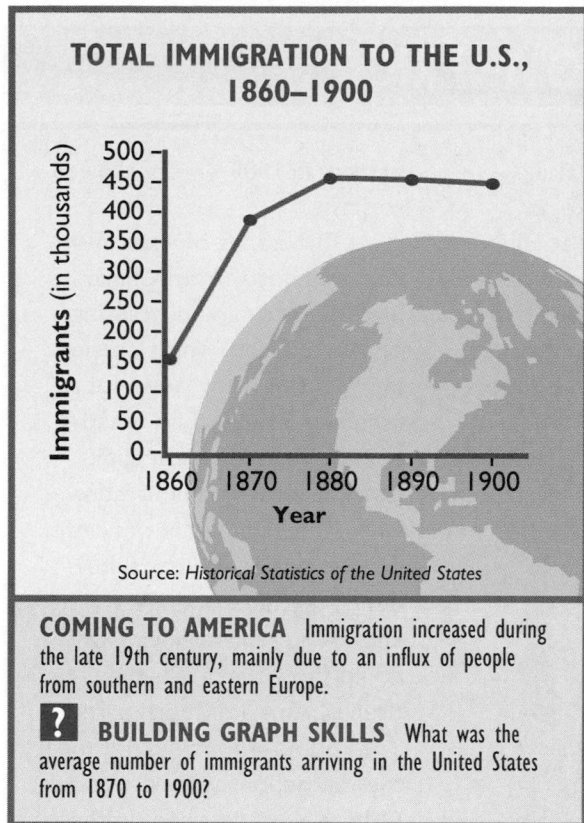

TOTAL IMMIGRATION TO THE U.S., 1860–1900

Immigrants (in thousands)

500
450
400
350
300
250
200
150
100
50
0

1860 1870 1880 1890 1900
Year

Source: *Historical Statistics of the United States*

COMING TO AMERICA Immigration increased during the late 19th century, mainly due to an influx of people from southern and eastern Europe.

? **BUILDING GRAPH SKILLS** What was the average number of immigrants arriving in the United States from 1870 to 1900?

opportunities in the United States that were scarce in their home countries. Most hoped to make enough money in the United States to return home and buy land. Many did just that. Others, however, put down roots and stayed. The eastern European immigrants included Hungarian and Polish farmers and Jews from many countries. Most of the Jewish families and Armenian families fled their homelands to escape religious or political persecution.

Many immigrants learned of the opportunities available in the United States from railroad and steamship companies. In fact, convincing foreigners that the United States was *the* land of opportunity became a major business activity in the late 1800s. The agents of steamship companies and railroads swarmed over Europe, one observer noted, "as the locusts covered Egypt!" They painted a tempting—and often false—picture of America. Some railroad companies exaggerated the employment opportunities available in the United States. And the steamship lines charged rock-bottom fares to attract passengers.

Most of the millions who yielded to this hard sell found the journey to the "Promised Land" difficult and dangerous. The ocean voyage, though faster, safer, and more comfortable than in the past, was no pleasure trip for those traveling

in the poorest accommodations, called steerage. One Italian immigrant asked:

❝ How can a steerage passenger remember that he is a human being when he must first pick the worms from his food . . . and eat in his stuffy, stinking bunk, or in the hot and fetid atmosphere of a compartment where 150 men sleep? ❞

A NEW LIFE

As with earlier immigrants, the vast majority of newcomers did not find paradise at the end of the voyage. Confined to dingy slums, they worked at menial jobs for low wages. Taken advantage of and harassed by some native-born Americans, newcomers often expressed disappointment. Reports about America, a Polish immigrant complained, were "all bluster [with] not a word of truth." Others, however, saw the United States as a great improvement over their home countries.

Immigrant communities. Many industrial cities of the Northeast and Midwest became a patchwork of ethnic neighborhoods as new immigrants settled among others from their homelands. Social reformer Jacob Riis (himself an immigrant from Denmark) suggested that an 1890s map of New York City, colored according to nationality, "would show more stripes than . . . a zebra, and more colors than any rainbow."

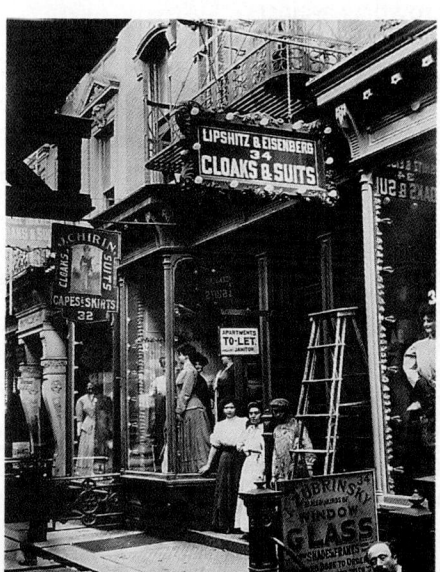

◀ The store signs in this 1910 photograph of a New York neighborhood reflect the ethnic diversity of the city.

Ellis Island in New York Harbor or Angel Island in San Francisco Bay was the first sight of America for millions of newcomers in the late 1800s and early 1900s. Both islands served as immigration stations during this period.

Ellis Island opened in 1892 to receive record numbers of European immigrants. Like many other immigrants, Italian Edward Corsi arrived full of hope:

> 66 My first impressions of the new world will always remain etched in my memory, particularly that hazy October morning when I first saw Ellis Island. . . . All of us . . . clustered on the foredeck for fear of separation and looked with wonder on this miraculous land of our dreams.
>
> Passengers all about us were crowding against the rail. Jabbered conversation, sharp cries, laughs and cheers—a steadily rising din filled the air. Mothers and fathers lifted up the babies so that they too could see, off to the left, the Statue of Liberty. 99

For most immigrants, however, these first feelings of joy were dampened by the confusion of the examination process. With thousands of newcomers arriving daily—many of whom spoke no English—processing at Ellis was hurried at best, impersonal and frightful at worst. Amid the noise and bustle, overworked officials sometimes misunderstood and changed immigrants' names: for example, Gardashian became Arness, and Mastroianni became Mister Yanni.

▲ **After it opened on January 21, 1910, Angel Island served as an immigration station on the West Coast.**

All newcomers who passed through Ellis were subjected to a physical exam. Those who had serious health problems, mental disorders, or contagious diseases like tuberculosis were deported. Those who passed the physicals entered a maze of crowded aisles where inspectors questioned them about their backgrounds, relatives, and job skills. Anyone with a prison record, or who could not support themselves in America, was sent back. But the vast majority—about 99 percent in 1905—were allowed to stay.

Thousands of Asian newcomers, mostly from China, underwent similar processing on Angel Island, which opened in 1910. But many were not as fortunate as their Ellis Island counterparts. Chinese applicants faced strict immigration laws, which limited entrance to certain groups—such as students, teachers, and merchants—or to individuals who could show they were the children of American-born parents.

Some who could not meet the restrictions were deported. Others were detained on the island—some for months or even years—as they awaited a determination in their cases. Some, while imprisoned there, carved poems into the barracks' walls recording their despair:

> 66 Who would have expected joy to become sorrow:
> Detained in a dark, crude, filthy room?
> What can I do?
> Cruel treatment, not one restful breath of air,
> Scarcity of food, severe restrictions—all unbearable.
> Here even a proud man bows his head low. 99

But for most immigrants, the anxiety they experienced on the islands soon gave way to a renewed sense of hope as they finally set foot on their adopted homeland to begin a new life.

▲ Jewish immigrants strived to maintain their religious heritage after arriving in the United States. By studying the Torah, boys learned the ancient wisdom and laws of Jewish Scripture.

In these close-knit neighborhoods, residents spoke the same languages and followed the customs of the old country. Neighborhood churches and synagogues helped immigrants maintain a sense of identity and belonging.

Foreign-language papers, too, eased immigrants' transition. In the early 1900s, more than 1,000 foreign-language papers were printed in the United States. The largest, with a peak circulation of 175,000 a day, was the *Jewish Daily Forward*. Published in Yiddish—a German dialect spoken by eastern European Jews—it primarily served New York's Jewish community.

Most cities also had **benevolent societies**, or support organizations, to aid newcomers. Some organizations offered new immigrants loans to start businesses. Others set up insurance plans that provided money for families whose breadwinners were sick or had died. "We visit our sick and bury our dead" was one society's slogan.

Aid from politicians. Newly arrived immigrants also received help from political **bosses**—powerful political party leaders. Bosses headed big-city **political machines**—party organizations that used patronage, or appointments to government jobs, to control elections. Machine politicians often welcomed immigrants at dockside or at railroad stations, ready to offer assistance. One observer described a boss's methods:

66 To this one he lends a dollar; for another he obtains a railroad ticket without payment; he has coal distributed in the depth of winter; . . . he sometimes sends poultry at Christmas time; he buys medicine for a sick person; he helps bury the dead. 99

Of course, the bosses expected something in return for their help—the immigrants' votes. Getting party candidates elected allowed bosses to control local government. Once in power, most bosses used any means necessary—the rigging of elections, bribery, even violence—to keep it. Many also ransacked city treasuries, lining their own and their friends' pockets.

▪▪ Ethnic neighborhoods, foreign-language newspapers, benevolent societies, and political machines helped immigrants adapt to American life.

Political bosses urged new immigrants to adopt American ways. However, the Americanization process often pitted parents against children. Many older immigrants cherished their ties to the old country. Children, however, tended to view their parents' old-world language, dress, and customs as old-fashioned. A second-generation Polish immigrant expressed bittersweet feelings about his parents' way of life. It was, he

Museum of the City of New York

◀ For immigrant children, the Americanization process began soon after they arrived in the United States. This photograph shows the children's playground at Ellis Island.

▪▪ 469

noted, "a slowly decaying world of aged folks living largely in a dream. One day it would pass and then there would remain only Americans whose forebears had once been Poles."

The immigrant worker.

Whether they adapted to American ways or remained tied to the old world, new immigrants had a common work experience. Many did the country's "dirty work"—or, as one observer put it, "the shoveling."

Certain ethnic groups gravitated toward certain jobs, mainly because earlier arrivals had established themselves in those lines of work. For example, many Italian and Polish men worked in the building trades. Eastern European men worked in mines or steel mills. French Canadians worked in New England textile mills. Many Jewish men and women and Italian women worked in the garment industry. Most Greeks and Chinese opened businesses such as laundries and restaurants, largely because discrimination closed off other opportunities.

Whatever they did, most immigrants found working life hard. The work itself was physically exhausting, hours were long, and wages low. Contract laborers—who, in return for passage to the United States, worked for a set period—were virtual prisoners of their employers. These workers, mostly young women laboring in the sweatshops of New York's garment industry, were literally locked in until they had finished the day's required work. Some immigrants worked as many as 15 hours a day to earn a living wage. Even the best-paid workers made little more than enough to support themselves and their families.

THE NATIVIST RESPONSE

While most immigrant workers enjoyed few of the rewards of their labor, they helped staff the factories that were responsible for the vibrant U.S. economy. Yet many native-born Americans saw immigration as a threat. They agreed with Thomas Bailey Aldrich, who in his poem "The Unguarded Gates" warned against a "wild motley throng" bringing "unknown gods and rites" and speaking "accents of menace." Many felt that these newcomers were just too different ever to fit in. Others went further, blaming immigrants for all society's ills.

Nativists also opposed immigration for economic reasons. Many charged that the immigrants' willingness to work cheaply robbed native-born Americans of jobs and pushed down wages for all. With the support of labor unions, nativist workers began pressing for restrictions on immigration. They gained the most supporters and achieved the most success in the West.

For years Chinese laborers had been tolerated—and exploited—on the West Coast, especially in California. But as unemployment mounted during the Panic of 1873, the new Workingmen's Party of California angrily cried, "The Chinese must go." Party leader Dennis Kearney, who was himself an Irish immigrant, addressed crowds all over the state, working them into a frenzy. White mobs attacked the Chinese, killing some and burning the property of others.

Leaders of California's Chinese community appealed to the authorities for protection. But help was not forthcoming. In fact, the state's political leaders responded by amending the state constitution to forbid Chinese residents to own property or work at certain jobs.

▶ Chinese immigrants formed their own communities and businesses after arriving in the United States. These two photographs are of San Francisco's Chinatown district.

Then in 1882 the U.S. Congress passed the **Chinese Exclusion Act**, which denied citizenship to people born in China and prohibited the immigration of Chinese laborers. This act made conditions worse for the Chinese in America. In 1885 a mob in Rock Springs, Wyoming Territory, murdered 28 Chinese and drove away hundreds more.

Neither the act nor the violence kept Chinese immigrants from coming to the United States. After 1906, some men—dubbed "paper sons" by the Chinese—entered the country by falsely claiming to be sons of Chinese American citizens. Immigration authorities could not disprove many of the claims because the 1906 San Francisco earthquake and fire had destroyed most of the Chinese community's birth records.

But even with the proper documents, Chinese arriving in the United States were held for months while their cases were investigated. One immigrant wrote this poem on the wall of his cell:

> 66 The day I am rid of this prison and
> attain success,
> I must remember that this prison
> once existed. . . .
> All my compatriots [fellow citizens]
> please be mindful.
> Once you have some small gains, return
> home [to China] early. 99

Other immigrants faced discrimination as organizations took up the anti-immigration banner. The **Immigration Restriction League**, founded in 1894 by a group of well-to-do Bostonians, sought to impose a literacy test on all immigrants. Congress passed such a measure, but President Grover Cleveland vetoed it in 1897, calling it

▲ This 1870 cartoon appeared in *Harper's Weekly* and satirizes the nativist reaction to Chinese immigration. A wall surrounds the United States that prevents immigrants from entering the country.

"illiberal, narrow, and un-American." Over the next 30 years, however, Congress tried several times—without success—to pass a similar measure.

Despite efforts to impose restrictions, immigration continued. Contrary to nativists' arguments, the new immigrants contributed to American society. America's rapid industrialization would have been impossible without immigrant workers. Their varied cultures, too, added new dimensions to American life.

▐▐ Prejudice and fear prompted nativists to try to restrict immigration.

SECTION 2 REVIEW

IDENTIFY and explain the significance of the following: old immigrants, new immigrants, benevolent societies, bosses, political machines, Chinese Exclusion Act, paper sons, Immigration Restriction League.

1. **MAIN IDEA** What changes occurred in immigration in the late 1800s?

2. **MAIN IDEA** What helped ease the new immigrants' adjustment to American life?

3. **RECOGNIZING BIAS** Why did nativists oppose the new immigrants? How did nativists demonstrate their bias against the new immigrants?

4. **WRITING TO EXPLAIN** Imagine you are a Chinese American citizen in 1906. Write a letter to a relative explaining how paper sons were able to come to the United States.

5. **EVALUATING** How were the new immigrants affected by new legislation?

URBAN LIFE

FOCUS

■ How did American cities change in the late 1800s?

■ How did urban life differ for the rich, the middle class, and the poor?

■ What was the aim of the settlement house and Social Gospel movements?

Spurred by industrialization and immigration, American cities grew dramatically during the second half of the century. In 1865 only 14 American cities had populations of more than 100,000, and only 20 percent of Americans lived in urban areas. By 1900 the nation was 40 percent urban and had 29 cities with populations in excess of 100,000. With growth came other changes, and a distinct urban culture developed.

Chicago's Masonic Temple

THE CHANGING CITY

The urban areas of the mid-1800s were compact. Few buildings were taller than two or three stories. And even in the largest cities, most people lived less than a 45-minute walk from the city center, where most businesses and industries were located. But by the late 1800s technological innovations and the great flood of people began to transform the urban landscape.

The impact of technology. Contributing to the transformation were steel, new building techniques, and Elisha Otis's mechanized elevator, all of which allowed cities to grow upward as well as outward. No longer restricted by the number of stairs people could comfortably climb, architects designed multistory buildings, or skyscrapers. Construction workers erected steel girders on which they "hung" walls of stone, brick, or concrete.

Moreover, the development of **mass transit**—trolley cars, commuter trains, and subways—made it possible for cities to spread out because workers no longer had to live within walking distance of their jobs. Frank J. Sprague, an electrical engineer who had worked with Thomas Edison, designed one of the first systems, an electric trolley that began serving Richmond, Virginia, in 1887. Other cities quickly adopted Sprague's

▶ Trolley cars were an important part of many urban mass transit systems. This photograph was taken in New York City around 1895.

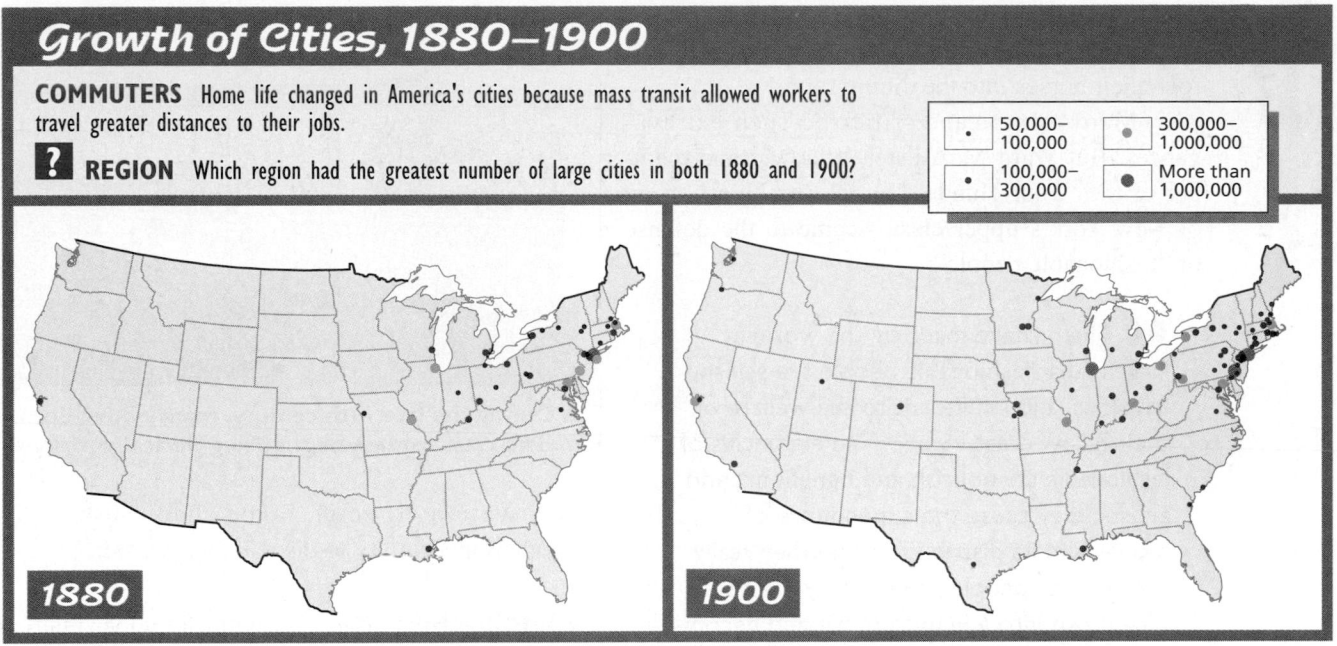

Growth of Cities, 1880–1900

COMMUTERS Home life changed in America's cities because mass transit allowed workers to travel greater distances to their jobs.

? REGION Which region had the greatest number of large cities in both 1880 and 1900?

| • 50,000–100,000 | • 300,000–1,000,000 |
| • 100,000–300,000 | ● More than 1,000,000 |

1880

1900

idea, and by 1895 the nation boasted over 10,000 miles of electric railways.

Mass transit led to the rise of **suburbs**, middle-class and wealthy residential areas beyond the city limits. Some social reformers applauded suburban development because it allowed people to live in "light and air." However, while middle-class and wealthy Americans could afford to enjoy the healthy life of the suburbs, many urban Americans remained trapped by poverty in crowded, and often unhealthy, tenement houses.

■■ **The skyscraper and mass transit helped American cities grow upward and outward.**

Upper-class life. The changing city also created a new group of wealthy city dwellers. There had been wealthy people in America since colonial times, but the urban upper class of the late 1800s was a new breed. The new rich made their money in the new industries, such as railroads, iron and steel, mining, or publishing. Their fortunes usually dwarfed those of the old upper-class merchants and bankers.

For the new rich, author William Dean Howells noted sarcastically, "the dollar is the measure of every value, the stamp of every success." And the new rich spent their dollars freely so that everyone knew how successful they were. Social scientist Thorstein Veblen labeled this behavior **conspicuous consumption**.

The new rich practiced conspicuous consumption by building houses that imitated extravagantly decorated Gothic castles or Italian Renaissance palaces. In the summer they fled their city homes for equally magnificent country estates. The new rich thought nothing of paying thousands of dollars to stage one night's amusement. One

▲ Cornelius Vanderbilt made his fortune by investing in railroads and steamship lines. With the help of his wife (left), Vanderbilt turned his New York City home into a magnificent palace.

wealthy man arranged a lavish—and unusual—party in which the guests wore riding gear and rode their horses into the dining room!

Many Americans criticized such extravagances. But Ward McAllister, a lawyer and member of the "Four Hundred"—the wealthiest group of New York's upper class—came to the defense of "fashionable people":

66 The mistake made by the world at large is that fashionable people are selfish, frivolous, and indifferent to the welfare of their fellow creatures. . . .The elegancies of fashionable life nourish and benefit art and artists; they cause the expenditure of money and its distribution; and they really prevent our people and country from settling down into a humdrum rut and becoming merely a money-making and money-saving people. 99

It is true that some wealthy people supported **philanthropy**—charitable efforts to promote public welfare. They financed libraries, museums, and art galleries; endowed universities; and established new theater groups, opera companies, and symphony orchestras. But, as critics quickly pointed out, not all rich men and women saw philanthropy

▲ During the late 19th century, many native-born, middle-class women began filling clerical positions.

as a way to do good. Some simply used it as another opportunity to display their wealth.

Middle-class life. As with the upper class, a middle class of doctors, lawyers, teachers, and small-business owners had existed since colonial times. However, by the late 1800s modern corporations had swelled the ranks of the middle class with managers, engineers, accountants, clerks, and salespeople. While a great show of wealth indicated success for the new rich, advancement at work measured middle-class achievement.

For the old middle class, work outside the home had been a male realm. But the rise of big

THE PRICE OF INDUSTRIALIZATION

In 1871 Austrian diplomat Joseph Alexander, Graf von Hübner, visited the United States. Von Hübner was impressed by the opportunities Americans enjoyed in an industrializing society. But he also saw that fierce competition in business took its toll on working people. Von Hübner said:

THROUGH OTHERS' EYES

66 *In the New World man is born to conquer. Life is a perpetual struggle, . . . a race in the open field across terrible obstacles, with the prospect of enormous rewards for reaching the goal. The American cannot keep his arms folded. He must embark on something, and once embarked he must go on and on forever; for if he stops, those who follow him would crush him under their feet. His life is one*

long campaign, a succession of never-ending fights, marches, and countermarches.

In such a militant existence, what place is left for the sweetness, the repose [rest], the intimacy of home or its joys? Is he happy? Judging by his tired, sad, exhausted, anxious, and often delicate and unhealthy appearance, one would be inclined to doubt it. Such an excess of uninterrupted labor cannot be good for any man. 99

business created a whole new range of jobs, such as stenographer, salesclerk, and secretary. Business owners increasingly hired young, single middle-class women to fill these positions, paying them lower wages than men. As a result, by 1910 nearly 35 percent of the more than 1.9 million clerical workers were women.

However, most married middle-class women worked at home. Smaller families, greater reliance on purchased goods, and new household technology such as running water, water closets, and home canning changed middle-class women's domestic work. For example, ready-made clothing lightened the sewing loads of many middle-class women. The advent of hot and cold running water meant that doing laundry no longer required pumping, hauling, and heating the water. Some middle-class families could also afford to hire servants to handle many household chores. In such families, women had more free time to take part in the city's growing number of cultural events. Many women joined reading and social clubs. Others participated in and led the reform movements of the late 1800s and early 1900s (see Chapter 17).

How the poor lived.
The servants who toiled in middle-class homes and the workers who labored in factories lived worlds away from the comfort of the middle class or the luxury of the wealthy. To make ends meet, working-class families often had to rent out parts of their homes or tiny apartments to boarders. The dark, airless tenement buildings sometimes housed as many as 12 families per floor. Jacob Riis described a tenement family of "honest, hard-working Germans":

> 66 All nine lived in two rooms, one about ten feet square that served as parlor, bedroom, and eating room, the other a small hall room made into a kitchen. The rent was . . . more than a week's wages for the husband and father. . . . That day the mother had thrown herself out of the window. . . . She was "discouraged," said some of the other women. 99

In New York City, a magnet for hundreds of thousands of immigrants and migrants from the countryside, some 43,000 tenement buildings housed more than 1.6 million poor people in 1900—nearly one half of the city's population.

▲ Crowded tenements, such as these lining Hester Street in New York City, sprang up as urban populations swelled.

Outside the tenements, raw sewage and piles of garbage fouled unpaved streets and alleys. Worse still, the slums usually adjoined industrial areas where factories belched pollution. "The stink is enough to knock you down," one New York resident complained. In such an environment, sickness and death were common. In some cities respiratory diseases like tuberculosis spread rapidly through tightly packed slums, killing many residents.

While the conditions faced by residents of poor neighborhoods were far from pleasant, those who experienced the greatest difficulties were African Americans. Because of widespread discrimination, most of them could get only poorly paid jobs. Moreover, African Americans had to pay outrageous rents for the most appalling apartments, and they faced almost constant police harassment. Yet many preferred the North to the South. As one African American journalist explained:

> 66 They sleep in peace at night; what they earn is paid them, if not they can appeal to the courts. They vote without fear of the shot-gun, and their children go to school. 99

■■ **The rich lived in grand style; the middle class in respectable comfort. But many city dwellers faced grinding poverty.**

THE DRIVE FOR REFORM

Few government programs helped the poor in the late 1800s. What assistance the poor received was limited to charitable handouts of food and clothing. Some idealistic young Americans realized that more needed to be done. To confront the problem of poverty head-on, they established and lived in **settlement houses**—community service centers—in poor neighborhoods. At the forefront of this effort was Jane Addams.

BIO GRAPHY

The settlement houses. Born in 1860 to a well-to-do family in Cedarville, Illinois, Jane Addams grew up in an atmosphere of politics and philanthropy. Her Quaker father was a passionate abolitionist, and as a state senator he had worked to pass social reform legislation. The young Addams set out to be a doctor, but a back problem put an end to her medical studies. Unsure about what career to pursue, she decided to recuperate and travel in Europe. Eventually, she decided to dedicate her life to helping the urban poor.

In time, Addams's work included other causes. She tirelessly worked for women's suffrage and served as president of the Women's International League for Peace and Freedom from 1919 to 1935. Worldwide recognition for her work came in 1931, when she and Nicholas Murray Butler won the Nobel Peace Prize.

Addams began her settlement-house work in 1889, when she and Ellen Gates Starr established a settlement at Hull House, a run-down mansion in one of Chicago's immigrant neighborhoods. Hull House's founding charter explained Addams's cultural and social-service mission:

Jane Addams

> 66 To provide a center for a higher civic and social life; to institute and maintain educational and philanthropic enterprises, and to investigate and improve the conditions in the industrial districts of Chicago. 99

Addams also hoped that Hull House would provide fulfilling careers for women. She expected that for "young women who had been given over too exclusively to study," Hull House "might restore a balance of activity" and help them "learn of life from life itself."

The volunteers who joined Addams were mostly young, college-educated women. They set up a day nursery and kindergarten for the children of working mothers and gave adult education classes. They offered recreational facilities and staffed an employment agency. And when the city failed to pick up garbage in poor neighborhoods, Addams secured an appointment as a garbage inspector to make sure the city provided the much-needed service.

Addams and other settlement workers improved services for the poor, but also learned much from their work. Addams's experiences taught her "that the things which make men alike are finer and better than the things that keep them apart, and that these basic likenesses . . . easily transcend [surpass] the less essential differences of race, language, creed, and tradition." The experience gained at settlement houses provided women such as Addams and many others with the skills

▼ As part of urban reform, settlement houses such as Hull House in Chicago improved services for immigrants and the poor.

and knowledge to make important contributions to social reform and politics.

Hull House served as a model for others hoping to aid the poor. In 1890 African American teacher Janie Porter Barrett founded one of the first African American settlement houses—the Locust Street Social Settlement—in Hampton, Virginia. Three years later, Lillian Wald started the Henry Street Settlement on New York's Lower East Side. By the end of the century, almost a hundred settlement houses had opened across the country.

The Social Gospel movement.

At the same time that the settlement houses began their work, a number of Protestant ministers joined the battle against poverty. They developed the idea of the **Social Gospel**, which called for people to apply Christian principles to address social problems. Washington Gladden, a Congregational minister in Columbus, Ohio, was an early leader of the Social Gospel movement. Arguing that the church had a moral duty to confront social injustice, Gladden led crusades to improve conditions for industrial workers.

Many churches attempted to implement the Social Gospel by providing libraries, classrooms, job training and counseling, and other social services. Caroline Bartlett's People's Church in Kalamazoo, Michigan, was one example of such a church. Bartlett became a Unitarian minister in 1889, the same year she began her work at the People's Church. Drawing on Social Gospel ideals, Bartlett threw open the doors of her church seven days a week. She established a free public kindergarten and a gymnasium and offered classes in domestic and industrial skills. Bartlett also set up a meals program for workers and sponsored creative activities, such as an orchestra and a literary society for African Americans.

Other religious groups joined the crusade to assist the urban poor. In 1880 the Salvation Army, an evangelical group founded in Great Britain, began offering food, clothing, and shelter to the poor to help put them on the path to physical and spiritual salvation.

■■ The settlement-house and Social Gospel movements fought poverty and other social problems.

▲ In this early 1900s photograph, nurses from New York's Henry Street Settlement House are on their way to help the poor and needy.

The "Gospel of Wealth."

Some Americans were troubled by the plight of the poor but viewed the Social Gospel and settlement-house movements as too radical. Steel baron Andrew Carnegie offered these people an alternative: the "Gospel of Wealth." In Carnegie's view the rich had been chosen as "stewards of wealth." Thus, they had an obligation to use their fortunes for the common good. "The man who dies thus rich," Carnegie argued, "dies disgraced."

Carnegie, however, was also a firm believer in Social Darwinism. He opposed handouts to the poor because, he argued, such handouts rewarded equally both the unworthy beggar and the worthy worker fallen on hard times. The best way to benefit the lower class, he said, was "to place within its reach the ladders upon which the aspiring can rise." Carnegie's "ladders" included universities and libraries. Carnegie gave some $350 million to such causes during his lifetime.

URBAN CULTURE

Carnegie's generosity and that of other philanthropists contributed greatly to urban cultural life during the late 1800s. Perhaps the greatest reform in this period, however, was the growth of free public education.

▲ African American students attended segregated schools, where educational resources or facilities rarely equaled those of white schools. This photograph shows an African American school around 1910.

Public education. The growth of public education went hand in hand with the growth of the cities. After 1860 more and more states passed compulsory school attendance laws and lengthened the school year from 78 to 144 days. From 1870 to 1900 the number of students in school grew from some 7 million to more than 15 million, and high school enrollment increased almost tenfold. Many of these new students were young women: in 1900 about 60 percent of high school graduates were women. In addition, more women joined the growing number of men attending college. As a result, the number of college graduates climbed from nearly 9,400 in 1870 to some 29,000 in 1900.

As enrollments increased, educational reformers proposed that schools do more than teach reading, writing, and arithmetic by rote. One of the main reformers was philosopher John Dewey. His "Laboratory School" at the University of Chicago stressed cooperative "learning by doing" and emphasized science, art, and history. Ella Flagg Young, superintendent of schools in Chicago, worked with Dewey to implement his ideas in her schools. Most urban schools, however, were slow to take up the new methods.

In this period most public schools remained segregated by race. Despite the expansion of support for public schools, most schools for African Americans were poorly equipped, since state and local governments spent little money on them.

Popular journalism. As a result of expanded education, by 1900 some 90 percent of Americans could read. The dramatic increase in the number of daily newspapers—from almost 600 in 1870 to some 2,600 by 1910—reflected this growth in literacy.

Daily newspapers in the same city often battled each other for a greater share of the reading public. The wildest circulation wars took place between Joseph Pulitzer's New York *World* and William Randolph Hearst's New York *Journal*. Pulitzer tried to win readers by running sensational news stories and by adding comic strips, advice columns, and a separate sports page. Hearst competed with even more-sensational stories under screaming headlines. The papers also vied for readers by publishing the popular cartoon series "Yellow Kid" by different artists. The cartoon provided the name for this style of reporting—**yellow journalism**.

Literature. In addition to newspapers, city dwellers read popular fiction—romances, mysteries, and westerns. Young boys favored Horatio Alger's success stories about hardworking street urchins who rose to middle-class respectability by courage—and luck. Similarly, Martha Finley's stories about the upright Elsie Dinsmore gained a huge following among young girls.

Older readers enjoyed realistic books about urban life. For example, Edith Wharton's *House of*

◄ Edith Wharton won the Pulitzer Prize in 1920 for the *Age of Innocence*.

Mirth (1905) described the conflicts between the new rich and the old elite. William Dean Howells's *Rise of Silas Lapham* (1885) wove a tale of greed and social ambition. Stephen Crane and Frank Norris depicted everyday life, including the grim side of urban experience.

Readers also favored local-color writers. The greatest of them was Samuel L. Clemens, better known as Mark Twain. In *The Adventures of Tom Sawyer* (1876) and *The Adventures of Huckleberry Finn* (1884), Twain vividly described rural adolescent life of the mid-1800s. African American writer Charles W. Chesnutt's *Conjure Woman* (1899) drew on tales told by freed slaves.

Leisure time. City dwellers also sought diversion in sports. For example, croquet and cycling—which enjoyed a great vogue in the 1890s—became especially popular activities for middle-class women. Men of all classes enjoyed playing and watching basketball, boxing, football, and baseball. Americans had been playing baseball since the 1840s, but in 1876, with the founding of the first professional league, it became a popular spectator sport as well. The *New York Times* noted that spectators "jumped like colts, clapped their hands, threw their hats into the air, slapped their companions on the back, . . . and . . . enjoyed themselves hugely."

Baseball had become, in one sportswriter's words, "the national game of the United States." But not all Americans were allowed to play in the professional leagues. In 1887 team manager

▲ Shown here is the 1866 championship game at Elysian Field, in Hoboken, New Jersey.

Adrian "Cap" Anson, a star player in his day, refused to let his team play against teams with African American players. Anson's action, and the widespread racism in the baseball leagues, led to the exclusion of African Americans from major league teams, a ban that lasted for 60 years.

For children, Barnum & Bailey's Circus provided "The Greatest Show on Earth." Also popular, especially among lower-class families, were amusement parks—such as Coney Island—with their roller coasters and Ferris wheels. Vaudeville shows, with roots in working-class variety acts, attracted middle-class as well as working-class audiences. Similarly, Yiddish theaters served as a source of nostalgia for Jewish immigrants.

■■ **An urban culture with diverse reading, entertainment, and leisure activities developed in the late 1800s.**

SECTION 3 REVIEW

IDENTIFY and explain the significance of the following: mass transit, suburbs, conspicuous consumption, philanthropy, settlement houses, Janie Porter Barrett, Lillian Wald, Social Gospel, yellow journalism.

LOCATE and explain the importance of the following: Hampton, Virginia; Columbus, Ohio.

1. **MAIN IDEA** In what ways did American cities change in the late 1800s?

2. **MAIN IDEA** Describe urban life for the rich, the middle class, and the poor.

3. **COMPARING** How were Jane Addams's work at Hull House and Caroline Bartlett's at the People's Church similar? How did they differ?

4. **WRITING TO INFORM** Imagine you are a journalist from outside the United States. Write an article informing your British readers about American urban culture.

5. **HYPOTHESIZING** What impact do you think John Dewey has had on modern public education in the United States?

Alexander Graham Bell patents telephone. Thomas Edison opens workshop in Menlo Park, New Jersey.

Lewis Latimer invents the incandescent light bulb.

Congress passes Chinese Exclusion Act.

Christopher Sholes invents typewriter.

Thomas Edison invents light bulb. Frank W. Woolworth founds first of his chain stores.

WRITING A SUMMARY
Using the essential points of the chapter as a guide, write a summary of the chapter.

REVIEWING CHRONOLOGY
Number your paper 1 to 5. Study the time line above, and list the following events in the order in which they happened by writing the first next to 1, the second next to 2, and so on. Then complete the activity below.

1. Standard Oil's profits reach some $45 million.
2. Alexander Graham Bell patents telephone.
3. Jane Addams establishes Hull House.
4. Sherman Antitrust Act passed.
5. Congress passes Chinese Exclusion Act.

Evaluating How did the establishment of Hull House contribute to social reform?

IDENTIFYING PEOPLE AND IDEAS
Explain the historical significance of each of the following people or terms.
1. trunk lines
2. Granville T. Woods
3. Lewis Latimer
4. new immigrants
5. bosses
6. Chinese Exclusion Act
7. Jane Addams
8. Janie Porter Barrett
9. yellow journalism
10. Charles W. Chesnutt

UNDERSTANDING MAIN IDEAS
1. How did technological advances in steel making promote changes in American cities in the 1800s?
2. How did urban daily life change in the late 1800s?
3. How did the government attempt to restrict big business?
4. Why did nativists oppose immigration, and what actions did they take to prevent it?
5. What goals were shared by benevolent societies and by reformers involved in the settlement-house and Social Gospel movements?

REVIEWING THEMES
1. **Economic Development** How did changes in technology affect the nation's economy in the late 1800s?
2. **Technology and Society** In what ways did innovations in communication and energy change American urban life?
3. **Cultural Diversity** How did increases in immigration affect social life in the late 19th century?

THINKING CRITICALLY
1. **Evaluating** What was the impact of the new industrial order on business organization?
2. **Analyzing** How did social change contribute to the growth of department and chain stores?
3. **Synthesizing** In what ways did the second industrial age both separate people and bring them together?

STRATEGY FOR SUCCESS
Review the Skills Handbook entry on Identifying Cause and Effect on page 989. Write a paragraph tracing the rise of big business from the development of the Bessemer process to the eventual government legislation limiting monopolies and trusts. Be sure to show the connections between causes and effects.

WRITING ABOUT HISTORY
Writing to Create
Among the best-selling books of the late 19th century were dime novels, books with paper covers that sold for 10 cents. Dime novels offered plots with lots of action and suspense. Using a 19th-century tycoon, immigrant, or African American migrant as a main character, write an outline for a dime novel.

| Mark Twain publishes *The Adventures of Huckleberry Finn.* | Frank J. Sprague starts an electric trolley service. | Jane Addams establishes Hull House. Caroline Bartlett begins work at the People's Church. | Sherman Antitrust Act passed. Janie Porter Barrett founds Locust Street Social Settlement. | Standard Oil's profits reach some $45 million. Charles W. Chestnutt publishes *The Conjure Woman.* | Edith Wharton publishes *House of Mirth.* |

| 1885 | 1890 | 1895 | 1900 | 1905 |

USING PRIMARY SOURCES

Author Frank Norris's eye for detail makes his novels fascinating records of urban life in the late 1800s. Norris was only 22 when he wrote his first novel, *McTeague* (1899), a story of a San Francisco dentist who becomes corrupted by city influences. In the following excerpt, Norris describes McTeague's neighborhood. Write a paragraph identifying aspects of the new urban culture.

> **66** *From noon to evening the population of the street was of a mixed character. The street was busiest at that time; a vast and prolonged murmur arose—the mingled shuffling of feet, the rattle of wheels, the heavy trundling of cable cars. . . . Evening began; and one by one a multitude of lights, from the demoniac [devilish] glare of the druggists' windows to the dazzling blue whiteness of the electric globes, grew thick from street corner to street corner. . . . The cable cars were loaded with theatre-goers—men in high hats and young girls in furred opera cloaks. On the sidewalks were groups and couples—the plumbers' apprentices, the girls of the ribbon counters, the little families . . . the dressmakers, the small doctors,* the harness makers—all the various inhabitants of the street were abroad, strolling idly from shop window to shop window. . . . The tamale men appeared.* **99**

Frank Norris

LINKING HISTORY AND GEOGRAPHY

Study the map on page 473. How did the movement of people to cities lead to urban economic growth?

BUILDING YOUR PORTFOLIO

Complete the following projects independently or cooperatively.

1. SOCIAL CONFLICT In Chapter 14 you were a Sioux living on the Pine Ridge Reservation in South Dakota. Building on that experience, imagine you are an immigrant who has just arrived from southern or eastern Europe. Create a series of poems and graphics that illustrate the problems you face in your new home and your hopes for the future.

2. TECHNOLOGY AND INDUSTRY In Chapter 14 you were a land speculator who hopes to establish a small railhead in Nebraska. Building on that experience, develop a plan to use new technologies—such as the telephone, the dynamo, and electric lighting—and innovations in transportation to attract residents and businesses.

3. REFORM Imagine you are a female settlement-house worker. Create a promotional banner that shows how the reform efforts of your organization serve the needs of the entire urban community. Banners might include mottos, symbols, or slogans.

CONQUERING DISTANCE

$\mathcal{T}$HE late 19th century was a period of massive population shifts for the United States. Between 1860 and 1910 some 23 million immigrants crossed the Atlantic and Pacific oceans to get here. Many of these immigrants joined the migration across country as millions of people settled the American West. This westward migration was aided by dozens of railroad lines, trails, and improved systems of communication. These means of transportation and communication linked numerous western cities together, forming the basis of a modern transcontinental economy that eventually lured some western immigrants to the East Coast.

Conquering Distance Overseas

IMMIGRATION TO THE U.S., 1860–1910

Other 28%
Japan <1%
China 1%
Germany 17%
Scandinavia 8%
Russia & Baltics 10%
Italy 13%
Ireland 10%
Great Britain 12%

$\mathbf{C}$ompared to European immigrants, immigrants from Asia had to travel twice as far to reach the United States. The vast majority of Chinese immigrants in the late 19th century came from the province of Guangdong. Although most initially settled along the Pacific coast, particularly in the San Francisco area, some eventually journeyed across the United States. In 1870 a Massachusetts factory owner began to recruit Chinese laborers from California to take the place of striking workers. As this practice caught on, more Chinese Californians made the trek to the east coast. Today the thriving Chinatowns of Boston, New York, and San Francisco are all the results of the 19th century journeys from Guangdong.

From Across the Pacific to the Atlantic Coast

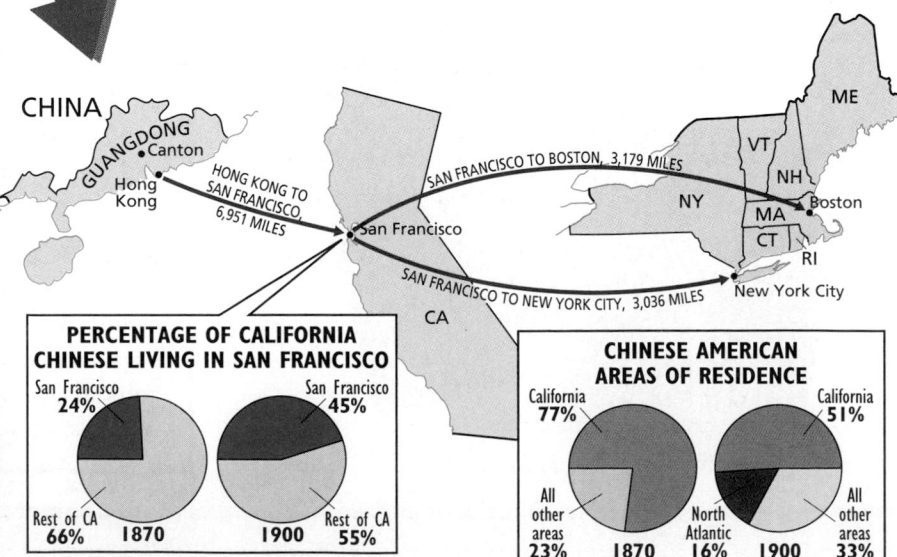

PERCENTAGE OF CALIFORNIA CHINESE LIVING IN SAN FRANCISCO

San Francisco 24%
Rest of CA 66%
1870

San Francisco 45%
Rest of CA 55%
1900

CHINESE AMERICAN AREAS OF RESIDENCE

California 77%
All other areas 23%
1870

California 51%
North Atlantic 16%
All other areas 33%
1900

Map labels (states/territories): WA, OR, CA, NV, ID, MT, ND, SD, WY, UT, AZ (ARIZONA TERRITORY), NEW MEXICO TERRITORY, CO, NE, KS, OKLAHOMA TERR., INDIAN TERR., TX, MN, IA, MO, AR, LA, WI, IL, IN, MI, KY, TN, MS, AL

Cities: Seattle, Walla Walla, Portland, Boise, Salt Lake City, Sacramento, San Francisco, Los Angeles, Yuma, Tucson, El Paso, Santa Fe, Pueblo, Cheyenne, Denver, Laramie, Ogallala, Omaha, St. Joseph, Kansas City, Abilene, Salina, Wichita, Dodge City, Coffeyville, Ft. Smith, Dallas, Ft. Worth, Houston, San Antonio, Des Moines, Minneapolis, St. Paul, St. Louis, Sedalia, Chicago, New Orleans, Bismarck, Ft. Buford, Miles City

Railroads/Trails labeled: NORTHERN PACIFIC, GREAT NORTHERN, SHORTLINE, OREGON, CENTRAL PACIFIC, UNION PACIFIC, PONY EXPRESS, OVERLAND STAGE, DENVER & RIO GRANDE, KANSAS PACIFIC, ATCHISON TOPEKA & SANTA FE, ATLANTIC & PACIFIC, SOUTHERN PACIFIC, BUTTERFIELD PACIFIC, OVERLAND MAIL, TEXAS & PACIFIC, MISSOURI, KANSAS, & TEXAS, ST. JOSEPH & GRAND ISLAND, HANNIBAL & ST. JOSEPH, GOODNIGHT-LOVING CATTLE TRAIL, CHISHOLM CATTLE TRAIL, WESTERN CATTLE TRAIL, SHAWNEE TRAIL, SANTA FE-FT. SMITH TRAIL, LOWER EMIGRANT TRAIL, SANTA FE TRAIL

Ethnic settlement areas: GERMAN, IRISH, NORWEGIAN, SWEDISH, FINNISH, POLISH, CZECH, DANISH, DUTCH, FRENCH, MEXICAN, CHINESE

Indian reservations: SIOUX, NEZ PERCÉ, SHOSHONE, PAIUTE, ARAPAHO, NAVAJO, HOPI, APACHE, CHEROKEE, CREEK, SEMINOLE, CHICKASAW, CHOCTAW

claimed by Texas

Legend

- ▬▬ Railroad
- ▬ ▬ Cattle trail
- ▬▬ Other trail
- ▨ Area settled by 1890
- DUTCH Ethnic settlement area
- SIOUX Indian reservation

N W E S

0 ——— 200 ——— 400 Miles
0 ——— 200 ——— 400 Kilometers
Albers Equal Area Projection

As the railroads and western population increased, many small towns grew into thriving cities within a few short years. Many followed the pattern of Omaha, Nebraska. The small settlement of Omaha, which was a popular stopping point for settlers headed to Colorado, officially became a town in 1857. After the first tracks of the Union Pacific Railroad were laid there in 1865, Omaha's population soared. Located in the heart of cattle country, the city developed a thriving meat-processing industry in the 1880s. This new industry attracted many settlers, particularly poor immigrants from southern and central Europe.

POPULATION OF OMAHA

Year	Population
1860	1,833
1900	102,555

Omaha

WESTERN POPULATION GROWTH, 1860–1910

Year	% Foreign born	% Native born	Total
1860	29%	71%	619,000 total
1870	32%	68%	991,000 total
1880	28%	72%	1,801,000 total
1890	25%	75%	3,134,000 total
1900	20%	80%	4,309,000 total
1910	20%	80%	7,082,000 total

■ 25% % Foreign born
□ 75% % Native born

Chart information from *Historical Statistics of the United States*, *World Book Encyclopedia*, and Ronald Takaki's *Strangers from a Different Shore*.

POLITICS AND PROTEST

FOCUS

UNDERSTANDING THE MAIN IDEA

Rapid industrialization and westward expansion helped transform the United States into a prosperous, modern nation. However, many Americans believed that they had not received their fair share of prosperity. Ignored by the major political parties, these Americans organized to protect their own interests or became involved in the political process to win reform.

THEMES

■ **DEMOCRATIC VALUES**
What actions might citizens take to bring about change in society?

■ **CULTURAL DIVERSITY**
How might political and economic conditions unite different groups in society? How might they divide groups?

1869	1883	1886	1892	1894
Knights of Labor founded.	Pendleton Civil Service Act passed.	Haymarket Riot occurs.	Populist party founded.	Pullman strike occurs.

By the late 1800s the promise of Jacksonian democracy was little more than a distant, vain hope for many Americans. To them it appeared that all political power lay in the hands of a few wealthy people. Winning a share of power and prosperity, they realized, would take action on their part.

Child factory laborers

In the 1873 novel *The Gilded Age,* by Mark Twain and Charles Dudley Warner, a Washington observer tries to explain to a young friend why Congress takes so long to get down to business each legislative session:

> ❝ The first preliminary it always starts out on, is to clean itself, so to speak. It will arraign [accuse] two or three dozen of its members, or maybe four or five dozen, for taking bribes to vote for this and that and the other bill last winter. . . . One of our Congresses can never rest easy until it has thoroughly purified itself of all blemishes. ❞

Astounded, his young friend asks whether Congress ever worries that it will expel so many members that it can no longer do business. "Why I did not say Congress would expel anybody," the man replies. "But good God we *try* them, don't we!"

> ❝ They appoint a committee to investigate, and that committee hears evidence three weeks. . . . They don't acquit, they don't condemn. They just say, "Charge not proven." It leaves the accused in a kind of a shaky condition before the country, it purifies Congress, it satisfies everybody. ❞

In real life, of course, it did not satisfy everyone. Many Americans were deeply troubled by the abuses of wealth and power that seemed to characterize the era. Some people called for political reform. Others—such as industrial workers and farmers—took matters into their own hands, organizing to protect their interests.

UMW emblem, 1890

Section 1

RESTORING HONEST GOVERNMENT

FOCUS

- Why did many Americans call for civil service reform?
- Why did critics believe that the Pendleton Civil Service Act would accomplish little?
- How did President Harrison deal with the reform programs of President Cleveland?

Few contemporary observers had anything good to say about the late-19th-century political scene. Historian Henry Adams noted that "the period was poor in purpose and barren in results." Many Americans agreed with Adams, viewing their elected representatives as little better than a bunch of crooks. Infuriated, these Americans demanded political reforms.

The Gilded Age

GRAFT AND CORRUPTION

Mark Twain and Charles Dudley Warner titled their novel about post–Civil War America *The Gilded Age* to make a point. Twain and Warner believed that, like the base material that hides beneath the glittering gold surface of a gilded picture frame, corruption and greed lurked below the polite and prosperous luster of late-19th-century American society. The image struck a chord, and the era became known as the **Gilded Age**.

The authors had ample evidence to support their view—particularly in the area of politics. Politicians of both parties—and at every level of government—made pious speeches about the great honor of holding public office. Yet they often showed more interest in taking advantage of their positions to plunder the public treasury than in serving the public good.

Twain and Warner took as their main target the national political scene. But corruption was no less widespread on state and local levels, where powerful political machines prevailed. Among the most notorious was Tammany Hall, the Democratic party machine that controlled New York City government. Tammany Hall's reputation for graft and corruption was launched by William Marcy Tweed, who along with his cronies—the **Tweed Ring**—robbed the city treasury of some $200 million between 1865 and 1871.

It is doubtful that any of the later bosses ever exceeded Tweed's take, but graft remained one of the Gilded Age's best roads to riches—one the bosses vigorously defended. "Everybody is talkin' these days about Tammany men growin' rich on graft," complained boss George Washington Plunkitt, "but nobody thinks of drawin' the distinction between honest graft and dishonest graft."

66 There's an honest graft, and I'm an example of how it works. . . . My party's in power in the city, and it's goin' to undertake a lot of public improvements. Well, I'm tipped off, say, that they're going to lay out a new park at a certain place. . . . I go to that place and I buy up all the land I can in the neighborhood. Then the board of this or

section of the transcontinental railroad. Crédit Mobilier overcharged Union Pacific by more than $20 million. These "excess profits" went straight into the pockets of Crédit Mobilier's stockholders, many of whom were members of Congress, including then–Speaker of the House Colfax. Although this scandal transpired before Grant became president, it tarnished his administration's image.

Critics charged that the corruption in Grant's administration was in large part the result of the spoils system (see Chapter 7). Rather than award civil service jobs on the basis of patronage, they asked, why not use ability as the deciding factor? Let applicants who received the highest grades on competitive examinations get the jobs, regardless of their party affiliation.

■■ **Convinced that the spoils system led to political corruption, many Americans called for civil service reform.**

that makes its plan public, and there is a rush to get my land. . . . Ain't it perfectly honest to charge a good price and make a profit on my investment and foresight? . . . Well, that's honest graft. **"**

SCANDAL IN THE WHITE HOUSE

Party bosses were not the only masters at graft and corruption, however. Politicians in Washington, D.C., played the same games—often for even higher stakes. This fact was brought home during Ulysses S. Grant's years in the White House.

Grant's first term in office was marred by several scandals. In 1869 his brother-in-law helped financier Jay Gould attempt to corner the gold market. The attempt failed, pushing several investors—though not Gould—into financial ruin. Then in 1872 an even greater scandal surfaced, one involving Grant's vice president, Schuyler Colfax. In 1867, directors of the Union Pacific Railroad had formed the Crédit Mobilier Company and then had awarded the company contracts to build a

Civil service reform was the battle cry of New York *Tribune* editor Horace Greeley, Grant's Liberal Republican opponent in the 1872 presidential race. The Liberal Republican party was formed by Republicans shocked over the Grant scandals and tired of Reconstruction. The Democrats, hoping to benefit from the split in the Republican party, threw their support to Greeley.

▼ **This New York newspaper cartoon satirized the corrupt politicians of the times.**

WHO STOLE THE PEOPLE'S MONEY?—DO TELL. NY.TIMES.   'TWAS HIM.

Liberal Republicans viewed the Crédit Mobilier scandal as a nail in Grant's political coffin. But Grant, playing once again on his image as a war hero, easily won reelection. Disheartened and worn out, Greeley died just three weeks after the election. His party did not last much longer, and it seemed that civil service reform, too, had been dealt a death blow. However, continued exposure of corruption in the second Grant administration breathed new life into the movement.

THE STRUGGLE FOR REFORM

Hoping to make the corruption of the Grant years a campaign issue, the Democrats nominated New York governor Samuel J. Tilden as their presidential candidate in 1876. Tilden had won national attention by helping break up the Tweed Ring. But the Republicans rode to victory with their nominee: Ohio governor Rutherford B. Hayes, known for his support of civil service reform (see Chapter 13 for details on election).

President Hayes's efforts at reform soon drew the wrath of his own party. The Republicans had split into two factions—nicknamed the Stalwarts and the Half-breeds—over the issue of patronage. The Stalwarts, led by the haughty Senator Roscoe Conkling of New York, strongly opposed reform. Conkling referred to the proposed merit system for government jobs as "snivel service." The Half-breeds, led by James G. Blaine of Maine, claimed to support reform, but they also wanted to control patronage jobs.

Hayes chose not to run for reelection in 1880. At the Republican Convention, the two factions battled to control the party ticket. The Half-breeds won, naming James A. Garfield as the party's presidential candidate. To appease the Stalwarts, they placed Conkling's friend Chester A. Arthur on the ticket as vice president.

Garfield edged out his Democratic rival, Civil War veteran General Winfield Scott Hancock, by fewer than 40,000 votes. But his victory was short-lived. On July 2, 1881, Charles Guiteau (guh-TOH), a disappointed and mentally unstable government job seeker, shot Garfield. The deranged Guiteau believed that killing Garfield would further the Stalwart cause. The shooting had the opposite effect. When Garfield died in September, Chester A. Arthur, though a Stalwart, sympathetically responded to the calls for reform.

In 1883 President Arthur helped gain passage of the **Pendleton Civil Service Act**, which established a Civil Service Commission to administer competitive examinations to those seeking government jobs. The act was an important step toward reform because it made into law the idea that federal jobs below the policy-making level should be filled by merit. Critics charged, however, that the act was of limited value because it covered only about 10 percent of federal jobs.

■■ Critics argued that the Civil Service Act covered too few federal jobs to be effective.

Angered by Arthur's reform efforts, many Stalwarts refused to support his bid for the 1884 Republican presidential nomination. Instead, they cast their lot with James Blaine, the leader of the Half-breeds. Blaine's nomination angered

PRESIDENTIAL LIVES

RUTHERFORD B. HAYES
1822–1893

in office
1877–1881

At the time of his election to the presidency, Rutherford B. Hayes was hardly a novice in politics. He had served as Cincinnati's city solicitor, as a U.S. congressman, and as governor of Ohio for three terms. But he found the presidency hard work. "I am heartily tired of this life of bondage, responsibility, and toil," he told his wife. After one term he gladly returned to private life.

JAMES A. GARFIELD
1831–1881

in office
1881

James A. Garfield was the last president to be born in a log cabin. Garfield enjoyed his years in Congress but did not look forward to life in the White House. He called the presidency "a bleak mountain" and forecast that "I am bidding good-bye to private life and to a long series of happy years which I fear terminate in 1880." The following year, Garfield lay dead from an assassin's bullet.

James A. Garfield.

CHESTER A. ARTHUR
1829–1886

in office
1881–1885

Chester A. Arthur much preferred the social side of the presidency to paperwork. Arthur loved life in the executive mansion. "He wanted the best of everything," an employee recalled, "and wanted it served in the best manner." Tall and handsome, with impeccable manners, Arthur was called Gentleman Boss by his political followers, and in the White House he became known as the Prince of Hospitality.

Chester A. Arthur

Republican reformers, who charged that the candidate "wallowed in spoils like a rhinoceros in an African pool." Dubbed **"mugwumps"** (the Algonquian word for big chiefs), these reformers threw their support to the Democratic candidate, Grover Cleveland. Like Tilden, Cleveland had gained national attention when, as governor of New York, he opposed Tammany Hall. Mudslinging, rather than a discussion of the issues, marked the campaign. But in the end Cleveland won.

ADVANCES AND SETBACKS

Proclaiming that "a public office is a public trust," Cleveland entered the White House determined to move political reform forward and end the days when government jobs were given only in reward for political favors. Toward this end, he doubled the number of federal jobs requiring civil service exams.

Despite angering some party leaders with his stand on reform, Cleveland won the Democratic presidential nomination in 1888. To oppose him, the Republicans chose Benjamin Harrison of Indiana, a grandson of the ninth president, William Henry Harrison. After a dirty campaign, Cleveland won the popular election by some 100,000 votes. But Harrison came out on top in electoral votes, thus winning the race.

The new president and Congress quickly set out to reward their supporters, thereby weakening the reform efforts of Cleveland. The Republicans filled practically every job not on the civil service list with members of their own party. The 1890 Republican Congress was also so free with money for pensions and other pet projects that it became known as the Billion Dollar Congress.

▪▪ President Harrison weakened the reform efforts of President Cleveland.

GROVER CLEVELAND
1837–1908

in office
1885–1889 and
1893–1897

Called Uncle Jumbo by his family, Grover Cleveland was a large and genial man. Because he was so insistent about government reform, however, his enemies called him His Obstinacy.

A bachelor, Cleveland was accused in the campaign of 1884 of fathering a child out of wedlock. Refusing to participate in the mud-slinging, Cleveland replied: "The other side can have a monopoly of all the dirt in this campaign." The New York *World* defended Cleveland, giving four reasons for supporting the candidate: "1. He is an honest man; 2. He is an honest man; 3. He is an honest man; 4. He is an honest man."

BENJAMIN HARRISON
1833–1901

in office
1889–1893

Grandson of a president and son of a congressman, Benjamin Harrison was often compared to earlier Harrisons, much to his displeasure. Once when he was introduced at a political gathering as the grandson of President William Henry Harrison, "Little Ben" immediately retorted, "I want it understood that I am the grandson of nobody. I believe that every man should stand on his own merits."

Indeed, as president, Harrison was unlike his grandfather. Although Harrison was an effective public speaker, close up he seemed aloof. One official dubbed him the "White House Iceberg."

SECTION 1 REVIEW

IDENTIFY and explain the significance of the following: Gilded Age, Tweed Ring, Schuyler Colfax, Samuel J. Tilden, Rutherford B. Hayes, James A. Garfield, Charles Guiteau, Chester A. Arthur, Pendleton Civil Service Act, mugwumps, Grover Cleveland, Benjamin Harrison.

1. **MAIN IDEA** What led many Americans to call for civil service reform?

2. **MAIN IDEA** Why was the Pendleton Civil Service Act criticized?

3. **CONTRASTING** How did President Harrison's reform record differ from that of President Cleveland?

4. **WRITING TO PERSUADE** Imagine you are Horace Greeley. Write an editorial stating what is wrong with the spoils system and why Grant should be defeated in the 1872 election.

5. **IDENTIFYING CAUSE AND EFFECT** Why did Charles Guiteau assassinate President Garfield? Why can it be said that Guiteau's action did not have its intended effect?

LABOR STRIVES TO ORGANIZE

FOCUS

■ What was working life like for industrial laborers in the late 19th century?

■ What weakened support for the labor movement?

■ How did the government respond to labor disputes in the 1890s?

*P*reoccupied with political reform, the government overlooked one of the major trends of the late 1800s—the growing gulf between the haves and the have-nots. By 1890 close to 75 percent of the nation's wealth was controlled by just 10 percent of the population. At the same time, nearly 50 percent of American industrial workers lived below the poverty line. Demanding the right to share in the country's prosperity, some workers organized labor unions.

South Carolina textile mill worker, c. 1890

THE NEW WORKING CLASS

The demand for labor soared under the new industrial order. Millions of workers were needed to staff factories, construct machines, furnish raw materials, and transport and sell finished goods. This great demand was met, in large part, by the flood of immigrants who came to the United States during the 1800s. By 1900 one third of the country's industrial workers were foreign-born.

These immigrant workers were joined by hundreds of thousands of rural Americans who moved to the cities in search of jobs. Among this group were thousands of African Americans from the South who came to the North in hope of securing industrial work. Though the postwar South was home to many industries—textiles, tobacco, lumber, coal, and iron—African Americans were barred

from most factory jobs. Almost all southern textile workers were white and native-born. Cigar factories did rely on African American workers—women cleaned and sorted the leaves, men made the cigars—but their numbers were few. In 1891, only some 7,400 southern blacks held industrial jobs. Most African Americans, like most southerners, remained tied to the land and impoverished.

▶ Sorting tobacco leaves in cigar factories was grueling, tedious work. The strong fumes often caused painful eye disorders.

Southern blacks hoped conditions would be better in the North. But industrial employment remained out of reach for most. The best jobs still went to native-born whites or to immigrants. African American men—even those with skills—generally found themselves confined to the dirtiest or most dangerous work or to such service-related jobs as gardening or driving coaches.

African American women in northern cities competed with poor immigrant women for domestic jobs and unskilled factory work. Most women—African American or immigrant—worked because they had to work. As a state official in Massachusetts noted, "a family of workers can always live well, but the man with a family of small children to support, unless his wife works also, has a small chance of living properly." The ranks of women workers more than doubled between 1870 and 1890 as wives, daughters, and sisters labored to put food on the table. By 1900, women accounted for about 15 percent of the labor force—some five million workers.

The number of children in the work force doubled during this period for the same reason. By 1890 close to 20 percent of American children between ages 10 and 15—some 1.5 million in all—worked for wages. In the textile mills of North Carolina, for example, one in every four workers was a child. The ratio was much lower in Massachusetts mills—1 in 20. In other places, countless boys and girls worked in garment factories or at home, making clothing or other items by the piece. Others labored in the nation's mines, canneries, and shoe factories, or they roamed the streets shining shoes, selling newspapers, collecting scrap, running errands, or delivering packages.

▲ In the 1870s the Knights of Labor campaigned for legislation to protect child workers. But children continued to experience wretched working conditions throughout the next few decades.

Working Conditions

Children in the labor force faced terrible conditions. In some textile mills, for instance, children worked 12-hour shifts—often at night—for pennies a day. But all industrial workers, regardless of age, sex, or race, labored long hours for little pay. Conditions were especially rough for unskilled workers. Most unskilled male laborers worked at least 10 hours a day, 6 days a week, for less than $10 a week. Many African American, Mexican American, and Asian American men worked the same number of hours for even lower wages. And employers made few allowances for women and children, expecting them to work the same number of hours as men for sometimes as little as half the pay.

Such long hours left workers exhausted at the end of the day. And fatigue increased the danger in already unsafe working surroundings. In 1881 alone, some 30,000 railroad workers were killed or injured on the job. Most employers felt no responsibility for work-related deaths and injuries and made little effort to improve workplace safety.

Workers who lived in a **company town**, a town where a company owned the housing and the businesses, faced special problems. These workers usually received their wages in **scrip**—paper money that could be used only to pay rent to the company or to buy goods at company stores. Prices at company stores were usually much higher than at regular stores, and workers often spent whole paychecks on necessities like food and clothing.

■■ **For most industrial laborers, working life meant long hours of toil for little pay and few benefits.**

ᴛHE KNIGHTS OF LABOR

As conditions worsened, workers clamored for change. They knew that alone they could do little. But if they banded together, the wealthy factory owners, the corrupt politicians, and the rich capitalists on New York's Wall Street would have to listen. Workers formed a number of local unions in the first half of the 1800s, but after 1850, organizing efforts went national.

One of the earliest national unions was the **Knights of Labor**, founded in 1869 by nine Philadelphia garment workers led by Uriah

▼ Terence V. Powderly is shown here surrounded by other influential leaders of the Knights of Labor.

Stephens. It remained largely a white male organization until 1879, when Terence V. Powderly, an Irish Catholic machinist and mayor of Scranton, Pennsylvania, became its leader. Under his leadership the Knights' membership mushroomed.

Powderly wanted the Knights of Labor to attract workers who were often excluded from other unions. He therefore opened the union's doors to both skilled and unskilled laborers. He also welcomed thousands of women into the union's ranks. A number of women, such as Mary Harris Jones, played prominent roles in the Knights of Labor.

Born in Cork, Ireland, in 1830, Mary Harris came to the United States as a young child. She married George Jones, a union supporter, in 1861. Widowed six years later, she devoted herself to the labor movement. In the 1870s, at the invitation of Powderly, she became an organizer for the Knights of Labor. Declaring that her place was "wherever there is a fight," she organized strikes, marches, and demonstrations. Her activities earned her the title "the most dangerous woman in America." But because she looked more motherly than radical, most people called her Mother Jones.

BIO GRAPHY

Mary Harris Jones

Jones was sentenced to 20 years in jail for her part in a 1912 West Virginia strike, but a public outcry caused the governor of the state to free her. Mother Jones continued fighting for the rights of America's working people until her death, at age 100, in 1930.

Powderly also opened the union to African Americans. By the mid-1880s the Knights claimed some 60,000 black members. At the Knights' 1886 national convention in Richmond, Virginia, African American delegate Frank Ferrell told the crowd:

❝ One of the objects of our Order is the abolition of these distinctions which are maintained by creed or color. . . . My experience . . . [has] taught me that we have worked so far successfully toward the extinction of these regrettable distinctions. ❞

Not all African American Knights, however, agreed with Ferrell's assessment. "The white Knights of Labor prevent me from getting employment because I am a colored man," complained a mason from North Carolina, "although I belong to the same organization." Still, the Knights did more than other early unions to try to meet the needs of African American workers.

The Knights were not equality-minded when it came to everyone, however. Although Powderly welcomed some European immigrants to the union, he, like many working-class Americans, actively opposed Chinese workers, claiming they stole jobs from white Americans. At his urging, for instance, West Coast branches of the Knights of Labor vigorously campaigned for passage of the Chinese Exclusion Act.

Powderly led the Knights of Labor for 15 years. Under his leadership, the union fought for temperance, the eight-hour workday, equal pay for equal work, and an end to child labor. By 1886, the union boasted a membership of more than 700,000.

THE GREAT UPHEAVAL

The Knights' phenomenal growth was due in part to the great railroad strike of 1877 and to a successful strike that the Knights had launched against railroad baron Jay Gould in 1884. Both strikes made workers more willing to press for the better working conditions being championed by the Knights. In 1886, as the nation entered a year of intense strikes and violent labor confrontations that would become known as the **Great Upheaval,** the Knights were riding the crest of immense popularity.

By 1886, American workers were primed for action. An economic depression in the early 1880s had led to massive wage cuts. Workers needed—and demanded—relief. When negotiations with management failed, many workers took direct action. By the end of 1886, some 1,500 strikes, involving more than 400,000 workers, had swept the nation. Many of these strikes turned violent, as angry strikers clashed head-on with their employers and the police. Perhaps the most notorious of these confrontations was the **Haymarket Riot**.

The seeds for the Haymarket Riot were sown when some 40,000 Chicago workers struck on May 1, 1886. The strike was launched by the local craft unions, but it soon fell under the leadership of a group of political radicals and **anarchists** (people who oppose all forms of government). On May 3 a confrontation between the police and the strikers picketing the McCormick harvester plant left two strikers dead. In protest, the strikers called a meeting for the next day in Chicago's Haymarket Square. Peaceful and sparsely attended, the rally was about to break up when nearly 200 police officers appeared. Suddenly a bomb exploded in the midst of the police. The police responded with gunfire. When the smoke cleared, more than 70 people lay wounded. The day's rioting also resulted in the deaths of seven police officers and one civilian.

The police arrested eight well-known anarchists—only one of whom had attended the meeting—charging them with incitement to murder. All eight

▼ Printed in both English and German, posters asked workingmen to "appear in full force" at Haymarket Square to protest the killing of two strikers. There, a confrontation with Chicago police quickly erupted into violence.

Labor Strikes, 1870–1900

STRIKES INCREASE The strike became the chief means for workers to improve wages and working conditions.

? **LOCATION** Where did the majority of railroad-related strikes occur?

1886 HAYMARKET RIOT
Bomb kills police breaking up labor rally; public turns against workers.

1875–1876 MOLLY MAGUIRES
Irish miners accused of murdering foreman; 24 convicted, 10 hanged.

1892 HOMESTEAD STRIKE
Skilled iron and steel workers' strike at Carnegie Steel Company fails.

Legend:
- Great railroad strike of 1877
- Miners' strike ✕
- Other railroad strike
- Other strike ✿
- Counties with strike activity, 1881–1900

were found guilty; four went to the gallows. On the final day of the trial, one of the defendants warned:

> **❝** I have told [Chicago Police] Captain Schaack, and I stand by it, "if you cannonade us, we shall dynamite you." You laugh! Perhaps you think, "you'll throw no more bombs"; but let me assure you I die happy on the gallows, so confident am I that the hundreds and thousands to whom I have spoken will remember my words; . . . they will do the bomb throwing! **❞**

But worker activism actually decreased by the close of the year. Emboldened by the Haymarket conviction, employers struck back. They drew up **blacklists**—lists of union supporters—that they shared with one another. Blacklisted workers found it almost impossible to get jobs. Many employers also made job applicants sign agreements—called **yellow-dog contracts** by the workers—promising not to join unions. When these measures failed and workers struck anyway, many companies instituted **lockouts**, barring workers from the plant, and brought in nonunion **strikebreakers**, often African

Americans or others who felt abandoned by the unions. As labor suffered repeated defeats and as the tide of public sentiment turned against workers, union membership—including the Knights'—shrank.

Many of the workers who remained in unions were in skilled trades. Alarmed by the violence of 1886 and by the response of the employers, these workers broke ranks with the unskilled and joined the newly formed **American Federation of Labor** (AFL), founded by Samuel Gompers in 1886. The AFL was a collection of independent skilled craft unions committed to working together to advance the interests of skilled workers (see Chapter 17).

■■ Support for the labor movement was weakened by the violence of the 1886 strikes.

THE HOMESTEAD AND PULLMAN STRIKES

After a few years of relative peace, industrial unrest broke out again in 1892. At Andrew

▲ Pullman strikers in 1894 blocked trains, sabotaged railroad switches, and drove engineers from railway cars to protest wage cuts.

Carnegie's Homestead steel plant in Pennsylvania, manager Henry Clay Frick announced a wage cut. In June the workers went on strike. Frick responded by instituting a lockout and hiring some 300 detectives to guard the plant. A violent clash between strikers and the detectives in early July resulted in 16 deaths. The violence soon spread to other plants. Order was restored only after state militiamen were called in.

Labor disputes sparked more violence in 1894. On May 11, 1894, workers at the Pullman sleeping-car factory in Chicago went on strike. The owner, George Pullman, had cut wages while refusing to lower rents or prices at the stores in his company town. Eugene V. Debs, head of the American Railway Union (ARU), backed the Pullman strikers. Urging other union members to boycott all trains that included Pullman cars, Debs proclaimed:

❝ The struggle . . . has developed into a contest between the producing classes and the money power of the country. We stand upon the ground that the workingmen are entitled to a just proportion of the proceeds of their labor. ❞

The railroad companies came to George Pullman's rescue by threatening to fire any worker who refused to handle Pullman cars. In response, railroad workers tied up rail traffic throughout the Midwest. The railroad companies quickly turned to the federal government for help. By attaching mail cars to the Pullman cars, the railroads gave the government a way to block the strike on the grounds that the strikers were preventing mail delivery. The government demanded that the ARU end the strike. When Debs and other ARU officials ignored the order, they were jailed.

Meanwhile, President Cleveland ordered federal troops into Chicago on July 4, sparking violence that left scores dead or wounded and produced hundreds of thousands of dollars in property damage. Within a few days, however, the troops had restored order. In the process, the Pullman strike had been broken and the ARU destroyed.

▪▪ During the 1890s the government sided with business against the labor unions.

SECTION 2 REVIEW

IDENTIFY and explain the significance of the following: company town, scrip, Knights of Labor, Mary Harris Jones, Frank Ferrell, Great Upheaval, Haymarket Riot, anarchists, blacklists, yellow-dog contracts, lockouts, strikebreakers, American Federation of Labor.

LOCATE and explain the importance of the following: Haymarket Square, Homestead steel plant, Pullman sleeping-car factory.

1. **MAIN IDEA** Describe working life for most industrial laborers in late-19th-century America.

2. **MAIN IDEA** How did the strikes of 1886 weaken the labor movement?

3. **ASSESSING CONSEQUENCES** How did business and the government respond to labor activism in the late 1800s?

4. **WRITING TO EXPRESS A VIEWPOINT** Imagine you are a member of an industrial workers' union in the late 1800s. Write a proposal for changes in work rules and conditions to present to management. State why you think these changes should be made.

5. **EVALUATING** Why might it be said that the Knights of Labor's recruitment policies under Powderly seem contradictory?

FARMERS, POPULISM, AND DEPRESSION

FOCUS

- **What problems did American farmers face during the late 1800s?**
- **What did the Grange and Alliance movements and the Populist party hope to achieve?**
- **Why did the Populists fail in the 1896 election?**

Farm family, 1881

America's farmers suffered many hardships during the late 1800s. Like industrial workers, farmers organized to win their share of prosperity. This drive to organize culminated in the founding of the People's, or Populist, party. A severe economic depression helped the Populists gain strength during the early 1890s. However, the party's later focus on a single issue—free silver—led to its downfall.

THE FARMERS' PLIGHT

The development of the new industrial order offered fresh opportunities for American farmers. The rapidly growing population in the industrial centers needed feeding. The farmers responded, each year raising more crops and animals. Unfortunately for the Americans, farmers in Great Britain, Russia, Canada, Argentina, Australia, and other nations did the same. Soon prices tumbled as supply exceeded demand. But railroad freight charges continued to spiral upward, as did the cost of new machinery. As farm profits plunged, many farmers bought more land and increased production. Greater production, however, only pushed prices even lower.

To make matters worse, almost all farm families had borrowed money to pay for their land or to buy new equipment, generally putting their farms up as security. Those who could not repay the loans lost their farms. Many ended up as tenant farmers, paying rent to the new owners. Others were forced to become farm laborers.

■■ **In the late 1800s, farmers were burdened with crushing debt as the prices of farm products fell and costs increased.**

To farmers, the situation seemed terribly unfair. The merchants who sold farm equipment and other supplies were making money. Also prospering were the bankers who lent farmers money and the railroads that hauled the farmers' grain and livestock to market. All that the farmers had to show for long days of backbreaking labor were rising debts. Something had to be done.

THE GRANGE MOVEMENT

In an effort to better their lot, farmers organized. The first major farmers' organization, the Patrons of Husbandry, or the **National Grange**, was founded by Oliver Hudson Kelley in 1867. Kelley set up the Grange primarily as a social organization. But as membership increased and farmers'

Agricultural Regions, 1900

AGRICULTURAL ABUNDANCE Due to its size and its varied soils and climates, the United States has been able to feed its own people and to produce a surplus for export.

? PLACE What kind of agriculture is found in the industrial states of the Northeast?

financial problems grew, the Grange began tackling economic and political issues.

To lower costs, some Grange members formed **cooperatives**. Cooperative members sold their products directly to big-city markets and bought farm equipment and other goods in large quantities at wholesale prices—thereby cutting costs. But the Grange's main focus was on forcing states to regulate railroad freight rates. In the early 1870s, responding to pressure from farmers, the state legislatures of Illinois, Iowa, Minnesota, and Wisconsin passed "Granger laws," which set up state commissions to fix maximum railroad rates.

Many railroads challenged the Granger laws in the courts. In a victory for farmers, the United States Supreme Court in *Munn* v. *Illinois* (1877) declared that state legislatures had the right to regulate businesses—like railroads—that involved the public interest. But 10 years later the Court, in *Wabash* v. *Illinois,* qualified its decision. State governments, the Court ruled, had no power to regulate traffic that moved across state boundaries. Only the federal government had that right.

This decision led directly to the passage of the **Interstate Commerce Act** in 1887. The act prohibited railroads from giving secret rebates, or refunds, to large shippers or from charging more for short hauls than for long hauls over the same line. It also stated that railroad rates had to be "reasonable and just." To monitor railroad activities, the act created the **Interstate Commerce Commission** (ICC). But the ICC had little power to enforce its rulings. When it took railroads to court for violating the law, the courts almost always ruled in the railroads' favor.

THE ALLIANCE MOVEMENT

While the Grange was struggling to win the fight for railroad legislation, a more powerful farm organization—the **Farmers' Alliance**—arose. Beginning in Texas in 1877, the Alliance movement quickly spread. Debt-ridden farm families grasped the Alliance message of solidarity and hope like a drowning person clinging to a log. By

▲ African American farmers joined the Colored Farmers' Alliance to protect their interests against monopolies and unfair freight prices. Shown here are Virginia homesteaders during the 1890s.

1890 the movement claimed some 400,000 members in three organizations: the National Farmers' Alliance of the Northwest, the all-white Southern Alliance, and the Colored Farmers' Alliance.

Alliance leaders traveled the country, urging people to take action. Among the most effective was Mary Elizabeth Lease from Kansas. "The great common people of this country are slaves, and monopoly is the master," she told her audiences:

66 The politicians said we suffered from overproduction. Overproduction, when 10,000 little children, so statistics tell us, starve to death every year in the United States. . . . We will stand by our homes and stay by our fireside by force if necessary, and we will not pay our debts to the loan-shark companies until the government pays its debts to us. 99

Like the Grange, the Alliance organized cooperatives to buy equipment and to market farm products. It also offered farmers low-cost insurance and lobbied for tougher bank regulations, government ownership of the railroads, and a **graduated income tax** that taxed higher incomes at a higher rate.

■■ The Grange and Farmers' Alliance movements sought economic and political gains for farmers.

THE MONEY QUESTION

The Alliance also echoed the demand that farmers had been making since the end of the Civil War: expand the money supply by printing more greenbacks, the paper money used during the war. The resulting inflation would benefit farmers by allowing them to charge more for their farm products and by making it easier for them to repay their bank loans.

Such prospects alarmed eastern bankers. They wanted the money supply tied to the **gold standard**. Under this system, each dollar was equal to and redeemable for a set amount of gold, and the amount of money in circulation was limited by the amount of gold held in the U.S. Treasury.

Siding with the bankers, the government began withdrawing greenbacks from circulation. Farmers responded by demanding that the government back the money supply with silver (which was plentiful in the West) as well as with gold. Bowing to pressure, Congress passed the **Bland-Allison Act** in 1878 and the **Sherman Silver Purchase Act** in 1890. Both acts required the government to buy silver each month and mint it into coins. But because the government bought so little silver, the money supply did not increase noticeably.

Disappointed, Alliance members threw themselves into the 1890 elections, supporting any candidate who accepted their pro-farmer programs. The results were remarkable. Alliance-backed candidates won 38 U.S. congressional seats, 4 southern governorships, and numerous other political offices.

THE POPULIST PARTY

Elated, Alliance leaders sought to build on these successes by forming a new political party. At a national convention in St. Louis in February 1892, a gathering of farmers, labor leaders, and reformers founded the People's party, which became more commonly known as the **Populist party**. Politician and author Ignatius Donnelly of Minnesota opened the convention with a thunderous address:

66 We meet in the midst of a nation brought to the verge of moral, political, and material ruin. Corruption dominates the ballot-box, the Legislatures, the Congress. . . . We seek to restore the government of the Republic to the hands of the "plain people." 99

WILLIAM McKINLEY
1843–1901

**in office
1897–1901**

William McKinley used presidential power so effectively that a Republican newspaper concluded: "No executive in the history of the country . . . has given a greater exhibition of his influence over Congress." Even his political enemies respected his tact and persuasiveness. Speaker of the House Tom Reed said of him, with envy, "My opponents in Congress go at me tooth and nail, but they always apologize to William when they are going to call him names."

A courteous manner characterized McKinley in private life as well. He was devoted to protecting and caring for his wife Ida, who suffered headaches and seizures that often kept her from fulfilling her role as First Lady. He stayed close to her during state dinners and receptions. If she fainted, he would tend to her and yet carry right on with conversation so as not to embarrass her.

William McKinley

The party platform echoed Grange and Alliance demands: a graduated income tax, bank regulation, government ownership of railroad and telegraph companies, and the free coinage of silver. Appealing to the labor and reform votes, the platform also called for immigration restrictions, a shorter workday, and voting reforms.

■■ **The Populist party platform addressed many of the concerns of farmers, laborers, and political reformers.**

The Populists nominated James B. Weaver to run in the 1892 presidential election against Republican Benjamin Harrison, the incumbent, and Democrat Grover Cleveland, the former president who had lost to Harrison in the 1888 election. Weaver had run for president—and lost—on the Greenback party ticket in 1880. Cleveland won the 1892 election. But the Populist party elected 3 senators, 11 congressmen, 3 governors, and numerous state legislators. And Weaver polled a very respectable one million popular votes, carrying four western states and 22 electoral votes.

DEPRESSION, DISCONTENT, AND GOLD

In May 1893, only two months after Cleveland took office, one of the country's leading railroad companies failed. The failure triggered a financial panic on Wall Street that sent stock prices plunging. The country quickly slid into an economic depression. By the end of 1893, some three million people were unemployed—100,000 in Chicago alone. In New York City 20,000 homeless people sought shelter in jails. Strikes and protests swept the country.

The depression had many causes, including a worldwide financial panic. But President Cleveland chose to focus on one—the Sherman Silver Purchase Act, which required the government to pay for silver purchases with Treasury notes redeemable in either gold or silver. As new silver finds decreased the value of the metal, people rushed to exchange their notes for gold. This action put a terrible strain on the Treasury's gold reserves. To protect the gold standard and to restore confidence in the economy, Cleveland called for repeal of the Sherman Silver Purchase Act. Congress complied in October 1893.

THE ELECTION OF 1896

Cleveland's actions salvaged the gold standard, but they did not end the debate on the money supply. Silver became a central issue in the 1896 election.

The Republicans gave the presidential nomination to Ohio governor William McKinley and adopted a conservative platform upholding the gold standard. A deeply split Democratic party

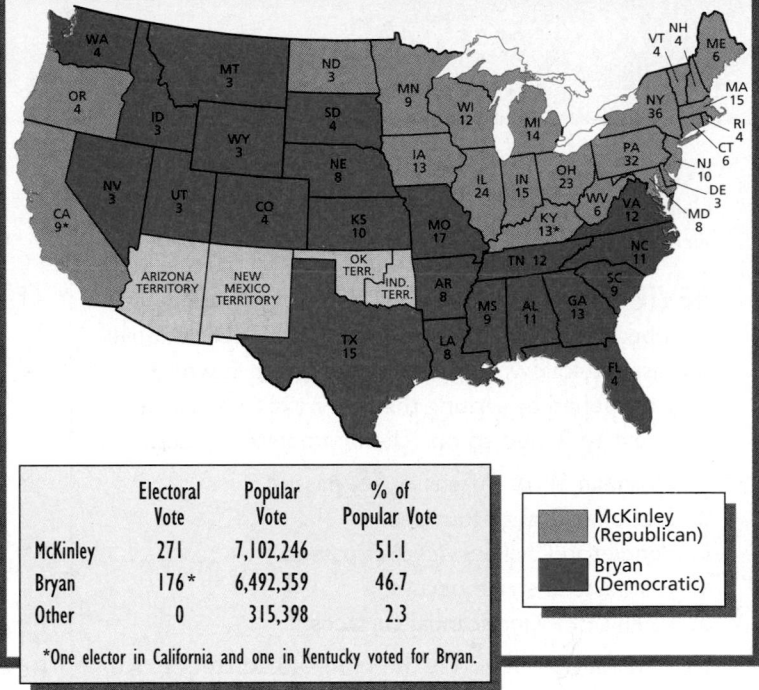

▶ While Bryan traveled 13,000 miles and gave 600 speeches during the 1896 campaign, McKinley stayed home and received visitors on the front porch of his Ohio home. Ribbons from McKinley's campaign are shown here.

Election of 1896

FREE SILVER The Democratic party's split over the issue of free silver enabled McKinley and the Republicans to capture the White House.

❓ **REGION** Which areas of the United States backed McKinley and his gold standard platform?

	Electoral Vote	Popular Vote	% of Popular Vote
McKinley	271	7,102,246	51.1
Bryan	176*	6,492,559	46.7
Other	0	315,398	2.3

*One elector in California and one in Kentucky voted for Bryan.

■ McKinley (Republican)
■ Bryan (Democratic)

rejected President Cleveland, finally nominating free-silver advocate William Jennings Bryan, a two-term congressman from Nebraska. The Populists—their free-silver platform taken up by the Democratic party—threw their support to Bryan.

Bryan swept the South and much of the West, but he made no headway at all in the urban industrial East or in the mixed industrial and farm states of the Midwest. When the popular votes were counted, McKinley had edged out Bryan by some 500,000 votes. The Populists were in shock—free silver had proved too weak an issue on which to base a national campaign.

The election defeat and the arrival of better times for farmers essentially ended the power of the Populist party. It nevertheless stands as the first example of a large-scale effort by a disadvantaged group in the modern industrial era to use the political process to advance its interests. Furthermore, the Populist platform laid the groundwork for

future reform (see Chapter 17). As the great Populist leader Mary Elizabeth Lease noted in 1914, "The seeds we sowed out in Kansas did not fall on barren ground."

∎∎ **New prosperity among farmers and the decline of the free-silver issue led to the collapse of the Populist party.**

SECTION 3 REVIEW

IDENTIFY and explain the significance of the following: cooperatives, Interstate Commerce Act, Interstate Commerce Commission, Mary Elizabeth Lease, graduated income tax, gold standard, Bland-Allison Act, Sherman Silver Purchase Act, Populist party, James B. Weaver, William McKinley, William Jennings Bryan.

1. **MAIN IDEA** What serious problems did American farmers face in the late 19th century?

2. **MAIN IDEA** What were the main goals of the Grange and Farmers' Alliance movements? What did the Populist party try to accomplish through its political platform?

3. **GEOGRAPHY: REGION** What regions of the nation did William Jennings Bryan win in the 1896 election? In what areas did he poll the fewest votes?

4. **WRITING TO EXPLAIN** Imagine you are Mary Elizabeth Lease in 1914. Write an essay explaining why the Alliance movement was necessary and describe the legacy of the Populist party.

5. **ANALYZING** Why did expansion of the money supply appeal to farmers but not to eastern bankers?

National Grange founded.

Knights of Labor founded.

Crédit Mobilier scandal surfaces.

Mark Twain and Charles Dudley Warner publish *The Gilded Age.*

Rutherford B. Hayes elected president.

1865   1870   1875

WRITING A SUMMARY

Using the essential points of the chapter as a guide, write a summary of the chapter.

REVIEWING CHRONOLOGY

Number your paper 1 to 5. Study the time line above, and list the following events in the order in which they happened by writing the first next to 1, the second next to 2, and so on. Then complete the activity.

1. Sherman Silver Purchase Act passed.
2. National Grange founded.
3. Pendleton Civil Service Act passed.
4. Homestead strike occurs.
5. Crédit Mobilier scandal surfaces.

Synthesizing How was the Homestead steel strike typical of many strikes of the period?

IDENTIFYING PEOPLE AND IDEAS

Explain the historical significance of each of the following people or terms.

1. *The Gilded Age*
2. Tweed Ring
3. Charles Guiteau
4. Grover Cleveland
5. Mary Harris Jones
6. Terence V. Powderly
7. lockouts
8. cooperatives
9. Mary Elizabeth Lease
10. gold standard

UNDERSTANDING MAIN IDEAS

1. What problems did American industrial workers and farmers face in the late 1800s?
2. Why did some Americans support civil service reform?
3. What position did the government take in the labor disputes of the late 1800s?
4. How did the Populist party represent the interests of farmers, laborers, and political reformers?
5. What caused the Populist party to lose the 1896 election?

REVIEWING THEMES

1. **Democratic Values** What steps did reformers take to bring about political and economic change in American society in the late 1800s?

2. **Cultural Diversity** How were different groups of people united by changing economic and political conditions? How were they divided?

THINKING CRITICALLY

1. **Hypothesizing** How might workers have gained more ground if the strikes of 1886 had not become so violent?
2. **Analyzing** Why did the Interstate Commerce Act and the Sherman Silver Purchase Act represent only partial victories for reformers?
3. **Evaluating** How did the focus of reform efforts change from the 1870s to the 1890s?

STRATEGY FOR SUCCESS

Review the Skills Handbook entry on Reading Charts and Graphs beginning on page 996. Then study the graph below. What might account for the dramatic change in Knights' membership before and after 1886?

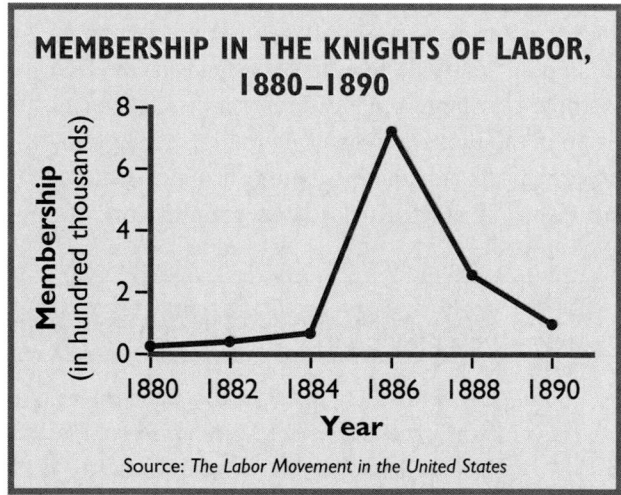

MEMBERSHIP IN THE KNIGHTS OF LABOR, 1880–1890

Source: *The Labor Movement in the United States*

WRITING ABOUT HISTORY

Writing to Explain Imagine you are Mary Harris Jones and have been invited to be the guest speaker at a rally for the Alliance movement. Write a speech explaining how the Alliance can use the techniques of unions such as the Knights of Labor.

| James A. Garfield elected president. | Grover Cleveland elected president. | | Sherman Silver Purchase Act passed. | Pullman strike occurs. |
| Pendleton Civil Service Act passed. | Haymarket Riot occurs. | Benjamin Harrison elected president. | Homestead strike occurs. Populist party founded. | William McKinley elected president. |

| 1880 | 1885 | 1890 | 1895 | 1910 |

USING PRIMARY SOURCES

In the late 19th century, farmers faced a variety of problems, from unpredictable weather and pests to railroad price-fixing. Read the poem below, written by a Georgia farmer in 1890. Then explain how it reflects the problems that led to the formation of farmers' groups. What was the most severe problem?

> ❝ *We worked through spring and summer,*
> *through winter and through fall;*
> *But the mortgage worked the hardest*
> *and the steadiest of them all;*
> *It worked on night and Sunday, it*
> *worked each holiday;*
> *It settled down among us and it never*
> *went away.*
>
> *Whatever we kept from it seemed*
> *almost as bad as theft;*
> *It watched us every minute and ruled*
> *us right and left*
> *The rust and blight was with us*
> *sometimes, and sometimes not;*
> *The dark brown scowling mortgage was*
> *forever on the spot.*
>
> *The weevil and the cut worm, they*
> *went as well they came;*
> *The mortgage stayed forever, eating*
> *hearty all the same*
> *It nailed up every window, stood*
> *guard at every door;*
> *And happiness and sunshine made their*
> *place with us no more.* ❞

LINKING HISTORY AND GEOGRAPHY

Review the map on page 495. In which region did most labor strikes take place? Why do you think this was so?

BUILDING YOUR PORTFOLIO

Complete the following projects independently or cooperatively.

1. **SOCIAL CONFLICT** In chapters 14 and 15 you explored social conflicts arising from westward expansion and immigration. Building on that experience, imagine you are an African American from the rural South seeking a job in a northern industrial city. Write a short play that describes the competition for urban jobs and the problems you are facing in securing employment.

2. **TECHNOLOGY AND INDUSTRY** In chapters 14 and 15 you were a land speculator planning a railhead in Nebraska. Building on that experience, imagine that your town is a reality and has become a thriving railroad hub linking cattle ranchers, farmers, and area manufacturers and merchants to eastern markets. Local members of the Grange are up in arms over the cost of shipping their products by rail. Prepare a speech to deliver to the state legislature supporting passage of a series of Granger laws.

3. **REFORM** In Chapter 15 you portrayed a settlement-house worker. Building on that experience, imagine you are a labor leader organizing a union in the late 1800s. Create a poster designed to persuade women, African Americans, and recent immigrants to join the union.

American Letters

Mark Twain's America

Samuel Langhorne Clemens—Mark Twain to generations of readers—remains one of America's greatest humorists and chroniclers of the American character. In the following two selections, Twain explores life in two very different settings—the Mississippi River and Washington, D.C.

▲ **Mark Twain**

From *Life on the Mississippi*

by Mark Twain

The river's earliest commerce was in great barges—keelboats, broadhorns. They floated and sailed from the upper rivers to New Orleans, changed cargoes there, and were tediously warped and poled back by hand. A voyage down and back sometimes occupied nine months. In time this commerce increased until it gave employment to hordes of rough and hardy men; rude, uneducated, brave, suffering terrific hardships with sailor-like stoicism; heavy drinkers, coarse frolickers in moral sties like the Natchez-under-the-hill of that day, heavy fighters, reckless fellows, every one, elephantinely jolly, foul-witted, profane, prodigal of their money, bankrupt at the end of the trip, fond of barbaric finery, prodigious braggarts; yet, in the main, honest, trustworthy, faithful to promises and duty, and often picturesquely magnanimous.

By and by the steamboat intruded. Then, for fifteen or twenty years, these men continued to run their keelboats downstream, and the steamers did all of the upstream business, the keelboatmen selling their boats in New Orleans, and returning home as deck-passengers in the steamers.

But after a while the steamboats so increased in number and in speed that they were able to absorb the entire commerce; and then keelboating died a permanent death. The keelboatman became a deckhand, or a mate, or a pilot on the steamer; and when steamer-berths were not open to him, he took a berth on a Pittsburgh coal-flat, or on a pine raft constructed in the forests up toward the sources of the Mississippi.

In the heyday of the steamboating prosperity, the river from end to end was flanked with coal-fleets and timber-rafts, all managed by hand, and employing hosts of the rough characters whom I have been trying to describe. . . .

By way of illustrating the keelboat talk and manners, and that now departed and hardly remembered raft life, I will throw in, in this place, a chapter from a book which I have been working at. . . . The book is a story which details some passages in the life of an ignorant village boy, Huck Finn, son of the town drunkard. . . . He has run away from his persecuting father, and from a persecuting good widow who wishes to make

▼ *Mississippi riverboat*

a nice, truth telling respectable boy of him; and with him a slave of the widow's has also escaped. They have found a fragment of a lumber-raft (it is high water and dead summer-time), and are floating down river by night, and hiding in the willows by day—bound for Cairo, [Illinois,] whence the Negro will seek freedom in the heart of the free states. But, in the fog, they have passed Cairo without knowing it. By and by they begin to suspect the truth, and Huck Finn is persuaded to end the dismal suspense by swimming down to a huge raft which they have seen in the distance ahead of them, creeping aboard under cover of the darkness, and gathering the needed information by eavesdropping: . . .

I swum down along the raft till I was most abreast the campfire in the middle, then I crawled aboard and inched along and got in among some shingles on the weather side of the fire. There was thirteen men there—they was the watch on deck of course. And a mighty rough-looking lot, too. . . .

The man they called Ed said the muddy Mississippi water was wholesomer to drink than the clear water of the Ohio; he said that if you let a pint of this yaller Mississippi water settle, you would have about a half to three-quarters of an inch of mud in the bottom, according to the stage of the river, and then it warn't no better than Ohio water—what you wanted to do was to keep it stirred up—and when the water was low, keep mud on hand to put in and thicken the water up the way it ought to be.

The Child of Calamity said that was so; he said there was nutritiousness in the mud, and a man that drunk Mississippi water could grow corn in his stomach if he wanted to. He says:

"You look at the graveyards; that tells the tale. Trees won't grow worth shucks in a Cincinnati graveyard, but in a Sent Louis graveyard they grow upwards of eight hundred foot high. It's all on account of the water the people drunk before they laid up. A Cincinnati corpse don't richen a soil any." ❖

From *The Gilded Age*

by Mark Twain and Charles Dudley Warner

Every individual you encounter in the City of Washington almost—and certainly every separate and distinct individual in the public employment, from the highest bureau chief, clear down to the maid who scrubs the Department halls . . . —represents Political Influence. Unless you can get the ear of a Senator, or a Congressman, or a Chief of a Bureau or Department, and persuade him to use his "influence" in your behalf, you cannot get an employment of the most trivial nature in Washington. Mere merit, fitness and capability, are useless baggage to you without "influence." The population of Washington consists pretty much entirely of government employés and the people who board them.

There are thousands of these employés, and they have gathered there from every corner of the Union and got their berths through the intercession (command is nearer the word) of the Senators and Representatives of their respective States. It would be an odd circumstance to see a girl get employment at three or four dollars a week . . . without any political grandee to back her, but merely because she was worthy, and competent, and a good citizen of a free country that "treats all persons alike." Washington would be mildly thunderstruck at such a thing as that. If you are a member of Congress, (no offence,) and one of your constituents who doesn't know anything, and does not want to go into the bother of learning something, and has no money, and no employment, and can't earn a living, comes besieging you for help, do you say, "Come, my friend, if your services were valuable you could get employment elsewhere—don't want you here?" Oh, no. You take him to a Department and say, "Here, give this person something to pass away the time at—and a salary"—and the thing is done. You throw him on his country. He is his country's child, let his country support him. There is something good and motherly about Washington, the grand old benevolent National Asylum for the Helpless. ❖

THINKING AND WRITING ABOUT LITERATURE

1. Toward which group does Mark Twain seem most sympathetic—the Mississippi boatmen or the public servants in Washington? Provide evidence to support your answer.
2. Twain and Charles Dudley Warner published *The Gilded Age* in 1873. What events in Washington might have influenced the tone of the book?

Strategies for Success

INTERPRETING ECONOMIC DATA

The ability to interpret economic data broadens your understanding of historical developments, such as the impact of new technologies. A great deal of information about the economy—production, prices, income, and so on—can be found in statistical charts and graphs. But data, to be useful, must be analyzed and interpreted. The data in a given chart or graph is like a snapshot that shows one specific angle on the economy or segment of the economy. When interpreting economic statistics, take into consideration what you know about the overall economy or that segment of the economy for the period under study.

How to Interpret Economic Data

1. **Read the chart or graph.** Identify the type of data included in the chart or graph and the categories, amounts, and time intervals in which the data are presented. Determine the purpose of the chart or graph. Review, if necessary, Reading Charts and Graphs beginning on page 996.
2. **Find significant trends.** Study the actual numbers or values, noting increases and decreases and looking for significant trends.
3. **Use the information.** Ask yourself: What do these statistics tell me? Compare and contrast the data in an effort to understand the trends and changes. Then draw conclusions and form hypotheses based on your analysis.

Applying the Strategy

Advances in the communications industry helped transform the U.S. economy in the late 19th century. As the chart on this page indicates, telegraph and telephone networks—measured in miles of telegraph wire laid and in number of telephones in use—saw dramatic expansion in the last 25 years of the century. Both means of communication depended heavily on the use of copper for wire. The graph shows that copper mining underwent a similar dramatic expansion during the last 30 years of the 19th century.

The fact that communications and copper mining both experienced rapid expansion during the late 1800s suggests an economic link between the two industries. Higher demand for copper may have spurred mining efforts and thus led to an increase in the available supply. But remember to keep in mind the bigger historical picture. Consider, for example, the possible roles of the expansion of the nation's railroad system, which helped link western mining regions to the rest of the country, and of the growth of the electric power industry, which was the largest user of copper.

Practicing the Strategy

Study the data in the graph on page 459. Then, on a separate sheet of paper, answer the following questions.

1. What type of information is presented in the graph?
2. What trend in the data does the graph show?
3. What possible conclusions can be drawn from the information presented in the graph?

EXPANSION OF COMMUNICATIONS INDUSTRY, 1875–1900

Year	Number of Telephones	Miles of Telegraph Wire
1875	3,000*	179,000
1880	48,000	234,000
1885	156,000	462,000
1890	228,000	679,000
1895	340,000	803,000
1900	1,356,000	933,000

*Data for 1876
Source: *Historical Statistics of the United States*

COPPER MINED IN THE U.S., 1870–1900

Source: *Historical Statistics of the United States*

BUILDING YOUR PORTFOLIO

Outlined below are three projects. Independently or cooperatively, complete one and use the products to demonstrate your mastery of the historical concepts involved.

1 SOCIAL CONFLICT

Westward expansion, immigration, and industrialization often created conflicts between different groups in American society. Using the portfolio materials you designed in chapters 14, 15, and 16, develop a series of dramatic sketches and monologues that address these conflicts and explore the *positive* consequences of cultural diversity for society.

2 TECHNOLOGY AND INDUSTRY

In the late 1800s technological advances and the growth of industry dramatically changed the appearance of the American city as well as the life-styles and work habits of its citizens. Using the portfolio materials you designed in chapters 14, 15, and 16, prepare a presentation highlighting the development of your Nebraska town from small railhead to thriving city. Be sure to include an indication of the problems that you faced and some of the solutions.

3 REFORM

American society changed rapidly at the end of the 19th century, leading to a host of social, economic, and political problems. Using the portfolio materials you designed in chapters 15 and 16, hold a meeting between business leaders, labor organizers, and urban reformers to discuss what social reforms are needed, and how these reforms can be accomplished with the cooperation of all the groups involved.

Videodisc Review

In assigned groups, develop an outline for a video collage of America in the years between 1860 and 1910. Choose images that best illustrate the major topics of the period. Write a script to accompany the images. Assign narrators to different parts of the script, and present your video collage to the class.

Further Reading

Andrist, Ralph K. *The Long Death: The Last Days of the Plains Indians.*
Macmillan (1993). History of the struggle of the Plains Indians.

Barth, Gunther. *City People: The Rise of Modern City Culture in Nineteenth-Century America.* Oxford (1980). Analysis of the spread of big-city culture.

Brown, Dee. *Bury My Heart at Wounded Knee.* Holt (1970). A history of the American West through Native American eyes.

Jones, Jacqueline. *The Dispossessed: America's Underclasses from the Civil War to the Present.* Harper-Collins (1992). An overview of poverty in America.

Katz, William L. *The Black West.* Open Hand (1987). History of the African American pioneers who helped develop the West.

Luchetti, Cathy, and Carol Olwell. *Women of the West.* Orion (1982). Firsthand accounts of women's lives in the West taken from photographs, diaries, and letters.

Schlereth, Thomas J. *Victorian America: Transformations in Everyday Life 1876–1915.* HarperCollins (1991). Detailed historical overview of the impact of immigration, expansion, and industrialization on American society.

American ALMANAC

▲ Harry Houdini

The American People

THE MOVE TO THE CITIES

1800
- 6%
- 94%

1900
- 40%
- 60%

1990
- 25%
- 75%

Rural

Urban

Source: *Bureau of the Census*

Off to Work

1900 Industry workers make about 29¢ per hour; farm workers earn $1 per day.

1900 Booker T. Washington organizes National Negro Business League.

1900 A 1,000-man logging camp consumes 1,200 lbs. of meat, 1 ton of fruit and vegetables, 900 lbs. of flour, 600 lbs. of sugar, 190 lbs. of butter, and 240 dozen eggs daily.

1900 Nearly 126,000 Americans serve in the U.S. armed forces at home and abroad.

1909 W.E.B. Du Bois helps found the new National Association for the Advancement of Colored People (NAACP).

1916 Montana representative Jeannette Rankin is first woman elected to Congress.

1916 Ezequiel de Baca elected governor of New Mexico—attaining highest elected office held by a Hispanic American to date.

▶ *Ezequiel de Baca*

At Your Leisure

1899 Scott Joplin's "Maple Leaf Rag" makes him "King of Ragtime."

1900 Eastman Kodak's $1.00 Brownie Box Camera boosts amateur photography.

1903 Baseball's Boston Americans win first World Series.

1904 Cy Young is first major league player to pitch a perfect game.

1908 Escape artist Harry Houdini attracts huge crowds.

1910 Boy Scouts and Camp Fire Girls founded.

1912 Fox-trot, crab step, kangaroo dip, chicken scratch, and bunny hug dances are big hits!

1912 Stores are bursting with consumer products: Crayola crayons, Campbell's soup, Pepsi-Cola, Jell-O, ice cream cones, Corn Flakes, Life Savers, and Oreos.

1915 Charlie Chaplin is sensation of the year; in his career he produces, directs, or acts in more than 80 films!

1920 National Negro Baseball League is formed—enabling African Americans to play professional baseball.

▶ *Naval Aviation Camp at Guantánamo Bay, Cuba, 1913*

UNIT

6

A World Power

1897–1920

▲ *Model T Ford*

❖ **The Automobile**

1900 People spend $1,250 for a new Oldsmobile; a horse and buggy costs $400.

1904 Official speed limits are set in New York: 10 mph in cities, 15 in villages, 20 on country roads.

1909 Ford produces the Model T, priced at $950; price drops to $290 by 1924.

1920 Auto sales climb to 1,905,500—up from 4,100 in 1900!

◄ *Wright brothers' airplane*

▼ *Blanche Stuart*

❖ **Firsts in Science and Technology**

1900 Only about 2% of U.S. households have a telephone; today about 95% have one.

1909 Robert E. Peary and African American Matthew Henson reach North Pole.

1909 U.S. Army buys its first airplane—from the Wright brothers.

1910 Blanche Stuart is first American woman to fly an airplane.

❖ **The Latest Looks**

1890s First factory-made clothes appear.

1907 Annette Kellerman is arrested for wearing "shocking" attire on a Boston beach: a bathing suit.

THE AGE OF REFORM

FOCUS

UNDERSTANDING THE MAIN IDEA

A new reform mood swept the United States during the early 1900s. With great optimism and faith in scientific efficiency, reformers set out to conquer the negative effects of industrialization and rapid urbanization: unsafe working conditions, long hours, poor wages, and slum housing.

THEMES

■ **ECONOMIC DEVELOPMENT** How might state governments justify regulating how businesses treat workers?

■ **DEMOCRATIC VALUES** How might reform groups help extend opportunities to all citizens?

■ **CONSTITUTIONAL HERITAGE** How might reform movements lay the groundwork for constitutional change?

1900	1904	1909	1912	1919
ILGWU established.	National Child Labor Committee formed.	NAACP founded.	Massachusetts passes minimum-wage law.	Eighteenth Amendment ratified.

While the Gilded Age had promoted industrial development and generated great profits for some, it had also created many problems. The Populist movement had brought to the nation's attention the plight of farmers and urban workers. Gilded Age reformers like Jane Addams and the men and women involved in the Social Gospel movement had worked to improve conditions for the urban poor.

*I*n 1906 Upton Sinclair published *The Jungle,* a novel about the meat-packing industry in Chicago. In an effort to alert the public to what he saw as the consequences of capitalist greed, Sinclair described industry practices in graphic detail:

66 There was never the least attention paid to what was cut up for sausage. . . . There would be meat that had tumbled out on the floor, in the dirt and sawdust. . . . There would be meat stored in great piles in rooms; and the water from leaky roofs would drip over it, and thousands of rats would race about on it. . . . These rats were nuisances, and the packers would put poisoned bread out for them, they would die, and then rats, bread, and meat would go into the hoppers together. 99

Sinclair's images were so vivid that they made some readers physically sick. "I aimed at the public's heart," Sinclair remarked, "and by accident I hit it in the stomach." In response to *The Jungle*, Americans demanded federal laws prohibiting unhealthful conditions in food-processing industries.

The Jungle was part of a reform movement that swept the country in the early 20th century. Most reformers recognized the benefits of industrialism, but they were intent on correcting its abuses.

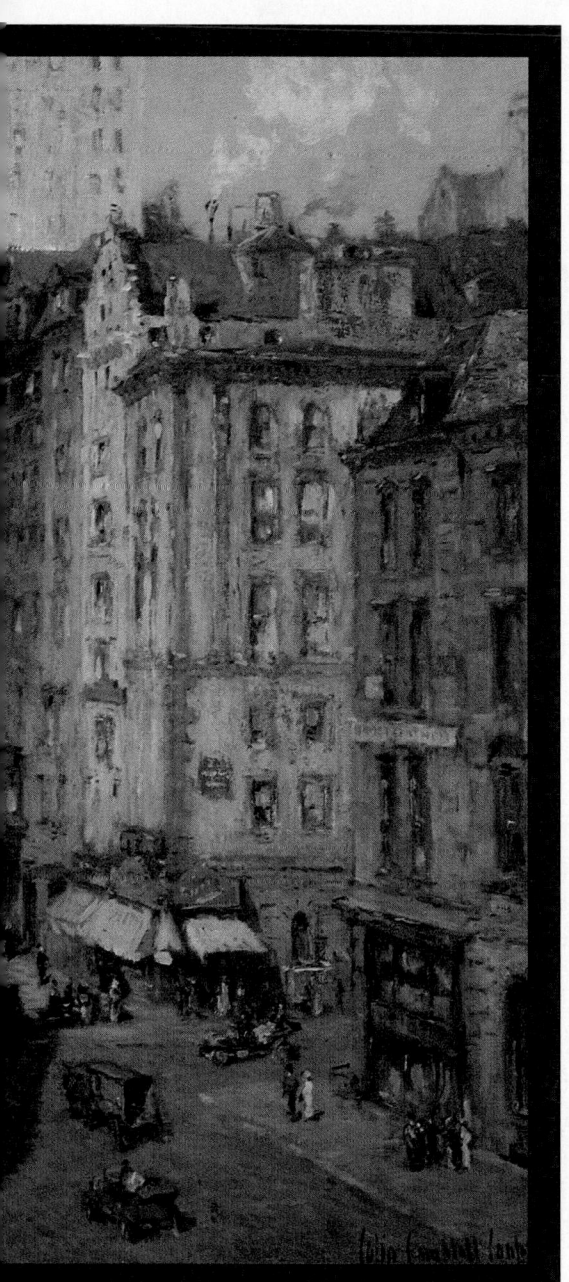

Fifth Avenue in New York, 1913

Urban child collecting firewood

THE PROGRESSIVE MOVEMENT

FOCUS

- What were some of the goals of progressivism?
- Why were many women attracted to the Progressive movement?
- What roles did muckrakers, writers, and intellectuals play in the Progressive movement?

In spite of its name, the Progressive movement—the reform effort that swept the nation between 1900 and 1920—was not a single movement united behind a single goal. Rather it was a collection of reform-minded individuals and groups dedicated to bettering life in the United States. Building on Populist efforts and the work of 19th-century reformers, the progressives publicized the ills of industrial society and sought to remedy them.

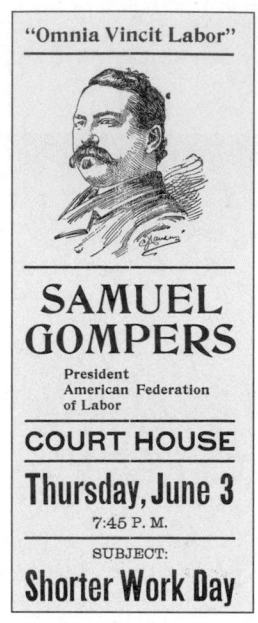

"Omnia Vincit Labor"

SAMUEL GOMPERS

President American Federation of Labor

COURT HOUSE

Thursday, June 3

7:45 P. M.

SUBJECT:

Shorter Work Day

Announcement of an AFL meeting, 1897

THE PROGRESSIVE SPIRIT

By the early 1900s industrialization had transformed the United States. Much of the transformation was positive: economic growth, new goods and services, and an expanding middle class. However, economic growth also widened the gap between the rich and the poor and contributed to unsafe working conditions and crowded cities. These ills led to a spirit of reform known as **progressivism**.

This concern over the effects of industrialization was by no means new. In the late 1800s Populists had protested unfair or corrupt corporate practices and had pressed for government legislation to stop them. Populism, however, was mainly a rural movement. Progressivism, on the other hand, focused on urban problems, such as unsafe working conditions, bad sanitation, and corrupt political machines.

Progressives carried on the Populists' struggle to "restore government to the people" by proposing election reforms that would enable people to participate more fully in running their government (see

◀ In the early 1900s most major labor unions excluded women, even though they made up nearly one fourth of the work force. Seamstresses, such as these shown here, often formed their own unions to fight for better working conditions.

The Granger Collection, New York

◄ The progressive spirit also influenced a new school of artists during the early 1900s. Known as the Ash Can School for the gritty and realistic subjects of their paintings, the movement included such artists as George Bellows, Robert Henri, John Sloan, George Luks, William Glackens, and Everett Shinn. Many of their paintings, such as George Bellows's *Lone Tenement* (1909), shown at left, depicted the ugly tenements and tough living conditions of poor urban neighborhoods.

Chapter 18). Progressives believed that the cure for democracy's ills was more democracy.

Progressives also carried on the Populists' demand for a curb on corporate power. Toward this end, they promoted legislation that prohibited monopolies and enabled smaller businesses to compete successfully in the economy.

Like Populists, progressives were inspired by the spirit of social justice. To cap the skyrocketing incomes of the rich, they took up the Populists' demand for a federal graduated income tax. They also supported the Populists' cry for an eight-hour workday. In addition, they sought to institute minimum wages, assure safe working conditions, and end child labor.

The progressive spirit was deeply infused with idealism. Theodore Roosevelt, who would become a leading progressive, aptly reflected this idealism when he wrote:

❝ If we wish to do good work for our country, we must be unselfish, disinterested, sincerely desirous of the well-being of the commonwealth, and capable of devoted adherence to a lofty ideal. ❞

This idealism extended to a firm belief in the power of science and technology to solve social problems. The progressive philosopher John Dewey urged reformers to gather data about society's ills through observation and experimentation and then test solutions. Progressives, assisted by universities, initiated many social research projects.

▪▪ Progressives sought a more democratic government, a check on corporate power, and solutions to social problems.

Although people from all walks of life participated in reform efforts during the Progressive Era, many progressives were native born, middle or upper class, and college educated. Men and women of the urban middle class—social workers, engineers, writers, teachers, doctors, ministers, lawyers, and small-business owners were particularly attracted to progressivism. This class had grown from some 750,000 in 1870 to around 10 million by 1910. In the words of Kansas editor William Allen White, by the 1900s Populism had "shaved its whiskers, washed its shirt, put on a derby, and moved up into the middle class."

Many middle-class women were attracted to the Progressive movement for the same reason earlier generations of women had assisted reform efforts: reform work provided them with one of the

▲ Shown here is a group of Vassar women from the 1920s.

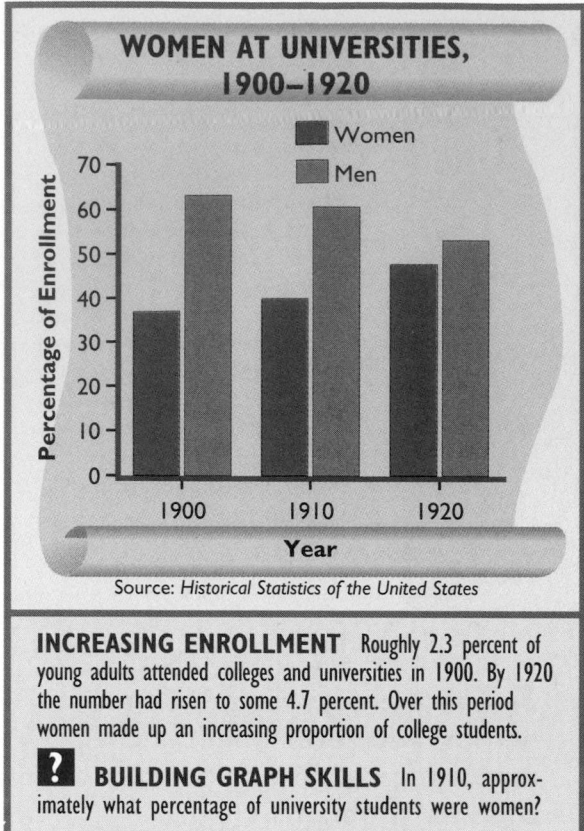

WOMEN AT UNIVERSITIES, 1900–1920

Legend:
- Women
- Men

Y-axis: Percentage of Enrollment (0, 10, 20, 30, 40, 50, 60, 70)

X-axis: Year (1900, 1910, 1920)

Source: *Historical Statistics of the United States*

INCREASING ENROLLMENT Roughly 2.3 percent of young adults attended colleges and universities in 1900. By 1920 the number had risen to some 4.7 percent. Over this period women made up an increasing proportion of college students.

? **BUILDING GRAPH SKILLS** In 1910, approximately what percentage of university students were women?

few acceptable avenues for influencing politics and society. Although the number of women enrolled in colleges increased during the early 1900s, women's career options were limited. Reform work provided college-educated women with a way to apply their knowledge of medicine, psychology, sociology, and other disciplines. Some women made careers of reform work; others volunteered their time through associations such as the General Federation of Women's Clubs, the Women's Trade Union League, and the National Association of Colored Women.

■■ **Not only did reform work provide women with a way to influence social change, it was one of the few career opportunities open to college-educated women.**

ℐNSPIRATION FOR REFORM

Progressive journalists helped spread the reform message. Newly founded mass-circulation magazines like *McClure's, Munsey's,* and *Cosmopolitan* filled their pages with stories that explored corruption in politics and business as well as such social problems as slums and child labor.

The progressive journalists were relentless in their assaults on social evils, leading Theodore Roosevelt to complain: "Men with a muck-rake are often indispensable to the well-being of society, but only if they know when to stop raking the muck." The vivid image stuck, and the journalists became known as **muckrakers**—a name they accepted with obvious pride.

▲ *McClure's* featured the work of many prominent authors and journalists, including Rudyard Kipling and Ray Stannard Baker.

McClure's publication of "Tweed Days in St. Louis" by journalists Lincoln Steffens and Claude Wetmore in October 1902 marked the beginning of the muckraking school of journalism. The article exposed the political machine in St. Louis, comparing corrupt city government there with New York City's government under Boss Tweed. *McClure's* went on to publish hundreds of articles on political and corporate corruption, poor working conditions, and slum life.

BIO GRAPHY In November 1902, *McClure's* ran the first installment of Ida Tarbell's "History of the Standard Oil Company." Tarbell, the daughter of an independent oil producer, was born in western Pennsylvania in 1857. She grew up admiring the independent oil man "whose ear was attuned to Fortune's call, and who had the daring and the energy to risk everything." Tarbell was deeply angered when John D. Rockefeller's Standard Oil Company began swallowing up independent oil companies. When her father went bankrupt and his partner committed suicide, 15-year-old Tarbell blamed Rockefeller.

In 1876 Tarbell entered Allegheny College, the only female in a freshman class of 40 "hostile or indifferent" males. Soon after graduation she moved to Paris and began her career

Ida Tarbell

▲ Standard Oil's practice of swallowing up independent oil companies is sharply criticized in this editorial cartoon.

as a writer. By the 1890s she was writing a popular biographical series for *McClure's*.

In 1900 the magazine's reform-minded founder, Scotch-Irish immigrant S. S. McClure, assigned her to investigate Standard Oil. "Out with you. Look, see, report," he urged. "Don't do it," warned her father, knowing too well the power of Standard Oil to punish its enemies. But she went ahead, publishing her findings in a series of 18 articles. Month after month she attacked Standard Oil's business practices:

66 One of the most depressing features . . . is that instead of such methods arousing contempt, they are more or less openly admired. . . . There is no gaming table in the world where loaded dice are tolerated, no athletic field where men must not start fair. Yet Mr. Rockefeller has systematically played with loaded dice. . . . Business played in this way loses all its sportsmanlike qualities. It is fit only for tricksters. 99

McClure's readers shared Tarbell's outrage, hailing her as "a modern Joan of Arc" and "the Terror of the Trusts." One reader even called her series "the *Uncle Tom's Cabin* of today." Later, Rockefeller biographer Allan Nevins would call it "the most spectacular success of the muckraking school of journalism, and its most enduring achievement."

Meanwhile, muckraking books poured off the presses. In *The Octopus* (1901) Frank Norris exposed the ways in which railroads misused their vast power. Lincoln Steffens continued to document political corruption in urban America in *The Shame of the Cities* (1904). Jack London wrote *The Iron Heel* (1907) to warn that bloody revolution might result if something was not done to curb capitalism's abuses.

Only a few progressives, however, concerned themselves with racial justice. One who did was Ray Stannard Baker. Baker traveled around the nation in 1904, examining the plight of African Americans. He found that African Americans were segregated, routinely robbed of their right to vote, and otherwise discriminated against. Worst of all, lynchings still took place. In *Following the Color Line* (1908), Baker described a lynching in Springfield, Ohio:

66 The worst feature of all in this Springfield lynching was the apathy of the public. No one really seemed to care. A "nigger" had been hanged: what of it? But the law itself had been lynched. What of that? . . . If ever there was an example of good citizenship lying flat on its back . . . , Springfield furnished an example of that condition. 99

■■ Muckrakers exposed political and corporate corruption, difficult working conditions, crowded slums, and racial injustice.

EXPLORING SOCIAL PROBLEMS

Like the muckraking journalists, novelists and intellectuals explored the darker side of the new industrial order's effect on people's behavior and values. Theodore Dreiser, in novels such as *Sister Carrie* (1900) and *The Financier* (1912),

▲ Slum life was a frequent target of muckrakers. This 1910 photograph shows a Jewish immigrant in the home he has made in a coal cellar.

◀ Jane Addams started the settlement-house movement in order to provide college-educated women like herself an opportunity to "learn of life from life itself." Her settlement house grew and became a model for social reforms in child labor, health care, urban renewal, and public education.

depicted workers brutalized by low wages and business owners driven by greed.

Progressive intellectuals proposed solutions. In *The Promise of American Life* (1909), political theorist Herbert Croly praised Alexander Hamilton's call, over a century earlier, for a strong, activist central government. But instead of promoting the interests of only the business class, as Hamilton had favored, Croly held that the government should promote the welfare of all its citizens by expanding opportunities.

Social thinkers urged citizens to take responsibility as well. Jane Addams, by now well known for her settlement-house work among Chicago's immigrants, argued in *Democracy and Social Ethics* (1902) that democracy meant more than the right to vote. It demanded a society in which all citizens showed concern for the poor:

❝ This is the penalty of a democracy— that we are bound to move forward or [slip backward] together. None of us can stand aside; our feet are mired in the same soil, and our lungs breathe the same air. ❞

■■ Progressive writers and intellectuals publicized social problems and offered theories on how to solve them.

Although progressives like Addams and Croly wanted to change American society, they remained committed to democracy. Most progressives sought reforms of local government, businesses, and city life to ensure that democratic freedoms were available to all citizens.

SECTION 1 REVIEW

IDENTIFY and explain the significance of the following: progressivism, John Dewey, muckrakers, Lincoln Steffens, Ida Tarbell, S. S. McClure, Ray Stannard Baker, Theodore Dreiser, Herbert Croly, Jane Addams.

1. **MAIN IDEA** In what ways did progressives hope to reform society?

2. **MAIN IDEA** What types of political and social evils did muckrakers expose through their writings?

3. **RECOGNIZING POINTS OF VIEW** Why were middle-class women attracted to the Progressive movement and reform activities?

4. **WRITING TO INFORM** Imagine you are a progressive writer or intellectual in the early 20th century. Write an article for *McClure's* proposing a solution to a social problem of the new industrial order.

5. **COMPARING** In what ways were the goals of Populists and progressives similar?

Section 2

REFORMING THE NEW INDUSTRIAL ORDER

FOCUS

- How did progressives try to reform the workplace?
- How did the Supreme Court respond to social legislation?
- Which labor organizations represented workers in the Progressive Era? How did these organizations differ?

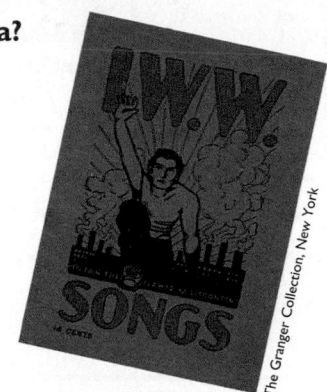

IWW songbook

The new industrial order changed American society in deep and disturbing ways. Many workers felt victimized by unhealthful working conditions, poor wages, and long workdays. At times progressive reformers and labor organizations joined forces, but more often they organized their own campaigns to improve conditions for workers.

REFORMING THE WORKPLACE

As progressives explored working conditions firsthand, they saw men and women laboring long hours, often in dangerous jobs. In 1900 the average laborer worked nearly 10 hours a day, 6 days a

▼ Child laborers, such as these shown in a textile mill, often worked in unsafe conditions.

week for about $1.50 a day. Women and children workers were paid even less.

Social reformers had long argued that the conditions women and children faced in the workplace undermined home and family life. Progressives and labor-union activists campaigned for laws prohibiting or limiting child labor and improving conditions for women workers. Florence Kelley was one of the women who worked tirelessly for this cause, helping to persuade the Illinois legislature in 1893 to prohibit child labor and to limit the number of hours women could work. In 1904 she helped organize the National Child Labor Committee, which worked to persuade state legislatures to pass laws against employing young children. By 1912 the committee had helped 39 states pass child labor laws. Some states even limited older children's employment to 8 or 10 hours a day and barred them from working at night or in dangerous occupations. But enforcement of such laws was lax. Many employers, claiming that their business success depended on cheap child labor, simply refused to obey the laws and continued to hire child workers.

Progressives also campaigned for laws that would force factories to limit the long hours employers demanded of their adult workers, men

WAGES OF WHITE URBAN WORKERS

Average Annual Wages (in dollars)

	1900		1920	
	Female	Male	Female	Male

Source: *Understanding the Gender Gap*

WOMEN IN THE WORK FORCE Even though the number of women workers increased in the early 1900s, women continued to earn less than their male counterparts.

? **BUILDING GRAPH SKILLS** In 1900, about how much more were white male workers earning than white female workers?

and women alike. In 1903, Florence Kelley helped lobby the Oregon legislature to pass a law limiting women laundry workers to 10 hours a day. Earlier, Utah had enacted a law that limited working days in dangerous occupations like mining and smelting to 8 hours. Other states passed similar laws.

Wages were another target for progressives. Of the some 30 million men and 8 million women employed in 1910, about one third lived in poverty. In 1912, in response to progressive agitation, Massachusetts passed the nation's first minimum-wage law—setting base wages for women and children. Gradually, other states followed suit.

But it would not be until 1938 that the nation passed a minimum-wage law for all workers.

Progressives also worked to improve workplace safety. Tragic events in March 1911 catapulted the need for such reforms onto the front pages of the nation's newspapers.

Late in the afternoon on Saturday, March 25, some 500 employees—most of them young Jewish or Italian immigrant women—were completing their six-day workweek at New York City's Triangle Shirtwaist Company. Shortly before quitting time, as they rose from their crowded worktables and started to leave, a fire erupted in a rag bin. Within moments the entire eighth floor of the 10-story building was ablaze. Escape quickly became impossible—there were only two stairways, and most of the exit doors were locked. Leaping from high windows became the last, desperate way out. Some 60 workers took it—to their death.

Through the night, weeping family members wandered among the crushed bodies on the sidewalk, looking for their loved ones. In all, more than 140 people perished in the Triangle fire, victims of a thoroughly unsafe workplace. Rose Schneiderman, a Women's Trade Union League organizer, argued that only a strong working-class movement could bring real change to the workplace. She noted:

66 This is not the first time girls have been burned alive in the city. Each week I must learn of the untimely death of one of my sister workers. Every year thousands of us are maimed. The life of men and women is so cheap and property is so sacred. There are so many of us for one job it matters little if 143 of us are burned to death. 99

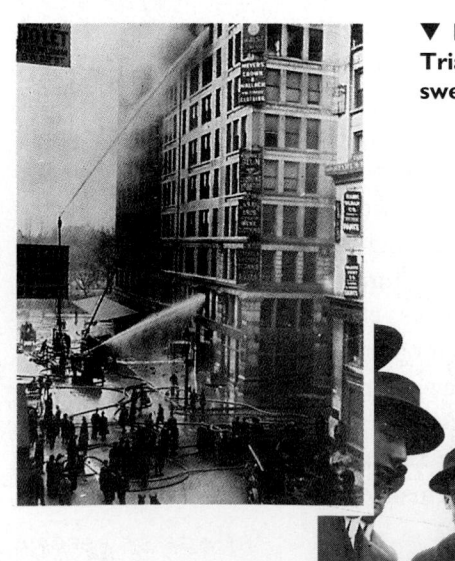

▼ Rose Schneiderman's impassioned speech (below) after the Triangle Shirtwaist Company's fire (left) marked the beginning of sweeping reforms that improved factory safety regulations.

BOOK-KEEPER'S STENOGRAPHER'S AND ACCOUNTANT'S UNION ·12646

But it did matter. The public outcry was so great that it pressured lawmakers to pass protective legislation. The New York legislature responded by enacting the nation's strictest fire safety code.

■■ **Progressives sought laws to end child labor, limit working hours, raise wages, and improve safety.**

THE COURT'S RESPONSE

As more states passed laws regulating the workplace, employers fought back through the courts—even to the Supreme Court. Employers appealed to the Fifth and Fourteenth amendments to the Constitution, which prohibit states from depriving any person of "life, liberty, or property, without due process of law." Owners claimed that laws that limited their businesses unfairly deprived them of their "property."

The Supreme Court sided with business owners and declared much of the early social legislation unconstitutional. The Court also ruled that some social legislation violated the constitutional "liberty" of workers by denying them **freedom of contract**. In 1905, for example, in *Lochner* v. *New York,* the Court overturned the New York law limiting bakers' workdays to 10 hours, declaring that the law robbed workers of their "liberty of contract." Workers, the Court argued, should be free to accept any conditions of employment that business owners required—including 14- or 16-hour workdays.

The Court did uphold some social legislation, however. In 1908, in *Muller* v. *Oregon,* an employer challenged the 10-hour workday law Florence Kelley had helped push through the Oregon legislature. Kelley and her co-worker, Josephine Goldmark, swung into action to convince the Court to uphold this hard-won law. Goldmark gathered data for the brief, or legal argument, to defend the law. Kelley recruited Goldmark's brother-in-law, the brilliant Boston lawyer Louis D. Brandeis, to argue the case. The "Brandeis Brief" broke new legal ground. In addition to making sound legal points, the brief included extensive evidence of the bad effects that working long hours had on women's health and well-being. This social research not only convinced the Court to uphold the Oregon law but became a model for the defense of other social legislation.

◀ **Josephine Goldmark**

▶ **Louis Brandeis**

■■ **On the grounds of property rights and freedom of contract, the Supreme Court struck down much—but not all—progressive legislation.**

LABOR UNIONS

Progressive reformers were not the only ones fighting for workers' rights. Labor unions continued to battle for better conditions and for the

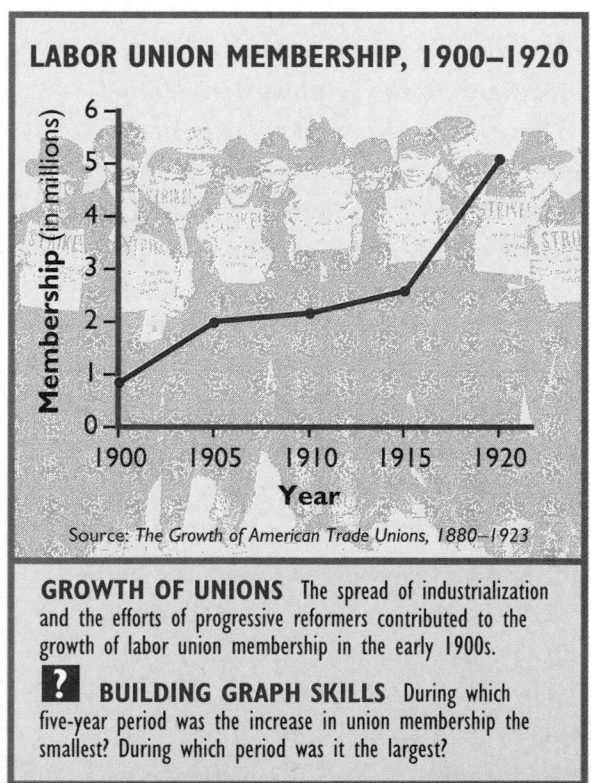

LABOR UNION MEMBERSHIP, 1900–1920

Membership (in millions) / Year

Source: *The Growth of American Trade Unions, 1880–1923*

GROWTH OF UNIONS The spread of industrialization and the efforts of progressive reformers contributed to the growth of labor union membership in the early 1900s.

? **BUILDING GRAPH SKILLS** During which five-year period was the increase in union membership the smallest? During which period was it the largest?

closed shop—a workplace where the employer hires only union members. Some union members favored "working within the system." They wanted to change how workers were treated, but they did not want to threaten capitalism's very existence. Others wanted to replace capitalism with an economic system that workers controlled. Many favored **socialism**, the system under which the government or worker cooperatives, not private interests, own factories, utilities, and transportation and communications systems.

The AFL. The major labor organization in these years remained the American Federation of Labor (AFL). The AFL stood firmly for working within the system. Under Samuel Gompers' leadership, AFL membership grew from some 500,000 in 1900 to about 2 million in 1914. But the AFL

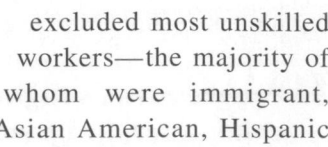

◀ AFL seal, about 1890

excluded most unskilled workers—the majority of whom were immigrant, Asian American, Hispanic American, or African American men and women. This left most urban workers without organized support.

One AFL union that did try to assist unskilled workers was the International Ladies' Garment Workers Union (ILGWU). Established in 1900 in New York City, it sought to unionize workers—mainly Jewish and Italian immigrant women—employed in sewing shops like the Triangle Shirtwaist Company.

In order to organize workers, union leaders generally planned a strike to establish the union's power to negotiate for workers. The International Ladies' Garment Workers Union used this tactic in November 1909 when it staged the "Uprising of the Thirty Thousand." Thousands of women garment workers walked off their jobs to demand that their companies recognize the ILGWU as their union.

The strike lasted through the bitter winter. Hard-pressed strikers received generous aid from progressive groups such as the Women's Trade Union League, an organization of well-to-do women who supported the efforts of working women to form unions.

The strike's results were mixed. Most employers agreed to many of the ILGWU's demands. The employers, however, were determined to run **open shops**—or nonunion workplaces. Thus, they refused to recognize the union.

The IWW. While Gompers and his AFL trade unions negotiated with business owners for worker gains, a new union emerged with a different agenda. The Industrial Workers of the World (IWW), founded in Chicago in 1905, opposed capitalism. Its leader, "Big Bill" Haywood, proclaimed IWW's aim:

> 66 Fellow workers, this is the continental congress of the working class. We are here to confederate the workers of this country into a working-class movement that shall have for its purpose the emancipation of the working class from the slave bondage of capitalism. 99

IMMIGRANT WORKERS

THROUGH OTHERS' EYES

*P*rogressive reformers won shorter workdays, better working conditions, and other improvements for many U.S. workers. But such changes were unknown to the immigrants who crossed the border from Mexico to work the railroads, mines, and fields of the southwestern United States. These immigrant workers experienced both poor working conditions and prejudice. In 1910 the Mexican newspaper **Diario del Hogar** wondered what drove "our workingmen, so attached to the land, to abandon the country [Mexico], even at the risk of the Yankee contempt with which they are treated on the other side of the Bravo [Rio Grande]." Indeed, some Mexican laborers were brutally assaulted or lynched. Venustiano Carranza, Mexico's president from 1917 to 1920, claimed that 114 Mexicans had been murdered across the border. And in 1922 the Mexican newspaper **Heraldo** charged that "Mexicans are still being killed without any effort by the American authorities to punish the murderers."

► Employers often used armed guards to remove picketing workers. This photograph shows local militiamen aiming their guns at strikers in Lawrence, Kansas.

Haywood denounced the AFL's cooperation with business owners and its failure to include unskilled workers. He vowed to organize migrant farm workers, miners, lumber workers, and textile workers to overthrow the capitalist system. In addition to enlisting African American, Hispanic American, and Asian American workers, the IWW actively recruited women workers and the wives of male workers. An IWW newspaper expressed optimism about the role of union women:

66 The advent of women side by side with men in strikes, will soon develop a fighting force that will end capitalism and its horrors in short order. . . . The industrial union movement seeks to develop the fighting quality of both sexes. 99

The Wobblies, as the members of the IWW came to be called, pursued their goals through general strikes, boycotts, and industrial sabotage. Their greatest hour came in 1912 when they led 20,000 workers in a strike against the textile mills of Lawrence, Massachusetts, to protest a 30-cent wage cut. After a bitter and much publicized two-month strike, the mill owners gave in.

Success was short-lived, however. Several later IWW-led strikes failed miserably. Most Americans grew fearful of IWW's aims, and the government cracked down on the union with increasing force. Disagreements among Wobbly leaders also weakened IWW's power. Within a few years the IWW collapsed and eventually faded from power. The AFL trade unions continued to flourish, but the majority of American industrial workers remained outside the union movement.

■■ The AFL worked within the system and focused on skilled workers, while the IWW opposed capitalism and focused on unskilled workers.

SECTION 2 REVIEW

IDENTIFY and explain the significance of the following: Florence Kelley, Rose Schneiderman, freedom of contract, Josephine Goldmark, Louis D. Brandeis, closed shop, socialism, Samuel Gompers, open shops, "Big Bill" Haywood.

1. **MAIN IDEA** What kinds of laws to improve the workplace did progressives seek?

2. **MAIN IDEA** What reasons did the Supreme Court use to justify striking down some progressive legislation?

3. **CONTRASTING** How did the goals of the AFL differ from those of the IWW?

4. **WRITING TO DESCRIBE** Imagine you are a worker in New York City's Triangle Shirtwaist Company in March 1911. Write a letter to a friend that describes work conditions before and after the fire.

5. **USING HISTORICAL IMAGINATION** If you were a progressive in the early 1900s, how would you balance the needs of employers with the needs of employees?

REFORMING SOCIETY

F O C U S

■ **What steps did reformers take to try to solve urban problems?**

■ **What actions did African American and Native American progressives take to address discrimination?**

■ **Why can it be said that the Progressive movement had mixed results for immigrants?**

Woman doing laundry, about 1910

Progressive reformers were convinced that as citizens they were responsible for the well-being of their communities. While most white progressives concentrated on improving housing, public health, and personal morality, African American and Native American progressives organized to fight discrimination. Other progressives, motivated by nativist sentiments, set out to change immigrants' cultures.

REFORMING CITY LIFE

By 1920, for the first time in U.S. history, more than 50 percent of Americans lived in cities. As urban populations soared, the ability of cities to provide garbage collection, safe and affordable housing, health care, police and fire protection, and adequate public education was stretched to the breaking point.

Cleaning up the city. What cities needed, some reformers announced, was "municipal house-keeping," a campaign to make the cities a more healthful and livable home for all residents. "The community is one great family," explained Louise DeKoven Bowen, the president of Chicago's Woman's City Club, and "each member of it is bound to help the other." The Woman's City Club, other women's clubs, various men's clubs, and reform organizations enlisted the aid of local governments to clean up the cities. Some organizations took the cleanup campaign literally, working to rid the cities of garbage. Other reform organizations worked for better housing or to improve public education.

Progressive reformers published articles and books documenting urban problems, even assigning blame for them in some cases. For example, Lawrence Veiller (VYL-uhr), a settlement-house worker, lashed out at irresponsible tenement owners "who for the sake of a large profit on their investments sacrifice the health and welfare of countless thousands."

Veiller campaigned tirelessly for improved housing. In 1901 he succeeded in getting the New York State Tenement House bill passed. The law banned construction of dark and airless tenements. New buildings had to be constructed around an open courtyard that would let in light and air. The law also required that new buildings contain one bathroom for each apartment or for every three rooms, rather than one or two for an entire floor, as was the common practice. Housing reformers in other states used the New York law as a model for their own legislative proposals.

In another campaign to make the cities more-healthful places to live, a group of physicians and reform-minded citizens formed the National Tuberculosis Association. The association focused on education and on lobbying the government to fund special hospitals to treat victims of tuberculosis. Thanks in part to this effort, by 1915 the death rate from TB had dropped significantly.

Other reformers campaigned for more city parks and playgrounds to provide safe places for children to play. The play-ground developed earlier at Jane Addams's Hull House in Chicago served as the model, and by 1920, millions of dollars had been spent establishing playgrounds.

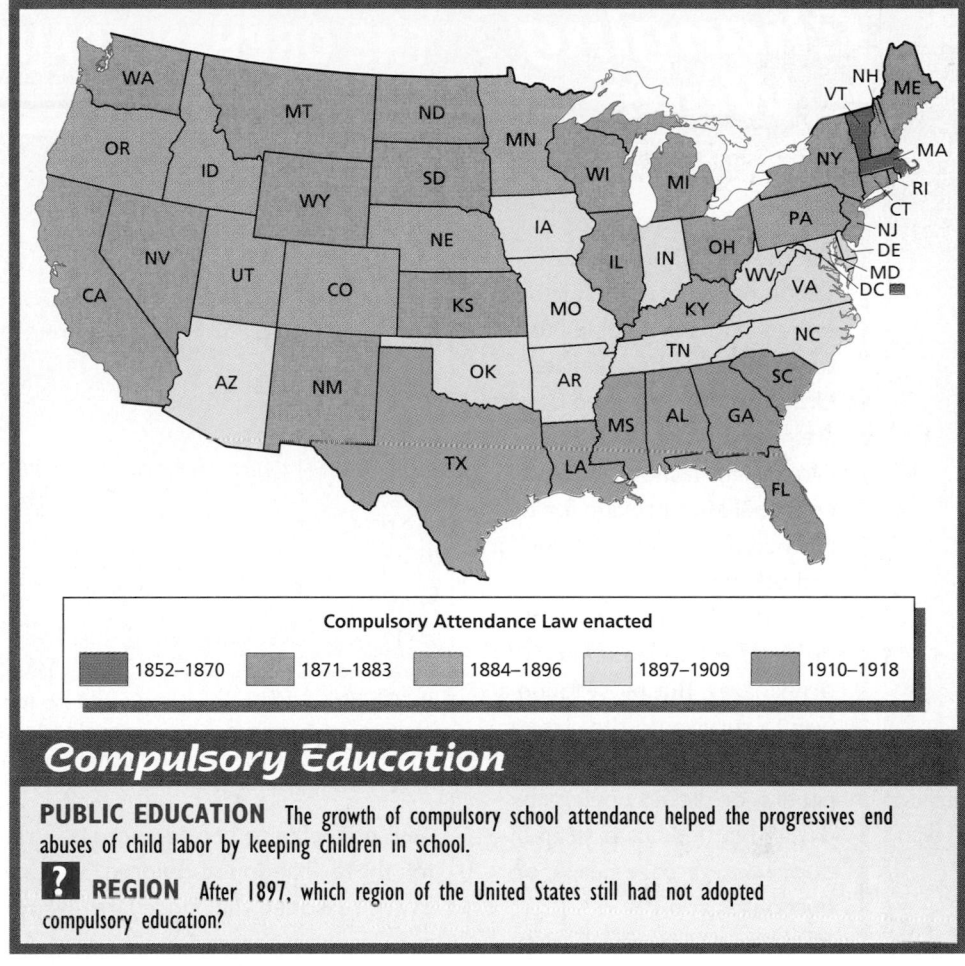

Compulsory Attendance Law enacted

| 1852–1870 | 1871–1883 | 1884–1896 | 1897–1909 | 1910–1918 |

Compulsory Education

PUBLIC EDUCATION The growth of compulsory school attendance helped the progressives end abuses of child labor by keeping children in school.

? REGION After 1897, which region of the United States still had not adopted compulsory education?

City planning. Progressives firmly believed that cleaned-up cities would produce better citizens. Out of this belief grew the city-planning move-ment. The first National Conference on City Planning was held in 1909. Through wise and careful planning, its members hoped, the spread of slums could be halted and cities could be beautified with lush green parks, sparkling fountains, and tree-shaded streets.

In 1909 Daniel Burnham, a leading architect and city planner, produced a magnificent plan for redesigning Chicago, the first comprehensive plan to redesign an American city. It portrayed a future Chicago of almost dreamlike harmony and beauty. The centerpiece of Burnham's vision for Chicago was a soaring city hall that would inspire all residents to be good citizens. "Make no little plans," said Burnham. "They have no magic to stir men's blood."

City-planning commissions in Washington, D.C., Cleveland, and San Francisco

◀ **Daniel Burnham**

◀ **Daniel Burnham's plan for Chicago included wide inter-secting streets similar to the ones he saw in Paris.**

In the late 1800s and early 1900s, periodic economic downswings left many people unable to provide for their families. Urban immigrants faced desperate poverty. Many children of broken families, or whose parents could not provide for them, roamed the streets of New York and other eastern cities.

Many of these children died; others ended up in orphanages. But most found a way to survive on the streets. They shined shoes, sold newspapers, or picked pockets by day and curled up to sleep in doorways, garbage heaps, or outhouses at night.

Progressives and other reformers pitied the abandoned children. But they also feared that without parents to teach them right from wrong, the children posed a danger to society. As the Children's Aid Society warned:

66 They will vote—they will have the same rights as we ourselves though they have grown up ignorant of moral principle. . . . Let society beware, when the vicious, reckless multitude of New York boys, swarming now in every foul alley and low street, come to know their power and use it! 99

The founding director of the Children's Aid Society, the minister Charles Loring Brace,

▲ Children whose parents could no longer care for them often were sent to orphanages. Some remained there until they were old enough to take care of themselves; others were placed in homes or ran away.

devised a plan to provide homes for these abandoned children. Brace reasoned that since farmers needed laborers and street urchins needed homes, why not bring these adults and children together? By 1914 the Society would help some 116,000 children leave eastern cities on "orphan trains" for a better life on farms in New England, the South, and the Midwest.

Photojournalist Jacob Riis, a supporter of the Society, described how "big-hearted farmers" came from miles away to meet the trains and choose from the "little troop[s]" of children. "Night falls," he wrote, "upon a joyous band returning home over the quiet country road, the little stranger snugly stowed among his new friends, one of them already, with home and life before him."

Despite the many success stories, there were problems. Some critics justifiably charged

that the Society failed to turn away farmers who were looking for no more than cheap labor. Others condemned the lack of adequate follow-up supervision. They argued that such safeguards were necessary to protect children from being taken advantage of economically or abused physically. Still others accused the Society of "dumping" New York's juvenile delinquents. As a result, some states passed laws restricting the placement of children in foster homes across state borders.

Whatever the shortcomings of the program, it provoked a long and fruitful debate on how the nation could provide for abandoned or orphaned children. Before the first orphan train departed in 1854, child-welfare workers saw institutionalization as the only option. By 1900 "placing out"— finding homes for children—had become the preferred solution.

also engaged Burnham to develop grand schemes for their cities. His plans were never fully realized, but some, such as those for Washington, were a success. Above all, his efforts helped people realize that city planning—building codes, sanitation standards, and zoning—was a necessary function of municipal government.

■■ **Progressives sought to clean up the cities by enlarging the function of government to include housing standards, public health, and city planning.**

URBAN MORAL REFORM

Progressives also wanted to "clean up" what they considered to be immoral behavior. Toward this end, they pushed for prohibition—a ban on the manufacture and sale of alcoholic beverages—and for the closing of the nation's saloons. Reformers believed that prohibition and the elimination of saloons would have several benefits. These reforms would lessen social problems by removing what reformers viewed as two of the chief causes of unemployment: crime and the breakup of families. Such actions would also limit the powers of brewery and liquor interests, groups that exercised considerable influence over the government.

▲ While serving as president of the WCTU, Frances Willard also helped organize the Prohibition party in 1882.

The Anti-Saloon League (ASL) and the **Women's Christian Temperance Union** (WCTU), an offshoot of the mid-19th-century temperance movement, led the crusade against alcohol. By 1902 the ASL had branches in 39 states with 200 paid staff members. It sent out thousands of volunteer speakers, many of them Protestant ministers, to spread the anti-saloon message in the nation's churches.

Billy Sunday, an ex-ballplayer and a Presbyterian minister, preached that the saloon was "the sum of all villainies," and "the parent of crimes and the mother of sins." Frances Willard, who presided over the WCTU from 1879 to 1898, described the zeal she felt as she led a prayer meeting in a saloon early in her career:

66 Kneeling on that sawdust floor, with a group of earnest hearts around me, and behind them, filling every corner and extending out into the street, a crowd of unwashed, unkempt, hard-looking drinking men, I was conscious that perhaps never in my life, save beside my sister Mary's dying bed, had I prayed as truly as I did then. 99

A brilliant organizer and magnetic public speaker, Willard eventually made the WCTU a powerful national force for temperance, moral purity, and the rights of women.

Drawing on Americans' spirit of patriotic sacrifice, prohibitionists achieved their goal during World War I. The **Eighteenth Amendment**, which Congress passed in 1917 and the states ratified in 1919, barred the manufacture, sale, or importation of alcoholic beverages. The amendment proved unpopular and difficult to enforce, however, and was repealed in 1933 (see Chapter 22).

The growing popularity of the newly invented motion picture gave urban reformers another source of danger to worry about. The first movie to tell a story, *The Great Train Robbery,* was

▼ Movie theaters attracted large crowds by showing action films such as *The Great Train Robbery.* Early cowboy stars gained worldwide fame from these movie westerns.

No. 201
EDISON FILM
COPYRIGHTED 1903
THE GREAT TRAIN
ROBBERY

produced in 1903, and by 1910, millions of Americans were attending the movies each week. In 1916 the *New York Times* could declare that films were the fifth-largest U.S. industry.

To the urban poor a 5- to 10-cent movie ticket provided cheap, readily available entertainment. But many middle-class Americans believed that movies—especially the steamy romances—and movie houses were immoral and sources of temptation, particularly for the young. As one writer of the time reported:

> 66 The pictures thrown upon the luminous curtain of the stage have been declared extremely corrupting to the idle young people lurking in the darkness before it. The darkness itself has been held a condition of inexpressible depravity and a means of allurement to evil. 99

Declaring that moviegoing "softens the mental fibre and saps the character," reformers demanded that motion pictures be censored. Several states and cities set up censorship boards to ban movies they considered immoral. In 1909 the movie industry began to censor itself.

■■ **Reformers sought to improve American morals by working for prohibition and censorship of movies.**

*T*HE LIMITS OF PROGRESSIVISM

For nonwhites the Progressive movement had mixed results. While most progressives were concerned about the plight of the poor, few white progressives devoted very much energy to addressing the problems of discrimination and prejudice against African Americans and Native Americans. Some progressives even expressed openly racist or nativist sentiments against these groups. Many African Americans and Native Americans, however, drew on progressive ideas to craft solutions appropriate to their own communities.

One of the most influential black leaders to emerge during this period was W.E.B. Du Bois (doo BOYS) Born in 1868 in Great Barrington, Massachusetts, Du Bois graduated from Fisk University, a black school in Nashville, Tennessee. He then studied history in Germany and at Harvard University. In 1895 he became the first African American to earn a doctorate from Harvard. Two years later he was hired as a professor of history and economics at Atlanta University, a leading African American college, where he taught until 1910.

By the early 1900s Du Bois was recognized as a brilliant thinker and strong advocate of African American civil rights and culture. He believed that a college education, rather than vocational training, would ensure greater progress for African Americans. He also believed that African Americans should be politically active in the struggle for racial equality.

Throughout his life Du Bois maintained a passionate interest in Africa, which he regarded as the spiritual homeland of all blacks. Du Bois eloquently expressed his dual identity as both African and American:

> 66 One feels his two-ness—an American, a Negro, two souls, two thoughts, two unreconciled strivings, two warring ideals. . . .
> The history of the American Negro is the history of this strife. . . . He would not Africanize America. . . . He would not bleach the Negro soul in a flood of white Americanism. . . . He simply wishes to make it possible for a man to be both a Negro and an American, without being cursed and spit upon. 99

W.E.B. Du Bois

In the 1920s, in an effort to forge greater unity among blacks and to promote pride in their African heritage, Du Bois organized a series of Pan-African congresses, which attracted black leaders from around the world.

During the 1930s and 1940s, Du Bois continued his career as a scholar and political activist. By the 1950s he had embraced socialism—which attracted many prominent American intellectuals, both black and white—for its promise of social justice. In 1961, at age 93, Du Bois joined the Communist party and moved to Ghana, where he died two years later.

The fight for racial justice. In 1909, in an effort to end racial discrimination, Du Bois, along with leading white progressives such as Jane Addams, helped found the **National Association for the Advancement of Colored People** (NAACP). Through its magazine, *The Crisis,* which Du Bois edited, the NAACP publicized cases of racial inequality and called for social reforms that would ensure equal rights for African Americans.

The NAACP also worked through the courts to end restrictions on voting and on other civil rights. In 1915 it won its first major victory in *Guinn* v. *United States.* In this case the Supreme Court outlawed the "grandfather clause" that southern states used to ensure that suffrage requirements designed to keep blacks from voting would not apply to whites. Two years later, in *Buchanan* v. *Warley,* NAACP lawyers successfully overturned a

▶ **Du Bois served as editor of *The Crisis* from 1910 to 1932. This monthly magazine focused on issues important to African Americans.**

Louisville, Kentucky, law requiring segregated housing. As a result, similar laws were struck down across the country. Since then the NAACP has continued to fight for African Americans' legal rights.

Another important organization in the struggle for racial justice during this period was the National Urban League. Founded in 1910 by concerned blacks and whites, the League worked to improve job opportunities and housing for urban

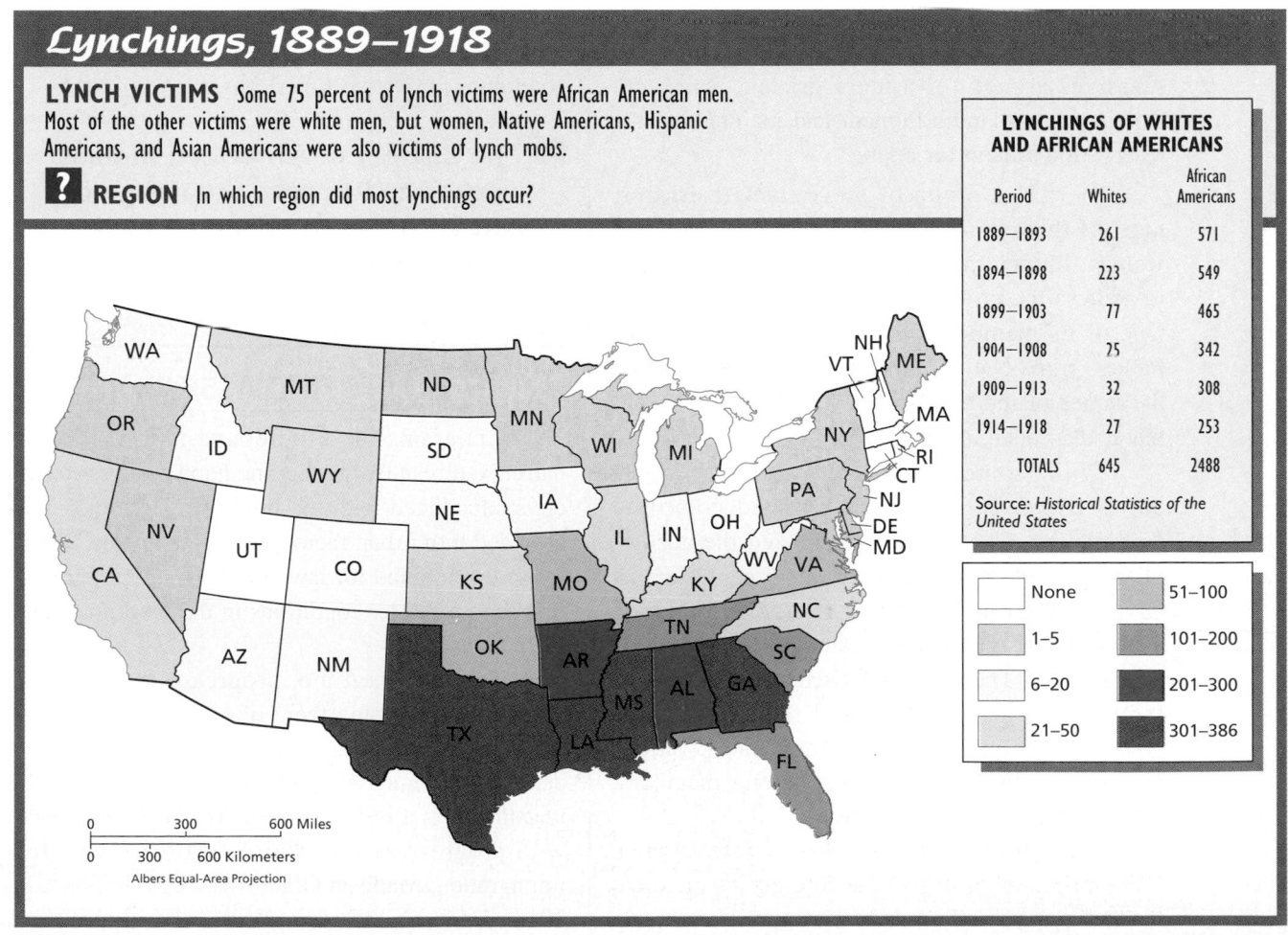

Lynchings, 1889–1918

LYNCH VICTIMS Some 75 percent of lynch victims were African American men. Most of the other victims were white men, but women, Native Americans, Hispanic Americans, and Asian Americans were also victims of lynch mobs.

? REGION In which region did most lynchings occur?

LYNCHINGS OF WHITES AND AFRICAN AMERICANS

Period	Whites	African Americans
1889–1893	261	571
1894–1898	223	549
1899–1903	77	465
1904–1908	25	342
1909–1913	32	308
1914–1918	27	253
TOTALS	645	2488

Source: *Historical Statistics of the United States*

None
1–5
6–20
21–50
51–100
101–200
201–300
301–386

0   300   600 Miles
0   300   600 Kilometers
Albers Equal-Area Projection

blacks. One of its chief goals was to help African American migrants from the South adjust to life in northern cities. Today the National Urban League carries on its efforts to end racial discrimination and to aid the disadvantaged.

The NAACP and the National Urban League made possible some important gains for black citizens. Nevertheless, most African Americans still faced discrimination, segregation, and denial of equal rights. The long struggle to eliminate racism continued.

■■ Black leaders and organizations such as the NAACP and the National Urban League fought for racial justice. But racism continued to haunt American life.

Native American progressives.

Most progressives supported the Dawes Act of 1887 (see Chapter 14), which encouraged Native Americans to abandon reservation life and become private landowners. However, progressives realized that this policy had led many Native Americans to lose their property to land speculators and fall deeper into poverty. Thus, many progressives argued for a more gradual approach: slowing down land allotment and maintaining the reservation system for a time.

In 1911 a group of 50 Native Americans, most of them middle-class professional men and women, formed the **Society of American Indians** to address the problems facing Native Americans. One of its members, Seneca historian Arthur C. Parker, urged Native Americans "to strike out into the duties of modern life and . . . find every right that had escaped them before."

While some members supported strengthening tribal values, most favored complete assimilation. The Society publicized the accomplishments of famous Native Americans such as Olympic gold medalist Jim Thorpe and lobbied against the use of such derogatory terms as "buck" and "squaw." They also discussed ways to improve Indian health, education, civil rights, and local government. But the Society's moderate positions on most issues led to disputes among members, thus weakening the organization.

One member, Dr. Carlos Montezuma, a Yavapai-Apache, urged the Society to criticize the Bureau of Indian Affairs for mismanaging

▲ As a founder of the Society of American Indians, Gertrude S. Bonnin fought to protect Native Americans in Oklahoma from exploitation. There, land speculators used every possible tactic to secure oil leases to valuable Indian property.

reservations. Most Society members refused to take such a strong antigovernment stand, and the group's influence dwindled after 1923. While the Society did not last long, it provided a forum for Indian leaders and a basis for later attempts to improve conditions for Native Americans.

■■ The Society of American Indians worked to improve the image of Native Americans and to solve the problems they faced.

𝓘MMIGRANTS AND ASSIMILATION

For immigrants the Progressive movement also had mixed results. On the one hand, many reformers sympathized with the plight of the newcomers crowded into urban factories and tenements. These reformers lobbied for laws to improve immigrants' lives and to better conditions in the workplace and in city slums.

At the same time, progressives criticized immigrants, accusing them of immoral behavior—of drinking, gambling, and other vices. They also denounced immigrant support for big-city political machines. As a result, some native-born Americans with progressive ideals also favored restricting immigration. Madison Grant was a case in point. In 1916 Grant, a prominent New Yorker, published

The Passing of the Great Race. In this book he expressed vicious racist opinions about African Americans, Jews, and immigrants from southern and eastern Europe. Only immigrants from England and northern Europe met Grant's standard of human worth. Yet Grant was also a progressive who supported urban planning and other reforms.

Many progressives, fearing the cultural diversity immigrants brought to American life, believed immigrants should be "Americanized" as quickly as possible. Americanizing, though, often meant denying the value of the immigrants' own culture and trying to reshape them in the mold of the native-born Protestant majority. Russian immigrant Eugene Lyons described the unsettling effects of this process in *Assignment in Utopia*:

▲ In 1890 Arnold Genthe photographed this Chinese immigrant family on an outing in San Francisco.

 We were "Americanized" about as gently as horses are broken in. . . . We sensed a disrespect for the alien traditions in our homes and came unconsciously to resent and despise those traditions . . . because they seemed [impossible] barriers between ourselves and the adopted land. 🙶

The immigrant poor and the political bosses who represented them did, however, support middle-class progressives when they fought for practical reforms such as worker protection,

public-health programs, or regulation of slum housing. On such issues the big-city political machines sometimes played a key role. For example, a New York State legislative committee set up to investigate factory conditions after the 1911 Triangle fire won strong backing from New York City's immigrant-based democratic political machine.

■■ **Immigrants supported progressive reformers on practical health and welfare issues.**

SECTION 3 REVIEW

IDENTIFY and explain the significance of the following: Lawrence Veiller, Women's Christian Temperance Union, Frances Willard, Eighteenth Amendment, W.E.B. Du Bois, National Association for the Advancement of Colored People, Society of American Indians.

1. **MAIN IDEA** What approach did progressives use to clean up American cities?

2. **MAIN IDEA** How did reformers attempt to improve American morality?

3. **MAIN IDEA** How did African Americans and Native Americans attempt to fight racism and discrimination?

4. **WRITING TO EXPLAIN** Imagine you are an immigrant. Write a brief pamphlet for other immigrants that attempts to explain why you do or do not support the Progressive movement.

5. **ANALYZING** Why did progressives support prohibition and the elimination of saloons?

CHAPTER 17
Review

Ida Tarbell's "History of the Standard Oil Company" begins publication in *McClure's*.

National Child Labor Committee formed.

Ray Stannard Baker's *Following the Color Line* and Upton Sinclair's *The Jungle* published.

ILGWU established.

IWW founded.

1897   1900   1905

WRITING A SUMMARY

Using the essential points of the chapter as a guide, write a summary of the chapter.

REVIEWING CHRONOLOGY

Number your paper 1 to 5. Study the time line above, and list the following events in the order in which they happened by writing the first next to 1, the second next to 2, and so on. Then complete the activity below.

1. Eighteenth Amendment ratified.
2. IWW founded.
3. Massachusetts passes minimum-wage law.
4. NAACP founded.
5. National Child Labor Committee formed.

Evaluating What effect did the Triangle Shirtwaist Company fire have on improving workplace safety?

IDENTIFYING PEOPLE AND IDEAS

Explain the historical significance of each of the following people or terms.

1. progressivism
2. Josephine Goldmark
3. muckrakers
4. Florence Kelley
5. freedom of contract
6. Daniel Burnham
7. socialism
8. Lawrence Veiller
9. Frances Willard
10. Society of American Indians
11. Lincoln Steffens

UNDERSTANDING MAIN IDEAS

1. In what ways did women work for progressive goals? Why were they so active in the Progressive movement?
2. What roles did muckrakers, writers, and intellectuals play in the reform movement?
3. Which labor issues did reformers hope to remedy through legislation?
4. What actions did progressive reformers take to improve conditions in cities?
5. What steps did African American and Native American progressives take to address the problems facing their communities?

REVIEWING THEMES

1. **Economic Development** Why did states pass laws to protect workers' rights?
2. **Democratic Values** How did progressives propose to extend opportunities to all citizens? Were they successful in these efforts? Why or why not?
3. **Constitutional Heritage** How did progressives help win passage of the Eighteenth Amendment?

THINKING CRITICALLY

1. **Analyzing** How did industrialization influence progressive reform efforts?
2. **Hypothesizing** How might the course of reform have been different if the Supreme Court had supported more early social legislation?
3. **Contrasting** How did the AFL and the IWW differ in their views on the scope and nature of labor reform?

STRATEGY FOR SUCCESS

Review the Strategies for Success on Interpreting Economic Data on page 506. Study the two graphs below. This information was compiled as an average for all industries in the period from 1900 to 1910. What conclusions can you draw from the graph data about the impact of progressivism?

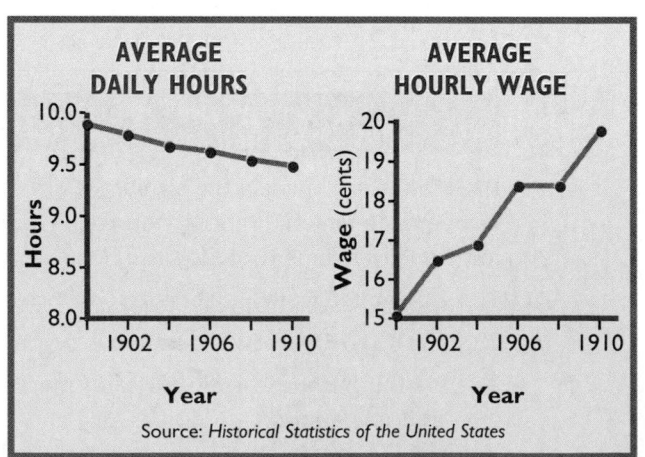

AVERAGE DAILY HOURS

AVERAGE HOURLY WAGE

Source: *Historical Statistics of the United States*

First National
Conference on
City Planning
held. NAACP
founded.

National
Urban
League
founded.

Society of
American
Indians
formed.

Massachusetts
passes minimum-
wage law. IWW
wins textile
workers' strike.

Supreme Court out-
laws "grandfather
clause" in *Guinn* v.
United States.

Eighteenth
Amendment
ratified.

1910   **1915**   **1920**

WRITING ABOUT HISTORY

Writing to Persuade Imagine you are the young Boston lawyer Louis D. Brandeis. Write a closing argument attempting to convince the Supreme Court to uphold laws that guarantee workers' rights. Include specific examples of working conditions to support your arguments.

USING PRIMARY SOURCES

In 1905 W.E.B. Du Bois wrote to an African American student who was discouraged about the career opportunities that would be available to her. Read the following excerpt from his letter and write a summary of his advice to her.

> 66 *I have heard that you are a young woman of some ability but that you are neglecting your school work because you have become hopeless of trying to do anything in the world. I am very sorry for this. . . .*
>
> *There are in the U.S. today tens of thousands of colored girls who would be happy beyond measure to have the chance of educating themselves that you are neglecting. If you train yourself as you easily can, there are wonderful chances of usefulness before you: you can join the ranks of 15,000 Negro women teachers, of hundreds of nurses and physicians, of the growing number of clerks and stenographers. . . . Ignorance is a cure for nothing. Get the very best training possible & the doors of opportunity will fly open before you as they are flying before thousands of your fellows. On the other hand every time a colored person neglects an opportunity, it makes it more difficult for others of the race to get such an opportunity. Do you want to cut off the chances of the boys and girls of tomorrow?* 99

LINKING HISTORY AND GEOGRAPHY

Review the map on compulsory education on page 523. Note that most states adopted compulsory attendance laws for school-aged children during the 19th century, but 19 states did not do so until after 1896. Where are most of these 19 states located? Drawing on what you have learned in previous chapters, what factors might help explain the link between geographic region and the timing of passage of compulsory attendance laws for school-aged children?

BUILDING YOUR PORTFOLIO

Complete the following projects independently or cooperatively.

1. **REFORM** Imagine you are a progressive reformer in the early 1900s. Write an editorial for *McClure's, Cosmopolitan,* or another progressive magazine that addresses an urban problem in government, business, the workplace, or the community. Be sure that your editorial suggests a possible solution to the problem. Editorials might examine political machines, corporate abuses, poor working conditions, or public-health concerns.

2. **DEMOCRATIC RIGHTS** Imagine you are a progressive reformer working to promote women's rights. Prepare a speech on women's rights to deliver at an Independence Day celebration. Be sure that the speech outlines the various problems and concerns faced by women in the early 1900s and indicates how progressive reformers intend to address these problems and concerns.

THE PROGRESSIVE PRESIDENTS

FOCUS

UNDERSTANDING THE MAIN IDEA

Many progressives sought to extend their reform efforts to government itself. They wanted to take power away from corrupt political machines and mobilize the power of the government to improve American life. On the national level, presidents Theodore Roosevelt, William Howard Taft, and Woodrow Wilson tried in varying degrees to implement the progressive reform agenda.

 THEMES

■ **DEMOCRATIC VALUES**
What are some ways in which government can restore political power to the people?

■ **ECONOMIC DEVELOPMENT** How can government regulate business practices without discouraging free enterprise?

■ **CONSTITUTIONAL HERITAGE** How might people use constitutional change to reform politics and society?

1901	1906	1910	1912	1914	1920
William McKinley assassinated.	**Pure Food and Drug Act** passed.	**Mann-Elkins Act** passed.	**Progressive party** formed.	**Federal Trade Commission** created.	**Nineteenth Amendment** ratified.

Various efforts to reform society had occupied American women and men throughout the 19th century. Reformers had campaigned to end slavery, to secure women's rights, and to correct the problems caused by industrialization and urbanization. Similar new efforts at reform engaged many middle-class Americans early in the 20th century.

Suffrage rally, 1912

On the morning of May 6, 1895, two progressive reporters, Jacob Riis and Lincoln Steffens, waited eagerly outside New York City police headquarters. The new head of the city's four-member police commission, Theodore Roosevelt, was due to arrive any minute. The reporters eagerly wished to find out Roosevelt's plans for reforming New York's notoriously corrupt police department.

Riis and Roosevelt were already friends and political allies. Five years before, Riis had gained national attention for his book *How the Other Half Lives,* in which he documented the grim reality of slum life in New York City. Roosevelt wrote to Riis, requesting a meeting, saying, "I have read your book, and I have come to help."

Now Roosevelt would have the chance to reform the nation's largest police force. Arriving at police headquarters, he called the two reporters into his office, leaving his fellow commissioners outside. Motioning Riis and Steffens to sit down, he said, "Now then, what'll we do?" As Steffens later recalled, "It was just as if we three were the Police Board." Within days Roosevelt had fired the police chief and had begun to clean up the department. By the end of the summer, fellow commissioner Avery Andrews noted, "The whole country . . . was talking about Theodore Roosevelt."

Six years later, Roosevelt was president of the United States. He brought to the White House the same boundless energy and progressive spirit he had demonstrated as police commissioner. Under Roosevelt's leadership progressivism moved from state and local politics into the national arena.

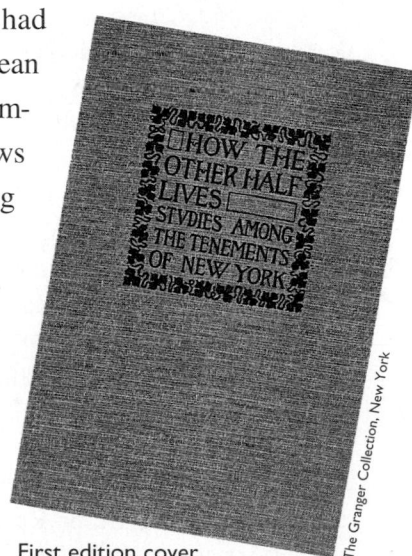

First edition cover of Riis's book

The Granger Collection, New York

REFORMING GOVERNMENT

FOCUS

- What forms did government corruption take?
- What election reforms did progressives support to make government more democratic?
- What reforms were enacted in city and state governments during the Progressive Era?

*P*rogressives did not limit their reform efforts to social ills. They also tackled the task of curbing the political power of the privileged few and removing the corrupt political machines that served them. Toward this end, progressives sought changes in the electoral process that would restore political power to the people.

New York political boss Charles Murphy voting, 1916

GOVERNMENT CORRUPTION

Theodore Roosevelt and other progressive reformers found corruption at all levels of government, from city hall to Washington, D.C. As Lincoln Steffens so graphically reported in *The Shame of the Cities,* urban political machines demanded bribes from anyone wanting to do business with city government.

In Philadelphia, for instance, in order to secure jobs teachers had to pay the political machine $120 of the first $141 they earned. In Pittsburgh, public jobs went to contractors who paid bribes. Of course, they were allowed to pad their bills to make up the losses. One Pittsburgh political boss even opened his own paving firm so that he could take the lion's share of contracts himself—at inflated prices.

Government corruption did not stop at the city level. City machines were often linked to Democratic or Republican state machines. The state machines catered to "special interests," making deals with the railroads, the lumber industry, or anyone else who wanted tax breaks or other favors

from state legislatures. In return, the machines expected generous gifts, often in the form of "campaign contributions."

At the federal level some U.S. senators, who were often put in power by state machines, accepted bribes to vote the way corporations wished. In 1906 the progressive writer David Graham Phillips began

▲ This 1926 cartoon, entitled *The National Gesture,* satirizes the widespread practice of receiving bribes among government officials.

publishing articles that described how special interests influenced American politics. In "The Treason of the Senate," he wrote:

> 66 The greatest single hold of "the interests" is the fact that they are the "campaign contributors." . . . Who pays the big election expenses of your congressman, of the men you send to the legislature to elect senators? Do you imagine those who foot those huge bills are fools? Don't you know that they make sure of getting their money back, with interest? 99

■■ Corrupt political bosses and machines accepted bribes from special interests in return for government favors.

ELECTION REFORMS

Government corruption outraged reformers. To restore honest government, they demanded, "Give the government back to the people!" Only when government heeded the public's voice, they believed, could the problems of American life be remedied.

One way progressives sought to break the powers of the bosses and the special interests was to reform the election process. First, they wanted to take the job of choosing candidates for office away from the machines. Therefore, progressives pushed for the **direct primary**—a nominating election in which voters choose the candidates who will later run in a general election. Wisconsin adopted the direct primary in 1903, and by 1916 most other states had followed suit.

Next, progressives proposed to change the method of electing U.S. senators. At the time, the U.S. Constitution mandated that state legislatures elect senators. To progressives, this law made it easy for the bosses to control government. By 1912 the progressive tide had grown strong enough to pass the **Seventeenth Amendment**, which was ratified the next year. The amendment authorized voters to elect their senators directly.

As another step toward more democratic government, the progressives sought to reform the voting process. At the time, each political party

▲ Progressives reformed the voting process by eliminating colored ballots. With the secret ballot, people could cast their vote without revealing their party preference.

printed its own ballot in a distinctive color. On Election Day the colored ballots made it easy to see how people voted. Without secrecy, voters could be pressured to support certain candidates. To lessen this threat, progressives proposed using the secret ballot. Developed in Australia, the ballot lists all candidates on a single sheet of paper and is printed at public expense. By 1910 most states had switched to the secret ballot.

Finally, progressives urged states to adopt three other election reforms: initiative, referendum, and recall. The **initiative** gives voters the power to initiate, or introduce, legislation. If a certain percentage of voters in a state (usually 5 to 15 percent) petition their legislature to enact a measure, the legislature has to consider it. The **referendum** is a companion to the initiative. By securing a specified number of signatures on a petition, voters can compel the legislature to place a measure on the ballot. The **recall** enables voters to remove an elected official from office by calling for a new election.

■■ Progressives supported the direct primary, the direct election of U.S. senators, the secret ballot, and the initiative, referendum, and recall.

REFORMING CITY GOVERNMENT

Efforts to reform government were not motivated solely by a desire for more democracy. Businesspeople supported reform because the costs of political corruption had become too great. John Patterson of the National Cash Register Company argued that individuals "skilled in business management and social service" should run "municipal affairs on a strict business basis." Many agreed. As a result, good-government campaigns put a large number of reform mayors into office. Two of the most successful were elected in Ohio: Samuel M. Jones and Tom Johnson. Both were self-made men who had amassed their fortunes early and then in mid-life had traded business for politics.

Samuel M. "Golden Rule" Jones got his nickname from his belief in the biblical Golden Rule—"Do unto others as you would have them do unto you." Seeking to apply this principle to government, Jones successfully ran for mayor of Toledo in 1897. Over the next seven years he overhauled the police force, improved municipal services, set a minimum wage for city workers, and opened kindergartens for children.

During this same period, Tom Johnson served as Cleveland's mayor. A former streetcar magnate, he knew personally how closely business interests were tied to political bosses, and he worked to sever those ties. His success led writer Lincoln Steffens to call Johnson "the best mayor of the best governed city in the United States."

▶ Samuel M. Jones pushed through so many reforms that his party refused to renominate him for mayor in 1899. He ran as an independent, however, and defeated both of his opponents. The photograph above shows a kindergarten in Toledo, Ohio, in the early 1900s.

A few charismatic mayors alone, however, could not conquer entrenched corruption. Many reformers came to believe that only a change in the structure of city government could break the political machines. The typical city government of the time consisted of a mayor and a city council made up of aldermen. Each alderman was the elected leader of one of the wards into which a city was divided. Under this system a political machine could easily elect its own people and thus run city affairs its own way.

Oddly enough, it was a natural disaster that produced an alternative to this system. In 1900 a hurricane struck Galveston, Texas, killing some 6,000 people and destroying the city. The city's government could not cope with the emergency, so

▶ The disastrous hurricane that struck Galveston, Texas, in 1900 led to a new structure of government.

the state legislature named a five-person city commission to rebuild the area. The commissioners were experts in their fields, not party loyalists. Thus they based their decisions on what would work best rather than on what would benefit the political machine. Citizens praised the commission as more honest and efficient than the previous city government. By 1913, city commissions ran more than 350 U.S. cities.

The desire for increased government efficiency also gave rise to city managers. These were expert administrators hired to run cities as they might run a business—with maximum efficiency.

■■ **Many American cities elected reform mayors, formed city commissions, and hired city managers to increase government efficiency.**

REFORMING STATE GOVERNMENT

The spirit of reform also affected many state governments. In Wisconsin, Governor Robert M. "Fighting Bob" La Follette instituted reforms that turned Wisconsin into what Theodore Roosevelt would call "the laboratory of democracy."

 Born in June 1855 in Primrose, Wisconsin, La Follette worked his way through college and law school. Although a loyal Republican, he found himself at odds with Wisconsin's Republican machine, which railroad and lumber interests dominated. After serving as a county district attorney and as a U.S. congressman

during the late 1800s, he signaled his break with the party machine by refusing an alleged bribe by a party boss.

La Follette emerged early in the progressive movement as one of its most energetic leaders. A spellbinding orator, he won farmers, the working class, and the middle class to progressivism.

Elected governor in 1900, he vigorously backed a reform program—soon known as the **Wisconsin Idea**—that became a model for other states. First, La Follette brought the direct primary to Wisconsin. He then prodded the state legislature to increase taxes on the railroads and the public utilities—gas, electric, and streetcar companies—and to create commissions to regulate these companies in the public interest. La Follette also got laws passed to curb excessive lobbying and backed labor legislation, the conservation of Wisconsin's natural resources, and other social legislation. In 1905 the Wisconsin legislature elected La Follette to the U.S. Senate, where he continued to battle for reform until his death in 1925.

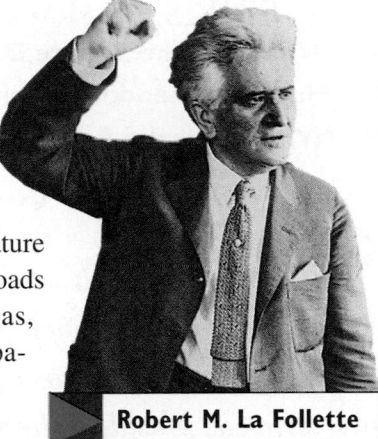

Robert M. La Follette

■■ **La Follette's Wisconsin Idea provided a model for reforming local and state government and regulating big business.**

SECTION 1 REVIEW

IDENTIFY and explain the significance of the following: direct primary, Seventeenth Amendment, initiative, referendum, recall, Samuel M. Jones, Tom Johnson, Robert M. La Follette.

LOCATE and explain the importance of the following: Wisconsin.

1. **MAIN IDEA** What measures did progressives suggest to make government more democratic?

2. **MAIN IDEA** How did many U.S. cities try to increase government efficiency and lessen corruption?

3. **GEOGRAPHY: HUMAN-ENVIRONMENT INTERACTION** How did the Galveston hurricane help produce a new political structure for cities?

4. **WRITING TO INFORM** Imagine you are David Graham Phillips. Write an article describing political corruption at the local, state, and federal levels.

5. **ANALYZING** What reforms made up the Wisconsin Idea? Why can it be said that these reforms are examples of the progressive spirit?

Section 2

ROOSEVELT AND THE SQUARE DEAL

FOCUS

■ **What was the Square Deal?**

■ **How did Theodore Roosevelt fight corruption in business?**

■ **What steps did Roosevelt take to protect the environment?**

$\mathcal{T}$heodore Roosevelt was the first progressive president of the United States. Taking office after the assassination of President William McKinley, Roosevelt was elected in his own right in 1904. During his two terms as president, he promoted the regulation of big business and helped preserve natural resources for future generations.

Assassination of
President McKinley, 1901

ROOSEVELT BECOMES PRESIDENT

In 1900 President McKinley ran for reelection with Theodore Roosevelt as his running mate. The Democrats again nominated William Jennings Bryan and made free silver their campaign issue. But in 1900 most Americans felt prosperous, and McKinley and Roosevelt sailed to victory. Then on September 6, 1901, anarchist Leon Czolgosz shot McKinley. A week later the president died, and Roosevelt became the nation's chief executive.

**BIO
GRAPHY** Theodore Roosevelt was born in 1858 into a wealthy New York family. A sickly child, he built up his strength through rigorous exercise. From his father, he acquired a love of the outdoors, a strong sense of fair play, and concern for the less fortunate. As a student at Harvard University, he developed a taste for history and politics. After graduating, Roosevelt won election to the New York state legislature, where he served from 1882 to 1884. As a legislator he earned a reputation as a moderate but energetic reformer.

Toward the end of his third term, Roosevelt's wife, Alice Lee,

Theodore Roosevelt

died following childbirth. Deeply saddened, he did not seek reelection. Instead he headed for his ranch in the Dakota Territory. Roosevelt spent much of the next two years ranching and writing history books, including what would become the four-volume *Winning of the West*. The harsh winter of 1885–86, however, forced him out of the cattle business and back to New York. In December 1886 he married childhood friend Edith Kermit Carow.

In the 1890s Roosevelt served in a variety of federal and state positions. Then, during the Spanish-American War in 1898 (see Chapter 19), he helped organize a volunteer cavalry unit—the Rough Riders—and went off to fight in Cuba. He returned a war hero that same year and was elected governor of New York.

As governor, Roosevelt worked to reform government and to regulate big business. Angered by the governor's progressive efforts, conservative Republican party leaders tried to ease Roosevelt out of state office by having him run as vice president on the McKinley ticket in 1900. Alarmed, the conservative senator Mark Hanna warned that there would be "only one life between

Theodore Roosevelt relished the limelight. As one of his children remarked, Roosevelt always wanted to be "the bride at every wedding."

This hero of the Rough Riders became a legend in his own time. Roosevelt always lived life to the hilt. "No President has ever enjoyed himself as much as I have enjoyed myself," he claimed. An old friend explained Roosevelt's great love of life: "You must

always remember that the President is about six [years old]."

His energy was legendary. For example, when the French ambassador once visited the White House, he and the president played tennis, jogged, and then worked out. Roosevelt turned to his guest and asked, "What would you like to do now?" "If it's just the same with you, Mr. President," said the ambassador, "I'd like to lie down and die."

Theodore Roosevelt

---

this madman and the Presidency." When Roosevelt moved into the White House a year later, Hanna exclaimed to a colleague, "My God, that . . . cowboy in the White House!"

Teddy, or TR, as he was now commonly called, loved hunting and sports. Only 42 years old, he brought a new style to the presidency. Journalist William Allen White described him as a "rumbling, roaring . . . tornado of a man." His no-nonsense style and toothy grin made him a favorite target of political cartoonists.

THE SQUARE DEAL

Unlike the presidents of the Gilded Age, who generally took a hands-off approach to government, Roosevelt believed that the president should use his office as a "bully pulpit" to speak out on vital issues. Roosevelt brought dynamic leadership to the progressive movement.

Soon after Roosevelt became president, a labor dispute helped define his approach to the office. In 1902 some 150,000 Pennsylvania coal miners struck for higher wages and recognition of the United Mine Workers union. But the mine owners—mostly railroad companies—would not negotiate.

Roosevelt urged the two sides to accept **arbitration**—to let a third party settle the dispute. When the mine owners refused, the president threatened to take over the mines. The mine

owners backed down. The arbitrators gave both the miners and the mine owners part of what they wanted. The compromise was a landmark: For the first time, the federal government had intervened in a strike to protect the interests of the workers and the public. Satisfied, Roosevelt pronounced the compromise a square deal.

The **Square Deal** became Roosevelt's 1904 campaign slogan. He promised to "see to it that every man has a square deal, no less and no more." This pledge summed up Roosevelt's belief in balancing the interests of labor, business, and consumers. Roosevelt's Square Deal called for limiting the power of trusts, promoting public health and safety, and improving working conditions.

The president was so popular with voters that no Republican dared challenge him for the 1904 nomination. In the election, Roosevelt easily defeated his Democratic opponent, Judge Alton Parker of New York.

▪▪ Roosevelt's Square Deal pledged fair treatment for business, workers, and the public.

REGULATING BUSINESS

One of Roosevelt's goals during both terms in office was to regulate large corporations. While he considered big business essential to the nation's growth, he also believed companies should behave responsibly.

"We don't wish to destroy corporations," he said, "but we do wish to make them subserve the public good."

Trustbusting. In 1902 the president put this philosophy into practice. He directed the attorney general to sue the Northern Securities Company, which monopolized railroad shipping in the Northwest. In 1904 the Supreme Court ruled that the monopoly violated the Sherman Antitrust Act and therefore ordered the corporation dissolved. Encouraged by this victory, Roosevelt's administration went on a "trustbusting" campaign, filing 44 suits against business combinations deemed "bad." It was not size that mattered, Roosevelt declared, but whether a trust was good or bad for the public as a whole. As he put it, "We draw the line against misconduct, not against wealth."

The Roosevelt administration also promoted railroad regulation. At the president's urging, Congress passed two laws that turned the Interstate Commerce Commission (ICC) into a significant regulatory agency. The first, the 1903 **Elkins Act**, forbade shippers from accepting rebates (money secretly given back to shippers in return for their business). The second, the 1906 **Hepburn Act**, authorized the ICC to set railroad rates and to regulate other companies engaged in interstate commerce, such as pipelines and ferries.

Protecting the consumer. Roosevelt was also concerned about the food and drug industries. By the early 1900s clear evidence existed that some drug companies, meat packers, and food processors were selling dangerous products. Some drug companies sold ineffective over-the-counter medicines that contained dangerous drugs such as cocaine or morphine. Exposing drug industry abuses, journalist Samuel Hopkins Adams wrote:

66 Gullible America will spend this year some seventy-five millions of dollars in the purchase of patent [over-the-counter]

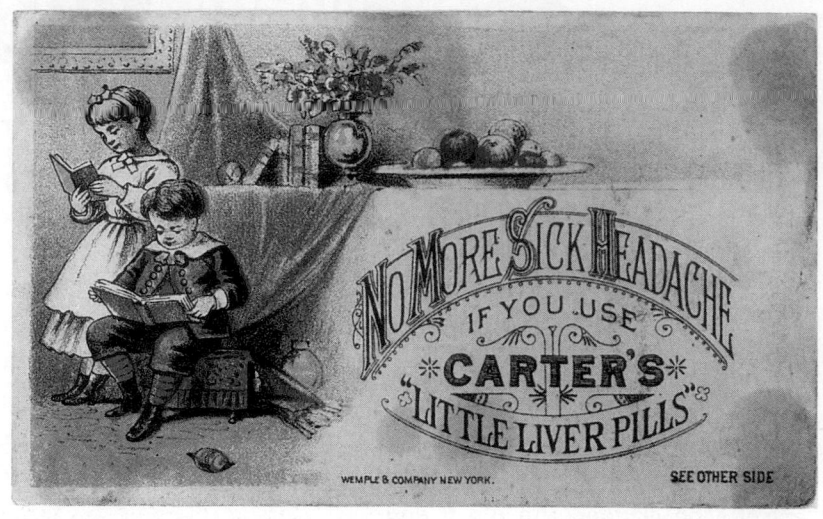

▲ The Pure Food and Drug Act tried to prevent drug manufacturers from making false or exaggerated claims about their products. This advertisement, for example, promises the user will be spared from headaches after taking Carter's liver pills.

medicines. . . . It will swallow huge quantities of alcohol, an appalling amount of opiates and narcotics. 99

The drug companies' claims that their "health tonics" could cure everything from baldness to cancer, Adams charged, amounted to fraud.

In response to these abuses and those of the food industry, Roosevelt and Congress enacted two consumer-protection laws in 1906. The **Meat Inspection Act** required government inspection of meat shipped from one state to another. The **Pure Food and Drug Act** forbade the manufacture, sale, or transportation of food and patent medicine containing harmful ingredients. The law also required that containers of food and medicines carry ingredient labels.

■■ Roosevelt fought corruption in business by breaking up illegal trusts and regulating railroads and the food and drug industries.

Protecting the environment. The president may have achieved his most enduring legacy in the field of conservation. He recognized that America's natural resources were limited and that the needs of business had always taken precedent over the environment. "In the past, we have admitted the right of the individual to injure the future of the Republic for his own present profit," he charged. "The time has come for a change."

Never content with mere talk, Roosevelt withdrew from sale millions of acres of public land and set aside some 150 million acres as forest reserves. At his urging, Congress created national parks and wildlife sanctuaries and in 1902 passed the **Newlands Reclamation Act**. The act allowed money from the sales of public land to be used for irrigation and **reclamation**—the process of making damaged land productive again. Moreover, a 1908 White House conference on conservation led to the creation of a National Conservation Commission to study natural resource issues and to the establishment of conservation agencies in 41 states.

■■ Roosevelt saved public lands from destructive development and created wildlife sanctuaries and national parks.

Then and Now   NATIONAL PARKS

In the late 1800s government, industry, and most Americans still believed there was no end to the nation's natural resources. Between the 1850s and the 1870s alone, millions of acres of public land were sold cheaply or even given away to mining, logging, and railroad companies for development.

However, an increasing number of Americans, including Theodore Roosevelt, believed the country's lands and wildlife were being recklessly destroyed. During his two terms in office, President Roosevelt fought for programs to protect public land and historic sites.

Many opposed Roosevelt's efforts, believing the economic value of the reserved land outweighed the need to conserve it. But in 1916, largely as a result of Roosevelt's efforts, Congress created the National Park Service to maintain and oversee the country's 10 national parks and 21 national monuments. Today, the National Park Service manages some 355 sites on 80 million acres of land.

Although the number and size of parks have increased tremendously since Roosevelt's day, one problem facing the Park Service remains unchanged. The agency is still caught between those who wish to preserve and expand park land and those who want to use the parks' resources.

▲ **Yellowstone National Park was established in 1872. Shown here is a detail from Thomas Moran's painting of the park, *Grand Canyon of the Yellowstone*.**

Conservationists charge that clear-cutting, strip mining, and overdevelopment are destroying wildlife habitats and old-growth forests. Logging and mining interests counter that the demand for wood and mineral products—not to mention the protection of thousands of industry jobs—requires the use of park resources. Lawmakers are caught in the middle, hoping to please voters on both sides of the issue.

Lawmakers—and Park Service officials—also face the problem of trying to maintain the parks while containing costs. More than 250 million people visit the national parks annually, and some officials argue that the visitors are literally "loving the parks to death." To counteract the strain on park resources, officials have proposed that visitation be limited in certain popular parks.

The future of the national parks is far from settled. But all sides in the debate might well consider Teddy Roosevelt's words: "A nation is obligated to manage its resources for the greatest good of the greatest number over the long run."

National Parks and Conservation

NATIONAL PARK SYSTEM The park system, which includes the national parks, national monuments, and national historic parks, protects the nation's cultural and historic sites as well as its natural wonders.

? PLACE Which state has the greatest land area set aside in national parks?

[Map of the United States showing National Parks, National Forests and grasslands, and National Monuments, with insets for Alaska, Hawaii, and Puerto Rico & Virgin Is.]

National parks (NP)

National forests and grasslands

National monuments (NM)

SECTION 2 REVIEW

IDENTIFY and explain the significance of the following: Theodore Roosevelt, Leon Czolgosz, arbitration, Square Deal, Judge Alton Parker, Elkins Act, Hepburn Act, Meat Inspection Act, Pure Food and Drug Act, Newlands Reclamation Act, reclamation.

1. **MAIN IDEA** What did Roosevelt pledge to accomplish through the Square Deal?

2. **MAIN IDEA** What actions did Roosevelt take against trusts and railroads?

3. **MAIN IDEA** How did the Meat Inspection Act and Pure Food and Drug Act try to protect consumers?

4. **WRITING TO EXPLAIN** Imagine you are a member of the National Conservation Commission. Write a report to the president, evaluating the impact that business has had on natural resources and offering a plan of action for protecting those resources.

5. **TAKING A STAND** Roosevelt's handling of the Pennsylvania coal miners' strike represented a new approach to labor relations. Take a stand either on the side of the miners or the mine owners and explain how that group might feel about Roosevelt's solution.

REFORM UNDER TAFT

FOCUS
- **What reforms did President Taft carry out?**
- **Why did Taft lose the progressives' support?**
- **What was the result of the 1912 election?**

Although a financial panic and sharp depression hit the nation in 1907, President Roosevelt remained popular. The Republican nomination was his for the asking, but having served almost two full terms, he chose not to run again. The Republicans then turned to William Howard Taft, who easily won the 1908 election. In some ways, Taft carried on Roosevelt's reform program. But as his term wore on, progressives became more and more unhappy with his actions.

Taft and Sherman
campaign banner, 1908

TAFT TAKES OFFICE

At the 1908 Republican convention, Roosevelt supported his secretary of war, William Howard Taft, who won the nomination on the first ballot. The Democrats again nominated William Jennings Bryan, whose prolabor platform won the backing of the American Federation of Labor. Despite labor's support, the Democrats lost the election by a wide margin.

From the start it was clear that Taft would be a different sort of president than Roosevelt. Roosevelt enjoyed being in the public eye. Taft was just the opposite. "I don't like politics," he once wrote. "I don't like the limelight."

A smart but cautious man, Taft stressed the limits on his power as president, rather than his potential for leadership. Nevertheless, he chalked up an impressive list of accomplishments. His administration filed 90 antitrust suits, more than twice the number begun under Roosevelt. At Taft's urging, Congress passed the **Mann-Elkins Act** in 1910, extending the regulatory powers of the Interstate Commerce Commission to telephone and telegraph companies.

Taft also advanced the cause of conservation. He added vast areas to the nation's forest reserves. Taft also supported reforms to aid working people. With his approval, Congress created the Department of Labor to enforce labor laws. It also passed mine-safety laws and established an eight-hour workday for employees of companies holding contracts with the federal government.

The Taft administration was partly responsible, too, for the adoption of the **Sixteenth Amendment**. Proposed in 1909 and ratified in 1913, the amendment authorizes a national tax

WILLIAM H. TAFT
1857–1930

in office
1909–1913

Bill Taft was an unhappy president—at heart a judge, not a politician. He seemed ill suited for public office, dozing off at official dinners or Cabinet meetings, forgetting names, procrastinating, and being tactless at the worst moments. When leaving the White House, he welcomed incoming President Woodrow Wilson by saying, "I'm glad to be going. This is the lonesomest place in the world."

What Taft really wanted was a seat on the U.S. Supreme Court. Taft had had a distinguished legal career, serving as U.S. solicitor general, as a federal judge, as a president of the American Bar Association, and as a law professor at Yale University. In 1921 Taft got his wish—he was appointed chief justice of the Supreme Court. "Presidents come and go," a happy Taft said, "but the Court goes on forever."

based on individual income. Progressives had long supported such a tax as a way to fund needed government programs in a fair manner.

■■ **Taft's administration supported the Mann-Elkins Act, conservation programs, labor reforms, and the Sixteenth Amendment.**

TAFT ANGERS THE PROGRESSIVES

Despite these reforms, Taft lost the support of progressive Republicans. The split between the

president and the progressives began in April 1909 with the passage of a tariff bill.

Both Taft and the progressives favored tariff reductions to lower the prices of consumer goods. Some members of Congress, however, wanted high tariffs to protect American industry. They won out when the House sent a low-tariff bill to the Senate, and Nelson Aldrich of Rhode Island turned it into a high-tariff measure.

Taft could have vetoed the bill, now called the Payne-Aldrich Tariff, or he could have pressured Aldrich to change the rates. But Taft lacked the political skill to oppose conservative Republicans in Congress. Despite his misgivings, he signed the bill. To make matters worse, he proceeded to call it the best tariff ever passed. Outraged progressives accused Taft of betraying the reform cause.

Progressives also attacked Taft for sabotaging Roosevelt's conservation program. The dispute revolved around Taft's secretary of the interior, Richard Ballinger, who believed that the Roosevelt administration had exceeded its authority when it stopped the sale of public land. Ballinger approved the sale of a vast tract of coal-rich Alaska timberland. The head of the U.S. Forest Service, Gifford Pinchot (PIN-shoh), an ardent conservationist and Roosevelt's friend, attacked Ballinger for favoring private interests over conservation. Taft warned Pinchot to stop criticizing Ballinger. When Pinchot did not stop, Taft fired him.

For progressives the Ballinger-Pinchot affair signaled Taft's weakness on conservation.

▼ This cartoon appeared in the *Tacoma News Tribune* in 1919 and satirizes Taft's awkward position in the Ballinger-Pinchot affair.

Although his administration later restored the Alaska land to the federal forest reserve, the episode hurt the Republicans in the 1910 congressional elections. For the first time in 16 years, the Republicans lost control of the House of Representatives.

Taft made one particularly dangerous enemy—Theodore Roosevelt, who broke with Taft over the Pinchot controversy. In the congressional elections of 1910, Roosevelt campaigned for progressive Republicans who opposed Taft and the party's conservative wing. In a speech at Osawatomie (oh-suh-WAHT-uh-mee), Kansas, Roosevelt offered his **New Nationalism**—a bold program of social legislation calling for tough laws to protect workers, ensure public health, and regulate business. He declared:

> 66 The true friend of property, the true conservative, is he who insists that property shall be the servant and not the master of the commonwealth. . . . The citizens of the United States must effectively control the mighty commercial forces which they have themselves called into being. 99

Government, Roosevelt said, must become the "steward of the public welfare." His call for a more activist federal government represented a far more liberal position than he had taken as president. Delighted, reformers hailed the New Nationalism as a revival of the progressive spirit.

THE REPUBLICAN PARTY DIVIDES

Not long before Roosevelt's speech, a bitter dispute in Congress had further deepened the gulf between Taft and the progressives. In the spring of 1910, progressive Republicans in Congress launched a major attack on Speaker of the House Joseph ("Uncle Joe") Cannon of Illinois, a conservative Republican.

◀ The Progressive, or Bull Moose, party held its convention in Chicago on August 5, 1912. Delegates paraded through the aisles, singing "Onward Christian Soldiers," and unanimously nominated Theodore Roosevelt for president. Souvenirs from the Bull Moose campaign are shown here.

Cannon, a 73-year-old tobacco-chewing poker player, was one of Washington's most powerful politicians. As Speaker he ruled the House with an iron hand, appointing all House committees and naming their chairmen. As head of the powerful Rules Committee, which determined the order of business in the House, Cannon prevented bills he opposed from even reaching the House floor for debate.

Progressives charged that Cannon used his great power to block reform legislation. ("Not one cent for scenery," he had growled in dismissing a call for environmental protection.) In March 1910 Congressman George Norris of Nebraska, a progressive, began an effort to break Cannon's power. Norris proposed that in the future, House members elect the Rules Committee and that the Speaker be excluded from membership.

After a heated debate, Norris's motion passed. A year later, the House also stripped the Speaker of the power to appoint members of the other committees—a major progressive victory. Throughout this bitter dispute, Taft refused to take sides, further alienating progressives.

By 1912 the conservative and the progressive wings of the Republican party were deeply divided. Theodore Roosevelt, by now completely at odds with Taft, decided to run again for the presidency. Borrowing a prizefighting term, he proclaimed: "My hat is in the ring." Roosevelt won almost every Republican state primary, including the one in Taft's own state, Ohio.

At the convention the Taft forces, firmly in control of the party machinery, refused to seat many of Roosevelt's delegates. When Taft won the nomination, Roosevelt's supporters angrily walked out, and held their own convention, adopting a platform based on the New Nationalism and nominating Roosevelt as their presidential candidate. Thus was born the Progressive party, also known as the Bull Moose party after Roosevelt declared that he felt "fit as a bull moose" to run.

▲ **Part of the speech
Theodore Roosevelt delivered on October 14,
1912, and the eyeglass case he carried are shown
here. Notice the bullet holes made during the
attempted assassination.**

Roosevelt's candidacy, however, almost
ended on October 14, 1912, when a deranged man
shot him in the chest during a campaign stop.
Roosevelt went ahead with his planned speech,
despite the bullet lodged in his body. This reckless
display of courage reinforced his image as a larger-
than-life hero.

∎∎ **When Roosevelt failed to win the
Republican presidential nomina-
tion from Taft, he formed the
Progressive party.**

A DEMOCRATIC VICTORY IN 1912

Although Roosevelt's campaign continued to pick
up steam, the division in the Republican party
practically assured a Democratic victory.
Roosevelt and Taft were likely to split the
Republican vote, while Democrats united behind
one candidate. Their choice was Governor
Woodrow Wilson of New Jersey, who ran on a
platform calling for tariff reduction, banking
reform, laws benefiting wage earners and farmers,
and stronger antitrust legislation.

Wilson, a native of Virginia and a political
newcomer, had long nurtured dreams of high office.
In college he had made calling cards proclaiming
"Thomas Woodrow Wilson, Senator from Virginia."
He eventually became a professor at Princeton
University in New Jersey and later served as its
president. He was elected governor in 1910. In his
short time as governor, he fought the state's
Democratic party bosses and pushed through laws
regulating business. As an outspoken reformer and
eloquent speaker, Wilson was the presidential
choice of progressives in the Democratic party.

In the 1912 campaign, Wilson brilliantly captured the nation's reform mood. His program, the
New Freedom, called for a revival of small business and a return to an America where the "little
guy" was free from the control of big business and
government. Wilson asserted:

❝ The only way that government is kept
pure is by keeping . . . channels open, so
that . . . there will constantly be coming
new blood into the veins of the body
politic. ❞

RISE OF THE SOCIALIST PARTY Number of Socialist Votes, 1900–1920						
Election Year	**1900**	**1904**	**1908**	**1912**	**1916**	**1920**
Presidential	87,814	402,283	420,793	900,672	585,113	919,799
Gubernatorial	0	73,914	13,694	386,828	125,907	230,907
Congressional	8,021	138,201	113,450	1,599,420	770,230	1,128,200

Sources: *Congressional Quarterly's Guide to U.S. Elections* (for gubernatorial and congressional),
Historical Statistics of the United States (for presidential)

THE SOCIALIST CHALLENGE Dramatic social changes at the turn of the century spurred the popularity of the prolabor,
reform-minded Socialist party.

❓ BUILDING CHART SKILLS In which year did Socialist candidates obtain the largest number of overall votes?

Although Wilson shared the progressive belief in government as an agent of reform, he believed that making government too strong could stifle individual freedom. He believed that the goal of reform should be to rid the system of corruption so that free competition could flourish, without significantly altering the system itself. In this regard he differed from Roosevelt and especially from another candidate for president, Eugene Debs of the Socialist party. The Socialist party supported worker control of the government and public ownership of all major industries. The party had done very well in the 1910 elections.

Among Debs, Wilson, and Roosevelt, American voters had a choice of three strong reform-minded candidates. Even Taft supported reform programs, although he appeared to represent a more conservative viewpoint.

As expected, Wilson won the election, receiving 435 electoral votes to 88 for Roosevelt and 8 for Taft. Debs won over 900,000 popular votes but no electoral votes. Out of more than 15 million votes cast, the three reform candidates received some 11 million. Some 1,200 Socialist candidates, including 79 mayors, were elected to offices across the country, reflecting the desire for new approaches to government. Although Wilson won just six million popular votes, he took office with a strong mandate for reform.

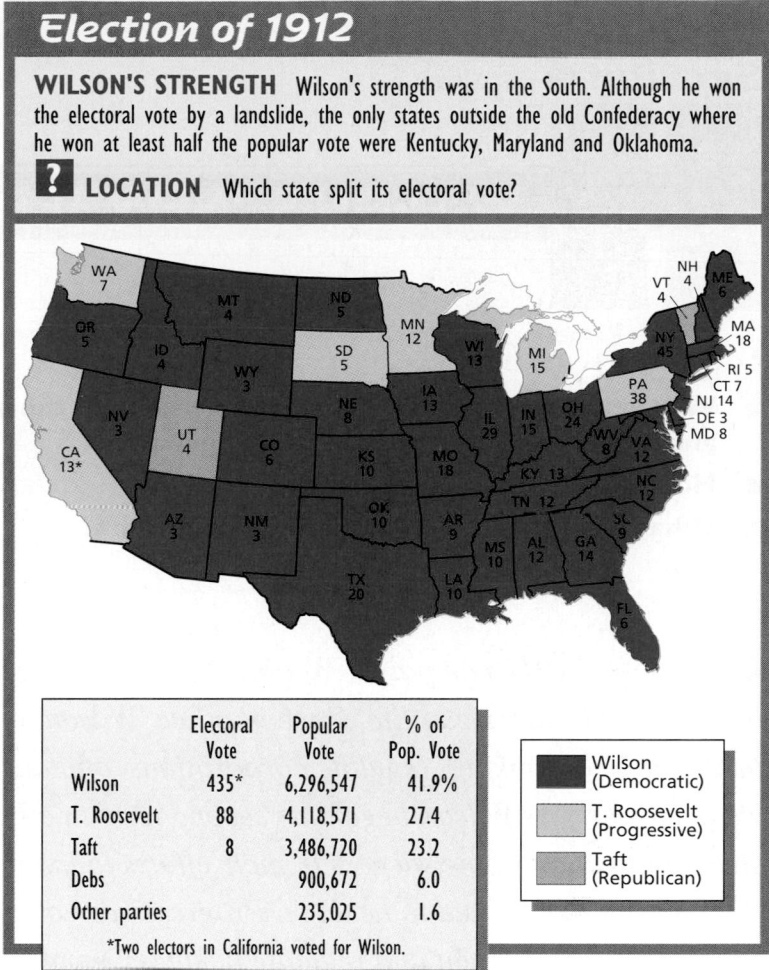

Election of 1912

WILSON'S STRENGTH Wilson's strength was in the South. Although he won the electoral vote by a landslide, the only states outside the old Confederacy where he won at least half the popular vote were Kentucky, Maryland and Oklahoma.

? LOCATION Which state split its electoral vote?

	Electoral Vote	Popular Vote	% of Pop. Vote
Wilson	435*	6,296,547	41.9%
T. Roosevelt	88	4,118,571	27.4
Taft	8	3,486,720	23.2
Debs		900,672	6.0
Other parties		235,025	1.6

*Two electors in California voted for Wilson.

Wilson (Democratic)
T. Roosevelt (Progressive)
Taft (Republican)

■■ **The split in the Republican vote and the public support for reform enabled Woodrow Wilson to win the 1912 presidential election.**

SECTION 3 REVIEW

IDENTIFY and explain the significance of the following: William Howard Taft, Mann-Elkins Act, Sixteenth Amendment, Nelson Aldrich, Richard Ballinger, Gifford Pinchot, New Nationalism, Joseph Cannon, George Norris, Woodrow Wilson, New Freedom, Eugene Debs.

1. **MAIN IDEA** What contributions did the Taft administration make to reform?

2. **MAIN IDEA** What actions caused Taft to lose the support of progressives?

3. **MAIN IDEA** How did the Progressive party help determine the outcome of the 1912 presidential election?

4. **WRITING TO EXPRESS A VIEWPOINT** Imagine you are Teddy Roosevelt. Write a speech explaining your plan of action and why you formed the Progressive party.

5. **DISTINGUISHING FACT FROM OPINION** Supporters of the Progressive party believed that Taft had not lived up to the progressive ideals of the Roosevelt administration. Comparing Taft's reform record to Roosevelt's, was this a fair assessment? Why or why not?

WILSON'S "NEW FREEDOM"

FOCUS

- What did the Wilson administration achieve in the areas of tariff and banking reforms and business regulation?
- How did women win the right to vote?
- What was the major success of progressivism?

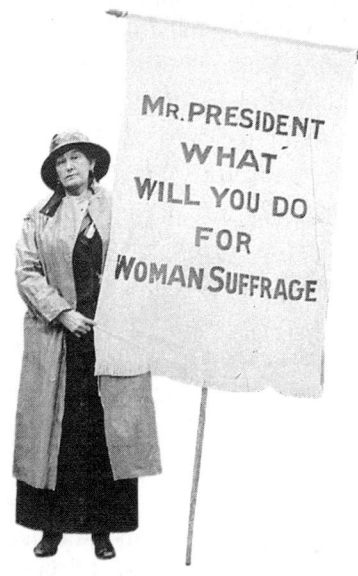

*D*uring the 1912 campaign, Woodrow Wilson pledged to restore opportunity in American life. Once in office, Wilson moved to lower tariffs, reform banking, regulate corporations, and aid farmers and wage earners. As Wilson began his second term in office, progressives could claim some success in their efforts to improve American life. Yet much remained to be done. Progressives had barely begun to clean up government and regulate business, women still did not have the right to vote, and the pledge of equal opportunity for all Americans remained unfulfilled.

Suffragist demonstrating in front of the White House, about 1916

REFORM ON MANY FRONTS

On March 4, 1913, President Wilson gave his first inaugural address in which he eloquently summed up the spirit of the progressive reform movement:

66 We have been proud of our industrial achievements, but we have not . . . stopped . . . to count the . . . fearful physical and spiritual cost to the men and women and children upon whom the . . . weight and burden of it all has fallen. . . . This is not a day of triumph; it is a day of dedication. Here muster, not the forces of party, but the forces of humanity. 99

A month later, Wilson presented his legislative agenda. It included tariff and banking reforms and stronger antitrust laws. Opposed by business groups and lobbyists, Wilson used all his skill to rally support for his program, both in Congress and among the American people.

Wilson's first priority was to lower tariffs. Well aware that big business had blocked tariff reduction during Taft's presidency, Wilson mounted a public campaign to undermine the business lobby and overcome Senate opposition. His

◀ Woodrow Wilson is shown delivering his first inaugural address on March 4, 1913.

WOODROW WILSON
1856–1924

in office
1913–1921

Woodrow Wilson had a reputation for being very serious and often inflexible. He hated political compromise and at times would oppose legislation he originally proposed if it was amended by someone else. He once told a political associate, "I am sorry for those who disagree with me. . . . Because I know they are wrong."

Yet, despite his public image, Wilson often surprised his close associates with

sudden displays of humorous behavior. Once when Wilson was riding in the country with a Secret Service agent, they passed a small boy on the road. "Did you see what that boy did?" Wilson said to the agent, very seriously "He made a face at me." Then the president asked, "Did you see what I did?" "No, Sir," said the agent. With a boyish grin, Wilson replied, "I made a face right back!"

---

strategy worked. In 1913 Congress passed the **Underwood Tariff Act**, which reduced tariffs to their lowest levels in 50 years. To make up for the lost revenue, the bill imposed a graduated income tax, taxing people with high incomes at a higher rate than those with low incomes.

Next on Wilson's agenda was banking. At the time, there was no central fund that banks could borrow from to prevent collapse during financial panics. Thus, when many people withdrew their deposits at the same time, banks commonly failed. Reform was clearly necessary, but Americans disagreed on how to change the banking system. Conservative business groups wanted to give the nation's large private banks more control. In contrast, many Democrats and progressive Republicans wanted the government to run the system.

The **Federal Reserve Act** of 1913, which Wilson helped pass, combined these two views. It created a three-level banking system. At the top was the Federal Reserve Board, a group appointed by the president and charged with running the system. At the second level were 12 Federal Reserve banks, under mixed public and private control. These "bankers' banks" served other banks rather than individuals. At the third level were private banks, which could borrow from the Federal Reserve banks at interest rates set by the Board.

:: Wilson worked to secure passage of the Underwood Tariff Act and the Federal Reserve Act.

WILSON AND BIG BUSINESS

Having achieved important tariff and banking reforms, Wilson turned to business regulation. He wanted to limit the power of monopolies, which he viewed as a threat to small business. Toward this end, he backed passage of the **Clayton Antitrust Act** of 1914. This act clarified and extended the 1890 Sherman Antitrust Act by clearly stating what corporations could not do. For example, companies could not sell goods below cost to drive competitors out of business. They also could not buy competing companies' stock to create a monopoly.

The Wilson administration also backed the creation of the **Federal Trade Commission** (FTC). The FTC, which Congress established in 1914, was

◀ This 1913 cartoon portrays Wilson's use of antitrust legislation to protect small businesses from the unfair competition of monopolies and other large corporations.

Changing Ways

THE 1913 ARMORY SHOW

The progressive reform spirit influenced art as well as economic policies in the early 1900s. Just as industry reformers attacked business trusts, progressive artists tackled the leading American museums' monopoly in determining which paintings and sculptures the public saw.

Resistant to change, the mainstream art community in America was hostile to the "radical" ideas and techniques of the growing modern art movement in Europe. Modernists such as Picasso, Van Gogh, Matisse, and Cézanne offered a new art style, which blurred the lines between reality and fantasy.

Resolved to introduce the American public to modern art, a small group of independent artists formed the Association of American Painters and Sculptors (AAPS) in 1912. The group planned an international exhibition, combing galleries and studios in Munich, Berlin, Paris, and the Hague for works to display. On February 17, 1913, the International Exhibition of Modern Art opened in the 69th

Regiment Armory in New York City. The Armory Show presented some 1,300 works by both European and American artists.

Newspaper reporters raved about the show, calling it "an event not to be missed."

▲ **The Armory Show introduced contemporary European artists and works of art, such as Marcel Duchamp's *Nude Descending a Staircase*, to a curious, but often puzzled, American public.**

Art critics were not so kind. They blasted Van Gogh as "unskilled" and Cézanne as "absolutely without talent." As for Duchamp's *Nude Descending*

a Staircase, they described it as "a lot of disused golf clubs and bags" and "an explosion in a shingle factory."

Ironically, the critics' remarks boosted attendance, which exceeded the organizers' wildest dreams. People came primarily to gape. "I remember one woman becoming so hysterical with laughter," an artist recalled, "that she actually rolled over on the floor—I also remember [AAPS president] Arthur B. Davies taking Teddy Roosevelt through the show—Roosevelt waved his arms and stomped through the Galleries pointing at pictures and saying 'That's not art!' 'That's not art!'"

Even if it failed to enchant Americans with modern art, the Armory Show was a huge success in terms of attendance and publicity. Before the show moved to Chicago, AAPS honored its "friends and enemies" in the press with a beefsteak dinner. Glasses were raised; speeches were made; diners sang and danced. One critic summed up the general mood: "It was a good show, but don't do it again."

authorized to investigate corporations and issue "cease and desist orders" to those engaged in unfair or fraudulent practices and to use the courts to enforce its rulings. Among the abuses the FTC targeted were mislabeled products and false claims.

■■ **Wilson backed passage of the Clayton Antitrust Act and creation of the Federal Trade Commission.**

WILSON AND WORKERS

The Wilson administration also supported legislation to aid working people. The **Federal Farm Loan Act** provided low-interest loans to farmers. The Clayton Antitrust Act included a provision that affirmed labor's right to strike so long as property was not irreparably damaged. The **Adamson Act** reduced the workday for railroad workers from 10 to 8 hours, with no cut in pay. This law not only won applause from reformers but avoided a threatened railroad strike. With Wilson's support, Congress also passed the **Federal Workmen's Compensation Act**, which provided benefits to federal workers injured on the job.

The Wilson administration was less successful in the campaign against child labor. For years progressives had wanted to get young children out of the mills, factories, and mines (see Chapter 17). As labor organizer Mother Jones later recalled:

66 Every day little children came into Union Headquarters, some with their hands off, . . . some with their fingers off at the knuckle. They were stooped little things, round shouldered and skinny. Many were not over ten years of age. 99

Faced with rising protests against child labor from the National Consumers' League and other groups, Congress passed the **Keating-Owen Child Labor Act** in 1916. This act, which had Wilson's backing, outlawed the interstate sale of products produced by child labor. In 1918, however, the Supreme Court declared the law unconstitutional because it restricted commerce instead of directly outlawing child labor. Another law, passed in 1919, met the same fate. Not until the 1930s would the United States outlaw child labor.

THE STRUGGLE FOR WOMEN'S SUFFRAGE

Another part of the progressive agenda—the campaign for women's suffrage—faced strong opposition. Liquor interests feared that women would vote for prohibition. Businesses feared that the vote would empower women to demand better wages and working conditions. When one state senator expressed the widely held belief that the vote would rob women of their beauty and charm, a suffragist retorted:

66 We have women working in the foundries. . . . Women in the laundries . . . stand for 13 or 14 hours in the terrible steam and heat with their hands in hot starch. Surely these women won't lose any

WOMEN'S SUFFRAGE *THROUGH OTHERS' EYES*

In 1902 the first International Woman Suffrage Conference was held in Washington, D.C. The United States was among the nations represented that had not yet granted women national suffrage. Swedish delegate Emmy Evald remarked that in her homeland women had voted on some level since 1736. She then went on to point out the contradictions in the American situation:

66 *You* can not trust the ballot into the hands of women teachers in the public schools but you give it to men who can not read or write. You can not trust the ballot to women who are controlling millions of [dollars] and helping support the country but you give it to loafers and vagabonds who know nothing, have nothing and represent nothing. You can not trust the ballot in the hands of women who are the wives and daughters of your heroes but you give it to those who are willing to sell it for a glass of beer and you trust it in the hands of anarchists. 99

more of their beauty and charm by putting a ballot in a ballot box once a year than they are likely to lose standing in foundries or laundries all year. 🙶

One leading force in the suffrage movement was the National American Woman Suffrage Association, or NAWSA, founded in 1890. Its first two presidents, Elizabeth Cady Stanton and Susan B. Anthony, took a local approach, trying to get state legislatures to grant women the vote. They achieved few successes in their first few years of lobbying, however.

In 1913 Alice Paul, a militant young Quaker suffragist, broke away from NAWSA and formed another organization, which in 1916 became the National Woman's party. It focused on passing an amendment to the Constitution guaranteeing

▲ Alice Paul

women the right to vote. When Wilson and the Democratic party failed to support woman suffrage in the 1916 election, the Woman's party campaigned against them. Wilson won, but narrowly. (See Chapter 20 for more on the election.)

Paul, who had studied in England, favored using the attention-getting protest tactics employed by British suffragists. For example, in January 1917, with Wilson reelected, the Woman's party began round-the-clock picketing of the White House in an effort to pressure Wilson to support a suffrage amendment. They held banners asking, "Mr. President, What Will You Do for Woman Suffrage?" and "How Long Must Women Wait for Liberty?" Many were arrested. Some went on hunger strikes in prison.

Meanwhile, the NAWSA, energized by the leadership of the highly skilled organizer Carrie Chapman Catt, continued to follow traditional political means to attain voting rights. Launching what came to be called her "Winning Plan" in 1916, the NAWSA won a string of successes for suffrage at the state level. After the United States entered World War I in 1917, leaders of the movement—along with millions of American women—lent strong support to the war effort. Their patriotism helped weaken opposition to women's suffrage. By 1919 thirty states had granted women full or partial voting rights. Finally, in 1919, the U.S. Congress passed the **Nineteenth Amendment**, granting women full voting rights. It was ratified in 1920.

Carrie Chapman Catt cautioned, however, that the vote was only an "entering wedge." Women still had to force their way through the "locked door" of political decision making.

■■ **In 1920, with ratification of the Nineteenth Amendment, American women won their long battle for the right to vote.**

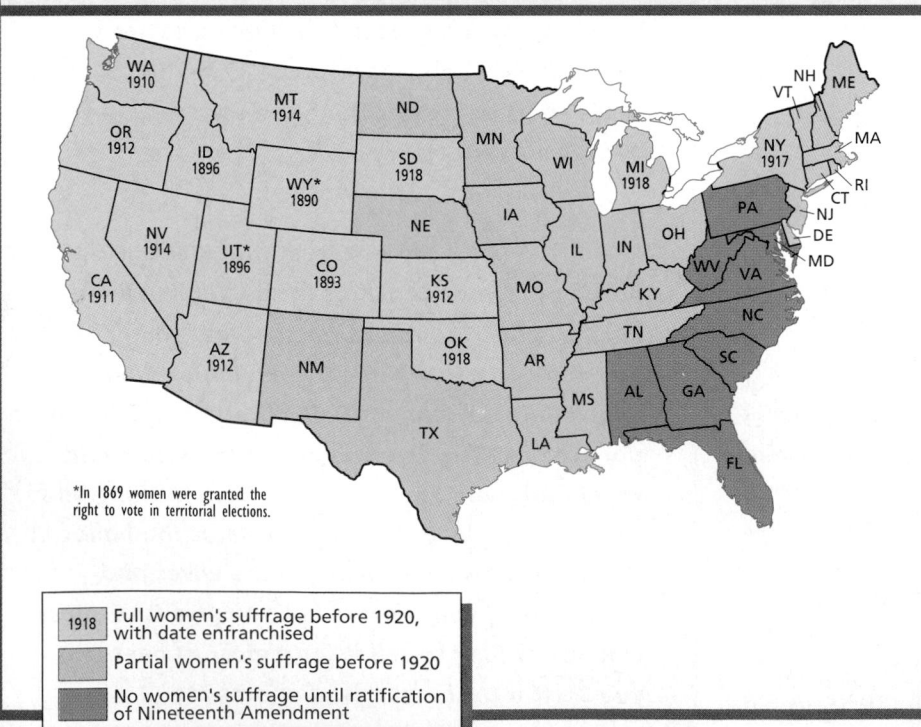

Women's Suffrage, 1920

FIGHTING FOR THE VOTE The National American Woman Suffrage Association worked to convince state legislatures to grant women the vote, while the National Woman's party campaigned for a constitutional amendment.

❓ **REGION** Which section of the United States took the lead in granting the vote to women?

WA 1910
OR 1912
MT 1914
ND
ID 1896
SD 1918
MN
WY* 1890
NV 1914
UT* 1896
CO 1893
NE
IA
CA 1911
AZ 1912
NM
KS 1912
OK 1918
MO
AR
TX
LA
WI
MI 1918
IL
IN
OH
KY
TN
MS
AL
GA
SC
NC
VA
WV
PA
NY 1917
NH
VT
ME
MA
RI
CT
NJ
DE
MD
FL

*In 1869 women were granted the right to vote in territorial elections.

1918 — Full women's suffrage before 1920, with date enfranchised

Partial women's suffrage before 1920

No women's suffrage until ratification of Nineteenth Amendment

The Progressive Legacy

Although scholars agree that the progressive movement left a lasting legacy, they often disagree over how to define that legacy. Many scholars have noted that progressivism was primarily supported by fairly conservative, middle-class, white Americans trying to maintain some level of political and economic power. Many of the successes and shortcomings of the movement can be tied to its origins in the white middle class.

Progressivism made great strides in many areas; however, some of the economic and political reforms of the movement failed to bring about the radical changes anticipated. Such policies as the creation of the Federal Reserve System and implementation of a federal income tax did improve the government's ability to regulate the economy and pay for new programs. Yet, many regulations on businesses fell short of changing the capitalist system; corporations were eventually able to use the regulations to their own advantage. On the political front, reforms such as the initiative, referendum, and recall were primarily used on the local level and thus had little impact on broad questions of public policy.

One of progressivism's most successful elements, the settlement-house movement, increased emphasis on education, improved opportunities for women, brought great urban reform, and eased the plight of European immigrants. However, the settlement-house workers neglected to address the problems of African Americans, many of whom were new migrants from the rural South. This was one of progressivism's greatest shortcomings.

The progressive presidents certainly showed little interest in racial issues. President Wilson was the least sympathetic to African American concerns. During his administration numerous bills designed to institute segregation were submitted to Congress. Although none passed, Wilson issued an executive order segregating eating and restroom facilities for federal employees. Wilson argued that this policy prevented friction between white and black workers, but African Americans strongly protested it as racist.

Despite these shortcomings, however, progressives took real strides toward making the new industrial society more just and orderly. Their greatest legacy was in demonstrating that America's democratic system could respond and adapt to changes in American life.

▪▪ Although progressivism fell short of some of its goals and failed to address racism, it made industrial society more just and humane.

SECTION 4 REVIEW

IDENTIFY and explain the significance of the following: Underwood Tariff Act, Federal Reserve Act, Clayton Antitrust Act, Federal Trade Commission, Federal Farm Loan Act, Adamson Act, Federal Workmen's Compensation Act, Keating-Owen Child Labor Act, Alice Paul, Carrie Chapman Catt, Nineteenth Amendment.

1. **MAIN IDEA** How did Wilson hope to reduce tariffs and reform the banking system?
2. **MAIN IDEA** How did the Wilson administration attempt to regulate business?
3. **MAIN IDEA** What did the passage of the Nineteenth Amendment accomplish?
4. **WRITING TO EVALUATE** Write a paragraph evaluating the legacy of progressivism.
5. **ANALYZING** How successful was Wilson in enlisting the "forces of humanity" to help farmers, railroad and federal workers, and child laborers?

William McKinley assassinated. Theodore Roosevelt becomes president.

Pennsylvania coal miners strike. Newlands Reclamation Act passed.

Elkins Act passed.

Theodore Roosevelt elected president.

Hepburn Act, Meat Inspection Act, and Pure Food and Drug Act passed.

1900

1905

WRITING A SUMMARY

Using the essential points of the chapter as a guide, write a summary of the chapter.

REVIEWING CHRONOLOGY

Number your paper 1 to 5. Study the time line above, and list the following events in the order in which they happened by writing the first next to 1, the second next to 2, and so on. Then complete the activity below.

1. Progressive party formed.
2. Nineteenth Amendment ratified.
3. Pennsylvania coal miners strike.
4. Federal Trade Commission created.
5. William Howard Taft elected president.

Analyzing How did the Sixteenth and Seventeenth amendments promote reform?

IDENTIFYING PEOPLE AND IDEAS

Explain the historical significance of each of the following people or terms.

1. initiative
2. Samuel M. Jones
3. Hepburn Act
4. reclamation
5. Richard Ballinger
6. New Nationalism
7. Joseph Cannon
8. Federal Reserve Act
9. Adamson Act
10. Alice Paul

UNDERSTANDING MAIN IDEAS

1. Why were city commissions effective at achieving efficiency in city government?
2. How did the Wisconsin Idea lay the foundation for further reforms?
3. In what ways were Theodore Roosevelt and William Howard Taft similar in their approaches to reform?
4. Why did Roosevelt challenge Taft in 1912?
5. What were the effects of the Clayton Antitrust Act and the creation of the Federal Trade Commission on the regulation of business?
6. What was the progressive movement's greatest legacy?

REVIEWING THEMES

1. **Democratic Values** How did reformers seek to curb political corruption and to make government more democratic in the early 20th century?
2. **Economic Development** How did President Roosevelt attempt to regulate business without discouraging free enterprise?
3. **Constitutional Heritage** How might reformers have used the Nineteenth Amendment as a means of accomplishing reform in politics and business?

THINKING CRITICALLY

1. **Synthesizing** How did Roosevelt bring dynamic leadership to the progressive movement at the city, state, and national levels?
2. **Evaluating** How did the controversy over tariffs contribute to Taft's defeat in the 1912 election?
3. **Analyzing** What interests worked against the campaign for women's suffrage in the early 20th century?
4. **Hypothesizing** How might life have been different for African Americans if Wilson had pursued a different racial policy?

STRATEGY FOR SUCCESS

Review the Skills Handbook entry on Reading a Time Line on page 991. Then study the time-line entries below, which focus on the years from 1908 to 1912. What cause-and-effect relationship is suggested by the sequence of events listed? How did the events of 1910 relate to those of 1912?

1908	William Howard Taft elected president.
1909	Payne-Aldrich Tariff passed. Taft fires Gifford Pinchot.
1910	Republicans lose control of House of Representatives.
1912	Roosevelt forms Progressive party. Woodrow Wilson elected president.

WRITING ABOUT HISTORY

Writing to Evaluate Write an essay evaluating the progressives' record on racial issues.

William Howard Taft elected president.

Mann-Elkins Act passed.

Progressive party formed. Woodrow Wilson elected president.

Sixteenth and Seventeenth amendments ratified. Underwood Tariff Act and Federal Reserve Act passed.

Clayton Antitrust Act passed. Federal Trade Commission created.

Woodrow Wilson reelected president.

Nineteenth Amendment ratified.

1910   1915   1920

USING PRIMARY SOURCES

In 1906 Upton Sinclair published *The Jungle,* a biting attack on the industrial practices and unsanitary conditions in the Chicago stockyards. Read the following excerpt, which describes the manufacture and processing of canned goods in "Packingtown" (Chicago). Then, in a paragraph, explain how publication of this book might have influenced the passage of the Meat Inspection Act.

66 *"Deviled ham" . . . was made out of the waste ends of smoked beef that were too small to be sliced by the machines; and also tripe, dyed with chemicals so that it would not show white, and trimmings of hams and corned beef, and potatoes, skins and all. . . . All this ingenious mixture was ground up and flavored with spices to make it taste like something. Anybody who could invent a new imitation had been sure of a fortune, . . . but it was hard to think of anything new in a place where . . . men welcomed tuberculosis in the cattle they were feeding, because it made them fatten more quickly; and where they bought up all the old rancid [stale] butter . . . rechurned it with skim milk, and sold it in bricks in the cities!* 99

Chicago stockyards, 1919

LINKING HISTORY AND GEOGRAPHY

Study the map on page 552. What might explain the link between geographic region and the granting of women's suffrage?

Sample ballot, 1892

BUILDING YOUR PORTFOLIO

Complete the following projects independently or cooperatively.

1. **REFORM** In Chapter 17 you portrayed a progressive reformer addressing a problem in your city. Building on that experience, write a platform for the Progressive party that translates the problems of political machines, women's suffrage, business regulation, and worker protection into specific reforms your party hopes to institute.

2. **DEMOCRATIC RIGHTS** In Chapter 17 you portrayed a progressive reformer preparing a speech on women's rights to deliver at an Independence Day celebration. Building on that experience, imagine you are the editor of a labor union newspaper. Write an editorial indicating why you believe that progressives are not adequately addressing the needs of working-class women.

Chapter 19

1898–1917

AMERICA AND THE WORLD

FOCUS

UNDERSTANDING THE MAIN IDEA

In the waning years of the 19th century, the United States established itself as a world power by defeating Spain and acquiring Spain's last colonies in the Western Hemisphere. The progressive presidents asserted a strong foreign policy, acting to promote U.S. economic and security interests in the Pacific, the Caribbean, Asia, and Latin America.

THEMES

■ **GLOBAL RELATIONS** Why might a country acquire overseas colonies? Why might a country resist becoming a colony?

■ **ECONOMIC DEVELOP-MENT** How might foreign investors influence a country's economy? What problems might arise from these investments?

■ **DEMOCRATIC VALUES** Does the acquisition of colonies conflict with democratic principles? Why or why not?

1898	1899	1904	1910	1915
Spanish-American War begins.	U.S. annexes Philippines.	Russo-Japanese War begins.	The Mexican Revolution starts.	Wilson sends marines into Haiti.

President James Monroe issued the Monroe Doctrine in 1823 as a warning to European powers to keep out of the Americas. But for much of the 19th century, the United States was too involved in domestic affairs to enforce the doctrine.

Battle of Manila Bay

D awn was just breaking as the American fleet, its flags flying, steamed across lovely Manila Bay, in the Philippines. It was early morning, May 1, 1898—just 11 days after the United States had declared war on Spain. Commodore George Dewey stood on the bridge of his flagship, *Olympia,* his eyes trained on the Spanish guns aimed at his ships from the shore and from the small Spanish fleet anchored in the harbor.

Sighting the Americans, the Spanish opened fire. Shortly after 5:30 A.M., Commodore Dewey gave an order to his flagship captain: "You may fire when you are ready, Gridley." The boom and flash of naval guns exploded through the bay. Shells crashed into several Spanish vessels, and they erupted into flames.

The Battle of Manila Bay had begun, the first battle of the Spanish-American War. It marked America's emergence on the world stage at the end of the 19th century. Throughout most of the century, Americans had followed George Washington's advice and remained aloof from foreign entanglements. Indeed, as late as 1889, Congressman Henry Cabot Lodge of Massachusetts wrote: "Our relations with foreign nations today fill but a slight place in American politics." But this would soon change as the United States became deeply involved in events abroad, from nearby Cuba and Mexico to distant China.

U.S. soldiers question Filipino women, 1899.

WAR WITH SPAIN

FOCUS

- What fueled the quest for overseas territory?
- Why did the United States declare war on Spain?
- What was the outcome of the Spanish-American War for the United States and Spain?

In the late 1800s the United States emerged as the world's leading industrial producer and agricultural exporter. This economic success encouraged the nation to establish overseas colonies, just as the European powers were doing. The United States hoped colonization would provide new markets for its goods and new sources of raw materials. U.S. involvement in Samoa and a short war with Spain in 1898 increased the American role in the Pacific and the Caribbean.

Recruiter, 1898

THE IMPULSE FOR IMPERIALISM

In March 1889 seven warships—one British, three German, and three American—faced off in the South Pacific harbor of Apia, in present-day Western Samoa. But before a shot could be fired, a typhoon struck, destroying all but the British ship. What brought these three powerful nations to the brink of war? **Imperialism**: the quest for colonial empires.

Between 1876 and 1915, vast areas of Africa, Asia, and Latin America fell under the control of a handful of industrialized nations locked in a race to acquire overseas colonies. Great Britain, the leading imperialist power, had colonies flung so far across the globe that the British could boast, "The sun never sets on the British Empire."

What lay behind this wave of imperialism? The desire for power and prestige played a role, but it was also a matter of economics. Industrial workers, aided by efficient machines and abundant capital, produced far more goods than could be consumed at home. In response, industrialists turned to Africa, Asia, and Latin America for new

◄ **Samoan families lived in grass-thatched huts, such as this one in Pago Pago.**

customers and new sources of raw materials. The telegraph, steamship, and railroad made even the remotest areas potential markets. To protect these new markets from competition, industrialized nations launched a campaign of colonization.

Although American enthusiasm for overseas expansion never matched that of the Europeans, support grew during the late 1800s. Some supporters, like Alfred Thayer Mahan of the U.S. Naval College, argued that overseas territories would make the United States more powerful and provide sites for naval bases and steamship fueling stations from which to conduct trade. Others claimed that the United States had a duty to spread its political system and the Christian religion to other parts of the world. This belief often went hand-in-hand with feelings of racial superiority. In his widely read book *Our Country* (1885), Josiah Strong, a Protestant minister and social reformer, proclaimed that Anglo-Saxons (people of English ancestry) had a special mission:

66 God, with infinite wisdom and skill, is training the Anglo-Saxon race for an hour sure to come in the world's future. . . .
Then this race . . . the representative, let us hope, of the largest liberty, the purest Christianity, the highest civilization . . . will spread itself over the earth. 99

■■ **The quest for empire was fueled by strategic, economic, and cultural motives.**

It was the desire for naval bases and fueling stations, rather than cultural concerns, that led the United States, Great Britain, and Germany to square off in Samoa in 1889. The Samoans realized that this competition put them in grave danger. In 1898 Te'o Tuvale, a government official, warned his fellow Samoans:

66 Be kind and don't start a war in Samoa, because if you do the Three Powers [Britain, Germany, and the United States] will take over the conduct of the country and your orators and Chiefs and things that you have been accustomed to will be of no further use. 99

Te'o Tuvale's prophecy was fulfilled the next year when, in the face of overwhelming European and U.S. military might, Samoans surrendered their government. The United States won control over Eastern Samoa, and Germany was granted control over Western Samoa. Today Western Samoa is independent, while Eastern (or American) Samoa remains a U.S. territory (see map on page 564).

CONFLICT IN CUBA

The Caribbean island of Cuba, just 90 miles from the Florida Keys, provided a testing ground for U.S. imperialism. In the late 1800s Cuba simmered with unrest. Along with its Caribbean neighbor Puerto Rico, it was the last of the Spanish colonies in the Americas. Since 1868, Cubans had launched a series of unsuccessful revolts against Spanish rule. To put down the rebellion, the Spanish government exiled many leaders of the independence movement. Foremost among these exiles was the brilliant Cuban poet José Martí, who was forced out of Cuba in 1871 and again in 1879.

From his exile in New York, Martí wrote poems and newspaper articles promoting Cuban independence. He also urged Cuban exiles to mount an invasion of Cuba:

▲ **José Martí**

66 Let us rise up at once with a final burst of heartfelt energy. . . . Let us rise up for the true republic, those of us who, with our passion for right and our habit of hard work, will know how to preserve it. 99

When Cubans launched another revolt in February 1895, Martí and other exiles joined them. Martí became a martyr for Cuban independence when he was killed a month later in a battle with Spanish soldiers.

In 1896 Spain sent General Valeriano Weyler to put down the uprising. Within days Weyler had imprisoned thousands of farmers in concentration camps to prevent them from supplying the rebels. Over the next two years, starvation and disease claimed the lives of perhaps 200,000 Cubans.

The American press branded Weyler "the Butcher." William Randolph Hearst's *Journal* and Joseph Pulitzer's *World,* two New York City newspapers, outdid each other in publicizing Spanish atrocities. (This type of sensationalized reporting was named yellow journalism after "The Yellow Kid," a comic strip published for a time in both papers.) In 1897 Hearst sent artist Frederic Remington to Cuba to send back drawings that documented Spanish cruelty. Hearst hoped to horrify Americans into agitating for war against Spain. Finding nothing to draw, Remington reportedly cabled Hearst: "EVERYTHING IS QUIET. THERE IS NO TROUBLE HERE. THERE WILL BE NO WAR. WISH TO RETURN." Hearst was said to have replied: "PLEASE REMAIN. YOU FURNISH THE PICTURES AND I'LL FURNISH THE WAR."

In addition to U.S. horror at Spanish atrocities, threats to U.S. investments in Cuba convinced many that the United States should aid the Cuban rebels. In the face of mounting war fever, President William McKinley, himself a veteran of the Civil War, struggled to remain neutral and to resist committing American troops. "I have been through one war. I have seen the dead piled up, and I do not want to see another," he explained.

But early in 1898, two shattering events forced his hand. First, on February 9 Hearst's *Journal* printed a letter written by Spain's minister to the United States, Enrique Dupuy de Lôme. Intercepted by a Cuban spy and sold to Hearst, the letter ridiculed President McKinley as "weak, and a bidder for the admiration of the crowd."

Americans were outraged at the Spaniard's remarks, which the *Journal* called "the worst insult to the United States in its history." Then on February 15 the American battleship *Maine*—sent to Havana, Cuba, to protect U.S. lives and property—blew up, killing 260 sailors. "DESTRUCTION OF THE WAR SHIP MAINE WAS THE WORK OF AN ENEMY!" screamed the *Journal*'s headline. Though it was later determined that a fire in a coal bin had probably caused

the explosion, many Americans blamed Spain. "Remember the *Maine*! And to hell with Spain!" became a familiar chant.

Spain tried to calm tensions by agreeing to a U.S.–proposed peace plan. But it was too late. On April 11 President McKinley bowed to public pressure and asked Congress to intervene in Cuba "in the name of humanity, in the name of civilization, and in behalf of endangered American interests."

On April 20 Congress recognized Cuban independence and voted to use U.S. military force to help Cuba attain it. Congress also adopted the **Teller Amendment**, which stated that the United States claimed no "sovereignty, jurisdiction, or control" over Cuba. Once Cuba won its independence from Spain, the amendment promised, the United States would "leave the government and control of the Island to its people."

■■ **To protect U.S. investments and to help Cuba overthrow Spanish rule, the United States declared war on Spain in April 1898.**

WAR WITH SPAIN

The first battles of the **Spanish-American War** were not fought in nearby Cuba, but halfway around the world, in the Spanish-held Philippine Islands. Weeks before war was declared, Assistant Secretary of the Navy Theodore Roosevelt had, without authorization, cabled Commodore George Dewey, commander of the U.S. Navy's Asiatic fleet anchored at Hong Kong. Roosevelt ordered Dewey to keep his ships ready to take offensive action in the Philippines.

On May 1, 1898, less than two weeks after war was declared, Dewey's fleet easily defeated the small Spanish fleet guarding the Philippine city of Manila. In order to capture the city itself, Dewey obtained the support of a rebel army of Filipino patriots led by Emilio Aguinaldo (ahg-ee-NAHL-doh). Filipinos had been fighting for independence from Spain for two years. Now, along with U.S. soldiers, they attacked and captured Manila. Cut off by Commodore Dewey's warships and surrounded by Aguinaldo's forces, Spanish forces in the Philippines surrendered on August 14, 1898.

863,956 **The World.** 863,956
WORLDS CIRCULATED YESTERDAY · "Circulation Books Open to All." · · "Circulation Books Open to All." · WORLDS CIRCULATED YEERDAY
VOL. XXXVIII. NO. 13,339. · NEW YORK, THURSDAY, FEBRUARY 17, 1898. · PRICE

MAINE EXPLOSION CAUSED BY BOMB OR TORPEDO?

Capt. Sigsbee and Consul-General Lee Are in Doubt---The World Has Sent a Special Tug, With Submarine Divers, to Havana to Find Out---Lee Asks for an Immediate Court of Inquiry---260 Men Dead.

IN A SUPPRESSED DESPATCH TO THE STATE DEPARTMENT, THE CAPTAIN SAYS THE ACCIDENT WAS MADE POSSIBLE BY AN ENEMY.

Dr. E. C. Pendleton, Just Arrived from Havana, Says He Overheard Talk There of a Plot to Blow Up the Ship---Zalinski, the Dynamite Expert, and Other Experts Report to The World that the Wreck Was Not Accidental---Washington Officials Ready for Vigorous Action if Spanish Responsibility Can be Shown---Divers to Be Sent Down to Make Careful Examinations.

▲ The United States found it difficult to maintain its neutrality in the Cuban-Spanish conflict amid the public outrage triggered by sensationalized news reports. This headline appeared in Joseph Pulitzer's *World*.

Spanish-American War, 1898

WAR AT SEA The Spanish-American War was primarily decided at sea. The Spanish fleets protecting Cuba and the Philippines were no match for the well-prepared U.S. Navy. Both Spanish fleets were destroyed, while the Americans suffered minimal casualties.

? MOVEMENT Where did Commodore George Dewey destroy the Spanish fleet?

(Map, left panel — Caribbean theater)

UNITED STATES
Gulf of Mexico
Tampa
FLORIDA
Miami
Nassau
Key West
Florida Keys
Sinking of *Maine* + Feb. 1898
Havana
Cienfuegos
CUBA (Spanish)
San Juan Hill July 1
El Caney July 1
Santiago
Daiquiri
Destruction of Spanish Fleet July 3
HAITI
Port-au-Prince
DOMINICAN REPUBLIC
Santo Domingo
Ponce
San Juan
PUERTO RICO (Spanish)
JAMAICA (British)
Kingston
BAHAMAS (British)
ATLANTIC OCEAN
Tropic of Cancer
CARIBBEAN SEA
25° N
20° N
15° N
85° W   80° W   75° W   70° W   65° W

0   150   300 Miles
0   150   300 Kilometers
Lambert Conformal Conic Projection

(Map, right panel — Pacific theater)

CHINA
Hong Kong (British)
TAIWAN (Japanese)
DEWEY
SOUTH CHINA SEA
PACIFIC OCEAN
LUZON
Manila Aug. 13
Manila Bay May 1
Dewey defeats Spanish fleet
MINDORO
PANAY
NEGROS
PALAWAN
SAMAR
LEYTE
MINDANAO
PHILIPPINES (Spanish)
20° N
10° N
120° E

0   200   400 Miles
0   200   400 Kilometers
Mercator Projection

(Locator globe inset)
ARCTIC OCEAN
NORTH AMERICA
EUROPE
ASIA
PACIFIC OCEAN
AFRICA
PACIFIC OCEAN
SOUTH AMERICA
ATLANTIC OCEAN
INDIAN OCEAN
AUSTRALIA
ANTARCTICA
Equator
Robinson Projection

Legend:
Spanish possession | U.S. forces | Spanish forces | Battle | U.S. naval blockade

---

Victory in Cuba would not come quite as easily as it had in the Philippines. With a regular army of only some 28,000 soldiers, the U.S. War Department was unprepared for land battles. Thousands of volunteers raced to enlist, but how could they be trained and equipped overnight? With little training and outfitted in heavy wool uniforms (the only ones that army storehouses could supply), U.S. troops sailed for tropical Cuba in mid-June. For rations, the men were issued canned corned beef that was supposed to keep in any weather. "Well," reported one soldier, "it commenced to explode. We had to throw it all overboard." Another soldier described life once the troops arrived in Cuba:

> 66 Heavy rains pouring down, no tents for cover, . . . standing in trenches in a foot of water and mud, day and night. . . . Ration issue consisting of a slice of sow belly, hardtack, and some grains of coffee. . . . Then came the issue of fleece-lined underwear in a 132 [degree] climate. . . . Then came on malaria. 99

▲ **Emilio Aguinaldo, shown wearing a vest, sat for this photograph with his advisers in 1896.**

▲ Soldiers of the African American 9th and 10th cavalries are shown here during the Battle of Las Guásimas on June 24, 1898. This victory paved the way for American forces to capture Santiago.

The major American land actions in Cuba began on July 1 as U.S. troops mounted an assault on the Spanish stronghold of Santiago. Their aim was to capture the heights above Santiago—El Caney and San Juan Hill—so that they could aim their guns down on Spanish troops. One U.S. division overcame Spanish forces at El Caney.

In what would become the war's most famous battle, Lieutenant Colonel Teddy Roosevelt (who had resigned his naval post) led a cavalry unit of some 1,000 men toward the garrison on San Juan Hill. Composed largely of athletes from eastern colleges, miners, cowboys, Native Americans, ranchers, and would-be adventurers, the unit was known as the Rough Riders.

Since their horses had not been shipped, the Rough Riders had to charge on foot under intense Spanish fire. The African American 9th and 10th cavalries cleared the way for the final surge. By nightfall U.S. troops controlled the ridge above Santiago. Then on July 3, the U.S. Navy sank the Spanish fleet off the coast of Cuba, resulting in more than 400 Spanish casualties. With their navy crushed, two weeks later, on July 17, Spanish troops in Cuba surrendered. Meanwhile, U.S. troops also defeated Spanish troops in Puerto Rico.

The war was costly for Spain. By the terms of the peace treaty, Spain granted Cuba its independence and ceded Puerto Rico and the Pacific island of Guam (see map on page 564) to the United States. Spain also gave up control of the Philippines in return for a U.S. payment of $20 million.

The United States also paid a price for the war. Some 5,400 soldiers died, nearly 400 in battle and the rest from dysentery, typhoid, malaria, yellow fever, or food poisoning. But the war also brought rewards. By gaining control of overseas territories, the United States secured its position as an imperialist and world power. Expansionists expressed delight, but many Americans were troubled by the quest for empire.

■■ **The United States gained most of Spain's overseas territory through victory in the Spanish-American War.**

■■ SECTION 1 REVIEW

IDENTIFY and explain the significance of the following: imperialism, Te'o Tuvale, José Martí, Valeriano Weyler, William Randolph Hearst, William McKinley, Enrique Dupuy de Lôme, Teller Amendment, Spanish-American War, George Dewey, Emilio Aguinaldo.

LOCATE and explain the importance of the following: American Samoa; Santiago, Cuba; Manila, Philippines; Puerto Rico; Guam.

1. **MAIN IDEA** What led the United States and other industrial powers to turn to imperialism?

2. **MAIN IDEA** What factors caused the United States to become involved in the Spanish-American War?

3. **GEOGRAPHY: PLACE** What territories did the United States gain as a result of the Spanish-American War? How did the war affect Spain?

4. **WRITING TO CREATE** Imagine you are Cuban revolutionary José Martí. Write a poem supporting Cuban independence from Spain.

5. **EVALUATING** How did publishers William Randolph Hearst and Joseph Pulitzer influence the United States to declare war on Spain in 1898?

EXPANSION IN THE PACIFIC

FOCUS

- How did the United States deal with Filipino calls for independence?
- Why did the U.S. government annex Hawaii?
- What role did the United States play in China?
- What kind of relationship developed between Japan and the United States in the late 1800s and early 1900s?

*A*merica's war with Spain began over Cuba. But, in addition to establishing a U.S. presence in the Caribbean, the war extended the U.S. presence in Asia and the Pacific. After the war, the United States established political control over the Philippines and added Hawaii to its colonial holdings. The United States also became further involved in affairs in China and took a new interest in Japan.

Hawaiian coin

UPROAR OVER THE PHILIPPINES

When Dewey's fleet steamed into Manila Bay in 1898, few Americans even knew where the Philippines were. President McKinley confessed that before he consulted a globe, he could not locate the islands "within two thousand miles." The Philippines—a group of islands—cover some 100,000 square miles in the Pacific Ocean, southeast of the Chinese coast. Now that the Philippines were "flung into [U.S.] arms by Dewey's guns," Americans faced an urgent question: Should Filipinos be forced to accept U.S. rule?

The debate over annexation. The debate over whether the United States should **annex**, or take control of, the Philippines was rooted in the larger controversy over imperialism raging across the country.

People questioned whether it was proper or wise for the United States to annex any foreign territory and rule its government and its people.

Expansionists argued forcefully in favor of annexation. In addition to making a case for annexation for commercial and naval reasons, some believed that the United States would bring democracy to the Philippines. Others held that the United States had to rule the Philippines to keep out European powers. Charles Denby, a former American

▶ Filipino women are shown winnowing, or separating, rice on Palawan Island.

foreign minister to China, warned opponents of annexation that times had changed:

> 66 I recognize the existence of a national sentiment in accordance with . . . Washington's Farewell Address, which is against the acquisition of foreign territory; but . . . circumstances are changed. . . . We have a great commerce to take care of. We have to compete with the commercial nations of the world in far-distant markets. Commerce, not politics, is king. 99

Opponents of American imperialism responded that, by annexing the Philippines and denying its independence, the United States would violate its own ideals expressed in the Declaration of Independence. In June 1898, opponents of U.S. imperialism formed the Anti-Imperialist League, which proclaimed:

> 66 We regret that it has become necessary in the land of Washington and Lincoln to reaffirm that all men, of whatever race or color, are entitled to life, liberty, and the pursuit of happiness. . . . We insist that the subjugation of any people is "criminal aggression" and open disloyalty to the distinctive principles of our Government. 99

After a fierce debate, the Senate narrowly approved the treaty annexing the Philippines on February 6, 1899. The vote was 57 to 27, barely reaching the two-thirds majority required.

Conquest and early rule. Filipinos, however, did not want to exchange one master for another—gaining independence from Spain only to lose it to the United States. Emilio Aguinaldo had already set up a provisional Filipino government and proclaimed himself president of the Philippine Republic. Now he warned that Filipinos would go to war if "American troops attempt to take forcible possession. Upon their heads will be all the blood which may be shed."

For the next three years, Filipino independence fighters and U.S. soldiers fought for control of the Philippines. U.S. forces captured Aguinaldo in March 1901. When Filipino resistance continued, however, U.S. forces implemented a concentration camp policy as Weyler had done in Cuba. By the time U.S. forces crushed the rebellion in 1902, the cost in Filipino lives was horrendous, estimated in the hundreds of thousands. More than 4,000 U.S. soldiers lost their lives.

In 1902 the U.S. Congress passed the **Philippine Government Act**, also known as the Organic Act. The act decreed that the Philippines would be ruled by a governor and a two-house legislature. The United States would appoint the governor and the legislature's upper house. After peace was

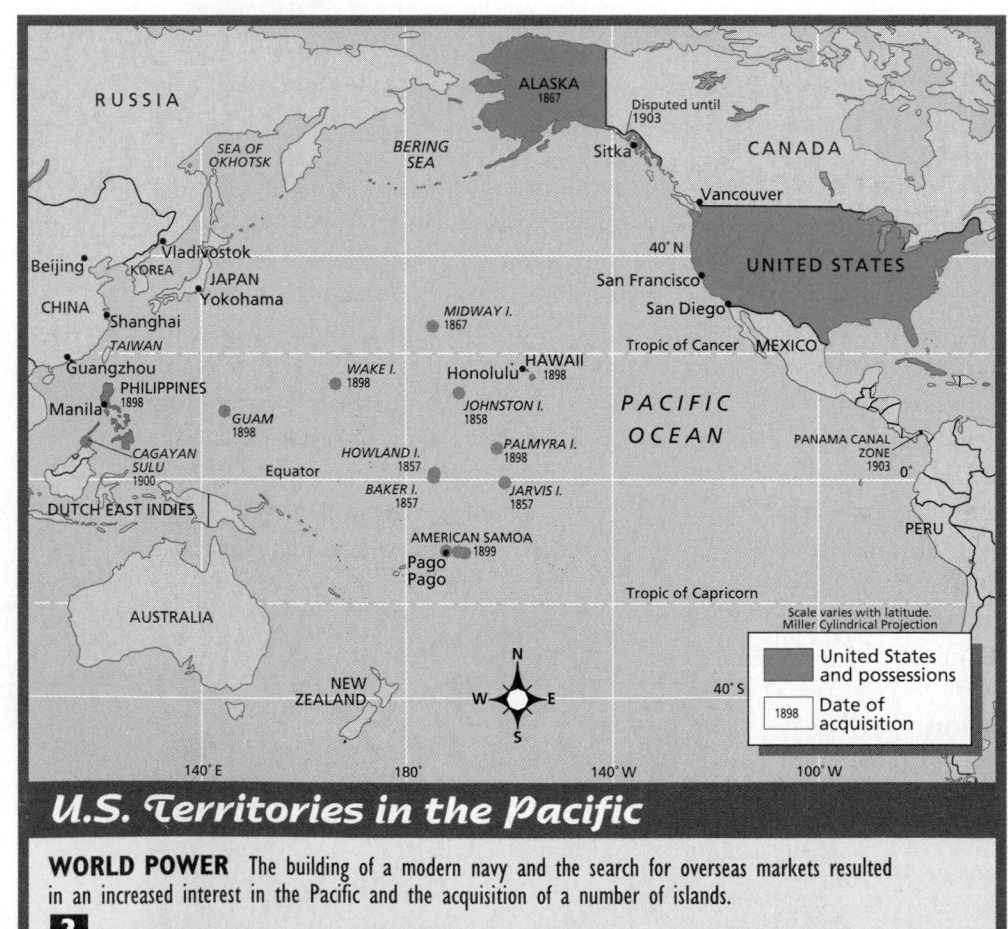

U.S. Territories in the Pacific

WORLD POWER The building of a modern navy and the search for overseas markets resulted in an increased interest in the Pacific and the acquisition of a number of islands.

❓ **LOCATION** Which U.S.—claimed islands lie well to the south of the equator?

▲ To suppress the Filipino uprising, the United States sent approximately 70,000 troops to the Philippines in 1899. This cartoon shows Emilio Aguinaldo's government crushed by American military might.

restored, Filipino voters would be allowed to elect the legislature's lower house.

Judge William Howard Taft became the first American governor of the Philippines. Taft authorized the construction of public schools, roads, and railroads and improved medical care and sanitation. As the United States reduced and then removed tariffs on Filipino products, U.S. trade with the Philippines flourished.

But Filipinos still lacked the independence for which they had fought so long. The **Jones Act of 1916** gave Filipinos the right to elect both houses of their legislature but stated that independence would have to wait until Congress declared that "a stable government" had been established. The wait would be a long one. The United States finally granted independence to the Philippines on July 4, 1946, nearly half a century after American and Spanish naval guns had shattered the early morning silence of Manila Bay.

■■ Despite Filipino calls for independence, the United States annexed the Philippines and delayed independence until 1946.

ACQUIRING HAWAII

Renewed interest in expansion after the Spanish-American War led to demands for U.S. annexation of the Hawaiian Islands, nearly 4,000 miles east of the Philippines. The United States had long been interested in Hawaii for its strategic location along trade routes to China and for its fertile lava-enriched soil. In the 1820s Protestant missionaries from New England traveled to the islands to convert Hawaiians to Christianity. The missionaries' descendants remained, becoming major landholders. By the 1870s Americans living in Hawaii controlled land and trade and exercised growing influence over the Hawaiian government.

When the Hawaiian king, Kalakaua (kah-LAH-KAH-ooh-ah), sought to restrict American influence in 1886, some 400 American businessmen, planters, and traders in Hawaii formed the secret Hawaiian League. Their aim was to overthrow the monarchy and persuade the United States to annex Hawaii.

In 1887 the League forced Kalakaua to sign a new constitution that made the Hawaiian monarch only a figurehead and limited native Hawaiians'

▼ After 1900, pineapples began to rival sugarcane as Hawaii's most important crop. Many of the laborers on Hawaiian plantations were from China, Japan, Korea, and the Philippines.

right to hold office in their own country. Hawaiians criticized what they called the "Bayonet Constitution." That same year, the United States succeeded in getting Kalakaua to grant rights to use Pearl Harbor for a U.S. naval base.

Hawaiian resentment intensified as American interests continued to lobby Washington to annex Hawaii. Then in 1891 Kalakaua died. Succeeding him was his sister, Liliuokalani (li-lee-uh-woh-kuh-LAHN-ee), champion of Hawaiian nationalism, who pledged to regain "Hawaii for Hawaiians."

Liliuokalani was born into a Hawaiian ruling family in 1838. As a young girl she saw the monarchy reclaim Hawaiian independence after a brief British takeover. She would never forget the pride she felt as the Hawaiian flag was again raised over her native land.

Queen Liliuokalani

Early in her reign, Queen Liliuokalani began working to overturn the Bayonet Constitution and replace it with one that would return power to native Hawaiians. In 1893 she announced her plans to publish a new constitution. The announcement caused the annexationists to swing into action. Forming a Committee of Safety, they forcibly occupied government buildings, declared the end of the monarchy, and set up a provisional government of their own. U.S. Marines stood by as the American foreign minister to Hawaii recognized the provisional government. A deeply saddened Queen Liliuokalani signed a paper giving up her throne:

> 66 I, Liliuokalani, . . . protest against any and all acts done against myself and the constitutional government of the Hawaiian kingdom. . . . Now, to avoid any collision of armed forces and perhaps the loss of life, I do, under this protest, and impelled by said forces, yield my authority until such time as the government of the United States shall . . . undo the action of its representatives and reinstate me. 99

▶ **Ivory vases and brightly colored fans were some of the many items sold through the lucrative China trade. The fan shows the seaport town of Huang-pu, where American ships took aboard Chinese goods.**

The U.S. government never reinstated Liliuokalani. But recognizing that native Hawaiians overwhelmingly opposed annexation, it did not annex Hawaii until 1898. Liliuokalani lived out the rest of her life in Honolulu, a proud reminder of Hawaii's past. She died in 1917 after a severe stroke and was buried in the Royal Mausoleum.

■■ **American settlers' response to Queen Liliuokalani's reforms and a renewed interest in overseas colonies led to the U.S. annexation of Hawaii.**

AMERICAN INVOLVEMENT IN CHINA

The United States had originally become interested in Hawaii because it was the gateway to the China trade. This trade had begun in 1784 when a U.S. trading ship, the *Empress of China,* sailed for the port of Guangzhou (Canton). In 1843 China officially opened five ports to trading ships from the United States and Europe.

For the next 50 years, China's rulers struggled to balance American and European interests to keep them from overrunning the country. In 1895, however, the Chinese government was overrun from another direction. Japan attacked and defeated China, winning from it the large island of Taiwan (Formosa), territory on China's Liaotung Peninsula, and control of Korea.

European powers quickly took advantage of China's weakened position. Great Britain, France, Germany, and Russia pressured the Chinese government to carve the country into separate **spheres of influence**—ports or regions where a particular country would have exclusive rights over trade, mines, and railroads.

Peabody and Essex Museum, Salem, Massachusetts

The United States feared it would be squeezed out of the China trade. In 1899 Secretary of State John Hay responded by inaugurating an **Open Door policy**, which called for all nations to have equal access to trade and investment in China. Senator Henry Cabot Lodge concluded: "We ask no favors; we only ask that we shall be admitted to that great market upon the same terms with the rest of the world."

In September 1899 Hay began sending a series of Open Door notes to the European powers and Japan. The notes asked them to agree to three principles: (1) to keep all ports in their spheres open to all nations; (2) to allow Chinese officials to collect all tariffs and duties; and (3) to guarantee equal railroad, harbor, and tariff rates in their spheres to all nations trading in China. When the European nations and Japan did not reject the principles outright, Hay announced that the Open Door policy had been accepted.

Chinese resentment of foreigners continued to grow, however. It erupted in the spring of 1900, when a Chinese secret society—the "Fists of Righteous Harmony"—launched a rebellion to drive the "foreign devils" out of the country. They attacked Western missionaries and traders in northern China, killing about 300. Supported by some Chinese government officials, the "Boxers"—the name Westerners gave them because of the "Fists" in their Chinese name—laid siege to the large walled-in foreign settlement in the capital at Beijing (Peking). For eight weeks the siege continued until finally, in August, an international force rescued the foreigners.

The **Boxer Rebellion** ended, but John Hay feared that Japan and other nations would use it as an excuse to seize more Chinese territory. In a second series of Open Door notes, he pressured the foreign powers to observe open trade throughout China and to preserve China's right to rule its own territory. China retained its territory but had to pay foreign powers $333 million in damages for losses sustained during the Boxer Rebellion.

■■ **The United States worked to maintain its trading rights in China through the Open Door policy.**

AN EMERGING JAPAN

Japan's 1894 invasion of China marked Japan's emergence as an imperial power. A mere 41 years earlier Japan had ended its almost complete isolation from the rest of the world. From 1639 to the 1850s Japanese rulers had allowed only one Dutch trading ship a year to enter the country. However, Japan's foreign policy had suddenly changed in 1853, when Commodore Matthew Perry of the United States sailed his squadron of black-hulled warships, bristling with guns, into Edo (Tokyo) Bay. President Millard Fillmore had ordered Perry to persuade Japan to open its doors to trade with the rapidly industrializing West. The gifts Perry presented to Japan's rulers symbolized the industrial age: a telegraph transmitter and a model train.

Perry's warships and industrial wonders forced the Japanese to yield to Western demands for trade. But they also convinced Japanese rulers that they must modernize their country—build up its military might and its industry. If they did not, they reasoned, foreigners might gain control of their nation.

Japan rapidly transformed itself into an industrial power and built up its army and navy. Within four decades Japan had become a winner in the struggle for empire rather than a victim of it, as its war with China, and later with Russia, proved.

Japan and Russia were rivals for Chinese territories—especially for Korea and for the fertile soil and mineral riches of Manchuria in northern

▲ Almost a year after Perry presented gifts to the Japanese, U.S. ships were allowed to trade in the ports of Hakodate and Shimoda.

U.S. IMPERIALISM

	U.S. Involvement	Interim Status	Current Status
Samoa	Agreement divides islands between U.S. and Germany (1899)	German Samoa achieves independence (1962)	American Samoa under U.S. control
Philippines	Ceded to U.S. (1898)	Philippine Government Act defines government (1902) Declared a commonwealth (1935)	Independent republic (1946)
Cuba	American forces occupy Cuba (1898)	Platt Amendment authorizes U.S. intervention (1902)	Independent republic (1934)
Puerto Rico	Ceded to U.S. (1898)	Foraker Act establishes government (1900) Application for statehood (1924)	Declared a commonwealth (1952)
Hawaii	U.S. annexation (1898)	Application for statehood (1937)	50th state (1959)

Sources: *An Encyclopedia of World History*, *Webster's New Geographical Dictionary*

AMERICAN EXPANSIONISM U.S. economic and security interests extended into Asia, the Pacific, the Caribbean, and Latin America at the turn of the century.

? **ASSESSING CONSEQUENCES** Using one of the countries on the chart as a case study, trace U.S. involvement and its consequences for the country's current status.

By May 1905 the Japanese had won a series of crucial battles, and they asked Roosevelt to negotiate peace with Russia. Roosevelt brought representatives of the two countries together at Portsmouth, New Hampshire, where they pounded out a treaty. It granted neither side all it wanted and left both dissatisfied. But it did end the war, and it won the Nobel Peace Prize for Roosevelt.

Aware that Japan might now turn its expansionist eye toward the Pacific, including the U.S.–held Philippines, Roosevelt decided to demonstrate American military might. In late 1907 he sent a fleet of 4 destroyers and 16 battleships, painted a dazzling white, on a 46,000-mile world cruise. The "Great White Fleet" sailed into the Japanese port of Yokohama, where it underscored Roosevelt's later boast that now "the Pacific was as much our home waters as the Atlantic."

China. In February 1904, Japanese troops attacked Russian forces in Manchuria, starting the **Russo-Japanese War**. President Theodore Roosevelt watched the war closely. If Japan won, it might grow dangerously strong. If Russia won, it might cut off U.S. trade with Manchuria.

■■ The United States came to see Japan, newly emergent as a modern world power, as a rival for influence in China and the Pacific.

SECTION 2 REVIEW

IDENTIFY and explain the significance of the following: annex, Philippine Government Act, Jones Act of 1916, William Howard Taft, Kalakaua, Liliuokalani, spheres of influence, John Hay, Boxer Rebellion, Matthew Perry, Russo-Japanese War.

LOCATE and explain the importance of the following: Hawaii; Taiwan; Korea; Beijing, China; Yokohama, Japan.

1. **MAIN IDEA** How did the United States respond to Filipino demands for independence?

2. **MAIN IDEA** What events led to the U.S. annexation of Hawaii?

3. **MAIN IDEA** What did the Open Door policy attempt to accomplish in China?

4. **WRITING TO EXPLAIN** Imagine you are a U.S. diplomat in Japan in 1905. Write a report to President Roosevelt, explaining why the United States should reevaluate its relationship with Japan.

5. **TAKING A STAND** Do you think the United States is ever justified in annexing a foreign territory? Give reasons for your answer.

Section 3

EXPANSION IN LATIN AMERICA

FOCUS

- How did the United States deal with Cuba and Puerto Rico after the Spanish-American War?
- What events cleared the way for construction of the Panama Canal?
- How did presidents Roosevelt, Taft, and Wilson enforce the Monroe Doctrine?

From 1898 onward, as American power grew in the Pacific, the U.S. role in Latin America expanded as well. Cuba came under strong U.S. control, while Puerto Rico became an out-and-out American possession. The United States built a canal across the Isthmus of Panama in these years, and the U.S. presence was felt throughout Latin America.

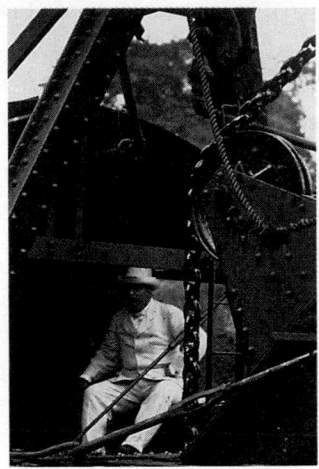

President Theodore Roosevelt at Panama Canal site

GOVERNING CUBA AND PUERTO RICO

Both Cuba and Puerto Rico hoped that the peace treaty ending the Spanish-American War would bring independence from Spain followed by the speedy departure of American troops. After all, the Teller Amendment had pledged to Cuba that the United States would allow Cubans to control their government. But Cubans and Puerto Ricans were disappointed. Wanting to restore order quickly in both countries and thus protect U.S. investments, President McKinley set up military governments to rule the islands.

McKinley appointed General Leonard Wood governor of Cuba in 1899. Wood authorized the construction of schools and a sanitation system. U.S. Army doctors Walter Reed and William Gorgas had called for the sanitation system to reduce the mosquito population. Carlos Finlay

▲ Carlos Finlay

(feen-LY), a Cuban doctor, had theorized that mosquitoes spread yellow fever. He was right. Once built, the system all but eliminated the disease.

Wood also presided over the writing of a new constitution that limited Cuba's independence. The U.S. Congress agreed to remove American troops only if Cuba made the **Platt Amendment** part of its constitution. The Platt Amendment (1) limited Cuba's freedom to make treaties with other countries; (2) authorized the United States to intervene in Cuban affairs as it saw necessary; and (3) required Cuba to sell or lease land to the United States for naval and fueling stations. This last clause eventually led to the establishment of the U.S. Navy base at Guantánamo Bay (see map on page 578). In effect, the Platt Amendment made Cuba an American **protectorate**: America promised to protect Cuba from other nations but reserved the right to intervene in Cuba's affairs.

In 1902, after Cuba reluctantly accepted the Platt Amendment, U.S.

troops left. But a U.S. presence remained at the naval base at Guantánamo Bay, which was leased in 1903. Over the next three decades, the United States intervened in Cuba several times. It pressured Cuba into accepting policies favorable to U.S. investors and sent in troops when it decided that the Cuban government could not keep order. The Platt Amendment remained in force until 1934, when America renounced its right to intervene in Cuba. Even then, however, U.S. influence over Cuban affairs remained great.

For Puerto Rico, U.S. policy followed a different course. No Teller Amendment guaranteed independence for Puerto Rico, so the United States ruled the island as a territory like Samoa or the Philippines in the Pacific. But just how these new territories were to be governed raised a thorny legal question for the United States. Were the people of these territories entitled to all the rights of U.S. citizens?

No, ruled the Supreme Court in 1901. The Court argued that the new territories were not fully part of the United States. Therefore, Congress could choose which rights to extend them. The Court affirmed the **Foraker Act** of 1900, which called for Puerto Rico's governor and upper house of the legislature to be appointed by the United States and a lower house to be elected by Puerto Ricans.

The **Jones Act of 1917** made Puerto Ricans American citizens and gave them the right to elect both houses of their legislature. In 1952 Puerto

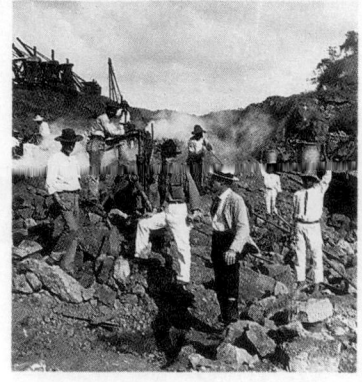

▶ The Panama Canal was built by the United States between 1904 and 1914. Shown here are laborers who helped construct the canal.

Rico became a self-governing commonwealth of the United States, which retains ties of citizenship and trade with the mainland.

■■ **After the Spanish-American War, the United States retained a strong influence in Cuba, and Puerto Rico became a U.S. territory.**

𝒯HE PANAMA CANAL

With such vital interests in both the Caribbean and the Pacific, the United States looked for a way to cut the travel time between the seas. The long and hazardous voyage around Cape Horn at the southern tip of South America took several weeks. In response the United States proposed digging a canal through a narrow neck of land in Central America to allow the U.S. Navy to police both seas.

Early steps toward a canal. The idea for such a canal was not new. As far back as 1517, Vasco Núñez de Balboa had proposed that a canal be dug across the 50-mile-wide Isthmus of Panama. In 1850 the United States and Great Britain had drawn up the **Clayton-Bulwer Treaty**, proposing an equal partnership to build and run a Central American canal, but they never acted on it. In the 1880s a French company actually worked on a canal across the Isthmus. But after less than 10 years and the loss of some 20,000 lives and more than $280 million, the French abandoned the effort. Deadly tropical diseases, repeated landslides, and bankruptcy killed the project.

Finally, in 1901 President Theodore Roosevelt decided that "after four centuries of conversation" by other countries, it was time for the United States to act. He instructed Secretary of State John Hay to negotiate with Great Britain

▲ After Puerto Rico became a U.S. territory, the government built new public schools such as the one shown here.

On August 15, 1914, the SS *Ancon* completed the first passage through the Panama Canal, a 51-mile-long ribbon of waters connecting the Caribbean Sea and the Pacific Ocean. The voyage marked the completion of what Theodore Roosevelt called "the greatest task of its own kind that has ever been performed in the world at all!"

Americans began working on the canal in 1904. Roosevelt was eager "to make the dirt fly" in Panama, but poor working conditions and shortages hampered U.S. efforts from the start. Then in late 1904 a large outbreak of yellow fever hit. By early 1905 the project was at a near standstill.

To put the project back on track, Roosevelt appointed John F. Stevens as chief engineer and architect. Stevens tackled the technical problems, while army colonel Dr. William C. Gorgas worked on improving living conditions. Gorgas, who had helped rid Cuba of tropical diseases, had drinking water purified and buildings screened. Then, to destroy the breeding places of the mosquitoes that transmit yellow fever and malaria, he had swamps drained and standing water coated with oil. By 1906 yellow fever had almost been eliminated. Malaria was under control by 1913.

Panama Canal Zone

STRATEGIC INTERESTS Because it took the U.S. naval vessel *Oregon* 66 days to sail from San Francisco around Cape Horn to Key West during the Spanish-American War, pressure increased to build a U.S.—controlled canal through Central America.

? LOCATION If you enter the Panama Canal from the Caribbean Sea on the Atlantic side, which direction will you travel to exit on the Pacific Ocean?

Canal construction soon resumed in force. More than 60 giant steam shovels bit into the land, digging out nearly 160 trainloads of earth each day. Workers numbered more than 43,000, many of whom were recruited from the British West Indies.

Originally, the canal was designed to be built at sea level, but the difficulty of moving millions of tons of dirt and rock prompted a new design—an elevated waterway using locks. One group of workers dredged an approach channel and built a dam and locks on the Atlantic side. Another group dredged a passage from the Pacific through the Bay of Panama and constructed two smaller sets of locks. The hardest job fell to another group, which had to blast an eight-mile-wide path through the mountainous Continental Divide. Geologic faults, heavy rains, and shifting earth caused frequent and often fatal avalanches. But finally, on October 10, 1913, President Wilson signaled crews to dynamite the protective dike at the south end of the canal. In a dramatic finale, water from the two sides rushed together—85 feet above sea level.

The human and economic costs of building the canal were staggering: some 6,000 workers died and about $366 million was spent. But the seemingly impossible had become a reality. The United States—and the rest of the world—now had a "Path Between the Seas."

to end the partnership set up by the Clayton-Bulwer Treaty. In the resulting **Hay-Pauncefote Treaty**, Britain agreed that the United States could build the canal by itself and have "exclusive management and policing of it." In return, the United States promised to keep the canal open to all the world's vessels in wartime as well as in peacetime.

Hay then began negotiations with the Republic of Colombia—of which Panama was then a part. In 1903 the **Hay-Herrán Treaty** was drafted. In return for a 99-year lease on a six-mile strip of land across the Isthmus, the United States agreed to pay Colombia $10 million and a yearly rental of $250,000. But holding out for better terms, Colombia's senate adjourned without ratifying the treaty. A furious President Roosevelt accused the Colombians of blackmail and swore that they must not be allowed "to bar one of the future highways of civilization."

▲ John Hay served as secretary of state from 1898 until his death in 1905.

Revolution in Panama. Events in Panama soon turned in Roosevelt's favor. Key Panamanian leaders who wanted the canal built began plotting revolution against the Colombian government. Helping them was Philippe Bunau-Varilla (boo-noh-vah-ree-yah), the former chief engineer for the French canal-building attempt.

Bunau-Varilla traveled to Washington to get American support for the revolution. On October 9, 1903, he met privately with President Roosevelt. Exactly what was said at the meeting remains unknown, but on November 2 the U.S. gunboat *Nashville* arrived in Panama. The following day, Panamanians began their rebellion. U.S. Marines prevented Colombian forces from reaching the rebels.

On November 4, 1903, the victorious rebels set up a new government and declared Panama an independent nation. Acting with lightning speed, the United States two days later recognized the

▲ This 1903 cartoon shows Roosevelt digging the Panama Canal and throwing dirt in the direction of Colombia, the country that had refused to ratify an earlier canal treaty.

Republic of Panama, and Hay began negotiating a new canal treaty with Panama's special envoy, Bunau-Varilla. The **Hay–Bunau-Varilla Treaty** gave the United States complete and unending sovereignty over a 10-mile-wide Canal Zone.

Did the United States engineer the Panamanian revolution? The facts remain obscure, but President Theodore Roosevelt later boasted, "I took the Canal Zone and let Congress debate." It is clear that U.S. aid to the Panamanian rebels and America's immediate recognition of Panama as an independent nation served American interests and made the Panama Canal possible. American trade and naval power grew stronger because of it, allowing the United States to extend its economic and political interests in Latin America.

■■ The Panamanian revolution and a favorable treaty cleared the way for the United States to build and retain control of the Panama Canal.

APPLYING THE MONROE DOCTRINE

The American interventions in Cuba, Puerto Rico, and Panama were only three instances in a long history of U.S. involvement in Latin America. As far back as 1823, the Monroe Doctrine had cast the United States as protector of the hemisphere. But for much of the century the doctrine was little more than an idle threat. This changed following the Spanish-American War, as presidents Theodore Roosevelt, William H. Taft, and Woodrow Wilson actively enforced the Monroe Doctrine in an effort to protect U.S. interests in Latin America (see map on page 578).

The Roosevelt Corollary.

Latin America, with its wealth of raw materials and potential consumers, attracted a flood of European and American capital during the late 1800s. Much of this capital was in the form of high-interest bank loans. Although many Latin American countries welcomed the loans, difficulty in repaying them often resulted in foreign intervention. In 1902, for example, Great Britain, Germany, and Italy blockaded and attacked Venezuelan ships and ports when the nation failed to repay its loans. President Roosevelt quickly warned the three European powers not to seize any Venezuelan land and convinced them to settle the issue through arbitration.

Roosevelt's actions sent a clear signal that he intended to enforce the Monroe Doctrine. Roosevelt underscored this point in 1904 when the Dominican Republic proved unable to repay its European lenders. Fearing that the Europeans would use force to collect the loans, he issued the **Roosevelt Corollary** to the Monroe Doctrine:

> 66 If a nation . . . keeps order and pays its obligations, it need fear no interference from the United States. Chronic wrongdoing . . . in the Western Hemisphere . . . may force the United States, however reluctantly, . . . to the exercise of an international police power. 99

Without seeking approval from any Latin American nation, Roosevelt assumed the role of "international police officer" in the Western Hemisphere. He had applied in practice the West African proverb he loved to quote: "Speak softly and carry a big stick; you will go far."

Next, Roosevelt convinced the Dominican government to accept U.S. assistance. The United States pledged to use American armed forces to stop any European country from seizing Dominican territory. In exchange, the Dominican government agreed to let the United States collect all Dominican customs duties and turn half over to

YANKEE IMPERIALISM

THROUGH OTHERS' EYES

Although much of Latin America had at first favored the Monroe Doctrine, support for the policy began to dwindle by the early 1900s. As Peruvian diplomat Francisco García Calderón noted, the Monroe Doctrine took "an aggressive form with Mr. [Theodore] Roosevelt, the politician of the 'big stick.'" Writing in 1913, García Calderón chronicled the list of recent U.S. interventions in Panama, Cuba, the Dominican Republic, and Venezuela. As a result of this "Yankee imperialism," he claimed, "everywhere the Americans of the North are feared" and "hostility against the Anglo-Saxon invaders assumes the character of a . . . crusade." In the view of Mexican scholar Luis Quintanilla, the Roosevelt Corollary had twisted the Monroe Doctrine "from a case of America vs. Europe" to one of "United States vs. America."

foreign creditors. In 1916, when civil disturbances racked the Dominican Republic, the United States government sent in marines. They did not leave until eight years later, in 1924.

▪▪ The Roosevelt Corollary established a greater U.S. role in Latin America.

Some Latin American countries objected to Roosevelt's policy. They argued that every country should maintain control over its own affairs. Some Latin American countries issued a declaration stating that debts owed to other countries could not be collected by force. But despite Latin American protests, intervention continued.

Dollar diplomacy.

Roosevelt's successor as president, William H. Taft, further extended U.S. influence in Latin America. Taft favored "substituting dollars for bullets"—economic influence for military force—as a means of protecting U.S.

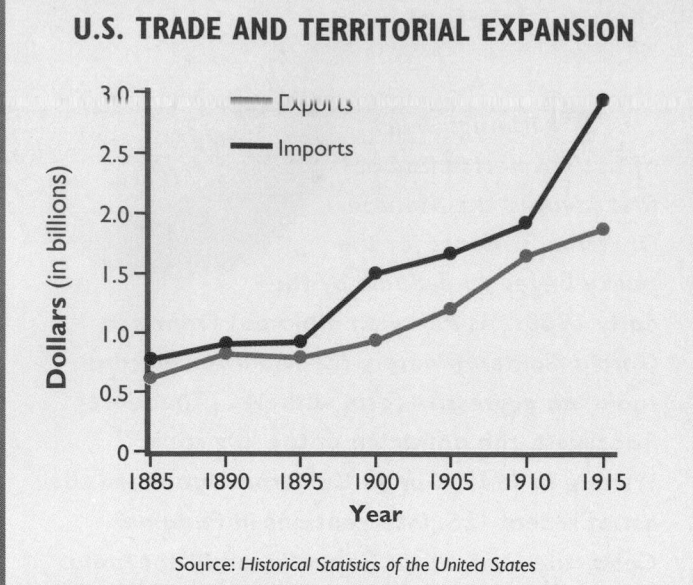

U.S. TRADE AND TERRITORIAL EXPANSION

Dollars (in billions)

— Exports
— Imports

Year

1885 1890 1895 1900 1905 1910 1915

Source: *Historical Statistics of the United States*

U.S. FOREIGN TRADE As the United States emerged as a world power, it began to acquire overseas colonies. One consequence of this territorial expansion was the rapid increase of U.S. exports and imports to and from these new overseas markets.

 BUILDING GRAPH SKILLS What was the difference in the value of U.S. exports and imports by 1915?

interests in Latin America (see map on page 578). To implement this policy, which came to be called **dollar diplomacy**, Taft suggested replacing European loans with American ones. Increasing U.S. economic power, Taft argued, would reduce the chances of European intervention. By 1914 U.S. capital in Latin America had grown to over $1.6 billion, mainly invested in railroads, mines, and banana and sugar plantations.

Nicaragua was one of the places that Taft put dollar diplomacy to the test. At the invitation of the Nicaraguan president, American bankers made loans totaling $1.5 million to Nicaragua in 1911. The following year, Taft sent more than 2,000 marines to crush a revolt and to protect the U.S. investments that had poured in.

Taft's successor, President Woodrow Wilson, believed that democratic governments, not U.S. dollars, would keep European powers out of Latin America. To keep Germany from taking control of strategic Caribbean territory, Wilson sent marines to several Caribbean countries to put down rebellions and establish constitutional governments. In 1915, when revolution shook Haiti, Wilson sent in marines. Haiti was forced to accept a treaty giving the United States powers in running the Haitian government, and the marines stayed until 1934. Some 1,500 Haitians died resisting U.S. control.

■■ **Taft's dollar diplomacy and Wilson's military interventions increased U.S. political and economic influence in Latin America.**

SECTION 3 REVIEW

IDENTIFY and explain the significance of the following: Leonard Wood, Carlos Finlay, Platt Amendment, protectorate, Foraker Act, Jones Act of 1917, Clayton-Bulwer Treaty, Hay-Pauncefote Treaty, Hay-Herrán Treaty, Hay–Bunau-Varilla Treaty, Roosevelt Corollary, dollar diplomacy.

LOCATE and explain the importance of the following: Guantánamo Bay, Panama Canal, Colombia, Venezuela, Dominican Republic, Nicaragua, Haiti.

1. **MAIN IDEA** How did the U.S. relationship with Cuba and Puerto Rico change after the Spanish-American War?

2. **MAIN IDEA** Why did the United States support the Panamanian rebels and recognize the Republic of Panama?

3. **CONTRASTING** How did presidents Roosevelt, Taft, and Wilson apply the Monroe Doctrine in Latin America?

4. **WRITING TO PERSUADE** Imagine you are a political leader in a Latin American country during this period. Write a speech seeking to persuade the U.S. government not to interfere in the affairs of your country.

5. **HYPOTHESIZING** How might U.S. policy toward Puerto Rico have been different if the Teller Amendment had been extended to apply to that territory?

Section 4

CONFLICT WITH MEXICO

FOCUS

- How did the Mexican Revolution affect relations between the United States and Mexico?
- Why did the United States intervene in Mexico?
- Why did tensions between the two countries remain strong during Carranza's presidency?

*D*ollar diplomacy played a significant role in another Latin American country: Mexico. Though many Mexicans uneasily referred to the United States as "the Colossus of the North," economic ties between the two countries increased in the late 19th century. But the Mexican Revolution of 1910 threatened these ties, bringing the two countries to the brink of war.

American artillery along the Mexican border, 1916

THE MEXICAN REVOLUTION

Dollars helped tie Mexico and the United States closer together in the late 19th century, thanks to Mexico's president, Porfirio Díaz. Díaz, who with the political support of wealthy landowners ruled Mexico for more than 30 years, offered special concessions to attract foreign investment. By 1908, U.S. companies controlled three quarters of all Mexican mining operations. Total U.S. investments amounted to almost $1 million by 1913.

Foreign investors helped develop Mexico's economy by building railroads that linked Mexico to U.S. and other foreign markets. But foreign investors and Díaz's friends profited the most from economic growth. Little trickled down to workers and peasants. Indeed, Díaz's policies helped wealthy Mexicans and foreigners take land away from peasants. As a result, most Mexicans—mainly landless peasants and struggling urban workers—lived in poverty.

In 1910 Díaz used force and fraud to defeat opposition candidate Francisco Madero. Peasants,

workers, and the middle class, angry at the lack of political democracy, rallied behind Madero in armed revolt against Díaz beginning in November. The rebels defeated Díaz's troops in key cities in northern and central Mexico, forcing Díaz into exile in Paris in 1911. In Mexico's first democratic elections in 30 years, Madero won the presidency.

Madero sought to establish a democratic government, but few agreed on the details. The revolutionary leaders who had supported Madero against

▼ Women served in military roles during the Mexican Revolution. This 1911 photograph shows a group of female revolutionaries armed with rifles.

Díaz thought Madero's plan did not go far enough in such areas as returning land to the peasants. Others, including conservative military officers and wealthy landowners, thought the plan went too far.

Complicating this situation was Henry Lane Wilson, the U.S. ambassador, who did not believe Madero could protect U.S. investments in Mexico. Wilson overstepped his diplomatic role by arranging for factions opposed to Madero to meet and discuss Madero's overthrow. In 1913, backed by wealthy landowners and foreign business interests, General Victoriano Huerta (WER-tah) seized control of the government and had Madero thrown into jail. Huerta's soldiers shot Madero when, they alleged, he attempted to escape.

Madero's murder outraged President Woodrow Wilson. He angrily refused to recognize Huerta, calling his regime a "government of butchers." Civil war raged in Mexico as revolutionary armies battled to drive Huerta out. President Wilson adopted a policy of "watchful waiting," hoping that the revolutionaries would be successful. He also authorized arms sales to the revolutionaries, while refusing to allow arms sales to Huerta's forces.

■■ The Mexican Revolution strained U.S.–Mexican relations as the fighting disrupted Mexico's government and society.

▲ Pancho Villa, center, and Emiliano Zapata, right, are shown with their followers in the presidential palace in Mexico City.

AMERICAN INTERVENTION

Four major revolutionary armies continued to fight Huerta. But their leaders—Venustiano Carranza (bay-noos-TYAHN-oh kahr-RAHN-sah), Francisco "Pancho" Villa, Emiliano Zapata, and Álvaro Obregón (oh-bray-GAWN)—were not united. Two of the leaders, Carranza and Villa, actually hated each other. Although the revolutionaries controlled territory throughout Mexico, Wilson worried that they would never be able to defeat Huerta.

In 1914 an incident occurred that gave Wilson an excuse to intervene directly. On April 9,

Huerta's soldiers arrested several crew members from the USS *Dolphin*. The U.S. sailors had gone ashore for supplies at the Mexican port of Tampico. The Americans were released unharmed, but Wilson pursued the matter. He backed the American admiral, who demanded an apology and a public ceremony in which Mexico would "hoist the American flag in a prominent position and salute it with twenty-one guns." Huerta made the apology but refused to perform the ceremony.

On April 20 President Wilson went before Congress:

❝ I . . . come to ask your approval that I should use the armed forces of the United States . . . to obtain from General Huerta and his adherents the fullest recognition of the rights and dignity of the United States, even amidst the distressing conditions now unhappily obtaining in Mexico. ❞

Before Congress could act, Wilson learned that a German ship bearing arms for Huerta was heading for the Mexican port of Veracruz. He ordered the U.S. Navy to land marines at Veracruz, take the customs house, and prevent the weapons from being delivered. By the time Congress voted Wilson the authority to use force, the order had been carried out.

At this critical stage Argentina, Brazil, and Chile—sometimes called the "ABC powers"—organized a conference at Niagara Falls, Ontario, to resolve the crisis. The conference urged Huerta to resign. Since his forces were losing, he complied and fled to Spain. In August 1914 Carranza marched into Mexico City. For the next year the revolutionary generals battled each other for control of the presidency.

■■ The United States intervened in Mexico to help overthrow the antirevolutionary Huerta government.

CARRANZA IN POWER

In 1915 Carranza assumed the presidency, and American forces withdrew from Veracruz. The United States recognized Carranza's government in the same year, after he guaranteed that Mexico would respect foreign lives and property.

BIO GRAPHY Venustiano Carranza, with his trim white goatee and his "gentlemanly bearing," hardly fit anyone's picture of a typical revolutionary. Born in 1859 in the state of Coahuila (koh-uh-WEE-luh) in northern Mexico, he

Venustiano Carranza

was over 50 years old when he took up the rebel cause.

Carranza, who owned a large, profitable ranch, had held many government offices under Díaz. But in 1908 Díaz and Carranza clashed, and three years later, Carranza joined Madero's fight to overthrow Díaz. After Madero was deposed, Carranza helped defeat Huerta's forces. He used his experience as head of a revolutionary army and his considerable political talents to gain the presidency of Mexico.

Carranza's presidency was marked by conflict. Pancho Villa, who had hoped for U.S. support against Carranza, decided to retaliate against the Americans for recognizing Carranza as president. Villa communicated his plans to rebel leader Emiliano Zapata:

66 We have decided not to fire a bullet more against Mexicans, our brothers, and to prepare and organize ourselves to attack the Americans in their own dens and make them know that Mexico is a land for the free and a tomb for thrones, crowns, and traitors. **99**

In March 1916 some 500 of Villa's men crossed the border to raid Columbus, New Mexico. Villa's men burned and looted the surprised town and army post. Seventeen Americans—nine civilians and eight soldiers—were killed, while more than a hundred Mexicans were killed. Villa hoped the raid would provoke American intervention in Mexico that would undermine Carranza's regime. He did not have to wait long for this result.

Without Carranza's approval President Wilson ordered an expedition into Mexico to capture Villa "dead or alive." A week after Villa's raid, General John J. Pershing led a force of some 5,800 men into Chihuahua, Villa's home state. Although Pershing later increased his troop size to more than 10,000 men, Villa eluded capture. The deeper Pershing pushed into Mexican territory, the more the Mexicans resented the Americans.

A battle between Mexican and U.S. troops in June brought the United States and Mexico to the brink of war. Carranza ordered Mexican troops to prevent U.S. soldiers from going any farther south. When one of Pershing's cavalry units attempted to pass through the town of Carrizal, the commander of the Mexican garrison refused passage. Instead of bypassing the town, the U.S. commander entered Carrizal, and a battle ensued.

▲ In 1916 President Wilson sent U.S. soldiers into Mexico to capture Pancho Villa, "dead or alive."

U.S. Interests in Latin America

DOLLAR DIPLOMACY American policy in Latin America aimed at protecting U.S. interests and investments and keeping European powers out. Ownership of the Panama Canal increased U.S. concerns that nearby countries not fall under the control of hostile forces.

? LOCATION Which areas were United States protectorates?

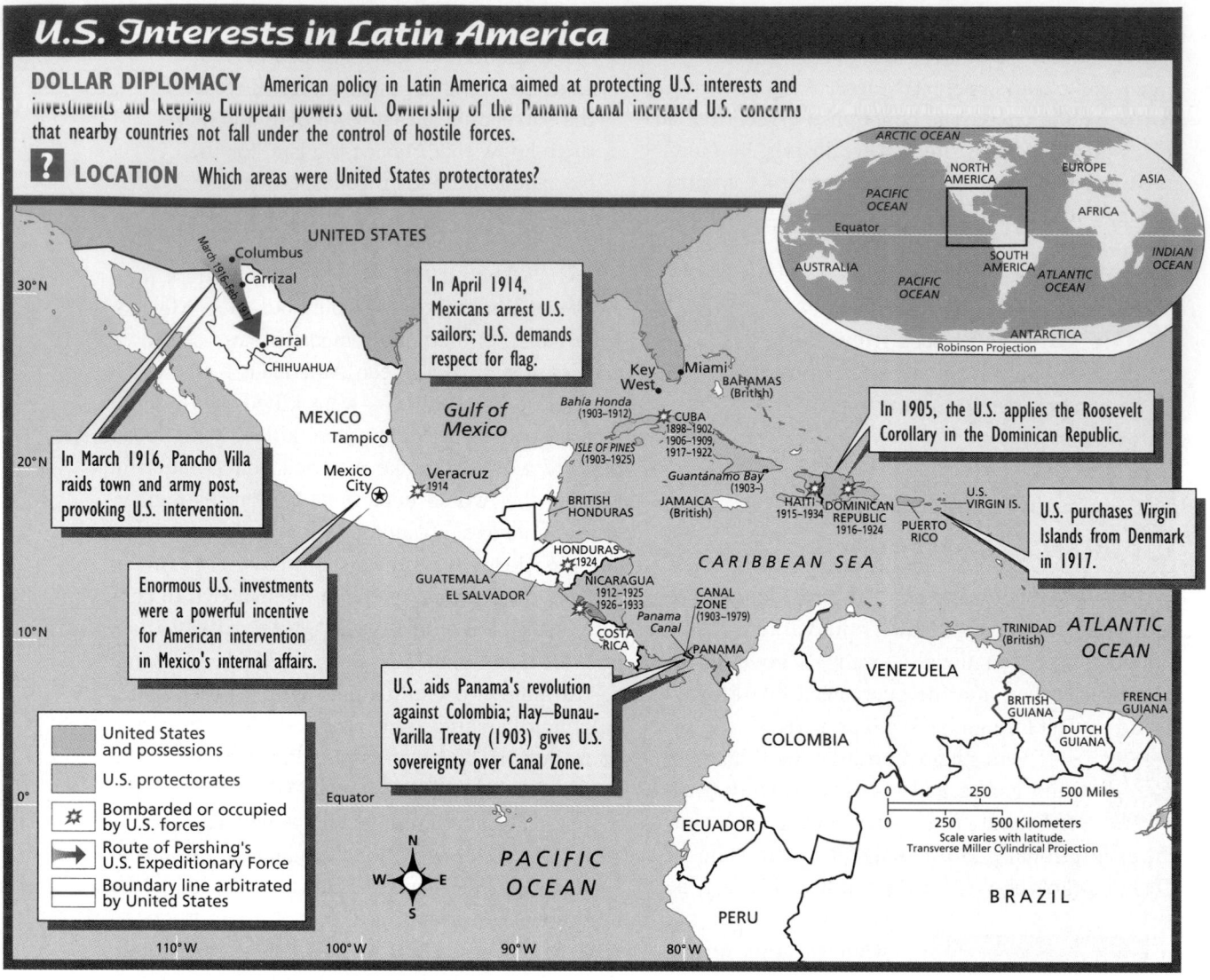

In April 1914, Mexicans arrest U.S. sailors; U.S. demands respect for flag.

In March 1916, Pancho Villa raids town and army post, provoking U.S. intervention.

Enormous U.S. investments were a powerful incentive for American intervention in Mexico's internal affairs.

In 1905, the U.S. applies the Roosevelt Corollary in the Dominican Republic.

U.S. purchases Virgin Islands from Denmark in 1917.

U.S. aids Panama's revolution against Colombia; Hay–Bunau-Varilla Treaty (1903) gives U.S. sovereignty over Canal Zone.

Legend:
- United States and possessions
- U.S. protectorates
- ✶ Bombarded or occupied by U.S. forces
- → Route of Pershing's U.S. Expeditionary Force
- Boundary line arbitrated by United States

By early September 1916 nearly 150,000 U.S. National Guardsmen were stationed along the Mexican border. But the prospect of armed conflict with Mexico was extremely unpopular in the United States, particularly since events in Europe and on the high seas threatened to pull the United States into World War I (see Chapter 20). Wilson backed down. In exchange for withdrawing U.S. troops, Wilson asked Carranza to adopt a measure that would allow the United States to intervene in Mexico to protect U.S. investments. Carranza refused to limit Mexican sovereignty in this way. Realizing that the threat of war increased with every day U.S. troops remained in Mexico, Wilson ordered U.S. troops withdrawn in January 1917.

In that same year, Carranza approved a sweeping new constitution for Mexico, but he would not have much time to put its provisions in place. In 1920 he was overthrown and killed by forces loyal to another revolutionary leader—Álvaro Obregón.

Obregón and subsequent Mexican presidents gradually implemented the new constitution, which would have important repercussions for U.S. oil companies in Mexico in the 1930s (see Chapter 25).

■■ **Villa's raid on a U.S. town raised tensions between the United States and Mexico to a dangerous pitch.**

COMMENTARY

Expansion in Perspective

In the years from 1890 to 1920, America's global involvement expanded enormously. In some cases this involvement meant actual military intervention and colonial rule of foreign territories. Although new territory and influence benefited the United States, many Americans believed that overseas expansion helped foreign countries as well. Many supporters of imperialism viewed Samoa, Cuba, Puerto Rico, and other non-European countries as economically backward and uncivilized. Using this doctrine, American imperialists asserted that Americans had a responsibility to bring democracy, prosperity, and order to nonindustrialized nations.

But did U.S. imperialism bring all of these benefits to foreign countries? In Cuba, Puerto Rico, and the Philippines, better sanitation, education, transportation, and public health followed the American flag. And in some cases, such as in Venezuela, U.S. diplomatic actions prevented European countries from colonizing Latin American territory.

U.S. economic and military interventions, however, rarely brought order or democracy to politically troubled countries. U.S. dollar diplomacy in Nicaragua did not prevent a revolt, and the United States brutally suppressed the Filipino independence movement. Although designed to create democracy, the U.S. military governments that were established in many countries often denied citizens a basic democratic principle: political representation.

U.S. attempts to spread American culture sometimes came at the expense of the other country's culture. In Puerto Rico, for example, the U.S. government ordered that English—instead of the native Spanish—be used in classrooms to make Puerto Ricans "good North American citizens." Manuel Maldonado-Denis, a Puerto Rican who grew up under this system, recalled that "Puerto Rican students had to daily swear loyalty to the North American flag in English" and sing "songs in English composed to inspire patriotism in North American students." In this way, Maldonado-Denis concluded, the United States attempted "to rob us of every source of identification with all that is Puerto Rican."

U.S. economic expansion also created resentment against the United States around the world. The millions of dollars that U.S. banks and businesses poured into oil wells, mines, plantations, and railroad projects in poor nations gave the United States control of those nations' natural resources. Poor nations grew angry as they watched their resources and the profits from them flow into the United States. Their struggle to regain control of their own resources would provide a continuing source of tension with the United States.

SECTION 4 REVIEW

IDENTIFY and explain the significance of the following: Porfirio Díaz, Francisco Madero, Victoriano Huerta, Venustiano Carranza, Francisco "Pancho" Villa, Emiliano Zapata, Álvaro Obregón, John J. Pershing.

1. **MAIN IDEA** How were relations between the United States and Mexico affected by the Mexican Revolution?

2. **MAIN IDEA** Why did President Wilson ask Congress for authority to use the armed forces in Mexico?

3. **IDENTIFYING CAUSE AND EFFECT** What event during Carranza's presidency provoked U.S. intervention in Mexico? What effect did this have on relations between the two countries?

4. **WRITING TO EXPLAIN** Imagine you are a landless peasant in Mexico after the overthrow of Porfirio Díaz. Write a letter to a relative in the United States explaining why you took part in the revolution.

5. **SYNTHESIZING** How did U.S. intervention both help and hurt other countries?

Spanish-American War begins. U.S. gains control of Puerto Rico, Guam, and Hawaii.

U.S. annexes Philippines. Open Door policy inaugurated.

Boxer Rebellion begins in China.

U.S. recognizes Republic of Panama. Hay–Bunau-Varilla Treaty negotiated.

Philippine Government Act passed.

1898   **1900**   **1902**

WRITING A SUMMARY

Using the essential points of the chapter as a guide, write a summary of the chapter.

REVIEWING CHRONOLOGY

Number your paper 1 to 5. Study the time line above, and list the following events in the order in which they happened by writing the first next to 1, the second next to 2, and so on. Then complete the activity below.

1. Panama Canal completed.
2. U.S. recognizes Republic of Panama.
3. Venustiano Carranza assumes power in Mexico.
4. Open Door policy inaugurated.
5. Russo-Japanese War begins.

Identifying Cause and Effect Select two events from the time line, and in a paragraph, explain the cause-and-effect relationship between them.

IDENTIFYING PEOPLE AND IDEAS

Explain the historical significance of each of the following people or terms.

1. imperialism
2. José Martí
3. Emilio Aguinaldo
4. Liliuokalani
5. spheres of influence
6. John Hay
7. Carlos Finlay
8. dollar diplomacy
9. Porfirio Díaz
10. Venustiano Carranza

UNDERSTANDING MAIN IDEAS

1. What led industrialized nations to seek overseas colonies in the late 19th and early 20th centuries? What arguments did imperialists use to justify the establishment of overseas colonies?
2. What positive and negative effects did U.S. intervention in the Philippines have on that country?
3. How did U.S. relations with Hawaii and Japan eventually lead to American involvement in China?
4. How did U.S. actions in the Dominican Republic, Nicaragua, and Haiti signify Roosevelt's, Taft's, and Wilson's willingness to apply and extend the Monroe Doctrine?

5. Why were the United States, Great Britain, and Germany interested in Samoa? Who finally won control of Samoa?

REVIEWING THEMES

1. **Global Relations** Why was the United States interested in controlling Cuba? Why was Cuba surprised and angered by the position of the American government?
2. **Economic Development** How did the presence of foreign investors in Mexico affect the economy of that country? What problems resulted from these investments?
3. **Democratic Values** Why might some people argue that U.S. actions in the Philippines conflicted with democratic principles?

THINKING CRITICALLY

1. **Evaluating** How did the United States government react to revolutionaries such as Emilio Aguinaldo and Venustiano Carranza?
2. **Analyzing** Why did Japan, unlike China, not come under European spheres of influence?
3. **Hypothesizing** What might have been the effect on U.S. relations with Cuba, Puerto Rico, and the Philippines if the United States had adopted an Open Door policy in each of those countries?

STRATEGY FOR SUCCESS

Review the Skills Handbook entry on Writing a Paper beginning on page 1001. Imagine you are a native Hawaiian in 1893 who has witnessed the overthrow of Queen Liliuokalani. What information will you need to collect if you are preparing an article for a local newspaper about this event? Suppose that you are writing a diary entry about the occupation. How will your approach to writing differ in this case?

WRITING ABOUT HISTORY

Writing to Explain Write an essay that traces the negotiations and events that helped the United States build and control the Panama Canal.

Russo-Japanese
War begins.

The Mexican
Revolution starts.

Panama Canal
completed. ⎯

Venustiano
Carranza assumes
power in Mexico.
Wilson sends
marines into Haiti.

Pancho Villa's
soldiers raid
Columbus,
New Mexico.

1904   **1910**   **1912**   **1914**   **1916**

USING PRIMARY SOURCES

At the height of the Mexican Revolution, American journalist John Reed traveled with the Mexican rebels under the command of Pancho Villa. Read the following excerpt from Reed's book, *Insurgent Mexico,* in which he evaluates Villa's leadership qualities. Why does Reed think that Villa's army will defeat the opposing troops of the Mexican Federal army?

66 *Villa had to invent an entirely original method of warfare, because he never had a chance to learn anything of accepted military strategy. . . . Secrecy, quickness of movement, the adaptation of his plans to the character of the country and of his soldiers . . . these are his characteristics. . . . One of the troubles of the Mexican Federal army is that its officers are thoroughly saturated with conventional military theory. [Villa's] soldier is still . . . , above all, a loose, individual, guerrilla fighter. . . . When Villa's army goes into battle he is not hampered by salutes, or rigid respect for officers, . . . or theories of . . . the function of cavalry, infantry and artillery in any particular position. . . . [Villa] does know that guerrilla fighters cannot be driven blindly in platoons around the field in perfect step, that men fighting individually and of their own free will are braver than long volleying rows in the trenches. . . . And where the fighting is fiercest . . . Villa is among them, like any common soldier.* 99

Pancho Villa

LINKING HISTORY AND GEOGRAPHY

Historians have noted that the Spanish-American War was primarily decided at sea. Study the map on page 561 and the text discussion on pages 560–62. Then write a paragraph supporting this view and describing how geography might have influenced U.S. military strategy.

Teddy Roosevelt and the Rough Riders

BUILDING YOUR PORTFOLIO

Complete the following projects independently or cooperatively.

1. **GLOBAL RELATIONS** Imagine you are a member of the State Department in the early 1900s. Write a memorandum to the president that addresses concerns about U.S. relations with Spain, China, Japan, Latin America, or Mexico. Your memorandum should mention specific issues dealing with annexation, colonization, construction of the Panama Canal, or protection of U.S. investments, and propose courses of action.

2. **WAR** Imagine you are a U.S. Army recruiting officer in 1898. Create a series of recruiting posters aimed at attracting a wide range of recruits—such as college students, Native Americans, cowboys, would-be adventurers—to serve in the Spanish-American War.

THE UNITED STATES AND THE WORLD

Foreign landholdings of the United States were very small compared to those of the European empires. The largest American territory, Alaska, appeared to many skeptics to be a useless, frozen wasteland. The discovery of gold, oil, and other useful minerals, however, would prove very valuable to the United States in years to come.

𝒯HE Industrial Revolution affected nations throughout the world. By 1914, the eve of World War I, many nations of the world were connected in a complex web of economic trade and investment. The vast majority of this trade and investment was controlled by European nations, particularly Great Britain, which had amassed a huge colonial empire. Japan was the only Asian nation to attempt significant foreign expansion in the early 20th century. Compared to the European empires, the United States had relatively little financial investment in other countries. Yet even the United States expanded its economic and political involvement in foreign nations during this period.

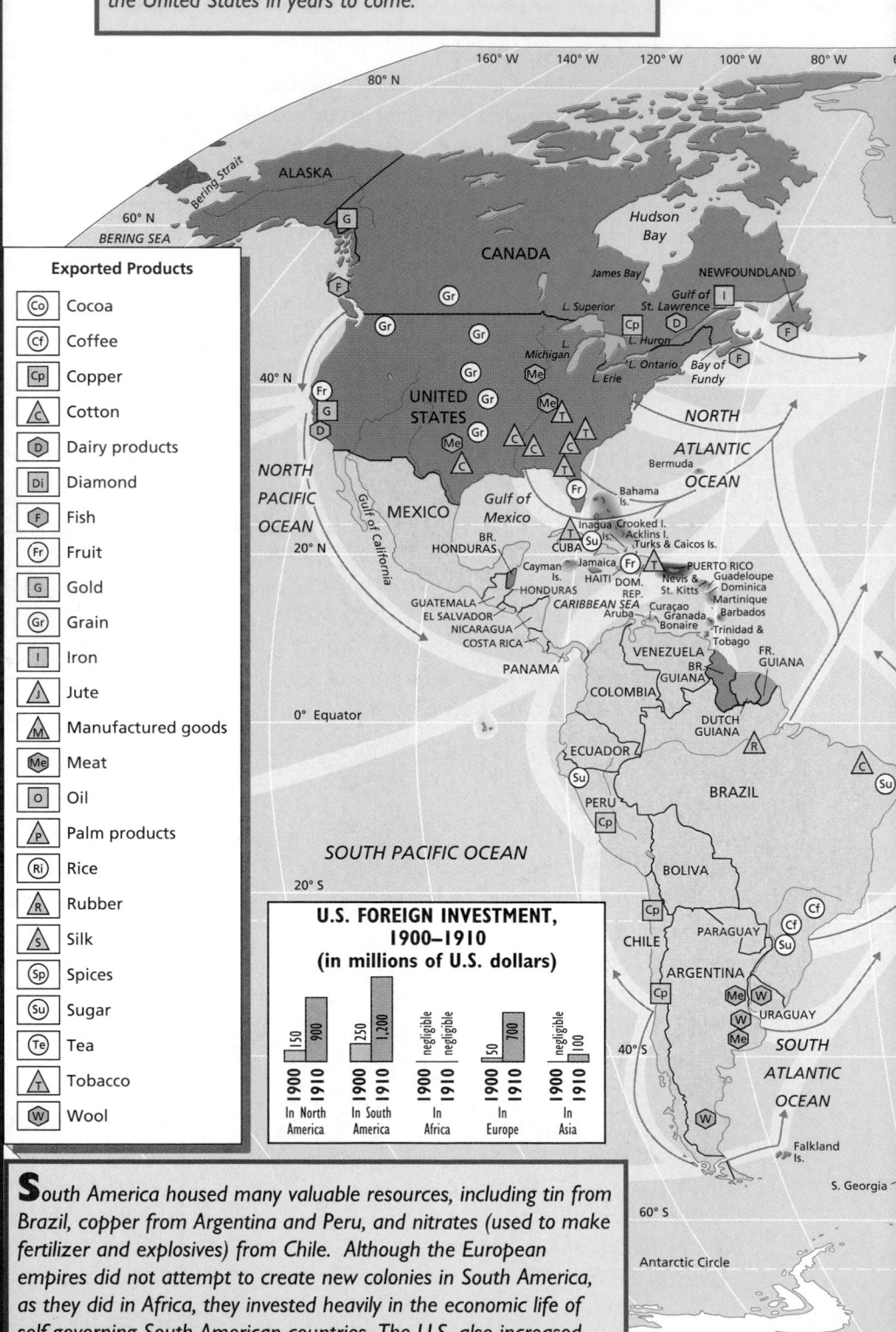

Exported Products

Co	Cocoa
Cf	Coffee
Cp	Copper
C	Cotton
D	Dairy products
Di	Diamond
F	Fish
Fr	Fruit
G	Gold
Gr	Grain
I	Iron
J	Jute
M	Manufactured goods
Me	Meat
O	Oil
P	Palm products
Ri	Rice
R	Rubber
S	Silk
Sp	Spices
Su	Sugar
Te	Tea
T	Tobacco
W	Wool

U.S. FOREIGN INVESTMENT, 1900–1910 (in millions of U.S. dollars)

	1900	1910
In North America	150	900
In South America	250	1,200
In Africa	negligible	negligible
In Europe	50	700
In Asia	negligible	100

South America housed many valuable resources, including tin from Brazil, copper from Argentina and Peru, and nitrates (used to make fertilizer and explosives) from Chile. Although the European empires did not attempt to create new colonies in South America, as they did in Africa, they invested heavily in the economic life of self-governing South American countries. The U.S. also increased investment in South America, but most of its investments were concentrated in Central America and the Panama Canal region.

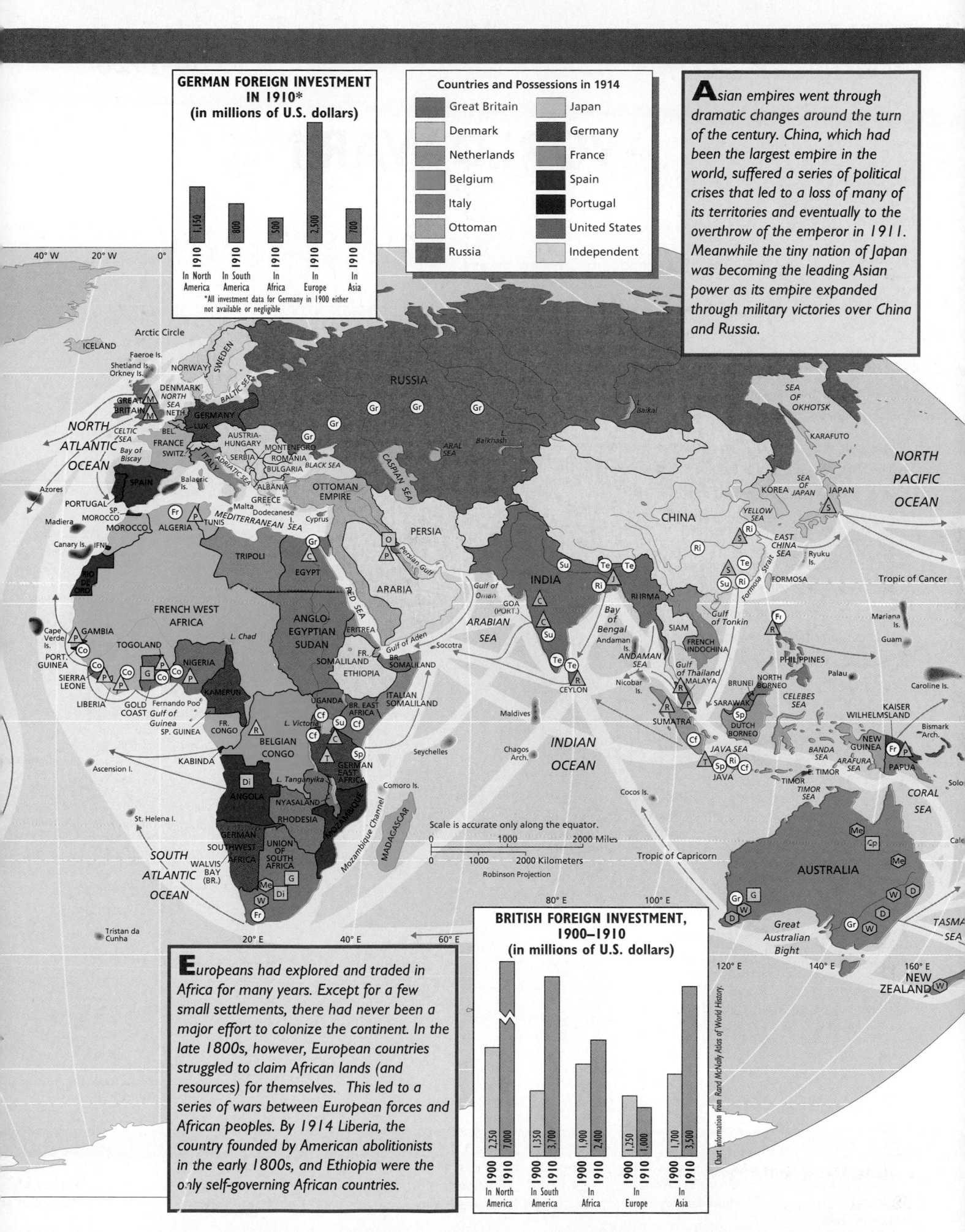

GERMAN FOREIGN INVESTMENT IN 1910*
(in millions of U.S. dollars)

1910	1910	1910	1910	1910
1,150	800	500	2,500	700
In North America	In South America	In Africa	In Europe	In Asia

*All investment data for Germany in 1900 either not available or negligible

Countries and Possessions in 1914

- Great Britain
- Denmark
- Netherlands
- Belgium
- Italy
- Ottoman
- Russia
- Japan
- Germany
- France
- Spain
- Portugal
- United States
- Independent

Asian empires went through dramatic changes around the turn of the century. China, which had been the largest empire in the world, suffered a series of political crises that led to a loss of many of its territories and eventually to the overthrow of the emperor in 1911. Meanwhile the tiny nation of Japan was becoming the leading Asian power as its empire expanded through military victories over China and Russia.

Europeans had explored and traded in Africa for many years. Except for a few small settlements, there had never been a major effort to colonize the continent. In the late 1800s, however, European countries struggled to claim African lands (and resources) for themselves. This led to a series of wars between European forces and African peoples. By 1914 Liberia, the country founded by American abolitionists in the early 1800s, and Ethiopia, were the only self-governing African countries.

BRITISH FOREIGN INVESTMENT, 1900–1910
(in millions of U.S. dollars)

1900	1910	1900	1910	1900	1910	1900	1910	1900	1910
2,250	7,000	1,350	3,700	1,900	2,400	1,250	1,000	1,700	3,500
In North America		In South America		In Africa		In Europe		In Asia	

Chart information from Rand McNally Atlas of World History.

Scale is accurate only along the equator.

0   1000   2000 Miles
0   1000   2000 Kilometers

Robinson Projection

WORLD WAR I

FOCUS

UNDERSTANDING THE MAIN IDEA

When war enveloped Europe, the United States tried to remain neutral. In 1917, however, the United States joined the Allied cause. The government quickly moved to mobilize the economy and to build public support for the war. Then when the fighting stopped, Wilson worked to shape a just peace. He failed, however, to win congressional support for the treaty he helped write.

THEMES

■ **GLOBAL RELATIONS** Why might a country be drawn into an international conflict in spite of efforts to remain neutral?

■ **ECONOMIC DEVELOPMENT** How might fighting a war affect a nation's economy?

■ **DEMOCRATIC VALUES** How might war affect a government's respect for its citizens' rights?

1914	1915	1917	1918	1919
Archduke Franz Ferdinand assassinated.	German U-boat sinks *Lusitania*.	Congress declares war.	Wilson introduces Fourteen Points.	Treaty of Versailles si

In his farewell address President Washington had warned against entangling American "peace and prosperity in the toils of European ambition." The United States had long heeded this advice and tried to remain neutral. But isolation became increasingly difficult as the nation emerged as a world power in the early 1900s.

Houplines, France, 1918

On the morning of July 29, 1914, Americans opened their newspapers to screaming headlines announcing the outbreak of war in Europe. The *New York Tribune* proclaimed: "AUSTRIA DECLARES WAR, RUSHES VAST ARMY INTO SERBIA; RUSSIA MASSES 80,000 MEN ON BORDER."

Most Americans reacted with stunned disbelief. Many were grateful that the Atlantic Ocean separated them from Europe. Urging Americans not to take sides, President Wilson attempted to steer a neutral course among the warring nations. With the passing months, however, neutrality became more difficult for the United States. Step by step, events pushed America closer to involvement. Finally, in the spring of 1917, the United States entered the fighting on the side of the Allies—one of some 30 nations on five continents formally to join the war. Before it ended, the war claimed the lives of over 8.5 million people and left some 21 million wounded or maimed.

World War I profoundly affected the American home front. It spurred government regulation of the economy, triggered a great northward migration of African Americans, and unleashed ugly forces of suspicion—even attacks—against dissenters.

President Wilson hoped that a new world order would arise from the ashes of the war. Yet, ironically, when the shooting stopped, the victors imposed a harsh peace on Germany, and the United States refused to join the League of Nations, the organization that embodied Wilson's hopes.

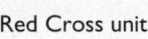

Red Cross unit

WORLD WAR I BREAKS OUT

FOCUS

- **What tensions helped bring about the war in Europe?**
- **What was life in the trenches like?**
- **Why did most Americans find it difficult to remain "impartial in thought" concerning the war?**
- **How did the warring nations' naval strategies challenge American neutrality?**

Soldier and horse in gas masks

*B*y the early 1900s nationalism, territorial rivalries, and militarism had turned Europe into a powder keg of hatred and petty jealousies. An assassination in a small Balkan state provided the spark that ignited this explosive mix. Within weeks, war gripped the whole continent. Everyone expected the conflict to end quickly, but it settled into a deadly stalemate. The United States declared neutrality, but the personal feelings of many Americans and the actions of the warring nations tested the country's stand.

THE ORIGINS OF THE WAR

While the Wilson administration grappled with the problems created by the Mexican Revolution, another dangerous international situation developed in Europe. On the surface Europe appeared peaceful—after all, no major conflicts had erupted since the 1870s. Furthermore, many European nations had endorsed the recommendations of two international peace conferences that arbitration be used to settle disputes among nations. But most European governments paid no more than lip service to arbitration and international cooperation. Fear, distrust, and petty jealousies often ruled their relations with other nations.

Nationalism and territorial rivalries.

At the root of the problem was the intense nationalism that engulfed Europe. Nationalism proved especially strong in northern, central, and eastern Europe. There the **Pan-German movement**, led by Germany, sought to unite all German-speaking peoples under one flag. In direct opposition, Russia supported the **Pan-Slavic movement**, which sought to bring together all the Slavic peoples of central and eastern Europe. These movements seemed destined to come into conflict, for many Slavs lived in Austria-Hungary, a part of the German world.

Another source of tension in Europe was imperialism. European nations, large and small, coveted land held by their neighbors. In 1908, for example, Austria-Hungary annexed Bosnia and Herzegovina. The annexation angered Serbia, which also had designs on the small Balkan province. Other countries, too, eyed neighboring territories. Russia wanted ice-free harbors in the Baltic Sea and access for Russian warships from the Black Sea into the Mediterranean. Germany, the major Baltic power, opposed Russia's ambitions. France wanted to recover Alsace-Lorraine, a

French area the Germans had conquered in 1871, and Italy desired nearby territories belonging to Austria-Hungary.

Militarism and alliances. This dizzying tangle of territorial claims helped generate a spirit of **militarism**, or glorification of armed strength, across the continent. Each nation built up its army and navy against the military threat posed by its neighbors. Military buildup quickly turned into an arms race as each nation tried to develop weapons more powerful than those of its neighbors.

European nations also sought to strengthen their military positions through alliances. Germany, Austria-Hungary, and Italy formed the **Triple Alliance**. Great Britain, France, and Russia joined in the **Triple Entente**. In the treaties that cemented these alliances, the members usually promised to aid any other member who came under attack from an outside power.

The spark that led to war. These alliances helped maintain a balance of power, but they also meant that even a minor incident could provoke a war. Many observers feared that if such an incident occurred, it would be in the Balkans—a region so unstable that some called it "the powder keg of Europe." Observers also agreed that the incident would likely involve nationalist rivalries. As German general Helmuth von Moltke (MAWLT-kuh) remarked in 1912:

66 A European war is bound to come sooner or later, and then it will . . . be a struggle between Teuton [German] and Slav. It is the duty of all states who uphold the banner of German spiritual culture to prepare for this conflict. But the attack must come from the Slavs. 99

The attack came in 1914. In June of that year, Archduke Franz Ferdinand, the heir to the Austro-Hungarian throne, paid a goodwill visit to Sarajevo (SAHR-uh-ye-voh), the capital of Bosnia and Herzegovina. As Franz Ferdinand's open motor car proceeded along the city's streets, Serbian nationalist Gavrilo Princip (PREENT-seep) stepped out of the crowd and fired two shots, killing the archduke and his wife, Sofie.

Suspecting—correctly—that the Serbian government knew of Princip's plans, Austria-Hungary declared war on Serbia. The declaration drew each side's allies into the conflict. Russia sided with Serbia; Germany, with Austria-Hungary. Within a week France and Great Britain had declared war on Austria-Hungary and Germany. Despite membership in the Triple Alliance, Italy remained neutral until 1915, when it joined France, Great Britain, Russia, and the other **Allied Powers** against the **Central Powers** of Germany, Austria-Hungary, the Ottoman Empire (Turkey), and Bulgaria. Eventually some 30 nations would take sides in the Great War.

▪▪ **Nationalism, territorial rivalries, militarism, and military alliances created tensions that led to war.**

▼ Archduke Franz Ferdinand, his wife, and their children pose for a royal family picture.

▶ Gavrilo Princip was 19 years old when he assassinated Franz Ferdinand. He was arrested and sentenced to 20 years—the maximum prison penalty for someone under 20 years old.

THE EARLY WEEKS OF THE WAR

In 1905, accepting the inevitability of a European war, German military leaders had developed a plan for swift victory. The plan called for German forces to skirt the heavily defended Franco-German border, march through then-neutral Belgium, and invade France across the practically unguarded Belgian border before Great Britain could move its forces across the English Channel. With France and Britain knocked out of the war, Germany could focus on defeating Russia.

On August 3, 1914, the Germans launched their plan, surging into Belgium. German military leaders expected to reach the French border quickly and then sweep across northern France toward Paris. Like their kaiser (ruler), Wilhelm II, they believed that the war would end "before the leaves have fallen from the trees." But thanks to

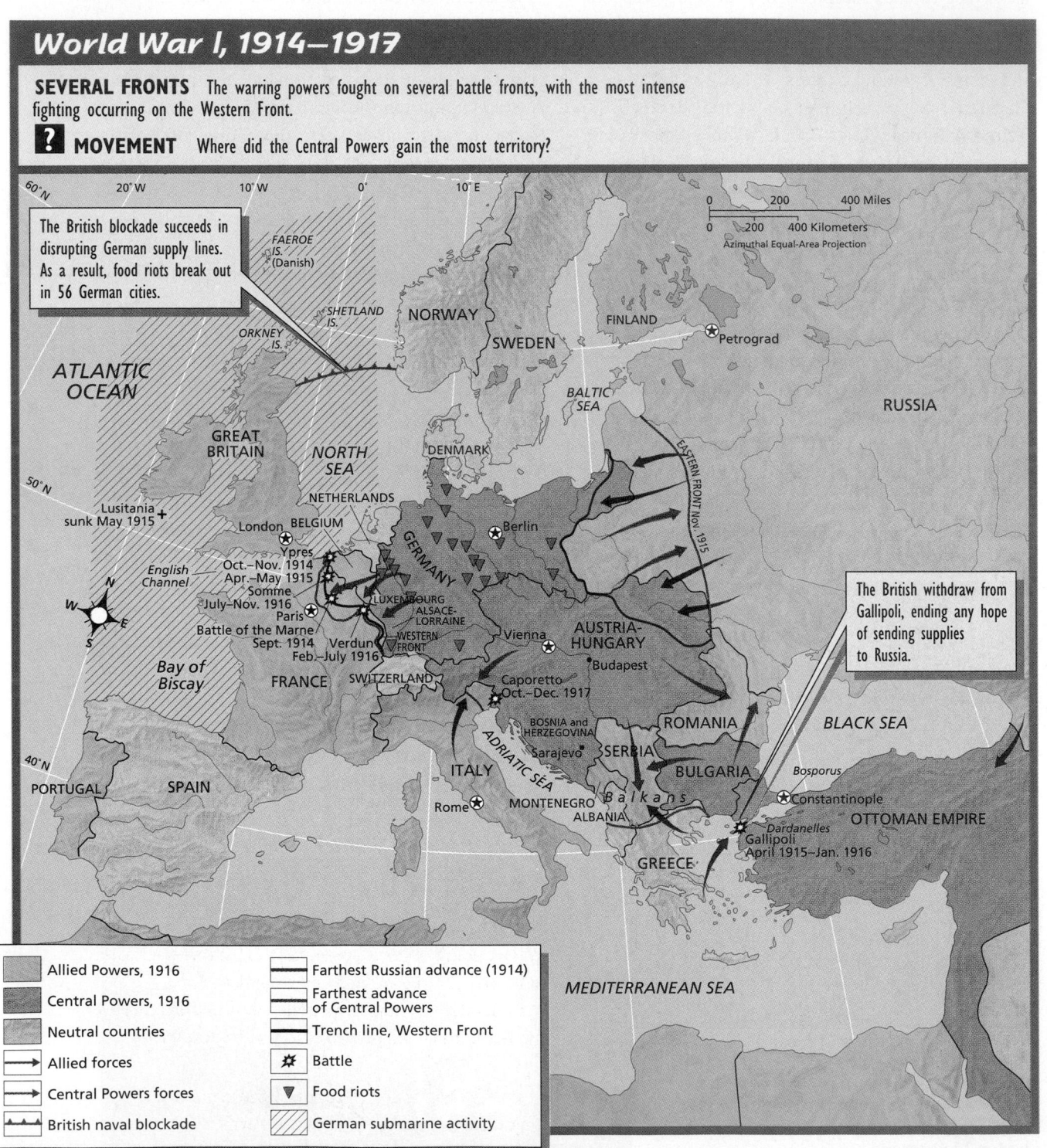

World War I, 1914–1917

SEVERAL FRONTS The warring powers fought on several battle fronts, with the most intense fighting occurring on the Western Front.

? MOVEMENT Where did the Central Powers gain the most territory?

The British blockade succeeds in disrupting German supply lines. As a result, food riots break out in 56 German cities.

The British withdraw from Gallipoli, ending any hope of sending supplies to Russia.

0   200   400 Miles
0   200   400 Kilometers
Azimuthal Equal-Area Projection

ATLANTIC OCEAN

FAEROE IS. (Danish)
SHETLAND IS.
ORKNEY IS.

NORWAY
SWEDEN
FINLAND
Petrograd

BALTIC SEA

RUSSIA

GREAT BRITAIN
NORTH SEA
DENMARK
NETHERLANDS
London
BELGIUM
Berlin
GERMANY

EASTERN FRONT Nov. 1915

Lusitania sunk May 1915
English Channel
Ypres Oct.–Nov. 1914 Apr.–May 1915
Somme July–Nov. 1916
Paris
Battle of the Marne Sept. 1914
LUXEMBOURG
ALSACE-LORRAINE
WESTERN FRONT
Verdun Feb.–July 1916
Vienna
AUSTRIA-HUNGARY
Budapest

Bay of Biscay
FRANCE
SWITZERLAND
Caporetto Oct.–Dec. 1917

BOSNIA and HERZEGOVINA
Sarajevo
SERBIA
ROMANIA
BLACK SEA

ADRIATIC SEA
ITALY
Rome
MONTENEGRO
ALBANIA
Balkans
BULGARIA
Bosporus
Constantinople
OTTOMAN EMPIRE

PORTUGAL
SPAIN

GREECE
Dardanelles
Gallipoli April 1915–Jan. 1916

MEDITERRANEAN SEA

Legend

- Allied Powers, 1916
- Central Powers, 1916
- Neutral countries
- → Allied forces
- → Central Powers forces
- British naval blockade
- Farthest Russian advance (1914)
- Farthest advance of Central Powers
- Trench line, Western Front
- ✿ Battle
- ▼ Food riots
- German submarine activity

the small Belgian army's fierce resistance, the Germans spent nearly three weeks fighting their way across Belgium. As a result, General Joseph Joffre (zhawfruh), the French commander, had time to rush troops to the Belgian border, and the British had time to transport some 90,000 troops to northern France.

These measures managed to slow the German advance but did not stop it. The Germans' superior military might pushed the French and the British back to the Marne River in northeast France. Against heavy odds, the French and the British stopped the Germans early in September 1914 at the **First Battle of the Marne.** From roughly Ypres (eepruh) to Verdun, the German line fell back some 40 miles (see map on page 588). The French and the British launched a counteroffensive but were unable to dislodge the Germans. The Germans had no better luck advancing against the Allies. As 1914 drew to a close, leaders of both sides realized that there would be no quick victory.

ALLIED AND CENTRAL RESOURCES, 1914–1918

Allied Powers | Central Powers

(Left graph — Number in thousands)
- Tanks Produced
- Aircraft Strength, 1918
- Major Naval Vessels, 1914

(Right graph — Number in millions)
- Troops Mobilized During the War

Sources: *Encyclopedia of Military History; A Concise History of WWI*

COMPARATIVE STRENGTHS At the beginning of the war, Germany had the majority of aircraft and was the second greatest naval power. However, the Allied countries mobilized more troops and were able to use their economic resources to surpass Germany in overall war production.

❓ BUILDING GRAPH SKILLS What was the total aircraft strength in 1918?

The Granger Collection, New York

▲ **This 1914 photograph shows German soldiers traveling to the western front in a train marked with the inscription "A trip to Paris—See you again on the boulevard."**

WAR REACHES A STALEMATE

By early 1915 both armies dug in along a front running some 400 miles from the North Sea to the Swiss border. Holed up in trenches and separated by a thin strip of territory called **no-man's land**, both sides struggled to advance.

Trench warfare. Even the most hardened soldier had never encountered anything like **trench warfare**. Britain's field marshal Lord Kitchener lamented, "I don't know what is to be done—this isn't war." In this war most battles began with deafening artillery fire. Then as the smoke and dust from the cannonade cleared, one army would charge the enemy trenches. Most soldiers who succeeded in getting through the barbed wire and land mines strewn across no-man's land were cut down by a hail of bullets from the enemy trenches. In the **Battle of the Somme** in 1916, for example, the British suffered some 60,000 casualties in a single day! All told, this four-month-long battle claimed more than a million dead and wounded.

Maneuvering in the trenches was disheartening. As British soldier Charles Carrington wrote:

❝ When moving about in the trenches you turn a corner every few yards, which makes it seem like walking in a maze. It is impossible to keep your sense of direction and infinitely tiring to proceed at all. When the trenches have been fought over the confusion becomes all the greater. Instead of neat, parallel trench lines, you make the best use of existing trenches which might run in any direction. **99**

Even during lulls in the fighting, life in the trenches proved frightful. Rats and lice plagued the soldiers. Rain flooded the trenches, drenching the soldiers in mud. Artillery fire frequently prevented burial of the dead for days, and exploding shells often unearthed corpses buried earlier. Such unsanitary conditions bred disease, and sickness claimed nearly as many men as bombs and bullets did. The only way out of the trenches, a British soldier observed, was on a stretcher.

New weapons. New weapons added to the horror of trench warfare. The Germans' machine guns fired hundreds of rounds per minute, felling advancing Allied troops like a scythe cutting wheat. The Allies introduced the tank partly to counter the machine gun's deadly impact. First used at the Battle of the Somme in September 1916, the tank produced the intended effect. It

▲ **A British tank force is shown here fighting near Amiens, France, in August 1918.**

scared the Germans "out of their wits," one British soldier reported, and made them "scuttle like frightened rabbits."

But perhaps the most feared new weapon introduced during World War I was poison gas. No whistling shell announced a gas attack. The green mist silently drifted over the trenches, and the soldiers had only seconds to slip on their gas masks. Any delay meant a slow, suffocating death. After watching a comrade die of poison gas, soldier-poet Wilfred Owen wrote:

66 But someone still was yelling out
    and stumbling,
And floundr'ring like a man in fire
    or lime . . .
Dim, through the misty panes and
    thick green light,
As under a green sea, I saw him
    drowning. **99**

■■ **Heavy casualties, unsanitary conditions, and fearful new weapons made trench warfare a horrible experience.**

▲ **Soldiers fought much of World War I from trenches. There they struggled to protect themselves from artillery fire, exposure to all types of weather, and disease and unsanitary conditions.**

Continued stalemate. While new military technology produced horrendous casualties on both sides, it did little to break the stalemate on the western front. From 1915 to the spring of 1917, both armies launched offensives that gained them a few miles of territory, which more often than not they quickly lost.

As the months passed, many people wondered whether the fighting would ever stop. They began to suggest that only the intervention of the United States could bring the war to an end.

AMERICAN NEUTRALITY

At the outbreak of the war, most Americans had expressed surprise and horror. After the initial shock, however, Americans tended to look on the war as a faraway conflict that did not involve the United States. As one American diplomat wrote: "Again and ever I thank Heaven for the Atlantic Ocean."

Not surprisingly, then, President Wilson received strong support when he announced a policy of neutrality. All Americans, he urged, ought to be "neutral in fact as well as in name . . . impartial in thought as well as action." Wilson thought that by taking a neutral stance, the United States might help to negotiate a settlement to the conflict. He pursued this goal throughout 1915 and 1916, but without success.

As the war dragged on, most Americans remained neutral in action, but few could claim to be impartial in thought. Some 28 million Americans—almost 30 percent of the population—were immigrants or the children of immigrants. Many men and women of German, Austrian, Hungarian, or Turkish background sympathized with the Central Powers. So did many Irish Americans anxious to free Ireland from Great Britain's rule.

Most Americans, however, backed the Allies. Ties of ancestry, language, and culture bound many Americans to Britain. Strong, long-established links to France also existed. After all, the French had helped Americans win their War of Independence. The British also bolstered American support for the Allies through a skillful propaganda campaign, which painted Germans as brutal warmongers.

■■ **The U.S. government remained neutral, but most Americans— because of ancestral ties or national sympathies—favored one side or the other.**

Challenges to American neutrality.

Despite its policy of neutrality, the United States could not remain untouched by the war. When the war began, the British navy blockaded the German coast and planted explosive mines across the North Sea. The British even stopped American ships bound for ports in neutral countries and examined cargos—including the mail—for goods that might ultimately be destined for Germany. The United States protested, charging that British actions violated American neutrality.

American hostility toward Great Britain faded, however, in the face of German submarine, or U-boat, warfare. Early in 1915 the Germans established a "war zone" around Great Britain. Any ships entering this zone, even those from neutral nations, were liable to U-boat attack. In response, Wilson warned that the United States would, in accordance with international laws of neutrality, hold Germany accountable for any injury to American lives or property on the high seas.

On March 28, 1915, a U-boat sank a British liner in the Irish Sea, killing more than 100 people, including an American. While the United States debated its response, a far more serious incident occurred. On May 7, 1915, a U-boat patrolling off the Irish coast torpedoed the British passenger liner *Lusitania*. The dead included 128 Americans. The *New York Herald* accused the Germans of "piracy on the high seas," and the *New York Times* called the Germans "savages drenched with blood." Outraged Americans agreed. German leaders justified their actions, declaring that they had placed advertisements in U.S. newspapers warning Americans against sailing into the war zone. They also charged that the *Lusitania* was carrying

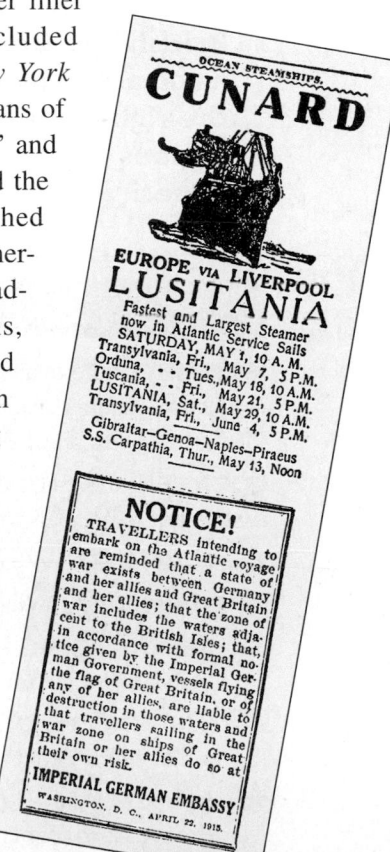

▶ The *Lusitania*'s 1915 voyage announcement carried a warning from the German Embassy against Atlantic sea travel.

▲ The *Lusitania* was photographed shortly before its fateful voyage from New York in 1915.

armaments for England—an accusation that later proved true.

Nevertheless, Wilson fired off an angry protest to the German government, demanding specific pledges against unrestricted submarine warfare. Secretary of State William Jennings Bryan, charging that the president's protest amounted to an ultimatum, resigned. Bryan argued that the United States could not issue ultimatums and remain neutral. The country, he warned, would eventually be drawn into the war.

■■ British and German naval activities violated the rights of neutral nations and led to American protests.

THE SINKING OF THE *LUSITANIA*

Germany's Baron von Schwarzenstein offered the following response to the outrage over the sinking of the *Lusitania*:

"❝*I*t was only after England declared the whole North Sea a war zone . . . that Germany with precisely the same right declared the waters around England a war zone and announced her purpose of sinking all hostile commercial vessels found therein. . . . In the case of the Lusitania the German Ambassador even further warned Americans through the great American newspapers against taking passage thereon. Does a pirate act thus? Does he take pains to save human lives? . . . Nobody regrets more sincerely than we Germans the hard necessity of sending to their deaths hundreds of men. Yet the sinking was a justifiable act of war. . . . The scene of war is no golf links, the ships of belligerent powers no pleasure places. . . . We have sympathy with the victims and their relatives, of course, but did we hear anything about sympathy . . . when England adopted her diabolical plan of starving a great nation?*❞"

SECTION 1 REVIEW

IDENTIFY and explain the significance of the following: Pan-German movement, Pan-Slavic movement, militarism, Triple Alliance, Triple Entente, Archduke Franz Ferdinand, Gavrilo Princip, Allied Powers, Central Powers, First Battle of the Marne, no-man's land, trench warfare, Battle of the Somme.

LOCATE and explain the importance of the following: Austria-Hungary, Bosnia and Herzegovina, Alsace-Lorraine, Balkans, Belgium.

1. **MAIN IDEA** What factors contributed to the outbreak of World War I?

2. **MAIN IDEA** What effect did Britain and Germany's naval strategies have on American neutrality?

3. **RECOGNIZING POINTS OF VIEW** Did the U.S. government's policy of neutrality reflect the views of most Americans? Why or why not?

4. **WRITING TO DESCRIBE** Imagine you are a British soldier in no-man's land during 1916. Write a diary entry that describes the conditions you experience during trench warfare.

5. **ANALYZING** How might trench warfare and new weapons have contributed to the stalemate on the western front?

THE UNITED STATES GOES TO WAR

FOCUS

- Why did the United States finally enter the war?
- Why did the United States institute a draft?
- What part did the American military play in the Allied war effort?

*G**ermany's continued violations of American neutrality drew the United States into World War I on the Allied side in 1917. The Americans' entry came none too soon for the Allies, who faced a desperate military situation. As U.S. forces poured into Europe the tide turned. The Germans slowly fell back, and in November 1918 the warring parties signed an armistice. The four-year nightmare had finally ended.*

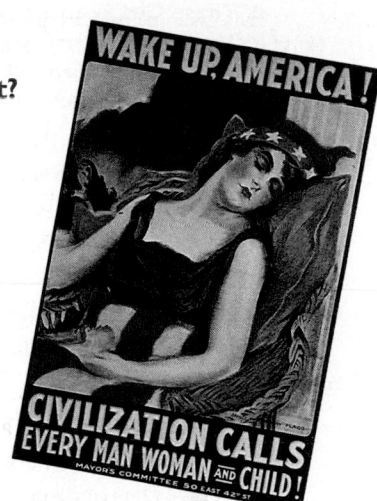

World War I poster

THE ROAD TO WAR

The sinking of the *Lusitania* brought the conflict in Europe closer to home for many Americans. Even so, most still hoped the United States could stay out of the war. Further challenges to American neutrality, however, were not long in coming. In August 1915 two Americans died when a German submarine sank the *Arabic,* another British liner. Then in March 1916 the French passenger vessel *Sussex* was attacked, injuring several Americans. In a sternly worded message to the German government, President Wilson threatened to sever diplomatic ties if Germany did not abandon unrestricted submarine warfare. The German government responded with the *Sussex* **pledge**, a renewal of an earlier promise not to sink liners without warning or without assuring the passengers' safety.

Wilson's actions criticized. Most Americans supported Wilson's approach. However, a number of prominent politicians, including former president Theodore Roosevelt, accused Wilson of not doing enough. Wilson, "that infernal skunk in the White House," Roosevelt complained, had adopted a course of inaction and was little better than a "coward and weakling."

Others accused Wilson of abandoning neutrality. Former secretary of state William Jennings Bryan argued that Wilson's commercial and trade policies helped the Allies. As secretary of state, Bryan had discouraged American bankers from

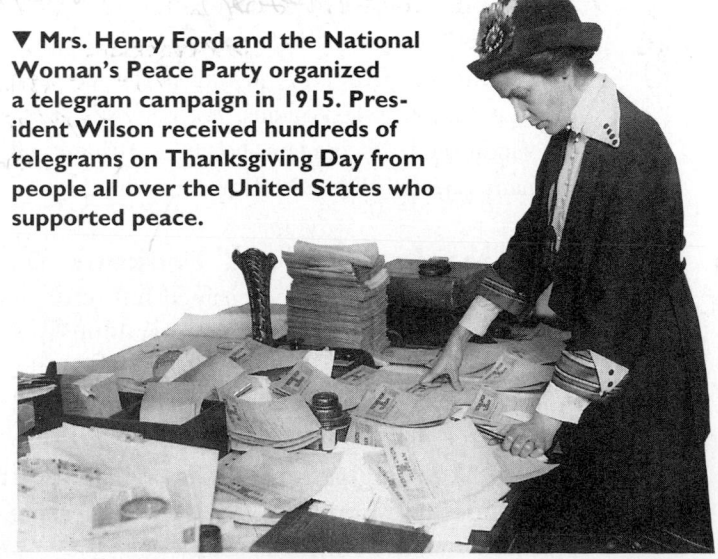

▼ **Mrs. Henry Ford and the National Woman's Peace Party organized a telegram campaign in 1915. President Wilson received hundreds of telegrams on Thanksgiving Day from people all over the United States who supported peace.**

▲ These Girl Scouts helped the war effort by collecting peach pits. The pits could be ground into a charcoal powder and placed in gas masks to help filter out the poisonous fumes during gas attacks.

making loans to either side, but this policy was soon abandoned. Bryan's successor at the State Department, Robert Lansing, encouraged trade in war materials, especially with the Allies. By 1916 arms sales to the Allies stood at some $500 million, about 80 times the amount sold in 1914.

Preparedness and peace. Bryan's fears increased when Wilson launched a military "preparedness" program. The **National Defense Act**, passed in June 1916, increased the number of soldiers in the regular army from some 90,000 to about 175,000, with an ultimate goal of about 223,000 men. It also set the size of the National Guard at some 450,000 troops and provided for their training. Another bill, passed two months later, appropriated $313 million to build up the navy.

President Wilson assured Americans that he had not abandoned neutrality. Running on the slogan "He Kept Us Out of War," Wilson won reelection in 1916, narrowly defeating the Republicans' Charles Evans Hughes.

Wilson still hoped to negotiate a settlement to the war. In a January 1917 speech, he called for "peace without victory." A lasting peace, he said, had to be one between equals, not between victor and vanquished. Once again, however, Britain and Germany rejected Wilson's effort to mediate.

Diplomatic relations broken. On February 1, 1917, Germany resumed full-scale U-boat warfare. The Germans were gambling that their U-boat fleet could defeat the Allies before the Americans joined the war. Wilson, as he had threatened, broke off diplomatic relations. He also ordered the arming of American merchant ships sailing into the war zone. Nonetheless, German torpedoes sank five American ships.

The publication on March 1, 1917, of an intercepted cable from German foreign secretary Arthur Zimmermann to the German minister in Mexico further heightened tensions. In the event that the United States declared war on Germany, the **Zimmermann Note**, as it was quickly dubbed, instructed the minister to propose to Mexico that it enter an alliance with Germany. With German support, the cable went on, Mexico could "reconquer the lost territory in New Mexico, Texas, and Arizona."

As the weeks passed, Wilson reluctantly concluded that the United States could not stay out of the conflict. On April 2, 1917, the president addressed Congress, asking them to vote on a declaration of war.

CONGRESS DECLARES WAR

A hushed Congress heard Wilson condemn Germany's submarine warfare for its "wanton and wholesale destruction." Wilson, however, did not rest his case solely on the evils of U-boat warfare. He summoned Americans to a crusade for a better world:

> 66 We are glad . . . to fight thus for the ultimate peace of the world and for the liberation of its peoples, . . . for the rights of nations great and small and the privilege of men everywhere to choose their way of life. . . . The world must be made safe for democracy. 99

At these words, cheers and applause rang through the Capitol. A somber Wilson later told an aide: "My message today was a message of death for our young men. How strange it seems to applaud that."

■ **U-boat activity and the interception of the Zimmermann Note led the United States to declare war on Germany.**

BIO GRAPHY The Senate declared war on April 4; the House, two days later. The vote was not unanimous—6 senators and 50 representatives opposed the declaration. Congresswoman Jeannette Rankin of Montana was among the opposition. "I want to stand by my country," she explained, "but I cannot vote for war."

Born in Missoula, Montana, in 1880, Rankin was a committed pacifist, social worker, and leader of the women's suffrage movement. In 1916 she became the first woman elected to Congress, and in 1918 she played a key role in the passage of the Nineteenth Amendment. However, with Allied victory only days away, Rankin lost her bid for a Senate seat in the November 1918 elections.

Jeannette Rankin

Elected to the House again in 1940, Rankin continued to speak out against the draft and military spending, casting the only vote against the United States' entry into World War II. That vote cost her reelection in 1942. She did not give up her pacifism, however. In January 1968, at age 87, Rankin led a march on Washington, D.C., to protest the Vietnam War.

MOBILIZING AMERICAN MILITARY POWER

In his war message on April 2, President Wilson pledged all the nation's "material resources" to the Allied war effort. But what the Allies most urgently needed were fresh troops. Few Americans, however, rushed to volunteer for military service.

On May 18, 1917, Congress responded by passing the **Selective Service Act**, which required men between ages 21 and 30 to register with local draft boards. (The age range was later changed to 18–45) By the end of the war, some 24 million men had registered, and some 2.8 million had been drafted. In fact, more than half of the almost 4.8 million Americans who served in the armed forces were draftees.

Many who supported conscription argued that the draft would help build a more democratic America by bringing together soldiers from different backgrounds. In reality, Native Americans, African Americans, Mexican Americans, and many foreign-born soldiers faced discrimination.

Most foreign-born soldiers, for example, were assigned to segregated units where they were taught civics and English. Congress did, however, offer citizenship to the some 10,000 Native Americans who served during the war.

The more than 370,000 African American recruits experienced particularly harsh discrimination. They were blocked from service in the marines and limited to kitchen duties in the navy. Most African Americans in the army were confined to all-black support units commanded by white officers. And African American draftees sent to army training camps in the South often faced harassment from local whites.

Pressure from the NAACP and other African American organizations convinced the army to open up more opportunities for black soldiers. A school was established to train African American officers, and more blacks were assigned combat duty. The army, however, made no effort to integrate blacks and whites in the same units.

■■ The United States instituted the draft to bring the armed services up to full force.

▲ Approximately 1,400 African American officers served during World War I. This officer was stationed in Saint-Dizier, France.

OVER THERE

With mobilization well under way, American troops sailed to France as part of the American Expeditionary Force (AEF). The first U.S. troops, under the command of General John J. Pershing, reached France in late June 1917. On July 4 thousands of "Yanks," cheered on by huge crowds, marched through Paris to the tomb of the Marquis de Lafayette, the French hero of the American Revolution. "Lafayette, we are here!" proclaimed one of Pershing's aides.

Lieutenant Edward F. Graham wrote home about the sense of purpose that he—and many other soldiers—felt:

66 The desperate contest between justice and empire . . . is now on. You should be proud to have me . . . participate in the

---

HISTORY in the Making

BY DR. PAUL BOYER

The Doughboy's Pack

History is much more than a study of dates, documents, or facts about influential people. Ordinary objects also leave a historical record about an event or an era. For example, common items provided to soldiers during a war tell a story about how that war was fought.

During World War I the American infantryman—or doughboy, as he was nick-named—wearily trudged across European battlefields carrying all his necessary equipment inside a canvas "field kit" strapped to his back. Some of the items provided to American soldiers in World War I are shown on these pages. Examine the photographs carefully. What can we learn about the combat experiences of World War I soldiers by studying what they carried?

Begin with the field kit. Examine the cartridge belt attached at waist level. Notice the individual pockets. Each compartment held 10 rounds of ammunition. The around-the-

▶ **Soldier equipped with gas mask and steel helmet**

waist design with pockets was adopted during World War I because of automatic weapons. Rifles could now fire as many as five bullets per minute, and a soldier needed easy access to large amounts of ammunition during the heat of battle. The cartridge belt served this purpose.

Next notice the shovel strapped to the field kit, with its blade encased inside a protective flap. Until 1918 most of the war on the western front was fought from the trenches. Consequently, digging equipment was a necessity. Each squad shared a variety of tools: shovels, hand axes, pickaxes, and wire cutters. Wire cutters were particularly essential to the needs of World War I infantry. Before a soldier could reach the enemy's trenches, he had to clear a path through coils of sharp barbed wire. Getting even a small cut from the rusty barbs could prove dangerous—infections in a minor wound often led to the amputation of an arm or a leg.

Now examine the photograph of the American soldier wearing the gas mask and steel helmet. Chlorine gas and mustard gas were highly feared weapons introduced during World War I. The gas mask struggle as a part of the human wall against a second Dark Ages. "

As the weeks went by, American troops arrived in France in ever-swelling numbers. To supply and maintain them, army engineers built docks and railroads and strung up networks of telephone and telegraph lines. They also constructed camps, ammunition dumps, storage sheds, and hospitals.

Some 10,000 American women worked in these hospitals. Emily Vuagniaux, an Army Medical Corps nurse, described life in a battlefield hospital:

"We . . . have worked . . . sometimes 18 hours straight. I have the operating room and they run four tables day and night and have between 200 and 300 patients right off the field, so you may know we are quite close in. "

filtered out poisonous fumes that could suffocate or blind a soldier. The odd-looking rubber contraption was hot and uncomfortable, but crucial to survival. The soldier's steel helmet, as you can see, extended to the top of the ear line. The helmet was designed to help prevent head wounds. A soldier was particularly vulnerable to such injuries when he first peered out from a trench—just before going "over the top."

Next look at a soldier's vital "mess" equipment. The oval "meat can" served as both a skillet and a plate. Sturdy metal containers protected two days' worth of rations from rain, rats, and insects. A doughboy carried two portions of hard biscuits called hardtack. The condiment can had separate compartments for coffee, sugar, and salt. Above the condiment can is a bacon tin. In addition to such supplies, a soldier carried emergency rations such as stringy beef, scornfully called "monkey

meat" by many soldiers. From this mess equipment and the simple nature of the rations, we can assume that a doughboy's supply lines were within a short distance of each squad. More-substantial meals were prepared by a company cook, who followed the combat units.

In addition to the items shown here, an infantryman carried a tent, tent poles, a rain poncho, a bayonet, a blanket, a sewing kit, socks, identification tags, a compass, and a flashlight. On a long march a World War I soldier might have cursed his heavy pack. But he also knew his burden could mean the difference between life and death.

▲ Field kit

◄ Bacon tin

◄ Condiment can

▲ Meat can

▲ Ambulance drivers were responsible for transporting wounded soldiers from the battlefield to hospitals behind the front lines. Many of the ambulance units included women drivers and mechanics.

Thousands more American women went to Europe as volunteers for the Red Cross, the YMCA, or other agencies.

Merchant vessels, escorted by American warships, transported troops, supplies, and volunteers through the submarine-infested North Atlantic. This **convoy system** proved quite effective. Of the more than two million American soldiers who crossed the Atlantic, not one died as the result of an enemy attack on the high seas. Other American warships patrolled the western Atlantic and laid some 70,000 mines in a lethal 240-mile necklace across the North Sea from Norway to the Orkney Islands off Great Britain. This barrier made life hazardous for German U-boats trying to return to their bases.

THE END OF THE WAR

The Americans' entry into the war came none too soon for the Allies. In an effort to break the deadlock on the western front, the Allies had launched an offensive in the summer of 1917. It failed, shattering the Allied troops' already shaky morale. That fall, mutinies broke out in French units all along the front. In October the Central Powers crashed through Italian lines at Caporetto, on the border between Italy and Austria-Hungary (see map on page 588). Only the arrival of Allied reinforcements saved Italy from collapse.

Worse news arrived from Russia. The Russian people, dissatisfied with working and living conditions, had overthrown the czar in March 1917. Political turmoil continued until November, when the **Bolsheviks**, a branch of the Russian Communist party, seized power. The Bolshevik leader, Vladimir Ilich Lenin, opposed the war. The Bolsheviks signed the **Treaty of Brest-Litovsk** with the Central Powers in March 1918, leaving the Central Powers free to mass their forces on the western front.

Germany's last bid for victory. On March 21, 1918, some one million German troops launched a do-or-die offensive against the Allies. The Germans were backed by some 6,000 heavy guns, including "Big Berthas" capable of firing 250- to 300-pound shells 74 miles. By late May the Germans had pushed the Allies back to the Marne River, only 50 miles from Paris.

General Pershing had originally insisted that American troops fight as a separate army under their own commanders. In light of the situation, however, he agreed to join a unified Allied army under the command of Marshal Ferdinand Foch of France. The introduction of American forces proved decisive. In a last-ditch defense of Paris, American troops helped the French stop the Germans at Château-Thierry on June 3–4. Nearby, a division of American marines counterattacked, recapturing Belleau Wood and two other villages. After fierce fighting, the German advance was halted, and Paris was saved.

On July 15 the Germans threw everything into a final assault around Reims. But the Allied lines held, and Foch ordered a counterattack three days later. The charge, spearheaded by American troops, pushed the Germans back. The tide had turned in favor of the Allies.

◾◾ With the assistance of American troops, the Allies turned the tide against the Germans.

Allied victory. In the late summer Foch seized the initiative, ordering a major offensive along the entire western front. Over the next three months, the Allies pushed deep into German-held territory.

In this offensive the Americans fought as a separate army under Pershing's command and led the attack that pushed the Germans back at Saint-Mihiel, France, in September 1918. The Americans next drove toward Sedan, the French rail center that the Germans had held since 1914. For more than a month the Americans pushed northward along the Meuse River and through the rugged Argonne Forest, facing artillery and machine-gun fire all the way. The Americans suffered some 120,000 casualties on this drive, but by November they had reached and occupied the hills around Sedan.

Lieutenant Edward Graham was one of the casualties. By the time he died, he no longer saw the war as a noble venture. In his last letter he described it as incomprehensible:

> 66 This is a cowering war—pigmy man huddles in little holes and caves praying to escape the blows of the giant who pounds the earth with blind hammers. 99

African American troops played a major role in the Argonne offensive. Members of the 369th Infantry, an African American regiment whose men hailed from New York, so distinguished

World War I: The Western Front, 1917–1918

GERMAN OFFENSIVE When the Germans signed the Treaty of Brest-Litovsk with Russia in March 1918, some 579,000 German soldiers were able to move to the Western Front.

? **PLACE** Which two countries were largely occupied by the Germans throughout World War I?

⚓ Naval mutinies

Army mutinies

German Mutinies

Allied Powers
Central Powers
Neutral countries
German forces
Allied forces

Front at beginning of German offensive, 1918
Farthest advance of German forces, 1918
Armistice line
✸ Battle
French army mutinies

Azimuthal Equal-Area Projection

0   25   50 Miles
0   25   50 Kilometers
Lambert Conformal Conic Projection

▲ The armistice ending the war was signed in this railway passenger car on November 11, 1918.

Mutinies broke out in both the German army and navy. German civilians took to the streets demanding food, not war. Realizing that the war was lost, Wilhelm II fled to the Netherlands in early November. The following day, Germany's new government agreed to an **armistice**, or cease-fire.

On November 8, 1918, German representatives were summoned to Compiègne (kohmp-YAYN), the Allied headquarters, to hear the armistice terms. The Allies demanded that the Germans evacuate France, Belgium, Luxembourg, and Alsace-Lorraine. They also insisted that Germany surrender an enormous amount of war materials, including much of their naval fleet. In addition, the Allies reserved the right to occupy German territory east and west of the Rhine. After brief negotiations the Germans agreed to these harsh terms.

Early on the morning of November 11, the warring parties signed the armistice, and at 11 A.M. the cease-fire went into effect. The constant crashing of guns was replaced, according to one American, by a "silence [that] was nearly unbearable." The Great War, at long last, had ended.

themselves that the French awarded them the *Croix de Guerre* (kwahd i GER), or "Cross of War," a French military honor.

Repeatedly hammered during the Allied offensive, the Central Powers began to disintegrate. Morale in the German military sagged. One soldier, anxious for peace, wrote home:

> 66 In what way have we sinned, that we should be treated worse than animals? Hunted from place to place, cold, filthy . . . we are destroyed like vermin. Will they *never* make peace? 99

SECTION 2 REVIEW

IDENTIFY and explain the significance of the following: *Sussex* pledge, Robert Lansing, National Defense Act, Zimmermann Note, Jeannette Rankin, Selective Service Act, John J. Pershing, convoy system, Bolsheviks, Treaty of Brest-Litovsk, Ferdinand Foch, armistice.

LOCATE and explain the importance of the following: Caporetto, Château-Thierry, St. Mihiel, Sedan, Meuse River, Compiègne.

1. **MAIN IDEA** What actions provoked the United States to declare war on Germany?

2. **MAIN IDEA** Why did the United States pass the Selective Service Act?

3. **GAINING A MULTICULTURAL PERSPECTIVE** What evidence suggests that conscription did not make America more democratic?

4. **WRITING TO INFORM** Imagine you are Secretary of State Robert Lansing. Write a memorandum to President Wilson that summarizes the effect the American entry into the war had on Allied efforts.

5. **HYPOTHESIZING** How might the war in Europe have been different if Germany had abandoned U-boat warfare?

Section 3

THE WAR AT HOME

F O C U S

- What steps did the federal government take to mobilize the economy for war?
- How did the labor force change during the war?
- How did the government stifle dissent and rally support for its wartime policies?

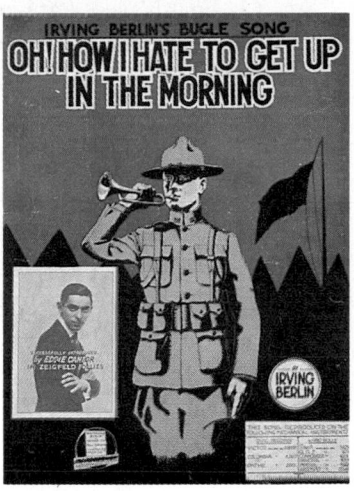

Irving Berlin song sheet, 1918

Once the United States entered the war, President Wilson quickly moved to mobilize the nation. The government set up programs to finance the war, to conserve scarce resources, and to redirect industry and labor toward wartime production. Wilson also launched a huge propaganda campaign to mobilize support for the war effort. But as the government whipped up enthusiasm for the war, intolerance of antiwar opinion spread across the land.

MOBILIZING THE ECONOMY

At the outset of the war, Wilson had noted that "there are no armies in this struggle; there are entire nations armed." To "arm" the nation, Wilson realized, the economy had to be put on a wartime footing.

The first step in this process was raising money to pay for the war, which eventually cost Americans more than $33 billion. The government raised money through four Liberty Bond issues during the war and one Victory Bond issue after the armistice. Posters, parades, and rallies promoted each bond issue. "Every person who refuses to subscribe . . . is a friend of Germany," declared William McAdoo, secretary of treasury and Wilson's son-in-law, and "is not entitled to be an American citizen." These promotions were a huge success, raising some $23 billion for the war.

The government also planned to raise money by increasing taxes. This, however, proved far more difficult than selling bonds. Congress heatedly debated a new tax program for months, finally reaching agreement in October 1917. The new taxes on business incomes and large personal incomes produced about $9 billion for the war—much less than expected.

Mobilizing the economy for war entailed more than raising money, however. It also involved coordinating the actions of government, business,

▲ Movie stars Douglas Fairbanks, Mary Pickford, and Charlie Chaplin lent their support to a Liberty Bond drive in Philadelphia.

WORLD WAR I ■■ 601

and industry. This was done through a multitude of federal war boards. While the federal government never took complete control of the economy, it exercised sweeping economic power through these various agencies. It set the prices and production levels of hundreds of commodities and regulated businesses crucial to the war effort.

CONSERVING FOOD AND FUEL

Among the most successful of the federal war boards were the **Food Administration** and the **Fuel Administration**, which were charged with regulating the production and supply of these essential resources. To direct the Food Administration, Wilson chose Herbert Hoover, a prosperous mining engineer who had managed a food-relief campaign for war-stricken Belgium. Hoover saw his task as twofold: to encourage increased agricultural production and to conserve existing food supplies.

To stimulate wartime production, Hoover guaranteed farmers high prices. Farm production soared. For example, farmers upped wheat production, harvesting some 921 million bushels in 1919—a dramatic increase over the 1917 figure of some 637 million bushels.

▲ Herbert Hoover, director of the Food Administration

Announcing that "food will win the war," Hoover called on Americans to reduce their food consumption by observing wheatless and meatless days. To supplement their diets, he suggested they plant "victory gardens" filled with vegetables. The campaign proved very effective—without, as Hoover proudly noted, forced rationing.

The Fuel Administration director, Harry Garfield, the son of the former president, took a similar course of action, encouraging people to observe heatless Mondays. Garfield was not averse to using force, however. When the nation ran short of coal in early 1918, he closed all factories east of the Mississippi for several days.

ORGANIZING INDUSTRY

Hundreds of other boards and agencies regulated industrial production and distribution. For example, the **Railroad Administration**, run by William McAdoo, reorganized the railroads, setting limits on transportation rates and workers' wages.

The work of all these boards was coordinated by the government's central war agency, the **War Industries Board** (WIB). Its director, Wall Street banker Bernard Baruch, had overall responsibility for allocating scarce materials, establishing production priorities, and setting prices. Baruch preferred to persuade business leaders to comply with his wishes. However, when steel owners refused to cut prices, the government threatened to take over their foundries and mills.

At first many business leaders were critical of Wilson's economic mobilization programs. Government intervention, they argued, would permanently damage the American free-enterprise system. As profits soared, however, they ceased to complain.

■ **The government mobilized for war by setting up programs to raise money, conserve scarce resources, and coordinate government, business, and industry.**

MOBILIZING LABOR

Organized labor moved quickly to gain its share of wartime prosperity. With hundreds of thousands of men drafted into the army and with European immigration slowed to a trickle, industry found itself desperately short of labor as it geared up for the war effort. Taking advantage of this situation, unionized workers across the country went on strike, demanding higher wages and other benefits. Nearly 4,500 strikes involving more than one million workers occurred in 1917 alone. The tactic worked—over the war years, working conditions substantially improved.

To ensure that the voice of labor received a hearing, President Wilson established the **National War Labor Board** (NWLB) in April 1918. Composed of representatives from business and labor, the NWLB arbitrated disputes between workers and employers. In the more than 1,200

▲ Many American women helped the war effort by working in munitions factories and other industries. Here, a woman loads cartridges for rifles.

cases that it heard, the board ruled in favor of labor more often than not. In this climate of official support, union membership grew rapidly. AFL membership, for instance, rose from some 2 million in 1916 to roughly 3.2 million by 1919. By the end of the decade, some 15 percent of the nonagricultural work force was unionized.

The labor shortage that helped strengthen unions also brought about changes in the work force. The number of women working outside the home grew by about 6 percent during the war. Many of these women took traditionally male jobs. They worked as automobile mechanics, truck drivers, bricklayers, metalworkers, or railroad engineers. In all, some 1.5 million American women worked in industry during the war. Like Norma B. Kastl, an interviewer with a women's service bureau, many women considered employment their patriotic duty:

❝ The navy is taking on women as yeomen to do shore duty. . . . Every girl that becomes a yeoman can have the satisfaction of knowing that she is releasing, as from prison, some sailor who had been fuming . . . because he had to spend his days in an office instead of on the deck of a destroyer. ❞

Women also helped plan wartime mobilization. Carrie Chapman Catt, a women's suffrage leader, sat on the Women's Committee of the Council of National Defense, a civilian agency organized to support the war effort. Harriot Stanton Blatch, the daughter of Elizabeth Cady Stanton, headed the Food Administration's Speakers' Bureau.

Women's war efforts helped produce one very important political change—the passage of the Nineteenth Amendment. President Wilson, who had wavered on woman suffrage, threw his support behind the amendment in recognition of women's wartime contributions. "The greatest thing that came out of the war," Carrie Chapman Catt later noted, "was the emancipation of women, for which no man fought."

ℸHE GREAT TREK NORTH

The labor shortage that drew women into the work force also spurred immigration from Mexico. Fleeing the Mexican Revolution and lured by southwestern employers who depended on Mexican labor, some 150,000 men and women migrated from Mexico to the United States during the war. Most took agricultural, mining, or railroad jobs in Arizona, California, Colorado, New Mexico, or Texas. But some headed northward for better-paying jobs in such industrial centers as Chicago and Cleveland.

Job opportunities and the prospect of higher wages also brought about one of the most important population shifts in American history—the **Great Migration** of African Americans from the South to northern cities between 1915 and 1930. Persuaded by recruitment agents sent by the Pennsylvania Railroad and other large employers, hundreds of thousands of African Americans moved northward during the war years (estimates range from 200,000 to 550,000). African American newspapers strongly encouraged the migration: "Get out of the South," declared an editorial in the Chicago *Defender*. "Come north . . . The *Defender* says come."

▪▪ **The wartime labor shortage brought large numbers of women, Mexican immigrants, and African Americans into the work force.**

▲ National guardsmen were called in to preserve the peace during the East St. Louis race riot in July 1917.

African Americans went to the North with great hope. But for many, life in the North proved harsh. Although they enjoyed a better standard of living than they had in the South, racial violence remained a serious problem. The most brutal wartime racial incident occurred in East St. Louis, Illinois, on July 2, 1917. White rioters—egged on by spectators—rampaged through black neighborhoods in an orgy of burning and shooting that left at least 39 dead. Shocked and angered, many African Americans asked themselves why they should fight for freedom in Europe when they enjoyed so little at home.

MOBILIZING ATTITUDES

Many Americans—for religious, political, or personal reasons—believed that the United States should have stayed out of the conflict. President Wilson, who wanted all Americans to support the war effort, established the **Committee on Public Information** (CPI) in the spring of 1917. Headed by George Creel, a progressive journalist, the CPI waged a vigorous propaganda campaign to sell the war to Americans.

At first much of the material that the CPI put out was based on fact but censored to present an upbeat picture of the war. Very quickly, however, the CPI began churning out raw propaganda, picturing the Germans as evil monsters. Hollywood joined in, producing movies such as *The Claws of the Hun, The Prussian Cur,* and *The Kaiser, the Beast of Berlin.* These titles vividly illustrate the message the CPI tried to convey.

CPI pamphlets warned citizens to be on the lookout for German spies. Dozens of "patriotic organizations," with names like the American Protective League and the American Defense Society, sprang up. These groups spied, tapped telephones, and opened mail in an effort to ferret out "spies and traitors."

These groups targeted almost anyone who called for peace, questioned the Allies' progress, or criticized the government's policies. They were particularly hard on German Americans, many of whom lost their jobs. Sometimes this anti-German sentiment took absurd turns. German books vanished from library shelves, schools stopped teaching German language courses, and German music disappeared from concert programs. People even renamed German-sounding items: sauerkraut became liberty cabbage, dachshunds became liberty pups, and hamburger became Salisbury steak.

Vigilantes publicly humiliated people of German heritage by forcing them to kiss the flag, recite the Pledge of Allegiance, or buy war bonds. Sometimes the vigilantes turned violent. In March 1918 John H. Wintherbotham, a midwestern representative for the government's Council of National Defense, reported:

66 All over this part of the country men are being tarred and feathered and some are being lynched. . . . These cases do not get into the newspapers nor is an effort

◀ Wartime posters inspired people to purchase savings stamps for their country.

ever made to punish the individuals concerned. In fact, as a rule, it has the complete backing of public opinion. **99**

SUPPRESSING DISSENT

Even in this hysterical atmosphere, some Americans continued to oppose the war. Quaker and Mennonite men, committed by faith to nonviolence, refused to take up arms. Considered traitors by many Americans, they faced violence and abuse.

Pacifists like Congresswoman Jeannette Rankin, Senator Robert La Follette, and settlement-house leader Jane Addams never stopped calling for peace. But such declarations held little sway with Wilson, who heaped contempt on the pacifists for their "stupidity."

The Socialist party, too, proclaimed its unalterable opposition to the war. To most party members, the war used the laboring masses as cannon fodder in a capitalist struggle for control of world markets. The Industrial Workers of the World (IWW), the radical labor union, had a similar view of the war and led strikes in a number of war-related industries.

To silence dissenters, Congress passed the **Espionage Act** in June 1917 and the **Sedition Act** a year later. These measures not only outlawed acts of treason but also made it a crime to "utter, print, write, or publish any disloyal . . . or abusive language" criticizing the government, the flag, or the military. Opposition to the draft, to war-bond drives, or to the arms industry also became a crime.

■■ The Committee on Public Information rallied support for the war, while the Espionage and Sedition acts crushed antiwar dissent.

More than 1,000 people—including some 200 members of the IWW—were convicted of violating these laws. Victor Berger, a Socialist congressman from Wisconsin, received a 20-year sentence for publishing antiwar articles in his newspaper, the Milwaukee *Leader.* The Socialist party leader Eugene V. Debs went to prison for 10 years for making a speech against the war.

Many Americans, even some who supported the war, believed that the Espionage and Sedition acts violated the First Amendment. The Supreme Court, however, disagreed. In the landmark case *Schenck* v. *United States* (1919), Justice Oliver Wendell Holmes wrote:

66 The question . . . is whether the words used are used in such circumstances and are of such a nature as to create a clear and present danger. . . . When a nation is at war many things that might be said in time of peace . . . will not be endured [and] no Court could regard them as protected by any constitutional right. **99**

This decision was meant to apply to extraordinary circumstances like war. Unfortunately, intolerance of unpopular ideas continued long after the war had ended.

SECTION 3 REVIEW

IDENTIFY and explain the significance of the following: William McAdoo, Herbert Hoover, Food Administration, Fuel Administration, Railroad Administration, War Industries Board, Bernard Baruch, National War Labor Board, Carrie Chapman Catt, Harriot Stanton Blatch, Great Migration, Committee on Public Information, Espionage Act, Sedition Act, Victor Berger.

1. **MAIN IDEA** How did the U.S. government mobilize the economy for war?

2. **MAIN IDEA** What effect did wartime labor shortage have on the work force?

3. **MAIN IDEA** What steps did the government take to shape and control public opinion during the war?

4. **WRITING TO EXPLAIN** Imagine you are an American opposed to the war. Write a newspaper editorial, outlining your reasons for opposing the Committee on Public Information.

5. **EVALUATING** Do you think the U.S. government was justified in taking control of the economy during the war? Why or why not?

THE LEAGUE OF NATIONS

FOCUS

■ What two major issues did Wilson's peace plan address?

■ Why was Wilson forced to compromise on his Fourteen Points?

■ Why did the Senate reject the Treaty of Versailles?

■ What impact did the war have on Europe and the Middle East?

President Wilson developed a program for a just peace even before the war ended. This program served as the focus of the Paris Peace Conference in 1919. Wilson had to compromise on many of the points, but the final treaty included the heart of his peace program—the League of Nations. The U.S. Senate, however, rejected the treaty. Without American membership, the League of Nations proved inadequate to solve the world's postwar problems.

Versailles, site of peace-treaty signing

WILSON'S FOURTEEN POINTS

News of the armistice on November 11, 1918, set off a joyful celebration in the United States. Wilson shared the people's great happiness at the Allied victory, but he knew that the task of forging a just peace lay ahead.

This challenge had long been on Wilson's mind. Late in 1917 he had invited a group of scholars to advise him on peace terms. Drawing from their work, Wilson had developed a program for world peace, which he had presented to Congress on January 8, 1918. He called his program the **Fourteen Points** because it contained 14 points, or principles.

Nine of the points dealt with the issue of **self-determination**—the right of people to govern themselves—and with the various territorial disputes created by the war. Other points focused on what Wilson considered the causes of modern war: secret diplomacy, the arms race, violations of freedom of the seas, and trade barriers. But the final point—the establishment of the League of Nations—was the heart of Wilson's program.

◄ **Jubilant Americans celebrate Armistice Day in Washington, D.C., in 1918.**

In his peace plan Wilson aimed to settle territorial disputes and to end the causes of modern war.

Congress and the American public warmly received the Fourteen Points. The reaction of the Allies, however, proved lukewarm. Moreover, the German government, labeling Wilson an "American busybody," rejected the program.

However, as the war turned against them, the Germans sued for a peace settlement based on the Fourteen Points. Wilson had to push and prod the Allies, but they eventually agreed. After the armistice a peace conference was set for January 1919 in Paris. To make sure that the talks focused on his peace program, Wilson attended the conference.

▲ Pictured here are David Lloyd George of England, Naron Sonnino of Italy, Georges Clemenceau of France, and Woodrow Wilson of the United States.

THE PARIS PEACE CONFERENCE

On December 4, 1918, Wilson boarded the *George Washington* for his precedent-setting trip to Europe—he was the first president to cross the Atlantic while in office. As the ship steamed out of New York harbor, a huge crowd gave Wilson a rousing send-off. His reception at the French port of Brest some nine days later proved no less enthusiastic. And on a triumphal tour through France, Britain, and Italy, people welcomed him as a conquering hero. Elated by the cheering throngs, Wilson convinced himself that he had a mandate to shape the peace according to the Fourteen Points.

While Wilson and his fellow leaders gathered to discuss peace, the world was far from peaceful. Across central and eastern Europe, various ethnic groups, now liberated from Austro-Hungarian or Russian rule, clashed over territory. Defeated, Germany teetered on the brink of civil war. In Russia, Bolsheviks fought off the czarists' challenge. The Allied powers—including America—had become entangled in the Russian conflict, sending troops to support the czarists' effort to overthrow the Bolsheviks.

The other delegates at the conference refused to let Wilson dictate the peace terms. Italy's prime minister, Vittorio Orlando, came to Paris only to make sure his nation got the territories it had been promised on entering the war in 1915. David Lloyd George, Britain's prime minister, had just won an election with such slogans as "Hang the Kaiser." He had no intention of showing generosity toward the Germans nor of giving up Britain's naval supremacy by accepting Wilson's idea of "freedom of the seas."

The French premier, Georges Clemenceau, wanted to ensure France's security by crushing Germany. Distrustful of Wilson's idealism, Clemenceau growled: "God gave us his Ten Commandments, and we broke them. Wilson gave us his Fourteen Points—we shall see."

As the conference opened on January 18, 1919, Wilson expressed great enthusiasm for the task ahead. But the demands of the other members of the **Big Four**—as Wilson, Orlando, Lloyd George, and Clemenceau became known—soon wore Wilson down. The others insisted that Germany bear the financial cost of the war by making huge payments, called **reparations**, to the Allies. They also wanted several secret spoils-of-war treaties honored. Such demands violated practically every one of the points of President Wilson's peace plan.

Wilson had two options: he could either compromise or walk out. Indeed, at one point he ordered the *George Washington* to stand by to return him to the United States. But he realized that leaving would be an admission of failure. He also feared that without a comprehensive peace agreement, the Bolshevik Revolution might spread from Russia into the already politically unstable regions of central and eastern Europe. More than anything else, however, he wanted to see the creation of the League of Nations. The League, he believed, would remedy any injustices the treaty might contain. Wilson stayed on.

■■ **Allied demands that Germany pay war damages and that secret treaties be honored forced Wilson to compromise.**

THE TREATY OF VERSAILLES

After six months of debate, the delegates agreed to a peace treaty. The official signing of the **Treaty of Versailles** took place in the magnificent palace of Versailles, just outside Paris, on June 28, 1919. Publicly, the American delegation expressed satisfaction with the document. In private, however, they voiced a different opinion. Secretary of State Robert Lansing confided that he felt "disappointment, . . . regret, and . . . depression." He continued:

66 The terms of peace appear immeasurably harsh and humiliating. . . . Resentment and bitterness, if not desperation, are bound to be the consequences of such provisions. . . . We have a treaty of peace, but it will not bring permanent peace because it is founded on the shifting sands of self-interest. 99

According to the treaty, Germany's colonies and the Ottoman Empire (Turkey) were divided among the Allied nations, as specified in the spoils-of-war treaties. At Wilson's insistence, however, the treaty established a **mandate system** that required the new colonial rulers to report on their administration to the League of Nations. To satisfy nationalist longings in central and eastern Europe, the peace treaty also created the new nations of Czechoslovakia and Yugoslavia. (Finland, Estonia, Latvia, Lithuania, and Poland also emerged from the war as independent nations— Poland after nearly 150 years of domination by outside powers.)

The treaty proved a bitter pill for the Germans. Not only did Germany lose its colonies, but France also reclaimed Alsace-Lorraine and won 15-year control of the Saar, an industrial region of Germany rich in coal

Lost by Germany
Lost by Bulgaria
Lost by Austria-Hungary
Lost by Russia
Lost by Ottoman empire
British mandate
French mandate
Occupied by Allies

In 1922 the Bolsheviks were firmly in control of Russia, and they organized the Union of Soviet Socialist Republics.

Europe and the Middle East After World War I

END OF EMPIRE Four empires had collapsed by the end of the First World War—the Russian, German, Austro-Hungarian, and Ottoman.

❓ **LOCATION** How many countries were created from or received land that had belonged to Russia before the war?

and iron. In addition, Germany was disarmed, forced to admit full guilt for the war, and assessed billions of dollars in reparations.

Harsh as this treatment was, it would have been much worse but for Wilson's moderating influence. He steadfastly opposed some of the more extreme Allied demands. And, above all, the president made sure that the treaty included a covenant creating the League of Nations.

▲ The first informal meeting of the League of Nations met in Geneva in 1920.

Headquartered in Geneva, the League consisted of a permanent administrative staff; an assembly, where each member nation had one vote; and a council, or executive body. The council was intended to have five permanent members—France, Great Britain, Italy, Japan, and the United States—and four other members that were periodically elected by the assembly.

The League Covenant required member nations to try to resolve disputes peacefully. If negotiations failed, the nations were to observe a waiting period before going to war. If any member nation failed to follow this procedure, the council could apply economic pressure and even recommend the use of force against the offending nation. The heart of the League Covenant—Article 10— required each member nation to "respect and preserve" the independence and territorial integrity of all other member nations.

THE TREATY IN THE SENATE

Returning to America in July 1919, President Wilson worked to win the Senate's consent to the Treaty of Versailles. He believed that he could count on the votes of most Democratic senators, but he would need solid support from Republicans to gain the required two-thirds majority. He faced a difficult task, for most Republican senators had doubts about the treaty. Fourteen of them—called the **irreconcilables**—would have nothing to do with the League of Nations and flatly rejected the treaty. The other 35 Republican senators—the

reservationists—said they could support the treaty if the League Covenant were amended. They particularly objected to Article 10, which seemed to commit the United States to go to war in defense of any League member that came under attack. The Senate's constitutional power to declare war must be protected, they insisted.

Wilson's only hope for consent was to win over close to 20 reservationists. Gaining their support, however, meant compromising on the League, which Wilson refused to do. The more his advisers urged compromise, the more rigid Wilson became.

Henry Cabot Lodge of Massachusetts, head of the Senate Committee on Foreign Relations and Wilson's longtime enemy, led the reservationists. Lodge, too, refused to budge. Playing for time, he bottled up the treaty in the Foreign Relations Committee through the summer of 1919. Angry and frustrated, Wilson took his case to the people. Although he was not feeling well, Wilson began a grueling 9,500-mile speaking tour on September 4. In city after city he ardently defended the treaty. To Wilson's satisfaction, the crowds grew more enthusiastic as the tour went on. Lodge, however, remained unmoved. "The only people who have votes on the treaty," he declared, "are here in the Senate."

On the night of September 25, after an impassioned speech in Pueblo, Colorado, Wilson complained of a splitting headache. His worried doctor ordered him back to Washington, D.C. A few days later, Wilson collapsed from a near-fatal stroke. Wilson lived out the rest of his term in seclusion in the White House, cut off from practically everyone except his wife and his closest aides. Moody, suspicious, and increasingly out of touch with reality, Wilson refused all suggestions of compromise on the treaty.

In November, Lodge presented the treaty, with a list of 14 reservations, to the Senate. Wilson ordered Democratic senators to vote no on the document, thereby rejecting it. The treaty without the list of reservations met the same fate at the hands of the irreconcilables and reservationists. In March

◀ On his 65th birthday in September 1919, Woodrow Wilson was photographed for the first time since his stroke.

1920 another vote on Lodge's version of the treaty failed, although a number of Democrats broke ranks and sided with the reservationists. A few weeks later, Wilson vetoed a congressional resolution declaring the United States at peace with the Central Powers. There would be no peace treaty, he insisted, without the League of Nations.

■■ Wilson's refusal to compromise on the League Covenant led to U.S. rejection of the Treaty of Versailles.

Wilson clutched at the 1920 election as his one remaining hope. He urged the nation to make the election a "great and solemn referendum" on the League Covenant. Americans, however, wanted to put the war and troublesome European problems behind them, and in November they gave the Republican party a landslide victory. By the time Wilson left office, the League of Nations had been established, but without the participation of the United States.

THE GLOBAL IMPACT OF THE WAR

While U.S. leaders debated whether or not to accept the Treaty of Versailles, the Europeans struggled to recover from the war. The destruction and human suffering were almost incomprehensible. In all, over 8.5 million died in battle, and another 21 million were wounded. Germany, with some 6 million dead and wounded, and Russia, with nearly 7 million casualties, suffered the greatest losses. (In contrast, the United States armed forces counted some 112,000 dead.) To add further misery, the influenza epidemic of 1918–1919 killed some 27 million worldwide.

The war had left the industry and agriculture of much of continental Europe in ruins. Northern France was completely destroyed. As British economist John Maynard Keynes observed:

66 For mile after mile nothing was left. No building was habitable and no field fit for the plow. . . . One devastated area was exactly like another—a heap of rubble, a morass of shell-holes, and tangle of wire. 99

Those businesses still operating could not produce enough to meet demand, and rampant inflation resulted. In Germany, food shortages were so extreme that it proved almost impossible to keep track of prices.

▼ Verdun was just one of the many cities reduced to rubble by bombing attacks during the war.

▼ American soldiers who fell in France are still remembered and honored in this cemetery.

Germany, reeling from the harsh terms of the treaty, seethed with unrest. Throughout the continent, nations vied with one another over territories they thought the treaty ought to have ceded to them. In the Middle East, Arab nations, which had sided with the Allies in hopes of winning their independence from the Ottoman Turks, found themselves living under French and British mandates. Tensions in the region heightened after Britain issued the **Balfour Declaration** in 1917, declaring British support for a Jewish homeland in Palestine.

The new world order, which so many hoped would arise from the ashes of World War I, never materialized. Instead, as historian J. M. Winter noted, "The old order reasserted its will, distributed the spoils of war, and left unresolved the problems which had led to . . . war in 1914."

 The war, which destroyed a generation of young men and left much of Europe in ruins, resolved few prewar issues.

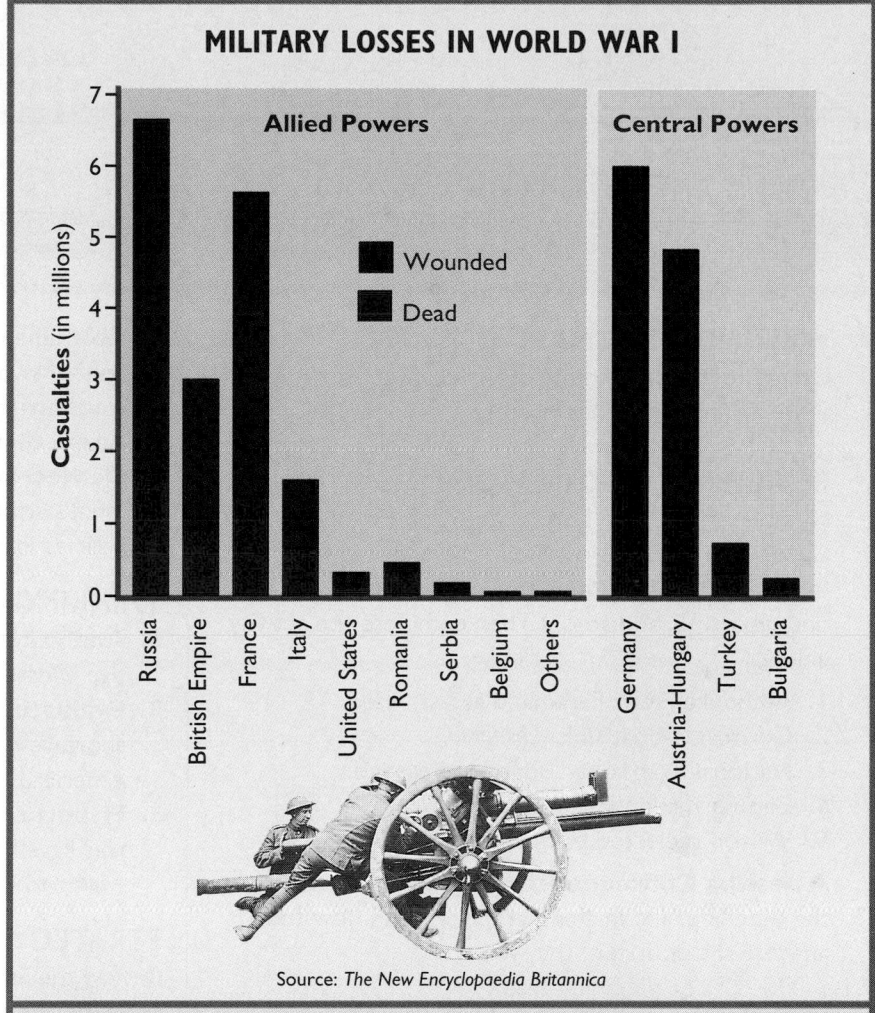

MILITARY LOSSES IN WORLD WAR I

Allied Powers

Central Powers

Casualties (in millions)

■ Wounded
■ Dead

Russia, British Empire, France, Italy, United States, Romania, Serbia, Belgium, Others

Germany, Austria-Hungary, Turkey, Bulgaria

Source: *The New Encyclopaedia Britannica*

A GLOBAL WAR It is estimated that more than 8.5 million soldiers died during World War I; an even higher number suffered from battle-inflicted wounds.

? BUILDING GRAPH SKILLS Which Allied power had the highest number of total casualties? Which Central power had the highest casualties?

SECTION 4 REVIEW

IDENTIFY and explain the significance of the following: Fourteen Points, self-determination, Vittorio Orlando, David Lloyd George, Georges Clemenceau, Big Four, reparations, Treaty of Versailles, mandate system, irreconcilables, reservationists, Henry Cabot Lodge, Balfour Declaration.

LOCATE and explain the importance of the following: Czechoslovakia, Finland, Estonia, Latvia, Lithuania, Yugoslavia, Poland, Saar.

1. **MAIN IDEA** What did Wilson's peace plan hope to accomplish?

2. **MAIN IDEA** What Allied demands forced Wilson to compromise on his Fourteen Points?

3. **ASSESSING CONSEQUENCES** What were some of the effects of the war on Europe and the Middle East?

4. **WRITING TO EXPRESS A VIEWPOINT** Imagine you are a reservationist in the U.S. Senate. Prepare a speech stating your reasons for not supporting ratification of the Treaty of Versailles.

5. **SYNTHESIZING** What aspects of the Treaty of Versailles lend support to Secretary of State Robert Lansing's observation that it was "founded on the shifting sands of self-interest"?

Archduke Franz Ferdinand assassinated. First Battle of the Marne fought.

Italy enters war on Allied side. German U-boat sinks *Lusitania*.

German government issues *Sussex* pledge. Wilson reelected president.

1914   **1915**   **1916**

WRITING A SUMMARY

Using the essential points of the chapter as a guide, write a summary of the chapter.

REVIEWING CHRONOLOGY

Number your paper 1 to 5. Study the time line above, and list the following events in the order in which they happened by writing the first next to 1, the second next to 2, and so on. Then complete the activity below.

1. Archduke Franz Ferdinand assassinated.
2. German U-boat sinks *Lusitania*.
3. National War Labor Board established.
4. Zimmermann Note published.
5. Wilson reelected president.

Assessing Consequences Select two events on the time line, and in a paragraph, explain how they affected the course of the war.

IDENTIFYING PEOPLE AND IDEAS

Explain the historical significance of each of the following people or terms.

1. militarism
2. Triple Entente
3. Gavrilo Princip
4. *Sussex* pledge
5. Jeannette Rankin
6. convoy system
7. Bernard Baruch
8. Great Migration
9. self-determination
10. Henry Cabot Lodge

UNDERSTANDING MAIN IDEAS

1. What tensions contributed to the outbreak of war in Europe?
2. What contributions did the United States make to the Allied war effort both before and after entry into the war?
3. What role did women play in the war effort?
4. What did President Wilson hope to accomplish through his Fourteen Points? Why was he forced to compromise?

REVIEWING THEMES

1. **Global Relations** What factors led the United States to declare war in 1917? Do you think U.S.

involvement in the conflict was inevitable? Explain your answer.
2. **Economic Development** How was the American economy mobilized for war?
3. **Democratic Values** How did the U.S. government's attempts to rally support for its wartime policies interfere with First Amendment rights?

THINKING CRITICALLY

1. **Analyzing** What were the positive and the negative effects of the draft in the United States?
2. **Evaluating** What effect did the wartime labor shortage have on unions, women, African Americans, and Mexican Americans?
3. **Hypothesizing** How might the outcome of the war have been different if Wilson had been more willing to compromise on his Fourteen Points?

STRATEGY FOR SUCCESS

Review the Strategies for Success on Interpreting Editorial Cartoons on page 332. Then study the following cartoon, which appeared shortly after the sinking of the *Lusitania*. What clues does the cartoonist give to suggest that Germany humiliated the United States in this incident?

WRITING ABOUT HISTORY

Writing to Persuade Imagine you are an African American soldier during the war. Write your commanding officer a letter that tries to convince the army to open up more opportunities for black soldiers.

USING PRIMARY SOURCES

In his classic novel about World War I, *All Quiet on the Western Front,* Erich Maria Remarque portrayed the horrible experiences of war through the eyes of German soldiers. Read the following excerpt, which describes an encounter between German and French soldiers. What point is Remarque trying to make about trench warfare?

The moment we are about to retreat three faces rise up from the ground in front of us. Under one of the helmets [I see] a dark pointed beard and two eyes that are fastened on me. I raise my hand, but I cannot throw into those strange eyes; for one mad moment the whole slaughter whirls like a circus round me, . . . then the head rises up, . . . and my hand-grenade flies through the air and into him.

 We make for the rear, pull wire cradles into the trench and leave bombs behind us with the strings pulled, which ensures us a fiery retreat. The machine-guns are already firing from the next position.

We have become wild beasts. We do not fight, we defend ourselves against annihilation. It is not against men that we fling our bombs, what do we know of men in this moment when Death is hunting us down—now, for the first time in three days we can see his face, now for the first time in three days we can oppose him. . . . No longer do we lie helpless, . . . we can destroy and kill, to save ourselves, . . . and to be revenged. "

LINKING HISTORY AND GEOGRAPHY

Refer to the map on page 588. After the French and the British stopped the German advance at the Marne in 1914, the German army retreated to the Aisne River, halted, and dug themselves into trenches. Why do you think the Germans chose trench warfare rather than retreat into Germany?

Soldiers in trench

BUILDING YOUR PORTFOLIO

Complete the following projects independently or cooperatively.

1. GLOBAL RELATIONS In Chapter 19 you portrayed a State Department official concerned with global relations. Building on that experience, imagine you are the U.S. ambassador to Germany in 1915. Write a letter to the Kaiser, protesting German violations of neutral shipping rights.

2. WAR In Chapter 19 you portrayed a recruiting officer during the Spanish-American War. Building on that experience, imagine you are a senator committed to U.S. neutrality in World War I. Write a speech that states why the United States should remain neutral.

American Letters

The Spanish–American War

As a result of the Spanish-American War, the United States won territories in the Caribbean and the Pacific. In the following selections, Cuban poet and essayist José Martí, Puerto Rican poet Lola Rodríguez de Tió, an anonymous Mexican American poet, and American writers Mark Twain and Edgar Lee Masters explore the meaning of the war for the Caribbean and the United States.

▲ **Lola Rodriguez de Tió**

Diary Entry

by José Martí

[April 25, 1895.] Day of combat. Straight through the woods we are drawing close, already in the claws of Guantanamo. . . . The breast swells with fond reverence and overpowering affection at the sight of the vast landscape of the loved river. We cross it, near a *ceiba* tree, and after greeting a patriot family, overjoyed to see us, we enter the open wood, with sweet sun, rain-washed leaves. As over a carpet go our horses, so thick is the grass. All is garland and leaf, and through the openings, to the right, the green of the cleared fields is visible on the other bank, sheltered and compact. . . . Here as everywhere I am touched by the affection with which we are received, and the unity of soul which will not be allowed to coalesce [grow together], and which will not be recognized, and which will be overridden, harming, at least with the harm of delay, the Revolution in the impulse of its first year. The spirit I sowed, is that which has borne fruit, and that of the Island, and with it, and guiding ourselves by it, we will soon triumph, and with a better victory and for a better peace. ❖

The Song of Borinquen

by Lola Rodríguez de Tió

Awake, Borinqueños,[1]
    for they've given the signal!

Awake from your sleep
    for it's time to fight!

Come! The sound of cannon
    will be dear to us.

At that patriotic clamor
    doesn't your heart burn?

Look! The Cuban will soon be free,
    the machete will give him freedom.

The drum of war announces in its beating
    that the thicket is the place, the meeting place!

Most beautiful Borinquen, we have to follow Cuba;
    you have brave sons who want to fight!

Let us no more seem fearful!
Let us no more, timid, permit our enslavement!

We want to be free already
    and our machete is well sharpened!

Why should we, then, remain so asleep
    and deaf, asleep and deaf to that signal?

▼ **General Toral surrenders the city of Santiago to General Shaftner in 1898.**

There's no need to fear, Ricans, the sound of cannon,
for saving the homeland is the duty of the heart!

We want no more despots! Let the tyrant fall!
Women, likewise wild, will know how to fight!

We want freedom and our machete will give it to us!

Let's go, Puerto Ricans, let's go already,
for LIBERTY is waiting, ever so anxious! ❖

---

1 Borinqueños are Puerto Ricans. The word is adapted from
 Borinquén, the Native American name for Puerto Rico.

The Voice of the Hispano

Anonymous

Many are the opinions
Against the Hispanic people
And they accuse them of betraying
The American government.

Making an experiment,
They will be disillusioned,
Our brave native men
Do not refuse to be soldiers.

It matters not what is said
Or how our fame is insulted,
As they will fight with pleasure
For the American eagle.

They accuse our native people
Of being rabble,
But they have not proven to be so
On the battlefield.

Like good countrymen
And faithful Americans,
We will free them from that yoke
The humble Cubans. ❖

From To the Person Sitting in Darkness

by Mark Twain

There have been lies; yes, but they were told in a good cause. We have been treacherous; but that was only in order that real good might come out of apparent evil. True, we have crushed a deceived and confiding people; we have turned against the weak and the friendless who trusted us; we have stamped out a just and intelligent and well-ordered republic; we have stabbed an ally in the back and slapped the face of a guest; we have bought a Shadow from an enemy that hadn't it to sell; we have robbed a trusting friend of his land and liberty; . . . but each detail was for the best. ❖

"Harry Wilmans" From Spoon River Anthology

by Edgar Lee Masters

I was just turned twenty-one,
And Henry Phipps, the Sunday-school superintendent,
Made a speech in Bindle's Opera House.
"The honor of the flag must be upheld," he said,
"Whether it be assailed by a barbarous tribe of
    Tagalogs[1]
Or the greatest power in Europe."
And we cheered and cheered the speech and the flag
    he waved
As he spoke.
And I went to the war in spite of my father,
And followed the flag till I saw it raised
By our camp in a rice field near Manila,
And all of us cheered and cheered it.
But there were flies and poisonous things;
And there was the deadly water,
And the cruel heat,
And the sickening, putrid food. . . .
Following the flag,
Till I fell with a scream, shot through the guts.
Now there's a flag over me in Spoon River!
A flag! A flag! ❖

---

1 a people of central Luzon, Philippines

THINKING AND WRITING ABOUT LITERATURE

1. José Martí had just returned to Cuba from his exile in New York when he wrote this diary entry. Which phrases show that he missed Cuba in his absence?
2. Like Martí, Lola Rodríguez de Tió lived in New York and wrote in support of independence from Spain. Whose model does she urge Puerto Ricans to follow?
3. In the anonymous poem, what does the author believe Mexican American soldiers will prove?
4. Mark Twain's controversial essay and Edgar Lee Masters's poem use irony to express the authors' views of the war. Describe both authors' perspectives on the war.

Strategies for Success

RECOGNIZING STEREOTYPES

A stereotype is a generalization or oversimplification about a group or culture. Stereotypes deny individual differences by attributing the same characteristics to every member in a group: All poor people are lazy. All Irish drink too much. All African Americans are good athletes. All girls have difficulty with math and science. Most stereotypes are negative and often lead to discrimination and prejudice.

How to Recognize Stereotypes

1. **Examine the message.** Pay close attention to how a person or group is portrayed. Identify generalizations that lack supporting facts. Ask yourself: Are the same qualities being attributed to all individuals in a group?
2. **Note words that signal stereotyping.** Watch for clue words such as *all, always, never,* or *every* that allow no exceptions; their use may signal stereotyping.
3. **Detect bias or prejudice.** Note any bias or tone that indicates prejudice toward the subjects being described.
4. **Use your knowledge.** In evaluating general statements about people, apply what you have learned from your studies or through direct experience with individual classmates, your family members, or others.

Applying the Strategy

In the following passage, Samuel Bryan, an Anglo American sociologist, describes Mexican immigrants in the United States in 1912:

> 66 Socially and politically the presence of large numbers of Mexicans in this country gives rise to serious problems. . . . They . . . are slow to learn English, . . . move readily from place to place, and do not acquire or lease land to any extent. But their most unfavorable characteristic is their inclination to . . . live in a clannish manner. 99

Bryan's description is an example of the kind of stereotyping that breeds prejudice. First, he lumps together all Mexican immigrants—and, by implication, all Mexican Americans. He ignores the fact that in many areas of the United States stable, prosperous Mexican American communities existed long before Anglo settlement. Second, he blames immigrants for conditions that are a product of their immigrant status. Like members of other immigrant groups, Mexicans often found many jobs closed to them. One area in which they could find work was farm labor. Because farm labor is seasonal, Mexican farm workers were forced to move often in search of crops to harvest. This migratory existence, coupled with the low wages typical of such farm work, made it difficult for many Mexican immigrants to buy land.

Practicing the Strategy

Study the song poster below. Then, on a separate sheet of paper, answer the following questions.
1. What group is pictured in this song poster?
2. Why can this song poster be considered an example of stereotyping?

BUILDING YOUR PORTFOLIO

Outlined below are four projects. Independently or cooperatively, complete one and use the products to demonstrate your mastery of the historical concepts involved.

1 REFORM

In the late 19th century the transformation of the United States from a rural economy to an industrialized, urban society created numerous social problems. In response, the Progressive party sought reforms. Using the portfolio materials you designed in chapters 17 and 18, create a series of Progressive party campaign posters that outline the party's reform goals.

2 DEMOCRATIC RIGHTS

Historians note that progressivism was primarily a white, middle-class movement and thus did not address many of the concerns of working-class women. Using the portfolio materials you designed in chapters 17 and 18, conduct a debate between a white, middle-class progressive and a working-class woman on whether the progressive emphasis on women's suffrage best serves the needs of all women.

3 GLOBAL RELATIONS

The expansionist policies of the United States in the 19th century led to the establishment of U.S. overseas colonies, increased foreign investment, and conflicts with foreign powers. Using the portfolio materials you designed in chapters 19 and 20, create a world map showing areas of U.S. colonization, investment, and conflict through World War I.

4 WAR

The Spanish-American War and World War I brought the United States onto the world stage. Using the portfolio materials you designed in chapters 19 and 20, prepare a speech for delivery to Congress, outlining some of the costs and benefits of America's international role.

Videodisc Review

In assigned groups, develop an outline for a video collage of America in the years between 1897 and 1920. Choose images that best illustrate the major topics of the period. Write a script to accompany the images. Assign narrators to different parts of the script, and present your video collage to the class.

Further Reading

Ettinger, Albert M., and A. Churchill Ettinger. *A Doughboy with the Fighting 69th.* White Mane (1992). Reminiscence of World War I by a soldier of the 69th Rainbow Division.

Hall, Linda B., and Don M. Coerver. *Revolution on the Border: The United States and Mexico, 1910–1920.* University of New Mexico Press (1990). Examines the role that trade and investment played in U.S.–Mexico relations.

Liliuokalani. *Hawaii's Story by Hawaii's Queen.* Charles E. Tuttle (1991). Firsthand account of 19th-century Hawaii.

Schneider, Dorothy, and Carl J. Schneider. *Into the Breach.* Viking (1991). Examines the participation of American women in World War I.

Tuchman, Barbara W. *The Guns of August.* Bantam (1989). Analysis of the events of August 1914 that propelled Europe into World War I.

American
ALMANAC

◄ Dance marathon

❖ America's Music and Dance

1922 Cornet player Louis "Satchmo" Armstrong helps popularize jazz.

1923 Couple dances over 90 hours, setting dance marathon record.

1927 Duke Ellington's band opens in Harlem's Cotton Club.

1937 About 3,000 teenagers wait in line to see Benny Goodman.

1938 Cuban Desi Arnaz performs in Miami and introduces the conga dance to America.

1942 Glenn Miller's "Chattanooga Choo Choo" is first "gold record," selling over 1 million copies.

❖ At Your Leisure

1924 Americans own 2.5 million radios—up from 2,000 in 1920. By 1937 they spend 4.5 hours a day listening.

1920s Donald Duncan puts his yo-yo on the market.

1930 Lone Ranger's first ride is heard on radio. Hi-yo, Silver!

1935 Americans buy and sell real estate in the board game Monopoly.

1936 Knock-knock jokes are knocked around.

1937 At your local grocery you can find Eskimo Pies, Betty Crocker cake mixes, Wrigley's gum, Rice Krispies, 7-Up, Snickers, Twinkies, Skippy peanut butter, and Spam.

1940 Dick Tracy, Flash Gordon, Superman, and Batman are in the comics.

1943 Teenagers are hot on slumber parties, beach parties, roller rinks, soda shops, and argyle sweaters.

❖ Fashion Plate

1920s Gideon Sundback's 1913 invention—the zipper—catches on!

1934 Clark Gable reveals his bare chest in movie; sales of men's undershirts drop.

1942 Pants are popular with women; sales of slacks are five times greater than in 1941.

❖ The Cost of Living

1920s Eggs cost 68¢ a dozen; milk 17¢ a quart; bread 12¢ a loaf; oranges 63¢ a dozen; coffee 47¢ a pound.

1927 Lawyers make $5,205 per year; teachers make $1,277.

1930 Sneakers cost 39¢; men's suits cost $15.50.

▼ Glenn Miller

► Desi Arnaz

UNIT 7

Prosperity and Crisis

1920–1945

▼ George Washington Carver

▼ Mickey Mouse

© The Walt Disney Company

❖ The Silver Screen

1921 Heartthrob Rudolph Valentino skyrockets to fame.

1928 Mickey Mouse makes first appearance—Donald Duck follows in 1934 and Bugs Bunny in 1940.

1931 Gangster and horror films rival westerns in popularity.

1936 Shirley Temple is year's biggest star.

1939 *Stagecoach* makes John Wayne a movie hero.

1946 A record 90 million people go to the movies on average each week!

▲ Shirley Temple

❖ Sports Extra

1935 Babe Ruth retires with home run record—714!

1936 Jesse Owens wins 4 Olympic gold medals in track and field in Berlin.

1937 Joe Louis is world heavyweight champion.

❖ Firsts in America

1927 Charles Lindbergh makes first solo flight across the Atlantic; in 1932, Amelia Earhart is first woman to do same.

1929 First truly national Hispanic organization—League of United Latin American Citizens, or LULAC—is founded in Texas.

1939 George Washington Carver receives Theodore Roosevelt Medal for extensive research in crop rotation and agricultural chemistry.

1940 Drs. Glenn Seaborg and Edwin McMillan of the University of California, Berkeley, discover plutonium.

▶ Jesse Owens

A TURBULENT DECADE

FOCUS

UNDERSTANDING THE MAIN IDEA

The end of World War I ushered in a period of economic and social instability. Voters, eager to return to "normalcy," elected probusiness Republican presidents, and as the 1920s progressed, prosperity returned. Not all, however, shared the benefits of this economic renewal. Organized labor lost ground, and Native Americans, African Americans, and immigrants faced discrimination.

THEMES

- **DEMOCRATIC VALUES** How might a democratic government respond to a perceived threat of revolution?

- **CULTURAL DIVERSITY** In what ways might ethnic and racial groups respond to acts of discrimination?

- **ECONOMIC DEVELOPMENT** What actions should the federal government take to promote economic prosperity?

1919	1921	1924	1927	1928
Palmer raids begin.	Congress limits immigration.	Congress grants Native Americans citizenship.	Sacco and Vanzetti executed.	Herbert Hoover elected president.

During World War I the government tried to stifle dissent, women took jobs traditionally held by men, and African Americans moved to northern cities. These and other changes in society continued to affect Americans after the war.

Aftermath of Wall Street bombing, 1920

The end of World War I brought joyous celebration. As author Malcolm Cowley wrote, "We danced in the streets, embraced old women and pretty girls, swore blood brotherhood with soldiers in little bars, drank with our elbows locked in theirs, reeled through the streets with bottles of champagne." But this joy proved short-lived.

For many Americans life after the war did not appear promising. War veterans returned home to find few jobs available. Those who did find work soon discovered that soaring prices ate up their earnings. Economic and social problems increased. Strikes broke out across the nation, and violent race riots exploded in many American cities. Fueled by wartime fears, anti-immigrant feelings raised social tensions. Looking back on the first years after the war, author and journalist Ray Stannard Baker remarked, "I can recall no period in which life in America looked bleaker."

World War I veteran with his family, 1919

POSTWAR TROUBLES

FOCUS

- What were economic conditions like after the war?
- How did workers react to hard times?
- Why did many Americans fear that a Communist revolution was at hand?
- What did the Sacco and Vanzetti case reveal about America in the early 1920s?

1916 strike sympathizers

*T*he horrors of World War I shocked and disillusioned many Americans. The war, wrote novelist John Dos Passos, had been a "waste of time, waste of money, waste of lives, waste of youth." In response, many Americans tried to return to the way things had been before the war. But there was no going back. Instead of a return to the "old ways," the nation faced economic hardship and social strife.

DEMOBILIZATION

Under the best of conditions, **demobilization**, the shift from a wartime to a peacetime footing, is not an easy task for a nation. The process is made more difficult when the shift is rapid, as was the case after World War I. The war's end caught the

American government by surprise—literally. Trains carrying new recruits to boot camp were stopped en route. Within a year some four million soldiers returned to civilian life.

Women were urged to give up their jobs to make room for returning veterans. "The same patriotism which induced women to enter industry during the war should induce them to vacate their positions," declared the New York labor federation. Most of the women who did not respond to patriotic appeals were forced out of jobs traditionally held by men. As a result, the percentage of women in the work force in 1920 fell slightly below what it had been in 1910.

Adding to employment worries was a skyrocketing cost of living. With peace at hand, consumers went on a spending spree, making purchases they had put off during the war. As the demand for goods outpaced supply, prices soared until the cost of goods and services in 1920 was about twice that of 1914.

Soon, however, this trend reversed as the deep but brief recession of 1920–1921 struck and

▲ After World War I, millions of veterans scrambled for available jobs. American Legion employment offices, such as this one in Los Angeles, tried to find work for veterans.

prices fell. Demobilization was one of the factors behind the recession. During the war millions of Americans worked in war industries. But at war's end the government canceled more than $2 billion in war contracts. Factories responded by cutting back production and laying off workers. By 1921 some 5 million workers—more than 10 percent of the labor force—were unemployed, and the economy was shrinking.

A farm crisis contributed to the economic problems. Farmers had benefited from wartime markets in Europe. As European farm production revived, however, these markets dried up and farm prices fell. According to the Department of Agriculture, wheat, for example, dropped from $2.16 a bushel in 1919 to less than a dollar a bushel in 1922. Burdened with debt, hundreds of thousands of American farmers lost ownership of their land during the 1920s.

■■ After the war the cost of living soared, but prices soon fell as a recession took hold and unemployment increased.

LABOR STRIFE

In 1919, however, Americans were still struggling with rapidly rising prices for food, clothing, and shelter. Workers watched in dismay as runaway inflation ate up their wartime financial gains. Angry and frustrated, they asked for higher wages and shorter hours. But management ignored labor's pleas. In response, many workers walked off the job. In 1919 alone, unions called more than 3,600 strikes—involving more than four million workers.

◀ Strikes became commonplace in the years after World War I, as workers demanded better wages and conditions. Here, mounted policemen break up a group of Philadelphia strikers in 1919.

The Seattle general strike. The first strike of 1919 occurred in January, when some 35,000 shipyard workers in Seattle, Washington, walked off the job, demanding higher wages and a shorter workday. Within two weeks 110 local unions voted to join the shipyard workers in a general strike.

The general strike began on February 6 at 10 A.M. An eerie calm fell over the city as 60,000 workers left their jobs. "It was," declared one shipyard worker, "the most beautiful thing I ever seen!"

Alarmed at such a show of unity, Seattle newspapers blamed immigrants, calling the strikers "muddle-headed foreigners" and "riffraff from Europe intent on terrorizing the community." Mayor Ole Hanson denounced the strike as the work of Bolsheviks and called in troops to prevent unrest. But no violent incidents occurred. Instead, the well-disciplined strikers took steps to preserve order and to make sure that food and essential services were available to the community. Nevertheless, the strikers came under increased public pressure to go back to work. After five days they ended the strike without winning any of their demands.

▲ The *Seattle Union Record* published a special edition on February 6, 1919, announcing the beginning of the general strike.

Although the strike had been peaceful, anti-labor forces tried to convince the public that Seattle had been on the brink of revolution. Mayor Hanson told the national press:

66 Revolution . . . doesn't need violence. The general strike . . . is of itself the weapon of revolution, all the more dangerous because quiet. To succeed, it must suspend everything. . . . That is to say, it puts the government out of operation. And that is all there is to revolt—no matter how achieved. 99

Many people believed these charges. In the end the Seattle strike helped turn public opinion against organized labor.

◀ An important issue during the Boston police strike was whether public employees had the right to strike. When policemen refused to report to work, civilians took over traffic control and other public safety jobs.

The Boston police strike.

In September 1919 another strike, this time by the Boston police force, further inflamed antilabor sentiments. The Boston police had recently formed a union to seek better pay and working conditions. Although police in other cities had unionized without incident, Boston's police commissioner, Edwin Curtis, refused to recognize the union. Instead, he fired 19 officers for engaging in union activities. In response, some 75 percent of the police force went on strike.

Public order collapsed. Journalist William Allen White described the first night of the strike:

66 The devil was loose in Boston. . . . Little knots of boys and young men began wandering through the streets. . . . By midnight, the . . . crowds had formed one raging mob, a drunken, noisy, irresponsible mob. . . . Someone threw a loose paving stone through a store window about one o'clock. The tension snapped. . . . By two o'clock, looting had begun. 99

After two nights of violence, Governor Calvin Coolidge called in the state militia to restore order. The city's newspapers denounced the strikers as "agents of Lenin" and the strike as a "Bolshevist nightmare." The public also came out firmly against the strike. Recognizing that their cause was doomed, the police voted unanimously to

return to work. Curtis, however, refused to reinstate them. Instead, he hired a new force made up of unemployed veterans. Union sympathizers protested. Unmoved, Coolidge backed the commissioner, proclaiming that "there is no right to strike against the public safety by anybody, anywhere, any time." Coolidge's words made him an overnight hero in conservative circles.

The steel strike.

Two weeks after the trouble in Boston, the most important strike of 1919 began. In late September some 365,000 steelworkers—many of them immigrants—walked off the job, demanding recognition of their union and protesting low wages and long working hours. This massive walkout threatened to shut down the steel industry.

For years the major steel companies had fought efforts to unionize steelworkers. Now the companies did everything in their power to break the strike. In an effort to divide labor along ethnic lines, they portrayed foreign workers as radicals and called on "loyal" Americans to return to work.

▼ During the steel strike, Pittsburgh policemen arrested dozens of protesters. In a notice printed in several languages, the *Pittsburgh Chronicle Telegraph* declared the strike a failure and urged strikers to go back to work.

The steel bosses also brought in thousands of African Americans and Mexican Americans as replacement workers, and they hired armed thugs to attack the strikers. Strikers were jailed, beaten, or shot. Faced with such tactics, union leaders called off the strike on January 9, 1920. Labor had suffered a crushing defeat. It would be 15 years before unions again tried to organize workers in heavy industry.

■■ **Workers responded to hard times by striking for higher pay and better working conditions, but their efforts largely failed.**

THE RED SCARE

The 1919 strikes were prompted primarily by labor's desire for a fair deal. However, many Americans saw labor unrest as proof that Russia's Bolshevik Revolution of 1917, with its call for a worldwide revolution of workers, was spreading to American shores. This fear of communism reached fever pitch in 1919 and 1920, a period of anti-Communist hysteria known as the **Red Scare**.

Although Communists and Socialists comprised only a tiny fraction of the country's population, some Americans saw "Reds" everywhere. They even implied that Communists controlled many women's organizations. Peace groups, such as the Women's International League for Peace and Freedom, came under particularly strong attack. Antiradical fears reached such heights that several elected members of the New York State Assembly were expelled because they were members of the Socialist party. As journalist Walter Lippmann sarcastically noted:

66 The people are shivering in their boots over Bolshevism, they are far more afraid of Lenin [the Bolshevik leader] than they ever were of the Kaiser [Wilhelm II, who ruled Germany during World War I]. We seem to be the most frightened lot of victors that the world ever saw. 99

■■ **The Bolshevik Revolution and the strikes of 1919 led many Americans to fear that a Communist revolution was at hand.**

▲ This cartoon entitled *Put Them Out & Keep Them Out* appeared in the *Philadelphia Inquirer* in 1919 and expressed the fear that Bolshevism was creeping into American society.

The Palmer raids. In 1919 a rash of bomb scares seemed to justify Americans' fears. In April, alert postal clerks discovered 36 bombs in the mail addressed to such prominent citizens as John D. Rockefeller, Supreme Court justice Oliver Wendell Holmes, and Postmaster General Albert Burleson. Then less than a month later, several bombings occurred, one of which damaged the front of Attorney General A. Mitchell Palmer's house. The assailant, an Italian anarchist, died in the blast.

Newspapers began demanding harsh action against radicals. One paper even called for "a few free treatments in the electric chair." Attorney General Palmer, hoping to further his presidential ambitions, responded by launching an anti-Red crusade. He created a special government office to

◀ A. Mitchell Palmer

gather information on radical activities and put J. Edgar Hoover, the future head of the FBI, in charge.

Palmer's most dramatic action was a series of raids to capture alleged radicals. The **Palmer raids** began in November 1919 and peaked on January 2, 1920, when federal officials arrested thousands of suspected radicals in 33 cities nationwide. As journalist Frederick Lewis Allen wrote:

> 66 Over six thousand men were arrested in all, . . . often without any chance to learn what was the explicit charge against them. . . . In Detroit, over a hundred men were herded into a bull-pen measuring twenty-four by thirty feet and kept there for a week. . . . In Hartford, while the suspects were in jail the authorities took the further precaution of arresting . . . all visitors who came to see them. 99

Most of those arrested were poor immigrants newly arrived in the country. In most cases, there was no real evidence against them. In fact, although the government claimed that radicals were "armed to the teeth," only three pistols were seized in the raids.

BIO GRAPHY **Emma Goldman.** During the Red Scare hundreds of foreigners suspected of radical activities were deported to Russia. Among the deportees was Emma Goldman, a noted feminist, writer, and speaker.

Goldman was born in 1869 in Lithuania, a nation that was then part of Russia. Raised in a traditional Jewish family, Goldman was an independent, determined girl who often clashed with her authoritarian father. When she was 15, her father arranged for her to marry a man she did not love. But as she later wrote, "I would not listen to his schemes; I wanted to study, to know life, to travel. Besides, I never would marry for anything but love." So at age 16, Goldman immigrated to the United States.

The young Goldman settled in Rochester, New York, where she took a factory job. Gradually she grew disillusioned with the treatment of foreigners and workers in the United States. In 1889 at age 20, she moved to New York City and entered the world of radical politics. She soon became famous for her fiery speeches. After one such speech in 1893, she was convicted of inciting a riot and sent to prison for a year.

In 1906 Goldman started a radical monthly called *Mother Earth*. In its pages she presented articles on a wide range of topics, from birth control to modern art and literature. Above all, she used the magazine as a forum to defend freedom of speech.

In 1917 Goldman was arrested again, this time for opposing the draft. Two years later, at the height of the Red Scare, she was released from prison and deported to Russia. Like many other radicals, she was eager to see revolutionary Russia up close. "At last . . . ," she wrote, "I would behold . . . the land freed from political and economic masters." Instead of a free land, however, she found a country where freedom of expression was severely limited. Disenchanted, Goldman left Russia in 1921 and spent the rest of her life speaking and writing in Europe.

By mid-1920 public hysteria over radicalism was dying down. The fearful predictions of A. Mitchell Palmer and others that a Communist revolution was close at hand proved to be unfounded. Furthermore, many Americans had never supported the witch-hunting tactics employed by many of the anti-Communist crusaders.

SACCO AND VANZETTI

Although the Red Scare passed, hostility toward foreigners and radicals persisted. This hostility was evident during the 1921 trial of two Italian anarchists, Nicola Sacco and Bartolomeo Vanzetti. Accused of committing murder during a payroll robbery at a factory outside Boston, they were convicted and sentenced to death.

The verdict outraged defenders of civil liberties. They argued that the two men had been

Emma Goldman

◄ American poet Edna St. Vincent Millay was one of many protesters during the Sacco and Vanzetti trial.

Free Them and Save Massachusetts! American Honor Dies With Sacco and Vanzetti!

convicted not because of the evidence presented but because they were immigrants and radicals. Even the trial judge had shown bias by declaring that the men's anarchist beliefs were grounds for conviction.

The verdict and subsequent appeals drew worldwide attention. In Paris, New York City, and elsewhere, thousands of people marched in protest. Noted writers and artists rallied to the cause. Calling them "victims of race and national prejudice and class hatred," labor unions contributed to Sacco and Vanzetti's defense fund. The protesters called for a new trial, but all these pleas failed. On August 23, 1927, Sacco and Vanzetti were executed.

Many Americans believed that radicals like Sacco and Vanzetti deserved to be punished for their views, while others saw them as heroes and martyrs. Historians still debate whether Sacco and Vanzetti were guilty or innocent. All agree, however, that the case reflected the deep divisions tearing at American society in the postwar era.

■■ **The Sacco and Vanzetti case underscored a hostility in the United States toward foreigners and radicals following the war.**

▶ In the early 1930s immigrant artist Ben Shahn created a series of paintings about the events surrounding the Sacco and Vanzetti trial.

Ben Shahn, *Bartolomeo Vanzetti and Nicola Sacco* (1931–1932)

SECTION 1 REVIEW

IDENTIFY and explain the significance of the following: demobilization, Ole Hanson, Edwin Curtis, A. Mitchell Palmer, Palmer raids, Emma Goldman, Nicola Sacco, Bartolomeo Vanzetti.

LOCATE and explain the importance of the following: Seattle, Washington; Boston, Massachusetts.

1. **MAIN IDEA** How did the end of World War I affect the economy?

2. **MAIN IDEA** How did workers respond to deteriorating economic conditions after the war? Were their efforts successful?

3. **IDENTIFYING CAUSE AND EFFECT** What events led to the Red Scare? What were some of the Red Scare's consequences?

4. **WRITING TO INFORM** Imagine you are a reporter covering the Sacco and Vanzetti case. Write an article exploring the public debate surrounding the anarchists' arrest and conviction.

5. **ANALYZING** Why can it be said that international events had a strong impact on American society in the postwar years?

The coal industry fell on hard times as oil became a popular fuel source. The producers of cotton and wool textiles suffered because of competition from new synthetic fabrics, such as rayon. These and other "sick industries" signaled that not all was well in the economy.

◼◼ The Harding administration's probusiness policies helped fuel an economic boom, but not all sectors of the economy benefited.

The Harding scandals. Midway through Harding's term, most Americans seemed happy with the nation's course. Yet talk of corruption had begun to haunt the Harding administration. A group of Harding's friends—known as the Ohio Gang—had followed him to Washington and were using their connections with the president to enrich themselves at the public's expense.

The first scandal came to light in the spring of 1923, when it was discovered that Charles Forbes, director of the Veterans' Bureau and Harding's close friend, had received millions of dollars as the result of corrupt schemes. Harding was deeply worried over the Forbes scandal and other signs of wrongdoing in his administration. In June 1923 he confessed to journalist William Allen White, "I have no trouble with my enemies. I can take care of my enemies all right. [It's my] friends . . . that keep me walking the floor nights." Soon after talking to White, Harding set out on an extended tour of the West. In San Francisco on August 2, he died.

After Harding's death other scandals surfaced. In 1924 Attorney General Harry Daugherty,

◀ Teapot Dome and other scandals tarnished the reputation of the Harding administration.

Harding's right-hand man, was forced to resign after it was discovered he had been taking bribes. Worse still was the **Teapot Dome scandal**, which took its name from a government oil reserve in Teapot Dome, Wyoming. According to a Senate investigation, Secretary of the Interior Albert Fall had received loans, cash, and cattle for leasing the oil reserve—along with another reserve in California—to private oil companies. Fall was convicted of accepting bribes and jailed in 1926—the first cabinet member to be imprisoned for crimes committed while in office.

COOLIDGE TAKES CHARGE

After Harding's death Vice President Calvin Coolidge succeeded to the presidency. Immediately he began working to limit the damage from the Harding scandals and to restore the reputation of the presidency.

Coolidge easily won the Republican presidential nomination in 1924. On the 103rd ballot the Democrats, divided between rural and urban wings and split over issues such as prohibition, chose John W. Davis, a corporate lawyer. Both parties faced strong opposition from the Progressive party's nominee, Robert La Follette. Backed by angry farmers and workers, the Progressive platform denounced federal policies favoring business and called for more aid to working people.

Despite these rumblings of discontent, Coolidge won by a landslide, receiving 15.7 million votes to Davis's 8.4 million. La Follette received about 4.8 million votes. Although the Progressive party faded from the scene when La Follette died soon after the election, its strong showing made it clear that not all Americans agreed with the Republicans' emphasis on big business.

In some ways Calvin Coolidge seemed an unlikely man to win the support of so many Americans. Stern

◀ Calvin Coolidge

CALVIN COOLIDGE
1872–1933

UNITED STATES POSTAGE

$5 CALVIN COOLIDGE 1923-1929 $5

Vermont-born Calvin Coolidge had a stern face and quiet, unemotional manner that made him seem the very picture of cold New England granite. According to his wife Grace, once at a Washington dinner party another guest told Coolidge she had bet that she could make him say at least three words to her. Tight-lipped as usual, Coolidge replied, "You lose."

"Silent Cal" could be as frugal—or even stingy—as he was quiet. Sometimes rather than buying presents, he sent out the boxes of cigars that he himself had received as gifts. Coolidge even refused to share the contents of the stream in front of his vacation home in South Dakota. One day he observed a stranger catching fish from the stream. Coolidge sent a Secret Service agent after the man to retrieve the fish, stating bluntly, "They are my fish."

and unemotional, he was known as Silent Cal. His often sour expression inspired one wit's comment that Coolidge looked as if he had been weaned on a pickle. Yet because Coolidge's no-nonsense manner and frugal habits recalled a simpler era, many Americans found him reassuring.

A staunch conservative, Coolidge was even more probusiness than Harding. "The business of America is business," he once declared. "The man who builds a factory builds a temple. The man who works there worships there." Coolidge favored legislation to aid business but generally opposed laws to help farmers or workers, arguing that such legislation stifled private initiative and harmed the economy.

Coolidge also took a tightfisted approach to government spending. In the name of economy, he vetoed a bonus bill designed to aid World War I veterans (Congress passed the bill over his veto). He also vetoed a bill designed to boost farm prices by authorizing the government to buy surplus crops and sell them abroad.

Despite these vetoes the president remained popular and almost certainly could have won reelection in 1928. Instead, to almost everyone's surprise, he announced he would not run.

■■ Coolidge was a conservative, probusiness president whose nononsense style won the support of most Americans.

THE ELECTION OF 1928

In 1928 the Republicans nominated Secretary of Commerce Herbert Hoover for president. Hoover had a reputation for skill and efficiency. His strongest asset, though, was the nation's apparent prosperity after eight years of Republican rule. In a campaign speech he declared:

HERBERT C. HOOVER FOR PRESIDENT

66 The poorhouse is vanishing from among us. We have not yet reached the goal, but, given a chance to go forward with the policies of the last eight years, we shall soon . . . be in sight of the day when poverty will be banished from this nation. 99

▲ By the 1928 election Herbert Hoover was known for his integrity and humanitarian ideals.

After a bitter fight the Democrats nominated Governor Alfred E. Smith of New York, a moderate progressive. The party's choice signaled a shift in Democratic strategy—a response, in part, to the Progressive party's strength in the 1924 election. Smith's core support came from urban immigrant voters. By nominating Smith, the Democrats hoped to be seen as "the party of progress and liberal thought," as Franklin Roosevelt put it. Yet Smith had several political liabilities. He was Roman Catholic, he opposed prohibition, and he had ties to New York City's Tammany Hall. All these points stirred strong opposition to Smith's candidacy, especially in the South.

Riding on Smith's handicaps and the economy's strength, Hoover won 58 percent of the popular vote. Smith lost his own state as well as several southern states that went Republican for the first time since Reconstruction. However, Smith did well in the nation's largest cities. His appeal to these voters offered the Democrats hope for the future.

■■ **Herbert Hoover sailed to victory in 1928 on the strength of the economy and his opponent's political liabilities.**

THE EFFECTS OF REPUBLICAN POLICIES

During the 1920s the Republican administrations' probusiness policies helped promote economic growth. Yet these policies also had negative effects on the environment and on many working people.

Business growth and prosperity. One reason for the economic boom that began in 1923 was the availability of surplus capital, in part due to tax cuts. This capital allowed old industries to grow rapidly and new ones to enter the ranks of the corporate giants. The 1920s also saw more than 1,000 **mergers**—the combining of two or more companies. Business favored mergers because they brought greater efficiency and higher profits. By 1930, some 200 corporations owned nearly half the nation's corporate wealth. The government, with its favorable attitude toward business, encouraged this process of consolidation and made little effort to enforce antitrust laws.

▲ **As early as 1917, the corner of 42nd St. and Madison Ave. in New York City was often congested with heavy auto traffic.**

This rapid industrial growth was not without its drawbacks, however. Chemical wastes poured into the nation's rivers and lakes. Cities witnessed increased traffic congestion and air pollution. Yet few Americans saw these consequences of industrial development as problems.

Labor and farming. Workers did not share significantly in business's good fortune during the 1920s. From 1923 to 1929, business profits increased some 60 percent. Over the same period, workers' incomes grew by only about 10 percent. Many workers in "sick industries" even faced pay cuts and unemployment. Farmers were also hit hard, as the postwar slump in farm prices continued into the 1920s.

To help farmers, Congress passed the **Fordney-McCumber Tariff Act** of 1922. The act levied high duties on imported farm products in an effort to boost domestic crop prices. But it brought little relief. Farmers still faced shrinking markets, low prices, high interest rates, and crushing debts.

Organized labor also suffered during the 1920s as the government and courts sought to roll back the gains of the Progressive Era. Federal courts, for example, upheld "yellow-dog contracts," which required employees to promise not to join a union. At the same time, business leaders promoted a policy known as the **American Plan**. The plan called for open shops—factories in which workers could choose not to join unions and management did not have to negotiate with union leaders. As a result, union membership shrank from a high of more than 5 million in 1920 to some 3.6 million in 1923. Without the backing of strong unions, many people continued to work long hours for low wages under often unsafe conditions.

■■ **Republican policies contributed to business growth and general prosperity, but many workers and farmers suffered.**

THE EQUAL RIGHTS AMENDMENT

Regulating hours, working conditions, and wages for women and children had been an important part of the progressive agenda. However, in the 1920s women debated the desirability of such protective legislation. This debate came about because of the National Woman's party's efforts on behalf of the

Equal Rights Amendment, introduced into Congress in 1923. Had it passed, the amendment would have given men and women "equal rights throughout the United States." One of the amendment's effects would have been to invalidate protective legislation.

The amendment drew most of its support from middle-class and professional women. They argued that protective legislation discouraged employers from hiring women. Furthermore, they argued, limitations on working hours kept women out of many highly paid jobs.

Opponents of the amendment supported protective legislation as necessary to protect women—few of whom belonged to unions—and their families. Mary Anderson, director of the U.S. Women's Bureau, asserted:

> 66 Women who are wage earners, with one job in the factory and another in the home, have little time and energy left to carry on the fight to better their economic status. They need the help of . . . labor laws. 99

Pauline Newman of the Women's Trade Union League observed that before protective legislation women "were 'free' and 'equal' to work long hours for starvation wages, or free to leave the job and starve!"

Protective legislation did hamper women working in male-dominated occupations. However, few working-class women were employed in such occupations. Thus, they withheld their support for the amendment, which they viewed as benefiting only middle-class and upper-class women who had the training to enter the professions or skilled trades.

The debate over these issues created deep divisions in the women's movement. It would continue to divide women's organizations until the 1960s.

■■ **The debate over the Equal Rights Amendment divided women's groups.**

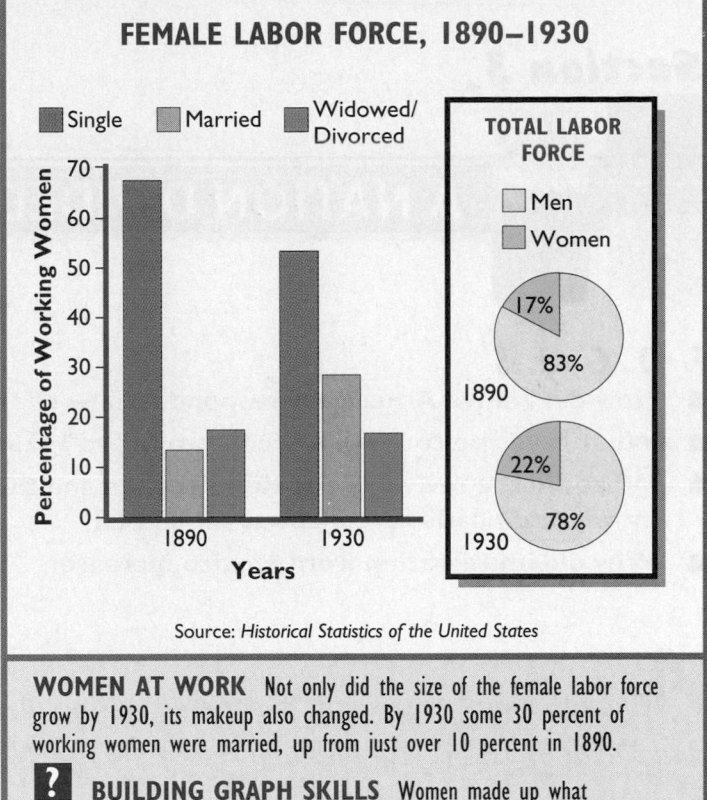

FEMALE LABOR FORCE, 1890–1930

■ Single   ■ Married   ■ Widowed/Divorced

TOTAL LABOR FORCE

□ Men   ■ Women

1890: 17% / 83%
1930: 22% / 78%

Source: *Historical Statistics of the United States*

WOMEN AT WORK Not only did the size of the female labor force grow by 1930, its makeup also changed. By 1930 some 30 percent of working women were married, up from just over 10 percent in 1890.

❓ **BUILDING GRAPH SKILLS** Women made up what percentage of the total labor force in 1890? in 1930?

 S E C T I O N 2 R E V I E W

IDENTIFY and explain the significance of the following: Warren G. Harding, Andrew W. Mellon, Herbert Hoover, Charles Dawes, Teapot Dome scandal, Albert Fall, Calvin Coolidge, Alfred E. Smith, mergers, Fordney-McCumber Tariff Act, American Plan.

1. **MAIN IDEA** Why did American voters elect a Republican president in 1920?

2. **MAIN IDEA** What qualities did President Coolidge possess that won the support of most Americans in the 1920s?

3. **ASSESSING CONSEQUENCES** What effect did the probusiness policies of Harding and Coolidge have on the economy?

4. **WRITING TO PERSUADE** Imagine you are a Republican campaigning for Herbert Hoover in 1928. Write a handbill you would distribute to urge other voters to support your candidate.

5. **ANALYZING** Why were women's groups divided over support of the Equal Rights Amendment?

A NATION DIVIDED

FOCUS

■ How did Native Americans respond to new efforts to seize tribal land?

■ What gave rise to black nationalism in the 1920s?

■ What did the revival of the Ku Klux Klan and the passage of new immigration laws reveal about the 1920s?

■ Why did immigration from Mexico increase?

Although many Americans prospered during the 1920s, deep social and racial divisions still plagued American life. Native Americans, African Americans, and Mexican immigrants all struggled for a place in American society. As African Americans continued to migrate to northern cities, racial tensions increased. The Ku Klux Klan encouraged bigotry not only against African Americans but also against foreigners. Responding to the national mood, Congress passed laws limiting immigration.

Ku Klux Klansman

NATIVE AMERICAN LIFE

For Native Americans the 1920s brought some recognition of the difficulties they faced. The Dawes Act, which attempted to "Americanize"

▲ Native Americans carry water from a government well in Arizona.

Indians by dividing tribal land into individual plots (see Chapter 14) had clearly failed. The act's allotment policies—as the Board of Indian Commissioners acknowledged—had often been "a short cut to the separation of . . . Indians from their land and cash."

In the 1920s Native Americans successfully organized to fight new efforts to take tribal land. Native American leaders stopped the Harding administration's attempt to buy back all tribal land. Then in 1922 the different Pueblo tribes of the Southwest organized against the Bursum Bill, which was designed to legalize non–Native American claims to Pueblo land. Furthermore, the bill would limit the power of tribal governments. The Pueblos appealed to all Americans:

66 This bill will destroy our common life and will rob us of everything which we hold dear—our lands, our customs, our traditions. Are the American people willing to see this happen? 99

Many Americans were not. The Pueblos won the support of the General Federation of Women's Clubs and of anthropologists, as well as the support of many other influential men and women. As a result, the *New York Times* could write in January 1923 that the bill was "happily, dead."

In 1924 Congress granted citizenship to all Native Americans, partly in recognition of those who had fought in World War I. But citizenship did not soften the harsh effects of poverty that many Native Americans continued to experience.

▪▪ **Native Americans organized to fight efforts to take their lands.**

AFRICAN AMERICANS MOVE NORTH

During the 1920s some 800,000 African Americans joined the hundreds of thousands who had moved to the North during World War I. By 1930 the North's African American population had reached almost 2.5 million, more than double its size in 1910. Large African American communities sprang up in Chicago, Detroit, New York City, and other

▲ A neighborhood strewn with rubble reveals the tragic aftermath of the Chicago race riots in 1919.

northern cities. Harlem, a section of New York City with a large African American population, was called "the capital of Black America."

The North, however, was not free of bigotry. African Americans who had risked their lives in Europe "to make the world safe for democracy" confronted lynch mobs. Others faced discrimination, and as demands for labor eased, African Americans were the first to lose their jobs.

At times, racial tensions erupted violently. One of the worst outbreaks occurred in Chicago in July 1919. The trouble began when a white man

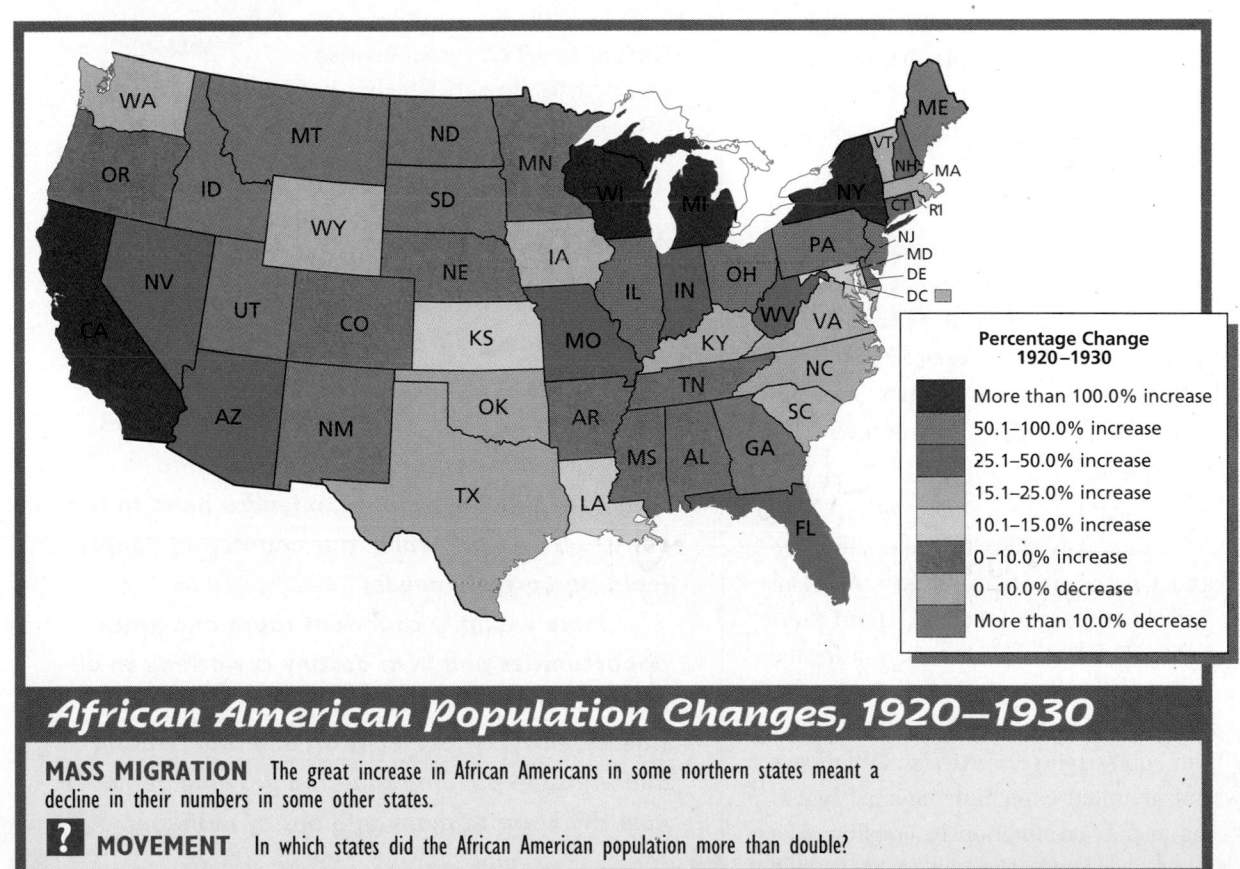

African American Population Changes, 1920–1930

Percentage Change 1920–1930

- More than 100.0% increase
- 50.1–100.0% increase
- 25.1–50.0% increase
- 15.1–25.0% increase
- 10.1–15.0% increase
- 0–10.0% increase
- 0 10.0% decrease
- More than 10.0% decrease

MASS MIGRATION The great increase in African Americans in some northern states meant a decline in their numbers in some other states.

? MOVEMENT In which states did the African American population more than double?

▲ The NAACP began as an interracial coalition fighting for African Americans' rights. James Weldon Johnson, seated behind the desk, served as executive secretary of the NAACP from 1920 to 1930. Johnson was also a noted author and songwriter.

threw rocks at an African American teenager swimming in Lake Michigan. The boy drowned. The fight that broke out between whites and blacks on shore spread to the rest of the city. The rioting continued for more than a week. White gangs fueled much of the violence as they prowled the slums, attacking African Americans and destroying property. By the time order was restored, 38 people had been killed and 537 injured.

By late 1919, some 25 race riots had erupted around the country. In June 1921, at least 30 people died during a race riot in Tulsa, Oklahoma. One resident described attacks on the black section of town:

> 66 People were seen to flee from their burning homes, some with babes in their arms and leading crying and excited children. . . . [A] machine gun . . . was raining bullets down on our section. 99

Faced with continued violence and discrimination, many African Americans organized to defend their rights. The National Association for the Advancement of Colored People (NAACP) stepped up its legal battle to win equal rights for African Americans and mounted campaigns against lynching and discrimination in housing. The unions' continued failure to help black workers led labor activist A. Philip Randolph to found the Brotherhood of Sleeping Car Porters in 1925. It became a powerful voice for black workers.

BLACK NATIONALISM

Frustrated by the slow pace of change, some African Americans lost hope of ever achieving equality in the United States. What African Americans needed, they said, was a nation of their own. Foremost among these black nationalists was Marcus Garvey.

BIOGRAPHY Garvey, a native of Jamaica, founded the Universal Negro Improvement Association (UNIA) in 1914. UNIA had two main goals: to foster African Americans' economic independence by establishing black-owned businesses and to create an independent

THROUGH OTHERS' EYES

THE BACK–TO–AFRICA MOVEMENT

Marcus Garvey's Back-to-Africa movement drew many followers both in America and in Africa. In 1922 a representative of the king of Abyssinia (Ethiopia) read the following message to a Universal Negro Improvement Association (UNIA) convention:

> 66 *Assure them [Garvey's followers] of the cordiality with which I invite them back to the home land, particularly those qualified to help solve our big problems and to develop our vast resources. Teachers, artisans, mechanics, writers, musicians, professional men and women—all who are able to lend a hand in the constructive work which our country so deeply feels, and greatly needs.*
>
> *Here we have abundant room and great opportunities and here destiny is working to elevate and enthrone a race which has suffered slavery, poverty, persecution and martyrdom, but whose expanding soul and growing genius is now the hope of many millions of mankind.* 99

black homeland in Africa. "We shall now organize," Garvey told the delegates to UNIA's first international convention, "to plant the banner of freedom on the great continent of Africa."

A charismatic speaker, Garvey urged African Americans to draw on their African heritage:

> 66 When Europe was inhabited by . . . a race of savages, . . . Africa was peopled with a race of cultured black men, who were masters in art, science and literature. . . . Why, then, should we lose hope? Black men, you were once great; you shall be great again. Lose not courage, lose not faith, go forward. 99

To foster economic independence, Garvey founded the Black Star Steamship Company in 1919. He urged African Americans to invest in his company so that they "may exert the same influence on the world as the white man does today." Garvey promised investors huge returns, but the company never turned a profit. In 1925 Garvey was jailed for mail fraud in connection with his fund-raising activities. President Coolidge pardoned him in 1927 but ordered him deported. He died in 1940, still clinging to his dream.

Garvey's movement declined after he was jailed. Nevertheless, as one newspaper said in 1927, "He made black people proud. . . . He taught them that black is beautiful." Although other African American leaders, such as W.E.B. Du Bois, shared Garvey's belief in racial pride and solidarity, they opposed his Back-to-Africa movement. They insisted that African Americans should fight for justice and equality in American society.

■■ **Continued discrimination and a growing sense of black pride led to the rise of black nationalism.**

*T*HE RETURN OF THE KU KLUX KLAN

To some degree, racism and discrimination during the 1920s reflected a broader repressive mood in American society. More and more, native-born Protestant Americans distrusted people who seemed different. One sign of this growing intolerance was the resurgence of the Ku Klux Klan.

Like the Klan of post–Civil War days, the new Klan, established in 1915 at Stone Mountain, Georgia, used kidnappings, beatings, and lynchings to terrorize African Americans in the South. However, the Klan also grew rapidly outside the South. In northern and midwestern towns and cities, the Klan targeted not only blacks but also radicals, immigrants, Catholics, and Jews, as well as such threats to traditional moral values as divorce.

The Klan grew slowly at first, but as the Red Scare took hold, membership soared. Reaching its peak in the mid-1920s, the Klan had perhaps as many as five million members. At mass rallies white-robed Klan members burned crosses and spoke out against people and ideas they considered "undesirable." Klan views also influenced politics, helping candidates win elections in such states as Louisiana, Oklahoma, Ohio, Texas—even Oregon. The Klan was particularly powerful in Indiana.

After 1925, however, the Klan declined, and by 1930 its membership had dropped to some 9,000. Rising prosperity and the end of the Red Scare diminished the Klan's appeal, but other factors also contributed. One was the conviction of a Klan leader—Grand Dragon David Stephenson—for second-degree murder. Another was the discovery that Klan promoters were getting rich from membership fees and the sale of regalia. Nevertheless, the Klan did not die out; it continues to spread its message of white supremacy.

▲ **Ku Klux Klan members taught racist attitudes to their children. Here, a baby is being enrolled into the Klan on Independence Day, 1927.**

IMMIGRATION RESTRICTIONS

During the 1920s the Klan also played on anti-immigrant feelings. Many Americans feared that the country was being overrun by immigrants—in 1920 nearly a quarter of the population was foreign-born or nonwhite. Furthermore, the number of immigrants, which had declined during the war, was once again rising, increasing from some 140,000 in 1919 to some 805,000 in 1921. This dramatic growth, coupled with the widespread belief that immigrants held radical views and took jobs from native-born Americans, led to demands for limits on immigration.

In 1921 Congress passed a law limiting the number of immigrants from each country allowed into the United States. The quota was set at 3 percent of each nationality already in the country in 1910, except for Asians, who were excluded

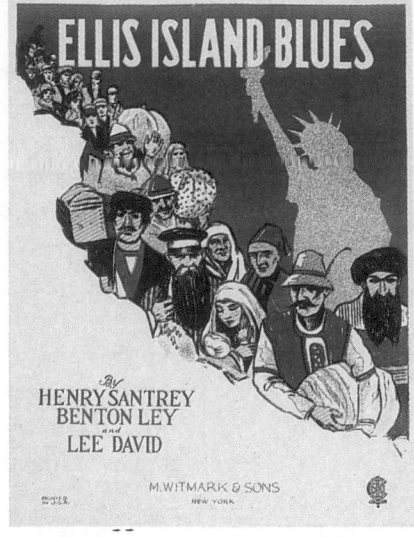

▲ "Ellis Island Blues" was one of many songs written in the 1920s about the flood of immigrants to the United States after World War I.

altogether. (Immigration from nations in the Western Hemisphere was not limited.) The **Immigration Act of 1924** reduced the quota to 2 percent of the 1890 figures for each national group. This change worked against southern and eastern Europeans because in 1890 most Americans traced their origins to England, Ireland, or northern Europe. While the 1924 law did not exclude Asians, it set the annual quota at only 100 Chinese and 100 Japanese immigrants. In 1925 the restrictions reduced the total number of new immigrants from Europe, Africa, Asia, and Australia to some 153,000.

■■ **The revival of the Ku Klux Klan and new limits on immigration revealed continued hostility toward racial and ethnic groups.**

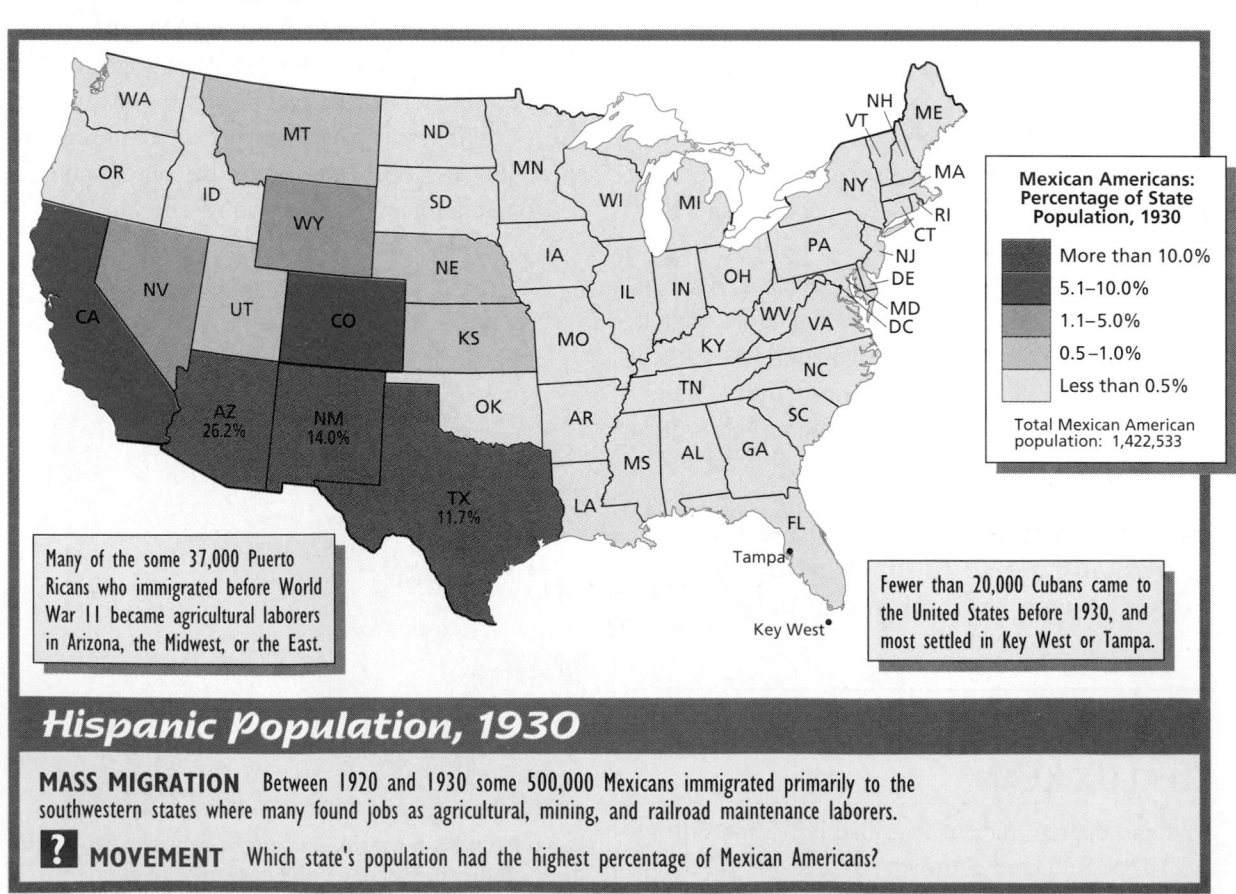

Mexican Americans: Percentage of State Population, 1930
- More than 10.0%
- 5.1–10.0%
- 1.1–5.0%
- 0.5–1.0%
- Less than 0.5%

Total Mexican American population: 1,422,533

AZ 26.2%
NM 14.0%
TX 11.7%

Many of the some 37,000 Puerto Ricans who immigrated before World War II became agricultural laborers in Arizona, the Midwest, or the East.

Fewer than 20,000 Cubans came to the United States before 1930, and most settled in Key West or Tampa.

Hispanic Population, 1930

MASS MIGRATION Between 1920 and 1930 some 500,000 Mexicans immigrated primarily to the southwestern states where many found jobs as agricultural, mining, and railroad maintenance laborers.

❓ **MOVEMENT** Which state's population had the highest percentage of Mexican Americans?

MEXICAN AMERICAN MIGRATION

In the Southwest, employers, particularly in agriculture, railroad construction, and mining, encouraged Mexican immigration, which was not affected by the restrictive legislation of the 1920s. Few people were arriving from Europe and Asia, and southwestern employers were eager to keep a steady flow of workers to fill low-wage jobs. As a result, during the 1920s some 500,000 immigrants arrived from Mexico, where wages were far lower.

Those who took agricultural jobs not only had to accept low pay but many also had to live in ramshackle labor camps. One observer noted:

 Shelters were made of almost every conceivable thing—burlap, canvas, palm branches. . . . We found one woman carrying water in large milk pails from the irrigation ditch. . . . This is evidently all the water which they have in camp. 99

In the 1920s many Mexican immigrants also moved into urban areas. Some were drawn to well-paying factory jobs in cities such as Chicago and Detroit and established new centers of Mexican population in the Midwest. Most, however, migrated to cities in the Southwest—particularly Los Angeles, El Paso, and San Antonio (see map on page 638). Usually the men came alone, and once established, they sent for their wives and children. Many brought other relatives as well, reestablishing extended family networks. These networks helped new arrivals find jobs and housing.

Because of economic hardship, many families allowed their young, unmarried daughters to work outside the home. Many found employment in bakeries, hotels, and laundries, while others worked as maids. Their newfound independence, as one Mexican immigrant woman sadly noted, brought young women "into conflict with their parents. They learn . . . about the outside world, learn how to speak English, and then they become ashamed of their parents who brought them up here." Despite such conflicts, these new immigrants contributed to the mosaic of cultures that helps define American life.

■■ **The promise of jobs drew Mexican immigrants, who were not subject to restrictive quotas, to cities in the Southwest and Midwest.**

▲ Mexican American Victor Villaseñor wrote *Rain of Gold,* a book about his family's experiences as immigrants to California in the 1920s. Shown here is the 1929 wedding of his parents, Juan Salvador and Lupe.

■■ SECTION 3 REVIEW

IDENTIFY and explain the significance of the following: A. Philip Randolph, Marcus Garvey, Immigration Act of 1924.

1. **MAIN IDEA** In what way did Native Americans fight government attempts to take tribal land?

2. **MAIN IDEA** What events in the 1920s revealed continued hostility toward racial and ethnic groups?

3. **GAINING A MULTICULTURAL PERSPECTIVE** What factors contributed to the rise of black nationalism?

4. **WRITING TO EXPLAIN** Imagine you are a Mexican immigrant in the 1920s. Write a diary entry that explains why you moved to the Southwest or to the Midwest.

5. **EVALUATING** What effect did the migration of African Americans have on the North?

Palmer raids begin. Marcus Garvey founds Black Star Steamship Company.

Warren G. Harding elected president.

Race riot breaks out in Tulsa, Oklahoma. Congress limits immigration.

Pueblos organize against Bursum Bill.

1919   1921

WRITING A SUMMARY

Using the essential points of the chapter as a guide, write a summary of the chapter.

REVIEWING CHRONOLOGY

Number your paper 1 to 5. Study the time line above, and list the following events in the order in which they happened by writing the first next to 1, the second next to 2, and so on. Then complete the activity below.

1. Palmer raids begin.
2. Calvin Coolidge elected president.
3. Congress limits immigration.
4. Sacco and Vanzetti executed.
5. Equal Rights Amendment introduced into Congress.

Hypothesizing How might political events have been different during the 1920s if President Harding had not died?

IDENTIFYING PEOPLE AND IDEAS

Explain the historical significance of each of the following people or terms.

1. demobilization
2. Edwin Curtis
3. Red Scare
4. Emma Goldman
5. Andrew W. Mellon
6. Teapot Dome scandal
7. mergers
8. American Plan
9. Marcus Garvey
10. Immigration Act of 1924

UNDERSTANDING MAIN IDEAS

1. Why did the cost of living soar after the war? How did demobilization lead to recession and an increase in unemployment?
2. What were the results of the 1919 strikes in Seattle and Boston?
3. How were Warren G. Harding and Calvin Coolidge alike in their approaches to government?
4. What were the "sick industries" during the 1920s? Why did they fail to benefit from the economic boom?
5. What events and attitudes led to increased social tensions during the 1920s?

REVIEWING THEMES

1. **Democratic Values** What steps did the federal government take during the 1920s to reduce the perceived threat of revolution?
2. **Cultural Diversity** In what ways did Native Americans, African Americans, and Mexican Americans respond to discrimination?
3. **Economic Development** How did Republican probusiness policies attempt to stimulate the economy?

THINKING CRITICALLY

1. **Synthesizing** Why did many Americans vote Republican in the 1920, 1924, and 1928 presidential elections?
2. **Analyzing** Why did many farmers fail to benefit from the economic boom of the 1920s?
3. **Evaluating** Do you think women's groups that opposed the Equal Rights Amendment were justified? Why or why not?

STRATEGY FOR SUCCESS

Review the Strategies for Success on Recognizing Stereotypes on page 616. Then read the following passage from a 1926 article by Hiram Wesley Evans, the Imperial Wizard of the Ku Klux Klan. What group is the subject of this passage? Why can Evans's characterization be considered an example of stereotyping?

> 66 The alien . . . is unalterably fixed in his instincts, character, thought, and interests by centuries of racial selection and development. . . . He thinks first for his own people, works only with and for them, . . . considers himself always one of them, and never an American. 99

WRITING ABOUT HISTORY

Writing to Evaluate Write an essay evaluating the impact of the Sacco and Vanzetti case on public opinion.

Harding dies.
Equal Rights
Amendment
introduced
into Congress.

Congress grants Native
Americans citizenship.
Immigration Act of
1924 passed. Calvin
Coolidge elected
president.

A. Philip Randolph
founds Brother-
hood of Sleeping
Car Porters.

Albert Fall
goes to prison.

Sacco and
Vanzetti
executed.

Herbert Hoover
elected president.

1923   **1925**   **1927**   **1929**

USING PRIMARY SOURCES

In 1925 more than 11,000 textile workers went on strike in Passaic, New Jersey, to demand better working conditions and higher wages. Read the following excerpt from "The War in Passaic" written by labor activist Mary Heaton Vorse. Then write a paragraph summarizing the author's views of the strike.

66 *Half the picket line is composed of young people. Mothers with children by the hand, older women and high-school boys and girls stream along, their heads thrown back, singing. . . . Passaic sprawling in its winter slush and snow watches its mill-workers make a full-hearted protest against the intolerable conditions in the mills, against the inhuman and unbearable wage cut. . . .*

The mayor of Passaic menaced the strikers with a force of three hundred mounted policemen. . . . They charged a crowd of 3,000 strikers, bludgeoned many men, women, and children, and smashed with deliberate intent the persons and cameras of the news photographers. . . . The strikers, armed with gas masks, helmets, and their unbending courage, defied the police successfully—and paraded in peace. . . .

The present Passaic strike is only a phase of the long fight of the textile workers for organization and a living wage. . . . When there is such want and suffering, when conditions of toil are so degrading, when the places that human beings live in are so indecent, it becomes the concern of the public at large to make its power felt and to see that this state of things is altered. **99**

LINKING HISTORY AND GEOGRAPHY

Study the African American and Hispanic population maps on pages 635 and 638. Write a brief summary of the population trends shown on each map. Then prepare a list of possible factors that might help explain the population distributions.

Passaic strikers

BUILDING YOUR PORTFOLIO

Complete the following projects independently or cooperatively.

1. THE ECONOMY Imagine you are a World War I veteran in 1919. Write a letter to your senator, explaining why you feel the federal government should help you secure a job. Your letter might mention your concerns about low wages, the high cost of living, and the few employment opportunities available in the postwar economy.

2. CULTURE AND SOCIETY Imagine you are an immigrant artist on the staff of Emma Goldman's radical magazine *Mother Earth* in the late 1920s. Create a cover illustration for an upcoming issue that expresses your views about one of the following: the Red Scare, the Sacco and Vanzetti case, labor strikes, or the Equal Rights Amendment.

LAND USE

FOR thousands of years Americans have used the land to grow crops. Many Native American groups cultivated crops on small plots of land long before the arrival of Europeans. In the early days of the republic, most farmers continued to grow food crops on small farms, although many large plantations in the South used the land to grow great quantities of tobacco and cotton. By the late 19th century, improved farm machinery and pesticides allowed farmers to grow larger quantities of food on smaller plots of land. Despite changes in farming techniques, some aspects of American farming have remained the same. For instance, corn is still the primary food crop grown in America—just as it was in the earliest civilizations.

Land Use Before 1492

Game
Fish
Wild plants
Cultivated plants
Balance of game and wild plants
Maize Primary crop

0 200 400 Miles
0 200 400 Kilometers
Albers Equal-Area Projection

Early Native American civilizations grew a variety of crops. Although maize was the most common domesticated crop, others included beans, squash, pumpkins, tomatoes, potatoes, sweet potatoes, peanuts, cashews, pineapples, papayas, avocados, sunflowers, chili peppers, cacao, vanilla, tobacco, indigo, and cotton.

The multipurpose, high-protein soybean has become the agricultural wonder of the 20th century. By 1991 it was the second most-popular crop in the United States. Soybeans are used in the processing of cattle feed, fertilizer, insect sprays, and paint, as well as in food products such as soy sauce, soy milk, baby food, cereals, processed meats, and tofu.

AGRICULTURAL PRODUCTION, 1910–1991

	1910	1991
CORN (in bushels)	2.85 billion	7.75 billion
WHEAT (in bushels)	625 million	1.98 billion
COTTON (in bales)	11.61 million	17.5 million
TOBACCO (in pounds)	1.05 billion	1.66 billion
SOYBEANS (in bushels)	< 50,000	1.99 billion

Sources: Historical Statistics of the United States, Statistical Abstract of the United States.

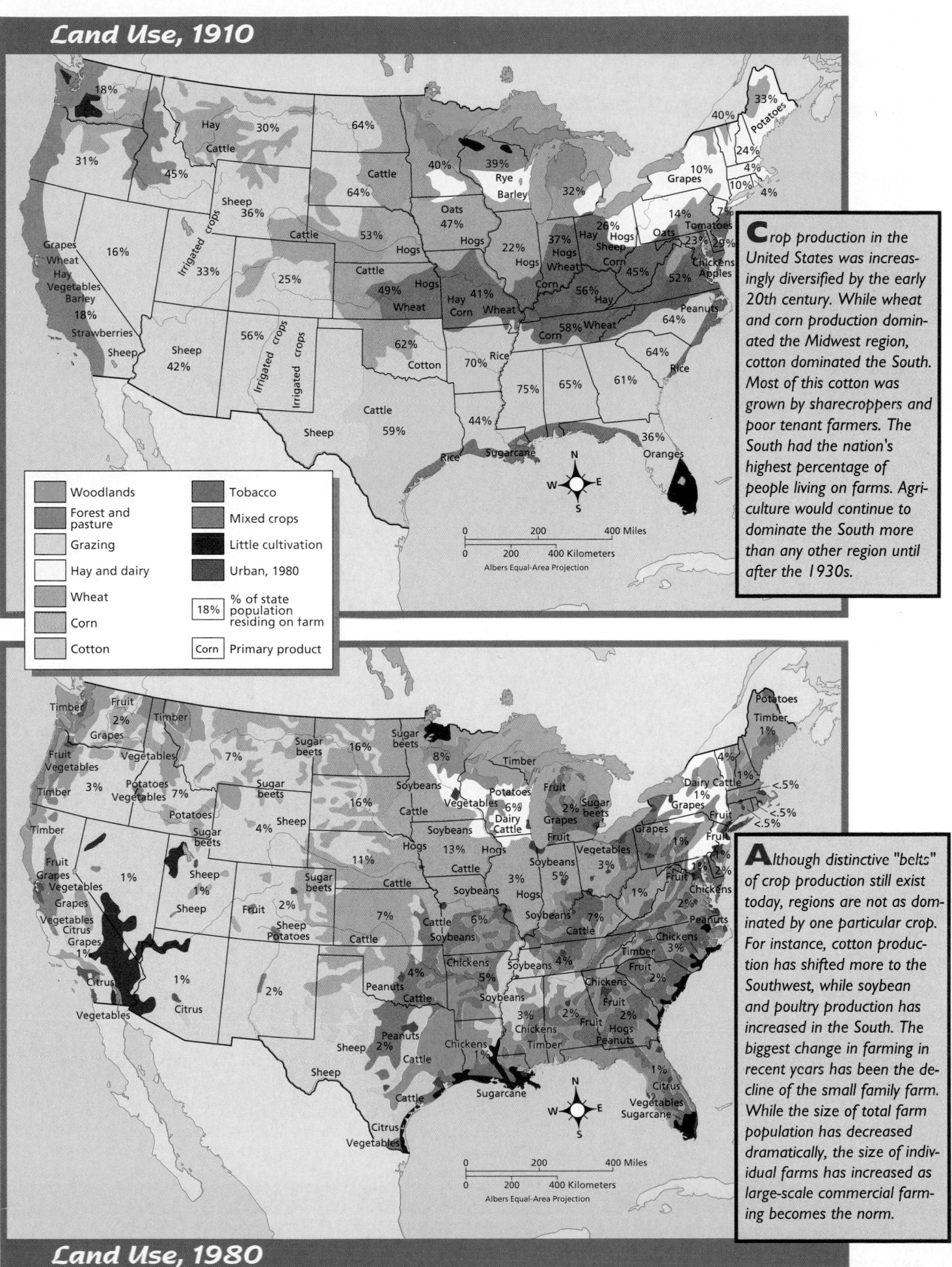

Land Use, 1910

Legend

- Woodlands
- Forest and pasture
- Grazing
- Hay and dairy
- Wheat
- Corn
- Cotton
- Tobacco
- Mixed crops
- Little cultivation
- Urban, 1980

18% — % of state population residing on farm

Corn — Primary product

Crop production in the United States was increasingly diversified by the early 20th century. While wheat and corn production dominated the Midwest region, cotton dominated the South. Most of this cotton was grown by sharecroppers and poor tenant farmers. The South had the nation's highest percentage of people living on farms. Agriculture would continue to dominate the South more than any other region until after the 1930s.

Although distinctive "belts" of crop production still exist today, regions are not as dominated by one particular crop. For instance, cotton production has shifted more to the Southwest, while soybean and poultry production has increased in the South. The biggest change in farming in recent years has been the decline of the small family farm. While the size of total farm population has decreased dramatically, the size of individual farms has increased as large-scale commercial farming becomes the norm.

Land Use, 1980

THE JAZZ AGE

FOCUS

UNDERSTANDING THE MAIN IDEA

Jazz, the upbeat musical form developed by African Americans, helped give the 1920s a unique character. The automobile, advertising, radio programs, and movies also influenced American life. Artists and writers portrayed an American society growing more urban and "modern." Many Americans found the changes of the 1920s unsettling, and the decade was marked by social conflict.

THEMES

■ **ECONOMIC DEVELOPMENT** How might increased consumer spending help improve a nation's economy?

■ **TECHNOLOGY AND SOCIETY** How might new technology transform people's lives?

■ **CULTURAL DIVERSITY** How might the cultural traditions of a particular area or group conflict with or contribute to a national culture?

1920	1925	1926	1927	1928
First radio stations go on the air.	Scopes trial held in Dayton, Tennessee.	Langston Hughes's *Weary Blues* published.	Charles Lindbergh completes first nonstop flight from New York to Paris.	Amelia Earhart crosses Atlantic Ocean by plane.

Americans had cut back on purchasing goods during World War I. With the war over, men and women were eager to buy the new products that postwar American industry offered in abundance.

An avalanche of new products transformed the lives of Americans in the 1920s—none more so than the automobile. The automobile changed the way Americans worked, socialized, and ran their households. It also helped change social roles for women. As early as 1907 a poem celebrated the growing independence of women who drove:

> **66** Like the breeze in its flight, or
> the passage of light,
> Or swift as the fall of a star.
> She comes and she goes in a nimbus
> of dust
> A goddess enthroned on a car.
> The maid of the motor, behold her
> erect
> With muscles as steady as steel.
> Her hand on the lever and always
> in front
> The girl in the automobile. **99**

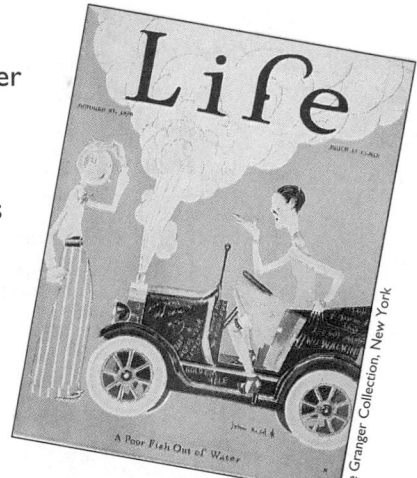

Life magazine cover, 1926

New forms of entertainment, including the wildly popular jazz bands, amused Americans in the generally prosperous 1920s. Radio programs, talking pictures, musical performances, and sporting events also entertained millions. But the decade was not all amusement. A small group of writers and artists revitalized American arts with their sober reflections on the war, race relations, and the nature of American society.

Jazz floor show in Chicago, 1924

BOOM TIMES

FOCUS

- **What factors led to the economic boom of the 1920s?**
- **Which processes changed work habits during the twenties?**
- **How did the automobile affect American life?**
- **What developments stimulated consumerism?**

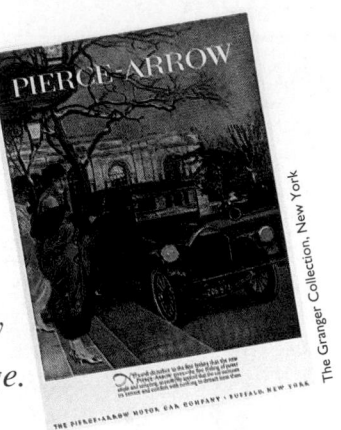

The economy prospered in the 1920s. In 1928 wages were a third higher than they had been in 1914. The gross national product climbed from $70 billion in 1922 to $100 billion just seven years later. Prosperity was accompanied by changes in the workplace and a new automobile age. Salespeople sold cars and a host of other products through aggressive campaigns that aimed to turn the United States into a nation of consumers.

Automobile advertisement, 1920

PROSPERITY AND PRODUCTIVITY

Many factors led to the boom times of the 1920s. One was the Republicans' probusiness stance. Another was abundant supplies of energy—coal, oil, natural gas, and waterpower, as well as a vast network of electrical power plants. Between 1920 and 1929 fuel oil output doubled, and annual electrical production went from some 56 billion to 114 billion kilowatt-hours. By 1930 over two thirds of all U.S. homes had electricity.

The widespread availability of electricity created a demand for a dizzying array of new electrical appliances—washing machines, sewing machines, cake mixers,

and food grinders. Radio and phonograph sales boomed. Chemical companies also tempted consumers, offering a variety of products made from plastic, rayon, acetate, and other new "wonder" materials. In 1930, textile mills produced more than 118 million pounds of rayon and acetate yarns—more than 13 times the 1920 production level.

A new production technique—the **assembly line**—helped factories churn out goods faster. Around 1913, after adapting techniques used in the slaughterhouses

▶ **The Ford Motor Company introduced assembly-line techniques in its factories as early as 1913. This photograph of a Ford factory was taken in 1924. Henry Ford is shown in the inset.**

ELECTRICAL PRODUCTION

Kilowatt Hours (in billions)
120
100
80
60
40
20
0

1920   1930
**Total U.S.
Consumption**

Percent
80
70
60
50
40
30
20
10
0

1920   1930
**Homes
with Electricity**

Source: *Historical Statistics of the United States*

ABUNDANT ENERGY The use of alternating electric current and powerful transformers allowed electricity to be transmitted over great distances. As a result, electrical use increased dramatically during the 1920s.

? IDENTIFYING CAUSE AND EFFECT By about what percentage did electrical consumption increase from 1920 to 1930?

The assembly line allowed manufacturers to reduce the prices of cars, bringing them within reach of ordinary American families. Automobile registrations during the twenties rose from 8 million to 26 million—an average of one car for every five citizens.

In the 1920s the auto industry was the nation's biggest business. This new industrial giant consumed huge quantities of steel, glass, rubber, and other materials. Gasoline, formerly a troublesome by-product of the petroleum industry, became the industry's most-valued product. By 1929 over one million people labored in the automobile industry or a related business.

▪▪ Probusiness policies, ample energy, new industries, and the assembly line fueled the economic boom of the 1920s.

of Chicago, Henry Ford introduced the assembly line in his Detroit automobile plant. Workers stood in one spot as partially assembled automobiles moved past them on a conveyor belt timed to advance precisely six feet per minute. Bit by bit, workers assembled the 5,000 parts of a Model T, or "Tin Lizzie," until the finished product could be driven out of the factory. Machinery did much of the work of producing individual parts and carrying them to workers. Boasted Ford:

66 Every piece of work in the shop moves; it may move on hooks, on overhead chains . . . it may travel on a moving platform, or it may go by gravity, but the point is that there is no lifting or trucking. . . . No workman has anything to do with moving or lifting anything. 99

The assembly line cut the engine assembly time for a Model T in half. Other large car manufacturers quickly followed Ford's lead and installed assembly lines. But few small companies could afford the expense of building or maintaining the new technology. Unable to compete, many were driven out of business. Soon the industry was dominated by three big corporations: Ford, General Motors, and Chrysler.

*C*HANGES IN WORK

Although assembly lines increased productivity, they had a human cost. Little technical skill was needed to "work the line." Thus, many higher-paid skilled laborers were thrown out of work. But even the people who found jobs on the line suffered. The work was deadening, leading many to quit within a few weeks. To counter the high turnover, Ford limited the workday to eight hours and doubled wages to an unheard-of $5 a day.

Both of these bold steps were welcomed. However, as the wife of one Ford worker noted, the pay increase did not change working conditions:

66 The chain system [assembly line] you have is a *slave driver! My God!* Mr. Ford. My husband has come home & thrown himself down & won't eat his supper—so done out! Can't it be remedied? . . . That $5 a day is a blessing—a bigger one than you know but *oh* they earn it. 99

The innovations of "Fordism" were more than matched by those of another movement, "Taylorism." The movement's creator, Frederick W. Taylor, called his approach **scientific management**.

◀ Frederick W. Taylor pioneered techniques used to increase workers' output.

It was based on the idea that every kind of work could be broken down into a series of smaller tasks. Trained observers conducted "time-and-motion" studies to identify these tasks and then set rates of production that people and machines had to meet. Soon "efficiency experts" were applying Taylor's methods to many areas of business.

The assembly line and scientific management changed the types of jobs available to workers. While the number of factory jobs grew only slightly during the 1920s, openings for such white-collar jobs as manager, clerical worker, and salesperson increased from slightly more than 10 million to more than 14 million. Because most of these jobs required that applicants have at least a high-school education, few newly arrived immigrants qualified. Discriminatory hiring practices also closed most of these jobs to African Americans.

Changes in technology affected domestic labor as well. Electrical appliances transformed housework for those who could afford them. Before the introduction of appliances, servants did the laundry and heavy cleaning in most middle- and upper-class homes. With the introduction of electrical appliances, many middle-class housewives took over the jobs they had previously supervised. As a result, many servants were forced to find new employment.

As more families bought cars, housewives also began taking over their families' transportation duties. Before many middle- and upper-class families had cars, their groceries and other supplies had been delivered to their homes. The automobile allowed housewives to assume these responsibilities as well. Thus, like household servants, delivery people often found their jobs in jeopardy.

■■ Scientific management and new technology transformed working conditions in the 1920s.

𝐴 LAND OF AUTOMOBILES

Just as the automobile assembly line transformed the world of work, so the automobile revolutionized the entire transportation system. By 1930 cars, trucks, and buses had almost completely replaced horse-drawn vehicles. Even railroads and trolley cars lost riders to Ford's "Tin Lizzie" and other automobiles.

To accommodate the increased traffic, more than 400,000 miles of new roads were built during the decade. Alongside the highways sprouted a host of new structures—filling stations, drive-in restaurants, tourist cabins, and billboards.

The automobile enabled rural residents to have greater contact with their neighbors and more access to shopping and leisure activities. Cars linked rural regions to urban areas, making it easier for rural residents to relocate to the booming cities and for city dwellers to visit the country. At the same time, however, the automobile contributed to the depopulation of America's inner

▼ With some nine million automobiles in use by 1920, more and more families explored the country in their cars. Shown here is an advertisement encouraging motorists to take the Apache Trail Motor Tour through Arizona's National Reserve.

APACHE TRAIL
120 MILE MOTOR TRIP THROUGH ARIZONA'S NATIONAL RESERVE

A thrilling day's journey in a comfortable motor car between Globe and Phoenix, Ariz., via Roosevelt Lake and Dam, the ancient Cliff Dwellings and the Canyon of the Salt River. Through tickets over Southern Pacific Lines will be honored via the APACHE TRAIL on payment of $15 additional.

Pullman Sleeping Cars in connection with the Sunset Limited are operated between El Paso, Tex., and Globe, Ariz., every Sunday, Tuesday and Friday. Also daily Pullman Sleeping Cars between Phoenix, Ariz., and Los Angeles, Cal.

Read the story of the APACHE TRAIL in this issue of Recreation.

Ask Southern Pacific ticket agents for information and literature.

SOUTHERN PACIFIC LINES
NEW YORK CITY, 366 Broadway   NEW ORLEANS, Metropolitan Bank Bldg.
SAN FRANCISCO, Flood Bldg.   HOUSTON, Southern Pacific Bldg.

In the 1920s, as millions of Americans purchased automobiles, a new craze swept the nation—the "autotouring" vacation. Guidebooks urged Americans to hit the road:

66 Does father crave to fish for trout and bass and pike and musky? Take him auto-touring. Does sister want to dip in the surf . . . or see the world? Take her automobile vacationing. . . . Does mother sigh for a rest from daily routines? Take her touring. . . . Does baby need fresh mountain air far from flies and heat? Take him auto-camping. 99

Freed from travel restrictions imposed by the schedules and routes of passenger trains, car owners took to the road to see America.

Most motor tourists were city dwellers who vacationed in the country to "get away from it all." But in getting away, they often took a lot of "it" with them. Camping gear for the typical autotourist included a tent, gas stove, heater, cooking utensils, pots and pans, folding table and chairs, spring beds, and blankets.

Autotourists tended to camp together and had a culture all their own. They often dressed in ways that led observers to marvel and to gawk at the same time. One reporter wrote:

▲ Families took advantage of new government autocamps while traveling on the road. This photograph shows a family camping in the 1920s.

66 It was amazing what colorful combinations the knickered rovers [autotourists] managed to attain. They wore veils of all descriptions, flowing Egyptian veils and even gas masks [to keep out road dust]. They wore paper hats that tied under their chins, caps trimmed with the tails of squirrels, skins of rattlesnakes, and quills of porcupines. 99

At first farmers welcomed these visitors from the city. Autotourists broke the isolation of rural life and seemed likely customers for farm produce. But instead of buying fruits and vegetables, vacationers often snitched them from trees and fields. Sometimes campers even milked farmers' cows! They also dumped their garbage on farmers' land. Soon signs banning autotouring appeared in rural areas. One such sign read:

66 Trespassers will B persecuted to the full extent of 2 mongrel dogs which neve was over sochible to strangers and I doubl brl shot gun which ain't loaded with sofa pillors. 99

National and state park services, along with town governments, stepped in to keep local people and visitors from clashing. These agencies set up free autocamps to provide tourists with welcome comforts, while keeping them off private land. Electric lighting made it possible for motorists to arrive and set up camp after dark, and gas ranges eliminated the need for firewood.

The heyday of autotourism passed as the prosperity of the 1920s gave way to the depression of the 1930s. But its legacy can be seen today in the continuing appeal of sight-seeing and camping vacations and in the popularity of recreational vehicles.

cities. Suburbs, now more accessible than ever, attracted thousands of middle-class families.

The automobile also transformed family life. Cars enabled families to enjoy simple drives in the country and elaborate camping trips. The automobile created new social opportunities for teenagers as well. Sociologists Robert Lynd and Helen Lynd, whose book *Middletown* (1929) chronicled life in Muncie, Indiana, wrote:

> 66 The extensive use of this new tool [the automobile] by the young has enormously extended their mobility and the range of alternatives before them; joining a crowd motoring over to a dance . . . twenty miles away may be a matter of a moment's decision, with no one's permission asked. 99

But the automobile had negative effects as well. Critics claimed that cars reduced people's sense of neighborliness. The Lynds observed that "since the advent of the automobile and the movies" Muncie families and neighbors no longer spent "long summer evenings and Sunday afternoons on the porch or in the side yard." Also, by the twenties, cars were already causing pollution, traffic jams, and parking problems. Most serious was the steadily climbing accident rate.

■■ **Cars revolutionized the nation's transportation system, eased rural isolation, aided suburban growth, and changed family and community relations.**

CREATING CONSUMERS

Advertising, which became big business in the 1920s, fueled the demand for cars and other consumer goods. Before World War I, money spent on advertising had totaled some $500 million yearly. By 1929 the total had soared to more than $3 billion. Ads were everywhere. Commercial messages bombarded potential buyers not only in magazines and newspapers but also on billboards and over the new medium of radio.

Advertisements, most of which targeted women, used psychology to play on consumers' hopes and fears. Ads for Borden's milk, for instance, warned mothers that "Hardly a family—well-to-do and poor alike—escapes the menace of malnutrition. Your own child may fall victim to this insidious evil."

Companies used slogans, jingles, and testimonials by celebrities to fix product names in

▶ Advertisements often stressed the ease of operation or low maintenance of the device being offered for sale. This ad for an "unusually quiet" refrigerator appeared in 1927.

▼ Salespeople proudly display a host of new home electrical appliances that proved wildly popular in the 1920s.

customers' minds. Eleanor Roosevelt (whose husband, Franklin D. Roosevelt, was then governor of New York) praised Cream of Wheat, which their son John had eaten since babyhood. The cereal, she was quoted as saying, "has undoubtedly played its part in building his robust physique."

As the number of products expanded to meet the growing demand, new chain stores sprang up around the country. For example, the A & P grocery chain grew from some 3,000 stores in 1922 to about 14,000 by 1925. The chain grocery stores, which slowly replaced the corner markets, stocked a wide variety of new products. The chain stores could do so because cellophane, a transparent wrapping material first produced in the United States in 1924, and quick-freezing techniques preserved fresh foods longer and allowed them to be shipped over longer distances.

Effective merchandising depended above all on clever salespeople. "There are always some people that you can sell anything to if you hammer them hard enough," claimed a car dealer. Door-to-door salespeople hawked everything from cleaning supplies to encyclopedias.

People also bought more because of easy credit. Before the 1920s, consumers bought only a few expensive items, such as pianos and sewing machines, on the installment plan. By mid-decade,

▲ Chain grocery stores did not completely replace the neighborhood grocery. Immigrants continued to shop at family-run groceries such as this one, owned by Antonio and Angeline Tortolano. At such stores customers could buy ethnic foods and talk to shopkeepers in their native language.

buyers purchased about 75 percent of cars on credit. The practice soon spread to many other items. As a car dealer noted:

> 66 To keep America growing we must keep Americans working, and to keep Americans working we must keep them wanting; wanting more than the bare necessities; wanting the luxuries and frills that make life so much more worthwhile, and installment selling makes it easier to keep Americans wanting. 99

■■ Advertising, merchandising, and installment buying encouraged consumerism.

SECTION 1 REVIEW

IDENTIFY and explain the significance of the following: assembly line, Henry Ford, Frederick W. Taylor, scientific management, Robert Lynd, Helen Lynd.

1. **MAIN IDEA** What factors contributed to the economic prosperity of the 1920s?

2. **MAIN IDEA** What innovations transformed working conditions in the late 1920s?

3. **ASSESSING CONSEQUENCES** How did the invention of the automobile change the way Americans lived?

4. **WRITING TO INFORM** Imagine you are the president of a chain store. Prepare for your board of directors a brief summary of how the company plans to attract new customers.

5. **ANALYZING** Why can it be said that the technological and business innovations of the 1920s had both positive and negative consequences for American society?

LIFE IN THE TWENTIES

F O C U S

■ What were the most popular forms of entertainment during the 1920s?

■ In what ways did young women of the 1920s depart from traditional female behavior?

■ What did the debate over Prohibition and Fundamentalism reveal about American society in the 1920s?

The decade of the 1920s has been called the gateway to modern America. For the first time a truly national mass culture emerged in the United States. Commercial radio linked Americans from coast to coast. Instant communications not only entertained people but also informed them about serious developments. The emerging mass culture also brought changes in women's roles and caused conflicts over traditional values.

Matinee idol Rudolph Valentino

POPULAR ENTERTAINMENT

Boom times in the United States meant that many—though not all—Americans had bigger paychecks and more free time than in years past. To help fill their leisure hours, many Americans turned to radio and movies.

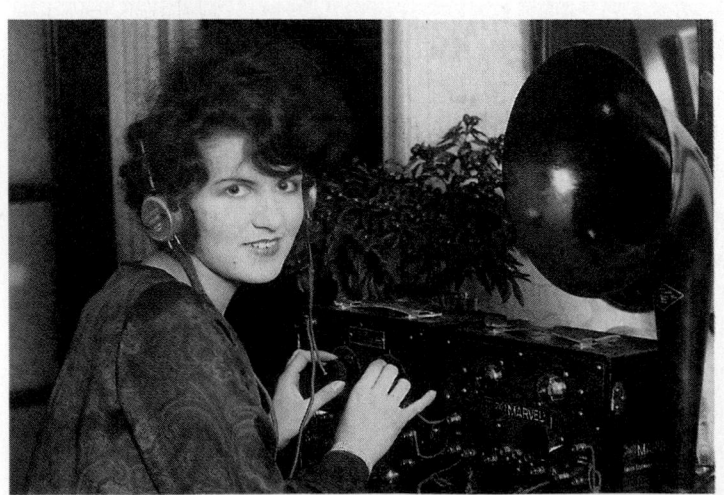

Commercial radio arose in the twenties. The first stations, Detroit's WWJ and Pittsburgh's KDKA, went on the air in 1920. By 1929, more than 800 stations reached some 10 million homes—more than a third of the nation's households. "There is radio music in the air, every night, everywhere," gushed a San Francisco newspaper. "Anybody can hear it at home on a receiving set." Along with music, radio stations broadcast sports events, news, and comedy shows.

By the end of the decade, two networks, the National Broadcasting Company (NBC) and the Columbia Broadcasting System (CBS), aired their programs nationwide. Households across the land tuned in to the same programs.

Movies proved equally popular, having grown in both length and complexity since their beginnings in the 1890s. The earliest movie

◀ **Advances in technology made radio more accessible to Americans during the 1920s. This photograph shows a young woman tuning in to a program on her radio set in 1922.**

▲ Moviegoers during the 1920s stood in line to see romance films starring John Gilbert and Greta Garbo, action films with Douglas Fairbanks, or comedies featuring Charlie Chaplin.

▶ As motion pictures grew in popularity, theater owners built lavish movie palaces with elaborate balconies, box seats, and a pit for live orchestral music.

theaters—called nickelodeons because of the five-cent admission—attracted mainly working-class and immigrant audiences. By the 1920s, lavish movie palaces with names like the Roxy, the Bijou, and the Ritz, were attracting middle-class audiences as well. The more-luxurious theaters had velvet drapes, plush carpets, uniformed ushers, and great theater organs to accompany the silent films. The mass appeal of movie theaters impressed journalist Lloyd Lewis:

    ❝ In the "de luxe" [movie] house every man is a king and every woman a queen. Most of these cinema palaces sell all their seats at the same price,—and get it; the rich man stands in line with the poor. . . . In this suave atmosphere, the differences . . . that determine our lives outside are forgotten. All men enter these portals equal, and thus the movies are perhaps a symbol of democracy. ❞

In 1927 Warner Brothers released the first feature-length "talkie," *The Jazz Singer,* starring Al Jolson. Silent-screen stars with high squeaky voices soon found themselves unemployed. In their places emerged new actors with distinctive and appealing voices, among them Gary Cooper and Clara Bow. The advent of sound also led to new film forms, including musicals and newsreels,

short films summing up the news of the day. In 1929 some 80 million Americans flocked to the theaters each week.

■■ Americans turned to radio and movies for entertainment during the 1920s.

CELEBRITIES AND HEROES

When movie star Rudolph Valentino died in 1926 at age 31, mourners lined up for blocks to view his body. In this era of mass culture, actors became instant celebrities. So did other figures in the public eye, especially athletes and pilots.

One sports favorite was Babe Ruth. Ruth dominated baseball from 1920 to 1935, during which time he led the New York Yankees to four World Series championships. In 1927 the spindle-legged, pigeon-toed ball player astounded the sports world with a record 60 home runs. Hard-hitting tennis star Helen Wills wowed audiences

▲ During his long career, Babe Ruth hit 714 home runs—a record not broken until 1974.

Richard Müller-Freienfels, a German professor and writer, studied industrialization and the mass culture that emerged in the early 20th century. Here is his description of American life in the 1920s:

THROUGH OTHERS' EYES

"*All the men seem to be clothed by the same tailor, and all the women seem to have bought their hats at the same shop. . . . The most remarkable thing is that even the people impress one as having been standardized. All these clean-shaven men, all these girls, with their doll-like faces, which are generally painted, seem to have been produced somewhere in a Ford factory, not by the dozen but by the thousand. In no other country are the individuals reduced to such a dead-level as in the United States, and this appears all the more remarkable when we reflect that nowhere [else] is there such a . . . mixture of races and peoples.*"

and captured more major tennis championships than any other woman in the world. Wills won the U.S. Open title seven times and Wimbledon eight times. Swimmer Gertrude Ederle broke the world record when she swam the English Channel in 1926 at age 19. She went on to set more than 20 U.S. swimming records and to win several medals in the 1924 summer Olympics.

Few athletes of the 1920s, however, enjoyed greater fame than Jim Thorpe. Born in 1888 in Oklahoma, he was of Sauk, Fox, Irish, and French ancestry. Thorpe attended the Carlisle Indian School in Pennsylvania. There he played every intercollegiate sport the school offered.

After he left Carlisle, Thorpe began training for the Olympics. At the 1912 games, held in Stockholm, Sweden, he became the first contestant to win both the pentathlon and the decathlon. "Sir, you are the greatest athlete in the world," said the Swedish king as he presented Thorpe with his gold medals. "Thanks, King," replied Thorpe with a grin.

A year later Thorpe's triumph turned to ashes. The news became public that he had played semiprofessional baseball for money. (At the time, Olympic athletes had to be amateurs.) Officials erased his name from Olympic record books and confiscated his awards. Many people felt that Thorpe had been treated unfairly; he had not realized that playing baseball for money would disqualify him from track competition.

Thorpe went on to a respectable career in major-league baseball and in the 1920s enjoyed several spectacular years playing professional football. In his later years, which were clouded by illness, he tried to become a movie actor. Not until 1982, 29 years after his death, did an Olympic committee restore his medals.

Probably the greatest celebrity of the 1920s was pilot Charles Lindbergh. In May 1927 he took off in a small single-engine plane, aiming to win a $25,000 prize that had been offered to the first pilot to

BIO
GRAPHY

Jim Thorpe

► Charles Lindbergh's solo flight across the Atlantic Ocean in 1927 in his plane, *The Spirit of St. Louis,* made him an international celebrity.

fly nonstop from New York to Paris. After flying solo for 33 1/2-hours, he landed in France. Americans were delirious with joy. New Yorkers threw a ticker-tape parade for Lindbergh, and President Coolidge received the modest young man at the White House. Lindbergh's flight offered exciting glimpses of a coming era of air travel. The next year, pilot Amelia Earhart became the first woman to cross the Atlantic Ocean by plane.

▲ Flapper styles spread all over the country, even to rural South Texas. Shown here are Idalia Canales and Rosenda García, two cousins who lived in a small town near the Rio Grande and copied the flapper look.

THE "NEW WOMAN"

Two of the many changes in the 1920s were in women's dress and behavior. Influenced by popular actresses and by the independence of working-class women, some young women exercised new freedom in how they dressed and behaved. These women stopped wearing heavy corsets and started wearing shorter skirts and transparent silk hose. Actress Colleen Moore explained that these changes in dress represented a new independence for women:

66 Long skirts, corsets, and flowing tresses have gone. . . . The American girl will see to this. She is independent, a thinker [who] will not follow slavishly the ordinances of those who in the past have decreed this or that for her to wear. 99

People began to call the era's "new women" **flappers**. Flappers enjoyed defying traditional standards of womanly behavior. They wore their dresses daringly short, bobbed their hair, and wore makeup. They also drove cars, participated in sports, and smoked cigarettes.

Flappers gloried not only in their social freedom but also in their economic independence. Young women increasingly worked outside the home, which gave them more freedom to meet people and save money for themselves. If they married, however, they were expected to quit their paid employment and to fulfill their roles as wives and mothers. As Samuel Gompers, leader of the AFL, made clear in 1921 when he described the winner of the first Miss America beauty pageant, the homemaker was still the ideal of American womanhood:

66 She represents the type of womanhood America needs— strong, red-blooded, able to shoulder the responsibilities of home-making and motherhood. It is in her type that the hope of the country resides. 99

■■ The "new woman" of the twenties defied conventions in dress and behavior.

A CRISIS OF VALUES

For some Americans the flapper symbolized the negative changes overtaking the country in the 1920s. With their unconventional dress and behavior, flappers rejected traditional values. To conservatives, the popularity of romantic movies and cheek-to-cheek dancing seemed signs of increasing immorality. Most critics blamed these "modern" habits on cities, noting with anxiety that radio and movies spread city ways to even the remotest rural areas. Anxiety increased when the census of 1920 revealed that for the first time, more than half of the U.S. population lived in metropolitan areas. In the face of these tremendous changes, arguments raged over such issues as alcohol and religion.

▲ Couples during the 1920s often held each other close in a cheek-to-cheek style while dancing to romantic music such as the tango.

▲ Federal agents such as Izzy Einstein and Moe Smith often went undercover and tried to purchase alcohol in speakeasies. When the alcohol was served, the agents made their arrests.

Prohibition. Progressive reformers had called for a ban on alcohol to combat such urban problems as family violence, crime, and poverty (see Chapter 17). Baptists, Methodists, and other Protestants also opposed drinking. After the Eighteenth Amendment made the manufacture, sale, and transportation of alcoholic beverages illegal in January 1919, Congress passed the **Volstead Act** in October 1919 to enforce the amendment. America entered the era of Prohibition.

In some regions Prohibition was strictly enforced, and drinking declined. But in many parts of the country, especially among immigrants, college students, and some city dwellers, Prohibition was extremely unpopular and widely ignored. Many people treated the reform as an annoyance, if not a joke. They frequented speakeasies, made their own wine or liquor, and bought bootleg (illegal) alcohol that had been smuggled from Canada or the West Indies.

Bootlegging became one of the decade's booming businesses. Criminal gangs in the large cities controlled liquor sales. Gang leaders gained the cooperation of law enforcement officials by bribing or threatening them. Al Capone, the boss of Chicago's underworld,

▼ Aimee Semple McPherson preached for nearly 20 years in a Los Angeles temple built for her by supporters at a cost of $1.5 million.

commanded a small army of heavily armed mobsters. He and other gangsters made millions of dollars.

Gangs branched out to seize control of gambling establishments, houses of prostitution, and dance halls. They also made money through "protection" rackets, collecting money from owners of stores and other businesses by threatening violence if their victims failed to pay.

Prohibition had some positive consequences. Alcoholism declined and so did the number of deaths from alcohol-related causes. Prohibition's negative results, however, drew more attention. Prohibition led to a widespread breakdown of law and order and turned millions of otherwise law-abiding citizens into lawbreakers. Prohibition would later be repealed with the ratification of the **Twenty-first Amendment** in 1933.

Fundamentalism. The increasing popularity of a Protestant movement called **Fundamentalism** also revealed deep cultural conflicts in 1920s America. Fundamentalists believed that every word of the Bible should be regarded as literally true. They attacked Christian "liberals" who had accepted modern scientific learning, such as the theory of evolution. This "modernism," said Fundamentalists, weakened Christianity and contributed to the moral decline of the nation.

Revivalist preachers of the "old-time religion" found an eager audience, both in rural areas and in urban areas where traditional values remained strong. Billy Sunday, who had long preached against alcohol, drew huge crowds to his tent revivals. People were spellbound by Sunday's showmanship and his rousing attacks on dancing, card playing, and drinking. When Prohibition went into effect, he held a funeral service for "John Barleycorn," who personified alcohol, and declared that "the reign of tears is over."

Another popular revivalist of the 1920s was Aimee Semple McPherson, whose practice of faith healing and message of love attracted thousands to her International Church of the Foursquare Gospel, headquartered in Los Angeles. Most of her followers were city dwellers of modest

The Roaring Twenties was a time of short skirts, bathtub gin, gambling, jazz, and the first talking movies. It was a time when old taboos were falling away one after the other. Alarmed and outraged by what they saw as the breakdown of the nation's moral standards, many community, religious, and government groups took action.

These activists pulled from library and store shelves books and magazines that used foul language, discussed sex frankly, or supported radical political ideas. U.S. Customs officials labeled many foreign books obscene and seized them, including the novel *Ulysses* by Irish author James Joyce.

Groups also targeted the movie industry. Several states and dozens of communities formed censorship boards to ban movies deemed unsuitable for young people. To both stem the tide of censorship and address public concerns over movie content, Hollywood set up in 1924 its own review board, a forerunner of today's movie-rating system, to screen movie content.

The American Civil Liberties Union and other groups opposed these growing

▲ Although James Joyce's *Ulysses* was initially banned, a later federal court ruling declared that it was not obscene and was a true work of literature.

restrictions on the content of movies and literature. They argued that such censorship violated the Constitution's First Amendment, which guarantees freedom of speech and freedom of the press.

Today the battle between censorship and freedom of speech continues. The National Endowment for the Arts (NEA), for example, has come under attack for funding artists whose works some consider obscene. But while some critics judge the art as obscene and unsuitable for public display, the artists defend their right to freedom of expression. The NEA and other agencies are caught in the middle of the battle.

Several rock and rap musicians have also come under fire for recording songs that contain sexually explicit or violent lyrics. In response, the Recording Industry Association of America has begun placing warning labels on any recordings that contain lyrics that might be unsuitable for minors. But many people believe voluntary labeling is not enough. In 1992, for instance, Washington State banned the sale and distribution of certain recordings to minors.

Is such censorship a violation of free speech or a needed form of protection? American society and U.S. courts continue to struggle with this question.

---

income, many of them recent migrants from the Midwest. Outfitted in her signature white dress, white shoes, and blue cape, McPherson addressed her followers' concerns about the new doctrines of "communism, socialism, and jazz-ism." McPherson also used radio and magazines to spread her fundamentalist message.

The Scopes trial. Fundamentalism went on trial in a famous court case in July 1925. Earlier that year the Tennessee legislature had outlawed the teaching of Charles Darwin's theory of evolution—a prime target of Fundamentalists—in the state's public schools. To test the law's constitutionality, the American Civil Liberties Union offered to defend any Tennessee schoolteacher who would challenge the statute. John Scopes, a shy high-school biology teacher from Dayton, accepted the offer.

The trial took place in a circus atmosphere. As the trial began in Dayton, the little town was overrun by reporters, farmers in mule-drawn wagons, and big-city lawyers. Scopes's chief defense attorney was salty Clarence Darrow, a famous criminal lawyer from Chicago. The prosecution's

► Clarence Darrow (right) devoted a large part of his legal career to defending the "underdog." This photograph shows him with John Scopes in 1925.

▼ Because the theory of evolution implied that human beings had descended from ape-like creatures, the Scopes trial became known as the "Monkey Trial."

THE CHICAGO DAILY NEWS.

FINAL EDITION | BOX SCORE •

TWO CENTS—SPRINT[...] 50TH YEAR—173. [...] TUESDAY, JULY 21, 1925. • HOME EDITION [...] 5 O'CLOCK

SCOPES "GUILTY" IN APE CASE

star witness was the elderly William Jennings Bryan, the former Democratic presidential candidate and secretary of state.

The Scopes trial exposed a deep division in American society between traditional religious values and new values based on scientific ways of thought. Bryan represented the many Americans who felt that the theory of evolution contradicted deeply held religious beliefs. Speaking before the trial to an audience of local admirers, Bryan declared:

66 Our purpose and our only purpose is to vindicate [uphold] the right of parents to guard the religion of their children against efforts made in the name of science to undermine faith in supernatural religion. 99

Darrow, on the other hand, expressed the views of many other Americans when he attacked the Tennessee law as a threat to free expression. In one of his courtroom speeches, he warned his listeners that "today it is the public school teachers, tomorrow the private, the next day the preachers and the lecturers, the magazines, the books, the newspapers."

Darrow's arguments, however, failed to sway the jury. They found Scopes guilty and fined him $100. The verdict was a victory for Fundamentalists. But press accounts of the trial, which often portrayed Bryan and his cause as narrow-minded, colored many people's views of Fundamentalism.

■■ **The debate over Prohibition and Fundamentalism revealed a crisis of values in 1920s America.**

SECTION 2 REVIEW

IDENTIFY and explain the significance of the following: Babe Ruth, Helen Wills, Gertrude Ederle, Jim Thorpe, Charles Lindbergh, Amelia Earhart, flappers, Volstead Act, Twenty-first Amendment, Fundamentalism, Aimee Semple McPherson, John Scopes.

1. **MAIN IDEA** What two forms of entertainment were most popular among Americans during the 1920s?

2. **MAIN IDEA** How did the flapper represent the "new woman" of the 1920s?

3. **IDENTIFYING VALUES** In what ways did the differing views of Clarence Darrow and William Jennings Bryan in the Scopes trial reflect the clash in values of 1920s America?

4. **WRITING TO INFORM** Write an essay explaining the negative and positive consequences of Prohibition.

5. **HYPOTHESIZING** What social factors might account for the popularity of sports figures and revivalists during the 1920s?

Section 3

A CREATIVE ERA

FOCUS

- How did African Americans contribute to the arts during the Harlem Renaissance?
- Who were the Lost Generation writers, and how did they get their name?
- How did the Mexican mural painters approach their art?
- How did mass media and advertising affect American culture in the 1920s?

𝒯he decade of the 1920s was a period of great creative energy. African American musicians transformed popular music by introducing the nation to jazz. A new generation of writers explored the problems of postwar American life and the experience of being black. Mexican muralists brought their paintings of social protest to the United States. And new currents in art and architecture swept the nation.

Louis Armstrong

MUSIC AND DANCE

The 1920s has been called the Jazz Age because this was the period when jazz, with its richly complex rhythms, first won a wide following. Jazz originated among African Americans in the South, especially in New Orleans. By the late 1800s, jazz had emerged from a blend of West African and Latin American rhythms, African American spirituals and blues, and European harmonies.

Joseph "King" Oliver, an early jazz great, helped spread jazz northward by moving from New Orleans to Chicago and founding the Creole Jazz Band. In 1922 the great jazz trumpeter Louis Armstrong joined Oliver in Chicago. Pianist and composer Ferdinand "Jelly Roll" Morton also moved north.

▶ Ferdinand "Jelly Roll" Morton began his career playing ragtime piano in New Orleans. Later, he moved to Chicago where he formed the recording group Red Hot Peppers.

As it became popular on a national level, jazz was adapted in various ways. White musicians—among them the cornetist and pianist Bix Beiderbecke—incorporated jazz rhythms in their music. George Gershwin's *Rhapsody in Blue,* which

THE JAZZ AGE ■■ 659

▲ During the 1920s jazz music such as "Tin Roof Blues" and "If You Knew Susie Like I Know Susie" became popular hits.

premiered in 1924, "translated" jazz into symphonic form. Jazz also influenced many classical musicians, including such noted composers as Igor Stravinsky and Aaron Copland.

The big bands, both black (Fletcher Henderson's and Duke Ellington's, for instance) and white (such as Paul Whiteman's), popularized jazz for dancing, creating faster and bouncier dances set to jazz rhythms. This new kind of jazz swept the nation via phonograph records, radio, and the movies. Young men and their flapper partners shocked their elders by dancing cheek-to-cheek fox-trots. The Charleston, originally an African dance performed by slaves, became *the* dance of the twenties.

While jazz became universal in the 1920s, it continued to express the particular sadness, pain, and joy of black America. African American poet Langston Hughes noted that through jazz, African Americans were saying "Why should I want to be white? I am a Negro—and beautiful!"

■■ **Jazz became widely popular during the 1920s, influencing many other forms of music.**

𝓐 BLACK RENAISSANCE

African American writers, artists, actors, and musicians in the 1920s expressed a growing black pride. Nowhere was this pride more evident than in the New York City neighborhood of Harlem, the nation's leading African American community. So many important African American writers, musicians, and artists lived in Harlem that this period of artistic development is known as the **Harlem Renaissance**.

The 1920s was a decade of achievement for African American musicians. They popularized not only jazz but also blues and religious songs known

▲ Although known for his work on stage, film, and radio, Paul Robeson also joined movements that fought for better working conditions, racial justice, and world peace.

as spirituals. In 1920 Mamie Smith's recording of "Crazy Blues" made popular the moody melodies of blues for white audiences. Bessie Smith, "the Empress of the Blues," toured widely and made many blues recordings. Marian Anderson, a gifted singer who began her operatic career in the 1920s, and Paul Robeson, singer and actor, incorporated spirituals in their repertoires.

In an era when African Americans were limited in the theatrical roles they were allowed to play, blacks produced and staged several enormously successful Broadway musicals, including Eubie Blake's *Shuffle Along* (1921). African American actors also achieved fame. Charles Gilpin played the title role in Eugene O'Neill's drama *Emperor Jones* in 1920. Paul Robeson made history in 1924 by becoming the first black actor to play a leading role opposite a white actress.

BIO GRAPHY A leading African American actor of the 1920s was Rose McClendon. Born in 1884 in South Carolina, McClendon moved to New York City as a child. She took part in church

Rose McClendon

plays but did not become a professional actress until her thirties, after winning a scholarship to the American Academy of Dramatic Art.

McClendon first won fame in *Deep River*, a "native opera with jazz" staged in 1926. Even the simple act of descending a staircase won her praise from critics and fellow actors alike. In later years she played in the Pulitzer Prize–winning tragedy *In Abraham's Bosom,* about a would-be reformer; the first production of *Porgy,* set in Charleston, South Carolina; and *Never No More,* the story of a lynching. Her last role was in Langston Hughes's *Mulatto.*

In addition to directing plays at the Harlem Experimental Theatre, Rose McClendon helped found the Negro People's Theatre in Harlem in 1935. The organization increased opportunities for black actors and playwrights.

As important and impressive as African American contributions to movie and stage were during the Harlem Renaissance, it was above all a literary movement. Black novelists and poets produced work marked by bitterness and defiance but also by joy and hope. In his novel *Home to Harlem* (1928), Jamaica-born Claude McKay explored the excitement and stresses of Harlem life for a returned black soldier. Nella Larsen, born in Chicago of West Indian and Danish ancestry, described the quest for racial identity in her novel *Quicksand* (1928).

Among the most-famous Harlem poets were Langston Hughes and Countee Cullen. Hughes's *Weary Blues* (1926) and Cullen's *Color* (1925) viewed African American life and the African cultural heritage with sensitivity. In the poem "I, Too," Hughes sums up black pride in a few powerful lines:

> 66 I, too, sing America.
>
> I am the darker brother.
> They send me to eat in the kitchen
> When company comes,
> But I laugh,
> And eat well,
> And grow strong.

Harlem Renaissance, 1920s

HARLEM'S EXPANSION Migrants came to New York City from the South and the islands of the West Indies. During the 1920s, some 25 percent of Harlem's black population was foreign born.

? PLACE What was the extent of African American settlement in Harlem in 1920?

Famous club where Duke Ellington and other black entertainers perform for whites-only audiences.

This branch library features exhibits by African American artists and poetry readings by Countee Cullen.

Site of Marcus Garvey's UNIA rallies

Countee Cullen's column, "The Dark Tower," provides the name for this Harlem literary salon.

W.E.B. Du Bois sometimes lectures here, and the Krigwa Players stage plays by African Americans.

Johnson's 1922 anthology, *The Book of Negro Poetry,* helps launch the Harlem Renaissance. His parties draw noted intellectuals, such as Paul Robeson and Clarence Darrow.

- Black settlement in Harlem, 1920
- Black settlement in Harlem, 1930
- Areas predominately African American
- ■ Point of interest

▲ Langston Hughes

Tomorrow,
I'll be at the table
When company comes.
Nobody'll dare
Say to me,
"Eat in the kitchen,"
Then.

Besides,
They'll see how beautiful I am
And be ashamed—

I, too, am America. **99**

∷ African American musicians, actors, and writers in the 1920s flourished, creating a cultural movement known as the Harlem Renaissance.

ᴛHE LOST GENERATION

The creative spirit of the 1920s expressed itself not only in jazz, but also in the literature of the decade. Many younger writers of the time were haunted by the death and destruction of World War I and scornful of middle-class consumerism and the superficiality of the postwar years. "You are all a lost generation," said poet Gertrude Stein to one such writer, Ernest Hemingway. The label stuck, and scholars refer to writers of the era as the **Lost Generation**.

Ernest Hemingway spent much of his life in France, Spain, and Cuba. An ambulance driver in World War I, he expressed his anger at war's

futility in such novels as *The Sun Also Rises* (1926) and *A Farewell to Arms* (1929). In a famous passage from the latter book, a war veteran explains what the war means to him:

66 I was always embarrassed by the words sacred, glorious, and sacrifice and the expression in vain. We had heard them . . . and had read them . . . now for a long time, and I had seen nothing sacred, and the things that were glorious had no glory and the sacrifices were like the stockyards at Chicago if nothing was done with the meat except to bury it. **99**

Disillusionment with World War I echoed in the works of other Lost Generation writers, including John Dos Passos's *Manhattan Transfer* (1925).

Another Lost Generation writer, F. Scott Fitzgerald, was the foremost chronicler of the youthful Jazz Age. In his first novel, *This Side of Paradise* (1920), Fitzgerald described the life of rich college students bored by fast living and hard liquor. In *The Great Gatsby* (1925), Fitzgerald portrayed the emptiness of life devoted to a frenzied struggle to make money and win social status in Prohibition-era America. Sinclair Lewis also criticized American society, satirizing middle-class life in *Main Street* (1920) and *Babbitt* (1922).

∷ Gertrude Stein called Ernest Hemingway and other postwar writers "a lost generation" because of their anger and disappointment.

ᴛHE MEXICAN MURALISTS

Another renaissance of the 1920s took place in Mexico and was later brought to the United States by its major artists. This artistic movement stressed Native American traditions and the ideals of the Mexican Revolution of 1910. The artists emphasized the nobility of ordinary people—peasants and other workers—and the tyranny of wealthy capitalists. Their favorite medium was the monumental public mural because, in the words of artist José Clemente Orozco (oh-ROHS-koh), "it cannot be hidden away for the benefit of a certain privileged few. It is for the people. It is for *ALL*."

▲ Diego Rivera painted many murals that focused on workers and their relationship to industrial production. Shown here is *Entry to the Mine.*

The movement's three major artists—known in Mexico as *los tres grandes,* or "the big three"—were Orozco, David Alfaro Siqueiros (see-KAY-rohs), and Diego Rivera. Each first became known in Mexico in the 1920s and painted murals in the United States in the early 1930s.

Orozco created several murals for American universities, many featuring heroic figures who helped humanity. At New Hampshire's Dartmouth College, Orozco's library murals painted in the early 1930s include the figure of Quetzalcoatl (ket-SAHL-kwaht-uhl), the god who brought the arts of civilization to the Toltecs.

In Los Angeles, Siqueiros painted large-scale murals outdoors, "in the free air," as he put it, "facing the sun, facing the rain, for the masses." His best-known work, *Tropical America* (1932), painted on a wall in a Mexican American section of Los Angeles, featured a crucified Indian. The mural expressed Siqueiros's belief that U.S. imperialism in Latin America was disastrous for Indians. The piece so angered U.S. officials that Siqueiros was deported and the work completely painted over.

Diego Rivera focused on workers' problems and industrial development in his U.S. murals. In his words:

❝ There is more beauty in an electrical plant, with its frank outline and its nervous system of steel transmitting the electric fluid indispensable to social life, than in the redundant Baroque imitations of European architecture that have contaminated the soil of America. ❞

In a mural at the Detroit Institute of Art, which Rivera painted in 1932, his subject was, fittingly, assembly-line workers in automobile factories.

■■ The Mexican muralists glorified ordinary people and created art that all could view.

OTHER CURRENTS IN ART AND DESIGN

Like Rivera, U.S. artists and designers confronted the machine age in their works. They chronicled factories, new technology, workers, and urban landscapes.

Painting and photography. Many American painters of the 1920s depicted urban, industrial settings. Edward Hopper's New York City scenes convey a sense of loneliness. *Early Sunday Morning* (1930) shows a row of darkened stores and a street empty of people. New York City intrigued Georgia O'Keeffe, too. In the 1920s she painted pictures of its factories and tenements. Later she would move to New Mexico and capture the stark beauty of the Southwest.

Photography came into its own as an art form in the early 1900s. Alfred Stieglitz (STEEG-luhts),

Addison Gallery of American Art, Phillips Academy, Andover, MA

▲ This 1928 painting by Edward Hopper is called *Manhattan Bridge Loop.*

more than anyone else, gave it new status. Stieglitz's New York gallery influenced many other American artists. His own subjects included airplanes, skyscrapers, and crowded city streets. Charles Sheeler, a photographer and painter, won fame for the "portraits of machinery" he produced for the Ford Motor Company, which commissioned him to photograph its plant near Detroit, Michigan, in 1927.

Industrial design. The machine age that inspired artists also gave rise to a new professional field: industrial design. Spreading from Germany to the United States in the 1920s, industrial design aimed to create objects that were pleasing to look at as well as functional.

Industrial designers, working with such new materials as stainless steel and plastics, developed a wide range of products with a "modern" look. The designers developed streamlining—contours that reduced resistance—for trains, planes, ships, and cars. They also applied streamlining to objects that did not even move, such as radios, clocks, and appliances.

Manufacturers soon learned that a new design for what was essentially the same product boosted sales. They had discovered what came to be called **planned obsolescence**—making products that are designed to go out of style. Auto manufacturers were among the first to take advantage of planned obsolescence. In the early 1920s General Motors introduced the ideas of the yearly model change and the trade-in. Thereafter, many American families routinely traded in their "old" models and bought new cars every year.

Architecture. Industrial design, which combined function and visual appeal, had its counterpart in the world of architecture. Louis Sullivan and Frank Lloyd Wright inspired many other architects to embrace the idea that a building ought to use the materials and follow the forms most suitable to the building's purpose. The structure that most clearly illustrated this principle was the skyscraper, with its clean-cut vertical lines, its use of steel and concrete, its many glass windows, and its relative freedom from ornamentation.

New York City, whose population density and expensive real estate made it more efficient to build upward than outward, witnessed a boom in skyscraper construction during the 1920s. Builders

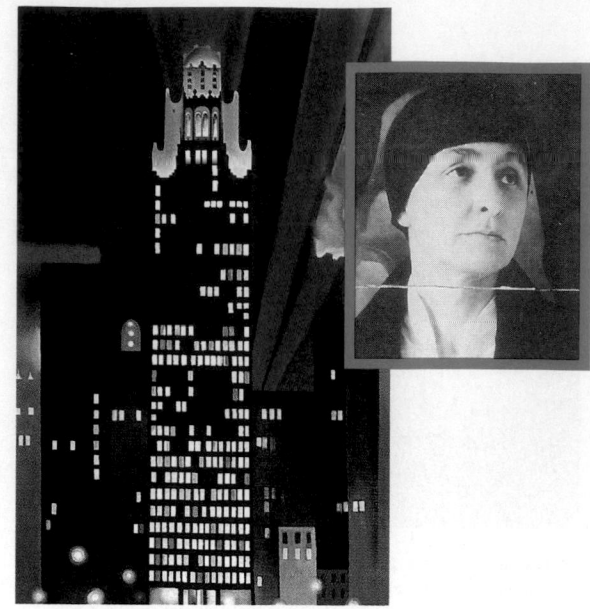

▲ Georgia O'Keeffe (inset) painted this scene, entitled *Radiator Building, Night, New York,* in 1927.

began construction of two landmarks—the Chrysler Building and the Empire State Building.

Civic boosters loved the skyscrapers, but critics had their doubts. A verse of the time protested:

> " THE
> SKY-
> SCRAPER
> TALL
> IS A
> WONDER
> TO ALL
> A THING
> TOADMIRE
> BEYOND
> QUESTION
> Butoh!downbelowwherepedestriansgo
> itcertainlyaddstocongestion "

COMMENTARY

A Standardized Culture?

What were the social effects of the new mass media and mass marketing of the 1920s? Most historians agree that mass media and mass marketing helped produce a standardized middle-class culture. Movies, radio, advertising, and magazines like The Saturday Evening

Post *and* Time *reached every corner of the nation. These new forms of media promoted middle-class ways by presenting an ideal world of hardworking middle-class families. Mass marketing promoted standardization by persuading people to drive the same model cars and buy the same brands of food, soap, and appliances.*

Historians recognize, however, that mass media and mass marketing also changed middle-class life. Many Americans—rich and poor, urban and rural—listened and danced to African American–influenced music and dance. Many middle-class women adopted forms of behavior previously associated with working-class women, such as wearing makeup and smoking.

The mass media also helped strengthen working-class, immigrant, and African American cultures. Musical recordings by African Americans, Mexican Americans, and others preserved traditional musical forms. Immigrant and working-class neighborhood movie theaters served as community meeting places. Some local radio stations devoted their programs exclusively to ethnic audiences, offering ethnic music and local news as well as news about the immigrants' homelands. Ethnic newspapers also helped preserve the immigrants' languages and ethnic identities.

While most middle-class families bought the same brands at chain stores, most working-class and immigrant families continued to buy from their local corner groceries. These local grocers, who usually shared the ethnicity of their patrons, extended credit to their customers. The grocers sold traditional ethnic ingredients such as Italian macaroni and Jewish kosher meats, which the chain stores rarely carried. These corner groceries thus allowed ethnic Americans to maintain traditional diets and served as places to swap news and gossip.

The mass media thus helped maintain ethnic cultures while they promoted middle-class values. And when middle-class Americans all over the country copied the style of life presented by the movies, network radio, and mass magazines, they were adopting ways influenced by different cultural perspectives. In short, the mass media and mass marketing supported traditional ways but also spread new ways of thinking and acting throughout the nation.

■■ **Mass media and advertising promoted new and standardized modes of behavior, but also helped sustain traditional cultures.**

SECTION 3 REVIEW

IDENTIFY and explain the significance of the following: Joseph "King" Oliver, Langston Hughes, Harlem Renaissance, Marian Anderson, Paul Robeson, Rose McClendon, Ernest Hemingway, Lost Generation, Diego Rivera, Alfred Stieglitz, planned obsolescence.

LOCATE and explain the importance of the following: Harlem.

1. **MAIN IDEA** In what ways did the artists of the Harlem Renaissance contribute to American culture?

2. **MAIN IDEA** Why were Ernest Hemingway and other young writers of the 1920s called "a lost generation"? Who coined this phrase?

3. **COMPARING** How was the work of José Clemente Orozco similar to that of Diego Rivera?

4. **WRITING TO EVALUATE** How did radio help people maintain long-held customs?

5. **ANALYZING** Why might black artists, writers of the Lost Generation, and Mexican muralists be considered social critics?

First radio stations go on the air.

Eubie Blake's *Shuffle Along* opens.

George Gershwin composes *Rhapsody in Blue*.

1920   1922   1924

WRITING A SUMMARY

Using the essential points of the chapter as a guide, write a summary of the chapter.

REVIEWING CHRONOLOGY

Number your paper 1 to 5. Study the time line above, and list the following events in the order in which they happened by writing the first next to 1, the second next to 2, and so on. Then complete the activity below.

1. Scopes trial held in Dayton, Tennessee.
2. Eubie Blake's *Shuffle Along* opens.
3. *The Jazz Singer* released.
4. Robert Lynd and Helen Lynd's *Middletown* issued.
5. George Gershwin composes *Rhapsody in Blue*.

Assessing Consequences How did *The Jazz Singer* influence the development of American entertainment?

IDENTIFYING PEOPLE AND IDEAS

Explain the historical significance of each of the following people or terms.

1. assembly line
2. scientific management
3. Helen Lynd
4. Jim Thorpe
5. Charles Lindbergh
6. Fundamentalism
7. Harlem Renaissance
8. Rose McClendon
9. Diego Rivera
10. planned obsolescence

UNDERSTANDING MAIN IDEAS

1. How was middle-class life in the 1920s changed by mass media and advertising?
2. What postwar problems did the Lost Generation deal with in their literature?
3. What influences led women to exercise new freedom in dress and behavior?
4. How did the prosperity of the 1920s influence American entertainment?
5. What contributions did African Americans make to the changing American culture of the 1920s?

REVIEWING THEMES

1. **Economic Development** How did advertising, merchandising, and installment buying help the nation's economy in the 1920s?

2. **Technology and Society** How did new technology affect Americans' lives at work and at home?
3. **Cultural Diversity** How did the Mexican muralists celebrate and criticize American culture?

THINKING CRITICALLY

1. **Analyzing** How did increased productivity and consumerism pave the way for future environmental problems?
2. **Synthesizing** Why might the Model T be an appropriate symbol for the 1920s?
3. **Evaluating** How did social changes contribute to the popularity of religious revivals?

STRATEGY FOR SUCCESS

Review the Skills Handbook entry on Taking a Test on page 1002. Below is a sample multiple-choice question that might be asked about Chapter 22. Write a paragraph summarizing how you would arrive at the correct answer.

The aspect of industrial design that most increased sales was
    a. scientific management.
    b. advertising.
    c. planned obsolescence.
    d. streamlining.

Ford automobile plant, 1921

Scopes trial held in Dayton, Tennessee.	Gertrude Ederle breaks world record for swimming English Channel. Langston Hughes's *Weary Blues* published.	*The Jazz Singer* released. Charles Lindbergh completes first nonstop flight from New York to Paris.	Amelia Earhart crosses Atlantic Ocean by plane.	Ernest Hemingway's *A Farewell to Arms* published. Robert Lynd and Helen Lynd's *Middletown* issued.

1926   **1928**   **1930**

WRITING ABOUT HISTORY

Writing to Explain Imagine you are a high school principal at the time of the Scopes trial. Write a letter to parents, outlining the issues involved in the trial and explaining how the verdict will affect next year's science curriculum.

USING PRIMARY SOURCES

Harlem was the social, cultural, and entertainment capital for many African Americans during the 1920s. In the following excerpt, Howard "Stretch" Johnson talks about the black basketball teams popular in the 1920s and about the influence of Paul Robeson, one of the Harlem Renaissance's major figures. Write a paragraph explaining how Robeson influenced African Americans in the 1920s.

 The Renaissance Big Five basketball team was a part of [the Harlem Renaissance]. . . .

My father was a very fine professional basketball player. He played with a group called the Puritans, which later became the Renaissance Big Five. . . .

Paul Robeson played with Alpha fraternity against my father when my father was playing with St. Christopher's, another semipro team that was popular in the '20s. Paul was a great figure. People used to swarm around him when he walked out on the street. He was the inspiration in every walk of life. Those blacks who went in for law had respect for his being a Phi Beta Kappa at Columbia University. Those who aspired to be successful in the athletic field had him as an exemplar [model] with his record at Rutgers, where he got fifteen varsity letters—more varsity A's than any individual who ever went to Rutgers—in football, basketball, track, and baseball.

LINKING HISTORY AND GEOGRAPHY

Refer to the map on page 661. What factors might explain the birth of the Harlem Renaissance during the 1920s?

Young women in Harlem

BUILDING YOUR PORTFOLIO

Complete the following projects independently or cooperatively.

1. **THE ECONOMY** In Chapter 21 you portrayed an unemployed veteran. Building on that experience, imagine you are a prosperous business owner in the 1920s. Create an advertisement for a new household product aimed at the expanding consumer market. Your ad might use psychology, slogans, jingles, or celebrity testimonials to sell your product.

2. **CULTURE AND SOCIETY** In Chapter 21 you portrayed an immigrant artist. Building on that experience, imagine you are an African American artist during the Harlem Renaissance. Create a dance, jazz poem, or painting that expresses cultural pride in your African American heritage.

THE GREAT DEPRESSION

FOCUS

UNDERSTANDING THE MAIN IDEA

In 1929 the stock market crashed, causing financial ruin for millions of Americans. The collapse of the stock market was one of several factors that gave rise to the Great Depression. When President Hoover's efforts to revive the economy failed, Americans elected a Democratic president, Franklin D. Roosevelt, to reverse the country's economic decline.

 THEMES

- **ECONOMIC DEVELOPMENT** What factors might cause an economic depression?

- **GEOGRAPHIC DIVERSITY** How might an economic crisis affect people's choices of where to live?

- **CULTURAL DIVERSITY** How and why might various ethnic groups be affected differently by an economic depression?

1929	1930	1931	1932
Stock market crashes.	Smoot-Hawley Tariff passed.	Scottsboro Boys case begins.	Franklin Roosevelt elected president.

The economic boom of the 1920s gave most Americans tremendous faith in the future. For many Americans, prosperity seemed limitless; however, the prosperity was unevenly distributed. The life-style of the Jazz Age also led to enormous debt.

Mexican American women bound for picket line, 1933

*T*hursday, October 24, 1929, dawned windy and cool in New York City. Employees of the New York Stock Exchange buttoned their overcoats as they hurried down Wall Street to work. In the first few hours of stock trading, share prices fell sharply. At first, investors remained calm. The market had been shaky in recent weeks but had always resumed its upward trend. Today was different, though. As prices continued to fall, panic struck. Frantic orders to sell stock came pouring in.

All across America, grim-faced investors watched as stock tickers reported the alarming news. The plunge in prices was wiping out the life savings of millions of Americans who had invested in stocks. "One saw men looking defeat in the face," said an eyewitness. "[It was] the smash-up of the hopes of years."

The economic prosperity of the 1920s was over, and the worst economic depression in U.S. history had begun. Over the next several years the American people faced widespread unemployment and poverty. By the time of the 1932 election, they were desperate for a change.

Ticker tape machine

PROSPERITY SHATTERED

FOCUS

- Why did many Americans invest in the stock market in the 1920s?
- What caused the stock market crash of 1929?
- What factors gave rise to the Great Depression?

Throughout the generally prosperous 1920s, isolated voices warned of problems with the American economy. Some people pointed to the farm crisis and to "sick" industries as problems in need of attention. Yet despite these warnings, most Americans believed that the economy would continue to thrive. Then came the stock market crash of 1929. Stock prices plunged, and investors lost billions of dollars. U.S. industries, already showing signs of weakness, almost ground to a halt.

Newspaper headline, October 1929

"GET RICH QUICK"

Few Americans other than farmers and the poor worried about the nation's economic health in the late 1920s. Many Americans agreed with Herbert Hoover that the nation was "nearer to the final triumph over poverty than ever before in the history of any land."

This sense of confidence was reflected in the stock market. Stock sales had risen steadily for several years. As demand rose, so did stock prices. Many experts saw no end to the **bull market**—the upward trend in stock prices (as opposed to a **bear market**, or downward trend). Business leaders, such as General Motors executive John J. Raskob, urged Americans to invest, claiming that anyone who put $15 a month in the stock market for 20 years would end up with $80,000—a fortune at the time.

By the late 1920s, stock speculation—"playing" the market by buying and selling to make a quick profit—was widespread. Although speculation fueled economic growth, it also created problems. Rapid buying and selling inflated the prices of stocks to the point that many stocks were selling for more than they were really worth. This speculative buying was fine as long as demand was high, but if investor confidence weakened, prices would tumble.

The situation was made shakier still by **margin buying**—purchasing stocks with borrowed money. Many speculators put up as little as 10 percent of the price of a stock, borrowing the rest. Margin buying worked as long as the bull market continued. If prices fell, though, investors would find themselves deep in debt with no way to pay off their loans. It was a very risky venture.

Although consumer confidence in the market remained high throughout the summer of 1929, a few gloomy voices were heard. In early September, stock analyst Roger Babson wrote: "Sooner or later a crash is coming, and it may be terrific." Some shrewd investors saw the writing on the wall and began to sell their stocks, but most people remained confident in the market. As one eyewitness wrote: "Money is king—but there is something else. It is a high, wild time, a time of riotous spirits and belief in magic rather than cold calculation."

■■ **Hoping to earn enormous profits from rising stock prices, many Americans invested in the stock market.**

THE STOCK MARKET CRASHES

The magic faltered on October 24, 1929—**Black Thursday**. Large investors, made nervous by various factors, including rising interest rates, suddenly began to sell their shares. The dumping of so much stock on the market jolted investor confidence and caused prices to plunge. Panic gripped Wall Street. A *New York Times* reporter described the crash:

> 66 It came with a speed and ferocity that left men dazed. The bottom simply fell out of the market. . . . The streets were crammed with a mixed crowd—agonized little speculators, . . . sold-out traders, . . . inquisitive individuals and tourists seeking . . . a closer view of the national catastrophe. . . . Where was it going to end? 99

Black Thursday was only the opening stage of a long downward spiral. Prices dropped still lower the following week, as more investors sold their stocks. On October 29—**Black Tuesday**—prices sank to a shocking new low as investors dumped over 16 million shares of stock on the market.

As prices plunged, brokers fired off frantic telegrams to the customers who owed them money. The brokers demanded cash to cover their loans. Unable to raise the funds, thousands of people were forced to sell their stocks at huge losses. Many investors were wiped out. By mid-November the average value of leading stocks had been cut in half, and stockholders had lost some $30 billion. By year's end stock losses exceeded the total cost of U.S. involvement in World War I.

■■ **Speculative buying drove stock prices above their real value. When large-scale selling occurred in October 1929, the market crashed.**

THE DEPRESSION BEGINS

In the first months after the stock market crash, business leaders and public officials insisted that the setback was minor and temporary. President Hoover declared: "We have now passed the worst and . . . shall rapidly recover." But optimistic statements could not conceal the grim truth. By late 1930 it was clear that a major economic depression was under way in the United States and throughout the rest of the world.

From late 1929 to 1933 the U.S. economy sank steadily. In 1929, the last boom year of the period, America's **gross national product**—the total value of all goods and services produced in a given year—reached $103 billion. In 1933, at the depth of the depression, it fell below $56 billion. Over that same period, average income for Americans fell by half. By 1932 the auto and steel industries were producing at just a small fraction of their capacity. Factories and mines stood idle. Railroad cars sat silent and empty. Many companies shut down, and millions of workers lost their jobs.

The banking industry was also hard hit by the

THE CRASH

Company	High Price Sept. 3, 1929	Low Price Nov. 13, 1929
American Telephone and Telegraph	304	197 1/4
General Electric	396 1/4	168 1/8
General Motors	72 3/4	36
Montgomery Ward	137 7/8	49 1/4
United States Steel	261 3/4	150
Woolworth	100 3/8	52 1/4

Source: Only Yesterday

FROM RICHES TO RAGS In the days following the stock market crash on October 29, 1929, stock prices continued to fall. Average stock prices reached their lowest point for the year on November 13, 1929, slightly two months after they had reached the high point for the year on September 3.

❓ **BUILDING CHART SKILLS** Which company's stock lost the greatest number of points between September 3 and November 13, 1929?

▲ Panicked by the 1929 stock market crash, many bank depositors stood in long lines to withdraw their money. This photograph was taken in New York City.

depression. After the stock market crash, many debt-ridden investors and businesses could not repay their loans, leaving banks with no incoming funds. Fearing bank failures, many depositors panicked and withdrew their savings. Under the combined weight of these factors, the banking system collapsed.

Between 1930 and 1932 more than 5,000 U.S. banks failed. Customers who went to their banks to withdraw savings often found the doors barred and their money gone. Because bank deposits were not insured, many people lost their life savings. The collapse of one big New York City bank in 1930 wiped out roughly $180 million in savings by some 100,000 depositors, including many poor immigrants.

WHAT CAUSED THE DEPRESSION?

The stock market crash of 1929 jolted the American economy and destroyed individual fortunes, but it alone did not cause the **Great Depression**, the deep economic downturn that gripped the United States between 1929 and the beginning of World War II. At the time, many observers, including President Hoover, blamed the depression on the state of the world economy following World War I. The global economy had suffered enormous setbacks because of the massive war debts incurred by European countries. But this, like the stock market crash, was only a contributing factor. Today economists and historians agree that the root causes of the Great Depression lay in numerous factors, including the American economic system itself.

The troubling twenties. Although the 1920s appeared to be a decade of unlimited

PRESIDENTIAL LIVES

HERBERT HOOVER
1874–1964

in office
1929–1933

As a young man Herbert Hoover was shy and awkward, but very hardworking. Born into a Quaker family in Iowa, he was left an orphan at age nine. He had few friends in college and would wander around with his eyes glued to the ground as if to avoid people. As one of his few friends noted, he had a habit of standing "with one foot thrust forward, jingling the keys in his trouser pocket," chuckling sometimes, but rarely laughing out loud. Even in the White House he remained self-conscious and shy.

After college Hoover rapidly built a career as a successful mining engineer and business consultant. By the age of 40 he was a millionaire. His role as coordinator of food relief during World War I also gave him a reputation as a kind and humanitarian leader. After his presidency he continued to work in public service and wrote many books and articles.

"There is little importance to men's lives," he wrote, "except the accomplishments they leave to posterity."

The Global Depression

UNEMPLOYMENT The worldwide depression created record levels of unemployment.

? **PLACE** In 1932 which countries had unemployment rates exceeding 30 percent?

United States
America remains determined to collect the war debts despite the European countries' inability to pay them.

Japan
Except from 1930 to 1932, Japan's rate of industrial production continues to climb. Military spending helps fuel this expansion.

France
Unemployment remains low because foreign workers are sent home, and many factory workers return to family farms.

Germany and Italy
Government economic policies and centralized control help bring these countries out of the depression.

South America
Dependent on selling raw materials, Chile, Bolivia, and Peru see exports fall by more than 69 percent from 1928–29 to 1932–33.

USSR
The Communists organize agriculture and build up heavy industry in order to become economically self-sufficient.

UNITED STATES 23.6% / 3.2%
CANADA 17.6% / 2.9%
BELGIUM 23.5% / 1.9%
NORWAY 15.4%
DENMARK 30.8% / 15.5%
GERMANY 31.7% / 13.1%
POLAND 30.1% / 4.9%
GREAT BRITAIN 22.5% / 11.0%
ITALY *20.5%* / 7.2%
15.6%

Azimuthal Equidistant Projection

Percentage of Work Force Unemployed
1929   1932
*Figure for Italy is from 1931

---

economic prosperity, many analysts place primary blame for the Great Depression on economic practices in the 1920s. These practices produced quick profits for some but in the long run contributed to economic chaos. Farm prices, for example, dropped in the 1920s. By the end of the decade, mining, textiles, construction, and other industries were also beginning to suffer.

Another disturbing trend was the widespread dependence on credit. In the late 1920s, the federal government encouraged borrowing by keeping interest rates low. The Republican administrations of the time reasoned that an easy-credit policy would promote business. Easy credit enabled consumers to buy goods when they did not actually have the money to pay for them. This was not a problem when the economy was booming. Once the economy began to slow and the government raised interest rates, however, many consumers could not pay their debts. After the crash many businesses stopped extending credit altogether.

In 1931 one department store even tried to turn the "credit crunch" to its advantage. While inviting customers to shop and spend as much as they wanted to, it advertised that it would accept only cash. The store claimed to be protecting its patrons from falling into debt. This approach depended on the hope that consumers would keep spending in the face of a depression.

Unfortunately, by 1931 few debt-ridden consumers had the cash to make any purchases. The illusion of prosperity had prevented many from realizing that the benefits of the economic policies of the 1920s had been unevenly distributed.

A mismanaged economy. Economists cite the unequal distribution of income in America as another central cause of the Great Depression. Between 1923 and 1929 the disposable income of the wealthiest 1 percent of the nation increased by 63 percent while the income of the poorest 93 percent of the nation decreased by 4 percent. As writer Upton Sinclair noted: "The . . . depression is one of abundance, not of scarcity. . . . The cause of the trouble is that a small class has the wealth, while the rest have the debts."

This income gap meant that a large portion of the population did not have the buying power needed to boost the economy. According to many economists, if workers had received better wages for their labor and farmers better prices for their crops, the depression would have been less severe or perhaps could have been avoided.

Even the global factors that Hoover blamed for the depression could have been eased by more-farsighted U.S. policies. Economists point out that the United States contributed to the worldwide economic downturn by placing high tariffs on imported goods. Even after the crash, Congress continued to pass high tariffs, including the highest in U.S. history, the **Smoot-Hawley Tariff** of 1930.

The business cycle. Some economists argue that better fiscal planning in the 1920s could not have prevented the onset of the Great Depression. These economists view depressions as an inevitable part of the **business cycle**—the regular ups and downs of business in a free-enterprise economy. According to business-cycle theory, industries increase production and hire more workers during prosperous times so that eventually surpluses pile up. Industries then cut back on production and lay off workers, causing the start of a recession or a depression.

Events in the Great Depression support the business-cycle theory in part. While a wave of new products fueled the economic growth of the 1920s, by the end of the decade fewer Americans were buying expensive goods. Most people who wanted such products, and could afford them, had already bought them. The inability to sell their goods caused many businesses to fail and contributed to the depression.

According to this theory, however, once the surplus goods are sold, industries again gear up for production and the depression comes to an end. But the *length* and *severity* of the Great Depression went far beyond the normal rhythms of the business cycle. Thus it seems impossible to blame the business cycle—or any one factor—for causing the most severe economic depression in U.S. history.

■■ **Many factors contributed to the Great Depression: the global economic downturn, debt, the unequal distribution of wealth, and overproduction.**

SECTION 1 REVIEW

IDENTIFY and explain the significance of the following: bull market, bear market, margin buying, Black Thursday, Black Tuesday, gross national product, Great Depression, Smoot-Hawley Tariff, business cycle.

1. **MAIN IDEA** What drove many Americans to participate in the bull market of the 1920s?

2. **MAIN IDEA** How did speculation affect stock prices?

3. **IDENTIFYING CAUSE AND EFFECT** What caused the large-scale selling of stocks in October 1929? What effect did this have on the stock market?

4. **WRITING TO EXPLAIN** Write an essay outlining the factors that contributed to the Great Depression.

5. **ANALYZING** Considering the economic developments of the 1920s, how accurate was Upton Sinclair's statement that the depression was "one of abundance, not of scarcity"?

Section 2

HARD TIMES

FOCUS

- How did unemployment affect Americans in the 1930s?
- What were urban and rural living conditions like during the Great Depression?
- What did Americans do for entertainment during the period?

he Great Depression of the 1930s was not the first depression in American history, but it was by far the worst. It lasted for most of the decade, and during that time millions of Americans lost their jobs and sank into poverty. In cities and in rural areas, many people suffered from hunger, homelessness, and despair. Life was not all bleak during the depression, though. Movies, radio, and popular fiction helped lift American spirits.

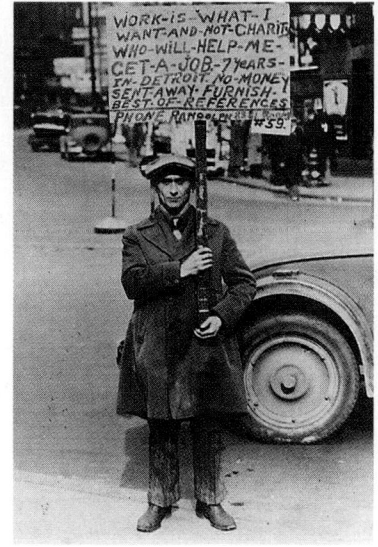

Unemployed worker, 1930

"WORK IS WHAT I WANT"

Perhaps the clearest sign of the deepening depression was a sharp rise in unemployment. In 1929 some 1.5 million Americans were unemployed; three years later that figure had risen to some 12 million, as ailing and failed businesses laid off their employees. To poet Langston Hughes, it seemed "everybody in America was looking for work."

By 1932, industrial output had fallen to about half that of 1929, resulting in massive layoffs. Even for those who managed to keep their jobs, wages fell dramatically—in some cases to as low as 10 cents an hour. Factory workers' average annual income fell by nearly one third between 1929 and 1933. For the first time in years, immigration to the United States greatly decreased. One despondent Slavic immigrant told a reporter in 1932: "If you had told me, when I come to this country that now I live like this, I shot you dead."

African Americans faced especially difficult times, as economic troubles added to the problem of racial discrimination they already faced. When factories laid off employees, black workers were often the first to go. In several cities as much as 25 to 40 percent of African Americans were out of work by 1933. One study of Chicago unemployment patterns noted the general view among whites that blacks "should not be hired as long as there are white men without work."

African American women, who made up the vast majority of domestic servants, also suffered

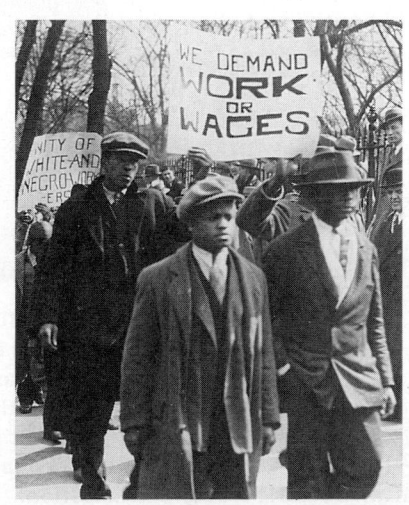

◄ Thousands of unemployed workers gathered before the White House on March 6, 1930, to protest for better unemployment policies.

Unemployment Relief

DOUBLE TROUBLE In the early 1930s a disastrous drought struck the agricultural states of the Great Plains, adding to the difficulties caused by the depression.

? **PLACE** Which state had the highest percentage of its people receiving unemployment?

Percentage of Total State Population Receiving Unemployment Relief

- More than 25 percent
- 21-25 percent
- 16-20 percent
- 11-15 percent
- Less than 11 percent

ND 29%
SD 41%
OK 28%
NM 31%

because of increased competition in domestic and agricultural work.

Some unemployed workers took to selling apples on the street, where on a good day a seller might earn $1.15, causing President Hoover to claim, "Many people have left their jobs for the more profitable one of selling apples." But few people in the depression had any choice over how or where they worked. Some even hitchhiked or hopped freight trains across the country to find jobs.

■■ **During the depression one fourth of the work force lost their jobs. Many had to seek work wherever they could find it.**

massive unemployment. Without regular work, many had to participate in degrading "slave markets," where they would stand on street corners and try to obtain work as maids. One observer of the "Bronx Slave Market" described the typical scene:

❝ Rain or shine, cold or hot, you will find them there—Negro women, old and young—sometimes bedraggled, sometimes neatly dressed . . . waiting expectantly for Bronx housewives to buy their strength and energy for an hour. ❞

Since many employers could hire women more cheaply than men, the percentage of women in the work force actually increased in the 1930s. Most were employed as office workers or domestic servants. But as the percentage of women in the work force rose overall, the percentage of employed African American women actually fell

▲ In the 1930s many couples participated in dance marathons to win money. Some marathons would last for days, until all but one couple dropped from exhaustion.

LIFE IN THE CITY

The impact of the depression spread all across America, hitting people in cities and on farms and disrupting family life. Some of the most-lasting images of the period came from urban America, as the depression hit many cities hard. During the early 1930s the federal government did little to aid local communities.

City governments and charitable organizations such as the Red Cross took on the burden of providing direct relief to the needy. Neighbors, especially those in ethnic communities, also helped one another. One elderly African American woman told a visitor: "My neighbors helps me, by bringin' me a little to eat, when they knows I ain't got nothin' in the house to cook."

Mexican American communities formed *mutualistas,* or mutual-aid societies, to help local residents. Some Chinese American communities set out open barrels of

▲ Shantytowns appeared outside many towns and cities during the early 1930s. Shown here is a Hooverville in New York City.

rice so that people could draw from them privately, without asking for handouts. Harlem residents organized "rent parties"—large social gatherings that charged a small admission to help pay someone's monthly rent.

Across the country, people struggled daily to feed themselves and their children. Haggard men and women waited in **breadlines** for bowls of watery soup and crusts of dry bread. When one hungry schoolchild was told to go home for lunch, she replied: "It won't do any good. . . . This is my sister's day to eat." By 1932 one out of every five children in New York City suffered from malnutrition. Some Americans suffered long-term health effects in the form of stunted growth, weak bones, and dental problems from these poor diets.

In addition to hunger, homelessness was a serious urban problem during the depression. **Shantytowns**—collections of makeshift shelters built out of packing boxes, scrap lumber, corrugated iron, and other thrown-away items—rose up outside most cities. Blaming an unresponsive president for their plight, the homeless mockingly referred to these shantytowns as Hoovervilles and the newspapers they often slept under as Hoover blankets.

■■ **With little help from the federal government, urban communities struggled to provide for the hungry and homeless.**

LIFE ON THE FARM

The depression also struck hard at rural America, as the farm crisis of the 1920s turned into a disaster in the 1930s. People in the cities needed food but could not pay for it. As demand for farm products shrank, prices plummeted, and farmers found themselves with more goods than they could sell. While people went hungry in the cities, farmers in some areas were forced to let crops rot in the fields and to slaughter excess livestock they could not afford to feed.

As their incomes fell, many farmers were unable to keep up their mortgage payments. While banks foreclosed on farms all across America, some communities banded together to fight back. Often when a bank held a foreclosure auction to sell off a family's possessions, neighbors would

DEPRESSION WORLDWIDE

THROUGH OTHERS' EYES

The depression of the 1930s knew no borders. In a radio talk in 1931, British economist John Maynard Keynes discussed its worldwide reach:

❝ *The slump in trade and employment and the business losses . . . are as bad as the worst which have ever occurred in the modern history of the world. No country is exempt. The privation [hardship] and—what is sometimes worse—the anxiety which exist today in millions of homes all over the world is extreme. In the three chief industrial countries of the world, Great Britain, Germany, and the United States, I estimate that probably 12 million industrial workers stand idle. But I am not sure that there is not even more human misery today in the great agricultural countries of the world—Canada, Australia, and South America, where millions of small farmers see themselves ruined by the fall in the prices of their products, so that their receipts after harvest bring them in much less than the crops have cost them to produce.* ❞

arrive and bid absurdly low prices, such as 25 cents for a plow. After the auction they would then give the goods back to the farm family.

Conditions were especially bleak for tenant farmers in the South, where most rural residents already faced crippling poverty. As cotton prices fell from 16 cents per pound in 1929 to below 6 cents in 1931, many tenant farmers, mostly African Americans, were virtually ruined. Some were even forced off the land they had lived on all their lives. While farmers in the Midwest faced an overabundance of food, southern cotton farmers faced scarcity due to poor soil and lack of money to buy food. Gracie Turner, a sharecropper's wife, testified to the hardships of tenant life in the 1930s:

▲ Shown here is a meeting of the Spanish-speaking Congress in Los Angeles, about 1940. This group, known as El Congreso, helped organize Hispanic migrants to fight for their rights.

66 That's all there is to expect—work hard and go hungry part time. . . . This year's been so hard we had to drop our burial insurance. . . . All it costs is twenty-five cents . . . but they don't come many twenty-five cents in this house. 99

Migrant farm workers in the Southwest, most of them recent immigrants, also faced great difficulties. As relief costs soared, local authorities chose the cheaper policy of paying Mexican migrants to return to their native land. During the 1930s some 500,000 people of Mexican descent—some of them U.S. citizens—were pressured into leaving the states. Those who remained often faced severe discrimination and poor working conditions.

Some of the Mexican American families who stayed during the depression helped organize resistance to discrimination in the Southwest. One such organizer was Josefina Fierro de Bright, the daughter of migrants who had fled revolution in Mexico to settle in

California. The experience of growing up during the depression in the midst of poverty and ethnic discrimination had a profound effect on the young Fierro. As with many children of the depression, her life was very unstable. Her family had to move often, causing Fierro to change schools eight times. But throughout the hard times her mother always encouraged her to strive for success. "Rely on yourself, be independent," Mrs. Fierro advised. She also emphasized the importance of getting an education.

In 1938, at age 18, Josefina Fierro entered the University of California at Los Angeles. She planned to study medicine, but activism on behalf of the Mexican American community soon took up most of her time. With the aid of her husband, activist Hollywood screenwriter John Bright, she began to lead boycotts of companies that did business in Mexican American communities but did not hire Mexican American workers. Enlisting financial support from a few well-known movie stars, Fierro de Bright also started a radio program for Spanish-speaking audiences.

Josefina Fierro de Bright

These activities brought her to the attention of a Mexican American group called El Congreso, which was organizing Hispanic migrants to stand up for their rights. In 1939 El Congreso leaders asked Fierro de Bright to help them establish a branch in Los Angeles. Over the next few years, she worked tirelessly, leading marches and hunger strikes, lobbying for expanded relief programs for Hispanic Americans, and encouraging bilingual education for migrant children. "I used to work so hard it used to kill me," she recalled. But throughout her life she never forgot the lessons her mother instilled in her during those early years of the depression. Those memories spurred her efforts to improve the lives of all working people.

■■ **Rural farm workers faced increased hardship during the depression. Some were forced to leave their land.**

₣AMILY LIFE IN THE 1930s

On farms and in cities, family members often pulled together and helped one another cope with their difficulties. They shared food and money and provided the support and encouragement their relatives needed to get through hard times. In many cases, relatives doubled up in small houses, and young adults moved back in with their parents.

Economic hardship took its toll on families, however. Some eventually broke apart under the strain. The divorce rate rose during the depression. Many young people put off getting married and starting their own families, which caused marriage

▼ Life was difficult for many families during the depression. Many mothers struggled to make ends meet, such as this wife of an Alabama factory worker who earned one dollar a day.

and birthrates to decline, especially during the early years of the depression. Looking back on those years, a Chicago schoolteacher remarked:

> 66 Do you realize how many people in my generation are not married? . . . It wasn't that we didn't have a chance. I was going with someone when the Depression hit. We probably would have gotten married. . . . Suddenly he was laid off. It hit him like a ton of bricks. And he just disappeared. 99

Life was certainly not easy for women during the depression. In the face of economic hardship, the mothers of hard-hit depression families often played roles of quiet heroism. The daily challenges of putting food on the table, using worn-out appliances, and making clothes and shoes last for one more year brought constant worry. As one woman remarked: "I figured every which way I could to make ends meet . . . but some of [those] ends just wouldn't meet. They just couldn't be stretched far enough to meet." In rural and small-town households, women revived old crafts such as soap making and bread making. Others took jobs outside the home to help support their families.

COMMENTARY

The Psychological Impact of the Depression

The Great Depression affected Americans in countless ways. Some of these effects—such as hunger and homelessness—were temporary for most people. When the depression ended, most Americans got back on their feet. Other effects, though, were longer lasting. In fact, the depression had a major long-term impact on the behavior and the outlook of the millions of Americans who struggled through hard times.

The term depression *could just as easily describe the mood of the country as well as the economy in the 1930s. More than 20,000 Americans committed suicide in 1932, a 28 percent increase over 1929. For middle-class and well-to-do Americans, many of whom had never* known poverty, the depression was a cruel blow. Many would never forget the shame they felt at being unemployed, losing their businesses or homes, and being unable to provide for their families. The attitude of an unemployed teacher in New Orleans was typical: "If with all the advantages I've had, I can't make a living, I'm just no good, I guess. I've given up ever amounting to anything. It's no use."

The depression had a devastating effect on the unemployed. Many men whose lives had been dominated by work did not know what to do without a job. They often spent their days just dawdling around the house or roaming the streets. The depression proved equally severe on working women who lost their jobs, especially those whose families depended on two incomes to survive. Many parents who could not support their families were consumed by guilt and self-doubt.

Even after the depression, the memories of those lean years remained vivid. Habits of scrimping and saving, of making every penny count, would stay with members of this generation for the rest of their lives. A strong desire for financial stability and material comforts shaped the outlook of many Americans who came of age during the depression.

POPULAR CULTURE IN THE THIRTIES

Even during hard times, Americans found ways to enjoy themselves. Many people took up inexpensive pastimes, such as reading and playing games at home. Movies and radio also offered a temporary release from economic worries.

The sound explosion. Movies were a big hit during the depression. Talking pictures, which had begun to replace silent films in the late 1920s, enthralled audiences, who flocked to the new movie theaters cropping up in nearly every town. Among the most popular movies of the early 1930s were gangster films, which portrayed tough guys fighting their way to the top against all odds.

▼ Bette Davis

▲ Greta Garbo

Likewise, strong women, such as Bette Davis, Greta Garbo, Mae West, and Marlene Dietrich, lit up the screen, reinforcing the theme of survival in a difficult world.

Meanwhile, upbeat musicals like *Gold Diggers of 1933,* featuring the song "We're in the Money," and comedies portraying the hilarious antics of comedians like the Marx Brothers proved very popular. Movie cartoons also brightened the 1930s, thanks to Walt Disney's Mickey Mouse and Donald Duck characters. Often, Disney cartoons were as popular with movie audiences as the feature films they preceded.

As the movie business flourished, radio also enjoyed its golden age. Radio was immensely popular because it offered free entertainment at home.

▲ Hollywood musicals flourished during the depression. In order to take their minds off their troubles, audiences flocked to see upbeat films such as *Gold Diggers of 1933.*

By the 1930s baseball was the country's favorite sport and a symbol of American culture, just as it is today. But baseball in the 1930s was in some ways much different from the game we know now.

To be a baseball fan in the 1930s meant taking trips out to the ballpark. Without television to bring the game into people's homes, fans either listened to games on the radio or headed for their local baseball stadium to root for the home team. Games were held only in the daytime until 1930—the year the first night game was held in a major-league park.

Depression-era fans watched such players as home-run king Babe Ruth and pitcher Walter "Boom Boom" Beck. They cheered players who had higher batting averages and hit more home runs than today's players. The ballparks were often smaller than today's stadiums. And the day games favored batters because they could see the ball more clearly during the day than today's players can at night.

However, the biggest difference between baseball then and now was who could play the game. Professional baseball was still racially segregated in the 1930s. White owners maintained a so-called gentleman's agreement not to sign black players. So African Americans formed clubs and leagues of their own.

The Negro National League (NNL) fielded teams in the East such as the Newark Eagles and the New York Black Yankees. The Negro American League (NAL) covered the South and Midwest with clubs like the Kansas City Monarchs and the Chicago American Giants. Players included Hall of Fame pitcher Satchel Paige and William "Judy" Johnson. Turnouts at Paige's games could be as large as any in the majors.

Although they would not sign black players, white club owners rented their ballparks to black teams when white teams were on the road. In fact, it was under just such an arrangement that the Kansas City Monarchs pioneered a portable lighting system and held the first night games in a major-league park. The Monarchs' night games drew such good crowds that within a few years scores of other ballparks also installed lighting.

In the off-season, Satchel Paige and many other baseball players—both black and white—played in Mexico, Cuba, and other countries. Like most Americans in the 1930s, baseball players needed all the money they could earn—their salaries, especially in the black leagues, provided just enough to get by. Today's off-season training camps and million-dollar contracts were unheard of during the depression. Salaries, team rosters, ballparks, and media coverage are all very different today. But the most important element—the enjoyment the game brings—remains the same.

▲ Baseball increased in popularity during the 1930s thanks to the skills of players such as Babe Ruth and Lou Gehrig. This painting by Morris Kantor, *Baseball at Night,* depicts a game from 1934.

During the 1930s the number of radio sets in the United States rose from some 12 million to about 28 million. The most popular programs allowed listeners to forget the hardships of reality. Like the voice of a comforting friend, the opening of a favorite program captured listeners:

66 Return with us now to those thrilling days of yesteryear . . . [sound of hoofbeats] . . . From out of the West comes a fiery horse with the speed of light, a cloud of dust, and a hearty 'Hi-yo Silver'—The Lone Ranger rides again! 99

Heroes such as the Lone Ranger, Little Orphan Annie, and the Shadow always triumphed over evil, offering a hopeful message to listeners.

Literature in the early 1930s. The public's desire for entertainment also gave rise to new forms of popular literature. Magazines and comic books offered cheap and accessible forms of entertainment, presenting fantastic heroes such as Superman and Tarzan. One of the best-selling magazines of the time, *Reader's Digest,* presented a selection of condensed articles from various magazines. For families on a limited budget, this "all-purpose" magazine seemed ideal.

Many of the most popular novels of the era also offered escapism. In James Hilton's *Lost Horizon* (1933), a weary traveler stumbles upon a peaceful, prosperous utopia hidden in the mountains of Tibet. The idea of discovering a perfect world appealed to many readers.

Not all fiction of the 1930s was escapist, however. James T. Farrell portrayed the grim

◀ **William Faulkner** used his experiences growing up in Oxford, Mississippi, to create the mythical Yoknapatawpha County—a setting that appeared frequently in his novels.

▶ **Book cover of** *The Sound and the Fury*

life of Chicago's Irish immigrants in his *Studs Lonigan* trilogy (1932–1935), while Nathanael West presented the American dream as a nightmare in *Miss Lonelyhearts* (1933). William Faulkner, in novels such as *The Sound and the Fury* (1929) and *As I Lay Dying* (1930), tragically portrayed small-town life in fictional Yoknapatawpha County, Mississippi. Faulkner's novels later earned him the Nobel Prize for literature in 1949 and two Pulitzer prizes—one in 1955 and another in 1963.

■■ **During the 1930s Americans enjoyed many forms of popular culture, including movies, radio programs, and literature.**

SECTION 2 REVIEW

IDENTIFY and explain the significance of the following: *mutualistas,* breadlines, shantytowns, Josefina Fierro de Bright, James Hilton, James T. Farrell, Nathanael West, William Faulkner.

1. **MAIN IDEA** How did the depression affect the work force?

2. **MAIN IDEA** What impact did the Great Depression have on living conditions in rural areas?

3. **MAIN IDEA** How were urban communities affected by the Great Depression? In what ways did individuals and communities try to cope?

4. **WRITING TO DESCRIBE** Imagine you are a magazine editor researching a story on popular culture during the 1930s. Write an outline for an article that describes popular forms of entertainment during this period.

5. **EVALUATING** How did economic hardship alter family life in the 1930s?

HOOVER FAILS

FOCUS

- What beliefs shaped President Hoover's response to the depression?
- What effect did the Hoover administration's economic policies have on the depression?
- Why did Hoover lose the election of 1932?

When the depression began, many Americans had great faith in Herbert Hoover. His skills as a businessman and as an administrator inspired confidence. Under his direction the government undertook some important measures to fight the depression. But they were not enough to end the crisis. As a result, voters in the election of 1932 rejected Hoover in favor of his Democratic opponent, Franklin D. Roosevelt.

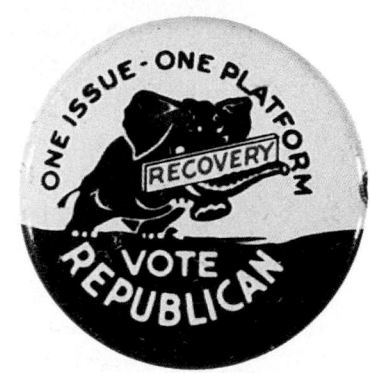

Republican campaign button, 1932

HOOVER'S PHILOSOPHY

The most urgent task confronting President Hoover was to ease the human suffering caused by the depression. Prior to the crash most Americans believed that the government should not interfere in the free-enterprise system. Immediately after the crash, the *New York Times* advised that "the fundamental prescriptions for recovery [are] such homely things as savings . . . and hopeful waiting for the turn." Within a few months, however, the worsening crisis led to calls for the federal government to provide direct relief—food, clothing, shelter, and money—to the needy. Hoover rejected the idea of such government aid, stating:

66 I do not believe that the power and duty of the [federal] Government ought to be extended to the relief of individual suffering. . . . The lesson should be constantly enforced that though the people support the Government the Government should not support the people. 99

Direct federal relief, Hoover argued, would create a vast bureaucracy, inflate the federal budget, and undermine the self-respect of people receiving the aid. Instead, Hoover urged Americans to lift themselves up through hard work and strength of character.

Hoover's political beliefs stemmed from the notion of **rugged individualism**—the idea that

▼ Unemployed workers protested in New York's Times Square in 1933. Demonstrators carried signs indicating they were willing to work for $1 a week.

▲ Private charities and organizations such as the Salvation Army helped families in need of assistance by bringing them food and clothing.

▼ Nurses, such as this one in Maryland, often went door-to-door offering people free medical assistance.

success comes through individual effort and private enterprise. He believed that private charities and local communities, not the federal government, could best provide for those in need. "A voluntary deed," said Hoover, "is infinitely more precious to our national ideals and spirit than a thousandfold poured from the Treasury."

Hoover was not alone in his beliefs. Millions of Americans agreed that voluntary efforts were preferable to government intervention. It soon became clear, however, that voluntary efforts alone could not deal with the scale of the depression. Communities and private charities lacked the resources to cope with the ever-rising tide of human misery. Local governments were forced to stretch already inadequate funds to cover growing numbers of needy families. By 1933, for example, families on public welfare in New York City were paid just $23 a month.

In 1930 Hoover appointed the Committee for Unemployment Relief to assist state and local relief efforts. The committee, however, did little beyond urging Americans to contribute more to charity. The human misery of the depression continued practically unchecked.

■■ **Hoover's belief in rugged individualism led him to oppose direct federal relief for those in need.**

BOOSTING THE ECONOMY

Although critics would later charge that Hoover's relief plans failed because he did not get the government involved, Hoover was not totally opposed to the government intervening in the economy. In fact, despite his opposition to direct public relief, Hoover's administration played a

▲ President Hoover addressed 250 leaders of finance, industry, and commerce in August 1932. In his speech, Hoover asked business leaders to assume more responsibility for improving the economy.

more active role in attempting to shape the economy than any previous administration had.

Stimulating the economy. Within weeks of the stock market crash, Hoover called a White House conference of top business, labor, and political leaders. The *New York Times* hailed the meeting as a step in the right direction, noting:

> 66 [It is] the largest gathering of noted heads of industrial and other corporations in Washington since the resources of the nation were marshalled for participation in the World War! 99

Hoover urged these leaders to maintain employment and wages voluntarily as a step toward reviving business activity and promoting recovery. At the same time, he issued cheerful public statements designed to boost confidence and get the economy going again.

Unfortunately, most people did not share Hoover's optimism. Many became very cynical toward the administration as trust in government and in business declined. Moaned the chairman of the Republican National Committee: "Every time an administration official gives out an optimistic statement about business conditions, the market immediately drops."

At Hoover's request, Congress funded several public-works programs, among them the giant Hoover Dam on the Colorado River. Hoover expected these projects to achieve two goals: (1) to stimulate business by providing contracts for construction and materials and (2) to provide relief by employing jobless workers. Overall, he approved some $800 million in public-works funding. Yet the crisis was so great that even this large amount had little impact on the depression.

Coping with the farm crisis. Hoover also took some steps to ease the plight of farmers. As crop prices fell, Hoover instructed the Federal Farm Board—created through the **Agricultural Marketing Act** of 1929—to buy up surplus wheat, corn, cotton, and other farm products. Officials believed that reducing crop supplies would cause prices to rise. The government could store these commodities and then sell them when prices were higher. The scheme did not work. Farmers at first refused to limit production. Instead, they reacted to low prices by growing more crops. In 1931 the Farm Board stopped buying surplus crops, having already spent some $180 million.

Just as he opposed direct relief for jobless factory workers, Hoover resisted giving direct aid to desperate farmers. He did try to aid farmers indirectly, though, by recommending passage of the **Home Loan Bank Act** in 1932. The act provided money to savings banks, building and loan associations, and insurance companies for low-interest mortgages. Hoover believed that the act would reduce foreclosures on homes and farms and thus allow more farmers to keep their land. He also believed that the act would encourage home construction, boosting employment and increasing the flow of money through the economy.

The Reconstruction Finance Corporation. Hoover also tried to stimulate the economy through the **Reconstruction Finance Corporation** (RFC), created by Congress in February 1932. The RFC lent large sums to railroads, insurance companies, banks, and other financial institutions. By strengthening these key businesses through federal loans, Hoover hoped to reduce bank failures and create more jobs.

By the end of Hoover's term, RFC loans had helped a number of large corporations avoid collapse. Yet the economy continued to decline, in part because the RFC offered too little, too late. It was created while the depression was in full swing, and it provided no direct aid to industries or

◀ Hoover Dam on the Colorado River was completed in 1936. It is the main source of hydroelectric power in the Southwest.

to small businesses, which continued to fail at an alarming rate.

Critics attacked the RFC's trickle-down approach to economic recovery. They argued that money lent to big business would not filter down quickly enough to help the real victims of the depression—ordinary citizens. As one economist put it, this was like putting fertilizer on the branches of a tree—rather than on the roots—to help the tree grow. A more effective approach, said critics, would be to funnel money directly to those in need. This would increase consumers' buying power and thereby stimulate business. Newspaper columnist Walter Lippmann reflected popular sentiments when he wrote:

> **66** It is hard for the country to realize that this era of easy finance is over. . . . In respect to government finance, as in respect to so many other things, Congress and the people of the country have radically to readjust their minds. **99**

Government activism. Although President Hoover's policies failed to end the Great Depression, the RFC and other measures—such as the Home Loan Bank Act and funding for public works—represented a major shift in government policy. To a greater degree than ever before, the president and Congress accepted the idea that the federal government can and should do something to boost the economy in times of crisis.

In the early 1930s Treasury Secretary Andrew Mellon had advised the traditional do-nothing approach. He even argued that a short depression would be good for the country because "it will purge the rottenness out of the system." But as the depression became more severe, the government took unprecedented steps to promote recovery. Unfortunately, these measures were not sufficient to halt the downward trend. As Americans continued to suffer, they increasingly blamed their plight on Herbert Hoover.

▲ **Andrew Mellon**

■■ **Hoover's limited measures to end the depression did little to ease the crisis.**

RUMBLINGS OF DISCONTENT

By 1932 Hoover was the most hated man in America. His appearance in movie newsreels provoked boos and catcalls from audiences. And he made little effort to win public support by changing his aloof manner or stiff, boring speeches. "This is not a showman's job," Hoover remarked. "I will not step out of character."

As confidence in Hoover eroded, radical political parties grew more vocal. Both the Communist party and the Socialist party condemned the capitalist system that they believed created the depression. Both parties helped organize several mass protests in the early 1930s. Socialist leader A. J. Muste gathered the jobless into Unemployed Leagues to demand work. The Communist party encouraged labor-union activism and led strikes by migrant farm workers.

A Most Vicious Circle

▲ **As the depression worsened, more and more people began to blame President Hoover for their troubles. This cartoon appeared June 1931 in the Albany News.**

▲ Shown here is lawyer Samuel Leibowitz (left) meeting with Heywood Patterson, one of the principal defendants in the Scottsboro case.

The party also helped expose racial injustice. In 1931 an all-white jury in Scottsboro, Alabama, sentenced eight of nine black youths aged 13 to 21 years to death on a highly questionable rape charge. The Communist party helped supply legal defense for the "Scottsboro Boys" and organized mass demonstrations to overturn the convictions.

Many desperate Americans responded to communist and socialist calls for direct action. Early in 1932, thousands of unemployed men demanding work participated in a hunger march on the Ford auto plant near Detroit. Four were killed when police opened fire. In Seattle, 5,000 unemployed protestors seized a public building. After two days local officials finally forced them out.

Some activism was spontaneous, reflecting the desperation of the times. In rural areas people armed with clubs, pitchforks, and shotguns confronted officials trying to foreclose on homes. Farmers destroyed crops and blocked roads to prevent food from being shipped to market, hoping that limiting food supplies would push prices up. "They say blockading the highway's illegal," an Iowa farmer said. "Seems to me there was a Tea Party in Boston that was illegal too."

The biggest protest was staged by more than 10,000 World War I veterans and their families in May 1932. They came to Washington, D.C., to support a veterans' bonus bill then before Congress. The bill would have granted the veterans—many of whom were unemployed—early payment of pension bonuses due to them for their service during the war. This group was soon dubbed the **Bonus Army**.

At first, officials allowed the Bonus Army demonstrators to live in empty government buildings and to camp in an open area across the Potomac River. When Congress rejected the bonus bill, most of the demonstrators returned home. But about 2,000 veterans stayed, defying orders to leave. In a clash with authorities, two veterans and two policemen were killed. The police requested aid, and President Hoover ordered the army to disperse the squatters.

In late July the army moved in with machine guns, tanks, and tear gas. One woman recalled her husband's experience that day:

> 66 My husband went to Washington. To march with . . . the bonus boys. He was a machine gunner in the war. He'd say them . . . Germans gassed him in Germany. And [then] his own government . . . gassed him and run him off the country up there with a water hose, half drowned him. 99

▲ More than 10,000 veterans marched to Washington, D.C., in May 1932 to petition Congress for full and immediate payment of pension bonuses earned during World War I.

Commanded by General Douglas MacArthur (later a hero in World War II), the troops drove the veterans from the buildings, broke up their encampment, and burned their shacks. Hundreds were injured and three killed, including an 11-week-old baby. Many Americans found the government's treatment of the veterans shocking. Across the nation, anger against Hoover grew. As the election of 1932 approached, Americans joked bitterly, "In Hoover we trusted and now we are busted."

■■ **Public unrest grew as the depression worsened and Hoover mishandled the Bonus Army protest.**

THE ELECTION OF 1932

In the summer of 1932, with elections scheduled for the fall, the Republicans reluctantly renominated Herbert Hoover as their presidential candidate. With public sentiment running strongly against the Republicans, no other member of the party was eager for the nomination. The Democrats, sensing victory, chose Franklin Delano Roosevelt of New York as their candidate.

The Democratic challenger. Roosevelt—who often went by his initials, FDR—was a determined and skillful politician. Born into a wealthy and prestigious family, his background suggested that he would be more likely to identify with the wealthy than with working-class citizens. He could easily have become a Wall Street power broker, but instead he chose a career in public service.

FDR was highly influenced by the progressivism of his distant cousin, former president Theodore Roosevelt, and by that of the former president's niece Eleanor Roosevelt, who married FDR in 1905. Her earnest belief in social reform impressed the young FDR. Mrs. Roosevelt would become one of his most important political assets. A fellow Democrat once said of the relationship between Franklin and Eleanor Roosevelt: "Any good things he may have done during his political career are due to her and any mistakes he may have made are due to his not taking up the matter with his wife."

FDR ran as a vice-presidential candidate in 1920, but his political career appeared to be over when he was paralyzed from the waist down by polio in 1921. Yet with the help of his wife, he overcame his physical challenges and was elected governor of New York in 1928. As governor he gained high marks for his imaginative state relief programs that had instituted unemployment benefits and supported failing industries. In accepting his party's nomination for president, Roosevelt issued a call for a new style of government, declaring:

▼ Franklin D. Roosevelt's support of innovative relief programs while governor of New York made him a strong contender for the 1932 Democratic party presidential nomination (below). The photograph at right shows him campaigning in 1932.

> 66 Republican leaders not only have failed in material things, they have failed in national vision, because in disaster they have held out no hope. . . . I pledge you, I pledge myself, to a new deal for the American people. 99

A change in leadership. The 1932 campaign had one key issue—the depression. While Hoover tried to defend his policies, he realized he had little chance of victory. Roosevelt continually attacked Hoover's record and called for major policy changes, including direct federal relief for the needy, a massive public-works program, and federal regulation of the stock market to prevent fraud. Roosevelt promised to seek a fairer distribution of wealth and to put the political and economic system at "the service of the people."

On election day, Roosevelt and his running mate, John Nance Garner of Texas, carried 42 states, capturing 23 million popular votes and 472 electoral votes to Hoover's 16 million popular votes and 59 electoral votes. The Democrats won decisive majorities in both houses of Congress, solidifying gains they had already made in the congressional election of 1930. As a result, Roosevelt was confident that his programs would have strong support in Congress.

In the 1920s most Americans had credited the Republicans for the era's glowing prosperity. In 1932, voters made it clear that the Republicans would have to take the blame for the depression.

▲ **These Roosevelt campaign artifacts were used during the 1932 presidential election.**

Many of those who voted for Roosevelt were really voting against Herbert Hoover. But other Americans saw in Roosevelt the kind of dynamic personality they believed could lead the country out of its troubles. Roosevelt had promised a "new deal." During the four months between Election Day and Roosevelt's inauguration on March 4, 1933, Americans waited hopefully to see how the new president would carry out his campaign pledge.

■■ **Hoover lost the election of 1932 because voters were upset by the Republicans' handling of the depression and were inspired by Franklin Roosevelt's confidence.**

SECTION 3 REVIEW

IDENTIFY and explain the significance of the following: rugged individualism, Agricultural Marketing Act, Home Loan Bank Act, Reconstruction Finance Corporation, Andrew Mellon, A. J. Muste, Bonus Army, Franklin Delano Roosevelt, Eleanor Roosevelt.

1. **MAIN IDEA** Why did President Hoover rely on local and voluntary efforts and oppose direct federal relief for those in need?

2. **MAIN IDEA** What measures did the Hoover administration support to end the depression? Why did they fail?

3. **MAIN IDEA** Why did public unrest grow during the Hoover administration?

4. **WRITING TO EXPRESS A VIEWPOINT** Imagine you are a campaign worker for Franklin Delano Roosevelt. Write a campaign poster explaining why voters should support your candidate in the 1932 election.

5. **HYPOTHESIZING** How might the events of the early 1930s have been different if the Hoover administration had supported direct federal relief?

Stock market crashes. William Faulkner's *The Sound and the Fury* published. Agricultural Marketing Act passed

Smoot-Hawley Tariff passed. William Faulkner's *As I Lay Dying* published.

1929

1930

WRITING A SUMMARY

Using the essential points of the chapter as a guide, write a summary of the chapter.

REVIEWING CHRONOLOGY

Number your paper 1 to 5. Study the time line above, and list the following events in the order in which they happened by writing the first next to 1, the second next to 2, and so on. Then complete the activity below.

1. Stock market crashes.
2. Bonus Army marches on Washington, D.C.
3. Scottsboro Boys case begins.
4. James Hilton's *Lost Horizon* and Nathanael West's *Miss Lonelyhearts* published.
5. Smoot-Hawley Tariff passed.

Evaluating How did Hoover's appointment of the Committee for Unemployment Relief show his support for rugged individualism?

IDENTIFYING PEOPLE AND IDEAS

Explain the historical significance of each of the following people or terms.

1. bear market
2. Andrew Mellon
3. Black Tuesday
4. *mutualistas*
5. shantytowns
6. Josefina Fierro de Bright
7. James T. Farrell
8. rugged individualism
9. Home Loan Bank Act
10. Bonus Army

UNDERSTANDING MAIN IDEAS

1. What factors led Americans to invest in the stock market during the 1920s? Why did the stock market crash in 1929?
2. How did the depression affect the banking industry?
3. What effect did the depression have on family life in the 1930s?
4. What measures did President Hoover take to stimulate the economy?
5. What are some of the ways in which people expressed their discontent during the depression?

REVIEWING THEMES

1. **Economic Development** What factors caused the Great Depression?
2. **Geographic Diversity** How did the depression influence where people lived during the 1930s?
3. **Cultural Diversity** How were African Americans and Mexican Americans affected differently by the depression?

THINKING CRITICALLY

1. **Evaluating** How did the depression affect the behavior and outlook of Americans who struggled through those hard times?
2. **Analyzing** Why did Hoover oppose direct federal relief to the needy?
3. **Synthesizing** What major policy changes did Franklin Roosevelt propose during the 1932 presidential campaign?

STRATEGY FOR SUCCESS

Review the Skills Handbook entry on Distinguishing Fact from Opinion on page 990. Then read the following excerpt, in which the editor of the Johnstown *Tribune* warns the city of dangers to be expected from the arrival of the Bonus Army. What opinions does the editor have about the marchers? How might they differ from the opinions of one of the marchers?

> **66** In any group of the size of the Bonus Army, made up of men gathered from all parts of the country, without discipline, without effective leadership in a crisis, . . . there is certain to be a mixture of undesirables—thieves, plug-uglies [thugs], degenerates. . . . The community must protect itself from the criminal fringe of the invaders. **99**

WRITING ABOUT HISTORY

Writing to Create Write a poem or lyrics for a song that would reflect the mood of Americans struggling with the depression.

USING PRIMARY SOURCES

As the depression continued into the winter of 1932, the growing numbers of unemployed forced to seek relief in soup kitchens became a familiar sight. In her poem "Bread Line," which was published in January 1932, Florence Converse attempted to make sense of this tragedy. Read the following excerpt from the poem. What point is the poet trying to make?

> ❝ *What's the meaning of this queue,*
> *Tailing down the avenue,*
> *Full of eyes that will not meet*
> *The other eyes that throng the street—*
> *The questing eyes, the curious eyes,*
> *Scornful, popping with surprise*
> *To see a living line of men*
> *As long as round the block, and then*
> *As long again? . . .*
>
> . . . .
>
> *What's the meaning in these faces*
> *Modern industry displaces,*
> *Emptying the factory*
> *To set the men so tidily*
> *Along the pavement in a row?*
> *Now and then they take a slow*
> *Shuffling step, straight ahead,*
> *As if a dead march said:*
> *"Beware! I'm not dead."*
>
> . . . .

> *A spark can creep, a spark can run;*
> *Suddenly a spark can wink*
> *And send us down destruction's brink.*
>
> . . . .
>
> *What if our slow-match have caught*
> *Fire from a burning thought?*
> *What if we should be destroyed*
> *By our patient unemployed?* ❞

LINKING HISTORY AND GEOGRAPHY

Refer to the map on page 676. Which states had the smallest percentage of people receiving unemployment benefits? What factors might account for variations in the number of people receiving unemployment assistance?

Breadline

BUILDING YOUR PORTFOLIO

Complete the following projects independently or cooperatively.

1. **THE ECONOMY** In chapters 21 and 22 you dealt with the postwar economic downswing and the upswing of the 1920s. Building on that experience, imagine you are a cartoonist in 1929. Create an editorial cartoon that criticizes the investment practices that led to the stock market crash.

2. **GLOBAL RELATIONS** Imagine you are a journalist in the 1930s at the height of the Great Depression. Create a series of newspaper headlines that describe the effects of the depression both in the United States and around the world. Headlines might mention stories about individual families, homelessness and food shortages, unemployment, Hoover's political problems, or international trade issues.

THE NEW DEAL

FOCUS

UNDERSTANDING THE MAIN IDEA

To help the nation recover from the Great Depression of the 1930s, President Franklin Roosevelt created a series of programs known as the New Deal. These reforms improved the economy and expanded the role of government in economic life. The government provided jobs to thousands of unemployed workers and provided direct relief to the needy.

THEMES

- **ECONOMIC DEVELOPMENT** How can the federal government aid economic recovery?

- **CONSTITUTIONAL HERITAGE** Why might government interference in the economy be considered unconstitutional?

- **CULTURAL DIVERSITY** What role might the arts play in reflecting ethnic and cultural diversity?

The prosperous economic times of the 1920s had come to a devastating end with the stock market crash of 1929 and the Great Depression. President Hoover's administration had been very cautious in dealing with the economic crisis. By electing Franklin Roosevelt in 1932, the nation appeared ready for the federal government to take a more active role in shaping the economy.

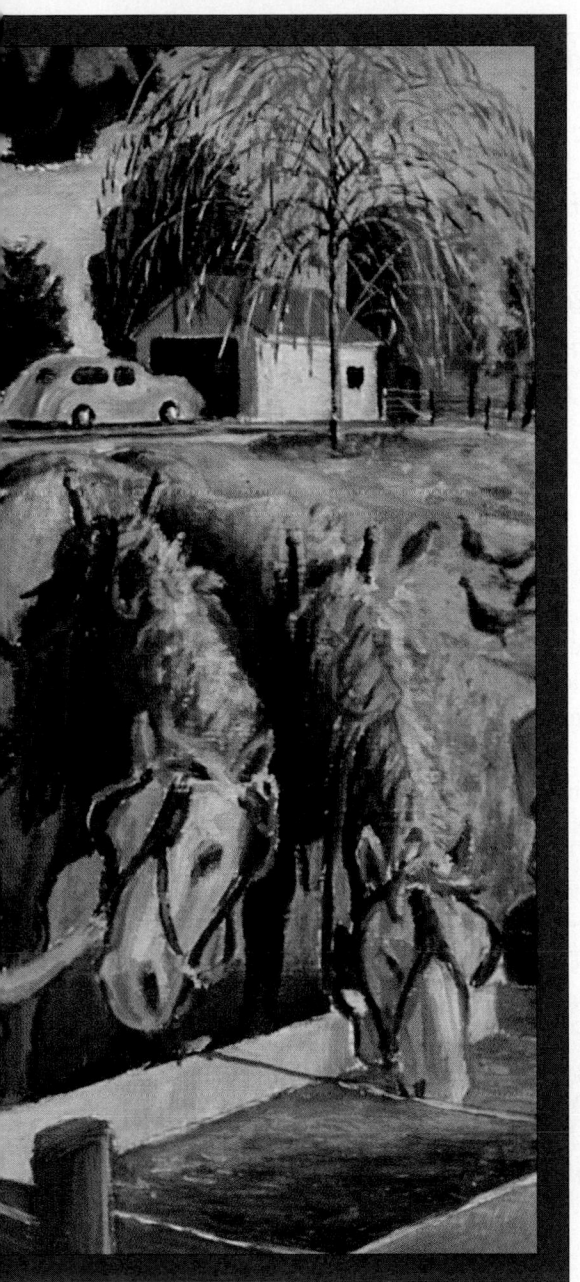

Post office mural, *Evening on the Farm,* by Orr C. Fisher

By 1933, Americans had endured three years of economic depression—each year more desperate than the last. On his last day in office, President Hoover was heard to sigh, "We are at the end of our string. There is nothing more we can do." But the new president, Franklin Delano Roosevelt, did not share this despair. In his inaugural address he offered the American people hope:

> ❝ First of all let me assert my firm belief that the only thing we have to fear is fear itself—nameless, unreasoning, unjustified terror which paralyzes needed efforts to convert retreat into advance. . . . This Nation asks for action, and action now. ❞

Roosevelt's words rang out across the land, lifting Americans from despair and stirring their hopes. Some half a million letters in support of the new president poured into the White House.

Roosevelt's program had three general aims: *relief,* to ease the plight of citizens in economic distress; *recovery,* to restore the economy to health; and *reform,* to correct ills and injustices in American society. Despite much confusion, inefficiency, and political conflict, Roosevelt's measures proved enormously powerful and far-reaching. They restored public hope, aided the unemployed, and gave the government a central role in regulating business and the economy and promoting public welfare.

National Recovery Administration symbol

RESTORING HOPE

F O C U S

■ **What New Deal programs tackled the banking, farm, and home owners' crises?**

■ **How did the New Deal provide relief for the unemployed?**

■ **What effect did the New Deal have on the Tennessee Valley region?**

New Yorker
magazine cover, 1933

*R*oosevelt wasted no time making good his pledge of "action, and action now." As soon as he arrived in the Oval Office, he confidently proposed programs that would strengthen the nation's teetering banking system and provide relief for the needy. Soon he moved on to attack the deep-seated problems that plagued agriculture and industry. One project would transform an entire region of the country.

*R*OOSEVELT CONFRONTS THE EMERGENCY

Roosevelt's optimism proved contagious. "The whole country is with him," noted humorist Will Rogers, "just so he does something. If he burned down the Capitol, we would cheer and say, 'Well, we at least got a fire started anyhow.'" People were ready for action, even if it meant making mistakes along the way.

Roosevelt did indeed get a fire started. With the help of the Brain Trust, the advisory group that he had formed in 1932 while still governor of New York, the energetic new president drew up 15 relief and recovery measures, his promised "new deal for the American people." Immediately after taking office on March 5, Roosevelt called Congress into special session. Over the next 100 days, Congress approved all

15 measures, which made up the heart of the president's **New Deal** program.

Roosevelt started with the nation's banks, which were in serious trouble. The day after his inauguration, he issued a proclamation closing every bank in the nation for a few days. This so-called **bank holiday** was designed to stop massive withdrawals. On Thursday, March 9, Congress took only a few hours to pass the **Emergency Banking Act**,

▶ **Americans listened as Roosevelt discussed important issues in one of his many radio broadcasts.**

J. B. Murray, a young
Australian, came to
the United States in
1926. He spent the
next 11 years working in
California orchards, oil fields,
and ranches. When Franklin Roosevelt was
nominated for the presidency in 1932,
Murray became an eager observer of
American politics.

"*For myself,*" he later wrote in a book
about his travels titled American Trails, "*I believed
in Roosevelt completely, and became engrossed
with his campaign. He travelled to distant cities,
and into the farming country, and wherever he
went left hope behind him. The man's charm of
manner and quiet confidence and strength were
irresistible.*" Murray noted that Roosevelt's "*personality flooded the countryside like warm sunshine. . . . The country listened spellbound to [his]
clear, confident voice, which assured all that a
new era was commencing.*" Murray concluded,
"*Listening to his radio talks, I had already marked
him down as the greatest man of the age.*"

Corporation (FDIC) in June 1933. This
reform insured each bank deposit up to
$2,500. (Today, the figure is $100,000
per account.)

Roosevelt then turned his attention
to the plight of the farmers. On March
28 he issued an executive order to create
the **Farm Credit Administration**, to
provide low-interest, long-term loans to
farmers. Congress obliged, and with
these loans, farmers paid off mortgages and overdue taxes, bought back
lost farms, and purchased needed
seed, fertilizer, and equipment. In
April, Roosevelt asked Congress to
create the **Home Owners Loan
Corporation** (HOLC) to address the
problem of home owners who could
not meet their mortgage payments.
Again, Congress obliged. By June 1936
the HOLC had saved the homes of
some one million American families by
granting them low-interest, long-term
mortgage loans.

■■ **The bank holiday and
FDIC restored public
trust in banks, while the
FCA and HOLC pro-
vided loans to farmers
and home owners.**

which authorized the government to examine all
banks and allow those that were financially sound
to reopen. Roosevelt hoped that the act would
restore public confidence in the banking system.

Caught without cash, Americans scrambled
to find substitutes for it during the bank holiday.
Many used subway and bus tokens, postage
stamps, and IOUs. On Sunday evening, March 12,
some 60 million anxious Americans tuned in their
radios to hear the president explain how the bank
holiday would protect their money. In this first of
many "fireside chats"—radio broadcasts from the
White House—Roosevelt urged people to reinvest
in banks. "I can assure you that it is safer to keep
your money in a reopened bank than under the
mattress," he advised.

The next morning, as banks began reopening,
more than $1 billion in deposits flowed into the sys-
tem. Confidence in banks increased still more when
Congress created the **Federal Deposit Insurance**

RELIEF FOR THE NEEDY

Along with these measures the Roosevelt administration also launched a large-scale program of
direct relief to the nation's 13 million unemployed.
In many ways Roosevelt's direct-relief program
completed the agenda that reformers had been trying to get the government to support since the
Progressive Era. Through the efforts of Eleanor
Roosevelt and Democratic National Committee
member Molly Dewson, the president brought in
many long-time reformers to direct his programs,
including Secretary of Labor Frances Perkins.

In May 1933, at Roosevelt's request, Congress
established the **Federal Emergency Relief
Administration** (FERA) with half a billion dollars
for relief aid to be funneled directly to state and
local agencies. One of FDR's most trusted advisers,
Harry L. Hopkins, headed the FERA program.

A Washington newspaper reported the eagerness of the FERA director to get relief to the needy:

66 The half-billion dollars for direct relief of States won't last a month if Harry L. Hopkins, the new relief administrator, maintains the pace he set yesterday in disbursing more than $5,000,000 during his first two hours in office. 99

By 1935 the total of such direct federal relief aid had risen to some $3 billion. At one point nearly eight million American families were surviving on public assistance.

Americans, however, disliked this kind of aid. They wanted jobs, not handouts. So Hopkins organized the **Civil Works Administration** (CWA) to create jobs. Most of these were "make-work" projects such as raking leaves and picking up park litter. From 1933 to 1934, the CWA paid some $750 million in wages to some four million men and women.

To aid unemployed young men between ages 18 and 25, Congress established the **Civilian Conservation Corps** (CCC) in 1933. Initially, some 250,000 young men left their homes and went to army camps for CCC training. Once trained, they spread out into the nation's forests, where they planted trees, cleared underbrush, laid out park trails, and developed campgrounds and beaches. For their efforts they earned a dollar a day. Most of their earnings were sent back home to help their families. Said one CCC veteran of the experience:

66 I really enjoyed it. I had three wonderful square meals a day. . . . They sure made a man out of ya, because you learned that everybody here was equal. There was nobody better than another in the CCC's. 99

During its nearly 10-year life, the CCC enrolled more than 2.5 million young men and planted millions of trees, most in the South and the Southwest. The program earned back much of its cost in the value it added to the nation's forests.

■■ **Through the FERA, the CWA, and the CCC, the New Deal granted direct relief to the unemployed and created jobs.**

HELPING THE NATION RECOVER

While New Deal relief programs aided needy Americans, the Roosevelt administration also pursued recovery programs to revive the economy. Roosevelt saw relief as a short-term remedy; recovery was his long-term goal.

To stimulate recovery in business and industry, the Roosevelt administration poured money into the economy through federal loans and government spending—a process sometimes called "priming the pump." Many of the New Deal recovery programs were based on the theories of noted economist John Maynard Keynes, who argued that for a nation to recover fully from a depression, the government had to spend money to create jobs and boost investment.

One of the chief ways in which the Roosevelt administration attempted to prime the economy's pump was through the **National Industrial Recovery Act** (NIRA), which Congress passed in June 1933. The act was designed to stimulate industrial and business activity and reduce unemployment by stabilizing prices, raising wages, limiting workers' hours, and providing jobs. To help achieve these goals,

◀ **Some 2.5 million jobless young men were employed by the CCC from 1933 to 1943. During the decade they worked on projects designed to preserve and restore the nation's natural resources.**

1882 1982 USA 20c
Franklin D. Roosevelt

"Mr. Roosevelt is a unique figure in the modern world: the one statesman . . . who seems able to relax," wrote one journalist about the charismatic leader. Indeed, FDR always appeared to be warm, energetic, and easygoing, despite the enormous pressures that faced his administration. His optimistic outlook may have helped in his recuperation from polio.

The president always hid his private thoughts behind his dazzling smile. One of his speech writers commented that you could never tell what was going on in FDR's "heavily forested interior." Yet, the president relied heavily on instinct and idealism in making decisions. Political philosophy held little value for him. His warm style and compassionate manner, expressed in his weekly "fireside chats," helped win support for many of his programs. Years after the depression many Americans would remember FDR almost as a beloved family member.

---

the NIRA created two new federal agencies—the **Public Works Administration** (PWA) and the **National Recovery Administration** (NRA).

The PWA, under the leadership of Secretary of the Interior Harold Ickes, provided jobs and stimulated business activity by contracting with private firms to construct roads, public buildings, and other public-works projects. Between 1933 and 1939, the PWA spent more than $4 billion on some 34,000 projects.

OF COURSE WE MAY HAVE TO CHANGE REMEDIES IF WE DONT GET RESULTS

FDR

NEW DEAL REMEDIES

CONGRESS

NRA

▲ Roosevelt's approach to government was to recommend a new program, try it, and if it failed, then "admit it frankly and try another." His approach is satirized in this 1934 cartoon.

The NIRA's other arm, the NRA, attempted to promote recovery by encouraging businesses to draw up "codes of fair competition." Under these codes, competing businesses agreed to work together to stabilize prices, wages, hours, and production levels. Businesses were able to do this because the NIRA had suspended antitrust laws. To help protect labor through this period of business self-regulation, Section 7(a) of the NIRA guaranteed workers the "right to organize and bargain collectively through representatives of their own choosing . . . free from the interference, restraint or coercion of employers."

Under the direction of former army general Hugh S. Johnson, the NRA took off on a wave of popular enthusiasm. Parades of workers marched through cities displaying the NRA banner—a blue eagle clutching lightning bolts in its claw, with the slogan "We Do Our Part." Johnson compared the NRA to a fighting army:

❝ This campaign is a frank dependence on the power and the willingness of the American people to act together as one person in an hour of great danger. . . . The Blue Eagle is a symbol of industrial solidarity and self-government. ❞

But enthusiasm soon faded. Businesses did not always obey the codes. Workers complained that the codes held their wages down, while consumers complained that the codes pushed prices up. As people lost confidence in the NRA, they joked that it stood for "National Run Around" and "No Recovery Allowed." In 1935 the Supreme Court declared the NIRA (and the NRA) unconstitutional.

AGRICULTURAL RECOVERY

To raise farm prices and increase farmers' purchasing power, Roosevelt proposed that farmers cut production. Congress passed the **Agricultural Adjustment Act** (AAA) in May 1933, which established the Agricultural Adjustment Administration (AAA). The AAA paid farmers to reduce their output of cotton, wheat, corn, hogs, rice, tobacco, dairy products, and other commodities. The money for these payments, or **subsidies**, came from taxes levied on food processors, including meat packers, canners, and flour millers.

In one year the plan reduced the cotton crop by more than three million bales, raising cotton prices. Such increased income gave cotton growers and large-scale farmers more cash to spend, thus stimulating overall economic recovery. New Deal

supporters pointed to these favorable results as proof of the value of sound federal planning. But critics of the New Deal farm program pointed out that the taxes on food processors were passed along to consumers in the form of higher prices. Thus, while farmers' incomes rose, the purchasing power of city dwellers declined.

Critics also charged that farmers with large land-holdings benefited far more from the AAA than did small farmers. Often when large landowners cut production, they forced sharecroppers off their land and kept all of the government payments for themselves. Thus, the poorest farmers were forced into deeper poverty. In response, a group of Arkansas sharecroppers, both black and white, formed the **Southern Tenant Farmers' Union** (STFU) in 1934. The union lobbied the government to halt tenant evictions and to force landowners to share payments with the farmers who rented land. Within one year the STFU had grown to more than 10,000 members.

Early in 1936, the Supreme Court struck down the AAA on the grounds that the processing tax was unconstitutional. This decision, like its ruling against the NIRA and NRA, reflected

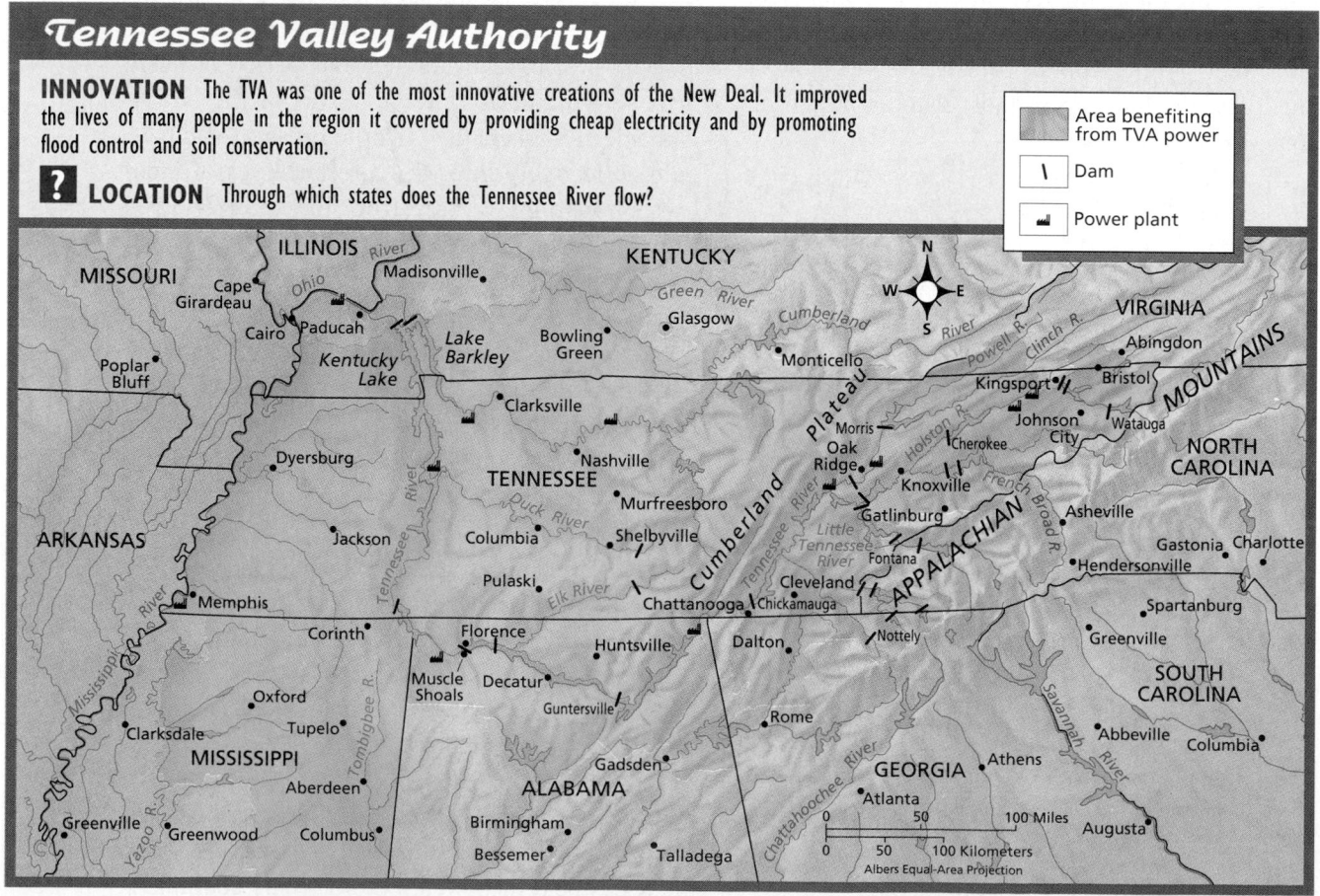

Tennessee Valley Authority

INNOVATION The TVA was one of the most innovative creations of the New Deal. It improved the lives of many people in the region it covered by providing cheap electricity and by promoting flood control and soil conservation.

? LOCATION Through which states does the Tennessee River flow?

Area benefiting from TVA power

Dam

Power plant

the Supreme Court's opposition to growing government power.

▪▪ To stimulate economic recovery, Congress passed the NIRA to help business and industry and the AAA to aid agriculture.

*R*EVITALIZING A REGION

The most monumental of all the early New Deal programs was the Tennessee Valley project, which sought to revitalize the seven-state region drained by the Tennessee River and its tributaries (see map on page 698). This rural area was scarred by over-cut forests and frequent flooding. Poverty, malnutrition, disease, and illiteracy plagued its two million residents.

The **Tennessee Valley Authority** (TVA), created in May 1933, transformed the economic and social life of the region. Under the guidance of David E. Lilienthal, the TVA built 38 dams and several power stations that provided electricity, flood control, and recreational facilities for the region. Other TVA projects combated malaria, illiteracy, and soil erosion and tried to improve the region's standard of living, which had barely changed since Reconstruction.

▲ The TVA's system of hydroelectric plants, dams, and navigation channels covers an area of some 41,000 square miles. Shown here is the construction of Norris Dam.

Critics denounced the TVA as overuse of government power. Shareholders in private utility companies, who feared it would cut into their dividends, brought several court cases against the TVA. The Supreme Court, however, refused to strike down the TVA. Probably the best known of the "alphabet soup" of programs created during Roosevelt's First Hundred Days, the TVA remains one of the New Deal's most enduring successes.

▪▪ The TVA transformed economic and social conditions throughout the Tennessee River Valley.

SECTION 1 REVIEW

IDENTIFY and explain the significance of the following: New Deal, bank holiday, Emergency Banking Act, Federal Deposit Insurance Corporation, Farm Credit Administration, Home Owners Loan Corporation, Frances Perkins, Federal Emergency Relief Administration, Harry L. Hopkins, Civil Works Administration, Civilian Conservation Corps, National Industrial Recovery Act, Public Works Administration, National Recovery Administration, Agricultural Adjustment Act, subsidies, Southern Tenant Farmers' Union, Tennessee Valley Authority.

LOCATE and explain the importance of the following: Tennessee River Valley.

1. **MAIN IDEA** How did the Roosevelt administration attempt to restore confidence in the banking system? What New Deal measures provided loans to farmers and home owners?

2. **MAIN IDEA** Which New Deal programs granted direct relief to the unemployed and created jobs? Which programs helped business, industry, and agriculture?

3. **GEOGRAPHY: REGION** Describe the physical characteristics of the Tennessee River Valley.

4. **WRITING TO INFORM** Imagine you are a resident of the Tennessee River Valley in 1935. Write a letter to a critic of the TVA, outlining the positive ways in which the TVA has transformed the region where you live.

5. **ANALYZING** How are the economic theories of John Maynard Keynes evident in the approach that the Roosevelt administration took toward reviving the economy?

NEW CHALLENGES

FOCUS

■ **What criticisms were aimed at the New Deal?**

■ **What enabled Roosevelt to win reelection easily in 1936?**

■ **How did Roosevelt try to prevent the Supreme Court from overturning his programs?**

■ **How did the Second New Deal benefit labor and agriculture?**

Once the furious activity of the First Hundred Days ended, the nation anxiously waited to see how well the New Deal would work. Critics were quick to speak out. Rather than slowing the New Deal down, however, these critics made the administration more determined to enact still another series of innovative programs that created jobs, provided security for older Americans, and improved labor and farming conditions.

Townsend Plan sign near Weslaco, Texas

CRITICS OF THE NEW DEAL

Criticism of the New Deal came from both the left and the right of the political spectrum. Liberal and radical critics on the left argued that the New Deal was not going far enough in providing relief, recovery, and reform. Conservatives on the right charged that the New Deal was going too far—pushing government into areas where it had no right to interfere. Conservatives were also concerned about the heavy costs of the New Deal. Although FDR had campaigned for a balanced budget in 1932, the federal deficit rose from roughly $1.3 billion in 1933 to some $3.5 billion in 1936.

Most conservative complaints came from the American Liberty League, made up largely of Republican business interests and disenchanted Democrats led by Al Smith, who accused New Deal supporters of "irresponsible ravings against millionaires and big business." The League complained that the New Deal measures were destroying both the Constitution and free enterprise and would drive the nation into bankruptcy.

Among the liberal opponents of the New Deal was Dr. Francis E. Townsend of California. Townsend wanted the government to grant a pension of $200 a month to every American over 60 years old. All recipients were to spend the pensions within 30 days and thus pump money into the

▲ Huey Long

economy. Father Charles E. Coughlin, the "radio priest," broadcast a similar message from his pulpit in Michigan. He urged the government to nationalize all banks and return to the silver standard.

Huey Long, "the Kingfish," a colorful but corrupt senator from Louisiana, probably had the most radical plan. Like Robin Hood, Long wanted to take from the rich and give to the poor. He claimed that he had done just that as governor of Louisiana, when he had helped the poor by building public housing, roads, and schools and by providing free textbooks to students. Actually, he had financed his state's public-works projects not by taking from the rich, but by imposing higher taxes on everyone—including the poor. In addition, Long and his friends had often profited personally from the projects.

In 1933 Senator Long proposed a radical new kind of relief program, which he called **Share-Our-Wealth**. The program would empower the government to confiscate wealth from the rich through taxes and then provide a guaranteed minimum income and a home to every American family. Long even had his own theme song:

> 66 Ev'ry man a king, ev'ry man a king,
> For you can be a millionaire,
> There's enough for all people to share.
> When it's sunny June and December too,
> Or in the wintertime or spring:
> There'll be peace without end,
> Ev'ry neighbor a friend,
> With ev'ry man a king. 99

In spite of Long's reputation for corruption, the Share-Our-Wealth program drew a great deal of popular support. Some critics suspected that Long harbored dreams of becoming a dictator. Such fears led the Communist party and the Socialist party to denounce Long even though his program promised to redistribute wealth. Bolstered by popular support, Long soon threatened to challenge Roosevelt as a third-party candidate in the 1936 election. But both this threat and the Share-Our-Wealth program died when an assassin killed Long in 1935.

■■ Some critics accused the New Deal of pushing government power too far, while others wanted to expand it further.

THE SECOND NEW DEAL

In the midterm elections of 1934, the Democrats picked up more seats in Congress. The victory, coupled with pressure from the left, encouraged New Deal planners to initiate more public-works programs, a social security plan, and wage and hour improvements for laborers. This series of programs would eventually come to be called the **Second New Deal**. While still providing relief and pursuing recovery, the Second New Deal would increasingly emphasize reform.

The Works Progress Administration. A works program, the **Works Progress Administration** (WPA), began in April 1935 under the direction of Harry Hopkins. The CWA had ended the previous year, yet unemployment was still high. Millions of American families remained on relief rolls. To create jobs for them, Congress allotted $5 billion for the WPA.

Over the eight years of its life, the WPA employed an estimated 14 million people, with about 2 million working for it at any given time. Workers engaged in a variety of tasks. Male blue-collar workers built or rebuilt a total of some 350 airports, more than 100,000 public buildings, some 78,000 bridges, and about 500,000 miles of roads. White-collar workers took on research projects and teaching jobs. The WPA had a special division for women, but the program often discriminated against women by paying them lower wages than men. On most projects male workers received $5 a day while female workers received only $3 for the same job.

▼ **The WPA employed many women, such as this weaver from Kansas, in a variety of jobs.**

The WPA tried to help struggling young people between the ages of 16 and 25 by establishing the **National Youth Administration** (NYA), a "junior WPA." The NYA gave young people part-time jobs that provided money to help them stay in school. Within a year the NYA was providing aid to half a million people.

Social Security. Another cornerstone of the Second New Deal was the **Social Security Act**, which Congress passed in August 1935. The act contained three major provisions. First, it provided unemployment insurance for workers who lost their jobs. The funds for this insurance came from a payroll tax on businesses. Second, the act provided pensions for retired workers over age 65. The money for these pensions came from two sources—a payroll tax on employers and a tax on employees' wages. Third, in a shared federal-state program, the act provided payments to the blind, disabled, and elderly and to wives and children of male workers who had died.

At first the Social Security Act covered only a limited segment of the work force. Farmers and the self-employed were excluded, as well as domestic workers, some 60 percent of whom were African American women. Over the years, however, coverage broadened, and the Social Security Act became the model for a wide range of public social welfare programs.

Other programs. Underlying Roosevelt's Second New Deal was the president's belief that the government had not yet "weeded out the overprivileged and . . . effectively lifted up the underprivileged." To help the underprivileged, Roosevelt issued an executive order in May 1935 establishing the **Rural Electrification Administration** (REA). The REA extended power lines into isolated rural areas. Within a few years, only 1 farm in 10 lacked electricity.

To help weed out the overprivileged, Roosevelt went after public utility companies, charging that many were able to set higher prices because they held monopolies over gas and electricity. To reform this system, Congress passed a law giving the government the right to regulate interstate production, transmission, and sale of gas and electricity.

Roosevelt also went after the rich, declaring that tax laws had not done enough "to prevent an unjust concentration of wealth and economic

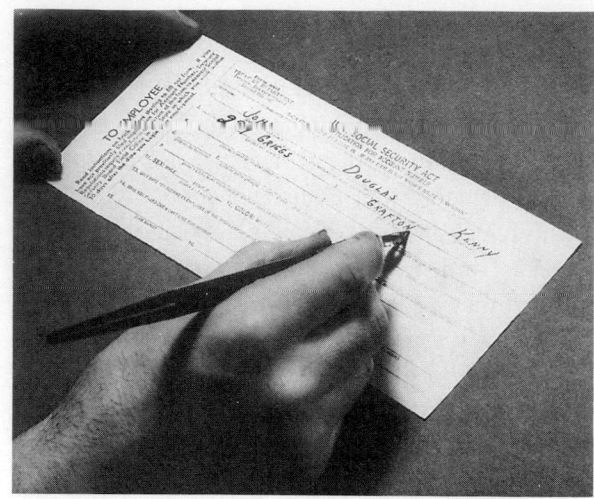

▲ **The Social Security Act marked an unprecedented step in providing relief to the unemployed and elderly. In this photograph, a man named John Kenny fills out one of the first applications for a social security number.**

power." In response, Congress passed the Revenue Act of 1935. Often referred to as the **Wealth Tax Act**, it sharply increased taxes on the nation's richest people. Corporations had to pay an "excess profits" tax if they made an annual profit greater than 10 percent. A year later, Congress increased corporate taxes again. Business complained bitterly that the tax increase discouraged business expansion.

𝒯HE ELECTION OF 1936

By 1936 the depression still lingered. Some 9 million workers lacked regular jobs, and 3.5 million remained on the WPA or the CCC rolls. Many factories remained closed or operated at far less than full capacity. Still, America had made some progress. Since 1932 the national income had jumped from roughly $43 billion to more than $80 billion and unemployment had dropped by nearly three million.

In June 1936 the Democrats enthusiastically nominated Roosevelt for a second term. Labor unions, farmers, those on relief, and even many Republicans also endorsed him. For the first time since Reconstruction, most African Americans living in the North abandoned their traditional ties to the Republican party—"the party of Lincoln"—to support the Democrats. The Republicans nominated the capable but unexciting governor of Kansas, Alfred M. Landon. The Republican platform condemned the New Deal,

NEW DEAL PROGRAMS

Year	First New Deal	Provisions
1933	Emergency Banking Act	Gave administration right to regulate banks.
1933	Farm Credit Administration (FCA)	Extended loans to farm owners to refinance loans.
1933	Economy Act	Aimed at balancing the budget.
1933	Civilian Conservation Corps (CCC)	Employed young men on public-works projects.
1933	Federal Emergency Relief Administration (FERA)	Provided relief to the needy.
1933	Agricultural Adjustment Act of 1933 (AAA)	Paid farmers to reduce crops; funded by processing tax later declared unconstitutional.
1933	Tennessee Valley Authority (TVA)	Constructed dam and power projects to improve Tennessee Valley Region.
1933	Home Owners Loan Corporation (HOLC)	Loaned money to home owners to refinance mortgages.
1933	Banking Act of 1933	Created FDIC and prohibited banks from selling stock or financing corporations.
1933	Federal Deposit Insurance Corporation (FDIC)	Insured individual bank deposits.
1933	National Industrial Recovery Act (NIRA)	Established NRA and a series of fair-competition codes for businesses.
1933	National Recovery Administration (NRA)	Regulated industry and raised wages and prices.
1933	Public Works Administration (PWA)	Set up public-works projects to increase employment and business activity.
1933	Civil Works Administration (CWA)	Provided federal jobs to the unemployed.
1934	Securities and Exchange Commission	Regulated securities market.
1934	Federal Housing Administration (FHA)	Insured bank loans for building and repairing homes.

Year	Second New Deal	Provisions
1935	Works Progress Administration (WPA)	Employed people to do public works, research, and artistic projects.
1935	Soil Conservation Service	Promoted control and prevention of soil erosion.
1935	Rural Electrification Administration (REA)	Provided electricity to rural areas lacking public utilities.
1935	National Youth Administration (NYA)	Provided job training and part-time jobs to students.
1935	National Labor Relations Act (Wagner-Connery Act)	Recognized rights of labor to organize and bargain collectively; regulated labor practices.
1935	Social Security Act	Provided unemployment benefits, pensions for the elderly, and survivor's insurance.
1935	Revenue Act of 1935 (Wealth Tax Act)	Increased taxes on the wealthy.
1937	Farm Security Administration (FSA)	Provided loans to help tenant farmers buy land.
1938	Agricultural Adjustment Act of 1938 (AAA)	Increased government regulation of crop production and payments to farmers.
1938	Revenue Act of 1938	Increased taxes on wealthy businesses.
1938	Fair Labor Standards Act	Established minimum wage of 40 cents per hour and maximum work week of 40 hours for businesses in interstate commerce.

Source: *Encyclopedia of American History*

RELIEF, RECOVERY, AND REFORM Franklin Roosevelt proposed a wide number of programs to aid in the nation's recovery after he assumed office in 1933. These programs became the First New Deal. Two years later he outlined a broader program of social reform in the Second New Deal.

? **BUILDING CHART SKILLS** Which New Deal programs were aimed primarily at helping farmers?

but called for few specific changes in New Deal programs. The Republicans did promise to balance the budget and to reduce federal power by returning more power to the states.

Roosevelt's opponents—mainly business interests upset by new regulations and corporate taxes, conservative newspaper editors, and rich Americans angered by high taxes—renewed their charges that Roosevelt ignored the Constitution. They pointed out that the Supreme Court had overturned the NRA, AAA, and five other key New Deal measures. American individualism, free enterprise, and private property, they insisted, were being abandoned for socialism. Some even charged falsely that the Social Security Act would require everyone to wear metal dog tags!

President Roosevelt entered the fight with great zest. In accepting renomination, he pledged to stay on the course the New Deal had set. He won a smashing victory—with some 28 million popular votes to Landon's 17 million. Roosevelt carried every state but Maine and Vermont—the most lopsided victory in more than a century. The Democrats increased their majorities in both houses of Congress. The coalition that Democrats forged in the election—farmers, southern whites, city dwellers, industrial workers, and northern blacks—would hold together for many elections to come.

■■ **The Democrats, forging a powerful coalition of groups who benefited from the New Deal, easily reelected Roosevelt in 1936.**

ROOSEVELT AND THE SUPREME COURT

Flushed with his triumph and convinced of the power that a solidly Democratic Congress gave him, Roosevelt moved to "reform" the Supreme Court. Angered that the Court had declared several New Deal measures unconstitutional, Roosevelt called attention to the ages of the justices, labeling them "Nine Old Men" (six were 70 or older), and accused them of being stuck in the "horse and buggy" days in their thinking.

In February 1937, two weeks after his second inauguration, Roosevelt asked Congress to grant him the power to appoint one new justice for each of those 70 or older, up to six new justices. The Supreme Court needed "a persistent infusion of new blood," he argued. Roosevelt's proposal triggered a storm of protest across the nation. Critics—Democrats as well as Republicans—charged that this unprecedented "court-packing" would tamper with the delicate balance of legislative, executive, and judicial powers. Dorothy Thompson, a popular political columnist, denounced Roosevelt's scheme as a move toward dictatorship:

    66 If the American people accept this last audacity of the President without letting out a yell to high heaven, they have ceased to be jealous of their liberties and are ripe for ruin. This is the beginning of a pure personal government. **99**

▶ The negative attitude that many members of the Supreme Court had toward New Deal reforms is satirized in the cartoon *Nine Old Men.*

Congress resoundingly denied Roosevelt's request. But this was just one battle in a war that FDR would eventually win. The Supreme Court soon upheld the Social Security Act and the National Labor Relations Act. Many Americans concluded that the justices had decided to become more agreeable to prevent a drastic reform of the Court itself. "A switch in time saves nine," people joked. Over the next four years, seven justices died or retired and were replaced by Roosevelt appointees. By 1945 eight of the nine justices were Roosevelt appointees.

■■ **Roosevelt tried to "pack" the Supreme Court with six new members in order to protect his New Deal programs.**

▲ As unions became better organized and membership grew, the number of strikes increased. A 1937 sit-down strike is shown above. Workers for a New York City vending company (right) also went on strike later that same year.

𝒯HE SECOND NEW DEAL AND LABOR

When the Supreme Court declared the NIRA unconstitutional in May 1935, it struck down Section 7(a), which protected the rights of labor unions. Two months later, however, Congress passed the National Labor Relations Act, also called the **Wagner-Connery Act**, to guarantee labor's right to organize unions and to bargain for better wages and working conditions.

The American Federation of Labor (AFL) continued its efforts to organize workers, including those in such mass-production industries as steel and automobiles. But the AFL did not move fast enough to please gruff, shaggy-browed John L. Lewis, the intimidating leader of the United Mine Workers union. In 1935 Lewis and several other like-minded labor leaders organized the **Congress of Industrial Organizations** (CIO), which tried to unite workers in various industries.

The new CIO unions included all workers, skilled and unskilled, in a given industry. For example, the United Auto Workers (UAW) represented all workers in automotive plants. Previously, different AFL craft unions had represented different types of autoworkers, such as electricians, welders, or metalworkers. Now all auto workers negotiated as a single powerful union. And in contrast to many AFL branches, the CIO welcomed African American, immigrant, and female members.

The organizing efforts of both the AFL and the CIO resulted in a wave of strikes. One of the most bitter strikes was waged against General Motors (GM) in the winter of 1936–37. The UAW had been trying to unionize GM factories, but the company had been fighting the union's efforts. Meanwhile, GM workers were growing increasingly frustrated with frequent layoffs, abuses of power by management, and work speedups. On December 31, 1936, this frustration led to a **sit-down strike**.

Instead of leaving the automotive plants, workers occupied the factories and pledged to remain until management met their demands. Wives, daughters, and female workers formed the Women's Auxiliary and the Women's Emergency

Brigade to picket outside the plants in support of the union. Many women felt their lives were changed by this experience. They soon took up the cause of equal pay for men and women in the auto industry. Said one female activist:

> 66 I'm living for the first time with a definite goal. . . . Just being a woman isn't enough anymore. I want to be a human being with the right to think for myself. 99

Finally, after six weeks, General Motors gave in and granted the UAW the right to organize GM workers. Within eight months the UAW membership grew to some 400,000. Owing in part to the Wagner-Connery Act, total union membership shot up from about 4 million in 1936 to some 9 million in 1939.

■■ **The Wagner-Connery Act guaranteed the rights of labor, increasing union membership and activity.**

⟋HE SECOND NEW DEAL AND FARMERS

The Second New Deal also brought relief for farmers. When the Supreme Court struck down the Agricultural Adjustment Act in January 1936, Congress created another program to replace it. Like the AAA, the new program aimed to keep farm prices high by cutting crop production. To avoid opposition from the Supreme Court, however, Congress combined crop reduction with a soil conservation plan—a legitimate governmental activity.

The Second New Deal also sought to help tenant farmers, sharecroppers, and migrant farm workers. The rise of the Southern Tenant Farmers' Union had brought a backlash of violence against sharecroppers by landowners and authorities in the South, forcing some union members to conduct their activities in secrecy. Then in 1936 the union organized

▲ The depression left many African Americans struggling to find work. This photograph shows people from Memphis, Tennessee, being transported to Arkansas for a day's work in the cotton fields.

a series of strikes by cotton pickers in five states. In 1937 Congress created the **Farm Security Administration** (FSA) to make low-interest, long-term loans to tenant farmers and sharecroppers to buy farms. The FSA also established camps where migrant farm workers could find shelter and medical care.

The Roosevelt administration recognized that the soil conservation program did not do enough to limit farm production. So in 1938 Congress passed a second Agricultural Adjustment Act. The government continued to pay farmers to withdraw land from production and to practice conservation, but it also authorized the Department of Agriculture to limit the amount of specific crops that could be brought to market each year. When harvests exceeded these limits, the government stored the surpluses until prices rose. Farmers cooperating in this program could get government loans based on the value of their stored crops.

▶ Migrant workers experienced grinding poverty and set up crude homes near where they worked. Shown here is a migrant Mexican family in Imperial Valley, California.

All in all, New Deal agricultural policy compiled a mixed record. Farm income did rise from 1933 to 1937, but critics pointed out that higher farm prices not only hurt consumers but also caused American farm products to lose out in highly competitive foreign markets. Critics also complained about the large cost of farm subsidies. But the farm legislation of the 1930s had some successes. It helped many farmers escape economic disaster, saved homes, and increased the fertility of millions of acres of land through conservation programs.

■■ **The Second New Deal increased farm income; aided tenant farmers, sharecroppers and migrant workers; and encouraged soil conservation.**

*B*USINESS SLUMP, POLITICAL SETBACKS

During 1936 and early 1937, the economy seemed to be improving, but in August 1937 it again plunged downward. Stung by criticism of excessive government spending, Roosevelt had begun cutting back on New Deal relief and public-works programs in 1936. Unfortunately, private industry was not yet strong enough to employ those dropped from government rolls because of the cutbacks. In addition, withholding Social Security taxes from workers' paychecks further reduced the flow of money into the economy. By the autumn of 1937, factories were closing and unemployment was rising. Republicans called this period of economic activity "Roosevelt's recession."

President Roosevelt and Congress again primed the economic pump by increasing government lending and spending. The Reconstruction Finance Corporation rescued troubled businesses. The Works Progress Administration quickly doubled the number of workers on its payroll from some 1.5 million to about 3 million. By the fall of 1938, unemployment had declined and industrial production had increased.

As the 1938 midterm elections drew near, Roosevelt decided to reenergize the New Deal (and to punish Democrats who had voted against his Supreme Court reform plan) by opposing conservative Democrats in Congress who did not support the Second New Deal. He actually urged voters to turn these Democrats out of office!

Just as his "court-packing" scheme had backfired, however, so did his attempt to "purge" the Democratic party. All but one member of Congress whom Roosevelt opposed won reelection. Moreover, voters elected still more Democrats who opposed New Deal programs. Adding to Roosevelt's dismay, the Republicans gained 7 seats in the Senate and 80 in the House. Though the Democrats still maintained majorities in both houses of Congress, their margin was much narrower. Faced with increasing criticism from all sides, FDR decided not to propose any new reforms in 1939, marking an end to the New Deal era.

SECTION 2 REVIEW

IDENTIFY and explain the significance of the following: Francis E. Townsend, Charles E. Coughlin, Share-Our-Wealth, Second New Deal, Works Progress Administration, National Youth Administration, Social Security Act, Rural Electrification Administration, Wealth Tax Act, Alfred M. Landon, Wagner-Connery Act, Congress of Industrial Organizations, sit-down strike, Farm Security Administration.

1. **MAIN IDEA** What charges did some critics level against the New Deal?

2. **MAIN IDEA** How did the Wagner-Connery Act benefit labor? How did other Second New Deal programs benefit agriculture?

3. **MAIN IDEA** Why did Roosevelt try to "pack" the Supreme Court with six new members?

4. **WRITING TO EXPRESS A VIEWPOINT** Imagine you are a Democratic campaign worker during the 1936 election. Write a campaign pamphlet aimed at the "Roosevelt coalition," explaining why you think FDR should be reelected.

5. **IDENTIFYING VALUES** How did criticisms of the New Deal reveal the values held by the left and the right?

LIFE IN THE NEW DEAL ERA

FOCUS

■ How did African Americans fare during the New Deal era?

■ What gains did Native Americans make during the 1930s?

■ What effect did the Dust Bowl have on the Southwest population?

African Americans, Native Americans, Mexican Americans, and displaced farmers remained among the nation's poorest groups during the depression years. They faced not only economic hardship but also prejudice and hostility. The New Deal, however, did make some efforts to help these groups.

Thomas Hart Benton's *Ploughing It Under*, 1939

A STRUGGLE FOR AFRICAN AMERICANS

New Deal programs succeeded to a large degree in helping African Americans economically. Some programs, however, were tainted by discrimination. The FERA and later the WPA became the greatest sources of relief and work for African American males. Some 200,000 young black men flocked to the CCC, where they found work and training, though they were strictly segregated from whites. The TVA employed black workers, but they were not allowed to live in the model towns built by the TVA. NRA codes often set lower wages for blacks than for whites, a practice that led some African American leaders to call the NRA the "Negro Run Around" or "Negroes Ruined Again." Social Security also discriminated indirectly against African Americans since most were agricultural or domestic workers not eligible for benefits.

The discrimination evident in the programs was reflective of social attitudes. The depression increased racial tensions in the country, especially in the South. Twenty-four black people were lynched in 1933 alone. Fearing political backlash from the South, Roosevelt did little to support legislation that might bring civil equality for African Americans, such as a federal antilynching law sponsored by the NAACP. Eleanor Roosevelt, however, became a champion of racial justice. Black leaders often commented on Mrs. Roosevelt's unusual ability to understand the struggles of African Americans. "We [whites] are largely to blame" for poverty among the black community, she once said. It was her goal to see educational and economic opportunities open up for African Americans.

Interior Secretary Harold Ickes, a former president of the Chicago NAACP, also tried to respond to the concerns of African Americans. When the Daughters of the American Revolution (DAR) refused to let the gifted black concert singer Marian Anderson perform in their

◀ When Marian Anderson (inset) was denied the use of concert facilities at Constitution Hall, she gave a free concert from the steps of the Lincoln Memorial on Easter Sunday, 1939.

Constitution Hall, both Ickes and Mrs. Roosevelt reacted strongly. Roosevelt resigned her longtime membership in the DAR, stating that "to remain as a member implies approval of that action." She and Ickes then arranged for Anderson to give a free concert at the Lincoln Memorial, which attracted an audience of some 75,000.

Long before this incident, Ickes had brought in several prominent African Americans to advise his department on racial matters, including Robert C. Weaver, the first African American to obtain a Ph.D. in economics from Harvard. Weaver was just one of many African Americans who received high-level government jobs during the New Deal era. FDR named more than 100 blacks to major departments of the federal government, more than any other president since Ulysses S. Grant. These appointees included a wide variety of experts, from legal scholars to educators, social workers, and newspaper editors.

A core group of African American government officials evolved into the Federal Council on Negro Affairs, which became known as the black cabinet or the black brain trust. According to Robert Weaver, their "common cause was to maximize the participation of blacks in all phases of the New Deal." They met weekly at the home of Mary McLeod Bethune, the dynamic director of the Division of Negro Affairs in the National Youth Administration.

BIO GRAPHY Mary McLeod Bethune's journey to prominence in Washington began in 1875 in Mayesville, South Carolina, where she was born the 15th of 17 children to farmers who had once been slaves. The young girl's chances for an education seemed slim, since the Mayesville school was for whites only. But with the aid of a Presbyterian mission school and a series of scholarships, she eventually attended the Moody Bible Institute in Chicago. Bethune originally intended to become a missionary in Africa but soon found her mission to be educating African American children. She once said of her decision:

> 66 The drums of Africa still beat in my heart. They will not let me rest while there is a single Negro boy or girl without a chance to prove his [or her] worth. 99

In 1904 she founded a primary school for black girls in Florida, which eventually evolved into Bethune-Cookman College, a four-year coeducational institution with a predominantly African American student body.

Bethune became involved with numerous African American groups, including the NAACP and the Urban League. In 1935 she helped unite all national organizations for African American women into the National Council of Negro Women. Through her work with this association, she became close friends with Eleanor Roosevelt, who insisted that Bethune be appointed to work with the NYA. Bethune fought hard, though not always successfully, to rid the NYA of

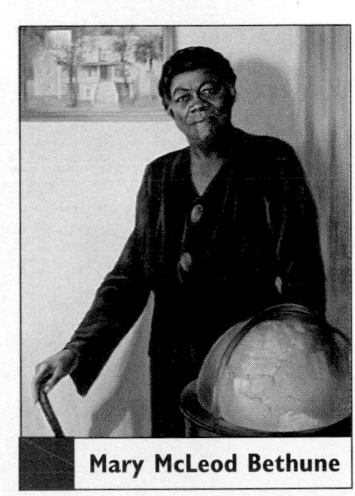

Mary McLeod Bethune

racism. Although Bethune left government service after the NYA ended in 1944, she continued to work on behalf of civil rights and educational opportunities for young African Americans until her death in 1955.

■■ **African Americans gained economic assistance and a voice in government during the New Deal. But little progress was made toward ending discrimination.**

A NEW DEAL FOR NATIVE AMERICANS

As the New Deal era began, life for many Native Americans was very bleak. A late 1920s report on Native American life across the country listed numerous problems that plagued their communities. Inadequate housing, poor health care, and malnutrition left many of the nation's more than 300,000 Native Americans easy prey for epidemics.

Native Americans argued that their culture had been stripped away by measures like the Dawes Act (see Chapter 14), which had ended tribal government and authorized the sale of tribal land to individuals. Antonio Luhan, a member of the Taos Pueblo in New Mexico, described how government policies and the Bureau of Indian Affairs commissioners who enforced them overwhelmed Native American culture:

66 We had Commissioners against us who tried to stop our ceremony dances and our [religious] dances. They nearly destroy us; call our ways bad or immoral or something, and put in the paper they are going to stop us. 99

In the 1920s Luhan had shown a white social worker named John Collier the poor living conditions in Native American communities. Deeply moved, Collier founded the **American Indian Defense Association**, which fought to protect religious freedom and tribal property for Native Americans. For the next decade Collier championed Indian reform efforts. In 1933 President Roosevelt appointed Collier as the new commissioner of Indian Affairs. Almost immediately Collier tried to change the government's direction by revitalizing Native American life and culture. "Anything less than to let Indian culture live on would be a crime against the earth itself," Collier declared.

To put these reform ideas into law, Congress passed the **Indian Reorganization Act** of 1934. Reversing the Dawes Act policy, the new law tried to revive tribal rule. The act provided funds to start tribal business ventures and to pay for the college education of young Native Americans. It also ordered Congress "to promote the study of Indian civilization and preserve and develop . . . Indian arts, crafts, skills, and traditions."

▲ The Indian Reorganization Act encouraged Native Americans to preserve their cultural traditions. Shown here is Angelia La Moose, a young girl in the Flathead tribe, wearing a traditional Native American dress.

◀ This 1930 photograph shows a Native American home on the San Xavier Indian Reservation in Arizona.

Critics complained that Collier had not obtained enough input from the tribes themselves in formulating policies and that the programs decreased the power of women in some tribes. Still, two thirds of the nation's Native American tribes voted to participate in the new programs.

■■ **New Deal policies encouraged Native Americans to reclaim and revitalize their cultural heritage.**

THE STRUGGLE FOR A PLACE IN THE SUN

Toward the end of the 1930s, a billboard appeared on Route 66 just outside Tulsa, Oklahoma, that proclaimed: "NO JOBS in California. If YOU are looking for work—KEEP OUT!" The message was clear. The market for migrant workers on the West Coast was glutted. The sign was directed at the thousands of migrant farmers from the Midwest who traveled to California in the mid-1930s. Driven off their land by the forces of nature, they sought a better life in the Southwest.

The Dust Bowl. In the mid-1930s a severe drought struck the Great Plains—the Texas and Oklahoma panhandles and parts of Colorado, New Mexico, and Kansas. As the topsoil loosened and dried, winds picked it up and turned this 50-million-acre region into a wasteland. Throughout the **Dust Bowl**, as the region came to be called, windswept dust clouds darkened the skies at noon and buried fences and farm machinery. Dust crept into houses through tiny cracks; ships reported great dust clouds hundreds of miles out to sea. One Texas farmer recalled:

❝ If the wind blew one way, here came the dark dust from Oklahoma. Another way and it was the gray dust from Kansas. Still another way, the brown dust from Colorado and New Mexico. Little farms were buried. And the towns were blackened. ❞

To prevent future dust bowls, the Department of Agriculture started extensive programs in soil-erosion control. The most dramatic was a shelter-belt of some 217 million trees that CCC workers planted. This windbreak stretched through the Great Plains from Texas to Canada.

By 1939 the amount of dried-out farmland had decreased dramatically. But it was too late to save the many Dust Bowl farmers who had already

(continued on page 714)

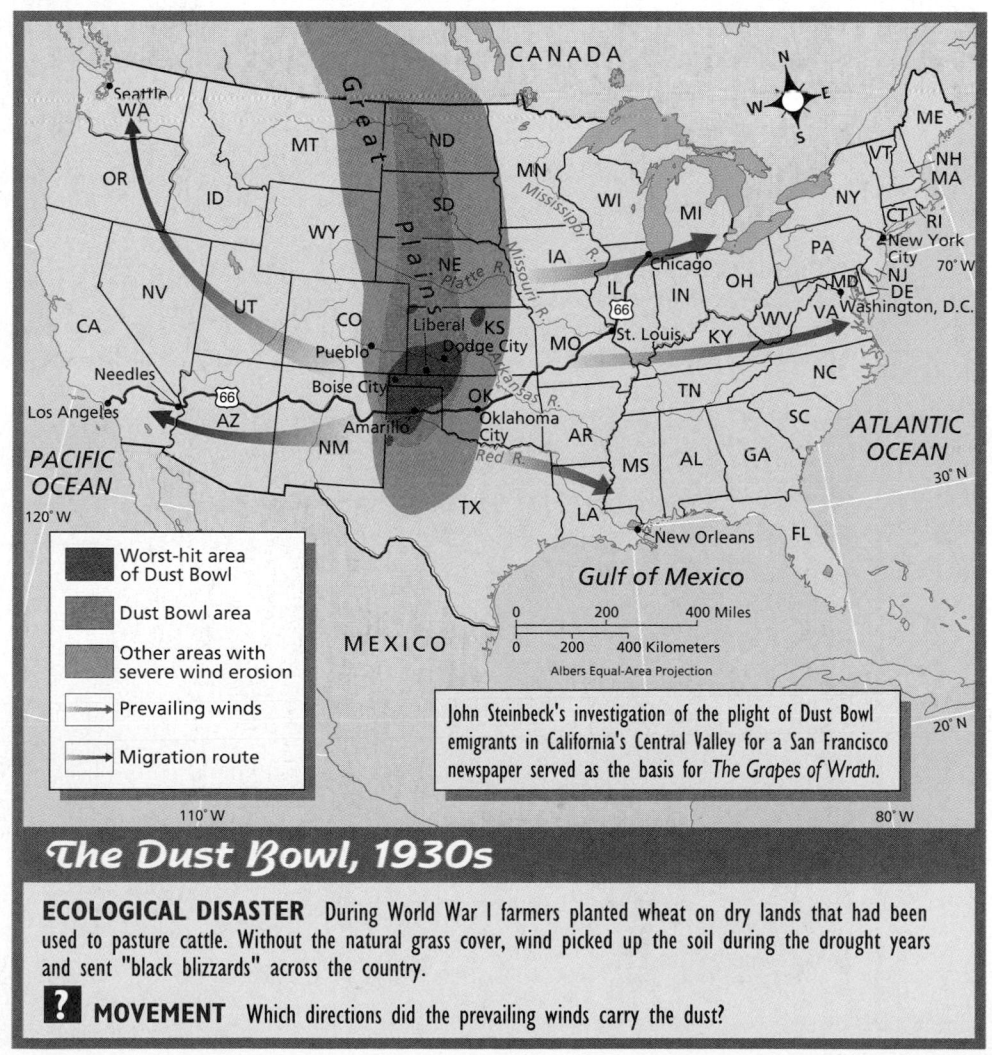

The Dust Bowl, 1930s

Worst-hit area of Dust Bowl

Dust Bowl area

Other areas with severe wind erosion

→ Prevailing winds

→ Migration route

John Steinbeck's investigation of the plight of Dust Bowl emigrants in California's Central Valley for a San Francisco newspaper served as the basis for *The Grapes of Wrath*.

ECOLOGICAL DISASTER During World War I farmers planted wheat on dry lands that had been used to pasture cattle. Without the natural grass cover, wind picked up the soil during the drought years and sent "black blizzards" across the country.

? **MOVEMENT** Which directions did the prevailing winds carry the dust?

Photographing the Depression

Many Americans at first were suspicious of the New Deal programs. The tradition of self-reliance ran deep in the United States. President Roosevelt believed that opponents of federal relief programs might change their minds if they saw the frightful conditions under which migrant farm workers and city dwellers lived. With Roosevelt's encouragement numerous federal agencies, including the Department of the Interior, the Works Progress Administration (WPA), the Department of Agriculture, and the Farm Security

Administration (FSA), hired photographers in the 1930s to travel across the country and document the lives of ordinary Americans.

No agency used photography more effectively than the FSA, whose staff amassed

more than 250,000 images of American life during the depression. Roy E. Stryker, head of the FSA historical section, assembled an all-star team of photographers that included Walker Evans, Ben Shahn, Arthur Rothstein, and Dorothea Lange.

▶ Russell Lee photographed these carrot field workers in Santa Maria, Texas, waiting to begin their day.

◀ In Missouri, 1939, Arthur Rothstein captured the mood of this sharecropper's child after the boy's family had been evicted from their land.

To make sure his photographers were prepared, Stryker often tutored them before sending them out on assignment. For example, former print journalist Carl Mydans was set to "go South and 'do cotton'" for the FSA. Learning that Mydans knew virtually nothing about the subject, Stryker postponed the trip. Mydans recalled what happened next:

66 We sat down and we talked almost all day about cotton. We went to lunch and we went to dinner, and we talked well into the night. He [Stryker] talked about cotton as an agricultural product, cotton as a commercial product, the history of cotton in the South, what cotton did to the history of the U.S.A. and how it affected areas outside the U.S.A. By the end of that evening, I was ready to go off and photograph cotton! 99

▶ *Migrant Mother* is one of Dorothea Lange's most famous photographs of the depression.

Other photographers, such as Dorothea Lange, were already well grounded in understanding the social and economic forces that shaped rural Americans' lives in the 1930s. Lange often traveled for weeks at a time, working up to 14 hours a day. One of her most famous photographs, *Migrant Mother,* showed an exhausted single mother whose children subsisted chiefly on vegetables they scavenged from California fields. When it appeared in 1936, *Migrant Mother* inspired Californians to defy powerful growers' associations and insist on decent, government-sponsored housing for seasonal harvesters.

Migrant Mother was not the only photograph to fulfill Roosevelt's goal of gaining support for government

programs. From 1936 to 1941, FSA photographs were widely published in government pamphlets and in *Time, Life,* and other magazines. The pictures prompted an outpouring of congressional and public support for federal relief.

Today, the FSA photographs are housed in the Library of Congress and provide an invaluable source of information for historians. They are a detailed visual record of the 1930s that allows researchers today to "see" life in depression America. These photographs have thus enabled historians and citizens alike to step back in time to a crucial period in our history.

◀ Ben Shahn photographed these rural West Virginia residents heading into Scotts Run to obtain food from relief workers in 1935.

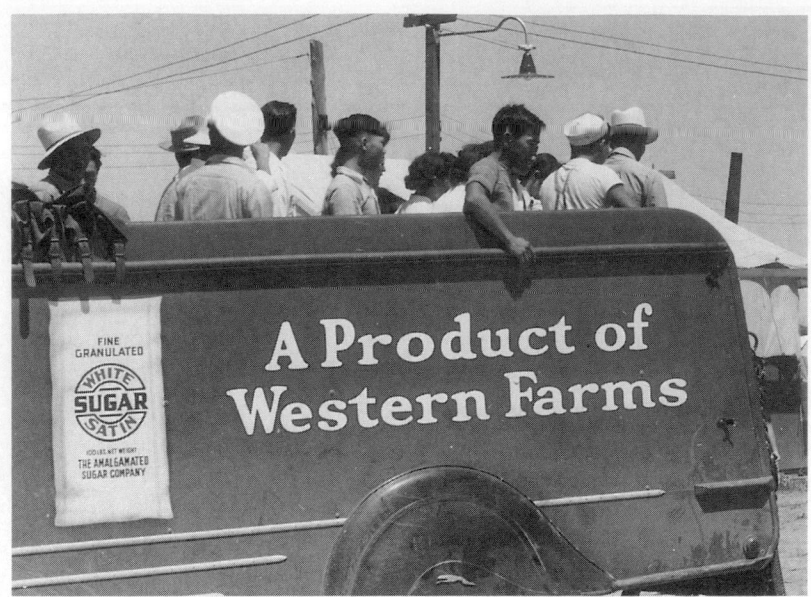

▲ Many Japanese Americans on the West Coast also worked as migrant field laborers. These men labored in sugar fields as far north as Oregon.

" When we moved to California, we would work after school. Sometimes we wouldn't go "Following the crops," we missed much school. Trying to get enough money to stay alive the following winter, the whole family picking apricots, walnuts, prunes. . . . We were taken advantage of quite a bit by the labor contractor and the crew pusher. "

lost their land. Packing their meager belongings into battered old cars or trucks, they headed west on Route 66, bound for what they saw as a land of promise—California and other parts of the West Coast. There they hoped to find work picking crops. Thousands of them made the trek, and since many came from Oklahoma, they picked up the nickname **Okies**. Once they reached the West Coast, however, they found themselves in desperate competition with other farm laborers looking for work.

Competition for migrant work. Even before the Dust Bowl refugees started arriving, Mexican Americans had been having a hard time finding work in the West. Like African Americans, Mexican Americans often found themselves the victims of discrimination in many New Deal programs. For example, although the CCC did not segregate Mexican Americans, some complained that they were harassed by camp officials, denied clothing, and assigned to kitchen duty more often than non-Hispanics.

Many families continued to seek what little work they could find as migrant farm laborers. A 1935 California survey found that the average income of Mexican American families had fallen below $300 a year. César Chávez, who later became a noted labor leader, recalled growing up in a depression-era migrant family:

Mexican Americans also faced job competition from Filipino laborers. During the 1920s the Filipino population of California had grown to more than 30,000. Like Mexican American migrants, most Filipinos worked in agriculture. When the depression hit, both groups faced tough economic times, but the Filipino workers attempted to combat decreasing wages by organizing. Throughout the early 1930s the Filipino Labor Union launched a series of strikes to protest wage reductions. In 1936 the American Federation of Labor sponsored the Field Workers Union, a combined organization for Mexican American and Filipino laborers.

The unions were able to keep wages from falling too much. However, as more Okies arrived, competition for migrant work increased. Thus life for all migrants remained difficult.

■ Dust Bowl refugees moved to the West, where they competed with Mexican Americans and Filipinos for migrant farm work.

*P*ICTURING THE FACE OF THE DEPRESSION

The grim experiences of migrants and others in rural America provided rich subject matter for documentary filmmakers and photographers. These artists created a memorable visual record of the New Deal era. Better than any words could do, their images of the slumped shoulders of

▲ FSA photographer Carl Mydans captured the devastation of soil erosion in Kentucky in 1936.

sharecroppers in rural Alabama; future African American filmmaker Gordon Parks; international photojournalist Margaret Bourke-White; and Dorothea Lange, probably the best-known of the FSA photographers.

BIO GRAPHY Lange was one of the most talented photographers of the depression era. Born in Hoboken, New Jersey, she decided in her late teens to become a photographer. After studying the craft for several years, she set out to tour the world and record her impressions. Lange was out of money by the time she reached San Francisco, however, so she stayed and opened a portrait studio.

When the depression struck, Lange began to take pictures of the homeless men wandering the streets of San Francisco. Soon the federal government hired her to photograph migrant farmers in California. Her pictures, which carry captions in the farmers' own words, revealed the migrants' poverty and suffering, as well as their great dignity. Lange's most famous picture, *Migrant Mother* (see page 713), is considered a masterpiece.

During World War II, Lange continued her documentary work by taking pictures of Japanese Americans in California internment camps. Later she produced photo essays for *Life* magazine and traveled the world taking pictures. By the time of her death in 1965, she ranked as one of the world's foremost photographers.

The Granger Collection, New York

Dorothea Lange

unemployed men, the staring faces of children, and the worried expressions of prematurely aged women conveyed the human suffering of the era.

In 1936 and 1937 the filmmaker Pare Lorentz directed two documentary films on the era. *The River* depicts the TVA and its effect on the surrounding regions, while *The Plow That Broke the Plains* portrays the devastation of the Dust Bowl. Using few images of people, the films rely heavily on background music and an unseen narrator to enhance the visual images of the depression's impact on the landscape.

In the late 1930s the Farm Security Administration recruited a group of photographers to record American rural life. These photographers included Walker Evans, who depicted life among

SECTION 3 REVIEW

IDENTIFY and explain the significance of the following: Marian Anderson, Robert C. Weaver, Mary McLeod Bethune, Antonio Luhan, John Collier, American Indian Defense Association, Indian Reorganization Act, Okies, Pare Lorentz, Dorothea Lange.

LOCATE and explain the importance of the following: Dust Bowl.

1. **MAIN IDEA** How did the New Deal affect African Americans during the 1930s?

2. **MAIN IDEA** How did the Indian Reorganization Act benefit Native Americans?

3. **LINKING HISTORY AND GEOGRAPHY** What factors caused the Dust Bowl during the 1930s?

4. **WRITING TO DESCRIBE** Imagine you are an Okie migrating west in 1939. Write a diary entry describing your experiences on the West Coast.

5. **ANALYZING** How did filmmakers, such as Pare Lorentz, and photographers, such as Dorothea Lange, serve as social critics during the 1930s?

THE NEW DEAL AND THE ARTS

FOCUS

■ How did Federal Project No. I aid writers and artists?

■ What were many novels like in the late 1930s?

■ What common themes were often heard and seen in music, plays, and paintings of the New Deal era?

In attempting to put Americans back to work, the Roosevelt administration did not forget about those who worked in the arts. The WPA established a series of programs to employ writers, actors, musicians, painters, and other artists. Meanwhile literature in the late 1930s began to turn from escapist fantasies to realistic portrayals of the depression, while musicians, playwrights, and painters searched for uniquely American subject matter.

1936 poster for
WPA production, *Macbeth*

THE WPA PROGRAMS

All workers struggled with unemployment in depression-era America, including artists. Without an audience that could afford to buy their work, most of the nation's writers, stage actors, musicians, and painters lost their means of earning an income. Like workers in other fields, they sought relief from the government. In February 1935 a few writers picketed federal offices in

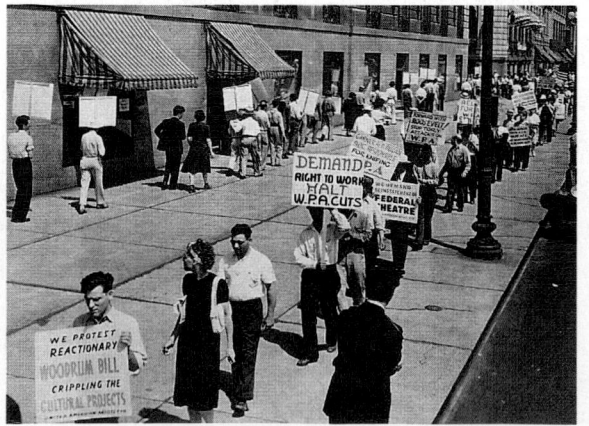

New York City, carrying signs that read "CHILDREN NEED BOOKS. WRITERS NEED BREAD. WE DEMAND PROJECTS."

Later that year, the WPA set aside some $300 million to create **Federal Project No. 1**. This program tried to encourage pride in American culture by aiding unemployed artists in the fields of writing, theater, music, and visual arts.

The WPA's **Federal Writers' Project** (FWP) hired some 6,600 unemployed writers to produce a variety of works, including state travel guides and histories of various ethnic groups. Others conducted oral-history interviews with hundreds of elderly former slaves. Historians still use these sources to study slave life. Members of the project also studied American folklore and wrote down folktales. These eventually became the basis for the best-selling *Treasury of American Folklore* (1944). The FWP eventually won praise as the "biggest literary project in history," producing more than 1,000 books

◄ **Unemployed and striking actors picketed outside the hotel where heads of the regional, state, and national offices of the WPA met in July 1939.**

and pamphlets. It also helped launch the careers of numerous writers who went on to great success, such as John Steinbeck and Richard Wright.

The WPA's Federal Theatre Project hired unemployed actors, directors, designers, stagehands, and playwrights to encourage theatrical productions. It entertained millions of Americans, bringing productions to many small towns that had never experienced live theater. The Federal Music Project hired musicians to form orchestras and present some 4,000 musical productions per month to audiences across the country. It also hired music researchers to write down popular American folk songs. The Federal Arts Project hired unemployed artists and designers to produce posters for New Deal programs and to teach art in public schools. Others painted murals on public buildings constructed by the PWA.

■■ Federal Project No. 1 employed various writers and artists and spread their work throughout the country.

LITERATURE IN THE LATE 1930s

American interest in romantic fiction continued into the late 1930s. One of the best-selling novels of the decade was Margaret Mitchell's *Gone with the Wind* (1936), a sweeping story of the Old South during the Civil War and Reconstruction. Many depression-era readers could relate to the turmoil faced by the novel's main character, Scarlett O'Hara, who survives war and economic chaos. Her uplifting closing line, "After all, tomorrow is another day," inspired readers of the 1930s.

By the end of the decade, many writers had incorporated the experiences of the depression into their works. John Steinbeck, a writer employed by the FWP, produced a gripping picture of the depression era in *The Grapes of Wrath* (1939). The story follows the fortunes of a desperately poor Dust Bowl family as they travel to California:

66 As the dark caught them, they clustered like bugs near to shelter and to water. And because they were lonely . . . , because they had all come from a place of sadness and . . . were all going to a new mysterious place, they huddled together. **99**

▲ Some three years in the planning, MGM's production of *Gone with the Wind* was the most eagerly awaited and top-grossing film of 1939.

As it was for the real Okies, life in California is lonely and harsh for Steinbeck's fictional migrant family. Like *Gone with the Wind,* however, Steinbeck's novel includes a hopeful note, as the head of the family, Ma Joad, optimistically states, "They ain't gonna wipe us out. Why, we're the people—we go on."

Other novels described the experiences of ethnic minorities in the era. African American anthropologist Zora Neale Hurston wrote *Their Eyes Were Watching God* (1937), which explores a black woman's search for fulfillment in rural Florida. Richard Wright offered a grim picture of black urban life in *Native Son* (1940), which

◀ *Native Son* by Richard Wright

▶ *Their Eyes Were Watching God* by Zora Neale Hurston

chronicles the journey of a young African American man lost in a racist world where he can never succeed. *Native Son* explores several themes that haunted the 1930s, including class differences, socialism, racism, and urban despair.

■■ **Many novels of the late 1930s reflected the experiences of the depression.**

*P*ERFORMING ARTS IN THE NEW DEAL ERA

American music of the late 1930s increasingly tried to capture uniquely American sounds. As WPA researchers wrote down American folk songs and folktales, composer Aaron Copland used these themes as the basis for his most popular compositions, including *Billy the Kid* (1938).

Interest in African American music continued throughout the 1930s. Black gospel, a cross between jazz and traditional spirituals, gained popularity through the work of African American composer Thomas A. Dorsey—whose songs included "Precious Lord, Take My Hand"—and singers such as Sister Rosetta Tharpe and Mahalia Jackson. Jackson recalled that some ministers initially objected to this new style of music:

▲ **Paper fan depicting singer Mahalia Jackson**

66 They didn't like the hand-clapping and the stomping and they said we were bringing jazz into the church and it wasn't dignified. Once at church one of the preachers got up in the pulpit and spoke out against me. I got right up, too. I told him I was born to sing gospel music. 99

Jazz continued its rise in popularity, largely because of the development of swing, a smooth big-band style popular in dance halls. The style derived its name from Duke Ellington's 1932 hit "It Don't Mean a Thing If It Ain't Got That Swing." White conductor Benny Goodman helped popularize swing in the late 1930s. He also broke new ground in popular music by integrating his shows with both black and white performers. Meanwhile, other bands, such as those of Count Basie and Glenn Miller, kept the swing sound alive throughout the 1930's.

On the theatrical stage, plays with social significance—that is, plays that dealt with the nation's labor and class problems—drew large audiences. Robert Sherwood's *The Petrified Forest* (1935) attacked the "petrified forest" of ideas destroying America. Lillian Hellman's *The Little Foxes* (1939) exposed the upper-class greed that many believed was undermining America. By the end of the decade, popular plays, like popular music, focused increasingly on American traditions and values. Two examples are Thornton Wilder's *Our Town* (1938), a heartwarming drama of life and death in a small American town around 1900, and William Saroyan's *The Time of Your Life* (1939), which celebrates the diversity of urban America.

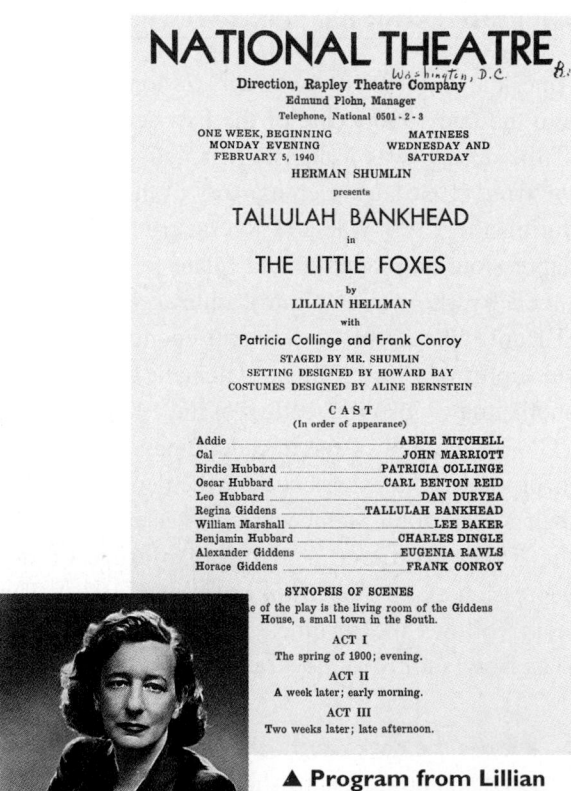

▲ **Program from Lillian Hellman's *The Little Foxes***

◄ **Lillian Hellman**

■ Music—folk songs, gospel, and jazz—and plays—socially significant and traditional—reflected uniquely American styles and themes.

PAINTERS EXAMINE LOCAL CULTURE

Like American writers, painters recorded a variety of memorable American images during the depression. Harlem artist Jacob Lawrence portrayed the daily lives of African American heroes, such as Frederick Douglass and Harriet Tubman, while New Mexico artist Georgia O'Keeffe painted haunting images of the southwestern desert landscape.

Perhaps reflecting the New Deal's focus on farmers' problems, many artists of the era looked to rural America for their subject matter. A group of midwestern artists known as the **regionalists** stressed local folk themes and customs. The regionalists included artists such as Thomas Hart Benton of Missouri, John Steuart Curry of Kansas, and Grant Wood of Iowa.

These artists reminded urban art lovers of America's rural traditions. Wood always insisted that his best ideas "came while milking a cow." The most famous of the regionalist paintings is probably Wood's *American Gothic,* which depicts a stern farmer, pitchfork in hand,

▲ Paintings of rustic scenes, such as *Sugaring Off* by Anna "Grandma" Moses, were typical of regionalists and other folk artists of the depression era.

Grandma Moses: *Sugaring Off.* Copyright © 1992 Grandma Moses Properties Co., New York

standing beside a sad-eyed woman in front of a humble farmhouse.

As interest in regional culture grew, people began to rediscover the richness of American folk art, such as handmade quilts and woodcarvings. Many obscure folk artists, including the elderly painter Anna "Grandma" Moses, became well-known during this period.

■ American painters, led by the regionalists, explored a diversity of local folk life.

SECTION 4 REVIEW

IDENTIFY and explain the significance of the following: Federal Project No. 1, Federal Writers' Project, Margaret Mitchell, John Steinbeck, Zora Neale Hurston, Richard Wright, Aaron Copland, Thomas A. Dorsey, Benny Goodman, Robert Sherwood, Lillian Hellman, Thornton Wilder, Jacob Lawrence, Georgia O'Keeffe, regionalists, Anna "Grandma" Moses.

1. **MAIN IDEA** Why was Federal Project No. 1 created?

2. **MAIN IDEA** What contribution did regionalists make to American painting?

3. **COMPARING** What common themes did music and plays of the 1930s share?

4. **WRITING TO CREATE** Write a promotional piece for *The Grapes of Wrath, Their Eyes Were Watching God,* or *Native Son* that shows how the novel reflects the experiences of the depression.

5. **GAINING A MULTICULTURAL PERSPECTIVE** How were the experiences of African Americans expressed artistically during the New Deal era?

FDR declares bank holiday. Congress passes 15 New Deal measures.

Southern Tenant Farmers' Union formed. Indian Reorganization Act passed.

Social Security Act, Wealth Tax Act, and Wagner-Connery Act passed. CIO organized. Mary McLeod Bethune helps form National Council of Negro Women. Federal Project No. 1 created.

1933   1935

WRITING A SUMMARY

Using the essential points of the chapter as a guide, write a summary of the chapter.

REVIEWING CHRONOLOGY

Number your paper 1 to 5. Study the time line above, and list the following events in the order in which they happened by writing the first next to 1, the second next to 2, and so on. Then complete the activity below.

1. Aaron Copland composes *Billy the Kid*.
2. CIO organized.
3. Richard Wright's *Native Son* published.
4. FDR declares bank holiday.
5. Indian Reorganization Act passed.

Assessing Consequences How did Mary McLeod Bethune help maximize the participation of African Americans in the New Deal?

IDENTIFYING PEOPLE AND IDEAS

Explain the historical significance of each of the following people or terms.

1. New Deal
2. Frances Perkins
3. subsidies
4. Zora Neale Hurston
5. Wealth Tax Act
6. sit-down strike
7. Robert C. Weaver
8. John Collier
9. Dust Bowl
10. Huey Long

UNDERSTANDING MAIN IDEAS

1. What was the purpose of the bank holiday and the FDIC?
2. How were the economic and social programs of the Second New Deal different from those of the First New Deal?
3. What steps did the government take in the 1930s to aid farmers?
4. How did the New Deal affect African Americans and Native Americans?
5. What contributions did Pare Lorentz and Dorothea Lange make to the New Deal era?

REVIEWING THEMES

1. **Economic Development** How did the Roosevelt administration attempt to promote economic recovery?
2. **Constitutional Heritage** Why might the Supreme Court have declared some New Deal measures unconstitutional?
3. **Cultural Diversity** How did writers and artists of the 1930s reflect the ethnic and cultural diversity of the nation?

THINKING CRITICALLY

1. **Analyzing** Why did some conservative and liberal critics oppose the New Deal?
2. **Evaluating** Do you think that Roosevelt was justified in trying to "pack" the Supreme Court? Why or why not?
3. **Assessing Consequences** How did WPA programs enrich American culture during the 1930s?

STRATEGY FOR SUCCESS

Review the Skills Handbook entry on Identifying the Main Idea beginning on page 988. Examine the photograph below, taken by Margaret Bourke-White in 1937. These residents of Louisville, Kentucky, are waiting in a relief line to receive aid. What contrasts can you see between the experiences of the people in the line and the message on the billboard behind them?

WORLD'S HIGHEST STANDARD OF LIVING

There's no way like the American Way

Margaret Mitchell's *Gone with the Wind* published. FDR reelected president.

FDR tries to "pack" Supreme Court. Farm Security Administration created. GM strike begins.

Second AAA passed. Aaron Copland composes *Billy the Kid*. Thornton Wilder's *Our Town* opens.

John Steinbeck's *The Grapes of Wrath* published. Lillian Hellman's play *The Little Foxes* opens.

Richard Wright's *Native Son* published.

1937

1939

WRITING ABOUT HISTORY

Writing to Classify Create a chart that classifies the programs of the New Deal according to whether they were designed primarily to help banks, farmers, labor, or business.

USING PRIMARY SOURCES

Jesse Perez worked for the meat-packing industry in Chicago in 1939, during a time when the CIO was attempting to organize workers in the stockyards. Read the following excerpt, which comes from an interview Perez did at that time with a member of the Federal Writers' Project. What does Perez have to say about the treatment of Mexican workers by the company during this time?

66 *The bosses in the yards never treat Mexican worker same as rest. I was first to wear CIO button; ever since I start wearing the button they start to pick. I can butcher, but they don't give me job. . . . So when I start telling the boys we have a union for them, almost all join right away. We talk all the time what the union going to do for us, going to raise wages, stop speed-up. The bosses watch and they know it's a union coming.*

    So every day they start saying we behind in the work. They start speeding up the boys more and more every day. . . . We told bosses we working too fast, can't keep up. The whole gang, thirteen men, all stop. Bosses say, we ain't standing for nothing like this. Four days later they fire the whole gang, except two. We took the case in the labor board and . . . now all who was fired got work.

    Now the bosses try to provoke strike before CIO get ready. . . . We know what they do, we don't talk back, got to watch out they don't play tricks like that. 99

LINKING HISTORY AND GEOGRAPHY

Describing the effects of the Dust Bowl, John Steinbeck wrote: "The Western States are nervous under the beginning change. . . . A half-million people moving over the country; a million more, restive [restless] to move; ten million more feeling the first nervousness." How did the Dust Bowl influence population shifts in the Southwest?

Scene from the film *The Grapes of Wrath*, 1939

BUILDING YOUR PORTFOLIO

Complete the following projects independently or cooperatively.

1. THE ECONOMY In chapters 21, 22, and 23, you examined the U.S. economy in the 1920s. Building on that experience, imagine you are a New Deal legislator. Write a proposal for a new public works project. Your proposal should describe what the project is, how workers and businesses will benefit, and why your project will be useful to society in terms of relief, recovery, or reform.

2. CULTURE AND SOCIETY In chapters 21 and 22 you explored U.S. society in the 1920s. Building on that experience, imagine you are an author in the 1930s. Write a short, realistic passage for your novel that describes the Dust Bowl's effect on your main character.

BETWEEN THE WARS

FOCUS

UNDERSTANDING THE MAIN IDEA

After World War I many Americans hoped to focus on matters at home. Unfortunately, the depression touched off global economic problems. The rise of dictators in Europe set the stage for another war. Dictators also came to power in several Latin American countries. Other countries in Latin America, such as Nicaragua and Mexico, attempted to reduce U.S. influence.

THEMES

- **GLOBAL RELATIONS** How might nations work together to promote world peace?

- **ECONOMIC DEVELOPMENT** What economic problems might wars create? What political problems might result from these economic difficulties?

- **DEMOCRATIC VALUES** What conditions might give rise to a dictatorship?

1921	1926	1931	1933	1939
Washington Conference begins.	**Augusto Sandino organizes revolt in Nicaragua.**	**Japan invades Manchuria.**	**Adolf Hitler becomes chancellor of Germany.**	**World War II starts.**

World War I and the depression created chaos in Europe. Germany was required to pay substantial war reparations, while other European countries owed the United States large war debts. After the war many Americans called for an end to foreign military involvements.

Nazi parade watchers, 1932

"One word . . . describes the whole feeling in America to-day, and that is *disillusionment* [disappointment]: disillusionment in the leaders, disillusionment in the business men, disillusionment in politics," wrote a friend to British prime minister David Lloyd George in January 1932. This feeling of pessimism arose from the economic strains of the depression and the international chaos caused by World War I. Instead of bringing peace, the end of the war ushered in a period of economic and political instability in Europe.

Many Americans feared that involvement in European affairs might draw the United States into another war. In 1937 the magazine *Christian Century* estimated that "ninety-nine Americans out of a hundred would today regard as an imbecile anyone who might suggest that, in the event of another European war, the United States should again participate in it." In general, the United States backed down from military intervention in foreign countries in the 1920s and 1930s. American efforts on the world stage focused on reducing weapons and improving relations with Latin America.

Nevertheless, conditions brewing in Europe and Asia would soon doom hopes for world peace. In Italy, Germany, and Spain, ruthless dictators came to power by promising to make their countries great through foreign conquest. In Japan, militaristic dreams of empire threatened U.S. interests in China and the Pacific. When the aggressor nations formed an alliance, the stage was set for global war.

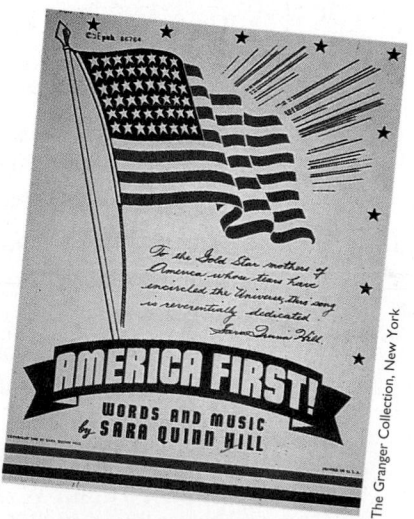

The Granger Collection, New York

Antiwar sheet music, 1940

THE SEARCH FOR PEACE

FOCUS

- Why did the United States pursue an isolationist foreign policy after World War I?

- How did the United States try to promote world peace in the 1920s and 1930s?

- How did war debts and reparations affect European countries after World War I?

Profoundly disillusioned by the Great War, the United States sought to promote world peace during the 1920s. Fear of becoming involved in another war caused Americans to try to avoid conflict at any cost. As the world slipped into an economic depression and dictators rose to power in Europe in the 1930s, however, the United States found it increasingly difficult to remain isolated from the world's problems.

Peace activists, 1940

LEGACIES OF WORLD WAR I

Over 8 million people, including more than 112,000 Americans, had died fighting in the Great War. Yet, because of the postwar chaos in Europe and the founding of a Communist government in the Soviet Union, Americans did not believe that the war had made the world "safe for democracy." The Women's International League for Peace and Freedom summed up the nation's doubts: "War to end war has proved a failure. The war is won, yet nowhere is there peace, security or happiness."

Americans worried about being dragged into another foreign conflict. "We ask only to live our own life in our own way, in friendship and sympathy with all, in alliance with none," declared Senator Hiram W. Johnson in 1922. Such sentiments led the United States to follow a policy of partial **isolationism**, or withdrawal from world affairs, in the 1920s and 1930s.

Isolationists did not want to cut off the United States completely from the affairs of the rest of the world. They merely wanted to avoid what Thomas Jefferson had called "entangling alliances" that could drag the United States into another war. Isolationists also supported U.S. **unilateralism**, that is, one-sided or independent action in foreign affairs.

Isolationism and unilateralism led the United States to shun membership in international organizations set up after the war, such as the League of Nations and the Permanent Court of International Justice (the World Court).

Presidents Coolidge, Hoover, and Roosevelt all proposed that the United States join the World Court, created to solve international disputes. Public opinion, however, ran strongly against membership. The Senate set strict terms for joining in order to guard its right to make treaties. The nations that already belonged to the World Court rejected the Senate's terms, and the matter was dropped.

■■ **To avoid being drawn into European wars, the United States pursued an isolationist foreign policy after World War I.**

PROMOTING PEACE

Instead of joining international peacekeeping organizations, the United States used diplomacy to promote world peace. American peace groups urged the U.S. government to bring world leaders together to negotiate **disarmament**, or limiting their weapons. Jane Addams, Emily Greene Balch, Jeannette Rankin, and other leaders of the women's movement played important roles in these peace efforts. For their organizing efforts in the United States and abroad, both Addams (in 1931) and Balch (in 1946) received the Nobel Peace Prize.

The Washington Conference. In Washington, D.C., beginning in November 1921, the United States hosted an international conference on naval disarmament and Pacific security. U.S. secretary of state Charles Evans Hughes surprised the other delegates with his bold proposal that the major powers scrap 78 large warships amounting to almost 1.9 million tons. He also called for a 10-year "naval holiday" during which no battleships or battle cruisers would be built.

Hughes proposed that the United States, Great Britain, and Japan scrap enough large warships to bring their naval strength into a ratio of 5:5:3. That is, Great Britain and the United States would be equal in naval strength, with a large-warship tonnage of roughly 525,000 each, while Japan would have some 315,000 tons. Italy and France would both be limited to some 175,000 tons. This plan became known as the **Five Power Agreement**. Marveled one observer: "Secretary

Hughes sank in 35 minutes more ships than all the admirals of the world have sunk in . . . centuries."

The Washington Conference produced other important agreements as well. In the **Four Power Treaty**, Japan, Great Britain, France, and the United States pledged to respect one another's territory in the Pacific. The **Nine Power Treaty**, which included the nations that signed the Five Power agreement as well as the Netherlands, Portugal, Belgium, and China, guaranteed China's territorial integrity and promised to uphold the Open Door policy.

Japan's navy minister, Admiral Kato Tomosaburo, declared that the conference had created "a new order of seapower." He explained Japan's support for disarmament:

❝ Japan is ready for the new order of thought—the spirit of international friendship and cooperation for the greater good of humanity—which the Conference has brought about. ❞

For a time the Washington Conference agreements eased tensions in Asia. Japan withdrew, at least partially, from the Shandong (Shantung) Peninsula it had invaded in 1914 and from parts of Siberia it had occupied during the Russian Revolution. In 1930 Japan's agreement to extend

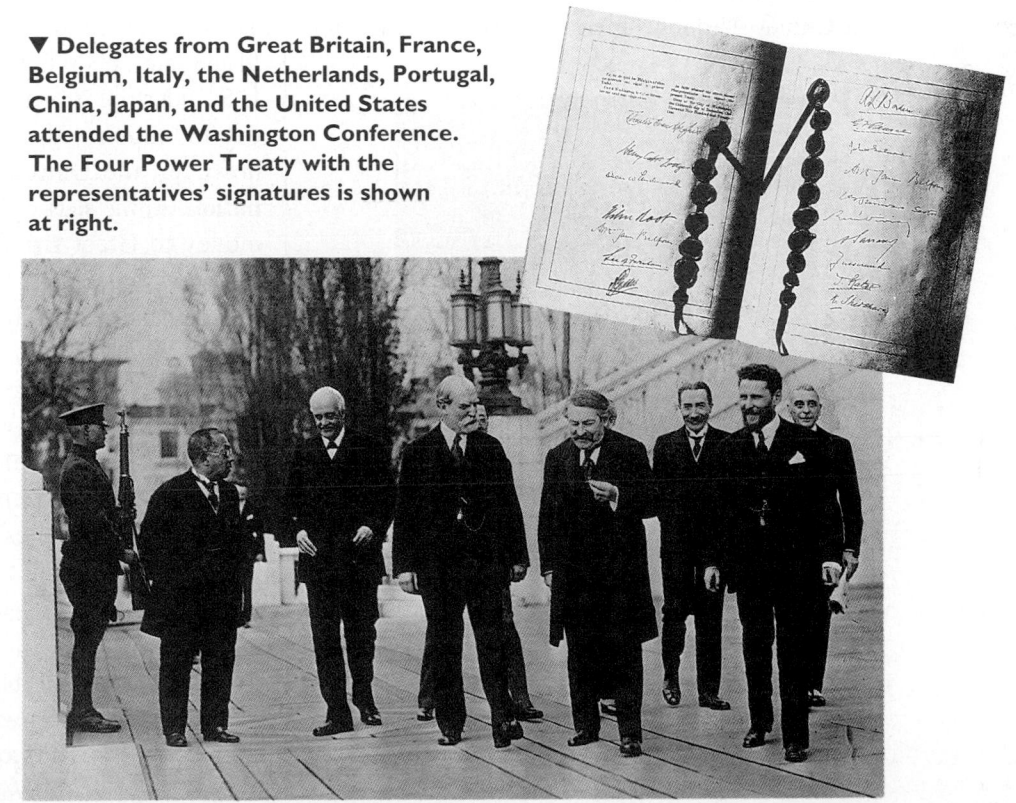

▼ Delegates from Great Britain, France, Belgium, Italy, the Netherlands, Portugal, China, Japan, and the United States attended the Washington Conference. The Four Power Treaty with the representatives' signatures is shown at right.

the holiday on warship construction marked the high point of postwar international cooperation.

Unsuccessful efforts. On April 6, 1927, the 10th anniversary of America's entry into World War I, the French foreign minister, Aristide Briand (ah-ree-steed bree-ahn), proposed that France and the United States enter into an agreement to outlaw war as a means of resolving their differences. The U.S. secretary of state, Frank Kellogg, made a counter-proposal that the pact include all nations. Sixty-two countries eventually signed the **Kellogg-Briand Pact**, which outlawed war "as an instrument of national policy" but allowed countries to go to war in self-defense. Unfortunately, the treaty lacked provisions for enforcement. One U.S. senator remarked that the treaty was "as effective to keep down war as a carpet would be to smother an earthquake."

■■ Through diplomatic conferences and international agreements the United States worked for world peace.

The pact's weaknesses became clear in September 1931. Japan, whose military leaders were gaining influence, violated all the international agreements and invaded the Chinese territory of Manchuria (see map on page 739). This invasion launched a bloody war between Japan and China. Although many Americans called for

▲ Suffragist and peace activist Carrie Chapman Catt praised the Kellogg-Briand Pact and lobbied Congress for its passage.

▲ These Japanese cavalrymen were photographed in Manchuria in December 1931, some three months after the war between China and Japan had begun.

an economic boycott of Japan, U.S. leaders refused to support sanctions against the Japanese. The failure of diplomacy to prevent Japanese aggression marked the end of attempts at international agreements. Preoccupied by the Japanese invasion and the worldwide economic depression, delegates of the League of Nations' 1932 World Disarmament Conference went home without agreeing to reduce weapons.

WAR DEBTS AND REPARATIONS

The issue of war debts also weakened peace efforts. In the late 1800s European investors had financed U.S. industrial growth, making the United States a **debtor nation** with respect to Europe. After 1914, however, the United States became a **creditor nation**. At the start of World War I, U.S. banks lent money to Great Britain and France so that they could buy armaments in the United States. The U.S. government granted billions more in credit to the Allies. By 1920 the Allies owed more than $10 billion to the United States.

The debtor nations argued that their debts to the United States should be wiped out. David Lloyd George, who had been the British prime minister when the United States entered the war, said:

66 The United States did not from first to last make any sacrifice or contribution remotely comparable to those of her European Associates, in life, limb, money, material or trade, towards the victory which she shared with them. **99**

U.S. officials rejected appeals from Great Britain, France, and Italy to cancel all their war debts. However, the U.S. government reduced the interest rates on the loans and canceled part of the debts. Still, the only way the Allies could pay their war debts to the United States was to collect reparations, or damages, from defeated Germany. In 1921 a reparations commission had set total German reparations at 132 billion gold marks ($32 billion). The Germans bitterly condemned the reparations as too harsh. Chancellor Joseph Wirth paid part of the reparations by borrowing money from Great Britain. The German government also printed paper money, causing massive inflation as the value of the German mark plunged.

In 1931, as the worldwide depression deepened, President Herbert Hoover declared a year's **moratorium**, or halt, on reparation and war-debt payments. The moratorium, however, only prolonged the crisis. Most of the war debts remained unpaid. By 1934 none of the debtor nations except Finland could make even a token payment.

America's efforts to collect the war debts sowed resentment in Europe. In Germany the economic hardships created by the reparations made people especially bitter. With his country near financial collapse, Adolf Hitler, a young German politician, hatched a plot to overthrow the German government in 1923. The plot failed, and Hitler was sent to jail. The next year, an international plan temporarily eased Germany's economic crisis by providing loans and extending German debt payments. Continuing German anger over reparations, however, would help bring Hitler to power 10 years later.

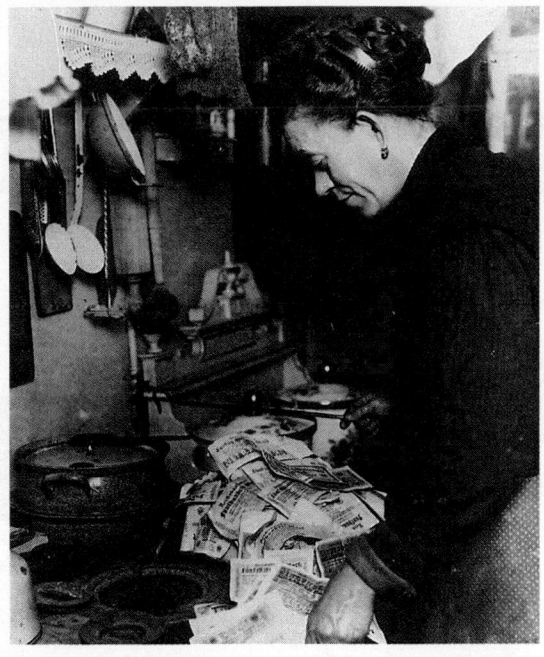

▲ During the 1920s rapid inflation in Germany made most currency worthless. This woman used several million-mark notes to start a breakfast fire.

■■ Europeans resented America's efforts to collect war debts. German anger over reparations helped Adolf Hitler gain support.

SECTION 1 REVIEW

IDENTIFY and explain the significance of the following: isolationism, unilateralism, disarmament, Emily Greene Balch, Charles Evans Hughes, Five Power Agreement, Four Power Treaty, Nine Power Treaty, Kato Tomosaburo, Kellogg-Briand Pact, debtor nation, creditor nation, moratorium.

LOCATE and explain the importance of the following: Manchuria.

1. **MAIN IDEA** Why did the United States partially withdraw from world affairs after World War I?

2. **MAIN IDEA** What steps did the United States take to work for world peace?

3. **ASSESSING CONSEQUENCES** How did war debts and reparations affect Germany and other European countries?

4. **WRITING TO INFORM** Imagine you are a delegate to the Washington Conference in 1921. Write an essay outlining the goals and accomplishments of the conference.

5. **ANALYZING** Why was the Kellogg-Briand Pact unsuccessful in resolving the conflict in Manchuria?

RELATIONS WITH LATIN AMERICA

FOCUS

■ How did U.S. relations with Latin America change in the 1930s?

■ How did the Great Depression affect Latin American countries?

■ What role did the United States play in Nicaraguan politics?

■ How did the United States respond when Mexico took over the Mexican oil industry?

In the 1920s and 1930s the United States preferred to use economic influence—dollar diplomacy—rather than military force to protect its interests in Latin America. For example, conflict between the Mexican government and U.S. oil companies was solved through diplomacy. However, when U.S. interests faced threats in Nicaragua, America sent in the marines.

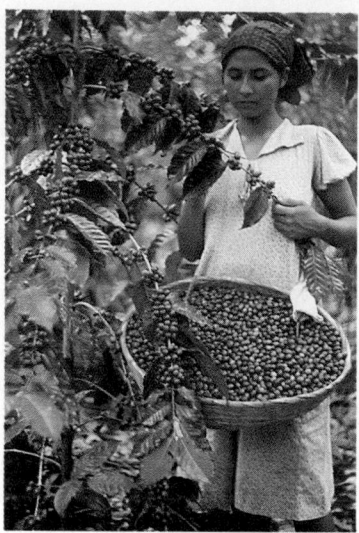

Woman picking coffee in El Salvador

THE GOOD NEIGHBOR

While the United States tried to avoid war in Europe, presidents Coolidge, Hoover, and Roosevelt all tried to improve relations with Latin American countries. Before his inauguration, Hoover toured Latin America to promote goodwill. Franklin D. Roosevelt spelled out the **Good Neighbor policy** in his inaugural speech of 1933:

❝ In the field of world policy I would dedicate this nation to the policy of the good neighbor—the neighbor who resolutely respects himself and, because he does so, respects the rights of others. ❞

To back up his words, Roosevelt in 1934 canceled the Platt Amendment, by which the United States had claimed the right to intervene in Cuba's affairs. Two years later he gave up the U.S. claim to intervene unilaterally in Panama. Roosevelt also withdrew marines from Haiti, where they had been stationed as an occupying force since 1915. However, in economic matters the United States often behaved more like an overbearing landlord than a good neighbor.

U.S. investors played a powerful, and sometimes negative, role in Latin America. After World War I, large U.S. companies increased their investments in banana, coffee, and sugar plantations in Central America and the Caribbean.

■■ **In the 1930s the United States pledged to reduce military intervention in Latin America. U.S. business investment continued, however.**

The largest of the American companies was the United Fruit Company, which owned millions of acres in Central America and the Caribbean. In Guatemala it was the largest landowner, exporter, and employer. Besides establishing plantations, United Fruit and other companies built roads and railroads and controlled the ports and shipping lines necessary to export their products. They also tied these regions to the world economy, though

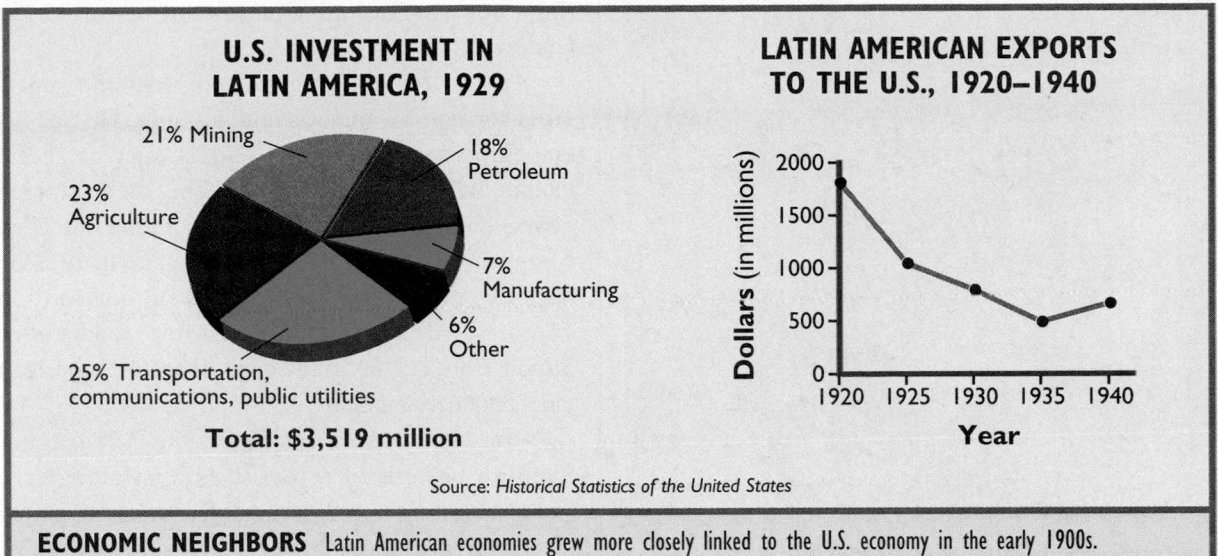

U.S. INVESTMENT IN LATIN AMERICA, 1929

21% Mining
18% Petroleum
23% Agriculture
7% Manufacturing
6% Other
25% Transportation, communications, public utilities

Total: $3,519 million

LATIN AMERICAN EXPORTS TO THE U.S., 1920–1940

Dollars (in millions)
Year

Source: *Historical Statistics of the United States*

ECONOMIC NEIGHBORS Latin American economies grew more closely linked to the U.S. economy in the early 1900s.

? BUILDING GRAPH SKILLS Approximately how much money did U.S. businesses invest in Latin American agriculture in 1929? In which five-year period did the value of Latin American exports to the United States decrease the most?

profits went mostly to the corporations and wealthy Latin Americans.

In addition to their economic importance in Latin America, the U.S. companies had political power. They made alliances with Latin American landowners and politicians and often played a role in governing the countries in which they operated. The economic and political powers of the large American companies earned them the resentment of many Latin Americans. Chilean poet Pablo Neruda (nay-ROO-thah) wrote:

66 The Fruit Company, Inc.
reserved for itself the most
    succulent,
the central coast of my own land,
the delicate waist of America.
It rechristened its territories
as the "Banana Republics." 99

"Banana republics" were countries run largely to serve the interests of the foreign companies that grew bananas and other crops.

THE RISE OF DICTATORS

The Wall Street crash of 1929 sent shock waves through Latin America. Worldwide depression meant lower prices for coffee, bananas, and other crops on which Latin American economies depended. In El Salvador, coffee prices fell so low

that some plantation owners did not bother to harvest the 1930 coffee crop. Farm wages dropped to eight cents a day.

As workers lost their jobs, the gulf between Latin America's small class of wealthy landowners and the large class of poor landless people widened. The U.S. diplomat Major A. R. Harris commented on the inequality he noted between the classes in El Salvador in 1931:

66 The first thing one observes . . . is the number of expensive automobiles on the streets. . . . There seems to be nothing between these high-priced cars and the ox-cart with its barefooted attendant. . . . Roughly 90 percent of the wealth of the country is held by about one-half of one percent of the population. 99

In countries throughout the region, the difficult 1930s brought **caudillos** (kow-THEE-ohs) to power. These caudillos were military leaders who used force to maintain order. In 1932 the caudillo Maximiliano Hernández Martínez brutally crushed a revolt by peasants in El Salvador's hard-hit coffee-growing region. Thousands of peasants were massacred.

During the 1930s caudillos also came to power in Cuba, the Dominican Republic, Guatemala, and Honduras. U.S. diplomats sometimes denounced the caudillos' methods of staying in power: bans on opposition parties and restrictions

▲ U.S. Army cooks are shown buying produce from Nicaraguan vendors. The baskets contain papayas and alligator pears.

on freedom of speech. However, the United States often supported the caudillos, since they created favorable environments for U.S. businesses.

■■ **The depression wrecked Latin American economies, caused social unrest, and helped bring caudillos to power in many countries.**

ꟷNTERVENTION IN NICARAGUA

The United States played a large role in Nicaraguan politics throughout the 1920s and 1930s. In 1925 General Emiliano Chamorro (chah-MAWR-roh) overthrew the government, sparking a bitter civil war.

The United States refused to recognize Chamorro. In May 1926 President Coolidge sent in the marines to protect U.S. commercial interests. He also sent Henry Stimson to negotiate an end to the civil war. Stimson brought the two sides together and they negotiated a peace treaty in May 1927. More important, Stimson called for the abolition of Nicaraguan armed forces. U.S. troops would then train a new Nicaraguan National Guard to maintain order after the withdrawal of U.S. forces.

Augusto César Sandino (sahn-DEE-noh), a general who opposed Chamorro, refused to accept Stimson's proposal. Born in 1893, Sandino was the son of an Indian woman and a well-to-do landowner.

After attending high school, Sandino supervised some of his father's landholdings. He fled his hometown in 1920 to avoid arrest after he shot a man in the leg during a fight. During the next three years, Sandino worked as a mechanic for U.S. companies in Honduras and Guatemala. In 1923 he began working for a U.S.–owned oil company in Tampico, Mexico. There Sandino read about Simon Bolívar, the great hero of Latin American independence struggles.

In 1926, after his return to Nicaragua, Sandino organized a revolt against Chamorro and Chamorro's successor, Adolfo Díaz. He hoped to rid Nicaragua of the Americans, whom he viewed as invaders, and to allow ordinary Nicaraguans to control their country's land and wealth. He planned to help workers and peasants "exploit our own natural resources for the benefit of the Nicaraguan family in general."

Sandino's army, which varied from as few as 30 to as many as 3,000, proved a tough adversary for the U.S. Marines. Although the Americans used aerial bombing for the first time against Sandino's forces, they could not completely destroy the army, which relied on sympathetic farmers to feed and house them.

The marines never defeated Sandino. The war became increasingly costly for the United States in the midst of the depression. In 1933 President Hoover withdrew the last of the U.S. troops. A year later, the commander of

Augusto César Sandino

the U.S.–trained National Guard, General Anastasio Somoza, ordered Sandino's assassination. With Sandino dead, organized resistance to Somoza and his military evaporated. Somoza forced out the Nicaraguan president in 1936 and took over the presidency the next year. With U.S. backing, Somoza and other members of his family ruled Nicaragua almost without interruption until the Sandinista revolution (named for Sandino) overthrew the dynasty in 1979.

BIO GRAPHY

■■ **The United States opposed Sandino and trained the National Guard, which helped bring Somoza to power.**

▲ **President Lázaro Cárdenas (center) is shown with Britain's minister to Mexico (left) and Mexico's secretary of foreign relations (right) shortly before diplomatic relations between Mexico and Great Britain were broken in May 1938.**

*R*ELATIONS WITH MEXICO

Perhaps the most severe test of the Good Neighbor policy came when Mexico's president, Lázaro Cárdenas (KAHR-thay-nahs), began to **nationalize**, or assert government control over, that country's oil industry in March 1938. Although the Mexican Constitution of 1917 proclaimed that Mexico controlled all its underground resources (see Chapter 19), U.S. and British firms had continued to own and operate oil companies in Mexico. When the foreign companies refused to meet the demands of Mexican oil workers for higher wages and better working conditions, however, President Cárdenas nationalized the oil fields.

U.S. oil companies hotly criticized the Mexican seizure of their property. They pressed the U.S. State Department to resist the nationalization. Some called for action to oust Cárdenas. Meanwhile, the U.S. ambassador to Mexico, Josephus Daniels, argued for a compromise between the Mexican government and the oil companies. He urged the United States to recognize Mexico's right to control its oil resources but added that U.S. companies should be compensated for the property they had lost.

Most Mexicans supported Cárdenas's bold action against the oil companies. Mexicans worried, however, that the United States might invade Mexico to restore U.S. oil companies' property rights. With events in Europe and Asia looking increasingly threatening, however, Roosevelt decided to maintain good relations with Mexico. He acknowledged Mexico's right to control its own resources and urged the oil companies to reach an agreement with the Mexican government for fair compensation. Mexico agreed to the compromise and began payments in 1939.

■■ **Roosevelt resisted calls from oil companies for U.S. intervention to protect their interests in Mexico.**

SECTION 2 REVIEW

IDENTIFY and explain the significance of the following: Good Neighbor policy, caudillos, Maximiliano Hernández Martínez, Emiliano Chamorro, Henry Stimson, Augusto César Sandino, Adolfo Díaz, Anastasio Somoza, Lázaro Cárdenas, nationalize, Josephus Daniels.

LOCATE and explain the importance of the following: El Salvador, Nicaragua.

1. **MAIN IDEA** How did the United States hope to secure its interests in Latin America after World War I?

2. **MAIN IDEA** What effect did the Great Depression have on Latin America?

3. **IDENTIFYING CAUSE AND EFFECT** How did the United States intervene in Nicaraguan politics throughout the 1920s and 1930s? What was the effect of this intervention?

4. **WRITING TO PERSUADE** Imagine you are Josephus Daniels in 1938. Write a memorandum to President Roosevelt recommending U.S. policy toward Mexico after the oil fields were nationalized.

5. **EVALUATING** Why did Augusto César Sandino organize a revolt against Díaz?

THE ROAD TO WAR

FOCUS

■ What led to the rise of dictatorships after World War I?

■ How did other countries respond to German aggression?

■ What caused World War II?

■ How did the United States move closer to becoming involved in World War II?

Japanese women raising money for the war in China

America's isolationist stand faced a severe test when dictators came to power in Italy, Germany, Spain, and Japan in the 1920s and 1930s. Americans tried to stay out of European affairs. Neutrality proved difficult, however, as France and other nations fell before German armies, Great Britain battled for its life, and Japan expanded its territory in Asia.

THE RISE OF DICTATORSHIPS

Most European nations after World War I faced inflation and unemployment, which caused political and social unrest. Disagreements over how to solve these problems led to violent clashes between Communists and conservatives. Right-wing military leaders came to power in several countries by promising to end the chaos.

Mussolini in Italy. Although Italy had been on the winning side when World War I ended, many Italians felt they had not benefited from the Treaty of Versailles. Thousands of Italian soldiers returned home after the war only to find themselves jobless. Many joined the Italian Communist party, which urged Italian peasants to take over land and Communist workers to seize factories.

To smash the Communist party and promote his own rise to power, Benito Mussolini founded the **Fascist party** in 1921. The Fascists believed that a military-dominated government should control all aspects of society. Beginning in 1921,

bloody clashes between Communists and Fascists created a situation bordering on civil war. In October 1922 Mussolini led an army of his followers, whose black uniforms gave them the name **Blackshirts**, in a march on Rome. With the support of nationalists, who wanted to strengthen Italy, and of businesspeople who opposed the Socialists and Communists, the Fascists occupied the city.

▲ Benito Mussolini (center), shown here with his followers during their march on Rome, was known as *Il Duce* (eel DOO-chay), or "the leader."

The king appointed Mussolini prime minister and granted him dictatorial powers. Mussolini limited freedom of speech, arrested political opponents, and restricted voting rights. Acting on a pledge to make Italy an imperial power, Mussolini sent Italian forces into the African nation of Ethiopia in 1935 (see map on page 736). The small, poorly equipped Ethiopian army proved no match for the Italian dive-bombers and machine guns. The U.S. Congress, fearful of being drawn into the conflict, passed a neutrality act banning arms shipments to both sides. Such an embargo hurt Ethiopia more than Italy, which continued to receive weapons from Germany and oil from U.S. companies.

African Americans raised money to send relief and medical aid to the Ethiopians. Thousands of African Americans volunteered to fight in Ethiopia, but pressure from the U.S. government forced Ethiopia to reject such support. This lack of support convinced other fascist countries, such as Germany, that aggression would go unpunished.

Hitler in Germany. In 1932 Adolf Hitler's National Socialist party, or **Nazi party**, won over 40 percent of the vote, and Hitler became chancellor the next year. While in prison, Hitler had written *Mein Kampf* (*My Struggle*), which laid out his plans to restore German power. Hitler blamed Jews, intellectuals, and Communists for Germany's decline. The book won him many supporters, especially among the middle class and the unemployed ruined by inflation and depression.

Hitler's government, called the Third Reich (the Third Empire), claimed dictatorial powers. Hitler prohibited Jews and non-Nazis from holding government positions, outlawed strikes, and made military service mandatory. Nazi storm troopers, known as **Brownshirts** because of the color of their uniforms, crushed all political opposition.

Hitler's tight control over German industry strengthened the economy and reduced unemployment, allowing him to rearm the country in violation of the Treaty of Versailles. Hitler declared:

66 The buildup of the armed forces is the most important precondition for . . . political power. . . . How is this political power to be used when it is won? . . . Maybe fighting for new export possibilities, maybe . . . conquest of new *Lebensraum* [space for expansion] in the East. 99

◀ **During the 1930s Nazi posters, such as the one shown here, appealed to those who longed to see Germany restored to its former position as a world power.**

In March 1936, German troops moved into the Rhineland (see map on page 736). Two years later they overran Austria. Hitler then turned toward the Sudetenland (soo-DAYT-uhn-land), in western Czechoslovakia, where more than three million German-speaking people lived. Hitler demanded that Czechoslovakia turn over the region to Germany. Czechoslovakia refused Hitler's demand.

Meanwhile, Hitler's **anti-Semitism**, or hatred of Jews, became official government policy. He deprived Jews of their German citizenship and authorized the destruction of Jewish property. On November 9, 1938, Nazi thugs burned down synagogues and destroyed Jewish businesses. Known as *Kristallnacht*, "the night of broken glass," the violence provided a chilling preview of the still more-terrible fate that awaited European Jews and others who fell victim to Hitler's murderous rule. Despite outrage at these events, however, Americans were not yet willing to intervene in Germany or to encourage Jewish immigration.

Franco in Spain. Spain did not escape the spread of fascism. In the 1930s Spain faced bitter political conflicts. In 1931 a constitution that limited the power of the military and the Catholic church went into effect. It called for such reforms as universal suffrage, nationalization of public utilities, and land for peasants.

Threatened by the liberal reforms, conservative military men united under the leadership of General Francisco Franco. In July 1936 the Fascist army officers tried to overthrow the government, starting the **Spanish Civil War** between Fascists and Loyalists.

After almost three years of fighting, Franco took over the national government with German and Italian military aid. The Soviet Union aided the Loyalists, but Roosevelt's fears of being drawn into a European war kept the United States from sending aid.

Individual Americans, however, did join the fight against fascism. Some 3,000 Americans joined the Abraham Lincoln Brigade, one of several international brigades made up of volunteers who went to Spain. Ernest Hemingway, who covered the Spanish Civil War, expressed his support for the Loyalist cause in the powerful novel *For Whom the Bell Tolls* (1940).

▲ Shown here are Spanish Loyalists leaving Madrid to fight a rebel army advancing on the city.

Militarists in Japan. As German aggression threatened Europe, Japanese expansion loomed in Asia (see map on page 739). Although Japan had moved toward democracy in the 1920s, the leaders of Japan's military forces remained independent of the government. These military men wanted to lessen Japan's reliance on foreign imports, to reduce the influence of Western countries in Asia, and to win for Japan control of new territory throughout Asia.

The creation of a Japanese empire in Asia would give Japan direct control over territories that produced rubber, petroleum, iron, and timber. Worsening economic conditions in Japan strengthened the appeal of the militarists' position.

Japan's 1931 invasion of Manchuria signaled its imperial ambitions. In 1934 and 1935, breaking their Washington Conference pledges, the Japanese began a rapid naval buildup. On July 7, 1937, Japanese and Chinese troops clashed near Beijing (Peking). This incident soon developed into a full-scale war. Japan occupied northern China and launched devastating bombing raids against Chinese cities. Although the League of Nations and the United States condemned Japan's actions, they failed to check Japanese expansion.

■■ In Italy, Germany, Spain, and Japan, postwar problems brought military dictators to power in the 1920s and 1930s.

THE RESPONSE TO FASCISM

The spread of fascism in Asia and Europe caused a shake-up in international diplomatic relationships. The most surprising of these realignments was the shift in U.S.–Soviet relations. The Soviets were concerned about curbing the Japanese, who had massed

THE SPANISH CIVIL WAR

THROUGH OTHERS' EYES

After the Spanish Civil War, many Loyalists remained bitter over the failure of Western nations to support their cause. In 1940 Julio Alvarez del Vayo, a wartime diplomat for the defeated Spanish Republic, charged that this lack of support had cost the Loyalists the war:

"*Apart from Russia, from whom she was able, for a time, to buy arms, Republican Spain had no great powers at her side to supply her with men and munitions. . . . Alone, abandoned to their fate, . . . the Spanish people fought for nearly three years against the armed might of the totalitarian states. . . .*

My one desire is to show what it would have meant to the Western democracies to have had in Spain a certain ally ready to defend the liberty and dignity of Europe against all attempts at domination and oppression. If . . . Republican Spain had not been defeated, the present war [World War II] would never have begun. . . .

No, it was not Spanish democracy that failed. It was the other democracies who failed to save democratic Spain, as they will one day learn to their cost."

troops in nearby Manchuria. Hoping "to avert the Japanese danger," Soviet foreign affairs commissar Maksim Litvinov mended diplomatic fences with the United States. In November 1933, after years of hostility between the two countries, the United States formally recognized the Soviet Union.

The fascist powers also formalized their ties. In 1936 the rest of Europe trembled when Germany and Italy formed a military alliance. The two countries became known as the **Axis powers**, which later included Japan.

Roosevelt called for European leaders to meet and resolve their conflicts peacefully. Hitler and Mussolini joined British prime minister Neville Chamberlain and French premier Édouard Daladier (dah-lahd-yay) at Munich in September 1938. The four leaders at the **Munich Conference** signed a pact giving Germany control of the Sudetenland. The European leaders had opted for a policy of **appeasement**, or giving in to demands in an effort to avoid larger conflicts. Many politicians underestimated Hitler's expansionist goals, believing that Hitler sought only to remedy what he considered wrongs created by the Treaty of Versailles. But other politicians, such as Winston Churchill of Great Britain, feared that appeasement would only encourage Hitler to take more territory. Britain and other nations in Europe sped up their rearmament.

◼ European leaders tried to appease Hitler to avoid war.

Most Americans denounced the actions of the Axis powers, but isolationism remained strong. American pacifists—religious groups such as the Mennonites and the Society of Friends (Quakers) and groups such as the Committee on the Cause and Cure of War—urged U.S. leaders to reject war as a means of solving conflicts.

A series of neutrality laws passed by Congress from 1935 to 1939 expressed Americans' desire for peace. The neutrality laws (1) prohibited the shipment of U.S. munitions to warring nations, (2) required warring nations that bought goods from America to transport these goods in their own ships, and (3) forbade Americans to travel on the vessels of warring nations.

Not all Americans endorsed neutrality. Many urged the United States to help the nations under attack. If America allowed aggression to go unpunished, they warned, the United States might one day find itself surrounded by powerful enemies.

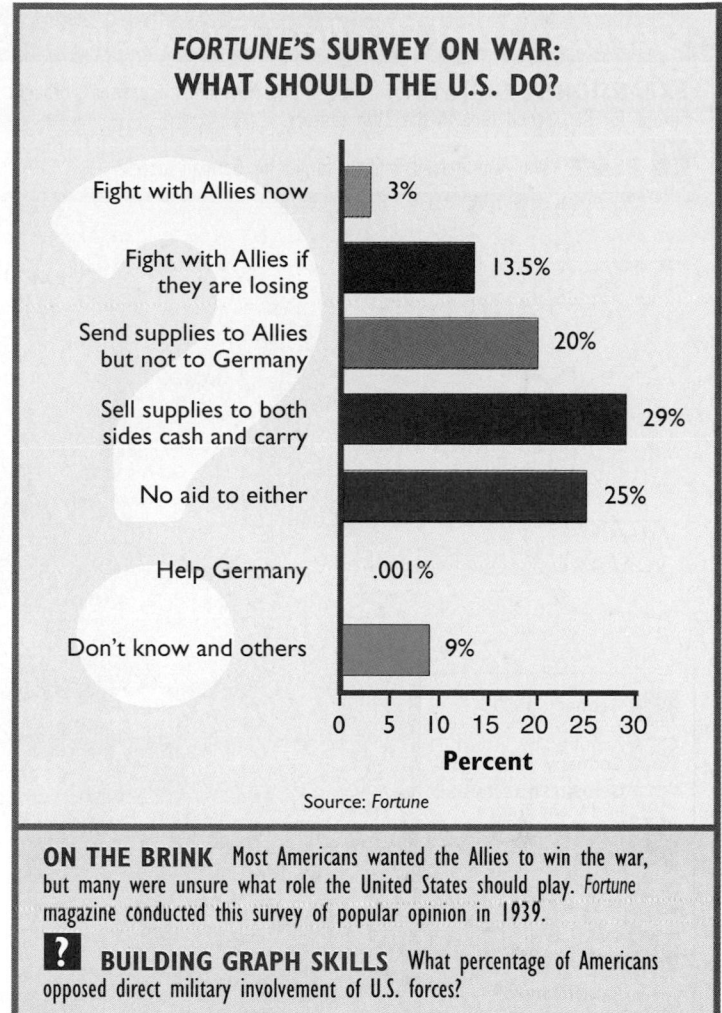

FORTUNE'S SURVEY ON WAR: WHAT SHOULD THE U.S. DO?

- Fight with Allies now — 3%
- Fight with Allies if they are losing — 13.5%
- Send supplies to Allies but not to Germany — 20%
- Sell supplies to both sides cash and carry — 29%
- No aid to either — 25%
- Help Germany — .001%
- Don't know and others — 9%

Percent

Source: *Fortune*

ON THE BRINK Most Americans wanted the Allies to win the war, but many were unsure what role the United States should play. *Fortune* magazine conducted this survey of popular opinion in 1939.

? **BUILDING GRAPH SKILLS** What percentage of Americans opposed direct military involvement of U.S. forces?

By 1937 President Roosevelt had become convinced that the United States must resist aggression. In October he urged other countries to quarantine, or isolate, expansionist countries. Most Americans, however, were not yet ready to accept U.S. involvement in the quarantine. Proof of this position came in December 1937, when Japanese planes attacked the U.S. gunboat *Panay* and three U.S. oil tankers on China's Yangtze (YANG-SEE) River (Chang Jiang). Several U.S. citizens were killed, and many were wounded. A public opinion poll showed that 54 percent of Americans thought the United States should withdraw from China, rather than risk becoming involved in a war.

WAR!

U.S. public opinion slowly changed, however, as German aggression continued. In March 1939, Hitler's armies occupied all of Czechoslovakia. Hitler also proposed to annex the Polish port city of

German and Italian Expansion, 1935–1941

EXPANSIONIST DICTATORS Hitler's and Mussolini's aggressions brought war to most of Europe for the second time in the 20th century.

? **PLACE** Why was Poland a likely target for German attack?

Danzig (DAN-sig), but the Poles refused. On April 7, Mussolini's troops invaded Albania.

Awakening at long last to their common peril, Great Britain and France announced that an attack upon Poland would mean war and called on the Soviet Union to join them in resisting further aggression. Instead, on August 23, 1939, the Soviet Union signed a **nonaggression pact** with Nazi Germany. This surprising union came about in part because of a secret clause in the pact in which the two nations agreed to divide Poland between them.

On September 1, 1939, German bombers and armored divisions crashed across the border into Poland. Two days later, Great Britain and France declared war on Germany. World War II had begun. Soviet troops, meanwhile, invaded Poland from the east, occupied the independent nations Estonia, Latvia, and Lithuania, and demanded the right to establish military bases in Finland. When Finland refused, the Soviet Union attacked the small nation and soon annexed part of its territory.

▪▪ **Allied appeasement failed to halt German aggression. In 1939 the German invasion of Poland sparked World War II.**

▲ This 1939 cartoon satirizes the lack of trust between Germany and the Soviet Union, even after the two nations signed the nonaggression pact.

Roosevelt took steps to aid the European countries under siege. Some three weeks after the German invasion of Poland, he urged Congress to amend the neutrality act that barred the export of munitions. After a six-week debate, Congress agreed on a compromise. The new law allowed any nation to buy munitions from the United States but required that the goods be shipped on foreign vessels.

The European conflict loomed as a major issue in the 1940 election. Both candidates—Roosevelt, who sought a third term, and Republican Wendell Willkie—promised to keep America out of the conflict. In a radio talk on September 3, 1939, Roosevelt pledged: "As long as it remains in my power to prevent, there will be no blackout of peace in the United States."

Roosevelt won his bid for an unprecedented third term. In spite of his public promises to pursue peace, however, he became increasingly alarmed by Japanese and German aggression. He began to view American involvement as unavoidable and started a campaign to prepare U.S. defenses for the likely conflict.

By the end of 1940, U.S. supplies flowed to Great Britain. The British, however, had little cash to pay for needed war materials. Roosevelt proposed that the United States lend or lease arms and other supplies to the British and the other Allies. Congress passed the **Lend-Lease Act** in March 1941. It appropriated $7 billion for ships, planes, tanks, and any other supplies to non-Axis countries.

■■ **The United States took its first step toward involvement in the growing European conflict by extending aid to the Allies.**

CONTINUING AGGRESSION

While Hitler carried on his **blitzkrieg** (BLITS-kreeg), or "lightning war," against Poland, the French mobilized. In May 1940, German armored divisions, supported by fighter planes and bombers, crossed the **Maginot Line**, a line of defenses along the French border with Germany. The Germans occupied France; the Netherlands, Belgium, Luxembourg (known as the Low Countries); Denmark; and Norway.

Germany established a puppet government in France headed by Philippe Pétain (pay-tan) and headquartered in the town of Vichy (VISH-ee). A secret French organization known as the Resistance continued to oppose the Germans. In London, French general Charles de Gaulle headed a committee called "Free France," which organized opposition against the Germans.

With the fall of France, Great Britain stood alone. On May 10, 1940, Winston Churchill

▲ Members of the Resistance continued to fight the Germans after the fall of France. This French girl was part of a patrol that hunted down German snipers in Paris late in 1944.

▲ RAF combat pilots are shown rushing to their planes to fight German bombers somewhere over French territory.

became prime minister. With a rare gift for leadership, Churchill rallied the British:

> 66 Hitler knows that he will have to break us in this island or lose the war. . . . Let us therefore brace ourselves to our duties, and so bear ourselves that, if the British Empire and its Commonwealth last for a thousand years, men will still say, "This was their finest hour." 99

On June 10 Italy declared war on France and Great Britain. In August, Hitler unleashed his bombers against Great Britain. The outnumbered British Royal Air Force (RAF) flew day and night to combat the German blitzkrieg.

TENSIONS MOUNT IN THE ATLANTIC

In the face of continuing German attacks, U.S. aid to the Allies gradually increased. By the spring of 1941, German and Italian submarines were turning the North Atlantic into a graveyard of ships. In April, U.S. airplanes and naval vessels began to patrol the Atlantic, notifying British warships of the location of German ships.

A few months later, Roosevelt issued "shoot-on-sight" orders to U.S. warships operating in the North Atlantic "safety zone" America had established in 1939. U.S. warships also began to accompany merchant vessels as far as Iceland. In November, Congress voted to allow U.S. merchant vessels to enter combat areas. Roosevelt armed the merchant vessels and provided them with gun crews.

With the United States moving rapidly toward undeclared war with Germany, Roosevelt and

Churchill met secretly off the coast of Newfoundland in August 1941. The two leaders agreed to a series of principles for international relations. Known as the **Atlantic Charter**, the agreement (1) pledged that the United States and Great Britain would forego territorial expansion, (2) affirmed their respect for the right of every nation to choose its own form of government, and (3) called for freedom of international trade and equal access to raw materials for all countries. Once the war was over, the charter declared, aggressor states should be disarmed, and all nations should work together to rid the world of fear and want.

THE GROWING THREAT FROM JAPAN

As war raged in Europe, Japan added to its conquests in Asia. In July 1941, Japanese troops occupied French Indochina (see map). President Roosevelt immediately froze all Japanese assets in the United States and approved an embargo on shipments of gasoline, machine tools, scrap iron, and steel to Japan. Japan retaliated by freezing all U.S. assets in areas under its control. As a result, trade between the United States and Japan practically ended. To help prevent further Japanese expansion in China, the United States had made China eligible for lend-lease aid earlier in the year.

As U.S. resistance to Japanese aggression grew stronger, Japan's war leaders planned an attack on the United States. Even as the plan went forward, however, a Japanese peace mission visited Washington. On November 20, 1941, this mission demanded that the United States (1) unfreeze Japanese assets, (2) supply Japan's gasoline needs, and (3) cease all aid to China.

The United States had no intention of giving in to the Japanese demands. However, U.S. diplomats kept up the appearance of continuing negotiations with Japan to allow more time to prepare U.S. defenses in the Pacific. By this time the United States had succeeded in breaking the secret code used to send messages between Tokyo and the Japanese mission in Washington, D.C. The Americans knew that the Japanese planned a strike against the United States. The challenge was, as Secretary of War Henry Stimson wrote in his diary, "how we should maneuver them into the position of firing the first shot without allowing too much danger to ourselves."

Japanese Expansion, 1931–1941

A PATH OF CONQUEST Japan's military leaders believed that conquering neighboring lands would solve the country's economic problems.

? PLACE What important Chinese cities had Japan captured by 1938?

Japanese-Soviet border clashes occur in 1938 and 1939.

Japan invades Manchuria in 1931.

Japanese attack U.S. ships in Dec. 1937.

UNION OF SOVIET SOCIALIST REPUBLICS

MONGOLIA

Nomenk'an 1939

MANCHURIA

Vladivostok
Chang–ku Feng 1938

Shenyang

Beijing

Tianjin

Lüshun (Port Arthur)

SAKHALIN

KURIL ISLANDS

SEA OF JAPAN

JAPAN

Tokyo

40° N

TIBET

Yan'an

Yellow R. (Huang He)

CHINA

Yangtze R. (Chang Jiang)

Shandong Peninsula

Qingdao

YELLOW SEA

KOREA

Nanjing 1937
Capital, 1928–1937

Shanghai

Hankou
Hangzhou

Chongqing
Capital, 1937–1946

EAST CHINA SEA

30° N

INDIA (British)

BURMA (British)

Xiamen
Shantou

Guangzhou

HONG KONG (British)

MACAO (Portuguese)

HAINAN

TAIWAN

RYUKYU ISLANDS

BONIN IS. (Japanese)

VOLCANO IS. (Japanese)

PACIFIC OCEAN

140° E

150° E

Bay of Bengal

THAILAND

SOUTH CHINA SEA

PHILIPPINE ISLANDS (U.S.)

20° N

CEYLON

FRENCH INDOCHINA

80° E

90° E

110° E

120° E

130° E

10° N

ARCTIC OCEAN

EUROPE

ASIA

PACIFIC OCEAN

NORTH AMERICA

ATLANTIC OCEAN

AFRICA

INDIAN OCEAN

AUSTRALIA

Equator

SOUTH AMERICA

PACIFIC OCEAN

ANTARCTICA

Robinson Projection

	Japanese empire in 1930
	Extent of Japanese empire by 1938
	Extent of Japanese empire, December 7, 1941
✵	Point of conflict

0   500   1,000 Miles
0   500   1,000 Kilometers

Orthographic Projection

SECTION 3 REVIEW

IDENTIFY and explain the significance of the following: Benito Mussolini, Fascist party, Blackshirts, Adolf Hitler, Nazi party, Brownshirts, anti-Semitism, *Kristallnacht,* Francisco Franco, Spanish Civil War, Axis powers, Munich Conference, appeasement, Winston Churchill, nonaggression pact, Lend-Lease Act, blitzkrieg, Maginot Line, Atlantic Charter.

LOCATE and explain the importance of the following: Ethiopia; Rhineland; Sudetenland; Munich, Germany; Yangtze River (Chang Jiang); Albania; Poland; Finland; French Indochina.

1. **MAIN IDEA** What policy did European countries follow in negotiations with Hitler? Why?

2. **MAIN IDEA** What factors led to war in 1939?

3. **MAIN IDEA** What step brought the United States closer toward involvement in the war?

4. **WRITING TO EVALUATE** Imagine you are an American reporter in Europe during the 1920s and 1930s. Write an article that accounts for the rise of dictatorships after World War I.

5. **HYPOTHESIZING** How might events in Europe have been different if European leaders had not decided on an appeasement policy with Hitler?

WRITING A SUMMARY

Using the essential points of the chapter as a guide, write a summary of the chapter.

REVIEWING CHRONOLOGY

Number your paper 1 to 5. Study the time line above, and list the following events in the order in which they happened by writing the first next to 1, the second next to 2, and so on. Then complete the activity below.

1. Spanish Civil War begins.
2. Washington Conference begins.
3. Lázaro Cárdenas nationalizes Mexican oil fields.
4. Kellogg-Briand Pact proposed.
5. World War II starts.

Assessing Consequences What effect did the Munich Conference have on events in Europe?

IDENTIFYING PEOPLE AND IDEAS

Explain the historical significance of each of the following people or terms.

1. unilateralism
2. Emily Greene Balch
3. Five Power Agreement
4. caudillos
5. Augusto César Sandino
6. nationalize
7. Adolf Hitler
8. *Kristallnacht*
9. nonaggression pact
10. Winston Churchill

UNDERSTANDING MAIN IDEAS

1. What factors encouraged the growth of isolationism in the United States after World War I? What events in the 1930s convinced U.S. leaders to abandon the policy?
2. What economic and political role did the United States play in Latin America?
3. Why did Lázaro Cárdenas nationalize Mexican oil fields in 1938?
4. Why did some European leaders favor a policy of appeasement toward Hitler? Why did others oppose it?
5. What were the provisions of the Atlantic Charter? Why was it adopted?

REVIEWING THEMES

1. **Global Relations** In what ways did countries promote world peace after World War I?
2. **Economic Development** What economic and political problems emerged after World War I?
3. **Democratic Values** How did the fascist dictatorships in Europe limit civil liberties?

THINKING CRITICALLY

1. **Analyzing** How did Benito Mussolini rise to power?
2. **Evaluating** What were the goals of Japan's militarists? Why did they want to create a Japanese empire in Asia?
3. **Synthesizing** How did American approaches to neutrality change between 1935 and 1941?

STRATEGY FOR SUCCESS

Review the Strategies for Success on Interpreting Editorial Cartoons on page 332. Then study the following cartoon, entitled *New Kind of Pump Priming*. What is the cartoonist's message?

Pump Priming—New Style

Japan invades Manchuria.	FDR announces Good Neighbor policy. Adolf Hitler becomes chancellor of Germany.	Italy invades Ethiopia.	German troops move into the Rhineland. Spanish Civil War begins.	Lázaro Cárdenas nationalizes Mexican oil fields. Jewish property destroyed during *Kristallnacht*.	Germany signs nonaggression pact with Soviet Union. World War II starts.	FDR elected to third term.	Lend-Lease Act passed. Atlantic Charter signed.

1930   **1935**   **1940**

WRITING ABOUT HISTORY

Writing to Describe Imagine you are a Loyalist during the Spanish Civil War. Write a letter to an American friend describing the events during that period.

USING PRIMARY SOURCES

President Roosevelt's proposal of the Lend-Lease Act aroused fierce debate in Congress. Read the following excerpt from isolationist Burton K. Wheeler, a Republican senator from Montana, who argued against passing the measure. What reasons does he give for his stand?

> 66 *Never before have the American people been asked or compelled to give . . . so completely of their tax dollars to any foreign nation. Never before has the Congress of the United States been asked by any President to violate international law. . . . Never before has the United States given to one man the power to strip this nation of its defenses. . . .*
>
> *Approval of this legislation means war, open and complete warfare. I, therefore, ask the American people before they . . . accept it—Was the last World War worthwhile?*
>
> *If it were, then we should lend and lease war materials. If it were, then we should lend and lease American boys. President Roosevelt has said we would be repaid by England. We will be. . . . Our boys will be returned—returned in caskets, maybe; returned with bodies maimed; returned with minds warped and twisted by sights of horrors and the scream and shriek of high-powered shells.* 99

LINKING HISTORY AND GEOGRAPHY

After World War I, France built the Maginot Line, a line of fixed fortifications to protect its border with Germany. French military commanders felt this series of forts would repel a German attack. Study the map below, which shows the German invasion of France in 1940. How did the German army defeat this French strategy?

BUILDING YOUR PORTFOLIO

Complete the following projects independently or cooperatively.

1. GLOBAL RELATIONS In Chapter 23 you portrayed a journalist examining the global effects of the Great Depression. Building on that experience, imagine your assignment is to evaluate the new political trends of the 1930s. Create a chart that compares the similarities and differences among fascist dictators around the world.

2. WAR Imagine you are a diplomat at the 1938 Munich Conference. Write a speech aimed at convincing the Allies to abandon their policy of appeasement toward Germany's Adolf Hitler. Your speech might mention *Kristallnacht*, Hitler's repressive domestic policies, German aggression into the Rhineland and Austria, and your opposition toward granting the Sudetenland to Hitler.

AMERICANS IN WORLD WAR II

UNDERSTANDING THE MAIN IDEA

In December 1941 the Japanese bombed Pearl Harbor, bringing the United States into World War II. Americans and their allies battled the Axis powers on land in Europe and North Africa and on sea in the Atlantic, Pacific, and Mediterranean. By August 1945 the Allies defeated the Axis powers, but only after heavy casualties and the atomic bombing of two Japanese cities.

THEMES

- **GLOBAL RELATIONS** How might nations coordinate civilian and military resources to win a global war?

- **CULTURAL DIVERSITY** Why might wartime patriotism lead to increased discrimination against certain groups?

- **TECHNOLOGY AND SOCIETY** What political and moral concerns might a government take into account when developing a potentially destructive technology?

1941	1942	1943	1944	1945
Japanese attack Pearl Harbor.	Bataan Death March occurs.	Zoot-suit riots break out.	D-Day invasion begins.	Japan surrenders.

The German invasion of Poland in 1939 launched World War II. By 1940, much of Western Europe had fallen to Germany, while Japan expanded its hold on Asia. For a time, the United States maintained its neutrality. Lend-lease aid to the Allies, beginning in 1941, however, marked an important step in U.S. involvement in the conflict.

Aftermath of Japanese attack on Hawaii, 1941

Shortly before 8:00 A.M. on December 7, 1941, the message *"Tora! Tora! Tora!"* was radioed to Japanese carrier ships approaching Hawaii. The signal "Tora," meaning "tiger," launched the long-planned Japanese air-and-sea attack on the U.S. naval base at Pearl Harbor. The heart of America's Pacific Fleet was anchored there, and more than a hundred U.S. planes lined nearby airfields.

In seconds after the attack began, explosions from bombs and torpedoes turned Pearl Harbor into a blazing inferno. When the assault ended less than two hours later, almost 20 American warships and nearly 200 aircraft had been destroyed. Among some 2,400 American dead were 1,103 sailors who were entombed on the *Arizona* when the battleship sank.

The bombing shocked and united Americans. Ann Hoskins, a Connecticut newspaper owner, noticed that before the attack "there was great tension and feelings between people not to intervene. But the minute Pearl Harbor happened, there was utter unity." The next day, a somber President Roosevelt described December 7 as "a date which will live in infamy" and called on Congress for a declaration of war against Japan.

Japanese American children during World War II

Section 1

EARLY DIFFICULTIES

FOCUS

- What obstacles did the United States face when it first entered the war?
- In which three battles did the Allies halt Japan's advance in the Pacific?
- What were two major turning points in the western theater of operations?
- What forms did Allied cooperation take?

Army nurses evacuated from Bataan

*D*eeply angered by the bombing of Pearl Harbor, Congress and the American people overwhelmingly supported President Roosevelt's call for war against Japan. Great Britain declared war on Japan as well. On December 11, Japan's allies, Germany and Italy, declared war on the United States, and Congress recognized a state of war with those two nations. World War II had now vastly expanded.

AXIS ADVANTAGES

When the United States entered the war, the Axis powers had two big advantages. First, Germany, Italy, and Japan had already secured firm control of the areas they had invaded. The United States thus faced a long, drawn-out fight on several fronts, including Western Europe, the Pacific, the Mediterranean, and Northern Africa.

Second, Germany was better prepared for war. Since 1933 it had been rearming itself and building airfields, barracks, and military training centers. By the mid-1930s, the Nazis had converted most of the German economy to military production. In contrast, the United States had not begun to prepare for war until 1940, when President Roosevelt called for more money to be devoted to military production. Even then, however, its preparations were limited.

■■ When the United States entered the war, it faced the problems of fighting on many fronts and a lack of preparation.

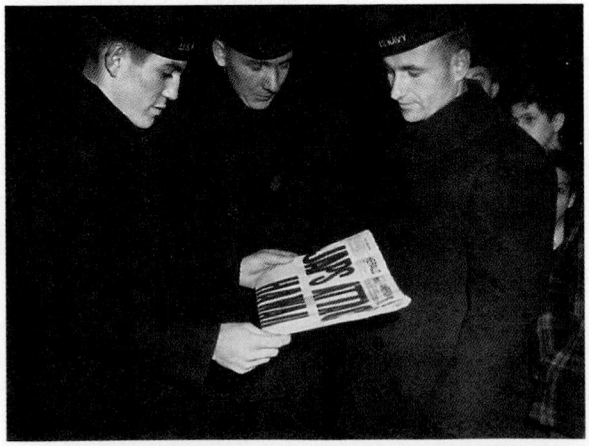

◀ Three U.S. sailors in Chicago read about the Japanese attack on Pearl Harbor.

Hitler, Mussolini, and the Japanese war leaders hoped they could win the conflict before the United States—fighting a two-ocean war—could mobilize its enormous resources. After the Pearl Harbor attack, one Hitler aide warned:

66 We have just one year to cut off Russia from her American supplies. . . . If we don't succeed and the munitions potential of the United States joins up with the manpower potential of the Russians, the war will enter a phase in which we shall only be able to win it with difficulty. 99

WAR IN THE PACIFIC

Japan's assault on Pearl Harbor was only part of a giant offensive throughout the Pacific region. In December the Japanese launched attacks on several other American islands, on the Philippines, and on various British possessions. By the end of the month, Japan controlled Guam, Wake Island, the British colony of Hong Kong, and Thailand.

The year 1942 brought more Japanese victories. In January, Japanese forces took Manila, the capital of the Philippines. The next month, they overran the British naval base at Singapore, and in the **Battle of the Java Sea**, they crushed a fleet of American, British, Dutch, and Australian warships (see map on page 746). By April, Japan had conquered most of the Netherlands East Indies, with its supplies of oil, tin, rubber, and other vital war materials. The Japanese were also driving the British out of Burma.

In the Philippines a small force of Americans and Filipinos under General Douglas MacArthur, commander of U.S. Army troops in the Far East, mounted a heroic but hopeless resistance against the Japanese. After the surrender of Manila, MacArthur's forces withdrew to the Bataan Peninsula across Manila Bay. In March, MacArthur was ordered to Australia but vowed, "I shall return."

Fighting against overwhelming odds, the hungry, sick, exhausted survivors who remained on Bataan surrendered in April. Japanese soldiers forced the some 70,000 survivors to march through the jungle on their way to prison camp. Some 10,000 died on what came to be called the **Bataan Death March** (see map on page 771). U.S. and Filipino soldiers received brutal treat-

JAPAN DECLARES WAR

The day after the Japanese attack on Pearl Harbor, Emperor Hirohito made a speech that was relayed around the world. In it he laid out Japan's reasons for declaring war on the United States and Great Britain:

66 *B*oth America and Britain . . . have aggravated the disturbances in East Asia. . . . These two powers, inducing other countries to follow suit, increased military preparations on all sides of Our Empire. . . . They have obstructed by every means Our peaceful commerce, and finally resorted to a direct severance [cutting off] of economic relations. . . . Patiently have We waited and long have We endured, in hope that Our Government might retrieve the situation in peace. But Our adversaries [enemies], showing not the least spirit of conciliation, have unduly delayed a settlement. . . . Our Empire for its existence and self defense has no other recourse but to appeal to arms and to crush every obstacle in its path. 99

ment at the hands of the Japanese: prisoners were beaten, shot, or prevented from drinking water. The bravery of the Filipino defenders at Bataan inspired thousands of Filipino Americans to enlist in the armed forces. In 1942 alone some 16,000 Filipino Americans in California joined the fight.

By the summer of 1942, the Japanese were poised to strike west at India, south at Australia, and east through Hawaii at the Pacific coast of the United States. At this crucial point, however, the Allies succeeded in halting the Japanese advance in the Pacific. The U.S. Pacific Fleet, commanded by Admiral Chester Nimitz, helped turn the tide with three battles.

The first battle began on May 7, 1942, in the Coral Sea, off the northeastern coast of Australia. A Japanese force on its way to attack Port Moresby, New Guinea, seized Tulagi (too-LAHG-ee) Island,

▲ Shown here are American and Filipino soldiers at the start of the grueling Bataan Death March in April 1942. Thousands died on the march to a Japanese prison camp.

one of the Solomons. But before the Japanese force could reach its destination, a joint British-American naval force intercepted it. Planes from U.S. carriers damaged a Japanese carrier and destroyed one carrier and several aircraft. The **Battle of the Coral Sea** was an important victory for the Allies. Although the Allies lost a carrier, the battle stopped the Japanese advance on Australia.

The second naval battle took place early in June 1942. Japan, with the objective of crushing the Pacific Fleet, launched a two-pronged attack. One unit succeeded in occupying two of the Aleutian Islands, near Alaska. This move was

World War II in the Pacific, 1941–1945

TURNING POINT The initiative in the Pacific war passed to the Allies after the Battle of Midway, which cost Japan four aircraft carriers and most of its skilled naval pilots.

? REGION What area did the Allies largely bypass in their island-hopping drive toward Japan?

Legend:
- Japanese controlled, 1942
- Farthest Japanese advance, May 1942
- Allied advance
- � Major battle

ALASKA (U.S.)

UNION OF SOVIET SOCIALIST REPUBLICS

60° N

BERING SEA

ALEUTIAN ISLANDS

SAKHALIN

ATTU (U.S.) KISKA (U.S.)

KURIL IS.

MONGOLIA

MANCHURIA

PACIFIC OCEAN

Beijing

SEA OF JAPAN

JAPAN

CHINA

KOREA

Tokyo

30° N

Nanjing

YELLOW SEA

Hiroshima
Nagasaki
Shanghai

MIDWAY I.
✪ Midway
June 1942

HAWAIIAN ISLANDS

RYUKYU IS.
✪ Okinawa
April–June 1945

Iwo Jima
Feb.–March 1945

Pearl Harbor
Dec. 1941

INDIA

TAIWAN

Hong Kong

BURMA

HAINAN

Rangoon

BATAAN

THAILAND

FRENCH INDOCHINA

Manila

Philippine Sea
June 1944

Saipan
June–July 1944

✪ Wake I.
Dec. 1941

PHILIPPINE ISLANDS (U.S.)

✪ Leyte Gulf
Oct. 1944

MARIANA IS.

✪ Guam
Dec. 1941
July–Aug. 1944

MARSHALL IS.

MALAYA

Singapore

CAROLINE IS.

TRUK IS.

TARAWA I.

BORNEO

NETHERLANDS EAST INDIES

ADMIRALTY IS.

✪ Gilbert I.
Nov. 1943

Equator 0°

SUMATRA

✪ Java Sea
Feb.–March 1942

JAVA

NEW GUINEA

✪ Guadalcanal
Aug.–Nov. 1942

INDIAN OCEAN

Scale varies with latitude.
Scale at Equator
0   1,000   2,000 Miles

0   1,000   2,000 Kilometers
Miller Cylindrical Projection

130° E

Darwin

Port Moresby

SOLOMON IS.

✪ Coral Sea
May 1942

NEW HEBRIDES

150° E

CORAL SEA

AUSTRALIA

180°

N
W   E
S

▲ Although U.S. forces won the Battle of Midway in June 1942, the islands did not escape damage. Japanese bombers hit military installations, including the oil tank shown here.

designed to divert American ships to the north while the Japanese carried out their second offensive, an attack on Midway, two small islands northwest of Hawaii. The United States, however, knew of the Japanese strategy because American experts had broken the Japanese fleet code. Nimitz was therefore able to assemble U.S. aircraft carriers and destroyers north of Midway to fend off the Japanese attack.

Americans and Japanese clashed from June 3 to June 6. U.S. fighters, dive-bombers, and torpedo planes sank four Japanese aircraft carriers and shot down many enemy planes. The American victory at the **Battle of Midway** proved crucial. Japan lost not only ships and planes but also a number of skilled pilots, many of whom had taken part in the Pearl Harbor attack. The battle provided the Americans with valuable experience in naval air warfare and gave people confidence in the carrier-based strike force.

After the Battle of Midway, the United States successfully launched its first offensive. In August 1942, American marines waded ashore at Guadalcanal, another of the Solomon Islands. For six desperate months, with a heavy loss of life, they clung to a toehold around the airport, repelling Japanese attacks from the air, the sea, and the surrounding jungle.

In November the Japanese sent a huge fleet to the Solomons, hoping to regain Guadalcanal. The American fleet defeated the Japanese in a bloody battle. Guadalcanal was secure. The tide of battle in the Pacific had finally turned in the Allies' favor.

■■ The Allies stopped the Japanese Pacific offensive in the battles of Coral Sea, Midway, and Guadalcanal.

FIGHTING IN EUROPE AND THE MEDITERRANEAN

By the time of the attack on Pearl Harbor, the Axis powers, which now included Hungary, Romania, and Bulgaria, were in firm control of much of the western theater of operations—Europe and the lands around the Mediterranean. Yugoslavia and Greece had been occupied, and southern Europe was firmly under the Axis boot. Throughout most of 1942, the Axis powers continued to achieve one victory after another.

The Germans and their allies scored victories on many different fronts. German submarines, or U-boats, controlled the Atlantic Ocean, sinking Allied military and merchant ships and nearly cutting off British supply lines. In the first half of 1942, German U-boats sank almost 500 ships off the eastern seaboard of the United States.

In Europe, German troops had penetrated far into the Soviet Union after their initial attack in June 1941. As the Germans advanced, the Soviets lost many industrial centers as well as rich grainfields in the Ukraine (see map on page 748). In the summer of 1942, the Germans pushed toward the oil fields of southern Russia. They also laid siege to Stalingrad (now known as Volgograd). The city mobilized its defenses. For months the men, women, and children defending the city suffered a nightmare of shell fire and starvation.

In North Africa, Italian forces had launched an invasion in 1940. When British troops later began to inflict heavy damage on the Italians, Hitler sent in the German *Afrika Korps* under commander Erwin Rommel.

▼ Erwin Rommel (left) was commander of the German *Afrika Korps* in North Africa.

World War II in Europe, 1942–1945

DESERT FOX After being battered at El Alamein, Rommel retreated some 1,250 miles to Tunisia in eight weeks. By May 1943 Africa was cleared of Axis forces, making the Mediterranean safe for Allied shipping and the invasion of Italy.

? LOCATION Where and when did the Allies open a second major front in Europe?

The German defeat at Stalingrad marked the turning point in the war in the East.

ICELAND

ATLANTIC OCEAN

NORTH SEA

NORWAY

SWEDEN

FINLAND

Leningrad

Moscow

GREAT BRITAIN

IRELAND

DENMARK

BALTIC SEA

London

Elbe

NETHERLANDS

BELGIUM

Berlin
Apr.–May 1945

Warsaw

Vistula

UNION OF SOVIET SOCIALIST REPUBLICS

English Channel

D-Day
June 1944

Leipzig

Dresden

Oder

Stalingrad
Nov. 1942–Feb. 1943

Paris

Rhine

GERMANY

Battle of the Bulge
Dec. 1944

UKRAINE

FRANCE

Vichy

SLOVAKIA

HUNGARY

SWITZERLAND

Milan

VICHY FRANCE

ROMANIA

Danube

PORTUGAL

SPAIN

CROATIA

SERBIA

BULGARIA

Yalta

BLACK SEA

ITALY

MONTENEGRO

CORSICA

Anzio
Jan. 1944

Rome

ALBANIA

Naples

Istanbul

SARDINIA

GREECE

AEGEAN SEA

TURKEY

Oran

Algiers

Tunis

SICILY

MALTA

SYRIA
(Vichy Fr.)

Casablanca

MOROCCO
(Vichy Fr.)

ALGERIA
(Vichy Fr.)

TUNISIA
(Vichy Fr.)

CRETE

LEBANON
(Vichy Fr.)

MEDITERRANEAN SEA

PALESTINE
(Br.)

Alexandria

Suez Canal

TRANS-JORDAN
(Br.)

Normandy Landings, June 6, 1944

GREAT BRITAIN   London

Portsmouth

English Channel

Calais

CHANNEL IS.
(Br.)

Cherbourg

Utah
(U.S.)

Omaha
(U.S.)

Gold
(Br.)

Caen

Le Havre

Juno
Sword
(Br.) (Br. & Canadian)

Rouen

NORMANDY

FRANCE

Paris

0   50   100 Miles

0   50   100 Kilometers

El Alamein
Oct.–Nov. 1942

Cairo

LIBYA
(Italian)

EGYPT

SAUDI ARABIA

	Axis controlled, Jan. 1942
	Allied controlled, Jan. 1942
	Neutral country
	Farthest Axis advance, 1942
→	Allied advance
✧	Major battle
	Invasion beach

0   200   400 Miles

0   200   400 Kilometers

Azimuthal Equal-Area Projection

Robinson Projection

ARCTIC OCEAN

EUROPE

NORTH AMERICA

ASIA

PACIFIC OCEAN

ATLANTIC OCEAN

AFRICA

PACIFIC OCEAN

Equator

SOUTH AMERICA

INDIAN OCEAN

AUSTRALIA

PACIFIC OCEAN

ANTARCTICA

◄ More than 100,000 Soviet women earned military honors for their participation in the war. Here two snipers, E. Novikova (left) and O. Mokshina (right), wait for hours in the snow to ambush German troops.

▼ Soviet forces laid siege to Stalingrad for 17 months before the German army surrendered in February 1943. Shown here is part of the ruined city shortly after it was liberated.

Rommel, known as the Desert Fox, had advanced as far as El Alamein, Egypt, by July 1942. His troops were ready for a final thrust at the Suez Canal and the oil fields of the Middle East (the European designation for Northeast Africa and Southwest Asia). At the same time, Axis aircraft all but forced British naval craft out of the Mediterranean. In order to reach Egypt, the Middle East, and India, Britain had to send its ships thousands of miles around Africa.

Despite the British forces' transport problems, it was Rommel who suffered most from shortages of men and supplies. The British, led by General Bernard Montgomery, turned this to their advantage. In October, Montgomery attacked, pushing Rommel's *Afrika Korps* steadily westward out of Egypt and into Libya by November. The British victory in the **Battle of El Alamein** helped turn the corner for the Allies in North Africa.

Another turning point came in the fall of 1942, when the Soviets attacked German troops in Stalingrad. Throughout a terrible winter the Germans hung on, forbidden by Hitler to surrender. Trapped in the ruined city with few supplies and little food, the Axis troops finally surrendered in February 1943. After the **Battle of Stalingrad**, less than one third of the original German force of almost 300,000 remained alive. Galina Utkina, a Russian woman, recalled the crucial role Soviet women played in defeating the Germans:

❝ Anti-aircraft battalions, air-force regiments and signalling units were made up entirely of women. When the battle reached the city itself, women fought alongside the men. ❞

The Allied victories at El Alamein and Stalingrad broke the momentum of the Axis advance. Said British prime minister Winston Churchill: "Before Alamein we never had a victory. After Alamein we never had a defeat."

■■ **Setbacks for the Axis powers at El Alamein and Stalingrad were turning points in World War II.**

ALLIED COOPERATION

How had the Allies managed to overcome the powerful offensives mounted by the Axis in both theaters of the war? The ability of the United States to harness its human and industrial resources helped the Allied effort. Through the lend-lease program the United States shipped vast quantities of munitions to its allies. By the end of the war, lend-lease aid totaled more than $50 billion. Of this vast sum, over 60 percent went to Great Britain.

Allied cooperation, which involved joint strategic planning, also helped turn the tide. Just two weeks after the assault on Pearl Harbor, Churchill and Roosevelt met in Washington, D.C., together with their top military commanders and technical aides. The two leaders and their staffs agreed that defeating the Axis powers in Europe would be the first Allied priority. For the time being, Allied strategy in the Pacific would be defensive rather than offensive.

To formalize their alliance, representatives of 26 Allied countries, calling themselves the United Nations, met in Washington, D.C. On January 1, 1942, they signed the Joint Declaration, which had been drafted by Roosevelt and Churchill. In it the Allies (1) promised full military and economic cooperation in the war effort, (2) agreed that none of them would make a separate peace with the Axis powers, and (3) endorsed the war aims outlined by Roosevelt and Churchill in the Atlantic Charter (see Chapter 25).

Throughout the war Churchill and Roosevelt met frequently. At Casablanca, Morocco, in January 1943, the two leaders agreed to demand the **unconditional surrender** of their enemies. In other words, if the Axis powers gave up, they would have to do so on the Allies' terms. Churchill and Roosevelt also agreed that the Allies should attack Hitler on a second front in order to relieve pressure on the Soviet Union (the first front). The Allies decided to open the second front by invading southern Europe by way of North Africa and the Mediterranean island of Sicily.

▲ **Chinese leader Chiang Kai-shek (left), President Roosevelt (center), and British prime minister Winston Churchill (right) are shown at the Cairo Conference in November 1943.**

At Cairo in November 1943, Roosevelt and Churchill met with Chiang Kai-shek of China. The leaders outlined Allied strategy against Japan and made plans to restore Japanese-held territories after the war. At Tehran, Iran, shortly afterward, Roosevelt and Churchill met for the first time with Soviet leader Joseph Stalin. Stalin gave his support for Allied war plans.

■ **Cooperation among the Allies took the form of lend-lease exchanges, joint strategic planning, and agreement on war aims.**

SECTION 1 REVIEW

IDENTIFY and explain the significance of the following: Battle of the Java Sea, Douglas MacArthur, Bataan Death March, Battle of the Coral Sea, Battle of Midway, Erwin Rommel, Bernard Montgomery, Battle of El Alamein, Battle of Stalingrad, unconditional surrender, Joseph Stalin.

LOCATE and explain the importance of the following: Pearl Harbor, Guam, Wake Island, Hong Kong, Thailand, Bataan, Coral Sea, Midway Islands, Guadalcanal, Ukraine, Stalingrad, El Alamein, Casablanca.

1. **MAIN IDEA** Where did the Allies stop the Japanese Pacific offensive?

2. **MAIN IDEA** What two German setbacks were turning points for the Allies in World War II?

3. **CONTRASTING** What advantages did the Axis powers have over the United States at the beginning of the war?

4. **WRITING TO INFORM** Imagine you are a participant in one of the early wartime conferences. Write a memorandum to the Allies, giving examples of cooperative efforts that could help them win the war.

5. **LINKING HISTORY AND GEOGRAPHY** What was the significance of the American victory at the Battle of Midway for both Japan and the United States?

Section 2

THE HOME FRONT

FOCUS

- How did the United States mobilize for war?
- Why were Japanese Americans interned during the war?
- What gains did African Americans and Mexican Americans make during the war?
- What changes did World War II bring for American women?

Although World War II was fought on the battlefields of Europe, Asia, and North Africa, American farms and factories also helped win the war. As the United States mobilized its resources for combat, the entertainment industry helped sustain morale. For Japanese Americans the war resulted in confinement in remote camps. For African Americans, Mexican Americans, and women, the conflict brought both new opportunities and reminders that discrimination and inequality still existed in American society.

Seamstresses making
flags and banners

MOBILIZING FOR WAR

After the Japanese attack at Pearl Harbor plunged the United States into war, America switched from a peacetime to a wartime economy. Engineer R. W. Danischefsky noted how quickly factory orders came in: "At the time of Pearl Harbor [December 7, 1941] we had five projects in Michigan. By the end of December we had forty-two." To fill these vital orders, union leaders agreed not to organize strikes during the war.

A production boom. The United States soon became the Allies' biggest armaments supplier. Between 1940 and 1945, U.S. war plants produced millions of planes, tanks, jeeps, and guns. Shipbuilders produced thousands of ships, creating a powerful navy and merchant marine.

War production helped create an economic boom. The number of jobless workers, still over 2.5 million in 1942, sank to fewer than 700,000 in 1944. Earnings nearly doubled between 1939 and 1945. People who had stood in breadlines a decade

◄ After the bombing of Pearl Harbor, many existing factories were converted to wartime production. The Firestone Tire & Rubber Company, for example, made antiaircraft guns, tank and submarine parts, and gas masks, as well as tires for all military vehicles.

earlier now worked overtime and brought home fat paychecks.

The boom also led to vast population shifts. More than four million workers left their homes to find work in war-industry locations in other states. Sharecroppers, tenant farmers, and others eking out a living on farms flocked to the centers of wartime production—shipyards on the Gulf and Pacific coasts and factories in the Midwest and West. The West especially witnessed phenomenal economic and population growth during the war. The federal government spent billions of dollars to build western factories and military bases. This wartime spending helped the West become a major industrial region after World War II.

American farms also achieved marvels of productivity. Although many agricultural workers went off to fight in the war or to work in wartime factories, productivity remained high. During the war years U.S. farmers produced enough food to supply the American people and the Allies overseas.

Government expansion. Mobilizing for war led to a greatly expanded federal government. The number of federal employees grew from almost one million in 1940 to nearly three million by 1945. The Office of War Mobilization (OWM) coordinated all government agencies involved in producing and distributing civilian goods. Its powerful director, James F. Byrnes, was sometimes called the "assistant president."

The **War Production Board** (WPB) directed the conversion of existing factories to wartime production and supervised the building of new plants. The WPB assigned raw materials to industry, including scrap iron from factories and recyclable tin, aluminum, and fats (used in bullets) from homes.

The WPB (and later the OWM) also coordinated the production and distribution of consumer goods. For instance, it diverted nylon to making parachutes. The WPB even regulated clothing styles in order to save fabric; canceled for the duration of the war were cuffs on men's trousers and pleats in women's skirts.

▶ After the war began, the government conserved valuable resources by establishing rationing programs. Students at Wilson Senior High in Washington, D.C., are shown learning how to use the latest ration book.

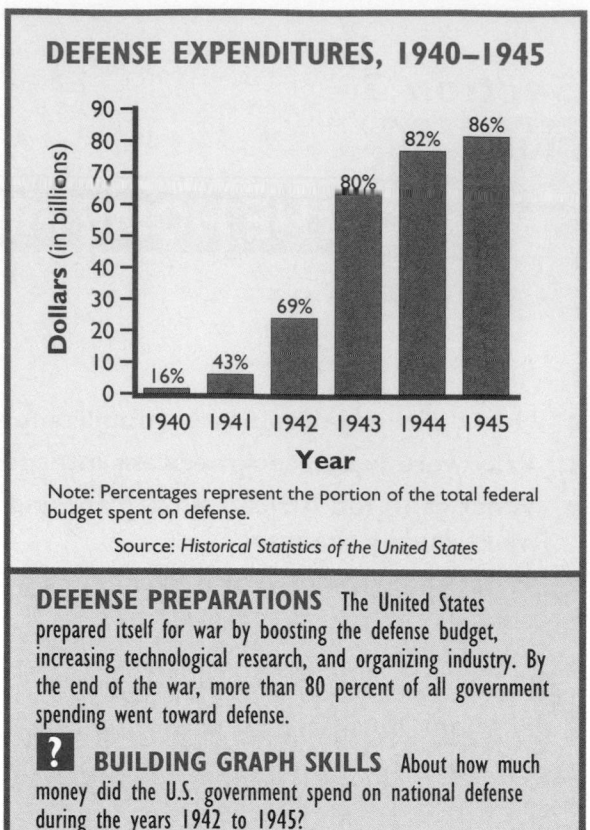

DEFENSE EXPENDITURES, 1940–1945

Dollars (in billions)

Year	
1940	16%
1941	43%
1942	69%
1943	80%
1944	82%
1945	86%

Note: Percentages represent the portion of the total federal budget spent on defense.

Source: *Historical Statistics of the United States*

DEFENSE PREPARATIONS The United States prepared itself for war by boosting the defense budget, increasing technological research, and organizing industry. By the end of the war, more than 80 percent of all government spending went toward defense.

? **BUILDING GRAPH SKILLS** About how much money did the U.S. government spend on national defense during the years 1942 to 1945?

Directing the economy. The government also extended its control over the economy. In order to pay for the war, the government increased by more than 10 times the number of Americans who had to pay income tax. The new taxes included most middle- and lower-income groups for the first time. The rest of the money came from borrowing, mainly through war bonds.

The sale of war bonds also helped the government deal with another major concern—keeping inflation down. When incomes remain high but few consumer items are available for people to buy, prices go up and inflation results. Selling war bonds offered one way of siphoning off excess income, thus keeping inflation down.

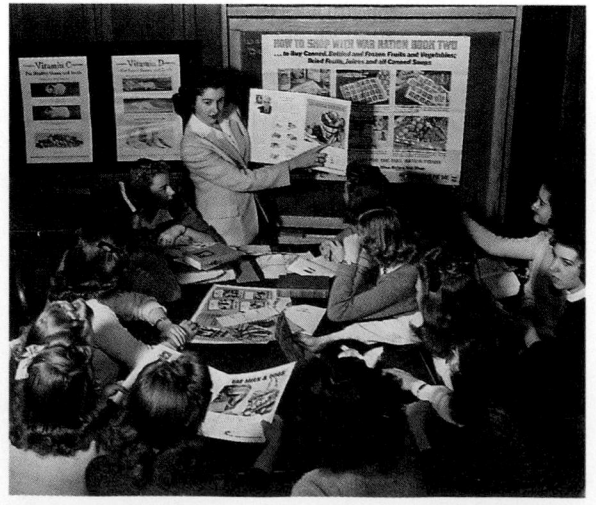

The government took other anti-inflationary steps as well. One was rationing, which reduced consumer demand by limiting how much people could buy. The measure also cut civilian purchases of products needed for the war effort. Rationed items included gasoline, heating fuel, tires, coffee, sugar, meat, butter, and canned goods. The government also tried to keep wages and prices down. At first it froze wages, but when the cost of living rose, the government allowed wages to rise by 15 percent.

Raising an army. Gearing up for war meant, along with increased production and expanded government controls, recruiting soldiers. In 1940, before the attack on Pearl Harbor, the United States passed the **Selective Training and Service Act**, which provided for the first peacetime draft in American history. The law required the registration of all men between ages 21 and 35 (age limits later extended from 18 to 37). Local draft boards determined fitness and deferred men for family, religious, or health reasons.

Of the some 15 million members of the armed services during World War II, about two thirds were draftees and the rest volunteers, including more than 300,000 women. Women enrolled in the Women's Auxiliary Army Corps (WAACs), Women's Airforce Service Pilots (WASPs), or auxiliary branches of the navy (WAVES), coast guard (SPARS), and marines. They worked as nurses, did office work, drove vehicles, and ferried planes in order to free men for active duty.

While most women military personnel served on the home front, women in the Army Nurse Corps (ANC) and Navy Nurse Corps (NNC) tended wounded soldiers overseas. Eunice Hatchitt, a nurse who served at Bataan, described the terrible conditions and heavy casualties:

66 Days and nights were an endless nightmare, until it seemed we couldn't stand it any longer. Patients came in by the hundreds, and the doctors and nurses worked continuously under the tents amid the flies and heat and dust. We had from eight to nine hundred victims a day. 99

■■ **The United States mobilized for war by increasing production, expanding government control of the economy, and raising an army.**

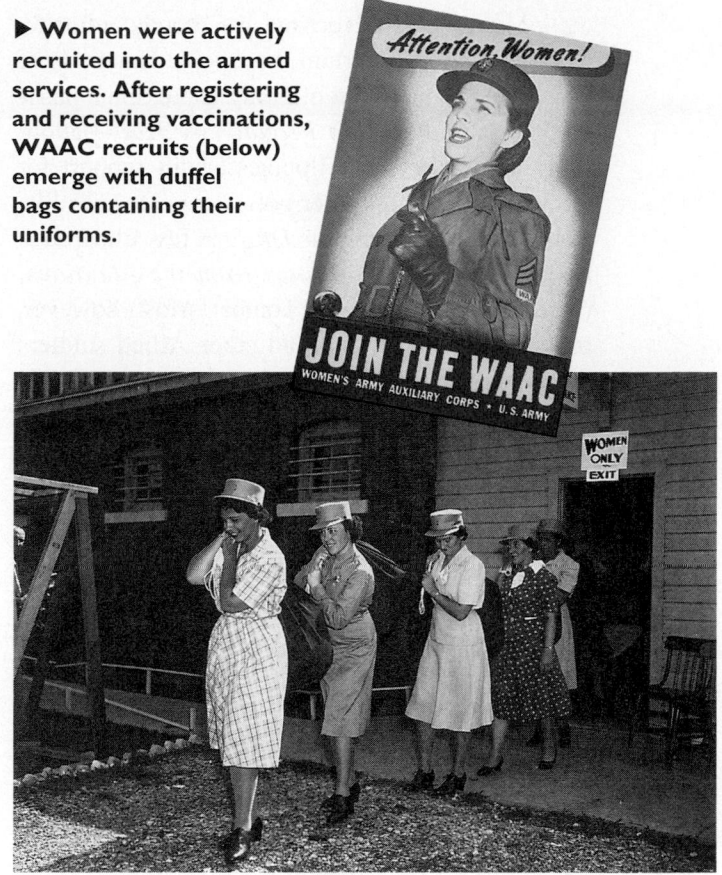

▶ Women were actively recruited into the armed services. After registering and receiving vaccinations, WAAC recruits (below) emerge with duffel bags containing their uniforms.

The urgency of the war effort convinced President Roosevelt, who had led the nation since 1933, to run for an unprecedented fourth term. As the 1944 campaign drew near, Roosevelt told an aide, "God knows I don't want to [run], but I may find it necessary." Roosevelt was nominated with little opposition; his vice-presidential candidate was a Missouri senator, Harry S. Truman.

The Republicans chose Thomas E. Dewey, governor of New York, who had won fame as a district attorney for prosecuting racketeers. However, he lacked Roosevelt's charisma and experience and was defeated by an electoral vote of 99 to Roosevelt's 432.

PROMOTING THE WAR

As it mobilized the nation's resources, the government also worked to keep morale high. This was especially important in the early days of the war, when Allied troops faced many setbacks. The government encouraged the media to do their part. Moviemakers, songwriters, and radio station programmers responded by urging all-out participation in the war effort.

Movie stars advertised war bonds and traveled overseas to entertain the troops. Hundreds of war movies poured out of Hollywood. Some patriotic films, such as *So Proudly We Hail*—about army nurses in the Philippines—built support for the war. Striking a lighter note were comedies like Bob Hope's *Caught in the Draft*. A few films, such as *Wake Island* and *Report from the Aleutians,* offered realistic views of combat. Most, however, romanticized American and other Allied soldiers and stereotypically portrayed the Japanese as treacherous, the Germans as fanatical, and the Italians as cowardly.

Radio stations broadcast both war news and entertainment. Radio correspondents such as Edward R. Murrow and Eric Sevareid gave on-the-scene accounts of war-ravaged Europe. A new federal agency, the Office of War Information (OWI), controlled the flow of war news at home.

Wartime musical hits included "Remember Pearl Harbor" and "Praise the Lord and Pass the Ammunition!" But the biggest hits of the period did not deal directly with the war. African American musicians—including trumpeter Dizzy Gillespie, sax player Charlie Parker, and piano player Thelonious Monk—popularized a new form of jazz, called bebop, or bop. Also popular were such sentimental songs as "White Christmas," which expressed Americans' longing for a return to peace.

The war also affected popular radio serials. Radio stations abandoned spy and sabotage programs for the duration of the war. Some even banned certain sound effects, such as wailing sirens, to avoid alarming listeners.

On the whole, World War II was a popular war. Most Americans put up with shortages, planted "victory gardens" to conserve food, and bought millions of dollars worth of war bonds. Many families proudly displayed window banners with a star—a blue one for a loved one in the service, a gold one to commemorate a death in combat.

JAPANESE AMERICAN RELOCATION

By and large, World War II did not produce the kind of home-front intolerance that occurred during World War I. One tragic exception was the forced relocation and imprisonment, or **internment**, of Japanese Americans living on the Pacific coast. In September 1945, U.S. State Department adviser Eugene Rostow called internment "a tragic and dangerous mistake" and argued that "its motivation and its impact on our system of law deny every value of democracy."

When Pearl Harbor was bombed, about 119,000 people of Japanese ancestry lived in Washington, Oregon, and California. Of these, about a third, the Issei (EE-SAY), had been born in Japan and were regarded by the U.S. government as aliens ineligible for U.S. citizenship. The rest, the Nisei (NEE-SAY), had been born in the United States and were thus American citizens.

People of Japanese ancestry had long suffered racial discrimination in the United States. Laws prevented Japanese immigrants from becoming citizens, and prejudice restricted the kinds of jobs they and their descendants could hold and the neighborhoods where they could live.

▶ This painting of the internment camp at Heart Mountain, Wyoming, was done by Japanese American artist Estelle Ishigo.

◀ Toyo Miyatake photographed this scene in Los Angeles in the early days of World War II. With their belongings piled high on the sidewalk, Japanese Americans wait for the buses that will take them to a relocation assignment center.

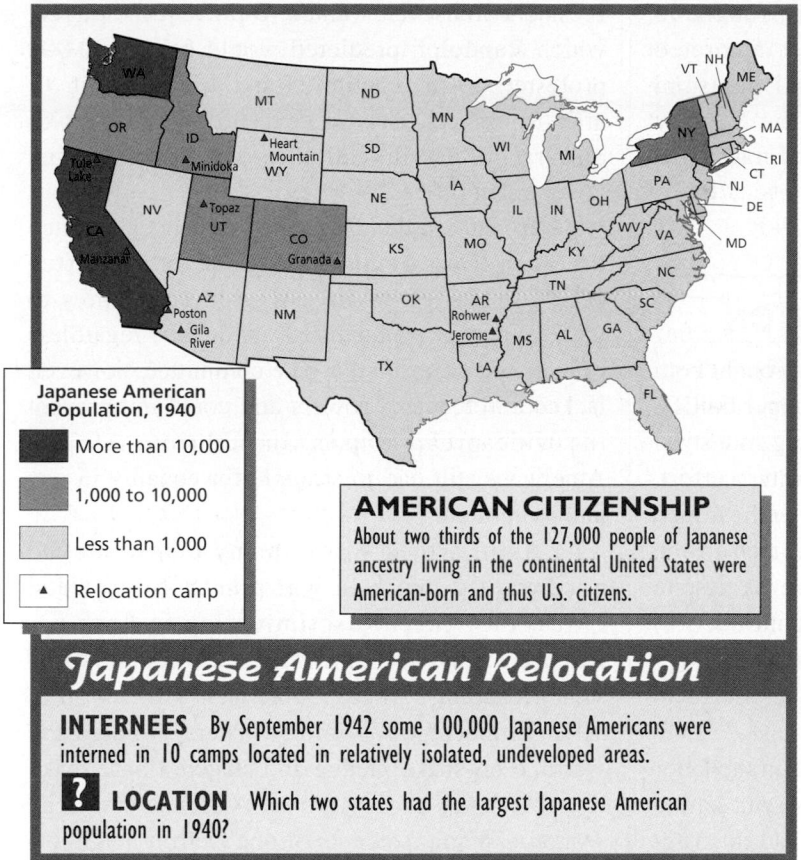

Japanese American Population, 1940

- ▮ More than 10,000
- ▮ 1,000 to 10,000
- ▯ Less than 1,000
- ▲ Relocation camp

AMERICAN CITIZENSHIP
About two thirds of the 127,000 people of Japanese ancestry living in the continental United States were American-born and thus U.S. citizens.

Japanese American Relocation

INTERNEES By September 1942 some 100,000 Japanese Americans were interned in 10 camps located in relatively isolated, undeveloped areas.

❓ LOCATION Which two states had the largest Japanese American population in 1940?

fearfully watched his neighbors being taken away for questioning by the FBI. He recalled bitterly that "they had done nothing; the only thing that they had done was to be born of Japanese ancestry."

He was 10 years old when his family was uprooted. Mineta wore his Cub Scout uniform on the train, hoping that it would show his loyalty to the United States. After six months in a barracks at the Santa Anita racetrack in southern California, Mineta's family was interned with some 10,000 others at a hastily built camp at Heart Mountain, Wyoming. "These camps were all barbed wire, guard towers, searchlights," recalled Mineta. "They were concentration camps. There's no question about it."

After the war Mineta attended college, became an insurance agent, and went into local politics in San Jose. In 1974 he was elected to the House of Representatives, where he served on several committees and introduced legislation seeking reparations for Japanese American internees.

Like most other internees, Mineta regretted what had happened, but his patriotism never wavered:

When war came, prejudice turned into near hysteria. There was no evidence of disloyalty on the part of any Issei or Nisei. Strong anti-Japanese sentiments among some vocal politicians and residents of western states, however, persuaded the federal government to remove people of Japanese descent from the West Coast. In February 1942 they were ordered to detention camps in Wyoming, Utah, and other states. Here they were imprisoned until 1945—an action upheld by the Supreme Court in 1944.

◼ Because of prejudice and war hysteria, Japanese Americans living on the West Coast were interned in relocation camps.

Relocation tragically disrupted the lives of Japanese Americans. They had to leave hurriedly, abandoning or selling their homes and businesses at rock-bottom prices. A government estimate later put Japanese American property losses at $400 million.

One imprisoned Japanese American was Norman Mineta, a Nisei from San Jose, California. On the day of the bombing, the young Mineta

❝ Despite the color of our hair and skin, despite the shape of our eyes, the U.S. was our country. I remember how my parents reminded us of that fact. Just before our family was evacuated, my father . . . said, "No matter what happens, *this* is your home." ❞

Patriotism, and the desire to disprove accusations of disloyalty, inspired many young men in the camps to volunteer for military duty (in segregated units).

Norman Mineta

One Nisei combat team, the 442nd, fought in Europe and became one of the most decorated units in the armed services. Several thousand Japanese Americans also served in the Military Intelligence Service as interpreters and translators in the Pacific.

THE MARCH ON WASHINGTON

For African Americans, World War II brought both continued discrimination and greater opportunities. Many blacks moved into better-paying industrial jobs and played a key role in the military effort. About a million black soldiers served in the armed forces, including several thousand women in the Women's Auxiliary Army Corps. However, despite their protests, African Americans continued to serve in segregated units and until 1943 were kept out of combat. Blacks were usually restricted to menial work.

The millions of black Americans in the labor force in the 1940s also played an important home-front role in the war effort. But they had to struggle to gain acceptance. Many war plants would not hire blacks or would employ them only as janitors. And despite labor leaders' no-strike pledge, some white workers staged strikes, called "hate strikes," to keep black workers out of high-paying factory jobs.

In 1941, before the United States entered the war, African American labor leader A. Philip Randolph planned a march on Washington, D.C., to protest discrimination against black workers.

▲ African Americans served with distinction during the war. These pilots at a training center in Tuskegee, Alabama, study a map before going aloft in 1943.

President Roosevelt wanted to prevent the march, which Randolph predicted would bring 100,000 protesters to the Capitol. Randolph called it off after Roosevelt issued an executive order forbidding racial discrimination in defense plants and government offices.

To enforce the order, the government created the **Fair Employment Practices Committee** (FEPC). The FEPC investigated companies to make sure that all qualified applicants, regardless of race, were considered. The committee, however, lacked enforcement powers and could not prevent the widespread abuses. In addition, African Americans still had to struggle for equality in pay and promotion.

As in World War I, many blacks moved northward to work in war plants. In crowded cities, they faced discrimination in housing. Resulting tensions sometimes led to outbursts of violence against African Americans. In Detroit in 1943, some 25,000 white workers violated the wartime no-strike pledge and staged a hate strike to protest the promotion of African American workers. White residents of one Detroit neighborhood tried to prevent blacks from moving into the newly constructed Sojourner Truth Housing Project. In June of the same year, 25 blacks and 9 whites died in several days of rioting after a fight between blacks and whites at Belle Isle, a popular Detroit park, spread to other parts of the city.

Despite these incidents, most African Americans supported the war. Educator and civil rights activist Mary McLeod Bethune noted that African Americans "feel that the fight against fascism is their fight too," because they realized "that their persecution would be even worse under Hitler."

THE ZOOT-SUIT RIOTS

For Mexican Americans, as for blacks, World War II brought both opportunities and problems. More than 300,000 Mexican Americans served in the military, and 17 earned the Congressional Medal of Honor. The 88th Division, an elite combat unit known as the "Blue Devils," consisted mostly of Mexican Americans.

Mexican Americans also helped meet home-front labor needs. University of Texas history professor Carlos E. Castañeda served as assistant to the chairman of the FEPC and worked to

▲ These Mexican American infantrymen are being trained to use the rapid-firing Garand rifle at a U.S. Army camp in the South. Because many of these soldiers spoke Spanish, army instructors gave instructions in both English and Spanish.

■■ **African Americans and Mexican Americans won better factory jobs during the war but continued to face wide-spread discrimination.**

improve working conditions for Mexican Americans in Texas. In 1945 the FEPC ordered a major Texas oil company to discontinue its hiring and promotion practices that discriminated against Hispanics.

As a result of similar FEPC actions, and the pressing need for workers, many factories opened up jobs to Mexican Americans. Many Mexican Americans moved from the Southwest to industrial centers in the Midwest and on the West Coast. Under a 1942 agreement between the United States and Mexico, thousands of Mexican farm and railroad workers—known as **braceros**—came north to work in the Southwest during World War II.

But prejudice and discrimination against Hispanics in jobs, housing, and recreation facilities caused bitter resentment. Relations grew especially hostile in Los Angeles. Mexican American youths had adopted the fad of wearing zoot suits—outfits with long jackets, pegged trousers, and wide-brimmed hats. In the summer of 1943, sailors roamed the city attacking zoot-suiters in what came to be known as the **zoot-suit riots**. The government eventually clamped down on the sailors, but not before they had viciously beaten many Mexican Americans.

A citizens' committee later determined that the attacks were motivated by racial prejudice. The committee also placed partial responsibility on the police, who had responded to the riots by arresting Mexican Americans, and on biased newspaper reports.

ROSIE THE RIVETER

During the depression, the government discouraged women, especially married women, from working. The government now urged them to enter the job market to replace departing servicemen and to help win the war against fascism. One government poster showed a woman worker in bandanna and overalls. The caption read: "I'm Proud . . . my husband <u>wants</u> me to do my part." Advertisements and a popular song promoted "Rosie the Riveter," the symbol of patriotic women defense workers.

From 1940 to 1944 the number of women in the labor force increased by more than four million. Women worked in war plants and replaced men in a host of jobs ranging from newspaper reporting to truck driving. Many of these new workers were married women who were taking jobs outside the home for the first time. Many women already in the paid work force left traditional "women's work" as domestics and other service jobs to work in factories.

■■ **World War II increased women's participation in the paid labor force and allowed them to move into traditionally male jobs.**

Women's participation in the war effort gave many of them a new sense of pride and self-worth. One woman aircraft worker finally felt a sense of achievement after feeling "average" at other jobs:

66 Foremen from other departments come to my machine to ask me to do some work for them if I have time because they say I'm the best countersinker in the vast building! At forty-nine I've at last become not better than average, but the best! 99

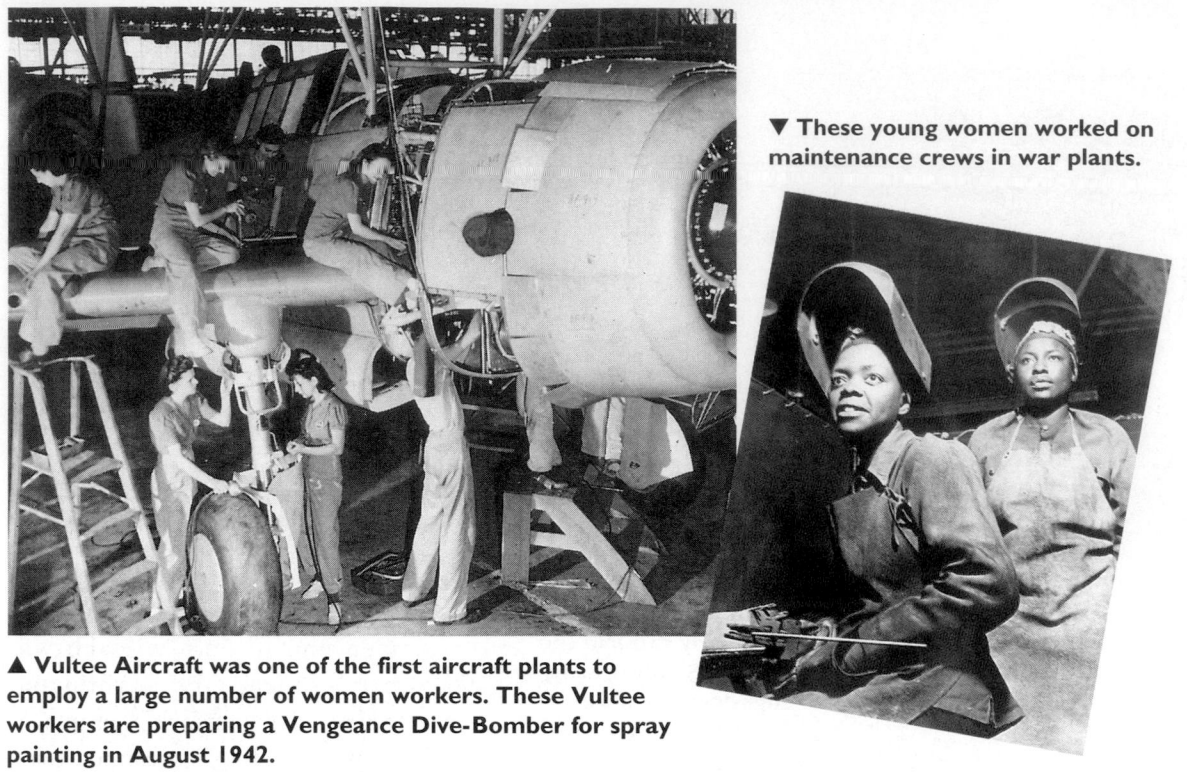

▼ These young women worked on maintenance crews in war plants.

▲ Vultee Aircraft was one of the first aircraft plants to employ a large number of women workers. These Vultee workers are preparing a Vengeance Dive-Bomber for spray painting in August 1942.

A government study in 1942 praised women workers, noting that factories "were practically unanimous in reporting that on the whole the work done by women was considered equal to that of men." Nevertheless, women encountered discrimination. Women workers continued to be paid less than men for the same work. African American women and women over 40 found few employers willing to hire them. Although Frances Perkins, long a supporter of women workers, continued to head the Department of Labor during the war years, wartime federal agencies did little to enforce equal treatment for women workers.

In spite of women's achievements, it was widely assumed—by many women as well as men—that most of the jobs women held during the war were temporary. A manager of a shipyard predicted that "these women who are willing . . . to lend a hand with the war will be the . . . office personnel of . . . the future." The message was clear: in traditionally "masculine" jobs, women were wanted as emergency helpers, not as competition.

SECTION 2 REVIEW

IDENTIFY and explain the significance of the following: James F. Byrnes, War Production Board, Selective Training and Service Act, Thomas E. Dewey, internment, Norman Mineta, A. Philip Randolph, Fair Employment Practices Committee, braceros, zoot-suit riots.

1. **MAIN IDEA** What steps did the United States take to shift from a peacetime to a wartime economy?

2. **MAIN IDEA** How did World War II change life for American women?

3. **RECOGNIZING BIAS** Why did the United States forcibly relocate and imprison Japanese Americans living on the West Coast?

4. **WRITING TO EVALUATE** Imagine you are either an African American or a Mexican American during World War II. Write a letter to your representative in Congress, evaluating the gains you have made during the war.

5. **IDENTIFYING CAUSE AND EFFECT** What did the U.S. government do to keep morale high during World War II? How did most Americans respond to the government's actions?

DEFEAT OF THE AXIS POWERS

FOCUS

- What did the Allied offensive in North Africa achieve?
- How did the Allies gain final victory in Europe?
- What was the chief objective of Allied assaults in the Pacific?
- Why and when did Japan surrender?

American supplies and troops began to make a difference in the war by late 1942. But it would take over two more years of hard fighting to defeat the Axis powers. The Allied invasions of North Africa, Italy, and France and the fierce bombardments of German cities forced Germany to surrender in May 1945. In the Pacific, meanwhile, the United States seized Japanese-held islands, including the Philippines. Atomic attacks devastated Japan, and it surrendered in August 1945.

Liberation of Paris, 1944

ALLIED ATTACKS IN THE MEDITERRANEAN

The Allies agreed soon after Pearl Harbor that they would open up a second front against the Axis powers in order to relieve pressure on the Soviet Union. At Churchill's urging, they focused this attack on the Mediterranean region—what Churchill called the "soft underbelly" of the Axis territory.

Axis surrender in North Africa. In November 1942, after the British had driven the Germans and Italians into Libya, another Allied force landed in French Northwest Africa in an invasion code-named Operation Torch (see map on page 748). General Dwight D. Eisenhower commanded the invasion force, which consisted of American and British soldiers. As the soldiers established beachheads in Morocco and Algeria, Allied planes and ships cut Axis supply lines from Italy. Then, during the winter of 1942–43, the two Allied land forces—one from the west and the other from the east—began squeezing the Axis troops into a trap between them.

Several fierce battles took place in Tunisia. Finally, in May 1943, the Axis force of some

◄ **"We are out to win the war in the quickest and most economical way,"** U.S. Army chief of staff George C. Marshall (right) declared in 1943. Marshall was photographed with General Dwight D. Eisenhower in North Africa in June 1943.

250,000 men surrendered. The Allies now controlled much of the Mediterranean. This victory also gave American troops valuable combat experience, especially in amphibious assaults.

▪▪ The conquest of North Africa gave the Allies increased control over the Mediterranean.

The invasion of Italy. From North Africa it was not far to the Italian island of Sicily. Allied leaders decided to invade it next in order to clear the Axis forces out of the central Mediterranean and acquire a launching pad for an invasion of the Italian mainland.

Amid high winds and difficult seas, almost half a million troops landed in July 1943 and subdued Sicily in a little over a month. The Italian king named a new prime minister to replace Benito Mussolini and ordered Mussolini's arrest. The Germans, however, were determined not to surrender the peninsula. They took Mussolini to Germany and then set up a base for him in northern Italy.

In September the Italian government signed an armistice with the Allies. Two days later the Allies invaded southern Italy to attack the Germans. Although the Allies took Naples on October 1, they soon bogged down. Hoping to outflank Nazi troops near Rome, they landed to the south at Anzio in January 1944 (see map on page 748); but their attack failed, and they were pinned down for months. Not until June 1944 did the Allies march into Rome, which became the first Axis capital to fall.

American and British forces then began driving slowly north. They were joined by small units of troops from more than 25 countries. After months of bitter mountain warfare, the German occupiers were finally defeated. Mussolini was captured in late April and shot by Italian partisans.

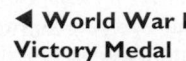

◀ **World War II Victory Medal**

VICTORY IN EUROPE

During the months of fighting in the Mediterranean region, the Allies were waging campaigns on several other fronts as well. Although they faced a determined enemy, they eventually overcame all resistance.

Sea and air assaults. In the Atlantic, German U-boats continued to take a staggering toll of Allied ships, lives, and supplies. Not until 1943 did the **Battle of the Atlantic** begin to turn in the Allies' favor. An important factor was the refinement of sonar equipment, which uses sound waves to detect underwater objects. The Allies also developed fast escort ships for convoys and air-bombed German U-boats and submarine yards. By 1944 the Allies had won the Battle of the Atlantic.

In the air, too, 1943 was an important year for the Allies. They intensified their campaign of strategic bombing aimed at destroying German military production and at undermining the morale of the German people. British Royal Air Force (RAF) planes flew chiefly at night, dropping their bombs in the general area of a given target. American aircraft concentrated on precision bombing in daylight raids. By 1944, bombers rained tons of explosives on German factories, supply lines, and military centers. Many German civilians died in these raids.

The invasion of France. Victory in the Battle of the Atlantic and air assaults on Germany paved the way for Operation Overlord—the long-awaited Allied invasion of German-occupied France. Commanded by General Eisenhower, it had involved years of planning. The Allies put in place a system of dummy installations and false clues to convince the Germans that the invasion would take place near Calais.

Instead, the Allies landed to the south, in Normandy. On **D-Day**, June 6, 1944, nearly 5,000 troop transports, landing craft, and warships carried some 150,000 American, British, and Canadian soldiers across the English Channel. Overhead, planes dropped close to 23,000 airborne troops and bombed roads, bridges, and German troop concentrations. Sergeant Ralph G. Martin recalled that "everything was confusion" during the landing made in pounding surf:

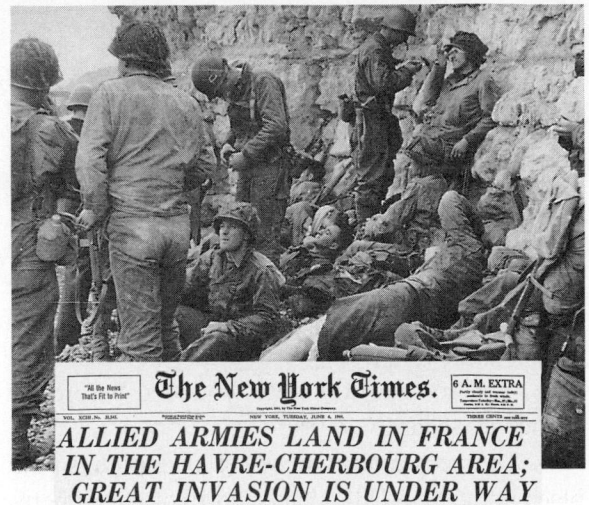

▲ The *New York Times* announced the Allied invasion of France on June 6, 1944. After landing at Normandy, these American members of the invasion force rest under a cliff before advancing inland.

> ❝ Units were mixed up, many of them leaderless, most of them not being where they were supposed to be. Shells were coming in all the time; boats burning; vehicles with nowhere to go bogging down, getting hit; supplies getting wet; boats trying to come in all the time, some hitting mines, exploding. ❞

The Germans had fortified the Normandy beaches with concrete bunkers, tank traps, and mines. But the Allied disinformation campaign had done its job. Hitler refused to send reinforcements, believing that the main invasion would occur elsewhere. Although the Allies met determined opposition, they penetrated 15 miles into France in less than a week. Aided by the French Resistance, the Allies drove steadily eastward. They liberated Paris on August 25, 1944. By early September they had landed over two million troops in western Europe. Another Allied force drove northward through France from the Mediterranean. Meanwhile, Soviet troops pressed Germany from the east.

A German counterattack.
Although Germany's situation was grave, Hitler would not give up. In September 1944 the Germans launched their first V-2s, long-range rockets aimed at cities in England and Belgium. Once launched, these bombs could not be shot down without causing considerable damage.

By September 1944 the Allies had crossed the German border. As they paused to bring in supplies and to regroup, the Germans launched their last counterattack. In heavy snow, they drove against the Allies in the thickly wooded Ardennes region of Belgium and northern France, pushing them westward to create a dangerous bulge in the Allied lines. In the resulting **Battle of the Bulge**, some 200,000 Germans attacked an initial American force of around 80,000. Because many of the regular troops had been transferred to other areas, much of the fighting was done by "cooks, clerks, mechanics, and radio operators."

Allied reinforcements were rushed to the front, and the Allies pushed the Germans back. Artilleryman Francis Tsuzuki, whose Japanese American battalion pursued the Germans, remembered that "the Germans were retreating so fast. At times we were moving . . . more than 100 miles a day." By January 1945 it was clear that the German offensive had failed. In February Roosevelt, Churchill, and Stalin met at the **Yalta Conference** to plan for the postwar peace. At the conference the leaders agreed to divide and occupy Germany and outlined plans for a new international peace organization.

Last days.   During the early months of 1945, Allied bombers continued to blast German industrial and population centers, including Dresden, Leipzig, and Berlin. One of the most devastating—and controversial—attacks hit Dresden in February. This beautiful old city, of little strategic value, was packed with refugees fleeing from the war-torn areas. In one massive two-day attack, Allied bombers caused the worst firestorms of the war. Total civilian deaths have been estimated at between 30,000 and 60,000.

▲ The Allied bombing of Dresden, Germany, left many famous buildings in ruins. Shown here is the damage to the inner court of the Zwinger Museum, which housed a priceless art collection.

In March, Allied troops from the west crossed the Rhine and drove into the heart of Germany. By then, Soviet troops occupied much of Eastern Europe. Churchill wanted the Allies to push east as far and as fast as possible because he was worried that the Russians might later lay claim to territories they seized. But Eisenhower, who did not want military strategy determined by political considerations, halted the Allied advance at the Elbe River in April. The Soviet army agreed to halt momentarily east of Berlin.

On April 30, 1945, Hitler committed suicide in his bunker deep under the ruins of Berlin. As Soviet troops occupied the city, German armies all over Europe stopped fighting. American sergeant Mack Morriss described the grim mood of the fallen city: "There is a feeling that here has ended not only a city but a nation, that here a titanic force has come to catastrophe." Germany surrendered unconditionally on May 7. The next day, known as V-E (Victory in Europe) Day, marked the formal end of the war in Europe. The next month the Allies divided defeated Germany into four occupation zones.

■■ **After winning the Battle of the Atlantic and bombing Germany, the Allies invaded France. Germany surrendered in May 1945.**

PACIFIC OFFENSIVES

In the Pacific, as in the western theater of operations, the Allies went on the offensive by 1943. The planned attack on Japan had two components: (1) air, land, and naval forces would seize Japanese-held islands in the central Pacific and set up air bases there; (2) combined forces would retake New Guinea and then the Philippines. The ultimate objective, of course, was to come within striking distance of Japan itself.

Island-hopping. As early as 1942, the American high command had adopted a policy of **island-hopping**. This meant that troops would attack and seize only certain strategic Japanese-held islands, rather than try to recapture all of them. Japanese garrisons on bypassed islands would be cut off from supplies and troop reinforcements.

In the central Pacific, an island-hopping offensive began in November 1943 in the Gilbert Islands (see map on page 746). Army troops easily took Makin Island. Tarawa Island proved more difficult. Because of a coral reef encircling the island, the marines who landed there, according to Sergeant John Bushemi, had to wade in to the beach "in the face of murderous Japanese fire, with no protection." Almost 1,000 marines lost their lives, and some 2,000 were wounded before the island was secure.

The next important series of landings took place in the Marshall Islands, north of the Gilberts. Here Americans captured several key bases from which they bombed the Truk Islands, the headquarters of the Japanese fleet.

By the summer of 1944, Americans advanced to the Mariana Islands. In June, under cover of intense air and naval bombardment from nearby carriers, landing craft swept in to the beaches of Saipan. The Japanese, determined to take a stand, sent out a big fleet to stop this offensive. In the resulting **Battle of the Philippine Sea**, the United States won a decisive victory, downing hundreds of Japanese planes while only losing some 80 U.S. planes.

Saipan and Guam fell in July and August, respectively. U.S. victories here were especially crucial. The islands provided airstrips from which American bombers could launch missions against the islands of Japan.

Reconquering the Philippines. Despite these setbacks, Japanese resistance proved just as fierce when the Allies began their New Guinea–Philippines campaign in June 1943. Douglas MacArthur, who had earlier evacuated the Philippines, commanded U.S. forces.

 MacArthur was born in 1880, the son of distinguished general Arthur MacArthur. After graduating first in his class from West Point, young MacArthur served in the Philippines and was wounded twice in World War I. From

Douglas MacArthur

THE NAVAJO CODE TALKERS

During World War II Native Americans served in several branches of the U.S. armed forces. Their languages allowed them to play a unique role in the Signal Corps, the communication units responsible for coding and sending classified military information. On the basis of the success of a few Native American army groups in code work, the Marine Signal Corps decided in March 1942 to organize a unit composed entirely of Navajos. The marines believed that the Navajo language would be unfamiliar to the Japanese, and thus would provide an unbreakable code. They quickly assembled a group of Navajo soldiers for the job.

The new unit devised and memorized a special Navajo dictionary containing 413 military terms. For example, the Navajo word for

"chicken hawk" meant dive-bomber in the code; "hummingbird" meant fighter plane; and "iron fish" meant submarine. Armed with this new code, the Navajo "Code Talkers" first went into action in the fall of 1942 in the Pacific.

Soon after the Code Talkers arrived on the front lines, U.S. field commanders reported that the Navajos' methods reduced the time

needed for decoding and encoding messages by half. As radio operators tracking Japanese movements, the Navajos often had to work in especially dangerous conditions behind enemy lines. "The Navajo Code Talkers have proved to be excellent Marines, intelligent, industrious, efficient," one officer wrote. Another remarked, "Were it not for the Navajos, the Marines would never have taken Iwo Jima."

By August 1943 nearly 200 Navajos were participating in the Code Talker program, and by the war's end more than 400 had served in the Marine Signal Corps. Their codes completely baffled the Japanese and were never broken. Though the Navajo Code Talkers made up only a small part of the Allied forces, their contributions to the war effort were invaluable.

▲ Corporal Henry Bake, Jr., (left) and Private George H. Kirk (right) were two members of the Navajo Code Talkers. They are shown operating a portable radio set behind front lines in the Solomon Islands in 1943.

1919 to 1922 he was superintendent of West Point. He took part in the attack on the Bonus Army marchers of 1932 (see Chapter 23), justifying the violence by claiming that Communists were behind this veterans' protest. After serving as a military adviser in the Philippines for several years, MacArthur was recalled to active duty in the summer of 1941. Eventually he was given command of all U.S. Army units in the Pacific.

In many respects, MacArthur was an excellent strategist. No one doubted his courage. But he was also arrogant, and though he demanded

absolute loyalty from his subordinates, he did not hesitate to disagree with his superiors.

In the Allied drive to recapture the Philippines, MacArthur led U.S. and Australian troops in a series of landings along the north coast of New Guinea. By late July 1944 they had reached the western end of this large island. Allied forces also took smaller islands nearby, such as the Admiralty Islands.

By the fall of 1944, with New Guinea secure and with its newly won bases in the Marianas, the United States was ready to invade the Philippines.

Allied forces poured onto the beaches of the island of Leyte in October. When the Japanese navy counterattacked, the result was the **Battle of Leyte Gulf**, the last, largest, and most decisive naval engagement in the Pacific. The battle was a disaster for the Japanese, who lost four carriers, two battleships, and several cruisers. From this time on, the Japanese fleet no longer presented a serious threat to the Allies.

Allied troops, aided by Filipino guerrillas, fanned out over the islands of the Philippines. Overcoming bitter opposition, they entered Manila in February 1945 and subdued most Japanese defense forces within weeks. "I'm a little late," said MacArthur, "but we finally came."

■■ Island-hopping and the reconquest of the Philippines brought the Allies within bombing distance of Japan's cities.

𝒱ICTORY IN THE PACIFIC

These Pacific victories gave the United States enough bases to launch B-29 bombers against the Japanese home islands. In a series of devastating night attacks, U.S. planes hit most of the country's major cities. The worst raid, over Tokyo in March 1945, created firestorms that destroyed much of the city.

▼ A few hours after U.S. Marines captured Iwo Jima, naval landing crafts delivered tons of supplies to the island. The slippery volcanic ash made it difficult for marines to keep their footing while carrying the heavy crates.

Japanese civilian morale sagged, but the country's military leaders refused to surrender. In February 1945, when marines attacked Iwo Jima—only 750 miles from Tokyo—they met strong resistance. U.S. marines struggled to take Mount Suribachi, which the Japanese held with a strong system of tunnels and bunkers. The **Battle of Iwo Jima** lasted nearly a month. Some 4,000 marines were killed, while the Japanese lost more than 20,000.

On April 1 the largest landing force in Pacific history invaded Okinawa, located about 350 miles from Japan. Allied soldiers drove the Japanese forces to the southern tip of the island. The **Battle of Okinawa** was perhaps the bloodiest battle of the Pacific war, with American casualties estimated at 49,000 and Japanese losses at over 100,000. Meanwhile, a 700-plane squad of **kamikaze**, or suicide planes, damaged 13 U.S. destroyers. (*Kamikaze* is a Japanese word meaning "divine wind.")

By early April 1945, however, American victory in the Pacific was near. But President Roosevelt did not live to see the end of hostilities with Japan. The world was stunned when he died suddenly on April 12. The new president, Harry S. Truman, wrote candidly about his bewilderment:

▲ The sudden death of President Roosevelt shocked many Americans. Overcome with grief, Sergeant Graham Jackson plays "Going Home" on his accordion while the president's casket passes by.

❝ I did not know what reaction the country would have to the death of a man whom they all practically worshiped. I was worried about the reaction of the Armed Forces. . . . I knew the President had a great many meetings with Churchill and Stalin. I was not familiar with any of these things. ❞

Truman had little time to ponder. In a few weeks he was faced with a tough decision. Although battered by relentless bombing, Japan still had a well-trained army and strong inner defenses. And Germany's surrender in May freed the Allied forces for the war in the Pacific.

By this time, however, the United States had a fearsome new weapon, the atomic bomb. In the top-secret **Manhattan Project**, scientists had been working on a bomb since 1942. They tested it successfully at Alamogordo, New Mexico, on July 16, 1945. The very next day, Truman met with Allied leaders at Potsdam, south of Berlin. On July 26 they demanded Japan's unconditional surrender, which Japan rejected.

Truman proceeded to give the order to use atomic weapons against Japan. On August 6 a U.S. plane called the *Enola Gay* dropped an atomic bomb on Hiroshima. It flattened a huge area of the city and killed more than 75,000. Three days later the United States dropped the second atomic bomb, on Nagasaki. The Japanese estimated that the total number of deaths caused by both bombs—including those who died later from burns and radiation poisoning—was 240,000.

A day before the bombing of Nagasaki, the Soviet Union had declared war on Japan and began

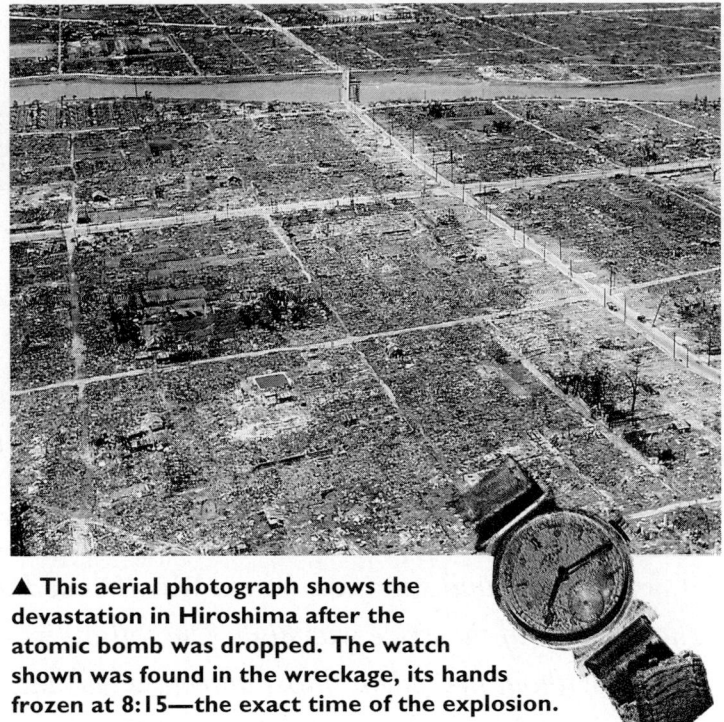

▲ This aerial photograph shows the devastation in Hiroshima after the atomic bomb was dropped. The watch shown was found in the wreckage, its hands frozen at 8:15—the exact time of the explosion.

an invasion of Manchuria. The Japanese soon offered to surrender. The formal surrender was signed on September 2, 1945, aboard the battleship *Missouri* in Tokyo Bay.

■■ **After the U.S. atomic bombings of Hiroshima and Nagasaki, Japan surrendered in August 1945.**

SECTION 3 REVIEW

IDENTIFY and explain the significance of the following: Dwight D. Eisenhower, Battle of the Atlantic, D-Day, Battle of the Bulge, Yalta Conference, island-hopping, Battle of the Philippine Sea, Battle of Leyte Gulf, Battle of Iwo Jima, Battle of Okinawa, kamikaze, Harry S. Truman, Manhattan Project.

LOCATE and explain the importance of the following: Sicily, Anzio, Normandy, Dresden, Elbe River, Gilbert Islands, Marshall Islands, Mariana Islands, New Guinea, Leyte, Iwo Jima, Okinawa, Hiroshima, Nagasaki.

1. **MAIN IDEA** What did the Allies accomplish through the military campaign in North Africa?

2. **MAIN IDEA** What events forced Germany to surrender in 1945?

3. **GEOGRAPHY: LOCATION** How did the Allies attempt to regain control of the Pacific? What was the overall aim of this military strategy?

4. **WRITING TO EXPLAIN** Write an essay that explains when and why Japan surrendered.

5. **USING HISTORICAL IMAGINATION** Imagine you are a soldier on either the European or the Pacific front. Write a diary entry that describes conditions you experienced in one of the battles mentioned in the text.

THE PRICE OF VICTORY

FOCUS

- What were some of the costs of World War II?
- What was the Holocaust? How did it affect European Jews?
- What were the international consequences of World War II?

Soviet civilians mourn dead soldiers.

After years of struggle and sacrifice, World War II ended in victory for the Allies. But the price was high. The toll in lives and property was without precedent. Most alarming was the knowledge—fully revealed only after the defeat of Germany—that Hitler had tried to exterminate all the Jews of Europe. Along with peace came many uncertainties about the future.

COSTS OF THE WAR

The United States and its allies achieved their war aims. Germany's murderous Nazi regime was destroyed. Japanese expansion in Asia was halted and the nation's military warlords overthrown. But the toll in death, suffering, and destruction was appallingly high.

World War II was the most devastating war the world has ever known. When it finally ended, hundreds of cities, from London to Tokyo, lay in ruins. Beautiful churches and palaces were reduced to rubble, and priceless works of art had gone up in smoke. Millions of people lacked heat, electricity, running water, adequate food, or means of traveling from one place to another. In some regions, mile upon mile of field and forest had been reduced to utter desolation.

There is no way of estimating the value of property loss, but two examples indicate its extent. In Düsseldorf, Germany, more than 90 percent of homes could not be lived in. The cities of Kiev and Minsk in the Soviet Union had to be completely rebuilt.

The war took more lives than any other conflict in history and brought untold suffering to civilians. According to one estimate, some 30 million noncombatants lost their lives from bombing, shelling, disease, or starvation. Millions more were injured, were weakened by malnutrition, or lost everything they owned. The Soviet Union and

◀ **Britain's Coventry Cathedral was one of many churches virtually destroyed by bombing attacks during the war. This ceremony was held among the church ruins in February 1941.**

DEATHS IN WORLD WAR II

Country	Military Deaths	Civilian Deaths
ALLIED POWERS		
British Commonwealth	373,372	92,673
France	213,324	350,000
Poland	123,178	5,675,000
Philippines	27,000	91,000
United States	292,131	6,000
Soviet Union	11,000,000	7,000,000
Yugoslavia	305,000	1,200,000
AXIS POWERS		
Bulgaria	10,000	10,000
Germany	3,500,000	780,000
Hungary	200,000	290,000
Italy	242,232	152,941
Japan	1,300,000	672,000
Romania	300,000	200,000

Source: *Encyclopedia Britannica*

THE WAR TO END ALL WARS World War II had an enormous global impact. Tens of thousands of men, women, and children died from causes directly related to the war, and untold numbers lost their homes and livelihoods.

? **BUILDING CHART SKILLS** Which country had the highest overall casualties?

China were especially hard hit. As in World War I, U.S. civilian losses were relatively light. In economic terms, armaments and other military costs probably totaled over $1 trillion.

■ World War II resulted in more deaths and destroyed more property than any other war in history.

THE HOLOCAUST

No other wartime civilian deaths caused more horror than those of the **Holocaust**, Nazi Germany's systematic slaughter of European Jews. Before the war, Hitler had forced Jews out of most professions and had stripped them of their civil rights (see Chapter 25). The Nazis' goal was a Germany that was *Judenrein*—free of Jews. The Nazi authorities at first encouraged emigration, and about two thirds of all German and Austrian Jews left their countries. Many of those who remained were imprisoned in concentration camps such as Dachau (DAHK-ow) and Buchenwald (BOO-kuhn-wawld).

When Germany occupied France and other countries of Western Europe, and attacked Poland and the Soviet Union, it extended its control over additional thousands of Jews. Now Hitler's war against this people entered a new phase—one of utter savagery. In many regions special squads of German soldiers rounded up Jews and shot them. Elsewhere, Jews were forced into cities and isolated in ghettos. In 1941 the Germans began constructing camps specifically for the purpose of **genocide**—the deliberate annihilation of an entire people. Hitler and senior Nazi officials called this extermination program the "final solution of the Jewish question."

Major death camps were Auschwitz (OWSH-vits), Treblinka, and Majdanek, all in Poland. Here Jewish men, women, and children were transported in sealed railroad cars, marched into rooms disguised as shower facilities, and gassed. Their bodies were then cremated. All told, some six million Jews—two thirds of the Jewish population of Europe—perished.

The Nazis' pitiless slaughter extended to other peoples, too. Other victims, numbering in the

▲ These starving survivors of Buchenwald were photographed in April 1945 after their liberation by Allied soldiers.

millions, included Gypsies, Poles, the mentally retarded, religious dissidents, and homosexuals. Communists, Socialists, and other political opponents of the Nazi regime faced imprisonment and death as well.

When the Allies liberated the death camps, they found thousands of starving survivors. One was Elie Wiesel, the Romanian-born American writer. Having been sent first to Auschwitz and then to Buchenwald, he was an emaciated youth of 16 when freed. Hospitalized for two weeks, he recovered. His writings, however, express the deep psychological scars left on concentration camp survivors:

> 66 One day I was able to get up, after gathering all my strength. I wanted to see myself in the mirror hanging on the opposite wall. I had not seen myself since the ghetto.
>
> From the depths of the mirror, a corpse gazed back at me.
>
> The look in his eyes, as they stared into mine, has never left me. 99

▪▪ The Holocaust took the lives of six million Jews—two thirds of European Jewry.

Why were the Nazis able to carry out the monstrous genocide? They built on a long history of anti-Semitism in Europe stretching back to the Middle Ages. A barrage of Nazi propaganda against Jews whipped up this anti-Semitism. Some non-Jews in countries occupied by the Nazis assisted or failed to prevent the Nazis from sending their Jewish fellow citizens off to the death camps. Others, however, heroically worked to save Jewish lives.

Another factor underlying the Holocaust was the lack of direct action by the Allies. Although reports of mass exterminations surfaced as early as 1941, the Allies believed the reports to be exaggerated. As a result, Allied nations did not open their doors to greater numbers of refugees or attempt to destroy rail lines that led to the death camps.

▶ **British prime minister Winston Churchill (left), President Roosevelt (center), and Soviet leader Joseph Stalin (right) met at Yalta in 1945 to discuss territorial divisions after the war.**

A NEW BALANCE OF POWER

By the time of the Yalta Conference, the political balance of power had clearly shifted. The United States had confirmed its position as the world's strongest nation. Its western European allies, notably Great Britain, had been weakened by the war. The Soviet Union, in spite of the devastation it had undergone, emerged from the war as a mighty force. For the next several decades, the United States and the Soviet Union, as **superpowers**, would dominate the world.

Much of the Soviet Union's new power was based on the territory it had occupied in Eastern Europe during the war. At the Yalta Conference, Roosevelt and Churchill had secretly agreed to accept the Soviet occupation of Polish territory in return for Stalin's vague promise of eventual free elections. When this agreement later became public, some critics blamed Roosevelt and Churchill for giving in to Stalin's demands. But with Soviet troops in control of Poland, they had little choice. Furthermore, Roosevelt wanted to assure Russia's entry into the war against Japan.

By the end of the war, the Soviet Union had absorbed the Baltic nations of Estonia, Latvia, Lithuania, and parts of Czechoslovakia and Romania. After Japan's surrender, the Soviet Union also took control of former Japanese territory, including the Kuril Islands and half of Sakhalin Island, which lie north of Japan. Defeated Japan also lost Inner Mongolia, Manchuria, and the islands of Taiwan (Formosa) and Hainan to China.

▪▪ Among the many consequences of World War II were the emergence of two superpowers and territorial realignments.

COMMENTARY

Using the Atomic Bomb

In the field of technology, the war brought several breakthroughs, including synthetic rubber, jet propulsion, and new methods of blood storage and transfusion. One frightening wartime scientific advance was the unleashing of atomic energy for military purposes. In the most controversial decision of World War II, President Truman approved the use of the atomic bomb against Japan. Was the United States justified? Or did it commit a grave error by using nuclear weapons, and against civilians at that?

The decision to fund research on an atomic bomb was made by President Franklin Roosevelt in 1941. He did so in response to fears of scientists in the United States, including Albert Einstein, that German physicists were working on such a weapon. By the time the bomb was successfully tested, Germany was defeated, Roosevelt was dead, and Truman was president.

In announcing the atomic bombing of Japan, Truman defended his decision by noting that Japan had refused to surrender. Truman claimed that dropping the two bombs had prevented an American invasion of Japan, scheduled for early 1946, that might have cost hundreds of thousands of American and Japanese lives. He also portrayed the atomic bomb as the American answer to the Japanese attack on Pearl Harbor. "The Japanese began the war," said Truman. "They have been repaid manyfold."

Some historians have questioned these explanations. (Since these historians have revised the previously accepted version of historical events, they are known as **revisionists**.) They have pointed to evidence that the Japanese were urgently seeking to end the war in the summer of 1945. These historians have suggested that the war could have been won without nuclear weapons and without an invasion of Japan. Some revisionists have argued that Truman and his advisers had another reason for dropping the bomb. They did so not only to end the war but also to demonstrate the power of atomic weapons and thus strengthen the hand of the United States in its postwar dealings with the Soviet Union.

While the debate over the American decision to use atomic weapons continues, all historians agree on the long-range effects of the decision. One result was a dangerous nuclear arms race. In the postwar period the United States, and the rest of the world, would face the challenges of controlling the creation and use of atomic weapons and of harnessing atomic power for peaceful uses.

SECTION 4 REVIEW

IDENTIFY and explain the significance of the following: Holocaust, genocide, Elie Wiesel, superpowers, revisionists.

LOCATE and explain the importance of the following: Sakhalin Island, Kuril Islands, Taiwan, Hainan.

1. **MAIN IDEA** Why was World War II the most devastating war the world has ever known?

2. **MAIN IDEA** How did the Holocaust affect European Jews?

3. **ASSESSING CONSEQUENCES** Summarize the international consequences of World War II.

4. **WRITING TO DESCRIBE** Imagine you are a soldier who has helped liberate one of the German death camps. Write a letter home that describes what you saw there.

5. **TAKING A STAND** Do you think the United States was justified in using the atomic bomb against Japan? Give reasons for your answer.

AMERICANS IN WORLD WAR II ■■ 769

Japanese attack Pearl Harbor.

Allies sign Joint Declaration. Bataan Death March occurs. Allies stop Japanese offensive in battles of Coral Sea, Midway, and Guadalcanal. Rommel defeated at Battle of El Alamein.

1941

1942

WRITING A SUMMARY

Using the essential points of the chapter as a guide, write a summary of the chapter.

REVIEWING CHRONOLOGY

Number your paper 1 to 5. Study the time line above, and list the following events in the order in which they happened by writing the first next to 1, the second next to 2, and so on. Then complete the activity below.

1. Allies sign Joint Declaration.
2. D-Day invasion begins.
3. Zoot-suit riots break out.
4. FDR dies.
5. Japanese attack Pearl Harbor.

Assessing Consequences What was the effect of the Allied victory at the Battle of Leyte Gulf?

IDENTIFYING PEOPLE AND IDEAS

Explain the historical significance of each of the following people or terms.

1. Douglas MacArthur
2. Battle of Midway
3. braceros
4. War Production Board
5. Norman Mineta
6. D-Day
7. island-hopping
8. kamikaze
9. genocide
10. Elie Wiesel

UNDERSTANDING MAIN IDEAS

1. How was the United States drawn into World War II? What advantages did the Axis Powers have over the United States at the beginning of the war?
2. What steps did the U.S. government take to mobilize for war? What did the media do to keep morale high?
3. What gains did African Americans, Mexican Americans, and women make during the war?
4. How did the Allies win the Battle of the Atlantic?
5. How did the Nazis carry out the Holocaust?

REVIEWING THEMES

1. **Global Relations** How did the Allies pool their resources to win World War II?
2. **Cultural Diversity** How did wartime conditions lead to increased discrimination against Japanese Americans?
3. **Technology and Society** What political and moral issues did the development of atomic weapons raise?

THINKING CRITICALLY

1. **Analyzing** What actions did the Allies take to win the war in Europe?
2. **Synthesizing** What were the final costs and consequences of World War II?
3. **Evaluating** Why was the atomic bomb used against Japan? What effect did the use of this weapon have on the war in the Pacific?

WRITING ABOUT HISTORY

Writing to Classify Create a time line listing the important battles and other events leading to the Allied victory in the Pacific.

STRATEGY FOR SUCCESS

Review the Skills Handbook entry on Identifying Cause and Effect beginning on page 989. Then study the poster below, which was issued by the U.S. government during World War II. What cause-and-effect relationship does the poster suggest?

Allied leaders meet at Casablanca, Cairo, and Tehran. Soviets defeat Axis troops at Stalingrad. Allies conquer North Africa. Zoot-suit riots break out.

Allies capture Rome. D-Day invasion begins. Japanese navy defeated at Battle of Leyte Gulf. Germans launch V-2 rockets. FDR reelected president. Allied and German troops clash at Battle of the Bulge.

Allies meet at Yalta. Allies win battles of Iwo Jima and Okinawa. FDR dies. Germany surrenders. U.S. drops atomic bombs on Hiroshima and Nagasaki. Japan surrenders.

1943   **1944**   **1945**

USING PRIMARY SOURCES

After the war, survivors of German concentration camps began to reveal to the world the horrors suffered by Jews and other prisoners. Read the following excerpt from *The Holocaust Kingdom* (1963), written by Alexander Donat, a survivor of Majdanek. Then write an essay expressing your feelings about what you have read.

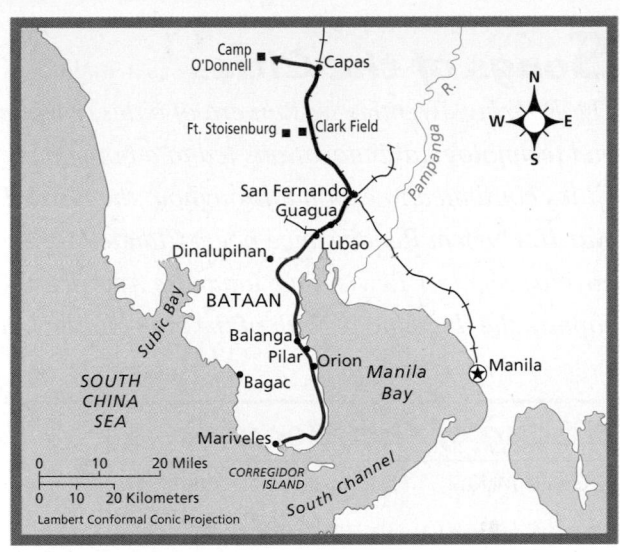

> *Usually they were taken there [to the gas chamber] at night, but once I saw the operation in broad daylight. . . . Through a crack in the wall we saw a long procession of living skeletons slowly emerging from Barrack Nineteen on their way to the gate. It was the way we would look in another two, four, or six weeks: it was the way it all ended. Majdanek was an industrial factory for producing corpses: death, the destruction of the greatest number of prisoners in the shortest time at the lowest cost was Majdanek's purpose. Life was treated as something . . . essentially worthless; in fact, contemptible. Death was our constant companion and not a terrible one, for quite often one wished passionately for it. It was life that was terrible, the long, agonizing process of parting from it after it had been shorn of dignity. Life in Majdanek was reduced to its basic elements.*

LINKING HISTORY AND GEOGRAPHY

After Allied forces on the Bataan Peninsula surrendered in April 1942, the Japanese ordered them to assemble at Mariveles and then march to San Fernando. From there the prisoners were shipped north by train. Study the map of the Bataan Death March in the next column. About how far did the prisoners have to march to reach San Fernando? About how far did they travel by train? What was their final destination? Why is it not possible to assess the difficulty of the journey from this map?

BUILDING YOUR PORTFOLIO

Complete the following projects independently or cooperatively.

1. GLOBAL RELATIONS In chapters 23 and 25 you portrayed a journalist. Building on that experience, imagine you are a member of a peace organization in the United States. Write an essay on ways to resolve international conflicts without war.

2. WAR In Chapter 25 you portrayed a diplomat at the beginning of the war. Building on that experience, imagine you are on a government committee examining the effects of the war. Compile statistics that illustrate the effects.

3. CULTURE AND SOCIETY In chapters 21, 22, and 24 you explored U.S. society in the 1920s and 1930s. Building on that experience, imagine you are a woman factory worker during World War II. Create a series of journal entries expressing your feelings about life on the home front.

American Letters

▲ Jean Toomer

Songs of the Cities

The Roaring Twenties was an era of cities, when economic prosperity and technological innovations led to a boom in skyscraper construction. Cities continued to expand throughout the Great Depression and World War II. Harlem Renaissance poets Claude McKay and Jean Toomer, novelist Sinclair Lewis, and Japanese American writer Toshio Mori capture the dynamic growth of the cities in the following selections.

A Song of the Moon

by Claude McKay

The moonlight breaks upon the city's domes,
And falls along cemented steel and stone,
Upon the grayness of a million homes,
Lugubrious[1] in unchanging monotone.

Upon the clothes behind the tenement,
That hang like ghosts suspended from the lines,
Linking each flat to each indifferent,
Incongruous[2] and strange the moonlight shines.

There is no magic from your presence here,
Ho, moon, sad moon, tuck up your trailing robe,
Whose silver seems antique and so severe
Against the glow of one electric globe.

Go spill your beauty on the laughing faces
Of happy flowers that bloom a thousand hues,
Waiting on tiptoe in the wilding spaces,
To drink your wine mixed with sweet drafts of dews. ❖

1 melancholy
2 not harmonious

From The Blue Meridian

by Jean Toomer

The prairie's sweep in flat infinity,
The city's rise is perpendicular to farthest star,
I stand where the two directions intersect,
At Michigan Avenue and Walton Place,[1]

Level with my countrymen,
Right-angled to the universe.

It is a new America,
To be spiritualized by each new American,
To be taken as a golden grain
And lifted, as the wheat of our bodies,
To matter uniquely man.
I would give my life to see inscribed
Upon the arch of our consciousness
These aims: Growth, Transformation, Love,
That we might become heart-centered towards
    one another,
Love-centered towards God, dedicated to the creation
    of a higher type of man, growing up to Him.
Let new eyes see this statue in the bay,
Let this be quarantine to unbend dreams,
Let old eyes see it in Wall Street and the Loop,[2]
And through this clearing house
Let all pass checks who may. ❖

1 streets in downtown Chicago
2 Chicago's downtown

From Babbitt

by Sinclair Lewis

The towers of Zenith aspired above the morning mist; austere [simple] towers of steel and cement and limestone, sturdy as cliffs and delicate as silver rods. They were neither citadels nor churches, but frankly and beautifully office-buildings.

The mist took pity on the fretted [eroded] structures of earlier generations: the Post Office with its shingle-tortured mansard,[1] the red brick minarets [towers] of hulking old houses, factories with stingy and sooted windows, wooden tenements colored like mud. The city was full of such grotesqueries,[2] but the clean towers were thrusting them from the business center, and on the farther hills were shining new houses, homes—they seemed—for laughter and tranquillity.

Over a concrete bridge fled a limousine of long sleek hood and noiseless engine. These people in evening clothes were returning from an all-night rehearsal of a Little Theater play. . . . Below the bridge curved a railroad, a maze of green and crimson lights. The New York Flyer boomed past, and twenty lines of polished steel leaped into the glare.

In one of the skyscrapers the wires of the Associated Press were closing down. The telegraph operators wearily raised their celluloid eye-shades after a night of talking with Paris and Peking. Through the building crawled the scrubwomen, yawning, their old shoes slapping. The dawn mist spun away. Cues [lines] of men with lunch-boxes clumped toward the immensity of new factories, sheets of glass and hollow tile, glittering shops where five thousand men worked beneath one roof, pouring out the honest wares that would be sold up the Euphrates[3] and across the veldt.[4] The whistles rolled out in greeting a chorus cheerful as the April dawn; the song of labor in a city built—it seemed—for giants. ❖

---

1 a sloping roof
2 things that are not harmonious
3 river in Southwest Asia
4 grassland of southern Africa

From *Lil' Yokohama*

by Toshio Mori

In Lil' Yokohama, as the youngsters call our community, we have twenty-four hours every day . . . and morning, noon, and night roll on regularly just as in Boston, Cincinnati, Birmingham, Kansas City, Minneapolis, and Emeryville.

When the sun is out, the housewives sit on the porch or walk around the yard, puttering with this and that, and the old men who are in the house when it is cloudy or raining come out on the porch or sit in the shade and read the newspaper. The day is hot. All right, they like it. The day is cold. All right, all right. The people of Lil' Yokohama are here. *Here, here,* they cry with their presence just as the youngsters when the teachers call the roll. And when the people among people are sometimes missing from Lil' Yokohama's roll, perhaps forever, it is another matter; but the news belongs here just as does the weather.

Today young and old are at the Alameda ball grounds to see the big game: Alameda Taiiku *vs.* San Jose Asahis. The great Northern California game is under way. Will Slugger Hironaka hit that southpaw from San Jose? Will the same southpaw make the Alameda sluggers stand on their heads? It's the great question. . . .

It is Sunday evening in Lil' Yokohama, and the late dinners commence. Someone who did not go to the game asks, "Who won today?" "San Jose," we say. "Oh, gee," he says. "But Slugger knocked another home run," we say. "What again? He sure is good!" he says. "Big league scouts ought to size him up." "Sure," we say.

Tomorrow is a school day, tomorrow is a work day, tomorrow is another twenty-four hours. In Lil' Yokohama night is almost over. On Sunday nights the block is peaceful and quiet. . . .

Something is happening to the Etos of the block. All of a sudden they turn in their old '30 Chevrolet for a new Oldsmobile Eight! They follow this with a new living-room set and a radio and a new coat of paint for the house. On Sundays the whole family goes for an outing. Sometimes it is to Fleishhacker Pool or to Santa Cruz. It may be to Golden Gate Park or to the ocean or to their relatives in the country. . . . They did not strike oil or win the sweepstakes. Nothing of the kind happens in Lil' Yokohama, though it may any day. . . . What then? ❖

THINKING AND WRITING ABOUT LITERATURE

1. What features of the city does Claude McKay describe? Why do you think he wants the moon to shine somewhere else?
2. What are the three things Jean Toomer wishes city dwellers to aspire to?
3. How does Sinclair Lewis describe Zenith's buildings? What do you think he means to show by contrasting the old and new buildings?
4. Why does Toshio Mori describe the daily activities of the Japanese American neighborhood of Lil' Yokohama?

Strategies for Success

RECOGNIZING PROPAGANDA

Propaganda is a form of mass communication designed to sway people's attitudes and actions. It appeals primarily to emotion, not reason, using language, symbols, and images. Propaganda is favored by totalitarian regimes, which use it to control the hearts and minds of their people. But propaganda is not always used for sinister purposes. Democracies employ propaganda to discredit their enemies and to gain citizen support for particular policies. Special-interest groups use it in lobbying for or against legislation, and politicians use it in campaigning for election. The following techniques are often used in propaganda:

- **Card-stacking** means presenting just one side of a story. Examples include the selective use of statistics and the parading of opinion as fact.
- **Name-calling** is attaching offensive labels to opponents to cast them in a negative light.
- **Sloganeering** is repetition of catchy, but often empty, statements instead of real arguments.
- **Bandwagon** involves begging support for a cause merely because it is popular. This technique relies on peer pressure to conform.
- **Endorsements** are testimonials by famous people who urge support of a cause. Propagandists hope that people will transfer their liking or respect for the celebrity to the cause.

How to Recognize Propaganda

1. **Look, listen, and read carefully.** Analyze the message being conveyed, noting the use of emotionally charged words. Also examine any imagery: propaganda can be visual.
2. **Recognize the technique used.** Identify the technique being employed (such as card-stacking or name-calling).
3. **Consider the purpose.** Ask yourself: Who is sending the message and why? Decide who is its intended audience and what reaction it is meant to provoke.

Applying the Strategy

During World War II the U.S. government used propaganda techniques to build support for the war. For example, patriotic posters used emotional appeals to encourage people to buy war bonds. The World War II poster in the next column pictures a women with her children. The picture and the words "I gave a man!" are meant to play on workers' emotions and to make them feel guilty if they do not buy war bonds.

The government also used propaganda techniques to recruit women for the nation's defense industry, sounding the theme that "it's a woman's war, too." A government brochure of the time, which used the bandwagon approach and one-sided descriptions of factory labor, read: "Millions of women find war work pleasant and as easy as running a sewing machine, or using a vacuum cleaner."

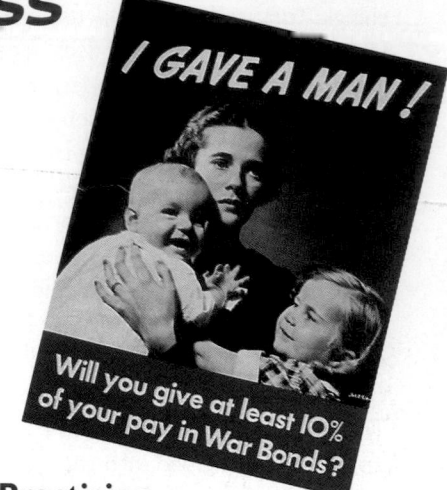

I GAVE A MAN !

Will you give at least 10% of your pay in War Bonds?

Practicing the Strategy

Read the statement below, made in 1927 by Joseph Goebbels (who later became Hitler's propaganda minister) in commemoration of the German soldiers who died in World War I. Then, on a separate sheet of paper, answer the questions that follow.

> **66** We think of the two million who grow pale in the graves of Flanders and Poland. . . . We think of . . . all those who gave their lives upon the altar of the future so that Germany might be established again. . . . Retaliation! Retaliation! The day is dawning! . . . We greet you, dead ones. Germany is beginning to glow anew in the dawn of your blood. . . . Let sound the march-beat . . . for freedom! The army of the dead marches with you, you storm troop soldiers, into a better future. **99**

1. What is the message of the excerpt? At whom is it aimed?
2. What clues identify this passage as propaganda?

BUILDING YOUR PORTFOLIO

Outlined below are four projects. Independently or cooperatively, complete one and use the products to demonstrate your mastery of the historical concepts involved.

1 THE ECONOMY
The excesses of the 1920s helped trigger the Great Depression. The federal government attempted to get the economy moving through the New Deal. Using the portfolio materials you designed in chapters 21, 22, 23, and 24, create a mural that depicts the economic trends between 1920 and 1940. Your mural might portray the effects of unemployment, consumerism, the depression, or the New Deal.

2 CULTURE AND SOCIETY
American society changed rapidly from the 1920s to the 1940s. Using the portfolio materials you designed in chapters 21, 22, 24, and 26, create a radio program that highlights the issues of the period. Shows might include news of the day, a jazz presentation from the 1920s, a book review from the 1930s, or an interview with women workers from the 1940s.

3 GLOBAL RELATIONS
The world experienced severe economic, political, and social unrest in the years leading up to World War II. Using the portfolio materials you designed in chapters 23, 25, and 26, conduct a debate with representatives from several nations about global relations after World War II. Debates should center around the issue of how the United States should respond in the future to the rise of dictators in other parts of the world.

4 WAR
World War II brought tragedy to millions of people around the world. Using the portfolio materials you designed in chapters 25 and 26, create a design for a war memorial to the victims of World War II. Memorials might commemorate soldiers, prisoners of war, victims of the Holocaust, or civilians killed in the war.

Videodisc Review

In assigned groups, develop an outline for a video collage of American life in the years between 1920 and 1945. Choose images that best illustrate the major topics of the period. Write a script to accompany the images. Assign narrators to different parts of the script, and present your video collage to the class.

Further Reading

Anderson, Jervis. *This Was Harlem: A Cultural Portrait, 1900–1950.* Farrar Straus Giroux (1993). Story of Harlem in the first half of the 20th century.

Berenbaum, Michael. *The World Must Know: The History of the Holocaust as Told in the United States Holocaust Memorial Museum.* Little, Brown (1993). Pictorial and eyewitness history of the Holocaust.

Cohen, Stan. *V for Victory:* Pictorial Histories (1991). Overview of the effect of World War II on Americans on the home front.

Cook, Haruko Taya, and Theodore F. Cook. *Japan at War.* New Press (1992). Accounts of war's effect on the Japanese .

McElvaine, Robert S. *The Great Depression: America, 1929–1941.* Times Books (1984). Overview of the Great Depression.

American ALMANAC

Between 1946 and 1964 the U.S. experiences a "baby boom"—about 76 million babies are born!

❖ The American People

BABY BOOM

Live Births (millions)

4.5
3.5
2.5
1.5
.5

1935   1945   1955   1965   1975

Year

Sources: *Historical Statistics of the United States; Statistical Abstracts of the United States.*

❖ America's Music

1949 Frank Sinatra's "New York, New York" is a smash hit.

1954 Elvis Presley releases his first record.

1958 Ritchie Valens—"the father of Latin/Chicano rock"—releases "La Bamba."

1963 At age 13 Stevie Wonder has his first hit—"Fingertips."

1964 The Beatles lead the British invasion.

1967 Aretha Franklin earns "Respect" with her #1 hit.

1970 The Jackson 5 release "ABC"—11-year-old Michael sings lead.

❖ In Style

In the 1960s women pile their hair high and spray it until it's stiff, resembling a "beehive."

In 1965 the miniskirt is all the rage!

The Afro, a hairstyle first worn by African Americans, is popular in the 1960s.

In the late 1960s and early 1970s hippie styles are "in"—peace signs, tie-dye, bangles, beads, and headbands.

Aretha Franklin ▶

❖ TV Generation

In 1945 less than 1% of American homes have a TV set; by 1975 this figure soars to 99.9%!

The Beatles ▼

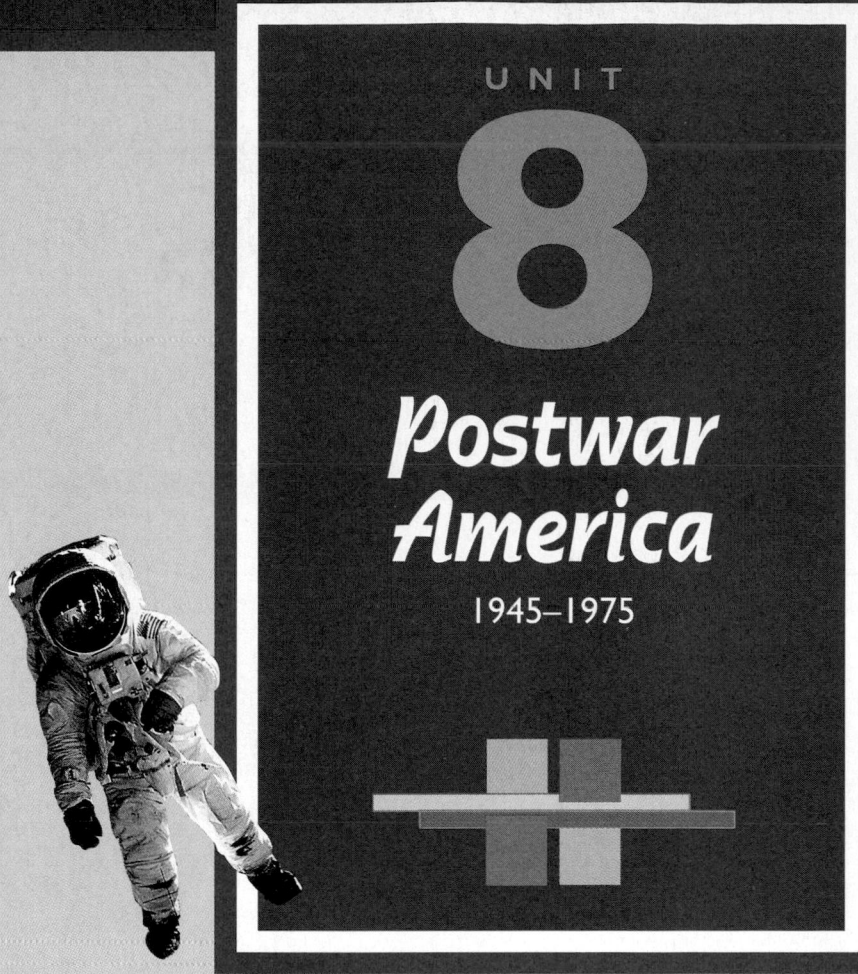

UNIT

8

Postwar America

1945–1975

❖ The Sporting Life

1947 Jackie Robinson signs on with Brooklyn Dodgers to become first African American in the majors.

1953 Maureen "Little Mo" Connolly becomes first woman to win tennis's Grand Slam.

1967 Football's first Super Bowl kicks off.

1972 Mark Spitz wins 7 Olympic gold medals in Munich.

1973 Nolan Ryan sets season strikeout record—383!

❖ Firsts on Earth and in Space

1945 First atom bomb is exploded.

1951 UNIVAC I, first mass-produced computer, is developed.

1953 James Watson and Francis Crick discover DNA.

1955 Dr. Jonas Salk announces successful polio vaccine.

1957 Soviets launch first satellite—*Sputnik I*—U.S. calls for increased math and science education.

1959 Daniel Inouye is first Japanese American and Hiram L. Fong is first Chinese American to serve in Congress; both represent Hawaii.

1962 Rachel Carson's *Silent Spring* helps launch the environmental movement.

1967 Amana introduces first home microwave.

1969 Neil Armstrong is first person to walk on the moon.

❖ The Shrinking Dollar

A pair of jeans costs $3.65 in 1955—by 1975 a pair costs $11.25.

A 16 oz. loaf of white bread in 1960 costs an average of 20.3¢.

▲ **Jackie Robinson**

◄ **Daniel Inouye**

THE POSTWAR YEARS

FOCUS

UNDERSTANDING THE MAIN IDEA

After World War II many nations struggled to rebuild their war-torn economies. In the United States, wartime production led to a postwar boom. On the international front, however, tensions between the United States and the Soviet Union grew. In 1950, in the midst of the increasing threat of nuclear disaster, the Korean War erupted.

THEMES

- **GLOBAL RELATIONS** What international and domestic problems might a rivalry between two powerful nations create?

- **TECHNOLOGY AND SOCIETY** How might a society respond to the development of a potentially destructive technology?

- **DEMOCRATIC VALUES** How might individuals be affected by a government's limitation of civil liberties?

1945	1947	1948	1950	1952
Nuremberg trials begin.	Truman Doctrine proposed.	Racial discrimination banned in military and in federal hiring.	North Korea invades South Korea.	U.S. occupation of Japan ends.

The Churchill-Roosevelt Atlantic Charter of 1941 had called for a free world in which all nations were able to choose their own governments. The agreement, however, did not end imperialism. It took World War II to end Japanese imperialism in Asia and to weaken European colonialism in Asia, Africa, and the Middle East.

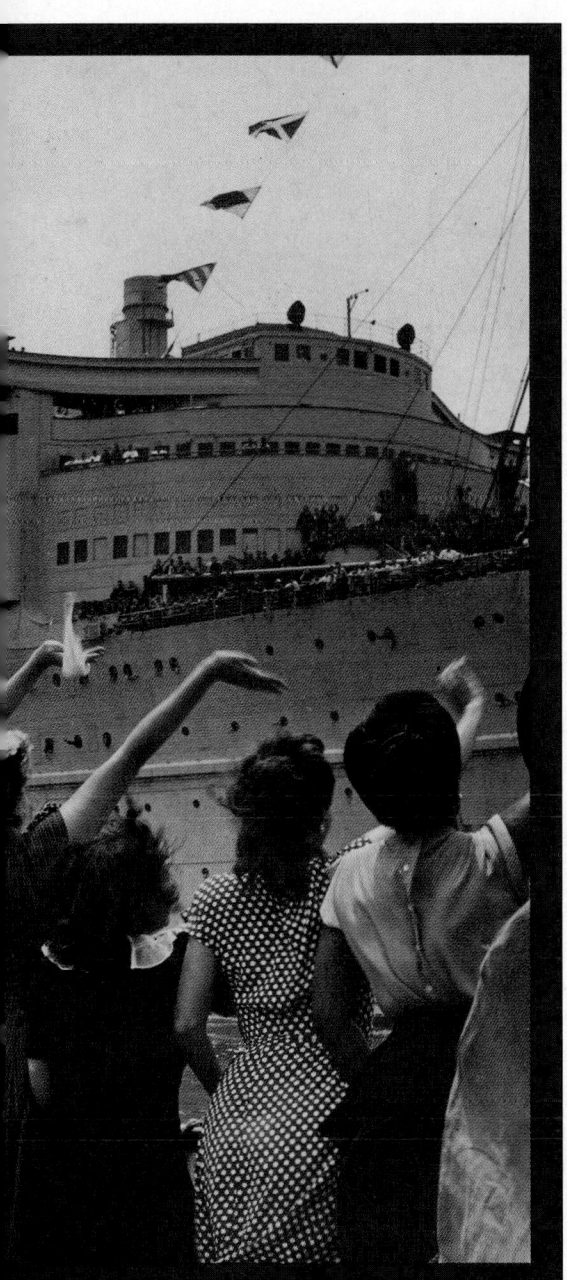

Returning U.S. soldiers, 1946

𝒯he United States emerged from World War II a world power. Americans realized, however, that with this new role came new challenges. Praising the "brave millions [of soldiers] homeward bound," General Douglas MacArthur in September 1945 urged all Americans "to preserve in peace what we won in war."

In their fight against fascism, American soldiers had helped liberate the surviving victims of Nazi concentration camps. Leon Bass, an African American soldier, believed that the Nazi death camps and the Holocaust had important lessons to teach Americans: "If this could happen [in Germany], it could happen anywhere. It could happen to me. It could happen to black folks in America." Horrified by the Holocaust and inspired by their advances during the war, many African Americans took up the fight for civil rights with increased energy.

The lessons learned from World War II, however, proved difficult to put into practice because of postwar economic chaos and the threat of an all-out nuclear war between the United States and the Soviet Union. Despite the creation of a new international organization to promote peace, Soviet-American tensions escalated and new conflicts broke out. By 1950 the United States was involved in yet another war, this time in Korea.

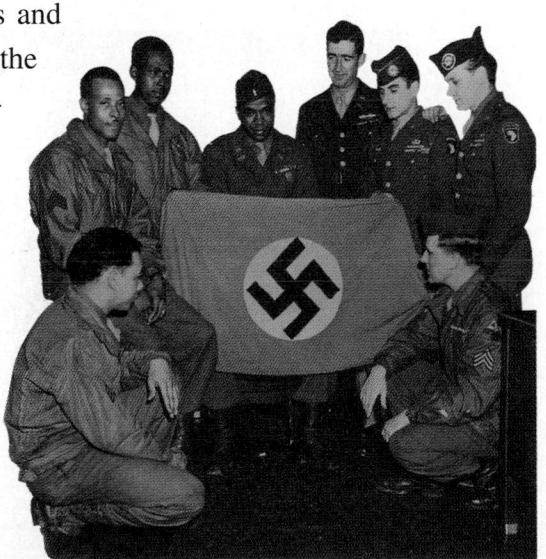

Soldiers with captured Nazi flag

HEALING THE WOUNDS OF WAR

FOCUS

■ How were Germany and Japan governed after the war?

■ What did the war crimes trials accomplish?

■ Why was the United Nations founded?

Many Americans gained confidence from the Allied victory. "The war and the victory showed us what we could do in the world," summed up Melville Grosvenor, a magazine editor. Americans now realized that the United States had to take a leading role in the world. One urgent task was dealing with the human suffering and political chaos resulting from the war. The United States worked with the other Allies to restore peace by occupying Germany and Japan and by creating a new international organization, the United Nations.

UN flag

OCCUPATION RULE

After the war Germany and Japan lay in ruins, their wartime governments shattered. A German actress, Hildegard Knef, described a German town "without houses, without windowpanes, without roofs; holes

Allied Occupation Zones, 1945

in the asphalt, rubble, rubbish, rats." An American GI noted that in the area around Tokyo "there was practically nothing left; the rubble did not even look like much." A Japanese American soldier remarked of the devastation: "Tokyo was all flattened, and people were living in holes with corrugated roofs. They were desperate for food." With the fighting over, Germany and Japan now faced the task of rebuilding their governments, economies, and cities under the watchful eyes of the Allies.

The occupation of Germany. The first overseas conference that President Harry S. Truman attended after Roosevelt's death—the **Potsdam Conference** in July 1945—laid the foundation for Germany's postwar status. Truman, Churchill (later replaced by new prime minister Clement Attlee), and Stalin met in Potsdam, Germany, to approve the details of their joint occupation of Germany. The leaders divided Germany into four occupation zones. The British, the French, and the Americans each took control of a zone in the western, industrialized part of Germany. The Soviets agreed to control the poorer,

▲ This 1946 photograph shows Emperor Hirohito (top) in the Japanese Diet, or legislature, in Tokyo. Hirohito unveiled the new constitution and announced the transfer of his power to the Japanese people and the abolition of the armed forces.

more rural, eastern zone. The four powers also set up occupation zones in Austria and agreed to administer jointly the city of Berlin.

In order to bring stability to the German zones, the occupying powers pledged to crush the Nazi party, reestablish local governments, and rebuild German industry. In addition, the Allies agreed to resettle German refugees.

The conference attendees recognized that the joint occupation of Germany would require cooperation. However, Soviet occupation of much of Eastern Europe created tensions among the Allies. Stalin demanded that the Allies recognize Soviet-backed Poland's claims to German territory it had occupied during the war. The other Allies reluctantly agreed but grew increasingly concerned about Soviet expansion in Eastern Europe. Another source of tension was the Soviet Union's demand for immediate reparations from Germany.

The occupation of Japan. Postwar Japan also faced incredible challenges in its attempts to rebuild. Its economy was in shambles, and Hiroshima and Nagasaki had been devastated by atom bombs. The United States administered

defeated Japan, occupying the island nation from 1945 to 1952.

In addition to helping rebuild the Japanese economy, the United States worked to end Japanese militarism and to create a democratic government. During the occupation Emperor Hirohito remained in the imperial palace, but he became merely a figurehead. Supreme Commander Douglas MacArthur, his staff, and the new Japanese congress ran the country.

Under MacArthur's direction, Japan demobilized more than five million troops and adopted a new constitution in 1947. The constitution set up a democratic system of government, which extended voting rights to women and established separation of church and state. The constitution abolished the Japanese army and navy and prohibited Japan from ever again becoming a military power. Although the constitution bore the clear stamp of American influence, it won support from the Japanese people.

The Japanese also undertook important economic reforms in this period. One program transferred land to Japanese farmers. The government also allowed labor unions to organize and broke up the *zaibatsu*, the huge corporations run by single families that had monopolized the Japanese economy. These political and economic reforms laid the foundation for Japan's tremendous economic recovery after the war.

■■ **After World War II the Allies occupied Germany and Japan and set up new governments in these countries.**

ᴛHE WAR CRIMES TRIALS

After the war the Allies also addressed the issue of war crimes. All agreed that convicted German war criminals had to be punished for starting the war and for the Holocaust. By the same token, Japanese war criminals were to be punished for the mistreatment of prisoners of war and for other atrocities committed in Bataan and China.

The German war crimes trials—known as the **Nuremberg trials** because they took place in Nuremberg, the former meeting place of Hitler's Nazi party—began in November 1945. Before an international military tribunal, witnesses gave chilling accounts of Nazi atrocities, including the torture and murder of millions of Jews, Gypsies,

▲ Allied judges at the Nuremberg trials brought German war criminals to justice. Hermann Göring, commander of the German air force during the war, is shown on the witness stand on May 13, 1946. He later committed suicide in jail.

and others. Marie Vaillant, a concentration camp survivor, testified:

> 66 For months, for years we had one wish only: the wish that some of us would escape alive, in order to tell the world what the Nazi convict prisons were like. . . . There was the systematic . . . urge to use human beings as slaves and to kill them when they could work no more. 99

In September 1946 the tribunal announced its first verdicts. The court had tried 21 Nazi leaders on four charges: planning the war, committing war crimes, committing other crimes against humanity, and conspiring to commit the crimes. Eleven Nazi leaders were sentenced to death; seven received jail sentences; and three were acquitted.

In other trials held in the U.S. occupation zone, thousands of former Nazi officials were tried and jailed, fined, or barred from public office. However, many Nazis—including Adolf Eichmann, the architect of the Jewish extermination program; Josef Mengele (MENG-ge-luh), Auschwitz's "Angel of Death"; and Klaus Barbie, known as the "Butcher of Lyons" for his cruel acts in that French city— escaped immediate prosecution by concealing their identities and fleeing to Latin America.

In the Tokyo war crimes trials, an international tribunal tried more than 20 war leaders. Seven were sentenced to death, including Hideki Tōjō, the wartime premier.

Many Americans, shocked by the evidence of war crimes, argued that more German and Japanese officials should have been punished. Nevertheless, the judges observed legal procedures and tried to avoid acting vengefully. In fact, the trials did set important precedents for international law and the conduct of war. The chief lesson was that nations and individuals can be held accountable for their actions during war. Many countries now accept the principle that war crimes cannot be excused on the grounds that those responsible were "just following orders."

▪▪ War crimes trials in Germany and Japan established the principle of individual responsibility for wartime conduct.

THE UNITED NATIONS

During the war, the Allies had met several times to map out strategies to defeat the Axis Powers. In

DECISION–MAKING BODIES OF THE UNITED NATIONS

Body	Function
General Assembly	Sets policies.
Security Council	Resolves diplomatic, military, and political disputes.
Economic and Social Council	Deals with human welfare and fundamental rights and freedoms.
International Court of Justice	Handles international legal disputes.
Trusteeship Council	Supervises territories that are not independent.
Secretariat	Performs routine administrative work of the UN.

Sources: *Encyclopedia of American History; Funk & Wagnalls New Encyclopedia*

MULTICULTURAL COOPERATION The United Nations was established in order to give every member nation a voice in international affairs. The General Assembly includes over 150 countries and uses five official languages—English, Russian, French, Spanish, and Chinese.

? **ANALYZING** Which body of the United Nations is responsible for monitoring military aggressions between nations?

1944, delegates from the United States, Great Britain, the Soviet Union, and China met at Dumbarton Oaks, an estate in Washington, D.C. There they worked out a proposal for a postwar international organization called the **United Nations** (UN). Through the UN, the Allies hoped to continue their alliance by working together to promote world peace.

In April 1945, delegates from 50 nations met in San Francisco to draw up the Charter of the United Nations. The delegates took just eight weeks to write the document. The charter established six bodies: (1) the General Assembly in which all countries shape policy, (2) the Security Council to address military and political problems, (3) the Economic and Social Council, (4) the International Court of Justice, (5) the Trusteeship Council to administer territories, and (6) the Secretariat—headed by the secretary-general—to administer the UN. As permanent members of the Security Council, the United States, the Soviet Union, Great Britain, France, or China could veto any action the UN proposed.

Soon afterward, the Senate overwhelmingly approved American membership in the UN. More than 60 percent of Americans approved of U.S. membership. On October 24, now observed as United Nations Day, the UN officially came into existence when the 29th country approved the UN charter. The UN established its headquarters in New York City. Trygve Lie (TRIG-vuh LEE) of Norway served as the UN's first secretary-general.

From the outset, UN delegates realized that building world peace required both diplomatic and economic cooperation. Eleanor Roosevelt, who, as a U.S. representative to the UN helped shape the Universal Declaration of Human Rights, explained:

▲ **Eleanor Roosevelt chaired the UN Human Rights Commission from 1946 to 1951. She helped draft the Universal Declaration of Human Rights in 1948.**

66 Security requires both control of the use of force and the elimination of want. No people are secure unless they have the things needed not only to preserve existence, but to make life worth living. . . . All peoples throughout the world must know that there is an organization where their interests can be considered and where justice and security will be sought for all. 99

Early critics of the UN insisted that it was doomed to fail because it had no real power to enforce its own decisions. Nevertheless, most Americans were as optimistic as President Truman, who noted in 1945: "This charter points down the only road to enduring peace. There is no other."

■■ **The United Nations was founded to promote peaceful cooperation among the nations of the world.**

SECTION 1 REVIEW

IDENTIFY and explain the significance of the following: Potsdam Conference, *zaibatsu,* Nuremberg trials, Adolf Eichmann, Josef Mengele, Klaus Barbie, Hideki Tōjō, United Nations, Trygve Lie, Eleanor Roosevelt.

1. **MAIN IDEA** What principle did the war crimes trials in Germany and Japan establish?

2. **MAIN IDEA** What was the purpose of the United Nations?

3. **COMPARING** How did the Allied powers govern Germany and Japan after World War II?

4. **WRITING TO DESCRIBE** Imagine you are a Japanese American soldier in Tokyo in 1946. Write a letter home that describes conditions in Japan after the war.

5. **ANALYZING** Why do you think the United Nations deals with economic and social issues in addition to its peacekeeping efforts?

THE CHALLENGES OF PEACE

FOCUS

- How did the American economy fare after the war?
- How did the Taft-Hartley Act affect unions?
- What were the most important issues in the 1948 election?

During the difficult transition from war to peace, Americans were apprehensive. Returning veterans were "worried sick about post-war joblessness," according to Fortune *magazine. Many African American, Mexican American, and women workers feared they would lose the economic gains they had made during the war.*

Homecoming, 1945

THE PROBLEMS OF DEMOBILIZATION

At war's end, troop ships headed home. By mid-1946 over nine million servicemen and women had been discharged. The troops received a hero's welcome, but their return also sparked concern. Could the economy absorb all these new workers? The government soon cancelled $23 billion in military contracts, hitting hard the shipyards, munitions factories, aircraft plants, and military bases.

Postwar measures. To prevent a depression and to help war-weary veterans make the difficult transition to civilian life, Congress passed the Servicemen's Readjustment Act of 1944, commonly known as the **GI Bill of Rights**. The act provided pensions and government loans to help veterans start businesses and buy homes or farms. Under the GI Bill, thousands of veterans also received money for tuition, books, and living expenses while they attended college.

▶ Under the GI Bill, many veterans received financial aid to pursue a college education or industrial training. Howard Timian of Milwaukee is shown here studying for an engineering course.

To ensure economic growth, Congress also passed the **Employment Act** of 1946. The act promised that the government would promote full employment and production. It also established the **Council of Economic Advisers** to counsel the president on economic policy.

Despite widespread fears, the postwar depression never materialized. Employment remained high, as plants that had been making tanks and bombers began to produce consumer goods. With world agricultural output shattered by the war, U.S. food exports also remained high. In addition, Americans now began spending the money they had saved from their wartime paychecks.

▲ A. Philip Randolph and Eleanor Roosevelt are shown here at a 1946 rally at Madison Square Garden to save the Fair Employment Practices Committee. Congress later abolished the committee.

Not all was rosy on the economic front, however. Government measures encouraged employers to give priority in hiring to veterans. The fears of many women, African Americans, and Mexican Americans were realized as they lost their jobs to returning veterans. During the war these workers had been encouraged to take jobs in vital defense factories. African Americans had been protected from job discrimination by the Fair Employment Practices Committee. Soon after the war, however, Congress abolished the committee.

Many workers were also hit hard by inflation. With the lifting of most wartime price controls in 1946, prices soared. Meat prices went so high that some markets began selling horsemeat. Blaming the Truman administration, angry consumers called the president "Horsemeat Harry."

■■ Despite fears of a depression, the American economy prospered after the war, though inflation hurt many workers.

Labor unrest. As inflation worsened, workers took matters into their own hands. Workers who had sacrificed during the depression and the war now craved a better standard of living. Freed of their wartime no-strike pledge, millions of workers walked off the job to win wage increases and to preserve some wartime price controls. In 1946—the most strike-filled year in U.S. history after 1919— almost five million workers walked the picket lines.

President Truman, though a backer of labor unions, opposed these strikes because he feared they would disrupt the economy. In April 1946, when some 400,000 coal miners went on strike, Truman ordered the army to establish government

control of the mines. United Mine Workers' president John L. Lewis responded: "You can't dig coal with bayonets." After the courts slapped heavy fines on the union, though, Lewis ordered the miners back to work. When confronted with striking railway workers, Truman threatened to end the strike by drafting the strikers into the army. Union leaders, however, negotiated an end to the strike without resorting to the draft.

To prevent further strikes, Congress—under Republican control since the 1946 elections— passed an antiunion bill in 1947. This law, known as the **Taft-Hartley Act**, allowed courts to end strikes, outlawed closed-shop agreements (which required union membership for employment), restricted unions' political contributions, and required union officers to swear they were not Communists. President Truman vetoed the bill, but Congress passed it over his veto.

The Taft-Hartley Act stirred angry debate. Conservative supporters argued that the law corrected unfair advantages granted to labor in the Wagner-Connery Act (see Chapter 24). Prolabor opponents denounced it as a "slave labor law."

The act limited the tactics unions could use. Despite these restrictions, however, organized labor continued to make some gains in the postwar years. For example, in 1948 General Motors and the United Automobile Workers (UAW) signed a contract tying wage increases to cost-of-living increases. Union contracts also began to include provisions for such benefits as retirement pensions and health insurance.

■■ The Taft-Hartley Act placed a variety of restrictions on labor unions.

◀ The cartoon *Three Men on a Horse* appeared on February 24, 1953. Union leaders John L. Lewis, Walter Reuther, and George Meany opposed the Taft-Hartley Act's restrictions on labor unions.

THE 1948 ELECTION

By 1948 inflation, high taxes, and labor unrest had eroded public support for Truman. His approval rating stood at 35 percent in March, down from 60 percent the previous year. "To err is Truman," people joked. But Truman was determined to prove his critics wrong. His stand on civil rights for African Americans proved to be an important issue in the 1948 campaign.

The Committee on Civil Rights. In 1946 African American civil rights groups urged Truman to take action against the racism that stained American society. They pointed out that most African Americans in the South were prevented from voting through the use of poll taxes.

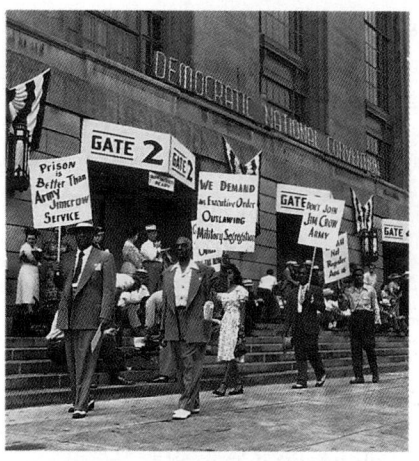

▲ Shown here are African American demonstrators outside the convention hall at the 1948 Democratic Convention in Philadelphia.

Blacks throughout the nation faced segregation in schools and buses and discrimination in housing and employment. And in many areas African Americans continued to be lynched, a crime that few local courts ever prosecuted. Efforts to battle these conditions met a wall of white resistance.

In December 1946 Truman, distressed by these reports, set up the **Committee on Civil Rights** to examine the issue. The committee's 15 members included African American lawyer Sadie Alexander; Dr. Channing Tobias, director of the Phelps-Stokes Fund, which supported educational opportunities for African Americans; General Electric's president Charles Wilson; and Franklin Roosevelt, Jr.

The committee issued its report, entitled "To Secure These Rights," in October 1947. The report documented widespread civil rights abuses, including discrimination against black veterans and an increase in Ku Klux Klan violence. The committee urged the government to pass an antilynching law and an anti-poll-tax measure and to end discrimination in federal agencies and the military. The report also called for an end to racial segregation in interstate transportation.

When Truman did not immediately act on the report's recommendations, African American leader A. Philip Randolph threatened to launch a campaign of civil disobedience if the military remained segregated. The tactic worked. In July 1948 Truman issued executive orders banning racial discrimination in the military and in federal hiring. He also took steps to end employment discrimination by companies working under government contracts.

White southern Democrats were outraged at African American demands for civil rights and at Truman's actions. Senator Olin Johnston of South Carolina angrily explained that the South's electoral votes "won't be for Truman. They'll be for somebody else. He ain't going to be re-elected."

The Democratic convention. Despite Senator Johnston's bluster, southern opposition did not prevent Truman from being nominated at the Democratic convention in July. Senator Alben W. Barkley of Kentucky was selected to be Truman's running mate. The Democrats hoped to appeal to the former New Deal coalition of farmers, unionized workers, big-city ethnic groups, and African Americans. The Democratic platform called for repeal of the Taft-Hartley Act; an increase in federal aid for housing, education, and agriculture; and broader social security benefits. It also included a strong civil rights plank.

The civil rights issue split the Democratic party. Southern delegates threatened to walk out of the convention. Declaring "LET 'EM WALK," the NAACP argued:

66 There is no room . . . for compromise. . . . Those Democrats who say the

▼ Due to Truman's poor showing in public-opinion polls during the 1948 campaign, the *Chicago Daily Tribune* published an early election-night edition announcing Dewey as the winner.

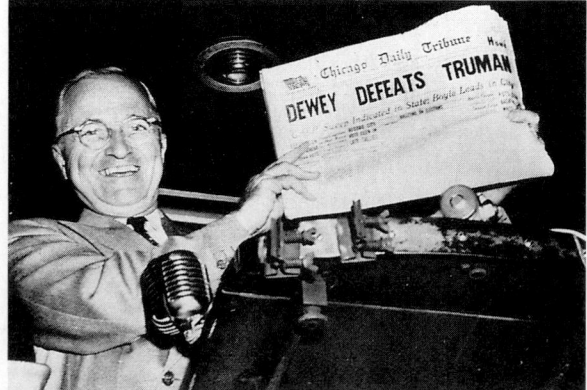

President's recommendation of such a program is a "stab in the back" of the South are saying they do not choose to abide by the Constitution. They are also saying . . . that the whole section of our nation believes as they do. . . . We *know* it is not true! "

After bitter debate the delegates adopted the civil rights plank. Southern delegates stormed out of the convention. They formed the States' Rights party—nicknamed the **Dixiecrats**—which called for continued racial segregation. The Dixiecrats nominated Governor J. Strom Thurmond of South Carolina as their presidential candidate. These explosive divisions were an opening skirmish in a mighty struggle against racism that would soon sweep over the nation.

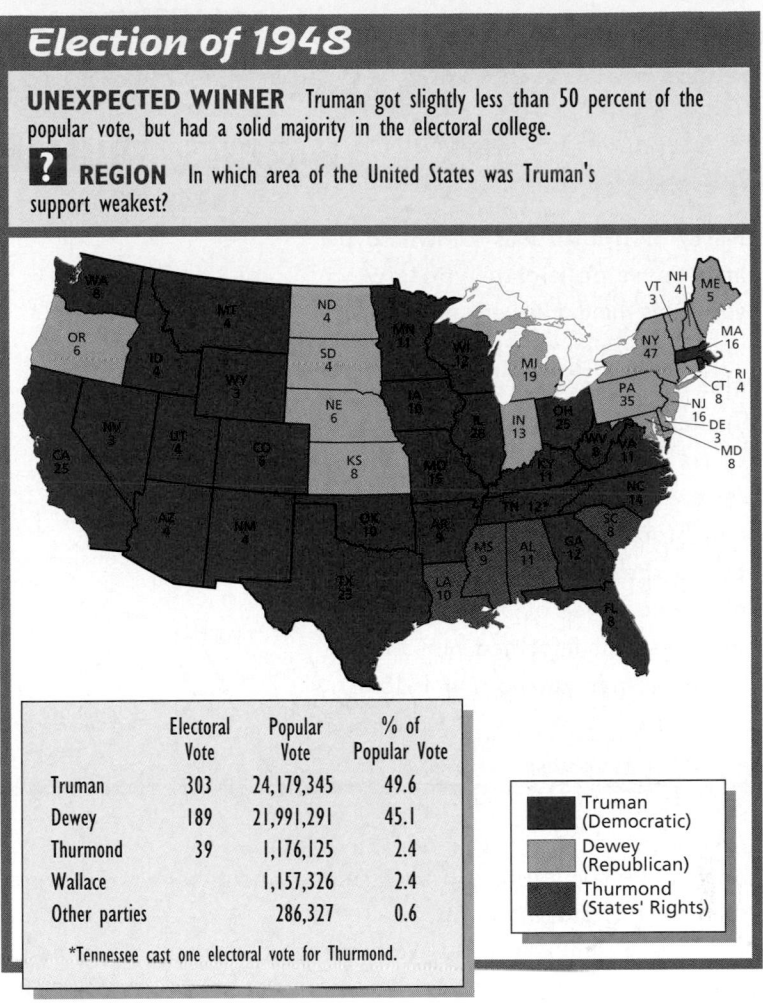

Election of 1948

UNEXPECTED WINNER Truman got slightly less than 50 percent of the popular vote, but had a solid majority in the electoral college.

? **REGION** In which area of the United States was Truman's support weakest?

	Electoral Vote	Popular Vote	% of Popular Vote
Truman	303	24,179,345	49.6
Dewey	189	21,991,291	45.1
Thurmond	39	1,176,125	2.4
Wallace		1,157,326	2.4
Other parties		286,327	0.6

*Tennessee cast one electoral vote for Thurmond.

■ Truman (Democratic)
■ Dewey (Republican)
■ Thurmond (States' Rights)

The race widens. A different issue caused another break within the Democratic party. Troubled by Truman's antilabor actions in 1946, former vice president Henry Wallace and other liberal New Dealers left the Democratic party to found the Progressive party. This group, which was not related to the Progressive party of the early 1900s, called for an extension of the New Deal and for friendly relations with the Soviet Union. The American Communist party supported the Progressive party.

With the Democrats' votes split three ways, the Republicans were confident of victory. They nominated Governor Thomas Dewey of New York as their presidential candidate and Earl Warren, the popular governor of California, as Dewey's running mate. Opinion polls and most newspapers predicted a Dewey victory.

But Truman ran an energetic campaign, attacking the conservatism of the Republicans and the radicalism of the Progressives. As he crisscrossed the country, criticizing the "do-nothing" Republican Congress, crowds began to chant, "Give 'em hell, Harry." In one of the great upsets of U.S. political history, Truman won, gaining 49

percent of the popular vote to Dewey's 45 percent. Black voters helped Truman carry several key states. Workers, farmers, and ethnic voters generally supported Truman, proving that the political coalition that had supported Franklin Roosevelt in the 1930s still held.

■■ **Civil rights and labor issues splintered the Democratic party. Truman, however, ran a tough campaign and won the 1948 election.**

THE FAIR DEAL

Heartened by his victory, Truman urged Congress to continue Roosevelt's New Deal reforms. Proclaiming that "every segment of our population . . . has a right to expect from our government a fair deal," Truman proposed new reforms, which he labeled the **Fair Deal**. Truman's Fair Deal proposed full employment, higher minimum wages, a national health insurance program, affordable

HARRY S. TRUMAN
1884–1972

Harry S. Truman was known to be an honest politician who always spoke his mind. His very direct manner of speaking shocked many people, but impressed others. Once Truman wrote a letter to a music critic who had written a harsh review of a recital by the president's daughter Margaret. In addition to calling the critic "a frustrated old man who never made a success," the president informed him that "I never met you, but if I do

Harry S. Truman

U.S. Postage 8 cents

you'll need a new nose." While some considered this response inappropriate, public opinion strongly supported Truman's defense of his daughter.

While Truman was quick to defend his family and others, he often downplayed his own abilities as president. Many years after he left office he told an interviewer, "I wasn't one of the great Presidents; but I had a good time trying to be one."

---

housing construction, aid to farmers, and the expansion of welfare benefits.

Most Republicans, and even conservatives in Truman's own party, opposed the president's program. Nevertheless, Truman managed to push through some of his reforms. Between 1949 and 1952 Congress extended social security benefits to some 10 million more people, raised the minimum wage from 40 to 75 cents an hour, and approved programs to clear slums. Congress also expanded federal programs to promote flood control, hydroelectric power, and irrigation.

Overall, though, the Fair Deal had limited success amid an increasingly conservative postwar political climate. Congress failed to repeal the Taft-Hartley Act or to pass a civil rights bill. Most of the New Dealers had resigned from Truman's cabinet in disappointment, leaving business leaders and military men who did not champion the Fair Deal. These domestic issues also unfolded against the backdrop of other pressing concerns that had international implications: conflict with the Soviet Union and almost hysterical fears of communism.

SECTION 2 REVIEW

IDENTIFY and explain the significance of the following: GI Bill of Rights, Employment Act, Council of Economic Advisers, John L. Lewis, Taft-Hartley Act, Committee on Civil Rights, Sadie Alexander, Alben W. Barkley, Dixiecrats, J. Strom Thurmond, Henry Wallace, Thomas Dewey, Fair Deal.

1. **MAIN IDEA** What effect did the end of World War II have on the U.S. economy?

2. **MAIN IDEA** What restrictions did the Taft-Hartley Act place on unions?

3. **GAINING A MULTICULTURAL PERSPECTIVE** How did the end of the war affect women, African American, and Mexican American workers?

4. **WRITING TO INFORM** Imagine you are a political correspondent covering the 1948 election. Write a magazine commentary that outlines the most important issues in the campaign.

5. **ANALYZING** What convinced Truman to desegregate the military and to end discrimination in federal jobs?

THE COLD WAR BEGINS

FOCUS

- What caused the Cold War?
- What did the United States hope to accomplish through the Marshall Plan?
- What effects did the Cold War have on American society?

*S*oon after World War II, the wartime alliance between the United States and the Soviet Union collapsed. The two countries, at odds because of competing global objectives and different economic and political systems, fought over control of Europe and access to atomic energy.

Berlin airlift, 1948

THE ROOTS OF THE COLD WAR

An intense rivalry between the United States and the Soviet Union began after World War II. With once-mighty Germany, Japan, and Great Britain in ruins, only the United States and the Soviet Union were left to struggle for international dominance. Their competition for global power and influence, which came to be known as the **Cold War**, was waged mostly on political and economic fronts rather than on the battlefield. Nevertheless, the threat of all-out war was always present.

The origins of the Cold War lay in the economic and political differences between the two nations and in each country's perception of the other. Most Americans opposed the foundations of the Soviet state: a state-controlled economy, one-party rule, suppression of religion, and the use of force to crush opposition. The Soviets, on the other hand, criticized American imperialism, racial discrimination, and the treatment of workers. Nikolai Novikov, the Soviet ambassador to the United States, expressed distrust of American international aims:

66 The foreign policy of the United States . . . is characterized in the postwar period by a striving for world supremacy. . . . Broad plans for expansion have been developed and are being implemented through diplomacy and the establishment of a system of naval and air bases . . . [and] through the arms race. **99**

Americans felt the same way about the Soviets. Soviet expansionism after World War II fueled American mistrust. During World War II the Soviets had taken over the Baltic states of Lithuania, Latvia, and Estonia. Then they captured large areas of Poland and Romania. By war's end the Soviets also controlled Manchuria.

After the war, Stalin made clear his determination to maintain Soviet influence in Eastern Europe, claiming the need for a buffer zone of "friendly nations" on the U.S.S.R.'s western border. He stripped eastern Germany of some 40 percent of its industrial equipment, installed pro-Soviet governments in Poland and Romania, and worked to establish Communist rule throughout Eastern Europe. The countries under Soviet control became known as **satellite nations**.

Concerned about Stalin's actions, the United States, Great Britain, and France solidified their control of West Germany and revived its industries. The United States also pressured Stalin to withdraw Soviet forces from Iran, the oil-rich Middle Eastern nation that the Soviets had occupied during the war. In April 1946 Stalin finally agreed to withdraw his troops.

In February of the same year, however, Stalin had made a tough speech—dubbed the "Declaration of World War III" by Supreme Court justice William Douglas—proclaiming that capitalism and communism could never coexist. Winston Churchill, Britain's wartime prime minister, answered Stalin in March with an equally tough speech delivered in Fulton, Missouri. Churchill declared that a Soviet "Iron Curtain has descended across the Continent," isolating Western Europe from Soviet-dominated Eastern Europe. Churchill called for closer cooperation between Great Britain and America to check Soviet power.

Churchill's speech was well received in Washington. At the time, George Kennan, a State Department official and Soviet expert, advised similar action. Kennan argued that the Soviet Union's long-term aim was to defeat capitalism and expand the Soviet sphere of influence. He believed that the Soviets would be persistent, yet cautious, expanding only when there were few risks. Kennan explained how American foreign policy could thus stop the spread of communism:

66 The Soviet pressure against the free institutions of the Western world is something that can be contained by the . . . vigilant application of counterforce at a series of constantly shifting geographical and political points. . . . The Russians look forward to a duel of infinite duration. 99

Kennan's **containment** doctrine, which aimed to contain, or restrict, Soviet expansion, became the basis for U.S. Cold War strategy. Many Americans, unwilling to return to the appeasement policy of the 1930s, applauded Kennan's stand against communism.

■■ The origins of the Cold War lay in U.S.–Soviet global competition, conflicting economic and political systems, and mutual distrust.

ℸHE DEADLOCK OVER ΛTOMIC WEAPONS

The United States and the Soviet Union soon became locked in a dispute over the control of atomic weapons. This standoff terrified many Americans, who feared a nuclear war. Most people shared lawyer David E. Lilienthal's 1946 assessment that "the awful strength of atomic power . . . directly affects every man, woman, and child in the world." Recognizing this fact, the UN early in 1946 created a commission to draw up a plan for the control of nuclear arms.

At the commission's first meeting, U.S. representative Bernard Baruch called for the creation of a special UN agency with the authority to inspect any nation's atomic-energy installations. This proposal, known as the **Baruch Plan**, would impose penalties on countries violating international controls. Until such a plan was in place, Baruch said, the United States would not reveal any atomic-energy secrets or give up its atomic weapons. At the time, American physicists were developing more-powerful nuclear bombs.

Working feverishly on its own bomb, the Soviet Union rejected all inspection and enforcement provisions. With neither country willing to compromise, hopes for international control of

▼ **In July 1946 the United States conducted atomic bomb tests in Bikini Atoll in the western Pacific Ocean. These tests were intended to measure the effects of atomic bombs on warships.**

atomic energy died. When the Soviet Union tested its first atomic bomb in 1949, fears of a nuclear-arms race became reality.

Despite the failure of the Baruch Plan, the United States achieved some success in controlling nuclear weapons. Atomic-energy scientists and U.S. peace organizations, such as the Women's International League for Peace and Freedom, urged the U.S. government to establish civilian, rather than military, control of atomic energy. Responding to these appeals, Congress in August 1946 passed the **Atomic Energy Act**. The act set up the Atomic Energy Commission (AEC) under civilian control to oversee nuclear weapons research and to promote peacetime uses of atomic energy. Its main activity, however, became supporting the government's nuclear weapons program.

Containment Around the World

As prospects for U.S.–Soviet cooperation dimmed, the Truman administration pursued a more aggressive policy toward the Soviet Union. The U.S. containment policy first took shape in Greece, where a civil war had broken out in 1946. Communist-led rebels battled the Greek monarchy, which relied on military and financial support from Great Britain. In early 1947, however, the British announced that they could no longer continue their aid to Greece. Without aid it seemed likely that Greece's pro-Western government would fall to the Communists and the country would come under Soviet control.

Containment in the Mediterranean. At the same time, the Soviet Union pressured Turkey to give up sole control of the Dardanelles, a narrow strait linking the Black Sea and the Mediterranean. President Truman knew that control of this area would give the Soviets a dominant position in the eastern Mediterranean and would threaten the security of the Suez Canal. In a somber speech before Congress on March 12, 1947, Truman declared: "It must be the policy of the United States to support free peoples who are resisting attempted subjugation [conquest] by armed minorities or by outside pressures."

This statement, which became known as the **Truman Doctrine**, made no mention of the Soviet Union, though clearly Truman had devised it with the Soviets in mind. Agreeing with Truman's sentiments, Congress soon voted $400 million to aid Greece and Turkey. This action was only a prelude, however, to the more massive foreign-aid program that soon followed.

Containment in Europe. After World War II, European economies were in shambles. In 1948 Germany produced only 45 percent of the goods it had produced before the war. To make matters worse, the winter of 1946–47 brought the worst blizzards in some 50 years. Starvation and chaos loomed. Some Americans believed that the United States should help Europe. They feared that such desperate economic conditions would make Europe more vulnerable to Soviet influence.

Secretary of State George C. Marshall shared this belief. Born in Uniontown, Pennsylvania, in 1880, Marshall graduated from Virginia Military Institute and joined the army. During World War I he served under General Pershing. As army chief of staff during World War II, he attended the Casablanca, Yalta, and Potsdam conferences.

After the war Marshall served briefly as a U.S. envoy to China before Truman appointed him secretary of state in 1947. In a speech at Harvard University on June 5, 1947, Marshall warned that if steps were not taken soon, Europe faced "economic, social, and political" collapse. He then called for a major U.S. effort to promote European recovery "to permit the emergence of political and social conditions in which free institutions can

George C. Marshall

exist." At the same time, Marshall warned that any attempt to block recovery or exploit Europe's difficulties for political ends would face strong American opposition.

After Marshall's speech, Truman asked Congress for $17 billion in economic aid for Europe. Truman's request sparked heated debate throughout the United States. Supporters argued that such aid would contain communism by restoring Europe's economic health and would help the U.S. economy as Europeans purchased American goods and military hardware. Opponents said the United States could not afford to "carry Europe on its back."

▲ The first cargo of sugar transported under the Marshall Plan is unloaded from the S.S. *Araby* in London in February 1949.

A turning point in the debate came early in 1948, when pro-Soviet Communists overthrew the government of Czechoslovakia. Moved to action by the coup, Congress passed the European Recovery Act, or **Marshall Plan**, in April 1948. The plan, based on Marshall's recommendations, provided some $12 billion in aid to Western Europe over the next four years. For his efforts Marshall won the Nobel Peace Prize in 1953.

■ **The Marshall Plan aimed to contain the spread of communism by easing economic hardship in Europe.**

CRISIS IN BERLIN

The non-Soviet zone of Germany grew stronger as a result of the Marshall Plan. In early June 1948, Great Britain, France, and the United States announced plans to combine their occupation zones and support the formation of a new West German government.

The Berlin airlift. The Soviets, deeply fearful of renewed German

power, opposed this action. On June 24, 1948, the Soviets suddenly blocked all roads, canals, and railways linking Berlin and western Germany, cutting off shipments of food, fuel, and other crucial supplies to the city. The Soviets hoped to drive the Western powers out of Berlin and to delay the formation of a West German government. Berlin had become a pawn in the Cold War chess game.

The British and the Americans responded to the Soviet action with the **Berlin airlift**. Over the next 10 months, U.S. and British planes carried more than two million tons of food and supplies to the people of West Berlin. As one Berliner recalled, the airlift became a lifeline to the rest of the world:

❝ Early in the morning, when we woke up, the first thing we did was listen to see whether the noise of aircraft engines could be heard. That gave us the certainty that we were not alone, that the whole civilized world took part in the fight for Berlin's freedom. ❞

The success of the Berlin airlift proved a huge embarrassment to the Soviet Union. In May

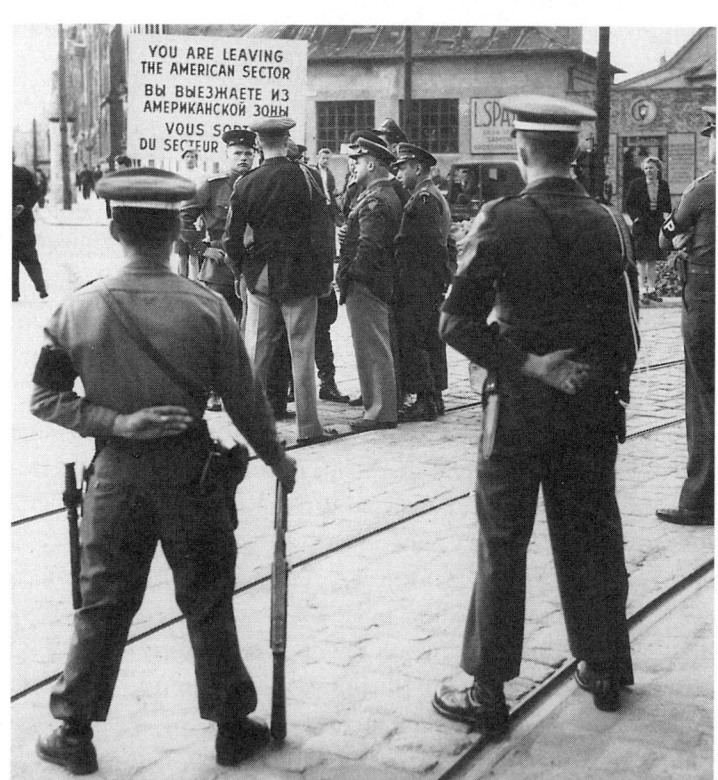

▲ As tensions mounted, American military police in Berlin warily faced their Soviet counterparts across the dividing line between the Allied and Soviet zones.

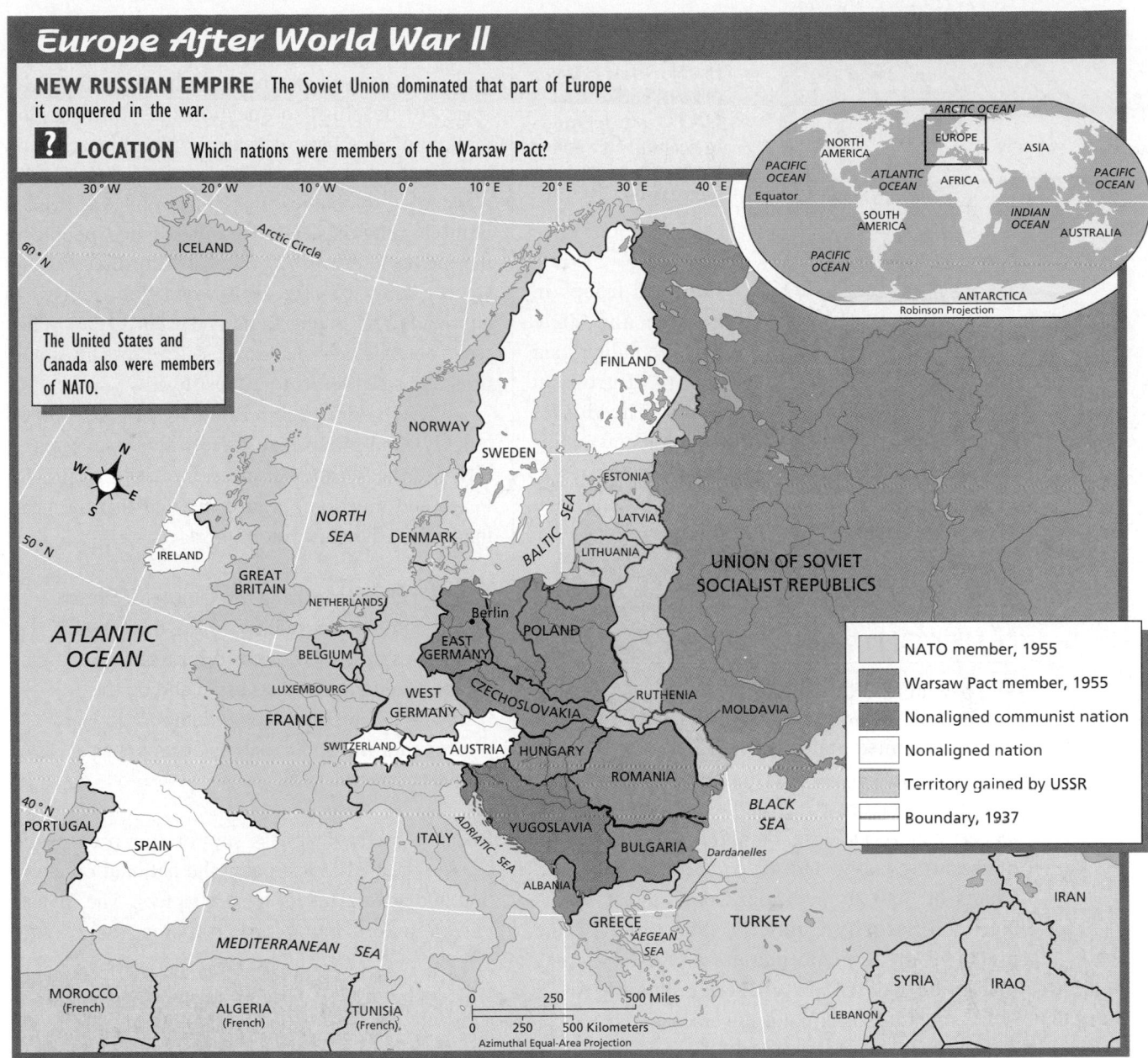

NEW RUSSIAN EMPIRE The Soviet Union dominated that part of Europe it conquered in the war.

? LOCATION Which nations were members of the Warsaw Pact?

The United States and Canada also were members of NATO.

Legend:
- NATO member, 1955
- Warsaw Pact member, 1955
- Nonaligned communist nation
- Nonaligned nation
- Territory gained by USSR
- Boundary, 1937

1949 the Soviets lifted the blockade. On May 9 the Federal Republic of Germany, known as West Germany, was founded. In response, the Soviets set up the German Democratic Republic—East Germany—in the Soviet zone. The division of Germany would last for more than 40 years as a result of Cold War rivalries.

The Western alliance. After the Berlin crisis the United States shifted its attention in Europe from economic recovery to military preparedness. In April 1949 nine Western European nations joined the United States, Canada, and Iceland in a military alliance called the **North Atlantic Treaty Organization**, or NATO.

Under the terms of the NATO treaty, known as the Atlantic Pact, each member nation pledged to defend the others in the event of an outside attack. When Truman submitted the treaty for Senate ratification, debate focused on whether the agreement would allow the United States to go to war without an act of Congress. Concern over this same issue had helped keep the United States out of the League of Nations. This time, however, fear of Soviet expansionism outweighed other concerns. In July 1949 the Senate ratified the treaty.

In 1951 General Dwight D. Eisenhower became the supreme commander of NATO forces. As its contribution to NATO, the United States

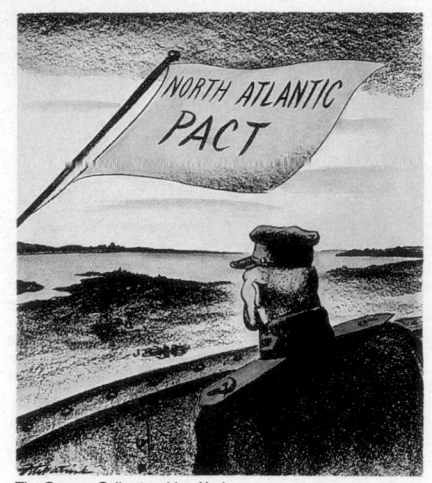

◄ This U.S. cartoon, entitled *Banner of the Non-Soviet Union* (1949), shows that NATO was formed in response to Allied fears of Soviet aggression.

stationed troops in Europe and gave massive military aid to its European allies. The Soviet Union responded in 1955 by forming its own military alliance with other Communist countries in Eastern Europe. This alliance came to be called the **Warsaw Pact**.

THE COLD WAR AT HOME

The Cold War had important consequences within the United States. As a result of Cold War pressures, the United States streamlined its military to allow for peacetime rearmament. In July 1947 Congress replaced the War Department with the Department of Defense, combining the leadership of the army, navy, and air force under the Joint Chiefs of Staff. In addition, Congress set up the **National Security Council** (NSC) to advise the president on strategic matters and established the **Central Intelligence Agency** (CIA) to gather information overseas.

Another Red scare. The Cold War also aroused fears of communism at home. Although Truman opposed communism abroad, some Republicans accused him of allowing Communists in the American government. Responding to such charges, Truman set up the Loyalty Review Board in 1947 to investigate all federal employees. By the end of 1951, more than 20,000 federal workers had been investigated, some 2,000 had resigned, and more than 300 had been fired as "security risks." In most cases the government did not allow dismissed employees to respond to the charges against them.

Meanwhile, Congress cracked down on the Communist party. Leading the anti-Communist crusade in Congress was the House Committee on Un-American Activities (HUAC), originally established in 1938 to investigate anti-American propaganda. HUAC held a series of hearings to question the political allegiances of members of peace organizations, liberal political groups, and labor unions. In 1947, responding to charges that Hollywood was riddled with Communists, HUAC investigated people in the movie industry. A group of film directors and writers, known as the **Hollywood Ten**, refused to answer HUAC's questions and went to jail. They were blacklisted—denied work in the film industry—and saw their careers destroyed.

The hysteria generated by HUAC spread quickly. One group that bravely spoke out against HUAC, the Women's International League for Peace and Freedom, argued in 1949 that the hearings violated democratic rights:

❝ Fully recognizing the danger of fascist and communist totalitarianism, the League believes that such forces can be best opposed by open discussion and by the strengthening of our own democratic procedures, rather than by attempts at direct control. ❞

Because of the league's support for progressive causes, the FBI investigated the national organization and several of its local chapters. The investigation scared many potential members away.

▲ A delegation of Hollywood personalities attended a meeting of HUAC on October 27, 1947. Humphrey Bogart, Lauren Bacall, and Sterling Hayden were among those present.

HUAC investigations had a similar effect on labor unions and many political groups.

The search for spies. HUAC also investigated individuals accused of spying for the Soviets. In 1948 Whittaker Chambers, who had been a member of the Communist party, accused Alger Hiss of being a Communist spy. Chambers told HUAC that Hiss, a New Deal lawyer who had joined the State Department in 1936, had given him secret State Department documents to pass on to the Soviets.

Hiss denied the charges, but persistent questioning by HUAC member Richard Nixon, a young Republican congressman from California, revealed apparent inconsistencies in Hiss's testimony. In 1950 Hiss was convicted of perjury (lying under oath) and sentenced to five years in prison.

Another notorious spy case also helped fuel domestic fears of communism. In 1951 a U.S. court convicted two Americans, Julius and Ethel Rosenberg, of giving the Soviets atomic-energy secrets during World War II. Defenders of the Rosenbergs claimed that the two were innocent victims of anti-Communist hysteria. Despite worldwide protests on their behalf, however, the Rosenbergs were executed in June 1953. Historians have found evidence for the guilty verdict but agree that the death sentences were extreme reactions in the poisonous Cold War climate.

Other anti-Communist measures included the **Internal Security Act**, passed in 1950. The act

▲ Escorted by a U.S. marshal (left), Julius and Ethel Rosenberg are shown outside of federal court on March 8, 1951, awaiting the result of their trial on charges of conspiracy to commit espionage.

required party members and organizations to register with the federal government. It also imposed strict controls on immigrants suspected of being Communist sympathizers. The anti-Communist hysteria of these years shattered many lives and careers. Today many historians look back on this period as one of the bleakest in American history.

■■ **Cold War anti-communism led to efforts to expose alleged Communists in the United States, creating a climate of fear and suspicion.**

SECTION 3 REVIEW

IDENTIFY and explain the significance of the following: Cold War, Nikolai Novikov, satellite nations, George Kennan, containment, Baruch Plan, Atomic Energy Act, Truman Doctrine, George C. Marshall, Marshall Plan, Berlin airlift, NATO, Warsaw Pact, National Security Council, Central Intelligence Agency, House Committee on Un-American Activities, Hollywood Ten, Internal Security Act.

LOCATE and explain the importance of the following: Greece, Turkey, Dardanelles, Federal Republic of Germany (West Germany), German Democratic Republic (East Germany).

1. **MAIN IDEA** What factors gave rise to the Cold War?

2. **MAIN IDEA** What was the purpose of the Marshall Plan?

3. **ASSESSING CONSEQUENCES** What impact did the Cold War have on U.S. society?

4. **WRITING TO EXPRESS A VIEWPOINT** Imagine you are a court reporter at either the Alger Hiss trial or the trial of Ethel and Julius Rosenberg. Write a letter to a friend abroad explaining the significance of one of the trials.

5. **SYNTHESIZING** How did the U.S. government put George Kennan's containment doctrine into practice?

Section 4

THE COLD WAR TURNS HOT

FOCUS

- Why did Israel and Arab nations go to war?
- How did Communists come to power in China?
- What led to the division of Korea?
- Who fought in the Korean War?

World War II had weakened the grip of European nations on their colonies and spheres of influence in the Middle East and Asia. After the war these former colonies struggled to set up their own governments. The United States became involved in the conflict between Israel and several Arab nations in the Middle East. Concerns over the spread of communism led the United States to support the Nationalists in their struggle against the Communists in China. By 1950 Cold War rivalries drew the United States into outright war in Korea.

U.S. soldiers in Korea, 1952

MIDDLE EAST TENSIONS

Soon after World War II, tensions flared in Palestine, a region at the eastern end of the Mediterranean claimed by both Jews and Arabs. Since World War I, Great Britain had ruled Palestine under a League of Nations mandate. Unable to resolve conflicting claims over the territory, Britain in 1947 turned the problem over to the United Nations. The UN came up with a plan to divide Palestine into two states—one for Jews, the other for Arabs—but Arabs rejected the proposal.

The proposal was a victory for **Zionism**, the movement calling for a Jewish homeland in Palestine. Zionist leader David Ben-Gurion

(ben-goohr-YAWN), born in Plonsk, Russia, in 1886, had fought for just this outcome since the early 1900s. Idealistic and determined, Ben-Gurion sailed to Palestine in 1906. Expelled in 1915 for Zionist activities, he went to the United States to raise money and recruit volunteers among the American Jewish community.

During World War II, Ben-Gurion supported the Allied struggle against Hitler but continued to organize Jewish resistance in Palestine. After the war, Ben-Gurion helped develop land, resettle Jewish refugees, and organize covert activities against British and Arab rule.

With the UN's decision to divide Palestine, Great Britain agreed to give up its control of the region. On May 14, 1948, the last

David Ben-Gurion

796　CHAPTER 27

Israel, 1949

Israel in June 1948

Territory Israel gained by January 1949

Territory Israel held after 1949 armistice

Boundary of British Mandate of Palestine, 1922–1948

★ Capital city

LEBANON

SYRIA

SEA OF GALILEE

Haifa
Nazareth

MEDITERRANEAN SEA

Nablus

WEST BANK (to Jordan)

Tel Aviv ★
Jaffa

Amman ★

Jerusalem

Bethlehem

Gaza
Hebron

GAZA STRIP (to Egypt)

DEAD SEA

EGYPT

ISRAEL

Negev

JORDAN

UN Partition

Israeli territory

Arab territory

Jerusalem (International Zone)

PALESTINE

EGYPT

1947

Sinai

Elat

0   20   40 Miles
0   20   40 Kilometers

Lambert Conformal Conic Projection

SUCCESS STORY The memory of the Holocaust and the struggle to create a Jewish state unified the Israelis in a common cause.

? PLACE Which river divides the West Bank from Jordan?

counted on an impressive arsenal bought in part with the millions of dollars that poured in from the American Jewish community.

◼◼ In 1948 war broke out between Israel and Arab nations over the disputed territory of Palestine.

In an effort to end the war, the UN sent a mediator, Count Folke Bernadotte of Sweden, to the Middle East. Bernadotte negotiated a shaky cease-fire, but within months he was assassinated by Israeli extremists. In 1949 a second UN mediator, the American diplomat Ralph Bunche, persuaded both sides to accept an armistice. For his efforts Bunche won the Nobel Peace Prize in 1950—

▲ **Ralph Bunche**

the first African American to receive that honor.

The 1949 agreement gave Israel more territory than the earlier UN partition plan had, but it divided Jerusalem into an Arab east and an Israeli west. The plan gave Egypt control of the Gaza Strip, while Jordan took over the West Bank of the Jordan River. The Arab countries, however, still refused to recognize the state of Israel. Also left unresolved was the fate of the Arabs remaining in Israel and the hundreds of thousands of Arabs who had fled or had been driven out of Israel.

Before the territorial agreements were finalized, Israel held its first parliamentary elections in January 1949. Ben-Gurion became prime minister, a post he held almost continuously until 1963. At his death in 1973, Ben-Gurion was hailed as the chief architect of the state of Israel.

COMMUNIST VICTORY IN CHINA

While the conflict between Arabs and Israelis escalated after World War II, tensions also came to a head in China. The seeds of the conflict were planted in the 1920s. Chiang Kai-shek's Kuomintang (KMT), or Nationalist party, battled the

of the British forces withdrew. Ben-Gurion and other Jewish leaders promptly proclaimed the new state of Israel. Both Truman and Stalin immediately recognized the new nation.

The Arab states, however, did not recognize Israel, since they wanted Palestine to remain an Arab country. Armies from the Arab states of Egypt, Lebanon, Jordan (called Transjordan until 1949), Syria, and Iraq attacked Israel. Although vastly outnumbered in the Arab-Israeli war, Israeli forces under Ben-Gurion's overall command captured and held much of Palestine. Israeli soldiers

THE ARAB RESPONSE

Musa Alami, an Arab lawyer and diplomat from Palestine, promoted Palestinian nationalism and unity among the Arab states. After the Arab-Israeli war, Alami published a book, *The Lesson of Palestine* (1949), which examined the causes of the war:

❝The British were the prime causers of the disaster. . . . They were assisted by the Americans and the Russians. . . . We found ourselves face to face with the Jews, and entered into battle with them to decide the future; and in spite of what the British, the Americans, and the Russians had done, it was still within our power to win the fight.

The Arabs failed to defend Palestine. . . . We worked on a local basis, without unity, without totality, without a general command, our defense disjointed and our affairs disordered, every town fighting on its own and only those in areas adjacent to the Jews entering the battle at all. . . . The natural result of all this was disaster and the loss of Palestine. ❞

Chinese Communists. KMT forces held most of northern China, and Communist soldiers controlled parts of southern and central China. But in 1931, when Japan invaded Manchuria, the KMT and the Communists declared a truce and joined forces against the Japanese.

In 1934, however, Chiang broke the truce when he launched what he hoped would be the final battles against the Communist-controlled areas of the south. The KMT forces were successful. From 1934 to 1935 some 100,000 Communists marched nearly 6,000 miles to northern China. Known as the **Long March**, this exodus

▲ Nationalist forces kidnapped Chiang Kai-shek in 1936. This photograph of Chiang with his wife was taken after his release.

helped cement Mao Zedong's leadership of the Chinese Communist party and led to the establishment of a strong base in the north.

Chiang's attacks on the Communists kept him from devoting full attention to stopping further Japanese aggression. By the early 1930s the Japanese controlled Manchuria, Inner Mongolia, and parts of northern China. To prevent the loss of more Chinese territory to the Japanese, a group of KMT soldiers kidnapped Chiang in 1936 and released him only after he agreed to join forces with the Communists against the Japanese. This cooperation continued throughout World War II.

At war's end, however, the conflict resumed. During World War II the Communists had prevented the Japanese from controlling all of northwest China. This effective resistance, plus the reforms that Mao instituted to give land to poor peasants, won more support for the Communists and recruits for their army.

The United States, which had long supported Chiang, did not want to see China become a Communist country. During and after World War II the United States sent economic and military aid, including troops, to China to unite the country under the KMT. Truman sent George Marshall to China in 1946 to arrange a truce, but neither side would compromise.

Although Chiang had helped modernize China by building railroads, roads, and factories, his government was becoming increasingly unpopular. The fight against the Japanese had wrecked the Chinese economy, and the Chinese people faced soaring inflation. Chiang seemed unresponsive to these economic problems. In addition, Chiang made no efforts at land reform to help the desperately poor peasants. Moreover, he presided over an increasingly corrupt and authoritarian government that banned all other political parties. As opposition to Chiang mounted, Mao's forces gained control of most of the country by 1949.

Realizing his defeat, Chiang and his army retreated to the island of Taiwan, off the coast of southeast China. The Chinese Communists established the People's Republic of China. Dismayed by the Communist victory, the United

States continued to recognize the Nationalists as China's legal government. The Chinese seat on the UN Security Council, granted to Chiang's Taiwan government after World War II, remained in Nationalist hands until 1971.

■■ **In 1949, after a long struggle with Nationalist forces, Chinese Communists under Mao Zedong won control of China.**

𝒯HE KOREAN WAR

Meanwhile, political tensions rose in Korea, a peninsula jutting southward from the northeast corner of China. The Japanese had ruled Korea from 1910 to 1945 but had been driven out by Soviet and American troops at the end of World War II. In 1945 the Allies divided Korea into two parts— North Korea and South Korea—with the border between the two countries set at the **38th parallel**. Soviet forces occupied the North, and American troops held the South.

This division was meant to be temporary, but Cold War tensions cemented it. In 1948 North Korea and South Korea set up separate governments, each claiming to rule the entire country. Communist North Korea, led by Kim Il Sung, became known as the People's Republic of Korea. Kim's government, a Communist dictatorship, redistributed land to poor peasants and nationalized most industries. Although Kim's government limited freedom of speech, it expanded education and established formal equality for women. South Korea, under President Syngman Rhee (SING-muhn REE), called itself the Republic of Korea. The southern republic faced economic and political instability after World War II.

Anxious that South Korea not fall to the Communists as China had, the United States built up the South Korean army as a counterbalance to the Soviet-trained northern forces. By 1949 both the United States and the Soviet Union had pulled their troops out of Korea. The pullout left only the two Korean armies tensely facing each other across the 38th parallel.

■■ **After World War II, Korea was divided into Soviet and American occupation zones. In 1948 North Korea and South Korea established separate governments.**

𝒯he Korean War

CHINESE INTERVENTION Fearing UN forces would cross the Yalu River into Manchuria, the Chinese entered the war and invaded Korea.

❓ MOVEMENT How far north of the 38th parallel did the UN forces advance?

The war begins. After repeated clashes between North Korean and South Korean troops, the North Korean army invaded South Korea on June 25, 1950. A perceived shift in American policy may have encouraged the invasion. Earlier that year Secretary of State Dean Acheson had given a speech defining America's "defensive perimeter" against the spread of communism in Asia. This perimeter, an imaginary line stretching from Alaska to the Philippines, did not include Korea. Thus it appeared that the United States would not defend South Korea against invasion.

In an emergency session the UN Security Council called for an immediate cease-fire. (At the time the Soviets were boycotting the Security Council over its refusal to admit Communist China, so their delegate was not on hand to veto the UN resolution.) Two days later, on June 27, President Truman pledged U.S. support for South Korea. That same day, the Security Council adopted a U.S.–sponsored resolution branding North Korea an "aggressor" and calling on UN members to come to South Korea's defense. Truman later explained: "I felt certain that if South Korea was allowed to fall, Communist leaders would be emboldened to override nations closer to our own shores."

Bitter fighting. Acting under the UN resolution, Truman ordered U.S. air and ground forces into action under the command of General Douglas MacArthur. Truman also ordered the U.S. Seventh Fleet to protect Taiwan. Although 15 other UN members contributed assistance, the United States and South Korea played the major role in resisting North Korea's aggression.

At first, however, the onslaught of North Korean forces and their Soviet-made tanks was overwhelming. Outgunned and outmanned, the U.S. and South Korean troops fell back. One soldier, Sergeant Raymond Remp, recalled his first encounter with the North Korean army:

66 Someone fired a green flare, and [the enemy] saw us. . . . They were right on top of us in the hills, firing down on us. . . .

Some colonel—don't know who— said, "Get out the best way you can." . . .

All day and night we ran like antelopes. We didn't know our officers. They didn't know us. We lost everything we had. 99

By August the North Koreans had overrun nearly all of South Korea. The U.S. and South Korean forces were backed into a small area around Pusan, in southeast Korea (see map on page 799).

On September 15, 1950, however, MacArthur launched a powerful counterattack. Coming ashore at Inchon, near the 38th parallel, MacArthur's forces swept inland, recapturing Seoul (SOHL), the capital of South Korea. At the same time, a strong UN army, now well equipped and supported from the air, attacked from the south. Caught in a huge trap, North Koreans surrendered by the thousands. Others fled north across the 38th parallel, with UN forces in hot pursuit. By late October the UN army had reached the Yalu River, the boundary between North Korea and China.

But again the tide turned. Late in November, China entered the war on North Korea's side, sending some 300,000 troops across the Yalu. Chinese foreign minister Zhou Enlai (JOH ENLY) explained why China had intervened:

66 The U.S. imperialists have adopted a hostile attitude towards us . . . while paying

MAJOR EVENTS OF THE COLD WAR	
Year	**Event**
1945	Korea divided into two zones, one occupied by United States and the other by Soviet Union.
1948	U.S. Congress approves Marshall Plan to provide some $12 billion in aid to Western Europe over next four years.
	Soviet Union blocks routes between Berlin and West Germany. Western powers meet blockade with Berlin airlift.
	North Korea and South Korea establish separate governments.
	United States and Soviet Union recognize Israel.
1949	NATO formed.
	Chinese Communists win control of China.
1950	Korean War begins when North Korea invades South Korea.
	China enters Korean War.
1955	Warsaw Pact signed.

Sources: *Encyclopedia of American History; Encyclopedia of World History*

STRUGGLE FOR SUPREMACY The United States and the Soviet Union fought to establish political supremacy across the globe through both diplomatic and military means.

? ANALYZING How did the United States attempt to counteract the influence of the Soviet Union?

lip service to non-aggression and non-intervention. From the information we got, they wanted to calm China first and after occupying North Korea, they will come to attack China. **99**

Outnumbered and with their lines dangerously extended, the UN forces fell back. After desperate fighting and heavy losses in the bitter winter cold, MacArthur's troops finally established a stable defensive line near the 38th parallel.

■■ During the Korean War, UN forces—mainly U.S. and South Korean soldiers—fought North Korean and Chinese troops.

The great debate. With China now involved, MacArthur called for a major expansion of the war. He proposed to blockade China's coast, bomb the Chinese mainland, and "unleash" Chiang's Nationalist forces to invade mainland China. This plan stirred fierce public debate. Supporters said it would bring victory in Korea and overthrow the Chinese Communists. Opponents argued that an attack on China could bring the Soviet Union into the conflict and trigger World War III.

President Truman strongly opposed MacArthur's plan because he did not want the war in Korea to lead to another world war. MacArthur, however, refused to accept the Korean War as a limited conflict. Publicly criticizing the president, MacArthur appealed to

▲ In September 1950, U.S. soldiers used hand grenades to remove the remaining North Korean forces from Seoul.

Republican leaders in Congress. He also delivered an ultimatum to the enemy—demanding unconditional surrender—thereby upsetting Truman's plans for peace negotiations. As commander in chief of the military, Truman removed MacArthur from his post in April 1951. General Matthew Ridgway replaced MacArthur as commander of the UN forces.

By the summer of 1951, the war had settled into a stalemate. Bitter fighting continued, but little territory changed hands. Combat in Korea's mountainous terrain became intensely frustrating as the American death toll mounted. Under these circumstances American public opinion gradually turned against the war. The Korean conflict would soon become a major issue in the 1952 presidential election.

SECTION 4 REVIEW

IDENTIFY and explain the significance of the following: Zionism, David Ben-Gurion, Ralph Bunche, Chiang Kai-shek, Long March, Mao Zedong, Kim Il Sung, Syngman Rhee, Dean Acheson, Douglas MacArthur, Zhou Enlai.

LOCATE and explain the importance of the following: Palestine, Israel, Gaza Strip, West Bank, Taiwan, People's Republic of China, 38th parallel, Pusan, Seoul, Yalu River.

1. **MAIN IDEA** Why did war break out between Israel and Arab states in 1948?

2. **MAIN IDEA** How did the end of World War II affect Korea?

3. **MAIN IDEA** What forces fought in the Korean War?

4. **WRITING TO EXPLAIN** Write an essay explaining how the Communists gained control of China in 1949.

5. **HYPOTHESIZING** How do you think the Korean War would have proceeded if MacArthur had been allowed to expand the war into China?

Potsdam Conference held. Nuremberg trials begin. UN charter drafted. Korea divided into two zones.

Employment Act and Atomic Energy Act passed. Coal miners go on strike. Committee on Civil Rights appointed. Baruch Plan proposed.

Japan adopts new constitution. Taft-Hartley Act passed. Truman Doctrine proposed. NSC and CIA established. HUAC investigates movie industry.

1945　　　　**1946**　　　　**1947**

WRITING A SUMMARY

Using the essential points of the chapter as a guide, write a summary of the chapter.

REVIEWING CHRONOLOGY

Number your paper 1 to 5. Study the time line above, and list the following events in the order in which they happened by writing the first next to 1, the second next to 2, and so on. Then complete the activity below.

1. Committee on Civil Rights appointed.
2. Israel declares its independence.
3. Truman Doctrine proposed.
4. North Korea invades South Korea.
5. UN charter drafted.

Identifying Cause and Effect Select two events on the time line, and in a paragraph, explain the cause-and-effect relationship between them.

IDENTIFYING PEOPLE AND IDEAS

Explain the historical significance of each of the following people or terms.

1. United Nations
2. Trygve Lie
3. GI Bill of Rights
4. Sadie Alexander
5. Dixiecrats
6. satellite nations
7. George Kennan
8. Atomic Energy Act
9. David Ben-Gurion
10. Mao Zedong

UNDERSTANDING MAIN IDEAS

1. How did the United States work with other Allies to restore peace after World War II?
2. Why did postwar fears of a depression never materialize? What effect did the lifting of wartime price controls have on the economy?
3. How did African Americans work for civil rights in the late 1940s? What effect did these actions have on the 1948 election?
4. What factors caused public support for President Truman to plunge by 1948? How did he win the 1948 election?
5. Why did China enter the Korean War on the side of North Korea?

REVIEWING THEMES

1. **Global Relations** What international and domestic tensions resulted from the conflict between the United States and the Soviet Union?
2. **Technology and Society** How did the development of atomic energy affect the United States?
3. **Democratic Values** How did the U.S. government's response to Cold War pressures lead to limitations on civil liberties?

THINKING CRITICALLY

1. **Problem Solving** What steps did the U.S. government take after World War II to make the transition from war to peace?
2. **Analyzing** How did the Taft-Hartley Act attempt to place restrictions on the tactics unions could use to win improvements?
3. **Synthesizing** What were the main causes of the Cold War? How did the Cold War get played out in Korea?

STRATEGY FOR SUCCESS

Review the Strategies for Success on Recognizing Propaganda on page 774. Then read the excerpt below, which comes from an address by J. Edgar Hoover warning of the dangers of communism. What clues identify this passage as propaganda?

66 The Communist Party of the United States . . . is far better organized than were the Nazis. . . . They [the Communists] are seeking to weaken America just as they did . . . when they were aligned with the Nazis. Their goal is the overthrow of our government. 99

WRITING ABOUT HISTORY

Writing to Explain Imagine you are an American diplomat in China during 1946. Write a memorandum to President Truman, explaining the reasons for the mounting opposition to Chiang Kai-shek after World War II.

Racial discrimination banned in military and in federal hiring. Marshall Plan passed. Berlin airlift begins. Israel declares its independence. Dixiecrats formed. Truman elected president.

NATO established. Middle East agreements reached. Communists gain control of China.

Alger Hiss convicted of perjury. Internal Security Act passed. North Korea invades South Korea.

Julius and Ethel Rosenberg convicted.

U.S. occupation of Japan ends.

1948   1949   1950   1951   1952

USING PRIMARY SOURCES

Attempts to find alleged Communists spread to every level of government. In 1946 President Truman nominated David Lilienthal to head the U.S. Atomic Energy Commission. During Lilienthal's confirmation hearings, Senator Kenneth D. McKellar of Tennessee accused the nominee of being a Communist sympathizer. In Lilienthal's eloquent reply below, how did he defend himself against the charge?

    66 *I believe—and I conceive the Constitution of the United States to rest . . . upon the fundamental proposition of the integrity of the individual. . . .*

    Any form of government, therefore, and any other institutions which . . . exalt the state or any other institutions above the importance of men, which place arbitrary power over men as a fundamental tenet [belief] of government are contrary to that conception, and, therefore, I am deeply opposed to them.

    The communistic . . . form of government falls within this category. . . . The fundamental tenet of communism is that the state is an end in itself, and that therefore the powers which the state exercises over the individual are without any ethical standard to limit them.

    That I deeply disbelieve. . . .

    I deeply believe in the capacity of democracy to surmount any trials that may lie ahead, provided only that we practice it in our daily lives.

    And among the things we must practice is this: that while we seek fervently to ferret out the subversive and anti-democratic forces in the country, we do not at the same time, by hysteria . . . and other unfortunate tactics, besmirch [soil] the very cause that we believe in. **99**

LINKING HISTORY AND GEOGRAPHY

Refer to the map on page 797. What effect did the 1949 armistice have on both Israeli and Arab territorial boundaries?

BUILDING YOUR PORTFOLIO

Complete the following projects independently or cooperatively.

1. THE COLD WAR Imagine that you are a U.S. delegate to the UN conference in San Francisco in 1945. Write a memorandum to the U.S. Senate, detailing world conditions in 1945 that call for the formation of an association of world nations and urging U.S. participation in such an association.

2. THE GOVERNMENT AND THE ECONOMY Imagine you are a member of the Department of Labor. Prepare a chart that shows how the U.S. government is assisting returning soldiers through programs designed to help them find civilian jobs, attain college educations, or own their own homes.

3. CIVIL RIGHTS Imagine you are a reporter covering the Committee on Civil Rights. Research and prepare a radio piece on why the committee was formed, who its members are, and what it has documented in its official report, "To Secure These Rights."

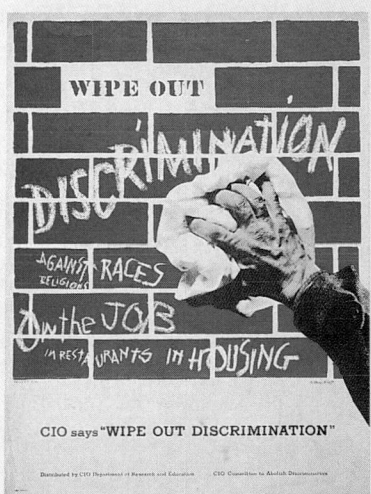

WIPE OUT DISCRIMINATION

AGAINST RELIGIONS RACES

On the JOB

IN RESTAURANTS   IN HOUSING

CIO says "WIPE OUT DISCRIMINATION"

DECADE OF CONTRASTS

FOCUS

UNDERSTANDING THE MAIN IDEA

Though the Korean War came to an end, the Cold War continued in the 1950s, increasing Americans' fears of communism and nuclear war. Meanwhile most Americans experienced economic prosperity, leading white middle-class Americans to move away from cities into suburbs. Popular culture, including television, encouraged conformity, but some groups challenged the practices of American society, especially discrimination against African Americans.

THEMES

■ **ECONOMIC DEVELOPMENT** How might an economic boom affect population growth and residential patterns?

■ **CULTURAL DIVERSITY** How can people demonstrate diversity in a society that emphasizes conformity?

■ **DEMOCRATIC VALUES** How might a group of people seek to change laws that discriminate against them?

The end of World War II renewed Americans' optimism about the future. Soon, however, the country was caught up in a Cold War with the Soviet Union. President Truman's commitment to contain the spread of communism led the United States into the Korean War and heightened suspicion that there were Communist spies in America.

United States airman at Atlanta Terminal Station, 1956

In 1952, after 20 years of Democratic rule in the White House, Americans chose Republican Dwight D. Eisenhower for president, echoing the campaign chant "We Like Ike." The Eisenhower era, which occupied much of the 1950s, saw continued conflict in many parts of the world. However, the emergence of new leadership in the Soviet Union raised hopes for a thaw in the Cold War. At home the 1950s brought widespread economic prosperity. The United States had long been the world's richest, most productive nation. Now millions of middle-class Americans enjoyed a rising standard of living, leading many to move away from cities and rural areas into suburbs.

American life was not all rosy, however. Cold War tensions and nuclear-war fears disturbed much of the nation. Moreover, economic prosperity was not shared equally. Rural residents, African Americans, Hispanic Americans, and Native Americans continued to endure poverty and prejudice. By the mid-1950s, however, a new generation of African Americans started to achieve some successes in the long struggle for the equality of opportunity promised in the Fourteenth Amendment.

Watching a 3-D movie, 1953

COLD WAR FEARS

FOCUS

- How did the outcome of the Korean War affect Korea?
- What led to Senator Joseph McCarthy's downfall?
- How did President Eisenhower handle threats to U.S. interests in Iran, Guatemala, and Egypt?
- How did the U-2 incident affect the arms race?

*S*oon after his victory in the 1952 presidential election, Dwight D. Eisenhower kept his campaign promise to end the Korean conflict. But the Cold War continued, generating fears of nuclear weapons and stirring suspicions that Communists had infiltrated every part of American life. On the world stage the Eisenhower administration developed an aggressive policy to fight the spread of communism, while taking steps to improve diplomatic relations with the Soviet Union.

Eisenhower campaign bumper sticker, 1952

THE GENERAL VS. THE EGGHEAD

As 1952 began, President Truman found himself confronted with a host of problems. The Korean War had ground to a bloody stalemate, and peace talks were making little progress. Republicans saw their chance to break the Democrats' 20-year hold on the White House by choosing popular World War II hero General Dwight D. Eisenhower as their presidential candidate. Conservative senator Richard M. Nixon of California served as his running mate.

Truman, recognizing that he had little support even within his own party, decided not to run for reelection. The Democrats selected Governor Adlai E. Stevenson of Illinois as their candidate. Stevenson defended the Fair Deal and Truman's foreign policies. Many voters, however, viewed him as an intellectual out of touch with the common people. Some jokingly referred to Stevenson as an "egghead"—"someone with more brains than hair."

Stevenson also could not match Eisenhower's patriotic appeal. Eisenhower reassured voters that America would remain strong throughout the Cold War. The hero of World War II promised to resist communism and end the Korean War. A triumphant Eisenhower received 55 percent of the popular vote and swept the electoral count 442 to 89.

▼ During the 1952 presidential election, Dwight Eisenhower had promised voters, "I shall go to Korea." Eisenhower fulfilled the promise a month after his presidential victory. Here he is shown eating lunch with his old army outfit.

KOREAN WAR ENDS, FEAR CONTINUES

The new president quickly fulfilled his promise to end the war. Eisenhower used military force to get peace negotiations moving. He stepped up bombing raids on North Korea in May 1953 and let it be known that he would use nuclear weapons, if necessary, to end the conflict.

On July 27, 1953, negotiators agreed to an armistice that divided Korea into two nations, Communist North Korea and anti-Communist South Korea, roughly at the 38th parallel—the prewar dividing line. Some Americans questioned whether this outcome in a distant war justified U.S. losses—some 54,000 dead and 103,000 wounded. More than 1.5 million Chinese and Koreans had also died in the conflict. For years after the war, U.S. relations with China and North Korea remained strained.

■■ **The armistice that ended the Korean War created two nations divided at the 38th parallel: North Korea and South Korea.**

The Korean conflict heightened the fears of some that communism was gaining ground in the United States. This anxiety continued even after the war ended. Many Americans became convinced that spies and Communist sympathizers were everywhere. Joseph McCarthy, a U.S. senator from Wisconsin, helped fuel these suspicions.

Senator McCarthy came to public attention in 1950, when he claimed to have a list of known Communists who worked at the State Department. Although he never produced the list, dozens of federal employees lost their jobs after being labeled as "security risks." McCarthy used his position as chairman of the Senate Permanent Subcommittee on Investigations to wage war against all suspected Communist sympathizers in the federal government. With almost no supporting evidence, McCarthy questioned the patriotism—and ruined the reputations—of hundreds of government workers. Many Americans, terrified of communism and the power of the Soviet Union, supported his crusade.

McCarthy's popularity and ruthlessness made many politicians wary of challenging him. One who did, however, was Margaret Chase Smith, a Republican senator from Maine. Smith was born in the small mill town of Skowhegan, Maine, in 1897. When her husband, Republican congressman Clyde Smith, died in 1940, voters chose her to complete his congressional term.

Margaret Chase Smith

After four full terms in the house, Smith won a seat in the Senate in 1948, becoming the first woman to be elected to both houses of Congress. Sixteen years later, she became the first woman to seek the Republican nomination for president. When she left the Senate in 1973, her colleagues praised her as a "woman of courage." Smith once said of public service:

> 66 It must be a complete dedication to the people and to the nation with full recognition that every human being is entitled to courtesy and consideration, that constructive criticism is not only to be expected but sought, that smears are not only to be expected but fought, that honor is to be earned but not bought. 99

MCCARTHY'S DOWNFALL

In 1950 Smith and several other senators issued the "Declaration of Conscience," which condemned those who had turned the Senate into "a forum of hate and character assassination." While she never mentioned McCarthy by name, everyone knew she was referring to him. Few others joined in the condemnation, however. Even President Eisenhower refused to criticize McCarthy.

Most of the critics who did speak out came from the arts or the media. In *The Crucible* (1953), playwright Arthur Miller drew parallels between McCarthyism and the Salem witchcraft trials of 1692. On the television program *See It Now,* newscaster Edward R. Murrow questioned McCarthy's tactics. "We cannot defend freedom abroad," Murrow cautioned, "by deserting it at home." While some viewers praised Murrow, others bombarded him with hate mail.

In 1954 McCarthy's committee investigated charges that Communists had gained a foothold in the U.S. Army. Each day a vast television audience, sometimes as many as 20 million people, tuned in to the Army-McCarthy hearings. McCarthy repeatedly interrupted the circus-like proceedings and frequently ridiculed witnesses. One victim of this treatment said McCarthy "acted like the gangster in a B movie rubbing out someone who had got in his way."

Television exposure of McCarthy's bullying tactics, contrasted with the calm, dignified behavior of army chief counsel Joseph Welch, soon turned public opinion against the senator. At one point when Welch took McCarthy to task for cruelty, the audience in the hearing room broke into applause. A few months later, the Senate—by a vote of 67 to 22—condemned McCarthy for conduct unbecoming a senator.

▲ In the 1950s schools across America frequently took the precaution of holding routine air-raid drills in case of a nuclear attack.

As concerns about nuclear war grew, the government launched a campaign to calm public fears. The federally sponsored book *How to*

■■ **McCarthy's behavior during the Army-McCarthy hearings cost him public support.**

NUCLEAR ANXIETY

Americans' fear of nuclear war heightened as the Soviet Union and the United States raced to develop more-powerful nuclear weapons. In 1950 American scientists began work on a **hydrogen bomb**, or H-bomb, which they said would be 1,000 times more powerful than the atomic bomb dropped on Hiroshima and Nagasaki in World War II. The first H-bomb test in 1952 completely vaporized a small island in the Pacific. Some nine months later, the Soviet Union tested their own H-bomb. J. Robert Oppenheimer, one of the creators of the atomic bomb, cautioned:

❝ [The United States and the Soviet Union] are like two scorpions in a bottle, each capable of killing the other but only at the risk of his own life. . . . The atomic clock ticks faster and faster. ❞

THE NUCLEAR ARMS RACE

THROUGH OTHERS' EYES

The testing of increasingly powerful and destructive nuclear weapons by the United States and the Soviet Union in the 1950s alarmed national leaders around the world. In April 1954 Jawaharlal Nehru, Prime Minister of India, voiced his fears:

❝ *The United States of America and the Union of Soviet Socialist Republics, we are told, possess this [nuclear] weapon and each of these countries has during the last two years effected test explosions, unleashing impacts which in every respect were far beyond those of any weapons of destruction known to man. . . . We know that its use threatens the existence of man and civilization as we know it. . . . There can be little doubt about the deep and widespread concern in the world . . . about these weapons and their dreadful consequences. But concern is not enough. . . . We must endeavor with faith and hope to promote all efforts that seek to bring to a halt this drift to what appears to be the menace of total destruction.* ❞

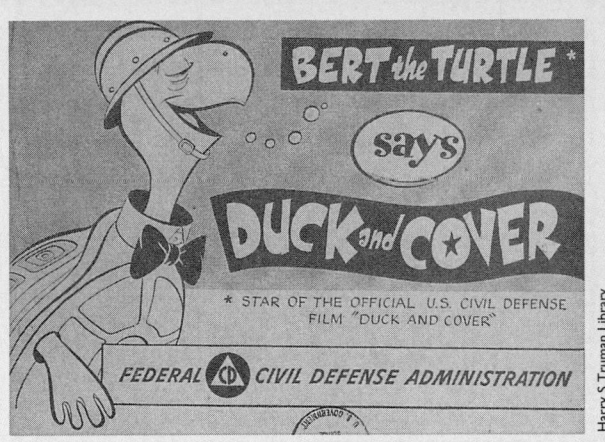

▶ During the 1950s many children learned about civil defense through the "Duck and Cover" program.

As Cold War tensions and Americans' fear of a Soviet nuclear attack increased in the 1950s, a civil defense craze swept the United States. In 1951 the Federal Civil Defense Administration began a campaign to educate the public on what to do in a nuclear attack. Pamphlets, films, television shows, magazines, and the "Duck and Cover" program for children all encouraged citizens to protect themselves. For example, the *Survival Under Nuclear Attack* booklet urged:

❝ You can live through an atom bomb raid and you won't have to have a Geiger counter, protective clothing, or special training in order to do it. The secrets of survival are: KNOW THE BOMB'S TRUE DANGERS. KNOW THE STEPS YOU CAN TAKE TO ESCAPE THEM. ❞

Americans' fear increased in 1954 when the U.S. *Bravo* hydrogen-bomb tests in the Pacific Ocean revealed the far-reaching effects of nuclear fallout. The crew of a Japanese fishing boat 85 miles away from the test site developed radiation sickness. People realized that no one would be safe in a nuclear attack. "The alternatives," one civil defense official said, "are to dig, die, or get out." No one wanted to die, and with little warning of incoming missiles, evacuating would not be possible. So Americans began to dig—constructing an estimated one million backyard fallout shelters by 1960.

Pamphlets like the *Family Fallout Shelter* promoted do-it-yourself home shelters. *Life* magazine even presented building a shelter as a father-and-son project. Shelter manufacturers also sprang up, selling their concrete and steel igloos at county fairs for about $1,500. The typical shelter contained flashlights, a first-aid kit, battery radio, chemical toilet, and two-week supply of food (mainly canned meats and vegetables) and water. Most shelters were furnished with only metal bunk beds or cots, a table, and chairs, but some had all the comforts of home. One man in Austin, Texas, spent $90,000 on his luxury shelter.

Many people also purchased guns to keep out anyone who tried to enter their shelter during a raid. This survivalist view led many to question the ethics of home bomb shelters. But before this issue could be resolved, the civil defense craze passed. In 1963 the United States, the Soviet Union, and Great Britain signed a treaty ending above-ground nuclear testing. The fear of fallout diminished, and demand for bomb shelters rapidly decreased.

Survive an Atomic Bomb, for example, offered suggestions on how to live through a nuclear attack. Thousands of Americans put these recommendations to use by building backyard bomb shelters. Schoolchildren went through air-raid drills in which they crawled under their desks to protect themselves from radiation.

While a nuclear attack remained only a possibility, radioactive fallout—a by-product of nuclear explosions—already posed a threat. American and Soviet H-bomb tests had spewed tons of radioactive material into the atmosphere. In 1957 Congress held a special hearing on the dangers of radioactive fallout. Defense officials

THE NUCLEAR THREAT, 1955–1960

Estimated Size of Nuclear-Weapon Stockpiles

- United States
- Soviet Union

Year: 1955, 1956, 1957, 1958, 1959, 1960

Source: *Nuclear Weapons Databook*

HEATING UP THE COLD WAR With the discovery of atomic power, the competition for superiority between the United States and the Soviet Union spilled over into a nuclear arms race.

? **BUILDING GRAPH SKILLS** In which year was the gap between the stockpiles of the United States and the Soviet Union the greatest?

claimed nuclear testing was perfectly safe, but many scientists argued that radiation released during the tests presented a serious danger to the environment and possibly increased the risk of cancer in human beings. Soon the fear of radiation led to an organized campaign against nuclear testing. In 1957 a group of Americans, including well-known doctor Benjamin Spock, organized the Committee for a Sane Nuclear Policy (SANE). SANE urged the United States to begin negotiations with the Soviet Union to end nuclear tests. Within a year SANE had grown to more than 25,000 members in some 130 chapters across the country.

The arms race surged on, however, especially after the Soviet Union launched the satellite *Sputnik* into orbit around the earth in October 1957. Many Americans feared that this launch proved the United States was falling behind the Soviets in technological development. Eisenhower urged Congress to expand American space technology by establishing the **National Aeronautics and Space Administration** (NASA). In 1958 NASA sent the first American satellite, *Explorer I*, into orbit. That same year Congress approved the **National Defense Education Act**, which appropriated millions of dollars to improve education in science, mathematics, and foreign languages.

FIGHTING COMMUNISM ABROAD

The Eisenhower administration viewed nuclear arms and technology as central to the government's priority of ending Communist expansion. Secretary of State John Foster Dulles called for the liberation of all nations that had fallen under Soviet control since 1945. To fulfill this aim, the United States would have to confront Communist aggression and not back down—even if that meant going all the way to the brink of war. "The ability to get to the verge without getting into war is the necessary art," Dulles said. This policy of **brinkmanship** rested on the threat of massive retaliation, including the use of nuclear weapons. Eisenhower, however, proved less confrontational than Dulles's policy might have suggested. Instead, he pursued U.S. aims by more covert—secret—means and by diplomacy.

Covert war and the CIA. Eisenhower tested his covert approach to the Cold War in Iran. Shortly after coming to power in 1951, Iranian premier Mohammad Mosaddeq (MAWS-ad-dek) nationalized British-owned oil fields in Iran. After Eisenhower took office he suspended aid to Iran, fearing that nationalization would endanger Western oil purchases. Eisenhower also authorized a covert action by the CIA to organize a military coup against the Iranian leader. The plan, called Operation Ajax, succeeded in having Mosaddeq arrested and replaced with the young pro-American Shah of Iran, Reza Pahlavi (ri-ZAH PAL-uh-vee). While Eisenhower achieved his goal of removing Mosaddeq, this interference in Iranian affairs sowed seeds of anti-American feelings in that country.

In 1954 Eisenhower ordered another covert action, this time in Latin America, where the United States had often intervened in the past. In

"Don't Be Afraid—I Can Always Pull You Back"

from *Herblock's Special For Today* (Simon & Schuster, 1958)

◄ The policy of brinkmanship was satirized in this 1956 cartoon. Secretary of State John Foster Dulles is shown pushing Uncle Sam to the brink of war.

1954 the Guatemalan president, Jacobo Arbenz Guzmán, took possession of uncultivated sections of Guatemala's largest plantations—including those of the American-owned United Fruit Company—to redistribute among the rural poor.

United Fruit Company executives accused the Guatemalan president of being a Communist sympathizer. Eisenhower called on the CIA to gather a small army to oust Arbenz. The CIA-led forces bombed the capital in May 1954 and installed a new pro-U.S. government, which quickly reversed Arbenz's reform program. But American intervention in Guatemala stirred up bitter resentment throughout Latin America.

The Suez crisis. In some cases, Eisenhower used diplomacy rather than covert actions to influence foreign policy. In 1955 the American government offered Egypt financial help to build a large dam at Aswan on the Nile River. However, when Egyptian leader Gamal Abdel Nasser also sought assistance from the Soviet Union, the United States canceled its promised aid. Nasser then seized the Suez Canal, a foreign-owned waterway that linked the Mediterranean and Red seas (see map on page 905). Egypt would use canal tolls to build the Aswan Dam, Nasser declared.

Nasser's nationalization of the canal posed many problems, including a threat to the Western

oil trade. Egypt also refused to allow ships bound for Israel to pass through the canal. Late in October 1956, Israel launched an attack into Egyptian territory toward the Suez Canal. Great Britain and France, claiming they were protecting

Cold War Defenses

CONTAINMENT The United States ringed the globe with alliances and military bases in an effort to prevent the spread of communism.

? LOCATION What system did the United States put into place to provide the first warning of a Soviet attack?

Legend:
- United States and allies
- Soviet Union and allies
- ⊙ Major U.S. base
- - - - North American Defense System (NORAD) Warning line or system
- ✸ Point of conflict

0   1,000   2,000 Miles
0   1,000   2,000 Kilometers
Azimuthal Equidistant Projection   Political status as of 1960.

Map labels: MALAYSIA, CAMBODIA, SOUTH VIETNAM, THAILAND, NORTH VIETNAM, LAOS, BURMA, EAST PAKISTAN, INDIA, INDIAN OCEAN, WEST PAKISTAN, Dhahran, SAUDI ARABIA, IRAN, Peshawar, 1953, EGYPT, Suez Canal 1956, Subic Bay, Clark, PHILIPPINES, TAIWAN, CHINA, MONGOLIA, TURKEY, Incirlik, Ankara, LIBYA, Okinawa, SOUTH KOREA, Kimpo, NORTH KOREA, Sasebo, Korean War 1950–1953, UNION OF SOVIET SOCIALIST REPUBLICS, U-2 Incident 1960, HUNGARY 1956, GREECE, YUGOSLAVIA, Wheelus, Yokosuka, JAPAN, Berlin 1958–1959, WEST GERMANY, Wiesbaden, Naples, ITALY, ALGERIA (French), FINLAND, SWEDEN, NORWAY, NATO HQ, FRANCE, Zaragoza, SPAIN, ARCTIC OCEAN, North Pole, Ballistic Missile Early Warning System, Holy Loch, UNITED KINGDOM, PORTUGAL, MOROCCO, Adak, GREENLAND (Danish), Keflavik, ICELAND, Thule, AZORES (Portuguese), Lajes, 180°, Midway, Unalaska, Sondrestrøm, ALASKA, Distant Early Warning Line, PACIFIC OCEAN, Goose, CANADA, ATLANTIC OCEAN, Mid-Canada Line, Pearl Harbor, HAWAII, Pinetree Line, Minot, Grand Forks, K.I. Sawyer, Grissom, BERMUDA (British), NORAD HQ, SAC HQ, UNITED STATES, U.S. Naval Space Surveillance System, Roosevelt Roads, PUERTO RICO (U.S.), MEXICO, CUBA, Guantánamo Bay, Howard, GUATEMALA 1954, PANAMA, CANAL ZONE the canal, seized the Mediterranean end of the waterway a few days later. The Soviet Union threatened war if the three nations did not withdraw from Egypt at once.

The United States faced the difficult task of choosing to support its allies—Britain, France, and Israel—or side with Egypt and the Soviet Union. In the end, Eisenhower supported a UN resolution calling for an immediate cease-fire and the withdrawal of the invading troops. He explained:

> 66 If the United Nations once admits that international disputes can be settled by using force, then we will have destroyed the foundation of the organization and our best hope of establishing a world order. 99

Grudgingly, Britain, France, and Israel withdrew their forces, and the crisis eased.

The Soviet Union's support of Egypt during the Suez crisis bolstered the Soviets' position among the Arab nations. To counter Soviet influence in the Middle East, the president issued the **Eisenhower Doctrine** in January 1957, offering military aid and in some instances American troops to any Middle East nation seeking help in resisting Communist aggression.

■■ Eisenhower used the CIA to protect U.S. interests in Iran and Guatemala. In the Suez Crisis, he relied on diplomacy.

Uprising in Eastern Europe. At the same time that the Suez crisis was unfolding, an equally dangerous situation was developing in Eastern Europe. In February 1956 Soviet leader Nikita Khrushchev stunned political observers by denouncing his predecessor, Joseph Stalin, who had died in 1953, for many ruthless crimes. Observers hoped that this move signaled a new era of reform for the Soviet Union and Eastern Europe. Later in 1956, Polish reformers tested Khrushchev by calling for greater political freedom.

Inspired by the example of Poland, thousands of Hungarians took to the streets in late October to demand reform. Moderates seized control of the Hungarian government and called for a Western-style democracy in their nation and for Hungary's secession from the Warsaw Pact. Khrushchev

▲ On November 2, 1956, Hungarian rebels triumphantly waved the tricolored Hungarian flag atop a captured Russian tank. Two days later Soviet troops occupied the main square in front of the Houses of Parliament, where this photograph was taken.

responded with crushing force. On November 4, heavily armed Soviet troops moved into the Hungarian capital, Budapest, and smashed the revolt within days. A new pro-Soviet government imposed martial law and executed or imprisoned the rebel leaders.

Throughout their struggle the Hungarian rebels pleaded for help from the West. Eisenhower worried, however, that intervention in Eastern Europe would lead to all-out nuclear war with the Soviets. He condemned the Soviets' actions but refused to aid the rebels. He did, however, help ease immigration laws to allow more Eastern European refugees into the United States. As a result, some 40,000 Hungarians fled to the United States after the uprising.

To some observers Eisenhower's lack of support for the rebels indicated a retreat from Dulles's talk of liberating Communist-controlled countries. But most of the American public supported Eisenhower, whom they reelected by a landslide against Adlai Stevenson in November 1956.

HOPES RAISED, HOPES DASHED

Near the end of the decade, the United States and the Soviet Union moved to improve their diplomatic relations. In 1959 Vice President Nixon

DWIGHT D. EISENHOWER
1890–1969

in office
1953–1961

U.S. 6ᶜ POSTAGE

DWIGHT D.
EISENHOWER

Dwight Eisenhower built his army career slowly. He graduated from West Point in 1915 and worked in an Army camp in Pennsylvania during World War I. Throughout the years between the first and second world wars he moved around the globe, from Panama to the Philippines, becoming a master organizer and coordinator.

In charge of Allied military forces in North Africa in 1943, "he now became," a British colleague explained, "the chairman of a company of great power and resources." As president, Eisenhower continued his military habits of shared leadership. "No man can be a Napoleon in modern war," the president once said. "I don't believe this government was set up to be operated by any one acting alone."

Dwight D. Eisenhower [signature]

---

visited the Soviet Union and Premier Khrushchev came to the United States. Touring Iowa farms, Pittsburgh steel plants, and Hollywood movie studios, the jovial Khrushchev charmed the American media. In Des Moines he jokingly told reporters, "We have beaten you to the moon, but you have beaten us in sausage making." He and Eisenhower agreed to meet at a summit conference in Paris the following year to discuss arms reductions.

In May 1960, however, just before the Paris conference was to open, Khrushchev announced that an American U-2—a high-altitude spy plane—had been shot down over the Soviet Union. At first American officials insisted that it was a weather-research plane that had strayed off course. But the captured pilot, Francis Gary Powers, admitted he had been on a spying mission.

Khrushchev refused to go ahead with the summit unless the United States halted such spying missions and apologized for past flights. Eisenhower promised that the U-2 flights would stop but did not apologize. Khrushchev refused to meet with Eisenhower again. The brief thaw in the Cold War had come to an abrupt end.

■■ **The U-2 incident halted arms-reduction talks between Khrushchev and Eisenhower.**

SECTION 1 REVIEW

IDENTIFY and explain the significance of the following: Dwight D. Eisenhower, Margaret Chase Smith, hydrogen bomb, *Sputnik,* National Aeronautics and Space Administration, National Defense Education Act, brinkmanship, Eisenhower Doctrine, Nikita Khrushchev.

LOCATE and explain the importance of the following: Iran, Guatemala, Suez Canal.

1. **MAIN IDEA** How did the armistice that ended the Korean War affect Korea?

2. **MAIN IDEA** What effect did the U-2 incident have on relations between the United States and the Soviet Union?

3. **COMPARING** What various tactics did Eisenhower use to protect U.S. interests abroad?

4. **WRITING TO PERSUADE** Imagine you are a reporter covering the Army-McCarthy hearings. Write a commentary explaining why Senator McCarthy should be removed from office.

5. **EVALUATING** What actions by the Soviet Union and the United States heightened Americans' fears of nuclear war?

THE AFFLUENT SOCIETY

FOCUS

■ **What was the economy like in the 1950s?**

■ **How did the population shift during the decade?**

■ **What was early television programming like?**

■ **How did the work force change in the 1950s?**

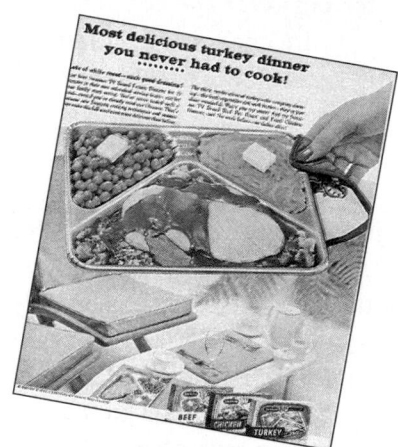

Advertisement for TV dinner

During Eisenhower's presidency a rapidly growing economy brought prosperity to many Americans. Newly prosperous whites left the cities for the suburbs, while the rural poor flocked to urban areas in search of jobs. The growth of the suburbs and the spread of television helped create a consumer culture that many of the poorer members of society could not enjoy. Changes in the workplace and the work force also helped transform American society during the 1950s.

MODERN REPUBLICANISM

President Eisenhower took office in 1953 determined to change the federal government. He pledged to cut the bureaucracy, to curb what he called the "creeping socialism" of the New Deal, to balance the budget, and to reduce government regulation of the economy.

In the first year of his presidency, Eisenhower cut thousands of government jobs and pared billions of dollars from the federal budget. To reduce government influence over the economy, he cut government farm subsidies and turned over federally owned coastal lands for private development.

But despite his pledge to curb "creeping socialism," Eisenhower left the basic social and economic programs of the New Deal–Fair Deal era intact. Under his administration, social security and unemployment benefits expanded, and the minimum wage increased. Eisenhower established the Department of Health, Education, and Welfare, under the supervision of Texan Oveta Culp Hobby. The president also supported the largest increase in educational spending up to that time. This approach to domestic affairs, which Eisenhower described as "conservative when it comes to money and liberal when it comes to human beings," became known as **modern Republicanism**.

Providing funding for social programs, defense, and other government obligations undermined Eisenhower's pledge to balance the federal budget.

◀ **As secretary of Health, Education, and Welfare, Oveta Culp Hobby lobbied for legislation providing for a national polio vaccination program.**

Only three of the eight budgets he presided over were balanced. Furthermore, during his years in office the federal debt grew by about 9 percent, to $291 billion.

THE "GOOD" YEARS

For many Americans the 1950s was a decade of economic prosperity. The post–World War II spending spree that began in the late 1940s continued into the 1950s. Defense spending, triggered by the Korean War, also boosted growth in the early 1950s. Unemployment and inflation rarely edged above 5 percent. By the mid-1950s more than 60 percent of Americans were earning a "middle-class" income, at that time considered $3,000–$10,000 annually. Never before, the popular media declared, had so many people enjoyed such prosperity. "This is a new kind of capitalism," declared the *Reader's Digest,* "capitalism for the many, not for the few."

Not everyone shared in the good times, however. A 1957 study found nearly 40 million Americans living below or near the poverty line of $3,000 for a family of four. Almost half of the nation's poor lived in rural areas, where they suffered from poor nutrition, inadequate medical care, and lack of education.

■■ **The 1950s saw rapid economic expansion and prosperity for many, but the prosperity was not evenly distributed.**

PEOPLE ON THE MOVE

The 1950s was a decade of geographic mobility. Millions of newly prosperous whites, especially young couples, moved to the suburbs that sprang up around the nation's cities. At the same time, many poor rural citizens migrated to the cities in search of a better life.

The urban communities. Most of the rural residents who moved to the cities to escape poverty found little improvement in their economic status. By 1960 more than 20 million city dwellers were living in poverty.

While large numbers of poor rural whites flocked to the cities, African Americans constituted

▲ **Puerto Rican immigrants developed strong community organizations in their New York neighborhoods. Here, Puerto Rican boys play in the game room of the Good Neighbor Church and Community Center located in Manhattan.**

the single largest group in the rural-to-urban movement. In a continuation of the Great Migration, which had begun during World War I (see Chapter 20), African Americans left the South for the industrial cities of the North. This northward movement peaked in the mid-1950s, with the African American population of some northern cities growing by about 2,000 each week.

Wide-scale unemployment caused many Puerto Ricans to leave the island for the mainland. Some 40,000–50,000 migrated annually in the 1950s. About 70 percent of Puerto Rican migrants settled in New York City. Many Mexicans also moved to the States in order to find work. While most immigrants from Mexico had previously settled in rural areas, the new immigrants tended to settle in cities such as Los Angeles, Denver, El Paso, Phoenix, and San Antonio. By 1960 about 80 percent of Hispanic Americans were living in cities.

Relocation under pressure. Thousands of Native Americans also moved to the cities in the 1950s. But unlike other migrants, Native Americans did so under federal pressure. To promote the assimilation of Native Americans into mainstream society, the Eisenhower administration supported passage of the **Relocation Act** of 1956. The act urged Native

▶ **In 1958, Native Americans protested when the federal government seized reservation land for a power project in Niagara Falls. This Tuscarora boy was photographed as he walked the picket line.**

Americans to move to urban areas. It even set up relocation offices in major cities to assist newcomers. Many feared that this would deplete the reservations of future leaders and destroy tribal cultures. Oglala Lakota activist Gerald One Feather recalled:

66 The relocation program had an impact on our . . . government at Pine Ridge [South Dakota]. Many people who could have provided [our] leadership were lost because they had motivation to go off the reservation to find employment or obtain an education. Relocation drained off a lot of our potential leadership. 99

To hasten relocation, the government adopted a policy of termination in 1953. **Termination** involved ending on a tribe-by-tribe basis the reservation system and most federal funding for Native Americans. Various tribal groups launched protests and lawsuits against the termination policy, considering it an attempt to wipe out Native American communities. By 1958 the Eisenhower administration backed down, saying it would no longer support legislation "to terminate tribes without their consent."

The suburbs. As more poor migrants settled in the cities, many more-prosperous city residents moved to the suburbs. By the end of the decade,

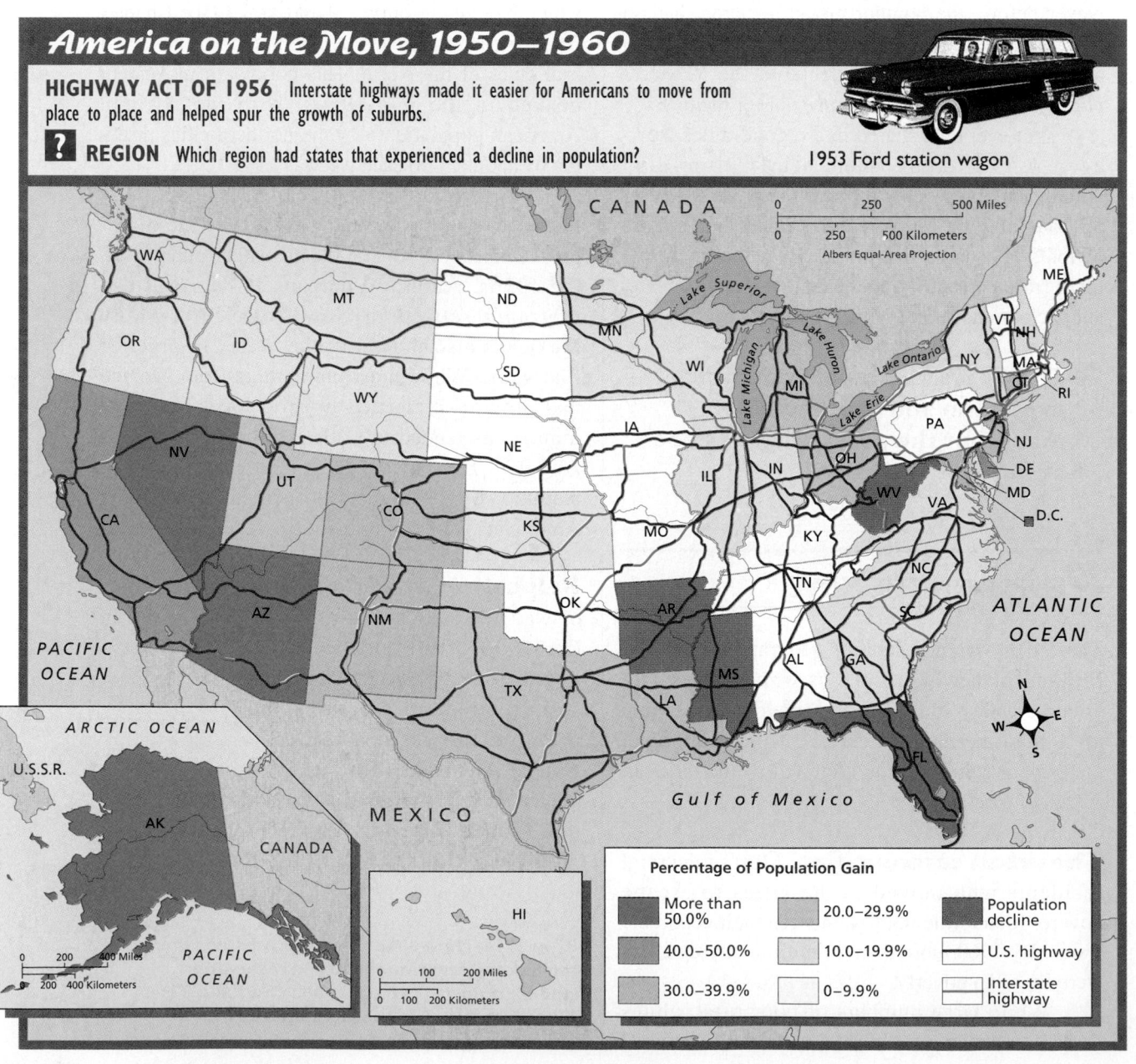

America on the Move, 1950–1960

HIGHWAY ACT OF 1956 Interstate highways made it easier for Americans to move from place to place and helped spur the growth of suburbs.

? REGION Which region had states that experienced a decline in population?

1953 Ford station wagon

Percentage of Population Gain
- More than 50.0%
- 40.0–50.0%
- 30.0–39.9%
- 20.0–29.9%
- 10.0–19.9%
- 0–9.9%
- Population decline
- U.S. highway
- Interstate highway

"I'm Mrs. Edward M. Barnes. Where do I live?"

Drawn by Robert Day ©1954, 1982
The New Yorker Magazine, Inc.

▲ **This cartoon satirizing life in the suburbs appeared in *The New Yorker* in 1954.**

close to 60 million Americans—one third of the total population—lived in the suburbs. Many of these suburbs were planned communities.

Suburban growth took off in part because more Americans could afford to purchase homes. Veterans had access to low-interest mortgages from such government agencies as the Veterans Administration (VA) and the Federal Housing Administration (FHA). Private savings and loan associations, too, offered mortgages on relatively easy terms. In addition, the **Highway Act** of 1956 greatly expanded the nation's highway systems, making it easier for suburban residents to commute to jobs in the cities.

The growth of suburbs was also spurred by an expanding population. During the depression and World War II years, many people had postponed getting married or starting a family. After the war, Americans began to get married at earlier ages and in greater numbers than they had for generations. They also had more children. The soaring birth rate accounted for more than 90 percent of the 30-million increase in the population during the 1950s. The decade, many observers said, had experienced nothing less than a **baby boom**.

■■ **Poor whites, African Americans, Hispanic Americans, and Native Americans moved to the cities, while many middle-class Americans moved to the suburbs.**

CONSUMPTION AND CONFORMITY

Suburbanization and prosperity changed the way many Americans lived. Seemingly secure in their jobs and confident of increasing incomes,

Americans went on a buying spree, purchasing between five and seven million new automobiles and an array of household appliances each year.

With an increase in consumerism came a rising emphasis on conformity. Suburban neighbors worked hard to "keep up with the Joneses," or rather, to make sure that they had as many modern conveniences as their neighbors. Scholar Henry Steele Commager noted how conformity affected American values: "What is the new loyalty? It is, above all, conformity. It is the uncritical and unquestioning acceptance of America as it is."

Children became an important focus of suburban life, largely because of the baby boom. Many social activities in the suburbs involved children, such as scouting, music lessons, and athletics. The number of children in schools increased by some 10 million in the 1950s.

The baby boom also led to an emphasis on child rearing, focusing on the role of mothers. Popular magazines, advertisements, and self-help books depicted the perfect wife and mother as a full-time homemaker who devoted all of her energy to making her family happy (and buying all the latest household gadgets). Contrary to these popular images, however, the number of working mothers actually *increased* during the 1950s, from about 3.6 million to some 6.6 million. By the end of the decade, over 39 percent of all women with children ages 6 to 17 worked for wages outside the home.

CHANGES IN MATERIAL STANDARDS OF LIVING, 1940–1955

Households Owning	1940	1955
Automobile	50.0%	71.0%
Television Set	0.0%	76.1%
Refrigerator	44.0%	94.1%
Washing Machine	46.0%	84.1%
Clothes Dryer	0.0%	9.2%
Vacuum Cleaner	38.0%	64.3%

Sources: *The Overworked American; 1956 Statistical Abstract; An Economic History of Women in America; The Proud Decades*

"THE GOOD LIFE" After World War II many American consumers rushed to buy the latest in modern conveniences.

❓ **BUILDING CHART SKILLS** Which item experienced the greatest increase in ownership?

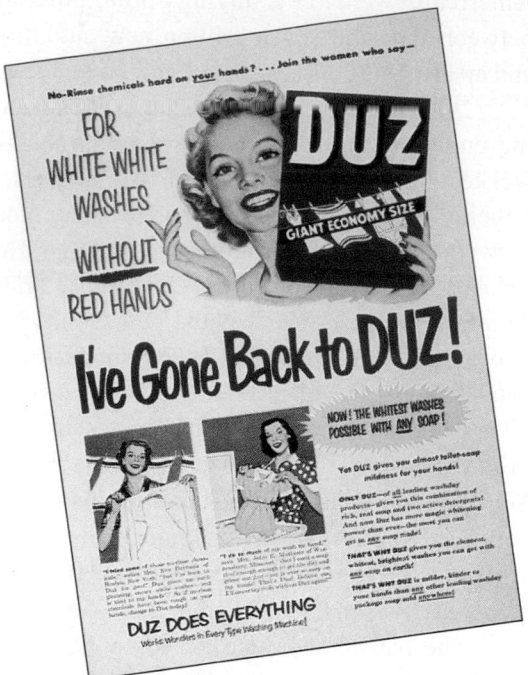

▲ The stereotypical "happy housewife" was often used in 1950s advertisements to sell household products to female shoppers.

While it had long been common for mothers of poor families to work for wages, an increasing number of women in the work force were middle-class suburban mothers. Despite the media's image of the typical middle-class family as a stay-at-home wife supported by a well-employed husband, many families needed a second income to share in the middle-class consumer culture. Many of the jobs held by these women were part-time or low-level jobs with little long-term career potential.

Just as the reality of working mothers conflicted with media images of the suburban housewife, so too did the reality of domestic life. Though advertisements portrayed the full-time suburban homemaker as happy and satisfied, many experts argued that isolation at home made women "bored stiff," especially after their children left home. Indeed, many stay-at-home suburban mothers longed to pursue career opportunities once their children were older. Writer Benita Eisler recalled:

66 For our generation of housewives and mothers, "getting it over with" was our promise to a future deferred. We would "do something" with our college education (or finish it) when we "got out from under" diapers, formulas, car pools. 99

THE GOLDEN AGE OF TELEVISION

Television helped to reinforce both consumerism and mythical images of American life. By the end of the 1950s, 46 million households owned at least one television set. According to a 1950 survey the average junior high student watched 27 hours of television per week.

Advertising played a major role in television programming. By 1960, advertisers were spending $1.6 billion trying to convince viewers to buy their products. Often one business would sponsor a show, such as *General Electric Theatre* and *Kraft Television Theatre,* so that viewers immediately connected the program with a company. This monopoly on advertising also gave many companies great control over program content. During the height of McCarthyism, many sponsors had actors and writers fired from shows because of their suspected political beliefs.

Sporting events, comedies, variety programs, and quiz shows—such as the World Series, *Your Show of Shows,* and *The $64,000 Question*—shared the airwaves with serious dramas in the early years of television. The most popular program of the decade was the comedy *I Love Lucy,* starring Lucille Ball and Desi Arnaz. Thousands of fans tuned in every week to witness Lucy's slapstick antics. Seventy percent of television viewers tuned in when the character gave birth to a baby boy in one episode.

Though television grew in popularity, it proved a very selective mirror, showing primarily white, middle-class, suburban experiences. Poverty, if shown at all, was a problem all but solved. Working women, ethnic minorities, and inner-city life rarely appeared. When they did, it was usually in a way that reinforced stereotypes.

▼ In 1993, *TV Guide* magazine rated the *I Love Lucy* show as the best sitcom in television history.

The 1950s was a decade in which science was king. New discoveries in biology, chemistry, and physics led many to believe that scientific research held the answers to all of the nation's, and even the world's, problems. This was especially the case in agriculture.

The production and use of chemical pesticides and fertilizers soared in the 1950s. One insecticide in particular was hailed as a modern miracle—dichlorodiphenyltrichloroethane (DDT). DDT and similar pesticides promised farmers increased crop yields and reduced labor expenses. Consumers would benefit as well with higher quality food at a lower cost. These modern chemicals seemed to be a dream come true.

But amid all the praise, Rachel Carson, a former biologist with the U.S. Fish and Wildlife Service, asked, "What has already silenced all the voices of spring in countless towns in America?" In 1962

Carson sent the world a startling message in her book *Silent Spring.* She warned that the indiscriminate use of pesticides, particularly DDT, killed wildlife and polluted the environment. Carson cited a Michigan town that sprayed DDT to kill beetles attacking the town's elm trees. When the elm leaves fell in the fall, they were eaten by worms, which were then eaten by robins. By early spring, almost all the robins in the city were dead.

▲ **Workers spray pesticides on fruit trees.**

Today, views on the use of DDT and other pesticides have changed dramatically. Public opinion and that of the scientific community now firmly stand behind many of Carson's ideas.

Since the 1960s, possible evidence of cancer and other health problems in field workers and children exposed to DDT has surfaced. And traces of DDT have been found in penguins and seals in Antarctica and in whales off the coast of Greenland—areas far removed from any application of the chemical.

As a result, in 1972 the Environmental Protection Agency (EPA) ordered a ban on domestic uses of DDT, and by the mid-1980s the agency had made addressing pesticide pollution a priority. Now the chemical industry, research scientists, and environmental groups are experimenting with a variety of natural biological controls, such as fungi, bacteria, and "beneficial" insects, to destroy harmful pests.

Carson died in 1964, too soon to see the results of her efforts. Her concerns and warnings inspired a generation of Americans to work toward finding ecologically safe pesticides and fertilizers.

One of the era's most controversial programs was the popular comedy about black urban life, *Amos 'n' Andy.* The show began as a radio program with two white men creating the voices of black characters. When the show moved to television, African American actors took over the roles; but to many viewers, the characters reflected white stereotypes of the black community. The NAACP launched a protest against the program, arguing that it portrayed African Americans as "lazy, dumb and dishonest." Others joined in the protest, and in 1953 *Amos 'n' Andy* left the air. In 1966 the network banned it from being shown in reruns.

■■ **Television provided a variety of programs but often reinforced stereotypes of ethnic groups, women, and American life.**

Changes in the Workplace

Many of the social shifts in America were related to shifts in the work force. Large corporations prospered during the decade. Some 5,000 companies merged together to form larger companies.

Automation. American factories were also changing. Throughout the 1950s companies introduced machines that could perform industrial operations faster and more efficiently than human workers could. This process of **automation** greatly increased productivity. But automation also reduced the number of manufacturing jobs. Many workers began to fear an automated future, as one popular song noted:

> 66 I walked, walked, walked into the
> foreman's office.
> To find out what was what.
> I looked him in the eye and said,
> "What goes?"
> And this is the answer I got:
> His eyes turned red, then green,
> then blue
> And it suddenly dawned on me—
> There was a robot sitting in the seat
> Where the foreman used to be. 99

Automation affected America's farms as well, as new machinery boosted production while reducing the labor force. While farm productivity increased from 1950 to the 1960s, the farm population shrank from 23 million to 15.6 million.

At the same time the number of manufacturing and farming jobs decreased, professional and service jobs increased. Huge new corporations required a multitude of managers, supervisors, and clerical workers. Furthermore, the spending spree of the 1950s created millions of retail jobs. Many of the newly created service jobs were in occupations traditionally filled by women, such as nursing, teaching, retail sales, and clerical work. By 1960, women made up about one third of the total work force. But many women continued to earn much less than men in the same fields, and few received promotions to management jobs.

The new union style. Changes in the work force also influenced organized labor. Boosted in part by the merger of the AFL and CIO in 1955, union membership grew steadily in the mid-1950s, peaking at some 18.5 million in 1956.

To help workers get their fair share of economic prosperity, union leaders abandoned efforts at economic, political, and social reforms in favor of achieving gains in wages and benefits. In order to do so, they sought accommodation, rather than confrontation, with management. George Meany, the AFL–CIO's first president, boasted that he had never led a strike. Further, he said he had no interest in reforming society. His only goal, he stated, was to ensure "an ever rising standard of living" for his members.

Many unions fought for and won guaranteed annual wages and cost-of-living adjustments—automatic pay raises linked to the rate of inflation. In return, unions made concessions, such as accepting automation plans or changes in work rules or production levels.

In the late 1950s newspapers reported corruption and links to organized crime among some union officials. Congress attempted to crack down on union corruption by passing the **Landrum-Griffin Act** of 1959, which banned ex-convicts from holding union offices, required frequent elections of officers, and regulated the investment of union funds. The negative publicity hurt union membership, which steadily declined after 1957.

■■ **The work force changed through automation, an increase in professional and service jobs, and a new approach by union leaders.**

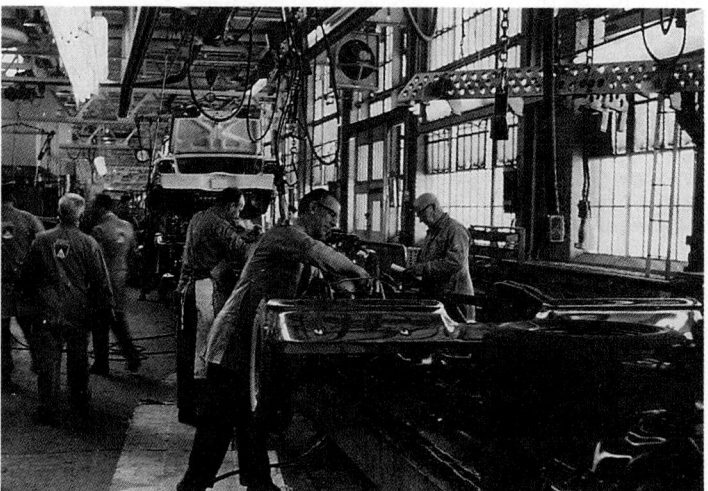

▲ Ford Motor Company closed its Somerville, Massachusetts, plant in 1958. Over 1,000 employees were directly affected by the decision.

URBAN RENEWAL

The changing work force also affected those moving to the cities. Automation had eliminated many of the semiskilled jobs traditionally taken by city newcomers. Skilled workers often found that their way to better jobs was blocked by discrimination.

Nowhere was discrimination more obvious than in housing. Prevented by poverty and by discriminatory real-estate practices from moving into newer neighborhoods, African Americans, Hispanics, and Native Americans were generally limited to crowded tenements and old housing in the poorest neighborhoods. Eventually, however, these neighborhoods provided a sense of community for those who lived there. Local stores, churches, and social clubs gave structure to the lives of those struggling to adjust to the cities. As one resident of El Barrio, New York's Puerto Rican neighborhood, observed:

66 This is our neighborhood. . . . We consider this part of the city to be ours. . . . The stores, barbershops, restaurants, butcher shops, churches, funeral parlors, . . . everything is all Latino. 99

Government officials, however, saw only neglected, shabby buildings. To improve inner-city housing, the federal government proposed **urban renewal** programs to replace old, run-down inner-city buildings with new ones. Across the country the government bulldozed older urban neighborhoods to

▲ A poor family crowds into the kitchen of a small tenement in Harlem, New York City.

make way for some 417,000 low-income public housing units. Most of these units were cramped apartments, so small, one resident said, "You feel like you can't breathe." The new buildings also had a cold, unfriendly atmosphere. The sense of community that people had felt in the old neighborhoods was gone.

SECTION 2 REVIEW

IDENTIFY and explain the significance of the following: Oveta Culp Hobby, modern Republicanism, Relocation Act, termination, Highway Act, baby boom, automation, George Meany, Landrum-Griffin Act, urban renewal.

1. **MAIN IDEA** Describe the shifts in population that occurred during the 1950s. How did these shifts affect city residents?

2. **MAIN IDEA** What changes occurred in the work force during the 1950s?

3. **IDENTIFYING CAUSE AND EFFECT** Why are the 1950s considered boom years? How were American values affected by the economic boom?

4. **WRITING TO EVALUATE** Imagine you are a television critic during the 1950s. Write an article for *TV Guide* that assesses the portrayal of ethnic groups, women, and families on television.

5. **GAINING A MULTICULTURAL PERSPECTIVE** What effect did discrimination in housing have on ethnic groups? Why were some ethnic communities upset with urban renewal programs?

VOICES OF DISSENT

FOCUS

■ Why were the *Brown* v. *Board of Education* decision and the Montgomery bus boycott major turning points for the civil rights movement?

■ What did the Central High School crisis demonstrate about some white southerners' attitudes toward desegregation?

■ How did teenagers rebel against the conformity of the 1950s?

Although politics and popular culture in the 1950s emphasized conformity, a few voices spoke out against the system. African Americans, tired of segregation and discrimination, launched the civil rights movement to demand equality. Meanwhile writers, including the Beats, and a new style of music called rock 'n' roll sowed the seeds of rebellion in teenagers.

Rebel Without a Cause
movie poster

BROWN v. BOARD

The NAACP had long waged a campaign against segregation in education, a practice upheld by the Supreme Court's 1896 "separate but equal" doctrine in *Plessy* v. *Ferguson* (see Chapter 13). The NAACP had been able to open some all-white universities and graduate schools to African American students by demonstrating that in most cases separate educational facilities for black students were far inferior to the facilities established for whites only. But the Court continued to maintain that segregation in and of itself was legal.

In 1952 a group of cases that challenged segregation in public schools came before the Supreme Court in the form of *Brown* v. *The Board of Education of Topeka*. The case involved Linda Brown, a young African American student from Topeka, Kansas. Segregation in Topeka's schools prevented her from attending an all-white elementary school a short walk from her home. Instead, she had to travel a long distance over dangerous railroad tracks to get to an all-black school.

Arguing on Brown's behalf, NAACP lawyer Thurgood Marshall introduced data that suggested segregation psychologically damaged African American students by lowering their self-esteem.

▼ **Thurgood Marshall (center) discussed legal strategies for fighting school segregation cases with other NAACP attorneys in 1954.**

Marshall's arguments greatly influenced the Court's ruling, which was issued on May 17, 1954. Written by Chief Justice Earl Warren, the unanimous decision declared that segregation generated

> 66 a feeling of inferiority . . . that may affect [children's] hearts and minds in a way unlikely ever to be undone. . . . In the field of education the doctrine of "separate but equal" has no place. Separate educational facilities are inherently unequal. 99

Many Americans praised the decision as a long overdue step toward ending segregation entirely. Scholar Allison Davis hailed it as the salvation of American industry because it would create more skilled black workers: "The survival of the United States seems to depend upon its developing the ability of millions of our citizens whose capacities have been crippled by segregation."

Some states moved quickly to end school segregation. Many white southern leaders, however, reacted to the decision with alarm. The governor of Virginia, for instance, vowed to use every legal means at his command to maintain segregated schools in his state. Because of the resistance from the South, the Supreme Court issued a ruling in 1955 calling on the federal district courts to end school segregation "with all deliberate speed."

THE MONTGOMERY BUS BOYCOTT

The NAACP next aimed at ending segregation on southern transportation systems, beginning their efforts in Montgomery, Alabama. Local NAACP leaders had been looking for a test case to challenge the practice of forcing African American citizens to ride in the back of buses. On December 1, 1955, Rosa Parks, a black seamstress, provided them with their case when she refused to give up her bus seat to a white passenger.

BIO GRAPHY Born in 1913 in Tuskegee, Alabama, Rosa Parks moved to the Montgomery area at a young age. Her mother was determined that Parks would receive a good education. Montgomery did not have a high school for black students, so her parents sent her to the laboratory school at Alabama State College. Because discrimination prevented her from finding a job that matched her education, she found work as a seamstress. She also became involved in the

Rosa Parks

civil rights movement, holding office in the Montgomery chapter of the NAACP.

In the late 1950s Parks moved to Detroit, where she began working for Congressman John Conyers in 1967. She has continued her commitment to civil rights action and has won numerous awards, including the NAACP's Spingarn Medal, recognizing the "highest or noblest achievement" by an African American.

Parks's refusal to give up her seat led to her arrest and conviction for violating the city's segregation laws. In protest, Montgomery's 50,000 African Americans organized a boycott against the bus system. The **Montgomery Improvement Association** (MIA), a group of local civil rights leaders, persuaded the community to continue the boycott while the NAACP and Parks fought her conviction in the courts.

The MIA chose as its spokesperson Martin Luther King, Jr., a 26-year-old Baptist minister who was new to the town. An energetic and charismatic speaker, King could inspire large audiences. His ability to move people helped hold the African American community together as the bus boycott dragged on for months.

White racists tried every method from intimidation to physical violence to break the boycott. White vigilantes attacked and beat boycotters and bombed the houses of King and other MIA leaders. Many boycotters—including Rosa Parks—lost their jobs. But King urged the black community not to respond to violence with more violence. Finally, the peaceful protest worked. In November 1956 the Supreme Court declared both the Montgomery and the Alabama segregation laws unconstitutional. By the end of the year, Montgomery had a desegregated bus system, and the civil rights movement had a new leader—Martin Luther King, Jr.

The successful struggle of thousands of Montgomery blacks to win their basic human rights marked a blow to conformity—and to the general fear of standing up against those in power engendered by Cold War hysteria in America. Not surprisingly, Martin Luther King, Jr., was accused of being a Communist by many who opposed the movement. Some southern whites, however, reluctantly accepted that change had to

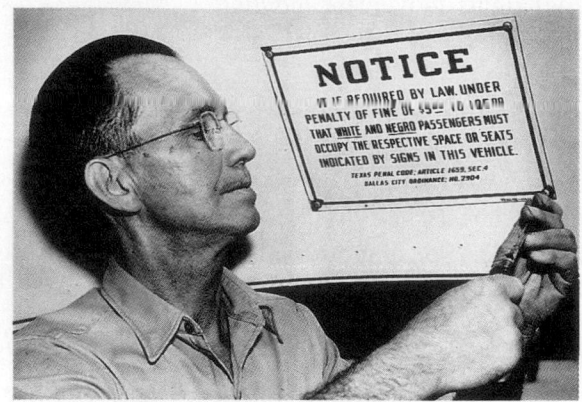

▲ In response to a 1956 court ruling, Dallas buses were ordered to end segregation. Shown here is an employee of the Dallas Transit Company removing a separate seating sign from the rear of a bus.

come. As a South Carolina newspaper declared, "Segregation is going—it's all but gone. . . . The South can't reverse the trend." Even so, other white southerners fought to delay change for as long as possible.

■■ *Brown* v. *Board of Education* and the Montgomery bus boycott marked the first steps toward ending segregation in the South.

SHOWDOWN IN LITTLE ROCK

Despite the Supreme Court rulings, school desegregation in the South moved slowly. By the end of the 1956–57 school year, the vast majority of southern school systems remained segregated. In Arkansas, however, school desegregation was progressing with relatively little opposition. Two of the three southern school districts that began desegregation in 1954 were in Arkansas. The Little Rock school board was the first

in the South to announce it would comply with the *Brown* decision.

Little Rock's desegregation plan was set to begin in September 1957 with the admission of nine black students to the all-white Central High School. However, Governor Orval Faubus, about to embark on a bid for reelection, came out against the desegregation plan. The night before school was to start, he ordered the Arkansas National Guard to surround Central High. He did so, he claimed, to protect the school from attacks by armed protesters. "It will not be possible to restore or to maintain order . . . if forcible integration is carried out tomorrow in the schools of this community," he warned.

No real danger existed, but Faubus's claims panicked the community. When the black students attempted to enter the school, a mob of angry whites and a line of armed National Guardsmen met them. One of the students, Elizabeth Eckford, described the ordeal:

66 When I got in front of the school, . . . I didn't know what to do. . . . Just then the guards let some white students through. . . . I walked up to the guard who had let [them] in. . . . When I tried to squeeze past him, he raised his bayonet, and then the other guards moved in. . . . Somebody [in the crowd] started yelling, *"Lynch her! Lynch her!"* 99

For nearly three weeks the National Guard prevented the students, now known as the "**Little Rock Nine**," from entering the school. Then under

▶ Elizabeth Eckford bravely walked alone through a crowd of angry, jeering whites before she was turned away from entering Little Rock's Central High School.

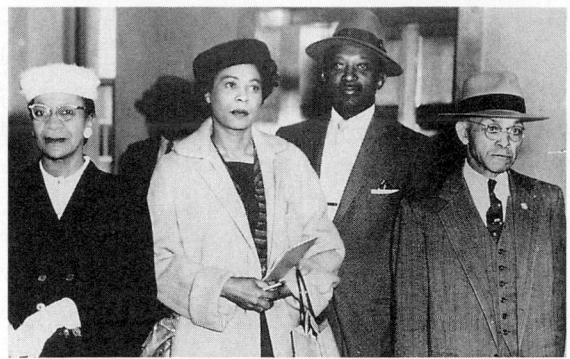

▲ On November 4, 1957, leaders of the Arkansas branch of the NAACP appeared in court to fight an ordinance forcing them to turn over confidential records. State president Daisy Bates (second from the left) played a central role in helping the Little Rock Nine integrate Central High School.

court order, Faubus removed the National Guard. When the nine attempted to enter the school on September 23, the white mob rioted. Deploring the "disgraceful occurrences" at Central High, President Eisenhower ordered some 1,000 federal troops to Little Rock. On September 25, 1957, under the troops' fixed bayonets, the Little Rock Nine finally entered Central High.

In the midst of the Little Rock crisis, President Eisenhower signed the **Civil Rights Act of 1957**. This act, the first civil rights law since Reconstruction, made it a federal crime to prevent qualified persons from voting. It also set up the federal Civil Rights Commission to investigate violations of the law. A follow-up law, passed in 1960, strengthened the courts' powers to protect blacks' voting rights. But prejudice and discrimination continued to be a fact of life for most African Americans. Much remained to be done before they could claim victory in the struggle for civil rights.

■■ The Central High crisis in Little Rock showed that some southern whites were not willing to comply with desegregation.

REBELS AMID CONFORMITY

While the African American community in the South was challenging segregation, other groups were beginning to question the American culture of consumption and conformity. One such group included a handful of writers and scholars who sought to expose what one called the "crack in the picture window" of society.

A number of novelists depicted the experiences of those facing poverty and discrimination. In Ralph Ellison's *Invisible Man* (1952), an African American man searches for his place in a society at once both hostile and indifferent to him. His struggle reflects that of many people left out of mainstream society:

❝ I am an invisible man. . . . I am a man of substance, of flesh and bone, fiber and liquids—and I might even be said to possess a mind. I am invisible, understand, simply because people refuse to see me. ❞

Other critics attacked suburban society and the corporate mentality of America. Harvard economist John Kenneth Galbraith warned privileged Americans in *The Affluent Society* (1958) that they were ignoring pressing social issues in their pursuit of material possessions and comfort.

Sociologists William Whyte, C. Wright Mills, and David Riesman criticized the new corporate system. Whyte in *The Organization Man* (1956) and Mills in *White Collar* (1951) argued that the need to conform in a large corporation was wiping out the independent spirit of workers. Riesman argued that the country was facing "a silent revolution against work" because work no longer had meaning for people. Many younger Americans were beginning to agree with him.

The **Beats**, a small but influential group of writers and poets, challenged both the literary

▲ Ralph Ellison received the National Book Award in 1953 for his novel *Invisible Man*.

conventions of the day and the life-styles of the middle class. Allen Ginsberg's poem "Howl," for instance, raged against the nuclear threat and the conventions of corporate America. The Beats wrote as they lived—without form, plot, planning, or revision. One of the best-known Beat works, Jack Kerouac's novel *On the Road* (1957), was written in a continuous three-week-long session at the typewriter. Kerouac celebrated the search for individual identity and the rejection of stability. One sentence in the novel caught the essence of the Beat philosophy: "We gotta go and never stop going till we get there."

A "SILENT GENERATION"?

Despite many parents' fears, the Beats never grew into a mass movement among young people. Indeed, many observers dubbed the middle-class youth of the 1950s the **silent generation** because of their seeming willingness to conform to consumer culture without protest. Despite the outward appearance of conformity, however, many young people were beginning to question society and to rebel in subtle ways.

Misunderstood rebels. Many young people discontented with suburban life found meaning in literature and films. Some identified with Holden Caulfield, the main character of J.D. Salinger's *The Catcher in the Rye* (1951). Disgusted by the hypocrisy of the adult world, Holden declared it "crumby" and "phony." Other young people turned

to satirical magazines, such as *MAD,* which dedicated itself to making fun of everything associated with "the American way of life." Many parents worried that reading such magazines would increase **juvenile delinquency**—antisocial behavior by the young.

Several of the most popular films of the decade reflected images of juvenile delinquency and young, angry rebels frustrated with life. Often their anger was directed not at any one particular thing, but at all of society in general. In the 1953 film *The Wild One,* a character asks the young gang leader played by Marlon Brando what he is rebelling against. Brando snarls back, "Whadda ya got?" This image of the rebel with no direction was reinforced in 1955's *Rebel Without a Cause,* starring James Dean, Natalie Wood, and Sal Mineo as teenagers confused about the values of their suburban families. Many teenagers could identify with that confusion.

The rock rebellion. Many teenagers tried to escape the conformity of suburbia through a new type of music called **rock 'n' roll**. This reworking of black rhythm and blues produced a raw sound very different from many tunes of the day, and teenagers claimed it as their own. Cleveland disc jockey Alan Freed coined the term *rock 'n' roll* in 1951, when he started a rhythm-and-blues show aimed at young white audiences. Soon the sound caught on across the country.

Elvis Presley, a truck driver from Memphis, Tennessee, emerged as rock's leading talent. With his sullen good looks, wild body movements, and blues-influenced vocal style, Presley sent shock waves through the white middle class. African American musicians such as Little Richard, Chuck Berry, and Fats Domino, as well as Hispanic performers like Ritchie Valens, profoundly influenced early rock 'n' roll.

Many parents immediately disliked rock 'n' roll. Some critics called it immoral. Others simply dismissed

◄ Teenagers tuned to Dick Clark's *American Bandstand* to listen to the latest rock 'n' roll records and watch the newest groups perform.

◀ Ritchie Valens

◀ Fats Domino

▲ Elvis Presley

it as useless noise, pointing out that the lyrics of many popular rock songs did not seem to make any sense, such as in the Silhouettes' 1957 hit "Get a Job":

 Sha da da da
Sha da da da da
Bah do
Bah yip yip yip yip yip yip yip yip
Mum mum mum mum mum mum
Get a job. 🙾

Rock 'n' roll also upset many people by seeming to break down the walls of racial segregation. White rockers such as Presley, Jerry Lee Lewis, and Buddy Holly shared the airwaves, and often the stage, with noted black artists. While southern officials were worried about sending black and white teenagers to school together, many of those same teens were listening to the same radio stations and sneaking off to attend the same integrated concerts.

■■ Teenagers rebelled against conformity through literature, films, and rock 'n' roll.

■■
■■

SECTION 3 REVIEW

IDENTIFY and explain the significance of the following: *Brown* v. *The Board of Education of Topeka,* Thurgood Marshall, Rosa Parks, Montgomery Improvement Association, Martin Luther King, Jr., Orval Faubus, "Little Rock Nine," Civil Rights Act of 1957, Ralph Ellison, Beats, Jack Kerouac, silent generation, juvenile delinquency, rock 'n' roll.

LOCATE and explain the importance of the following: Topeka, Kansas; Montgomery, Alabama; Little Rock, Arkansas.

1. **MAIN IDEA** What impact did the decision in *Brown* v. *Board of Education* and the Montgomery bus boycott have on the civil rights movement?

2. **MAIN IDEA** What did events in Little Rock show about attitudes of some southern whites toward school desegregation?

3. **RECOGNIZING POINTS OF VIEW** What arguments did members of the civil rights movement use to help overturn the "separate but equal" doctrine?

4. **WRITING TO EXPRESS A VIEWPOINT** Write a short story involving a teenage character who expresses his or her view of 1950s society.

5. **USING HISTORICAL IMAGINATION** Imagine you are a member of the Montgomery Improvement Association in 1956. Write a speech you would deliver to the community urging them to continue the boycott against the bus system.

Dwight D. Eisenhower elected president. First H-bomb test held. *Invisible Man* published.

I Love Lucy debuts.

Korean War ends.

Army-McCarthy hearings held. Supreme Court issues ruling in *Brown v. Board of Education.*

1950   **1952**   **1954**

WRITING A SUMMARY

Using the essential points of the chapter as a guide, write a summary of the chapter.

REVIEWING CHRONOLOGY

Number your paper 1 to 5. Study the time line above, and list the following events in the order in which they happened by writing the first next to 1, the second next to 2, and so on. Then complete the activity below.

1. U-2 incident occurs.
2. Montgomery bus boycott begins.
3. First H-bomb test held.
4. Army-McCarthy hearings held.
5. *On the Road* published.

Assessing Consequences How did the launch of *Sputnik* affect the United States?

IDENTIFYING PEOPLE AND IDEAS

Explain the historical significance of each of the following people or terms.

1. Margaret Chase Smith
2. brinkmanship
3. Mohammad Mosaddeq
4. Eisenhower Doctrine
5. Landrum-Griffin Act
6. baby boom
7. termination
8. Thurgood Marshall
9. "Little Rock Nine"
10. Beats

UNDERSTANDING MAIN IDEAS

1. How did the end of the Korean War affect Korea and the United States?
2. What factors led to the rise of McCarthyism? What events brought about McCarthy's downfall?
3. How did the economic prosperity of the 1950s affect both domestic life and the workplace?
4. What were some of the major successes and setbacks in ending segregated education in the 1950s?
5. How did literature, films, and music affect middle-class teenagers in the 1950s?

REVIEWING THEMES

1. **Economic Development** How were population shifts affected by the economic boom of the 1950s?

2. **Cultural Diversity** How did some people attempt to rebel against the conformity of the 1950s?
3. **Democratic Values** How did Native Americans and African Americans fight discrimination during this decade?

THINKING CRITICALLY

1. **Analyzing** What strategies did President Eisenhower use to fight the spread of communism? Where were these strategies used?
2. **Evaluating** What events contributed to Americans' fears of nuclear war? How were these fears reduced?
3. **Synthesizing** What was the popular image of a mother's role in society during the 1950s? How did this image conflict with reality?

STRATEGY FOR SUCCESS

Review the Strategies for Success on Recognizing Fallacies in Reasoning on page 220. Examine the following excerpt, written by a white southerner opposed to the forced integration of schools. Then analyze the excerpt for a fallacy in reasoning.

66 Much of the legislation enacted in the Southern states . . . has been aimed basically at preserving domestic tranquillity as well as racial integrity. This is especially true in the fields of education and recreation, where indiscriminate mingling of the races is bound to bring discord and strife. . . . The closing of such institutions in many cases would be the sensible alternative to the emotional, social, and physical upheaval which would follow on the heels of forced race mixing. 99

WRITING ABOUT HISTORY

Writing to Classify Create a time line that lists the important events of the civil rights movement in this period.

| AFL merges with CIO. Montgomery bus boycott begins. | Suez crisis occurs. Soviet troops invade Budapest, Hungary. | *Sputnik* launched. Federal troops ordered to Little Rock. *On the Road* published. | *Explorer I* launched. | U-2 incident occurs. |

1956   **1958**   **1960**

USING PRIMARY SOURCES

Rock 'n' roll music of the 1950s often reflected a desire to break away from old traditions and be more daring. Read the following lyrics from Chuck Berry's "Roll Over Beethoven" (1956). Who are Beethoven and Tchaikovsky? How do the lyrics of the song reflect rebellion and a break from the past?

> 66 *Well, I'm gonna write a little letter,*
> *gonna mail it to my local D.J.*
> *Yes, it's a jumpin' little record I want*
> *my jockey to play*
> *Roll over Beethoven, I gotta hear it*
> *again today*
> *You know my temp'rature's risin' and*
> *the juke box blowin' a fuse*
> *My heart's beatin' rhythm and my soul*
> *keeps a singin' the blues*
> *Roll over Beethoven and tell*
> *Tchaikovsky the news.* 99

Chuck Berry

LINKING HISTORY AND GEOGRAPHY

Alaska and Hawaii became the 49th and 50th states of the union, respectively, in 1959. Study the map in the next column. What strategic advantages of these two areas might have lent support for their statehood during the Cold War?

Alaska and Hawaii

BUILDING YOUR PORTFOLIO

Complete the following projects independently or cooperatively.

1. **THE COLD WAR** In Chapter 27 you served as a UN conference delegate. Building on that experience, prepare a speech outlining UN goals.

2. **CIVIL RIGHTS** In Chapter 27 you were a reporter covering the Committee on Civil Rights. Building on that experience, develop an outline of the civil rights movement from 1945 to 1960.

3. **POPULAR CULTURE** Imagine you are a magazine editor. Create a photo essay that reflects cultural changes in the 1950s.

Chapter 29

1960–1970

THE SIXTIES

FOCUS

UNDERSTANDING THE MAIN IDEA

The 1960s marked a decade of great change in America. The promise of President John Kennedy's administration was cut short by his assassination. But the new president, Lyndon Johnson, ushered in major social reforms through the Great Society programs, while civil rights leaders finally gained some ground in the struggle for equality. Their success inspired other groups, including some middle-class women and college students, to challenge traditional society.

THEMES

- **GLOBAL RELATIONS** How might foreign policy decisions undermine domestic programs?

- **DEMOCRATIC VALUES** How might protests help expand democracy?

- **CULTURAL DIVERSITY** What are some institutions and traditions that might come under fire by groups questioning conformity?

1960	1962	1964	1968	1969
John F. Kennedy elected president.	Cuban missile crisis erupts.	Freedom Summer launched.	Martin Luther King, Jr., assassinated.	Woodstock Music Festival occurs.

During the Eisenhower era the Cold War intensified. On the domestic front the civil rights movement gained momentum from the Supreme Court ruling on school desegregation and from the success of the Montgomery bus boycott. By the end of the 1950s, the popular culture's emphasis on conformity and consumerism came under attack from the Beats and rock 'n' roll.

March on Washington for civil rights, 1963

*I*n 1960, voters chose the youngest man ever elected president, the 43-year-old John F. Kennedy, to succeed one of the oldest presidents up to that time, the 70-year-old Dwight Eisenhower. Kennedy brought a spirit of youth and hope to the nation—a spirit reflected in the dramatic changes of the 1960s. The civil rights movement continued its success, winning expansion of voting rights for African Americans and further breaking down the walls of segregation in the South. Other groups, such as Mexican Americans, Native Americans, and women, also pressed for fairer treatment. Throughout America the generation raised after World War II started to question traditional society through organized protests, music, and the creation of a counterculture.

On the foreign front, the Cold War reached its most dangerous crisis when the United States and the Soviet Union came to the brink of nuclear war in Cuba. Afterward, both nations worked to ease tensions between them. During this period, the United States also increased its involvement in Latin America and Vietnam. As the Vietnam conflict shifted funding from domestic programs, such as President Lyndon Johnson's Great Society reforms, discontent grew within American society. By the end of the 1960s, much of the idealism that began the decade was lost in the wake of violence and division.

African dashiki, worn by American youths in the 1960s

THE NEW FRONTIER

FOCUS
- How did the Kennedy administration try to boost the economy?
- What was the purpose of flexible response?
- What events sparked the Cuban missile crisis? How did the crisis change Soviet-American relations?

*P*resident Eisenhower's successor, the 43-year-old John F. Kennedy, brought fresh vigor to the office, promising that his administration would be a "new frontier." On the domestic front, he boosted the economy, mostly by increasing spending on defense and space exploration. Internationally, he first stood firm against the Soviets, then tried to ease Soviet-American tensions. In November 1963, Kennedy's presidency ended suddenly and tragically, its bright promise largely unfulfilled.

President John F. Kennedy and Jacqueline Kennedy in 1961

A NEW BEGINNING

As 1960 began, many voters were looking for someone to inject new life into the White House. Economic recession in the late 1950s, coupled with the Soviet Union's advances in space technology, led many people to fear that the country was falling behind its counterparts.

As expected, the Republicans chose Richard Nixon as their presidential candidate in the upcoming election. His solid performance as Eisenhower's vice president had won him wide support among Republican party members. Trying to appeal to a wide variety of voters, he downplayed his past roles in conservative causes such as the investigations of the House Committee on Un-American Activities.

Senator John F. Kennedy of Massachusetts eventually emerged as the Democratic candidate. The Irish American Kennedy promised to "get America moving again." Voters were impressed with his charm, wit, good looks, and war record. But as a Roman Catholic, he faced falling victim to the same prejudices that had hurt Al Smith's presidential bid in 1928. To neutralize concerns about his religion, Kennedy assured voters that he believed firmly in the separation of church and state.

◀ **The second of four televised debates between Senator John F. Kennedy and Vice President Richard Nixon took place on October 7, 1960.**

Nixon led in the polls until the first of four televised debates. Tired and gaunt after an illness, Nixon seemed nervous and uneasy before the cameras. Kennedy, on the other hand, appeared fit, confident, and relaxed. The election was close. Kennedy and his running mate, Lyndon B. Johnson of Texas, defeated Nixon and his running mate, Henry Cabot Lodge, Jr., of Massachusetts, by a margin of fewer than 120,000 popular votes. Their electoral victory was more decisive—303 to 219.

Kennedy was the youngest person ever elected president. His youth helped provide the theme to his inaugural address:

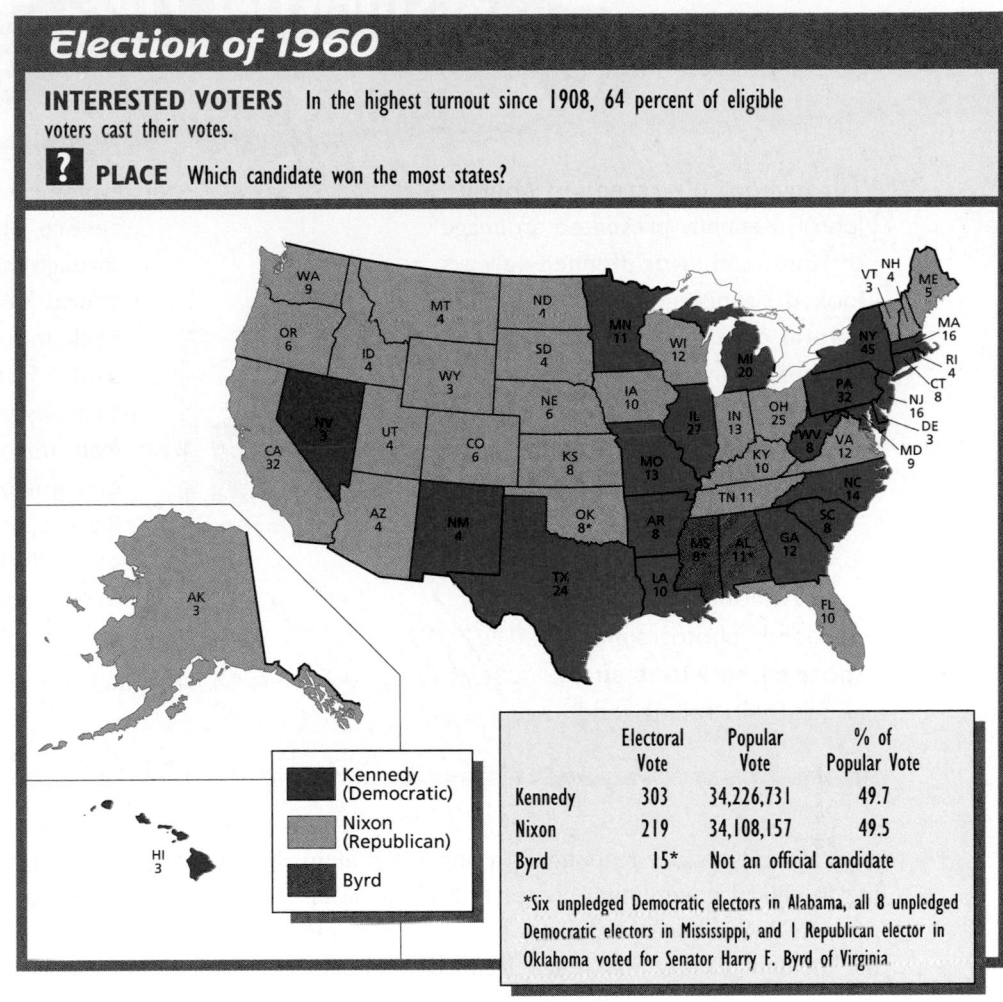

Election of 1960

INTERESTED VOTERS In the highest turnout since 1908, 64 percent of eligible voters cast their votes.

? PLACE Which candidate won the most states?

- Kennedy (Democratic)
- Nixon (Republican)
- Byrd

	Electoral Vote	Popular Vote	% of Popular Vote
Kennedy	303	34,226,731	49.7
Nixon	219	34,108,157	49.5
Byrd	15*	Not an official candidate	

*Six unpledged Democratic electors in Alabama, all 8 unpledged Democratic electors in Mississippi, and 1 Republican elector in Oklahoma voted for Senator Harry F. Byrd of Virginia.

66 Let the word go forth . . . that the torch has been passed to a new generation of Americans. . . . The energy, the faith, the devotion which we bring to this endeavor will light our country and all who serve it. . . . And so, my fellow Americans—ask not what your country can do for you—ask what you can do for your country. 99

THE DOMESTIC FRONTIER

Kennedy stocked his cabinet with young, well-educated men, including his brother Robert as attorney general. These advisers shared the belief that government should offer solutions to national and global problems. Since Kennedy had once compared these problems to a "new frontier," his agenda became known as the **New Frontier**.

One of the first domestic challenges that Kennedy faced was stimulating the economy. To help revive the economy, the president called for an increase in government spending, giving defense and space programs top priority. This emphasis reflected Cold War concerns. In April 1961 Soviet cosmonaut Yuri Gagarin had completed the first orbital space flight, sparking fears that the United States was falling behind in the space race. In late May 1961 Kennedy responded by challenging the nation to "commit itself to achieving the goal, before this decade is out, of landing a man on the moon and returning him safely to earth."

By the end of 1961, inflation was down, but unemployment was still relatively high. Kennedy hoped to keep inflation down and further the recovery by getting labor and business to agree to informal wage and price controls. Businesses had been granting higher wages to workers and then passing the costs on to consumers in the form of higher prices. Kennedy urged businesses to limit prices in return for workers agreeing to fewer pay raises. When U.S. Steel dramatically raised prices in 1962 after workers had agreed to accept small

JOHN F. KENNEDY
1917–1963

Throughout his career in politics, John F. Kennedy presented an image of youth and vigor. Kennedy always looked younger than his years. On several occasions after he entered Congress he was mistaken for a page boy. Once, while he was a senator, a guard tried to stop him from using a special telephone with the warning: "Sorry, mister, these are reserved for the Senators."

Although Kennedy was frequently photographed in sporting activities such as football, sailing, and

JOHN F. KENNEDY

13¢ UNITED STATES

swimming, his athletic image hid the severe physical pain he suffered through most of his adult life. During World War II he suffered a severe back injury after his naval vessel sank. For the rest of his life, Kennedy would endure extreme pain from this injury and from the effects of Addison's disease. His brother Robert once recalled that "at least one half of the days that he spent on this earth were days of intense physical pain." Publicly, however, he seldom displayed signs of physical strain.

pay raises, Kennedy responded in anger, threatening to cancel government contracts with the company. U.S. Steel soon withdrew the price hike, but the incident further weakened Kennedy's already shaky relationship with the business community.

■■ Kennedy helped boost the economy through increased spending, especially in space and defense programs.

Kennedy also had problems getting cooperation from Congress. A coalition of southern Democrats and conservative Republicans in Congress blocked about two thirds of the president's domestic programs. Early in 1963 Kennedy proposed a $13.5 billion reduction in personal and corporate taxes to boost spending. Congress, however, was not convinced that tax cuts were wise. As 1963 drew to a close, the tax-cut proposal remained tied up in the Senate.

One area of domestic policy that Congress did support involved women's rights. Kennedy appointed a presidential commission to examine the status of women in America. The commission report, completed in 1963, noted that while the number of working women in America had increased in recent years, women still faced discrimination in hiring and received less pay than men for the same jobs.

The president responded by issuing an order requiring the civil service to grant jobs "solely on the basis of ability to meet the requirements of the position, and without regard to sex." The commission report also led to passage of the **Equal Pay Act** in June 1963, which made it illegal for employers to pay female workers less than male workers for the same job.

▼ On June 10, 1963, President Kennedy signed into law the Equal Pay Act, which required that women receive pay equal to that of men for performing the same job.

KENNEDY AND THE COLD WAR

In foreign affairs Kennedy tended to follow the Cold War policies of his predecessors. As a World War II veteran, he shared Eisenhower's belief in the need for military strength; but unlike his predecessors, Kennedy did not want to rely solely on the threat of nuclear weapons to deter Communist expansion. He preferred to have a range of options open in case of international crises—a strategy called **flexible response**. To expand the nation's options, the Kennedy administration continued the nuclear arms buildup started under Eisenhower and strengthened conventional forces. In addition, the government established special military units like the Green Berets to assist nations struggling to combat communism.

▲ By 1967 some 10,200 Peace Corps volunteers worked in rural communities throughout the world. Shown here is Molly Heit, a schoolteacher in Peru who taught her students how to earn extra money by weaving simple tapestries for tourists.

■■ Flexible response offered a variety of options for dealing with international conflict.

Kennedy also supported nonmilitary options to prevent Communist expansion. Offering a helping hand to developing countries, he realized, could serve to strengthen their dependence on the United States and block Soviet intervention. Toward this end, he introduced a number of assistance programs designed to help the developing nations of Africa, Asia, and Latin America. Foremost among these programs was the **Peace Corps**, which sent volunteers to work for two years in developing countries.

The president also introduced a program to expand economic aid to Latin America. The **Alliance for Progress** offered billions of dollars in aid to participating nations. In exchange for money, the countries were expected to develop democratic reforms and encourage capitalism. The alliance was a disappointment, however. By 1963 most of the money that had been given to participating countries was in the hands of corrupt politicians, and few Latin American leaders had enacted reforms. One Latin American writer, Victor Alba, blamed the program's failure on its inability to mobilize the poor majority in Latin American countries:

66 We know who killed the Alliance: the oligarchic governments of Latin America. . . . We know who supplied the poison: the bureaucrats and technicians. And we know who would have defended it if anyone had bothered to let them know that it existed and needed defenders: the people. 99

THE BAY OF PIGS

Latin America was a special target for aid from the United States because the Soviet Union had recently gained a foothold there. In 1959 an uprising led by Fidel Castro succeeded in overthrowing the Cuban dictator, Fulgencio Batista. Many Americans applauded Castro's success, believing he would bring democracy to Cuba. Castro, however, quickly established a Communist-style dictatorship with strong ties to the Soviet Union.

Fidel Castro

When Kennedy took office, a plan to overthrow Castro was already in the works. The plan called for an invasion of Cuba by a group of anti-Castro Cuban refugees trained and financed by the Central Intelligence Agency (CIA). Kennedy gave the green light for the plan to proceed.

The invasion was a disaster. When the nearly 1,500 rebels came ashore at Cuba's Bay of Pigs on April 17, 1961, they were quickly pinned down by Cuban forces. The U.S. naval and air support that the rebels expected never materialized—at the last minute Kennedy vetoed any direct U.S. involvement. Equally damaging, the invasion failed to spark a popular uprising among the Cuban people. It took Cuban military forces less than 72 hours to crush the invasion and take some 1,200 surviving rebels prisoner.

Kennedy accepted full responsibility for the failed invasion, but his gesture did little to quiet criticism. One American journalist complained that the Bay of Pigs had made the United States look "like fools to our friends, rascals to our enemies, and incompetents to the rest." The invasion also drove Cuban leaders closer to the Soviets.

▲ To halt the flow of refugees into West Berlin, East Germans set up blockades along subway and elevated rail lines and cut off key crossing points between both sectors. This photograph shows one view of the Berlin Wall in October 1961.

THE BERLIN CRISIS

The Bay of Pigs convinced Soviet leader Nikita Khrushchev that Kennedy was weak and could be intimidated. During a summit meeting in June 1961, Khrushchev issued an ultimatum: the West must recognize the sovereignty of Communist East Germany and remove all troops from West Berlin.

Kennedy refused, saying that he intended to honor the United States' commitment to defend West Berlin. The situation worsened in mid-August, when the East Germans threw up a barbed-wire barrier across Berlin, cutting off traffic between East and West Berlin. Kennedy responded by sending more American troops to the city. The Soviets also bolstered their military forces there. For a few days American and Soviet soldiers eyed each other nervously across the barbed wire.

Tensions gradually eased when it became clear that the real goal of Khrushchev's ultimatum had been fulfilled. The barrier had halted the exodus of East Germans, who during the summer of 1961 had fled to the West through Berlin at a rate of some 1,000 per day. In time the East Germans replaced the barbed wire with a wall of gray concrete and watchtowers. The **Berlin Wall** became the most recognizable symbol of the Cold War.

THE MISSILES OF OCTOBER

After Berlin, Khrushchev continued to try to test America's commitment to containment, leading to the Cold War's greatest crisis. To ward off another invasion, Fidel Castro asked the Soviet Union to provide him with defensive weapons. The Soviets complied and also offered *offensive* weapons—nuclear missiles that could reach major cities of the eastern United States.

CIA officials monitored the Soviet arms buildup in Cuba throughout the summer of 1962. But they did not grasp the full extent of the buildup until October 14, when an American U-2 spy plane photographed numerous missile launching pads near the Cuban town of San Cristobal. Additional U-2 flights over the island located more missiles, all of which appeared to be aimed at the United States.

On October 22 Kennedy ordered a naval blockade of Cuba to prevent further deliveries of Soviet weapons. He also demanded that the Soviets remove the missiles. Khrushchev promised to challenge the blockade, calling it "outright banditry." Over the next two days, nuclear war loomed on the horizon. In a frenzy of activity, Soviet military advisers armed the missiles in Cuba. American B-52 bombers armed with nuclear weapons prepared for battle. Meanwhile, Soviet ships sailed toward the blockade line.

Suddenly, on October 24, many of the Soviet ships stopped short of the blockade line, turned, and sailed home. "We're eyeball to eyeball," said Secretary of State Dean Rusk, "and I think the other fellow just blinked." On October 28 Khrushchev agreed to dismantle the missile bases in response to Kennedy's promise not to invade Cuba. Kennedy also secretly agreed to remove American missiles from some foreign sites.

The event marked a historic turning point in Soviet-American relations. Sobered by their brush with nuclear war, Kennedy and Khrushchev sought to ease tensions between their countries. Kennedy declared that it was time to write a new chapter in the Cold War:

> 66 If we are to open new doorways to peace, if we are to seize this rare opportunity for progress, if we are to be as bold and farsighted in our control of weapons as we have been in their invention, then let us now show all the world on this side of the wall and the other that a strong America also stands for peace. 99

In 1963 the United States, the Soviet Union, and Great Britain signed a **Limited Nuclear Test**

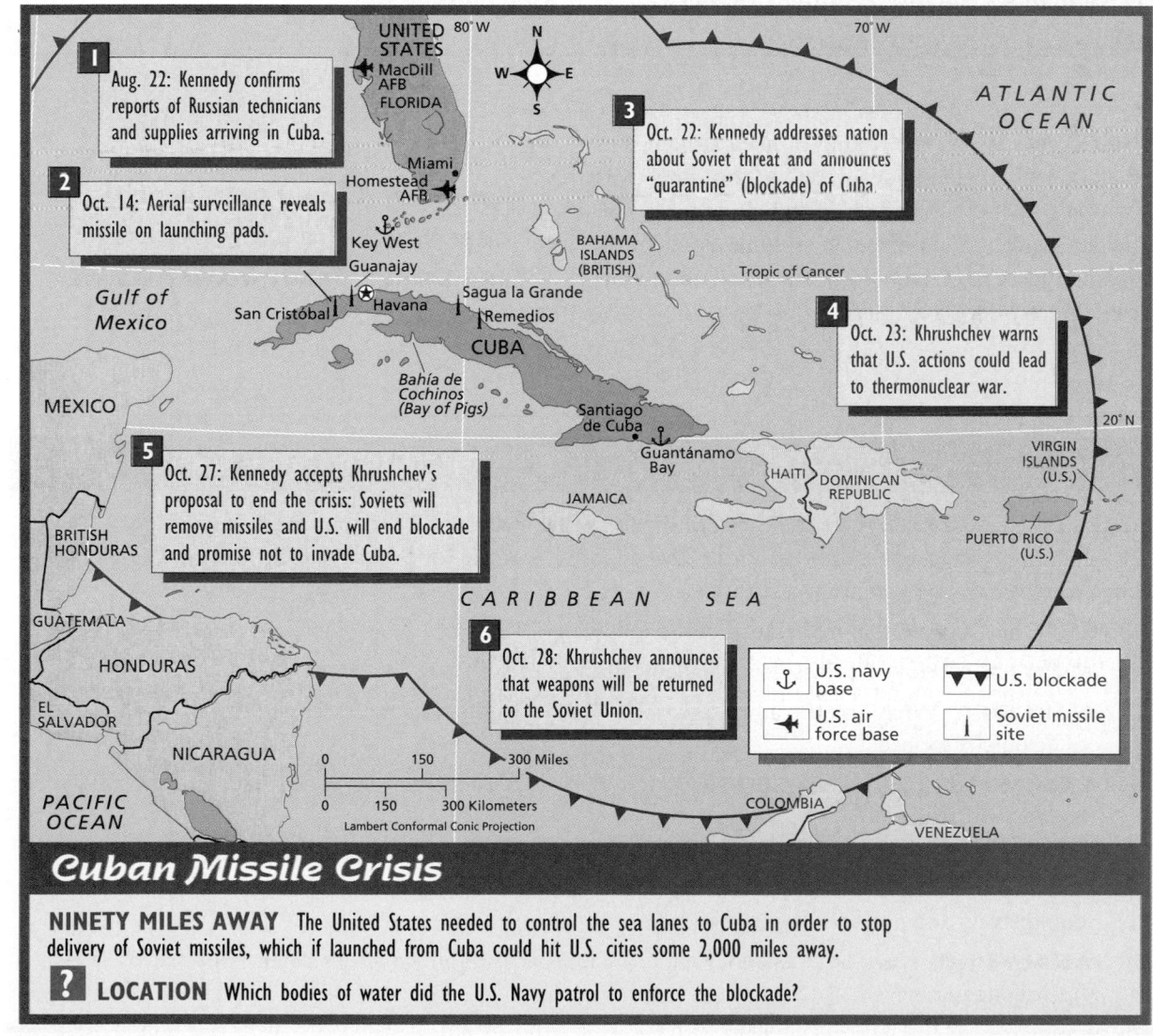

1 Aug. 22: Kennedy confirms reports of Russian technicians and supplies arriving in Cuba.

2 Oct. 14: Aerial surveillance reveals missile on launching pads.

3 Oct. 22: Kennedy addresses nation about Soviet threat and announces "quarantine" (blockade) of Cuba.

4 Oct. 23: Khrushchev warns that U.S. actions could lead to thermonuclear war.

5 Oct. 27: Kennedy accepts Khrushchev's proposal to end the crisis: Soviets will remove missiles and U.S. will end blockade and promise not to invade Cuba.

6 Oct. 28: Khrushchev announces that weapons will be returned to the Soviet Union.

Legend:
⚓ U.S. navy base
✈ U.S. air force base
▼▼ U.S. blockade
⎮ Soviet missile site

0 150 300 Miles
0 150 300 Kilometers
Lambert Conformal Conic Projection

Cuban Missile Crisis

NINETY MILES AWAY The United States needed to control the sea lanes to Cuba in order to stop delivery of Soviet missiles, which if launched from Cuba could hit U.S. cities some 2,000 miles away.

? **LOCATION** Which bodies of water did the U.S. Navy patrol to enforce the blockade?

CUBAN MISSILE CRISIS

THROUGH OTHERS' EYES

In October 1962 President Kennedy issued an ultimatum to the Soviet Union, demanding that it remove all its missiles from Cuba. For several days the world held its breath as it teetered on the brink of nuclear war. In the end, the Soviets agreed to remove the missiles. Soviet Premier Nikita Khrushchev relates his memory of the crisis:

❝ **I**t had been, to say the least, an interesting and challenging situation. The two most powerful nations of the world had been squared off against each other, each with its finger on the button. You'd have thought that war was inevitable. But both sides showed that if the desire to avoid war is strong enough, even the most pressing dispute can be solved by compromise. . . . I'll always remember the late President [Kennedy] with deep respect because, in the final analysis, he showed himself to be sober-minded and determined to avoid war. He didn't let himself become frightened, nor did he become reckless. He didn't overestimate America's might, and he left himself a way out of the crisis. . . . It was a great victory for us, though, that we had been able to extract from Kennedy a promise that neither America nor any of her allies would invade Cuba. ❞

Ban Treaty to end the testing of nuclear bombs in the atmosphere and under water. A "**hot line**" was also set up between the United States and the Soviet Union. This direct telephone connection enabled leaders of the two countries to communicate directly during a crisis.

■■ **The Bay of Pigs and Berlin crises led to the Cuban missile crisis, after which the United States and Soviet Union worked harder for peace.**

SECTION 1 REVIEW

IDENTIFY and explain the significance of the following: Richard Nixon, John F. Kennedy, New Frontier, Equal Pay Act, flexible response, Peace Corps, Alliance for Progress, Fidel Castro, Berlin Wall, Limited Nuclear Test Ban Treaty, "hot line."

LOCATE and explain the importance of the following: Cuba, Bay of Pigs, San Cristobal.

1. **MAIN IDEA** How did President Kennedy attempt to stimulate the economy?

2. **MAIN IDEA** What was the advantage of the Kennedy administration's foreign-policy strategy of flexible response?

3. **LINKING HISTORY AND GEOGRAPHY** Why were Americans so concerned with the missile buildup in Cuba?

4. **WRITING TO INFORM** Imagine you are a member of the presidential commission assigned to examine the status of women in America. Write a report that summarizes the findings of the commission and presents recommendations for change.

5. **ANALYZING** How did President Kennedy's approach to foreign affairs differ from that of his predecessors?

JOHNSON'S GREAT SOCIETY

FOCUS

■ **What were the four major concerns of the Great Society programs?**

■ **How did the Warren Court decisions affect individual rights?**

■ **How did foreign policy concerns affect President Johnson's domestic programs?**

On November 22, 1963, John Kennedy's presidency ended when he was gunned down in Dallas. The new president, Lyndon Johnson, pledged himself to the "ideas and ideals" that Kennedy had "so nobly represented." Johnson sponsored a series of social programs designed to transform American society. These triumphs on the domestic scene, however, were soon overshadowed as foreign policy problems caused Johnson's presidency to unravel.

LBJ taking the presidential oath in Dallas, 1963

TRAGEDY IN DALLAS

Kennedy knew he would have to campaign hard to win reelection in 1964. In November 1963 he traveled to Texas to try to bolster his support there. In Dallas on November 22, enthusiastic crowds lined the route of Kennedy's open-car motorcade from the airport. At about 12:30 P.M., as the motorcade moved through the downtown area, shots rang out. Kennedy slumped over, mortally wounded. Within hours Vice President Lyndon Johnson was sworn in as president. Over the next four days, the nation came together to mourn the dead president. Millions watched the funeral on television. Many Americans felt that the death of the youthful, vibrant Kennedy had also killed something in them. "We'll never be young again," Kennedy staffer Daniel Patrick Moynihan sadly observed.

Within hours of the shooting, the Dallas police had seized Lee Harvey Oswald as a suspect. Two days after his arrest, while he was being moved from one jail to another, Oswald was shot to death by nightclub owner Jack Ruby.

This strange turn of events caused many people to question whether Oswald had acted alone in killing the president or whether he had been part of a larger conspiracy. To end speculation, President Lyndon Johnson named a commission, headed by Chief Justice Earl Warren, to investigate the assassination. The **Warren Commission**, which spent 10 months reviewing the evidence, concluded that there was no evidence of conspiracy: both Oswald and Ruby had acted alone.

JOHNSON TAKES OVER

President Lyndon Johnson appeared very different from the wealthy, charismatic Kennedy. Born in the hill country of central Texas, Johnson grew up in a household that knew, in turn, poverty and relative prosperity. Brash, ambitious, and hardworking, Johnson rose rapidly through the Democratic party ranks. By the time he won election to the Senate in 1948, he was a major power in the party.

A master of compromise, Johnson seemed to always find the middle course on which most people could agree. This mastery of the political process, coupled with his years of experience in Washington, enabled Johnson to manage the transition of power with considerable skill and tact. Kennedy's cabinet and advisers stayed on to lend continuity to the Johnson administration.

Announcing in his first cabinet meeting in January 1964 that "the day is over when top jobs are reserved for men," Johnson pledged to add 50 more women to high government offices. Some of his choices included consumer advocate Betty Furness, economists Alice Rivlin and Penelope Thunberg, and Texas legislator Barbara Jordan. Although Johnson was able to appoint only 27 women to high offices, his strong support for women's rights marked a significant break with past administrations.

The new president also promised to appoint more Mexican Americans to high positions. He assigned Vicente T. Ximenes (he-MAY-nays) to chair a presidential committee on Mexican American affairs. Other top appointments went to Héctor P. García, a Texas advocate for Mexican American veterans, and to Raul H. Castro, a noted attorney who later became the first Mexican American governor of Arizona.

As 1964 began, Johnson focused his legislative efforts on three areas: tax cuts, civil rights, and poverty. Within weeks he had persuaded Congress to adopt Kennedy's tax program, which cut personal and corporate income taxes by 4 percent. He then pressured members of Congress to enact the long-stalled civil rights bill (see Section 3) and a comprehensive program to fight poverty.

THE WAR ON POVERTY

In 1962, social activist Michael Harrington published *The Other America,* a well-documented study of poverty in the United States. The best-selling book shattered the popular notion that all Americans had benefited from the prosperity of the 1950s. Harrington reported that more than 42 million Americans lived on less than $1,000 per year. He issued a direct challenge for leaders to face the reality of poverty:

66 [The poor exist] within the most powerful and rich society the world has ever known. Their misery has continued while the majority of the nation talked of itself as being "affluent." . . . In this way tens of millions of human beings became invisible. They dropped out of sight and out of mind. . . . How long shall we ignore this underdeveloped nation in our midst? 99

Harrington also noted that racism still kept many ethnic groups, especially African Americans, in poverty. He warned that the end of legalized segregation would not change the economic condition of most poor blacks. "The laws against color can be removed," he wrote, "but that will leave the poverty that is the historic . . . consequence of color. As long as this is the case, being born a Negro will continue to be the most profound disability that the United States imposes upon a citizen."

President Johnson responded to such concerns by declaring an "unconditional war on poverty in America." To launch his **War on Poverty**, Johnson sent to Congress a bill calling for the establishment of the **Office of Economic Opportunity** (OEO), with a budget of $1 billion, to coordinate a series of new antipoverty programs. These programs included the Job Corps, a work training program for young people between the ages of 16 and 21; Head Start, an education program for preschoolers from low-income families; and VISTA (Volunteers in Service to America), a domestic version of the Peace Corps. The bill passed Congress in late August 1964.

Whereas Kennedy had trouble pushing legislation through Congress, Johnson fulfilled all the major legislative goals of his first term within eight months. Comparing the two administrations, Texas journalist Liz Carpenter concluded: "Kennedy

▲ VISTA volunteers donated their time and talent to aid poor Americans in the United States and in U.S. territories having limited public services. Shown here is an elementary schoolteacher in the U.S. Virgin Islands.

inspired . . . Johnson delivered." Opinion polls showed that Americans were overwhelmingly impressed with Johnson's achievements.

JOHNSON'S VISION FOR AMERICA

Riding this wave of popularity, Johnson easily won the Democratic presidential nomination for the 1964 election. He selected Hubert Humphrey, a liberal senator from Minnesota, as his running mate. Adopting a platform that rejected Eisenhower's modern Republicanism, the Republicans chose Barry Goldwater, a conservative senator from Arizona, as their presidential nominee, with New York congressman William E. Miller as his running mate.

Goldwater and Johnson campaign dolls, 1964

Johnson won by a landslide, taking 61 percent of the popular vote and 486 electoral votes to Goldwater's 52. The Democrats further increased their majority in both the House and the Senate. The last president to receive such a mandate was Franklin Roosevelt in 1936.

The plan. Long before the election, Johnson had mapped out plans for his presidency. He saw his major task as building a **Great Society**. In this Great Society, he said, poverty and racial injustice would end. All children would have access to an education that enriched their knowledge and enhanced their talents. The cities would serve not only people's physical needs, but also their desire for culture and their "hunger for community." In short, in the Great Society people would be "more concerned with the quality of their goals than the quantity of their goods."

After his election Johnson moved quickly to make the Great Society a reality. While civil rights was a major part of the Great Society legislation, other issues included health care, education, and urban renewal.

The programs. In 1965 Johnson persuaded Congress to establish **Medicare**, a national health insurance program for people over age 65.

PRESIDENTIAL LIVES

LYNDON B. JOHNSON
1908–1973

Lyndon B. Johnson
United States
8 cents

in office
1963–1969

Many observers saw Lyndon Johnson as the stereotypical Texas politician—loud, brash, and slightly uncouth. Johnson loved to intentionally shock observers with his language, stories, and behavior. Once during an interview he lifted up his shirt for a photographer to display his scar from gall bladder surgery.

Johnson was also a very physical politician. He would shake people's hands until his own bled and slap others on their backs in a friendly gesture. Fellow senators joked that Johnson had two techniques for getting another senator's attention. There was the Half-Johnson—"when he just put a hand on your shoulder"—and the Full-Johnson—"when he put his arm clear around you and thrust his face close to yours." But Johnson's techniques got results.

He was known as a workaholic who drove himself and his staff to exhaustion to complete multiple tasks. "What's the hurry?" one senator asked another about Johnson's busy schedule. "Rome wasn't built in a day." The other senator replied, "No, but Lyndon Johnson wasn't foreman on that job."

Congress also authorized funds for states to set up **Medicaid** to provide free health care to the needy. Johnson traveled to Independence, Missouri, to sign the bill in front of 81-year-old Harry Truman, who had first proposed federally funded health insurance in his Fair Deal program.

Johnson also asked Congress to take action on funding for education. In a moving speech, he recalled:

> 66 My first job after college was as a teacher in Cotulla, Texas, in a small Mexican American school. . . . Somehow you never forget what poverty and hatred can do when you see its scars on the hopeful face of a young child. . . . It never even occurred to me in my fondest dreams that I might have the chance to help the sons and daughters of those students and to help people like them all over this country.
>
> But now I do have that chance—and I'll let you in on a secret: *I mean to use it.* 99

Congress responded by passing the **Elementary and Secondary School Education Act** of 1965, which provided $1.3 billion in aid to schools in impoverished areas.

Johnson also persuaded Congress to pass the **Omnibus Housing Act** in 1965, followed by the **Housing and Urban Development Act** of 1968. The acts authorized billions of dollars for urban renewal and housing assistance for low-income families. They also established the Department of Housing and Urban Development (HUD) to oversee all federal housing programs. Robert C. Weaver, a member of the New Deal's "black brain trust" headed this new department, making him the first African American member of a presidential cabinet. Weaver declared that the new programs had made Americans aware that "our cities were filled with poorly housed, badly educated, underemployed, desperate, unhappy Americans."

▲ President Johnson congratulates Robert Weaver after he is sworn in as secretary of HUD.

■■ Civil rights, health care, education, and urban renewal were the major concerns of the Great Society programs.

Great Society laws poured out of Congress at an incredible rate. It was the most hectic period of legislative activity since Franklin Roosevelt's first 100 days.

𝒯HE WARREN COURT DECISIONS

Like the Johnson administration, the Supreme Court of the 1960s reflected a spirit of activism. Under the leadership of Chief Justice Earl Warren, the Court tried to continue the trend begun with the 1954 desegregation decision in *Brown* v. *Board of Education* of defining and extending individual rights.

In addition to outlawing segregation across the nation, the Court tried to extend equality in the voting booth with the "one person, one vote" principle. In many congressional districts, sparsely populated rural areas were granted the same number of representatives as densely populated urban areas. In *Baker* v. *Carr* (1962), however, the Court declared that election districts had to be divided by population in order to offer fairly equal representation for everyone.

The Court also issued a series of decisions protecting the rights of those accused of crimes. *Gideon* v. *Wainwright* (1963) declared that the states had to provide lawyers, at public expense, for impoverished defendants charged with serious crimes. *Escobedo* v. *Illinois* (1964) stated that the accused had the right to have a lawyer present during police interrogations. *Miranda* v. *Arizona* (1966) said that accused persons had to be informed of their rights at the time of their arrests.

Many people saw the Supreme Court's actions as an attempt to build a country free of prejudice and inequality, but many others were outraged by such decisions. The Court had overstepped its authority, critics charged, by making law rather than interpreting it. Some went so far as to accuse the chief justice of "high crimes and misdemeanors," erecting billboards that proclaimed "IMPEACH EARL WARREN!" One critic declared:

> 66 Earl Warren has sinned too grandly for [impeachment]. He has defiled our jurisprudence and made war against the public order. . . . The bench over which he presides has made a mockery of the Supreme Court's appointed function. 99

■ The Warren Court's controversial decisions strengthened
individual rights.

FOREIGN POLICY AND THE GREAT SOCIETY

While the Great Society was taking shape, foreign affairs also drew President Johnson's attention. In addition to dealing with the Vietnam conflict inherited from Kennedy (see Chapter 30), he became involved in the affairs of the Dominican Republic (see map on page 837). The nation's democratically elected president, Juan Bosch, had been ousted by a military coup in 1963. The new leader never really gained control of the country, and in April 1965, factions within the military rebelled, demanding Bosch's return. The American ambassador, believing that Bosch had fallen under Communist influence, insisted that Johnson intervene to "prevent another Cuba."

Johnson responded promptly, sending in a force of some 22,000 marines. With American support, troops loyal to the military government gained the upper hand and the situation stabilized. In 1966, after relatively free and fair elections put a conservative, pro-American government in power, Johnson withdrew the marines.

Many people in Latin America condemned American intervention in the Dominican Republic, labeling it gunboat diplomacy. Even those who

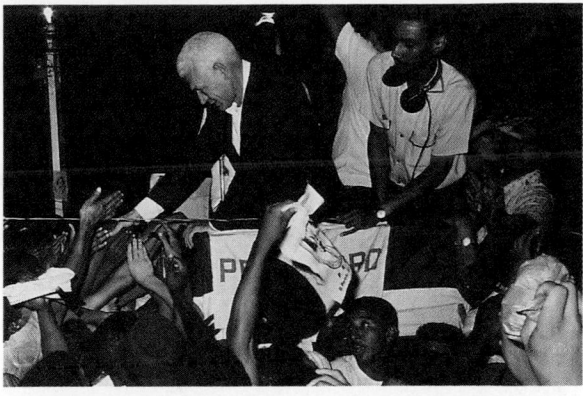

▲ Juan Bosch is shown here on December 18, 1962, two days before being elected president of the Dominican Republic. A military coup removed him from power less than one year later.

supported Johnson's action did so reluctantly. In the United States, however, the majority of the public backed Johnson, praising his aggressive stand against the threat of Communist expansion.

By the spring of 1965 Johnson was also focusing more of his attention on the Vietnam War. As the conflict in Vietnam consumed more of his time, his attention to Great Society programs decreased. In 1966 the government spent about 18 times more on the Vietnam War than it did on the War on Poverty. Citing such statistics, civil rights leader Martin Luther King, Jr., declared that the Great Society had been "shot down on the battlefields of Vietnam."

■ Foreign policy concerns drew
federal funding and President
Johnson's attention away from
Great Society programs.

SECTION 2 REVIEW

IDENTIFY and explain the significance of the following: Lyndon Johnson, Lee Harvey Oswald, Warren Commission, War on Poverty, Office of Economic Opportunity, Great Society, Medicare, Medicaid, Elementary and Secondary School Education Act, Omnibus Housing Act, Housing and Urban Development Act, Juan Bosch.

LOCATE and explain the importance of the following: Dominican Republic.

1. **MAIN IDEA** What four major concerns did the Great Society programs address?

2. **MAIN IDEA** How did events in Vietnam and Latin America affect President Johnson's domestic programs?

3. **IDENTIFYING VALUES** How did President Johnson's programs reflect values from his early life?

4. **WRITING TO EXPLAIN** Write an essay explaining how the Warren Court decisions strengthened individual rights.

5. **EVALUATING** Why do you think Michael Harrington believed that ending legalized segregation would not change the economic condition of most poor African Americans?

THE CIVIL RIGHTS MOVEMENT

FOCUS

■ What was the major tactic of the early civil rights movement? How did it generate public support for the movement?

■ What events helped expand legislation on civil rights and voting rights?

■ How was African American frustration expressed in the late 1960s?

■ What other civil rights movements were inspired by the African American civil rights movement?

As the 1960s began, southern civil rights leaders called for new efforts in the struggle for racial equality. These efforts won passage of important civil rights and voting rights laws in 1964 and 1965. However, some young members of the movement believed that progress was too slow. In the mid-1960s, frustration over the lack of progress exploded into violence in black neighborhoods. Meanwhile, other groups, inspired by African American activism, fought for their rights.

Martin Luther King, Jr., 1963

NONVIOLENCE IN ACTION

After the success of the Montgomery bus boycott (see Chapter 28), southern civil rights leaders met in Atlanta, Georgia, in 1957 to discuss future strategy. They expanded the Montgomery Improvement Association (MIA) into the **Southern Christian Leadership Conference** (SCLC), an alliance of church-based African American organizations dedicated to ending discrimination. The leader of the MIA, the Reverend Martin Luther King, Jr., led the new organization. The SCLC pledged to use **nonviolent resistance** in its protests. Nonviolent resistance required that protesters never resort to violence, even when others attacked them. King called it meeting "the forces of hate with the power of love."

Many non-SCLC members soon took up nonviolent protests on their own. On February 1,

1960, four African American college students sat down at the "whites only" lunch counter of a Greensboro, North Carolina, department store. The management refused to serve them, but they returned the following day, vowing to continue the **sit-in** protest until they received service. News of the Greensboro sit-in quickly spread, and within weeks students began similar demonstrations in cities throughout the South. In April 1960 the leaders of these demonstrations founded the **Student Nonviolent Coordinating Committee** (SNCC, pronounced "snick"), a loose association of student activists from throughout the South.

White response to the sit-ins tested the students' commitment to nonviolence. White racists taunted the demonstrators, dumping food and drinks on them. Sometimes the harassment escalated into physical attacks. But the demonstrators never resorted to violence. By the end of the year, many restaurants and other eating establishments across the South had been integrated.

■■ Early civil rights activists used nonviolent resistance to fight for equal rights.

𝒯HE FREEDOM RIDES

The success of the sit-ins inspired the **Congress of Racial Equality (CORE)**, a northern-based civil rights group, to launch a protest against segregation in interstate transportation. In May 1961 an integrated group of **Freedom Riders** set off from Washington, D.C., for a trip through the South.

Outside the town of Anniston, Alabama, a white mob firebombed one of the two buses carrying the group members and beat the riders as they tried to escape. The riders on the other bus were attacked in Birmingham. When the bus company refused to carry the passengers any farther, CORE called off the ride. Immediately, Nashville SNCC members stepped in to complete the rest of the trip. SNCC leader Diane Nash explained why:

> 66 If the Freedom Riders had been stopped as a result of violence, I strongly felt that the future of the movement was going to be cut short. The impression would have been that whenever a movement starts, all [you have to do] is attack it with massive violence and the blacks [will] stop. 99

Legend:
→ CORE route
→ SNCC route
☆ Arrests
✹ Violence

After leaving Anniston, one bus was firebombed on the outskirts of town.

The Freedom Rides

TESTING THE BAN The Freedom Riders planned to travel in buses to New Orleans to test observance of a Supreme Court ban on segregation in public places, but the trip ended in Jackson when the riders were arrested and sent to prison.

? LOCATION In which cities were the Freedom Riders attacked?

SNCC sent additional Freedom Riders to Birmingham, where they were quickly arrested by the city commissioner of public safety, T. Eugene "Bull" Connor, and dumped across the state line. The students made their way back to Birmingham and convinced the bus line to take them to Montgomery, where they were once again attacked by a mob. Under pressure from civil rights leaders, Attorney General Robert Kennedy sent federal marshals to protect the riders on the rest of their journey. In Jackson, Mississippi, however, state officials arrested the riders. Outraged by the arrests, hundreds of other protesters tried to carry on the rides. Over the summer more than 300 Freedom Riders traveled the South to protest segregation. In response, Robert Kennedy pressured the Interstate Commerce Commission (ICC) into strengthening its desegregation regulations.

◄ **Stunned Freedom Riders gather outside their bus after it was firebombed by a white mob. In all, 12 people were taken to an Anniston hospital for treatment.**

Successes and Setbacks

The civil rights movement saw many successes; it also saw many setbacks. Despite Supreme Court rulings, many educational institutions remained segregated. In 1962 the NAACP obtained a court order requiring the University of Mississippi to admit African American applicant James Meredith. President Kennedy dispatched federal marshals to ensure that Meredith arrived safely at school. When word got out on the evening of September 30 that Meredith was on campus, a riot broke out that left two people dead. Meredith registered the next day and attended classes the rest of the year under the protection of armed guards.

Events elsewhere tested the effectiveness of nonviolent resistance as a protest tactic. In Albany, Georgia, civil rights organizations staged numerous nonviolent protests against discrimination, but Police Chief Laurie Pritchett was prepared for them. Calling his method of law enforcement meeting "nonviolence with nonviolence," Pritchett quietly arrested all of the protesters without resorting to violence. He arranged to fill all the jails in the surrounding areas with prisoners and continued to fill them for as long as possible, causing the Albany movement to virtually stall out.

Nonviolent resistance proved more effective in Birmingham. In April 1963 the SCLC launched a series of boycotts, sit-ins, and marches to protest the city's segregation laws. Hundreds of demonstrators, including Martin Luther King, Jr., were arrested and jailed. The protests continued to grow until May, when Bull Connor ordered the police to attack the marchers, many of them schoolchildren, with high-pressure fire hoses, dogs, and nightsticks. Scenes of these attacks appeared in newspapers and on television throughout the world, increasing support for the civil rights movement.

■■ **Mob violence against civil rights activists increased public support for the movement.**

The March on Washington

Early in June, President Kennedy urged the passage of a broad new civil rights act designed to end segregation. To show support for Kennedy's civil rights bill, African American leaders called for a huge march on Washington, D.C. On August 28, 1963, more than 200,000 people gathered at the Lincoln Memorial where they heard Martin Luther King, Jr., deliver one of the most moving speeches

Civil Rights

MARCH TO FREEDOM

The Granger Collection, New York

Engraving observing passage of the Civil Rights Act of 1875

1865 Thirteenth Amendment passed.

1866 Fourteenth Amendment passed. ◆ Civil Rights Act passed.

1875 Civil Rights Act passed.

1881 First Jim Crow laws passed.

1860   1865   1870   1875   1880   1885

1863 Emancipation Proclamation issued.

1873 *Slaughterhouse Cases* limit protection of African American rights under Fourteenth Amendment.

The Granger Collection, New York

1869 Fifteenth Amendment passed.

Detail from the Emancipation Proclamation

1883 Civil Rights Act of 1875 declared unconstitutional.

Freedmen voting in Richmond, Virginia, 1871

in American history. Repeating the phrase "I have a dream," King spoke of a nation in which all Americans would live in harmony (see page 1010).

Other speakers, such as A. Philip Randolph, gave eloquent testimony to the long struggle for civil rights in America. SNCC leader John Lewis warned that the younger generation of demonstrators were determined not to give up their struggle until equality was a true reality:

> 66 By the force of our demands, our determination and our numbers, we shall splinter the segregated South into a thousand pieces, and put them back together in the image of God and democracy. 99

The success of the **March on Washington** raised the spirits of civil rights workers everywhere. But their joy proved short-lived. In mid-September a bomb exploded in a Birmingham church, killing four young African American girls. Then in November an assassin's bullet cut down President Kennedy. The new president, Lyndon Johnson, urged Congress to pass Kennedy's civil rights bill. The **Civil Rights Act of 1964** barred discrimination in employment and in public accommodations and gave the Justice Department the power to bring lawsuits to enforce school desegregation.

■■ The March on Washington helped bring about passage of the Civil Rights Act of 1964.

ℱREEDOM SUMMER AND SELMA

As Congress debated the Civil Rights Act, movement leaders turned their attention to voter registration. In June 1964 they launched **Freedom Summer**, a campaign to register African American voters. It involved nearly 1,000 volunteers, many of them white northerners. Freedom Summer focused on Mississippi, a state with a black population of 45 percent, but where only 5 percent of African Americans were on the voting rolls.

Mississippi had a reputation for racial violence, growing out of the state's many lynchings in the early 20th century and the murder of 14-year-old African American Emmett Till in 1955. Violence quickly struck the Freedom Summer campaign. On June 21 Michael Schwerner and Andrew Goodman, two white New Yorkers, and James Chaney, a black Mississippian, were abducted and killed. Shocked volunteers carried on, but many local blacks feared they would also become the victims of violence if they registered.

Students at Tuskegee Institute

1900 New York City race riot occurs.

1909 NAACP founded.

1908 Ray Stannard Baker's *Following the Color Line* published.

1890 1895 1900 1905 1910

1895 Ida Wells-Barnett publishes lynching study.

1896 *Plessy* supports segregation.

1906 Teddy Roosevelt discharges entire black regiment in Brownsville, Texas.◆Atlanta race riot occurs.

1910 National Urban League founded.

The Granger Collection, New York

Ida Wells-Barnett

By the end of the summer, only 1,600 African Americans had been added to the voting rolls.

In early 1965, civil rights workers launched a similar registration drive in Selma, Alabama. They invited King, who had won the Nobel Peace Prize the previous year, to lead them. For days African Americans attempted to register at election commission offices in the Selma area, only to face beatings and arrests. Civil rights leaders responded by calling for a protest march from Selma to Montgomery. On Sunday, March 7, some 600 people started on the 50-mile trek.

Just outside Selma, police attacked the marchers. One eight-year-old girl in the march recalled the scene: "I saw those horsemen coming toward me and they had those awful masks on; they rode right through the cloud of tear gas. Some of them had clubs, others had ropes, or whips, which they swung about them like they were driving cattle." Stunned by the fierceness of this attack, thousands of Americans poured into Selma to show support for the marchers. President Johnson was also shocked by Selma's "Bloody Sunday." On March 15, before a joint session of Congress, he asked for speedy passage of a voting rights bill. All Americans, he said, ought to take up the struggle for civil rights, for "it's . . . all of us who must overcome the crippling legacy of bigotry and injustice. And we *shall* overcome."

A week later, under the protection of federal marshals and the National Guard, the marchers completed their journey. Five months later Congress passed the **Voting Rights Act** of 1965, which put the entire registration process under federal control. Within days of the act's passage, federal examiners descended on the South to sign up new African American voters. By 1968 over half of all eligible African Americans in the South were registered.

■■ Freedom Summer, Selma's Bloody Sunday, and the Voting Rights Act of 1965 expanded African American voter registration.

BLACK POWER

As the civil rights movement grew, many African Americans questioned the effectiveness of nonviolence. Some felt that they should be able to use violence for self-defense. Others began to question the desirability of integration altogether. Using the slogan **Black Power**, many of these leaders argued that African Americans should mobilize to gain

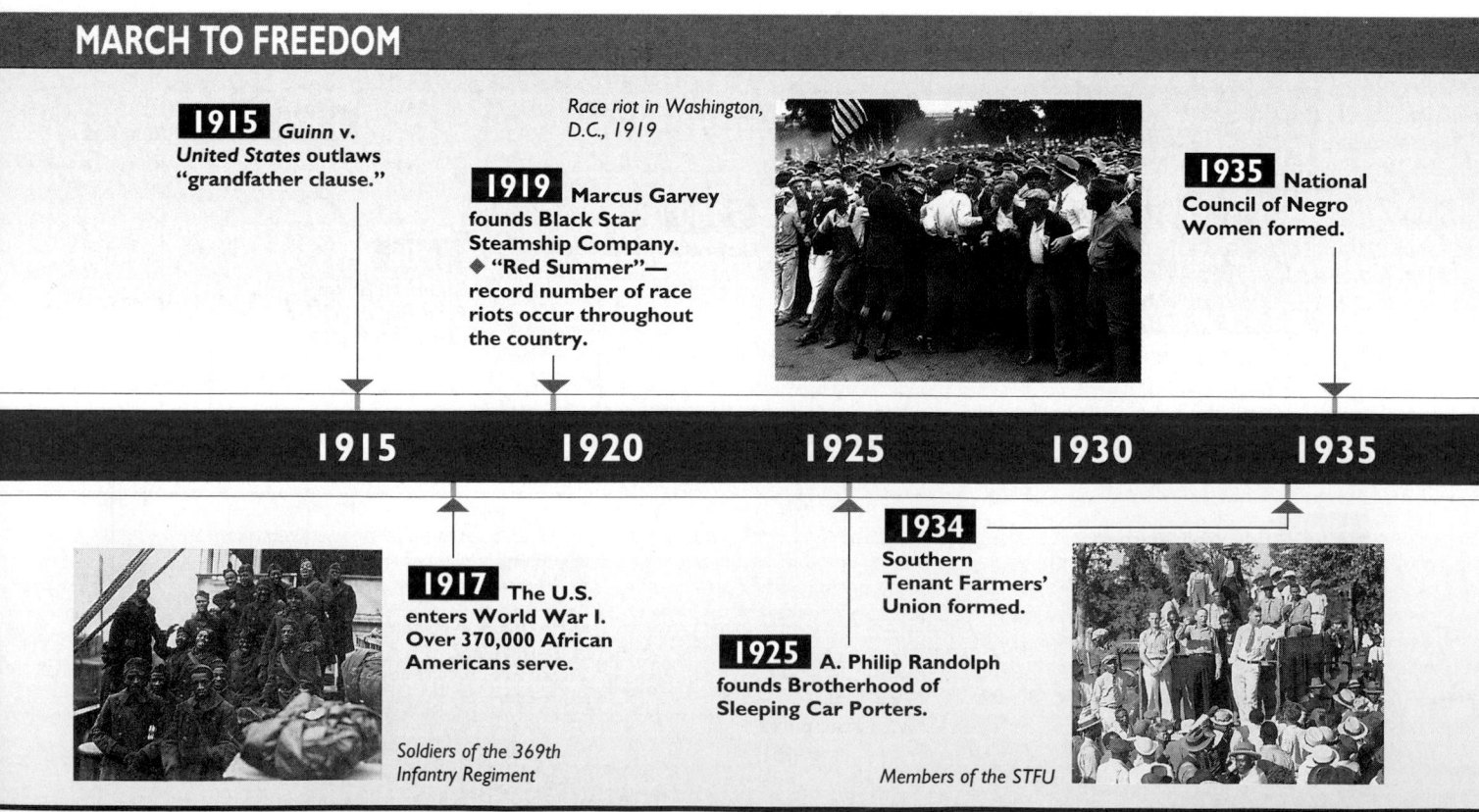

MARCH TO FREEDOM

1915 *Guinn v. United States* outlaws "grandfather clause."

Race riot in Washington, D.C., 1919

1919 Marcus Garvey founds Black Star Steamship Company. ◆ "Red Summer"— record number of race riots occur throughout the country.

1935 National Council of Negro Women formed.

1915　　1920　　1925　　1930　　1935

1917 The U.S. enters World War I. Over 370,000 African Americans serve.

Soldiers of the 369th Infantry Regiment

1925 A. Philip Randolph founds Brotherhood of Sleeping Car Porters.

1934 Southern Tenant Farmers' Union formed.

Members of the STFU

control of economic and political power. Some also argued that since white society caused racism, only separation from white society would help African Americans obtain such power. Although the Black Power slogan was not widely used until the late 1960s, it represented the ideas of many earlier African American leaders, including Marcus Garvey (see Chapter 21) and Malcolm X, a black nationalist who rose to prominence in the early civil rights era.

BIO GRAPHY Malcolm X was born Malcolm Little in 1925. His father was a Baptist minister and organizer for Marcus Garvey. After his father died at the hands of whites, the young Malcolm drifted into a life of crime, eventually ending up in prison. While in prison, he embraced the teachings of Elijah Muhammad's Nation of Islam, or Black Muslims, an offshoot of the orthodox Islamic faith.

Freed in 1952, Malcolm rejected the name Little, handed down to him from some former slaveholder, and used "X" to symbolize his lost African surname. He soon became a leading minister for the Nation of Islam. A powerful orator, Malcolm X championed black separatism and called for freedom to be brought about "by any means necessary." The time for nonviolence had passed, he argued:

" You're getting a new generation that has been growing right now, and they're beginning to think with their own minds and see that you can't negotiate up on freedom nowadays. If something is yours by right, then fight for it or shut up. If you can't fight for it, then forget it. **"**

Malcolm X

Malcolm X broke with the Black Muslims in 1964 after a pilgrimage to the Islamic holy city of Mecca. Turning away from separatism, he converted to orthodox Islam and began calling for unity among all people. This break set off a bitter struggle between Malcolm X and the Nation of Islam. In February 1965, Black Muslim assassins gunned down Malcolm X.

Other young activists, however, carried on some of his ideas. In 1966, college students Huey P. Newton and Bobby Seale founded the Black Panther party in Oakland, California, to promote self-determination in the black community. Asserting that blacks could not trust white police officers to protect them, the Black Panthers armed themselves and established citizen patrols to monitor the streets. "War can only be abolished through war," they

Workers in wartime plant

1941 The U.S. enters World War II. Some one million African Americans serve. ◆ Racial discrimination banned in defense industries and government.

1946 Truman appoints Committee on Civil Rights.

The "Little Rock Nine" and NAACP leaders

1957 Arkansas's "Little Rock Nine" enroll at Central High School. ◆ SCLC founded.

1940   **1945**   **1950**   **1955**   **1960**

1945 Smith v. Allright outlaws "white primaries."

1948 Racial discrimination banned in federal hiring and military.

Civil rights activist Ella Baker

1955 ICC bans segregation on interstate travel. ◆ Montgomery bus boycott begins.

1960 Sit-ins begin in Greensboro, N.C. ◆ SNCC founded. ◆ Civil Rights Act passed. ◆ *United States v. Raines* outlaws literacy tests for voting.

declared. Although the Black Panthers were involved in numerous confrontations with police, many African Americans admired their boldness.

FIRE IN THE STREETS

Frustration fueled much of the support for the Black Power movement. Despite the successes of the civil rights movement, discrimination still ruled the lives of most African Americans. In August 1965 frustration became revolt when a routine arrest by Los Angeles police in the black neighborhood of Watts broke into a riot that raged for six days. When the National Guard finally restored order, 34 people were dead, hundreds were injured, and almost 4,000 had been arrested.

Over the next two years, more than 100 riots broke out in cities across the country. The worst came in Detroit, where 43 people lost their lives. A federal report by the **Kerner Commission** charged that white racism was largely responsible for the tensions that led to the riots. "Our nation," the report warned, "is moving toward two societies, one black, one white—separate and unequal."

Seeking to address the frustration of the late 1960s, Martin Luther King, Jr., started to embrace some of the Black Power movement's ideas, such as the need for African Americans to gain economic power. He also became increasingly upset that funding that should have gone for the War on Poverty was being used for the war in Vietnam (see Chapter 30). In March 1968 he called for a Poor People's March on Washington to protest this misuse of government funding.

Before the Poor People's March took place, King went to Memphis, Tennessee, to show his support for a garbage workers' strike. On the evening of April 4, 1968, the man who was the symbol of nonviolence met a violent end when a sniper killed him. Within hours of King's death, black neighborhoods all over the country exploded in outrage. A week of rioting left 46 dead and thousands injured.

■■ **The Black Power movement and the riots of the late 1960s demonstrated growing frustration among African Americans.**

OTHERS INSPIRED BY THE MOVEMENT

King's tragic death and the divisions within the civil rights movement during the 1960s sometimes

MARCH TO FREEDOM

James Meredith attempting to enter Ole Miss

1962 James Meredith enrolls at Ole Miss.

1965 Demonstrators attacked in Selma. ◆ Voting Rights Act passed. ◆ Malcolm X assassinated. ◆ Watts riots occur.

1968 Martin Luther King, Jr., assassinated. ◆ Kerner Report blames white racism for riots.

Coretta Scott King at funeral service, 1968

1965   1970

1967 Nearly 100 race riots occur in the U.S. ◆ Kerner Commission appointed.

1963 SCLC launches Birmingham protests.

Lunch counter sit-in, 1963

1964 Freedom Summer project launched in Mississippi. ◆ Civil Rights Act passed. ◆ Mississippi Freedom Democratic party founded. ◆ Twenty-fourth Amendment outlawing poll taxes passed.

1961 CORE sponsors Freedom Rides. ◆ Albany Movement launched.

obscure the gains the movement made, including inspiring other groups, such as Mexican Americans and Native Americans, to fight for their rights. During the 1960s a group that would become the **United Farm Workers** (UFW), led by César Chávez, began to organize migrant workers, most of whom were Mexican Americans, to win better wages and working conditions. Chávez knew that many landowners exploited migrant labor. In 1965 Chávez called a strike of California grape pickers and launched a nationwide boycott of grapes picked by nonunion workers. By 1970 the UFW had won most of its demands. Throughout this struggle Chávez remained committed to using nonviolent resistance.

As in the African American movement for civil rights, many younger members of the Mexican American movement started calling for more-radical action. Young Mexican American college students organized the **Chicano movement**—also known as Brown Power—which emphasized pride in Mexican culture and heritage. Such pride was reflected in the numerous Mexican American political parties that sprang up around the country, most notably *La Raza Unida* ("the united race"), founded in Texas in 1970.

Some Native Americans organized into the Red Power movement, which demanded, among other things, that the U.S. government pay tribes for lands that had been taken from them illegally. In 1968 three Minnesota Chippewas organized the **American Indian Movement** (AIM), which would become the major force in the Red Power movement during the 1970s (see Chapter 31).

In 1969 a group of Red Power advocates occupied the abandoned federal prison on Alcatraz Island near San Francisco. The protesters offered to buy the island from the government with beads and cloth—the same price paid by the Dutch for Manhattan Island. The occupation of Alcatraz lasted for many months, until federal authorities finally removed the protesters by force.

All of these movements shared the African American movement's emphasis on ethnic pride and history. Just a few years earlier, popular culture had emphasized that to be American meant to be white and middle class. Black Power, Brown Power, and Red Power said that all Americans should be proud of their heritages and should fight to correct past injustices against them.

■■ **The civil rights movement inspired other groups, such as Mexican Americans and Native Americans, to fight for their rights.**

SECTION 3 REVIEW

IDENTIFY and explain the significance of the following: Southern Christian Leadership Conference, nonviolent resistance, sit-in, Student Nonviolent Coordinating Committee, Congress of Racial Equality, Freedom Riders, March on Washington, Civil Rights Act of 1964, Freedom Summer, Voting Rights Act, Black Power, Malcolm X, Kerner Commission, United Farm Workers, César Chávez, Chicano movement, American Indian Movement.

LOCATE and explain the importance of the following: Greensboro, North Carolina; Birmingham, Alabama; Albany, Georgia; Selma, Alabama; Memphis, Tennessee.

1. **MAIN IDEA** What tactic did members of the early civil rights movement use to fight for equal rights? What effect did this tactic have on public opinion?

2. **MAIN IDEA** What event helped bring about passage of the Civil Rights Act of 1964? What incidents helped expand African American voter registration?

3. **MAIN IDEA** How did the African American civil rights movement affect other ethnic movements?

4. **WRITING TO EXPRESS A VIEWPOINT** Imagine you are a Freedom Rider. Write a letter to the editor of a southern newspaper explaining why you feel it is necessary to complete the rides.

5. **TAKING A STAND** Take a stand in support of either Martin Luther King, Jr.'s method of negotiation and nonviolent resistance or Malcolm X's method of separation and self-defense. State the strengths and possible effects of that method on the civil rights movement.

CULTURE AND COUNTERCULTURE

FOCUS

■ How did hippies rebel against traditional society?

■ What did the revived women's movement do for women?

■ How did rock music impact the 1960s?

"*The times they are a-changin'*" *declared singer Bob Dylan in 1963. He was not referring to the civil rights movement alone. Many young people, rejecting the values of their parents' generation, embraced new styles of music and dress and new ways of life. Others challenged American traditions, including religious practices and the role of women in society. The result was a reinvention of culture that eventually affected the entire nation.*

Hippie, 1967

THE COUNTERCULTURE

The youth rebellion that began in the 1950s with the Beats and rock 'n' roll evolved into a broad movement in the 1960s that challenged the beliefs and traditions of older generations. Growing up during an era of Cold War fears, massive civil rights protests, and the Vietnam War led many children of the baby boom to question the values of American society and to blame their parents for creating the problems that plagued the country. This **generation gap** between the baby boomers and their elders grew ever wider as the decade wore on.

Shaking the ivory tower. The first audible rumblings of the 1960s youth movement occurred on college

campuses among white middle-class students. Many felt frustrated by the conservative curriculum offered at universities. To them, traditional courses seemed out of touch with the real world.

In 1964 discontent exploded into protest at the University of California at Berkeley. Some 70 percent of the students went on strike. Instead of attending classes, they rallied, held sit-ins, and picketed university administration buildings. Their intention, they declared, was to "Shut This Factory Down." By 1965 such chants were echoing from college campuses across the nation. Many students inspired by this experience

◀ Five hundred policemen were present during the Berkeley student protests in December 1964. Some demonstrators who staged a sit-in were arrested and hauled off to jail.

became involved in the political movements of the time. One woman who participated in the student movement at Columbia University recalled the mood of the students:

66 There was an incredible exhilaration, that here we were making history, changing the world. . . . Everybody believed that this university would never be the same, that society would be . . . changed, that there'd be a revolution in the United States within five years, and a whole new social order. 99

While some students wanted to change the world, others rebelled by rejecting everything connected with mainstream America, what they called the Establishment. Instead, these **hippies**—as they soon became known—sought to create an alternative life-style, a **counterculture**.

Elements of the counterculture. Like the Beats before them, hippies rejected the materialism and work ethic of past generations in favor of simplicity and doing "your own thing." Many hippies indulged in behavior intended to shock older Americans, such as public displays of nudity and the use of profanity. Most searched for new physical experiences by engaging in permissive sexual behavior or by experimenting with mind-altering drugs, such as LSD (lysergic acid diethylamide), or "acid."

Timothy Leary, a Harvard professor who was fired in 1963 for using LSD on his students, became the drug's leading advocate. Leary invited people to "tune in, turn on, drop out." Many followed his advice. But there was a high price to pay for the experimentation of the era, as reported cases of sexually transmitted diseases and drug addiction increased at an alarming rate.

Some hippies "dropped out" of society by joining rural communes, where they attempted to live collectively in harmony with nature. They rejected most modern conveniences, grew their own food, and shared all property. Some formed their own hippie neighborhoods in run-down urban areas, such as the **Haight-Ashbury** district of San Francisco.

■■ **Hippies rebelled against traditional society by forming their own counterculture.**

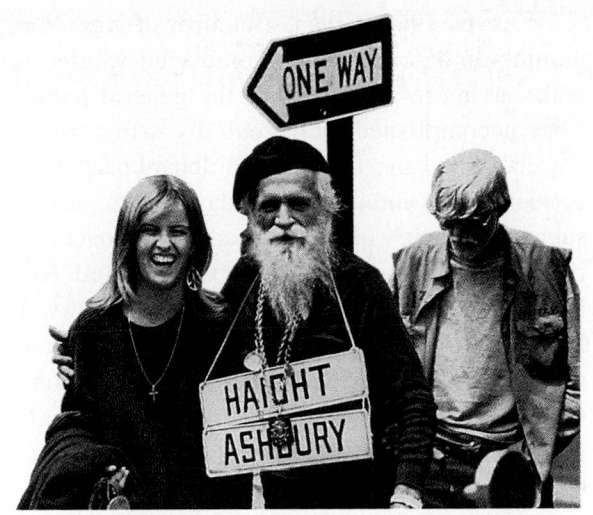

▲ **The Haight-Ashbury district of San Francisco attracted hippies of all ages. This photograph was taken in May 1968.**

QUESTIONING AMERICAN SOCIETY

The counterculture movement reflected a growing sense of skepticism in America. In the 1960s many Americans, even those not active in the counterculture movement, were beginning to question the value of conformity. Many institutions, including traditional churches, came under scrutiny. In the mid-1950s, over 80 percent of Americans said religion could answer all or most of modern society's problems. By 1969, however, 70 percent said that religion was *losing* its influence on American life, leading *Time* magazine to ask, "Is God Dead?"

Americans, especially the young, did not necessarily lack spiritual faith, but many came to lack faith in the ability of the old, established churches to provide spiritual growth in the modern world. The challenges of the nuclear age, some felt, had made conventional religious answers irrelevant. Reflecting the search for alternative answers, the number of college courses in religion—and enrollment in them—grew dramatically, as did interest in Eastern religions such as Zen Buddhism.

The questioning of tradition even extended into the art world. Many new visual artists argued that the art world had become a slave to elite tastes and prejudices. Artists created works only to please a few cultured critics, not to appeal to the majority of non-artists.

As the 1960s began, a number of New York painters and sculptors emerged who wanted to make art more accessible to the general public. They accomplished their goals by using "found objects"—tin cans, furniture, cardboard packaging, cartoon strips, and other everyday articles—as the subjects of their works. The leading proponents of this method, called **pop art**, included Roy Lichtenstein and Claes Oldenberg. Many of Lichtenstein's huge paintings were done in comic-strip style, complete with speech balloons. Oldenberg used a variety of materials to make giant sculptures of such things as hamburgers, toothpaste tubes, and clothespins.

The best-known pop artist, however, was Andy Warhol. His most notable paintings included oversize soup cans, rows of green soda bottles, and a garishly colored rendering of a photograph of Marilyn Monroe reproduced multiple times. Initially, Warhol painted by hand. However, he soon switched to a stencil-printing process called silk screen. Finally, he simply did designs that an army of assistants then reproduced. Warhol's message, that everything—even art—can be mass-produced, both glorified and mocked consumerism. Warhol once predicted that "In the future everyone will be famous for 15 minutes," reflecting consumers' constant desires for new products.

A REVIVED WOMEN'S MOVEMENT

One of the most lasting legacies of the 1960s was its challenge to traditional views of women. After years of inaction, the women's movement experienced a widespread revival.

Sparks of unrest. This revival was sparked in part by the publication of Betty Friedan's *The Feminine Mystique* (1963), which rejected the popular notion that women were content with the roles of wife, mother, and homemaker. Many women, she charged, felt stifled by the "comfortable concentration camp" of domestic life:

> 66 Each suburban wife struggled with it alone. As she made the beds, shopped for groceries, matched slipcover material, ate peanut butter sandwiches with her children, chauffeured Cub Scouts and Brownies, . . . she was afraid to ask even of herself the silent question—"Is this all?" 99

Other women agreed with Friedan. Her book helped motivate women to demand greater opportunities and fairer treatment in the workplace. Although the Civil Rights Act of 1964 outlawed sexual discrimination in employment, the government seemed reluctant to deal with women's grievances. As a result, in 1966 Friedan and other feminists founded the **National Organization for Women** (NOW) to lobby for women's rights. Women began to stand up for themselves in a variety of ways. Some held consciousness-raising sessions to improve their self-esteem. Others took direct action. In 1968, for example, some feminists disrupted the Miss America pageant, charging that beauty contests degraded women.

▶ Pop artists helped make art more accessible to the general public by selecting images that reflected everyday life. Andy Warhol, for example, painted these oversize soup cans in 1965.

Andy Warhol, Campbell's Soup, 1965

Roy Lichtenstein

◀ Many of Roy Lichtenstein's paintings were drawn in a flamboyant, comic-strip style.

Social History

Until relatively recently, most American history textbooks focused on political history, recounting the deeds of the nation's political, military, and social leaders. Today, however, textbooks have begun to place a greater emphasis on social history.

What is social history? Some 50 years ago the well-known British historian G. M. Trevelyan described social history as "the history of a people with the politics left out." Social historians studied people's private lives rather than political events. They concentrated on the household, giving details about the daily lives of men, women, and children. Though colorful, this history failed to explain larger historical themes.

But social history changed in the 1960s. The civil rights movement, antiwar protests, and the women's movement inspired a new generation of historians. In order to explain how these protest movements arose, historians began studying how African Americans, women, and ethnic groups other than white Protestants contributed to American history. Focusing on ordinary people—workers, women, city dwellers, farmers, immigrants—social historians set out to rewrite the history of the United States.

To do so, these historians sought out new sources and used new methods to reconstruct the daily lives and thoughts of ordinary people. Earlier historians had analyzed only written sources left by political and intellectual leaders. The new social historians uncovered new sources—workers' speeches and letters, oral histories, autobiographies, songs, folklore, reports of chari-

▲ *Roll, Jordan, Roll,* an example of social history by Eugene D. Genovese, explores plantation life in the pre–Civil War South.

table societies, and ethnic and immigrant newspapers. These historians used statistical methods to study how people voted, where they moved, what they ate and drank, how they spent and saved their money, and the size of their families.

The new social historians have created a body of work whose strength lies in its respect for cultural diversity. Their work explores the values and ideas that Americans of different racial, ethnic, and class backgrounds share and do not share. For example, Julia Kirk Blackwelder's *Women of the Depression: Caste and Culture in San Antonio, 1929–39* (1984) shows how people's racial and ethnic backgrounds helped them cope with economic distress.

The new social history also explores the social institutions—families, schools, churches, and so on—that both preserve traditional values and help introduce new ones. This history, however, goes beyond the "old" social history by using social institutions to help explain broader political, economic, or technological changes. For example, Kenneth Jackson's *Crabgrass Frontier* (1985) explains that American families' preference for detached homes of their own helped lead to the growth of suburbs—an important economic and geographic change.

The best social history combines research on political and economic institutions with research on how ordinary people think and act. This combination helps us understand politics and the forces that ultimately create change. In doing so, the new social historians can rightly claim to have updated Trevelyan's definition of social history by creating a history of all Americans with the politics mixed in.

A new generation. Many young women who had participated in the civil rights movement and counterculture realized that they faced just as much sexual discrimination in those realms as they did in mainstream society. One activist recalled a friend telling her that "you'll never be a radical as long as you don't see how the system affects *you*. You always think it affects other people." By the late 1960s more women inspired by other movements were beginning to stand up for their own rights. One woman who became so inspired was journalist Gloria Steinem.

Gloria Steinem was born on March 25, 1934, in Toledo, Ohio. In 1946 her parents divorced. She spent most of her teenage years taking care of her invalid mother. In 1952 Steinem entered Smith College, where she graduated with honors. "I loved Smith," she recalled. "They gave you three meals a day to eat, and all the books you wanted to read—what more could you want?" Steinem's love of reading and writing led to her desire to become a journalist.

Gloria Steinem

In 1968 she started writing a political column for *New York* magazine, which brought her into contact with activists such as César Chávez and African American Communist Angela Davis. Later that year she wrote her first openly feminist article, "After Black Power, Women's Liberation," which established her as an advocate of the movement. In 1971 she helped found the National Women's Political Caucus to encourage women to run for political office. That same year, she became editor of a new magazine for women entitled *Ms.*

"There is nothing outside of [the movement]," Steinem said. "I once thought I would do this for two or three years and go home to my real life." But she has continued to be a leader in the women's movement, writing several books, lobbying for causes such as the passage of the Equal Rights Amendment (see Chapter 31), and helping found numerous organizations for women, including the Coalition of Labor Union Women and Women Against Pornography.

■■ **The 1960s revival of the women's movement challenged traditional views of women.**

MUSICAL REVOLUTION

All of the social and political movements of the 1960s marched to new forms of music. A compelling influence on the youth rebellion of the 1950s, rock 'n' roll continued to reflect social change in the 1960s, while it branched out into a variety of new forms.

The year 1964 marked the musical **British Invasion**—the arrival of such English bands as the Beatles and the Rolling Stones. Looking back to rock 'n' roll and to African American blues for inspiration, these bands created a vibrant, powerful new style of music. Meanwhile, African American artists, many sponsored by Motown Records of Detroit, were experimenting with enhanced blendings of traditional black music. The unique and widely popular style they created became known as the "Motown sound."

The use of electrically amplified instruments, especially the electric guitar, inspired musicians to try innovative—and very loud—sounds on audiences. Seattle native Jimi Hendrix was the master

▼ Jimi Hendrix, shown here performing at the Isle of Wight in 1970, was one of the most innovative rock 'n' roll guitarists to emerge during the late 1960s.

▲ Folk music by artists such as Joan Baez was also popular during the 1960s.

of the electric guitar in the 1960s. Folk music also inspired a new type of rock sound as singers such as Joan Baez and Bob Dylan created lyrics that sent a political message to listeners, such as in this 1962 Dylan hit:

> 66 How many years can a mountain exist
> before it's washed to the sea?
> Yes, 'n' How many years can some
> people exist
> before they're allowed to be free?
> Yes, 'n' How many times can a man
> turn his head
> pretending he just doesn't see?
> The answer, my friend, is blowin'
> in the wind,
> The answer is blowin' in the wind. 99

Dylan brought folk music fully into the rock realm in 1965, when he abandoned the acoustic guitar, traditionally used in folk music, in favor of the electric guitar.

Rock music would be the focal point of an event that marked the beginning of the end for the counterculture movement—the Woodstock Music Festival. In August 1969 some 300,000 young people descended on rural upstate New York for the three-day festival, closing the New York State Thruway in the process. Despite driving rain, knee-deep mud, and severe shortages of food and drink, the concert remained a peaceful gathering as listeners reveled in the music of rock's top performers.

▲ In spite of traffic jams, water shortages, lack of public conveniences, and rain, the Woodstock Music Festival in August 1969 was an overwhelming success.

Woodstock was more than just a rock concert. It was a celebration of the era, marking the high point of the counterculture movement. Some four months later, at a free concert held at Altamont Raceway near San Francisco, a security team beat a young African American fan to death in full view of the stage. The idealistic spirit of the youth movement seemed to die with him.

■■ **Rock music followed the movements of the 1960s and marked the high point of the counterculture at Woodstock.**

 SECTION 4 REVIEW

IDENTIFY and explain the significance of the following: generation gap, hippies, counterculture, Timothy Leary, pop art, Roy Lichtenstein, Claes Oldenberg, Andy Warhol, Betty Friedan, National Organization for Women, Gloria Steinem, British Invasion, Jimi Hendrix, Bob Dylan, Woodstock.

1. **MAIN IDEA** Why did hippies form their own counterculture?

2. **MAIN IDEA** What effect did the revival of the women's movement have on traditional views of women?

3. **ASSESSING CONSEQUENCES** What consequences did the youth rebellion of the 1960s have on society?

4. **WRITING TO EVALUATE** Imagine you are a music critic in 1969. Write an article that evaluates the relationship between rock 'n' roll music and the events of the 1960s.

5. **SYNTHESIZING** How did the various works of pop artists reflect American culture in the 1960s?

SNCC founded. John F. Kennedy elected president.

Yuri Gagarin makes first manned space flight. Bay of Pigs invaded. Freedom Rides begin. Berlin Wall built.

Michael Harrington's *The Other America* published. Cuban missile crisis erupts.

Equal Pay Act passed. Betty Friedan's *The Feminine Mystique* published. March on Washington occurs. Kennedy assassinated.

1960   **1962**

WRITING A SUMMARY

Using the essential points of the chapter as a guide, write a summary of the chapter.

REVIEWING CHRONOLOGY

Number your paper 1 to 5. Study the time line above, and list the following events in the order in which they happened by writing the first next to 1, the second next to 2, and so on. Then complete the activity below.

1. Woodstock Music Festival occurs.
2. American Indian Movement organized.
3. Betty Friedan's *The Feminine Mystique* published.
4. Freedom Rides begin.
5. Medicare and Medicaid established.

Evaluating How did Michael Harrington's book *The Other America* influence American domestic policy?

IDENTIFYING PEOPLE AND IDEAS

Explain the historical significance of each of the following people or terms.

1. New Frontier
2. Peace Corps
3. Fidel Castro
4. Warren Commission
5. Juan Bosch
6. nonviolent resistance
7. Voting Rights Act
8. Chicano movement
9. generation gap
10. Gloria Steinem

UNDERSTANDING MAIN IDEAS

1. How did the Kennedy administration propose to deter Communist expansion?
2. What was the purpose of the Great Society? How did President Johnson propose to make the Great Society a reality?
3. What did the Brown Power, Red Power, and Black Power movements have in common?
4. How did young people rebel against conformity during the 1960s?
5. What gains did women make during the 1960s? How did they make these gains?

REVIEWING THEMES

1. **Global Relations** How did events overseas undermine the Great Society programs?
2. **Democratic Values** How did the Freedom Rides, sit-ins, and other peaceful civil rights protests help expand democracy?
3. **Cultural Diversity** What institutions and traditions were challenged in the late 1960s?

THINKING CRITICALLY

1. **Evaluating** How did the Warren Court's decisions in *Gideon* v. *Wainwright*, *Escobedo* v. *Illinois*, and *Miranda* v. *Arizona* strengthen individual rights?
2. **Synthesizing** In what ways did African Americans express frustration over their slow progress in achieving civil rights?
3. **Analyzing** What contribution did music and pop art make to society in the 1960s?

STRATEGY FOR SUCCESS

Review the Skills Handbook entry on Reading Charts and Graphs beginning on page 996. Study the graph below, which shows the number of drug arrests reported between 1960 and 1970. In which year did the number of arrests first exceed 100,000? About how many arrests were reported in 1970?

URBAN DRUG ARRESTS, 1960–1970

Source: *Information Please Almanac*

War on Poverty declared. OEO established. Freedom Summer launched. Civil Rights Act passed.

Medicare and Medicaid established. Malcolm X assassinated. Selma's Bloody Sunday occurs. U.S. intervenes in Dominican Republic. Voting Rights Act passed.

NOW founded. Supreme Court decides *Miranda* v. *Arizona*.

Martin Luther King, Jr., assassinated. American Indian Movement organized.

Woodstock Music Festival occurs.

1964　　　**1966**　　　**1968**

WRITING ABOUT HISTORY

Writing to Evaluate Write an essay that evaluates the different leadership styles of Lyndon Johnson and John F. Kennedy.

USING PRIMARY SOURCES

Native Americans were one ethnic group in the 1960s whose problems were not addressed by the U.S. government. Read the following excerpt, which comes from an article published in the *New Republic* in 1965, describing conditions on the Pine Ridge Reservation in South Dakota. Then write a paragraph summarizing what you have read.

> 66 *Practically none of the houses on the reservation has electricity. Half of the houses are without wells nearby; Poverty-Program workers are discovering people hauling water fifteen miles. Indoor plumbing or telephone service is rare. . . .*
>
> *There is a great deal of illness at Pine Ridge. . . . The infant mortality rate is twice that of the nation's, and infectious diseases among small children are a major problem. The incidence of tuberculosis is seventeen times that for the rest of the country. The life expectancy for a person at Pine Ridge is thirty-eight years, compared with sixty-two years nationally. . . .*
>
> *The solution to the Indian problem still is dimly seen to lie in pouring the Indians into the big cities where they will intermingle with everyone else. But the city planners are trying to figure out how to get people out of the cramped city and back into the countryside. If the administration does not pull hard to redevelop these rural areas, it will end up merely fanning the flames in the cities.* 99

LINKING HISTORY AND GEOGRAPHY

Refer to the map on page 837. How did geography influence U.S. policy toward Cuba and the Dominican Republic?

BUILDING YOUR PORTFOLIO

Complete the following projects independently or cooperatively.

1. CIVIL RIGHTS In chapters 27 and 28 you served as a reporter covering the civil rights movement. Building on that experience, write a memorandum to the manager of your station explaining why the station should provide coverage of the civil rights efforts of African Americans, Hispanic Americans, Native Americans, and women.

2. THE GOVERNMENT AND THE ECONOMY In Chapter 27 you prepared a chart of government programs designed to help WWII veterans. Building on that experience, imagine you are a member of Johnson's Great Society. Prepare an illustrated pamphlet that describes government efforts in areas such as health care, urban renewal, or education.

3. POPULAR CULTURE In Chapter 28 you prepared a photo essay on American culture during the 1950s. Building on that experience, imagine you are a reporter for *Rolling Stone*, assigned to write an article about the first two decades of rock 'n' roll. Prepare a family tree of rock music, using photos to trace the influence of rhythm and blues, jazz, folk, country, and the British Invasion on American music up to 1970.

URBAN AMERICA

As more people moved into the cities and suburbs after World War II, metropolitan areas —large cities or groups of cities and their surrounding areas—arose. The city of Los Angeles is typical of the 20th-century metropolis. In the 1920s most of the land inside the official city limits was not developed. As the city grew, it engulfed numerous surrounding areas. By the 1980s the Los Angeles metropolitan area encompassed some 80 smaller cities. Like many urban-dwellers, Los Angeles–area residents generally live outside the city and commute to work. This has led to the observation that Los Angeles, like many other metropolitan areas, is in fact "a hundred suburbs in search of a city."

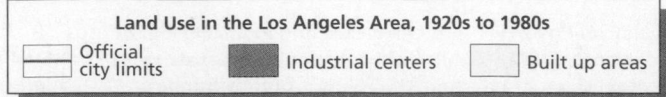

Land Use in the Los Angeles Area, 1920s to 1980s		
Official city limits	Industrial centers	Built up areas

Los Angeles Area, 1920s

Los Angeles River

Burbank

Hollywood

Beverly Hills

San Gabriel River

San Bernardino

Los Angeles

Santa Monica

Watts

PACIFIC OCEAN

Anaheim

Long Beach

Santa Ana

Santa Ana River

N W E S

| 0 | 10 | 20 Miles |
| 0 | 10 | 20 Kilometers |

Lambert Conformal Conic Projection

Transportation

Electric trolleys

Steam trains

Ethnic neighborhoods

10% or more African American

10% or more African American and 20% or more foreign-born Mexican

Los Angeles was at the forefront of creating the suburban housing system that grew popular in the 1950s. In the early 20th century, as eastern cities grew more crowded, Los Angeles built the nation's most extensive electric railway system to encourage people to live outside the city and commute to work.

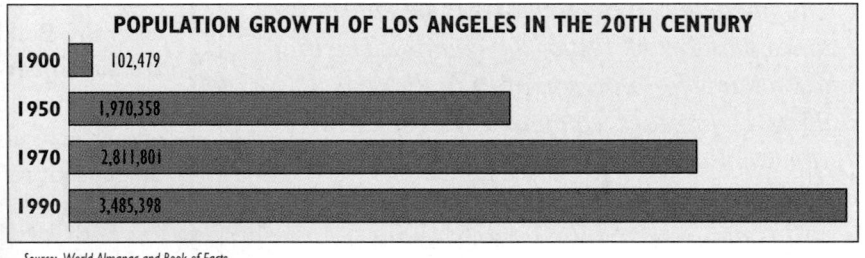

POPULATION GROWTH OF LOS ANGELES IN THE 20TH CENTURY

1900	102,479
1950	1,970,358
1970	2,811,801
1990	3,485,398

Source: World Almanac and Book of Facts

POPULATION OF LOS ANGELES IN 1990

53%	White
14%	Black
.5%	Native American, Alaskan, or Aleut
10%	Asian
40%	Hispanic origin*
23%	Other

*Hispanic origin may include persons of any race, thus chart represents more than 100%.

Source: Information Please Almanac

Los Angeles has been one of the most ethnically diverse cities in the country, yet years of discrimination in housing have left many ethnic groups limited to ghettos in the center of the city. In 1949 Ed Roybal, a Hispanic member of the Los Angeles city council, could not buy a house in the suburbs because the realtors would not sell to Hispanics. Such discrimination fueled racial unrest in the later 20th century, sparking numerous riots, such as the Watts riot of 1965 and the south central riots of 1992.

Los Angeles Area, 1950s

Transportation
- Freeway completed
- Freeway under construction
- Federal or state highway

Ethnic neighborhoods
- 40% or more African American
- 40% or more Hispanic
- 30% or more Asian

Burbank
Hollywood
Beverly Hills
Los Angeles
Santa Monica
Watts
Los Angeles River
San Gabriel River
San Bernardino
Santa Ana River
PACIFIC OCEAN
Anaheim
Santa Ana
Long Beach

0   10   20 Miles
0   10   20 Kilometers
Lambert Conformal Conic Projection

By the 1940s automobiles had replaced the railway system as the preferred means of transportation in Los Angeles. Construction of a huge freeway network encouraged automobile use, but it also led to a rise in smog pollution—a problem that plagues many cities today. While Los Angeles has grown rapidly, it has also faced numerous problems caused by its geography. The dry climate has contributed to several brush fires in recent years. Lack of an adequate water supply led to the construction of Owens River Aqueduct in 1913, followed by the California Aqueduct in 1973. Los Angeles also lies in an area of heavy earthquake activity. The city has been rocked by numerous earthquakes, including one in January 1994 that killed more than 50 people.

Los Angeles Area, 1980s

Average traffic flow per day
- 200,000 or more vehicles
- 100,000–199,000 vehicles
- 50,000–99,999 vehicles
- 49,999 or fewer vehicles
- Other major road

Ethnic neighborhoods
- 40% or more African American
- 40% or more Hispanic
- 30% or more Asian
- Mixed ethnic population

Burbank
Hollywood
Beverly Hills
Los Angeles
Santa Monica
Watts
Los Angeles River
San Gabriel River
San Bernardino
Santa Ana River
PACIFIC OCEAN
Anaheim
Santa Ana
Long Beach

0   10   20 Miles
0   10   20 Kilometers
Lambert Conformal Conic Projection

By the mid–1980s Los Angeles was the second-largest city in America. Many citizens, worried that the city was growing too rapidly, campaigned for measures to slow growth and improve urban conditions. In 1986 the city passed a measure that cut in half the amount of land available to developers for construction. Also in the mid–1980s the city began working on plans to improve public transportation with a new train and subway system.

WAR IN VIETNAM

FOCUS

UNDERSTANDING THE MAIN IDEA

Most U.S. leaders expected the war in Vietnam to end quickly once U.S. troops and equipment entered the conflict. They did not dream that some 2.6 million Americans would serve in a war that dragged on for more than a decade. Nor did they imagine that antiwar protests would grow to the proportions they did.

THEMES

■ **GLOBAL RELATIONS** How might global conditions lead one nation to intervene in the affairs of another?

■ **CONSTITUTIONAL HERITAGE** Why might one branch of government fear another branch becoming too strong?

■ **DEMOCRATIC VALUES** What are the limits to the government's responsibility to keep the public informed? In a democracy, what limits are there to a people's right to protest government actions?

1954	1955	1965	1973	1975
▼	▼	▼	▼	▼
Geneva Conference held.	Diem comes to power in South Vietnam.	U.S. sends combat troops to Vietnam.	Cease-fire declared.	Saigon falls.

The United States had taken the position of opposing the spread of communism anywhere in the world. U.S. troops had recently fought against Communist forces in Korea. Now Americans became involved in a similar war in Vietnam, where the Vietnamese had won their independence from the French a few years earlier.

In Graham Greene's novel *The Quiet American* (1955), the narrator sits in a Vietnamese café thinking about a new arrival, the American "adviser" Alden Pyle. According to the narrator, the young American "seemed incapable of harm":

> 66 Perhaps only ten days ago he had been walking back across the Common in Boston, his arms full of the books he had been reading in advance on the Far East and the problems of China. He didn't even hear what I said; he was absorbed already in the dilemmas of Democracy and the responsibilities of the West; he was determined—I learnt that very soon—to do good, not to any individual person but to a country, a continent, a world. 99

Greene's Alden Pyle closely resembles the American advisers sent to South Vietnam in the 1950s. This "quiet American," wading into the rough sea of post–World War II Southeast Asia, typifies the early American self-image in Vietnam: confident, serious, and eagerly committed to building a model democracy.

This sense of idealism was grounded in the effort to save Vietnam and the rest of the world from communism, even at great cost to America. The eventual cost—years of war and more than 60,000 Americans dead or missing—was higher than most believed possible. And despite the sacrifices, Vietnam was not "saved." In the war's wake, Americans were left to ponder how early idealism ended in what has been called "a tragedy of epic dimensions."

A U.S. Marine officer takes cover.

Vietnam Women's Memorial

BACKGROUND TO CONFLICT

FOCUS

- Why did China and then France want to control Vietnam?
- Why did the United States refuse to back Vietnamese independence in the 1940s and 1950s?
- Why did President Kennedy increase U.S. involvement in Vietnam?

For centuries invaders coveted the fertile river deltas and coastal lowlands of Vietnam. First China and later France conquered and ruled Vietnam. But the deep desire of the Vietnamese people to be free could not be overcome. During World War II, France began to lose its grip on Vietnam. And as the war came to a close, Vietnamese Communists fought for power, hoping to establish an independent nation. This threat of a Communist takeover soon drew the United States into the conflict.

French colonial occupation in Saigon

THE GEOGRAPHIC SETTING

Fishhook-shaped Vietnam is the easternmost country of Southeast Asia—8,000 miles across the Pacific from the west coast of the United States. It is slightly smaller than California, covering 127,207 square miles of mostly hills and dense forests. Lying south of China, Vietnam is bordered on the west by Laos and Cambodia. Its coastline stretches along the Gulf of Tonkin, the South China Sea, and the Gulf of Thailand (see map on page 865).

The population of Vietnam is centered mostly in two areas: the Red River Delta in the far north and the Mekong (MAY-KAWNG) Delta in the south. The Mekong Delta is Vietnam's richest agricultural region, specializing in rice cultivation. Hanoi is the major city of the north and the country's capital, while Ho Chi Minh City (previously South Vietnam's capital, Saigon) is the largest city in the south. Other cities, such as the ports Da Nang and Hue (WAY), are located on the narrow coastal lowlands of central Vietnam.

To the north of the Mekong Delta are the central highlands, sparsely populated and mostly covered by forest. Farther north, the Annamite Mountains form the jagged backbone of Vietnam. Their rugged peaks and dense rain forest separate much of Vietnam from neighboring Laos.

▲ **Vietnam is one of the world's largest producers of rice, cultivating more than 12 million acres each year.**

CHINESE OCCUPATION

The moist tropical climate of the deltas and coastal lowlands has allowed Vietnamese farmers to grow several crops of rice a year. It was this agricultural abundance that tempted China to invade the Red River Delta around 200 B.C. For more than a thousand years, the Chinese struggled to maintain control over northern and central Vietnam. But the Vietnamese resisted, finally winning limited independence from China in A.D. 939.

In the 1400s China tried to reassert control over Vietnam. A Vietnamese military leader named Le Loi employed guerrilla warfare to defeat the Chinese invaders. Using tactics similar to those later used against the French and Americans, Le Loi's rebels worked as peasants by day; by night they took up arms to attack the Chinese. By 1428 the rebels had driven the Chinese from the country and won independence for Vietnam. Le Loi became the new emperor.

FRENCH OCCUPATION

Vietnam again lost its independence in the surge of European imperialism in the mid-1800s. This time the invaders were French, attracted by the promise of gaining access to Asian trade and of making new Catholic converts.

Despite the stubborn resistance of the Vietnamese, French military power ultimately won out. In 1883 the Vietnamese were forced to grant France complete control of the country. France later combined Vietnam with Laos and Cambodia to form French Indochina, one of France's richest possessions.

▪▪ The Chinese and later the French sought control of Vietnam's rich farmlands and trade.

Ho Chi Minh and Vietnamese independence.
Like the Chinese, the French gained control of the land but not the hearts of the Vietnamese. Nationalist feelings remained strong.

Indochina

A TROPICAL PENINSULA The nations of Indochina occupy a peninsula stretching from the mainland of Southeast Asia deep into the tropical waters of the South China Sea.

? RELATIVE LOCATION How might Vietnam's location have contributed to its long history of foreign invasion?

Foremost among the nationalists was Nguyen That Thanh (en-gy-EN TAHT TAHN), a world wanderer and man of many names, whose last alias was Ho Chi Minh (HOH CHEE MIN)—"He Who Enlightens."

Ho was born in central Vietnam in 1890, the son of a poor country scholar. In 1911, calling himself Van Ba (Third Son), he got a job as cook on a French merchant ship. After spending a few years at sea, he decided to settle in London. There, while working as a pastry cook in a hotel, Ho learned the English language (he was already fluent in French).

From London, Ho went to Paris, where he soon emerged as a leader of Vietnamese nationalists living in France. Ho joined the French socialists but

Ho Chi Minh

soon left them to help organize the French Communist party. Later, Ho claimed that "it was patriotism and not Communism that originally inspired" his quest for Vietnamese independence. By 1923, though, he was convinced that a worldwide Communist revolution was Vietnam's only hope and left Paris to study revolutionary tactics in Moscow.

During the 1920s and 1930s Ho organized and plotted for Vietnamese independence. One French comrade described him as "taut and quivering, with only one thought in his head, his country, Vietnam." Hunted as a Communist, Ho donned disguises as he moved from country to country—sometimes a Chinese journalist, at other times a Buddhist monk with flowing robes.

What Ho awaited was a chance to launch his plan. That chance came during World War II. In 1940 the Japanese army swept down from China to occupy all of French Indochina, the Philippines, Malaya, and Indonesia. In Vietnam the Japanese left the French colonial government in place but controlled it. Early in 1941 Ho slipped secretly into Vietnam to organize a resistance. He called the movement the League for the Independence of Vietnam, or **Vietminh** (vee-ET-MIN). When the Japanese withdrew from Indochina after surrendering to the Allies in August 1945, the Vietminh declared independence.

In Hanoi on September 2, more than half a million people gathered at an independence celebration to hear Ho speak. In an effort to gain American support, the Vietminh leader echoed America's Declaration of Independence: "We hold the truth that all men are created equal, that they are endowed by their Creator with certain unalienable rights, among them life, liberty, and the pursuit of happiness."

At another celebration that day, American army officers joined Vietnamese leaders on the reviewing stand as a Vietnamese band played "The Star-Spangled Banner." U.S. warplanes flew over the gathering in a salute to Vietnam's independence. The French were sure to resist, but the United States seemed poised to prevent them from reclaiming colonial rule over Vietnam.

France and the Vietminh go to war.

American policy toward Vietnam was soon put to the test. By 1946 the French and the Vietnamese were once again locked in battle. Would America stand with the Vietnamese in this conflict? The answer was no. Not only did President Truman ignore Ho's pleas for assistance, he threw U.S. support behind France.

Why did Truman side with France? First, he viewed France as a vital ally in the struggle against the spread of communism in postwar Europe. Second, he was unwilling to back the Vietminh because of Ho's Communist connections. U.S. advisers feared that communism would engulf Asia (see Chapter 27). This fear was reinforced in 1949 when Mao Zedong's Communists took over China—Asia's most populous country and a former U.S. ally. By 1950 the United States was locked in a bloody ground war to turn back Communist North Korea's invasion of South Korea. Meanwhile, Communist-led nationalist revolts rocked Indonesia, the Philippines, and Malaya.

Because of these developments the focus of America's containment policy broadened to include East Asia. There, U.S. policymakers vowed to hold the line against communism. Truman's successor, Dwight D. Eisenhower, shared this resolve, especially in regard to Southeast Asia. Besides possessing abundant raw materials essential to modern industry, the region was considered of strategic importance in containing the Chinese Communists. Eisenhower warned that if Vietnam fell to communism, the rest of

▶ At Dien Bien Phu a weary French soldier awaits further shelling by Vietminh guerrillas in early 1954.

Southeast Asia would soon follow. The president illustrated his point by saying, "You have a row of dominoes set up. You knock over the first one, and what will happen to the last one is a certainty that it will go over very quickly." This idea came to be called the **domino theory**.

■■ Believing that communism would spread throughout Asia if it took hold in Vietnam, the United States turned down Ho's pleas for help against the French.

President Eisenhower's commitment to a non-Communist Vietnam was even stronger than Truman's. By 1954 America was paying much of the cost of France's war effort. But even with massive aid, the French suffered defeat after defeat.

Money and military equipment were of limited use against Vietminh guerrilla tactics. The Vietminh chose when and where to attack, struck without warning, and then disappeared into the jungle. In a comment to an American journalist in 1946, Ho Chi Minh had expressed his people's determination to prevail, characterizing the fight as "a war between an elephant"— the French—"and a tiger"—the Vietnamese:

> **66** If the tiger ever stands still, the elephant will crush him with his mighty tusks. But the tiger does not stand still. . . . He will leap upon the back of the elephant, tearing huge chunks from his hide, and then the tiger will leap back into the dark jungle. And slowly the elephant will bleed to death. That will be the war of Indochina. **99**
> From *America Inside Out* by David Schoenbrun © 1984

Frustrated, the French tried to lure the Vietminh into a conventional battle at Dien Bien Phu (dyen byen FOO), deep within Vietminh-held northern Vietnam. The plan backfired. Some 13,000 French soldiers soon found themselves encircled by more than 50,000 Vietminh troops. The French commander urged his war-weary soldiers to hold out—offering them the hope of a rescue: "The Americans will not let us down; the free world will not let us down."

Help did not come. Although willing to commit money, Eisenhower was reluctant to become directly involved in another Asian war so soon after the Korean War. As a result, the Vietminh defeated the French and on May 7, 1954, forced their surrender.

The Geneva Conference. In the spring of 1954, just one day after the French surrender at Dien Bien Phu, an international conference to settle the Indochina conflict began in Geneva, Switzerland. There, representatives of the French and the Vietminh attempted to map out Indochina's future. The People's Republic of China (Communist China), the United States, Great Britain, the Soviet Union, Laos, and Cambodia joined the discussions.

The Communist Chinese, who had begun aiding the Vietminh in 1950, hoped to limit U.S. influence in the region. They also wished to prevent the establishment of a strong, unified Vietnam on their southern border. The Americans,

◀ **A French newspaper reports the fall of Dien Bien Phu.**

meanwhile, did not want to see Vietnam handed over completely to the Communists.

A cease-fire was agreed to, but no definite political settlement was achieved. Vietnam was temporarily divided at the 17th parallel (17° north latitude). North of the 17th parallel, the Vietminh held undisputed power; south of the line, remnants of the French-controlled government resumed authority. Vietminh forces would withdraw to the north; French forces would withdraw to the south. General elections to reunify the country were scheduled for July 1956. Alarmed that the Communists would likely win a nationwide election, the United States refused to endorse the agreement.

THE REGIME OF NGO DINH DIEM

President Eisenhower estimated that Ho might win a general election by as much as four to one. Still, he hoped that southern Vietnam, at least, might be kept non-Communist. Who could stand against Ho? One possibility was Ngo Dinh Diem (en-GOH DIN de-EM), a former government official under the French. Though lacking Ho's charisma, Diem was enough of a nationalist to be a credible Vietnamese leader.

Diem takes power in the south. Ngo Dinh Diem was strongly anti-Communist. He had spent several years in the United States, where his political views attracted powerful backers. In 1955 Diem became president of the newly established Republic of Vietnam (South Vietnam) following a rigged election—in Saigon, Diem got more than 605,000 votes from the 450,000 registered voters! But Diem knew that he had no chance of winning a nationwide election against Ho. Thus, he refused to call an election in the south when the July 1956 date set by the Geneva Conference rolled around.

Diem, a Roman Catholic, was unpopular from the start. The large Buddhist population resented the favoritism he showed toward Catholics. Peasants disliked his land policies, which favored wealthy landholders. And almost everyone objected that power was solely in the grip of Diem's family. Above all, people feared his ruthless efforts to root out his political enemies. Diem's hated security forces routinely tortured and imprisoned opponents.

By the late 1950s armed revolution had erupted in the south. In 1959, military assistance began

flowing from the north to the Vietminh who had stayed in the south. In 1960 the southern Vietminh formed the National Liberation Front (NLF). The NLF's main goal was the overthrow of the Ngo Dinh Diem regime. Members of this rebel force were called **Vietcong** (Vietnamese Communists) by their opponents, but not all NLF supporters were Communists.

Many peasants joined the ranks of the NLF, some because of government repression. Others joined out of fear: the NLF, like Diem's forces, used terrorist tactics, assassinating hundreds of government officials. Soon much of the countryside was under Vietcong control.

America's involvement deepens. John F. Kennedy, who became president in 1961, fully subscribed to the domino theory. He also was eager to bolster America's image in the world—an image that had been tarnished by the failed Bay of Pigs invasion and the Soviets' raising of the Berlin Wall early in his presidency (see Chapter 29). Coming to the aid of South Vietnam, which Kennedy had once called the "cornerstone of the Free World in Southeast Asia," provided America with a chance to assert its power.

When Kennedy took office, some 700 U.S. military advisers were in South Vietnam training

▼ Ngo Dinh Diem paces the floor of his Saigon palace after crushing an attempt to overthrow his regime in the spring of 1955.

Diem's army. Over the course of his administration, Kennedy increased that number to more than 16,000. As Vietcong attacks mounted, Kennedy authorized U.S. forces to engage in direct combat. As a result, the number of Americans killed or wounded climbed from 14 in 1961 to nearly 500 in 1963.

■■ **President Kennedy saw U.S. involvement in Vietnam as a way to halt the spread of communism and strengthen America's image in the world.**

Diem's overthrow. The situation was also escalating politically. South Vietnam's Buddhist leaders now openly opposed Diem's regime. Diem was waging a brutal campaign of repression against Buddhists. Hundreds had been arrested, and many had been killed in the crackdown. In response, several Buddhist monks publicly set themselves on fire. These grisly protests shocked Americans, and U.S. officials in Saigon threatened to withdraw support for Diem unless he ended the repression.

When Diem refused to comply, U.S. leaders gave quiet encouragement to a group of young South Vietnamese army officers plotting Diem's overthrow. The plotters struck in November 1963, murdering both Diem and his brother. Diem's violent assassination upset U.S. advisers, who had been prepared to fly Diem out of the country.

▲ On June 11, 1963, Quang Duc set himself on fire at a busy intersection in Saigon. He was the first of several Buddhist monks who killed themselves to protest Diem's policies.

Kennedy's doubts increase. Diem's overthrow did nothing to ease Kennedy's growing concern over America's involvement in Vietnam. In an interview shortly before Diem's fall, Kennedy had said of the South Vietnamese: "In the final analysis it is their war. They are the ones who have to win or lose it." But we will never know how Kennedy might have handled the situation. Three weeks after Diem's murder, Kennedy himself was assassinated in Dallas.

SECTION 1 REVIEW

IDENTIFY and explain the significance of the following: Ho Chi Minh, Vietminh, domino theory, Ngo Dinh Diem, Vietcong.

LOCATE and explain the importance of the following: Vietnam, China, Red River Delta, Mekong Delta, Hanoi, Saigon, central highlands, Annamite Mountains, Dien Bien Phu.

1. **MAIN IDEA** Why did President Truman refuse Ho's requests for help against the French?

2. **MAIN IDEA** What led President Kennedy to increase U.S. involvement in Vietnam?

3. **LINKING HISTORY AND GEOGRAPHY** What attracted the Chinese and the French to Vietnam?

4. **WRITING TO PERSUADE** Imagine you are an adviser to President Eisenhower in 1959. On the basis of what you would know at the time, prepare a statement outlining the pros and cons of U.S. involvement in Vietnam. Then, in a paragraph, make a policy recommendation.

5. **USING HISTORICAL IMAGINATION** In the 1941 Atlantic Charter, President Roosevelt and British Prime Minister Churchill pledged "to see sovereign rights and self-government restored to those who have been forcibly deprived of them." Imagine that you are Ho. Write a letter to President Truman explaining why America should honor this pledge in Vietnam.

THE WAR ESCALATES

FOCUS

■ **Why did the Tonkin Gulf Resolution raise a constitutional issue?**

■ **What factors frustrated U.S. military efforts in Vietnam?**

"*I am not going to be the President who saw Vietnam go the way China went,*" *vowed Lyndon Baines Johnson, the next American president to inherit the Vietnam War. Throwing U.S. air power and thousands of young American troops into the conflict, Johnson hoped to end the war quickly. But the war in Vietnam would dominate the nation's consciousness for nearly a decade.*

LBJ

THE TONKIN GULF RESOLUTION

The new South Vietnamese government was just as corrupt and ineffective as Diem's, and the NLF continued to gain ground against the South's army (called the ARVN, for Army of the Republic of Vietnam). Secretary of Defense Robert McNamara, a cabinet member held over from the Kennedy administration, returned from a quick trip to Vietnam in December 1963 to give his new boss a sobering report. To prevent a Communist victory, McNamara advised, Johnson would have to increase the American commitment.

A Communist victory in Vietnam was an unthinkable prospect for Johnson. Like previous presidents, he firmly believed it was necessary to stop Communist expansion. Before increasing the U.S. commitment, however, Johnson planned to get congressional backing. Events on the seas off North Vietnam soon gave him the opportunity.

In August 1964 President Johnson announced that U.S. ships had been attacked twice in the Gulf of Tonkin. The president asked

Congress to authorize the use of military force "to prevent further aggression." In an overwhelming show of patriotism, Congress passed the **Tonkin Gulf Resolution**, giving the president authority to take "all necessary measures to repel any armed attack against forces of the United States."

Johnson claimed that the attacks in the Gulf of Tonkin were "unprovoked." Later it was revealed that one of the ships, the destroyer *Maddox,* had been engaged in spying in support of South Vietnamese raids against North Vietnam and had fired first. Thus, the first North Vietnamese attack was not without cause. The second, moreover, probably never occurred: it appeared that nervous sailors, caught in stormy weather, had misinterpreted interference on their radar and sonar as enemy ships and torpedoes. Nonetheless, Johnson and his advisers got what they wanted: authority to expand the war as they saw fit. As Johnson admitted later, the resolution was "like Grandma's nightshirt—it covered everything."

Only a few in Congress voiced caution. Wayne Morse of Oregon, one of only two senators to vote against the Tonkin Gulf Resolution, warned: "I believe that history will record we have made a great mistake. . . . We are in effect giving the President war-making powers in the absence of a declaration of war." In other words, in passing the resolution, Congress had given up its constitutional power to declare war.

■■ **The Tonkin Gulf Resolution allowed American presidents to fight an undeclared war in Vietnam—contrary to the intent of the U.S. Constitution.**

AMERICAN FORCES IN VIETNAM

With the Tonkin Gulf Resolution in his pocket, President Johnson responded to his advisers' call for a buildup, or **escalation**, of American military forces in Vietnam. He ordered the Selective Service, the agency charged with carrying out the military draft, to begin calling up young men to serve in the armed forces. In April 1965 the Selective Service notified 13,700 draftees, and by December some 40,000 had received "greetings" from their local draft boards.

During the war more than 2.6 million Americans served in Vietnam. In the beginning most were professional soldiers, already enlisted in the armed forces. But as the demand for troops grew, more and more draftees were shipped to Vietnam. At the height of the war, American soldiers in Vietnam were, on average, younger (19), poorer, and less educated than those who had served in World War II or in the Korean War.

All young men who registered for the draft did not have an equal chance of serving in Vietnam. One out of four was excused from service for health reasons. Another 30 percent received non-health-related exemptions or deferments (postponements of service), most often for college enrollment. Mainly because of college deferments, young men from higher-income families were the least likely to be drafted. As a result, the poor served in numbers far greater than their proportion in the general population—as they had in most of the previous wars.

African and Hispanic Americans served in combat in especially high numbers, particularly during the early years of the war. Some of these soldiers protested that black and Hispanic soldiers were being asked to do more than their share of the fighting—and dying. In 1965, for example, African Americans accounted for almost 24 percent of all battle deaths, even though they made up only 11 percent of the U.S. population.

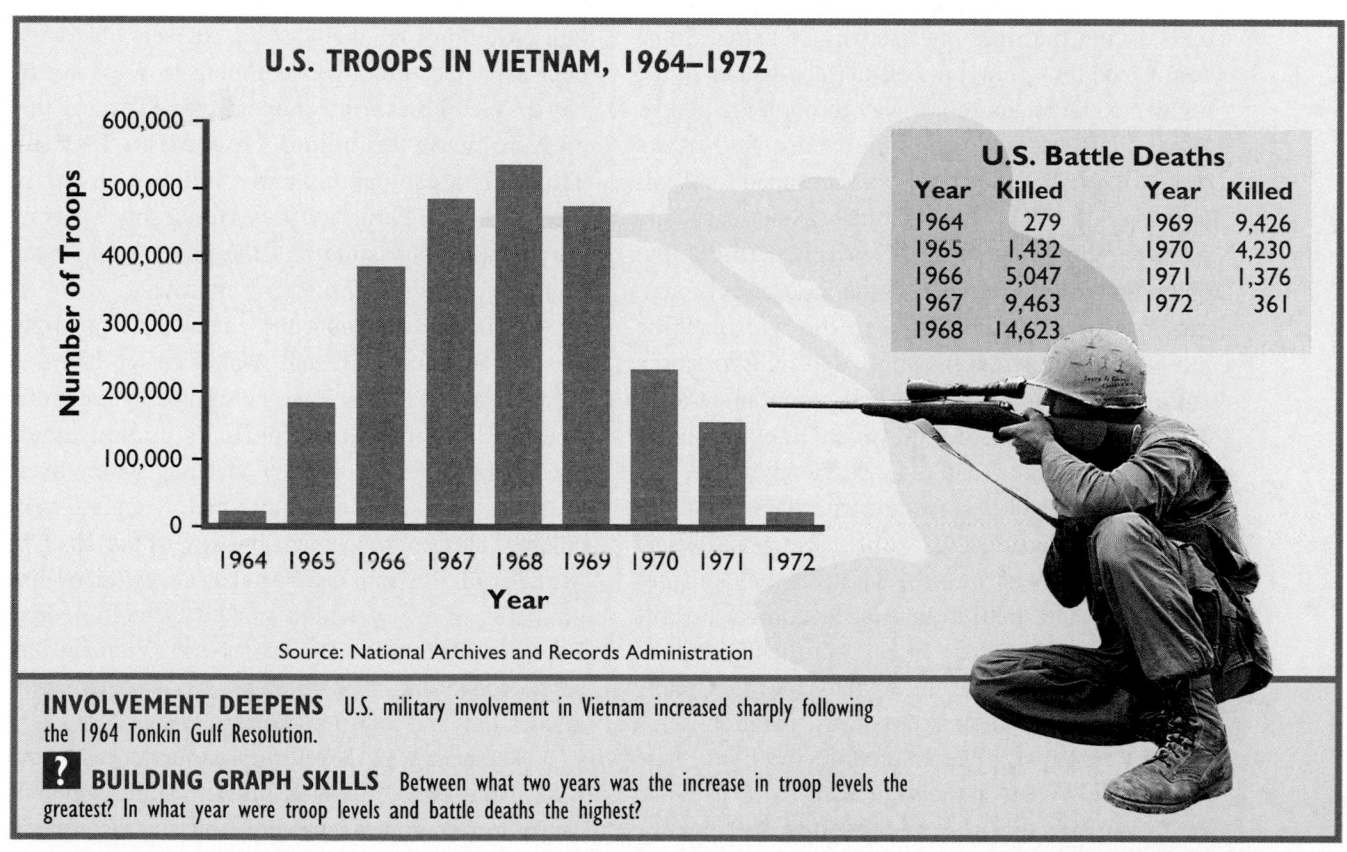

U.S. TROOPS IN VIETNAM, 1964–1972

U.S. Battle Deaths			
Year	Killed	Year	Killed
1964	279	1969	9,426
1965	1,432	1970	4,230
1966	5,047	1971	1,376
1967	9,463	1972	361
1968	14,623		

Source: National Archives and Records Administration

INVOLVEMENT DEEPENS U.S. military involvement in Vietnam increased sharply following the 1964 Tonkin Gulf Resolution.

❓ **BUILDING GRAPH SKILLS** Between what two years was the increase in troop levels the greatest? In what year were troop levels and battle deaths the highest?

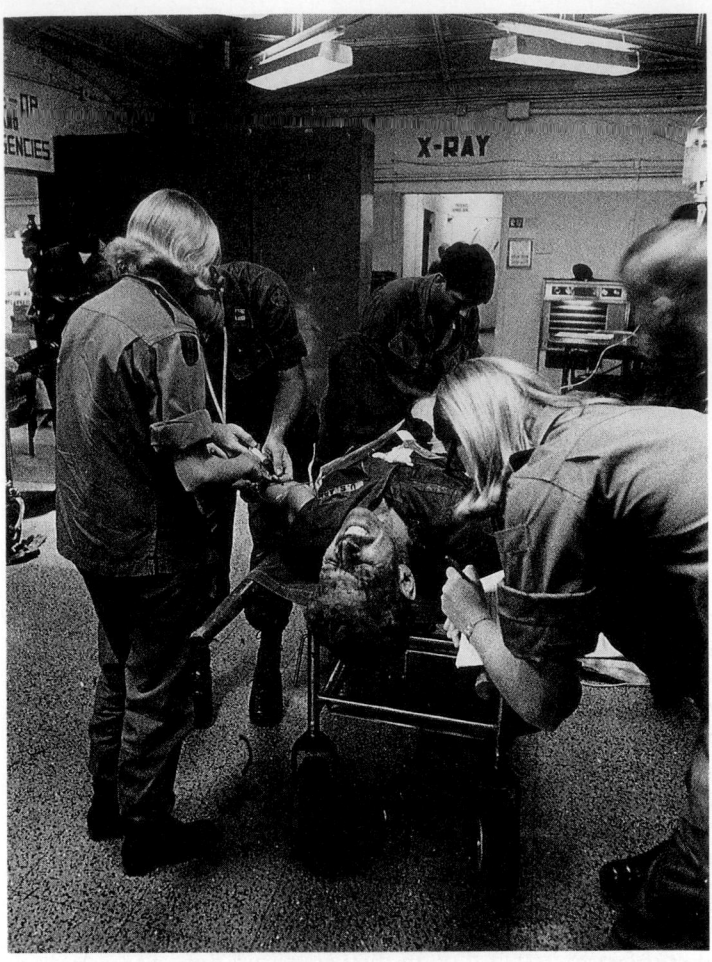

Navarra Rhoads, who served in the Army Nurse Corps, later described how complete this detachment could become:

❝ I remember I had completed this amputation and I had the soldier's leg under my arm. I was holding the leg because I had to dress it up and give it to graves registration. . . . This nurse came in and she was scheduled to take the place of another nurse. When she saw me, I went to greet her and I had this leg under my arm. She collapsed on the ground in a dead faint. I thought, "What could possibly be wrong with her?" There I was trying to figure out what's wrong with her, not realizing that here I had this leg with a combat boot still on and half this man's combat fatigue still on, blood dripping over the exposed end. ❞

THE AIR WAR

When Johnson sent troops to Vietnam in 1965, he did not anticipate the type of war that Rhoads described. He hoped to use air power to secure a quick victory. Like many of his advisers, the president expected prolonged bombing to pressure the North Vietnamese into negotiating. Toward this end, Johnson launched **Operation Rolling Thunder**, a campaign against military targets in the North, in February 1965. He closely oversaw the operation, boasting that the pilots "can't even bomb an outhouse without my approval."

Though weakening the enemy's will to fight was the air war's eventual goal, Johnson had two more-immediate aims. First, he wanted to assure the South Vietnamese of America's commitment. Second, he wanted to destroy Vietcong supply lines. Weapons and supplies from North Vietnam were coming into South Vietnam by way of the **Ho Chi Minh Trail**. The trail had begun as a network of jungle paths, some of which snaked through nearby Laos and Cambodia. By 1965 North Vietnam had begun converting the trail into a sophisticated communications and transportation system.

Johnson was therefore anxious to bomb the trail. Roads and bridges built to handle heavy trucks were bombed repeatedly, but the resourceful

The most vivid images of the war are of soldiers facing the rigors and terrors of battle. Some confronted the enemy in well-defined battles in the highlands. Others cut their way through the jungle, hearing but seldom seeing the enemy. Still others waded through rice paddies and searched rural villages for guerrilla bands. But most Americans who went to Vietnam were not assigned to combat units. Instead, they served in the thousands of support positions needed to keep the war machine moving: administration, supply and transportation, engineering, medical care, and communications. They were hardly safe, however. Enemy rockets and mortars could—and did—strike anywhere.

Some 10,000 servicewomen were among those who functioned in noncombat positions in Vietnam, most as nurses. Though they did not carry guns into battle, they faced combat horrors daily; eight gave their lives. Another 20,000 to 45,000 women worked in civilian capacities, many as volunteers for humanitarian organizations such as the Red Cross. Like soldiers in the field, these women had to detach themselves from the pain and suffering of war in order to cope. Jacqueline

Vietcong quickly repaired them or made do without them. They constructed many facilities underground as protection against bombing. Some 300,000 people, armed primarily with shovels, worked full time to maintain and expand the Ho Chi Minh Trail.

The U.S. military had estimated that the bombing would bring about North Vietnam's collapse within weeks. When this did not happen, Johnson increased the bombing. By 1967 U.S. fighter bombers were dropping an average of 800 tons of bombs on North Vietnam daily—bombing so heavy that in areas the landscape resembled the cratered surface of the moon. But each escalation failed to bring about the desired results. Frustrated, President Johnson broadened the air war to include strikes against areas of bordering Laos and much of South Vietnam.

In this wider air war, U.S. forces used a variety of deadly weapons, such as napalm—a jellied gasoline mixture used in firebombs—and the "cluster bomb"—which sprayed razor-sharp metal fragments when it exploded. America's arsenal also included **defoliants**, chemicals designed to strip the land of vegetation. The most widely used of these chemicals was Agent Orange. U.S. planes sprayed defoliants over thousands of acres in efforts to expose jungle supply routes and enemy hiding places and to rob the Vietcong of food.

THE GROUND WAR

Although the air war was designed to bring U.S. involvement in Vietnam quickly to an end, it had the opposite effect: North Vietnam—rather than surrendering—sent more troops and supplies south. Because of the widespread bombing, increasing numbers of South Vietnamese joined the ranks of the NLF. Soon the opposition forces included more South Vietnamese than North Vietnamese. The United States countered by launching a ground war. Between March 1965 and the end of 1967, U.S. troop strength grew from some 3,500 to some 486,000.

But sheer numbers were not enough to defeat an enemy who seemed to be everywhere. The NLF, aided by regulars of the North Vietnamese Army (NVA), struck at U.S. patrols or government-held villages and then melted back into the jungle. Vietnamese peasants who appeared peaceful during the day sided with the Vietcong at night.

The Americans conducted thousands of **search-and-destroy missions** in attempts to flush the Vietcong from their hideouts. U.S. ground patrols first located the enemy and then called in air

The Vietnam War

THE HO CHI MINH TRAIL U.S. efforts to destroy the Ho Chi Minh Trail caused the war to spill over into neighboring Laos and Cambodia.

? PLACE How did the geography of Vietnam help make the Ho Chi Minh Trail an effective weapon against U.S. and ARVN forces?

▶ Trip-wire-activated crossbow traps were one of many kinds of booby traps faced by combat soldiers in the jungles of Vietnam.

support to eliminate them. Once an area was "cleared," the patrols moved on in search of more Vietcong. Snipers and booby traps—from mines to animal snares to pits lined with stakes—made these missions extremely dangerous and frustrating. And villages seldom remained cleared of the NLF.

To deny the enemy any territorial gain, American forces targeted many villages for **pacification**: they moved the residents to refugee camps or cities and then burned the villages. In such warfare, progress could not be shown on a map. Instead, the daily body count of enemy dead became the sole measure of success—and a questionable measure at that. The U.S. military regularly guessed at or inflated the numbers. Said one officer responsible for body-count statistics: "If it's dead and Vietnamese, it's Vietcong."

AMERICAN MORALE EBBS

The first U.S. troops had arrived in a hopeful mood. As surely as they carried their packs and rifles, one soldier recalled, they held the "conviction that the Vietcong would be quickly beaten." Most also believed that the cause—defeating communism in South Vietnam—was honorable. This optimistic mood began to fade as the hazards of fighting a nearly invisible foe in an alien landscape sank in.

Equally frustrating was the enemy's will to fight on despite mounting casualties. U.S. war planners believed that superior American technology would win the war. Yet as 1967 ended, success seemed no closer than in 1963. Ho's earlier ominous warning to the French now seemed applicable to Americans: "You can kill ten of my men for every one I kill of yours, but even at those odds, you will lose and I will win."

■■ **U.S. forces were frustrated by their inability to disrupt Vietcong supply lines or make progress against an enemy that melted into the jungle.**

SECTION 2 REVIEW

IDENTIFY and explain the significance of each of the following: Tonkin Gulf Resolution, escalation, Operation Rolling Thunder, Ho Chi Minh Trail, defoliants, search-and-destroy missions, pacification.

LOCATE and explain the importance of the following: Gulf of Tonkin.

1. **MAIN IDEA** Why did Senator Wayne Morse believe Congress had made a grave mistake in passing the Tonkin Gulf Resolution?

2. **RECOGNIZING POINTS OF VIEW** Why did some people believe the draft was unfair?

3. **GEOGRAPHY: PLACE** How did Vietnam's geography contribute to the U.S. military's inability to defeat the Vietcong?

4. **WRITING TO DESCRIBE** Imagine you are a reporter in Vietnam in 1966. Write a short article describing the conditions faced by U.S. military and civilian personnel in Vietnam.

5. **ANALYZING** Why can it be said that Johnson's attempt to end the war quickly had the opposite effect?

Section 3

AMERICANS DIVIDED

FOCUS

■ What were the main reasons some Americans opposed the war?

■ Why did some Americans label antiwar protesters as disloyal?

By the end of 1967, over 16,000 Americans had been killed in Vietnam. Thousands more had been injured or disabled. And despite the government's optimistic forecasts, a U.S. victory seemed increasingly distant, if not out of reach. The fighting dragged on, frustrating soldiers and citizens alike. Gruesome TV images of terrified Vietnamese civilians and dead or injured soldiers brought the fighting home. Some people responded by demanding that the military be allowed to do whatever it took to win; others wanted America to pull out of Vietnam.

Peace button

THE MEDIA AND THE WAR

The Vietnam War invaded American homes in ways no previous conflict had. Free of the tight press restrictions imposed by the military during previous wars, war correspondents, photographers, and TV camera crews accompanied soldiers on patrol and interviewed people throughout South Vietnam. Television beamed footage and reports of the war into people's homes on a nightly basis. As a result, Americans saw images that seemed to contradict the government's optimistic reports.

Although such reporters as David Halberstam of the *New York Times* and Neil Sheehan of United Press International did not, in the beginning, question the goal of containing communism, they did criticize the government's optimism. As early as 1962 they argued that the war was not being won and could not be won so long as America supported the unpopular and corrupt Diem. They also reported on the ineffective-

ness of ARVN troops and accused the U.S. government of inflating enemy body counts to show progress.

▲ Television images of the war, compellingly reported by correspondents such as Morley Safer, shown here, became a nightly feature of news programs.

THE ANTIWAR MOVEMENT

A variety of pacifist, religious, civil rights, and student groups shaped the antiwar movement. Among these were peace groups such as Women Strike for Peace and the National Committee for a Sane Nuclear Policy and radical student groups like Students for a Democratic Society (SDS). The movement attracted a broad range of people. Doctors, teachers, ministers, and other professionals joined housewives, retired citizens, and students to protest the war.

SDS and campus protests. By the end of 1965, the SDS had members on 124 college campuses. Though it was only one of many groups opposing the war, in the minds of many Americans, the SDS *was* the antiwar movement. At colleges across the United States, the SDS and other student groups and faculty members held antiwar rallies and debates. These groups particularly criticized the involvement of universities in research and development for the military. They also protested the draft, the presence of the Reserve Officers Training Corps (ROTC) on campus, and the recruitment efforts by the armed services, the CIA, and such defense contractors as Dow Chemical, the manufacturer of napalm.

The antiwar movement builds. The SDS organized the first national antiwar demonstration—held in Washington, D.C., on April 17, 1965. More than 20,000 people participated. After an afternoon of speeches and singing, the crowd marched on the Capitol and delivered to Congress a petition demanding that lawmakers "act immediately to end the war." Because it drew far more people than expected, the march spurred on the antiwar movement. Over the next decade, countless demonstrators, employing tactics largely borrowed from the civil rights movement, protested U.S. involvement in Southeast Asia.

Linking the war to poverty and racism. Civil rights activists were among the most outspoken critics of the war. In 1967 the Reverend Martin Luther King, Jr., spoke of how the war was stealing resources from poverty pro-

HAWKS VERSUS DOVES

As the gap between what the government said and what people saw and read widened, doubts at home increased. The administration found itself criticized by both **doves**—people who opposed the war—and **hawks**—people who supported the war's goals. Hawks criticized the way the war was being fought, arguing for more U.S. troops and heavier bombing. Air Force general Curtis LeMay expressed the frustration of many hawks: "Here we are at the height of our power. The most powerful nation in the world. And yet we're afraid to use that power, we lack the will."

Doves opposed the war on many grounds. Pacifists, such as the Reverend Martin Luther King, Jr., believed that all war was wrong. Some doves, such as diplomat George Kennan, were convinced that Vietnam was not crucial to national security. Others objected to the Vietnam War in particular, fearing that the United States might resort to nuclear weapons. Prominent among the war's opponents was the respected pediatrician and author Dr. Benjamin Spock. He and others argued that America was fighting against the wishes of a majority of Vietnamese.

grams and how that fact heightened his opposition to U.S. involvement in Vietnam:

> 66 I watched the program broken and eviscerated [gutted] as if it were some idle political plaything of a society gone mad on war, and I knew that America would never invest the necessary funds or energies in rehabilitation of its poor so long as Vietnam continued to draw men and skills and money like some demonic, destructive suction tube. 99

Many civil rights activists voiced concern that the U.S. government was sending young African American men off to war in great numbers yet doing little to end racism at home. The Student Nonviolent Coordinating Committee (SNCC), founded in 1960 by African Americans to promote racial equality, expressed the views of growing numbers of blacks:

> 66 We take note of the fact that 16 percent of the draftees from this country are

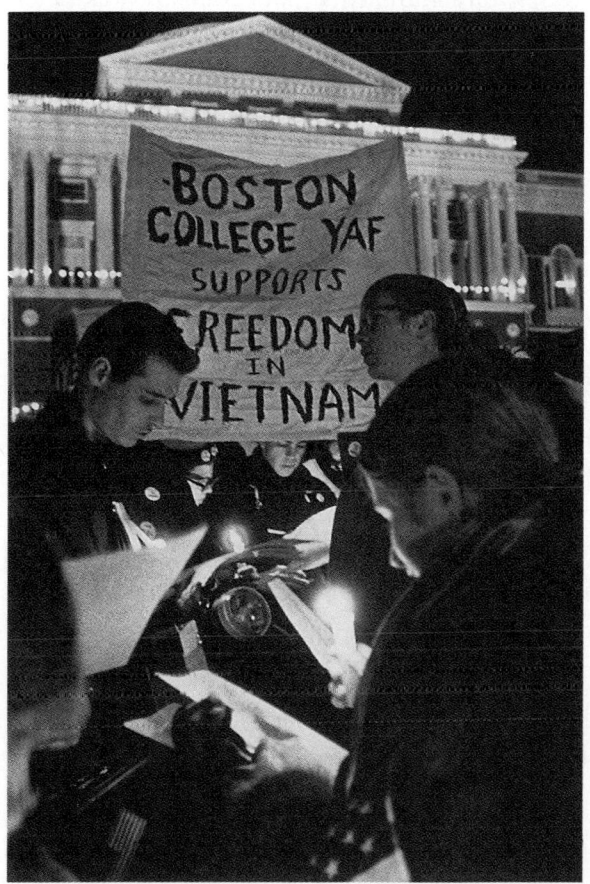

▲ Demonstrations were also organized by those in favor of U.S. politics in Vietnam, such as this rally of the Young Americans for Freedom.

Negro, called on to stifle the liberation of Vietnam, to preserve a "democracy" which does not exist for them at home. We ask: Where is the draft for the freedom fight in the United States? 99

By 1968 blacks were twice as likely as whites to label themselves as doves.

■■ **The antiwar movement focused on two points: Did we have the right to be in Vietnam? Were the sacrifices in lives and domestic programs worth our being there?**

PROTEST VERSUS LOYALTY

Despite their high visibility, antiwar protesters made up a small percentage of the U.S. population. Many Americans opposed the movement, especially its more extreme factions. Some believed that fighting for one's country was a patriotic duty. Others objected to the movement's tactics. People found certain acts of protest, such as burning the American flag, occupying buildings, and burning draft cards, particularly upsetting. Many veterans of past wars were angered by young men who went to prison rather than serve in the military or who fled to Canada to avoid the draft.

Though most Americans who disagreed with the antiwar movement expressed their opposition in private, some organized counterdemonstrations. Demonstrators at these rallies often carried signs proclaiming "America, Love It or Leave It" or "My Country, Right or Wrong."

■■ **Many Americans saw protesters as disloyal. Some believed it was a citizen's patriotic duty to serve in the armed forces. Others objected to antiwar tactics.**

GOVERNMENT CONFLICT

President Johnson and his advisers responded to antiwar protesters by insisting that the United States was helping to defend its ally in Saigon against aggression. If America failed to support

South Vietnam, asked Secretary of State Dean Rusk, what U.S. ally would ever trust us again?

But the administration also faced criticism in Congress. Doves, such as Senator J. William Fulbright of Arkansas, head of the Foreign Relations Committee, sharply criticized the Johnson administration's policies as too extreme. Fulbright held congressional hearings in 1966 to give the war's critics a forum. These televised hearings gave the antiwar position more credibility with mainstream Americans.

Even within Johnson's circle of advisers, gnawing doubts surfaced. Several senior staffers expressed misgivings about the administration's conduct of the war. Most troubling to the president was the turnabout of his secretary of defense, Robert McNamara.

By age 44 Robert S. McNamara had already reached the top of the corporate ladder. He was the new president of the Ford Motor Company, the first person to hold that position who was not a descendant of Henry Ford. Then in 1960, after only 34 days in his new job, McNamara received a call inviting him to become secretary of defense for the Kennedy administration.

With his impressive analytical skills, the intense, bespectacled secretary of defense persuaded

Robert McNamara

generals, legislators, national security advisers—and presidents—to follow his military advice. During the policy debates that led to the escalation of the war, it was McNamara—perhaps more than any other individual—who set America's course. Said Clark Clifford, who later succeeded him as secretary of defense: "McNamara held the key to the President's decision" to grant the military's 1965 request for more troops.

McNamara's many recommendations had failed, however, to achieve their results. As each optimistic forecast proved to be no more than wishful thinking, his confidence slipped; by October 1967 it had eroded altogether. McNamara leveled with President Johnson, telling him that "continuation of our present course of action in Southeast Asia would be dangerous, costly in lives, and unsatisfactory to the American people." But the policy that McNamara had helped shape was firmly entrenched, and Johnson was determined to stay with it. Within days Johnson had eased McNamara out of his cabinet position.

▶ McNamara sits alone after a presidential press conference announcing further troop shipments to Vietnam.

Lyndon Baines Johnson Library

SECTION 3 REVIEW

IDENTIFY and explain the significance of each of the following: doves, hawks, Reverend Martin Luther King, Jr., J. William Fulbright, Robert S. McNamara.

1. **MAIN IDEA** Why did some Americans oppose the war?

2. **MAIN IDEA** Why did the antiwar movement trouble some Americans?

3. **WRITING TO PERSUADE** Imagine you are a U.S. senator in 1967 and are either a hawk or a dove. Write the president a letter persuading him to support your view and to change his policies accordingly.

4. **EVALUATING** What roles do you think television coverage and economic and social conditions at home played in shaping American views toward the Vietnam War?

Section 4

WAR AT FULL TIDE

FOCUS

- Why did the Tet offensive weaken many Americans' confidence in their government?
- What were the key events of the 1968 presidential campaign?
- How did Nixon set out to end the war? How did Americans react to this plan?

The year 1968 was a troubled one. It began with a massive military offensive by the NLF and the North Vietnamese that shattered many Americans' confidence in Johnson's handling of the war. Demonstrations and violent riots followed. By year's end some 15,000 more Americans had died in Vietnam, and LBJ's political career lay in ruin. Republican Richard Nixon, who claimed to have a plan to end the war and "win the peace," won the White House. U.S. troops were slowly withdrawing from Vietnam, but the pace of U.S. bombing increased. And when Nixon ordered the invasion of Cambodia in 1970, war protests at home surged to a new high.

Captured NVA weapons

THE TET OFFENSIVE

January 30, 1968, was the start of Tet, the Vietnamese New Year. In past years the holiday had been honored by a lull in fighting. However, late that night, as most South Vietnamese and their U.S. allies slept, NLF guerrillas and North Vietnamese troops sprang from their jungle camps and city hideouts to execute a carefully planned strike. Within hours countless villages, more than 100 cities, and 12 U.S. military bases came under attack from nearly 70,000 Communist soldiers (see map, page 873). Heavy fighting raged in such U.S. strongholds as Saigon and Da Nang. At one point the Vietcong even occupied the courtyard of the U.S. Embassy.

North Vietnam expected the **Tet offensive** to bring down the government in the South as the people rallied behind their "liberators." But Hanoi was disappointed. When the assault was over, more than a month later, an estimated 40,000 Communist soldiers lay dead.

General William Westmoreland, commander of U.S. forces in Vietnam, hastened to describe the offensive as a Vietcong defeat. In a military sense, the general had a point. At a cost of 2,000 American and 4,000 ARVN lives, most of the attackers had been repelled. But despite suffering heavy losses, the NLF remained strong in many places. They had faced overwhelming U.S. firepower and were still standing—more determined than ever to fight on.

Even more important was the political effect the offensive had on the United States. Tet jarred American confidence by showing that no part of South Vietnam was secure—not even downtown Saigon. Walter Cronkite, anchor of the *CBS*

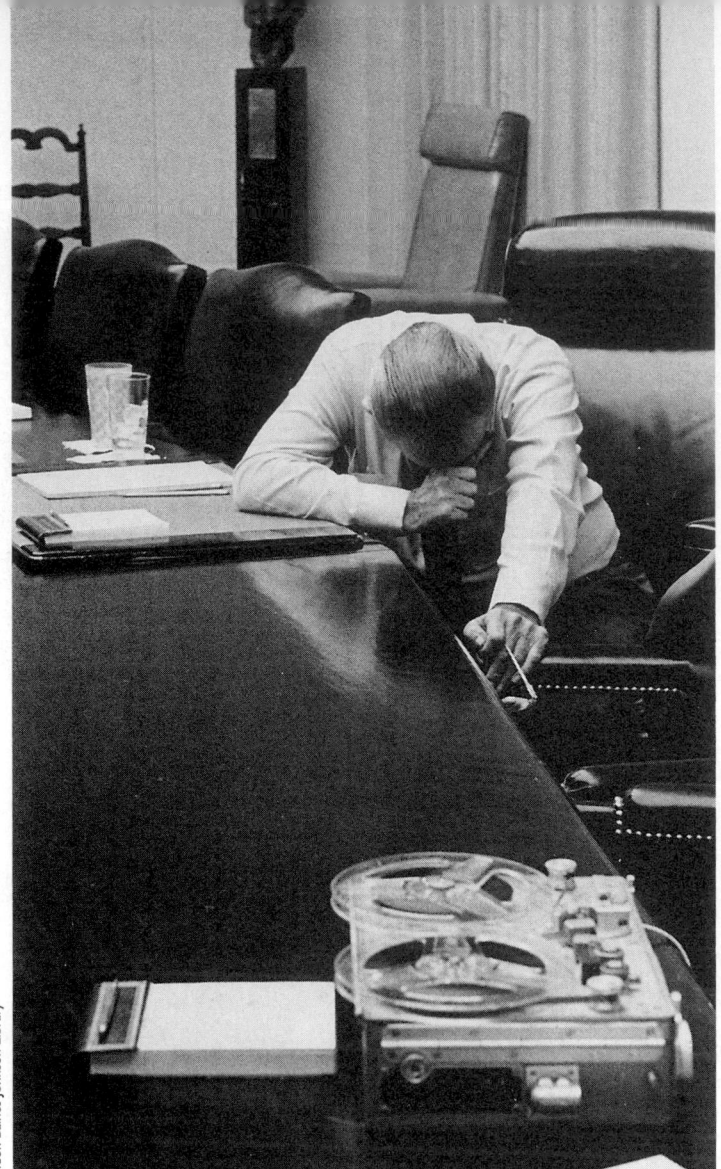

▲ An emotionally drained Johnson listens to a tape recording made by his son-in-law describing his duty in Vietnam.

THE ELECTION OF 1968

In the wake of the Tet offensive, three out of four Americans disapproved of Johnson's conduct of the war. Early in the 1968 Democratic presidential campaign, antiwar candidate Senator Eugene McCarthy of Minnesota took advantage of this growing dissatisfaction and challenged LBJ. In the March New Hampshire primary, McCarthy won almost as many votes as Johnson.

McCarthy's impressive showing drew another leading critic of the war into the race: Senator Robert F. Kennedy of New York (former U.S. attorney general). RFK's large national following, especially among African Americans, Hispanics, the young, and the poor, made him a strong contender for the Democratic nomination. Shaken by the division within his party, LBJ shocked the nation on March 31. Physically and emotionally exhausted, Johnson announced he would not seek reelection, saying he wished to spend his last months in office trying to end the war.

LBJ's withdrawal from the race left it wide open. Senators McCarthy and Kennedy and Vice President Hubert Humphrey went head-to-head in several state primaries. Kennedy won most of them, particularly the crucial California primary in June. He seemed destined to be the Democratic nominee. But on the night of his California victory, after delivering a speech in a hotel ballroom, RFK was shot. The next day he died—victim of a bullet fired by Sirhan Sirhan, a young Jordanian immigrant. A nation already in shock over the murder of the Reverend Martin Luther King, Jr., two months earlier (see Chapter 29) now had to come to grips with another assassination.

Society seemed to be spinning out of control. Amid the turmoil, the Democrats met in Chicago to settle on a candidate for the November election. The convention was a dispirited affair. President Johnson did not even attend, fearful of the reaction he would cause. And throughout the convention memories of the fallen Robert Kennedy remained hauntingly alive for the demoralized delegates. Vice President Humphrey, despite his close identification with Johnson, received the nomination. He chose Senator Edmund Muskie of Maine as his running mate.

The Democrats' difficulties were underscored by the chaos on the streets outside the convention. Some 10,000 antiwar protesters had massed in the city and camped in Grant Park,

Evening News, expressed America's bewildered mood: "I thought we were winning the war! What the hell is going on?" To one of his aides, President Johnson groaned: "If I've lost Walter, then it's all over. I've lost Mr. Average American."

After Tet, public criticism of the war rose dramatically. Such influential magazines as *Time* and *Newsweek* not only expressed misgivings about the war but also called for its end. Largely because of the shift in public opinion, Johnson denied Westmoreland's urgent request for 206,000 more troops. Though granting a small increase, LBJ made it clear there would be no more.

■■ **The Tet offensive dealt a double blow: it indicated that U.S. leaders had misled the public, and it exposed severe flaws in U.S. military operations in Vietnam.**

across from the hotel where many delegates were lodged. Of all the college students, longtime activists, and ordinary citizens opposed to the war, perhaps a few hundred came prepared for violent confrontation. In the sweltering August heat, they held rallies, chanting "Hell No! We Won't Go!" and taunting police with shouts of "Pig!"

Outraged to see his city overrun by people he viewed as dangerous revolutionaries, Chicago mayor Richard J. Daley ordered helmeted Chicago police to clear out the protesters. The police attacked on the night of August 28, clubbing protesters and using tear gas to disperse the crowd. Hundreds were injured; hundreds more were hauled to jail. Reporters, passersby, and police were also injured in the fray.

The violent spectacle of protest and police brutality at the Chicago convention raised Republicans' hopes of capturing the White House. At their convention in Miami Beach, the upbeat mood of Republican delegates matched the Florida sunshine. A familiar figure dominated the convention: Richard Nixon. After his defeat by Kennedy in 1960, Nixon also lost a bid for the governorship of California. But since then he had kept in the public eye.

Richard Nixon easily won the nomination. He chose Maryland governor Spiro Agnew as his running mate. Promising a "law-and-order" crackdown on urban crime, Nixon appealed for support to those Americans who neither approved of the disorderly antiwar protests nor wanted a U.S. defeat in Vietnam. Nixon told voters he had a plan to end the Vietnam War, though he revealed no details.

■■ LBJ's withdrawal and RFK's assassination left Humphrey in an uphill struggle against Nixon in the 1968 presidential campaign.

As Election Day neared, Humphrey's campaign picked up steam, boosted somewhat by LBJ's announcement in late October of a bombing halt. But time ran out for the Democrats, though the results were close: of 73 million votes cast, Richard Nixon received only some 500,000 more than Hubert Humphrey. Nixon's margin in the electoral college was much wider, however: he carried 32 states to Humphrey's 13. Former Alabama governor George Wallace, who campaigned as the candidate of the newly formed American

▼ Outside the Democratic Convention, Chicago police battled antiwar demonstrators.

Independent party, got some 10 million votes and won 5 states of the Deep South.

NIXON, VIETNAMIZATION, AND CAMBODIA

President Nixon gave foreign affairs his top priority. His key foreign-policy adviser was Henry Kissinger. Together they took important steps to improve relations with Communist China and the Soviet Union (see Chapter 31). But in 1969 Vietnam loomed as the most urgent problem, and Americans watched to see whether Nixon could fulfill his campaign pledge to end the war.

Part of Nixon's end-the-war plan was called **Vietnamization**. It involved turning over the fighting to the South Vietnamese as U.S. troops were gradually pulled out. This strategy, said Nixon, would bring "peace with honor." At best, Nixon hoped, Vietnamization might produce a stable anti-Communist South Vietnam. At worst, it would delay a collapse long enough to spare America the humiliation of outright defeat.

Nixon also hoped that Vietnamization was the key to removing a major obstacle to a peace agreement. The North Vietnamese had warned first Johnson and then Nixon that the United States would have to set a date for troop removals if peace talks were to continue. In February 1970, as U.S. troop withdrawals mounted, Henry Kissinger began meeting secretly in Paris with Le Duc Tho (layd uhk TOH) of North Vietnam.

When Nixon took office, U.S. troop strength in Vietnam stood at about 540,000. He soon ordered a withdrawal of some 25,000 soldiers. Over the next four years, many more came home. But the process was slow. At the end of 1972, about 24,200 Americans still remained in Vietnam.

Publicly, Nixon emphasized Vietnamization; secretly, however, he planned to widen the war—into Cambodia. North Vietnam had been staging troops along the border in neutral Cambodia—safe from U.S. attack—while sending supplies and troops south through Cambodia on the Ho Chi Minh Trail.

Early in 1969 Nixon ordered the widespread bombing of Cambodia. He hoped to destroy North Vietnamese supplies and trails—in line with Johnson's original war aims. He also wanted to send a signal to Hanoi that the United States was willing to respond with force to continued Communist aggression. The air strikes were concealed from Congress, the American people, and key military leaders—even the secretary of the air force.

Because of Cambodia's neutrality, Nixon feared an international uproar. But when a coup ousted Cambodia's ruler in March 1970, Nixon's policy changed. Since the new Cambodian government was pro-American, he made his policy public and justified the air strikes as defense of a friendly nation. Nixon then sent some 80,000 U.S. and ARVN troops into Cambodia.

The invasion destroyed the delicate balance that had kept Cambodia out of the war. NVA troops were forced into the interior of Cambodia, where battles with U.S. and ARVN forces destroyed much of the countryside.

ANTIWAR SENTIMENT INCREASES

News of the bombing and invasion of Cambodia provoked outrage in the United States, particularly on college campuses. When students at Kent State University in Ohio set fire to the campus ROTC building, Ohio's governor vowed to "eradicate" the protesters. On May 4, 1970, National Guard troops sent to control demonstrators shot into a group of students, killing four and injuring nine—some of whom were merely walking across campus.

Ten days later, state police in Jackson, Mississippi, fired at protesters in a dormitory at Jackson State College, killing two students and wounding nine. In outrage at these brutalities, students and faculty on hundreds of college campuses went on strike.

The Cambodian invasion also shocked members of Congress. They too had believed that American involvement in Southeast Asia was ending. Questioning Nixon's constitutional right to extend the war, Congress repealed the Tonkin Gulf Resolution in December 1970. Nixon insisted, however, that this action did not affect his authority to carry on the war. Congressional leaders responded by developing plans to stop the war by ending funding once troop withdrawals were finalized.

In 1971 another incident sparked the antiwar movement. The *New York Times* began publishing a collection of secret government documents relating to the war. Known as the **Pentagon Papers**, they showed that the government had frequently misled the American people about the course of the war. The documents were leaked to the press by Daniel Ellsberg, a former Defense Department official, who had been strongly prowar until

◀ **Four Kent State students were killed during a confrontation between National Guardsmen and some 3,000 rioters.**

spending time in Vietnam studying the effects of the war. While there, he found that few South Vietnamese supported their government. President Nixon tried to block publication of the Pentagon Papers but was unsuccessful.

■■ **Many Americans responded in anger when President Nixon coupled Vietnamization with an invasion of Cambodia.**

𝒯HE WAR GOES ON

As commander in chief, President Nixon ordered not only the invasion of Cambodia but also the renewed bombing of North Vietnam, which President Johnson had stopped. Extending the bombings into areas that had been off-limits was part of what the president called the "Madman Theory." As Nixon explained to his chief of staff, H. R. (Bob) Haldeman:

❝ I call it the Madman Theory, Bob. I want the North Vietnamese to believe that I've reached the point where I might do anything to stop the war. We'll just slip the word to them that, "for God's sake, you know Nixon is obsessed about Communists. We can't restrain him when he's angry—and he has his hand on the nuclear button"—and Ho Chi Minh himself will be in Paris in two days begging for peace. ❞

▲ **Nixon visits U.S. troops in Vietnam.**

Nixon's method was based on his belief that Eisenhower's hints that he might use the atomic bomb had helped end the Korean War. But Nixon miscalculated the opposition's endurance. Rather than ending, the war suddenly grew more fierce.

Hoping to reveal the weaknesses of Nixon's Vietnamization strategy, North Vietnam staged a major invasion of the South in March 1972. NVA troops drove deep into South Vietnam. Nixon responded by ordering heavy bombing of the North, including Hanoi. He also ordered the mining of Haiphong Harbor to prevent Soviet ships from delivering military supplies. Despite these steps, the opposition now held more territory in South Vietnam than ever.

SECTION 4 REVIEW

IDENTIFY and explain the significance of each of the following: Tet offensive, William Westmoreland, Eugene McCarthy, Robert F. Kennedy, Richard Nixon, Henry Kissinger, Vietnamization, Le Duc Tho, Kent State University, Jackson State College, Pentagon Papers.

LOCATE and explain the importance of the following: Haiphong Harbor.

1. **MAIN IDEA** How did Richard Nixon plan to end the war?

2. **MAIN IDEA** How did the 1968 election signal American dissatisfaction with the war effort?

3. **MAIN IDEA** What Nixon policies led to renewed antiwar protests?

4. **WRITING TO INFORM** Imagine you are Nixon's press agent. Write a news release explaining the reasons for bombing Cambodia.

5. **TAKING A STAND** In wartime, should the U.S. government make all information about the war available to its citizens? Why or why not?

Section 5

THE CEASE–FIRE AND AFTER

FOCUS

- Why did the United States agree to a cease-fire in January 1973?
- What factors contributed to America's inability to win the war?
- What long-term effects did the war have on the Vietnamese and American people?

In 1972 Vietnam again dominated the presidential campaign. Although the war was not yet over, Richard Nixon overwhelmed his antiwar opponent, Democratic senator George McGovern. By early 1973 a cease-fire was signed, finally ending America's most bitterly divisive episode since the Civil War. But the Vietnam War's painful legacy remains.

The fall of Saigon, April 1975

NIXON'S REELECTION

Senator George McGovern of South Dakota campaigned in the 1972 Democratic presidential primary as an antiwar candidate. An air force pilot in World War II, McGovern had been a history professor before going into politics. His opposition to the war ran deep. In one emotional Senate speech he declared in a trembling voice: "This chamber reeks of blood." George Wallace opposed McGovern for the Democratic nomination. While at a political rally in Maryland in May, however, Wallace was shot. The injury paralyzed him from the waist down, and he withdrew from the race.

After the disastrous 1968 convention, the Democrats adopted new rules that increased representation of minorities, women, and young people in party organizations. The **Twenty-sixth Amendment**, passed in 1971, had lowered the voting age from 21 to 18. McGovern drew much of his support from these groups, and at the convention he easily captured the nomination.

The Republicans renominated Nixon and Agnew. Nixon again stressed his strong commit-

ment to law and order at home and assured voters the war would soon be over. In fact, a few weeks before the election, Henry Kissinger announced a breakthrough in the negotiations to end the war. "Peace is at hand," he declared.

Nixon won the election by a landslide—47 million votes to 29 million for McGovern. In the electoral college, McGovern carried only Massachusetts and the District of Columbia.

A CEASE-FIRE AT LAST

For more than three years Henry Kissinger and North Vietnam's Le Duc Tho had engaged in difficult peace negotiations. Finally, in October 1972 North Vietnam offered a peace plan that Kissinger and President Nixon found generally acceptable. The plan included a cease-fire and pullout of all foreign troops from Vietnam, an end to U.S.

military aid, and the creation of a new government in South Vietnam that included Nguyen (en-gy-EN) Van Thieu (the current president), representatives of the NLF, and "neutrals." Thieu, who had not been included in the negotiations, objected to the proposed government, seeing it as a loss of power. Rather than abandon Thieu, the United States rejected the agreement.

When North Vietnam demanded that the agreement be reinstated, Nixon responded by ordering around-the-clock bombing of Hanoi and Haiphong. A furious Nixon declared to the chairman of the Joint Chiefs of Staff: "This is your chance to use military power to win this war, and if you don't, I'll consider you responsible." Some 40,000 tons of bombs rained on the two cities for nearly two weeks, with the barrage only halting for Christmas Day. But the intensive bombing did not sway the North Vietnamese. At the end of December, Nixon called off the bombing and agreed to resume talks.

On January 27, 1973, the negotiators in Paris announced a cease-fire. Although the plan scarcely differed from the one hammered out in October, minor changes allowed each side to claim a diplomatic victory. The United States pledged to withdraw its remaining forces from South Vietnam and to help rebuild Vietnam. The peace settlement also included a prisoner-exchange agreement. It did not, however, address the major issue behind the war—the political future of Vietnam. In urging Thieu to accept the cease-fire, Nixon secretly pledged that if fighting resumed, the United States would come to South Vietnam's aid.

▪▪ The United States agreed to a cease-fire in January 1973, after heavy bombing failed to sway the North Vietnamese from their demands.

Two years after U.S. forces withdrew, Saigon's military regime collapsed. In January 1975, North Vietnamese troops overran the northern part of South Vietnam. South Vietnamese troops retreated in panic, and new waves of refugees poured into Saigon.

In early April the noose around Saigon tightened. The U.S. military hastily evacuated the several thousand Americans still in the city. Some escaped from the U.S. Embassy roof by helicopter

REMEMBERING VIETNAM

Le Ly Hayslip spent the first 20 years of her life in Vietnam. After the war she reflected on what life in a constant state of war had been like:

"It was as if life's cycle was no longer birth, growth, and death but only endless dying brought about by endless war. I realized that I, along with so many of my countrymen, had been born into war and that my soul knew nothing else. I tried to imagine people somewhere who knew only peace—what a paradise! How many souls in that world were blessed with the simple privilege of saying good-bye to their loved ones before they died? And how many of those loved ones died with the smile of a life well lived on their lips—knowing that their existence added up to more than a number in a "body count" or another human brick on a towering wall of corpses? Perhaps such a place was America, although American wives and mothers, too, were losing husbands and sons every day in the evil vortex between heaven and hell that my country had become."

as North Vietnamese troops stormed the compound. Some 120,000 Vietnamese who had worked for the Americans were flown to the United States. On April 30, 1975, the Saigon government surrendered unconditionally.

For Americans the Vietnam War was over. The long, costly effort to prevent the creation of a united, independent Vietnam under Communist rule had failed. The war had spread to Cambodia and Laos, which had been ravaged. But the predicted collapse of all Southeast Asia—the falling dominoes—did not happen. Quarrels soon broke out between the Communist leaders of Vietnam and those of China and Cambodia. International communism was not as unified a world force as U.S. policymakers had feared—or had claimed.

COMMENTARY

Why Did the North Prevail?

Though some people argue that the United States did not lose the Vietnam War, the nation obviously did not achieve its goal—an independent, non-Communist South Vietnam. What contributed to this failure?

People have put forward many reasons to explain why the Communists were able to prevail against ARVN and U.S. forces. Without doubt the Communists' fierce desire for a united Vietnam gave them the will to fight on in the face of overwhelming military opposition. Like the French, American strategists underestimated the strength of this nationalist feeling among the Vietnamese people. For the Vietnamese the war against America was a continuation of their decades-long anticolonial crusade. At the same time, ineffective South Vietnamese leadership undercut the Americans' war effort. A succession of U.S.-sponsored political leaders, most of whom were generals, failed to inspire popular support among the South Vietnamese.

As the war dragged on, a growing number of Americans began doubting that the fall of South Vietnam to communism would seriously threaten America's interests or standing in the world. The climbing death toll and the failure of American leaders to admit the lack of progress resulted in a loss of public trust in the government and a steep decline in support for the war.

Some analysts claim that political and military strategies were at fault—that the United States was not aggressive enough in pursuing its war aims. Others point out that U.S. advisers trained the South Vietnamese forces in conventional warfare rather than in tactics better suited to Vietnam's geography and the enemy's guerrilla tactics. Some even argue that any use of military power to solve an essentially political problem was doomed to failure.

■■ **A determined foe, ineffective South Vietnamese leadership, and inappropriate military strategy and tactics all contributed to America's inability to win the war.**

𝒱IETNAM AFTER THE WAR

The war ravaged the Vietnamese people. According to Saigon government figures, some 185,000 ARVN soldiers died in combat. Estimates put the number of South Vietnamese civilian dead at nearly a half million. The exact number of Vietcong and North Vietnamese Army war casualties is unknown, but estimates place the total at nearly 1 million dead. In addition, approximately 879,000 Vietnamese were orphaned and 181,000 were disabled. Among the disabled were those exposed to Agent Orange. These people have been plagued by high rates of liver cancer and other illnesses.

Nearly 1.5 million Vietnamese fled Vietnam after the fall of Saigon. Desperate to escape economic and social hardships, many braved the rough South China Sea and Gulf of Thailand in tiny, crowded boats. They were joined by thousands of other Southeast Asian refugees, such as the Hmong

▲ **Many Vietnamese were forced to flee their homes following the Vietnam War. This photograph shows a small boat packed with Vietnamese refugees arriving in Hong Kong.**

(MUHNG) of Laos, also fleeing grave postwar conditions. More than 730,000 of these refugees have settled in the United States since the war.

VIETNAM VETERANS AFTER THE WAR

More than 2.6 million Americans were involved in the Vietnam War. More than 58,000 of them died; over 300,000 were wounded, and nearly 2,300 are missing and presumed dead. Improved emergency medical services saved many soldiers with severe wounds that in previous wars would have been fatal. As a result, there are an unprecedented number of paralyzed and otherwise severely disabled Vietnam veterans.

More than 600 Americans were prisoners of war (POWs). Some POWs spent six years or more in North Vietnamese jails, where they endured long periods of solitary confinement and torture.

One of the most visible tragedies of the war has been the fate of its veterans. No ticker-tape parades celebrated the return of soldiers from the Vietnam conflict. On the contrary, veterans often became like lightning rods for the anger, guilt, or shame of fellow citizens frustrated by the war; other Americans met them with stony silence.

The public's negative reaction enraged and demoralized many veterans. They had faced a life-and-death struggle, obeying orders in what they trusted was their country's national interests. In the book *Born on the Fourth of July* (1976), Vietnam veteran Ron Kovic recalled his pain over this lack of support:

> 66 I didn't want to believe it at first—people protesting against us when we were putting our lives on the line for our country. . . . How could they do this to us? Many of us would not be coming back and many others would be wounded or maimed. 99
>
> From *Born on the Fourth of July* by Ron Kovic ©1976

Thousands of Vietnam veterans turned to drugs or failed to kick the drug habits they had developed during the war. Many others had trouble finding jobs or settling down and starting families. Recent estimates indicate that between 250,000 and 350,000 homeless Americans are Vietnam veterans.

Soldiers who were involved in the spraying of defoliants later developed certain forms of can-

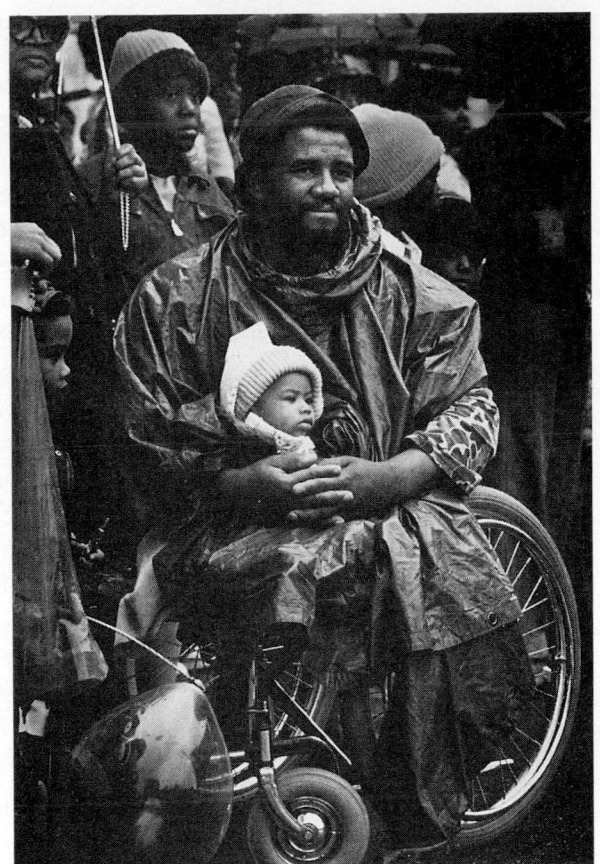

▲ One of the legacies of the Vietnam War was the number of paralyzed and severely disabled veterans. Shown here is veteran Earl Robinson as he watches an Armed Forces Day parade in 1976.

cer at an unusually high rate, and children of these veterans had a very high rate of birth defects. Research in the 1970s linked their medical problems to Agent Orange. In 1984 the manufacturers of the chemicals created a relief fund for the veterans and their families, and in 1991 the federal government extended permanent disability benefits to these veterans.

■■ The war left economic, emotional, and physical scars on the people of Vietnam and on many of the Americans who served there.

PUBLIC POLICY LEGACIES

The war shook Americans' confidence in their government. Many were shocked to discover that their leaders had misled them during the war. The actions of Johnson and Nixon raised a crucial constitutional question: under what authority can

During the 1991 Persian Gulf War, politicians and commentators often compared it with previous wars—particularly Vietnam. As President George Bush considered using military force to push the Iraqi army out of Kuwait, he assured the nation: "This will not be another Vietnam."

To fulfill this promise, Bush first insured that the Persian Gulf War would not be only America's war. In the United Nations and through direct diplomacy, Bush pushed for international support, including commitments of troops and money from U.S. allies. At home, he asked Congress to authorize the use of force.

With the bulk of world opinion and Congress firmly behind him, Bush then launched a military operation that reflected the lessons learned in Vietnam. Determined to avoid a drawn-out war, he rushed massive numbers of troops, equipment, and supplies to the Gulf. America's military assault would be quick and deadly. And in further contrast to Vietnam, Bush avoided Johnson's tendency to keep tight control on military operations. Instead, he left tactical decisions to his military commanders.

Bush also took a page from the Vietnam War in his approach to media coverage. He did not intend to allow the flow of information from the war zone to erode public support as

it had in Vietnam. The U.S. military therefore put tight restrictions on media access to the front lines. It also closely screened what was broadcast so that Americans would not be exposed to the kind of grisly images and grim statistics that fueled the Vietnam antiwar movement.

The president believed that the willingness to use U.S. military power was important to keeping international peace. At the same time, he felt sure that a clear victory over Iraq would rid the nation of the stigma of the Vietnam failure. Most of the news media and general public shared this view. In a special issue about the Persian Gulf victory, *Newsweek* proclaimed that "America's troops exorcised the ghosts of Vietnam."

With the ghosts banished, the men and women returning from the Persian Gulf received a very different welcome than their Vietnam-era counterparts. A surge of gratitude and respect toward all American veterans followed the Gulf War. Even many Americans who opposed the war against Iraq stressed their support for the troops and the sacrifices they made.

presidents wage an undeclared war? To prevent "another Vietnam," Congress passed the **War Powers Act** in 1973. The act reaffirms Congress's constitutional right to declare war by setting a 60-day limit on the presidential commitment of U.S. troops to foreign conflicts.

The Vietnam War also left a dismal economic legacy. The war cost American taxpayers about $150 billion, adding greatly to the national debt and fueling inflation. The war also siphoned off funding that might otherwise have gone to domestic programs, such as those that help the poor.

Above all, Americans learned that there are limits—imposed both by public opinion and by international threats, such as fear of a nuclear war—that can restrict the use of military force. Since Vietnam, leaders have been hesitant to commit U.S. troops in far-off regions without being certain of the consent of the American people and the nation's political allies.

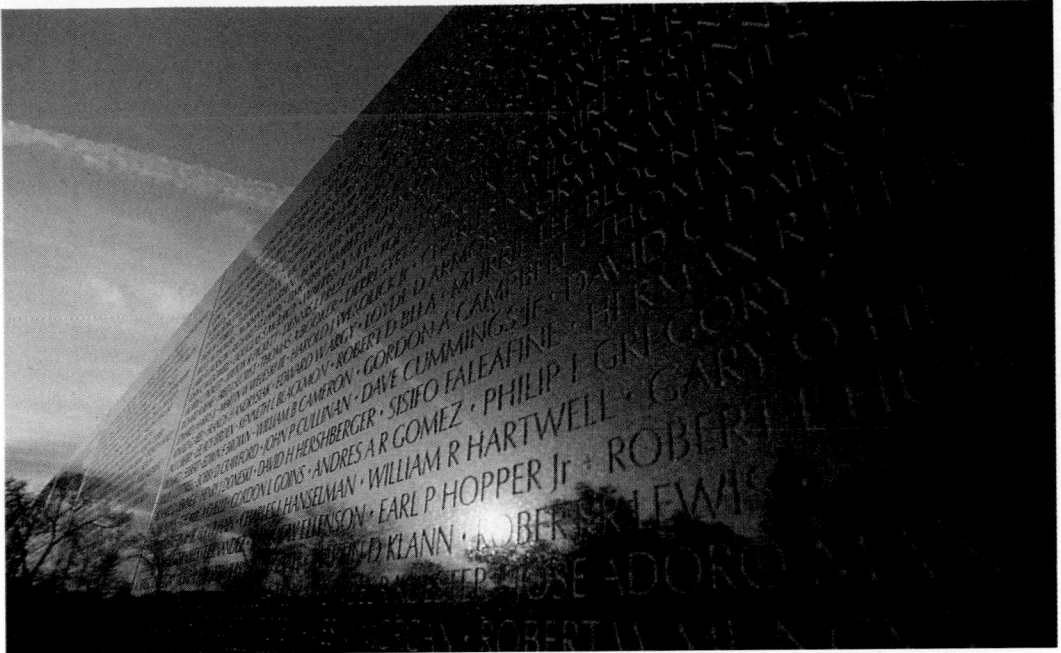

► The Vietnam Veterans Memorial—the "Wall"—serves as a tribute to Americans who died in the war.

■■ **The furor surrounding U.S. involvement in Vietnam led Congress to limit the president's war-making powers.**

*H*EALING THE WOUNDS OF THE WAR

Long after the war's end, Americans are still seeking ways to come to terms with the war and its legacies. Perhaps the most moving attempt to heal the rift caused by the war is the Vietnam Veterans Memorial in Washington, D.C., designed by Maya Ying Lin. Lin, a Chinese American, was a young architecture student at Yale when her design was chosen for the national monument. Of the healing aspects of the memorial, she said: "To overcome grief you have to confront it. An honest memorial makes you accept what happened before you overcome it. I think the memorial makes people accept."

Inscribed on a huge wall of black granite are the names of the more than 58,000 Americans who died in Vietnam. Lin insisted that the names be listed in chronological order—not in alphabetical order or by rank—so that "if you were in the war, you could find your time and a few people you knew." Hundreds visit the memorial daily. Some weep or leave flowers or written messages. Others simply ponder what the memorial—by its dark silence—has to tell them.

SECTION 5 REVIEW

IDENTIFY and explain the significance of each of the following: George McGovern, Twenty-sixth Amendment, War Powers Act, Maya Ying Lin.

1. **MAIN IDEA** What factors led the United States to agree to a cease-fire?

2. **MAIN IDEA** Discuss the effects the war has had both on the Vietnamese people and on many Vietnam veterans.

3. **ASSESSING CONSEQUENCES** What factors helped prevent the United States from achieving its goals in Vietnam? What might the United States have done differently to reach those goals?

4. **WRITING TO PERSUADE** Write a letter to your local chamber of commerce to persuade it to honor local Vietnam veterans in some way.

5. **EVALUATING** What have been some of the long-term effects of the Vietnam War on U.S. foreign and economic policy? Support your answer with specific examples.

War between Vietminh and French begins.

U.S. aids France in Indochina.

French surrender at Dien Bien Phu. Geneva Conference divides Vietnam.

Diem comes to power in South Vietnam.

1945   1950   1955

WRITING A SUMMARY

Using the essential points of the chapter as a guide, write a summary of the chapter.

REVIEWING CHRONOLOGY

Number your paper 1 to 5. Study the time line above, and list the following events in the order in which they happened by writing the first next to 1, the second next to 2, and so on. Then complete the activity below.

1. Students killed at Kent State and Jackson State.
2. Cease-fire declared.
3. Congress passes Tonkin Gulf Resolution.
4. Nixon begins bombing of Cambodia.
5. Tet offensive launched.

Identifying Cause and Effect Select two events on the time line, and in a paragraph, explain the cause-and-effect relationship between them.

IDENTIFYING PEOPLE AND IDEAS

Explain the historical significance of each of the following people or terms.

1. Ho Chi Minh
2. domino theory
3. Ngo Dinh Diem
4. Vietcong
5. Tonkin Gulf Resolution
6. defoliant
7. pacification
8. doves
9. Tet offensive
10. Vietnamization

UNDERSTANDING MAIN IDEAS

1. What were the main reasons the United States became involved in Vietnam?
2. Why did the United States increase its involvement in Vietnam after 1964?
3. What were the main reasons for Americans' opposition to the war?
4. Why did Richard Nixon win the 1968 election?
5. How has the Vietnam War influenced Americans?

REVIEWING THEMES

1. **Global Relations** How did the United States' stance on world communism lead to U.S. involvement in Vietnam?
2. **Constitutional Heritage** During the war the executive branch (the president) assumed increasing power. Why did this alarm Congress? What steps did Congress eventually take to safeguard its constitutional powers?
3. **Democratic Values** How did the antiwar protests illustrate American democratic values?

THINKING CRITICALLY

1. **Problem Solving** Imagine you are an adviser to President Kennedy, who is considering sending U.S. combat troops to Vietnam. Write him a memorandum suggesting at least two noncombat ways the United States might contain communism and support South Vietnam.
2. **Evaluating** Do you think LBJ had good reasons to escalate the U.S. war effort? Why or why not?
3. **Hypothesizing** Suppose the United States had won a decisive victory in Vietnam. How might life be different in Vietnam? in America?

STRATEGY FOR SUCCESS

Number your paper 1 to 8. Study the map at the right, noting the numbers on it. Then identify each place on the map by selecting from the names listed below. Write the correct name of each place next to its corresponding number on your paper. There are two extra names on the list.

Mekong River   *Vietnam*   *Laos*
Gulf of Tonkin   *Hanoi*   *Cambodia*
South China Sea   *China*   *Soviet Union*
Ho Chi Minh City

WRITING ABOUT HISTORY

Writing to Create The Vietnam War is reaching its peak, and you have just been drafted. Write a poem or song that expresses your feelings.

NLF formed to oppose Diem.

Congress passes Tonkin Gulf Resolution.

First official U.S. combat troops sent to Vietnam. First national antiwar demonstration held.

Tet offensive launched. Nixon elected president.

U.S. troop withdrawals begin. Nixon begins bombing of Cambodia.

Students killed at Kent State and Jackson State.

Pentagon Papers published.

Cease-fire declared.

Saigon falls.

1960   1965   1970   1975

USING PRIMARY SOURCES

One of the most difficult features of the war for U.S. troops was not knowing who the enemy was. The following poem by a marine who served in Vietnam describes one reaction. Read the poem and in a brief essay state your reaction to it.

Guerrilla War

*It's practically impossible
to tell the civilians
from the Vietcong.*

*Nobody wears uniforms.
They all talk
the same language
(and you couldn't understand them
even if they didn't).*

*They tape grenades
inside their clothes,
and carry satchel charges
in their market baskets.*

*Even their women fight;
and young boys,
and girls.*

*It's practically impossible
to tell civilians
from the Vietcong;*

*after awhile
you quit trying.*

—William Ehrhart

LINKING HISTORY AND GEOGRAPHY

In Vietnam, U.S. forces encountered a physical setting ill suited for motor vehicles and advanced tanks—conventional U.S. war machinery. Review the chapter discussion of Vietnam's physical characteristics and read the following description from Michael Herr's *Dispatches*. Then in a paragraph explain why such terrain made fighting difficult.

> 66 The Highlands of Vietnam are spooky, unbearably spooky, spooky beyond belief. They are a run of erratic mountain ranges, gnarled valleys, jungled ravines and abrupt plains where Montagnard [aborigines living in the Highlands] villages cluster, thin and disappear as the terrain steepens. 99

BUILDING YOUR PORTFOLIO

Complete the following projects independently or cooperatively.

1. **THE COLD WAR** In chapters 27 and 28 you served as a U.S. delegate to the UN conference. Building on that material, create a chart, photo essay, videotape, or other visual presentation showing the structure of the United Nations. Then write a short statement indicating how the UN might have been used to lessen U.S. military involvement in Vietnam.

2. **CIVIL RIGHTS** In chapters 27, 28, and 29 you served as a reporter covering civil rights movements. Building on that material, write a script for a 15-minute news program that relates the specific concerns of one of the movements to the Vietnam War. Your comments should examine economic and social factors at home, government policies, and conditions in Vietnam.

American Letters

Voices of Change

In many ways the postwar years were a troubled time. Americans confronted serious issues, from Cold War fears and war to racial prejudice and social injustice. Singer-songwriter Bob Dylan, San Francisco Beat poet Lawrence Ferlinghetti, African American poet Naomi Long Madgett, and Native American poet-novelist James Welch were among the writers who explored these problems and tensions.

The Times They Are A-Changin'

by Bob Dylan

Come gather 'round people
Wherever you roam
And admit that the waters
Around you have grown
And accept it that soon
You'll be drenched to the bone.
If your time to you
Is worth savin'
Then you better start swimmin'
Or you'll sink like a stone
For the times they are a-changin'.

Come writers and critics
Who prophesize with your pen
And keep your eyes wide
The chance won't come again
And don't speak too soon
For the wheel's still in spin
And there's no tellin' who
That it's namin'.
For the loser now
Will be later to win
For the times they are a-changin'.

Come senators, congressmen
Please heed the call
Don't stand in the doorway
Don't block up the hall

For he that gets hurt
Will be he who has stalled
There's a battle outside
And it is ragin'.
It'll soon shake your windows
And rattle your walls
For the times they are a-changin'.

Come mothers and fathers
Throughout the land
And don't criticize
What you can't understand
Your sons and your daughters
Are beyond your command
Your old road is
Rapidly agin'.

Please get out of the new one
If you can't lend your hand
For the times they are a-changin'.

The line it is drawn
The curse it is cast
The slow one now
Will later be fast
As the present now
Will later be past
The order is
Rapidly fadin'.
And the first one now
Will later be last
For the times they are a-changin'. ❖

▼ *Civil rights demonstrators attacked with high-pressure water hoses, 1963*

▼ *Flower power, 1967*

▲ Voter registration march to Montgomery, Alabama, 1965

From *I Am Waiting*

by Lawrence Ferlinghetti

I am waiting for my number to be
    called
and I am waiting
for the living end
and I am waiting
for dad to come home
his pockets full
of irradiated silver dollars
and I am waiting
for the atomic tests to end
and I am waiting happily
for things to get much worse
before they improve
and I am waiting
for the Salvation Army to take
    over
and I am waiting
for the human crowd
to wander off a cliff somewhere
clutching its atomic umbrella
and I am waiting
for Ike to act
and I am waiting
for the meek to be blessed
and inherit the earth. . .
and I am waiting for forests and
    animals
to reclaim the earth as theirs
and I am waiting
for a way to be devised
to destroy all nationalisms
without killing anybody
and I am waiting
for linnets[1] and planets to fall like
    rain
and I am waiting for lovers and
    weepers
to lie down together again
in a new rebirth of wonder. . . . ❖

1 birds of the finch family

Midway

by Naomi Long Madgett

I've come this far to freedom and
    I won't turn back.
I'm climbing to the highway from
    my old dirt track.
    I'm coming and I'm going
    And I'm stretching and
    I'm growing
And I'll reap what I've been
    sowing or my skin's not
    black.

I've prayed and slaved and waited
    and I've sung my song.
You've bled me and you've starved
    me but I've still grown
    strong.
    You've lashed me and you've
    treed me
    And you've everything but
    freed me
But in time you'll know you need
    me and it won't be long.

I've seen the daylight breaking
    high above the bough.
I've found my destination and I've
    made my vow;
    So whether you abhor me
    Or deride me or ignore me,
Mighty mountains loom before me
    and I won't stop now. ❖

Plea to Those Who Matter

by James Welch

You don't know I pretend my
    dumb.
My songs often wise, my bells
    could chase
the snow across these whistle-
    black plains.
Celebrate. The days are grim. Call
    your winds
to blast these bundled streets and
    patronize
my past of poverty and 4-day
    feasts.

Don't ignore me. I'll build my face
    a different way,
a way to make you know that I am
    no longer
proud, my name not strong
    enough to stand alone.
If I lie and say you took me for a
    friend,
patched together in my thin bones,
will you help me be cunning and
    noisy as the wind?

I have plans to burn my drum,
    move out
and civilize this hair. See my nose?
    I smash it
straight for you. These teeth? I
    scrub my teeth
away with stones. I know you help
    me now I matter.
And I—I come to you, head down,
    bleeding from my smile,
happy for the snow clean hands of
    you, my friends. ❖

THINKING AND WRITING ABOUT LITERATURE

1. Why do you think "The Times They Are A-Changin'" became an anthem for the youth movement of the 1960s?
2. What image does Lawrence Ferlinghetti paint of life in the 1950s?
3. To whom are the speakers in Naomi Long Madgett's and James Welch's poems addressing their message? How are the speakers' attitudes similar? How are they different?

Strategies for Success

CONDUCTING AN INTERVIEW

Historians often conduct interviews with people who witnessed or participated in historical events. Such interviews are called oral histories and are considered primary sources.

One of the largest oral history collections was compiled in the 1930s by the Federal Writers' Project of the WPA. Project members interviewed former slaves to gather their recollections of life in the South under slavery and during Reconstruction. The accounts were first published in 1944 in *Lay My Burden Down.* Historian Charles A. Beard described the accounts as "literature more powerful than anything I have read in fiction."

Effective interviewing involves more than just talking to people. To get the most from an interview, conduct it carefully and accompany it with prior research as well as follow-up analysis.

How to Conduct an Interview

1. **Identify and research the topic.** Gather information on your topic as the basis for questions.
2. **Set up an interview.** Contact the interviewee; identify yourself, state clearly the purpose of the interview, and schedule a convenient time and place to conduct it. Ask whether you may tape-record the interview.
3. **Prepare questions.** Formulate questions to get at the information you need. Plan the interview so that questions logically follow one another.
4. **Conduct the interview.** Be an active listener. Allow responses that go beyond your specific questions, but keep the interview on the topic.
5. **Analyze the interview.** Review and summarize the interview's content, noting what was said with emphasis. Identify statements that are representative of the person's overall views.

Applying the Strategy

Read the following excerpt from Studs Terkel's oral history *Working.* The speaker is Nora Watson, a staff writer for a publisher of health-care literature. Then decide what questions Terkel might have asked to obtain such responses.

> **❝** Jobs are not big enough for people. It's not just the assembly line worker whose job is too small for his spirit, you know? . . .
>
> I had expected to put the energy and enthusiasm and the gifts that I may have to work—it isn't happening. They expect less than you can offer. Token labor. . . . I know I'm vegetating and being paid to do exactly that. . . . But then you walk out with no sense of satisfaction. . . . I'm being had. Somebody has bought the right to you for eight hours a day. . . . You know what I mean? **❞**

Terkel probably began his interview with a question like "How do you spend your workday?" He then may have inquired about how demanding and rewarding the job is. Given Nora Watson's dissatisfaction, his follow-up questions probably encouraged her to reflect further on feeling "underemployed."

Practicing the Strategy

Several oral histories have been written based on interviews with ground and air troops, nurses, support personnel, reporters, and other people who were in Vietnam. But the war can be remembered from many points of view. Prepare a list of questions to use in conducting interviews with people who participated in the antiwar movement. Use chapters 29 and 30 as background for the period.

▼ **Studs Terkel**

BUILDING YOUR PORTFOLIO

Outlined below are four projects. Independently or cooperatively, complete one and use the products to demonstrate your mastery of the historical concepts involved.

1 THE COLD WAR

In 1945, representatives of 50 world nations created the United Nations. Using the portfolio materials you designed in chapters 27, 28, and 30, write a report to President Nixon in 1973 recommending or condemning continued U.S. membership in the United Nations. Your report should explain why the United States originally joined the United Nations and evaluate the decision in light of world events between 1945 and 1973.

2 CIVIL RIGHTS

To many Americans, the greatest strides in civil rights came in the 30 years after World War II. African Americans, Hispanic Americans, Americans with disabilities, women, and other groups made progress in securing rights long guaranteed others. Using the portfolio materials you designed in chapters 27, 28, 29, and 30, rehearse and then present your 15-minute news program to the class, making sure the program accomplishes the goals you set and follows your plan of production.

3 THE GOVERNMENT AND THE ECONOMY

In the postwar era, the United States government became increasingly involved in managing and influencing the American economy. Using the portfolio materials you designed in chapters 27 and 29, create a visual display of the different areas of the economy in which the government plays a role. Make sure your display shows how each type of government involvement affects the lives of average citizens.

4 POPULAR CULTURE

In the 1950s and 1960s, advances in science and technology, population growth and shifts, and a rising standard of living helped transform the daily lives of Americans. Using the materials you designed in chapters 28 and 29, present to the class a slide show documenting the changes in everyday life from the 1950s to the 1960s.

Videodisc Review

In assigned groups, develop an outline for a video collage of postwar America. Choose images that best illustrate the major topics of the period. Write a script to accompany the images. Assign narrators to different parts of the script, and present your video collage to the class.

Further Reading

Chafe, William H. *Civilities and Civil Rights.* Oxford (1981). Overview of the formative years of the civil rights movement.

Hampton, Henry, and Steve Fayer. *Voices of Freedom.* Bantam (1990). Oral history of the civil rights movement.

Knox, Donald. *The Korean War: Uncertain Victory.* Harcourt (1988). Oral history of war.

O'Neil, Doris C., ed. *Life—The '60s.* Bullfinch Press (1989). An overview of the 1960s from a social history perspective.

Thompson, Robert Smith. *The Missiles of October.* Simon & Schuster (1992). The story of the Cuban missile crisis.

Young, Marilyn B. *The Vietnam Wars, 1945–1990.* HarperCollins (1991). History of the Vietnam War and its aftermath.

American
ALMANAC

❖ The American People

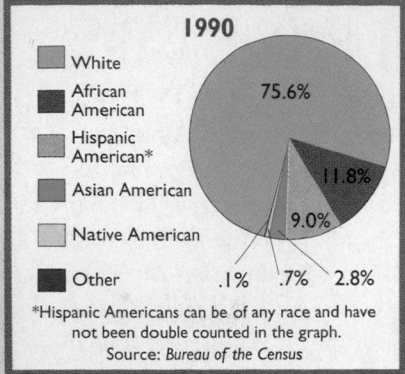

1990

- White
- African American
- Hispanic American*
- Asian American
- Native American
- Other

75.6%
11.8%
9.0%
.1% .7% 2.8%

*Hispanic Americans can be of any race and have not been double counted in the graph.
Source: *Bureau of the Census*

❖ A Healthy Body

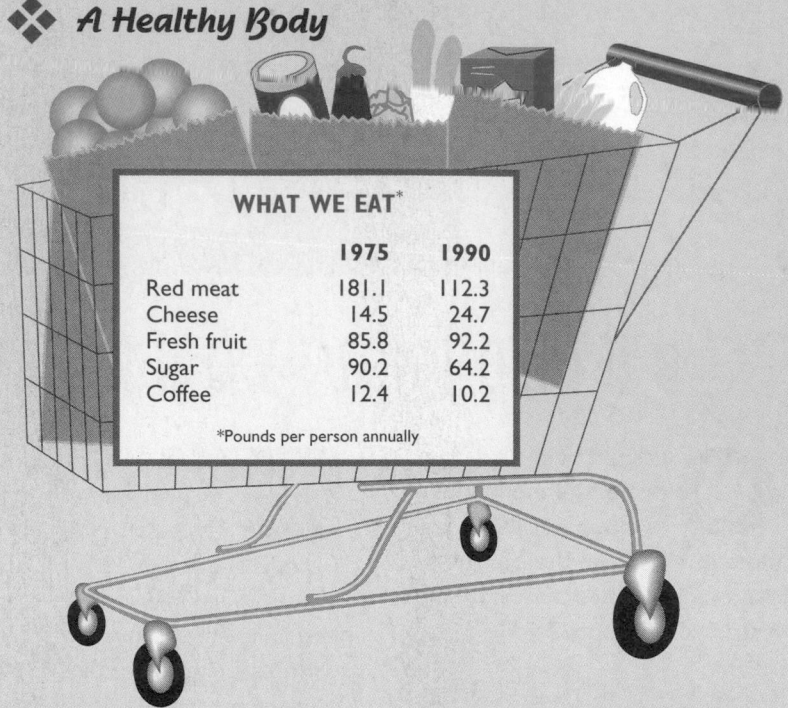

WHAT WE EAT*	1975	1990
Red meat	181.1	112.3
Cheese	14.5	24.7
Fresh fruit	85.8	92.2
Sugar	90.2	64.2
Coffee	12.4	10.2

*Pounds per person annually

❖ The Environment

1975 Oregon is first state to ban sale and use of aerosols containing chlorofluorocarbons.

1982 Crowd of about 550,000 gathers in New York for largest antinuclear rally.

1989 Cars are more efficient, averaging 20.5 miles per gallon—up from 13.5 in 1970.

1990 On Earth Day, people leave behind 100 tons of garbage in Central Park.

1971 Cigarette ads are banned from television.

1976 Sales climb 20% for bran cereals.

1989 U.S. surgeon general reports that over 40 million Americans have quit smoking since 1964.

1990 Americans eat 557% more broccoli than in 1971; 7% of the country eats at McDonald's each day.

◀ **Photo of galaxy taken by Hubble telescope**

❖ Up in the Sky

1973 Aboard first piloted SkyLab, 3 men spend 28 days in space.

1983 Guion Bluford is first African American astronaut; Sally Ride is America's first female astronaut.

1986 Richard Rutan and Jeana Yeager are first to fly around the world without refueling.

1990 Hubble telescope is launched, sending back never-before-seen pictures of the galaxy.

▼ **Earth Day, 1990**

UNIT
9

Modern Times

1970–the Present

▼ *Jenny Fille playing Little League baseball, 1974*

❖ *The Wide World of Sports*

1974 Hank Aaron hits his 715th home run, breaking Babe Ruth's record. Girls play Little League baseball for first time.

1984 Olympic games in Los Angeles attract record crowd—5.5 million—despite boycott by Soviets.

1993 Michael Jordan and the Chicago Bulls win their third consecutive NBA championship; playoff series sets NBA record for number of TV viewers.

❖ *Changing Times*

1972 Andrew Young is first African American congressman from the South since Reconstruction.

1976 Studies show 3 out of 5 marriages end in divorce; 1 out of 5 children lives in single-parent home.

1981 Sandra Day O'Connor is first woman appointed to U.S. Supreme Court.

1984 Geraldine Ferraro is first woman nominated for vice president on a major party ticket.

1988 In Los Angeles 55% of residents speak Spanish.

1980s Number of homeless is estimated at nearly 3 million.

▲ *Sandra Day O'Connor*

❖ *At Your Leisure*

1971 Disney World opens at a cost of more than $500 million; by 1990 70% of Americans have visited Disney World or Disneyland.

1975 99.9% of American homes have a TV; by 1990 the average American watches almost 7 hours each day.

1990 For every movie ticket bought, 6 videocassettes are rented.

1990 Americans purchase almost $2 billion worth of goods via TV shopping channels.

◀ *Michael Jordan*

FROM NIXON TO CARTER

FOCUS

UNDERSTANDING THE MAIN IDEA

Vice President Gerald Ford became president when the Watergate scandal forced Richard Nixon to resign in 1974. Ford lost the 1976 presidential election, however, to Democrat Jimmy Carter. The legacy of the civil rights movement continued through affirmative action programs and busing, which brought about a white backlash, and through activism by numerous groups that had faced discrimination.

THEMES

- **ECONOMIC DEVELOPMENT** How might a nation's choice of energy sources affect its economy?

- **GLOBAL RELATIONS** How might opening relations with one nation help improve relations with another nation?

- **CONSTITUTIONAL HERITAGE** Why is it dangerous for one branch of government to withhold information from another branch of government?

1970	1974	1976	1979
First Earth Day celebration held.	Nixon resigns presidency.	Jimmy Carter elected president.	Iran hostage crisis begins.

Throughout the 1960s the United States increased its involvement in the Vietnam War. As the war escalated, so did criticism of it. A weary Lyndon Johnson decided not to run for reelection in 1968. Republican Richard Nixon won the election, promising to end the war in Vietnam and to restore "law and order" to society.

Scene from 1976 bicentennial celebration

"*G*ood evening. This is the thirty-seventh time I have spoken to you from this office." President Richard Nixon's voice cracked with emotion as he addressed the American people on August 8, 1974. Less than two years earlier, he had won reelection in a landslide victory. Now he was announcing his resignation. Facing impeachment for his role in the Watergate affair, the most serious scandal ever to hit the White House, Richard Nixon became the first U.S. president to resign.

Vice President Gerald Ford served out the remainder of Nixon's term. In 1976 the nation elected a Democratic president, Jimmy Carter—a Washington outsider whose promise of honesty in government appealed to many Americans. Carter's popularity soon plummeted, however, and he was voted out of office after just one term.

Amid these political twists and turns, American society changed rapidly as many people moved to the Southwest and new waves of immigrants arrived from Latin America and Asia. In addition, the African American civil rights movement continued to influence other groups seeking equal rights—particularly women, Hispanic Americans, people with disabilities, and Native Americans.

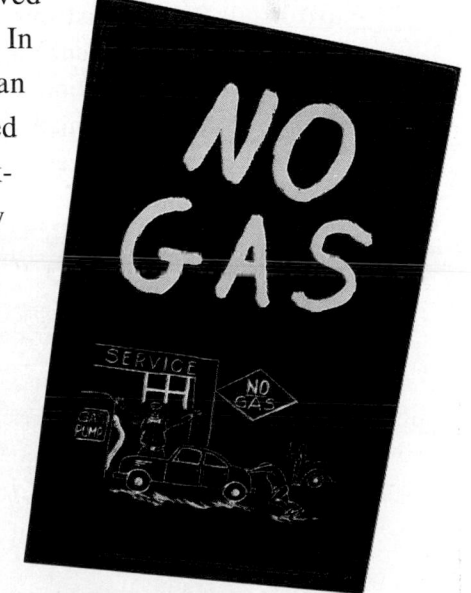

Gas station sign, 1973

THE NIXON YEARS

FOCUS

- How did President Nixon try to reverse the liberal trends of the Kennedy-Johnson years?
- What caused the energy crisis of the early 1970s?
- What factors contributed to the growth of the environmental movement?
- What was President Nixon's main foreign-policy goal?

President Nixon tried to steer the nation away from the liberalism of the Kennedy-Johnson years. His conservative agenda, however, was undermined by a Democratic Congress and by serious domestic problems, including a stagnant economy. In foreign affairs, though, the president had greater success. Nixon chalked up his most important achievement by easing tensions with the Communist world.

Chinese leader Mao Zedong and President Richard Nixon

COURTING THE SILENT MAJORITY

On July 20, 1969, Americans cheered as *Apollo 11* astronauts Neil Armstrong and Edwin "Buzz" Aldrin landed their lunar module on the moon. Stepping onto the moon's surface, Armstrong declared, "That's one small step for man, one giant leap for mankind." President Nixon and many other Americans hoped that the leap signaled a shift away from the troubles of the 1960s.

Much of Nixon's support came from middle-class voters weary from the social upheaval of the 1960s. Nixon called these people the **silent majority**—"the forgotten Americans, the non-shouters, the non-demonstrators." He won their votes by pledging to restore law and order and to cut back Democratic programs. Many critics of Johnson's Great Society policies charged that the programs had failed to significantly decrease poverty in America. Instead, critics insisted, these policies had created a complex, inefficient bureaucracy that made people dependent upon the federal government. The welfare system came under particular attack, as the number of welfare recipients climbed from some 3.1 million in 1960 to some 9.7 million in 1970.

◄ Astronauts Neil Armstrong and Edwin "Buzz" Aldrin made the first lunar landing in 1969. By 1973, five additional Apollo flights had explored the surface of the moon.

Under the existing welfare system, most families received the bulk of aid in the form of services, such as Medicaid. Nixon proposed replacing this system with the **Family Assistance Plan** (FAP), which would guarantee families a minimum income. Supporters of FAP argued that giving money directly to families would cut down on government service programs and the bureaucracy that went with them. Critics, however, charged that such direct aid would only make poor families even more dependent on the federal government. After a heated battle, the Senate voted down the FAP.

In addition to trying to reform the federal bureaucracy, Nixon promised not to ask for any new civil rights legislation. This move was part of the Republicans' **southern strategy**—a plan to woo conservative southern white voters away from the Democratic party. As part of this plan, Nixon also delayed pressuring southern schools to desegregate. When the Supreme Court ruled in 1971 that busing could be used to integrate schools, Nixon denounced the ruling.

The southern strategy also influenced the president's choice of justices for the Supreme Court. Nixon claimed that the liberal rulings of the Warren Court had encouraged lawlessness in America. Such lawlessness, he argued, was demonstrated by a series of prison riots in the late 1960s and the early 1970s. Among the most serious of these was the 1971 rebellion at New York's Attica prison, which resulted in the death of 40 prisoners and guards. When Chief Justice Warren retired in 1969, Nixon appointed a conservative justice, Warren Burger, to head the Court. Two other Nixon nominees to the Court were rejected by the Senate, but the president eventually appointed three more conservative justices: Harry Blackmun, Lewis Powell, and William Rehnquist.

■■ **Nixon tried to reverse liberal trends by cutting back on civil rights legislation and appointing conservative justices to the Supreme Court.**

TACKLING THE ECONOMY

Reversing the liberal policies of the 1960s was not the only challenge Nixon faced. He also had to tackle a faltering economy. Although the

United States had enjoyed an economic boom during the 1960s, by the time Nixon took office the economy was in trouble. High government spending on social programs and on the Vietnam War had led to a recession and growing unemployment. Normally in times of high unemployment, inflation goes down. Yet in the 1970s,

PRESIDENTIAL LIVES

RICHARD M. NIXON
1913–1994

FOR PRESIDENT RICHARD M. NIXON

in office 1969–1974

Richard Milhous Nixon rose to the top ranks of the Republican party through hard work and intense ambition. Growing up in a poor family in California made Nixon determined to be a success and to never give up.

One of the most famous examples of Richard Nixon's ability to bounce back from political challenges came during the 1952 presidential election. Nixon, who was Dwight Eisenhower's vice presidential running mate, had been accused of accepting personal gifts from wealthy businessmen. He went on national television to deny the charges. In what came to be called the "Checkers speech," Nixon admitted to accepting one personal gift. "You know what it was?" the candidate asked. "It was a little cocker spaniel dog . . . black, white, and spotted, and our little girl Tricia, the six-year-old, named it Checkers. . . . And I just want to say this, right now, that regardless of what they say about it, we're going to keep it." The Checkers speech won wide public support and saved Nixon from being dropped from the Republican ticket.

Richard Nixon

inflation and unemployment both rose. This phenomenon is called **stagflation**.

In August 1971 Nixon took a drastic step to curb inflation by imposing wage and price controls—temporary freezes on wages, prices, and rents. Many people were surprised by the action, since Nixon had long opposed the use of such controls. Labor leaders feared that wage freezes would hurt those earning the lowest wages. AFL–CIO president George Meany called it "Robin Hood in reverse, because it robs from the poor and gives to the rich."

Nixon, however, was bowing to political reality. Only by taking bold action on the economy could he hope to win the upcoming presidential election. The strategy worked. Inflation slowed, and Nixon was reelected in 1972. When he eased controls the following year, though, inflation shot up again. By August 1974 inflation had reached 12 percent. A homemaker from Chicago reflected public sentiments about the economy:

> 66 You always used to think in this country that there would be bad times followed by good times. Now, maybe it's bad times followed by hard times followed by harder times. 99

THE ENERGY CRISIS

The surging cost of oil was a major cause of inflation during the 1970s. Since World War II the U.S. economy had become increasingly dependent on foreign oil. By the early 1970s the United States was importing one third of its oil needs.

To get higher prices for their oil, several oil-exporting nations, mainly Arab countries, had formed the **Organization of Petroleum Exporting Countries** (OPEC) in 1960. In the fall of 1973, amid a new Arab-Israeli war, OPEC quadrupled oil prices. Many Arab countries cut off oil shipments to the United States as punishment

THE ENERGY CRISIS: OIL PRICES, 1973–1981

U.S. EXPENDITURE ON FOREIGN OIL, 1973–1981

Sources: *World Energy: the Facts and the Future*; inset: *Statistical Abstract of the United States*

OPEC'S OIL Throughout the 1970s the U.S. government struggled to ease the problems caused by skyrocketing oil prices. These efforts were largely unsuccessful because American dependence on foreign oil continually increased.

? **BUILDING GRAPH SKILLS** Between which two-year period did the United States experience its biggest increase in oil prices? Approximately how many barrels of foreign oil were purchased in 1975?

for U.S. support of Israel. Although the Arabs lifted their embargo after a few months, the price of oil remained high. Some Americans charged that oil companies were keeping prices artificially high to boost their profits.

The oil embargo and the price hikes caused an energy crisis in the United States during the winter of 1973–74. As the cost of gasoline, heating oil, and electricity soared, some parts of the country experienced severe hardship. One Detroit hospital told its patients to stay in bed to keep warm. "We had so little oil left that we just had to cut back the thermostats," noted one hospital official. "In storage rooms and areas with no patients, it got as low as 40 degrees."

Responding to the crisis, President Nixon announced a program to make the United States less dependent on foreign oil. He called for energy conservation and signed a bill authorizing construction of a pipeline to bring oil south from Alaska. Nevertheless, America's dependence on oil imports grew throughout the 1970s.

The Arab oil embargo and price hikes of 1973 helped provoke an energy crisis in the United States.

CLEANING UP THE ENVIRONMENT

When Nixon took office, few Americans seemed worried about the environment. Two events soon helped increase concern, however. The first was a massive oil spill off the coast of Santa Barbara, California, in 1969. The second was the first Earth Day celebration in April 1970. Across the country huge crowds took part in "teach-ins" and other activities designed to raise awareness of environmental problems. At an Earth Day event in New York City's Central Park, Episcopal priest Paul Moore told a group of schoolchildren: "Unless we stop stealing, exploiting, and ruining nature for our own gain, we will lose everything."

In 1970 Congress responded to growing public concern over the environment by approving the creation of the **Environmental Protection Agency** (EPA), a federal agency with power to enforce environmental laws. Congress also approved the creation of the **Occupational Safety and Health Administration** (OSHA) to make sure that workers were not exposed to unhealthy working conditions. That same year, Congress passed two laws to limit pollution. The **Clean Air Act** set air-quality standards and tough emissions guidelines for car manufacturers. The **Water Quality Improvement Act** made oil companies pay some of the cleanup costs of oil spills and set limits on the discharge of industrial pollutants into water.

■■ **Public concern over air and water quality, coupled with events like Earth Day, fueled the growth of the environmental movement in the 1970s.**

The government also increased support for the use of nuclear energy to replace oil and coal sources. As a relatively clean source of energy that did not rely on limited natural resources, nuclear power seemed to many energy experts to be "the only practicable energy source in sight adequate to sustain our way of life and to promote our economy." By January 1974, 42 nuclear power plants were in operation and over 160 more were under construction or in the planning stages. Yet many critics worried that the risks of a nuclear accident outweighed the advantages of nuclear power.

◀ As concerns over the environment grew, U.S. cities began to stage Earth Day celebrations. Shown here is the 1970 Earth Day event in New York City's Central Park.

FOREIGN AFFAIRS UNDER NIXON

Although domestic issues demanded much of Nixon's attention, his main interest was foreign affairs. Working closely with his national security adviser, Henry Kissinger, Nixon sought to reshape U.S. foreign policy and leave his mark on world affairs.

The Nixon–Kissinger approach. Nixon and Kissinger shared a belief in **realpolitik** ("practical politics")—an approach to foreign policy that emphasized national interests over moral or ethical concerns. Nixon believed that national interests, rather than ideals such as democracy and human rights, should be the guiding force in American foreign policy. Therefore, governments allied with the United States should receive American support, even if they violated human rights.

The chief goal of the Nixon-Kissinger foreign policy was to establish a balance of power among the world's five major powers: the United States, the Soviet Union, Western Europe, Japan, and Communist China. As Nixon explained in 1972:

❝ The only time in the history of the world that we have had any extended period of peace is when there has been a balance of power. It is when one nation becomes infinitely more powerful in relation to its potential competitors that the danger of war arises. ❞

■■ **Nixon's main foreign-policy goal was to achieve a balance of power that would help reduce international conflict.**

Relations with China and the Soviets.

As part of his plan, President Nixon sought improved relations with the People's Republic of China. By the 1970s China and the Soviet Union—though both still Communist—had become bitter enemies. Nixon believed that improved ties with China would enhance American power in Asia and further divide the Communist world.

Nixon visited China in 1972 in an effort to ease more than 20 years of hostility. The two nations agreed to work together to promote peace in the Pacific region and to develop trade relations and cultural and scientific ties. Furthermore, Nixon promised eventual withdrawal of U.S. forces from Taiwan. This move helped decrease Chinese support for the North Vietnamese. Although many American conservatives were shocked by Nixon's trip, it gave the president leverage to promote a new policy with the Soviet Union.

In May 1972, three months after visiting China, Nixon flew to Moscow for talks with Soviet leader Leonid Brezhnev (BREZSH-nef). The two agreed to promote trade and to cooperate on other issues of mutual concern. At the time, Nixon declared, "There must be room in this world for two great nations with different systems to live together and work together."

Nixon and Brezhnev also signed a treaty limiting nuclear weapons. This treaty, the product of the **Strategic Arms Limitation Talks** (SALT), limited the number of intercontinental nuclear missiles—those capable of traveling long distances to other continents—each nation could have. Although the SALT treaty did not end the arms race, it was a small first step in reducing the nuclear threat. As a result of the peace talks, the United States and the Soviet Union entered into a period of **détente**—the lessening of military and diplomatic tensions between countries.

Trouble spots.

In general, Nixon and Kissinger paid little attention to countries that were not of direct strategic importance to the United States. One exception was the South American nation of Chile. In 1970 Chile elected a Socialist president, Salvador Allende (ah-YAYN-day). Fearing that Allende planned to turn Chile into "another Cuba"—a Communist ally to the Soviet Union—Nixon tried to topple the Allende government. He cut off aid to Chile and provided funds to Allende's opponents in the Chilean military. He also instructed the CIA to disrupt economic and political life in the country. In September 1973 the Chilean army killed Allende and set up a military dictatorship. To many observers, American actions in Chile represented a serious abuse of power.

Shortly after the Chilean coup, conflict erupted in the Middle East. Six years earlier, in 1967, Israel had crushed its Arab neighbors—Egypt, Jordan, and Syria—in the Six-Day War. Embittered by their defeat, the Arab states continued to harass Israel, and Israel continued to strike back. Israeli prime minister Golda Meir recalled the tension between her country and its Arab neighbors:

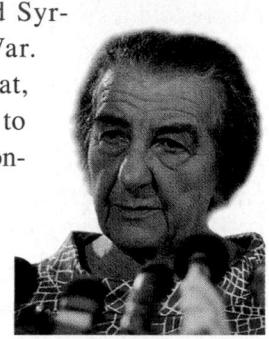

▲ **Golda Meir**

66 For years we had been shouting "peace" and hearing the echo "war" come back from the other side. . . . The only time that Arab states were prepared to recognize the existence of . . . Israel was when they attacked it in order to wipe it out. 99

This simmering conflict was fueled by Cold War competition, with the Soviets providing aid to their Arab allies and with the United States giving most of its support to Israel. Then, in October 1973, Egypt and Syria invaded Israel, seeking to recover land lost in the 1967 war. The attack, which came during the Jewish holiday of Yom Kippur, caught the Israelis by surprise. They soon launched a counterattack, however, that threatened Egypt's capital, Cairo. Facing defeat, Egypt called on the Soviet Union for help.

When the Soviets threatened to send troops into the region, President Nixon put all U.S. forces on alert. A major military confrontation seemed possible. Within days, however, the superpowers persuaded the Arabs and the Israelis to accept a cease-fire. Détente had survived its first critical test, but prospects for a lasting peace in the Middle East remained in doubt.

The Middle East

ANTI-AMERICANISM Growing U.S. dependence on foreign oil required good relations with oil-producing Arab states, a situation complicated by hostility between the Arabs and Israelis.

? **RELATIONSHIPS WITHIN PLACES** Not all conflicts in the Middle East were between Arabs and Israelis. According to the map, what other conflicts began in 1979?

*Map labels:*

ARCTIC OCEAN
EUROPE ASIA
NORTH AMERICA
ATLANTIC OCEAN
PACIFIC OCEAN
AFRICA
SOUTH AMERICA
INDIAN OCEAN
Equator
AUSTRALIA
ANTARCTICA
Robinson Projection

EUROPE
U.S.S.R.
BLACK SEA
Istanbul
Ankara
TURKEY
CAUCASUS MTS.
CASPIAN SEA
40° N
Tunis
TUNISIA
MEDITERRANEAN SEA
CYPRUS
Kurdistan
Iran hostage crisis 1979–1981
Khomeini seizes power 1979
Tehran
ASIA
HINDU KUSH
Kabul
SYRIA
Euphrates R.
Tigris R.
ZAGROS MTS.
IRAN
AFGHANISTAN
Soviet invasion 1979
Yom Kippur War, 1973
Beirut
LEBANON
Damascus
Baghdad
20° E
Tripoli
Suez Canal
Tel Aviv
Amman
Jerusalem
JORDAN
IRAQ
Basra
Failed helicopter rescue, 1980
PAKISTAN
Indus R.
Cairo
Sinai
ISRAEL
Neutral Zone
Kuwait
KUWAIT
LIBYA
EGYPT
Nile River
BAHRAIN
Riyadh
Persian Gulf
Strait of Hormuz
Gulf of Oman
INDIA
ALGERIA
Medina
SAUDI ARABIA
Mecca
QATAR
UNITED ARAB EMIRATES
OMAN
Muscat
20° N
AFRICA
RED SEA
San'a
YEMEN
SOUTH YEMEN
ARABIAN SEA
N W E S
SUDAN
Aden
Gulf of Aden
SOMALIA
ETHIOPIA
0 500 1,000 Miles
0 500 1,000 Kilometers
Scale varies with latitude. Scale at 10° N
Miller Cylindrical Projection
60° E 70° E 10° N

Legend:
- Member of OPEC
- Area of conflict
- Oil fields
- Capital city

SECTION 1 REVIEW

IDENTIFY and explain the significance of the following: silent majority, Family Assistance Plan, southern strategy, Warren Burger, stagflation, Organization of Petroleum Exporting Countries, Environmental Protection Agency, Occupational Safety and Health Administration, Clean Air Act, Water Quality Improvement Act, realpolitik, Leonid Brezhnev, Strategic Arms Limitation Talks, détente, Salvador Allende, Golda Meir.

LOCATE and explain the importance of the following: Israel, Egypt, Jordan, Syria.

1. **MAIN IDEA** What steps did President Nixon take to reverse the liberal policies of the Kennedy and Johnson administrations?

2. **MAIN IDEA** What factors provoked an energy crisis in the United States in 1973?

3. **IDENTIFYING CAUSE AND EFFECT** What events fueled the growth of the environmental movement in the 1970s?

4. **WRITING TO EVALUATE** Imagine you are a member of the National Security Council. Write a memorandum that outlines President Nixon's main foreign-policy goal and evaluates how this goal was threatened by events in the Middle East.

5. **ANALYZING** What was unique about the economy during the early 1970s? How did Nixon propose to deal with this situation?

FROM WATERGATE TO FORD

FOCUS

- What was the Watergate scandal?
- Why did President Nixon resign?
- What problems did President Ford face during his presidency?

Nixon's second term, which began with a sweeping reelection victory, ended less than two years later with his resignation from office. Just as the words Teapot Dome *sum up the scandals of Warren Harding's presidency, the word* Watergate *represents the political abuses of the Nixon years. With Nixon's departure from office, President Gerald Ford tried to restore credibility to the White House.*

Headline announcing Nixon resignation, 1974

CRISIS IN THE PRESIDENCY

Years after Richard Nixon left office, Henry Kissinger reflected on the presidency of his former boss:

> 66 Nixon had three goals: to win by the biggest electoral landslide in history; to be remembered as a peacemaker; and to be accepted by the "Establishment" as an equal. He achieved all these objectives at the end of 1972 and the beginning of 1973. And he lost them all two months later—partly because he turned a dream into an obsession. 99

This obsession began before Nixon won his landslide victory in the 1972 election. Nixon increasingly behaved as though there should be no limitations on his power. He shifted much of the authority of the cabinet, whose appointment required Senate approval, to his personal White House staff. He also hid vital information from Congress and the public. When the news media

criticized Nixon's actions, the White House charged them with biased reporting.

Nixon's public actions were nothing compared to what he did in secret to help ensure his reelection. In 1969 he ordered his staff to compile an "enemies list"—made up of critics opposed to his policies—and then tried to smear their reputations. Two years later, in reaction to Daniel Ellsberg's leak of the Pentagon Papers (see Chapter 30), Nixon set up a secret unit called "the plumbers." This group, which included former agents of the CIA and FBI, was ordered to stop leaks and carry out a variety of illegal actions in the name of "national security."

By 1972 these secret activities had mushroomed into a full-scale effort to ensure Nixon's reelection—no matter what it took. This campaign of criminal activity and electoral "dirty tricks," along with subsequent attempts to cover them up, became known as **Watergate**. The scandal took its name from the Watergate building in Washington, D.C. In June 1972 five men carrying wiretap equipment and other spying devices were caught breaking into the Watergate offices of the Democratic National Committee. It was soon

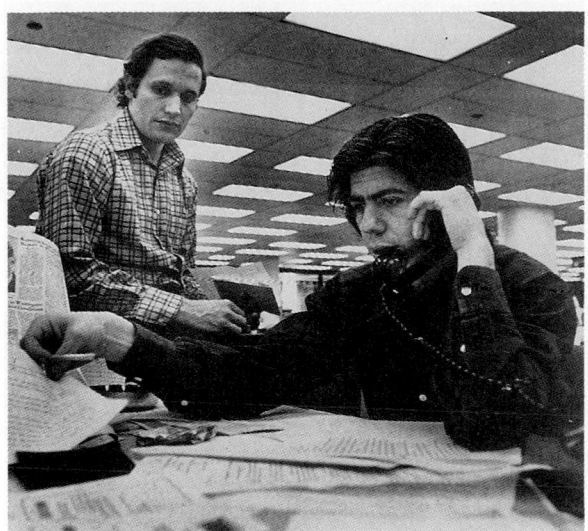

▲ Bob Woodward (left) and Carl Bernstein (right) were two *Washington Post* reporters who investigated the link between the Nixon White House and the Watergate break-in. This photograph was taken in April 1973.

discovered that these men had ties to the White House and were being paid with funds from Nixon's campaign organization, the Committee to Re-elect the President (CREEP).

The administration denied any link to the break-in, calling it a "third-rate burglary." But two *Washington Post* reporters, Bob Woodward and Carl Bernstein, kept digging for the truth. A high-level source, known only as "Deep Throat," revealed that White House officials and CREEP had hired 50 agents to sabotage the Democrats' chances in the 1972 election.

■■ **The Watergate scandal implicated the Nixon administration in illegal activities, which officials later tried to cover up.**

𝒯HE WATERGATE INVESTIGATION

As astonishing as Woodward and Bernstein's revelations were, they did not prevent Nixon's reelection. But by the spring of 1973, both the judicial and the legislative branches of government were investigating Watergate. Senator Sam Ervin of North Carolina led the investigations for the Senate. One of the first witnesses to testify was James McCord, an ex-CIA agent who had taken part in the Watergate break-in. McCord admitted that top White House officials had helped plan the

break-in and later tried to cover it up. This testimony broke the case wide open.

The biggest bombshells were yet to come. In May, live television coverage of the Senate hearings began. Across the nation millions of Americans sat glued to their sets as senators grilled witnesses and compiled evidence of official misconduct. Eventually several top White House officials were sent to jail. Still, Nixon's role in Watergate remained unclear. Time and again, a key member of the Watergate committee, Senator Howard Baker of Tennessee, asked: "What did the president know and when did he know it?" In June, Nixon's former White House counsel John Dean gave the stunning answer: the president himself had ordered the cover-up.

Nixon denied the charge, and there seemed to be no way to prove it. Then another witness revealed that Nixon had secretly tape-recorded his conversations in the White House. In the tapes, investigators believed, lay the truth behind Watergate. The Justice Department's special prosecutor, Archibald Cox, demanded that Nixon turn over the tapes. Citing "executive privilege," Nixon refused on the grounds that release of the tapes would endanger national security.

In the midst of this controversy, the Justice Department dealt the administration another blow. In October 1973 it charged Vice President Spiro Agnew with income-tax evasion. Agnew pleaded no contest and resigned in exchange for minimal punishment. Nixon then nominated Gerald Ford, the Republican leader in the House of Representatives, as vice president.

NIXON RESIGNS

Shortly before Agnew resigned, a federal judge ordered Nixon to release the tapes. The president refused to comply. On October 20, after Special Prosecutor Cox demanded that he obey the judge, Nixon ordered Attorney General Elliot Richardson to fire Cox. Both the attorney general and Deputy Attorney General William Ruckelshaus resigned rather than obey the order. The task of firing Cox then fell to Robert Bork, the solicitor general, who complied. This series of events, known as the **Saturday Night Massacre**, outraged the public and led to increased calls to impeach Nixon.

Nixon finally agreed to release some of the White House tapes. Vital segments were missing, however, and Nixon again resisted turning over the whole set. It was only months later—after the Supreme Court ordered Nixon to turn over all the tapes—that Americans found out the truth: Nixon had directed the Watergate cover-up and had authorized illegal activities. Still, Nixon refused to step down. Congress responded by recommending impeachment charges against him. Facing almost certain conviction, Nixon finally accepted his fate. On August 8, 1974, he spoke to the nation:

▲ **Gerald Ford is sworn in as the nation's 38th president as his wife, Betty, watches.**

66 I have never been a quitter. To leave office before my term is completed is opposed to every instinct in my body. But as president I must put the interests of America first. . . . Therefore, I shall resign the presidency effective at noon tomorrow. 99

■■ **President Nixon resigned rather than face impeachment for his role in covering up the Watergate affair.**

On August 9, 1974, Vice President Gerald Ford was sworn in as the 38th president of the United States. He then nominated Governor Nelson Rockefeller of New York for vice president, and Congress confirmed his choice. For the first time in history, both the president and the vice president held office by appointment.

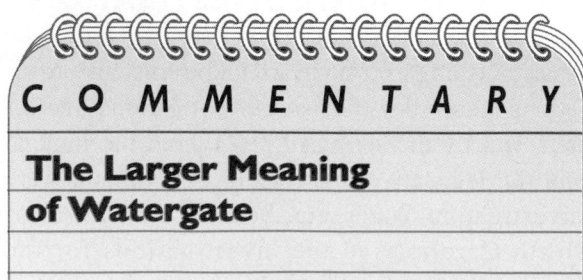

COMMENTARY

The Larger Meaning of Watergate

Watergate was not the first scandal to taint the presidency. The administration of Ulysses S. Grant, a century before Nixon, was stained by *financial scandal. So, too, was the presidency of Warren G. Harding. But Watergate was different. Nixon was the first president to resign from office and the first since Andrew Johnson in 1868 to face a serious threat of impeachment. Unlike Johnson, Nixon's troubles did not result from a power struggle with Congress but from charges of criminal activity.*

Furthermore, Watergate did not involve typical political misconduct, such as taking bribes. It challenged the very basis of our constitutional government. Nixon tried to place the presidency above the rule of law and above the constitutional system of balance of powers. Afterward, Congress would try to clean up government corruption by passing several laws, including some limiting the amount of money individuals and corporations could contribute to a political candidate.

Watergate tested our system of constitutional government to the limit, but the system held firm. Vigorous investigative journalism and strong action by the courts and Congress exposed the criminal activities of the Watergate conspirators and forced a president to resign. Watergate underscored the fact that the United States is a government of law, not of individuals.

FORD TRIES TO REUNITE THE NATION

The new president, Gerald Ford, was gifted with the common touch. As leader of the Republicans in the House, he had won the respect of colleagues in both parties for his honesty and unassuming manner. "I'm a Ford, not a Lincoln," he once joked.

But President Ford lost much of this early goodwill when, a month after taking office, he granted Nixon a full pardon. Overnight Ford's popularity rating dropped from 72 percent to 49 percent. His critics charged that now the full truth about Watergate would never emerge. They pointed to the double standard that allowed Nixon to go free while his co-conspirators were punished. Many people suspected that the pardon had been agreed upon in advance in exchange for Nixon's

resignation. President Ford denied this charge. He defended the pardon by saying that a public trial would have prolonged the bitterness and division produced by Watergate. He had acted, he said, to heal "the wounds of the past."

A week later, Ford took another controversial step by offering partial amnesty to Vietnam draft evaders and military deserters who agreed to reaffirm their allegiance to the United States and spend two years performing public service. Supporters of the Vietnam War felt the pardon was unfair to soldiers who had served their country. Meanwhile, only a handful of people accepted the president's offer. Some war resisters, like Dee Knight, contrasted the conditional pardon with the full pardon granted Nixon:

> **66** We knew the clemency was proclaimed just to offset the Nixon pardon, which was an insult. We weren't criminals, and Nixon was, but Ford proposed to pardon Nixon unconditionally while offering "alternative punishment" to us. **99**

FORD'S TROUBLES CONTINUE

Ford soon ran into other problems, including conflicts with the Democratic majority in Congress. A moderate conservative, Ford vetoed a number of social-welfare bills sponsored by Democrats. In fact, he vetoed more bills than any other president had in such a short time. As Ford's relations with Congress worsened, he found it increasingly difficult to implement his policies.

One of Ford's main goals was to combat inflation, which was being fueled by the energy

▶ **The energy crisis and the rising cost of oil drove the prices of many consumer goods higher in the United States. To win public support for his anti-inflation program, President Ford issued buttons with initials representing "Whip Inflation Now."**

GERALD R. FORD
1913–

in office
1974–1977

Gerald Ford faced the difficult task of restoring the nation's confidence in government after the Watergate crisis. Most observers believed that Ford was uniquely qualified to remove the taint of scandal from the White House. Throughout his career he had been known as an honest and likable politician. "The nicest thing about Jerry Ford," said Senator Robert P. Griffin, "is that he doesn't have any enemies." Indeed, when Ford first heard about President Nixon's "enemies list," he responded that "anybody who can't keep his enemies in his head has too many enemies."

EXPERIENCE COUNTS
Elect Gerald R. FORD in '76

Unlike many politicians, Ford made friends because he always maintained a fair-minded attitude. He was never vengeful when he lost or arrogant when he won. He acquired this attitude from years of playing sports, especially football. He had been a star player for the University of Michigan and received several offers to play for professional teams. Instead he worked his way through law school as a coach and entered politics. Sports remained an influential part of his life, however. He was the most athletic president in the White House since Teddy Roosevelt.

Gerald R. Ford

crisis and the soaring cost of oil. Like Nixon, Ford tried to curb inflation by cutting federal spending, but this threw the country into a recession and prolonged the nation's economic woes.

In foreign affairs, Ford also continued many of Nixon's policies, including détente. Gradually, however, U.S.–Soviet relations began to unravel. One problem was Soviet emigration policy, which restricted the freedom of Jews and political dissidents to leave the country. When members of Congress criticized this policy, the Soviets canceled a proposed U.S.–Soviet trade pact. Over the next few years, relations continued to sour.

Ford also tried to maintain American influence in Southeast Asia. Toward that end, he requested $722 million in military aid for Cambodia and South Vietnam. But Congress, opposed to further military ventures in Southeast Asia, turned down Ford's request. Then, in May 1975, Cambodian Communists

seized the *Mayaguez,* an unarmed U.S. cargo ship. In response, Ford launched a military action to free the vessel and its crew. Forty-one Americans were killed in the effort to release the 39 crew members. While some applauded the president's actions, others criticized it as hasty and ill-timed. As facts later revealed, the *Mayaguez* crew had already been released when the troops were sent.

▼ **Cambodian Communists seized an unarmed U.S. cargo ship, the *Mayaguez,* in May 1975. President Ford called the action piracy and sent U.S. Marines to free the vessel and its crew.**

■■ Ford clashed with Congress over domestic and foreign policy. During his term U.S.–Soviet relations began to unravel.

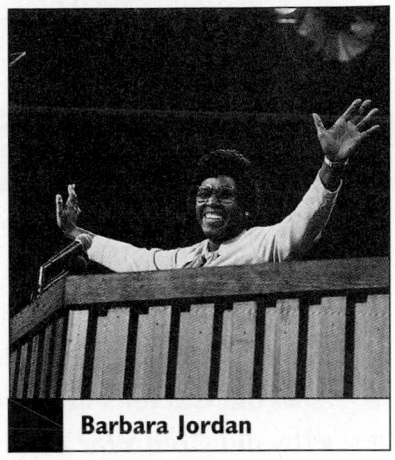

Barbara Jordan

THE ELECTION OF 1976

At the 1976 Republican convention, Ford narrowly won the party's nomination over his more conservative challenger, Ronald Reagan of California. To balance the ticket, the convention nominated conservative senator Robert Dole of Kansas for vice president. At the Democratic convention, Jimmy Carter—a former governor of Georgia—won the nomination, with Senator Walter Mondale of Minnesota as his running mate. Giving the keynote address at the Democratic convention was Congresswoman Barbara Jordan of Texas.

Jordan brought a strong sense of moral authority to the Democratic party. Born in 1936, she grew up in Houston, Texas. She excelled in school and eventually received a law degree from Boston University. In 1966 Jordan became the first African American woman elected to the Texas senate. There her tireless efforts on behalf of social reform won praise from President Lyndon Johnson, who noted, "She proved that black is beautiful before we knew what it meant."

In 1972 Jordan was elected to the U.S. House of Representatives, where she soon gained a reputation as a skilled legislator and brilliant orator. She played a key role in drawing up impeachment charges against President Nixon. At one point

Jordan declared: "I am not going to sit here and be an idle spectator to the . . . destruction of the Constitution." Despite her outstanding record in Congress, in 1978 Jordan announced that she would not run for a fourth term. As a political analyst and adviser, however, she played a prominent role in national affairs until her death in 1996.

In her speech to the 1976 Democratic convention, Jordan declared:

66 We cannot improve on the system of government handed down to us by the founders of the Republic, but we can find new ways to implement that system and realize our destiny. **99**

The idea of a new approach to government was central to Jimmy Carter's campaign. Little known outside the South, Carter ran as a Washington outsider untainted by Watergate. He promised never to lie to the American people and openly noted that he was a born-again Christian whose religious ethics strongly shaped his political actions. "You can't divorce religious beliefs and public service," he said. In a close election, he captured 297 electoral votes to Ford's 240. After eight years of Republican rule, the Democrats returned to the White House. Many hoped that Carter would be able to reverse the public's mistrust of government.

SECTION 2 REVIEW

IDENTIFY and explain the significance of the following: Watergate, Bob Woodward, Carl Bernstein, Sam Ervin, James McCord, John Dean, Archibald Cox, Gerald Ford, Saturday Night Massacre, Jimmy Carter, Barbara Jordan.

1. **MAIN IDEA** Why did President Nixon choose to resign from office in 1974?

2. **MAIN IDEA** What difficulties did President Ford face during his time in office?

3. **ASSESSING CONSEQUENCES** What was the significance of the Watergate investigation?

4. **WRITING TO INFORM** Imagine you are an investigative reporter for the *Washington Post,* covering the Watergate scandal. Write an article that outlines the major events in the scandal and the investigation leading up to President Nixon's resignation.

5. **HYPOTHESIZING** How might events have been different if Ford had not pardoned Nixon?

CARTER: THE OUTSIDER AS PRESIDENT

FOCUS

- What critical domestic issues faced the Carter administration?
- How did Carter's foreign policy differ from Nixon's?
- Why did Cold War tensions rise under President Carter?
- How did the Iran hostage crisis affect Carter's presidency?

*O*n January 20, 1977, Jimmy Carter took the oath as the 39th president of the United States. Initially a popular president, Carter enjoyed some notable successes. But serious problems—including persistent inflation and conflict in the Middle East—eventually helped erode the president's popularity. In 1980 he lost his bid for a second term.

Family member awaiting return of hostages in Iran

*A*N "OPEN ADMINISTRATION"

During the presidential campaign, Carter had promised, if elected, to stay in touch with the people. He quickly showed his intentions to keep that promise. Following his inauguration, the president and his family walked down Pennsylvania Avenue to the White House, rather than make the trip in a limousine surrounded by Secret Service.

The Carter style. Carter brought a folksy style to the White House, abandoning much of the pomp and ceremony of previous presidents. Contributing to this informal tone was his colorful family, who became the subject of much public interest. The news media reported on the activities of Carter's young daughter, Amy, and on the views of his outspoken mother, Miss Lillian. Carter's wife, Rosalynn, received even more attention as one of his most trusted advisers. Although critics questioned his wife's influence on policy, the president insisted that she play a prominent role in White House affairs.

Early on, Carter took several steps that indicated a new approach to government. On his first full day in office, he announced an unconditional pardon for most Vietnam-era draft evaders, moving beyond the conditional pardon offered by President Ford. This gesture helped heal lingering divisions over the war. Carter also held several

◀ The Carter family attracted almost as much media attention as the president. Shown here are President Carter with his wife, Rosalynn, and his young daughter, Amy.

The common reaction to Georgia governor Jimmy Carter's announcement that he was running for president was "Jimmy who?" Few people outside of his home state were familiar with this peanut farmer from Plains. Soon, however, voters began to discover that there was much more to this southern politician than his large grin. A highly ranked graduate of the United States Naval Academy, Carter had worked as a nuclear engineer before entering politics.

One of the most surprising things about Carter was his modern relationship with his wife. Rosalynn Carter took an active and public role in political affairs, traveling around the world to represent her husband's views. Meanwhile Jimmy Carter shared in the household chores, such as cooking, caring for their children, and grocery shopping. One interviewer was shocked to see the candidate sewing a button onto his own jacket during the presidential campaign. When asked if he always did his own sewing, Carter simply mumbled with thread in mouth, "Uh-huh."

"town meetings" and radio and television call-in sessions to keep in touch with the people. Unlike Richard Nixon, Jimmy Carter seemed determined to keep his administration open to public view.

Carter's economic policy.
One of Carter's first tasks was to stimulate the economy, which was just beginning to emerge from several years of recession. Some eight million Americans—7.8 percent of the work force—were out of work. The unemployment rate among African Americans and Hispanic Americans was a staggering 13 percent.

To revive the economy and create jobs, Carter implemented a series of economic measures, including a corporate tax cut. The Carter administration's policies helped reduce unemployment slightly, but they also fueled inflation, which reached 13.3 percent by 1979. To curb inflation, Carter called for voluntary wage and price controls, along with cuts in funding for social services. But Carter's anti-inflation program produced more unemployment. By the summer of 1980, the economy was once again in recession.

Facing the energy crisis.
A major cause of the nation's economic woes was the high cost of imported oil. To reduce the nation's oil dependence, Congress created the **Department of Energy** in 1977. The following year it passed the **National Energy Act** to relax controls on the price of natural gas. Despite these efforts, world events continued to affect the nation's energy supply.

In January 1979 a revolution in Iran disrupted world oil shipments. A few months later, OPEC raised the price of oil 50 percent, leading to another U.S. energy crisis (see the chart on page 902). As gasoline supplies dwindled, many gas stations closed or reduced their hours. Tempers flared as frustrated drivers had to wait hours to fill

▼ High energy costs hurt many groups during the late 1970s, especially farmers. On February 6, 1979, protesting farmers drove their tractors down Pennsylvania Avenue to demonstrate in front of the White House.

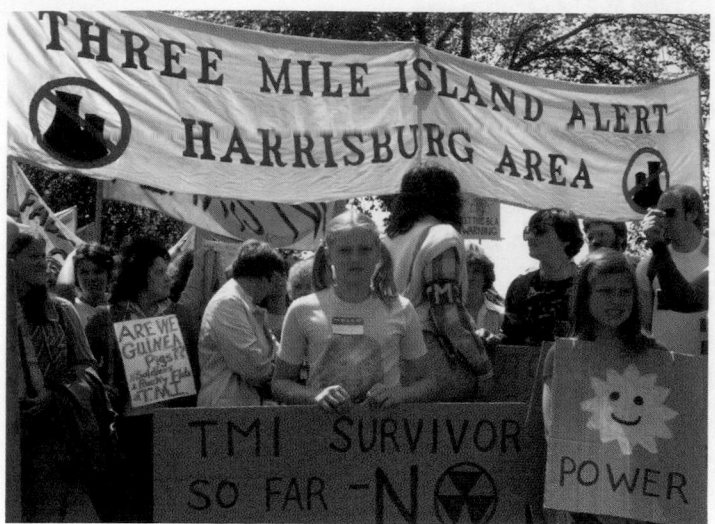

▲ After the disaster at Three Mile Island, residents staged protests that questioned the safety of nuclear power. Protesters urged the government to explore alternative energy research, such as solar power.

their gas tanks. Some people responded by driving less and by embracing other energy-saving measures, such as installing solar heaters in their homes.

In the midst of the oil crisis, another event dramatized America's energy problems. In late March 1979 a nuclear reactor failed at the Three Mile Island power plant in Pennsylvania, nearly causing a catastrophic nuclear meltdown—the melting of the reactor's core. This incident stirred public doubts about nuclear power.

■■ **An economic recession and an energy crisis were among the serious domestic issues facing the Carter administration.**

*H*UMAN RIGHTS AND FOREIGN POLICY

While Carter was struggling with difficult domestic issues, he was also charting a new course in foreign affairs. Rejecting the realpolitik of the Nixon years, Carter tried to inject moral principles into American foreign policy. Reflecting on past administrations, he declared:

❝ We are deeply concerned . . . by the . . . subtle erosion in the focus and morality of our foreign policy. Under the Nixon-Ford administration, there has evolved a kind of secretive "Lone Ranger" foreign policy—

a one-man policy of international adventure. This is not an appropriate policy for America. ❞

Carter's new approach was most evident in the area of **human rights**—the rights of all people to freedom from unlawful detention or torture. Declaring that "our commitment to human rights must be absolute," Carter called for strong diplomatic and economic pressure on countries that violated human rights.

Not surprisingly, many dictatorships that repressed the rights of their people strongly opposed Carter's policy. Some American diplomats also had doubts. They warned that such meddling in the domestic affairs of other countries might increase world tensions. The United States would resent meddling by other nations in *its* domestic affairs, they pointed out.

■■ **Carter moved away from Nixon's foreign policy of realpolitik to emphasize moral principles and respect for human rights.**

Carter's stand on the Panama Canal caused even greater controversy. He supported Panama's right to control the Canal Zone and pushed for passage of the **Panama Canal treaties**, which granted Panama control over canal operations by the year 2000. Critics charged that Carter was "giving away" the canal. "We built it, we paid for it, it's ours, and . . . we are going to keep it!" declared conservative Republican Ronald Reagan.

Gradually, however, public opinion shifted in Carter's favor, and after a long and bitter debate, the Senate narrowly ratified the treaties in 1978. In

▲ Through the Panama Canal treaties, President Carter proposed that the United States give control of the Canal Zone to Panama by the year 2000.

Latin America, where U.S. control over the canal had long been a sore point, the treaties met with general approval.

CARTER AND THE COLD WAR

Carter's stance on the Panama Canal issue signaled a more flexible approach to relations with developing countries. Carter hoped the approach would improve America's image and diminish the appeal of communism. His policy was evident in Africa, where the United States and the Soviet Union were jockeying for influence among the continent's newly independent states.

Unlike Nixon and Ford, who showed little interest in Africa, Carter tried to win friends among African nations by helping them sort out their problems in their own way. One Carter official noted, "It is not a sign of weakness to recognize that we alone cannot dictate events elsewhere. It is rather a sign of maturity in a complex world."

Carter's ambassador to the United Nations, former civil rights activist Andrew Young, tried to reach out to black African states. He criticized white imperialism in Africa, condemned South Africa's policy of **apartheid** (racial segregation), and supported black majority rule in Rhodesia (now Zimbabwe).

Carter's flexible approach helped smooth relations in Africa and ease Cold War conflict. The easing of tensions was short-lived, however. In December 1979, Soviet troops invaded the country of Afghanistan to install a pro-Soviet leader. The invasion put Soviet troops within striking distance of major oil routes.

Labeling the invasion a threat to peace, President Carter warned the Soviets to withdraw. When they refused, he cut grain sales to the Soviet Union and announced a boycott of the 1980 Summer Olympics in Moscow. Congress also postponed the signing of a key U.S.–Soviet arms-control treaty. Finally, the president warned that any Soviet military action in the Persian Gulf would provoke a military response by the United States.

■■ **Although the U.S. improved relations with developing countries, Cold War tensions increased when the Soviets invaded Afghanistan.**

CARTER AND THE MIDDLE EAST

Not long before the Soviet invasion of Afghanistan, Carter engineered his chief foreign-policy triumph: a Middle East peace accord. Carter had taken office in 1977 amid fears of another Egyptian-Israeli war. Egyptian president Anwar Sadat (sah-DAHT) and Israeli premier Menachem Begin (muh-NAHK-uhm BAY-gin) met for peace talks, but those talks deadlocked.

BIO GRAPHY Anwar Sadat received a great deal of criticism from the leaders of other Arab nations for attempting any peace talks with Israel. Sadat was born in the small village of Mit Abu-Kum on the Nile Delta in 1918. His childhood was heavily influenced by his close-knit family and the local Imam (religious leader), who taught him the principles of the Islamic faith. Soon after graduating from the Egyptian Military Academy in 1938, Sadat joined a group of rebels who wanted to rid Egypt of its constitutional monarchy, which was under British control.

Anwar Sadat

Sadat went to prison in the 1940s for his efforts to liberate Egypt. After being released from prison, he joined the rebel forces who finally overthrew the monarch in 1952. Thereafter Sadat played a central role in shaping Egyptian policy, finally

◄ As U.S. ambassador to the United Nations, Andrew Young condemned apartheid and sympathized with the concerns of developing nations. His actions made him a controversial figure, and he was forced to resign in 1979.

becoming president in 1970. As president he played a key role in Middle East events, including trying to pave the road to peace. When Sadat visited Israel in 1977, Premier Begin remarked:

66 The time of the flight between Cairo and Jerusalem is short . . . [but] the distance between them . . . until yesterday, quite large. . . . Sadat passed this distance with heartfelt courage. . . . We, the Jews, know how to appreciate this courage. 99

But Sadat always downplayed his own role in bringing about peace. He considered his actions a collective effort by the entire country. To him, all Egyptians shared responsibility for the nation's future. He once said:

66 Responsibility cannot be relegated to certain individuals, no matter how good your opinion of them might be; neither can it be confined to groups of people, however good their intentions may be. Responsibility is the entire people's property. 99

In September 1978 Sadat met with Begin and Carter at Camp David, the presidential retreat in Maryland. There, after 12 days of negotiations, the three agreed on a framework for peace, which became known as the **Camp David Accords**. As a result of their efforts, Sadat and Begin shared the Nobel Peace Prize for 1978. The following year, the two leaders signed a formal peace treaty ending 30 years of war between Egypt and Israel. At the emotion-filled ceremony, each quoted the prophet Isaiah: "And they shall beat their swords into plowshares and their spears into pruning hooks."

The accords did not meet universal approval. Some supporters of Israel accused President Carter of favoring the Arabs in order to appease Arab oil-exporting nations, such as Saudi Arabia. Sadat drew the wrath of other Arab nations, furious at his "betrayal" for making peace with Israel. In 1981, members of an Islamic fundamentalist group within the Egyptian army assassinated Sadat while he was reviewing a military parade.

CARTER'S POPULARITY FALLS

Although Carter had chalked up some notable successes as president, by 1980 only 21 percent of Americans approved of his performance. Nixon's approval rating had not fallen this low even during the depths of Watergate. Carter's drop in popularity was partly due to his lack of political experience. But his troubles also lay in the nature of the problems he faced. The energy crisis, inflation, unemployment, Middle East conflict, and Cold War tensions were highly complicated issues that defied simple solutions. Of all the difficulties he faced, however, none was more damaging than the **Iran hostage crisis**.

Iran had long been regarded as critical to U.S. security in the Middle East. In the 1950s the United States had helped overthrow Iran's leader and restore Shah Reza Pahlavi to power (see Chapter 28). Although the shah's regime was very repressive, the United States always supported him. In 1979, however, followers of a militant Islamic leader, the Ayatollah Khomeini (eye-uh-TOH-luh koh-MAY-nee), forced the shah to flee the country. The new government was outraged when President Carter allowed the shah into the United States for medical treatment. On November 4, 1979, in an effort to force the shah's return to Iran for trial, Iranian militants seized 53 American hostages at the U.S. embassy in Tehran, Iran's capital.

Month after month, the hostage crisis dragged on. In April 1980 a rescue mission failed when U.S. military helicopters crashed in the Iranian desert, killing eight Americans. As frustration over the crisis mounted, public anger at Carter also grew. Many felt that his inability to free the hostages signaled America's decline as a symbol of power. Even one Carter aide admitted that "Khomeini would not have touched the Soviet Embassy."

Echoing these thoughts during the 1980 presidential election campaign, the Republican candidate, Ronald Reagan, attacked Carter as a weak president who had presided over a decline in American power. Reagan's promise to "make America strong

▶ **American hostage in Iran**

again" struck a chord with voters. He and his running mate, George Bush, easily won the election, capturing 489 electoral votes to Carter and Mondale's 49. An independent candidate, John Anderson, failed to capture any electoral votes, but did win almost 7 percent of the popular vote, further reflecting public frustration with the administration. For the first time since 1952, the Republicans won control of the Senate, while the Democrats' hold on the House was reduced somewhat.

After his defeat Carter continued to negotiate for the release of the hostages. On January 20, 1981, after 444 days in captivity, the hostages were finally freed, just moments after Ronald Reagan was sworn in as president.

Election of 1980

REPUBLICAN LANDSLIDE Carter's difficulties at home and abroad doomed his chances for reelection.

? LOCATION Which states did Carter win west of the Mississippi River?

	Electoral Vote	Popular Vote	% of Popular Vote
Reagan	489	43,904,153	50.7
Carter	49	35,483,883	41.0
Anderson		5,720,060	6.6
Other candidates		1,407,793	1.6

Reagan (Republican)

Carter (Democratic)

■■ **The Iran hostage crisis contributed to Carter's defeat in the 1980 election.**

SECTION 3 REVIEW

IDENTIFY and explain the significance of the following: Rosalynn Carter, Department of Energy, National Energy Act, human rights, Panama Canal treaties, Andrew Young, apartheid, Anwar Sadat, Menachem Begin, Camp David Accords, Iran hostage crisis, Ayatollah Khomeini, Ronald Reagan, John Anderson.

LOCATE and explain the importance of the following: Iran, South Africa, Rhodesia (Zimbabwe), Afghanistan.

1. **MAIN IDEA** What two serious domestic issues did President Carter face?

2. **MAIN IDEA** How did the Carter administration's approach to the Cold War influence events overseas? What event caused Cold War tensions to increase?

3. **CONTRASTING** Contrast the Carter administration's approach to foreign policy with the Nixon administration's approach.

4. **WRITING TO EXPLAIN** Imagine you are a political analyst covering the 1980 presidential election. Write an essay explaining why Carter has been defeated.

5. **TAKING A STAND** Was Carter right in supporting the Panama Canal treaties? Why or why not?

A DECADE OF SOCIAL CHANGE

FOCUS

■ How did the civil rights movement continue in the 1970s? How did some whites respond?

■ What did Native American leaders fight for during the 1970s?

■ What issues both encouraged and divided the women's movement during the 1970s?

■ How did the new immigrants in the 1970s help shape society?

A woman with visual impairment demonstrating for civil rights

During the 1970s American society underwent important social changes. African Americans made further gains, despite a growing white backlash. Hispanic Americans, Native Americans, people with disabilities, and women also made legal and economic strides. Amid these changes, society as a whole was evolving as Americans were living longer and moving more often, and new immigrants were swelling the population.

THE LEGACY OF THE CIVIL RIGHTS MOVEMENT

The 1970s brought some progress in the area of civil rights. Though a 1975 Civil Rights Commission report found that many African Americans were still being kept from voting by various means, by the end of the 1970s over 4,500 African Americans held elective office—three times the number in 1969. The roster of elected black officials in 1978 included 16 members of the House of Representatives and 170 mayors, including those of Los Angeles, Atlanta, Detroit, and Washington, D.C.

As new African American leaders gained political experience, they formed strong alliances and effective lobbies. They also worked hard to get out the black vote, a key factor in Jimmy Carter's electoral victory in 1976. As president, Carter helped open the doors of the federal government to African Americans, naming more blacks to federal jobs than any previous president. In addition to his choice of Andrew Young as UN ambassador, Carter appointed the first African American woman to a cabinet post—Patricia Harris as secretary of Housing and Urban Development.

During the 1970s Hispanic Americans also began to reap some rewards for their political struggles of the previous decade. Between 1974 and 1987 the number of elected Hispanic officials in the United States more than doubled. Growing numbers of Hispanic Americans were appointed to federal jobs, while Hispanic groups such as LULAC—**League of United Latin American Citizens**—mounted lobbying efforts and helped raise national awareness of Hispanic concerns. In California the United Farm Workers won a key victory in 1975 with the passage of a state law extending legal protection to migrant farm workers. In addition, the Southwest Voter Registration Education Project helped Hispanic Americans register to vote.

Americans with disabilities also made their voices heard in the 1970s. Why, they asked, should

▲ These demonstrators in San Francisco protested lack of access to public transportation by blocking buses during rush hour.

their tax dollars help build public facilities that people in wheelchairs or people with visual disabilities could not easily use? In response to protests, state and local governments passed laws requiring wheelchair ramps and special parking spaces at public facilities. Many public facilities also put up signs in braille to help people who are visually impaired. Congress joined these efforts by passing the **Rehabilitation Act** in 1973, which forbade discrimination in jobs, education, or housing because of physical disabilities. In 1975 it passed the **Education for All Handicapped Children Act**, which required public schools to provide education for children with physical and mental disabilities.

■■ **The legacy of the civil rights movement continued in the growing political clout of African Americans, Hispanic Americans, and people with disabilities.**

A WHITE BACKLASH

The expansion of civil rights during the 1970s was the result of both public and private efforts. In an effort to uphold federal laws against discrimination, the Civil Rights Division of the Department of Justice sued corporations and labor unions to end unfair employment practices. Many schools and businesses also instituted **affirmative action** programs, whereby ethnic minorities and women were given preference in hiring and admission

to make up for previous discrimination.

But the 1970s also brought a white backlash against the civil rights movement. Some white citizens complained that civil rights reform was depriving them of their own rights. One of the first targets of white anger was court-ordered busing to achieve school desegregation. Busing met with strong opposition in a number of cities, most notably Boston. One angry white Bostonian, Jimmy Kelley, warned: "You heard of the Hundred Years War? This will be the eternal war. It will be passed down from father to son."

By the fall of 1974, violent protests against busing had erupted in Boston. Many people were injured in the riots. Yet despite the risks, many

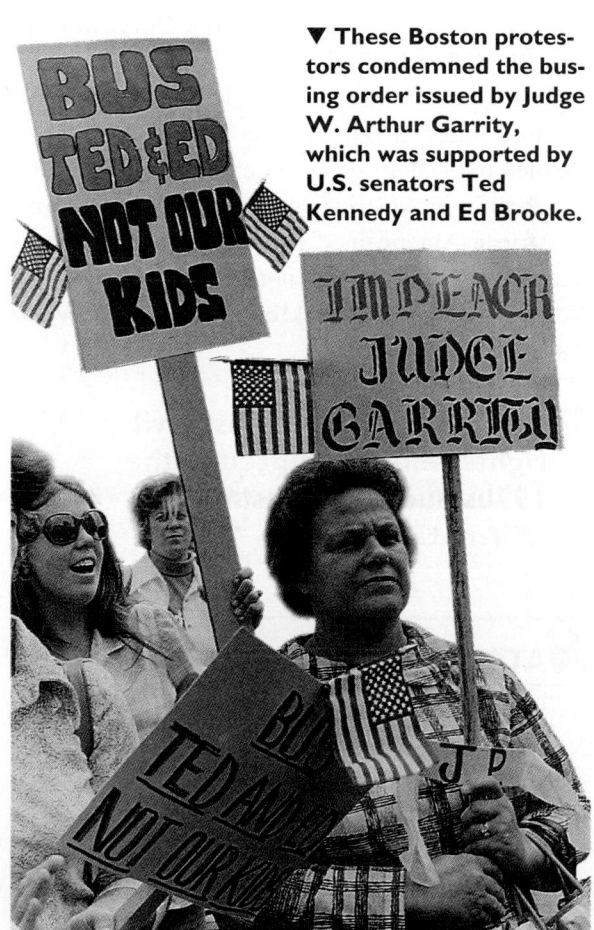

▼ These Boston protestors condemned the busing order issued by Judge W. Arthur Garrity, which was supported by U.S. senators Ted Kennedy and Ed Brooke.

black parents believed that busing was necessary. As one African American woman, Rachel Twymon, told her two children who were being bused to a previously all-white school:

66 I'm afraid this isn't going to be an easy year for either of you. You're going to be called a lot of ugly names. You're going to be spat at, maybe pushed around some. But it's not the first time this has happened and it won't be the last. It's something we have to go through—something *you* have to go through—if this city is ever going to get integrated. 99

By the late 1970s the busing controversy had quieted down, but anger over affirmative action continued. Many whites argued that affirmative action programs led to reverse discrimination. In 1978 the Supreme Court handed down an important ruling on affirmative action. In *University of California* v. *Bakke*, the Court ruled that a white man, Allan Bakke, had been unfairly denied admission to medical school on the basis of quotas—systems that set aside a fixed number of places for certain groups of people, in this case, African Americans. Although the Court did not rule out all forms of affirmative action, it did strike down quotas as a means of achieving racial equality. In a bitter dissent Justice Thurgood Marshall recalled the history of three centuries of racial discrimination in America and its toll on generations of African Americans: "The dream of America as the great melting pot has not been realized for the Negro; because of his skin color he never even made it into the pot."

∎∎ White backlash against civil rights reform erupted in the 1970s, fueled by busing and affirmative action.

NATIVE AMERICANS ORGANIZE

As part of the broad movement for civil rights, Native Americans also began to organize. Young urban Indians launched the American Indian Movement (AIM) in 1968, calling for a renewal of Native American culture and recognition of Native American rights. In 1972, some 500 AIM members, protesting what they called the "Trail of Broken Treaties," temporarily occupied the Bureau of Indian Affairs (BIA) in Washington, D.C.

BIO GRAPHY One of the leaders of the BIA occupation was Russell Means, a longtime Indian activist. Born in 1940 on the Pine Ridge Sioux Reservation of South Dakota, Means spent much of his childhood in the San Francisco Bay area. By 1970 he had become a prominent figure in AIM. That year, he gained national attention when he led an AIM occupation of the *Mayflower II*—a replica of the Pilgrim ship—during Thanksgiving Day celebrations in Plymouth, Massachusetts. In a 1971 interview, Means gave his justification for AIM's aggressive tactics:

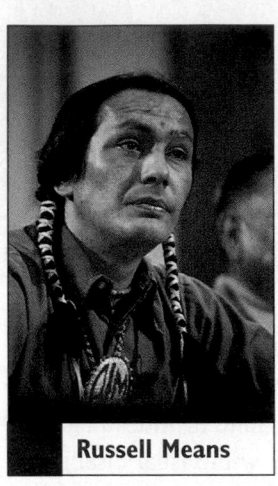

Russell Means

66 In all our demonstrations we have yet to hurt anybody or destroy any property. However, . . . we have found that the only way the white man will listen is by us creating a disturbance in his world. 99

In 1973 Means helped lead AIM's most dramatic action—the seizure of the trading post on the Sioux reservation in Wounded Knee, South Dakota. Here in 1890, U.S. cavalry units had brutally massacred more than 300 Sioux. Now Means declared that the government had two choices: "Either they attack and wipe us out like they did in 1890, or they negotiate our reasonable demands." Means wanted the government to initiate hearings on past broken treaties and investigate alleged misconduct in the Bureau of Indian Affairs.

For 71 days AIM members and U.S. marshals engaged in a grim standoff. Finally, after two people had been killed and one wounded, the government agreed to consider AIM's grievances, and the siege came to an end. The following year, Means and other AIM leaders were put on trial for the Wounded Knee incident. The case was dismissed, however, when defense lawyers presented evidence of government misconduct against AIM.

While AIM's confrontational tactics captured headlines and television attention, other Native American leaders worked to renew tribal life by

◀ Frustrated over government delays in addressing Native American grievances, AIM leaders resorted to more aggressive tactics. This photograph was taken on March 6, 1973, after members seized the trading post on Wounded Knee reservation.

quieter means, including court action. The Taos Pueblo Indians of New Mexico recovered 48,000 acres of land, including the sacred Blue Lake. Native Americans in Maine, claiming that more than half of the state had been illegally taken from them, won from Congress an $81.5 million award and the right to purchase up to 300,000 acres.

■■ During the 1970s Indian leaders fought to improve conditions for Native Americans and to take back tribal lands.

𝒯HE WOMEN'S MOVEMENT GAINS MOMENTUM

The women's movement made many advances in the 1970s as leaders worked to shape public policy and elect more women to public office. Many all-male colleges opened their doors to women, while other universities instituted courses in women's studies. In 1972 Congress passed the **Education Amendments Act**, which outlawed sexual discrimination in higher education.

The following year, the Supreme Court handed down a landmark decision affecting women. In the case ***Roe* v. *Wade***, the Court overturned a state law limiting women's access to abortion. The Court ruled that a woman and her doctor, not the state, should make such decisions. While most feminists hailed *Roe* v. *Wade* as a victory, opponents protested that the ruling violated the right to life of the unborn.

The 1970s also saw a major battle over the **Equal Rights Amendment** (ERA), the proposed

constitutional amendment barring discrimination on the basis of sex (see Chapter 21). The ERA received strong support from the National Organization for Women (NOW) and other women's groups. In testimony before Congress, feminist leader Gloria Steinem asserted:

❝ Women suffer second-class treatment from the moment they are born. They are expected to *be* rather than achieve, to function biologically rather than learn. A brother, whatever his intellect, is more likely to get the family's encouragement and education money, while girls are often pressured to conceal ambition and intelligence. ❞

Congress passed the ERA in 1972, but the amendment still required the approval of at least 38 states. At first, ratification seemed certain, but by

▼ During a news conference, National Women's Political Caucus leaders Bella Abzug, Gloria Steinem, Shirley Chisholm, and Betty Friedan announced their goal to increase the number of women delegates to the 1972 presidential conventions.

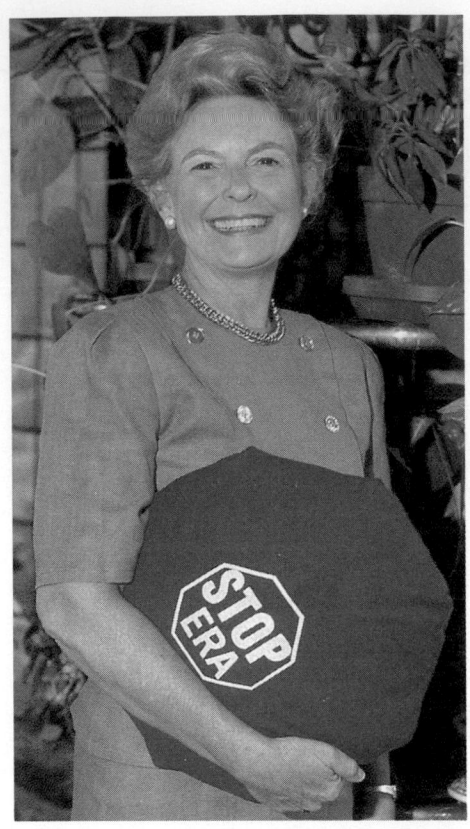

◀ Phyllis Schlafly was one of the most vocal critics of the ERA during the 1970s and the 1980s.

the 1982 deadline set by Congress, the ERA was still three states short of ratification. As a result, it failed to become law.

The women's movement made many political gains; however, it also alienated many women who viewed it as a movement primarily for privileged white women. Many women from working-class and ethnic communities felt that the leaders of NOW simply could not identify with the problems they faced every day.

The movement also alienated many middle-class women who felt that it downgraded the family and condemned women who chose to be full-time homemakers. These women viewed *Roe* v. *Wade* and the ERA as threats to traditional family life. Critics warned that the ERA would "nullify any laws that make any distinction between men and women." Eventually, they argued, men and women would even be forced to share public restrooms! When the ERA failed to win ratification, conservative critic Phyllis Schlafly proclaimed: "The defeat of the Equal Rights Amendment is the greatest victory for women's rights since the woman's suffrage movement of 1920."

■■ The women's movement was encouraged by *Roe* v. *Wade* and the ERA, but the issues alienated many women from the movement.

A CHANGING POPULATION

As different groups in American society worked for change, the society itself was evolving. Thanks to medical advances, Americans were living longer, a phenomenon referred to as the "graying of America." At the same time, the birthrate was dropping sharply, to an average of two births per woman. For years, experts had been promoting this level of **zero population growth** (ZPG)—a birthrate that replaces the existing population but does not increase it—in hopes of preventing overpopulation.

The divorce rate continued to rise during the 1970s. In 1979, 5.3 divorces were registered per 1,000 Americans, up from 2.2 in 1960. Increasingly, many Americans were abandoning the idea that marriage was necessarily a lifelong commitment.

Americans also moved more often in the 1970s than in the past. During the decade a growing number of Americans migrated from the North and the East to the **Sunbelt** states of the South and the West, seeking a warmer climate and a more suburban life-style. This migration caused the population growth of California, Texas, and Florida to outpace that of the rest of the nation.

Another key factor in America's evolution during this period was continued immigration, mostly from Asia and Latin America. Most Latin American immigrants came from Mexico, but a sizable number also came from the Caribbean. In 1980, for example, nearly 120,000 Cubans fled the

▲ Many multigenerational Asian families, such as the one pictured here, immigrated to the United States in the 1970s.

Communist island for the United States, settling mainly in the Miami area. Economically successful, Cuban Americans became an important interest group in American politics.

China, which opened the way for emigration after President Nixon's visit, supplied some of the new Asian population. Many of these Chinese immigrants were highly skilled and well-educated professionals fleeing political persecution. Despite their backgrounds, however, many found that discrimination and their lack of English skills kept them from obtaining well-paying jobs. The experiences of Wei-Chi Poon, a biology professor from China, and her husband, a skilled architect, were not unique. Neither knew any English when they immigrated to the United States. As a result, she had to toil in a laundry factory for $1.85 an hour, while he took on two low-paying jobs. "We were so busy working and so tired," she recalled, "we had no time and energy to study English."

Congress tried to aid such immigrants by passing two new laws. The **Voting Rights Act of 1975** required states and communities with large numbers of non-English speakers to print voting materials in various foreign languages. The **Bilingual Education Act** of 1974 encouraged public schools to provide instruction to students in their primary languages while they learned

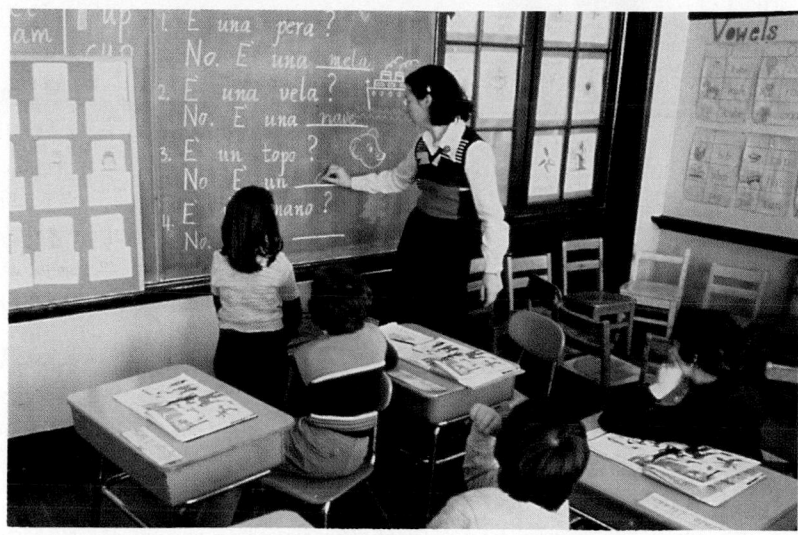

▲ The Bilingual Education Act of 1974 encouraged public schools, such as the one shown here, to provide students with instruction in their primary languages while they learned English.

English. Although some critics opposed bilingual education—claiming that it slowed the assimilation of immigrants into American life—there was little question that the United States was becoming an increasingly multicultural society. Coping with new immigrants, both legal and illegal, would remain an important issue for America.

■■ Large-scale Asian and Latin American immigration during the 1970s prompted support for bilingual education.

SECTION 4 REVIEW

IDENTIFY and explain the significance of the following: Patricia Harris, League of United Latin American Citizens, Rehabilitation Act, Education for All Handicapped Children Act, affirmative action, *University of California* v. *Bakke*, Russell Means, Education Amendments Act, *Roe* v. *Wade*, Equal Rights Amendment, zero population growth, Sunbelt, Wei-Chi Poon, Voting Rights Act of 1975, Bilingual Education Act.

1. **MAIN IDEA** Why did Native Americans begin to organize during this period?

2. **MAIN IDEA** What influence did the Asian and Latin American immigrants in the 1970s have on American society?

3. **IDENTIFYING CAUSE AND EFFECT** How did the impact of the civil rights movement continue into the 1970s? How did some whites respond to this legacy?

4. **WRITING TO EXPRESS A VIEWPOINT** Imagine you are a political observer of the women's movement. Write an essay that summarizes the impact of *Roe* v. *Wade* and the ERA on the movement.

5. **LINKING HISTORY AND GEOGRAPHY** Why did many Americans move to the Sunbelt states during the 1970s? What effect did this migration have on population patterns?

CHAPTER 31
Review

First Earth Day celebration held. Salvador Allende elected president of Chile. EPA and OSHA created.

Wage and price controls imposed.

Nixon visits China. SALT treaty signed. Watergate break-in occurs. ERA passed. Nixon reelected president.

Roe v. Wade decided. Egypt and Syria invade Israel. Saturday Night Massacre occurs.

1970

1972

WRITING A SUMMARY
Using the essential points of the chapter as a guide, write a summary of the chapter.

REVIEWING CHRONOLOGY
Number your paper 1 to 5. Study the time line above, and list the following events in the order in which they happened by writing the first next to 1, the second next to 2, and so on. Then complete the activity below.

1. Bilingual Education Act passed.
2. First Earth Day celebration held.
3. Watergate break-in occurs.
4. Panama Canal treaties ratified.
5. Iran hostage crisis begins.

Evaluating How did the Arab-Israeli war affect the United States?

IDENTIFYING PEOPLE AND IDEAS
Explain the historical significance of each of the following people or terms.

1. silent majority
2. Clean Air Act
3. Salvador Allende
4. Saturday Night Massacre
5. Barbara Jordan
6. apartheid
7. Anwar Sadat
8. Rehabilitation Act
9. Russell Means
10. *Roe v. Wade*

UNDERSTANDING MAIN IDEAS
1. How did Nixon's domestic and foreign policies differ from those of his predecessors?
2. What was the origin of the Watergate scandal? What long-term effects did this scandal have on the United States?
3. What domestic and foreign problems did Ford face during his administration?
4. How did Carter attempt to keep his pledge of an "open administration"? Why did he fail to win reelection in 1980?
5. How did the expansion of the civil rights movement during the 1970s affect ethnic groups, women, and people with disabilities? What caused white backlash during this period?

REVIEWING THEMES
1. **Economic Development** How did U.S. dependence on foreign oil affect the economy?
2. **Global Relations** What effect did Nixon's visit to China have on U.S.–Soviet relations?
3. **Constitutional Heritage** Why did Nixon refuse to turn over his White House tapes to the Justice Department? How did his refusal challenge the basis of constitutional government?

THINKING CRITICALLY
1. **Analyzing** What steps did the government take during the 1970s to clean up the environment?
2. **Synthesizing** What domestic and foreign policy actions by Nixon interfered with democratic rights?
3. **Evaluating** Do you think a government is justified in basing a policy of foreign affairs on the principle of human rights? Explain your answer.

WRITING ABOUT HISTORY
Writing to Create Imagine you are a member of the environmental movement. Design a poster for the first Earth Day celebration that illustrates your concerns about the environment.

STRATEGY FOR SUCCESS
Review the Strategies for Success on Conducting an Interview on page 894. Imagine you are a reporter covering the Camp David Accords during 1978. Prepare a list of three questions to use in conducting an interview with either Anwar Sadat or Menachem Begin.

Sadat, Carter, and Begin signing the Camp David Accords, 1978

| Nixon resigns presidency. Bilingual Education Act passed. | Mayaguez seized. | Jimmy Carter elected president. | Department of Energy created. | National Energy Act passed. Panama Canal treaties ratified. Camp David Accords reached. | Iran hostage crisis begins. Soviet Union invades Afghanistan. | Ronald Reagan elected president. |

1974   **1976**   **1978**   **1980**

USING PRIMARY SOURCES

During the 1970s, court-ordered busing was seen as one way of overcoming racial segregation. Read the following excerpt from an account about the effect of busing on West Charlotte High School in Virginia. What is the message of this piece?

> ❝ *The district judge . . . made it clear that he wanted socioeconomic integration as well as racial integration. . . .*
>
> *We are presently operating under [a court] order which forbids any change in assignment of a lottery-chosen white student assigned to West Charlotte High even if his family moves away from the area in which he was chosen. This has resulted in some bizarre transportation problems. In one case, we had to assign a driver and bus to pick up one pupil whose family built a new home and moved to the far northerly end of the county, more than 25 miles from West Charlotte High School.* ❞

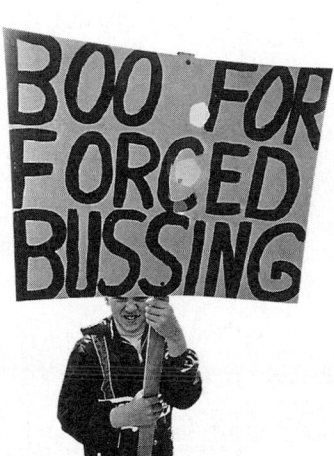

Young antibusing protester

LINKING HISTORY AND GEOGRAPHY

Study the map in the next column, which shows population changes in the United States from 1970 to 1980. Which states had the greatest population growth? Which regions were most affected by population growth?

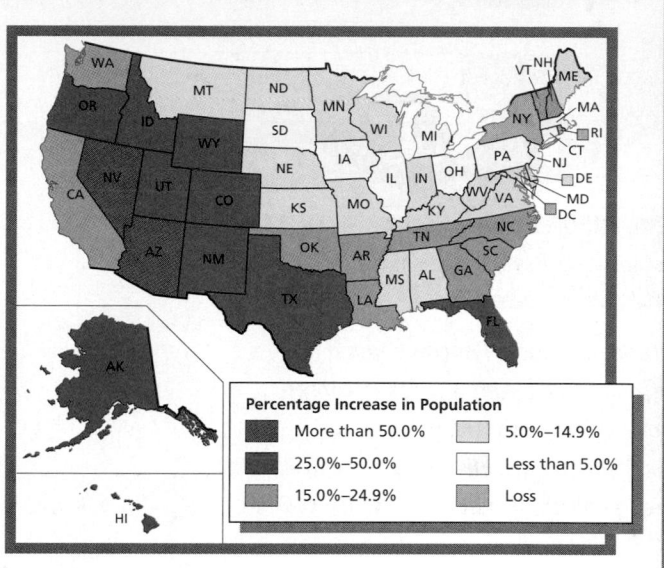

Percentage Increase in Population

More than 50.0%	5.0%–14.9%
25.0%–50.0%	Less than 5.0%
15.0%–24.9%	Loss

BUILDING YOUR PORTFOLIO

Complete the following projects independently or cooperatively.

1. POLITICS Imagine you are a *Washington Post* reporter covering the Senate investigations into the Watergate affair. Write a short article outlining the constitutional issues involved in the Watergate break-in, cover-up, and news coverage.

2. THE ECONOMY Imagine you are an economist in the 1970s. Create a flow chart that shows how increases in oil prices overseas ultimately affect the cost of consumer goods in the United States.

3. GLOBAL RELATIONS Imagine you are a United Nations delegate from an emerging nation. Conduct an interview with the secretary-general on the role the United Nations should play in establishing a world balance of power amid Cold War conflicts.

REAGAN, BUSH, AND CLINTON

FOCUS

UNDERSTANDING THE MAIN IDEA

President Ronald Reagan entered office in 1981 with a series of conservative reforms for the economy and foreign relations. His vice president, George Bush, won the presidency in 1988. Plagued by economic problems that his administration could not address to the satisfaction of voters, Bush lost to Democrat Bill Clinton in the 1992 election. In addition to the economy, issues such as increased immigration to the United States, urban racial tensions, and the spread of AIDS troubled Americans near the end of the century.

 THEMES

- **ECONOMIC DEVELOPMENT** What positive and negative effects might measures that cut taxes, social programs, and business regulations have on a nation's economy?

- **DEMOCRATIC VALUES** How might the use of modern technology increase democratic participation in an election?

1981	1984	1986	1988	1991	1992
Sandra Day O'Connor appointed to Supreme Court.	Ronald Reagan reelected president.	Tax Reform Law passed.	George Bush elected president.	Operation Desert Storm launched.	Bill Clinton elected president.

Public frustration with government grew in the 1970s as the Watergate scandal broke, the energy crisis emerged, and the economy continued to weaken. As a result, Democrat Jimmy Carter, who promised to reform government, was elected president. The Iran hostage crisis and runaway inflation, however, undermined his presidency, contributing to a Republican victory in the 1980 election.

Operation Desert Storm, 1991

*E*ntering the White House on a wave of discontent rising since the Vietnam War, Ronald Reagan promised to set the nation on a new course with his conservative political agenda of lower taxes, fewer federal regulations, cuts in social programs, and increased military spending. Reagan was an ideal president for the television age. Often called "the Great Communicator," he projected a sense of strength and patriotism that reassured Americans troubled by the nation's mounting economic problems and weakened image on the world stage. Television observer John Corry noted of Reagan: "His voice is his greatest weapon. It is not an orator's voice. It is husky, and sometimes it fades to a whisper. Meanwhile, it is extraordinarily intimate. Mr. Reagan does not speak to audiences; he speaks to individuals."

Reagan's vice president, George Bush, was elected president in 1988. Bush's greatest achievements were on the international front. Under his administration, the United States launched a successful invasion of Panama and played a primary role in crushing the Iraqi takeover of Kuwait. Bush's domestic record was less impressive, however. By the time the president ran for reelection in 1992, the country was beset by an ailing economy and other domestic problems. In a campaign that saw the rise of independent candidate H. Ross Perot and an increased role for women, Bush lost to baby-boom Democrat Bill Clinton.

Campaign button for presidential candidate H. Ross Perot, 1992

THE REAGAN MOVEMENT

FOCUS

- What was Reaganomics? How did it affect the country?
- Why did the Reagan administration consider events in Nicaragua and El Salvador important?
- What economic problems plagued the country during the late 1980s?
- What was the Iran-contra affair?

President Ronald Reagan and First Lady, Nancy

Ronald Reagan's 1980 presidential victory reflected the growing conservative mood of the nation. Adopting Reagan's conservative programs, Congress cut taxes and reduced federal regulation of the economy. As a result, the economy boomed in the mid-1980s. By the end of the decade, however, numerous political scandals and a soaring federal deficit troubled the nation.

THE NEW RIGHT

A former liberal Democrat turned conservative Republican, Ronald Reagan appealed to a wide range of voters who were disenchanted with liberal politics. Many moderate and conservative Democrats threw their support behind Reagan, proudly proclaiming themselves Reagan Democrats. Some of Reagan's strongest support, however, came from the political conservatives of the **New Right**. At the forefront of the New Right was Reverend Jerry Falwell's **Moral Majority**—a fundamentalist Christian organization founded in 1978.

Ronald Reagan and the New Right shared the same political goals. Both supported school prayer, a strong defense, and free-market economic policies. Both opposed abortion, the Equal Rights Amendment, gun control, and busing to end racial segregation in schools. To gain support for their causes, the New Right established research centers such as the Heritage Foundation and launched direct mail campaigns.

In addition to helping elect Ronald Reagan president, New Right conservatives were largely responsible for the Republicans gaining control of the Senate in 1980. They also played a significant role in shaping Republican policy throughout the decade. Although Jerry Falwell disbanded the Moral Majority in the late 1980s, New Right conservatives have continued to exert a strong influence in the Republican party.

◀ The Reverend Jerry Falwell's Moral Majority encouraged churchgoers to register to vote and support conservative causes.

REAGANOMICS IN ACTION

Ronald Reagan entered office with a comprehensive economic program already mapped out. The program, dubbed **Reaganomics**, was based on the supply-side economics argument that lowering the top income tax rates would spur economic growth. Supporters of Reaganomics claimed that people would use their tax savings to invest in businesses, thereby creating jobs, increasing consumer spending, and generating higher tax revenues. Congress responded by passing a three-year plan to cut federal income taxes by 25 percent.

Congress also supported another part of Reagan's economic plan—drastic cuts in government regulation of industries such as television, trucking, airline, and banking. The Reagan administration's probusiness, antiregulation stance was typified by the Department of Interior's handling of public lands. Against the angry objections of environmentalists, Secretary of the Interior James Watt leased huge areas of the seafloor to private companies searching for oil and gas. He also leased federal lands to coal companies. In Watt's words, the country should "mine more, drill more, cut more timber."

To Congress's and the public's pleasure, Reaganomics seemed to work. By 1983 the inflation rate had dropped to a manageable 4 percent. With inflation halted, Americans went on a shopping spree similar to those in the 1920s and 1950s. Business revived, the stock market soared, and the future looked bright.

Critics were quick to point out that not all Americans benefited equally from the recovery. Deep cuts in social programs—an important element in Reaganomics—hurt the poor. And although employment rose overall, joblessness remained high among African Americans and Hispanic Americans, especially unskilled workers in the inner cities. Unemployment among factory workers in the Midwest, once America's industrial heartland, also remained high. As a result, homelessness increased dramatically. Critics charged that Reagan's tax cuts favored the wealthy and that spending cuts and deregulation weakened programs that assisted those in need and protected consumers and the environment. They also warned that big tax cuts combined with increased military spending (another important element of Reaganomics) would produce enormous deficits in the federal budget.

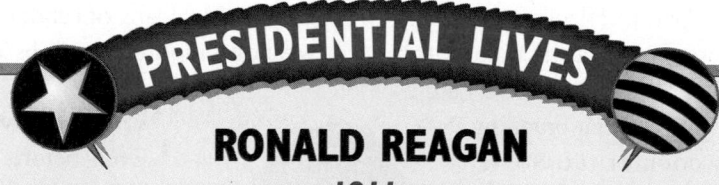

PRESIDENTIAL LIVES

RONALD REAGAN
1911–

in office
1981–1989

Unlike most presidential hopefuls, Ronald Reagan did not begin his political career early in life. Reagan was elected governor of California at age 55, the only office he held until being elected president at age 69. As president, Reagan always projected a young, confident image. One of his particular gifts was a sharp wit. After his first debate with Jimmy Carter in the 1980 election, a reporter asked if he had been nervous appearing on stage with the president. "No, not at all," he replied, then referred to his past

career as an actor: "I've been on the same stage with John Wayne."

Reagan's wit helped reassure the nation after a lone gunman shot him on March 30, 1981. As the wounded president was wheeled into the operating room, he looked around at the surgeons and quipped, "Please assure me that you are all Republicans!" While he was recuperating in intensive care, Reagan sent several humorous notes to his staff members, including one that read, "If I had had this much attention in Hollywood, I'd have stayed there!"

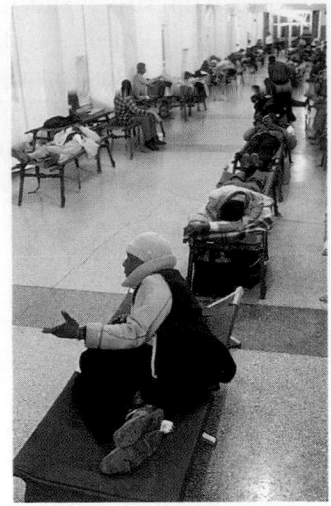

► Homelessness increased during the 1980s. This homeless shelter is located in Washington, D.C.

■■ Reaganomics stimulated the economy by cutting taxes and regulations on industries, but critics claimed the policies hurt the poorest Americans and increased the federal deficit.

*R*EAGAN AND THE COLD WAR

The Reagan administration's emphasis on increased military spending was in part a reflection of Ronald Reagan's strong anti-Communist views. Like British prime minister Margaret Thatcher, he took a hard line against the Soviet Union, even branding it an "evil empire." To counter the Soviet threat, Reagan called for new weapons systems and an increased U.S. presence in such areas as the Indian Ocean and the Persian Gulf.

New weapons. From 1981 to 1985 the Pentagon's budget grew from some $150 billion to about $250 billion. Critics charged that much money was wasted as military contractors padded their bills and officials

► Shown here is an antinuclear protester demonstrating in Copley Square, Boston, 1979.

invested too much in costly weapons that often failed to perform as promised. The MX, a new nuclear missile system, was one program that drew heavy criticism. Reagan's first secretary of state, Alexander Haig, heightened opposition when he suggested that "nuclear warning shots" might be useful in a conventional war.

The talk of nuclear war stirred public fear. In town meetings and state referendums, voters urged a superpower freeze on the testing and deployment of nuclear weapons. Many Americans marched in rallies to show their support for the freeze proposal.

To blunt the nuclear-freeze movement, Reagan proposed the **Strategic Defense Initiative** (SDI), a space-based missile-defense system. SDI stirred controversy. Critics labeled it "Star Wars," after the popular 1977 movie, saying it rested on untested technology and was probably unworkable. They warned that SDI research would intensify the arms race. Reagan countered that SDI would be a weapon for peace—one that killed weapons, not people. He proclaimed in a national address:

❝ I call upon the scientific community in our country, those who gave us nuclear weapons, to turn their great talents now to the cause of mankind and world peace: to give us the means of rendering these nuclear weapons impotent and obsolete. ❞

U.S.–Soviet relations. Even before Reagan took office, U.S.–Soviet relations had cooled because of the Soviet Union's 1979 invasion of Afghanistan (see map on page 905). Relations deteriorated further when, in August 1980, Polish workers in Gdańsk and Szczecin (SHCHET-seen) staged a series of massive strikes to protest high prices and to demand the right to form trade unions free from government or Communist party control. At first, things went well for the strikers. In late August, faced with the threat of a nationwide general strike, the Polish government legalized independent union activity. Labor

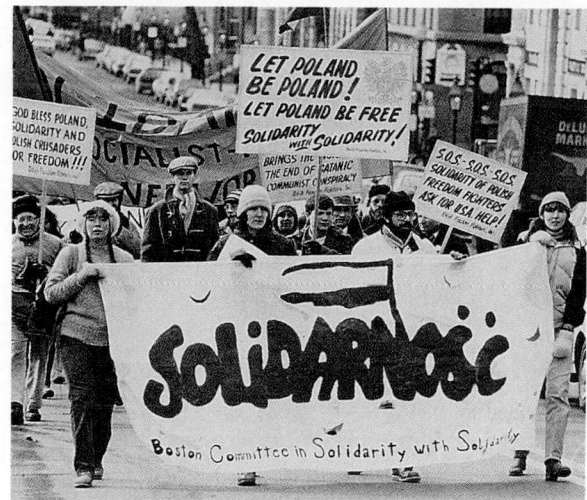

▲ Many Americans, particularly those of Polish descent, supported the Solidarity movement. These Boston residents marched to show their support.

nuclear missiles to England and Germany, the Soviets walked out of arms-control talks. When the Soviets boycotted the 1984 Summer Olympics in Los Angeles, relations between the two superpowers sank to their lowest point since the early 1970s.

REAGAN AND LATIN AMERICA

Fearing that the developing nations of Latin America would fall under the influence of the Soviet Union, Reagan pledged to increase U.S. involvement in the region. Of particular interest were the Central American countries of Nicaragua and El Salvador.

In 1979, Nicaraguan rebels known as **Sandinistas** had overthrown the dictatorship of Anastasio Somoza Debayle, whose family had ruled Nicaragua since the 1930s. Soon after Reagan took office, he cut all U.S. aid to Nicaragua on the grounds that the Sandinistas were backed by the Soviet bloc. The Sandinistas, he charged, were exporting revolution by shipping Cuban and Soviet weapons to rebels in El Salvador. When Nicaragua reacted to U.S. pressure by strengthening its ties to the Soviet bloc, Reagan decided that the Sandinista government must go. The assignment of overthrowing the Sandinistas went to the **contras**, a large army recruited, financed, and armed by the CIA. President Reagan called the contras "freedom fighters" and compared them to the founders of the United States.

activists responded by voting on September 17 to form the independent trade union **Solidarity**, under the leadership of Lech Walesa (vah-LEN-suh), an electrician at a Gdańsk shipyard who had helped launch the initial series of stikes.

Then in December 1981 the Soviet-backed government changed its stand and instituted martial law. Government troops shut down Solidarity centers and arrested union leaders. Expecting resistance, Soviet troops prepared to "restore order" as they had in Hungary in 1956 and in Czechoslovakia in 1968. Warning the Soviet Union not to invade Poland, Reagan called for new trade restrictions against the Soviets by the United States and its allies. The Soviet Union heeded the warning and stayed out of Poland.

Tensions flared again in 1983. On September 30, the Soviets shot down a Korean airliner over Soviet airspace, killing all 269 passengers, including many Americans. Despite international outcries, the Soviets refused to apologize for the incident, claiming the plane had been spying. Later that year, when the United States sent new

Many Americans opposed the CIA–sponsored war against the Sandinistas. They foresaw another Vietnam in Central America. Reflecting such fears, Congress began restricting funds for the contras late in 1984. But as the nation would soon

▶ The surrender of the Nicaraguan National Guard to the Sandinistas in July 1979 marked the end of the Somoza regime. Citizens celebrated the rebel victory by dragging a statue of Somoza through the streets of downtown Managua.

▲ José Napoleón Duarte is shown in 1984 speaking to a crowd during his election campaign in El Salvador.

learn, the White House continued to finance the contras despite the congressional ban, using funds secretly contributed by wealthy conservatives and foreign governments.

The Reagan administration also found itself pulled into events in El Salvador. In 1979 a group of young military officers seized power in the country. Though they promised reform, their government proved brutally repressive. The army and special death squads killed and tortured opposition leaders. Soon fighting erupted between government forces and rebels demanding radical reform.

In 1984, José Napoleón Duarte, a moderate, won election by promising to institute reforms and end the civil war. Eager to prevent a rebel victory that might allow El Salvador to fall under Soviet influence, the Reagan administration offered Duarte military and economic aid and sent advisers to train government troops. Duarte met with the rebels as promised, but as he later noted, he never expected success:

66 My government was not out to gain anything, nor would we give anything up. There was little hope for agreement on what each side visualized as the political future of El Salvador. . . . The important thing was to try talking. 99

The civil war raged on until intense international pressure forced both sides to sign a peace treaty in 1992.

Central America and the Caribbean, 1980s

SPREAD OF COMMUNISM The domino theory influenced Reagan's policy in Latin America.

? LOCATION Which countries did the United States invade or send troops to during the 1980s?

1986: Duvalier is ousted; political instability follows; Aristide is ousted in 1991.

1980–1992: Civil war between U.S.–backed government and leftist guerrillas supported by Cuba and Nicaragua.

1981–1987: United States aids the anti-Sandinista Contras in Nicaragua; civil war ends in 1990.

Communist country

Guerrilla activity or civil war

U.S. military presence or intervention

Capital city

Scale at Equator:
0   500   1,000 Miles
0   500   1,000 Kilometers
Scale varies with latitude.
Miller Cylindrical Projection

■■ Latin America, especially Nicaragua and El Salvador, became a crucial interest in the struggle between the United States and the Soviet Union.

REAGAN TRIUMPHS

Despite criticisms of his policies, Reagan's personal popularity remained high. His emphasis on patriotism and national pride struck a responsive chord with many Americans. While Carter was haunted by his errors, the public seemed quick to forgive and forget any mishaps or scandals in Reagan's administration. Congresswoman Patricia Schroeder once said of the president, "He's just like a Teflon frying pan: Nothing sticks to him."

Among the events that added to Reagan's popularity was a small-scale military action in 1983. On the tiny Caribbean island of Grenada, a military group overthrew the government and killed the prime minister. Several Caribbean nations requested U.S. intervention. On October 25, 1983, some 2,000 U.S. Marines and Army Rangers went ashore on Grenada, overthrew the coup leaders, and set up a government favorable to the United States. The U.S. action in Grenada provided some evidence for Reagan's claim that after the defeat in Vietnam, America was again "standing tall" in the world.

Soon after the Grenada invasion, Reagan announced that he would seek a second term in 1984, with George Bush again as his running mate. Former vice president Walter Mondale won the Democratic nomination. Mondale picked Congresswoman Geraldine Ferraro of New York as

his running mate. Ferraro thus became the first woman to run on a major party presidential ticket. Some predicted Ferraro's presence would increase support for the Democratic party among women.

Republicans had been taking steps to increase the presence of women in their own ranks. Reagan appointed several women to high public offices, including Elizabeth Dole as secretary of transportation, Margaret Heckler as secretary of health and human services, and Jeane Kirkpatrick as head of the U.S. delegation to the United Nations—the first woman to hold the post. In 1981 Reagan had also appointed the first woman ever to serve on the Supreme Court—conservative justice Sandra Day O'Connor. Republicans also made a special effort to win the support of women who felt abandoned by the feminist movement. The percentage of female delegates to the Republican convention increased from 24 percent in 1980 to 44 percent in 1984. In the end, Ferraro's presence did not add many votes for the Democrats. On election day, Reagan received 54.5 million popular votes to Mondale's 37.6 million. The Republicans swept the electoral vote, 525 to 13.

TROUBLE SIGNS

One issue that arose during the election was the shifting conservative emphasis of the Supreme Court. When Chief Justice Warren Burger retired in 1986, Reagan elevated Associate Justice William Rehnquist to chief justice. To fill Rehnquist's position, Reagan nominated conservative Antonin Scalia. When another justice retired in 1987, Reagan nominated Robert Bork, a federal judge and law professor who held a far narrower interpretation of the Bill of Rights than the Court had upheld in recent years.

Bork believed that much of the vast body of civil rights law was unconstitutional. Such views alarmed many people, including many senators. By a 58–42 vote, the Senate rejected Bork, handing Reagan a crushing loss. His next choice, Douglas Ginsberg, withdrew after press reports that he had smoked marijuana as a law professor. At last Reagan found a conservative judge who could also win Senate confirmation, Anthony Kennedy of California.

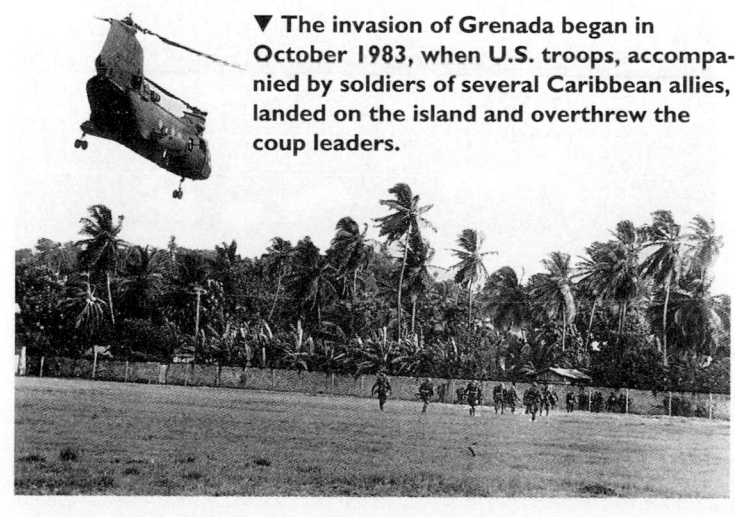

▼ The invasion of Grenada began in October 1983, when U.S. troops, accompanied by soldiers of several Caribbean allies, landed on the island and overthrew the coup leaders.

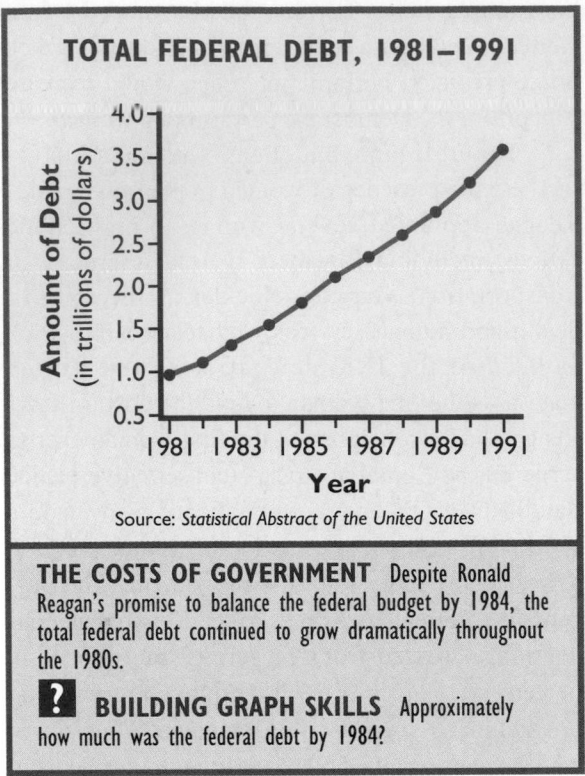

TOTAL FEDERAL DEBT, 1981–1991

Amount of Debt (in trillions of dollars)

4.0
3.5
3.0
2.5
2.0
1.5
1.0
0.5

1981 1983 1985 1987 1989 1991
Year

Source: *Statistical Abstract of the United States*

THE COSTS OF GOVERNMENT Despite Ronald Reagan's promise to balance the federal budget by 1984, the total federal debt continued to grow dramatically throughout the 1980s.

? **BUILDING GRAPH SKILLS** Approximately how much was the federal debt by 1984?

The failure of the Bork nomination was just one of several signs that the "Reagan Revolution" was starting to weaken. Of special concern was the federal deficit, which reached over $200 billion in 1985. Seeking to balance the budget with forced spending cuts, Congress passed the Balanced Budget and Emergency Control Act in 1985. Called the **Gramm-Rudman-Hollings Act** after its sponsors, the law required automatic across-the-board cuts in government spending when the deficit exceeded a certain amount. Other legislation took aim at specific problems. The **Tax Reform Law** of 1986, for example, wiped out many rules that gave certain groups special tax breaks.

The stock market also showed signs of trouble. Reagan's tax cuts and business deregulation had stimulated a stock market boom, but with this boom came a wave of illegal **insider trading**—the use of confidential financial information by stockbrokers for personal gain. Several large brokerage firms pleaded guilty to illegal activities and faced severe penalties. These scandals eroded investor trust in stockbrokers.

Then, on October 19, 1987, after several years of growth, the stock market crashed. On paper, stock losses totaled almost $1 trillion. Eastman Kodak saw the value of its stock fall by more than 30 percent. Many other major corporations experienced similar sharp drops in their stocks' values.

Another sign of economic trouble was the crisis that hit the nation's savings and loan (S&L) and banking industries in the late 1980s and early 1990s. Freed of federal regulation, banks and S&Ls, especially in the Southwest, had made risky loans to developers to build office towers, shopping malls, and other projects. In the late 1980s the real-estate market collapsed, and hundreds of S&Ls and banks that had loaned money to developers failed. Since the federal government insures S&L and bank depositors, it had to pay billions of dollars to cover these losses, further straining the federal budget. The federal deficit, the S&L and banking crisis, and other economic problems all remained after Reagan left office.

■■ **By the late 1980s the economy was suffering from a huge federal deficit, the stock market crash, and failures of S&Ls and banks.**

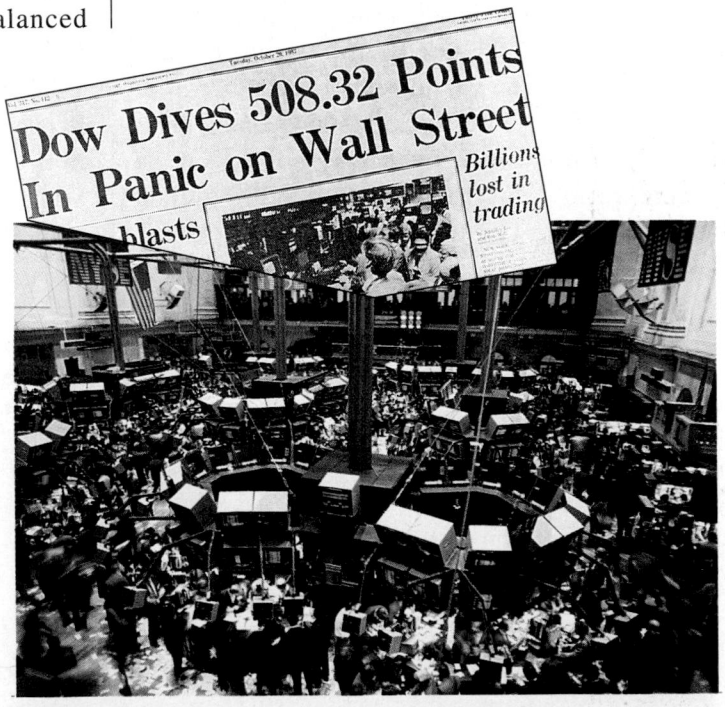

▲ Investors lost billions of dollars during the stock market crash of October 1987. Shown here is the frantic scene on the floor of the New York Stock Exchange on the day of the crash, as traders tried to sell shares and cut losses.

BEFRIENDING "THE EVIL EMPIRE"

President Reagan—and the American people—had much more to cheer about on the international front. The most significant event of Reagan's second term was a dramatic easing of Cold War hostilities. When Mikhail Gorbachev became leader of the Soviet Union in 1985, a new era of Soviet history began. With his nation troubled by a failing economy, a repressive political system, and heavy military costs, Gorbachev introduced a policy of openness, called *glasnost* (GLAZS-nuhst), that promised more freedom for the Soviet people.

Equally dramatic was *perestroika* (per-uh-STROY-kuh)—Gorbachev's plan to restructure the Soviet economy and government. On the economic front, he called for increased foreign trade and reduced military spending. The revenues from these changes were to be used to modernize factories. In a startling example of *perestroika,* the Soviet people in 1989 elected representatives to the newly created Congress of People's Deputies, the supreme governing body. It was the first election in Soviet history between competing candidates and the first by secret ballot.

To help achieve his goals at home and focus energy away from Cold War pursuits, Gorbachev pursued détente with the United States. In 1987 after a series of meetings between Gorbachev and President Reagan, the Soviet Union and the United States signed the **Intermediate-range Nuclear Forces** (INF) **Treaty**. This treaty eliminated all medium-range nuclear weapons from Europe and set up inspection procedures to ensure observance of the treaty's terms. Gorbachev also withdrew Soviet troops from Afghanistan. Addressing the United Nations in 1988, Gorbachev said:

> 66 The use or threat of force no longer can or must be an instrument of foreign policy. . . . All of us, and primarily the stronger of us, must exercise self-restraint and totally rule out any outward-oriented use of force. 99

In May 1988, as the Senate prepared to ratify the INF Treaty, Reagan boarded a jet for Moscow. In a glare of media attention, the U.S. president and the Soviet leader embraced like old friends.

▲ On June 1, 1988, President Ronald Reagan and Soviet leader Mikhail Gorbachev embraced during a Moscow ceremony celebrating ratification of the INF Treaty.

■■ **During Reagan's second term U.S.–Soviet relations improved dramatically as Gorbachev instituted *glasnost* and *perestroika*.**

THE IRAN-CONTRA AFFAIR

While relations with the Soviet Union were improving, the Reagan administration continued to face frustrating problems in the Middle East and Latin America. These frustrations led to the most serious crisis to hit the Reagan White House—the **Iran-contra affair**.

After Congress cut off funds for the contras' war against Nicaragua's Sandinista government, the Reagan administration sought other sources of funding. At the time, the White House was secretly bargaining with Iran for the release of U.S. hostages held in Lebanon by pro-Iranian groups. As part of the bargain, the administration shipped more than 500 antitank missiles to Iran by way of Israel. Without informing Congress, the administration used the profits from these arms sales to pay for weapons and supplies for the contras.

When the arms sales became public in 1986, Reagan appointed a committee to investigate. The committee cleared Reagan of any direct involvement but heavily criticized other White House officials, some of whom resigned. The secret funding of the contra war soon became known also. It was revealed that Lieutenant Colonel Oliver North, a White House aide, had funneled millions of dollars from the Iranian arms sales to the contras after Congress had forbidden aid.

In 1987, House and Senate committees investigated the affair. North admitted that he and his secretary, Fawn Hall, had destroyed key documents. But North emotionally insisted that he had acted out of loyalty and patriotism. North testified: "I'm not in the habit of questioning my superiors. . . . I don't believe that what we did even under those circumstances is wrong or illegal."

In its report the congressional committee denounced North's activities and criticized the loose White House management style that had allowed North to operate as he did. The chairman of the Senate committee, Senator Daniel Inouye of Hawaii, countered North's claim that he was just following orders. Said Inouye:

66 [The] colonel was well aware that he was subject to the Uniform Code of Military Justice. . . .

And that code makes it abundantly clear that orders of a superior officer must be obeyed by subordinate members—but it is lawful orders. . . . In fact, it says members of the military have an obligation to disobey unlawful orders. 99

In 1988 a court-appointed special prosecutor filed criminal charges against North and President Reagan's national security adviser, Admiral John Poindexter. North was convicted on various charges, including the destruction of government documents and lying to Congress. The conviction was later reversed on a legal technicality.

■■ **The Iran-contra affair involved illegal actions by White House aides to provide funding for the Nicaraguan contras through arms sales to Iran.**

◀ **Fawn Hall was called to testify before the congressional committee investigating the Iran-contra affair in 1987.**

SECTION 1 REVIEW

IDENTIFY and explain the significance of the following: New Right, Moral Majority, Reaganomics, Strategic Defense Initiative, Solidarity, Sandinistas, contras, José Napoleón Duarte, Geraldine Ferraro, Sandra Day O'Connor, Gramm-Rudman-Hollings Act, Tax Reform Law, insider trading, *glasnost*, *perestroika*, Intermediate-range Nuclear Forces Treaty, Iran-contra affair.

LOCATE and explain the importance of the following: Nicaragua, El Salvador, Grenada.

1. **MAIN IDEA** How did Reagan's economic policies both help and hurt the country?

2. **MAIN IDEA** What factors weakened the U.S. economy during the late 1980s?

3. **GAINING A MULTICULTURAL PERSPECTIVE** Imagine you are a citizen of El Salvador in the early 1980s. Describe the political situation in your country and explain why you think the United States is intervening in your country's affairs.

4. **WRITING TO INFORM** Imagine you are a member of the congressional committee appointed to investigate the Iran-contra affair. Write a letter to your constituents that summarizes the results of the investigation.

5. **ASSESSING CONSEQUENCES** How did each political party try to appeal to women voters in the 1984 presidential election?

Section 2

FROM BUSH TO CLINTON

FOCUS

■ **How did Operation Desert Storm differ from previous American military conflicts?**

■ **What were some of the domestic problems President Bush faced?**

■ **How did the 1992 election and President Clinton's early policies reflect voter concerns?**

*I*n 1988 Vice President George Bush was elected president. Bush's popularity soared after U.S. troops defeated the Iraqis in the Persian Gulf War. But Bush faced many challenges at home, including a persistent recession that contributed to his defeat by Democrat Bill Clinton in 1992. Clinton entered office in 1993 to the optimistic theme song "Don't Stop Thinking About Tomorrow." The youthful Democrat had reason to be optimistic, having just won a close, hard-fought election.

Female soldier during Operation Desert Storm

THE 1988 ELECTION

With the popular Reagan unable to run for a third term, the Democrats hoped to regain the White House in 1988. African American leader Jesse Jackson, who had run in 1984, was among a large group seeking the Democratic nomination. Jackson hoped to attract a "Rainbow Coalition"—a diverse group of voters representing all races, classes, and creeds. Few political observers had taken

Jackson's candidacy seriously in 1984, although he helped generate the largest turnout of African American voters ever for a Democratic primary.

By the 1988 election, Jackson's appeal had expanded to encompass a wide range of voters. On "Super Tuesday," the largest single day of primary voting, Jackson won more votes than any other candidate. Governor Michael Dukakis of Massachusetts, however, won the largest number of delegates and eventually gained the nomination. Dukakis, the son of Greek immigrants, selected Senator Lloyd Bentsen of Texas as his running mate. Vice President George Bush won the Republican presidential nomination with young Indiana senator Dan Quayle as his running mate.

The 1988 presidential campaign proved to be one of the dirtiest in recent years. Initially, Bush tried to appeal to voters' sense of optimism

◀ Seeking to unite a "Rainbow Coalition" of voters, Jesse Jackson ran for the Democratic party's presidential nomination in both 1984 and 1988.

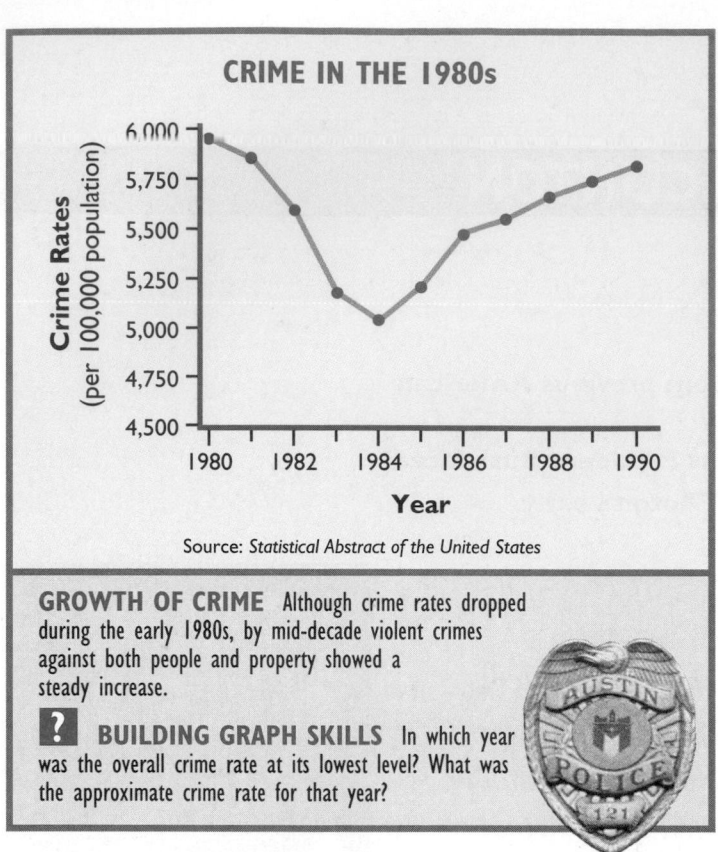

CRIME IN THE 1980s

Crime Rates (per 100,000 population)

Source: Statistical Abstract of the United States

GROWTH OF CRIME Although crime rates dropped during the early 1980s, by mid-decade violent crimes against both people and property showed a steady increase.

? BUILDING GRAPH SKILLS In which year was the overall crime rate at its lowest level? What was the approximate crime rate for that year?

by promising "a kinder and gentler nation." In the final weeks of the campaign, however, most of the Republican ads focused on negative issues. For instance, one commercial attacked Dukakis's record on the environment by showing scenes of Massachusetts' heavily polluted Boston Harbor.

The most controversial advertising campaign, however, was designed to sway voters troubled by the rising crime rate, which had jumped by over 12.5 percent between 1984 and 1988 (see chart). In a series of commercials and print ads, the Republicans painted Dukakis as weak on crime by associating him with convicted murderer Willie Horton and a Massachusetts prison program that provided prisoners with weekend passes. While out on a pass, Horton had escaped and attacked a Maryland couple.

Although some critics charged that the ads were racist (Horton was African American), Dukakis resisted using similarly negative ads in his own campaign. Instead, he tried to win the support of voters with his skills as a manager, arguing that the election should be about competence. This approach did not work, however. In the November election, the Bush-Quayle ticket won 426 electoral votes to the Dukakis-Bentsen ticket's 112. But the Democrats did increase their majorities in both houses of Congress and kept control of most state legislatures.

Election of 1988

LOW VOTER TURNOUT Only some 50 percent of those eligible voted in 1988, the lowest percentage since the election of 1924.

? LOCATION Which candidate carried Washington, D.C.?

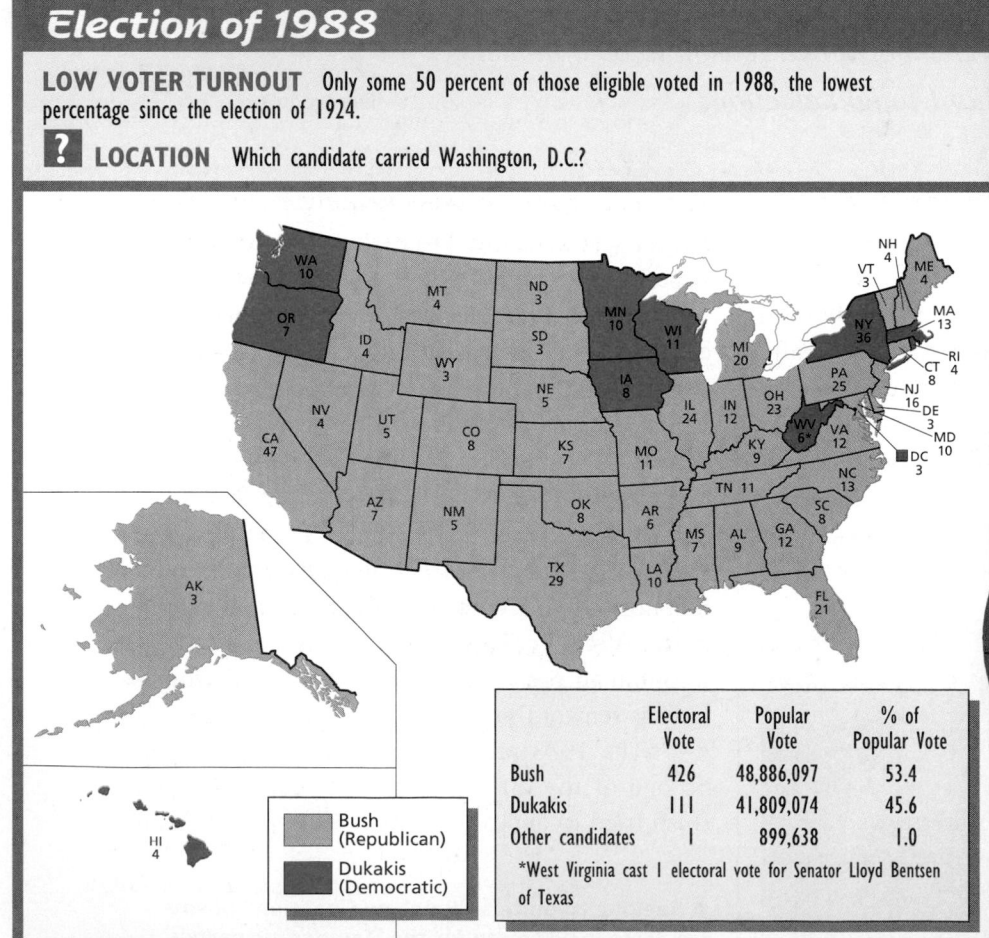

	Electoral Vote	Popular Vote	% of Popular Vote
Bush	426	48,886,097	53.4
Dukakis	111	41,809,074	45.6
Other candidates	1	899,638	1.0

*West Virginia cast 1 electoral vote for Senator Lloyd Bentsen of Texas

- Bush (Republican)
- Dukakis (Democratic)

▲ **1988 campaign button**

THE PERSIAN GULF WAR

Bush, who had served in numerous appointed government positions, including director of the CIA and representative to China, concentrated much of his attention on foreign affairs. He was determined to prove America's world leadership. Bush had his first chance in Panama, when in December 1989 he sent U.S. troops to arrest Panama's president Manuel Noriega, who was wanted on drug charges in the United States.

Operation Desert Storm. Bush again assumed a leadership role in August 1990 when Iraq, led by ruler Saddam Hussein, invaded neighboring Kuwait, a major oil producer. The United Nations condemned the attack, imposed economic sanctions on Iraq, and set a deadline for Iraq's withdrawal from Kuwait. As the January 15, 1991, deadline neared, military forces representing the United States, Britain, France, Egypt, and Saudi Arabia prepared for war. In all, some 690,000 allied troops—including some 540,000 Americans—amassed along the border of Kuwait. On January 16, the allied forces began bombing attacks on Iraqi forces and military and industrial installations.

The ground assault began on February 23. Within days the Iraqis had been driven back, and Kuwait's ruling al-Sabah family returned to power. American casualties included some 150 killed and 450 wounded. An estimated 100,000 Iraqis died. U.S. air attacks also severely damaged the Iraqi capital, Baghdad, and other cities. Many hailed the success of **Operation Desert Storm** and applauded the leadership of General Colin Powell and Secretary of Defense Richard Cheney. The commander of U.S. forces, General H. Norman Schwarzkopf, received a hero's welcome in New York City. Bush's approval rating soared to nearly 90 percent following the war.

A unique war. Operation Desert Storm was different from previous American military engagements. It was won almost entirely by the use of high-tech weaponry. Television reporters also provided unprecedented coverage of the war, including live coverage of the air war. Millions of Americans sat glued to their television sets as news correspondent Bernard Shaw reported the first allied bombings on Iraq:

66 This is [pause] something is happening outside. . . . The skies over Baghdad have been illuminated. We're seeing bright flashes going off all over the sky. 99

Military technology quickly became the star of the show as coverage of the war expanded. The technological nature of the war highlighted another

THE GULF WAR

THROUGH OTHERS' EYES

Although the Persian Gulf War was brief, many people were caught in the crossfire, including the residents of Israel. To retaliate against UN forces, Iraq launched an attack on Israel. Sari Nusseibeh, a Palestinian philosopher living in Israel when fighting broke out, recalled his impressions as the war raged around him and his family:

66 *It was January 29, 13 days since the aerial bombardment in the Gulf War had started. For fully two weeks we had been placed under a total 24-hour curfew, interspersed only by three two-hour intervals in which we were allowed to do our shopping. All of us—my wife, my three children, and myself—had taken to sleeping together on the floor of the sitting-dining area of our apartment. This way we kept each other company through the Scud [missile] scares (yes, even we Palestinians felt tense whenever the sirens blew, as we wondered each time where the rockets would fall, and what deadly poison they might be carrying). . . .*

For almost two weeks we lived in a state of suspension between TV scenes of missiles hitting Iraqi targets and footage of missiles flying over our heads. We were but one family in a population of 1.5 million Palestinians who had been confined to their homes. But Palestinian sufferings and fears were not aired on TV screens during that period—only the children giving vent to their primitive instincts of joy as missiles of destruction missed them and flew toward the enemy. 99

Desert Storm, 1991

IRAQI STRATEGY Saddam Hussein peppers Israel with Scud missiles in an effort to draw Israel into the war, and thereby drive Arab countries out of the coalition against him.

? MOVEMENT How did Allied strategy defeat Iraq?

1 Jan. 17: Operation Desert Storm begins with massive bombing of strategic targets in Iraq and Kuwait.

3 Iraqis set oil fields and storage tanks ablaze and pump oil into the Persian Gulf in an effort to foul a Saudi desalinization plant.

2 Deployment of U.S. Marines off the coast makes the Iraqis expect an amphibious landing.

4 Feb. 23: The four-day ground war begins.

7 Feb. 27: Allies liberate Kuwait City from retreating Iraqi invaders. Bush announces cease-fire.

6 Feb. 26: Helicopters bring in the 101st Air Assault Division to block the escape of Iraqi forces.

5 Feb. 25: Iraqi Scud missile kills 28 U.S. service personnel in their barracks.

Legend:
- Allied countries
- Neutral countries
- U.S. base
- Allied bombing
- Scud missile attack
- Iraqi nuclear site
- Allied advance
- Iraqi forces
- U.S. naval vessels
- Oil field

0 150 300 Miles
0 150 300 Kilometers
Lambert Conformal Conic Projection

---

unique aspect of Operation Desert Storm—the significant role played by women. More than 35,000 American women served in the Persian Gulf conflict—some 6 percent of U.S. troops. Eleven American women soldiers were killed and two taken prisoner. Though the U.S. military banned women from serving as combat pilots, they served in almost every other capacity—including flying support planes and working on missile crews.

The role of women in Desert Storm and the nature of the war caused many people to question the usefulness of banning women from combat. Critics argued that, with technology playing an increasingly significant role in modern warfare, physical strength—and the differences between men and women—would become less important than technological skill. Over the past few years the number of women in the military had increased to the point that U.S. Air Force colonel Douglas Kennett commented that his branch of the service "couldn't go to war without women and we couldn't win without them." In August 1991 the Senate removed the ban on women serving as combat pilots, but continued to limit service in ground battles.

■■ **Operation Desert Storm was unique for its use of high-tech weaponry, live television coverage, and use of women soldiers.**

PROBLEMS AT HOME

Bush's successes in foreign affairs won him much popularity and international praise, but some critics charged that he was neglecting problems at home.

As the 1992 presidential campaign approached, several domestic issues began to concern the public and undermine the president's support.

The Thomas-Hill hearings. Bush continued Reagan's efforts to move the Supreme Court in a conservative direction. In 1990 he filled a vacancy on the Court with David Souter, a conservative New Hampshire judge. In 1991 when Thurgood Marshall announced his retirement, Bush nominated Clarence Thomas, a conservative African American judge and former head of the federal Equal Employment Opportunity Commission (EEOC), to take his place.

During the confirmation hearings, law professor Anita Hill, a former associate of Thomas's at the EEOC, accused the nominee of **sexual harassment**—the use of unwelcome sexual language or behavior that creates a hostile working environment. In televised hearings, the Senate Judiciary Committee investigated her charges. The tactics used by some members of the committee, which included suggestions that Hill could be "destroyed and belittled" for testifying, outraged many women. After the Senate narrowly approved the Thomas nomination, female activists vowed to show their disapproval in the next election.

▲ During confirmation hearings for Supreme Court nominee Clarence Thomas (left), law professor Anita Hill (right) accused Thomas of sexual harassment. The Senate approved Thomas's nomination, in spite of an outcry by female activists.

Across the country the hearings stirred debate about sexual harassment. Many women told of experiencing harassment as they tried to succeed in male-dominated fields. One senate aide explained why some women, including herself, tolerated harassment:

66 You know what the code is, and if you want to be involved, you know what you have to tolerate. It's happened to me, and I never call anyone on it. You have to show you are tough enough to take a certain kind of harassment. 99

PRESIDENTIAL LIVES

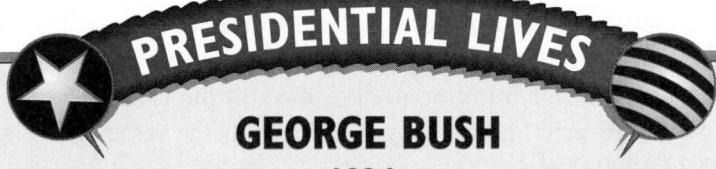

GEORGE BUSH
1924–

*in office
1989–1993*

Following a popular and charismatic president such as Ronald Reagan was not easy for George Bush. Throughout the 1988 campaign he was constantly fighting "the wimp factor"—the accusation that he was a weak politician and a better follower than leader. This charge seemed particularly ironic for Bush, who had served bravely as a pilot in World War II.

At the age of 18, George Bush became one of the youngest commissioned pilots in the navy. He flew 58 missions in all

and was shot down once. Bush's experiences in war may have contributed to his strong interest in foreign affairs. During his presidency, memories of World War II came back to him when he considered committing troops to battle. "When it came time for me to send our kids . . . to the Middle East," he once said, "I thought back on my own experiences in combat and what it was like to be shot at. . . . Having been in combat rounded out my awareness of the human cost of war."

The debate became more heated after news broke of wide-scale sexual harassment of female officers at a naval convention in September 1991. An earlier Pentagon study had revealed that two thirds of the women in the military had been sexually harassed by colleagues. Such revelations prompted the military to increase punishment of sexual harassment.

The economy. Many women reported that they tolerated sexual harassment because they could not afford to lose their jobs. Many people could relate to such feelings as the nation became more concerned with the economy. The 1991 federal deficit surged to $282 billion, with more than $350 billion predicted for 1992. The costs of the Persian Gulf War and the bailout of the S&L and banking industries added to the deficit.

The trade gap persisted as well. Though the trade deficit had declined from its 1990 high of almost $102 billion, in 1991 it still stood at about $66 billion. Japan's massive annual sales of automobiles and electronic goods to U.S. consumers accounted for a large portion of the gap. On a 1992 trade mission to Japan, President Bush and U.S. business leaders tried with little success to persuade the Japanese to increase imports from the United States.

Adding to these economic woes, a recession hit in 1990. As the economy continued to falter, unemployment rose. States facing budget deficits cut their welfare programs. The number of Americans living below the poverty line grew by more than two million in 1990. Despite repeated predictions of recovery, the recession hung on throughout 1992, complicating President Bush's reelection hopes.

■■ **Domestically, Bush faced troubles over the Thomas-Hill hearings and the sagging economy.**

WINDS OF CHANGE

As 1991 ended, most political observers expected Bush to win reelection despite the nation's economic woes. The president was still riding a wave of popularity from the Persian Gulf War. Only a handful of Democrats were willing to challenge him. Among these Democrats was Governor Bill Clinton of Arkansas.

 William "Bill" Clinton was born in Hope, Arkansas, on August 19, 1946, shortly after the death of his father. His mother, Virginia, later married Roger Clinton, an abusive alcoholic who adopted young Bill. Clinton's childhood experiences of dealing with poverty and a troubled home life greatly shaped his outlook on the world. Determined to improve society, he became a leader in school and civic affairs. When he met President John Kennedy in 1963, Clinton decided to make a career out of public service. After receiving a bachelor's degree in international affairs from Georgetown University, he went on to study at Oxford University in England, and to gain a law degree from Yale University.

At Yale he met Hillary Rodham, a brilliant young law student who later served as counsel to the House Judiciary Committee considering the impeachment of Nixon. Rodham and Clinton married in 1975. Three years later Clinton became the nation's youngest governor when he was elected to lead Arkansas. As a baby boomer, Clinton reflected many traits of his generation. He opposed the war in Vietnam and for a time tried to avoid being drafted. He was also heavily influenced by the idealism of the Kennedy era. Reflecting the impact of the civil rights movement, he believed strongly in the value of diversity and equality.

The impact of the women's movement on the baby-boom generation was noted most clearly in Clinton's relationship with his wife. One friend of the couple observed, "I know brighter people singly, but I do not know any married couple with their combined strengths." In the early 1990s Hillary Rodham Clinton was rated one of the top lawyers in the United States. As first lady of Arkansas, she served on several influential committees, including one that developed a ground-breaking education-reform program.

▲ **Hillary Rodham Clinton advised her husband on a number of key issues during the 1992 presidential campaign.**

Some observers noted that Hillary Rodham Clinton was qualified to run for president herself. Acknowledging this fact, Bill Clinton said during the 1992 campaign that voters would be getting "two for the price of one" if he were elected president.

THE 1992 ELECTION

The 1992 election proved to be different from any in recent history. After years of low voter participation, people turned out in droves to make their voices heard. Candidates used public forums such as television talk shows and radio call-in programs to answer questions directly from the public. A master of this electronic format was independent presidential candidate H. Ross Perot.

Perot, a billionaire from Texas, ran as an outsider to the political process. He promised to bring a populist reform movement to Washington, D.C., by decreasing the influence of political lobbyists and by giving the public a greater voice in government. He also promised to use his skills as a businessman to reform the economy. Perot's message appealed to many voters who were growing frustrated with President Bush's inability to improve the economy.

Perot's appeal reflected the feelings of many voters that politicians were out of touch with the concerns of many segments of society. One group of voters who insisted on being heard were women, especially those outraged by the Thomas-Hill hearings. Shortly after the hearings, activist Eleanor Smeal had declared: "The Senate did more in one week to underscore the critical need for more women in the Senate than feminists have been able to do in 25 years." Women responded by running for public office in record numbers.

The increase in women candidates led the press to dub 1992 "the year of the woman." Many of these candidates achieved success in the election. Four prominent women Democrats won U.S. Senate seats, including Patty Murray of Washington and African American Carol Moseley Braun of Illinois. California filled both of its Senate seats with women—Barbara Boxer and Dianne Feinstein.

Elsewhere, other candidates and issues were also making history. Cheyenne chief Ben Nighthorse Campbell of Colorado became the only Native American in the U.S. Senate. Californian Lynn Woolsey, a divorced mother of three, became the first member of the House to have ever received welfare. Fourteen states passed laws limiting the number of terms politicians can serve.

▶ **Ben Nighthorse Campbell** became the only Native American in the U.S. Senate after his victory in the 1992 senatorial election.

In the national election, Bill Clinton's message of economic and social reform paid off with a big win. Clinton and his running mate, Senator Al Gore of Tennessee, won 43 percent of the popular vote and 370 electoral votes to the Bush-Quayle ticket's 38 percent of the popular vote and 168 electoral votes. Although Perot and his running mate, Admiral William Stockdale, did not win any electoral votes, they captured 19 percent of the popular vote—the most of any independent presidential campaign since that of Theodore Roosevelt in 1912.

■■ **The 1992 election saw increased voter participation, numerous reform candidates, and the presidential election of baby boomer Bill Clinton.**

CLINTON TAKES OVER

Once in office Clinton quickly set about implementing the reforms he had promised during the campaign. To help him achieve his vision of change, Clinton put together the most racially diverse and gender-balanced cabinet in U.S. history. His appointees included Mexican American Henry Cisneros as secretary of housing and urban affairs and African Americans Ron Brown and Joycelyn Elders as secretary of commerce and surgeon general, respectively. Other women appointees included Press Secretary Dee Dee Myers, Attorney General Janet Reno, and Secretary of Health and Human Services Donna Shalala. After a long search, Clinton also chose distinguished judge Ruth Bader Ginsburg to fill a vacancy on the Supreme Court.

Clinton's biggest challenge during his first months in office was tackling the economy. He proposed a radical budget plan that would cut

BILL CLINTON
1946–

in office 1993–

Bill Clinton's presidency marked many firsts in the White House. He was the first president born in the post–World War II era and the first president from Arkansas. Clinton was also the first president to play the saxophone at his own inaugural celebration.

Clinton's career goal as a young teenager was to become a jazz musician. He was heavily influenced by African American jazz artists and early rock 'n' roll stars such as Elvis Presley. He excelled at playing the

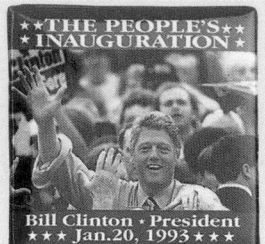

★★THE PEOPLE'S★★
★ INAUGURATION ★
Bill Clinton · President
★★★ Jan.20, 1993 ★★★

saxophone and was offered numerous music scholarships to college after he graduated from high school. Although Clinton went on to make a career in politics, he frequently used his musical talents in campaigns, such as during the 1992 presidential election when, wearing dark glasses, he played the saxophone on a popular late-night talk show. Despite his love of music, Clinton believes that he made the right career choice. "I would have been a very good musician," he has noted, "but not a great one."

government spending, raise some taxes, and overhaul the health-care system. Hillary Rodham Clinton took on the critical task of helping to reform health care. Clinton's most controversial budget proposal, an energy tax, was killed in Congress. Overall, however, most of Clinton's budget proposals won congressional approval.

Critics accused Clinton of moving too slowly on some issues. But his presidency marked the beginning of an experiment that would lead the country into the next century. As Clinton expressed in his inaugural address:

> 66 As we stand at the edge of the 21st century, let us begin anew with energy and hope, with faith and discipline. And let us work until our work is done. . . . We have heard the trumpets, we have changed the guard. And now each in our own way . . . we must answer the call. 99

SECTION 2 REVIEW

IDENTIFY and explain the significance of the following: Jesse Jackson, Michael Dukakis, George Bush, Saddam Hussein, Operation Desert Storm, Clarence Thomas, Anita Hill, sexual harassment, Bill Clinton, Hillary Rodham Clinton, H. Ross Perot, Ben Nighthorse Campbell, Ruth Bader Ginsburg.

LOCATE and explain the importance of the following: Kuwait, Persian Gulf.

1. **MAIN IDEA** What was unique about Operation Desert Storm?

2. **MAIN IDEA** What were two domestic issues that plagued President Bush?

3. **CONTRASTING** Why was the 1992 election different from any other in recent history?

4. **WRITING TO EXPLAIN** Analysts refer to 1992 as "the year of the woman." Considering women's roles in events during 1991, 1992, and 1993, write an essay explaining why the early 1990s might be called "the years of the women".

5. **ASSESSING CONSEQUENCES** What impact did Jesse Jackson's "Rainbow Coalition" campaign have on the 1984 and 1988 elections? How were the Jackson campaigns similar to that of H. Ross Perot in 1992?

AMERICA IN THE 1990s

FOCUS

■ How did immigration patterns of the 1990s affect the United States?

■ What were some problems urban Americans confronted?

■ How did government and businesses attempt to help working parents?

■ What health challenges did the nation face?

Leaving behind the 1980s, Americans faced an ailing economy and pressing social problems. The 1990 U.S. census revealed a population that was increasingly urban, southern and western, and immigrant. Americans struggled to overcome the economic problems and racial divisions that fractured many cities in the 1990s. Meanwhile, the rising costs of health care and the spread of AIDS contributed to the nationwide health-care crisis.

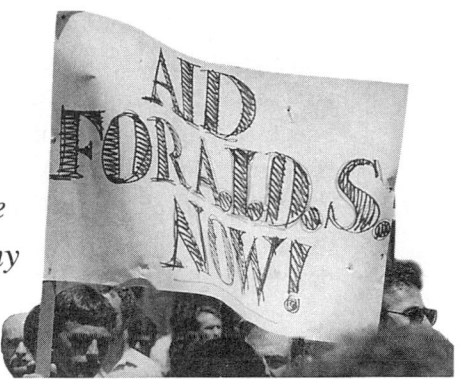

Rally supporting AIDS research

A NEW WAVE OF IMMIGRATION

In November 1991, U.S. Coast Guard vessels intercepted boatloads of Haitians bound for the United States. A military coup in September had ousted Haiti's first democratically elected president, Jean-Bertrand Aristide. Fleeing the growing political and economic chaos in their country, thousands of Haitians sailed to the United States.

However, bound by a 1981 agreement with Haiti and facing economic troubles of its own, the United States began to return the Haitians to their home country. Many politicians criticized the government's policy. "Returning Vietnamese, Russian Jews, Cubans, Nicaraguans and others back to the repressive countries from which they were fleeing

would have been unthinkable," declared Senator Connie Mack of Florida. "How can we justify it for Haitians?"

The Haitian issue underscored the continuing debate within the United States over immigration. The 1990 census revealed that immigrants had come to the United States in greater numbers in the

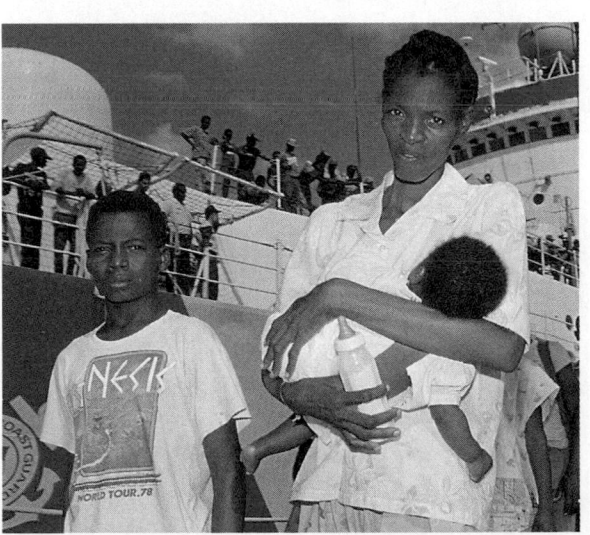

▶ The U.S. Coast Guard intercepted Haitian refugees, such as the family shown here, and took them to a temporary "tent-city" at Guantánamo Bay Naval Base. Some 2,500 refugees were housed at this base before being returned to Haiti.

1980s than in any decade since 1910, mostly from Asia, Latin America, and the Caribbean. This influx of immigrants alarmed many native-born Americans. Sixty-eight percent of the respondents to a 1992 *Business Week* poll thought that immigration was bad for the country. Many of those polled blamed immigrants for taking jobs away from native-born residents.

Supporters of immigration offered a different view. They argued that immigrants created new businesses that revitalized urban areas, helped increase U.S. exports by starting their own export companies, and, as employees, helped U.S. companies become more competitive globally. In addition, supporters of immigration noted that many recent immigrants, most notably those from India, the Philippines, China, and Korea, on average had more years of schooling than either native-born Americans or European immigrants. These well-educated immigrants contributed to many U.S. high-tech industries. Asian immigrants, they pointed out, made up about one third of all engineers in California's center of computer technology, the Silicon Valley.

▼ **New immigrants contribute to U.S. industry in many ways. Shown clockwise from upper left is a Korean bookstore owner, a Filipino travel agent, and an Indian businessperson.**

■■ **Opposition to immigration increased in the 1990s, although immigrants made many contributions to U.S. businesses and industries.**

President Bush recognized these benefits when he signed the **Immigration Act** of 1990, noting that "immigration is not just a link to America's past, it is also a bridge to America's future." The new law updated U.S. immigration policy by increasing the number of immigrants and doubling the number of skilled workers allowed into the United States each year. The act also authorized special visas for foreign investors interested in establishing businesses in economically depressed areas of the country.

As the United States witnesses increased immigration in the coming years, Americans will continue to grapple with the question of whether to welcome immigrants. Bette Bao Lord, a novelist who immigrated as a child to the United States from China, has urged Americans, native-born and immigrant alike, to unite:

> ❝ I do not believe that the loss of one's native culture is the price one must pay for becoming an American. On the contrary, I feel doubly blessed. I can choose from two rich cultures those parts that suit my mood or the occasion best. And unbelievable as it may seem, shoes tinted red, white and blue go dandy with them all. ❞

CITIES OF DIVERSITY

Conflicts experienced by immigrants included the riots that erupted in April 1992 in south central Los Angeles. The area exploded in violence after the acquittal of four white police officers accused of beating Rodney King, an African American. Most of the violence affected neighborhood residents and businesses as many people were beaten and robbed. Some looters specifically targeted Korean-owned businesses.

The riots disheartened people who had worked to improve relations among African Americans, Hispanic Americans, and Asian Americans in Los Angeles. Sylvia Castillo, a

Mexican American community activist who was a target of the violence, noted, "I knew I was outraged by the verdict and had always struggled against racism. All I could think was: 'Why are they [rioters] doing this to me?'" Rodney King himself urged people to "try to work it out" peacefully, asking, "Can we all get along?" In reality the majority of residents in south central Los Angeles did not take part in the riots, and many people braved the violence to rescue victims.

Miami, Florida, deemed the "new Ellis Island" by psychologist Marvin Dunn, also experienced increased immigration and racial tensions. In 1992 Miami had more foreign-born residents—including Cubans, Haitians, Nicaraguans, and Peruvians—than any other city in the United States. Boosted by a thriving tourist industry, the city's economy had boomed in recent years, but it had also seen three riots since 1980.

Tension in Miami was particularly strong between Cuban Americans and African Americans. In 1990, black leaders began a national boycott of Miami's convention facilities after Cuban American city officials snubbed African National Congress leader Nelson Mandela. Mandela had made favorable remarks about Fidel Castro, Cuba's Communist leader whose regime many Cuban Americans had fled. People from both communities tried to bridge the differences between them. After Hispanic American businesspeople agreed to hire more African Americans and patronize black-owned businesses, black leaders ordered an end to the boycott.

Throughout the nation, economic problems compounded many urban problems. Some analysts argued that bad economic conditions contributed to the Los Angeles riots. Once home to major companies such as Bethlehem Steel and Goodyear, Los Angeles in the 1980s and early 1990s witnessed the loss of many high-paying factory and defense-industry jobs. In 1991 alone the city lost over 200,000 jobs. Such loss of inner-city jobs was repeated across the country. Many of the companies that left the inner cities relocated to the suburbs, changing the faces of both the cities and the suburbs. Many of these suburban areas, termed "edge cities" by journalist Joel Garreau, now contain more office space than midtown Manhattan. While this development means more jobs for suburban areas, inner-city residents despair of being able to again attract the industries that could reduce unemployment in their communities.

▲ Tension flared between the African American and Cuban American communities in Miami after Nelson Mandela, shown here, spoke favorably of Fidel Castro.

■■ Inner cities experienced racial conflicts and lost jobs to the suburbs in the 1980s and 1990s.

WORK AND FAMILY

In May 1992 Vice President Dan Quayle sparked a public debate when he criticized a popular television program, *Murphy Brown,* for featuring a career woman who decided to raise her child alone. Quayle accused the fictional Brown of "mocking the importance of fathers, by bearing a child alone, and calling it just another 'life-style choice.'"

While some applauded the vice president's attempt to encourage two-parent families, others accused him of being out of touch with social conditions. "If the Vice President wants to say that a struggling unmarried 18-year-old and her newborn

◄ The television show *Murphy Brown* stirred controversy in May 1992 when the lead character, played by Candice Bergen, decided to raise her child alone.

The economic problems facing the United States in the 1980s and 1990s presented special problems for the nation's nearly two million Native Americans, more than 20 percent of whom lived on or near reservations. As in earlier years, joblessness, lack of education, and poor health care made life hard for many Native Americans. But cultural renewal, economic ventures, and successful claims of treaty rights offered promise.

The Shoshone-Bannock Indians of Fort Hall Reservation in Idaho were among the Native Americans who successfully pressed their treaty claims. In 1990, using the terms of an 1868 treaty with the United States, the Shoshone-Bannock Indians won the right to use water from the Snake River to irrigate their farmlands. The decision was the result of more than 25 years of Native American efforts to win greater political autonomy and economic self-sufficiency.

 BIO GRAPHY Wilma Mankiller, chief of the 108,000–strong Cherokee Nation, launched one of the most significant renewal efforts. Mankiller was born in Tahlequah, Oklahoma, in 1945. She spent her early years on a farm, where her family faced economic hardships and lived without indoor plumbing or electricity.

When Mankiller was 12, the farm failed after two drought years. Her family then moved to San Francisco, California, under the Bureau of Indian Affairs' relocation program. The adjustment to city life was difficult for Mankiller, who recalled, "One day I was [in Oklahoma] and the next day I was trying to deal with the mysteries of television, indoor plumbing, neon lights and elevators."

She soon became active in the American Indian Movement, which inspired her to become more involved in her community. In the mid-1970s Mankiller moved back to Oklahoma. She completed college and began working to promote economic growth in the Cherokee Nation. Stressing self-esteem and community self-help, Mankiller helped develop rural water systems, improve housing, and develop new businesses.

In 1985 Mankiller became the first woman principal chief, and in 1987 she won a tough four-way race and a subsequent runoff election. Mankiller compared her job to "running a small country, a medium-size

Wilma Mankiller

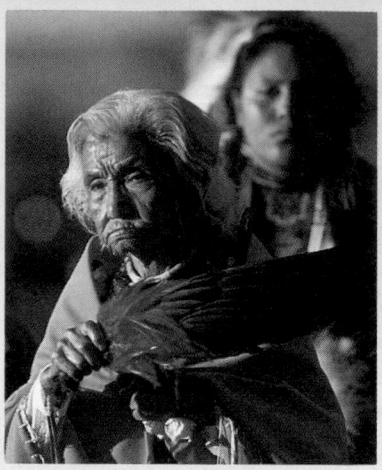

▲ The Shoshone-Bannock Indians successfully sued the U.S. government in 1990 to reclaim irrigation rights that had been guaranteed to them in an 1868 treaty.

corporation, and being a social worker." In addition to helping Cherokee communities create new jobs and provide better health care, the Cherokee Nation sponsored a program to teach students how to read and write the Cherokee language. "I can't help but feel hopeful about our future," Mankiller noted in her 1990 State of the Nation address:

❝ I think the strongest thing I see as I travel around to Cherokee communities and talk with people is their tenacity [persistence]. Despite everything that's happened to our people throughout history we've managed to hang on to our culture, we've managed to hang on to our sense of being Cherokee. ❞

are not a family," journalist Anna Quindlen argued, "then he has no idea what this country needs at this moment."

Anna Quindlen's remarks acknowledged the growing rate of single-parent families. From 1970 to 1991 the number of children living in single-parent households more than doubled. In 1991 some 20 percent of all white children, 60 percent of all African American children, and 30 percent of all Hispanic children lived with one parent, most often with their mothers. Most single parents faced the burden of parenting alone with only one income. Patricia Mull, a Los Angeles seamstress who stretched her income to send her daughter to private school, described the daily stress she faced: "I worry about the rent. I worry if I can make the payment in time. I worry if I have enough money left for other things. I worry about money every day, every night."

Many two-parent families shared Mull's concerns, as they struggled to balance job and family responsibilities. More than half of married women worked outside the home in 1988, up from about one third in 1960. The growing number of families with both parents in the work force and the growing number of single-parent families created the need for affordable day care. Employers increasingly began to realize that family responsibilities affected the job performance of their employees. To help employees balance work and family, a coalition of businesses in September 1992 announced a program to build more day-care and elder-care centers across the country.

The U.S. government also recognized the need to help working families. In February 1993, two weeks after his inauguration, President Bill Clinton signed into law the **Family and Medical Leave Act**, which President Bush had twice vetoed. The legislation requires large companies to provide workers up to 12 weeks of unpaid leave for family and medical emergencies without losing their medical coverage or their jobs.

THE GROWTH OF SINGLE-PARENT FAMILIES, 1970–1991

White children
African American children
Hispanic American children

Percentage of Children Within Each Group Living in Single-Parent Families

Year

1970*   1980   1991

* Data not available for Hispanic children.
Note: Hispanic children can be of any race.
Source: *Statistical Abstract of the United States*

POOR CHILDREN, 1990

15%
White

44%
African American

40%
Hispanic American

Percentage of children living below the poverty line

POVERTY RATE Single-parent families are more likely to live in poverty. In 1990 the poverty rate for single-parent Hispanic families was 68 percent, for single-parent African American families about 67 percent, and for single-parent white families nearly 45 percent.

? **BUILDING GRAPH SKILLS** What was the percent increase in African American children living in single-parent families from 1970 to 1980? What percent of Hispanic American children lived below the poverty line in 1990?

This legislation reflected the significant changes in attitudes toward work and family that have occurred in the 1990s. Florence Skelly, the vice chairperson of a market-research firm, noted in 1993 that "rather than trying to climb the economic ladder, people are becoming more concerned with relationships and family and community involvement."

■■ **Government and businesses issued new policies to help working parents juggle home and work life.**

HEALTH IN THE 1990s

Between 1970 and 1989, U.S. spending on health care rose from more than $74 billion to some $600 billion. The aging population, soaring physicians' fees, higher insurance costs, and more-expensive medical equipment accounted for much of this increase. Rising medical costs hit the poor and those without health insurance especially hard.

Fueling the health crisis in the 1990s was the alarming spread of Acquired Immune Deficiency

Syndrome, or **AIDS**. This is the final deadly stage of an illness believed to be caused by the human immunodeficiency virus, or HIV. By March 1993, AIDS had claimed the lives of more than 180,000 Americans, and some one million people had been infected with HIV. In 1993 it was reported that AIDS was the leading cause of death among men ages 25–44 in 64 U.S. cities and that new AIDS cases reported for women had more than tripled between 1986 and 1990.

AIDS has left almost no continent untouched. In the African nation of Zambia, President Kenneth Kaunda's son died of AIDS. In November 1991, basketball star Earvin "Magic" Johnson of the Los Angeles Lakers announced that he had tested positive for HIV. Other celebrities struck by the disease have included movie star Rock Hudson and tennis legend Arthur Ashe.

The World Health Organization (WHO) estimated in 1993 that some 2 million persons worldwide had full-blown AIDS and that some 13 million were carrying HIV. WHO expects some 400,000 to 550,000 adult cases of AIDS in the United States by the mid-1990s, with the number continuing to rise after that. The organization predicts that some 40 million people will be carriers of HIV by the year 2000. Other global health organizations place this number above 100 million infected people.

Some activists accused the United States government of responding too slowly and with too little research money to the AIDS crisis. The Food and Drug Administration responded to these criticisms

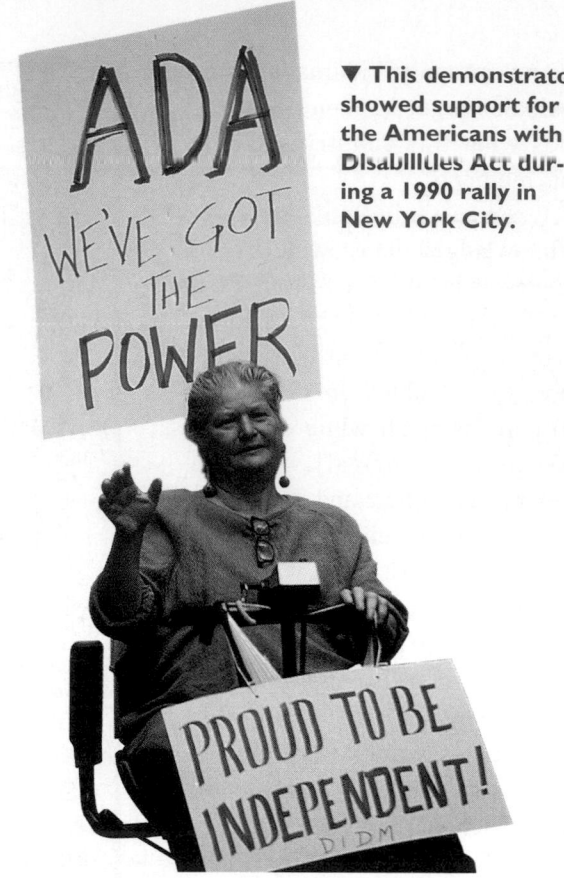

▼ This demonstrator showed support for the Americans with Disabilities Act during a 1990 rally in New York City.

by speeding up the approval of several drugs for the treatment of AIDS. Passage of the **Americans with Disabilities Act**, which George Bush signed into law in July 1990, also helped people suffering from AIDS. The act prohibits discrimination against people with mental or physical disabilities—including diseases such as AIDS—in employment, transportation, telephone services, and public buildings. The act also requires companies with 25 or more employees to remove structural barriers in offices.

▪▪ The rising costs of health care and the spread of AIDS led to a health crisis in the 1990s.

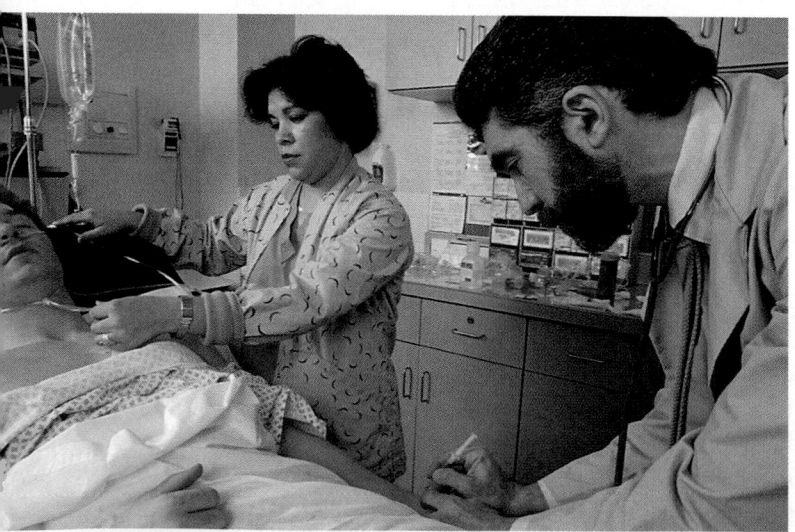

▲ The rising costs of health insurance, doctor's fees, and improved medical equipment created a health-care crisis during the 1990s.

𝒯ECHNOLOGY AND SOCIETY

Although Americans faced many economic and social challenges during the 1980s and 1990s, they also benefited from advances in technology. By the 1990s computers had become vital to American life. Computers guided robot welders on auto assembly lines and controlled the operations of car engines. Computerized money machines provided Americans with round-the-clock access to their checking and savings accounts. In 1991, one in four American homes had

▶ In 1986 NASA witnessed its greatest tragedy when the space shuttle *Challenger* exploded shortly after lift-off. All seven crew members were killed, including social studies teacher Christa McAuliffe (back row, second from left), who would have been the first civilian space passenger.

a computer for games, word processing, and financial planning.

Computers also helped make the workplace accessible for people with disabilities. Engineer Dillip Emmanuel developed an enhanced telecommunications device for the deaf (TDD) that allows people with hearing problems to receive telephone calls through a computer. Other engineers developed a flexible, customized keyboard, a computerized arm that allows people with disabilities to manipulate computer hardware, and software that can translate material into Braille.

Many of the advances in computers and technology could not have been possible without the work of the National Aeronautics and Space Administration (NASA). In 1981 NASA launched the first reuseable space vehicle—a **space shuttle**. Boosted by Reagan's support for space technology, NASA expanded its research efforts in the 1980s.

But NASA's research has not been limited to space flight. It has also been responsible for developing the communication satellites now used to link people worldwide. NASA has also been a leader in computer technology and robotics. Many technological advances once thought to be entirely science fiction—including **bionics**, the use of electronic devices to enhance biological functions—have become realities because of NASA's research. With the end of the Cold War, NASA has focused more of its efforts on technology for public rather than military use.

SECTION 3 REVIEW

IDENTIFY and explain the significance of the following: Immigration Act, Bette Bao Lord, Rodney King, Nelson Mandela, Dan Quayle, Family and Medical Leave Act, Wilma Mankiller, AIDS, Americans with Disabilities Act, space shuttle, bionics.

LOCATE and explain the importance of the following: Haiti, Los Angeles, Miami.

1. **MAIN IDEA** Why did opposition to immigration increase in the 1990s?

2. **MAIN IDEA** What economic and urban problems did inner-city workers and families face?

3. **MAIN IDEA** How did AIDS impact the nation?

4. **WRITING TO PERSUADE** Imagine you are the owner of a medical clinic. Write a speech that convinces listeners in your community that a health-care crisis exists in the 1990s.

5. **EVALUATING** How has NASA impacted science and technology?

WRITING A SUMMARY

Using the essential points of the chapter as a guide, write a summary of the chapter.

REVIEWING CHRONOLOGY

Number your paper 1 to 5. Study the time line above, and list the following events in the order in which they happened by writing the first next to 1, the second next to 2, and so on. Then complete the activity below.

1. U.S. troops invade Grenada.
2. Bill Clinton elected president.
3. Tax Reform Law passed.
4. Solidarity formed.
5. Thomas-Hill hearings occur.

Analyzing What was the purpose of the Gramm-Rudman-Hollings Act?

IDENTIFYING PEOPLE AND IDEAS

Explain the historical significance of each of the following people or terms.

1. Solidarity
2. contras
3. Geraldine Ferraro
4. insider trading
5. Saddam Hussein
6. Rodney King
7. Immigration Act
8. Wilma Mankiller
9. AIDS
10. Bette Bao Lord

UNDERSTANDING MAIN IDEAS

1. How did the Reagan administration fight the Cold War?
2. What challenges did President Bush face during his term?
3. What important issues did Americans discuss during the 1992 election campaign?
4. What benefits did the arrival of immigrants in the 1990s have for the United States?
5. What urban problems and health challenges did Americans face during the early 1990s?

REVIEWING THEMES

1. **Economic Development** What effects did Reaganomics have on the country?

2. **Democratic Values** In what ways might technological advances help increase voter participation in the election process?

THINKING CRITICALLY

1. **Comparing and Contrasting** How did the scandal surrounding the Iran-contra affair prove both similar to and different from the Watergate scandal?
2. **Analyzing** How did improved relations affect the United States and the Soviet Union?

STRATEGY FOR SUCCESS

Review the Strategies for Success entry on Comparing Points of View on page 420. Then read the following two excerpts from the 1984 presidential campaign. The first is from a speech by Jesse Jackson. The second is from a Republican commercial for Ronald Reagan. How do these two selections reflect different views of America?

> 66 Our flag is red, white and blue, but our nation is rainbow—red, yellow, brown, black and white. . . . America is not like a blanket—one piece of unbroken cloth, the same color, the same texture, the same size. America is more like a quilt—many patches, many pieces, many colors, many sizes, all woven and held together by a common thread. . . .
>
> Even in our fractured state, all of us count and fit somewhere. . . . We have not proven that we can win or make progress without each other. We must come together. 99

> 66 In a town not too far from where you live, a young family has just moved into a new home. Three years ago, even the smallest house seemed completely out of reach. Right down the street, one of the neighbors has just bought himself a new car, with all the options. The factory down the river is working again. Not long ago, people were saying it probably would be closed forever. . . . Life is better. America is back. 99

| Tax Reform Law passed. | | | | | | | Los Angeles riot occurs. Bill Clinton elected president. | Family and Medical Leave Act signed. Ruth Bader Ginsburg appointed to Supreme Court. |

Gramm-Rudman-Hollings Act passed. Mikhail Gorbachev becomes leader of Soviet Union.

Congress investigates Iran-contra affair. Stock market crashes.

INF Treaty ratified. George Bush elected president.

Immigration Act and Americans with Disabilities Act passed. Iraq invades Kuwait.

Operation Desert Storm launched. Thomas-Hill hearings occur.

| 1985 | 1986 | 1987 | 1988 | 1990 | 1991 | 1992 | 1993 |

WRITING ABOUT HISTORY

Writing to Explain Write an essay that explains the significance of the passage of the Americans with Disabilities Act.

USING PRIMARY SOURCES

After the Los Angeles riot, African American Willie L. Williams became the city's new chief of police. In an interview shortly after the riots, Williams expressed his impressions of African American concerns in Los Angeles. Read the following excerpt from the interview. According to Williams, what do African Americans want from police, and how has crime affected their neighborhoods?

 The African-American community wants strong, tough, honest, fair policing. There is no African-American community in America that does not want to see police there. The people want to be treated fairly. They want to be treated honestly and with dignity. . . .

Crime also has a long-term effect on the community because it drives out the mom-and-pop businesses, the corner stores, where a lot of shopping is done. It drives out the source of income for the teenagers and the young adults who don't have a lot of skills or are just going to school to learn skills. It often drives out the source of income for parents who may be living and working at home and working in the area. The cost of crime in the African-American community cannot be underestimated. **99**

LINKING HISTORY AND GEOGRAPHY

Refer to the maps on page 917 and page 938. Which states did the Democratic party win in 1988 that it did not win in 1980?

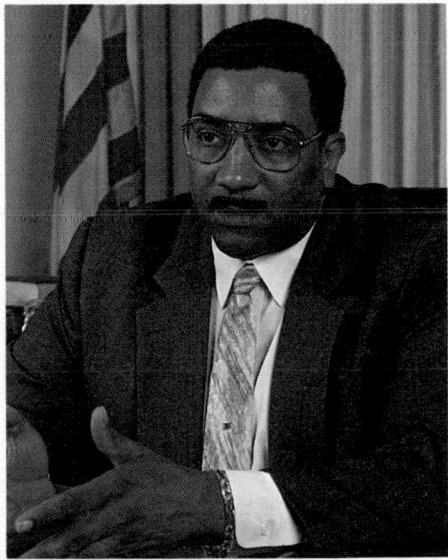
Willie L. Williams

BUILDING YOUR PORTFOLIO

Complete the following projects independently or cooperatively.

1. **POLITICS** In Chapter 31 you were a reporter covering Watergate. Building on that experience, imagine you are covering the Iran-contra affair. Create a flow chart that traces the Iran-contra transfer of weapons, money, and supplies.

2. **BUSINESS AND TRADE** Imagine you are the director of a private agency that assists immigrant businesspeople. Prepare a speech on how immigrant businesses are helping to boost your city's economy.

3. **THE ECONOMY** In Chapter 31 you examined oil prices and inflation. Building on that experience, imagine you are one of President Reagan's economic advisers. Prepare a pamphlet describing the principles and goals of Reaganomics.

A MULTI-CULTURAL COUNTRY

▪▪

EVEN before the founding of the United States, immigrants flocked to America from around the world. The origins of the immigrants have changed over time, however. The original Native Americans emigrated from Asia across Beringia. In colonial times the vast majority of immigrants came from Europe and Africa. Although Europe continued to provide the bulk of immigrants throughout the 19th century, more and more were from southern and eastern Europe. After World War II, immigration patterns changed dramatically as more people began to come from Latin America and from Asia. All of these immigrant groups have contributed to the diversity of American culture.

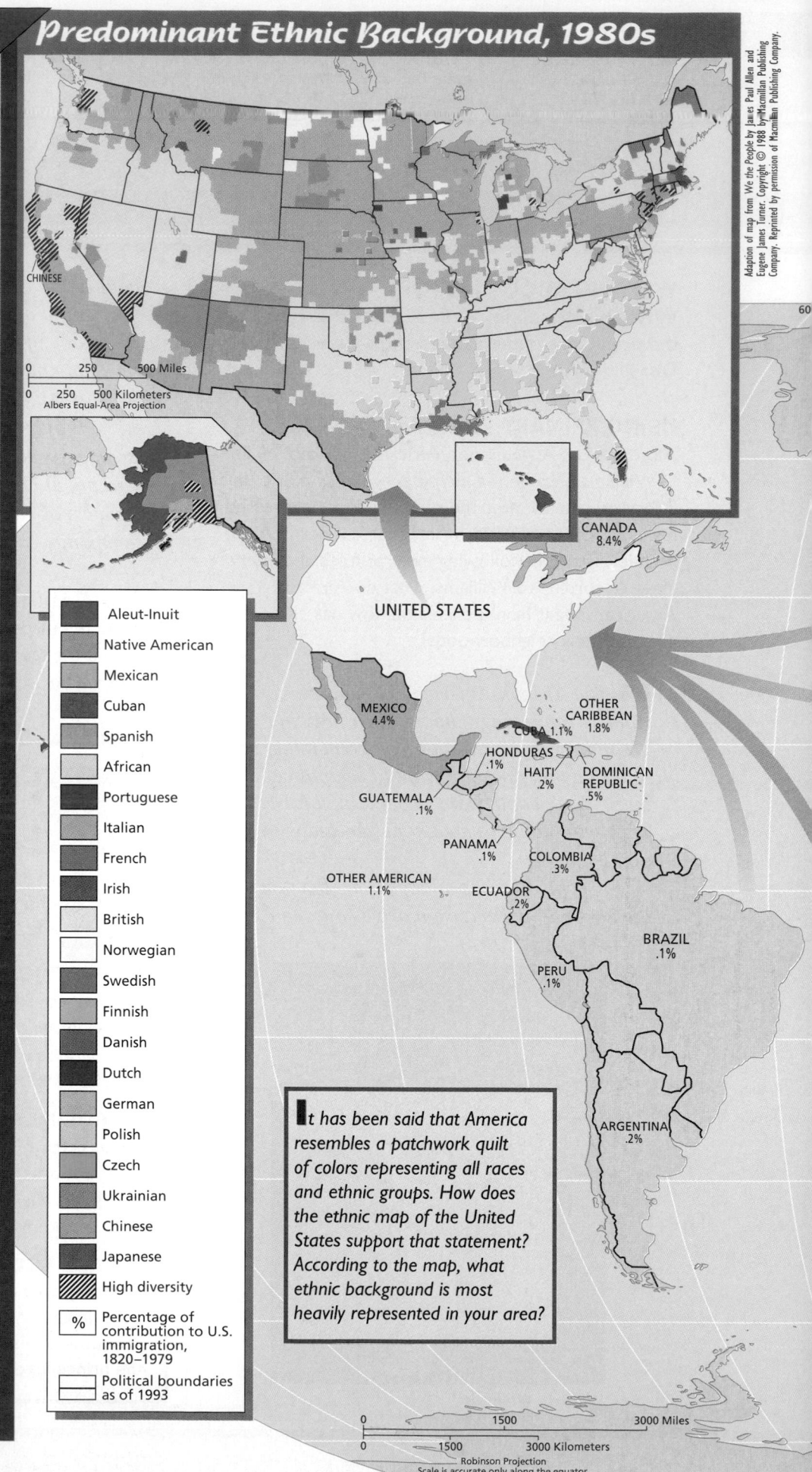

Predominant Ethnic Background, 1980s

Adaption of map from *We the People* by James Paul Allen and Eugene James Turner. Copyright © 1988 by Macmillan Publishing Company. Reprinted by permission of Macmillan Publishing Company.

CHINESE

0   250   500 Miles
0   250   500 Kilometers
Albers Equal-Area Projection

Legend:
- Aleut-Inuit
- Native American
- Mexican
- Cuban
- Spanish
- African
- Portuguese
- Italian
- French
- Irish
- British
- Norwegian
- Swedish
- Finnish
- Danish
- Dutch
- German
- Polish
- Czech
- Ukrainian
- Chinese
- Japanese
- High diversity
- % Percentage of contribution to U.S. immigration, 1820–1979
- Political boundaries as of 1993

UNITED STATES

CANADA 8.4%

MEXICO 4.4%

CUBA 1.1%

OTHER CARIBBEAN 1.8%

HONDURAS .1%

HAITI .2%

DOMINICAN REPUBLIC .5%

GUATEMALA .1%

PANAMA .1%

COLOMBIA .3%

OTHER AMERICAN 1.1%

ECUADOR .2%

BRAZIL .1%

PERU .1%

ARGENTINA .2%

It has been said that America resembles a patchwork quilt of colors representing all races and ethnic groups. How does the ethnic map of the United States support that statement? According to the map, what ethnic background is most heavily represented in your area?

0   1500   3000 Miles
0   1500   3000 Kilometers
Robinson Projection
Scale is accurate only along the equator.

Contributions to U.S. Immigration

Every day new residents arrive in the United States from throughout the world. In recent years many very small countries, such as Jamaica and El Salvador, have been huge contributors to U.S. immigration. Between 1981 and 1990, some 213,800 Jamaicans immigrated to the U.S.—close to 10 percent of Jamaica's total population in 1982!

TOP TEN CONTRIBUTORS TO U.S. IMMIGRATION, 1981–1990

Country	Percentage of U.S. Immigration
Mexico	23%
Philippines	7%
Vietnam	5%
China	5%
Korea	5%
India	4%
Dominican Republic	3%
El Salvador	3%
Jamaica	3%
Cuba	2%

Chart information from *The World Almanac and Book of Facts 1993* by Mark S. Hoffman. Copyright © 1992 by Pharos Books.

Map labels

OTHER EUROPE .6%
NORWAY 1.7%
SWEDEN 2.6%
FINLAND .1%
DENMARK .7%
GREAT BRITAIN 10.1%
IRELAND 4.5%
NETHERLANDS .7%
BELGIUM 4%
POLAND 1.1%
GERMANY 14.2%
(UKRAINE) .3%
FRANCE 1.5%
SWITZERLAND .7%
FORMER YUGOSLAVIA .2%
AUSTRIA AND HUNGARY 8.8%
PORTUGAL .9%
SPAIN .5%
ITALY 10.8%
GREECE 1.3%
LEBANON .1%
ISRAEL .1%
JORDAN .1%
TURKEY .8%
IRAN .1%
RUSSIA AND THE FORMER STATES OF THE SOVIET UNION 6.9%
AFRICA .3%
INDIA .4%
CHINA 1.1%
HONG KONG .4%
VIETNAM .3%
PHILIPPINES .9%
KOREA .6%
JAPAN .8%
OTHER ASIA .5%
AUSTRALIA & NEW ZEALAND 2%

AFRICAN SLAVE ARRIVALS TO THE UNITED STATES, 1701–1810

Period	Arrivals
1701–1720	19,800
1721–1740	50,400
1741–1760	100,400
1761–1780	85,800
1781–1810	91,600

Chart information from *The Atlantic Slave Trade* by Phillip D. Curtin. Copyright © 1969 by The University of Wisconsin Press.

The U.S. Census Bureau did not begin to keep track of immigrant origins until 1820. Since this was after the closing of the African slave trade, census figures on foreign arrivals do not account for the large numbers of Africans who arrived before 1820. The first U.S. census, conducted in 1790, counted African Americans as representing roughly 20 percent of the population.

In recent years immigration to the United States has become much more diverse. Whereas Europe contributed 90 percent of immigrants in the 1880s, it only contributed 10 percent in the 1980s. Germany, Ireland, Scandinavia, and Great Britain alone accounted for 68 percent of immigrants in the 1880s, more than the top ten countries combined in the 1980s!

CONTRIBUTIONS TO U.S. IMMIGRATION

1821–1830
- Asia <1%
- S. America <1%
- N. America 8%
- Africa <1%
- Other or unknown 23%
- Europe 69%

1881–1890
- Asia 1%
- Other or unknown <1%
- N. America 8%
- Africa <1%
- S. America <1%
- Europe 90%

1931–1940
- Asia 3%
- S. America 3%
- Africa <1%
- Other or unknown <1%
- N. America 28%
- Europe 66%

1981–1990
- Europe 10%
- Other or unknown <1%
- Africa 3%
- S. America 6%
- N. America 42%
- Asia 38%

Due to rounding, percentages do not total 100%.
Chart information from *Statistical Abstract of the United States 1992* and *Historical Abstract, 1975.*

AMERICA IN THE NEW WORLD ORDER

FOCUS

UNDERSTANDING THE MAIN IDEA

In the 1990s, world leaders faced the task of reorganizing relations in the post–Cold War world. As Japan and other countries gained economic power, many Americans feared that the United States would lose its place as the leading world power. Meanwhile, many world leaders worried about the effects of global pollution and health hazards such as drugs, overpopulation, and famine.

THEMES

- **ECONOMIC DEVELOPMENT** How might economic influence be more important than military strength in determining the political power of nations?

- **GLOBAL RELATIONS** What might nations do to resolve global conflicts in other regions?

- **TECHNOLOGY AND SOCIETY** How might technological advances both hinder and help the environment?

1972
Terrorists attack Israeli athletes at Munich Olympics.

1986
Chernobyl nuclear accident occurs.

1989
Berlin Wall falls.

1992
Operation Restore Hope launched.

1993
NAFTA ratified.

Cold War tensions decreased somewhat in the 1970s as President Nixon negotiated détente with Soviet leaders. But in the early 1980s U.S.–Soviet relations deteriorated as the Soviets became embroiled in turmoil in Poland, and the United States increased its activities in Central America. Relations began to improve, however, after the reform-minded Mikhail Gorbachev became leader of the Soviet Union in 1985.

Dismantling the Berlin Wall, 1989

*G*lasnost and *perestroika* marked the beginning of the end of the Cold War. World leaders now face the task of reshaping the international order in a new era—an era that is hardly peaceful. Bitter conflicts have erupted in many countries, and urgent economic and social problems spill beyond national borders. The most serious of these problems include nationalist conflicts in the former Soviet Union, conflicts over trade, an exploding world population, dwindling energy resources, and environmental hazards. And while industrialized nations continue to enjoy high standards of living, the developing world faces grinding poverty, malnutrition, and even famine. The task of deciding how the United States will address these global concerns is one of the greatest challenges facing American leaders today.

Although the world's problems are great, encouraging signs have emerged that the global community is prepared to tackle important issues. Organizations such as the United Nations and Amnesty International have tried to bring people together from around the globe to find solutions to pressing problems. Meanwhile brave individuals throughout the world are speaking out for justice and peace. As the leading superpower in the world, the United States is at the forefront of these efforts.

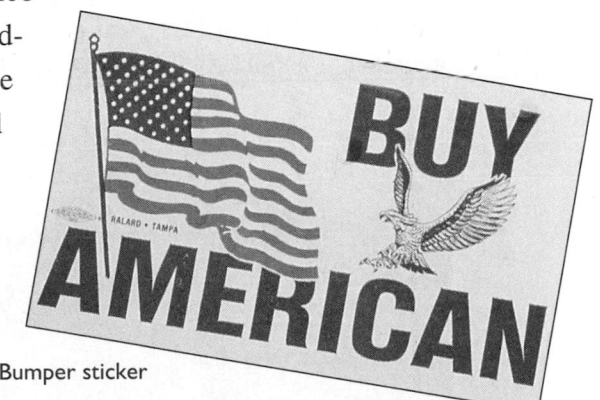

Bumper sticker

A NEW WORLD ORDER

FOCUS

- What events marked the end of the Cold War?
- How did the end of the Cold War affect regional conflicts?
- How did terrorist activity change in the 1990s?
- What role has the United Nations played in the post–Cold War era?

Mikhail Gorbachev's reform efforts in the Soviet Union led to the end of the Cold War—and eventually to the breakup of the Soviet Union. In early 1991, President Bush reflected on the promise of a new era free from Cold War pressures. "Now we can see . . . the very real prospect of a new world order," he declared, "a world in which freedom and respect for human rights find a home among all nations." But in recent years, conflict, crisis, and disorder have often seemed the norm.

Confrontation in Tiananmen Square, China, 1989

THE OLD ORDER FADES

Historians are still debating how far Mikhail Gorbachev really intended to go with the economic and political reform of the Soviet system. Undoubtedly, he meant to institute real change. But many argue that it is unlikely he foresaw the end result—the breakup of the Soviet Union and the collapse of Communist rule. Once set in motion, however, Gorbachev's reforms took on a course all their own.

Gorbachev's efforts to modernize and expand the Soviet economy led to a dramatic easing of Cold War tensions with the United States (see Chapter 32). They also indirectly assisted the democratic movements that swept Eastern and Central Europe in 1989 and 1990. No longer willing or able to bear the costs of propping up Communist regimes around the world, the Soviet Union announced in 1989 that it was adopting a policy of nonintervention in Eastern Europe. Thus the Soviets did nothing when Poland and Hungary moved toward free elections and the Communist governments in Czechoslovakia and Romania fell.

◀ Pro-democracy demonstrations, such as the one shown here, helped bring on the collapse of Communist party rule in Russia.

The Breakup of the Soviet Sphere

NATIONALISM The Soviets had kept a firm lid on nationalist sentiments. The collapse of the Soviet empire unleashed bitter ethnic and religious conflicts.

❓ LOCATION The U.S.S.R. and some of the nations in the former Soviet sphere broke up. Which nation was reunited?

Legend:
- Former Soviet republic
- Former East European satellite of Soviet Union
- ✪ Capital city
- Boundary of former Soviet Union

0 500 1,000 Miles
0 500 1,000 Kilometers
Lambert Conformal Conic Projection

The Soviets also did nothing to assist Communist leaders when pro-democracy demonstrations broke out in East Germany in the fall of 1989. Throughout the fall, tens of thousands of East Germans fled to the West through Hungary. Then in October demonstrators forced Communist leader Erich Honecker to resign. In an attempt to restore calm, the East German government opened the Berlin Wall on November 9 and lifted restrictions on travel to the West. But it was already too late; the pressure for **German reunification**—the reuniting of East and West Germany as one nation—was too great. After free elections, the two nations were united as the Federal Republic of Germany on October 3, 1990, without opposition from Gorbachev.

By 1991 Gorbachev had problems of his own in the Soviet Union. Alarmed by the pace of reforms, Communist hard-liners attempted to oust him. On August 18, 1991, they placed Gorbachev under house arrest at his vacation home on the Crimean Sea. The coup collapsed by August 21, but Gorbachev's days in power were numbered. On December 1 the Ukrainians voted for independence. A week later the presidents of Ukraine, Russia, and Belarus declared that the Soviet Union was "ceasing its existence" and that they were forming the **Commonwealth of Independent States** (CIS). Gorbachev announced on December 25 that he was resigning as president of the Soviet Union. On the same day, he turned over control of the armed forces to Boris Yeltsin, the president of Russia. By the end of 1991 the Soviet Union had completely disbanded. Eventually the former Soviet republics of Armenia, Azerbaijan, Kazakhstan, Kyrgyzstan,

Moldova, Tajikistan, Turkmenistan, Uzbekistan, and Georgia joined the CIS.

■■ The collapse of communism in Eastern Europe, the fall of the Berlin Wall, and the breakup of the Soviet Union marked the end of the Cold War.

In another part of the Communist world, however, pro-democracy reformers met a much different fate. In the spring of 1989, students and others took to the streets of Beijing, China, to protest Communist party policies. The government responded with force, sending soldiers and tanks against the peaceful protesters gathered in Tiananmen Square. Estimates of the number of protesters killed in the crackdown range from a few hundred to more than a thousand.

*R*EGIONAL CONFLICTS

As the threat of global war between nuclear-armed superpowers fades, regional conflicts have intensified. The end of Communist rule in Eastern Europe unleashed bitter ethnic and local disputes that had formerly been kept in check by Communist authorities. The region that was once the nation of Yugoslavia has been particularly torn by fighting between Serbs, Croatians, and Slovenes.

In the former Soviet Union itself, the 15 newly independent republics have experienced conflict as different groups struggle for power and self-rule. Russia and Ukraine have argued over

▲ In December 1992, UN forces helped stabilize the political situation in Somalia to ensure that food and supplies reached starving people.

control of the Black Sea fleet, while Christians in the former Soviet republic of Armenia have battled with Muslims in neighboring Azerbaijan (az-uhr-by-JAI IN). By September 1993 Russia was so unstable that Boris Yeltsin temporarily suspended the constitution and dissolved Parliament, sparking a major power struggle in the republic.

Unrest has not been confined to the former Soviet Union and Eastern Europe. In Africa the end of white-dominated rule in South Africa has brought a new upsurge of violence between rival political groups. Nelson Mandela, as leader of the African National Congress (ANC), played a central role in keeping negotiation over majority rule alive amid the violence. The African nations of Zambia, Liberia, Mali, and Somalia also have been torn by civil wars. In some countries these civil wars have increased social problems such as famine and poverty. In December 1992, United Nations forces, including many Americans, launched **Operation Restore Hope** to provide relief to famine-stricken Somalia. Fighting among rival clans in that country had prevented relief workers from getting food and other supplies to the starving Somali people.

■■ Regional conflicts in the former Soviet Union and in Africa have increased since the end of the Cold War.

In the Middle East hopes for peace between Palestinians and Israelis were renewed in September 1993, when Palestinian leader Yasir Arafat and Israeli prime minister Yitzhak Rabin signed a new peace accord. President Clinton, who oversaw the signing of the accord at the White House, called it a "historic and honorable compromise." Though the Clinton administration hosted the signing, the event capped years of efforts to bring peace to the Middle East. Cyrus Vance, the U.S. secretary of state during the signing of the 1978 Camp David Accords, declared of the 1993 agreement: "It is, at long last, what all of us who worked on the issue hoped and dreamed might one day come about. But we feared we would not see it in our lifetime." Such optimism was short-lived, however. On February 25, 1994, a Jewish gunman opened fire on Muslim worshipers in the West Bank town of Hebron, leaving some 30 people dead. Violence rocked the area in the wake of the massacre.

The Freedom of Information Act

Under the Freedom of Information Act (FOIA), anyone is supposed to be able to examine the records of U.S. federal agencies. Many people expected the FOIA to be particularly useful for scholars of political history. In reality, however, many scholars have found their use of the law severely limited by government red tape.

The congressional call for the Freedom of Information Act originated during the 1950s, when Senator Joseph McCarthy accused numerous government employees of harboring Communist sympathies. Several members of Congress began to push for an act that would allow easy access to government files on people accused of being Communists. By the time Congress passed the law in 1966, all government files were supposed to be open to the public unless national security needs clearly justified their exclusion.

Many government officials, however, claimed that the FOIA interfered with Cold War politics. In some circumstances, they argued, foreign agents might be reluctant to pass information on to American agencies for fear that the information might be made public through the FOIA. As a result of such concerns, numerous amendments were made to the FOIA to grant agencies exemptions from the law. Critics argue that such exemptions, coupled with the complicated way the government handles FOIA requests, have made the law virtually useless. This situation has been particularly troubling to scholars of political history, who cannot fairly evaluate government actions without inside information.

In the post–Cold War era, many observers have begun to press for an overhaul of the FOIA. One strong supporter of FOIA reform has been former Middle East journalist Terry Anderson. Anderson was captured by Islamic terrorists in 1985 and held hostage until December 1991. After his release, Anderson attempted to use the FOIA to research a book about his captivity. Anderson wrote to 10 agencies requesting information on himself, his fiancée, two other hostages held with him, and an Islamic group implicated in the hostage crisis.

Anderson received no useful information from his requests. Some agencies tried to delay answering for as long as possible. Others sent him information that did not relate to his requests or that came from public news reports he could easily have obtained elsewhere. In some cases, when he did receive classified documents, they were so heavily edited that they were useless. For example, one agency sent him 62 pages of documents, of which, Anderson found, "26 were totally blank, 20 showed only addresses with all the text [blacked out], 3 were newspaper reports, and 3 were reports on terrorism outside the Middle East."

As more people push for reform of the law they say is "outmoded by Cold War assumptions," scholars are hopeful that government documents will become more accessible. If reform of the FOIA opens new files to researchers, it may allow historians to examine and evaluate the Cold War period in a new light.

▲ **Terry Anderson tried to use the FOIA to obtain information for his 1993 book *Den of Lions.***

TERRORISM

Another effect of the end of the Cold War has been an increase in terrorist activity throughout the world. According to one group of experts, the number of terrorist acts rose by 11 percent from 1991 to 1992. Terrorism has been a global problem for many years. The 1972 Summer Olympics in Munich, West Germany, were marred when eight Arab terrorists killed two Israeli athletes and took nine others hostage. The standoff ended in a gun battle that left 15 people dead.

Over the past few decades, much terrorist activity has been highly organized and sponsored by the government of a particular country against an enemy nation. American leaders have been quick to respond to international terrorism linked directly to a particular nation. In 1986 President Reagan ordered a bombing attack on Libya after evidence tied that country's leader, Muammar Qaddafi (kuh-DAHF-ee), to an attack on a West Berlin nightclub that killed one American serviceman and injured many others. In the summer of 1993, President Clinton ordered the bombing of Iraqi Intelligence Service headquarters after the FBI uncovered an Iraqi plot to assassinate former president George Bush.

In recent years, however, terrorism by small groups and individuals has grown dramatically. Some of this terrorist activity has been directed at the United States. Americans were stunned on February 26, 1993, when a bomb blast rocked the World Trade Center in New York City, killing six people and injuring more than a thousand. The suspects arrested in the bombing were all tied to an Egyptian fundamentalist leader linked to several terrorist acts. In the summer of 1993, New York police prevented an even more severe attack when they arrested a group that was planning to bomb the United Nations, FBI offices, and the Lincoln and Holland tunnels under the Hudson River. Bruce Hoffman, a terrorism expert for the Rand Corporation, predicts that terrorism "is going to join . . . crime as one of the things we have to worry about in American cities."

■■ **Terrorist activity by small groups has been increasingly aimed at the United States.**

PROMOTING PEACE

With the end of the Cold War, many hope that the United Nations will at last become the international force for peace that its planners had envisioned. By 1992, thousands of UN forces were serving on peacekeeping missions throughout the world. By 1993, however, the United Nations had compiled a mixed record in dealing with the most-dangerous situations. UN forces in Somalia were not able to defeat the ill-equipped clans that were preventing relief efforts in that country. In Bosnia and Herzegovina, a former state of Yugoslavia, ethnic fighting among Serbs, Croatians, and Muslims left some 150,000 people dead or missing by the end of 1993. Although the United Nations sent peacekeeping forces to the area and launched an investigation into alleged war crimes of Serbian leaders, UN efforts seemed to do little to stop the fighting. In places such as Cambodia and El Salvador, however, UN peacekeepers played a more successful role.

NEGOTIATING WITH TERRORISTS

THROUGH OTHERS' EYES

*O*ne of the most-active terrorist organizations of the late 20th century has been the Irish Republican Army (IRA), a nationalist group protesting British control over Northern Ireland. In 1993 it was revealed that the British government had been trying to secretly negotiate peace with the Irish Republican Army, despite a long-standing policy against negotiating with terrorists. Although critics predicted the move would fail, Prime Minister Albert Reynolds of the Republic of Ireland cautioned, "This is the time for all political leaders to exercise calm, clear thinking, and courage to insure . . . peace." Added Sir Patrick Mayhew, the British secretary of state for Northern Ireland, "Peace, properly attained, is a prize worth risks."

Leaders in the United States criticized UN handling of the Bosnian crisis as President Clinton debated whether to commit U.S. troops to the mission. After peace talks fell apart in September 1993, Clinton vowed that any U.S. military intervention would have to be part of a major NATO operation, similar to Operation Desert Storm.

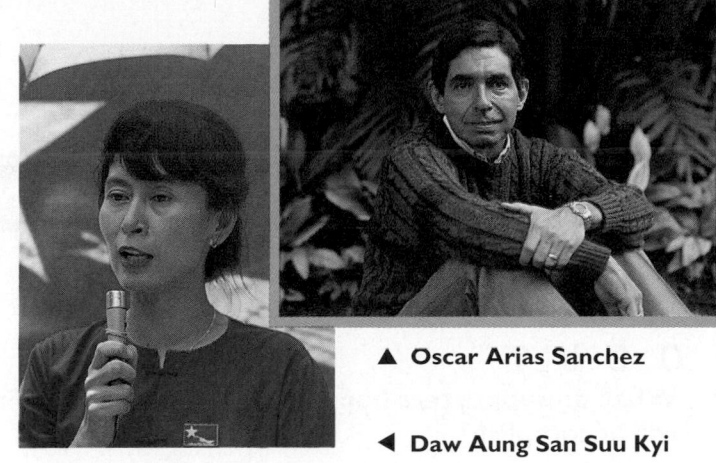

▲ Oscar Arias Sanchez

◄ Daw Aung San Suu Kyi

■■ The United Nations has played the role of peacekeeper in the post–Cold War era, with mixed results.

Efforts at promoting world peace have not been limited to the UN. Since the end of the Cold War, many private organizations have also pursued efforts to build a more peaceful and just world order. From 1945 to 1990, the number of private organizations concerned with international issues grew from under 3,000 to more than 13,000. The London-based Amnesty International, for example, publicizes cases of political repression, torture, and the imprisonment of people for their political beliefs throughout the world.

Individuals have also played vital roles in this effort, sometimes at great personal risk. The roster of men and women who have won the Nobel Peace Prize reflects the international nature of the struggle to create a better world. Recent winners have ranged from Costa Rican president Oscar Arias Sanchez, who tried to bring peace to Central America, to Daw Aung San Suu Kyi (daw awng sahn sue chee) of Burma, who resisted the military leaders who had seized power in her country. Her vision of the ideal government was similar to that of many other political reformers throughout the world:

> 66 To provide the people with . . . peace and security, rulers must observe . . . the concepts of truth, righteousness, and loving kindness. It is government based on these very qualities that the people of Burma are seeking in their struggle for democracy. 99

Ironically, she was unable to attend the awards ceremony in Oslo, Norway, because the military was holding her under house arrest.

SECTION 1 REVIEW

IDENTIFY and explain the significance of the following: German reunification, Commonwealth of Independent States, Boris Yeltsin, Operation Restore Hope, Yasir Arafat, Yitzhak Rabin, Oscar Arias Sanchez, Daw Aung San Suu Kyi.

LOCATE and explain the importance of the following: Azerbaijan, Bosnia and Herzegovina, Somalia.

1. **MAIN IDEA** What three events signaled the end of the Cold War? What effect did the end of the Cold War have on regional conflicts?

2. **MAIN IDEA** How has terrorism changed in recent years?

3. **MAIN IDEA** How has the United Nations worked to promote peace in the post–Cold War era? Why can it be said that the United Nations has had a mixed record in achieving its goal?

4. **WRITING TO PERSUADE** Imagine you are a member of the Nobel Prize committee. Write a speech to persuade members of the committee to nominate Oscar Arias Sanchez or Daw Aung San Suu Kyi for the Nobel Peace Prize.

5. **TAKING A STAND** Do you think it is best for groups such as the United Nations to handle international crises in the post–Cold War period? Why or why not?

A GLOBAL ECONOMY

FOCUS

■ What do supporters hope the North American Free Trade Agreement will accomplish?

■ How have some Americans proposed to combat foreign economic competition?

■ What has been the effect of the exportation of U.S. mass culture?

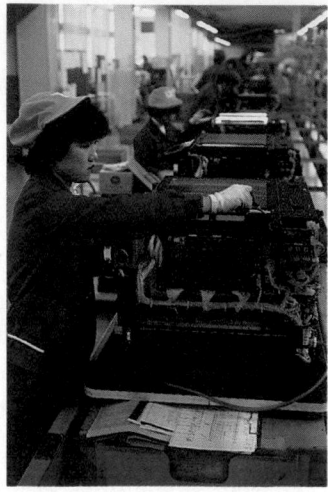

Japanese assembly worker

*B*illions of dollars' worth of international trade links the major industrial nations. This interweaving of economies has sometimes led to problems and tensions. As the U.S. trade deficit grows, many U.S. government and business leaders have argued that the answer lies in uniting North American countries into a unified trading alliance. Others have argued for protectionist legislation.

INTERNATIONAL TRADE

In the fall of 1992, American journalist Bruce W. Nelan observed:

66 Just as wars—two World Wars and, equally important, the Cold War—dominated the geopolitical map of the 20th century, economics will rule over the 21st. All the big questions confronting the world in the century ahead are basically economic. **99**

There is ample evidence to support this view. Today the United States is only one of several economic superpowers. The nations of the Pacific Rim and the European Union, in particular, provide stiff competition.

The nations of the **Pacific Rim**, which include Australia,

▲ As president of the EC's European Commission, Jacques Delors pushed for passage of the Maastricht Treaty.

China, Indonesia, Japan, Macao, Malaysia, New Zealand, Papua New Guinea, Philippines, Singapore, South Korea, and Taiwan, have played an increasingly central role in the global economy in recent decades. In 1991, for instance, goods from the Pacific Rim accounted for 39 percent of all imports to the United States. Japan alone provided for 19 percent of U.S. imports. The Pacific Rim's reputation for producing high-quality, low-priced automobiles, computers, telecommunications equipment, TVs, VCRs, radios, and other goods helped spur demand.

The **European Union**—the Western European trading bloc created by the European Community (EC)—was formed in 1993 with ratification of the Treaty on European Union, or **Maastricht Treaty**. By the terms of the treaty, the members of the European Union—at the time of ratification, Belgium, Denmark, France, Germany, Great

▲ In recent years high-quality Japanese products such as televisions, radios, and other electronic equipment have captured a large share of the U.S. market.

Britain, Greece, Ireland, Italy, Luxembourg, the Netherlands, Portugal, and Spain—relate to one another somewhat like the individual states of the United States do. The Union is designed to allow for the free movement of goods, labor, and capital among member nations. The treaty also calls for greater cooperation on such matters as health, education, foreign policy, culture, and crime. Some predict that a full political union—the "United States of Europe," which could include as many as 20 member states by the year 2000—will eventually form. If this were to happen, the European Union would be the world's largest trading bloc.

By 1993, concern over economic competition from Europe and the Pacific Rim led to growing support for U.S. ratification of the **North American Free Trade Agreement** (NAFTA). The agreement, which President Bush signed in December 1992 and Congress ratified in November 1993, provides for a lowering of trade barriers between the United States, Mexico, and Canada.

■■ Supporters hope that the North American Free Trade Agreement will help counter economic competition from the European Union and the Pacific Rim.

ᴍULTINATIONAL CORPORATIONS

Many Americans also worry about the increased impact of foreign investment in the United States. The global economy is becoming increasingly dominated by **multinational corporations** that invest money in a variety of business ventures all around the globe. U.S. media and entertainment companies have been a favorite of foreign investors. For example, in 1989 Japan's SONY Corporation bought Columbia Pictures, a major Hollywood movie studio, for $3.4 billion. Not to be outdone, Japan's Matsushita Electric Industrial Company, a leading electronics company, bought MCA, Inc., a major U.S. entertainment company, for some $6.5 billion.

In 1992, Japanese investors offered to buy the financially troubled Seattle Mariners baseball team. Meanwhile, a German corporation bought RCA Records, and Australian tycoon Rupert Murdoch gained control of the 20th-Century Fox film studio and of a media empire that included *TV Guide* magazine.

Sometimes it is difficult to gauge the economic effects of these multinational corporations. Leading Japanese corporations, for example, have opened factories in the United States. Honda operated a major plant in Marysville, Ohio. The U.S. branch of Mitsubishi, a Japanese electronics giant, employed 50,000 American workers. Such plants boost the U.S. economy, although most of the profits go to the parent corporations in Japan.

While some Americans complain of foreign investment in the United States, many American businesses are expanding their investments in other countries. For example, the New York–based International Telephone and Telegraph (ITT),

▲ Multinational corporations have opened several manufacturing plants in the United States. Shown here are workers in the Honda automobile factory in Marysville, Ohio.

U.S. BALANCE OF TRADE, 1991

Dollars (in billions)

120
100
80
60
40
20
0

Japan Canada EC (EU) OPEC

Imports
Exports

Source: *The World Almanac and Book of Facts*

FOREIGN TRADE The difference in value between a country's exports and its imports is called its balance of trade. A balance of trade may be either positive or negative in value.

? **BUILDING GRAPH SKILLS** From which country or group did the United States earn more in exports than it spent on imports?

which began as a communications company, expanded its investments in the 1970s and 1980s. By the 1990s ITT held major interest in such diverse businesses as hotels, parking facilities, food processing, insurance, and real estate. Its investments were spread throughout the world—from Bolivia to France. Other corporations such as General Motors, Texaco, and International Business Machines (IBM) also operate worldwide.

DEBATING ECONOMIC POLICY

The complex trading relationships that link the industrialized nations are not always friendly. When trade between nations falls out of balance, political strains often result. The most striking example of such strain has been the troubled relationship between the United States and Japan.

In 1988 the U.S. trade deficit with Japan soared to an all-time high of $5.4 billion as Japanese imports grabbed a bigger and bigger share of the U.S. market. In 1970, for example, Japanese imports accounted for only 5 percent of the U.S. auto market. By 1990 the Japanese held 28 percent of the market. The trade gap narrowed somewhat in the late 1980s, dropping to about $3.4 billion by 1991. The United States fared better in trading competition with the European Community. From 1988 to 1990, U.S. exports to Western Europe rose by 28 percent. In 1991 the United States enjoyed a surplus of almost $17 billion in its trade with EC nations.

These economic trends are urgently challenging Americans to look to the future. The task of revitalizing the U.S. economy and competing successfully in the world trade market is a very large one. Some Americans have advocated **protectionism**—higher tariffs and stricter barriers against foreign imports—to encourage American consumers to purchase domestic goods.

In a 1992 poll, 56 percent of Americans said that protecting U.S. industry and jobs from foreign competition should be the nation's top priority. Another poll showed that Americans considered Japan "the greatest threat to the U.S.'s dominant position in world affairs in the 21st century." As "Buy American" has become a popular slogan, some people have resorted to "Japan bashing," blaming all of America's economic woes on Japan. One U.S. congressman even charged that the recession of the early 1990s was "made in Japan." Reflecting such sentiments, Los Angeles in 1992 canceled a $122 million contract with a Japanese firm to build a commuter rail line.

Protectionist sentiments also fueled opposition to the ratification of the North American Free Trade Agreement. Such critics as former

▼ Some 1,000 members of the United Auto Workers Union Local 595 in Linden, New Jersey, attended a rally to protest both foreign imports and Japanese criticism of U.S. workers.

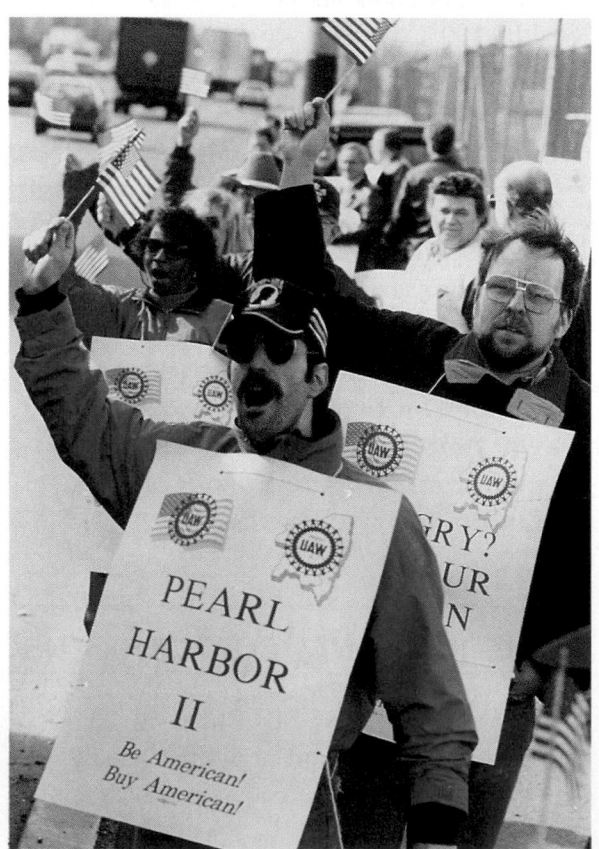

presidential candidates H. Ross Perot and Jesse Jackson opposed NAFTA, arguing it would encourage American businesses to invest more money in Mexico, where labor is cheaper and there are fewer environmental restrictions. They claimed that many Americans would lose their jobs. Yet over 60 percent of U.S. business executives polled in 1992 said that the advantages of free trade in promoting economic activity and efficiency outweighed the costs.

Many observers have urged the United States to imitate its competitors. For example, although Japan's economy is only about two thirds the size of the U.S. economy, Japanese businesses invest more in new plants and updated equipment than U.S. companies do. In America a larger slice of corporate profits goes directly to stockholders. Many critics have suggested Americans cut back on consumption and invest more wealth in new factories and modern technology.

Other observers emphasize a close connection between domestic policy and America's global economic competitiveness. These critics have zeroed in on American schools. Authors Marvin Cetron and Owen Davies note in their book *Crystal Globe:*

66 In a world whose workers require ever more basic education, technological savvy and specialized skill, America's schools are the least successful in the Western world. **99**

Some critics of American education look to Japan for ideas on improving the U.S. school system. Students need more instruction in basic skills and technical training, critics argue. Some have advocated year-long schooling, rather than the long summer vacations typical of the present system.

Japan is not without its own problems, however. By 1993 Japan was facing a severe recession, caused in part by an economy tightly

▲ The Japanese model of education has attracted many admirers in the United States. Shown here are students from Kojimachi Junior High School.

controlled by powerful monopolies. In order to get the economy moving, Prime Minister Morihiro Hosokawa, who took office in August 1993, proposed deregulation of the nation's key industries to foster competition.

:: **Protectionism and improved education have been some remedies proposed to combat foreign economic competition.**

EXPORTING U.S. MASS CULTURE

While America's international trade deficit has remained high in the early 1990s, one U.S. product is increasingly in demand. American mass culture—movies, pop music, and television shows—has won fans throughout the world. By 1990, mass culture was one of America's most profitable exports, with annual sales of over $5 billion. The sales of American TV shows in Europe alone totaled some $600 million a year. The U.S. music industry earned about 70 percent of its revenues from overseas sales. Said a British economics journal in 1989: "America is to entertainment what South Africa is to gold and Saudi Arabia is to oil."

American consumer products from McDonald's hamburgers and Coca-Cola to Levi's blue jeans have been snapped up by people the

▲ American consumer products such as fast food, clothing, and movies have spread throughout the world. This American restaurant, for example, is in Bangkok, Thailand.

They also worry that the rest of the world is getting a distorted impression of life in the United States from Hollywood movies and television shows. Deploring the impact of American television on the values and views of his fellow citizens, a Jamaican journalist wrote:

66 Because of what they see on television, everyone in Jamaica thinks . . . that everything in America is wonderful. Shows like *Dallas* make it look like the land of milk and honey. It makes people think that money and material wealth are the only ways to be rich in this world. 99

world over. The overseas division of the McDonald's Corporation, for instance, has grown enormously. Of McDonald's $20 billion sales in 1991, over $7 billion was generated by its some 3,600 restaurants in foreign nations. In 1992, McDonald's opened more restaurants overseas than it did in the United States, including one in Beijing, China.

Some foreign intellectuals worry that U.S. mass culture will suffocate their own cultures.

But the shared global culture has advantages as well. Television links the entire world through orbiting communications satellites. Events in one nation are instantly transmitted around the globe. Thus events like natural disasters quickly produce a global outpouring of sympathy and help.

▪▪ **The export of U.S. mass culture has helped the U.S. economy, but critics worry that it distorts images of the United States.**

SECTION 2 REVIEW

IDENTIFY and explain the significance of the following: Pacific Rim, European Union, Maastricht Treaty, North American Free Trade Agreement, multinational corporations, protectionism, Morihiro Hosokawa.

1. **MAIN IDEA** How have U.S. economic policies been affected by the European Union and by the Pacific Rim nations?

2. **MAIN IDEA** What remedies have been proposed to fight foreign economic competition?

3. **MAIN IDEA** What effect has the export of U.S. mass culture had on the United States and other countries?

4. **WRITING TO EXPLAIN** Imagine you are a U.S. economic adviser on trade with Japan. Write a memo that summarizes some of the economic reasons for the strained relationship between the United States and Japan.

5. **ANALYZING** Why might multinational corporations have both positive and negative effects on the global economy?

Section 3

ENERGY AND THE ENVIRONMENT

FOCUS

- What has led to renewed interest in alternative energy sources and conservation?
- What are some of the major environmental problems facing the world today?
- What are some of the solutions that have been proposed to deal with environmental concerns?

Of the many problems facing the United States and the rest of the world in the 1990s, some of the most pressing relate to energy use and the environment. Environmentalists warn that the earth's reserves of oil, gas, and coal—the fossil-based energy sources that once seemed unlimited—threaten to run out someday. Many also note that industrialization has taken a toll on the natural environment. In future decades, the combination of population growth and environmental pollution could make life more difficult.

Cleaning waterfowl after the Alaska oil spill, 1989

ENERGY CONSUMPTION

It was in the 1970s, during the presidencies of Richard Nixon, Gerald Ford, and Jimmy Carter, that a sense of crisis about the world's energy supply first gripped America (see Chapter 31). Spurred by government regulations, research went forward on more energy-efficient cars, furnaces, and air conditioners. But despite conservation efforts, global consumption of energy continues to rise under the pressure of population growth, urbanization, and industrial expansion. In 1991 the world consumed an amount of energy equivalent to that of over 535 billion barrels of oil. The United States, which is home to about 5 percent of the

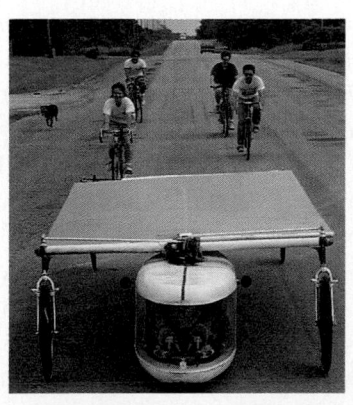

world's population, accounted for nearly 25 percent of this consumption. Some 40 percent of U.S. energy came from oil, 23 percent from natural gas, 22 percent from coal, 8 percent from alternative sources such as solar or hydroelectric power, and 7 percent from nuclear power.

In the early post–World War II years, nuclear power seemed an answer to the nation's energy needs. Enthusiastic journalists predicted that nuclear-power plants would generate electricity "too cheap to meter." But the nuclear-power industry was in serious trouble by the 1990s. In 1986 an accident at the Chernobyl nuclear-power plant

◄ **Some environmentalists suggest that solar-powered automobiles, such as the one shown here, may one day replace those fueled by gasoline.**

near Kiev, Ukraine (see map on page 971), left the plant a smoldering ruin, sent a cloud of radioactivity drifting across Europe, and made the surrounding land unsafe for human life. The Chernobyl disaster pumped 50 times more radioactive material into the environment than the bombs dropped on Hiroshima and Nagasaki combined during World War II.

The Chernobyl incident heightened public anxiety over nuclear power, leading some to call for increased funding for research on alternative energy sources such as solar power, **geothermal power** (geysers and hot springs), wind power, **biomass** (materials such as wood or waste products that can be burned or used to make fuel), and hydrogen. In addition, many of the nation's utility companies have launched successful energy conservation programs. These programs focus on reducing consumer demand and increasing the efficiency of energy production. The government has helped spur such efforts by providing tax breaks and other economic incentives to utility companies that institute conservation programs.

■■ Increases in global energy use and concern over the safety of nuclear-power plants have led to renewed interest in alternative energy sources and conservation measures.

ℱOREST LIFE

As scientists search for new forms of energy, many environmentalists focus on protecting the world's remaining forests and wildlife. Battered by population growth, industrialization, and expanding commercial agriculture and livestock operations, forests are disappearing at an alarming rate. The United Nations Food and Agriculture Organization reports that almost 42 million acres of tropical forests were lost per year between 1981 and 1990. The areas of greatest annual deforestation were in Latin America (some 20.5 million acres), Asia (some 8.9 million acres), and Africa (some 12.4 million acres).

Experts warn that forests play a vital role in the larger **ecosystem**—the interaction of living beings with their environment. Forests prevent floods and soil erosion. Trees also absorb carbon dioxide; therefore, as forests vanish, more carbon

▲ **Deforestation of the Amazon rain forest is proceeding at an alarming rate, as is evident in this photograph.**

dioxide is released into the atmosphere, contributing to atmospheric pollution and global warming (see page 972). Of special concern is the disappearance of tropical rain forests. Environmentalists point out that these rain forests are home to about half the world's plant and animal species. As the forests vanish, some species may be lost forever.

The debate over this disappearance of the rain forests is not a simple one. In poor nations, rain-forest lands are viewed as sources of jobs and revenue. Business and agricultural interests in developing nations argue that it is unfair for environmentalists in the industrialized world to ask poor nations to make economic sacrifices to preserve the rain forests.

BIO GRAPHY The conflict over the rain forests can be bitter and even deadly. In the 1980s, Chico Mendes, whose family made their living from tapping the sap from rubber trees in the rain forest of Brazil, organized a campaign against the destruction of the Amazon rain forest by ranchers seeking grazing land for their cattle. Mendes, who was born Francisco Alves Mendes Filho in 1944, grew up with a deep appreciation and understanding of things in nature. "I became an ecologist long before I had ever heard the word," he once recalled.

In the 1960s, South American leaders instituted a plan to burn off much of the rain forest in order to make room for industrialization and

Chico Mendes

large-scale agriculture. Mendes opposed this destruction by organizing workers who tapped rubber trees and otherwise utilized the rain forest in environmentally responsible ways. Using nonviolent methods of resistance, such as human blockades to stop heavy equipment, the protesters were able to focus worldwide attention on the disappearing Amazon rain forest.

Still, the burning of the rain forest continued. In 1988 Mendes declared:

66 In the last half century Amazônia has never seen so many fires as in 1988. They are burning everything. Our airports were closed one week in 1987 because of the smoke. This year they were closed one

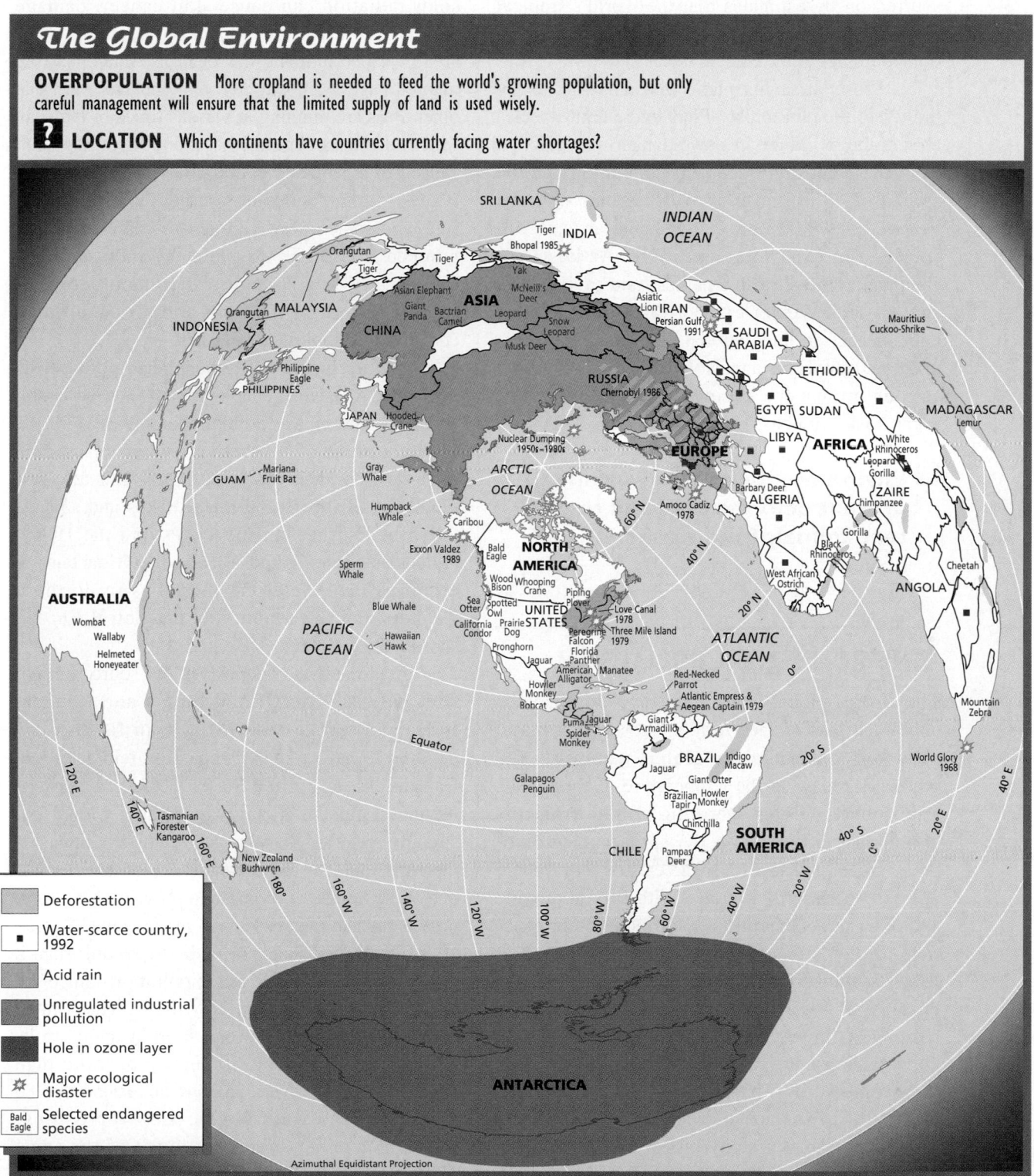

The Global Environment

OVERPOPULATION More cropland is needed to feed the world's growing population, but only careful management will ensure that the limited supply of land is used wisely.

? **LOCATION** Which continents have countries currently facing water shortages?

Legend:
- Deforestation
- Water-scarce country, 1992
- Acid rain
- Unregulated industrial pollution
- Hole in ozone layer
- Major ecological disaster
- Bald Eagle: Selected endangered species

Azimuthal Equidistant Projection

month for the same reason. When you look down from the airplane, Amazônia is nothing but smoke. How it hurts! **"**

In 1988 Mendes was assassinated. A rancher and his son were convicted of the crime, but many believe that the murder was part of a large-scale conspiracy among ranchers. The battle to save the Amazon and other forests continues, however, spurred on by estimates that the world's tropical forests will be gone within 115 years if deforestation continues at the current rate.

Efforts at saving plants and animals are not limited to the rain forests. Plant and animal species around the world are in grave danger of extinction from the explosion of human population and the spread of cities and industry (see map on page 971). One 1992 report claimed that at least 140 species were vanishing each day! Activists are campaigning to slow this process and save at least some species from extinction. For example, Greenpeace, an international environmental organization, campaigns against whaling. Other organizations protest the killing of animals for their horns, tusks, or pelts.

■■ Environmentalists are working to prevent deforestation and to protect animals from extinction and abuse.

ENVIRONMENTAL POLLUTION

The rise in global energy consumption and the continued loss of the world's forests have led to growing concerns over **global warming**, the gradual increase in the temperature of the earth's atmosphere. Global warming results from the greenhouse effect. With the spread of automobiles, cities, and factories, the earth's atmosphere has become heavily polluted with carbon dioxide and other gases that allow solar radiation to penetrate to the earth's surface while preventing heat from escaping. This process is intensified by the burning of fossil fuels and by the cutting and burning of forests. Scientists warn that over time the greenhouse effect could cause temperate areas to become so hot that crops would wither. The melting of the polar ice caps could flood coastal areas, jeopardizing many cities. Some scientists charge that the greenhouse effect is already

seriously harming the environment. The earth's surface was warmer in 1990 than in any other year since such statistics were first kept in the mid 1800s. Six of the hottest years on record were between 1980 and 1991.

A related danger is the thinning of the **ozone layer**—the thin veil of molecules some 10 to 30 miles above the earth's surface that protects against **ultraviolet solar radiation** (UV rays). Ultraviolet solar radiation can cause skin cancer, damage marine life, and harm crops. To date, the greatest area of ozone thinning has been in Antarctica (see map on page 971). But environmentalists warn that other areas are thinning at various times of the year. Much of the damage to the ozone layer has been caused by chemicals called **chlorofluorocarbons** (CFCs)—combinations of carbon, chlorine, fluorine, and sometimes hydrogen—which have been pumped into the atmosphere by industrialized nations. CFCs are used in the manufacture of aerosol sprays, refrigerator and air-conditioner coolants, electronics, and plastics.

A third hazard of atmospheric pollution is **acid rain**. As factories and automobiles spew chemical pollutants, these pollutants combine with the moisture in the atmosphere and later fall as rain, often far from their places of origin. This acid rain gradually kills trees and makes lakes and streams unfit for fish life. In the 1980s and the 1990s, regions as distant as the Appalachian Mountains in eastern North America, the lakes in northern Canada, and the mountains of central Europe showed the effects of acid rain.

Acid rain has become a major source of conflict between the United States and Canada. Industrial smoke from Michigan factories is believed to have a major impact on rain acidity in Canada. As the United States weakened environmental standards during the 1980s, Canadians strongly protested that this action unfairly impacted their environment. As a result, Canada has become one of the leaders in trying to improve global awareness about acid rain, especially in the United States.

The United States has a better record when it comes to dealing with water pollution. Since the Clean Water Act became law in 1972, the United States has made great progress in cleaning up its rivers and lakes. A 1990 survey of more than 656,000 miles of rivers and streams found that 80 percent of the waters were safe for fishing. Environmentalists note that much of the some 129,000 miles of water that were found unsafe were

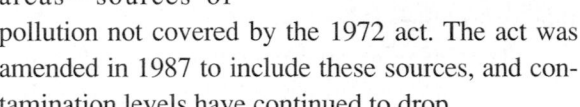

▶ Acid rain not only injures trees and lakes but also damages buildings and monuments. This statue in St. Peter's Square, Rome, has gradually deteriorated from being exposed to acid rain.

contaminated by fertilizers, pesticides, and animal waste washing from farmlands and residential areas—sources of pollution not covered by the 1972 act. The act was amended in 1987 to include these sources, and contamination levels have continued to drop.

Pollution from oil spills also presents serious problems. Spills, such as the 1989 Exxon *Valdez* accident along the coast of Alaska, kill countless fish and waterfowl and cost millions of dollars to clean up. As a result, environmentalists and many government leaders are calling for stricter controls.

■■ **Environmentalists and government leaders are working to reverse the effects of global warming, ozone depletion, acid rain, and water pollution.**

Recycling and Urban Growth

As environmental awareness grows, **recycling**—the collection and processing of used items for reuse—has been winning support. Recycling serves two important purposes: it reuses scarce natural resources, and it reduces the mountain of solid waste that must be burned in incinerators, buried in overflowing landfills, dumped into the sea, or shipped to disposal facilities in poorer nations.

By 1991 there were some 3,955 curbside recycling programs in the United States, a 250 percent increase over the 1989 figure. It is estimated that the nation recycled about 14 percent of its solid waste in 1991. The United States lags behind other industrialized nations in recycling, however. Japan, for example, recycles 50 percent of its paper and 54 percent of its glass. Still, Keisuke Amagusa, editor of the Japanese magazine *Technology and People,* argues that Japan and other countries should focus on conservation as well as on recycling. "The

[Japanese] government is focusing on garbage collected and not doing anything to reduce the garbage created," he complains.

Much of the concern over recycling is related to urban growth. Experts predict that by the year 2000, there will be at least 21 cities with populations of 10 million or more. Eighteen of these cities will be in poor, developing nations. The enormous amount of garbage created in these urban areas threatens the future of the residents. One expert estimates that an excess of garbage is risking the health of 40 percent of the urban population in the developing world.

Many cities are instituting innovative waste-management systems to save energy and recycle as much garbage as possible. In Cairo, Egypt, some 30,000 Zabaleens (Christians from southern Egypt) use horse-drawn carriages to collect garbage from the city. They then sort through the garbage and sell the reusable material. Thrown-away food goes to feed pigs. Waste products are used to fertilize crops. Scrap metal, glass, paper, and plastic are recycled.

One recycling expert notes that Cairo's system has great economic as well as environmental benefits:

66 Zabaleens make as much as three times the average income in Cairo. In many developing countries, up to 2 percent of the population is supported directly or indirectly by refuse from the upper 20 percent of the population. 99

▲ Growing populations have overburdened the sanitation resources of many cities. Some cities have loaded their garbage on barges and tried to export it to other areas—often without success. The governor of Florida, for example, refused to allow this New York barge to dock in his state.

Other cities, such as Juarez City, Mexico, have instituted similar systems. As a result, many urban planners, such as systems analyst Donella Meadows, are optimistic about the future. "If humans manage brilliantly starting very soon," she advises, "it is possible the world might look better than it does now."

THE WORLD RESPONDS

Growing environmental dangers have stirred the international community to action. For instance, in the 1982 agreements issued by the **Third UN Conference on the Law of the Sea**, participating nations pledged to protect the marine environment of coastal waters and to make the oceans "the common heritage of mankind."

Confronted with the urgent danger of ozone depletion, the international community again took action. The **Montreal Protocol on Ozone Depletion**, signed in Montreal, Canada, in 1987, set standards for reducing the emission of CFCs and other gases that threatened the ozone layer. In 1990, as evidence of ozone depletion grew more alarming, this agreement was made even stricter. Ninety-three nations pledged to halt CFC production entirely within the decade and more ozone-damaging chemicals were added to the banned list. In addition, the industrialized nations agreed to contribute $240 million to enable developing nations to purchase alternatives to CFCs.

In 1992, the 20th anniversary of the first United Nations conference on the environment, the UN sponsored the United Nations conference on Environment and Development—dubbed the **Earth Summit**—in Rio de Janeiro, Brazil. The conference attracted some 35,000 participants, including delegations from 178 nations and some 1,200 private environmental organizations. President Bush debated attending the conference, leading some to accuse him of foot-dragging on environmental issues. At the conference, U.S. representatives hedged on supporting several proposals, including a promise to cut carbon dioxide emissions to a certain level by the year 2000. Yet the conference yielded some significant compromises and increased hopefulness for future agreements.

The rise in environmental awareness has also been evident in the growth of private organizations and lobbying groups, such as the international Worldwatch Institute. In Europe, environmentalist political parties, such as the **Green parties** of Britain and Germany, have gained influence as public concern over the environment has increased. These groups have tried to work together to promote international cooperation and concern about the environment. As the Worldwatch Institute noted in 1992: "In an environmentally interdependent world, no country can separate its fate from that of the world as a whole."

■■ **New waste-management systems, recycling, and international cooperation are among the solutions promoted to control global environmental hazards.**

SECTION 3 REVIEW

IDENTIFY and explain the significance of the following: geothermal power, biomass, ecosystem, Chico Mendes, global warming, ozone layer, ultraviolet solar radiation, chlorofluorocarbons, acid rain, recycling, Third UN Conference on the Law of the Sea, Montreal Protocol on Ozone Depletion, Earth Summit, Green parties.

LOCATE and explain the importance of the following: Chernobyl, Antarctica.

1. **MAIN IDEA** How did utility companies, the public, and the government respond to global increases in energy consumption and to fears over the safety of nuclear power?

2. **MAIN IDEA** What are some of the environmental problems facing the world in the 1990s?

3. **WRITING TO PERSUADE** Imagine you are a member of the Worldwatch Institute. Write a letter to the head of a foreign nation, outlining possible solutions to control environmental hazards.

4. **IDENTIFYING VALUES** Provide support for the view that the international community values a healthy environment.

ADDRESSING GLOBAL ILLS

F O C U S

- **What has contributed to a worldwide increase in crime in recent decades?**
- **What are some of the countries that are experiencing particularly high rates of population growth?**
- **What are some of the causes of famine in the developing world?**

*W*hile protection of the environment is an urgent global task, humankind faces many other problems as well. The expansion of the international drug trade has contributed to a worldwide increase in crime. Meanwhile, many developing nations are suffering from famine and the effects of overpopulation—a problem experts predict will worsen in the next century. Many nations continue to look to the United States for help and guidance in solving these problems.

Afghan farmer collecting opium

DRUGS AND CRIME

As urbanization has increased worldwide, so has drug use and violent crime. The international drug trade is a multibillion dollar operation. The coca plant, the raw material of cocaine, is Peru's largest cash crop. In that country, as well as in countries such as Colombia, Burma, Laos, and Thailand, drug lords often amass great wealth, exert vast political influence, and control their own military forces. In the early 1990s, one Burmese drug lord had a 6,000-person private army. Consequently, many governments have had trouble combating the drug business. For example, in 1992 the United States convicted Panamanian president Manuel Noriega for large-scale drug trafficking. This conviction, however, has done little to slow the flow of drugs through Central America.

Drug use varies from country to country. A 1992 United Nations report noted: "Abuse of heroin is soaring in a number of regions, and cocaine, once abused mainly in the Americas and Europe, now threatens Africa, the Near and Middle East, South and Southeast Asia and the South Pacific." While overall drug use in the United States declined somewhat in the 1980s, the use of a cheap but deadly form of cocaine called crack has increased. Use of injected drugs, particularly heroin, has been responsible for the increased spread of AIDS in many countries. Two thirds of the AIDS patients in Italy and France have been heroin addicts.

As the worldwide drug traffic has grown, so has crime. A 1986 UN survey found a 120 percent increase in drug-related crimes worldwide from the preceding decade. The same report found a 30 percent increase in murder worldwide and a 22 percent increase in thefts. The trend has not stopped. In the United States, for example, violent crime rose by almost 33 percent from 1982 to 1991. Crime also has risen dramatically in the former Soviet Union since the end of Communist party rule. Violent crime in Moscow jumped nearly 90 percent in 1989. Said one Moscow citizen,

The State of the World

POPULATION GROWTH At the current rate of growth—1.7 percent—the world's population will double to some 10.5 billion people in 41 years. In Africa, where the annual growth rate is 3 percent, the population will double in less than 25 years.

? LOCATION Which continent has the highest rate of population growth and the most countries with an average calorie supply 25 percent below recommended levels?

Infant Mortality Rates for Selected Nations
(deaths per 1,000 live births)

Netherlands	11
United States	18
Romania	35
China	55
Brazil	94
Algeria	128
India	139
Gabon	227

Rich Nations and Poor Nations, 1991

Per Capita GNP, 1991
- Less than $300
- $300–$750
- $751–$2,500
- $2,501–$6,000
- $6,001–$9,000
- $9,001–$20,000
- $20,001–$30,000

▼ Calorie supply 25% below recommended levels, 1988

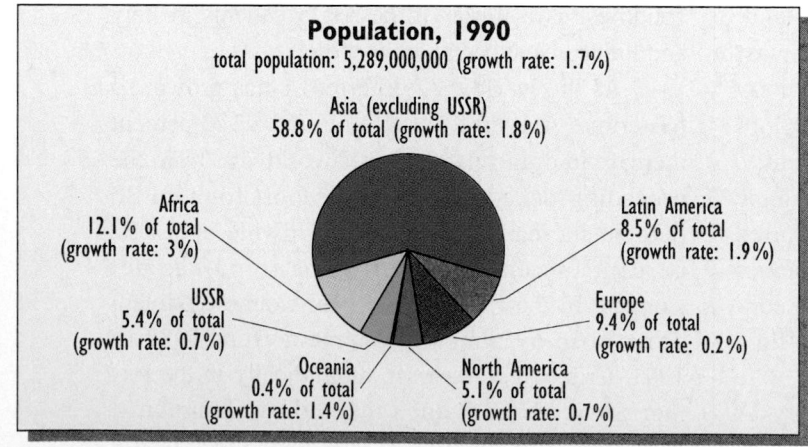

Population, 1990
total population: 5,289,000,000 (growth rate: 1.7%)

- Asia (excluding USSR) 58.8% of total (growth rate: 1.8%)
- Africa 12.1% of total (growth rate: 3%)
- USSR 5.4% of total (growth rate: 0.7%)
- Oceania 0.4% of total (growth rate: 1.4%)
- North America 5.1% of total (growth rate: 0.7%)
- Europe 9.4% of total (growth rate: 0.2%)
- Latin America 8.5% of total (growth rate: 1.9%)

Estimated Cumulative Adult HIV Infections, 1992

North America	1 million +
Central America, South America, & Caribbean	1 million +
Western Europe	500,000
North Africa & Middle East	75,000 +
Sub-Saharan Africa	7.5 million +
Australia, New Zealand, & Indonesia	25,000 +
India & Southeast Asia	1.5 million +
China, Japan, & Pacific	25,000 +
Eastern Europe, Russia, & Central Asia	50,000

echoing sentiments often heard in American cities: "Moscow was a safe city when I was growing up, but it isn't any more. There are thieves on the streets these days, all kinds of criminals."

■■ **An increase in the international drug trade has led to an increase in crime worldwide.**

POPULATION EXPLOSION

Many of the world's toughest problems have been made worse by a massive increase in population. By 1991 the world's population stood at 5.4 billion, and it was growing by a rate of three people every second. Much of this growth has been concentrated in the developing world. While the population of the industrialized nations grew by only 0.7 percent from 1983 to 1988, in many developing nations the population grew by 2 or 3 percent a year. Experts predict that India's population will jump from 866 million in 1991 to 1.3 billion by 2020; Mexico's, from 90 million to 152 million; and Bangladesh's, from 116.6 million to 210 million. By 2020, Africa is expected to account for about 18 percent of the world's population, in contrast to 9 percent in 1950.

Some argue that one of the keys to limiting population growth in developing countries is to advance the status of women. Former Indian prime minister Indira Gandhi, who was assassinated in 1984, wrote in 1980:

66 Men and most women are unaware of the potential ability of women. Their lives are entrapped by pre-conceived notions and attitudes from birth onwards. . . . A lower status for women, or lesser opportunity for women, is a handicap for the growth of mankind as a whole. **99**

Gandhi believed that if women are granted equality of rights and opportunity, they will no longer be valued primarily for their ability to produce children.

■■ **India, Mexico, Bangladesh, and the developing nations of Africa are expected to experience high rates of population growth in the coming decades.**

WORLD HUNGER

Rapid population growth has added to the problem of food shortages in some countries. In addition, variations in wealth produce wide variations in diet and nutrition within countries and between countries. In the United States, malnutrition is still a problem among the poor, particularly those in rural areas, even though most Americans enjoy a high standard of living.

By contrast, famine plagues many countries, including Bangladesh and the African countries of Ethiopia, Sudan, and Somalia. From the 1950s to the 1990s, rainfall declined sharply in northern Africa. Civil wars in some countries hit by famine have made the situation even worse and have prevented relief workers from reaching victims. Worldwide in the early 1990s, an average of 37,000 children under age five died *each day* of starvation, diarrhea, and diseases associated with malnutrition and poor health care. Some young survivors of famine may never completely recover.

The situation is made worse by the fact that the world's grain production actually declined in the late 1980s, despite advances in agricultural productivity in some nations. This was due in part to the fact that in Latin America and elsewhere, commercial meat operations producing beef, pork, and poultry for the world market expanded into rain-forest lands or into agricultural acreage

POVERTY AND NUTRITION

State	% Below Poverty Line	% Receiving Food Stamps/ Lunch Programs
Mississippi	25.7	19.5
Louisiana	23.6	16.8
New Mexico	20.9	10.0
Arkansas	19.6	9.5
Alabama	19.2	11.2

Source: *Statistical Abstract of the United States*

WHEN ENDS DON'T MEET In 1990 some 14 percent of the U.S. population was living below the poverty line, while 9 percent participated in the Federal Food Stamp and National School Lunch programs.

? **BUILDING CHART SKILLS** In which state was the percentage of population living below the poverty line but not receiving food assistance the greatest?

When President John F. Kennedy launched the Peace Corps program in 1961, hundreds of young Americans eager to help the United States win the Cold War joined the program. In its first year some 900 volunteers served in 16 host countries, where they started projects to improve agricultural output, literacy rates, and sanitation. At its height in the mid-1960s, the Peace Corps had more than 10,000 volunteers, serving in over 50 countries in Asia, Africa, and Latin America. During the 1970s, budget cuts and decreased recruitment efforts caused the number of Peace Corps volunteers to drop to some 6,000 recruits.

In the 1980s the agency reorganized and increased its emphasis on helping people gain skills in technology and free enterprise. This reorganization led to a change in the kind of volunteer recruited by the Peace Corps. The typical Peace Corps volunteers in the 1960s tended to be a young person in his or her twenties, fresh out of college, who volunteered for a stint before going on to other careers. Few volunteers in the 1960s had any previous work experience. The Peace Corps often served as a training ground for the volunteers, many of whom continued to work in public service. One such volunteer was Julia Chang Bloch, who joined the Peace Corps in 1964 after graduating from the University of California at Berkeley. Bloch later became a Peace Corps recruiter and continued to work in overseas service. In 1981, as assistant administrator of the Food for Peace and Voluntary

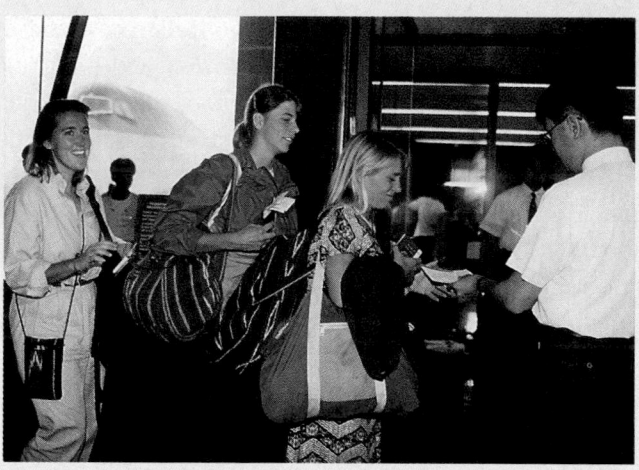

▲ Peace Corps volunteers in the Philippines

Assistance program, she became the highest-ranking Asian American in the Reagan administration.

"Certainly the Peace Corps was the first step for me in . . . a career in overseas aid and development," Bloch notes. "When I was an undergraduate . . . I had thought I might be a journalist, having majored in communications and public policy. But there are several hundred like me that I could point to."

In recent years, fewer Peace Corps volunteers have been recent college graduates. The Peace Corps has increased its efforts to recruit older volunteers, including retired persons, who possess special skills and experience needed in developing countries. In the 1960s as many as 85 percent of Peace Corps volunteers were under age 26. Today that figure has dropped to just over 50 percent.

The ending of the Cold War in the 1990s has also brought about a shift in the program's focus. The Peace Corps is now being invited into countries that were once part of the Soviet bloc. In November 1992 the first group of volunteers went to Russia. Many of them are teaching the Russians about capitalism and how to run small businesses. One of the first volunteers to go to Russia was a retired U.S. military officer, Charles Bennett, who had once trained as a navigator for nuclear-bombing missions against the Soviet Union. Bennett reflected on the changing times: "I had a military flavor to my life. The idea was to . . . kill the enemy and not be friends. But now the big threat is over. . . . Here I am now eating dinner [with] people I was willing to turn into dust."

formerly devoted to grain growing. The grain that continues to be raised in these nations increasingly goes to feed livestock rather than human populations.

■■ **Overpopulation, drought, civil wars, and a decreased grain supply have contributed to severe famines in the developing world.**

COMMENTARY

America's Role in the New Order

The end of the Cold War has not ended the world's problems. Solving these global problems will take a huge effort by all people working together democratically. Yet in many parts of the world, true democracy remains simply the dream of a few. A key question of the 1990s has been whether democratic nations can convince the rest of the world of democracy's appeal as they try to help solve social and economic ills. This goal will be accomplished not by military or economic might, but by the power of ideas.

In this effort the United States must play a central role. Some of the earliest English settlers in America believed they were lighting a beacon that would show the way to a new era in human history. With the American Revolution and the establishment of a new republic governed by elected officials who are guided by a written constitution and a bill of rights, the idea of America as a world leader took on new meaning.

Of course, the nation has often failed to live up to its professed ideals. Many groups have been excluded from the promise of democracy. But gradually, over the years, the United States has slowly and painfully tried to achieve a fuller and more complete understanding of the meaning of democracy and individual freedom. Despite a shifting balance of global power and changing economic realities, the appeal of the ideas of individual freedom, democratic self-government, and opportunity for all remains as strong as ever, especially to those denied them by repressive rulers or by grinding poverty. From South Africa to Eastern Europe to Southeast Asia to Latin America, the vision of democracy and freedom can still inspire men and women to acts of great courage and heroism.

As has always been true in our history, the shape of the future will be determined by the willingness of men and women to plunge into the fray and grapple with tough problems. In this book you have learned of our nation's history up to the present. The next chapters in this still-unfolding story will be written by you.

SECTION 4 REVIEW

IDENTIFY and explain the significance of the following: Indira Gandhi, Peace Corps.

LOCATE and explain the importance of the following: Peru, Bangladesh, Ethiopia, Sudan.

1. **MAIN IDEA** What has contributed to the worldwide increase in crime in recent decades?

2. **MAIN IDEA** How are the populations of India, Mexico, Bangladesh, and the developing nations of Africa expected to change in the coming years?

3. **IDENTIFYING CAUSE AND EFFECT** What factors have contributed to severe famines in the developing world?

4. **WRITING TO INFORM** Write an essay that explores the reasons why the drug trade became an international phenomenon during the 1990s.

5. **EVALUATING** What role do you think the United States should play in the new world order? Give reasons for your answer.

WRITING A SUMMARY

Using the essential points of the chapter as a guide, write a summary of the chapter.

REVIEWING CHRONOLOGY

Number your paper 1 to 5. Study the time line above, and list the following events in the order in which they happened by writing the first next to 1, the second next to 2, and so on. Then complete the activity below.

1. NAFTA ratified.
2. Berlin Wall falls.
3. Commonwealth of Independent States formed.
4. Chernobyl nuclear accident occurs.
5. Operation Restore Hope launched.

Analyzing Why do you think Indira Gandhi believed it was important to establish family-planning programs in India?

IDENTIFYING PEOPLE AND IDEAS

Explain the historical significance of each of the following people or terms.

1. Boris Yeltsin
2. Operation Restore Hope
3. Maastricht Treaty
4. protectionism
5. Morihiro Hosokawa
6. Chico Mendes
7. global warming
8. acid rain
9. Green parties
10. Indira Gandhi

UNDERSTANDING MAIN IDEAS

1. What events marked the end of the Cold War? What impact did the end of the Cold War have on conflicts around the world?
2. What various ways did the American government and public propose to deal with increasing foreign economic competition?
3. What are some alternative energy sources scientists proposed during the 1990s? Why were these energy sources necessary?
4. What global environmental problems divided nations during this period? What solutions were offered?
5. What were some of the problems that developing nations experienced during the 1990s?

REVIEWING THEMES

1. **Economic Development** How might economic influence increase the political power of the European Union and Pacific Rim nations?
2. **Global Relations** What role did the United Nations play in resolving global conflicts during the 1990s?
3. **Technology and Society** In what ways has technology proved both beneficial and harmful to the environment in recent decades?

THINKING CRITICALLY

1. **Analyzing** How did the end of the Cold War affect old global divisions?
2. **Evaluating** How might environmental policies possibly endanger jobs and the economy?
3. **Hypothesizing** What global problems might leaders in the 21st century need to face?

STRATEGY FOR SUCCESS

Review the Strategies for Success on Interpreting Editorial Cartoons on page 332. Then study the following cartoon, which appeared in the *Los Angeles Times* in 1975. What is the cartoonist's message?

WRITING ABOUT HISTORY

Writing to Inform Write a pamphlet that describes one contribution made to world peace or the environment by an international organization.

Montreal Protocol on Ozone Depletion signed.

Berlin Wall falls.

Commonwealth of Independent States formed. Maastricht Treaty signed.

"Earth Summit" held in Brazil. Operation Restore Hope launched.

New York's World Trade Center bombed. Yasir Arafat and Yitzhak Rabin sign Middle East peace accord. NAFTA ratified.

1987   1989   1991   1992   1993   1995

USING PRIMARY SOURCES

In the early 1980s a new environmental movement, symbolized by groups such as Earth First!, emerged. The movement abandoned conservative protests against corporations in favor of more-radical actions, such as tree sitting, inserting spikes into trees, and destroying logging equipment. Read the following excerpt from the book *Green Rage,* which profiles this movement. How do radical environmentalists justify the methods they use?

66 *In general, however, radical environmentalism has no pretensions of being a mass movement and does not expect the huge demonstrations the civil rights and antiwar movements produced. It aims to harass more than obstruct, with the hope that the public awareness it generates will do the rest. . . .*

A more important difference in strategy stems from the extreme urgency of the environmental crisis. . . . For the "constituency" of the biocentric civil rights movement, however, there is often no tomorrow. Once an old-growth forest is cut, it will not grow back for hundreds of years, if ever. Once a species becomes extinct the battle is lost. This sense of urgency often motivates the use of ecological civil disobedience, not to make far-reaching changes in society's views of the environment, but merely to buy time for legal redress or for the emergence of public pressure. 99

LINKING HISTORY AND GEOGRAPHY

Study the map in the right column, which shows the number of nations in Africa affected by hunger and food shortages, as measured by daily calorie intake. How many African nations have food supplies averaging less than 1,950 calories per person per day?

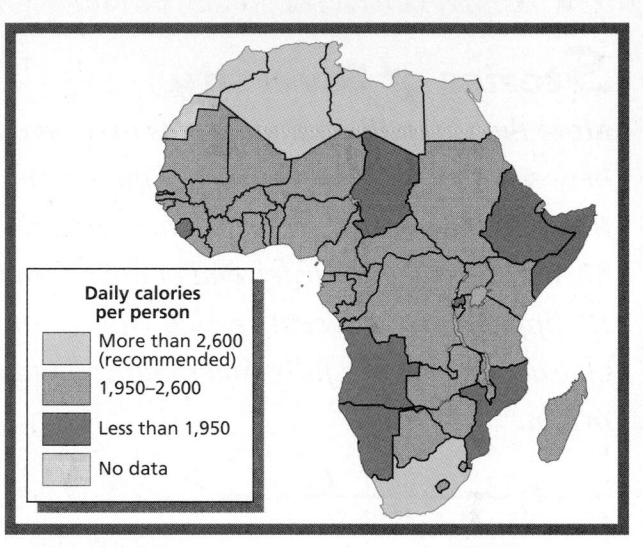

Daily calories per person

☐ More than 2,600 (recommended)
☐ 1,950–2,600
☐ Less than 1,950
☐ No data

BUILDING YOUR PORTFOLIO

Complete the following projects independently or cooperatively.

1. **GLOBAL RELATIONS** In Chapter 31 you portrayed a delegate to the United Nations. Building on that experience, write a speech explaining what effects the end of the Cold War has had on your nation. Your speech should indicate both the benefits of the end of the Cold War and any negative consequences—such as increased regional or local conflicts—for your nation.

2. **BUSINESS AND TRADE** In Chapter 32 you portrayed the director of a private agency assisting immigrant businesspeople. Building on that experience, imagine you are advising your clients on international trade. Research the advantages and disadvantages of free-trade agreements, such as the North American Free Trade Agreement, and then develop a policy statement to deliver to your clients.

American Letters

Stories of Diversity

More than 10 million immigrants arrived on American shores between 1970 and 1989, most of them from Asia or Latin America. In the following selections, Chinese American author Gish Jen, Mexican American writer and poet Sandra Cisneros, and Philippine-born novelist Jessica Hagedorn explore the struggles of characters who are fully American yet retain ties to their country of origin.

▲ **Sandra Cisneros**

From *Typical American*

by Gish Jen

"We are family," echoed Helen.

"Team," said Ralph. "We should have name. The Chinese Yankees. Call Chang-kees for short."

"Chang-kees!" Everyone laughed.

Ball games became even more fun. Theresa explained how the

▼ **Portrait of a Chinese Family (1985), by Tomie Arai**

Yankees had lost the Series to the Dodgers the year before; they rooted for a comeback. "Let's go Chang-kees!" This was in the privacy of their apartment, in front of their newly bought used Zenith TV; the one time they went to an actual game, people had called them names and told them to go back to their laundry. They in turn had sat impassive as the scoreboard. Rooting in their hearts, they said later. Anyway, they preferred to stay home and watch. "More comfortable." "More convenient." "Can see better," they agreed.

These were the same reasons Ralph advocated buying a car.

"*Seems like someone's becoming*[1] one-hundred-percent Americanized," Theresa kidded.

"*What's so American? We had a car, growing up. Don't you remember?*" Ralph argued that in fact this way they could avoid getting too Americanized. "*Everywhere we go, we can keep the children inside. Also they won't catch cold.*"

"*I thought we agreed the children are going to be American,*" puzzled Helen.

Ralph furrowed his brow. When Callie turned three they had decided that Mona and Callie would learn English first, and then Chinese. This was what Janis and Old Chao were planning on doing with Alexander; Janis didn't want him to have an accent. For Ralph and Helen, it was a more practical decision. Callie had seemed confused by *outside people* sometimes understanding her and sometimes not. Playing with other children in the park, she had several times started to cry, and once or twice to throw things; she had lost a doll this way, and a dragon. Also, one grabby little boy had, in an ensuing ruckus, lost some teeth. . . .

Now Ralph drummed his fingers. He stopped and smiled.

"*And what better way to Americanize the children than to buy a car!*" ❖

---

1 Italics indicate words spoken in Chinese.

"My Name"
from *The House on Mango Street*
by Sandra Cisneros

In English my name means hope. In Spanish it means too many letters. It means sadness, it means waiting. It is like the number nine. A muddy color. It is the Mexican records my father plays on Sunday mornings when he is shaving, songs like sobbing.

It was my great-grandmother's name and now it is mine. She was a horse woman too, born like me in the Chinese year of the horse—which is supposed to be bad luck if you're born female. . . .

My great-grandmother. I would've liked to have known her, a wild horse of a woman, so wild she wouldn't marry until my great-grandfather threw a sack over her head and carried her off. Just like that, as if she were a fancy chandelier. That's the way he did it.

And the story goes she never forgave him. She looked out the window all her life, the way so many women sit their sadness on an elbow. I wonder if she made the best with what she got or was she sorry because she couldn't be all the things she wanted to be. Esperanza. I have inherited her name, but I don't want to inherit her place by the window.

At school they say my name funny as if the syllables were made out of tin and hurt the roof of your mouth. But in Spanish my name is made out of a softer something like silver, not quite as thick as my sister's name Magdalena which is uglier than mine. Magdalena who at least can come home and become Nenny. But I am always Esperanza.

I would like to baptize myself under a new name, a name more like the real me, the one nobody sees. Esperanza as Lisandra or Maritza or Zeze the X. Yes. Something like Zeze the X will do. ❖

"Luna Moth"
from *Dogeaters*
by Jessica Hagedorn

Without warning, [my mother] cheerfully announces she is sending me to school in America and moving there with me for an indefinite period. I am ecstatic, at first. Everyone else is stunned. My father cannot stop her—my mother has inherited money from her father and pays for our passage to America. We settle first in New York, then Boston. I convince myself I am not homesick, and try not to bring up my father or brother when I speak. My mother actually sells a few paintings. The months turn into years. "Are we going to stay here forever?" I finally ask her. She looks surprised. "I don't know about you, but I love the cold weather. Go back to Manila if you want. Tell Raul I miss him more than he could ever imagine." She smiles one of her cryptic smiles. "But he'll have to visit me here if he wants to see me—" her voice trails off. . . .

When I finally come home to Manila to visit, my father warns me not to bother visiting our old house. "You'll be disappointed. Memories are always better." Smiling apologetically, he tells me reality will diminish the grandeur of my childhood image of home. I take his picture with my new camera, which later falls in the swimming pool by accident. The camera is destroyed, along with my roll of film. I decide to visit our old house . . . anyway, borrowing a car from Mikey. Pucha goes with me; she loves riding around in cars and doesn't need any excuse. . . .

My father is right. The house with its shuttered windows looks smaller than I remember, and dingy. The once lush and sprawling garden is now a forlorn landscape of rocks, weeds, and wild ferns. The bamboo grove has been cut down. "Let's go," Pucha whispers, impatient and uninterested. An old man with bright eyes introduces himself as Manong Tibo, the caretaker. He unlocks door after door for us, pulling aside cobwebs, warning us to be careful. Rotting floorboards creak under the weight of our footsteps. "My bedroom," I say to the old man, who nods. I am overwhelmed by melancholy at the sight of the empty room. A frightened mouse dashes across the grimy tiled floor. ❖

THINKING AND WRITING ABOUT LITERATURE

1. How do Gish Jen's characters become "Americanized"? What aspects of Chinese culture do they retain?
2. What aspects of Mexican and American culture does Sandra Cisneros's character associate with her name? Why does she want to change her name?
3. Why is Jessica Hagedorn's character disappointed when she sees her old home? Do you think she is happy in the United States?

Strategies for Success

EVALUATING NEWS STORIES

Information today comes at us in a flood—from talk shows to tabloids, from the morning headlines to the nightly news. Today's news reporting will become the basis of tomorrow's history, so evaluating news stories contributes to your understanding of current history. News sources, which collectively are called the news media, can be divided into two groups: *broadcast media* and *print media.*

▲ **Bill Clinton jamming on *The Arsenio Hall Show,* 1992**

Broadcast Media

Broadcast media include television and radio. Television is, by far, the dominant medium for news. Surveys show that Americans are much more inclined to watch TV news than to read a daily newspaper. Television, like no other medium, presents the opportunity to witness history in the making. TV and radio can provide on-the-spot, around-the-clock coverage, creating a sense of immediacy. Also, both increasingly offer "instant analysis" to go with their reporting. Broadcasters like CNN, the 24-hour all-news cable network, and "talk radio" have greatly expanded the amount and kind of news available over the air.

Print Media

Print media include newspapers, weekly newsmagazines like *Newsweek* and *Time,* and other publications that cover current events. Newspapers, particularly such big-city dailies as the *New York Times* or the *Chicago Tribune,* give detailed accounts of national and world events as they occur. Newsmagazines, which have more time to prepare their stories, specialize in in-depth analyses of issues.

How to Evaluate News Media

To evaluate news reporting, ask questions like the following:

- **Coverage.** Is the subject treated superficially or in-depth? Does the reporting include information on the background to a story? Does it explore long-range implications of events?
- **Fairness and accuracy.** Does the reporting stick to the facts? Is it fair and balanced? Is there any recognizable bias in the coverage?
- **Immediacy and interest.** How close in time is the reporting to the event? Have there been new developments since the story was written or broadcast? Is the news presented in an interesting way?

Applying the Strategy

Choose a topic that is frequently in the news and that has been covered both in print and on radio and TV. Evaluate recent reporting on the issue in terms of the categories listed above. First, examine how well the reporting covers the *why* and *how* of the event, as well as the *who, what, when,* and *where.* Remember that each story has a wider context, a past and a future; good reporting will bring out these connections. Second, consider whether the story is told objectively. Every reporter has a point of view, so be alert for any expression of bias. Finally, note whether any late-breaking developments have changed the situation as last reported. Evaluate the reporting for the level of interest it creates, keeping in mind that a complex subject such as a financial scandal may be hard to present in exciting images or film footage.

Practicing the Strategy

Choose another current topic and examine reporting about it by each of the following: a TV network news program, a major daily newspaper, a public-radio program, and a national weekly newsmagazine. Write a brief essay evaluating the treatment of the issue or event by the different news media, describing the depth of the coverage offered by each, the presence of bias in any of the reporting, and the impact of the story on you.

UNIT 9 Review

BUILDING YOUR PORTFOLIO

Outlined below are four projects. Independently or cooperatively, complete one and use the products to demonstrate your mastery of the historical concepts involved.

1 POLITICS

The Watergate scandal and the Iran-contra affair challenged the foundation of constitutional government. Using the portfolio materials you designed in chapters 31 and 32, write an editorial that examines the ways in which the Watergate scandal was both similar to and different from the Iran-contra affair.

2 THE ECONOMY

Stagflation and the effects of the energy crisis are only two of the economic problems presidents Nixon, Ford, and Carter struggled with in the 1970s. In the 1980s President Reagan attempted to stimulate the economy through conservative reforms. Using the portfolio materials you designed in chapters 31 and 32, discuss the different ways in which economic actions affect people by presenting your chart and pamphlet to the class.

3 GLOBAL RELATIONS

During the 1970s and 1980s, the United States opened negotiations with China, improved relations with the Soviet Union, and witnessed the end of the Cold War and the breakup of the Soviet Union. Regional and local conflicts emerged, however, as new nations were torn apart by ethnic and religious struggles. Using the portfolio materials you designed in chapters 31 and 33, conduct a panel discussion about the new world order that highlights the sometimes conflicting interests of the superpowers, industrialized nations, and developing nations.

4 BUSINESS AND TRADE

In the last several decades, the U.S. economy has become increasingly global in scope. Using the portfolio materials you designed in chapters 32 and 33, prepare a presentation on the role of immigrants and immigrant businesses in strengthening America's position in the global economy.

Videodisc Review

In assigned groups, develop an outline for a video collage of America in the years between 1970 and the present. Choose images that best illustrate the major topics of the period. Write a script to accompany the images. Assign narrators to different parts of the script, and present your video collage to the class.

Further Reading

Edelstein, Andrew J., and Kevin McDonough. *The Seventies: From Hot Pants to Hot Tubs.* Dutton (1990). Social history of the 1970s.

Johnson, Haynes. *Sleepwalking through History: America in the Reagan Years.* Norton (1991). Overview and critical analysis of the Reagan years.

Moore, Jim, with Rick Ihde. *Clinton: Young Man in a Hurry.* The Summit Group (1992). Biography detailing the rise of Bill Clinton to become the 42nd president of the United States.

Virga, Vincent. *The Eighties: Images of America.* Edward Burlingame Books (1992). Photographic essay on life in the United States during the 1980s.

Woodward, Bob, and Carl Bernstein. *The Final Days.* Simon & Schuster (1976). Chronicle of the last days of Richard Nixon's presidency.

TODD & CURTI'S

THE AMERICAN NATION

*Y*our understanding and appreciation of the past will grow as your study skills improve. This Skills Handbook contains instruction on critical thinking strategies and social studies skills that will help you gain a fuller understanding of American history. It explains, for example, how to identify cause and effect and how to distinguish fact from opinion. The lessons in the Handbook equip you to handle historical sources, time lines, maps, and graphs, as well as build your vocabulary and sharpen your research, writing, and test-taking abilities.

1 IDENTIFYING THE MAIN IDEA

In the study of history, the ability to identify what is central is a key to understanding any complex event or issue. *Todd & Curti's The American Nation* is designed to help you focus on the main ideas in American history. The paragraph titled Understanding the Main Idea that introduces each chapter and the Focus Questions that begin each section are intended to guide your reading. The essential points—the red summary statements placed throughout the text—highlight and reinforce the main ideas presented.

But not everything you read is structured like *Todd & Curti's The American Nation*. Applying the following guidelines will help you identify the main ideas in what you read.

HOW TO IDENTIFY THE MAIN IDEA

1. **Read introductory material.** Read the title and the introduction, if there is one. They often point to the main ideas to be covered.

2. **Have questions in mind.** Formulate questions that you think might be answered by the material. Having such questions in mind will focus your reading.

3. **Note the outline of ideas.** Pay attention to any headings or subheadings. They may provide a basic outline of the major ideas.

4. **Distinguish supporting details.** As you read, distinguish sentences providing supporting details from the general statements they support. A trail of facts may lead to a conclusion that expresses a main idea.

APPLYING YOUR SKILL

Read the following paragraph, from the subsection in Chapter 3 titled "The Pilgrims," to identify its main idea.

The Metropolitan Museum of Art

66 Conflicts over religious doctrine had raged in England since 1534 when Henry VIII broke with the Roman Catholic church to form the Church of England (Anglican church). Henry's motives had been primarily personal—the pope had refused to grant him a divorce from his first wife. At heart still a Roman Catholic, he had created a

church that remained largely Catholic in form. This deeply troubled the Pilgrims, who longed for a truly Protestant church. **99**

As the lead sentence indicates, the paragraph focuses on religious conflicts in England. Details about Henry VIII and the origin of the Anglican church are included to provide a background to the disputes. The main idea is best captured in the concluding sentence: There was no "truly Protestant church" in England, and this fact greatly upset the Pilgrims.

PRACTICING YOUR SKILL

Now read the last paragraph of the subsection on the Pilgrims (pages 66–67), then answer the following questions.

1. What is the paragraph's main idea? How does the author support that idea?
2. What is the relationship of the main ideas of this paragraph and the paragraph on the Church of England? Combine them into one statement that summarizes the subsection.

2 IDENTIFYING CAUSE AND EFFECT

Identifying and understanding cause-and-effect relationships is crucial to the study of history. To investigate why an event took place, and what else happened as a result of that event, historians ask questions such as: What is the immediate activity that triggered the event? What is the background leading up to the event? Who were the people involved?

HOW TO IDENTIFY CAUSE AND EFFECT

1. **Look for clues.** Certain words and phrases are immediate clues to the existence of a cause-and-effect relationship. Note the examples that follow:

CLUE WORDS AND PHRASES

Cause	Effect
as a result of	aftermath
because	as a consequence
brought about	depended on
inspired	gave rise to
led to	originating from
produced	outcome
provoked	outgrowth
spurred	proceeded from
the reason	resulting in

2. **Identify the relationship.** Read carefully to identify how events are related. Writers do not always state the link between cause and effect. Sometimes a reader of history has to infer the cause or the effect.

3. **Check for complex connections.** Beyond the immediate cause and effect, check for other, more complex connections. Note, for example, whether (1) there were additional causes of a given effect, (2) a cause had multiple effects, and (3) these effects themselves caused further events.

APPLYING YOUR SKILL

The diagrams on page 990 present an important cause-and-effect relationship among the events leading up to the American Revolution. Because of the costs incurred in the French and Indian War, Parliament levied taxes on the colonies to raise revenue—taxation that led colonists

The Granger Collection, New York

Cause	Effect
Britain incurs huge debt from the French and Indian War.	Parliament raises taxes on the colonies.

Cause	Effect/Cause	Effect
Britain incurs huge debt from the French and Indian War.	Parliament raises taxes on the colonies.	Colonists protest taxation without representation in Parliament.

to cry, "No taxation without representation!" A diagram of the first part of this relationship is shown above. The diagram at the top of the next column adds the relationship between the British taxation of colonists and the colonial protests, showing how an effect may in turn become a cause. Such diagrams provide a graphic way of seeing complex relations of events.

PRACTICING YOUR SKILL

From your knowledge of recent American history, choose a sequence of events shaped by cause-and-effect relationships. Draw a chart showing the relationships between the actions and the outcomes. Then write a paragraph that explains the connections.

3 DISTINGUISHING FACT FROM OPINION

Historical sources may contain facts and opinions. Sources such as letters, diaries, and speeches usually express personal views. The ability to distinguish facts from opinions is essential to judge the soundness of an argument or the reliability of a historical account.

HOW TO DISTINGUISH FACT FROM OPINION

1. **Identify the facts.** Ask yourself: Can it be verified? Determine whether the idea can be checked for accuracy in a source such as an almanac or encyclopedia. If so, it is probably factual; if not, it probably contains an opinion.

2. **Identify the opinions.** Look for clues that signal a statement of opinion: phrases such as *I think* and *I believe,* comparative words like *greatest* and *more important,* and value-laden words like *extremely* and *ridiculous* imply a judgment, and thus an opinion.

APPLYING YOUR SKILL

Read the following description of George Washington by Thomas Jefferson:

❝ His mind was great and powerful, without being of the very first order; . . . no judgment was ever sounder. It was slow in operation, being little aided by invention or imagination, but sure in conclusion. **❞**

Jefferson's assessment—that Washington was neither brilliant nor particularly imaginative as a thinker, but that he possessed sound judgment and decisiveness—is clearly an opinion. Note the comparative words and phrasing: *great . . . without being of the first order, . . . sounder, . . . slow in operation.*

PRACTICING YOUR SKILL

Read the excerpt below, in which Jefferson further evaluates Washington as a commander in battle. Then answer the questions that follow.

❝ . . . Hence the common remark of his officers, of the advantage he derived from councils of war, where hearing all suggestions, he selected whatever was best; certainly no General ever planned his battles more judiciously [carefully]. But if deranged [disrupted] during the course of the action, . . . he was slow in re-adjustment. **❞**

1. What fact (or facts) does Jefferson mention in his description of Washington?
2. Which words provide clues to Jefferson's opinion of Washington as a commander?

4 READING A TIME LINE

Chronology has been called "the skeleton of history." Knowing the chronological order of historical events—that is, the sequence in which they occurred—is essential to understanding them. A time line is a visual framework representing the chronology of a particular historical period. It enables you to see at a glance what happened when. Studying a time line involves seeing relationships between events as well as remembering important dates.

HOW TO READ A TIME LINE

1. **Determine its framework.** Note the years covered and the intervals of time into which the time line is divided.

2. **Study the sequence of events.** Study the order in which the events appear on the time line, noting especially the length of time between events.

3. **Supply missing information.** Think about the people, places, and other events associated with each item on the time line. In this way you can "flesh out" the framework.

4. **Note relationships.** Ask how an event relates to earlier or later events. Look for cause-and-effect relationships and long-term developments.

APPLYING YOUR SKILL

Study the time line below. It lists important events in the history of World War II in the Pacific.

1941	1942	1945
Japan invades Indochina. U.S. declares embargo against Japan. Japanese attack Pearl Harbor.	Battle of Midway occurs.	U.S. drops bombs on Hiroshima and Nagasaki. Japan surrenders.

When more than one event is listed for the same year, they are stacked with the earliest on top. The entries for 1941 illustrate the background to the surprise attack on Pearl Harbor.

PRACTICING YOUR SKILL

From the time line above, answer the following.

1. What other events might belong on this time line for the years between the attack on Pearl Harbor and the dropping of the atomic bombs?

2. What cause-and-effect relationship is suggested by the sequence of entries for 1945?

5 BUILDING VOCABULARY

In your study of history, you may encounter many new and unfamiliar words. But with regular effort you can master unfamiliar words and turn reading history into an opportunity to enlarge your vocabulary. Following the steps outlined here will assist you in building your vocabulary.

HOW TO BUILD VOCABULARY

1. **Identify unusual words.** As you read, list words that you cannot pronounce or define.

2. **Study context clues.** Study the sentence and paragraph where you find the new term. This setting, or context, may give you clues to the word's meaning through examples or a definition using more familiar words.

3. **Use the dictionary.** Use a dictionary to learn how to say the words on your list and what they mean.

4. **Review new vocabulary.** Look for ways to use the new words—in homework assignments, conversation, or classroom discussions. The best way to master a new word is to use it.

PRACTICING YOUR SKILL

1. What is context? How can it provide clues to a word's meaning?

2. As you read the next chapter, list any unusual words that you find. Write down what you think each word means, then check your definitions against those in a dictionary.

6 | REVIEWING MAP BASICS

Questions about history as well as geography can be answered by consulting maps. Maps convey a wealth of varied information through colors, lines, symbols, and labels. To read and interpret maps, you must be able to understand their language and symbols.

TYPES OF MAPS

A map is an illustration drawn to scale of all or part of the earth's surface. Types of maps include *physical maps, political maps,* and *special-purpose maps.* Physical maps illustrate the natural landscape of an area—the landforms that mark the earth's surface. Physical maps often use shading to show relief—the existence of mountains, hills, and valleys—and colors to show elevation, or the height above or below sea level. The map of the United States on pages 1014–15 is a physical map.

Political maps illustrate political units such as states and nations, employing lines to mark boundaries, dots for major cities, and stars or stars within circles for capitals. The map of the United States on pages 1016–17 is a political map. Political maps are used also to show information such as territorial changes or military alliances. Special-purpose maps present specific information such as the routes of explorers, the outcome of an election, regional economic activity, or population density. The "Election of 1860" and "The Underground Railroad" maps on these pages are special-purpose maps.

MAP FEATURES

Most maps have a number of features in common. Familiarity with these basic elements makes reading any map easier.

Titles, legends, and labels. A map's title tells you what the map is about. It often includes information on what area is shown and what time period is being represented. The *legend,* or key, explains any special symbols, colors, or shadings used on the map. Labels designate things such as political and geographic place-names as well as physical features like mountain ranges, oceans, and rivers.

Directions and distances. Most maps in this textbook have a *compass rose,* or directional indicator, like the one on "The Underground Railroad" map. The compass rose indicates the four cardinal points: *N* for north, *S* for south, *E* for east, and *W* for west. You can also find intermediate directions—northeast, southeast, southwest, and northwest—using the compass rose. This helps in describing the *relative location* of a place—its location relative to another point of reference. (If a map has no compass rose, assume that north is at the top, east is to the right, and so on.)

Many maps in this textbook include a scale, showing both miles and kilometers, to help you relate distances on the map to actual distances on the earth's surface. You can use a scale to find the distance between any two points.

The global grid. The *absolute location* of any place on the earth is given in terms of *latitude* (number of degrees north or south of the equator) and *longitude*

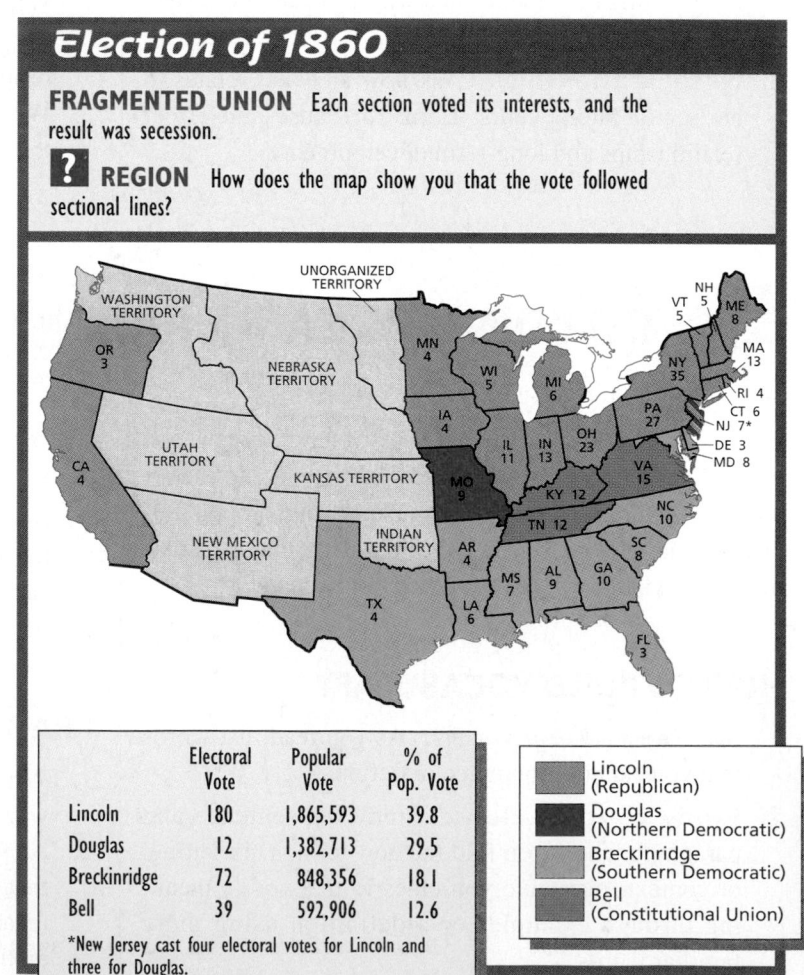

Election of 1860

FRAGMENTED UNION Each section voted its interests, and the result was secession.

? REGION How does the map show you that the vote followed sectional lines?

	Electoral Vote	Popular Vote	% of Pop. Vote
Lincoln	180	1,865,593	39.8
Douglas	12	1,382,713	29.5
Breckinridge	72	848,356	18.1
Bell	39	592,906	12.6

*New Jersey cast four electoral votes for Lincoln and three for Douglas.

Lincoln (Republican)
Douglas (Northern Democratic)
Breckinridge (Southern Democratic)
Bell (Constitutional Union)

(number of degrees east or west of the prime meridian). The *global grid* is created by the intersecting lines of latitude *(parallels)* and lines of longitude *(meridians)*. In *Todd & Curti's The American Nation,* grid lines sometimes are indicated by tick marks near the edge of the map. Many maps also have *locator maps* (right), which place the area of focus in a larger context, showing it in relation to the entire United States, or the world.

▶ **The maps on these two pages are special-purpose maps. On the page opposite is an Albers projection. Above right is a locator map, and below is an example of a tilted perspective.**

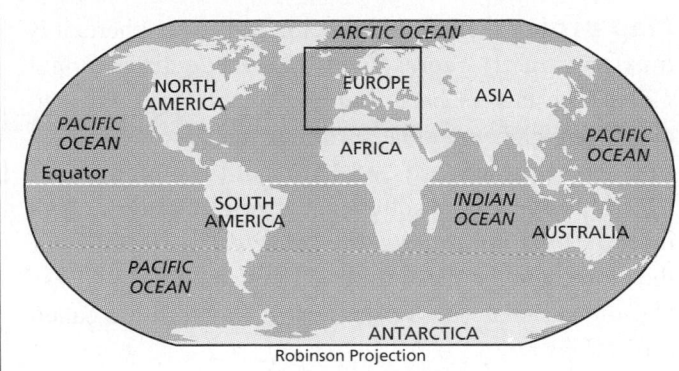

Robinson Projection

The Underground Railroad

Legend:
- Counties with slave population 50% or more
- Counties with slave population 10%–49%
- Counties with slave population <10%
- → Escape route

Tilted Perspective Projection

ROAD TO FREEDOM It is estimated that the more than 3,000 members of the Underground Railroad helped from 50,000 to 75,000 enslaved African Americans escape to freedom.

❓ LOCATION Why do you think Cairo, Illinois, and Cincinnati, Ohio, were important stops on the Underground Railroad?

Map projections. Because the earth is a sphere, it is most accurately represented by a three-dimensional globe. The task of *cartographers,* or mapmakers, is to depict that globe on a flat surface as accurately as possible—to, in the words of 16th-century mapmaker Gerardus Mercator, square the circle. Cartographers do this by transferring the curved coordinates of the globe onto the flat surface in a systematic way. These two-dimensional views of the earth's surface are called *projections.*

To flatten the curved coordinates of a globe, cartographers must squeeze or stretch the global grid of parallels and meridians. Thus every map projection, and therefore every map, distorts to some extent at least one of the following aspects: (1) the shape of land areas, (2) their relative sizes, (3) directions, or (4) distances. Mapmakers choose the projection that least distorts what they wish to show. Most projections in *Todd & Curti's The American Nation* fall into two broad categories: conformal and equal area.

Conformal projections preserve the shape and scale of small areas around a point or a line. They cannot, however, preserve the shape of large countries or continents because scale varies from point to point. For example, in a world map using a Mercator conformal projection, sizes and shapes are accurate along the equator but distorted toward the poles. As a result, Greenland and South America appear to be the same size even though South America is actually nine times as large as Greenland. The Transverse Mercator projection used on the "French and Indian War" map on page 92 and the "Lexington and Concord" map on page 114 are examples of conformal projection.

Equal-area projections show the relative sizes of different countries or continents quite accurately—a square inch or centimeter of paper represents the same number of square miles or kilometers of ground at any point on the map. But the price for this standardization is a distortion of distances and shapes. Most of the maps in *Todd & Curti's The American Nation* are equal-

area projections, with Albers Equal-Area projections being the most common. The Albers projection is used on most of the U.S. maps—including all of the special-purpose maps like the "Election of 1860"—because it is effective in showing, with a minimum of distortion, large countries with east-west orientations.

Not all of the projections used in this textbook are conformal or equal area. The Robinson projection, used for the locator maps, is an effective compromise between the two categories. It minimizes distortions in size, shape, distance, and direction, although without preserving complete accuracy in any aspect. Other projections are used to give unique perspectives. "The

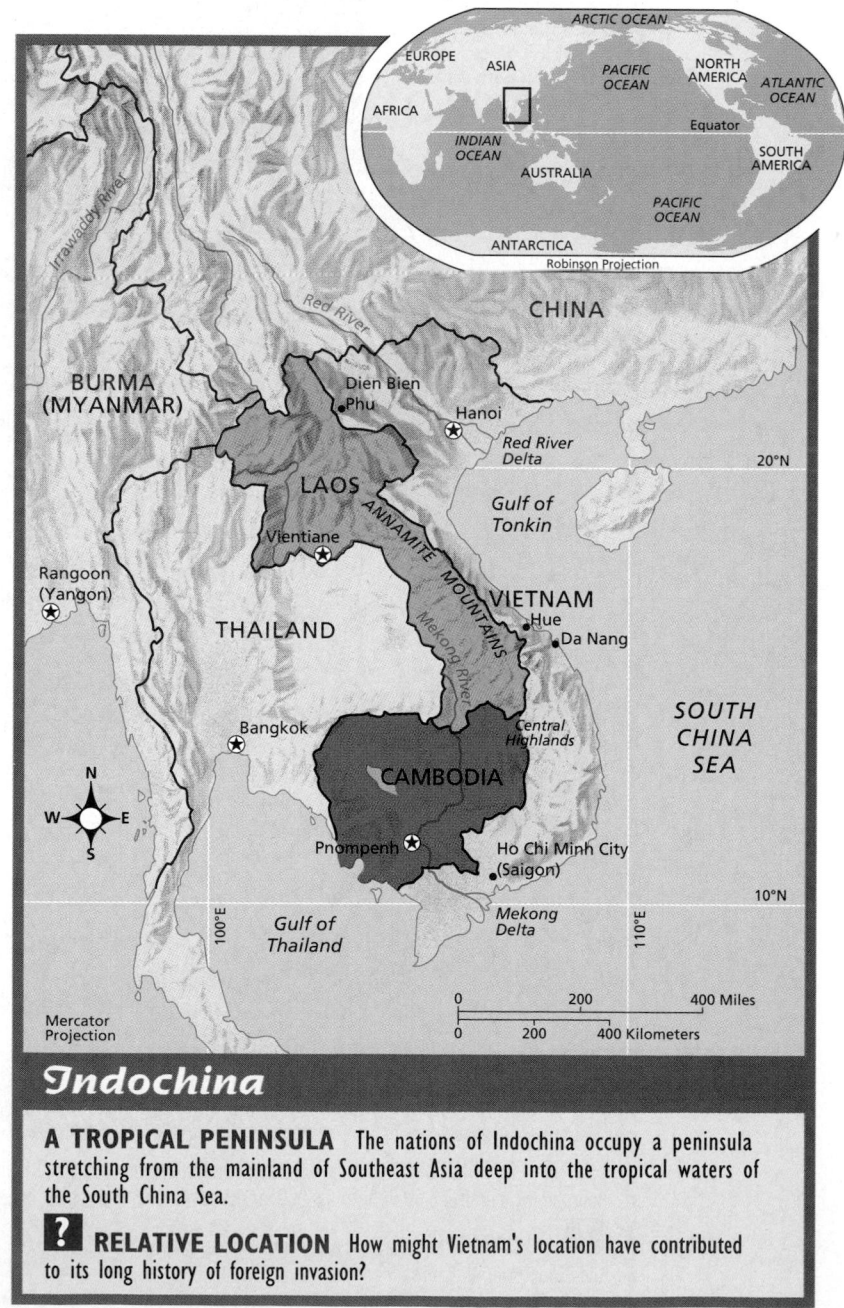

Indochina

A TROPICAL PENINSULA The nations of Indochina occupy a peninsula stretching from the mainland of Southeast Asia deep into the tropical waters of the South China Sea.

? RELATIVE LOCATION How might Vietnam's location have contributed to its long history of foreign invasion?

Underground Railroad" map on page 993 uses a *tilted perspective*. Compare the map to the Albers projection "Election of 1860" map on page 992. Note how the size and shape of the southern states are fairly accurate while the states and territories to the north and west are distorted on the tilted-perspective map. The perspective serves to draw attention to the southern states, the primary focus of the map.

HOW TO READ A MAP

1. **Determine the focus of the map.** Read the map's title and labels to determine the map's focus—its subject and the geographic area it covers.

2. **Study the map legend.** Read the legend and become familiar with any special symbols, lines, colors, and shadings used on the map.

3. **Check directions and distances.** Use the directional indicator and scale as needed to determine direction, location, and distance.

4. **Check the grid lines.** Refer to lines of longitude and latitude, or to a locator map, to fix the area in its larger context.

5. **Determine the projection.** Determine what projection is being used for the map, especially whether it is an equal area or a conformal projection. Ask yourself why this kind of projection has been chosen for the particular map, keeping in mind what its advantages or drawbacks are.

6. **Study the map.** Study the map's basic features and details, keeping its purpose in mind. If it is a special-purpose map, study the specific information being presented.

APPLYING YOUR SKILL

Study the map of Indochina on the opposite page. Use the locator map to determine the region's global location and to help you understand why the region is also called Southeast Asia. The locator map allows you to determine that Indochina is across the Pacific Ocean from the United States. Note that because the map has lines of longitude and latitude and a scale, you can find the absolute locations of each of the national capitals and compare the relative sizes of the countries. The scale even allows you to compare the size of the countries to your state.

This map combines both physical and political features in one map. Note how the use of relief clearly shows the mountains and coastal lowlands. Trace the Red River and Mekong River to their deltas and determine into what bodies of water each flows.

The California Gold Rush

FORTY-NINERS The discovery of gold at Sutter's sawmill on the California Trail drew thousands of people from all over the world.

? PLACE Why did Sacramento and Stockton become important during the gold rush?

Study the borders of the countries that make up Indochina. Note for which countries the Mekong River serves as a border. Also note that Laos is an entirely landlocked country, while Vietnam, on the other hand, has hundreds of miles of coastline on the Gulf of Tonkin, South China Sea, and Gulf of Thailand. Vietnam also has a lengthy mountainous border to its north and west—a geographic fact that has been very important in its history.

PRACTICING YOUR SKILL

For each of the special-purpose maps in this lesson—"Election of 1860" on page 992, "The Underground Railroad" on page 993, and "The California Gold Rush" on this page—answer the following questions.

1. What is the special focus of the map?
2. How is a map helpful in presenting this information?
3. What special symbols, if any, are used on the map?
4. What do the color variations or different lines indicate?

7 READING CHARTS AND GRAPHS

Charts and graphs are used to organize and present information visually. They categorize and display data in a variety of ways, depending on the type of chart or graph being used and the subject matter of the data. Several different types of charts and graphs are used in this textbook.

CHARTS

You are already familiar with the time line, which is a chart that lists historical events according to their chronological order. For an example of another kind of chronological chart, see the chart "Major Events of the Cold War" on page 800.

Other charts include flowcharts, organizational charts, and tables. A *flowchart* shows a sequence of events or the steps in a process. Cause-and-effect relationships are often shown by flowcharts (see page 990). An *organizational chart* displays the structure of an organization, indicating the ranking or function of its internal parts and the relationships between them. "Decision-Making Bodies of the United Nations" (below left) is an example

of an organizational chart. A *table* is a single, or more often, multicolumn chart that presents data in categories that are easy to understand and compare. Tables, such as "Changes in Material Standards of Living, 1940–1955" (below right), are effective in displaying statistics that vary greatly or would be cumbersome in graph form.

HOW TO READ A CHART

1. **Read the title.** Read the title to identify the focus or purpose of the chart.

2. **Study the chart's parts.** Read the chart's headings, subheadings, and labels to identify the categories used and the specific data given for each category.

3. **Analyze the details.** When reading quantities, note increases or decreases in amounts. When reading dates, note intervals of time. When viewing an organizational chart, follow directional arrows or lines.

4. **Put the data to use.** Form generalizations or draw conclusions based on the data.

DECISION–MAKING BODIES OF THE UNITED NATIONS

Body	Function
General Assembly	Sets policies.
Security Council	Resolves diplomatic, military, and political disputes.
Economic and Social Council	Deals with human welfare and fundamental rights and freedoms.
International Court of Justice	Handles international legal disputes.
Trusteeship Council	Supervises territories that are not independent.
Secretariat	Performs routine administrative work of the UN.

Sources: *Encyclopedia of American History; Funk & Wagnalls New Encyclopedia*

MULTICULTURAL COOPERATION The United Nations was established in order to give every member nation a voice in international affairs. The General Assembly includes over 150 countries and uses five official languages—English, Russian, French, Spanish, and Chinese.

? **ANALYZING** Which body of the United Nations is responsible for monitoring military aggressions between nations?

CHANGES IN MATERIAL STANDARDS OF LIVING, 1940–1955

Households Owning	1940	1955
Automobile	50.0%	71.0%
Television Set	0.0%	76.1%
Refrigerator	44.0%	94.1%
Washing Machine	46.0%	84.1%
Clothes Dryer	0.0%	9.2%
Vacuum Cleaner	38.0%	64.3%

Sources: *The Overworked American; 1956 Statistical Abstract; An Economic History of Women in America; The Proud Decades*

"THE GOOD LIFE" After World War II many American consumers rushed to buy the latest in modern conveniences.

? **BUILDING CHART SKILLS** Which item experienced the greatest increase in ownership?

◀ The chart "Decision-Making Bodies of the United Nations" is an organizational chart. "Changes in Material Standards of Living, 1940–1955" is a table.

GRAPHS

There are several types of graphs; each has certain advantages in displaying data for a particular emphasis. A *line graph* plots changes in quantities over time. A line graph has a horizontal axis and a vertical axis. One axis generally lists numbers or percentages, while the other axis is marked off in periods of time. The line is created by plotting data on the grid formed by the intersecting axes and then connecting the dots. "Total Immigration to the U.S., 1860–1900" is an example of a line graph. A *bar graph* can be used to display changes in quantities over time. But most often bar graphs are used to compare quantities within categories. For example, the bar graphs in the "Allied and Central Resources, 1914–1918" chart on this page compare the military resources of the Allied and Central powers during World War I. A *pie graph,* or *circle graph,* displays proportions by showing sections of a whole like slices of a pie, with the whole equaling 100 percent. "Population in the South, 1860" on page 998 features two pie graphs.

HOW TO READ A GRAPH

1. **Read the title.** Read the title to identify the subject and purpose of the graph. Note the kind of graph, remembering what each kind is designed to emphasize.

2. **Study the labels.** To identify the type of information presented in the graph, read the labels that define each axis, bar, or section of the graph.

3. **Analyze the data.** Note increases or decreases in quantities. Look for trends, relationships, and changes in the data.

4. **Put the data to use.** Use the results of your analysis to form generalizations and to draw conclusions.

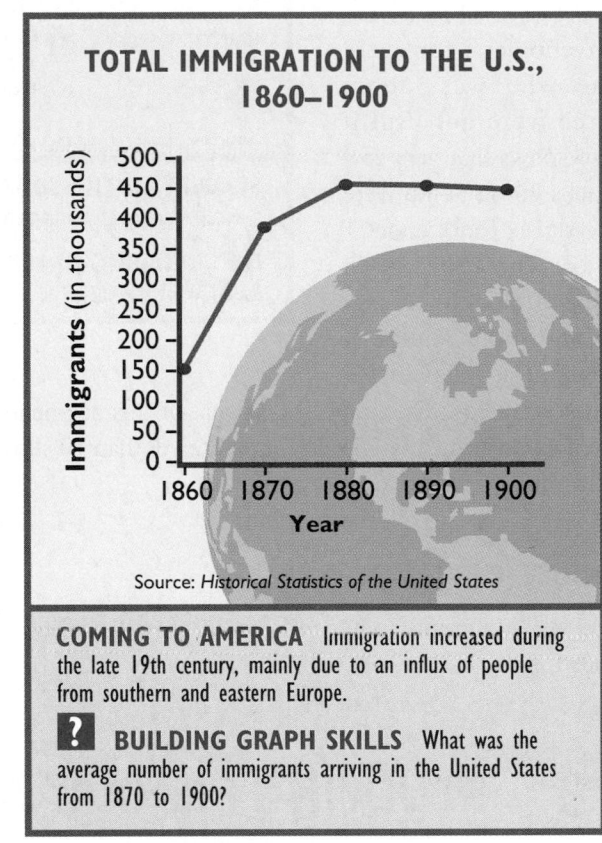

COMING TO AMERICA Immigration increased during the late 19th century, mainly due to an influx of people from southern and eastern Europe.

? **BUILDING GRAPH SKILLS** What was the average number of immigrants arriving in the United States from 1870 to 1900?

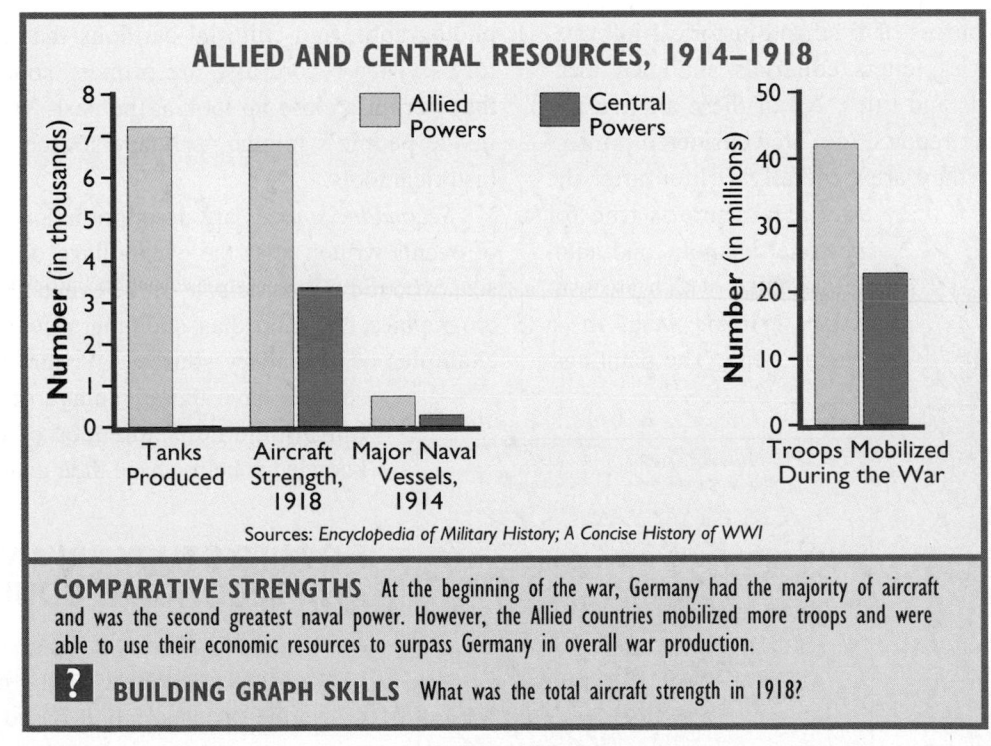

COMPARATIVE STRENGTHS At the beginning of the war, Germany had the majority of aircraft and was the second greatest naval power. However, the Allied countries mobilized more troops and were able to use their economic resources to surpass Germany in overall war production.

? **BUILDING GRAPH SKILLS** What was the total aircraft strength in 1918?

APPLYING YOUR SKILL

Study the pie graphs on the South's population on the eve of the Civil War. From the first graph you can see that relatively few whites were slaveholders; for every one who was, about three were not. But it also shows that very few blacks in the South were *not* slaves (only about 1 in 17). The second graph focuses on a small segment of the southern population—slaveholding households. The graph shows that of this segment of the population nearly 75 percent had fewer than 10 slaves, while only 3 percent had 50 or more.

POPULATION IN THE SOUTH, 1860

Total Population
1%
2%
47%
16%
34%

Slaveholding Households
1%
2%
72%
25%

Nonslaveholding whites
Slaveholding whites
Slaves
Free blacks
Others

Less than 10 slaves
10–49 slaves
50–99 slaves
100 or more slaves

Sources: *Historical Statistics of the United States; Slavery and the Southern Economy; The Black American Reference Book*

SLAVERY IN THE SOUTH Although slavery played an important part in the southern economy, only a small minority of southerners owned slaves.

? BUILDING GRAPH SKILLS Which group made up the largest section of the population in the South? What percent of all slaveholders owned 50 or more slaves?

PRACTICING YOUR SKILL

Use the line graph on page 997 to answer the following questions.

1. What type of data is illustrated, and what intervals are used for the horizontal axis and the vertical axis?
2. Which decade shows the greatest increase in immigration to the United States? At what number (approximately) does the level of immigration begin to level out? In what year does this occur?
3. What generalizations or conclusions can you draw from the information in this graph?

---

8 STUDYING PRIMARY AND SECONDARY SOURCES

There are many sources of firsthand historical information, including diaries, letters, editorials, and legal documents such as wills and titles. All of these are *primary sources*. Newspaper reports, too, are considered primary sources, although they are generally written after the fact. The same is true for personal memoirs and autobiographies, which are usually written late in a person's life. The paintings, photographs, and editorial cartoons that comprise history's visual record also are primary sources. Because they permit a close-up look at the past—a chance to get inside people's minds—primary sources are valuable historical tools.

Secondary sources are descriptions or interpretations of events written after the events have occurred by persons who did not participate in the events. History books, biographies, encyclopedias, and other reference works are examples of secondary sources. Writers of secondary sources have the advantage of knowing the long-range consequences of events. This knowledge helps shape their analyses.

HOW TO STUDY PRIMARY AND SECONDARY SOURCES

1. **Study the material carefully.** Consider the nature of the material. Is it verbal or visual? Is it based on firsthand

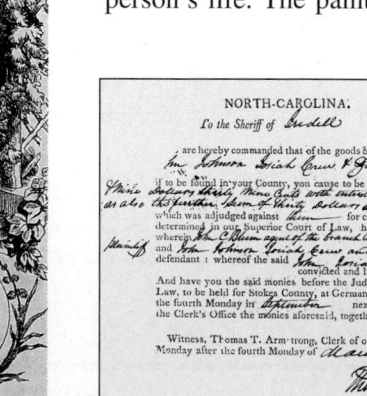

information or on the accounts of others? Note the major ideas and supporting details.

2. **Consider the audience.** Ask yourself: For whom was this message meant originally? Whether a message was intended, for instance, for the general public or for a specific, private audience may have influenced its style or content.

3. **Check for bias.** Watch for words or phrases that signal a one-sided view of a person or event.

4. **When possible, compare sources.** Study more than one source on a topic if available. Comparing sources gives you a more complete, balanced account.

PRACTICING YOUR SKILL

1. What distinguishes secondary sources from primary sources?

2. What advantage do secondary sources have over primary sources?

3. Why should you consider the original audience of a historical source?

4. Of the following, identify which are primary and which are secondary sources: a newspaper, a private journal, a biography, an editorial cartoon, a deed to property, a snapshot of a family on vacation, a magazine article about the history of the West, an autobiography.

9 CREATING AN OUTLINE

An outline is a tool for organizing information. It is a logical summary that presents the main points of what you have read or plan to communicate. An outline is an important part of preparing to write a paper. An essay outline, for example, would highlight the main ideas that you intend to express and sketch the details that you want to include for support. An outline is only a skeletal structure. It must be fleshed out in use. But if an outline is thorough and well thought out, it makes writing the final product much easier.

HOW TO CREATE AN OUTLINE

1. **Order your material.** Decide what you want to emphasize or focus on. Order or classify your material with that in mind. Determine what information belongs in an introduction, what should make up the body of your paper, and what to leave for the conclusion.

2. **Identify main ideas.** Identify the main ideas to be highlighted in each section. Make these your outline's main headings.

3. **List supporting details.** Determine the important details or facts that support each main idea. Rank and list them as subheadings, using additional levels of subheadings as necessary. Subheadings must come in pairs, at the least: no *A*'s without *B*'s, no *1*'s without *2*'s.

4. **Put your outline to use.** Structure your essay or report according to your outline. Each main heading, for instance, might form the basis for a topic sentence to begin a paragraph. Subheadings would then make up the content of the paragraph. In a more lengthy paper, each subheading might be the main idea of a paragraph.

The sample outline below could have been used in preparation for writing about the Louisiana Purchase. Note the several levels of headings that rank the parts of the outline.

I. Republicans favor westward expansion
    A. Settlement of the Trans-Appalachian West
    B. Access to the Mississippi River
        1. Importance of the port of New Orleans
        2. France regains control of Louisiana
            a. Threat to American trade
            b. Obstacle to U.S. westward expansion
II. Jefferson negotiates with France
    A. U.S. diplomats purchase Louisiana
    B. Why France made the sale
        1. Napoléon fails to build empire
            a. Need for naval base in West Indies
            b. Revolt in Saint Domingue (Haiti)
            c. French fail to regain Haiti
        2. Napoléon needs money for war plans

PRACTICING YOUR SKILL

Read the subsection in Chapter 17 titled "Urban Moral Reform" (pages 525–26). Then, using the information you have gained here, create an outline that you could use in writing about this subject.

To complete research papers or special projects, you may need to use resources other than this textbook. Conducting research generally requires you to seek out the resources available in a library.

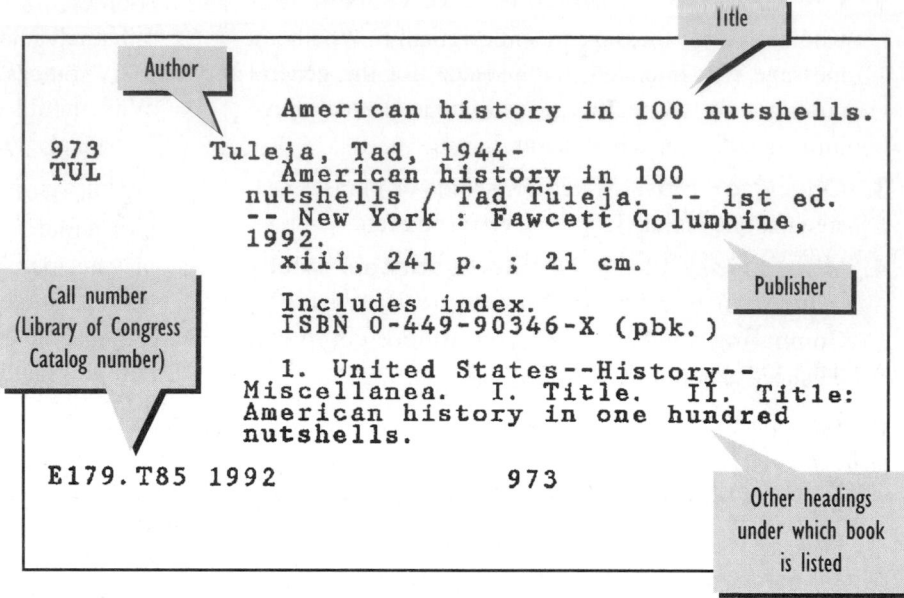

Author

Title

Call number (Library of Congress Catalog number)

Publisher

Other headings under which book is listed

```
                    American history in 100 nutshells.
973       Tuleja, Tad, 1944-
TUL            American history in 100
          nutshells / Tad Tuleja. -- 1st ed.
          -- New York : Fawcett Columbine,
          1992.
               xiii, 241 p. ; 21 cm.

               Includes index.
               ISBN 0-449-90346-X (pbk.)

               1. United States--History--
          Miscellanea.   I. Title.   II. Title:
          American history in one hundred
          nutshells.

E179.T85 1992                      973
```

FINDING INFORMATION

To find a particular book, you need to know how libraries organize their materials. Books of fiction are alphabetized according to the last name of the author. To classify nonfiction books, libraries use the Dewey decimal system and the Library of Congress system. Both systems assign each book a *call number* that tells you its classification.

To find the number, look in the library's *card catalog*. The catalog lists books by author, by title, and by subject. If you know the author or title of the book, finding it is simple. If you do not know this information, or if you just want to find any book about a general subject, look up that subject heading. Some libraries have computerized card catalogs, which can make searching for specific information easier.

Librarians can assist you in using the card catalog and direct you to a book's location. They can also suggest additional resources.

USING RESOURCES

In a library's reference section, you will find encyclopedias, specialized dictionaries, atlases, almanacs, and indexes to recent material in magazines and newspapers. Encyclopedias often will be your best resource. Encyclopedias include biographical sketches of important historical figures; geographic, economic, and political data on individual nations, states, and cities; and discussions of historical events and religious, social, and cultural issues. Entries often include cross-references to related articles.

Specialized dictionaries exist for almost every field. Historical dictionaries such as *The Concise Dictionary of American History* include definitions of historical terms as well as brief descriptions of important laws, court cases, social movements, and more. Geographical dictionaries—or *gazetteers*—list significant natural physical features and place-names. Pronunciation guides, statistical data, and brief descriptions are also included. *Atlases* contain maps and visual representations of geographic data.

To find up-to-date facts about a subject, you can use almanacs, yearbooks, and periodical indexes. References like *The World Almanac and Book of Facts* include historical information and a variety of statistics about population, the environment, sports, and so on. Encyclopedia yearbooks keep up with recent, significant developments not fully covered in encyclopedia articles.

Periodical indexes, especially *The Readers' Guide to Periodical Literature,* can help you locate articles published in magazines. The *New York Times Index* catalogs the news stories published in the *Times,* the U.S. daily newspaper with perhaps the most in-depth coverage of national and world events.

PRACTICING YOUR SKILL

1. In what two ways are nonfiction books classified?
2. What kinds of references contain information about geography?
3. Where would you look to find recent coverage of a political or social issue?
4. Would you look in an encyclopedia, an atlas, or an American history dictionary to find each of the following items? (a) the latitude of Guatemala (b) a biography of Julius Caesar (c) the purpose of the Taft-Hartley Act (d) the major industries of Cleveland, Ohio

Todd & Curti's The American Nation provides you with numerous writing opportunities. Section reviews have writing exercises (labeled Writing to Inform, Writing to Persuade, and so on) that give you the chance to write about a historical subject with a particular focus in mind. Chapter reviews contain additional opportunities for writing.

WRITING WITH A PURPOSE

Always keep your purpose for writing in mind. That purpose might be to analyze, to evaluate, to synthesize, to inform, to persuade, to hypothesize, or to take a stand. As you begin, your purpose will determine the most appropriate approach to take; and when you are done, it will help you evaluate how well you have succeeded.

Each different purpose for writing requires its own form, tone, and content. The point of view you are adopting will shape what you write, as will your intended audience. For example, you would take a different tone when writing to a president from the tone you would use with a relative.

HISTORICAL IMAGINATION

Many writing opportunities in *Todd & Curti's The American Nation* ask you to create a specific type of writing, such as a diary entry, a letter, a newspaper editorial, a poem, or an advertisement. Often such writing about history involves using historical imagination—that is, writing from the perspective of a person living *then* rather than *now*. An assignment may require, for instance, that you address a particular historical figure, such as a former president, or that you write as if living through a specific historical crisis.

HOW TO WRITE A PAPER

Each writing opportunity provided in this textbook will have specific directions about what and how to write. But whether you are writing a diary entry describing your experiences as a western pioneer or an essay about the significance of the frontier, you should follow certain basic steps. The guidelines outlined in the second column (which apply especially to longer papers) can help you plan and improve your writing.

SOME TYPES OF WRITING

- A **diary** is an informal, personal log of your experiences and recollections (or those of someone else in history). Entries are dated and consist of brief accounts of the day's happenings and your reactions.

- A **letter** is a personal communication meant for a specific individual.

- An **advertisement** is an announcement to promote a product or event. Effective ads are direct and to the point, using memorable language, such as jingles and slogans, to highlight important features.

- A newspaper **editorial** is a public statement of an opinion or point of view. It takes a stand on an issue and gives reasons for that stand.

1. **Identify your purpose in writing.** Read the directions carefully to identify the purpose for your writing. Keep that purpose in mind as you plan and write your paper.

2. **Consider your audience.** When writing for a specific audience, choose the tone and style that will best communicate your message.

3. **Create an outline.** Think and plan before you begin writing your first draft. Organize themes, main ideas, and supporting details into an outline.

4. **Collect information.** Do research if necessary. Your writing will be more effective if you have many details at hand.

5. **Write a first draft and evaluate it.** In your first draft, remember to use your outline as a guide. Each paragraph should express a single main idea or set of related ideas, with details for support. Be careful to show the relationships between ideas and to use proper transitions—sentences that build connections between paragraphs.

6. **Review and edit.** Revise and reorganize your draft as needed to make your points. Improve sentences by adding appropriate adjectives and adverbs. Make your writing clearer by changing the length or structure of awkward sentences. Replace inexact

wording with more precise word choices. Then check for proper spelling, punctuation, and grammar.

7. **Write your final version.** Prepare a neat, clean final version. Appearance is important; it may not affect the quality of your writing itself, but it can affect the way your writing is perceived and understood.

PRACTICING YOUR SKILL

1 What factor—more than any other—should affect how and what you write? Why?

2. Why is it important to consider the audience for whom you are writing?

3. What steps should you take to edit a first draft?

12 TAKING A TEST

When it comes to taking a test, for history or any other subject, nothing can take the place of preparation. A good night's sleep added to consistent study habits give you a far better chance for success than hours of late-night, last-minute cramming.

But keeping your mind focused on the test and free from distractions is not all you can do to improve your test scores. Mastering some basic test-taking skills can also help. Keeping up with your daily reading assignments and taking careful notes as you read can turn taking a test into a mere matter of review. Reviewing material that you already know takes less time—and causes less stress—than trying to learn something new under pressure.

Canajoharie Library & Art Gallery, Canajoharie, New York

▲ *Homework* by **Winslow Homer**

You will face several basic types of questions on U.S. history tests: multiple choice, matching, and essay. In answering multiple-choice questions, eliminate any answers that you know are wrong; this will narrow your field of choice. When doing a matching exercise, first go through the entire list, matching those that you are sure of. Then study any that remain.

Read essay questions carefully so that you know exactly what you are being asked to write. If time permits, make an outline of the main ideas and supporting details that you plan to include in your essay. Keep your answer clear and brief, but cover all necessary points.

HOW TO TAKE A TEST

1. **Prepare beforehand.** This all-important step not only involves studying and reviewing the material prior to the test. It also means being physically rested and mentally focused on the day of the test.

2. **Follow directions.** Read all instructions carefully. Listen closely, particularly if you are being told the directions rather than being given written instructions.

3. **Preview the test.** Skim through the entire test to determine how much time you have for each section. Try to anticipate which areas of the examination will be the most difficult for you. You may wish to allow yourself more time to work on the more difficult sections.

4. **Concentrate on the test.** Do not "watch the clock," but stay aware of the time. If you do not know an answer, move on to the next question. It is best to answer as many questions as you can within the time limit.

5. **Review your answers.** If you have time, return to questions that you skipped or were unsure of and work on them. Review your essays to catch and correct any mistakes in spelling, punctuation, or grammar.

PRACTICING YOUR SKILL

1. How can you improve your chances on multiple-choice questions?

2. Why is it important to skim through the entire test before you begin?

3. Name three things that can help you in taking a test.

Thomas Jefferson's First Inaugural Address

March 4, 1801

Friends and Fellow Citizens...

All ... will bear in mind this sacred principle, that though the will of the majority is in all cases to prevail, that will to be rightful must be reasonable; that the minority possess their equal rights, which equal law must protect, and to violate would be oppression. Let us, then, fellow citizens, unite with one heart and one mind. Let us restore to social intercourse [dealings] that harmony and affection without which liberty and even life itself are but dreary things. And let us reflect that, having banished from our land that religious intolerance under which mankind so long bled and suffered, we have yet gained little if we countenance [allow] a political intolerance as despotic, as wicked, and capable of as bitter and bloody persecutions. . . . But every difference of opinion is not a difference of principle. We have called by different names brethren of the same principle. We are all Republicans; we are all Federalists. If there be any among us who would wish to dissolve this Union or to change its republican form, let them stand undisturbed as monuments of the safety with which error of opinion may be tolerated where reason is left free to combat it. I know, indeed, that some honest men fear that a republican government cannot be strong, that this government is not strong enough; but would the honest patriot, in the full tide of successful experiment, abandon a government which has so far kept us free and firm on the theoretic [hypothetical] and visionary fear that this government, the world's best hope, may by possibility want energy to preserve itself? I trust not. I believe this, on the contrary, the strongest government on earth. I believe it the only one where every man, at the call of the law, would fly to the standard of the law, and would meet invasions of the public order as his own personal concern. Sometimes it is said that man cannot be trusted with the government of himself. Can he, then, be trusted with the government of others? Or have we found angels in the forms of kings to govern him? Let history answer this question.

Let us, then, with courage and confidence pursue our own Federal and Republican principles, our attachment to union and representative government. Kindly separated by nature and a wide ocean from the exterminating havoc of one quarter of the globe; too high-minded to endure the degradations of the others; possessing a chosen country, with room enough for our descendants to the thousandth and thousandth generation; entertaining a due sense of our equal right to the use of our own faculties, to the acquisitions of our own industry, to honor and confidence from our fellow citizens, resulting not from birth, but from our actions and their sense of them; enlightened by a benign religion, professed, indeed, and practiced in various forms, yet all of them inculcating [implanting] honesty, truth, temperance, gratitude, and the love of man; acknowledging and adoring an overruling Providence, which by all its dispensations proves that it delights in the happiness of man here and his greater happiness hereafter—with all these blessings, what more is necessary to make us a happy and a prosperous people? Still one thing more, fellow citizens—a wise and frugal government, which shall restrain men from injuring one another, shall leave them otherwise free to regulate their own pursuits of industry and improvement, and shall not take from the mouth of labor the bread it has earned. This is the sum of good government, and this is necessary to close the circle of our felicities [good intentions].

About to enter, fellow citizens, on the exercise of duties which comprehend [include] everything dear and valuable to you, it is proper you should understand what I deem the essential principles of our government and consequently those which ought to shape its administration. I will compress them within the narrowest compass they will bear, stating the general principle, but not all its limitations. Equal and exact justice to all men, of whatever state or persuasion religious or political; peace, commerce, and honest friendship with all nations, entangling alliances with none; the support of the state governments in all their rights, as the most competent administrations for our domestic concerns and the surest bulwarks [defenses] against anti-republican tendencies; the preservation of the general government in its whole constitutional vigor, as the sheet anchor [main support] of our peace at home and safety abroad; a jealous care of the right of election by the people—a mild and safe corrective of abuses which are lopped by the sword of revolution where peaceable remedies are unprovided; absolute acquiescence in [submission to] the decisions of the majority, the vital principle of republics, from which [there] is no appeal but to force, the vital principle and immediate parent of despotism; a well-disciplined militia, our best reliance in peace and for the first moments of war, till regulars may relieve them; the supremacy of the civil over the military authority; economy in the public expense, that labor may be lightly burdened; the honest payment of our debts and sacred preservation of the public faith; encouragement of agriculture, and of commerce as its handmaid; the diffusion of information and arraignment [bringing up] of all abuses at the bar of the public reason; freedom of religion; freedom of the press; and freedom of person under the protection of the *habeas corpus,** and trial by juries impartially selected. These principles form the bright constellation which has gone before us and guided our steps through an age of revolution and reformation. The wisdom of our sages and blood of our heroes have been devoted to their attainment. They should be the creed of our political faith, the text of civic instruction, the touchstone by which to try the services of those we trust; and should we wander from them in moments of error or of alarm, let us hasten to retrace our steps and to regain the road which alone leads to peace, liberty, and safety.

I repair, then, fellow citizens, to the post you have assigned me. With experience enough in subordinate offices to have seen the difficulties of this the greatest of all, I have learned to expect that it will rarely fall to the lot of imperfect man to retire from this station with the reputation and the favor which bring him into it. Without pretensions to that high confidence you reposed in our first and greatest revolutionary character [Washington] whose pre-eminent services had entitled him to the first place in his country's love and destined for him the fairest page in the volume of faithful history, I ask so much confidence only as may give firmness and effect to the legal administration of your affairs. I shall often go wrong through defect of judgment. When right, I shall often be thought wrong by those whose positions will not command a view of the whole ground. I ask your indulgence for my own errors, which will never be intentional, and your support against the errors of others, who may condemn what they would not if seen in all its parts. The approbation [approval] implied by your suffrage is a great consolation to me for the past, and my future solicitude [concern] will be to retain the good opinion of those who have bestowed it in advance, to conciliate [win over] that of others by doing them all the good in my power, and to be instrumental to the happiness and freedom of all.

Relying, then, on the patronage of your good will, I advance with obedience to the work, ready to retire from it whenever you become sensible how much better choice it is in your power to make. And may that Infinite Power which rules the destinies of the universe lead our councils to what is best, and give them a favorable issue for your peace and prosperity. ❖

**Habeas corpus:* legal provision guaranteeing a prisoner or detainee the right to be informed of the cause of his or her detention, as a protection against illegal imprisonment.

The Monroe Doctrine

December 2, 1823

At the proposal of the Russian Imperial Government, made through the minister of the Emperor residing here, a full power and instructions have been transmitted to the minister of the United States at St. Petersburg to arrange by amicable negotiations the respective rights and interests of the two nations on the northwest coast of this continent. A similar proposal had been made by His Imperial Majesty to the government of Great Britain, which has likewise been acceded [agreed] to. The government of the United States has been desirous by this friendly proceeding of manifesting the great value which they have invariably attached to the friendship of the Emperor and their solicitude to cultivate the best understanding with his government. In the discussions to which this interest has given rise and in the arrangements by which they may terminate the occasion has been judged proper for asserting, as a principle in which the rights and interests of the United States are involved, that the American continents, by the free and independent condition which they have assumed and maintain, are henceforth not to be considered as subjects for future colonization by any European powers. . . .

The citizens of the United States cherish sentiments the most friendly in favor of the liberty and happiness of their fellow men on that side of the Atlantic [in Europe]. In the wars of the European powers in matters relating to themselves we have never taken any part, nor does it comport with our policy to do so. It is only when our rights are invaded or seriously menaced that we resent injuries or make preparation for our defense. With the movements in this hemisphere we are of necessity more immediately connected, and by causes which must be obvious to all enlightened and impartial observers. The political system of the allied powers [Holy Alliance]* is essentially different in this respect from that of America. This difference proceeds from that which exists in their respective governments; and to the defense of our own, which has been achieved by the loss of much blood and treasure, and matured by the wisdom of their most enlightened citizens, and under which we have enjoyed unexampled felicity, this whole nation is devoted. We owe it, therefore, to candor and to the amicable relations existing between the United States and those powers to declare that we should consider any attempt on their part to extend their system to any portion of this hemisphere as dangerous to our peace and safety. With the existing colonies or dependencies of any European power, we have not interfered and shall not interfere. But with the governments who have declared their independence and maintained it, and whose independence we have, on great consideration and on just principles, acknowledged, we could not view any interposition for the purpose of oppressing them, or controlling in any other manner their destiny, by any European power in any other light than as the manifestation of an unfriendly disposition toward the United States. In the war between those new governments and Spain, we declared our neutrality at the time of their recognition, and to this we have adhered, and shall continue to adhere, provided no change shall occur which,

in the judgment of the competent authorities of this government, shall make a corresponding change on the part of the United States indispensable to their security.

The late events in Spain and Portugal show that Europe is still unsettled. Of this important fact no stronger proof can be adduced [offered] than that the allied powers should have thought it proper, on any principle satisfactory to themselves, to have interposed by force in the internal concerns of Spain. To what extent such interposition may be carried, on the same principle, is a question in which all independent powers whose governments differ from theirs are interested, even those most remote, and surely none more so than the United States. Our policy in regard to Europe, which was adopted at an early stage of the wars which have so long agitated that quarter of the globe, nevertheless remains the same, which is, not to interfere in the internal concerns of any of its powers; to consider the government *de facto* [such as it is] as the legitimate government for us; to cultivate friendly relations with it, and to preserve those relations by a frank, firm, and manly policy, meeting in all instances the just claims of every power, submitting to injuries from none. But in regard to those continents [North and South America] circumstances are eminently and conspicuously different. It is impossible that the allied powers should extend their political system to any portion of either continent without endangering our peace and happiness; nor can anyone believe that our southern brethren [Latin Americans], if left to themselves, would adopt it of their own accord. It is equally impossible, therefore, that we should behold such interposition in any form with indifference. If we look to the comparative strength and resources of Spain and those new governments and their distance from each other, it must be obvious that she can never subdue them. It is still the true policy of the United States to leave the parties to themselves, in the hope that other powers will pursue the same course. . . . ❖

*Holy Alliance: alliance between France, Austria, Russia, and Prussia.

The Seneca Falls Declaration of Sentiments

July 19–20, 1848

When, in the course of human events, it becomes necessary for one portion of the family of man to assume among the people of the earth a position different from that which they have hitherto occupied, but one to which the laws of nature and of nature's God entitle them, a decent respect to the opinions of mankind requires that they should declare the causes that impel them to such a course.

We hold these truths to be self-evident: that all men and women are created equal; that they are endowed by their Creator with certain inalienable rights; that among these are life, liberty, and the pursuit of happiness; that to secure these rights governments are instituted, deriving their just powers from the consent of the governed. Whenever any form of government becomes destructive of these ends, it is the right of those who suffer from it to refuse allegiance to it, and to insist upon the institution of a new government, laying its foundation on such principles, and organizing its powers in such form, as to them shall seem most likely to effect their safety and happiness. Prudence, indeed, will dictate that governments long established should not be changed for light and transient causes; and accordingly all experience has shown that mankind are more disposed to suffer while evils are sufferable [bearable], than to right themselves by abolishing the forms to which they were accustomed. But when a long train of abuses and usurpations [seizures] pursuing invariably the same object evinces [reveals] a design to reduce them under absolute despotism, it is their duty to throw off such government, and to provide new guards for their future security. Such has been the patient sufferance [suffering] of the women under this government, and such is now the necessity which constrains them to demand the equal station to which they are entitled.

The history of mankind is a history of repeated injuries and usurpations on the part of man toward woman, having in direct object the establishment of an absolute tyranny over her. To prove this, let facts be submitted to a candid world. . . .

Having deprived her of this first right of a citizen, the elective franchise [right to vote], thereby leaving her without representation in the halls of legislation, he has oppressed her on all sides.

He has made her, if married, in the eye of the law, civilly dead. . . .

Now, in view of this entire disfranchisement [loss of right to vote] of one half of the people of this country, their social and religious degradation—in view of the unjust laws above mentioned, and because women do feel themselves aggrieved, oppressed, and fraudulently deprived of their most sacred rights, we insist that they have immediate admission to all the rights and privileges which belong to them as citizens of the United States.

In entering upon the great work before us, we anticipate no small amount of misconception, misrepresentation, and ridicule; but we shall use every instrumentality [means] within our power to effect our object. We shall employ agents, circulate tracts [pamphlets], petition the state and national legislatures, and endeavor to enlist the pulpit and the press in our behalf. We hope this convention will be followed by a series of conventions embracing every part of the country. . . .

Resolutions

Resolved, That all laws which prevent woman from occupying such a station in society as her conscience shall dictate, or which place her in a position inferior to that of man, are contrary to the great precept of nature, and, therefore, of no force or authority.

Resolved, That woman is man's equal—was intended to be so by the Creator, and the highest good of the race demands that she should be recognized as such. . . .

Resolved, That woman has too long rested satisfied in the circumscribed [narrow] limits which corrupt customs and a perverted [misdirected] application of the Scriptures have marked out for her, and that it is time she should move in the enlarged sphere which her great Creator has assigned her.

Resolved, That it is the duty of the women of this country to secure to themselves their sacred right to the elective franchise.

Resolved, That the equality of human rights results necessarily from the fact of the identity [sameness of essential character] of the race in capabilities and responsibilities. . . .

Resolved, therefore, That, being invested by the Creator with the same capabilities, and the same consciousness of responsibility for their exercise, it is demonstrably the right and duty of woman, equally with man, to promote every righteous cause by every righteous means; and especially in regard to the great subjects of morals and religion, it is self-evidently her right to participate with her brother in teaching them, both in private and in public, by writing and by speaking, by any instrumentalities proper to be used, and in any assemblies proper to be held. . . .

Resolved, That the speedy success of our cause depends upon the zealous and untiring efforts of both men and women, for the overthrow of the monopoly of the pulpit, and for the securing to women an equal participation with men in the various trades, professions, and commerce. ❖

The Emancipation Proclamation

January 1, 1863

**BY THE PRESIDENT OF
THE UNITED STATES OF AMERICA**

A Proclamation

Whereas on the twenty-second day of September, A.D. 1862, a proclamation was issued by the President of the United States, containing, among other things, the following, to wit [namely]:

"That on the first day of January, A.D. 1863, all persons held as slaves within any state or designated part of a state, the people whereof shall then be in rebellion against the United States, shall be then, thenceforward, and forever free; and the executive government of the United States, including the military and naval authority thereof, will recognize and maintain the freedom of such persons and will do no act or acts to repress such persons or any of them, in any efforts they may make for their actual freedom.

"That the Executive will on the first day of January aforesaid, by proclamation, designate the states and parts of states, if any, in which the people thereof, respectively, shall then be in rebellion against the United States; and the fact that any state or the people thereof shall on that day be in good faith represented in the Congress of the United States by members chosen thereto at elections wherein a majority of the qualified voters of such states shall have participated shall, in the absence of strong countervailing [opposing] testimony, be deemed conclusive evidence that such state and the people thereof are not then in rebellion against the United States."

Now, therefore, I, Abraham Lincoln, President of the United States, by virtue of the power in me vested as Commander-in-Chief of the Army and Navy of the United States in time of actual armed rebellion against the authority and government of the United States, and as a fit and necessary war measure for suppressing said rebellion, do, on this first day of January, A.D. 1863, and in accordance with my purpose so to do, publicly proclaimed for the full period of one hundred days from the first day above mentioned, order and designate as the states and parts of states wherein the people thereof, respectively, are this day in rebellion against the United States the following, to wit:

Arkansas, Texas, Louisiana (except the parishes of St. Bernard, Plaquemines, Jefferson, St. John, St. Charles, St. James, Ascension, Assumption, Terrebonne, Lafourche, St. Mary, St. Martin, and Orleans, including the city of New Orleans), Mississippi, Alabama, Florida, Georgia, South Carolina, North Carolina, and Virginia (except the forty-eight counties designated as West Virginia, and also the counties of Berkeley, Accomac, Northampton, Elizabeth City, York, Princess Anne, and Norfolk, including the cities of Norfolk and Portsmouth), and which excepted parts are for the present left precisely as if this proclamation were not issued.

And by virtue of the power and for the purpose aforesaid, I do order and declare that all persons held as slaves within said designated states and parts of states are, and henceforward shall be, free; and that the executive government of the United States, including the military and naval authorities thereof, will recognize and maintain the freedom of said persons.

And I hereby enjoin [order] upon the people so declared to be free to abstain from all violence, unless in necessary self-defense; and I recommend to them that, in all cases when allowed, they labor faithfully for reasonable wages.

And I further declare and make known that such persons of suitable condition will be received into the armed service of the United States to garrison forts, positions, stations, and other places, and to man vessels of all sorts in said service.

And upon this act, sincerely believed to be an act of justice, warranted by the Constitution upon military necessity, I invoke the considerate judgment of mankind and the gracious favor of Almighty God. ❖

Abraham Lincoln's Gettysburg Address

November 19, 1863

Four score and seven years ago our fathers brought forth on this continent a new nation, conceived in liberty, and dedicated to the proposition that all men are created equal.

Now we are engaged in a great civil war, testing whether that nation, or any nation so conceived and so dedicated can long endure. We are met on a great battle-field of that war. We have come to dedicate a portion of that field as a final resting place for those who here gave their lives that that nation might live. It is altogether fitting and proper that we should do this.

But, in a larger sense, we cannot dedicate—we cannot consecrate [make holy]—we cannot hallow—this ground. The brave men, living and dead, who struggled here, have consecrated it far above our poor power to add or detract. The world will little note nor long remember what we say here, but it can never forget what they did here. It is for us, the living, rather, to be dedicated here to the unfinished work which they who fought here have thus far so nobly advanced. It is rather for us to be here dedicated to the great task remaining before us—that from these honored dead we take increased devotion to that cause for which they gave the last full measure of devotion; that we here highly resolve that these dead shall not have died in vain; that this nation, under God, shall have a new birth of freedom; and that government of the people, by the people, for the people, shall not perish from the earth. ❖

The Fourteen Points

January 8, 1918

Gentlemen of the Congress:

It will be our wish and purpose that the processes of peace, when they are begun, shall be absolutely open and that they shall involve and permit henceforth no secret understandings of any kind. The day of conquest and aggrandizement is gone by; so is also the day of secret covenants entered into in the interest of particular governments and likely at some unlooked-for moment to upset the peace of the world. It is this happy fact, now clear to the view of every public man whose thoughts do not still linger in an age that is dead and gone, which makes it possible for every nation whose purposes are consistent with justice and the peace of the world to avow now or at any other time the objects it has in view.

We entered this war because violations of right had occurred which touched us to the quick and made the life of our own people impossible unless they were corrected and the world secured once for all against their recurrence. What we demand in this war, therefore, is nothing peculiar to ourselves. It is that the world be made fit and safe to live in; and particularly that it be made safe for every peace-loving nation which, like our own, wishes to live its own life, determine its own insti-tutions, be assured of justice and fair dealing by the other peoples of the world as against force and selfish aggression. All the peoples of the world are in effect partners in this interest, and for our own part we see very clearly that unless justice be done to others it will not be done to us. The program of the world's peace, therefore, is our program; and that program, the only possible program, as we see it, is this:

I. Open covenants of peace, openly arrived at, after which there shall be no private international understandings of any kind but diplomacy shall proceed always frankly and in the public view.

II. Absolute freedom of navigation upon the seas, outside territorial waters, alike in peace and in war, except as the seas may be closed in whole or in part by international action for the enforcement of international covenants.

III. The removal, so far as possible, of all economic barriers and the establishment of an equality of trade conditions among all the nations consenting to the peace and associating themselves for its maintenance.

IV. Adequate guarantees given and taken that national armaments will be reduced to the lowest point consistent with domestic safety.

V. A free, open-minded, and absolutely impartial adjustment of all colonial claims, based upon a strict observance of the principle that in determining all such questions of sovereignty the interests of the populations concerned must have equal weight with the equitable claims of the government whose title is to be determined.

VI. The evacuation of all Russian territory and such a settlement of all questions affecting Russia as will secure the best and freest cooperation of the other nations of the world in obtaining for her an unhampered and unembarrassed opportunity for the independent determination of her own political development and national policy and assure her of a sincere welcome into the society of free nations under institutions of her own choosing; and, more than a welcome, assistance also of every kind that she may need and may herself desire. The treatment accorded Russia by her sister nations in the months to come will be the acid test of their good will, of their comprehension of her needs as distinguished from their own interests, and of their intelligent and unselfish sympathy.

VII. Belgium, the whole world will agree, must be evacuated and restored, without any attempt to limit the sovereignty which she enjoys in common with all other free nations. No other single act will serve as this will serve to restore confidence among the nations in the laws which they have themselves set and determined for the government of their relation with one another. Without this healing act the whole structure and validity of international law is forever impaired.

VIII. All French territory should be freed and the invaded portions restored, and the wrong done to France by Prussia in 1871 in the matter of Alsace-Lorraine, which has unsettled the peace of the world for nearly fifty years, should be righted, in order that peace may once more be made secure in the interest of all.

IX. A readjustment of the frontiers of Italy shall be effected along clearly recognizable lines of nationality.

X. The peoples of Austria-Hungary, whose place among the nations we wish to see safeguarded and assured, should be accorded the freest opportunity of autonomous development.

XI. Rumania, Serbia, and Montenegro should be evacuated; occupied territories restored; Serbia accorded free and secure access to the sea; and the relations of the several Balkan states to one another determined by friendly counsel along historically established lines of allegiance and nationality; and international guarantees of the political and economic independence and territorial integrity of the several Balkan states should be entered into.

Em[...] oth[...] shou[...] absolutel[...] opment, and [...] opened as a free [...] of the present Ottoman [...] secure sovereignty, but the [...] now under Turkish rule [...] security of life and an [...] autonomous development[...] all nations under inter[...]

XIII. An independe[...] be permanently erected which should include[...] commerce of indisputably Polish populations, should be assured a free and secure access to the [...] abited by political and economic independence an[...] be integrity should be guaranteed by international c[...] whose [...] nant.

XIV. A general association of nations m[...] be formed under specific covenants for the purpose of affording mutual guarantees of political independence and territorial integrity to great and small states alike.

In regard to these essential rectifications [righting] of wrong and assertions of right we feel ourselves to be intimate partners of all the governments and peoples associated together against the Imperialists. We cannot be separated in interest or divided in purpose. We stand together until the end.

For such arrangements and covenants we are willing to fight and to continue to fight until they are achieved; but only because we wish the right to prevail and desire a just and stable peace such as can be secured only by removing the chief provocations to war, which this program does not remove. We have no jealousy of German greatness, and there is nothing in this program that impairs it. We grudge her no achievement or distinction of learning or of pacific [peaceful] enterprise such as have made her record very bright and very enviable. We do not wish to injure her or to block in any way her legitimate influence or power. We do not wish to fight her either with arms or with hostile arrangements of trade if she is willing to associate herself with us and the other peace-loving nations of the world in covenants of justice and law and fair dealing. We wish her only to accept a place of equality among the peoples of the world—the new world in which we now live,—instead of a place of mastery.

Neither do we presume to suggest to her any alteration or modification of her institutions. But it is necessary, we must frankly say, and necessary as a preliminary to any intelligent dealings with her on our part, that we should know whom her spokesmen speak for when they speak to us, whether for the Reichstag [German legislature] majority or for the military party and the men whose creed is imperial domination.

We have spoken now, surely, in terms too concrete to admit of any further doubt or question. An

evident princi... ...one another, whether
have outlined ...s this principle be made
ples and na... structure of international
terms of li...people of the United States
they be st...
its found...
justice

...e program I
...tice to all peo-
...t to live on equal

could act upon no other principle; and to the vindica-
tion of this principle they are ready to devote their
lives, their honor, and everything that they possess.
The moral climax of this the culminating and final war
for human liberty has come, and they are ready to put
their own strength, their own highest purpose, their
own integrity and devotion to the test. ❖

Martin Luther King, Jr.'s "I Have A Dream" Speech

August 28, 1963

Five score years ago, a great American, in whose symbolic shadow we stand, signed the Emancipation Proclamation. This momentous decree came as a great beacon light of hope to millions of Negro slaves who had been seared in the flames of withering injustice. It came as a joyous daybreak to end the long night of captivity.

But one hundred years later, we must face the tragic fact that the Negro is still not free. One hundred years later, the life of the Negro is still sadly crippled by the manacles of segregation and the chains of discrimination. One hundred years later, the Negro lives on a lonely island of poverty in the midst of a vast ocean of material prosperity. One hundred years later, the Negro is still languished in the corners of American society and finds himself an exile in his own land. So we have come here today to dramatize an appalling condition.

In a sense we have come to our nation's Capital to cash a check. When the architects of our republic wrote the magnificent words of the Constitution and the Declaration of Independence, they were signing a promissory note to which every American was to fall heir. This note was a promise that all men would be guaranteed the unalienable rights of life, liberty, and the pursuit of happiness.

It is obvious today that America has defaulted on this promissory note insofar as her citizens of color are concerned. Instead of honoring this sacred obligation, America has given the Negro people a bad check; a check which has come back marked "insufficient funds." But we refuse to believe that the bank of justice is bankrupt. We refuse to believe that there are insufficient funds in the great vaults of opportunity of this nation. So we have come to cash this check—a check that will give us upon demand the riches of freedom and the security of justice.

We have also come to this hallowed spot to remind America of the fierce urgency of *now*. This is no time to engage in the luxury of cooling off or to take the tranquilizing drug of gradualism. *Now* is the time to make real the promises of democracy. *Now* is the time to rise from the dark and desolate valley of segregation to the sunlit path of racial justice. *Now* is the time to open the doors of opportunity to all of God's children. *Now* is the time to lift our nation from the quicksands of racial injustice to the solid rock of brotherhood.

It would be fatal for the nation to overlook the urgency of the moment and to underestimate the determination of the Negro. This sweltering summer of the Negro's legitimate discontent will not pass until there is an invigorating autumn of freedom and equality. Nineteen sixty-three is not an end, but a beginning. Those who hope that the Negro needed to blow off steam and will now be content will have a rude awakening if the nation returns to business as usual. There will be neither rest nor tranquility in America until the Negro is granted his citizenship rights. The whirlwinds of revolt will continue to shake the foundations of our nation until the bright day of justice emerges.

But there is something that I must say to my people who stand on the warm threshold which leads into the palace of justice. In the process of gaining our rightful place we must not be guilty of wrongful deeds. Let us not seek to satisfy our thirst for freedom by drinking from the cup of bitterness and hatred. We must forever conduct our struggle on the high plane of dignity and discipline. We must not allow our creative protest to degenerate into physical violence. Again and again we must rise to the majestic heights of meeting physical force with soul force.

The marvelous new militancy which has engulfed the Negro community must not lead us to a distrust of all white people, for many of our white brothers, as evidenced by their presence here today, have come to realize that their destiny is tied up with our destiny and their freedom is inextricably bound to our freedom. We cannot walk alone.

And as we walk, we must make the pledge that we shall march ahead. We cannot turn back. There are those who are asking the devotees of civil rights, "When will you be satisfied?"

We can never be satisfied as long as the Negro is the victim of the unspeakable horrors of police brutality.

We can never be satisfied as long as our bodies, heavy with the fatigue of travel, cannot gain lodging in the motels of the highways and the hotels of the cities.

We cannot be satisfied as long as the Negro's basic mobility is from a smaller ghetto to a larger one.

We can never be satisfied as long as a Negro in Mississippi cannot vote and a Negro in New York believes he has nothing for which to vote.

No, no, we are not satisfied, and we will not be satisfied until justice rolls down like waters and righteousness like a mighty stream.

I am not unmindful that some of you have come here out of great trials and tribulations. Some of you have come fresh from narrow jail cells. Some of you have come from areas where your quest for freedom left you battered by the storms of persecution and staggered by the winds of police brutality. You have been the veterans of creative suffering. Continue to work with the faith that unearned suffering is redemptive.

Go back to Mississippi, go back to Alabama, go back to South Carolina, go back to Georgia, go back to Louisiana, go back to the slums and ghettos of our Northern cities, knowing that somehow this situation can and will be changed. Let us not wallow in the valley of despair.

I say to you today, my friends, that in spite of the difficulties and frustrations of the moment I still have a dream. It is a dream deeply rooted in the American dream.

I have a dream that one day this nation will rise up and live out the true meaning of its creed: "We hold these truths to be self-evident; that all men are created equal."

I have a dream that one day on the red hills of Georgia the sons of former slaves and the sons of former slaveowners will be able to sit down together at the table of brotherhood.

I have a dream that one day even the state of Mississippi, a desert state sweltering with the heat of injustice and oppression, will be transformed into an oasis of freedom and justice.

I have a dream that my four little children will one day live in a nation where they will not be judged by the color of their skin but by the content of their character.

I have a dream today.

I have a dream that one day the state of Alabama, whose governor's lips are presently dripping with the words of interposition and nullification, will be transformed into a situation where little black boys and black girls will be able to join hands with little white boys and white girls and walk together as sisters and brothers.

I have a dream today.

I have a dream that one day every valley shall be exhalted, every hill and mountain shall be made low, the rough places will be made plain, and the crooked places will be made straight, and the glory of the Lord shall be revealed, and all flesh shall see it together.

This is our hope. This is the faith with which I return to the South. With this faith we will be able to hew out of the mountain of despair a stone of hope. With this faith we will be able to transform the jangling discords of our nation into a beautiful symphony of brotherhood.

With this faith we will be able to work together, to pray together, to struggle together, to go to jail together, to stand up for freedom together, knowing that we will be free one day.

This will be the day when all of God's children will be able to sing with new meaning, "My country 'tis of thee, sweet land of liberty, of thee I sing. Land where my fathers died, land of the Pilgrims' pride, from every mountainside, let freedom ring."

And if America is to be a great nation, this must become true. So let freedom ring from the prodigious hilltops of New Hampshire. Let freedom ring from the mighty mountains of New York. Let freedom ring from the heightening Alleghenies of Pennsylvania!

Let freedom ring from the snowcapped Rockies of Colorado! Let freedom ring from the curvaceous peaks of California! But not only that; let freedom ring from Stone Mountain of Georgia! Let freedom ring from Lookout Mountain of Tennessee!

Let freedom ring from every hill and molehill of Mississippi. From every mountainside, let freedom ring.

When we let freedom ring, when we let it ring from every village and every hamlet, from every state and every city, we will be able to speed up that day when all of God's children, black men and white men, Jews and Gentiles, Protestants and Catholics, will be able to join hands and sing in the words of the old Negro spiritual, "Free at last! Free at last! Thank God Almighty, we are free at last!" ❖

ATLAS

The World: Political

ARCTIC OCEAN

GREENLAND (Denmark)

Arctic
ICELAND

ALASKA (US)

CANADA

Godthab •

Aleutian Islands

Vancouver •   • Winnipeg

NORTH AMERICA

Ottawa • Montreal
Toronto

Chicago •   New York

ATLANTIC

UNITED STATES

Washington, D.C. ⊛

OCEAN

Los Angeles •

BERMUDA (UK)

Rabat ⊛
Casablanca ⊛

MOROCCO

Houston •

MEXICO

WESTERN SAHARA (Sovereignty disputed)

Tropic of Cancer

THE BAHAMAS

20°N

HAWAII (US)

Havana ⊛   CUBA

DOMINICAN REPUBLIC

PUERTO RICO (US)

MAURITANIA   MALI

Mexico City ⊛

JAMAICA   HAITI

VIRGIN ISLANDS (US, UK)

ST. KITTS AND NEVIS
ANTIGUA AND BARBUDA

Nouakchott ⊛

GUATEMALA   BELIZE
HONDURAS

DOMINICA

CAPE VERDE   SENEGAL
Dakar ⊛

Guatemala City ⊛

NICARAGUA

ST. LUCIA
GRENADA

BARBADOS

GAMBIA   Bamako ⊛
GUINEA-BISSAU   GUINEA

BURKINA FASO

EL SALVADOR

ST. VINCENT AND THE GRENADINES

Managua ⊛

COSTA RICA   PANAMA

TRINIDAD AND TOBAGO

SIERRA LEONE   CÔTE D'IVOIRE

GHANA

Caracas ⊛

LIBERIA

VENEZUELA   GUYANA

Bogotá ⊛   Georgetown ⊛
Paramaribo ⊛   SURINAME

N

COLOMBIA

FRENCH GUIANA (France)

W ⊕ E

PACIFIC

Galápagos Islands (Ecuador)

Quito ⊛
ECUADOR

S

0°   Equator

KIRIBATI

OCEAN

PERU

SOUTH AMERICA

BRAZIL

WESTERN SAMOA   AMERICAN SAMOA

• Lima

BOLIVIA

Brasília ⊛

La Paz ⊛

20°S   TONGA

Sucre ⊛

Rio de Janeiro

Tropic of Capricorn

PARAGUAY

São Paulo

CHILE

Asunción ⊛

ATLANTIC

ARGENTINA

URUGUAY

OCEAN

Santiago ⊛

Buenos Aires ⊛   Montevideo ⊛

40°S

FALKLAND ISLANDS (UK)

SOUTH GEORGIA (UK)

SOUTH SANDWICH ISLANDS (UK)

60°S

160°W   140°W   120°W   100°W   80°W   60°W   40°W   20°W

Antarctic Circle

 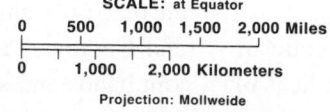

⊛ **National capitals**

• **Other cities**

SCALE: at Equator

0   500   1,000   1,500   2,000 Miles

0   1,000   2,000 Kilometers

Projection: Mollweide

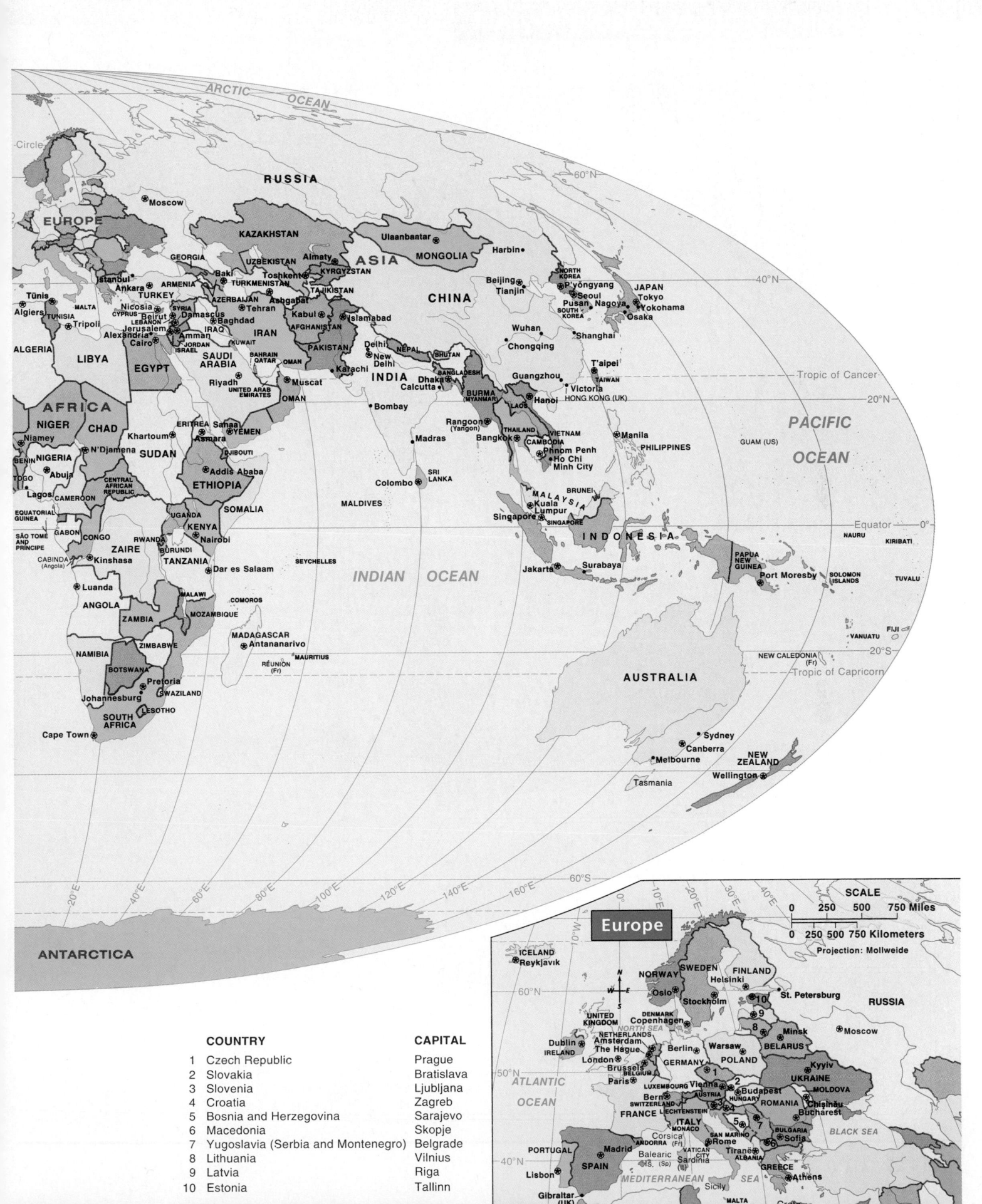

ARCTIC OCEAN

Circle

RUSSIA

⊛ Moscow

EUROPE

KAZAKHSTAN

⊛ Ulaanbaatar

ASIA

MONGOLIA

Harbin •

GEORGIA
UZBEKISTAN   Almaty
Baki⊛ Toshkent⊛ **KYRGYZSTAN**
ARMENIA   **TURKMENISTAN**
Istanbul ⊛ Ankara ⊛
TURKEY   **AZERBAIJAN**   **TAJIKISTAN**
Ashgabat⊛   Kabul⊛   **CHINA**
Beijing ⊛
Tianjin •

NORTH KOREA
P'yŏngyang ⊛   **JAPAN**
Seoul ⊛ Tokyo ⊛
Pusan Nagoya ⊛
SOUTH KOREA   Yokohama
Osaka ⊛

Tünis ⊛
TUNISIA   **MALTA**
Algiers ⊛   Nicosia ⊛ **SYRIA**
Tripoli ⊛   **CYPRUS**   Damascus⊛ **IRAN** Islamabad ⊛
LEBANON   Tehran⊛ **AFGHANISTAN** **PAKISTAN**
Beirut⊛ ⊛Baghdad
Jerusalem ⊛ **IRAQ**
Alexandria • Amman⊛ **KUWAIT**   Karachi •
ISRAEL   **JORDAN**   Delhi •
Cairo ⊛   **NEPAL**
BAHRAIN **QATAR**   **New**   **BHUTAN**
Delhi
LIBYA   **SAUDI**   **OMAN**   **INDIA** **BANGLADESH**
EGYPT   **ARABIA**   Dhaka⊛
UNITED ARAB   Calcutta • **BURMA**
Riyadh ⊛   **EMIRATES**   **(MYANMAR)**
⊛ Muscat   **LAOS**

Wuhan •
Chongqing •   Shanghai •

Guangzhou •   T'aipei ⊛
TAIWAN
• Victoria
HONG KONG (UK)

Tropic of Cancer

20°N

PACIFIC

OCEAN

ALGERIA

AFRICA
NIGER   **CHAD**
Niamey ⊛
BENIN   N'Djamena ⊛
NIGERIA   **SUDAN**
Abuja ⊛
TOGO   **CENTRAL**
Lagos •   **AFRICAN**
CAMEROON   **REPUBLIC**

ERITREA Sanaa ⊛
Khartoum ⊛   Asmara ⊛ **YEMEN**
DJIBOUTI
⊛ Addis Ababa
ETHIOPIA
SOMALIA

• Bombay

OMAN

Rangoon ⊛ **VIETNAM**
(Yangon)   **THAILAND**
Madras •   Bangkok ⊛ **CAMBODIA**
Phnom Penh ⊛
• Ho Chi
Minh City

Hanoi •

PHILIPPINES
⊛ Manila

GUAM (US)

EQUATORIAL
GUINEA   **GABON**
SÃO TOMÉ   **CONGO**
AND
PRINCIPE   **RWANDA**
UGANDA
ZAIRE   **KENYA**
Kinshasa ⊛ **BURUNDI** Nairobi ⊛
CABINDA   **TANZANIA**
(Angola)

SRI
LANKA
Colombo ⊛
MALDIVES

SEYCHELLES

Dar es Salaam •

INDIAN   OCEAN

BRUNEI
MALAYSIA
Kuala ⊛
Lumpur
Singapore ⊛
SINGAPORE

Equator   0°

NAURU
KIRIBATI

⊛ Luanda
ANGOLA   **MALAWI**
ZAMBIA   **MOZAMBIQUE**
COMOROS
ZIMBABWE
MADAGASCAR
Antananarivo ⊛
NAMIBIA   **RÉUNION** **MAURITIUS**
BOTSWANA   (Fr)
Pretoria ⊛
Johannesburg • **SWAZILAND**
SOUTH   **LESOTHO**
AFRICA
Cape Town ⊛

INDONESIA
Jakarta ⊛ • Surabaya

PAPUA
NEW
GUINEA
Port Moresby ⊛

SOLOMON
ISLANDS

TUVALU

VANUATU

FIJI ⊛

NEW CALEDONIA
(Fr)   20°S

AUSTRALIA   *Tropic of Capricorn*

• Sydney
⊛ Canberra   **NEW**
ZEALAND
• Melbourne

Tasmania   Wellington ⊛

ANTARCTICA

20°E   40°E   60°E   80°E   100°E   120°E   140°E   160°E   60°S

60°N   40°N

COUNTRY		CAPITAL
1	Czech Republic	Prague
2	Slovakia	Bratislava
3	Slovenia	Ljubljana
4	Croatia	Zagreb
5	Bosnia and Herzegovina	Sarajevo
6	Macedonia	Skopje
7	Yugoslavia (Serbia and Montenegro)	Belgrade
8	Lithuania	Vilnius
9	Latvia	Riga
10	Estonia	Tallinn

SCALE
0 250 500 750 Miles
0 250 500 750 Kilometers
Projection: Mollweide

Europe

ICELAND
⊛ Reykjavík

NORWAY   **SWEDEN**   **FINLAND**
Helsinki ⊛
⊛ 10
Oslo ⊛ ⊛ St. Petersburg   **RUSSIA**
UNITED   Stockholm ⊛ ⊛ 9
KINGDOM   **DENMARK**   ⊛ 8   **Minsk**
Copenhagen ⊛ ⊛ Moscow
NETHERLANDS   **BELARUS**
Dublin ⊛ Amsterdam ⊛ Berlin ⊛ Warsaw ⊛
IRELAND   The Hague   **GERMANY**   **POLAND**
London ⊛ Brussels ⊛ ⊛ 1   Kyyiv ⊛
BELGIUM   Vienna⊛ **UKRAINE**
Paris ⊛ **LUXEMBOURG**   ⊛ 2   **MOLDOVA**
Bern ⊛ **AUSTRIA** Budapest⊛ Chişinău ⊛
SWITZERLAND **HUNGARY** **ROMANIA** Bucharest ⊛
FRANCE   **LIECHTENSTEIN**   ⊛ 3
⊛ 4   ⊛ 5   ⊛ 7   **BULGARIA**
ITALY   **SAN MARINO**   ⊛ 6   Sofia ⊛
MONACO   Rome ⊛ Tiranë ⊛ **BLACK SEA**
Corsica   **VATICAN CITY**   **ALBANIA**
(Fr)
PORTUGAL   Madrid ⊛ **ANDORRA**
Balearic Sardinia
Is. (Sp)   (It)   **GREECE**
SPAIN   Athens ⊛
Lisbon ⊛
MEDITERRANEAN   SEA
Gibraltar   Sicily   **MALTA**
(UK)

NORTH SEA
ATLANTIC
OCEAN

60°N   50°N   40°N
10°W   0°   10°E   20°E   30°E   40°E

United States of America: Physical

PACIFIC OCEAN

Cape Mendocino

SAN FRANCISCO BAY

MONTEREY BAY

COAST RANGES

CASCADE RANGE

COLUMBIA PLATEAU

SALMON RIVER MTS

SAWTOOTH MTS

BITTERROOT RANGE

LEWIS RANGE

ROCKY MOUNTAINS

SIERRA NEVADA

CENTRAL VALLEY

GREAT BASIN

Pyramid Lake

Lake Tahoe

Mount Whitney (14,494 ft. 4418 m)

DEATH VALLEY

Great Salt Lake

Utah Lake

WASATCH RANGE

UINTA MTS

CONTINENTAL DIVIDE

Garnett Peak (13,804 ft. 4207 m)

Grand Tetons

Yellowstone Lake

Mount Elbert (14,433 ft. 4399 m)

Pikes Peak 14,110 ft. 4301 m

FRONT RANGE

DIVIDE

SANGRE DE CRISTO MTS

SAN LUIS VALLEY

COLORADO PLATEAU

GRAND CANYON

Lake Mead

Lake Powell

PAINTED DESERT

MOJAVE DESERT

Salton Sea IMPERIAL VALLEY

Channel Islands

SONORA DESERT

Gila River

GULF OF CALIFORNIA

GREAT INTERIOR PLAINS

Fort Peck Lake

Milk River

Missouri River

Yellowstone River

BIGHORN MTS

Bighorn River

Powder River

Lake Sakakawea

Red River

Lake Oahe

Cheyenne River

BLACK HILLS

White River

North Platte River

South Platte River

Niobrara River

Platte River

Republican River

Smoky Hill River

Kansas River

Arkansas River

Keystone Lake

Eufaula Lake

Lake Texoma

Canadian River

Pecos River

Rio Grande

Amistad Reservoir

Nueces River

Falcon Lake

Padre Island

Brazos River

Trinity River

Colorado River

GULF

MEXICO

To understand the relative locations of Alaska and Hawaii as well as the vast distances separating them from the rest of the United States, see the world map.

Kauai
Niihau
Oahu
Molokai
Lanai
Kahoolawe
Maui
Mauna Kea (13,796 ft. 4206 m)
Hawaii

PACIFIC OCEAN
SCALE
0   75   150 Miles
0   75   150 Kilometers

ARCTIC OCEAN
Arctic Circle
RUSSIA
BROOKS RANGE
Bering Strait
St. Lawrence Island
St. Matthew Island
Nunivak Island
Yukon River
Tanana River
Kuskokwim River
ALASKA RANGE
Mount McKinley (20,320 ft. 6194 m)
CANADA
Kodiak Island
GULF OF ALASKA
Alexander Archipelago

BERING SEA
Attu Island
Aleutian Islands
PACIFIC OCEAN

SCALE
0   250   500 Miles
0   250   500 Kilometers
Projection: Albers Equal Area

CANADA

MESABI RANGE

Isle Royale
Lake Superior

Lake Huron

Lake Michigan

Mississippi River
Wisconsin River

Des Moines River

P L A I N S

Illinois River

Wabash River

Scioto River

Lake of the Ozarks

OZARK PLATEAU

White River

Lake Barkley

Kentucky Lake

Cumberland River

OUACHITA MTS.

Red

Sebine River

Toledo Bend Reservoir

Tombigbee River

Alabama River

Coosa River

Pearl River

C O A S T A L   P L A I N

Chandeleur Islands
Mississippi Delta

GULF OF MEXICO

Chattahoochee River

Flint River

Apalachicola River

Okefenokee Swamp

FLORIDA PENINSULA

Lake Okeechobee

The Everglades

Cape Sable

Florida Keys

STRAITS OF FLORIDA

CUBA

St. Lawrence River
St. Lawrence Seaway

Lake Ontario

Lake Erie

Finger Lakes

ALLEGHENY PLATEAU

Allegheny River

Susquehanna River

A P P A L A C H I A N   M O U N T A I N S

ADIRONDACK MTS.

CATSKILL MTS.

GREEN MTS.
WHITE MTS.
LONGFELLOW MTS.

St. John River

Connecticut River

Cape Cod

LONG ISLAND SOUND
Long Island

Hudson River

Delaware River

DELAWARE BAY

CHESAPEAKE BAY

Potomac River

James River

Roanoke River

PIEDMONT

CUMBERLAND PLATEAU

GREAT SMOKY MTS.

BLUE RIDGE MOUNTAINS

Tennessee River

Catawba River

Savannah River

Ogeechee River

Altamaha River

Sea Islands

A T L A N T I C   C O A S T A L   P L A I N

PAMLICO SOUND

Cape Hatteras

ATLANTIC OCEAN

Cape Canaveral

THE BAHAMAS

ELEVATION

Feet	Meters
13,120	4,000
6,560	2,000
1,640	500
656	200
(Sea level) 0	0 (Sea level)
Below sea level	Below sea level

Ice cap

SCALE

0   250   500 Miles

0   250   500 Kilometers

Projection: Albers Equal Area

N
W   E
S

ATLAS ■■ 1015

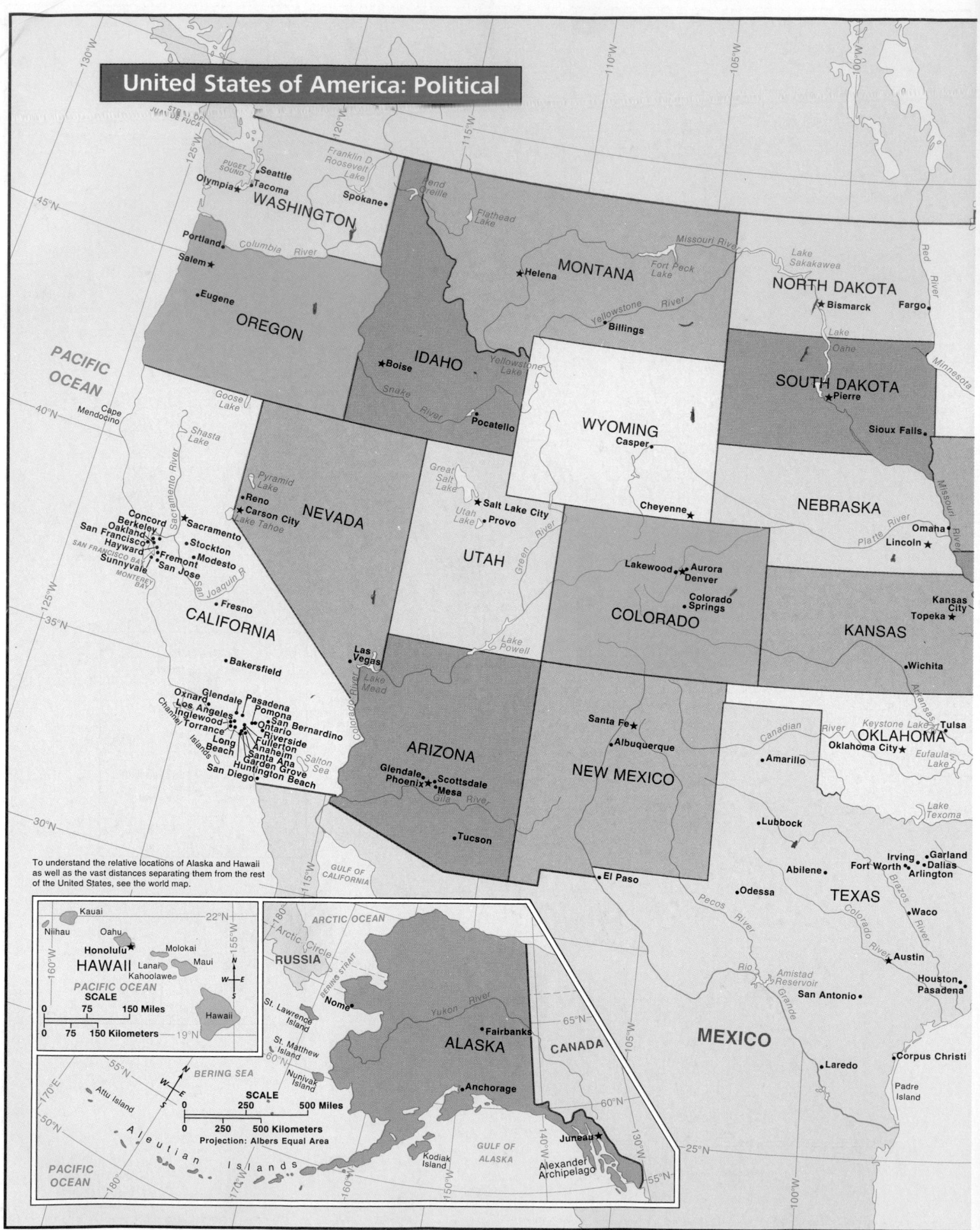

United States of America: Political

PACIFIC OCEAN

WASHINGTON
Seattle
Tacoma
Olympia ★
Spokane

OREGON
Portland
Salem ★
Eugene

Cape Mendocino

CALIFORNIA
Concord
Berkeley
Oakland
San Francisco
Hayward
Sunnyvale
Fremont
San Jose
Stockton
Modesto
Sacramento ★
Fresno
Bakersfield

Oxnard
Glendale
Pasadena
Pomona
Los Angeles
San Bernardino
Inglewood
Ontario
Torrance
Riverside
Long Beach
Fullerton
Anaheim
Santa Ana
Garden Grove
Huntington Beach
San Diego

Channel Islands

MONTEREY BAY
SAN FRANCISCO BAY

Shasta Lake
Goose Lake

NEVADA
Reno
Carson City ★
Lake Tahoe
Pyramid Lake

Las Vegas

IDAHO
Boise ★
Pocatello

Snake River

Great Salt Lake
UTAH
Salt Lake City ★
Provo
Utah Lake

Green River

Lake Powell

Lake Mead

Colorado River

ARIZONA
Glendale
Phoenix ★
Scottsdale
Mesa
Gila River
Tucson

Salton Sea

GULF OF CALIFORNIA

MONTANA
Helena ★
Billings
Yellowstone River
Yellowstone Lake
Flathead Lake
Fort Peck Lake
Pend Oreille
Franklin D. Roosevelt Lake
Columbia River
Missouri River

WYOMING
Casper
Cheyenne ★

COLORADO
Lakewood
Aurora
Denver
Colorado Springs

NEW MEXICO
Santa Fe ★
Albuquerque

El Paso

NORTH DAKOTA
Bismarck ★
Fargo
Lake Sakakawea
Red River

SOUTH DAKOTA
Pierre ★
Sioux Falls
Lake Oahe
Missouri River
Minnesota

NEBRASKA
Omaha
Lincoln ★
Platte River

KANSAS
Kansas City
Topeka ★
Wichita
Arkansas River

OKLAHOMA
Tulsa
Oklahoma City ★
Amarillo
Keystone Lake
Eufaula Lake
Canadian River

TEXAS
Lubbock
Abilene
Odessa
Fort Worth
Irving
Dallas
Arlington
Garland
Waco
Austin ★
Houston
Pasadena
San Antonio
Laredo
Corpus Christi
Padre Island
Pecos River
Brazos River
Colorado River
Lake Texoma
Rio Grande
Amistad Reservoir

MEXICO

To understand the relative locations of Alaska and Hawaii as well as the vast distances separating them from the rest of the United States, see the world map.

HAWAII
Kauai
Niihau
Oahu
Honolulu ★
Molokai
Lanai
Maui
Kahoolawe
Hawaii
PACIFIC OCEAN
SCALE
0   75   150 Miles
0   75   150 Kilometers

RUSSIA
ARCTIC OCEAN
Arctic Circle
Nome
St. Lawrence Island
St. Matthew Island
Nunivak Island
BERING STRAIT
Yukon River
Fairbanks
ALASKA
Anchorage
Kodiak Island
GULF OF ALASKA
Juneau ★
Alexander Archipelago
CANADA
BERING SEA
Attu Island
Aleutian Islands
PACIFIC OCEAN
SCALE
0   250   500 Miles
0   250   500 Kilometers
Projection: Albers Equal Area

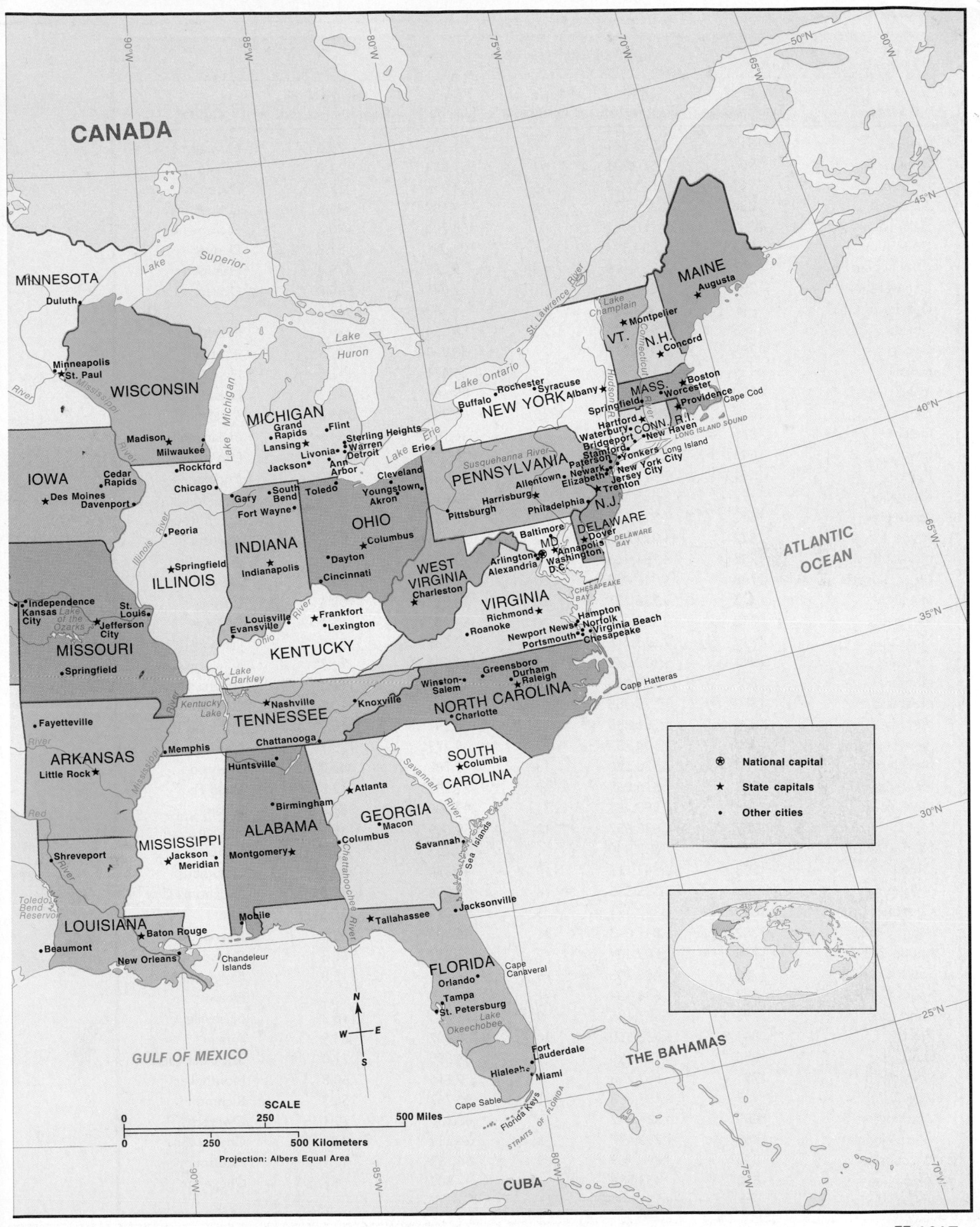

CANADA

MINNESOTA
• Duluth

• Minneapolis
★ St. Paul

WISCONSIN

Madison ★
Milwaukee •
• Rockford

IOWA
• Cedar Rapids
★ Des Moines
• Davenport

MICHIGAN
Grand Rapids • • Flint
Lansing ★ • Sterling Heights
Livonia • • Warren
Jackson • Ann • Detroit
Arbor

MAINE
• Augusta

★ Montpelier
VT. N.H.
★ Concord

MASS. • Boston
Springfield ★ • Worcester
Hartford • Providence
Waterbury • CONN. R.I.
Bridgeport • • New Haven
Stamford • LONG ISLAND SOUND
Paterson • Yonkers • Long Island
Newark • • New York City
Elizabeth • Jersey City
Trenton ★
N.J.

NEW YORK
Buffalo • • Rochester • Syracuse
★ Albany

Lake Champlain

St. Lawrence River

Lake Superior

Lake Huron

Lake Michigan

Lake Ontario

Lake Erie

• Chicago

Gary • • South Bend
Fort Wayne •

ILLINOIS
Springfield ★

• Peoria

INDIANA
Indianapolis ★

• Toledo

OHIO
• Columbus
• Dayton
Cincinnati •

Youngstown •
Akron •
Cleveland •

PENNSYLVANIA
Susquehanna River
Harrisburg ★
Pittsburgh •
Philadelphia •
Allentown •
Baltimore •
MD.
★ Dover
DELAWARE
DELAWARE BAY

WEST VIRGINIA
Charleston ★

Arlington • Annapolis ★
Alexandria • Washington, D.C. ⊛
CHESAPEAKE BAY

MISSOURI
• Independence
• Kansas City
St. Louis •
Lake of the Ozarks
★ Jefferson City
• Springfield

• Fayetteville

ARKANSAS
Little Rock ★

KENTUCKY
Louisville •
Evansville •
Frankfort ★
Lexington •
Ohio River

Lake Barkley

Kentucky Lake

Memphis •

TENNESSEE
★ Nashville
Chattanooga •
• Knoxville

VIRGINIA
Richmond ★
• Roanoke
Hampton •
Norfolk •
Newport News • Virginia Beach
Portsmouth • Chesapeake

NORTH CAROLINA
Winston-Salem • • Greensboro
Durham •
• Raleigh
• Charlotte

Cape Hatteras

Huntsville •

MISSISSIPPI
Jackson ★
Meridian •

ALABAMA

Birmingham •

Montgomery ★

Mobile •

GEORGIA
Atlanta •
Macon •
Columbus •
Savannah •
Savannah River
Sea Islands

SOUTH CAROLINA
★ Columbia

Shreveport •

LOUISIANA
Baton Rouge ★
• Beaumont
New Orleans • Chandeleur Islands

Red River
Mississippi River
Chattahoochee River

Tallahassee ★
Jacksonville •

FLORIDA
Orlando •
Tampa •
St. Petersburg •
Lake Okeechobee
Fort Lauderdale •
Hialeah • • Miami
Cape Sable
Florida Keys

Cape Canaveral

ATLANTIC OCEAN

THE BAHAMAS

GULF OF MEXICO

STRAITS OF FLORIDA

CUBA

Toledo Bend Reservoir

⊛ National capital
★ State capitals
• Other cities

N
W   E
S

SCALE
0   250   500 Miles
0   250   500 Kilometers
Projection: Albers Equal Area

FACTS ABOUT THE STATES

State	Year of Statehood	1990 Population	Reps. in Congress	Area (sq. mi.)	Population Density (sq. mi.)	Capital
Alabama	1819	4,040,587	7	51,705	79.6	Montgomery
Alaska	1959	550,043	1	591,004	1.0	Juneau
Arizona	1912	3,665,228	6	114,000	32.3	Phoenix
Arkansas	1836	2,350,725	4	53,187	45.1	Little Rock
California	1850	29,760,021	52	158,706	190.8	Sacramento
Colorado	1876	3,294,394	6	104,091	31.8	Denver
Connecticut	1788	3,287,116	6	5,018	678.4	Hartford
Delaware	1787	666,168	1	2,045	340.8	Dover
District of Columbia	—	606,900	—	69	9,882.8	—
Florida	1845	12,937,926	23	58,664	239.6	Tallahassee
Georgia	1788	6,478,216	11	58,910	111.9	Atlanta
Hawaii	1959	1,108,229	2	6,471	172.5	Honolulu
Idaho	1890	1,006,749	2	83,564	12.2	Boise
Illinois	1818	11,430,602	20	56,345	205.6	Springfield
Indiana	1816	5,544,159	10	36,185	154.6	Indianapolis
Iowa	1846	2,776,755	5	56,275	49.7	Des Moines
Kansas	1861	2,477,574	4	82,277	30.3	Topeka
Kentucky	1792	3,685,296	6	40,410	92.8	Frankfort
Louisiana	1812	4,219,973	7	47,752	96.9	Baton Rouge
Maine	1820	1,227,928	2	33,265	39.8	Augusta
Maryland	1788	4,781,468	8	10,460	489.2	Annapolis
Massachusetts	1788	6,016,425	10	8,284	767.6	Boston
Michigan	1837	9,295,297	16	58,527	163.6	Lansing
Minnesota	1858	4,375,099	8	84,402	55.0	St. Paul
Mississippi	1817	2,573,216	5	47,689	54.9	Jackson
Missouri	1821	5,117,073	9	69,697	74.3	Jefferson City
Montana	1889	799,065	1	147,046	5.5	Helena
Nebraska	1867	1,578,385	3	77,355	20.5	Lincoln
Nevada	1864	1,201,833	2	110,561	10.9	Carson City
New Hampshire	1788	1,109,252	2	9,279	123.7	Concord
New Jersey	1787	7,730,188	13	7,787	1,042.0	Trenton
New Mexico	1912	1,515,069	3	121,593	12.5	Santa Fe
New York	1788	17,990,455	31	49,108	381.0	Albany
North Carolina	1789	6,628,637	12	52,669	136.1	Raleigh
North Dakota	1889	638,800	1	70,702	9.3	Bismarck
Ohio	1803	10,847,115	19	41,330	264.9	Columbus
Oklahoma	1907	3,145,585	6	69,956	45.8	Oklahoma City
Oregon	1859	2,842,321	5	97,073	29.6	Salem
Pennsylvania	1787	11,881,643	21	45,308	265.1	Harrisburg
Rhode Island	1790	1,003,464	2	1,212	960.3	Providence
South Carolina	1788	3,486,703	6	31,113	115.8	Columbia
South Dakota	1889	696,004	1	77,116	9.2	Pierre
Tennessee	1796	4,877,185	9	42,144	118.3	Nashville
Texas	1845	16,986,510	30	266,807	64.9	Austin
Utah	1896	1,722,850	3	84,899	21.0	Salt Lake City
Vermont	1791	562,758	1	9,614	60.8	Montpelier
Virginia	1788	6,187,358	11	40,767	156.3	Richmond
Washington	1889	4,866,692	9	68,139	73.1	Olympia
West Virginia	1863	1,793,477	3	24,232	74.5	Charleston
Wisconsin	1848	4,891,769	9	56,153	90.1	Madison
Wyoming	1890	453,588	1	97,809	4.7	Cheyenne

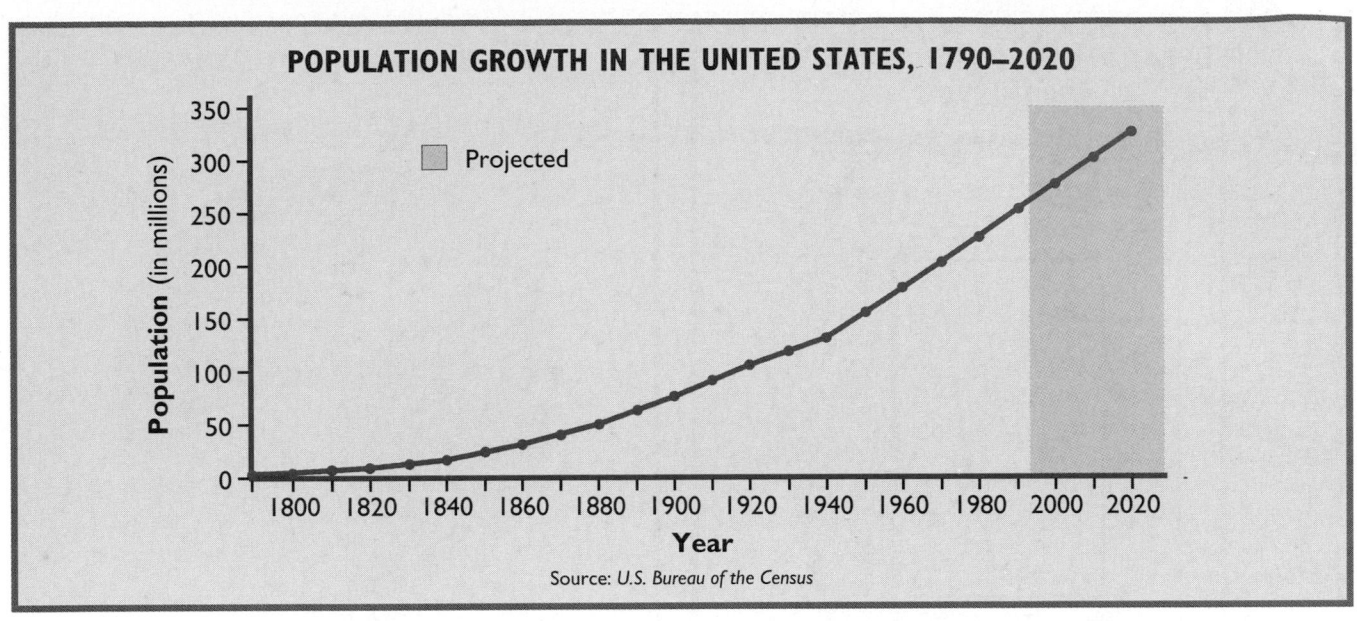

POPULATION GROWTH IN THE UNITED STATES, 1790–2020

Source: *U.S. Bureau of the Census*

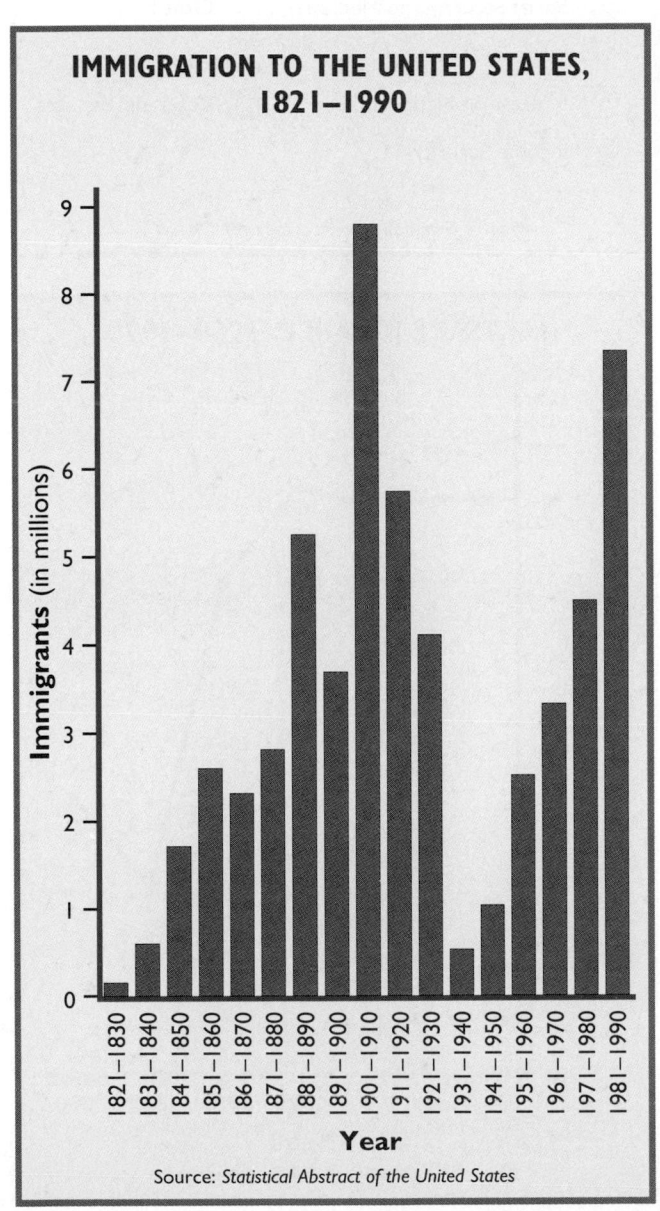

IMMIGRATION TO THE UNITED STATES, 1821–1990

Source: *Statistical Abstract of the United States*

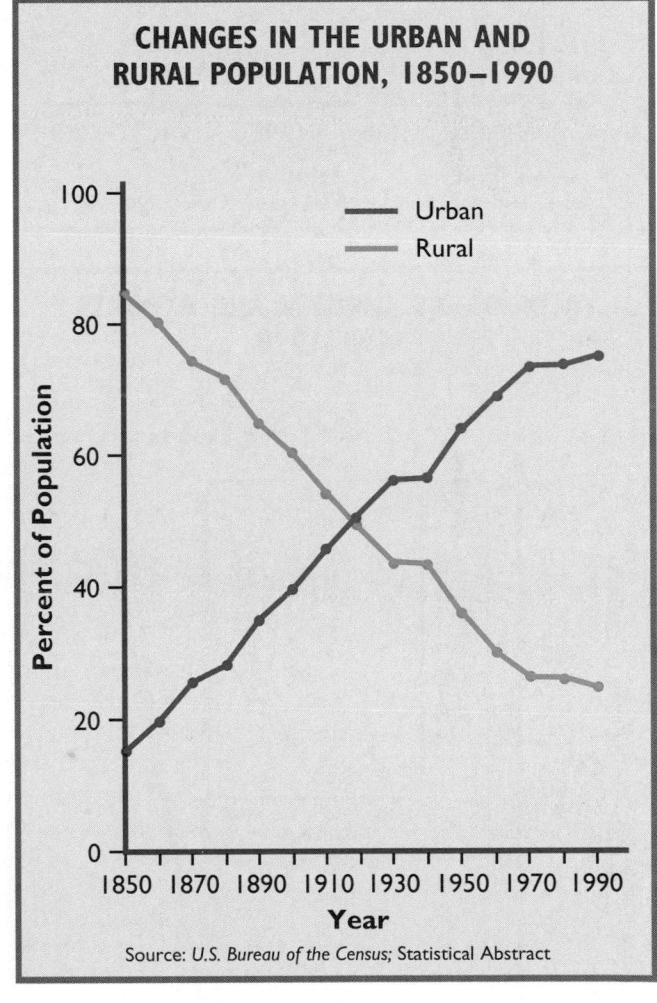

CHANGES IN THE URBAN AND RURAL POPULATION, 1850–1990

Source: *U.S. Bureau of the Census; Statistical Abstract*

FEDERAL RECEIPTS AND OUTLAYS, 1900–1990

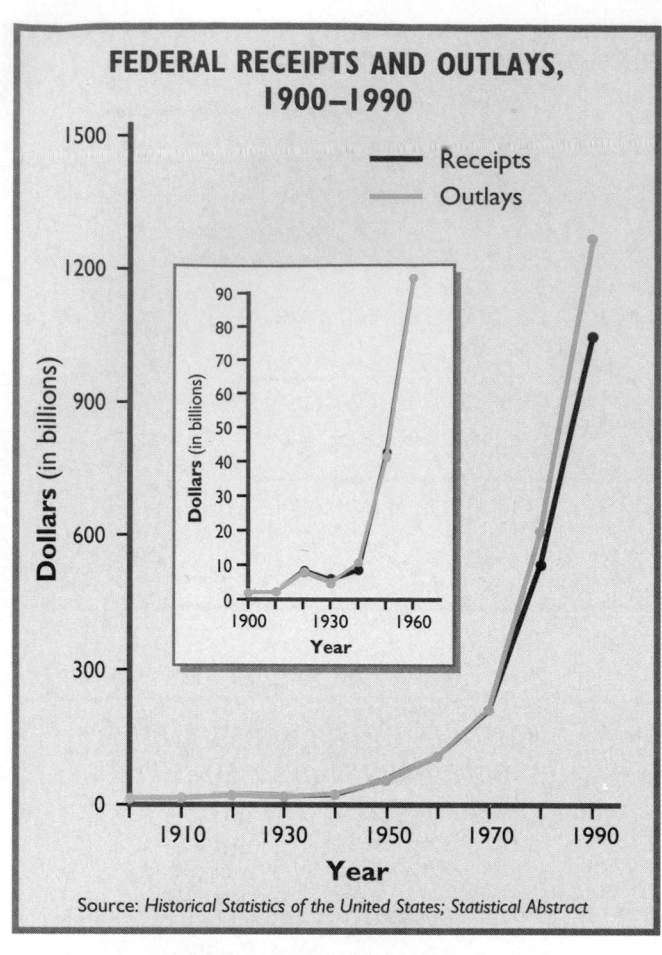

Source: *Historical Statistics of the United States; Statistical Abstract*

DISTRIBUTION OF OUTLAYS, 1992

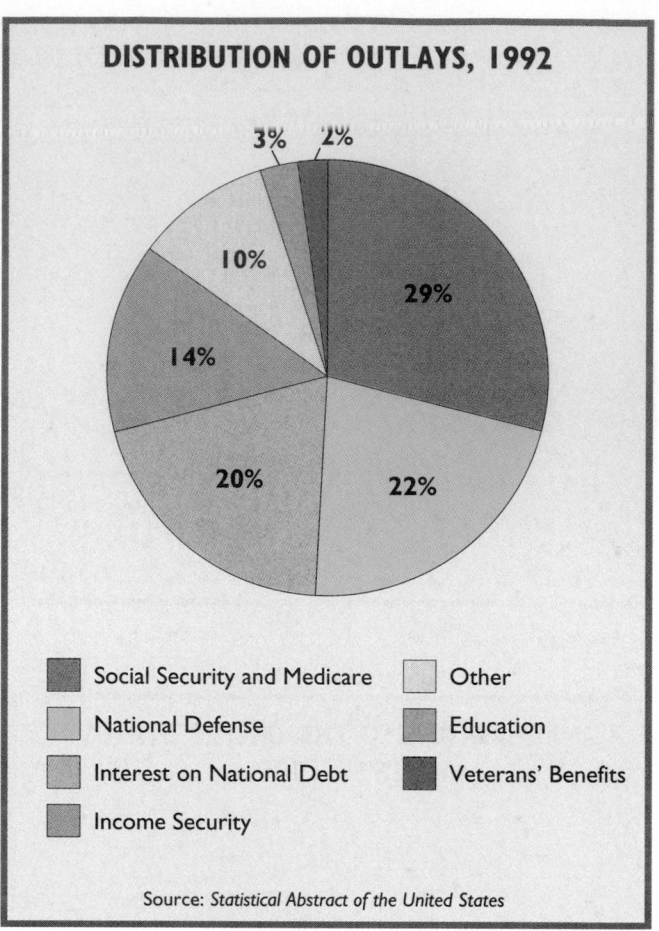

- Social Security and Medicare
- National Defense
- Interest on National Debt
- Income Security
- Other
- Education
- Veterans' Benefits

Source: *Statistical Abstract of the United States*

VALUE OF U.S. IMPORTS AND EXPORTS, 1900–1990

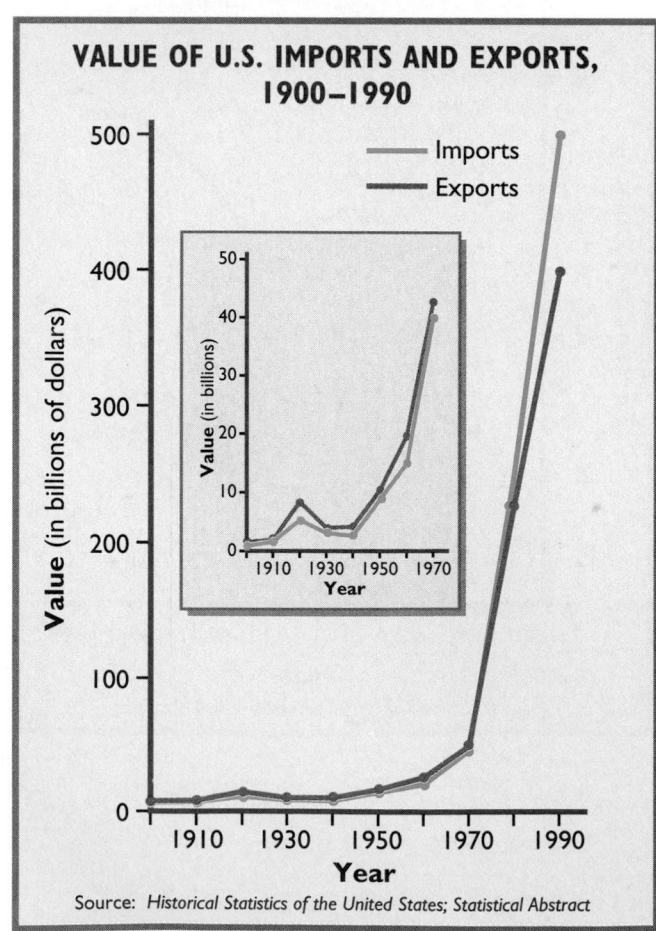

Source: *Historical Statistics of the United States; Statistical Abstract*

U.S. TRADE BALANCE, 1960–1990

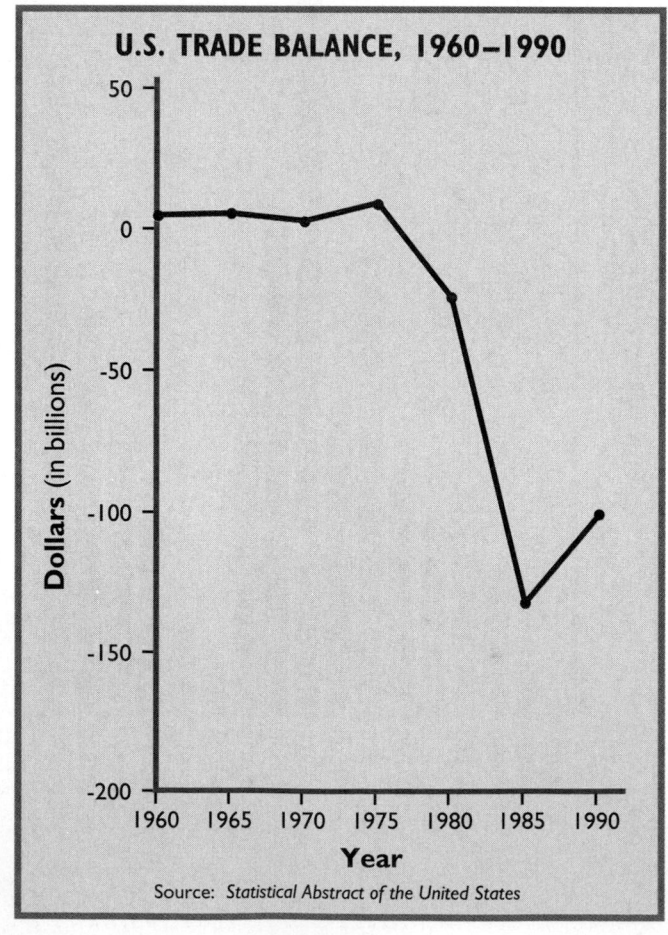

Source: *Statistical Abstract of the United States*

PRESIDENTS OF THE UNITED STATES

No.	Name	Born–Died	Years In Office	Political Party	Home State	Vice President
1	George Washington	1732–1799	1789–97	None	VA	John Adams
2	John Adams	1735–1826	1797–1801	Federalist	MA	Thomas Jefferson
3	Thomas Jefferson	1743–1826	1801–09	Republican*	VA	Aaron Burr
						George Clinton
4	James Madison	1751–1836	1809–17	Republican	VA	George Clinton
						Elbridge Gerry
5	James Monroe	1758–1831	1817–25	Republican	VA	Daniel D. Tompkins
6	John Quincy Adams	1767–1848	1825–29	Republican	MA	John C. Calhoun
7	Andrew Jackson	1767–1845	1829–37	Democratic	TN	John C. Calhoun
						Martin Van Buren
8	Martin Van Buren	1782–1862	1837–41	Democratic	NY	Richard M. Johnson
9	William Henry Harrison	1773–1841	1841	Whig	OH	John Tyler
10	John Tyler	1790–1862	1841–45	Whig	VA	
11	James K. Polk	1795–1849	1845–49	Democratic	TN	George M. Dallas
12	Zachary Taylor	1784–1850	1849–50	Whig	LA	Millard Fillmore
13	Millard Fillmore	1800–1874	1850–53	Whig	NY	
14	Franklin Pierce	1804–1869	1853–57	Democratic	NH	William R. King
15	James Buchanan	1791–1868	1857–61	Democratic	PA	John C. Breckenridge
16	Abraham Lincoln	1809–1865	1861–65	Republican	IL	Hannibal Hamlin
						Andrew Johnson
17	Andrew Johnson	1808–1875	1865–69	Republican	TN	
18	Ulysses S. Grant	1822–1885	1869–77	Republican	IL	Schuyler Colfax
						Henry Wilson
19	Rutherford B. Hayes	1822–1893	1877–81	Republican	OH	William A. Wheeler
20	James A. Garfield	1831–1881	1881	Republican	OH	Chester A. Arthur
21	Chester A. Arthur	1830–1886	1881 85	Republican	NY	
22	Grover Cleveland	1837–1908	1885–89	Democratic	NY	Thomas A. Hendricks
23	Benjamin Harrison	1833–1901	1889–93	Republican	IN	Levi P. Morton
24	Grover Cleveland		1893–97	Democratic	NY	Adlai E. Stevenson
25	William McKinley	1843–1901	1897–1901	Republican	OH	Garrett A. Hobart
						Theodore Roosevelt
26	Theodore Roosevelt	1858–1919	1901–09	Republican	NY	
						Charles W. Fairbanks
27	William Howard Taft	1857–1930	1909–13	Republican	OH	James S. Sherman
28	Woodrow Wilson	1856–1924	1913–21	Democratic	NJ	Thomas R. Marshall
29	Warren G. Harding	1865–1923	1921–23	Republican	OH	Calvin Coolidge
30	Calvin Coolidge	1872–1933	1923–29	Republican	MA	
						Charles G. Dawes
31	Herbert Hoover	1874–1964	1929–33	Republican	CA	Charles Curtis
32	Franklin D. Roosevelt	1882–1945	1933–45	Democratic	NY	John Nance Garner
						Henry Wallace
						Harry S. Truman
33	Harry S. Truman	1884–1972	1945–53	Democratic	MO	
						Alben W. Barkley
34	Dwight D. Eisenhower	1890–1969	1953–61	Republican	KS	Richard M. Nixon
35	John F. Kennedy	1917–1963	1961–63	Democratic	MA	Lyndon B. Johnson
36	Lyndon B. Johnson	1908–1973	1963–69	Democratic	TX	
						Hubert H. Humphrey
37	Richard M. Nixon	1913–1994	1969–74	Republican	CA	Spiro T. Agnew
						Gerald R. Ford
38	Gerald R. Ford	1913–	1974–77	Republican	MI	Nelson A. Rockefeller
39	Jimmy Carter	1924–	1977–81	Democratic	GA	Walter F. Mondale
40	Ronald Reagan	1911–	1981–89	Republican	CA	George Bush
41	George Bush	1924–	1989–1993	Republican	TX	J. Danforth Quayle
42	Bill Clinton	1946–	1993–	Democratic	AR	Albert Gore, Jr.

*The Republican party of the third through sixth presidents is not the party of Abraham Lincoln, which was founded in 1854.

BIOGRAPHIES

Abzug, Bella (1920–). Lawyer, politician. U.S. representative, 1971–77; supported legislation to promote federal jobs programs, public transportation, individual right to privacy. Strong advocate of women's rights; helped found the National Women's Political Caucus, 1971. (p. 921)

Adams, Abigail (1744–1818). First lady. Outspoken supporter of women's rights and opponent of slavery. During Revolutionary War, provided information on British troop activities in Boston to husband John Adams; urged him to support women's rights in Constitution. (p. 118)

Adams, John (1735–1826). The 2nd president, 1797–1801. On committee to draft Declaration of Independence; helped negotiate peace after Revolutionary War. Washington's vice president. Died same day as Jefferson, on 50th anniversary of Declaration of Independence. (pp. 132, 201)

Adams, John Quincy (1767–1848). The 6th president, 1825–29. Diplomat; U.S. senator, 1803–08; helped negotiate treaty ending War of 1812; Monroe's secretary of state, 1817–25; negotiated northern U.S. boundary with Britain; wrote much of Monroe Doctrine. U.S. representative, 1831–46. (p. 238)

Adams, Samuel (1722–1803). Revolutionary politician. Led agitation that resulted in Boston Tea Party. Signed Declaration of Independence. (p. 107)

Addams, Jane (1860–1935). Social worker. Opened social settlement Hull House, Chicago, 1889. (pp. 476, 516)

Aguinaldo, Emilio (1869–1964). Filipino leader. Took part in unsuccessful revolt against Spanish rule, 1896. Led Filipino troops against Spain in Spanish-American War; declared president of Philippine Republic, 1899. Led revolt against U.S. occupation until captured, 1901. (p. 560)

Allende, Salvador (1908–1973). President of Chile until his assassination in 1973. Became Marxist activist in college; helped found Chilean Socialist party; elected senator four times. After losing presidential race three times, won as candidate of Popular Unity, a bloc of Socialists, Communists, Radicals, and others, 1970. (p. 904)

Anderson, Marian (1902–1993). African American opera singer; toured Europe 1930–35; sang at Lincoln Memorial, 1939. In 1955 became first African American soloist with NY's Metropolitan Opera. Served as U.S. delegate to United Nations, 1958. Awarded UN Peace Prize, 1977. (pp. 660, 708)

Anthony, Susan B. (1820–1906). Women's suffrage leader; advocate of temperance, abolition of slavery. Helped found National Woman Suffrage Association, 1869; president of National American Woman Suffrage Association, 1892–1900; co-author

Jane Addams

Susan B. Anthony

History of Woman Suffrage, 1881–1902. (pp. 300, 552)

Arthur, Chester A. (1829–1886). The 21st president, 1881–85. Collector at port of NY, 1871–79; vice president, 1881. Became president at death of Garfield. (p. 489)

Atahuallpa (1502?–1533). Last Incan king of Peru. Fought with half-brother for control of empire following death of father, Huayna Capac, 1525; won control of kingdom, 1530. Held prisoner by Francisco Pizarro after refusing to convert to Christianity. Executed, 1533. (p. 48)

Austin, Stephen F. (1793–1836). Colonizer of Texas. Governed American colony in Mexican Texas, 1822–32; imprisoned in Mexico, 1833, for requesting separate government for Texas. Appointed secretary of state of Republic of Texas, 1836. (p. 307)

Bagley, Sarah G. (dates unknown). First female telegraph operator; first female labor leader. Began work in cotton mill, Lowell, MA, 1836. Helped organize Female Labor Reform Association to achieve 10-hour day, 1845; organized union branches in MA and NH. (p. 258)

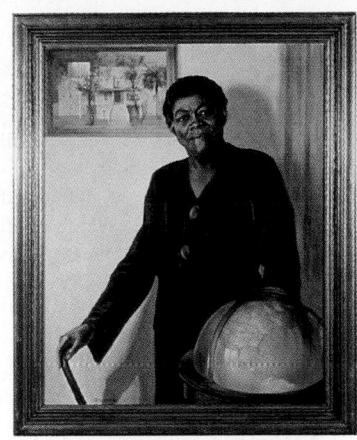

Mary McLeod Bethune

Baker, Ella (1903–1986). Civil rights activist; worked with Harlem youth groups and *Negro National News*, 1930s. Worked on national recruitment campaign for NAACP, 1940s; president of New York NAACP, 1954; leader in SCLC; helped found SNCC, MS Freedom Democratic party. (p. 849)

Ball, Lucille (1911–1989). One of America's best-loved slapstick comedians and actors. Moved to Hollywood, 1930s; performed in more than 50 films and four TV series. Best known for TV comedy *I Love Lucy* (with husband Desi Arnaz) in 1950s. Owned, directed TV production companies. (p. 818)

Barrett, Janie Porter (1865–1948). African American social reformer. Founded Locust Street Social Settlement, first settlement house for blacks in VA, 1890; helped found and run VA Industrial School for Colored Girls (renamed Janie Porter Barrett School for Girls, 1950). (p. 477)

Barton, Clara (1821–1912). Founder, American Red Cross. Civil War nurse, called "Angel of the Battlefield." Served with International Red Cross during Franco-Prussian War, 1870–71; founded American branch, 1881. Wrote *The Red Cross*, 1898. (p. 369)

Bates, Daisy (1922–). African American civil rights leader; publisher, *Arkansas State Press* newspaper. Became president of Arkansas NAACP, 1952; played key role in Central High School crisis; led protest against cuts in economic opportunity programs in state, 1972. (p. 825)

Ben-Gurion, David (1886–1973). Proclaimed independence of Israel. The 1st Israeli prime minister, 1949–53. (p. 796)

Bethune, Mary McLeod (1875–1955). Director of National Youth Administration's Division of Negro Affairs, 1936–44. (p. 709)

Blackwell, Elizabeth (1821–1910). Physician; first woman in U.S. to receive medical degree. Founded NY Infirmary for Women and Children, 1857, which was expanded to include medical school for women, 1868. Professor, London School of Medicine for Women, 1869–1907. (p. 369)

Bloch, Julia Chang (1941–). Asian American diplomat. Emigrated from China, 1951. Peace Corps volunteer to Sabah, 1960s; chief minority counsel for Senate Select Committee on Nutrition and Human Needs, 1970s; assistant administrator for Food for Peace and Voluntary Assistance, 1980s. (p. 978)

Bourke-White, Margaret (1906–1971). American photojournalist. Associate editor, *Fortune* magazine; staff member, *Life*. Covered events throughout the world, including Great Depression, World War II battles, conditions in Nazi concentration camps. (p. 715)

Brandeis, Louis D. (1856–1941). Lawyer and jurist; Associate Justice for Supreme Court, 1916–39. Known as "the people's attorney" for taking on cases involving social reform; wrote "Brandeis brief." (p. 519)

Buchanan, James (1791–1868). The 15th president, 1857–61. U.S. representative, 1821–31; minister to Russia; U.S. senator, 1834–45; Polk's secretary of state; helped draft Ostend Manifesto, 1854. (pp. 349, 357)

Bunche, Ralph (1904–1971). African American diplomat. Chairman political science, Howard University; contributor, Gunnar Myrdal's *An American Dilemma*, 1944. United Nations mediator in Palestine, Africa, Yemen, Cyprus; Nobel Peace Prize, 1950. (p. 797)

Bush, George H.W. (1924–). The 41st president, 1989–93. U.S. representative, 1966–70; appointed UN representative, chairman Republican National Committee by Nixon; appointed director of CIA by Ford. Reagan's vice president, 1981–89. (pp. 927, 941)

Cabeza de Vaca, Álvar Núñez (1490?–1560?). Spanish explorer. Treasurer, Narváez expedition to Florida; shipwrecked off Texas coast, 1528; explored Mexico; led later expeditions by de Niza, Coronado, De Soto. Colonial governor, Paraguay, 1542–44; deposed, banished to Africa. (p. 46)

Cárdenas, Lázaro (1895–1970). Mexican president, 1934–40. In revolutionary army of Carranza, 1913. As president, began Six-Year Plan of social reform, including redistribution of land, seizure of foreign oil properties. Supported Allied efforts during WWII. (p. 731)

Carranza, Venustiano (1859–1920). President of Mexico, 1917–20. (p. 577)

Carter, James Earl "Jimmy" (1924–). The 39th president, 1977–81. Governor of GA. Known for his campaign for global human rights and Camp David Accords between Egypt and Israel. (p. 913)

Castro, Fidel (1926–). Communist dictator of Cuba. Lawyer, early 1950s. Arrested for leading attempted revolt against dictator Batista, 1953; released from prison, 1955; formed "26th of

Ralph Bunche

Fidel Castro

July Movement"; overthrew Batista, 1959. During Cold War formed close ties with USSR. (p. 835)

Castro, Raul H. (1916–). Mexican American lawyer and statesman. U.S. ambassador to El Salvador, Bolivia, Argentina. First Mexican American governor of AZ, 1975. (p. 840)

Catt, Carrie Chapman (1859–1947). Women's suffragist, peace activist. President, National American Woman Suffrage Association; president International Woman Suffrage Alliance; founded National League of Women Voters, 1920, and National Committee on the Cause and Cure of War, 1925. (pp. 552, 726)

Chávez, César (1927–1993). Mexican American labor leader. Founded Farm Workers United, 1962; led strikes, boycotts against grape growers, lettuce growers; brought about CA Agricultural Labor Relations Act. (pp. 714, 851)

Chesnut, Mary Boykin (1823–1886). Confederate diarist. Kept journal of experiences in Richmond during Civil War. Diaries, first published 1905, became popular as *Mary Chesnut's Civil War*, 1981; regarded as finest literary work of Confederacy. (pp. 372, 395)

Chief Joseph. See Joseph, Chief

Chisholm, Shirley (1924–). African American politician; NY teacher, educational adviser. Elected to NY state assembly, 1964. First black female U.S. representative, 1969–83; first black woman to run for president, 1972 Democratic primary. (p. 921)

Churchill, Winston (1874–1965). British prime minister, 1940–45, 1951–1955. Joined House of Commons, 1901; served in numerous government positions, wrote several books before becoming prime minister, 1940, during WWII. Nobel Peace Prize, 1953. (pp. 737, 790)

Cleveland, Grover (1837–1908). The 22nd and 24th president. President, 1885–89; lost reelection, 1888, to Benjamin Harrison; again president, 1893–97. (p. 490)

Clinton, Hillary Rodham (1947–). First lady. Graduate, Yale Law School; Helped develop 1993 health-care reform package. (p. 942)

Clinton, William Jefferson "Bill" (1946–). The 42nd president. Nation's youngest governor (of AR). (p. 942)

Columbus, Christopher (1451–1506). Explorer credited with European discovery of Americas. (p. 38)

Coolidge, Calvin (1872–1933). The 30th president. Vice president, 1921–23; became president at death of Harding, 1923; elected president, 1924, served full term 1925–29; declined to run for reelection. (pp. 624, 631)

Cortés, Hernán (1485–1547). Spanish explorer. Sailed to Santo Domingo, 1504; in Velásquez expedition; explored Mexico, founded Veracruz. Defeated Aztecs, 1520; took over what is now Mexico City, 1521. Wealthiest person in early Spanish America. (p. 46)

Crazy Horse (1842?–1877). Oglala Sioux chief. Led Fetterman Massacre and Wagon-Box fight in Red Cloud's War, 1866–68. Led Sioux war of resistance against forced removal to reservation, 1876; victory at Battle of Little Big Horn against Custer, 1876; surrendered, 1877; killed while resisting imprisonment. Called "Strange One" by Sioux. (p. 429)

Cruz, Juana Inés de la (1651–1695). Mexican nun, poet. Prodigy; entered convent of San Jeronimo, 1669; studied science and humanities. Collected large library, which she donated, 1693.

Wrote several famous lyric poems. (p. 55)

Custer, George Armstrong (1039–1876). Army officer. Served in Civil War. Joined 7th Calvary Regiment in West; fought many battles against Indians; led Black Hills expedition; killed in Battle of Little Big Horn, "Custer's Last Stand." (p. 429)

Davis, Bette (1908–1990). Film actor. Gained fame playing strong, independent women. Received 10 Academy Award nominations; won twice for Best Actress, 1935 and 1938. Inspired numerous imitations and popular tune "Bette Davis Eyes." (p. 680)

Davis, Jefferson (1808–1889). President of Confederacy, 1862–65. Pierce's secretary of war, 1853–57; twice elected U.S. senator. Strong advocate of slavery and secession. Arrested for treason after Civil War; indicted but never tried. (p. 356)

Daw Aung San Suu Kyi (1945–). Burmese political activist, scholar. Studied at Oxford and London universities. Led protests against rulers of Burma Socialist Program party, 1988–89; helped found National League for Democracy; placed under house arrest in 1989. Nobel Peace Prize, 1991. (p. 963)

Daw Aung San Suu Kyi

W.E.B. Du Bois

Debs, Eugene V. (1855–1926).
Socialist and labor leader. Organizer, American Railway Union, International Workers of the World; imprisoned for role in Pullman strike. Founded Social Democratic party; ran for president five times. (p. 547)

Delany, Martin (1812–1885). African American physician, social reformer, journalist, soldier. Attended Harvard Medical School. Cofounder, coeditor *North Star*. Active abolitionist; worked with Underground Railroad. Attempted to establish African American colony in Nicaragua. (p. 385)

Díaz, Porfirio (1830–1915). President of Mexico, 1877–80, 1884–1911. Gained fame in Mexican War against U.S. Lost election to Juárez, 1871; overthrew Lerdo de Tejada, 1876. Exiled to France following Mexican Revolution, 1911. (p. 575)

Dickinson, Emily (1830–1886). Poet, recluse. Wrote some 1,700 poems; published only seven during her lifetime. Poems are deceptively simple in appearance; some reveal alienation from society. (p. 330)

Dix, Dorothea (1802–1887). Teacher, social reformer, humanitarian. Obtained reform in the care of mentally ill. (p. 286)

Douglass, Frederick (1817–1895). African American abolitionist, lecturer, author. Born a slave, escaped and settled in MA, 1838. Agent of MA Anti-Slavery Society. Published autobiography, 1845. Lectured in Great Britain and Ireland, 1845–47. Founder, abolitionist newspaper *North Star*. (pp. 294, 384)

Du Bois, W.E.B. (1868–1963). African American educator, historian, author. Leader, Niagara Movement; helped found NAACP; editor of *Crisis*, 1910–34. (p. 526)

Edison, Thomas Alva (1847–1931). "The Wizard of Menlo Park"; founded company that became General Electric. Patented more than 1,000 inventions. (p. 461)

Eisenhower, Dwight David "Ike" (1890–1969). The 34th president, 1953–61. WWII commander in chief of Allied forces, Western Europe, 1943; planned and led defeat of Germany, 1944–45. President, Columbia University, 1948–53. Supreme commander, NATO forces in Europe, 1951–52. (pp. 759, 813, 866)

Ellison, Ralph (1914–1994). African American writer. Editor, *Negro Quarterly*, 1940s. Novel *Invisible Man* (1952) polled as "the most distinguished single work" published in the United States between 1945 and 1965. Later works include *Shadow and Act*, 1964, *Going to the Territory*, 1986. (p. 825)

Emerson, Ralph Waldo (1803–1882). Author, Unitarian minister. Became popular writer and lecturer after publication of *Nature*, 1836, which expressed philosophy of transcendentalism. Best-known lectures include "The American Scholar," 1837, and "The Divinity School Address," 1838. (p. 285)

Equiano, Olaudah (1750?–1797). African American seaman, writer, abolitionist. (p.78)

Ferraro, Geraldine (1935–). Lawyer, politician. U.S. representative 1978–84. Chosen by Democratic presidential candidate Walter Mondale as running mate, 1984; first woman to run for vice president on a major political party's ticket. (p. 933)

Fierro de Bright, Josefina (1920–). Mexican American activist; fought for rights of Spanish-speaking citizens. (p. 678)

Josefina Fierro de Bright

Fillmore, Millard (1800–1874). The 13th president. U.S. representative, 1833–35, 1837–43. U.S. vice president, 1849–50. President, 1850–53, at death of Taylor. Sent Matthew Perry to Japan, 1853. (p. 342)

Fitzgerald, F. Scott (1896–1940). Author. Known for his novels chronicling the Jazz Age (1920s). Worked as scriptwriter in Hollywood, 1937. Work was popular during his lifetime but did not receive critical recognition until long after his death. (p. 662)

Ford, Betty (1918–). First lady. Dancer, Martha Graham Concert Group 1939–41; dance teacher, 1932–48. As first lady promoted adoption of Equal Rights Amendment. Founded Betty Ford Center for Treatment of Drug and Alcohol Abuse. (p. 908)

Ford, Gerald R. (1913–). The 38th president. U.S. representative, 1948–73; House Republican leader, 1965. Chosen by Nixon as vice president when Agnew resigned, 1973. Became president when Nixon resigned, 1974. (p. 910)

Franklin, Aretha (1942–). African American recording artist. Made first record at age 12. Recorded for Columbia, Atlantic, Arista records; released around 50 albums since her first in 1961. Recipient of Grammy Awards for rhythm and blues, soul-gospel. (p. 776)

Franklin, Benjamin (1706–1790). Statesman, scientist, author. Publisher *Poor Richard's Almanac.* Founded what became University of PA. Invented stove, bifocal eyeglasses, lightning rod; experimented with electricity. On committee to draft Declaration of Independence; diplomat to France, 1776–85. (pp. 132, 146)

Friedan, Betty (1921–   ). Author, feminist. Wrote *The Feminine Mystique,* 1963, which revealed that many American women longed for more in life than being wives and mothers. Founded National Organization for Women (NOW), 1966; led campaigns to end discrimination against women. (p. 854)

Fuller, Margaret (1810–1850). Writer, literary critic. Taught at Bronson Alcott's school, Boston. Editor of *The Dial,* transcendentalist publication; literary critic, *New York Tribune;* gained reputation as one of best critics in U.S. Settled in Italy. (p. 285)

Gandhi, Indira (1917–1984). Indian politician. Official hostess for father, Prime Minister Jawaharlal Nehru. President of Congress party; elected prime minister, 1966; defeated, 1977; again elected, 1980; assassinated by Sikh extremists, 1984. (p. 977)

García, Héctor P. (1914–   ). Mexican American physician, civil rights activist. In U.S. Medical Corps, WWII. Organized American G.I. Forum, to defend civil rights of Mexican Americans, especially veterans. First Mexican American member, U.S. Commission on Civil Rights. (p. 840)

Garfield, James A. (1831–1881). The 20th president, 1881. U.S. representative, 1863–80; Republican leader from 1876; U.S. senator, 1880. Assassinated, 1881. (p. 489)

Garland, Hamlin (1860–1940). Writer, advocate of literary realism. Won Pulitzer Prize for *A Daughter of the Middle Border,* 1921. (p. 443)

Garvey, Marcus (1887–1940). Pan-Africanist leader. Born Jamaica. Founded Universal Negro Improvement Association, 1914. Came to U.S., 1916; established UNIA branches in North; held UNIA convention in NY, 1920. Led movement to establish black-governed country in Africa; preached black pride. (p. 636)

Geronimo (1829–1909). Apache chief. Born AZ. Admitted to warriors' council, Chiricahua Apaches, 1846; nicknamed Geronimo by Mexicans. Led campaign against whites, 1885–86; was captured, escaped; surrendered. Settled at Fort Sill, OK. (p. 432)

Goldman, Emma (1869–1940). Toured and lectured on anarchism and free speech; arrested for lecturing on birth control, 1915. Deported to Russia, 1919. (p. 626)

Goldwater, Barry M. (1909–   ). Public official. U.S. senator from AZ, 1953–65 and 1968–87. Leader of conservative wing of Republicans. Published *The Conscience of a Conservative,* 1960. Republican presidential candidate, 1964. (p. 841)

Gorbachev, Mikhail (1931–   ). Soviet leader. Became head of USSR's Communist party, 1985; president of USSR, 1989. Instituted programs of economic and political restructuring (*perestroika*) and of openness (*glasnost*), which led to breakup of Soviet Union. (pp. 935, 958)

Grant, Ulysses S. (1822–1885). The 18th president, 1869–77. As general in Civil War, broke Confederate control of MS by capturing Vicksburg. Despite heavy losses finally wore down Confederates. Accepted Lee's surrender, 1865. (pp. 380, 386, 403)

Greenhow, Rose O'Neal (1815?–1864). Confederate spy. Prominent social figure in Washington, D.C. Secured and passed information on Union troop movement; imprisoned, exiled to Confederacy. Unofficial Confederate spy in Great Britain, 1863–64. Drowned trying to run blockade off NC coast. (p. 369)

Marcus Garvey

Grimké, Angelina (1805–1879) and **Sarah (1792–1873).** Sisters, abolitionists, women's rights pioneers. Became active in abolitionist movement, 1830s; among first women in U.S. to lecture in public. Began fight for women's rights when criticized for their "shocking" abolitionist behavior. (p. 297)

Angelina Grimké

Hamilton, Alexander (1755–1804). Helped write *The Federalist.* First secretary of the treasury, 1789–95. Fatally wounded in duel with Aaron Burr. (p. 192)

Harding, Warren G. (1865–1923). The 29th president, 1921–23. U.S. senator, 1915–21. Presidential term marked by corruption of his appointees, "the Ohio Gang." Died on speaking tour; succeeded by Coolidge. (p. 629)

Harrison, Benjamin (1833–1901). The 23rd president, 1889–93. Grandson of W. H. Harrison. U.S. senator, 1881–87. (p. 490)

Harrison, William Henry (1773–1841). The 9th president, 1841. Led military campaigns against Indians; won Battle of Tippecanoe Creek in War of 1812; defeated Tecumseh. U.S. representative, 1816–19; U.S. senator, 1825–28. Died of pneumonia, 1841. (pp. 212, 248)

Hayes, Rutherford B. (1822–1893). The 19th president, 1877–81. Ran against Samuel J. Tilden, 1876; contest decided by electoral commission. To keep peace with Southern Democrats, agreed to end military Reconstruction. (pp. 408, 488)

Hellman, Lillian (1905–1984). Playwright. Wrote psychological and social themes. Most famous works of the 1930s and 1940s, such as *The Little Foxes*, focused on dangers of greed, selfishness, and power. Involved in leftist politics. (p. 718)

Hemingway, Ernest (1899–1961). Writer. Ambulance driver, WWI; correspondent, Spanish Civil War. Created "Hemingway hero," who displays unusual courage. Pulitzer Prize for *The Old Man and the Sea,* 1952. Nobel Prize for Literature, 1954. (p. 662)

Henry "the Navigator" (1394–1460). Prince of Portugal; established school of navigation, directed voyages of exploration along African coast. (p. 30)

Henry "the Navigator"

Hobby, Oveta Culp (1905–1995). Military leader, statesman. First director of Women's Army Corps, WWI; first woman promoted to colonel, first to receive Distinguished Service Medal. Secretary health, education, and welfare, 1953–55. Publisher, *The Houston Post.* (p. 814)

Ho Chi Minh (1890–1969). Vietnamese Communist leader, president of N. Vietnam, 1945–69. (p. 865)

Hoover, Herbert (1874–1964). The 31st president, 1929–33. U.S. secretary of commerce under Harding and Coolidge, 1921–29. As president secured creation of Federal Farm Board and Reconstruction Finance Corporation. (pp. 631, 672, 683)

Houston, Sam (1793–1863). Soldier, politician. Lived with Cherokees. Served in army under A. Jackson. Practiced law, TN. U.S. representative, 1823–27; governor of TN, 1827–29. General; won Texas war for independence at Battle of San Jacinto, 1836. President, Republic of Texas, 1836–38 and 1841–44. U.S. senator, 1846–49; TX governor, 1859–61. (p. 309)

Hughes, Langston (1902–1967). African American author. Wrote volumes of poetry, short stories, plays, operas. Most popular character, Jesse B. Semple, expressed black views on social issues. Awarded NAACP Spingarn Medal, 1960, as "poet laureate of the Negro race." (p. 660)

Hurston, Zora Neale (1889–1968). African American writer, anthropologist. Studied black folklore in the South and the Caribbean. Wrote novels, folklore collections, radio scripts; taught drama at North Carolina College. (p. 717)

Hutchinson, Anne (1591–1643). Religious leader. Preached salvation through individual understanding of God's grace and love, regardless of obedience to laws of church and state. Banished from Massachusetts Bay Colony. Moved with family to RI, later to NY. (p. 73)

Inouye, Daniel (1924–   ). Asian American statesman. Veteran WWII.

U.S. representative, 1950s. First elected to Senate, 1962. Gained national attention during televised Senate investigation of Watergate. (pp. 777, 936)

Isabella I (1451–1504). Spanish monarch. Marriage to Ferdinand united largest Spanish kingdoms. Support of Columbus led to Spanish American empire. Staunch Catholic; supported reform of secular clergy, society; banished non-converting Jews. (pp. 22, 39)

Jackson, Andrew "Old Hickory" (1767–1845). The 7th president, 1829–37. In War of 1812, defended New Orleans; became national hero. U.S. representative, 1796–97; U.S. senator, 1797–98 and 1823–25. (pp. 214, 239, 246)

Anne Hutchinson

Jackson, Helen Hunt (1830–1885). Writer, reformer. Books include *A Century of Dishonor,* 1881, which showed government abuses of Native Americans. Investigated conditions of CA Indians, 1882; wrote *Ramona,* 1884, about Spaniards and Indians in early CA. (p. 433)

Jackson, Jesse (1941–). African American minister, civil rights leader. Worked with Martin Luther King, Jr., 1960s; organized several black self-help projects in Chicago, including Operation Breadbasket and People United to Save Humanity (PUSH). Founder of Rainbow Coalition; presidential candidate. (p. 937)

Jackson, Mahalia (1911–1972). Gospel singer, "the Queen of the Gospel Song." Her 1945 recording, "Move on up a Little Higher," brought international fame, won new audiences for gospel music. (p. 718)

Mahalia Jackson

Jefferson, Thomas (1743–1826). The 3rd president, 1801–09. Drafted Declaration of Independence. Governor of VA, 1779–81; minister to France; first secretary of state, 1790–93; John Adams's vice president, 1797–1801. Founder and designer of University of VA. Died same day as John Adams, on 50th anniversary of the Declaration. (pp. 118, 193, 210)

Johnson, Andrew (1808–1875). The 17th president, 1865–69. Self-educated, tailor. U.S. representative, 1843–53; governor of TN, 1853–57; U.S. senator, 1857–62; Lincoln's vice president, 1865; succeeded to presidency on Lincoln's death. Reconstruction policies led to impeachment, 1868; acquitted. Again U.S. senator, 1875. (p. 397)

Johnson, Lyndon Baines "LBJ" (1908–1973). The 36th president, 1963–69. U.S. representative, 1937–49; U.S. senator, 1949–61; JFK's vice president, 1961–63, succeeded to presidency on Kennedy's death. As president secured passage of Civil Rights Act of 1964 and Voting Rights Act of 1965. Popularity declined as civil conflicts grew over Vietnam War; did not run for reelection. (pp. 831, 841, 870)

Jones, Mary Harris "Mother" (1830–1930). Labor leader; appeared wherever there was a strike or labor dispute. (pp. 493, 551)

Jordan, Barbara (1936–1996). First African American woman from a Southern state in U.S. Congress; first black keynote speaker, Democratic national convention. (p. 911)

Joseph, Chief (c. 1840–1904). Nez Percé leader. From Wallowa Valley, OR. Fought U.S. troops to retain Nez Percé lands, 1877. Won battles, but when faced with U.S. Army strength, ordered retreat to Canada. Surrendered, resettled in Indian Territory; later returned to Northwest. (p. 432)

Chief Joseph

Kelley, Florence (1859–1932). Labor reformer. Early resident of Hull House. Her reports about women and child workers helped persuade Illinois legislature to reform working conditions. Earned law degree 1894. Secretary, National Consumers League, 1899–1932. (p. 517)

Kennedy, John Fitzgerald "JFK" (1917–1963). The 35th president, 1961–63. U.S. representative, 1947–53; U.S. senator, 1953–60. First Roman Catholic president; assassinated in Dallas, TX, 1963. Wrote *Why England Slept,* 1940; won Pulitzer Prize for *Profiles in Courage,* 1956. (pp. 831, 834, 868)

Kennedy, Robert Francis "RFK" (1925–1968). Politician. U.S. attorney general, 1961–64. U.S. senator, 1964–68. Assassinated while campaigning for Democratic presidential nomination, 1968. Wrote *Pursuit of Justice,* 1964. (pp. 833, 880)

Khrushchev, Nikita (1894–1971). Soviet leader. Communist premier, USSR, 1958–64. Promoted space exploration, increase in Soviet standard of living, "peaceful coexistence" with Western nations. Installed Soviet missiles in Cuba, 1962; later withdrew them to end the Cuban missile crisis with President Kennedy. (pp. 812, 836)

King, Coretta Scott (1927–). Civil rights leader. Carried on legacy of her husband, the Reverend Martin Luther King, Jr., after his death, 1968. As president of Martin Luther King, Jr., Memorial Center, promotes prison reform, voter registration, and other civil rights reforms. (p. 850)

King, Martin Luther, Jr. (1929–1968). Minister, civil rights leader. Led Montgomery bus boycott; founded Southern Christian Leadership Conference, 1957. Helped organize March on Washington, 1963. Won Nobel Peace Prize, 1964. Assassinated in Memphis, TN. (pp. 823, 844, 850)

Kirkpatrick, Jeane (1926–). Political scientist, stateswoman.

Mary Harris "Mother" Jones

Ambassador to United Nations, 1981–85. Took tough anti-Communist stance, supported pro-American authoritarian countries; influenced Reagan's foreign policy. (p. 933)

Kissinger, Henry (1923–   ). Statesman, political scientist. Harvard professor and government consultant, 1950s–60s. Nixon's principal adviser on foreign policy; helped settle end of Vietnam War. Won Nobel Peace Prize, 1973. (pp. 881, 903)

La Follette, Robert M. (1855–1925). Politician from WI. Leader of Progressive Republicans. (p. 537)

Lange, Dorothea (1895–1965). Photographer best known for documentary photographs of Great Depression. (pp. 712, 715)

Dorothea Lange

Las Casas, Bartolomé de (1474–1566). Spanish priest, reformer. Preached against the *encomienda* system in Spanish colonies; helped win laws to protect Native Americans. Bishop of Chiapas, 1544–47. (p. 41)

Lease, Mary Elizabeth (1850–1933). Activist. Farmed in Kansas, became involved in farmers' and workers' struggles. Helped found Populist party; worked for women's suffrage. Fiery speaker for the Farmers' Alliance and Populist party, 1890s. (p. 499)

Lee, Robert E. (1807–1870). Civil War general. President of Washington College (now Washington and Lee University), 1865–70. (p. 368)

Liliuokalani (1838–1917). Queen of Hawaiian Islands. Wrote *Hawaii's Story by Hawaii's Queen*, 1898. (p. 566)

Lin, Maya Ying (1959–   ). Architect. Designed Vietnam Veterans Memorial, Washington, D.C., dedicated 1982; designed Civil Rights Memorial, Montgomery, AL, opened 1989. (p. 889)

Lincoln, Abraham (1809–1865). The 16th president. Term spanned Civil War, 1860–65. Wrote Emancipation Proclamation, 1863. Assassinated in 1865. (pp. 351, 374, 396)

Livermore, Mary Ashton (1820–1905). Reformer. Led Chicago branch of U.S. Sanitary Commission, which raised money and supplies for Union army. President American Woman Suffrage Association, 1875–78, and of MA Woman's Christian Temperance Union, 1875–85. (p. 363)

L'Ouverture, Toussaint (c. 1743–1803). Haitian general. Led a slave insurrection, 1791. Won a civil war, 1799; invaded Santo Domingo (Dominican Republic), 1801, freed the slaves. Ruled entire island until 1802, when defeated by French troops and imprisoned in France. (p. 206)

Toussaint L'Ouverture

Lyon, Mary (1797–1849). Educator, pioneer of higher education for women. In 1837 opened Mount Holyoke Seminary, which later became Mount Holyoke College. Remained president of the seminary until her death. (p. 291)

MacArthur, Douglas (1880–1964). Army general. Allied supreme commander in Southwest Pacific, WWII; supreme commander of UN forces in Korea, 1950–51. (pp. 688, 745, 762)

Madero, Francisco (1873–1913). Mexican revolutionary, politician. Began successful revolt to oust dictator Porfirio Díaz, 1910; elected president, 1911. Overthrown by Victoriano Huerta, 1913; shot while under arrest. (p. 575)

Madison, Dolley (1768–1849). First lady. Graciously served as White House hostess during presidencies of Jefferson and Madison. Noted for saving Washington's portrait, important papers, and other treasures when British burned presidential mansion, 1814. (p. 214)

Madison, James (1751–1836). The 4th president, 1809–17. Helped write *The Federalist*. U.S. representative, 1789–97. Sponsored Bill of Rights. Jefferson's secretary of state, 1801–09. (pp.147, 213)

Malcolm X (1925–1965). African American leader. Black Muslim; preached black pride, black nationalism. Converted to orthodox Islam. Assassinated in 1965. (p. 849)

Malcolm X

Mandela, Nelson (1918–). South African anti-apartheid leader. Joined African National Congress (anti-apartheid group), 1944; led protests against South African government, 1950s–60s; sentenced to life in prison. Many groups attempted to effect his release; was not freed until 1990. (pp. 947, 960)

Mankiller, Wilma (1945–). Cherokee chief; first woman to be installed as principal chief of a major Native American tribe. (p. 948)

Mao Zedong (1893–1976). Chinese leader. Chairman Communist party, 1949–76, and of People's Republic of China, 1949–59. Began Great Leap Forward to improve Chinese economy, 1957; began Cultural Revolution to revitalize Communist values, 1966–69. (p. 798)

Marshall, George C. (1880–1959). U.S. Army officer, statesman. Truman's secretary of state, 1947–49; originated Marshall Plan, 1947. (p. 791)

Marshall, John (1755–1835). Chief Justice, U.S. Supreme Court. Lawyer and leading Federalist politician from VA. Member of commission sent to France during XYZ Affair. Member House of Representatives, 1799–1800; secretary of state, 1800–01. (p. 204)

Marshall, Thurgood (1908–1993). Supreme Court justice, 1967–91. Attorney for NAACP, 1938–61; successfully argued *Brown* v. *Board of Education* before Supreme Court. Served on U.S. Court of Appeals, 1961–65; appointed solicitor general, 1965. (p. 822)

Golda Meir

Martí, José (1853–1895). Cuban writer, revolutionary. Took part in uprising against Spanish government, 1868. Often exiled; lived and wrote in New York City. Founded Cuban Revolutionary party, 1892; died fighting for Cuban independence. Noted for poems and essays on independence. (pp. 559, 614)

McClendon, Rose (1884–1936). African American actor. Worked in NY theater; toured U.S. and Europe. (p. 660)

McKay, Claude (1890–1948). Harlem Renaissance poet, writer. Moved to U.S. from Jamaica, 1912. First books, *Songs of Jamaica* and *Constab Ballads*, used Jamaican dialect. Also wrote *Harlem Shadows*, 1922; *Banana Bottom*, 1933; *A Long Way from Home*, 1937. (p. 661)

McKinley, William (1843–1901). The 25th president, 1897–1901. U.S. representative, 1877–83 and 1885–91. Under direction of Marcus Hanna, elected governor of Ohio, 1892–96. Assassinated in 1901. (pp. 500, 560)

McNamara, Robert (1916–). Secretary of defense under Kennedy and Johnson, 1961–68; advised on military strategy in Vietnam. (p. 878)

McPherson, Aimee Semple (1890–1944). Revivalist. Founded International Church of the Foursquare Gospel, 1927; missionary to China. Crossed U.S. several times conducting revivals; gained thousands of followers through her dramatic radio broadcasts. (p. 656)

Means, Russell (1940–). Leader of the American Indian Movement of the 1970s. Led takeover of Bureau of Indian Affairs building, occupation of Wounded Knee. (p. 920)

Meir, Golda (1898–1978). Prime minister of Israel, 1969–74. Born in Ukraine; grew up in U.S.; moved to Palestine in 1921. Author of *My Life*, 1975. (p. 904)

Mendes, Chico (1944–1988). Brazilian rubber tapper. Led campaign against destruction of Amazonian rain forest. Assassinated in 1988. (p. 970)

Metacom (1639?–1676). Native American chief. Called King Philip by colonists. Sachem of Wampanoags. Waged war (King Philip's War) against colonists because of their takeover of Indian lands and execution of his men. War ended with his death, as did Native American resistance to white settlement in New England. (p. 90)

Mineta, Norman (1931–). Japanese American politician. U.S. representative, 1974–1995; sponsor of Japanese American redress bill. (p. 755)

Moctezuma II (1466–1520). Emperor of Aztecs. Seized by Cortés in Tenochtitlán and held hostage. (p. 46)

Moctezuma II

Monroe, James (1758–1831). The 5th president, 1817–25. Fought in Revolution; member Continental Congress. U.S. senator, 1790–94; helped negotiate Louisiana Purchase. Madison's secretary of state, 1811–17, and war, 1814–15. Issued Monroe Doctrine, 1823. (p. 230)

Moseley-Braun, Carol (1947–). First African American female senator, elected 1992. Lawyer, assistant U.S. attorney, 1973–77. IL state representative, 1978–88. Served as recorder of deeds, Cook County, IL, 1989–92. (p. 943)

Moses, Anna Mary "Grandma" (1860–1961). Regionalist painter. Began painting when in her 70s; captured country life of 19th- and 20th-century America in simple, primitive paintings. Published *My Life's History*, 1952. (p. 719)

Lucretia Mott

Mott, Lucretia (1793–1880). Quaker minister, abolitionist, women's suffrage leader. Helped found Swarthmore College. Active in the Underground Railroad. With Stanton, called Seneca Falls Convention. Founder and first president, American Equal Rights Association, 1866. (p. 298)

Murray, Judith Sargent (1751–1820). Writer. Published essays on women's rights during American Revolution. Wrote popular poetry and plays on religion, politics, education, social life in the 1790s. (p. 140)

Mūsā, Mansa (?–1337?). Emperor of Mali, West Africa. Ascended throne around 1312. Conquered Songhai; expanded trade; patron of arts, education, architecture. Made notable pilgrimage to Mecca by way of Cairo around 1324. (p. 26)

Nash, Diane (1938–). Civil rights leader. An organizer of SNCC's southern sit-in movement. Field organizer for Southern Christian Leadership Conference, 1960s. Protested against war in Vietnam. (p. 845)

Nixon, Richard Milhous (1913–1994). The 37th president, 1969–74. Eisenhower's vice president, 1953–61. In heat of televised Senate investigation of his role in Watergate scandal, and under threat of impeachment, was first president to resign. (pp. 832, 881, 901)

O'Connor, Sandra Day (1930–). Supreme Court justice. Became first female justice when appointed by Reagan in 1981. In home state of AZ, served as assistant attorney general, state senator, and judge. (p. 933)

O'Keeffe, Georgia (1887–1986). Artist. Developed her painting technique in 1920s when living in NY, with paintings of urban scenes. Won biggest acclaim late in life for her paintings of enormous flowers and Southwest desert and mountain scenes. (pp. 663, 719)

Paige, Satchel (1906–1982). African American baseball player. Pitched in Negro League, 1924–47. Became one of first African American pitchers in American League when he joined Cleveland Indians, 1948. Elected to Baseball Hall of Fame, 1971. (p. 681)

Parks, Gordon (1912–). African American photographer, filmmaker. Made award-winning photographs of Chicago's South Side, 1930s. Photographer for Farm Security Administration and Office of War Information. First African American to direct a film (*Shaft,* 1972) for a major studio. (p. 715)

Parks, Rosa Lee (1913–). African American who helped launch the civil rights movement by refusing to give up her bus seat to a white passenger. (p. 823)

Rosa Lee Parks

Paul, Alice (1885–1977). Women's suffrage leader. Founded Congressional Union for Woman Suffrage (later the National Woman's party), 1913. Submitted the first Equal Rights Amendment to Congress, 1923. (p. 552)

Perkins, Frances (1882–1965). Stateswoman. Secretary of labor, 1933–45; first female cabinet member. Researched and publicized conditions in sweatshops and factories, 1910s–20s. Helped draft and carry out FDR's labor legislation. Member of Civil Service Commission, 1946–52. (pp. 695, 758)

Pierce, Franklin (1804–1869). The 14th president, 1853–57. Born in NH. U.S. representative, 1833–37; U. S. senator, 1837–42. In Mexican War, 1846–48. As president opened Northwest for settlement. (p. 344)

Francisco Pizarro

Pizarro, Francisco (c. 1475–1541). Spanish conquistador. Explored northern South America and Central America, 1509. Accompanied Balboa's expedition to Pacific Ocean, 1513. Gained wealth in Panama. Conquered Incas. (p. 48)

Pocahontas (c. 1595–1617). Native American princess. Aided Jamestown settlers. Converted to Christianity; married colonist John Rolfe, 1614. Went to England and received by English monarchs, 1616; died of smallpox. (p. 60)

Polk, James K. (1795–1849). The 11th president, 1845–49. U.S.

representative, 1825–39; governor of TN, 1839–41. First "dark horse" candidate. During his presidency the U.S. acquired CA and most of Southwest. (p. 312)

Pontiac (1720?–1769). Ottawa leader. Supported French in French and Indian War. Led Native Americans against British in Pontiac's Rebellion, 1763; made peace with British, 1766, but alienated his followers. Murdered by a Peoria, 1769. (p. 105)

Powell, Colin (1937–   ). U.S. Army general. First African American to head National Security Council, 1987–89; also first to be named Chairman of the Joint Chiefs of Staff, 1989–93. Highly decorated officer in Vietnam War; helped plan successful U.S. strategy for Gulf War. (p. 939)

Randolph, A. Philip (1889–1979). African American labor leader. Organized railroad porters, 1925; convinced FDR to ban discrimination in defense industries and federal bureaus. Vice president AFL–CIO. Led largest civil rights demonstration in U.S. history: March on Washington for Jobs and Freedom, 1963. (pp. 756, 785)

Rankin, Jeannette (1880–1973). Suffragist, pacifist. First female member of Congress: U.S. House of Representatives, 1917–19 and 1941–43. (p. 594)

Reagan, Ronald Wilson (1911–   ). The 40th president, 1981–89. Contract movie actor, Hollywood; in 52 films, 1937–57. Spokesman and host of weekly TV series for General Electric, 1952–62. Governor of CA, 1966–74. (pp. 928, 929, 933)

Red Cloud (1822–1909). Native American chief. Led Bad Face band of Oglalas, also Sioux and Cheyenne, to resist federal development of Bozeman Trail in WY and MT, 1865–67. Signed Treaty of Fort Laramie, 1868. (p. 432)

Revels, Hiram R. (1822–1901). African American clergyman, educator, politician. Chaplain to Union black troops stationed in MS, 1864–65.

Settled in MS after war. First African American elected to U.S. Senate, 1870–71. (p. 406)

Rivera, Diego (1886–1957). Mexican painter. Leader, with Orozco and Siqueiros, of political-social school of painting, especially murals, 1920s–40s. Painted several large works in U.S., such as at Detroit Institute of Arts, 1932. (p. 663)

Robeson, Paul (1898–1976). African American actor, singer. Stage plays include *Emperor Jones*, 1923; *Show Boat*, 1926; *Othello*, 1943–44. Made first concert appearance, singing spirituals in New York City in 1925. Toured U.S., Europe, Russia. Starred in films, 1930s. (p. 660)

Roosevelt, Eleanor (1884–1962). First lady, author, diplomat, humanitarian. Married Franklin Roosevelt, 1905. Active in Democratic party. Delegate to United Nations; led its Commission on Human Rights; helped draft Universal Declaration of Human Rights and secure its adoption, 1948. (pp. 688, 708, 783)

Roosevelt, Franklin Delano "FDR" (1882–1945). The 32nd president, 1933–45. Married Eleanor Roosevelt, 1905. Nominee for vice president, 1920; contracted polio, 1921,

A. Philip Randolph

Governor of NY, 1929–33. Only president elected for third, fourth terms; presidency spanned Great Depression and WWII. (pp. 688, 697, 753)

Roosevelt, Theodore (1858–1919). The 26th president, 1901–09. Governor of NY, 1899–1900; McKinley's vice president, 1901; succeeded to presidency on McKinley's death. Served in Cuba with "Rough Riders." Progressive candidate, 1912. (pp. 538, 539, 562)

Rosenberg, Julius (1918–1953) and Ethel (1915–1953). Communist spies. Arrested for receiving nuclear weapons data from her brother—a sergeant stationed at Los Alamos, NM—and passing it on to Soviets. Convicted; first U.S. civilians executed for espionage. (p. 795)

Ruth, George Herman "Babe" (1898–1948). Baseball player. Nicknamed "Bambino" and "Sultan of Swat." With Boston Red Sox, 1915–19; NY Yankees, 1920–35; Boston Braves, 1935. Hit a record 60 home runs in 1927, a record 714 in career. Elected to Baseball Hall of Fame, 1936. (p. 653)

Sacagawea (1786?–1812?). Shoshone guide, interpreter for Lewis and Clark expedition. Captured by Hidatsas; sold around 1800 to Canadian trapper Toussaint Charbonneau, whom she married. Gave birth to baby boy during expedition. (p. 208)

Sandino, Augusto César (1893–1934). Nicaraguan rebel leader. Waged guerrilla warfare on U.S. Marines, 1927–32. (p. 730)

Santa Anna, Antonio López de (1794–1876). Mexican general, politician, president. Attempted to crush Texas Revolution; captured Alamo; defeated by Sam Houston at San Jacinto, 1836. Also lost Mexican War to General Scott, 1847. (p. 308)

Schlafly, Phyllis (1924–   ). Opponent of women's liberation movement; helped defeat ratification of proposed Equal Rights Amendment (ERA). Founded Stop ERA organization, 1972;

founded Eagle Forum, group that supports traditional roles of women, 1975. (p. 922)

Seale, Robert G. "Bobby" (1937–). African American activist. With Huey Newton in CA, founded Black Panther party, which emphasized black self-defense, education, and black power. Joined by Eldridge Cleaver, 1967. Opposed by law-enforcement groups. (p. 849)

Seguín, Juan Nepomuceno (1806–1890). Tejano politician, soldier. Recruited volunteers against Santa Anna. Fought at battle of San Jacinto. (p. 310)

Sequoya (1770?–1843). Cherokee artisan, scholar. Created a syllabary that helped teach Cherokee people to read and write Cherokee. (p. 242)

Serra, Junípero (1713–1784). Spanish missionary; Franciscan. Founded Catholic missions in CA, 1769–82, including San Diego (first European settlement in Upper CA), San Francisco de Assisi, San Juan Capistrano. Defender of Native Americans. (p. 52)

Sitting Bull (1831?–1890). Legendary Sioux leader. Head of entire Sioux nation around 1867; leader in war against U.S. Army, 1876–77; with Crazy Horse at battle of Little Big Horn against Custer. Surrendered, 1881. Gained world fame in Buffalo Bill's Wild West Show, 1880s. (p. 428)

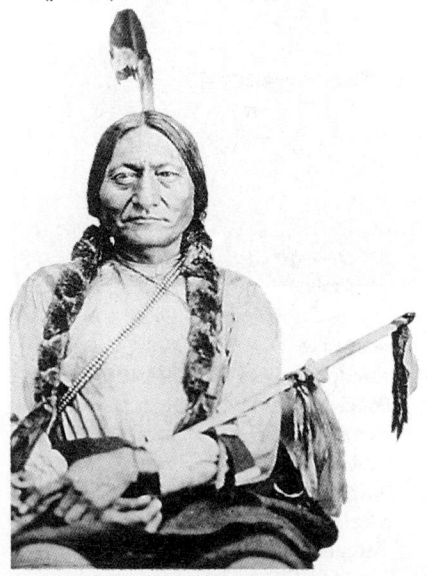

Sitting Bull

Smith, Bessie (1898?–1937). African American blues singer. Known for her emotional intensity and earthy realism of style. Recorded almost 200 songs (from 1923), often with major musicians such as Louis Armstrong. Wrote songs such as "Back Water Blues." (p. 660)

Margaret Chase Smith

Smith, Margaret Chase (1897–1995). Only woman to be elected to, and to serve in, both houses of Congress. Completed unexpired term of her late husband in House, 1940; elected to full term at next regular election. U.S. senator, 1948–72. Nominated as presidential candidate, 1964. (p. 807)

Stanton, Elizabeth Cady (1815–1902). Suffragist leader. With Lucretia Mott organized first woman's rights convention, Seneca Falls, NY, 1848; launched suffrage movement. President National Woman Suffrage Association, 1869–90; from 1851 worked with Susan B. Anthony for the cause. (pp. 298, 404, 552)

Stein, Gertrude (1874–1946). Author. Moved to Paris, 1903, where leading writers, artists of the day met in her home; wrote experimental prose, poems, operettas. Author of *Tender Buttons*, 1915; *Four Saints in Three Acts*, 1934. (p. 662)

Steinbeck, John (1902–1968). Novelist. Best known for works about agricultural workers: *Of Mice and Men*, 1937; *The Grapes of Wrath*, 1939 (Pulitzer Prize). Other works include *East of Eden*, 1952; *The Winter of Our Discontent*, 1961. Won Nobel Prize, 1962. (p. 717)

Steinem, Gloria (1934–). Feminist, writer. Founder of *Ms.* magazine. Author of *Revolution from Within*, 1992. (p. 856)

Stowe, Harriet Beecher (1811–1896). Author. Became abolitionist while living in Ohio 1833–50. Wrote *Uncle Tom's Cabin*, first published as serial in antislavery newspaper, 1851–52; in book form, 1852, it helped solidify antislavery feeling in North and contributed to the Civil War. (p. 344)

Taft, William Howard (1857–1930). The 27th president, 1909–13. Professor of law, Yale, 1913–21; Chief Justice of Supreme Court, 1921–30. (pp. 544, 565, 573)

Tarbell, Ida (1857–1944). Journalist. Best known for muckraking exposé *The History of the Standard Oil Company*, 1904. (p. 514)

Taylor, Zachary "Old Rough and Ready" (1784–1850). The 12th president, 1949–50. Entered army, 1808; fought in War of 1812 and Second Seminole War. Defeated Santa Anna at Buena Vista, ending war in northern Mexico. Died in office. (pp. 312, 339)

Tecumseh

Tecumseh (1768–1813). Shawnee chief. Spokesman for Indians of Ohio Valley; after Battle of Tippecanoe, joined British in War of 1812. (p. 212)

...argaret (1925–). ...e Minister, 1979–1990. ...e leader of a Western polit-...r party (Conservative party); first woman in the West to head a national government. (p. 930)

Thoreau, Henry David (1817–1862). Writer. Through Ralph Waldo Emerson met transcendentalists, including Bronson Alcott and Margaret Fuller. Helped edit *The Dial*, 1842–44. Best known for essay "Civil Disobedience," 1849, and book *Walden*, 1854. (p. 285)

Thorpe, James Francis "Jim" (1886–1953). Native American athlete. Won decathlon and pentathlon in Olympic Games, 1912. (pp. 528)

Truman, Harry S. (1884–1972). The 33rd president, 1945–53. U.S. senator, 1935–45. FDR's vice president, 1945; succeeded to presidency on FDR's death. As president established containment policy against USSR, Truman Doctrine, NATO, CIA, and Berlin Airlift; engaged U.S. in Korean War. (pp. 753, 764, 788)

Truth, Sojourner (1797?–1883). African American abolitionist, evangelist. Born enslaved; when freed, became itinerant preacher. (p. 294)

Tubman, Harriet (1820?–1913). Abolitionist. Escaped from slavery around age 39; became a leading abolitionist; helped more than 300 slaves escape to North by Underground Railroad. During Civil War served as nurse, launderer, and spy for Union in SC; later settled in NY. (p. 274)

Booker T. Washington

Turner, Nat (1800–1831). Slave leader. Led uprising that killed many whites and that contributed to southern white fear of slave revolts. (p. 272)

Tyler, John (1790–1862). The 10th president, 1841–45. U.S. representative, 1817–21; governor of VA, 1825–27; U.S. senator 1827–36. W. H. Harrison's vice president, 1841; succeeded to the presidency on Harrison's death. Texas was annexed during his term. (p. 249)

Van Buren, Martin (1782–1862). The 8th president, 1837–41. U.S. senator, 1821–28; governor of NY, 1829; Jackson's secretary of state, 1829–31, and vice president, 1833–37. Lost bid for reelection in 1840 and in 1848 as Free-Soil party candidate. (247)

Villa, Francisco "Pancho" (1878–1923). Mexican revolutionary. Active in Madero and Carranza revolutions; governor of Chihuahua, 1913; helped defeat Huerta, 1914. Raided Columbus, NM, killing 16; pursued by U.S. troops 1916; assassinated in 1923. (p. 576)

Warren, Earl (1891–1974). Jurist. Governor of CA, 1943–53; candidate for vice president (with T. Dewey), 1948; chief justice, U.S. Supreme Court, 1953–69; noted for opinions in *Brown* v. *Board of Education*, *Miranda* v. *Arizona*. (pp. 823, 839)

Warren, Mercy Otis (1728–1814). Author. Correspondent and friend of many leading colonial figures, such as John Adams, Samuel Adams, and Thomas Jefferson. Wrote political satires, and plays ridiculing British policies and persons and a history of the American Revolution. (p. 218)

Washington, Booker T. (1856–1915). African American educator. Born enslaved. Chosen to establish, and head Tuskegee Institute, AL, for training of blacks in trades and professions. Conservative viewpoint

opposed by W.E.B. Du Bois. Author of *Up From Slavery*, 1901. (p. 414)

Washington, George (1732–1799). The 1st president, 1789–97. Commander in chief of Continental Army, Revolutionary War. Set precedents for presidents. (pp. 114, 193)

Wells-Barnett, Ida (1862–1931). African American activist. Published *Red Record*, about lynching, 1895; founder Negro Fellowship League, 1910. (p. 415)

Wharton, Edith (1862–1937). Novelist. Born New York City; wrote finely crafted novels depicting rich New York society and its conventions, such as *The Age of Innocence* (Pulitzer Prize, 1920); most famous work is *Ethan Frome*, 1911; also wrote numerous short stories. (p. 478)

Wheatley, Phillis (1753?–1784). African American poet. Brought to Boston on slave ship; companion to wife of John Wheatley. Began writing poetry in English at age 13. Visited England, 1773; there published first book of poems, achieved fame. (p. 101)

Frances Willard

Willard, Frances (1839–1898). Educator, reformer. Dean of women and professors, Northwestern University, 1873–74. From 1874, devoted to temperance movement; president U.S. Women's Christian Temperance Union, 1879–98, and world WCTU, 1891–98; helped organize Prohibition party, 1882. (p. 525)

Wilson, Woodrow (1856–1924).
The 28th president, 1913–21. Tried but failed to keep U.S. out of WWI; domestic policies produced three amendments, including women's suffrage, 1920. Author of League of Nations; won Nobel Peace Prize, 1919. Wrote *A History of the American People*, 1902. (pp. 546, 549, 606)

Winnemucca, Sarah (1844–1891).
Paiute teacher, writer, guide. Lectured on behalf of Paiutes. Opened school in NV for Paiute children. (p. 433)

Woods, Granville T. (1856–1910).
African American inventor. Took college courses in electrical and mechanical engineering. Invented a steam-boiler furnace, telephone transmitter (bought by Bell), and induction telegraph system for trains. Registered more than 50 patents. (p. 459)

Wovoka (1858?–1932). Paiute religious leader. Following mystical experience in 1888 or 1889, began preaching message to Indians that gave rise to the Ghost Dance frenzy, especially among Sioux. Followers viewed him as a messiah. (p. 429)

Wright, Frank Lloyd (1867–1959).
Architect. Began practice in 1893 in Chicago, producing strikingly original designs. Worked in several styles, all showing mastery of space, form, and design. Structures include homes and public buildings, such as Guggenheim Museum, NY. (p. 664)

Wright, Richard (1908–1960).
African American author. Participated in Federal Writers' Project, 1935–37. Settled in Paris, 1946. Known for fiction dealing with prejudice, alienation, and suffering of urban blacks. Novel *Native Son*, 1940, marked him as a major American writer. (p. 717)

X, Y

X, Malcolm. *See* Malcolm X

Young, Andrew J., Jr. (1932–).
African American clergyman. First black U.S. representative from GA since Reconstruction (1972). Worked with National Council of Churches, Southern Christian Leadership Conference. Ambassador to United Nations, 1977–79. (p. 915)

Young, Brigham (1801–1877).
Religious leader. Converted to Mormon faith, 1832; traveling missionary from 1833. Directed Mormon settlement, Nauvoo, IL, 1838. Succeeded Joseph Smith as head of Mormon church; directed Mormon migration to Great Salt Lake Valley, UT, and settlement there. (p. 285)

Andrew J. Young, Jr.

Abilene   Town in east-central Kansas. Railhead town during the cattle boom of the late 19th century. (39°N 97°W) *m445*

Afghanistan   Country of southwest-central Asia. Invaded by the Soviet Union in 1979. Capital: Kabul. (33°N 63°E) *m905, m1012–13*

Alabama (AL)   State in the southern U.S. Admitted as a state in 1819. Capital: Montgomery. (33°N 87°W) *m1016–17*

Alaska (AK)   U.S. state in northwest North America. Became a territory in 1912 (first organized in 1884) and a state in 1959. Capital: Juneau. (64°N 150°W) *m1016–17*

Albania   Country in southeast Europe on the Adriatic Sea. Invaded by Italy in 1939. Capital: Tiranë. (41°N 20°E) *m736, m959, m1012–13*

Albany   City in southwestern Georgia. Scene of civil rights protests in the 1960s. (31°N 84°W) *m845*

Alsace-Lorraine   Region between France, Germany, Belgium, and Switzerland. Part of the German Empire, 1871–1918; returned to France by the Treaty of Versailles, 1919. (48°N 7°E) *m588*

American River   River in north-central California whose gold-bearing waters started the gold rush of 1849. (38°N 120°W) *m325*

American Samoa   Unincorporated territory of the U.S. in the southern Pacific Ocean. Administered by the U.S. since 1899. (14°S 170°W) *m564*

Annamite Mountains   Range of mountains that runs north-south through Vietnam. (17°N 105°E) *m865*

Anzio   Town in central Italy. In World War II Allied troops landed at Anzio in January 1944. (41°N 12°E) *m748*

Appomattox Courthouse   Virginia town where General Lee surrendered to General Grant, ending the Civil War. *m387*

Arizona (AZ)   State in southwestern U.S. Became a territory in 1863 and a state in 1912. Capital: Phoenix. (34°N 113°W) *m1016–17*

Arkansas (AR)   State in south-central U.S. Admitted as a state in 1836. Capital: Little Rock. (35°N 93°W) *m1016–17*

Armenia   Republic; member of the Commonwealth of Independent States. Formerly part of the USSR. Independent in 1991. Capital: Yerevan. (41°N 44°E) *m959, m1012–13*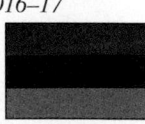

Atlanta   Major southern city, capital of Georgia. During the Civil War it was captured and burned by General Sherman, 1864. (33°N 84°W) *m387*

Austria-Hungary   Former monarchy in central Europe. Consisted of Austria, Hungary, Bohemia, and parts of Poland, Romania, Yugoslavia, and Italy. Formed in 1867; lasted until 1918. (47°N 12°E) *m588*

Azerbaijan   Republic; member of the Commonwealth of Independent States. Formerly part of the USSR. Independent in 1991. Capital: Baki. (40°N 47°E) *m959, m1012–13*

Baghdad   Capital of Iraq. Scene of U.S. bombings during the Persian Gulf War. (33°N 44°E) *m940*

Bahamas   Country in the Atlantic Ocean consisting of hundreds of islands. Gained independence from Great Britain in 1973. Capital: Nassau. (26°N 76°W) *m41, m1012–13*

Balkans   Countries that occupy the Balkan Peninsula, including Albania, Bulgaria, Greece, Romania, the former Yugoslavia, and northwestern Turkey. (43°N 24°E) *m588*

Baltimore   Maryland city northeast of Washington, D.C., on upper Chesapeake Bay. (39°N 76°W) *m75*

Bangladesh   Country in southern Asia. Formerly part of Bengal, it became part of Pakistan in 1947. In 1971 it became a separate nation. Capital: Dacca. (24°N 90°E) *m1012–13*

Barbary states   North African states of Algiers, Tunis, Tripoli, and Morocco. Some warred with the U.S. in the early 1800s. *m212*

Bataan   Peninsula of western Luzon, Philippines. In World War II U.S. and Philippine troops surrendered to the Japanese, April 1942. U.S. forces recaptured the peninsula in February 1945. *m746*

Bay of Pigs   Bay on southwest coast of Cuba. Site of the failed 1961 invasion by Cuban exiles trained by the CIA. (22°N 81°W) *m837*

Beijing   Capital of China. (40°N 116°E) *m25, m564*

Belarus   Republic in Eastern Europe; member of the Commonwealth of Independent States. Formerly part of the USSR. Independent in 1991. Capital: Minsk. (53°N 25°E) *m959, m1012–13*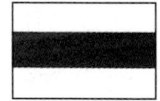

Belgium   Country in northwest Europe. Invaded by Germany in 1914 and 1940. Scene of the Battle of the Bulge. Capital: Brussels. (51°N 3°E) *m588, m1012–13*

Beringia   Land bridge formed during the last Ice Age between Siberia and what is today Alaska. (65°N 170°W) *m4*

Berlin   Capital and largest city of Germany. Divided into East Berlin and West Berlin in 1945. Reunited in 1989. (52°N 13°E) *m736, m780, m793*

Birmingham   City in north-central Alabama. Scene of several civil rights protests. (33°N 86°W) *m845*

Black Sea   Inland sea between Europe and Asia. (43°N 32°E) *m29*

Bosnia and Herzegovina   Country annexed to Austria-Hungary in 1908 and Yugoslavia in 1918. Capital: Sarajevo. (44°N 17°E) *m588, m959, m1012–13*

Boston   Massachusetts capital on Massachusetts Bay founded in the 17th century. Leading center of anti-British sentiment in the 18th century and antislavery thought in the 19th century. (42°N 71°W) *m129*

Brazil Republic in eastern South America. Largest country on the continent; ruled by Portugal from 1500 to 1822. Empire until 1889. Capital: Brasília. (9°S 53°W) *m971, m1012–13*

Buffalo City in western New York at the eastern end of Lake Erie on the Canadian border. End point of the Erie Canal. (43°N 79°W) *m233*

Cahokia Settlement founded by the Mississippian culture near present-day St. Louis, Missouri. (38°N 90°W) *m15*

California (CA) State in western U.S. Admitted as a free state in 1850. Capital: Sacramento. (38°N 121°W) *m1016–17*

Cambodia Republic in southeast Asia. Independent in 1954. Scene of fighting during Vietnam War. Capital: Pnompenh. (12°N 104°E) *m865, m1012–13*

Canada Country in northern North America. Settled by English and French colonists. Ceded to Great Britain in 1763. Declared equal partner of Great Britain, 1931. Capital: Ottawa. (50°N 100°W) *m214, m1012–13*

Cape of Good Hope Cape on southern tip of Africa. First rounded by Bartolomeu Dias in 1488. (34°S 18°E) *m29*

Cape Verde Islands Group of islands in Atlantic Ocean that were settled by the Portuguese in the mid-15th century; became a colony in 1495. Gained independence in 1975. Capital: Praia. (15°N 26°W) *m29, m1012–13*

Caporetto Town in Slovenia. Scene of World War I defeat of Italian troops in December 1917. *m588*

Casablanca City in northwest Morocco. Founded by the Portuguese in the 16th century. Scene of World War II Allied conference. (33°N 7°W) *m748*

Chancellorsville Town in northeastern Virginia where a major Civil War battle was fought in May 1863. Union forces were defeated by Confederate troops. *m377*

Chapultepec Fort in Mexico City, Mexico; scene of U.S. victory during the Mexican War. (19°N 99°W) *m313*

Château-Thierry Town in northern France where Allied forces stopped German advance in World War I. (49°N 3°E) *m599*

Chernobyl City in north-central Ukraine where a nuclear power plant exploded in 1986. (51°N 30°E) *m971*

Chesapeake Bay Inlet of Atlantic Ocean in Virginia and Maryland. (38°N 76°W) *m75*

Cheyenne Wyoming state capital since 1869. Railhead town during the cattle boom of the 19th century. (41°N 104°W) *m445*

Chicago City in northeastern Illinois on Lake Michigan. Major port and third largest U.S. city. (41°N 87°W) *m233, m495*

Chile Country in southwest South America colonized by Spain in 1541; became independent in 1818. Capital: Santiago. (35°S 72°W) *m582, m1012–13*

China (Official name: People's Republic of China) Country in eastern Asia. After a bitter civil war (1946–49), became a Communist republic; nationalists fled to Taiwan. Capital: Beijing. (36°N 93°E) *m564, m865, m1012–13*

Cincinnati City in southwestern Ohio. (39°N 84°W) *m253*

Colombia Country in northwest South America. Capital: Bogotá. (3°N 72°W) *m578, m1012–13*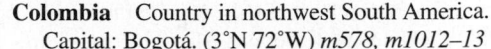

Colorado (CO) State in southwestern U.S. Became a territory in 1861 and a state in 1876. Capital: Denver. (39°N 107°W) *m1016–17*

Columbus Capital of Ohio. (40°N 83°W) *m1016–17*

Compiègne City in northern France. Armistice ending World War I signed nearby on November 11, 1918. (49°N 2°E) *m599*

Concord Town in northeastern Massachusetts in which (along with Lexington) the first fighting of the Revolutionary War was fought. (42°N 71°W) *m114*

Connecticut (CT) State in northeastern U.S., one of the original Thirteen Colonies. Admitted as a state in 1788. Capital: Hartford. (41°N 73°W) *m1016–17*

Coral Sea Part of the southwest Pacific Ocean. Scene of Allied naval victory during World War II. (13°S 150°E) *m746*

Cuba Island country in the Caribbean about 90 miles south of Florida. Capital: Havana. (22°N 79°W) *m837, m1012–13*

Cuzco Former capital of Inca Empire in Peru. (13°S 72°W) *m15*

Czechoslovakia Country in central Europe formed in 1918. Communist forces gained control of it in 1948 and kept power until 1989. In 1993 peacefully divided into Czech Republic (Capital: Prague) and Slovakia (Capital: Bratislava). (49°N 16°E) *m608, m736, m959, m1012–13*

Dardanelles Strait dividing Europe and southwest Asia. (40°N 26°E) *m793*

Deadwood City in western South Dakota. Founded after gold was discovered in Deadwood Gulch in 1876. (44°N 103°W) *m450*

Delaware (DE) State in eastern U.S., one of the original Thirteen Colonies. In 1787 became first state to ratify the Constitution. Capital: Dover. (38°N 75°W) *m1016–17*

Dien Bien Phu Town in northwestern Vietnam where French troops were defeated by Vietminh troops in 1954, leading to the end of French involvement in Indochina. (21°N 102°E) *m865*

District of Columbia (DC) Federal district of the U.S., seat of federal government since 1800. (39°N 77°W) *m1016–17*

Dodge City Kansas cattle town during the cattle boom of the 19th century. (37°N 100°W) *m445*

Dominican Republic Island country in the Caribbean. Makes up eastern part of island of Hispaniola. Capital: Santo Domingo. (19°N 70°W) *m578, m1012–13*

Dresden City in east-central Germany. Bombed during World War II. (51°N 13°E) *m748*

Dust Bowl Drought-ridden region in the 1930s that included parts of Texas, Oklahoma, Colorado, New Mexico, and Kansas. *m711*

East Berlin *See* Berlin.

Egypt Country in northeast Africa on the Mediterranean Sea. Capital: Cairo. (27°N 27°E) *m797, m905, m1012–13*

El Alamein   Town in northern Egypt on the Mediterranean Sea. Scene of World War II defeat of German Afrika Korps. *m748*

Elbe River   River in central Europe. (52°N 11°E) *m748*

El Salvador   Country in Central America. Capital: San Salvador. (14°N 89°W) *m578, m932, m1012–13*

England   Region of the United Kingdom, comprising most of the southern part of the island of Great Britain. Capital: London. (51°N 1°W) *m19*

Estonia   Country in northeast Europe. Annexed to the USSR in 1940. Became independent in 1991. Capital: Tallinn. (59°N 25°E) *m608, m959, m1012–13*

Ethiopia   Country in eastern Africa; formerly Abyssinia. Capital: Addis Ababa. (7°N 38°E) *m736, m976, m1012–13*

Federal Republic of Germany   *See* Germany

Finland   Country in northeast Europe. Capital: Helsinki. (62°N 26°E) *m608, m736, m1012–13*

Florida (FL)   State in southeastern U.S. Became a territory in 1822 and a state in 1845. Capital: Tallahassee. (30°N 84°W) *m1016–17*

Fort Duquesne   Scene of French defeat by the British in 1758. Eventually became Pittsburgh. *m92*

Fort Sumter   Fort in Charleston, South Carolina, harbor. Attack here by Confederate forces began the Civil War. (32°N 80°W) *m366*

France   Country in western Europe. French Revolution of 1789 overthrew the monarchy. Capital: Paris. (46°N 0°) *m19, m588, m748*

Fredericksburg   City in northeastern Virginia. Scene of Civil War battle in 1862. Union forces defeated by Confederate army. (38°N 77°W) *m377*

French Indochina   Former French territory in southeast Asia, 1946–55. (17°N 105°E) *m739*

Gaza Strip   Narrow coastal strip along the Mediterranean Sea. Controlled by Egypt, 1948–67, and by Israel, 1967–present. (31°N 34°E) *m797*

Genoa   City in northwestern Italy. Major trading center since Roman times. (44°N 10°E) *m29*

Georgia (GA)   State in southeastern U.S., one of the original Thirteen Colonies. Admitted as a state in 1788. Capital: Atlanta. (32°N 84°W) *m1016–17*

Georgia   Republic; member of the Commonwealth of Independent States. Formerly part of the USSR. Independent in 1991. Capital: T'bilisi. (42°N 43°E) *m959, m1012–13*

German Democratic Republic   *See* Germany

Germany   Country in western Europe. Fascist during the 1930s and 1940s. Divided into German Democratic Republic (East Germany) and Federal Republic of Germany (West Germany) after World War II. Reunified in 1990. Capital: Berlin. (51°N 8°E) *m736, m793, m959, m1012–13*

Gettysburg   Town in southern Pennsylvania. Scene of major Union victory in the Civil War. Abraham Lincoln delivered Gettysburg Address here in 1863. (40°N 77°W) *m377*

Ghana   Republic in western Africa. Ancient African trading kingdom. Capital: Accra. (8°N 2°W) *m26, m1012–13*

Gila River   River with source in western New Mexico; flows across southern Arizona. (33°N 110°W) *m315*

Gilbert Islands   Group of islands in the central Pacific Ocean. Scene of World War II battle. Capital: Tarawa. (0°174°E) *m746*

Goliad   Town in south-central Texas. Mission and *presidio* established by the Spanish in 1749. Texas forces defeated near here by Mexican troops during the Texas Revolution. (28°N 97°W) *m308*

Great Britain   Kingdom in western Europe. Consists of England, Scotland, and Wales. Capital: London. (54°N 4°W) *m1012–13*

Greece   Balkan country in southern Europe with numerous islands. Fought civil war, 1946–49. Capital: Athens. (39°N 21°E) *m793, m1012–13*

Greensboro   City in northern North Carolina. Scene of first 1960s sit-in to protest segregation. (36°N 79°W) *m845*

Grenada   Country in the Caribbean made up of the island of Grenada and the southern Grenadines. Capital: St. George's. (12°N 61°W) *m932*

Guadalcanal   One of the Solomon Islands in the Pacific Ocean. Scene of heavy fighting during World War II. (9°S 158°E) *m746*

Guam   Pacific island that became U.S. territory after the Spanish-American War. Capital: Agana. (14°N 143°E) *m746*

Guangdong   Province in southeast China. (23°N 113°E) *m482*

Guantánamo Bay   Bay on southeastern coast of Cuba. U.S. naval station established in 1903. (19°N 75°W) *m578*

Guatemala   Republic in Central America. Capital: Guatemala City. (15°N 91°W) *m811, m1012–13*

Gulf of Tonkin   Part of the South China Sea east of northern Vietnam. (20°N 108°E) *m873*

Hainan   Island located in the South China Sea, separated from Leizhou Peninsula by a narrow strait. Part of the Chinese province of Guangdong. (19°N 109°E) *m746*

Haiphong Harbor   Harbor of a city in northeast Vietnam on the Red River delta near the Gulf of Tonkin. Mined by U.S. forces during the Vietnam War (1972). (21°N 107°E) *m873*

Haiti   Island country in the Caribbean located on the western part of the island of Hispaniola. Former U.S. protectorate. Capital: Port-au-Prince. (19°N 72°W) *m578, m932, m1012–13*

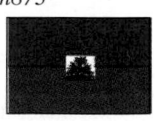

Hampton   City in southeastern Virginia opposite Norfolk on Hampton Roads, the outlet of three rivers into Chesapeake Bay. Settled by colonists from Jamestown in 1610, the city was sacked by the British in the War of 1812. (37°N 76°W) *m1016–17*

Hanoi   Capital of Vietnam. (21°N 106°E) *m865*

Harlem   Section of New York City in northern Manhattan bordering on the Harlem and East rivers. Influx of blacks beginning in 1910 made it one of America's largest African American communities. (40°N 74°W) *m661*

Hawaii (HI)   U.S. state in the central Pacific Ocean comprising the Hawaiian Islands. Admitted as a state in 1959. Capital: Honolulu. (20°N 157°W) *m564, m1016–17*

Hiroshima   Japanese city; U.S. dropped the first atomic bomb used in warfare on the city in August 1945. (34°N 132°E) *m746*

Hispaniola   Columbus and his crew established the colony of La Navidad here in 1492; today comprises the countries of the Dominican Republic and Haiti. (17°N 73°W) *m41*

Hong Kong   British crown colony located on the coast of China southeast of Guangzhou. Will become administrative region of China at end of the 20th century. Capital: Victoria. (21°N 115°E) *m746*

Iberian Peninsula   Peninsula of southwest Europe comprising Spain and Portugal. Separated from the rest of Europe by the Pyrenees and from Africa by the Strait of Gibraltar. (40°N 5°W) *m19*

Idaho (ID)   State in northwestern U.S. Admitted as a state in 1890. Capital: Boise. (44°N 115°W) *m1016–17*

Illinois (IL)   State in north-central U.S. Admitted as a state in 1818. Capital: Springfield. (40°N 90°W) *m1016–17*

Indiana (IN)   State in north-central U.S. Admitted as a state in 1816. Capital: Indianapolis. (40°N 86°W) *m 1016–17*

Indian Territory   Former territory in south-central United States. In 1834 it was set aside by the government as a homeland for forcibly displaced Native Americans. Western section, which became Oklahoma Territory, was opened to white settlement in 1889. In 1907 Indian Territory was merged with Oklahoma Territory to form the state of Oklahoma. (36°N 98°W) *m244*

Iowa (IA)   State in north-central U.S. Admitted as a state in 1846. Capital: Des Moines. (42°N 94°W) *m1016–17*

Iran   Country in southwest Asia where 53 Americans were held hostage during the Carter administration and which fought a long war with Iraq. Capital: Tehran. (31°N 53°E) *m905, m1012–13*

Iraq   Country in southwest Asia. Iraq's invasion of Kuwait led to UN–imposed economic sanctions and to war with the U.S. and the Allies in 1991. Capital: Baghdad. (32°N 43°E) *m905, m940, m1012–13*

Ireland   Located in the British Isles, Ireland is divided between Northern Ireland (Capital: Belfast), which is part of Great Britain, and the independent Republic of Ireland (Capital: Dublin). (54°N 8°W) *m1012–13*

Israel   Country in southwest Asia on the eastern Mediterranean coast that Jews established after the UN division of Palestine in 1948. Capital: Jerusalem. (32°N 34°E) *m797, m905, m1012–13*

Italy   Country in southern Europe, which fought on the side of the Allies in World War I. During World War II it was allied with Germany. Capital: Rome. (44°N 11°E) *m1012–1013*

Iwo Jima   Small Pacific island that the Americans captured in World War II after heavy fighting with the Japanese. *m746*

Jamaica   Island country in the Caribbean, which Columbus visited in 1494. It became a British colony in 1655 and an important sugar producer. Capital: Kingston. (18°N 78°W) *m41, m1012–13*

Jamestown   First successful English colony in America. *m57*

Japan   Chain of islands in the western Pacific Ocean. World War II military ally of Germany and Italy. Two of its cities devastated by atomic bombs. Since the war, has played a central role in the global economy. Capital: Tokyo. (37°N 134°E) *m739, m746, m1012–13*

Jerusalem   Capital of Israel, located in the east-central part of the country in the West Bank. Considered a holy place by Jews, Moslems, and Christians, the city was occupied as far back as the fourth millennium B.C. (31°N 35°E) *m25, m797*

Jordan   Country of southwest Asia. Capital: Amman. (30°N 38°E) *m797, m905, m1012–13*

Jordan River   River of southwest Asia rising in Syria and flowing about 200 miles south through the Sea of Galilee to the northern end of the Dead Sea. (32°N 36°E) *m797*

Kansas (KS)   Territory in central U.S., created by Kansas-Nebraska Act in 1854 in which the issue of slavery was to be determined on the basis of popular sovereignty. Admitted to the Union as a free state in 1861. Capital: Topeka. (38°N 99°W) *m345, 1016–17*

Kazakhstan   Republic; member of the Commonwealth of Independent States. Formerly part of the USSR. Independent in 1991. Capital: Almaty. (49°N 59°E) *m959, m1012–13*

Kentucky (KY)   State in east-central U.S. Admitted as a state in 1792. Capital: Frankfort. (37°N 87°W) *m1016–17*

Kings Mountain   Site of Tory defeat in South Carolina (1780). (35°N 81°W) *m129*

Korea   Peninsula and former country of eastern Asia between the Yellow Sea and the Sea of Japan. Officially divided into two independent nations, North Korea and South Korea, in 1945. (38°N 128°W) *m564, m799*

Kuril Islands   Island chain of extreme eastern Russia extending about 750 miles in the Pacific Ocean between Kamchatka Peninsula and northern Hokkaido, Japan. (46°N 149°E) *m746*

Kuwait   Oil-rich country on the northeast Arabian Peninsula at the head of the Persian Gulf. Invaded by Iraq, it was liberated by the Allies in the Persian Gulf War (1991). Capital: Al Kuwait. (29°N 48°E) *m940, m1012–13*

Kyrgyzstan   Republic; member of the Commonwealth of Independent States. Formerly part of the USSR. Independent in 1991. Capital: Bishkek. (42°N 28°E) *m959, m1012–13*

La Navidad   First Spanish settlement established by Columbus and named in honor of Christmas Day—the day it was founded in 1492. (19°N 72°W) *m41*

Lake Erie   One of the Great Lakes, linked with the Hudson River by the New York State Barge Canal. *m214*

Latin America   Central and South America; settled by Spain and Portugal. *m231*

Latvia   Country of northern Europe on the Baltic Sea. Capital: Riga. (57°N 24°E) *m1012–13*

Lexington   One of two northeastern Massachusetts towns (along with Concord) where the first fighting of the Revolutionary War took place. (42°N 71°W) *m114*

Leyte   Island of the east-central Philippines, north of Mindanao. (10°N 125°E) *m746*

Liberia   Country on west coast of Africa founded in 1817 by the American Colonization Society for the resettlement of freed African Americans. Capital: Monrovia. (6°N 10°W) *m1012–13*

Line of Demarcation   Line established in 1493 to divide the claims in the Americas of Spain and Portugal. *m45*

Lithuania   Country of northern Europe on the Baltic Sea; declared independence from USSR in March 1990. Capital: Vilnius. (55°N 23°E) *m959, m1012–13*

Little Rock   Capital of Arkansas, located in the central part of the state. Federal troops were sent there in 1957 to enforce a 1954 U.S. Supreme Court ruling against segregation in the public schools. (34°N 92°W) *m1016–17*

Los Angeles   City of southern California. Center of a sprawling metropolitan area. (34°N 118°W) *m1016–17*

Louisiana (LA)   One of the southeastern states carved out of the Louisiana territory. Admitted as a state in 1812. Capital: Baton Rouge. (31°N 93°W) *m1016–17*

Lowell   Massachusetts city on the Merrimack River northwest of Boston. (42°N 71°W) *m253*

Madeira Islands   Archipelago in the northeast Atlantic Ocean west of Morocco. Islands are a part of Portugal. (33°N 16°W) *m29*

Maine (ME)   State in the northeastern U.S. Admitted as a state in 1820. Capital: Augusta. (45°N 70°W) *m1016–17*

Mali   Country of western Africa. Capital: Bamako. (15°N 0°) *m26, m1012–13*

Manchuria   Region of northeast China, which was invaded by Japan in 1931. (48°N 125°E) *m739*

Manila   Capital and largest city of the Philippines, located on southwest Luzon Island and Manila Bay, inlet of the South China Sea. (14°N 121°E) *m564*

Mariana Islands   Group of 15 islands in the western Pacific Ocean, east of the Philippines. Guam, the largest island of the group, is a U.S. territory; other islands are a self-governing commonwealth under U.S. protection. *m746*

Marshall Islands   Self-governing island group in the central Pacific Ocean. Capital: Majuro. (10°N 165°E) *m746*

Maryland (MD)   State in east-central U.S., one of the original Thirteen Colonies. Admitted as a state in 1788. Capital: Annapolis. (39°N 76°W) *m1016–17*

Massachusetts (MA)   State in northeastern U.S., one of the original Thirteen Colonies. Admitted as a state in 1788. Capital: Boston. (42°N 72°W) *m1016–17*

Mediterranean Sea   Large sea bordered by southern Europe, southwest Asia, and northern Africa. (32°N 13°E) *m1012–13*

Mekong Delta   Located in northern Vietnam, the delta has formed where the Mekong River empties into the South China Sea. Fertile rice-growing region. (18°N 104°E) *m865*

Memphis   Tennessee city on the Mississippi River near the Mississippi border. Founded and named (1819) by Andrew Jackson. (35°N 90°W) *m1016–17*

Meuse River   River in western Europe flowing from northeast France through southern Belgium and the southeast Netherlands to the North Sea. (50°N 5°E) *m599*

Mexican Cession   Area that Mexico ceded to the U.S. at the end of the Mexican War, comprising the present-day states of California, Nevada, and Utah, and parts of Arizona, Colorado, and New Mexico. *m315*

Mexico   Republic in North America, bounded on the north by the U.S. and on the south by Guatemala and British Honduras. Capital: Mexico City. (23°N 104°W) *m1012–13*

Miami   City in southeastern Florida located on Biscayne Bay. (25°N 80°W) *m1016–17*

Michigan (MI)   State in north-central U.S. Admitted as a state 1837. Capital: Lansing. (46°N 87°W) *m1016–17*

Midway Islands   Islands northwest of Hawaii occupied by the United States Navy in 1867; site of an important U.S. naval victory in World War II. (28°N 179°W) *m746*

Minnesota (MN)   State in north-central U.S. Admitted as a state in 1858. Capital: St. Paul. (46°N 90°W) *m1016–17*

Mississippi (MS)   State in southeastern U.S. Admitted as a state in 1817. Capital: Jackson. (32°N 89°W) *m1016–17*

Missouri (MO)   State in central U.S. Admitted as a state in 1821. Capital: Jefferson City. (38°N 93°W) *m237, m1016–17*

Mogadishu   Located on the Indian Ocean; capital and largest city of Somalia. *m25*

Moldova   Republic; member of the Commonwealth of Independent States. Formerly part of the USSR. Independent in 1991. Capital: Chișinău. *m959, m1012–13*

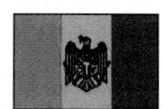

Montana (MT)   State in northwestern U.S. Admitted as a state in 1889. Capital: Helena. (47°N 112°W) *m1016–17*

Monterey   City in western California, south of San Francisco on Monterey Bay. (36°N 122°W) *m313*

Montgomery   Capital of Alabama. Capital of the Confederate States of America, February to May 1861. (32°N 86°W) *m1016–17*

Munich   City in southeastern Germany founded in 1158, long the center of Bavaria. City was largely rebuilt after extensive Allied bombing in World War II. (48°N 11°E) *m736*

Nagasaki   Japanese city; 1945 site of the second atom-bombing by the U.S., ending World War II. (32°N 130°E) *m746*

Nebraska (NE)   State in central U.S. Admitted as a free state in 1867. Capital: Lincoln. (41°N 101°W) *m1016–17*

Nevada (NV)   State in western U.S. Organized as a separate territory in 1861 and admitted as a state in 1864. Capital: Carson City. (39°N 117°W) *m1016–17*

New Guinea   Island in the southwest Pacific Ocean north of Australia. Western half is part of Indonesia; eastern half forms the major portion of Papua New Guinea. (5°S 140°E) *m746*

New Hampshire (NH)   State in northeastern U.S., one of the original Thirteen Colonies. Admitted as a state in 1788. Capital: Concord. (44°N 71°W) *m1016–17*

New Jersey (NJ)   State in eastern U.S.; one of the original Thirteen Colonies. Admitted as a state in 1787. Capital: Trenton. (40°N 75°W) *m1016–17*

New Mexico (NM)   State in southwestern U.S.; originally Zuni country, ceded to the U.S. by Mexico in 1848; organized as a territory that included Arizona and part of Colorado in 1850; admitted as a state in 1912. Capital: Santa Fe. (34°N 107°W) *m1016–17*

New Orleans   City in southeastern Louisiana between the Mississippi River and Lake Pontchartrain. Founded in 1718, it became the capital of a French colony in 1722 and passed to the U.S. as part of the Louisiana Purchase of 1803. (30°N 90°W) *m209*

New York (NY)   State in northeastern U.S. One of the original Thirteen Colonies. Admitted as a state in 1788. Capital: Albany. (42°N 78°W) *m1016–17*

Nicaragua   Country of Central America on the Caribbean Sea and the Pacific Ocean. Columbus spotted its Caribbean coastline in 1502, and the first European settlements were made by Spain in 1524. Capital: Managua. (12°N 86°W) *m578, m932, m1012–13*

Nogales   City in southern Arizona, south of Tucson on the Mexican border and adjacent to Nogales, Mexico. (31°N 111°W) *m52*

Normandy   Northern French province that was the site of the D-Day invasion during World War II. (49°N 0°) *m748*

North Carolina (NC)   State in southeastern U.S. One of the original Thirteen Colonies. Admitted as a state in 1789. Capital: Raleigh. (35°N 81°W) *m1016–17*

North Dakota (ND)   State in north-central U.S. Admitted as a state in 1889. Capital: Bismarck. (47°N 102°W) *m1016–17*

North Korea   (Official name: Democratic People's Republic of Korea) Country on east coast of Asia, bounded on north by China, on east by Sea of Japan, on south by South Korea, and on west by the Yellow Sea and Korea Bay. Capital: P'yongyang. (40°N 127°E) *m799, m1012–13*

North Vietnam   *See* Vietnam

Northwest Territory   Region of the north-central U.S., extending from the Ohio and Mississippi rivers to the Great Lakes. Area was ceded to the U.S. in 1783; became a territory in 1787 and later was split up into the present-day states of Ohio, Indiana, Illinois, Michigan, Wisconsin, and part of Minnesota. Control over the territory was a major issue in the War of 1812. *m142*

Nueces River   Texas river that Mexicans claimed was the boundary between Mexico and Texas. (28°N 98°W) *m313*

Ogallala   Nebraska city on the South Platte River, 52 miles west of North Platte. (41°N 101°W) *m445*

Ohio (OH)   State in north-central U.S. Originally part of the Northwest Territory; admitted as a state in 1803. Capital: Columbus. (40°N 83°W) *m1016–17*

Okinawa   Japanese island captured by U.S. forces in World War II after heavy losses on both sides. (26°N 128°E) *m746*

Oklahoma (OK)   State in south-central U.S. Except for its panhandle, Oklahoma formed part of the Louisiana Purchase; was organized as a territory in 1890 and became a state in 1907. Capital: Oklahoma City. (36°N 98°W) *m1016–17*

Oregon (OR)   State in northwestern U.S. Admitted as a state in 1859. Capital: Salem. (43°N 122°W) *m1016–17*

Oregon Country   Region encompassing all the land from the California border to Alaska and from the Pacific Ocean to the Rocky Mountains; held jointly by Great Britain and the U.S., 1818–46, when the international boundary was fixed at the 49th parallel. *m229*

Oswego   City in north-central New York at the mouth of the Oswego River on Lake Ontario northwest of Syracuse. (43°N 76°W) *m92*

Palestine   Often called the Holy Land, historical region in Southwest Asia between the eastern Mediterranean and the Jordan River, now divided between Israel and Jordan. (31°N 35°E) *m797*

Panama   Country in southern Central America occupying the Isthmus of Panama. Capital: Panama City. (8°N 81°W) *m578, m1012–13*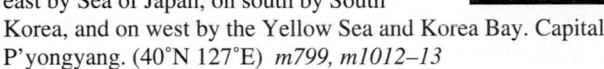

Panama Canal   Ship canal, about 51 miles long, crossing the Isthmus of Panama in the Canal Zone and connecting the Caribbean Sea with the Pacific Ocean. Opened to traffic on August 15, 1914. *m571*

Pearl Harbor   Port in the Hawaiian Islands where the American Pacific fleet was destroyed by a Japanese surprise attack in 1941. (21°N 158°W) *m746*

Pennsylvania (PA)   State in eastern U.S., one of the original Thirteen Colonies. Admitted as a state in 1787. Capital: Harrisburg. (41°N 78°W) *m1016–17*

People's Republic of China   *See* China

Persian Gulf   Arm of the Arabian Sea between the Arabian Peninsula and southwestern Iran in southwest Asia. (27°N 50°E) *m940*

Peru   Republic in western South America, bounded on north by Ecuador and Colombia, on east by Brazil and Bolivia, on southern tip by Chile, and on west by the Pacific Ocean. Capital: Lima. (10°S 75°W) *m976, m1012–13*

Philippines, Republic of the   Archipelago of about 7,100 islands, lying approximately 500 miles off the southeast coast of Asia. Capital: Manila. (14°N 125°E) *m561, m1012–13*

Pikes Peak   Mountain, 14,110 feet high, in Rocky Mountains in central Colorado. (38°N 105°W) *m450*

Pittsburgh   City in Pennsylvania, located at the point where the joining of the Allegheny and Monongahela rivers forms the Ohio River. Fort Duquesne was built on the site by the French c. 1750 and fell to the British in 1758, when it was renamed Fort Pitt. (40°N 80°W) *m233*

Plymouth   Site in Massachusetts where the Pilgrims first landed in North America in 1620. (42°N 70°W) *m69*

Poland   Country of central Europe bordering on the Baltic Sea. Capital: Warsaw. (52°N 17°E) *m608, m736, m959, m1012–13*

Portugal   Country of southwest Europe on the western Iberian Peninsula. It includes the Madeira Islands and the Azores in the Atlantic Ocean. Capital: Lisbon. (38°N 9°W) *m19, m1012–13*

Puerto Rico (PR)   Island east of Cuba and southeast of Florida, ceded to the U.S. after the Spanish-American War; self-governing commonwealth. Capital: San Juan. (18°N 67°W) *m561, m1012–13*

Pusan   City in southeastern South Korea on Korea Strait. Developed into a major port during the Japanese occupation of Korea, 1910–45. (35°N 129°E) *m799*

Quebec   First permanent French settlement in North America, now a city in eastern Canada on the St. Lawrence River. (47°N 71°W) *m92*

Red River   River of southeast Asia that rises in southern China and flows about 730 miles, generally south, through Vietnam to a fertile delta on the Gulf of Tonkin. (22°N 104°E) *m865*

Rhineland   Region along the Rhine River in western Germany. (50°N 6°E) *m736*

Rhode Island (RI)   State in northeastern U.S., one of the original Thirteen Colonies. Admitted as a state in 1790. Capital: Providence. (41°N 71°W) *m1016–17*

Rhodesia   Region of south-central Africa south of Zaire, comprising modern-day Zambia and Zimbabwe. (18°S 29°E) *m1012–13*

Richmond   State capital, in the east-central part of Virginia on the James River. Strategically important in the American Revolution. Capital of the Confederacy in the Civil War and major objective of the Union Army; fell in 1865. (37°N 77°W) *m366*

Rio Grande   "Great River" that forms the border between Texas and Mexico. (26°N 98°W) *m313*

Roanoke   Island off the coast of North Carolina where two early English settlements failed. (36°N 77°W) *m57*

Russia   Country in Eastern Europe and Northwest Asia. Formerly part of USSR. Independent in 1991. Member of the Commonwealth of Independent States. Capital: St. Petersburg, formerly Leningrad. (61°N 60°E) *m1012–13*

Saar   River, about 150 miles long, rising in northeast France and flowing north and northwest to the Moselle River in western Germany. River's valley is also known as the Saar Basin. *m608*

Sagres   Portuguese town in which Prince Henry ("the Navigator") built a school of navigation in the 15th century. *m29*

Sahara   Vast desert of northern Africa extending east from the Atlantic coast to the Nile Valley and south from the Atlas Mountains to the region of the Sudan. (23°N 1°E) *m26*

Saigon   Present-day Ho Chi Minh City. Largest city of Vietnam, in the southern part of the country near the South China Sea; formerly capital of South Vietnam. (10°N 106°E) *m865*

St. Augustine   City in northeastern Florida on the Atlantic Ocean, south-southeast of Jacksonville. Founded by the Spanish in 1565, it is the oldest permanent European settlement in the U.S. (30°N 81°W) *m52*

St. Lawrence River   River in southeast Canada flowing about 750 miles northeast from Lake Ontario along the Ontario–New York border and through southern Quebec to the Gulf of St. Lawrence. (48°N 69°W) *m57, m92*

St. Mihiel   Village in northeast France on the Meuse River east of Paris. World War I battle here (1918) was the first major American offensive led by General John J. Pershing. (49°N 5°E) *m599*

Sakhalin Island   Island of southeast Russia in the Sea of Okhotsk north of Hokkaido, Japan. (52°N 144°E) *m746*

Salem   City northeast of Boston. Founded in 1626, it is noted as the site of witchcraft trials, 1692, and of Nathaniel Hawthorne's *House of the Seven Gables*. (42°N 71°W) *m69*

San Antonio   City in south Texas. (29°N 98°W) *m308*

San Diego   City in southern California on San Diego Bay, an inlet of the Pacific Ocean near the Mexican border. (33°N 117°W) *m52*

San Francisco   City in western California on a peninsula between the Pacific Ocean and San Francisco Bay. Discovery of gold nearby in 1848 changed the city from a small community into a thriving boomtown. (37°N 122°W) *m52*

Santa Fe   Capital of New Mexico, in the north-central part of the state northeast of Albuquerque. Important city in Spanish America, it became the territorial capital in 1851 and state capital in 1912. (35°N 106°W) *m52*

Santiago   Cuban seaport captured by American forces during the Spanish-American War. (20°N 76°W) *m561*

Saudi Arabia   Country on the Arabian Peninsula in southwest Asia, bordered on the north by Jordan, Iraq, and Kuwait; the world's second-largest producer of oil. Capital: Riyadh. (22°N 46°E) *m940, m1012–13*

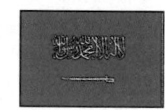

Savannah   U.S. city on east coast of Georgia captured by General Sherman during Civil War, 1864. (32°N 81°W) *m387*

Seattle   Washington city bounded by Puget Sound and Lake Washington. First settled in the 1850s; prospered after the coming of the railroad in 1884 and became a boomtown during the Alaskan gold rush of 1897. (47°N 122°W) *m445*

Sedan   Town of northeast France on the Meuse River near the Belgian border. Site of important battle in World War I. (50°N 5°E) *m599*

Selma   Alabama city west of Montgomery. In 1965 was the site of a voter-registration drive led by Rev. Martin Luther King, Jr. (32°N 87°W) *m845*

Seoul   Capital and largest city of South Korea, in the northwest section of the country. Twice occupied by Communist forces during the Korean War. (37°N 127°E) *m799*

Shiloh   Locality in southwestern Tennessee east of Memphis. Site of civil war battle, 1862, which claimed more than 10,000 casualties on both sides. *m382*

Sicily   Italian island in the Mediterranean taken by Allied forces prior to the occupation of Italy during World War II. (37°N 13°E) *m748*

Sierra Leone   Country in western Africa on the Atlantic coast. First visited by the Portuguese in the 1460s; region became a British protectorate in 1896 and achieved independence in 1961. Capital: Freetown. (8°N 12°W) *m29*

Somalia   Country of extreme eastern Africa on the Gulf of Aden and the Indian Ocean. Capital: Mogadishu. (3°N 44°E) *m1012–13*

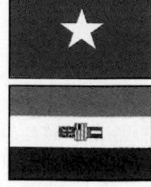

South Africa   Country of southern Africa on the Atlantic and Indian oceans. Pretoria is the administrative capital, Cape Town the legislative capital, and Bloemfontein the judicial capital. (28°S 25°E) *m1012–13*

South Carolina (SC)   State in southeastern U.S., one of the original Thirteen Colonies. Admitted as a state in 1788. First state to secede from the Union (1860). Capital: Columbia. (34°N 81°W) *m1016–17*

South Dakota (SD)   State in north-central U.S. Constituted the southern part of the Dakota Territory; admitted as a state in 1889. Capital: Pierre. (44°N 102°W) *m1016–17*

South Korea (Official name: Republic of Korea) Country on east coast of Asia, bounded on north by North Korea, on east by the Sea of Japan, on south by the Korea Strait, and on west by the Yellow Sea. Capital: Seoul. (36°N 128°E) *m1012–13*

South Vietnam   *See* Vietnam

Spain   Country in southwest Europe, occupying the greater part of the Iberian Peninsula and including the Balearic and Canary islands. Capital: Madrid. (40°N 4°W) *m1012–13*

Spice Islands   Present-day Moluccas. Group of islands in eastern Indonesia between Celebes and New Guinea. Islands were settled by the Portuguese but taken in the 17th century by the Dutch, who used them as the base for their monopoly of the spice trade. *m29*

Stalingrad   Present-day Volgograd (renamed in 1961). City of southwest Russia on the Volga River. (48°N 42°E) *m748*

Sudan   Country in northeast Africa south of Egypt. Capital: Khartoum. (14°N 28°E) *m976, m1012–13*

Sudetenland   Historical region of northwest Czechoslovakia along the Polish border. Seized by the Germans in September 1938, it was restored to Czechoslovakia in 1945. *m736*

Suez Canal   International waterway in the Middle East seized by Egypt in 1956. British, French, and Israeli troops unsuccessfully attempted to end Egyptian control. (31°N 32°E) *m811*

Sutter's Fort   Fortified town built by John Sutter on California's American River in 1839. *m325*

Syria   Country in southwest Asia on the eastern Mediterranean coast. Capital: Damascus. (35°N 37°E) *m905, m1012–13*

Taiwan   (Official name: Republic of China) Formerly Formosa. Country off the southeast coast of China made up of the island of Taiwan, the Pescadores, and other smaller islands. Capital: Taipei. (37°N 112°E) *m564, m746, m1012–13*

Tajikistan   Republic; member of the Commonwealth of Independent States. Formerly part of the USSR. Independent in 1991. Capital: Dushanbe. (39°N 69°E) *m1012–13*

Tennessee (TN)   State in south-central U.S. Admitted as a state in 1796. Capital: Nashville. (36°N 88°W) *m1016–17*

Tenochtitlán   Ancient name of Mexico City, which with Texcoco and Tlacopán formed the Aztec confederacy and became the capital of the Aztec empire. (19°N 99°W) *m15*

Texas (TX)   State in south-central U.S., bounded on south by Gulf of Mexico and Mexico. Known as the Lone Star State because it was an independent republic (1836–45) whose flag featured a single star. Capital: Austin. (31°N 101°W) *m1016–17*

Thailand   Formerly Siam. Country in southeast Asia on the Gulf of Thailand. Was occupied by the Japanese in World War II and was a strong supporter of the U.S. in the Vietnam War. Capital: Bangkok. (16°N 101°E) *m746, m1012–13*

Tikal   Ancient Mayan city, in present-day northern Guatemala, northeast of Petén Itza; excavation and restoration of ruins began in 1956. *m15*

Tombouctou   Town in Mali, in western Africa near the Niger River; reached height of prosperity as commercial and cultural center under Songhai rule c. 1500. (16°N 3°W) *m26*

Topeka   Capital of Kansas, in the northeastern part of the state west of Kansas City. (39°N 95°W) *m1016–17*

Turkey   Country in southwest Asia and southeast Europe between the Mediterranean and the Black seas. Capital: Ankara. (38°N 32°W) *m793, m1012–13*

Turkmenistan   Republic; member of the Commonwealth of Independent States. Formerly part of the USSR. Independent in 1991. Capital: Ashgabat. (40°N 56°E) *m959, m1012–13*

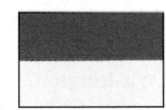

Ukraine   Republic; member of the Commonwealth of Independent States. Formerly part of the USSR. Independent in 1991. Central theater of warfare in both world wars. Capital: Kiev. (49°N 30°E) *m748, m959, m1012–13*

United Kingdom of Great Britain and Northern Ireland   *See* Great Britain

United States of America   Federal republic, North America, bounded on north by Canada and (in Alaska) by Arctic Ocean, on east by the Atlantic Ocean, on south by Mexico and the Gulf of Mexico, and on west by the Pacific Ocean. Capital: Washington, D.C. (38°N 110°W) *m1012–13, m1016–17*

Utah (UT)   State in western U.S. First explored by Coronado expedition, 1540. Admitted as a state in 1896. Capital: Salt Lake City. (39°N 112°W) *m1016–17*

Uzbekistan   Republic; member of the Commonwealth of Independent States. Formerly part of the USSR. Independent in 1991. Capital: Toshkent. (42°N 60°E) *m959, m1012–13*

Venezuela   Country in northern South America on the Caribbean Sea. Capital: Caracas. (8°N 65°W) *m578, m1012–13*

Venice   City in northeast Italy on islets within a lagoon in the Gulf of Venice, wide inlet of the northern Adriatic Sea. (45°N 12°E) *m29*

Vermont (VT)   State in northeastern U.S., one of the original Thirteen Colonies. Admitted as a state in 1791. Capital: Montpelier. (44°N 73°W) *m1016–17*

Vicksburg   City in western Mississippi on bluffs above the Mississippi River west of Jackson. During the Civil War it was besieged (1862–63) and finally captured by Union troops led by Ulysses S. Grant. (42°N 85°W) *m382*

Vietnam   Southeast Asian country (divided into North Vietnam and South Vietnam between 1954 and 1975) where United States and South Vietnamese forces fought a war against the Communist North Vietnamese. Capital: Hanoi. (18°N 107°E) *m865, m1012–13*

Virginia (VA)   State in eastern U.S., one of the original Thirteen Colonies. Admitted as a state in 1788. Capital: Richmond. (37°N 80°W) *m1016–17*

W

Wake Island   Island in the western Pacific Ocean between Hawaii and Guam. Annexed by the U.S. in 1898, it was a commercial air base and later a military base, held by the Japanese from 1941 to 1945. (19°N 167°E) *m746*

Waltham   Massachusetts city west of Boston. Site of first paper mill in U.S. and first power loom for manufacture of textiles. (42°N 71°W) *m253*

Washington (WA)   State in northwestern U.S., bounded on north by Canadian province of British Columbia and on west by the Pacific Ocean. Admitted as a state in 1889. Capital: Olympia. (47°N 121°W) *m1016–17*

Washington, D.C.   Capital of the United States, on the Potomac River between Virginia and Maryland and coextensive with the District of Columbia. Leading international political and educational center. (39°N 77°W) *m214*

West Berlin   *See* Berlin

West Virginia (WV)   State in east-central U.S. Admitted as a state in 1863. Part of Virginia until the area refused to endorse the Ordinance of Secession in 1861. Capital: Charleston. (39°N 81°W) *m1016–17*

Willamette Valley   Fertile agricultural region of Oregon, first settled in the 1830s by pioneers traveling west along the Oregon Trail. *m319*

Wisconsin (WI)   State in north-central U.S. Admitted as a state in 1848. First settled by the French, region was ceded to Great Britain in 1763 and became part of the Northwest Territory in 1787. Capital: Madison. (44°N 91°W) *m1016–17*

Wyoming (WY)   State in northwestern U.S. Organized as the Wyoming Territory in 1868 and admitted as a state in 1890. Capital: Cheyenne. (43°N 108°W) *m1016–17*

Y

Yalu River   River forming part of the North Korea–China border. (41°N 126°E) *m799*

Yangtze River   Longest river of China and of Asia, flowing about 3,450 miles from Xizang (Tibet) to the East China Sea. (30°N 117°E) *m739*

Yokohama   Japanese city in southeast Honshu, on the western shore of Tokyo Bay. Almost entirely destroyed by an earthquake and fire in 1923, again largely destroyed by U.S. bombing in World War II. (35°N 139°E) *m564*

Ysleta   First permanent Spanish colony in Texas, founded in 1681. (31°N 106°W) *m52*

Yugoslavia   Former country in southeast Europe bordering on the Adriatic Sea. It was formed in 1918 as the Kingdom of Serbs, Croats, and Slovenes after the collapse of the Austro-Hungarian Empire and renamed Yugoslavia in 1929. Today the name is claimed by Serbia and Montenegro. (44°N 17°E) *m608, m959, m1012–13*

Yukon Territory   Territory of northwest Canada east of Alaska. Region first explored by fur traders in the 1840s and acquired by Canada from the Hudson Bay Company in 1870. Capital: Whitehorse. (63°N 135°W) *m450*

GLOSSARY

This Glossary contains terms you need to understand as you study American history. After each term there is a brief definition or explanation of the meaning of the term as it is used in *Todd & Curti's The American Nation*. The page number refers to the page on which the term is introduced in the textbook.

Phonetic Respelling and Pronunciation Guide

Many of the key terms in this textbook have been respelled to help you pronounce them. The letter combinations used in the respellings throughout the narrative are explained in the following phonetic respelling and pronunciation guide. The guide is adapted from *Webster's Ninth New Collegiate Dictionary, Webster's New Geographical Dictionary,* and *Webster's New Biographical Dictionary.*

MARK	AS IN	RESPELLING	EXAMPLE
a	alphabet	a	*AL-fuh-bet
ā	Asia	ay	AY-zhuh
ä	cart, top	ah	KAHRT, TAHP
e	let, ten	e	LET, TEN
ē	even, leaf	ee	EE-vuhn, LEEF
i	it, tip, British	i	IT, TIP, BRIT-ish
ī	site, buy, Ohio	y	SYT, BY, oh-HY-oh
	iris	eye	EYE-ris
k	card	k	KARD
ō	over, rainbow	oh	oh-vuhr, RAYN-boh
u̇	book, wood	ooh	BOOHK, WOOHD
ȯ	all, orchid	aw	AWL, AWR-kid
ȯi	foil, coin	oy	FOYL, KOYN
au̇	out	ow	OWT
ə	cup, butter	uh	KUHP, BUHT-uhr
ü	rule, food	oo	ROOL, FOOD
yü	few	yoo	FYOO
zh	vision	zh	VIZH-uhn

A syllable printed in small capital letters receives heavier emphasis than the other syllable(s) in a word.

A

abolitionists   People who wanted to put an end to slavery. **78**

acid rain   Atmospheric pollution that gradually kills trees and makes lakes unfit for marine life. **972**

Adamson Act   Federal law reducing the workday for railroad workers from 10 to 8 hours with no decrease in wages. **551**

Adams-Onís Treaty (1819)   Agreement in which Spain transferred East Florida to the U.S. for $5 million and the U.S. promised to drop its claim to Texas. **230**

affirmative action   Programs giving preference to ethnic minorities and women in jobs or school admission to make up for past discrimination. **919**

African diaspora   Forcible resettlement of millions of African people to the Americas from the 1500s through the 1800s. **30**

Agricultural Adjustment Act (AAA)   Federal law passed in 1933 to reduce farmers' output, increase crop prices, and establish the Agricultural Adjustment Administration. **698**

Agricultural Marketing Act (1929)   Federal law that created the Federal Farm Board, an agency to help ease the plight of farmers by buying farm surpluses. **685**

AIDS   Acquired Immune Deficiency Syndrome, the final deadly stage of an illness believed to be caused by the human immunodeficiency virus (HIV). **950**

Albany Plan of Union (1754)   Benjamin Franklin's plan to unite the colonies through a loose confederation aimed at promoting their defense. **91**

Alien and Sedition Acts (1798)   Series of laws passed by the Federalists to protect the country from foreign influence, limit Republican power, and silence government critics. **202**

Alliance for Progress   President Kennedy's policy of sending economic aid to Latin America; designed to encourage democratic reforms and to promote capitalism. **835**

Allied Powers   World War I alliance that included France, Great Britain, Russia, Italy, and later the United States. **587**

American Anti-Slavery Society   First national antislavery organization devoted to immediate abolition, formed in 1833 by both black and white abolitionists. **294**

American Colonization Society Group founded by prominent northerners and southerners in 1817 to persuade slaveholders to free their slaves and transport them to Liberia. **265**

American Federation of Labor (AFL) Organization of independent skilled craft unions founded in 1886 by Samuel Gompers. **495**

American Indian Defense Association Organization that fought to protect religious freedom and tribal property for Native Americans. **710**

American Indian Movement (AIM) Organization, founded in 1968 by Minnesota Chippewas, that became the major force in the Red Power movement during the 1970s. **851**

American Plan Policy, promoted by business leaders during the 1920s, that called for open shops. **632**

Americans with Disabilities Act (1990) Federal law that prohibits discrimination against people with mental or physical disabilities. **950**

American System Henry Clay's federal program for economic development; it included a national bank, a protective tariff, and a national transportation system. **227**

amnesty Official pardon for crimes committed against the government. **395**

anarchists People who oppose all forms of government. **494**

annex Action by which one country takes control of another country or territory. **563**

Antifederalists Individuals who feared a powerful national government and opposed ratification of the U.S. Constitution. **150**

anti-Semitism Hatred of Jews. **733**

apartheid Racial segregation; former racial policy in South Africa. **915**

appeasement Policy of giving in to demands of a country or countries in an effort to avoid major conflicts. **735**

arbitration Hearing in which a third party settles a dispute. **539**

armistice Cease-fire. **600**

Articles of Confederation Agreement, ratified in 1781, in which the 13 colonies established a government of states with each state retaining power over its own affairs. **140**

assembly line Manufacturing technique in which a product is passed along a line of workers and assembled in stages. **646**

assimilation Cultural absorption of a group. **434**

Atlantic Charter (1941) Joint declaration of principles for international relations, agreed to by the United States and Great Britain. **738**

Atomic Energy Act (1946) Federal law that placed the Atomic Energy Commission under civilian control to oversee nuclear weapons research and to promote peacetime uses of atomic energy. **791**

automation Manufacturing process that used machines to perform industrial operations faster and more efficiently than human labor. **820**

Axis powers Military alliance of Germany, Italy, and Japan during World War II. **735**

B

baby boom Soaring birth rate between 1946 and 1964. **817**

Bacon's Rebellion (1676) Uprising by Virginia settlers, disgruntled over taxes and land, that included attacking Indians, looting wealthy plantations, and burning Jamestown. **77**

balance of trade Difference in value between trade exports and imports. **83**

Balfour Declaration (1917) Statement issued by Great Britain declaring its support for a Jewish homeland in Palestine. **611**

bank holiday (1933) New Deal proclamation that temporarily closed every U.S. bank to stop massive withdrawals. **694**

bank notes Paper money issued by banks in place of gold or silver. **192**

Baruch Plan (1946) Proposal submitted to the UN Atomic Energy Commission for international control of atomic energy. **790**

Bataan Death March (1942) Forced march of Allied prisoners on the Bataan peninsula to a Japanese detention camp, during which thousands died. **745**

Battle of Antietam (1862) Civil War battle that helped bolster northern confidence while dashing Confederate hopes of winning European support. **378**

Battle of Bunker Hill (1775) Revolutionary War battle in which British troops defeated Patriot forces atop two hills overlooking Boston Harbor. **116**

Battle of Camden (1780) Revolutionary War battle in which British troops defeated Patriot forces in South Carolina. **131**

Battle of Chancellorsville (1863) Confederate victory during the Civil War that resulted in the death of General Stonewall Jackson. **379**

Battle of El Alamein (1942) British victory in Egypt during World War II that broke the momentum of the Axis advance in North Africa. **749**

Battle of Fallen Timbers (1794) Decisive battle in the Northwest Territory in which U.S. troops defeated a confederation of Native Americans, weakening Indian resistance on the frontier. **197**

Battle of Fredericksburg (1862) Confederate victory during the Civil War that cost Union troops more than 12,000 casualties and led to General Burnside's replacement. **378**

Battle of Gettysburg (1863) Union victory during the Civil War that halted General Lee's invasion of the North. **379**

Battle of Iwo Jima (1945) Allied victory in the Pacific during World War II in which Japanese forces lost more than 20,000 troops. **764**

Battle of Leyte Gulf (1944) Decisive naval victory for the Allies during World War II that eliminated the Japanese fleet as a threat in the Pacific. **764**

Battle of Midway (1942) Allied naval victory that helped halt the major Japanese offensive in the Pacific during World War II. **747**

Battle of New Orleans (1815) Battle in which American troops defeated British forces after the War of 1812 had officially ended. **214**

Battle of Okinawa (1945) Allied victory in the Pacific during World War II in which Japanese forces lost more than 100,000 troops. **764**

Battle of Rosebud (1876) Battle against U.S. Army in which Native Americans gained confidence in their fighting force. **429**

Battle of San Jacinto (1836) Texan victory over Mexican troops that resulted in the Mexican government granting Texas its independence. **309**

Battle of Saratoga (1777) Patriot victory, during Revolutionary War, that convinced France to support the American fight for independence. **130**

Battle of Seven Pines (1862) Civil War battle in which Confederate general Johnston was seriously wounded and succeeded by Robert E. Lee. **377**

Battle of Shiloh (1862) Costly Civil War battle in which General Grant's troops defeated Confederate forces. **381**

Battle of Stalingrad (1942–43) Soviet defeat of German troops during World War II that broke the momentum of the Axis advance in Europe. **749**

Battle of the Atlantic World War II naval war fought between German U-boats and the Allied navy and air force. **760**

Battle of the Bulge (1944)   World War II battle in which Allied forces repulsed the final German offensive. **761**

Battle of the Coral Sea (1942)   Allied naval victory during World War II in which a joint British-American naval force stopped the Japanese advance on Australia. **746**

Battle of the Java Sea (1942)   World War II naval battle in which the Japanese navy defeated a fleet of American, British, Dutch, and Australian warships. **745**

Battle of the Little Bighorn (1876)   Native American victory that resulted in the death of U.S. Army general Custer and all the men in his detachment. **429**

Battle of the Philippine Sea (1944)   Decisive Allied naval and air victory over the Japanese during WorldWar II. **762**

Battle of the Somme (1916)   World War I battle in which the British lost some 60,000 troops in a single day. **589**

Battle of the Thames (1813)   American victory during the War of 1812 that helped break the British hold on the Northwest Territory. **214**

Battle of Tippecanoe (1811)   Battle in Indiana Territory between U.S. troops and a confederation of Native Americans; ended in defeat for the Indians and made William Henry Harrison a hero. **212**

Battle of Trenton (1776)   Revolutionary War battle in which Washington's army attacked and defeated Hessian soldiers stationed at Trenton, New Jersey. **128**

Battle of Vincennes (1779)   Revolutionary War battle in the West in which Patriot troops recaptured a British fort and went on to take control of western lands. **131**

Battle of Yorktown (1781)   Revolutionary War battle in which Patriot troops defeated British forces under General Cornwallis, effectively ending the war. **132**

Bear Flag Revolt (1846)   Uprising by U.S. settlers in California against Mexican rule in which they declared California an independent republic. **313**

bear market   Downward trend in stock prices. **670**

Beats   Small but influential group of writers and poets who challenged literary conventions and the life-style of the middle class in the 1950s. **825**

benevolent societies   Organizations formed during the turn of the century to support and aid new immigrants. **469**

Beringia   Former land bridge between Siberia and present-day Alaska used by Paleo-Indians to cross from Asia into North America. **4**

Berlin airlift (1948)   Joint effort by U.S. and British air forces to deliver food and supplies into West Berlin after the Soviets blocked all routes into the city. **792**

Berlin Wall   Concrete barrier built in 1961 to cut off traffic between East Berlin and West Berlin. **836**

bicameral   Legislature made up of two houses. **147**

Big Four   During World War I, term for U.S. president Wilson, French premier Clemenceau, Italian prime minister Orlando, and British prime minister Lloyd George. **607**

Bilingual Education Act (1974)   Federal law encouraging public schools to provide instruction to students in their native languages until they learned English. **923**

bill of attainder   Law that punishes a person by fine, imprisonment, or seizure of property without a court trial. **163**

Bill of Rights (1791)   First 10 amendments to the Constitution that protect individual liberties. **191**

biomass   Materials, such as wood or waste products, that can be burned or used to make fuel. **970**

bionics   Electronic devices to enhance biological functions. **951**

black codes   Laws adopted by former Confederates after the Civil War to limit the freedom of former slaves. **398**

blacklists   Lists of union supporters drawn up by employers for the purpose of denying jobs to union workers. **495**

Black Power   African American movement that focused on gaining control of economic and political power to achieve equal rights, by force if necessary. **848**

Blackshirts   Followers of Benito Mussolini. **732**

Black Thursday   October 24, 1929; day investors caused a panic on Wall Street by selling their shares. **671**

Black Tuesday   October 29, 1929; day the stock market crashed. **671**

Bland-Allison Act (1878)   Federal law passed in response to pressure from farmers; required the government to buy and mint silver each month. **499**

blitzkrieg   German word for war carried on with great speed and force, used to describe Hitler's "lightning war" against Poland in World War II. **737**

Bolsheviks   Branch of the Russian Communist party that seized power in 1917 following the overthrow of the czar. **598**

bonanza farm   Large-scale farm usually owned by a large company and run like a factory. **441**

Bonus Army   Name given to World War I veterans who marched on Washington, D.C., in 1932 to support a bill granting veterans early payment of pension bonuses. **687**

bosses   Powerful political party leaders who used political machines and patronage to control elections. **469**

Boston Massacre (1770)   Clash in Boston between an angry crowd of colonists and British soldiers that resulted in the death of five colonists. **110**

Boston Tea Party (1773)   Protest against British tax on tea in which colonists dumped tea into Boston Harbor. **111**

bourgeoisie   The middle class; originated in the Middle Ages and was made up of merchants and bankers. **20**

Boxer Rebellion (1900)   Revolt by a Chinese secret society attempting to drive foreigners out of China. **567**

braceros   Mexican farm workers who came to work in the Southwest during World War II and after. **757**

breadlines   Lines formed by people waiting for free food, such as those that occurred during the Great Depression. **677**

brinkmanship   Policy promoted by Secretary of State Dulles during the 1950s, which called for threatening all-out war in order to confront Communist aggression. **810**

British Invasion   Revolution in popular music inspired by the 1964 arrival of English rock bands such as the Beatles and the Rolling Stones. **856**

Brownshirts   Nazi storm troopers. **733**

Brown v. The Board of Education of Topeka (1952)   Supreme Court case challenging segregation in public schools; in it the Court ruled that separate educational facilities were unequal. **822**

bull market   Upward trend in stock prices. **670**

Bureau of Indian Affairs   Federal agency established within the War Department in 1824 to administer Native American reservations. **427**

business cycle   Regular ups and downs of business in a free-enterprise economy. **674**

cabinet   Heads of government departments who are appointed by, and serve as advisers to, the president. **191**

Camp David Accords (1978)   Middle East peace agreement drafted by the U.S., Egypt, and Israel. **916**

capitalism   Economic system based on a free market and private ownership of property. **192**

carpetbaggers Northern Republicans who moved south after the Civil War to help freedpeople or to profit financially from unsettled conditions under Reconstruction governments. **406**

caudillos Latin American military leaders during the 1930s who used force to maintain order. **729**

Cayuse War First of a series of Indian wars in Oregon Country that began in 1847 after the murder of missionaries Marcus and Narcissa Whitman and 12 others by Cayuse Indians. **322**

Central Intelligence Agency (CIA) Federal agency created to gather information overseas. **794**

Central Powers World War I alliance led by Germany, Austria-Hungary, the Ottoman Empire (Turkey), and Bulgaria. **587**

Charter of 1606 Document, issued by King James I of England, that licensed the Plymouth Company and the London Company to organize settlements in Virginia. **59**

checks and balances System giving each branch of the federal government the means to restrain the powers of the other two branches. **155**

Chicano movement Brown Power movement organized by young Mexican American college students to emphasize pride in Mexican culture and heritage. **851**

Chinese Exclusion Act (1882) Federal law that denied U.S. citizenship to people born in China and prohibited the immigration of Chinese laborers. **471**

chlorofluorocarbons (CFCs) Compounds, containing carbon, chlorine, fluorine, and sometimes hydrogen; they are suspected of damaging the ozone layer. **972**

circumnavigate To sail around the world. **45**

Civilian Conservation Corps (CCC) New Deal agency established in 1933 to employ men on conservation projects. **696**

civil liberties People's rights as individuals against the power of the government. **163**

Civil Rights Act of 1866 Federal law that granted full civil rights, but not voting rights, to everyone born in the U.S. **400**

Civil Rights Act of 1957 Federal law that made it a federal crime to prevent qualified persons from voting. **825**

Civil Rights Act of 1964 Federal law that barred discrimination in employment and public facilities and gave the Justice Department the power to enforce school desegregation. **847**

Civil Rights Bill of 1875 Federal law that prohibited discrimination by businesses serving the public. **408**

Civil Works Administration (CWA) New Deal agency designed to create jobs during the Great Depression. **696**

Clayton Antitrust Act (1914) Federal law that clarified and extended the 1890 Sherman Antitrust Act. **549**

Clayton-Bulwer Treaty (1850) Agreement between the U.S. and Great Britain that proposed an equal partnership in building and running a Central American canal. **570**

Clean Air Act (1970) Federal law that set air-quality standards and tough emissions guidelines for car manufacturers. **903**

closed shop Workplace where the employer hires only union members. **520**

Cold War Competition between the U.S. and the Soviet Union for global power and influence. **789**

Columbian exchange Transfer of people, ideas, plants, animals, and diseases among the Americas, Europe, Asia, and Africa; initiated by Columbus's voyages. **44**

Committee of Correspondence Massachusetts group formed in the 1770s to inform the colonies about British policies. **111**

Committee on Civil Rights Group established by President Truman in 1946 to document civil rights abuses. **786**

Committee on Public Information (CPI) Agency established in 1917 that waged a vigorous propaganda campaign to convince Americans to support the war effort. **604**

commonwealth Political unit founded on law in which members are expected to work together for the common good. **69**

Commonwealth of Independent States (CIS) International organization of sovereign states organized in 1991 by Russia, Ukraine, and Belarus. Other former Soviet republics later became members. **959**

company town Community where housing and businesses are owned by one firm. **493**

Compromise of 1850 Resolution proposed by Henry Clay that temporarily settled differences between the North and the South over slavery issues. **342**

Compromise of 1877 Deal between leading Republicans and southern Democrats that gave the presidency to Rutherford B. Hayes in 1876 in exchange for a promise not to use the military to enforce Reconstruction laws in the South. **408**

Comstock Lode Rich Nevada silver vein that was the center of frantic prospecting beginning in 1859. **449**

concurrent powers Powers granted jointly in the United States Constitution to the federal government and the state government. **154**

Congress of Industrial Organizations (CIO) Labor group organized in 1935 to unite workers in various industries. **705**

Congress of Racial Equality (CORE) Northern-based civil rights group that launched a protest against segregation in interstate transportation in 1961. **845**

conquistadors Spanish soldiers who helped conquer the Americas. **46**

conscription Compulsory draft into military service. **368**

conspicuous consumption Lavish spending to increase social prestige. **473**

Constitutional Convention Meeting called in 1787 and held in Philadelphia to strengthen the government, during which delegates wrote and adopted the U.S. Constitution. **145**

containment Cold War strategy proposed by George Kennan to stop the spread of communism. **790**

contras Nicaraguan army recruited, financed, and armed by the CIA to overthrow the Sandinistas. **931**

Convention of 1818 Agreement by which Great Britain and the U.S. set the U.S.–Canadian border at the 49th parallel west to the Rocky Mountains. **229**

convoy system Use of armed escort vessels to accompany unarmed vessels transporting troops or supplies. **598**

cooperatives Groups that pool members' resources to sell products directly to urban markets and buy goods at wholesale prices. **498**

Copperheads Northern Democrats who sympathized with the South during the Civil War. **375**

corporation Type of business in which the money needed to run the company is obtained by selling shares of stock. **462**

cotton gin Machine invented by Eli Whitney in 1793 to separate seeds from cotton fiber. **234**

Council of Economic Advisers Federal agency created by the Employment Act of 1946 to counsel the president on economic policy. **784**

counterculture Culture that holds values and beliefs different from those of established society; for example, the culture of the hippies in the 1960s. **853**

covenant Contract. **69**

creditor nation Country that loans money to other nations. **726**

Crittenden Compromise Civil War–era plan to resolve conflict between North and South by calling for the westward extension of the Missouri Compromise line through the remaining territories. **364**

crop-lien system Arrangement in which sharecroppers offered crops to merchants in exchange for supplies. **411**

Crusades Series of wars between 1096 and the late 1200s in which Christian crusaders fought Muslims for control of the Holy Land. **19**

cultural diffusion Process of spreading cultural practices or beliefs from one group to another. **8**

Dawes General Allotment Act (1887) Federal law that established private ownership of Indian land. **434**

D-Day June 6, 1944; day when Allied soldiers crossed the English Channel to begin their invasion of France. **760**

debtor nation Country that owes money to other nations. **726**

Declaration of Independence (1776) Document adopted by the Second Continental Congress that justified and outlined reasons for the American separation from Great Britain. **118**

Declaratory Act (1766) Law passed by Parliament that asserted the right of Great Britain to make laws governing its American colonies. **108**

defoliants Chemicals designed to strip land of vegetation. **873**

delegated powers Powers granted to the federal government in the U.S. Constitution. **154**

demobilization Shift from wartime preparations to a peacetime economy. **622**

denominations Religious groups consisting of a number of local congregations. **283**

Department of Energy Federal agency created in 1977 to reduce U.S. dependence on oil. **913**

depression Sharp drop in business activity accompanied by rising unemployment. **143**

détente Lessening of military and diplomatic tensions between countries. **904**

direct primary Nominating election in which voters choose candidates to run in a general election. **535**

disarmament Reduction or limitation in the amount of a nation's military weapons. **725**

dissenters People who disagree with opinions expressed by the majority. **68**

dividends Portions of a company's profits received by its stockholders. **462**

Dixiecrats States' Rights party formed by southern Democrats in 1948; supported continued racial segregation. **787**

doctrine of nullification Theory of the states' right to refuse to obey any act passed by Congress that they consider unconstitutional. **245**

dollar diplomacy President Taft's policy of using economic influence, rather than military force, to protect U.S. interests in Latin America. **574**

domestication Adaptation and control of plants and animals. **8**

domino theory Foreign policy principle of the 1950s and the 1960s stating that if one country fell to communism, neighboring countries would also fall. **867**

doves People who support negotiation and compromise and who oppose war. **876**

***Dred Scott* decision** (1857) Supreme Court case in which Scott, a slave, was declared not to be a citizen and therefore not able to bring a suit for his freedom in U.S. courts. **350**

drivers Slave assistants who helped overseers supervise other slaves. **269**

dry farming Techniques to conserve moisture in areas of little rainfall. **440**

Dust Bowl Fifty-million–acre region in the Great Plains that suffered a severe drought in the mid-1930s. **711**

duty Tax on imports. **106**

Earth Summit (1992) United Nations Conference on Environment and Development held in Rio de Janeiro, Brazil, in 1992. **974**

economies of scale Principle of buying supplies in bulk and producing goods in large quantities to lower production costs and increase profits. **463**

ecosystem Interaction of living beings with the environment. **970**

Education Amendments Act (1972) Federal law prohibiting sexual discrimination in higher education. **921**

Education for All Handicapped Children Act (1975) Federal law requiring public schools to provide education for children with physical and mental disabilities. **919**

Eighteenth Amendment (1919) Constitutional amendment that barred the manufacture, sale, or importation of alcoholic beverages; repealed by Twenty-first Amendment. **525**

Eisenhower Doctrine (1957) Policy designed to counter Soviet influence in the Middle East by offering military aid to those nations seeking help in resisting Communist aggression. **812**

elastic clause "Necessary and proper" clause that allows Congress to expand its powers beyond those limits outlined in the U.S. Constitution. **157**

electors People selected by state legislatures to cast electoral votes for president and vice president. **150**

Elementary and Secondary School Education Act (1965) Federal law that provided $1.3 billion to aid schools in impoverished areas. **842**

Elkins Act (1903) Federal law that prohibited shippers from accepting rebates. **540**

Emancipation Proclamation Decree freeing all slaves living in those areas of the Confederacy that were still in rebellion against the U.S. as of January 1, 1863. **384**

Embargo Act (1807) Measure that stopped shipments of food and other American products to all foreign ports in an effort to maintain U.S. neutrality in European conflicts. **211**

Emergency Banking Act (1933) Federal law authorizing only banks that were financially sound to reopen after the New Deal bank holiday. **694**

Employment Act (1946) Post–World War II law that established the Council of Economic Advisers and pledged the promotion of full employment and production. **784**

empresarios Businesspeople who agreed to recruit and take responsibility for new settlers in Texas in return for land grants from Mexico. **307**

encomienda System that gave Spanish colonists the right to have a certain number of Indians work for them. **40**

Enforcement Acts Three acts passed by Congress between 1870 and 1871 allowing the government to use military force to stop violence against African Americans. **407**

Enlightenment Intellectual movement of the 18th century that rejected traditional political, social, and religious ideas and emphasized human reason and progress. **84**

environment Physical surroundings. **5**

Environmental Protection Agency (EPA) Federal agency created in 1970 to enforce environmental laws. **903**

Equal Pay Act (1963) Federal law that made it illegal for employers to pay female workers less than male workers for the same job. **834**

Equal Rights Amendment (ERA) Proposed constitutional amendment barring discrimination on the basis of sex. **921**

escalation Increase or buildup of military forces or weapons. **871**

Espionage Act (1917) Federal law designed to silence dissenters during World War I. **605**

European Union Western European trading bloc formed by the European Community in 1993 with ratification of the Maastricht Treaty. **964**

Exodusters Black settlers who moved west during the late 1800s to find economic and political freedom. **439**

ex post facto **law** Law passed "after the deed"; sets a penalty for an act that was not illegal when committed. **163**

ƒ

factory system Manufacturing system that cuts costs and increases output by relying on machines to do the work. **235**

Fair Deal President Truman's proposed reforms after the 1948 election; for example, a national health insurance program. **787**

Fair Employment Practices Committee (FEPC) Federal commission created in 1941 to prevent job discrimination based on race or ethnic background. **756**

Family and Medical Leave Act (1993) Federal law requiring large companies to provide workers up to 12 weeks of unpaid leave for family and medical emergencies without losing their medical coverage or jobs. **949**

Family Assistance Plan (FAP) President Nixon's proposal to replace the welfare system with a plan that would guarantee families a minimum income. **901**

Farm Credit Administration New Deal agency created in 1933 to give farmers low-interest, long-term loans. **695**

Farmers' Alliance Powerful farm organization formed in 1877 that lobbied to help farmers economically and politically. **498**

Farm Security Administration (FSA) New Deal agency created in 1937 to help tenant farmers and sharecroppers buy farms through low-interest, long-term loans. **706**

Fascist party Political party, founded by Benito Mussolini in 1921, that supported a military-dominated government in control of all aspects of Italian society. **732**

Federal Deposit Insurance Corporation (FDIC) New Deal agency created in 1933 to insure bank savings deposits. **695**

Federal Emergency Relief Administration (FERA) New Deal agency created in 1933 to funnel relief aid directly to state and local agencies. **695**

Federal Farm Loan Act Federal law proposed during President Woodrow Wilson's administration that provided low-interest loans to farmers. **551**

federalism Division and sharing of powers between a strong central government and state governments. **146**

Federalist, The Essays written to support ratification of the U.S. Constitution; also called *Federalist Papers*. **150**

Federalists Members of a political party who advocated strong national government and favored ratification of the U.S. Constitution. **149**

Federal Project No. 1 New Deal program established in 1935 to aid unemployed artists. **716**

Federal Reserve Act (1913) Federal law that created a three-level banking system controlled by both private banks and the government. **549**

Federal Trade Commission (FTC) Government agency established in 1914 to enforce antitrust laws and to investigate corporations engaged in unfair or fraudulent practices. **549**

Federal Workmen's Compensation Act Federal law providing benefits to federal workers injured on the job. **551**

Federal Writers' Project (FWP) Program that hired unemployed writers to produce a variety of cultural works. **716**

feudalism System in the Middle Ages in which nobles pledged military assistance and loyalty to rulers in return for land and protection. **17**

Fifteenth Amendment (1869) Constitutional amendment that guaranteed that the right to vote could not be denied because of race. **404**

First Battle of Bull Run (1861) Confederate victory at Manassas Junction, outside of Washington, D.C., that proved the Civil War would last longer than a few months. **371**

First Battle of the Marne (1914) World War I battle in which French and British forces stopped the German advance in northeast France. **589**

First Continental Congress (1774) Meeting of delegates from 12 colonies to discuss grievances against Great Britain, including those resulting from the Intolerable Acts. **113**

Five Power Agreement (1921) Arrangement between the U.S., Great Britain, France, Italy, and Japan to set limits on each nation's naval strength. **725**

flappers "New women" whose dress and conduct after World War I defied traditional standards of womanly behavior. **655**

flexible response Strategy adopted by the Kennedy administration of keeping a range of options open for dealing with international crises. **835**

Food Administration Government agency responsible for regulating production and supply of food during World War I. **602**

Foraker Act (1900) Federal law outlining the organization of Puerto Rico's government. **570**

Fordney-McCumber Tariff Act (1922) Federal law that placed high duties on imported farm products in an effort to boost domestic crop prices and to help farmers. **632**

forty-niners Nickname for gold-seekers who went to California, beginning in 1849, to seek their fortune. **324**

Four Power Treaty (1921) Agreement between the U.S., Great Britain, France, and Japan to respect one another's territory in the Pacific. **725**

Fourteen Points (1918) President Wilson's program for world peace after World War I that contained 14 principles, including the creation of the League of Nations. **606**

Fourteenth Amendment (1866) Constitutional amendment that granted full citizenship, civil rights, and equal protection under the law to African Americans. **401**

Freedmen's Bureau Organization established by Congress in 1865 to aid southerners left homeless by the war and to help ex-slaves. **400**

freedom of contract Right of workers and employers to agree to certain conditions of employment. **519**

Freedom Riders Integrated group who protested segregation in interstate transportation in 1961. **845**

Freedom Summer Campaign to register African American voters during the summer of 1964. **847**

freedpeople Emancipated slaves after the Civil War. **394**

freemen People who enjoy full political and civil liberties. **69**

Freeport Doctrine (1858) Position, held by Stephen Douglas, that people in a territory have the power to prohibit slavery by refusing to pass local laws necessary to make a slave system work. **353**

Free-Soil party Political party, formed by antislavery Whigs and Democrats in 1848, that opposed the expansion of slavery into the territories. **339**

French Revolution Revolt beginning in Paris in 1789 that led to the overthrow of the monarchy and the creation of a new French Republic. **195**

Fuel Administration Government agency responsible for regulating production and supply of fuel during World War I. **602**

Fugitive Slave Act Law passed as part of the Compromise of 1850 that made it a federal crime to assist runaway slaves. **343**

Fundamental Orders of Connecticut (1639) First written constitution in the colonies; adopted by Thomas Hooker's congregation in its Connecticut Valley settlement. **72**

Fundamentalism Protestant movement whose followers believe in a literal interpretation of the Bible. **656**

Gadsden Purchase (1853)   Agreement by which the U.S. acquired Mexico's territory south of the Gila River in present-day Arizona and New Mexico for $10 million. **315**

gang labor   Work system in which groups of slaves performed specialized jobs. **270**

General Court   Massachusetts Bay Colony's elected legislature, which made laws for the colony. **69**

generation gap   Difference in years, attitudes, and cultural beliefs between generations; applied to baby boomers and their elders during the 1960s. **852**

genocide   Deliberate annihilation of an entire people. **767**

geothermal power   Alternative energy source from the earth's interior, such as from geysers and hot springs. **970**

German reunification   Reuniting of East Germany and West Germany as one nation in 1990. **959**

GI Bill of Rights (1944)   Servicemen's Readjustment Act, which provided pensions and government loans to help veterans start their own businesses, buy homes or farms, and attend college. **784**

Gilded Age   Name applied to post–Civil War America to describe the corruption and greed that lurked below the surface of industrial society. **486**

glasnost   Policy of openness introduced in the Soviet Union by Mikhail Gorbachev in 1985. **935**

global warming   Gradual increase in the temperature of the earth's atmosphere. **972**

Glorious Revolution (1688)   Bloodless English rebellion in which the Catholic king James II was replaced by the Protestant rulers Mary and William. **84**

glyph   Picture or symbol used in the Olmec and other picture writing systems. **11**

gold standard   Monetary system in which each dollar is equal to and redeemable for a set amount of gold. **499**

Good Neighbor policy   FDR's policy of promoting goodwill toward Latin America. **728**

government bonds   Certificates issued by a government in exchange for loans. **192**

graduated income tax   System in which the rate of taxation varies according to income. **499**

Gramm-Rudman-Hollings Act (1985)   Federal law requiring across-the-board cuts in government spending when the deficit exceeds a certain point. **934**

Great Awakening   Period of religious revival that swept through the colonies in the mid-18th century. **84**

Great Compromise (1787)   Plan approved at the Constitutional Convention in which each state, regardless of size, was given an equal voice in the upper house, while representation in the lower house was determined by population. **147**

Great Depression   Deep economic downturn that gripped the U.S. between 1929 and the beginning of World War II. **672**

Great Migration   Mass movement of Puritans from England to the Americas beginning in 1630. **68**   Mass movement of African Americans from the South to the North between 1915 and 1930. **603**

Great Society   President Lyndon Johnson's economic and social programs during the 1960s. **841**

Great Upheaval (1886)   Year of intense worker strikes and violent labor confrontations in the U.S. **494**

Green parties   Environmentalist political parties in Europe. **974**

gross national product   Total value of all goods and services produced by a country in a given year. **671**

guerrilla warfare   Military tactic of using hit-and-run skirmishes while avoiding direct battles. **131**

Haight-Ashbury   San Francisco district known for its hippie population during the mid-1960s. **853**

hajj   Pilgrimage. **26**

hard-rock mining   Technique that involved sinking deep mine shafts to get at ore in quartz veins. **452**

Harlem Renaissance   Period of African American artistic development during the 1920s in New York City's Harlem. **660**

Hartford Convention (1814)   Meeting of New England Federalists who debated seceding from the Union and negotiating a separate peace with Great Britain during the War of 1812. **215**

hawks   People who support war or a warlike policy. **876**

Hay–Bunau-Varilla Treaty (1903)   Agreement with Panama giving U.S. control over a 10-mile-wide Canal Zone. **572**

Hay-Herrán Treaty (1903)   Proposed agreement with Colombia that would have given the U.S. a lease to build a canal in Panama. **572**

Haymarket Riot (1886)   Violent confrontation in Chicago between workers, anarchists, and police that helped turn public support against the labor movement. **494**

Hay-Pauncefote Treaty (1901)   Agreement with Great Britain by which the U.S. could build and control a Central American canal. **572**

Hepburn Act (1906)   Federal law that authorized the Interstate Commerce Commission to set railroad rates and to regulate other companies engaged in interstate commerce. **540**

Highway Act (1956)   Federal law that expanded the nation's highway systems. **817**

hippies   Name given to people in the 1960s who rejected everything connected with mainstream America. **853**

Ho Chi Minh Trail   Network of jungle paths used by the North Vietnamese to move weapons and supplies to the Vietcong in South Vietnam. **872**

Hollywood Ten   Group of film directors and writers who went to jail rather than answer questions from the House Committee on Un-American Activities. **794**

Holocaust   Systematic slaughter of European Jews by the Nazis during World War II. **767**

Home Loan Bank Act (1932)   Federal law that provided money to savings banks, building and loan associations, and insurance companies for low-interest mortgages. **685**

Home Owners Loan Corporation (HOLC)   New Deal agency created in 1933 to grant low-interest, long-term mortgage loans to home owners. **695**

Homestead Act (1862)   Federal law that gave public land to any citizen willing to live on the Great Plains and cultivate the land for five years. **436**

horizontal integration   Method of expanding a company by buying other companies involved in the same business. **463**

"hot line"   Telephone connection between the U.S. and the Soviet Union that allowed leaders to communicate directly during a crisis. **838**

House Committee on Un-American Activities (HUAC)   Congressional committee established in 1938 to investigate anti-American propaganda. **794**

House of Burgesses   Virginia's colonial governing assembly. **77**

Housing and Urban Development Act (1968)   Federal law that, along with the Omnibus Housing Act, provided money for urban renewal and created the Department of Housing and Urban Development. **842**

human rights   Basic rights and freedoms to which all people are entitled, including freedom from unlawful detention or torture. **914**

hunter-gatherers People who moved from place to place in search of game and edible plants. **5**

hydraulic mining Technique that uses water pressure to remove mountains of gravel, exposing the minerals underneath. **452**

hydrogen bomb Weapon approximately 1,000 times more powerful than the atomic bomb. **808**

I

Immigration Act (1990) Federal law that updated U.S. immigration laws from the 1960s and increased the number of immigrants allowed into the United States each year. **946**

Immigration Act of 1924 Federal law reducing the immigration quota for each nationality to 2 percent of the 1890 figures. **638**

Immigration Restriction League Group founded in 1894 by well-to-do Bostonians who sought to impose a literacy test on all immigrants. **471**

impeachment Formal charge of wrongdoing or misconduct brought against a government official. **155**

imperialism Practice of extending the power of a nation by direct territorial acquisition of colonial empires. **558**

impressment Practice of kidnapping and forcing people into public service; used by Great Britain in the late 1700s and early 1800s to secure sailors for the British navy. **196**

indentured servant Person who agreed to work for a specified time for the person who paid his or her way to America. **61**

Indian Removal Act (1830) Federal law that provided for the relocation of Indian nations living east of the Mississippi River to Indian Territory in present-day Oklahoma. **243**

Indian Reorganization Act (1934) Federal law that sought to revive tribal rule by funding tribal business ventures and paying for the college education of Native Americans. **710**

Industrial Revolution Shift from hand production to machine production that began in Great Britain in the mid-1700s. **234**

inflation Rise in prices resulting from an increase in the amount of money in circulation relative to the amount of goods available for sale. **58**

initiative Election reform that gives voters the power to introduce legislation. **535**

insider trading Use of confidential financial information by stockbrokers for personal gain. **934**

interchangeable parts Parts made in large quantities that can be substituted for other parts during construction of a final product. **234**

Intermediate-range Nuclear Forces (INF) **Treaty** (1987) Agreement that eliminated all medium-range nuclear weapons from Europe and set up inspection procedures to enforce provisions of the treaty. **935**

internal improvements Advances in transportation networks such as roads and canals, undertaken at public expense. **228**

Internal Security Act (1950) Federal law that required Communist party members and organizations to register with the federal government. **795**

internment Imprisonment; practice of forced relocation applied to Japanese Americans living on the West Coast after Pearl Harbor. **754**

Interstate Commerce Act (1887) Federal law that regulated railroad freight rates and created an agency to monitor railroad activities. **498**

Interstate Commerce Commission (ICC) Organization created by the Interstate Commerce Act to oversee railroad companies, but having little power of enforcement. **498**

Intolerable Acts (1774) Series of laws passed by Great Britain to punish Massachusetts for the Boston Tea Party, while strengthening British control over the colonies; also called the Coercive Acts. **111**

Iran-contra affair Name given to the illegal actions taken by White House aides in the 1980s to fund Nicaraguan contras. **935**

Iran hostage crisis (1979–81) Period during which 53 Americans in Iran were seized by followers of militant Islamic leader Ayatollah Khomeini in an attempt to force the return of Shah Reza Pahlavi from exile in the U.S. **916**

Iroquois League Confederation of Indian tribes formed in the 15th or 16th century; also called the Six Nations. **91**

irreconcilables Fourteen Republican senators who opposed the League of Nations and rejected the Treaty of Versailles after World War I. **609**

island-hopping Allied military tactic during World War II in which certain strategic Japanese-held islands in the Pacific were seized, while others were bypassed. **762**

isolationism Policy of avoiding international political or economic alliances; followed by the U.S. during most of the 1920s and 1930s. **724**

J

Jay's Treaty (1794) Treaty in which Great Britain agreed to abandon its forts in the Northwest Territory in exchange for U.S. payment of debts owed to the British. **197**

Jim Crow laws State laws adopted in the South that were designed to enforce segregation. **413**

joint-stock companies Companies in which investors share the start-up and maintenance costs as well as profits or losses. **59**

Jones Act of 1916 Law that gave Filipinos the right to elect both houses of their legislature, but delayed independence until a stable government was established. **565**

Jones Act of 1917 Law that granted U.S. citizenship to Puerto Ricans and gave them the right to elect both houses of their legislature. **570**

judicial review Supreme Court's right to determine whether laws violate the U.S. Constitution. **157**

Judiciary Act (1789) Law that created the federal court system, including district courts, circuit courts of appeals, and the Supreme Court. **191**

juvenile delinquency Antisocial behavior by the young that is subject to legal action. **826**

K

kamikaze Japanese planes during World War II assigned to suicide missions against Allied ships. **764**

Kansas-Nebraska Act (1854) Federal law that established popular sovereignty in newly organized territories and overturned the Missouri Compromise. **347**

Keating-Owen Child Labor Act (1916) Proposed federal law that outlawed the interstate sale of products produced by child labor. **551**

Kellogg-Briand Pact (1927) Agreement signed by 62 nations that outlawed war as an instrument of national policy but allowed countries to declare war in self-defense. **726**

Kentucky and Virginia Resolutions State resolutions passed between 1798 and 1799 that declared states should be the final judge of whether a law was unconstitutional. **202**

Kerner Commission Federal Commission that investigated the 1960s riots and reported that white racism was responsible for the violence. **850**

Klondike Gold Rush Flood of prospectors to the Klondike district of Canada's Yukon Territory in the late 1890s in search of gold. **450**

Knights of Labor National union founded in 1869 that consisted of skilled and unskilled workers. **493**

Know-Nothings Name given to members of the nativist American party prominent during the 1850s. **262**

Kristallnacht "Night of broken glass," November 9, 1938, when Nazis burned down synagogues and destroyed Jewish businesses in Germany. **733**

laissez-faire capitalism Theory that opposes government regulation of economic matters. **462**

Land Ordinance of 1785 Federal law that established a system for surveying western lands by townships and selling smaller parcels to the public. **141**

Landrum-Griffin Act (1959) Federal law designed to reduce corruption in labor unions. **820**

land speculators People who buy land expecting a quick profit from its resale. **91**

League of United Latin American Citizens (LULAC) Hispanic group that lobbied for national awareness of Hispanic concerns and issues. **918**

Lecompton Constitution (1857) Proslavery Kansas constitution that gave voters the right to decide whether more slaves could enter the territory, but not the means to interfere with slavery already present. **349**

Lend-Lease Act (1941) Law that appropriated money for the U.S. to lend or lease arms and other supplies to non-Axis countries. **737**

Lewis and Clark expedition (1804–06) Expedition responsible for mapping the boundaries of the Louisiana Territory and cataloging its natural resources. **208**

limited liability Legal guarantee whereby stockholders are not held responsible for a corporation's debt. **462**

Limited Nuclear Test Ban Treaty (1963) Agreement by the U.S., the Soviet Union, and Great Britain to end the testing of nuclear bombs in the atmosphere or under water. **837**

literacy tests Tests requiring proof of a person's ability to read in order to vote; used in southern states to deny voting rights to African Americans. **412**

"Little Rock Nine" Name given to the African American students who were admitted to an all-white school in Arkansas in 1957. **824**

lockouts Tactic used by employers of barring workers from plants until concessions from workers are obtained. **495**

long drives Overland treks on which cowboys herded cattle from ranches to rail lines. **444**

Long March Exodus of 1934–35 when Communist Chinese marched nearly 6,000 miles to northern China, helping cement Mao Zedong's leadership of the party. **798**

Long Walk Forced march of Navajos to Bosque Redondo, a reservation in eastern New Mexico, following their surrender in early 1864. **435**

loose construction Theory set forth by Alexander Hamilton that the federal government possesses all powers not specifically forbidden by the U.S. Constitution. **193**

Lost Generation Name given by Gertrude Stein to writers of the 1920s whose works expressed disillusionment after World War I. **662**

Louisiana Purchase (1803) U.S. purchase from France of Louisiana for some $15 million. **206**

Lowell girls Single women who worked in the textile mills of Lowell, Massachusetts, in the early 19th century. **257**

Loyalists Americans loyal to Great Britain during the Revolutionary War; also called Tories. **119**

Maastricht Treaty Agreement between European countries that weakened economic barriers and made plans to create a unified monetary system in Europe; ratified in 1993. **964**

Maginot Line Line of defenses built by the French after World War I along their border with Germany. **737**

Magna Carta (1215) Charter signed by King John that limited the power of the English monarch, guaranteed basic liberties for nobles, and protected trade. **20**

mandate system Provision of the Treaty of Versailles that required new colonial rulers to report to the League of Nations on their administration of former Central Power territories. **608**

Manhattan Project Top-secret U.S. project begun in 1942 in which scientists developed the first atomic bomb. **765**

manifest destiny Phrase coined in 1845 to express the belief that the U.S. was destined to extend its boundaries westward to the Pacific Ocean. **306**

Mann-Elkins Act (1910) Federal law that extended the regulatory powers of the Interstate Commerce Commission to telephone and telegraph companies. **543**

manor Land a noble received from the ruler under the feudal system in exchange for military assistance and loyalty. **17**

Marbury v. *Madison* (1803) Legal case in which the Supreme Court first exercised its right of judicial review. **204**

March on Washington (1963) Demonstration in Washington, D.C., called by African American leaders to show support for President Kennedy's civil rights bill. **847**

margin buying Purchasing stock with borrowed money. **670**

Mariposa War (1850–51) California raids by the Miwoks and the Yokuts to reclaim Native American lands taken over by miners. **327**

market revolution Creation of profitable national markets during the 1800s brought about by new transportation systems and regional specialization. **234**

Marshall Plan (1948) U.S. program that provided some $12 billion in economic aid to Western Europe after World War II; also called the European Recovery Act. **792**

mass production Manufacture of large quantities of goods, usually by machines. **234**

mass transit Public transportation systems, such as commuter trains and subways, that made it possible for workers to live farther away from their jobs. **472**

Mayflower Compact (1620) Document that established Plymouth Colony as a self-governing colony based on the majority rule of male church members. **67**

Meat Inspection Act (1906) Federal consumer-protection law that required the government inspection of interstate meat shipments. **540**

Medicaid State programs established in 1965 and funded by Congress to provide free health care to the needy. **842**

Medicare Great Society program established in 1965 to provide national health insurance for people over age 65. **841**

mercantilism Economic policy based on the view that a nation's power depended on maintaining a favorable balance of trade by exporting more goods than it imported. **83**

merger Combining of two or more companies to achieve greater efficiency and higher profits. **632**

Mesoamerica Area that includes Central America and the southern and central regions of Mexico; also called Middle America. **10**

Mexican Cession (1848) Area surrendered by Mexico to the U.S. in the Treaty of Guadalupe Hidalgo; included the present-day states of California, Nevada, and Utah, and parts of Arizona, Colorado, and New Mexico. **315**

Mexican War (1846–48) Conflict between Mexico and the U.S. brought about by the U.S. annexation of Texas and its quest for more territory. **312**

middle class Social class that occupies a position between the wealthy and the poor. **256**

Middle Passage Voyage made by slave ships from Africa across the Atlantic Ocean during which many slaves suffered and died. **78**

militarism Glorification of armed strength and aggressive military preparedness. **587**

minutemen Members of the colonial militia who promised to be ready at a minute's notice. **114**

Missouri Compromise (1820) Act that maintained the balance of slave and free states in Congress by admitting Missouri as a slave state and Maine as a free state, while prohibiting the spread of slavery in the territories to areas north of latitude 36°30´. **238**

modern Republicanism Name given to President Eisenhower's attempt to balance liberal domestic reforms with conservative spending during the 1950s. **814**

monopoly Exclusive control, such as in trade or industry, that eliminates competition. **28, 462**

Monroe Doctrine (1823) U.S. government policy statement in which the Americas were declared off-limits to European expansion. **231**

Montgomery Improvement Association (MIA) Group of civil rights leaders in Montgomery, Alabama, whose members included Martin Luther King, Jr. **823**

Montreal Protocol on Ozone Depletion (1987) International agreement that set standards for reducing the emission of CFCs and other gases. **974**

Moral Majority Fundamentalist Christian political organization founded in 1978 by Reverend Jerry Falwell. **928**

moratorium Authorized period of delay in paying a debt or fulfilling a legal obligation. **727**

Morrill Act (1862) Federal law that gave land to states to establish agricultural colleges. **436**

mountain men Name given to fur trappers in the Far West. **318**

muckrakers Nickname given by President Theodore Roosevelt to progressive journalists in the early 1900s who exposed political and social evils. **514**

"mugwumps" Nickname for Republican reformers who supported Democratic candidate Grover Cleveland in the 1884 presidential election. **489**

multinational corporations Companies that invest money in a variety of international business ventures. **965**

Munich Conference (1938) Meeting attended by government leaders from Great Britain, Italy, France, and Germany in which a pact was signed giving Germany control of the Sudetenland. **735**

mutualistas Mutual-aid societies formed by Mexican American communities to help local residents. **676**

National Aeronautics and Space Administration (NASA) Federal agency established in 1958 to direct American space exploration. **810**

National Association for the Advancement of Colored People (NAACP) Civil rights organization founded in 1909 to work for various social reforms that would benefit African Americans and end racial discrimination. **527**

national bank Central bank with branches in major cities. **192**

national debt Money owed by the federal government to its creditors. **192**

National Defense Act (1916) Military "preparedness" program established prior to World War I that increased the size of the National Guard and the U.S. regular army. **594**

National Defense Education Act (1958) Federal law that appropriated money to improve education in science, math, and foreign languages. **810**

National Energy Act (1978) Federal law that relaxed controls on the price of natural gas in an effort to ease U.S. dependence on foreign oil. **913**

National Grange Farmers' group founded in 1867 as a social organization that grew into a political force; also called Patrons of Husbandry. **497**

National Industrial Recovery Act (NIRA) Federal law passed in 1933 to stimulate industrial and business activity and to reduce unemployment. **696**

nationalism Sense of pride or loyalty to a nation. **226**

nationalize To assert government control or ownership over a business or industry. **731**

National Organization for Women (NOW) Group founded by feminists in 1966 to promote equal rights for women. **854**

National Recovery Administration (NRA) Federal agency that encouraged businesses to draw up "codes of fair competition" as one means of achieving business recovery during the Great Depression. **697**

National Security Council (NSC) Organization created in 1947 by Congress to advise the president on strategic matters. **794**

National War Labor Board (NWLB) Group of representatives from business and labor who arbitrated disputes between workers and employers during World War I. **602**

National Youth Administration (NYA) New Deal agency that provided part-time jobs to people between the ages of 16 and 25. **702**

nativism Policy of favoring native-born Americans over immigrants. **261**

Navigation Acts (1651) Series of mercantilist laws designed to increase English merchants' profits by limiting direct trade between English colonies and other European nations. **83**

Nazi party Political party, led by Adolf Hitler, that controlled Germany from 1933 to 1945; also called the National Socialist party. **733**

New Deal President Franklin Roosevelt's program of providing relief and recovery to the U.S. during the Great Depression. **694**

New England Way Cooperation between church and state that was the basis for the Puritan commonwealth. **69**

New Freedom Name given to Woodrow Wilson's progressive program of reform as proposed during the 1912 presidential election. **546**

New Frontier President John Kennedy's political, social, and economic programs of the early 1960s. **833**

new immigrants People, mostly southern and eastern Europeans, who came to the United States in the late 1800s and early 1900s. **466**

Newlands Reclamation Act (1902) Federal law that allowed money from the sale of public land to be used for irrigation and reclamation. **541**

New Nationalism Name given to Theodore Roosevelt's program of social legislation first proposed during the 1910 congressional elections. **545**

New Right Conservatives who showed increased political influence during the 1980s. **928**

Nine Power Treaty (1921) Agreement arising from the Washington Conference that guaranteed China's territorial integrity and promised to uphold the Open Door policy. **725**

Nineteenth Amendment (1920) Constitutional amendment that granted women full voting rights. **552**

no-man's land Thin strip of territory along the Western Front that separated opposing armies during World War I. **589**

nonaggression pact (1939) Temporary alliance in which Germany and the Soviet Union agreed to divide Poland between them. **736**

nonimportation agreements Documents signed by colonial merchants promising not to buy or import British goods. **107**

Non-Intercourse Act (1809) Federal law that prohibited U.S. trade with Great Britain and France. **212**

nonviolent resistance Strategy of peaceful protest. **844**

North American Free Trade Agreement (NAFTA) International treaty ratified in 1993 to relax trade barriers between the U.S., Canada, and Mexico. **965**

North Atlantic Treaty Organization (NATO) Alliance formed in 1949 whose member nations agreed to protect one another in the event of attack. **793**

Northwest Ordinance (1787) Federal law that established a system for governing the Northwest Territory; also called the Land Ordinance of 1787. **142**

northwest passage Northern water route from Europe to Asia sought by early European explorers. Many European claims in North America resulted from the search for such a route. **56**

Northwest Territory Area organized in 1787 that extended north of the Ohio River to the Great Lakes and west of Pennsylvania to the Mississippi River. **142**

Nuremberg trials Trials of Nazi war criminals by the Allies that began in 1945. **781**

Occupational Safety and Health Administration (OSHA) Federal agency created in 1970 to protect workers from unhealthful working conditions. **903**

Office of Economic Opportunity (OEO) Government agency formed in 1964 to coordinate antipoverty programs, including the Job Corps, VISTA, and Head Start. **840**

Okies Negative term for farmers, many from Oklahoma, who migrated in 1939 to the West Coast to find work. **714**

old immigrants People, generally Protestants from northwestern Europe, who came to the U.S. between 1800 and 1880. **466**

Olive Branch Petition (1775) Final plea for peace sent by the Second Continental Congress to King George III. **116**

Omnibus Housing Act (1965) Federal law that, together with the Housing and Urban Development Act of 1968, provided money for urban renewal and housing assistance for low-income families. **842**

Open Door policy (1899) U.S. policy, proposed by Secretary of State John Hay, that called for all nations to have equal access to trade and investment in China. **567**

open range Grazing land that the government allowed cattle ranchers to use in the late 1800s. **446**

open shops Nonunion workplaces. **520**

Operation Desert Storm (1991) U.S. military mission that joined allies in driving Iraqi forces from Kuwait. **939**

Operation Restore Hope (1992) United Nations plan to ensure that relief efforts reached famine-stricken Somalia. **960**

Operation Rolling Thunder U.S. bombing campaign against military targets in North Vietnam that began in 1965. **872**

Orders in Council (1807) British acts that forbade neutral vessels from trading with France or from entering ports under French control. **211**

Oregon Country Disputed area of Pacific Northwest occupied jointly by the U.S. and Great Britain after the War of 1812. **229**

Oregon Trail Route to Oregon Country during the 1800s. **318**

Organization of Petroleum Exporting Countries (OPEC) Group of oil-producing countries, mainly Arab, formed in 1960 to get higher prices for oil exports. **902**

override Constitutional power that allows Congress to overrule a presidential veto with a two-thirds vote. **155**

overseers People who supervise workers. **269**

ozone layer Thin veil of molecules, located some 10 to 30 miles above the earth's surface, that protects the earth from UV rays. **972**

pacification Military tactic used by U.S. troops during the Vietnam War that involved moving residents to refugee camps and burning their villages. **874**

Pacific Railway Act (1862) Federal law that gave land for development of a transcontinental railroad. **436**

Pacific Rim Countries on the western edge of the Pacific Ocean. **964**

Paleo-Indians First people who crossed Beringia into North America during the last Ice Age. **4**

Palmer raids (1919–20) Raids to capture alleged radicals; launched by Attorney General A. Mitchell Palmer during the Red Scare. **626**

Panama Canal treaties (1978) Agreements granting Panama control over canal operations by the year 2000. **914**

Pan-German movement German plan prior to World War I to unite all German-speaking peoples under one flag. **586**

Panic of 1819 Economic collapse caused in part by the Second Bank of the United States' attempt to curb lending policies of state banks. **236**

Pan-Slavic movement Russian plan to bring together all Slavic peoples of central and eastern Europe, in direct opposition to the Pan-German movement of the early 1900s. **586**

partnerships Business enterprises that are owned by two or more people who are responsible for the businesses' debts. **462**

patio **process** Mining technique developed in Mexico and South America during the 1700s that used mercury to extract silver from ore; used in the western U.S. **449**

Peace Corps Program established by President John Kennedy in the early 1960s that sends volunteers to developing countries. **835**

Pendleton Civil Service Act (1883) Federal law that created a Civil Service Commission to administer competitive examinations to those seeking government jobs. **488**

Pentagon Papers Secret government documents, published in 1971, that showed how the government had misled Americans about the Vietnam War. **882**

peons Landless laborers, mostly Indians, who worked on Spanish haciendas. **53**

perestroika Mikhail Gorbachev's plan to restructure the Soviet economy and government during the late 1980s. **935**

pet banks State banks that received deposits of federal funds because of their officers' loyalty to the Democratic party and to President Andrew Jackson. **247**

philanthropy Charitable efforts to promote public welfare, such as financing libraries, museums, and art galleries; endowing universities; and establishing theater or music groups. **474**

Philippine Government Act (1902) Federal law decreeing that the Philippines would be ruled by a governor and a two-house legislature. **564**

Pilgrims People who left England because of religious conflict and sailed aboard the *Mayflower* to North America, where they founded Plymouth Colony in 1620. **66**

Pinckney's Treaty (1795) Agreement negotiated with Spain that set the southern boundary of the U.S. near Florida at the 31st parallel. **197**

planned obsolescence Practice of making products that are designed to go out of style. **664**

Platt Amendment Addition to Cuba's constitution, enacted in 1902 and renounced in 1934, that gave the U.S. greater control over Cuban affairs. **569**

Plessy v. *Ferguson* (1896) Supreme Court case in which the court upheld segregation by ruling that "separate but equal" facilities did not violate the Fourteenth Amendment. **414**

political machines Political organizations, headed by bosses, that used appointments to government jobs to control elections. **469**

poll taxes Fixed taxes imposed on every voter by southern states in an effort to deprive African Americans of the right to vote. **412**

Pontiac's Rebellion (1763) Indian war led by Ottawa chief Pontiac against settlers of western lands. **105**

pop art Art form begun in the 1960s that uses everyday objects as subject matter or in the works themselves. **854**

popular sovereignty Right of the people to rule, used as an argument for letting citizens of each new territory decide whether to permit slavery there. **339**

Populist party Political party founded by farmers, labor leaders, and reformers in 1892; also called the People's party. **499**

Potsdam Conference (1945) Overseas meeting attended by the U.S., Britain, and the Soviet Union that laid the foundation for Germany's postwar status. **780**

Pottawatomie Massacre (1856) Revenge attack by antislavery raiders, led by John Brown on proslavery settlers along Pottawatomie Creek in Kansas. **348**

precedent Action that may serve as a guide for future, similar actions. **190**

Proclamation of 1763 Declaration issued by Great Britain that barred settlement west of the Appalachian Mountains. **105**

progressivism Reform movement concerned with curing the ills caused by industrialization. **512**

prohibition Legal ban on the manufacture, transportation, and sale of alcoholic beverages. **289**

proprietorships Small businesses owned by individuals or families. **462**

protectionism Practice of imposing higher tariffs and stricter barriers against foreign imports in an effort to encourage Americans to purchase domestic goods. **966**

protectorate Country dependent on another for protection. **569**

Protestant Reformation Religious upheaval in Europe begun by Martin Luther in 1517 to protest corruption in the Roman Catholic church. **57**

Public Works Administration (PWA) New Deal agency established in 1933 that contracted with private firms to construct roads, public buildings, and similar projects. **697**

Pueblo Revolt (1680) Attacks by the Pueblo Indians that temporarily drove the Spanish from New Mexico. **51**

Pure Food and Drug Act (1906) Federal consumer-protection law that provided for government inspection of food and drugs. **340**

Puritans English Protestants who sought to "purify" the Anglican church of Catholic rituals and traditions. **66**

Quartering Act (1765) Law enacted by Parliament requiring the colonists to house and supply British troops. **109**

Quebec Act (1774) Law enacted by Parliament extending Quebec's boundaries south to the Ohio River and granting full religious rights to French Roman Catholics. **112**

Qur'an Holy book of Islam. **23**

railhead Town located along a railroad; long cattle drives usually ended there. **445**

Railroad Administration Federal agency that reorganized railroads and set limits on transportation rates and workers' wages during World War I. **602**

Reaganomics President Ronald Reagan's economic program built on big tax cuts to encourage business investment. **929**

realpolitik Approach to foreign policy, adopted by Henry Kissinger and President Richard Nixon, that emphasized national interests over moral or ethical concerns. **903**

recall Election reform that allows voters to remove an elected official from office by calling for a new election. **535**

reclamation Process of making damaged land productive. **541**

Reconquista Ongoing battle to recapture Spanish lands from the Moors that ended in 1492. **22**

Reconstruction Rebuilding of the former Confederate states to reunite the nation. **395**

Reconstruction Acts (1867) Federal laws that gave radical Republicans military control of the South. **402**

Reconstruction Finance Corporation (RFC) Federal agency created in 1932 to stimulate the economy by lending money to railroads, insurance companies, banks, and other financial institutions. **685**

recycling Collection and processing of used items for reuse. **973**

Red Scare (1919–20) Period of anti-Communist hysteria after the Bolshevik Revolution in Russia. **625**

referendum Election reform that allows voters to place a measure on the ballot. **535**

regionalists Midwestern artists popular in the 1930s who stressed local folk themes and customs in their work. **719**

rehabilitation Treatment to restore someone to a useful and constructive place in society. **287**

Rehabilitation Act (1973) Federal law forbidding discrimination in education, in jobs, or in housing because of physical disabilities. **919**

Relocation Act (1956) Federal law passed to relocate Native Americans to urban areas. **815**

Renaissance Rebirth of European art and learning spurred by the Crusades. **20**

rendezvous system Arrangement to cut costs and increase profits in the Rocky Mountain fur trade by having trappers gather once a year to sell furs and buy supplies. **318**

reparations   Payments of damages. **607**

republic   Form of government in which leaders receive authority from citizens to make and enforce laws. **138**

reservationists   Republican senators who would support the Treaty of Versailles only if the League Covenant were amended. **609**

reserved powers   Powers kept by the states because they are not specifically granted to the federal government or denied to the states by the U.S. Constitution. **154**

revisionists   Historians who revise the previously accepted version of historical events. **769**

right of deposit   Right to temporarily unload goods at a port without paying a duty. **198**

rock 'n' roll   Popular music introduced in the 1950s that reworked black rhythm and blues. **826**

Roe v. Wade   (1973)   Supreme Court case that overturned a state law limiting a woman's access to an abortion. **921**

Roosevelt Corollary   (1904)   Policy that extended the Monroe Doctrine by allowing the U.S. a greater role in maintaining peace and order in the Western Hemisphere. **573**

rotation in office   Periodic replacement of officeholders. **241**

rugged individualism   Idea that success comes through individual effort and private enterprise. **683**

Rural Electrification Administration (REA)   New Deal agency that brought electricity to isolated rural areas. **702**

Rush-Bagot Agreement   (1817)   Disarmament plan between the U.S. and Great Britain that limited each nation's military presence on the Great Lakes to a few armed ships. **229**

Russo-Japanese War   (1904–05)   War between Russia and Japan that began with a Japanese attack on Russian forces in Manchuria. **568**

S

Sand Creek Massacre   (1864)   Slaughter of Cheyenne Indians by U.S. troops in Colorado Territory. **427**

Sandinistas   Nicaraguan rebels who overthrew the dictatorship of Anastasio Somoza Debayle in 1979. **931**

Santa Fe Trail   Trail between Missouri and Santa Fe, New Mexico, important for taking merchandise to the West. **317**

satellite nations   Countries under the control of the Soviet Union. **789**

Saturday Night Massacre   (1973)   Resignation and firing of top government officials who refused to aid President Richard Nixon in the Watergate cover-up. **908**

scalawags   Southern whites who backed the Union and supported Reconstruction after the Civil War. **406**

scientific management   Theory, promoted by Frederick W. Taylor, that every kind of work could be broken into a series of smaller tasks for which rates of production could be set. **647**

scrip   Paper money that workers in company towns received as wages. **493**

search-and-destroy missions   Military attacks that involve looking for and annihilating hidden enemy troops. **873**

Second Battle of Bull Run   (1862)   Union defeat during the Civil War that led to General McClellan's appointment as commander of Union forces in the east. **377**

Second Continental Congress   (1775)   Convention held in Philadelphia in which delegates established the Continental Army and chose George Washington as its commander. **114**

Second Great Awakening   Renewal of religious faith that swept the U.S. beginning in the 1790s. **282**

Second New Deal   Government programs passed after the 1934 elections that provided relief and recovery but emphasized reform. **701**

Second Seminole War   (1835–1842)   Resistance by the Seminoles to their removal from Florida; cost more money and lives than any other Indian war in U.S. history. **244**

sectionalism   Loyalty to a particular area of the country. **198**

sedition   Act of stirring up discontent or rebellion against a government or other lawful authority. **202**

Sedition Act   (1918)   Federal law enacted during World War I that made written criticism of the government a crime. **605**

segregation   Separation of the races. **413**

Selective Service Act   (1917)   Federal law that required men to register with local draft boards. **595**

Selective Training and Service Act   (1940)   Federal law that provided for America's first peacetime draft. **753**

self-determination   Right of people to govern themselves. **606**

Seneca Falls Convention   (1848)   Meeting held in Seneca Falls, New York, that marked the birth of the organized women's rights movement in the U.S. **298**

separation of powers   Allotment of powers between the legislative, executive, and judicial branches of government to prevent any one branch from becoming too powerful. **155**

Separatists   Radical group of Puritans, including the Pilgrims, who separated from the Church of England and came to North America seeking religious freedom. **66**

serfs   People who lived on a feudal manor and worked the lord's land in exchange for crops and protection. **17**

settlement houses   Community centers in poor neighborhoods that provided food, shelter and other services. **476**

Seven Days' Campaign   (1862)   Civil War battle in which Confederate troops forced General McClellan to retreat before he could take Richmond. **377**

Seventeenth Amendment   (1913)   Constitutional amendment that provided for the direct election of United States senators. **535**

sexual harassment   Use of unwelcome sexual language or behavior that creates a hostile working environment. **941**

shantytowns   Makeshift shelters built by homeless people; for example, the Hoovervilles that were built during the Great Depression. **677**

sharecropping   Arrangement under which a sharecropper agreed to work a parcel of land in return for a share of the crop, a cabin, seed, tools, and a mule. **410**

Share-Our-Wealth   (1933)   Radical relief program proposed by Senator Huey Long to empower the government to confiscate wealth from the rich through taxes and provide a guaranteed minimum income and home to every family. **701**

Shays's Rebellion   (1786–87)   Farmers' revolt against high taxes and heavy debts, led by Daniel Shays. **144**

Sherman Antitrust Act   (1890)   Federal law that declared monopolies and trusts illegal. **464**

Sherman Silver Purchase Act   (1890)   Federal law that required the government to buy silver each month and mint it into coins. **499**

silent generation   Name given to middle-class youth of the 1950s who seemed willing to conform to consumer culture without protest. **826**

silent majority   Name given by President Richard Nixon to middle-class voters weary from the social upheaval of the 1960s. **900**

sit-down strike   Work stoppage in which workers occupy factories until management meets their demands. **705**

sit-in   Strategy of nonviolent protest in which a group enters a public place and refuses to leave. **844**

Sixteenth Amendment   (1913)   Constitutional amendment that authorized an individual income tax. **543**

Smoot-Hawley Tariff (1930)   High-tariff law that contributed to the global economic downturn of the 1930s. **674**

Social Darwinism   Theory, proposed in the late 1800s, that society progressed through competition, with the fittest rising to positions of wealth and power. **462**

Social Gospel   Movement by Protestant ministers in the late 1800s that called for people to apply Christian principles to address social problems. **477**

socialism   System under which government or worker cooperatives own all means of production and distribution. **520**

Social Security Act (1935)   Federal law that provided a system of unemployment compensation and retirement pensions. **702**

Society of American Indians   Organization formed by Native Americans to address Indian problems. **528**

Solidarity   Polish independent trade union and social movement that was formed in 1980. **931**

Sons of Liberty   Secret groups of Patriots formed in 1765 to oppose the Stamp Act and to protest British authority in the colonies. **107**

Southern Christian Leadership Conference (SCLC)   Alliance of church-based African American organizations formed in 1957 and dedicated to ending discrimination. **844**

southern strategy   President Richard Nixon's plan to woo conservative southern white voters away from the Democratic party by cutting back on new civil rights legislation. **901**

Southern Tenant Farmers' Union (STFU)   Arkansas sharecroppers who lobbied government in 1934 to halt tenant evictions and to force landowners to share payments with tenants. **698**

space shuttle   Reusable space vehicle first launched by NASA in 1981. **951**

Spanish-American War (1898)   War declared by the U.S. on Spain to protect U.S. investments and to help Cuba overthrow Spanish rule. **560**

Spanish Armada   Spanish naval force defeated by England in 1588. **58**

Spanish Civil War   War that began in 1936 between Fascists and Loyalists in Spain. **733**

specie   Gold or silver coins that a bank held to back up its notes. **226**

Specie Circular (1836)   Executive order issued by President Andrew Jackson instructing the Treasury to accept only gold and silver as payment for public land. **247**

spheres of influence   Ports or regions in a nation where a foreign country retains exclusive rights over trade, mines, and railroads. **566**

spirituals   Songs that are rich in Biblical lore. **275**

spoils system   Political practice, introduced by Andrew Jackson, of giving government jobs to supporters. **241**

Sputnik (1957)   Satellite launched by the Soviet Union that led the U.S. to focus more on technological development. **810**

Square Deal   Theodore Roosevelt's 1904 presidential campaign slogan pledging fair treatment for business, workers, and the public. **539**

stagflation   Economic condition in which inflation is accompanied by unemployment. **901**

Stamp Act (1765)   Law enacted by Parliament that placed a tax on all printed matter in the colonies. **106**

Stamp Act Congress (1765)   Delegates from nine colonies who gathered in New York City to seek repeal of the Stamp Act and to deny Parliament's right to tax the colonies. **107**

stock   Certificates of ownership in a company. **462**

stockholders   Owners of certificates in a corporation who receive a certain percentage of the corporation's profits through dividends. **462**

Strategic Arms Limitation Talks (SALT)   Agreement between the U.S. and the Soviet Union, limiting the number of intercontinental nuclear missiles each nation could have. **904**

Strategic Defense Initiative (SDI)   Space-based missile-defense system proposed by President Ronald Reagan in the 1980s to blunt the nuclear-freeze movement; also called "Star Wars." **930**

strict construction   Theory set forth by Thomas Jefferson that the federal government possesses only those powers that the U.S. Constitution specifically allows. **193**

strike   Tactic used by labor unions in which workers refuse to work until employers meet union demands. **258**

strikebreakers   Nonunion workers brought in by a company to replace striking workers. **495**

Student Nonviolent Coordinating Committee (SNCC)   Association formed in 1960 by student activists from throughout the South. **844**

subsidies   Payments made to farmers to reduce their production of a crop or commodity. **698**

subsistence farming   Growing just enough crops for survival. **8**

suburbs   Residential areas beyond city limits that came about partly as a result of mass transit. **473**

suffrage   Right to vote. **299**

Sugar Act (1764)   Law enacted by Parliament that set an import tax on foreign sugar, molasses, and other goods to the colonies. **106**

Sunbelt   Southern and western states having warm climates and suburban life-styles. **922**

superpowers   Nations that possess great power and become dominant in global politics. **768**

supremacy clause   Clause in the U.S. Constitution stating that the federal constitution and all federal laws outrank state constitutions and state laws. **155**

Sussex pledge (1916)   Promise by Germany not to sink ocean liners without warning or without assuring the passengers' safety. **593**

Swahili   Bantu language spoken by people in East Africa. **25**

Taft-Hartley Act (1947)   Federal law that extended government regulation of labor unions and included a provision allowing courts to end strikes. **785**

Tariff Act of 1816   Federal law that placed a 25 percent duty on most imported factory goods. **227**

tariffs   Taxes on goods. **148**

task system   System in which plantation slaves were given specific duties each day. **81**

Tax Reform Law (1986)   Federal law that eliminated special tax breaks for certain groups. **934**

Tea Act (1773)   Law enacted by Parliament that allowed the British East India Company to sell tea directly to American agents without paying certain duties. **111**

Teapot Dome scandal (1926)   Scandal in which Secretary of the Interior Albert Fall was convicted of accepting bribes for leasing the government oil reserve in Teapot Dome, Wyoming, to private oil companies. **630**

Teller Amendment (1898)   Act that stated the U.S. claimed no sovereignty, jurisdiction, or control over Cuba. **560**

temperance movement   Reform efforts to curb or limit alcohol consumption. **288**

Tennessee Valley Authority (TVA)   New Deal agency created in 1933 to develop power stations and dams throughout the Tennessee River Valley. **699**

termination   Government policy during the 1950s designed to end the reservation system. **816**

Tet offensive (1968)   North Vietnamese attack on South Vietnam during Tet, the Vietnamese New Year. **879**

Texas longhorn Hardy breed of cattle developed by the 1850s that helped make long drives possible. **444**

Texas Revolution (1835) Revolt against Mexico by Tejanos and American settlers in Texas after the loss of state power. **308**

Third UN Conference on the Law of the Sea (1982) International conference in which participating nations agreed to protect the world's oceans. **974**

Thirteenth Amendment (1865) Constitutional amendment that abolished slavery. **398**

38th parallel Border between North Korea and South Korea set by the Allies in 1945. **799**

Three-Fifths Compromise (1787) Agreement made at the Constitutional Convention that counted only three fifths of the slave population in determining total state population. **148**

Toleration Act (1649) Maryland colonial law that guaranteed religious freedom to all Christians. **74**

Tonkin Gulf Resolution (1964) Act that gave the president authority to take all necessary measures to repel an armed attack against U.S. forces. **870**

total war Strategy used in the Civil War of striking at the enemy's economic resources in addition to fighting enemy troops. **387**

Townshend Acts (1767) Law enacted by Parliament that placed duties on goods imported by the colonies. **109**

Trail of Tears (1838) Forced relocation of Cherokees from Georgia to Indian Territory, during which many died. **244**

Trans-Appalachian West Area between the Appalachian Mountains and the Mississippi River. **205**

transcendentalists New England intellectuals who believed people could attain perfection and could acquire knowledge about God, self, and the universe. **285**

treason Offense of openly attempting to overthrow a government to which a person owes allegiance, or of killing or personally harming the head of that government or his or her family. **164**

Treaty of Brest-Litovsk (1918) Agreement signed by the Bolsheviks in which Russia made a separate peace with the Central Powers and withdrew from World War I. **598**

Treaty of Fort Laramie (1851) Agreement that set boundaries for Native American groups and allowed the U.S. government to build roads and forts through Indian Territory. **321**

Treaty of Ghent Agreement signed in 1814 that ended the War of 1812. **214**

Treaty of Greenville (1795) Agreement with Native Americans that gave the U.S. title to Native American lands that make up much of present-day Ohio and part of Indiana. **197**

Treaty of Guadalupe Hidalgo Agreement ending the Mexican War in 1848 by which Mexico ceded Texas and the rest of its western territory. **313**

Treaty of Medicine Lodge (1867) Agreement that ended a long-standing war between the Sioux and the U.S. **428**

Treaty of Paris (1783) Agreement signed by Great Britain and the U.S. granting the U.S. independence, territory, and fishing rights. **132**

Treaty of Tordesillas (1494) Agreement that divided control over new territories in the Americas between Spain and Portugal. **45**

Treaty of Versailles (1919) Agreement ending World War I that provided for the establishment of the League of Nations. **608**

trench warfare Strategy used during World War I in which opposing armies fought from behind fixed fortifications. **589**

Triple Alliance Military alliance formed by Germany, Austria-Hungary, and Italy prior to World War I. **587**

Triple Entente Military alliance formed by Great Britain, France, and Russia prior to World War I. **587**

Truman Doctrine U.S. policy of giving military and financial aid to those countries resisting Communist rule. **791**

trunk lines Major railroads connected to surrounding areas by feeder or branch lines. **459**

trust Group of companies that give control of their stock to a board of directors, which then runs the companies as a single enterprise. **462**

Tweed Ring Corrupt political organization that controlled New York City government during the Gilded Age. **486**

Twelfth Amendment (1804) Constitutional amendment that requires electors to vote for presidential and vice-presidential candidates on separate ballots. **203**

Twenty-first Amendment (1933) Constitutional amendment that repealed Prohibition. **656**

Twenty-sixth Amendment (1971) Constitutional amendment that lowered the voting age from 21 to 18. **884**

u

ultraviolet solar radiation (UV rays) Radiation from the sun that can cause skin cancer, damage marine life, and harm crops. **972**

unconditional surrender Arrangement whereby the loser agrees to the terms of the victor. **750**

Underground Railroad Network that helped slaves escape to the North or Canada before the Civil War. **273**

Underwood Tariff Act (1913) Federal law that reduced tariffs to their lowest levels in 50 years. **549**

unilateralism One-sided or independent action in foreign affairs. **724**

United Farm Workers (UFW) Organization of migrant workers formed to win better wages and working conditions. **851**

United Nations (UN) International organization formed in 1945 to work for world peace. **783**

University of California v. *Bakke* (1978) Supreme Court decision that struck down quotas as a means of achieving racial equality; in institutions of higher learning, for example. **920**

urban renewal Programs designed to replace or restore run-down inner-city buildings. **821**

U.S. Department of Agriculture Government agency created in 1862 to help farmers. **440**

utopias Ideal communities. **284**

v

vertical integration Strategy whereby one company acquires other companies that provide materials and services necessary to the first company. **463**

veto Power to reject a proposed law. **155**

viceroy Governor who rules a country in place of a king. **39**

Vietcong Vietnamese Communists. **868**

Vietminh Resistance movement organized by Ho Chi Minh in 1941; also known as the League for the Independence of Vietnam. **866**

Vietnamization President Richard Nixon's plan to end the Vietnam War by turning over the fighting to the South Vietnamese army and withdrawing U.S. troops. **881**

Virginia Plan James Madison's proposal during the Constitutional Convention of shifting power away from the states toward a central government. **146**

Virginia Statute for Religious Freedom (1786) Virginia state law that called for separation of church and state. **139**

Volstead Act (1919)   Federal law that enforced the Eighteenth Amendment (Prohibition). **656**

Voting Rights Act (1965)   Federal law that put voter registration under government control. **848**

Voting Rights Act of 1975   Federal law requiring states and communities with large numbers of non-English speakers to print voting materials in various foreign languages. **923**

Wagner-Connery Act (1935)   Federal law that guaranteed labor's right to organize unions and bargain for better wages and working conditions. **705**

War Industries Board (WIB)   U.S. agency during World War I responsible for allocating scarce materials, establishing production priorities, and setting prices. **602**

war of attrition   Civil War strategy of wearing down the Confederates through constant attack. **386**

War on Poverty   President Lyndon Johnson's Great Society programs designed to end poverty in the U.S. **840**

War Powers Act (1973)   Federal law limiting the president's power to send U.S. troops to foreign conflicts. **888**

War Production Board (WPB)   Government agency during World War II that directed the conversion of existing factories to wartime production. **752**

Warren Commission   Group assigned in 1963 to investigate the assassination of President John Kennedy. **839**

Warsaw Pact (1955)   Alliance formed by the Soviet Union and other Communist countries in Eastern Europe. **794**

Water Quality Improvement Act (1970)   Federal law requiring oil companies to pay some oil spill cleanup costs and setting limits on discharge of industrial pollutants into water. **903**

Watergate   Name given to government scandal that began in 1972 and led to President Richard Nixon's resignation in 1974. **906**

Wealth Tax Act (1935)   Federal law that sharply increased taxes on the rich. **702**

Whiskey Rebellion (1794)   Uprising by western Pennsylvania farmers against a tax on whiskey. **194**

Wilmot Proviso (1846)   Proposed constitutional amendment that would have banned slavery in all lands acquired from Mexico. **339**

Wisconsin Idea   Program of progressive reforms proposed by Wisconsin governor Robert M. "Fighting Bob" La Follette during the early 1900s. **537**

Women's Christian Temperance Union (WCTU)   Reform group in favor of temperance, moral purity, and the rights of women. **525**

Woodstock (1969)   Three-day rock concert in upstate New York that was one of the high points of the counterculture movement. **857**

Worcester v. Georgia (1832)   Supreme Court decision that forbade the state of Georgia to seize Cherokee lands. **244**

Works Progress Administration (WPA)   New Deal agency formed in 1935 to create jobs for people on relief. **701**

Wounded Knee Massacre (1890)   Massacre that occurred between the Sioux on Wounded Knee Creek and the army sent to confiscate the Indians' rifles. **432**

writ of habeas corpus   Legal document that forces a jailer to release a person from prison unless the person has been formally charged with, or convicted of, a crime. **164**

writs of assistance   Search warrants issued to aid customs officers in the search for smuggled goods. **109**

XYZ affair (1797)   Foreign policy scandal in which the French sought bribes from U.S. diplomats before beginning treaty negotiations. **201**

Yalta Conference (1945)   Postwar peace meeting between the U.S., Britain, and the Soviet Union in which plans were made to divide and occupy Germany. **761**

yellow journalism   Newspaper stories that featured sensationalized reporting. **478**

yellow-dog contracts   Agreements many job applicants signed, promising not to join unions. **495**

yeoman farmers   Small farmers who own and cultivate their own land. **267**

z

zaibatsu   Huge corporations run by single families that had monopolized the Japanese economy prior to World War II. **781**

zero population growth (ZPG)   Birthrate that replaces existing population but does not increase it. **922**

Zimmermann Note (1917)   Document that showed that Germany was trying to establish a military alliance with Mexico. **594**

Zionism   Movement, originally intended to promote the founding of a Jewish national state, that called for a Jewish homeland in Palestine. **796**

zoot-suit riots (1943)   Racial attacks by U.S. sailors on Mexican American youths in Los Angeles. **757**

Freedom Riders (1961), 845, *m845*
Freedom's Journal, 222, 293
Freedom Summer (1964), 847-48
freedpeople, 394
Freeman, Daniel, *p436*
freemen, 69
Freeport Doctrine (1858), 353
Free-Soil party, 348; in election of 1848, 339
Frémont, John C., 313, 349
French and Indian War, 91-93, *m92*
French Huguenots, 81
French Indochina: Japanese occupation of, 738, *m738*
French Revolution, 195-96, *p195*
Frick, Henry Clay, 496
Friedan, Betty, 854, *p921*, 1026
Fuel Administration, 602
Fugitive Slave Act (1850), 343, 344-45, *p344, p345*
Fulbright, J. William, 878
Fuller, Margaret, 285, 1026
Fulton, Robert, 232-33
Fundamentalism, 656-57
Fundamental Orders of Connecticut (1639), 72
Furness, Betty, 840

Gable, Clark, 618
Gadsden, James, 315
Gadsden Purchase (1853), 315, *m315*
Gagarin, Yuri, 833
Gage, Thomas, 110, 114
Galbraith, John Kenneth, 825
Galveston, TX, reforms in, 536-37, *p536*
Gálvez, Bernardo de, *m129,* 130, *p130*
Gam Saan (Gold Mountain), 326
Gandhi, Indira, 977, 1026
gang labor, 270
Gannett, Deborah Sampson, 125
Garbo, Greta, 680, *p680*
García Calderón, Francisco, 573
García, Héctor P., 840, 1026
Garfield, Harry, 602
Garfield, James A., 489, *p489,* 1026; and election of 1880, 488; and Reconstruction, 408
Garland, Hamlin, 443, *p443,* 454, 1026
Garner, John Nance, 689
Garnet, Henry Highland, 292, *p292*
Garreau, Joel, 947
Garrison, Nicholas, painting by, *p64-65*
Garrison, William Lloyd: and equal rights for women, 296; launch of the *Liberator,* 293; opposition to, 294-95; and passage of Fifteenth Amendment, 404
Garrity, W. Arthur, *p919*
Garvey, Marcus, 636-37, *p637,* 1026
gazetteers, 1000
Gehrig, Lou, 681

General Court, 69
General Federation of Women's Clubs, 514, 635
generation gap, 852
Genet, Edmond, 196, *p196*
Geneva Conference (1954), 867-68
Genoa, Italy, 20, 28-29, *m29*
genocide, 767
Genthe, Arnold, photograph by, *p529*
Gentilz, Theodore, painting by, *p316*
geography: of Africa, *m583;* of agriculture, 642-43, *m642-43;* of Asia, *m583;* of Australia, *m583;* of cities, *m860, m861;* of Europe, *m583;* five themes of, 9; and immigration, 482, *m482-83, m954-55;* and imperialism, 582-83, *m582-83;* and industrialization, 252-53, *m252-53;* of North America, *m582;* and railroads, 253, *m253;* regions, 360-61, *m360-61;* and schools, *m360-61;* of South America, 582, *m582;* of the West, 186-87, *m186-87, m483*
George, Henry, 457
George III (England), 113-14, *p113,* 116, 118, 146
Georgia (CIS), *m959,* 960
Georgia (U.S.): in Civil War, 386-88; Great Awakening in, 85; secession of, 356, 364; scttlement of, 83, *p83*
geothermal power, 970
German Americans, 81, 82, *c259,* 260-62, 309-10, 466, 469, *c482, m482, m483,* 591, *m954*
German reunification (1990), 959
Germany: and Berlin airlift, *p789,* 792, *p792;* foreign investment in, *c582-83;* Green party in, 974; and Holocaust, 767-68; impact of war debt and reparations on, 726-27, *p727;* inflation in, 727, *p727;* involvement in China, 566-67; and Maastricht Treaty, 964-65; Nazis in, *p722-23,* 733, *p733,* 734-35, *m736;* post–World War II occupation of, 780-81, 789; reunification, 959; signing of nonaggression pact with Soviet Union, 736; and World War I, 587, 588-89, *m588,* 591-92, 593, *p612;* in World War II, 735-38, 747, *p747, m748,* 749, *c767,* 761-62
Geronimo, *m428,* 432-33, 1026
Gershwin, George, 659-60
Gettysburg Address, The (Lincoln), 380, 1008
Gettysburg, Battle of (1863), 379-81, *p379, p381*
Ghana, 26, *m26*
Ghost Dance, 429, *p429,* 432
GI Bill of Rights (1944), 784, *p784*
Gideon **v.** *Wainright* (1963), 842
Gilbert, Sir Humphrey, 59
Gilded Age, The (Twain and Warner), 485, 486, *p486,* 505
Gillespie, Dizzy, 754
Gilpin, Charles, 660
Ginsberg, Douglas, 933
Ginsburg, Ruth Bader, *p165,* 943
Gladden, Washington, 477

glasnost, 935, 957
Glass, Hugh, 318
Glidden, Joseph, 448
global grid, 993
global warming, 972
Glorious Revolution (1688), 84
Glory-Hunter (Van de Water), 431
glyph, 11
Golden Hind (ship), 58
Goldman, Emma, 626, *p626,* 1026
Goldmark, Josephine, 519, *p519*
gold rush, in California, 323, 324-27, *p324, m325, p325*
gold standard, 499, 500
Goldwater, Barry M., 841, 1026
Gompers, Samuel, 495, 520, 655
Gone with the Wind (Mitchell), 717, *p717*
Goodman, Andrew, 847
Goodman, Benny, 618, 718
Good Neighbor policy, 728-29
Gorbachev, Mikhail, 935, *p935,* 957, 958-59, 1026
Gordon, John B., 377
Gore, Al, 943
Gorgas, William C., 569, 571
"Gospel of Wealth," 477
Gould, Jay, 487, 494
government bonds, 192
graduated income tax, 499, 500
Grady, Henry W., 411
Graf von Hübner, Joseph Alexander, 474
Gramm-Rudman-Hollings Act (1985), 934
Grange movement, 497-98
Graniteville, SC, 252, *m252*
Grant, Madison, 528-29
Grant, Ulysses S., 1026; in Civil War, 380-82, 386, *p386, m387,* 388, *p388,* 403, *p403;* and corruption, 487-88; elected president (1868), 403, *p403;* Reconstruction policies of, *p406*
Grapes of Wrath, The (Steinbeck), 717
Grasse, François de, 132
Gravier, Charles, 103
"graying of America," 922
Great Awakening, 84-85, 115; Second, 282-84, *p282, c284*
Great Britain: and early Republic, 137, 143; and Atlantic Charter, 738; and blitzkrieg, 737-38, *p738;* and border settlement, 320; foreign investment and trade of, *c582-83, m582-83;* Green party in, 974; and impressment, 196; involvement in China, 566; and Jay's Treaty, 197; and Lend-Lease Act, 737; and Maastricht Treaty, 964-65; and Panama Canal, 570, 572; post–War of 1812 relations with, 228-29, *m229;* response to facism, 735; and the South, 266, 372-73; and War of 1812, 211-15, *m214, p215;* at Washington Conference, 725, *p725;* and World War I, 587-89, *m588, p590,* 591, *c611;* in World War II, *p766. See also* England

Great Compromise (1787), 147
Great Depression, *p668-69;* beginning of, 671-72; causes of, 670, 672-74; family life in, 679, *p679;* farm crisis in, 685; global impact of, *m673,* 677; Hoover's philosophy on, 683-89, *p684;* migrant labor during, 711, 712-13, *p712,* 714, *p714;* photographing, 712-13, *p712, p713,* 714-15, *p715;* psychological impact of, 679-80; rural life in, 677-79; stock market crash in, 671, *c671;* unemployment in, 675-76, *p675, m676;* urban life in, 676-77, *p677*
Great Gatsby, The (Fitzgerald), 662
Great Migration, 68; of African Americans, 603-04
Great Plains: geography of, 5; Native Americans in, 16; Pike's description of, 209; trunk lines crossing, 459
Great Serpent Mound, *p14*
Great Society, 841-42, 843, 900
Great Train Robbery, The (movie), 525-26, *p525*
Great Upheaval (1886), 494-95
"Great White Fleet," 568
Greece: and Maastricht Treaty, 964-65; in World War II, 747
Greek Americans, 466, 470, 937, *m954*
Greeley, Horace, 372, 383, 487
Greenback party, 500
Green Berets, 835
Greene, Graham, 863
Greene, Nathanael, 131
greenhouse effect, 972
Greenhow, Rose O'Neal, 369, 1026
Green parties, 974
Greenpeace, 972
Green Rage (Manes), 981
Greensboro, NC, 844
Grenada, U.S. invasion of, *m932,* 933
Griffith, D. W., 409
Grimké, Angelina, 297-98, *p297,* 1026
Grimké, Sarah, 281, 297-98, *p297,* 1026
gross national product, 671
Grundy, Felix, 212
Guacanagarí, 40
Guadalcanal, in World War II, *m746,* 747
Gualdape, San Miguel de, 50
Guam, in World War II, 745, *m746,* 762
Guanahani, 39, 40
Guangdong, 326, 482, *m482*
Guantánamo Bay, 569, 570; Naval Aviation Camp at, *p508*
Guatemala: coffee plantations in, *p54;* population growth of, *m976;* rise of military dictatorship in, 729; U.S. intervention in, 811
"Guerilla War" (Ehrhart), 891
guerrilla warfare: in American Revolution, 131; in Vietnam War, 872
Guinea, *m976*
Guinea-Bissau, *m976*
Guiteau, Charles, 488
Gulf of Thailand, 864, *m865*
Gulf of Tonkin, 864, *m865,* 870
Gullah, 81, 412

gun control, 928
Gutenberg, Johannes, 21
Gypsies, 781

hacienda, 53, 54
Hagedorn, Jessica, 983
Haig, Alexander, 930
Haight-Ashbury, 853, *p853*
Hainan, post–World War II, 768
Haiphong Harbor, 883
Haiti: revolt in (1791), 206, 208; U.S. policy toward, 574, 945, *p945;* withdrawal of U.S. marines from, 728
Haitians: immigration of, 945, *p945;* in Miami, 947
hajj, 26
Halberstam, David, 875
Haldeman, H. R. (Bob), 883
Half-breeds, 488
Hall, Thomas, 411
Halsall, William, painting by, *p66*
Hamilton, Alexander, 137, 1026; as delegate to Constitutional Convention, 146; duel between Burr and, 203, *p203;* and election of 1796, 200; federalist views of, 150; and Jefferson, 207; and judicial review, 157; letter from, 135; as secretary of treasury, 169, 191-94, *p192*
Hamlin, Hannibal, *p354, p355*
Hammond, James, 354
Hammond, Jesse, 284
Hammond, Matthew, 411
Hancock, Winfield Scott, 488
Hanna, Mark, 538-39
Hanoi, Vietnam, 864, *m865,* 866, 879, 883
Hanson, Ole, 623
Harding, Warren G., 628-30, *p629,* 1026; death of, 630; domestic policies of, 629-30; election of, in 1920, 628; scandals under, 630, *p630*
hard-rock mining, 452
Hargreaves, James, *p234*
Harlan, John Marshall, 414
Harlem Experimental Theatre, 661
Harlem Renaissance, 660-62, *m661;* literature of, 772
Harper, Frances Ellen, 419
Harpers Ferry, 353, 354
Harper's Weekly (magazine), *p401*
Harrington, Michael, 840
Harris, Charles, 409
Harris, Joel Chandler, *p277*
Harrison, Benjamin, 437, 486, *p486,* 489, 490, *p490,* 500, 1027
Harrison, Jesse Burton, 264-65
Harrison, William Henry, 212, 248-49, *p248,* 1027
Harris, Patricia, 918
"Harry Wilmans" (Masters), 615

Hartford Convention (1814), 215
Hartford Female Seminary, 291
Hart, Nancy, *p126*
Harvard College, 107
Hawaii: Japanese attack on, 743, *p742-43, m746;* labor in, *p565;* and statehood, *m829;* U.S. acquisition of, 565-66
Hawaiian League, 565-66
hawks, 876
Hay–Bunau-Varilla Treaty (1903), 572
Hayden, Sterling, *p794*
Hayes, Rutherford B., 408, 433, 488, *p488,* 1027
Hay-Herrán Treaty (1903), 572
Hay, John, 567, 570, 572, *p572*
Haymarket Riot (1886), 494-95, *p494*
Hayne, Robert, 245
Haynes, Lemuel, *p281*
Hay-Pauncefote Treaty (1901), 572
Hayslip, Le Ly, 885
Haywood, "Big Bill," 520-21
Head Start, 840
health: and cigarettes, 896; and food, 896, *c896*
health care: crisis in, 949-50, *p950;* and national health insurance, 787; reform, 944
Hearst, William Randolph, 478, 559-60
Heckler, Margaret, 933
Heit, Molly, *p835*
Helena, MT, 451
Hellman, Lillian, 718, *p718,* 1027
Hemingway, Ernest, 662, 734, 1027
Henderson, Fletcher, 660
Hendrix, Jimi, 856-57, *p856*
Henry VII (England), 21
Henry VIII (England), 66
Henry, Edward L., painting by, *p232*
Henry of Portugal, 30, *p30,* 1027
Henry, Patrick, 115, 146, 161
Henry Street Settlement, 477, *p477*
Henson, Matthew, 509
Hepburn Act (1906), 540
Heritage Foundation, 928
heroin, 975
Herzegovina: ethnic fighting in, 962-63; and World War I, 586
Hessians, in American Revolution, 116, 128
Hessing, Valjean, painting by, *p245*
Hickok, Wild Bill, 451
Hicks, Edward, painting by, *p82*
Hidalgo, Father Miguel, *p230*
Highway Act (1956), *m816,* 817
Hill, Anita, 941, *p941*
Hilton, James, 682
hippies, 853
Hirohito, Emperor, 745, 781, *p781*
Hiroshima, *m746,* 765, *p765,* 781, 808, 970
Hispanic Americans: and civil rights movement, 899, 918; and riots, 946-47; in 1930s, *m638;* and poverty, 805; unemployment of, 913, 929; and urban renewal, 821; in Vietnam War, 871; in World War II, 757. *See also* Cuban Americans; Mexican Americans; Puerto Ricans

Montgomery Improvement Association
(MIA), 823, 844
Monticello, *p207*
Montreal, Canada: in French and Indian
War, *m92,* 93; and ozone layer, 974
Montreal Protocol on Ozone Depletion
(1987), 974
Moody, Deborah, 73
Moral Majority, 928, *p928*
moratorium, 727
Morgan, J. P., 463
Mori, Toshio, 773
Mormons, 284-85, 360
Morocco, 26, 211
Morrill Act (1862), 436
Morris, Gouverneur, 149
Morriss, Mack, 762
Morristown, NJ, 124
Morse, Samuel F. B., 223, 459
Morse, Wayne, 870-71
Morton, "Jelly Roll," 659, *p659*
Mosaddeq, Mohammad, 810
Moscow, Russia, 975, 977
Moseley-Braun, Carol, 943, 1031
Moses, Anna "Grandma," 719, 1030;
painting by, *p719*
Moss, Alfred, A., Jr., 210
Mother Earth (magazine), 626
Motown Records, 856
Mott, Lucretia, 298, *p298,* 1031
mound builders, 14, *p14*
mountain men, 318
Mountain of Gold, (Sung), 329
Mount Holyoke Female Seminary, 291,
p291
movement, 9
movies: before 1920, 525-26; in 1920s,
619, 652-53, *p653;* in 1930s, 619,
680, *p680;* in 1940s, 619; in 1950s,
826; on videocassettes, 897, *p897;* in
World War II, 754
Moynihan, Daniel Patrick, 839
muckrakers, 514-15
"mugwumps," 489
Muhammad, 23
Müller-Freienfels, Richard, 654
Muller v. Oregon (1908), 519
Multicultural Perspective, Gaining a,
xxi
multinational corporations, 965-66
Mum Bett, *p118*
Munich, Germany, 735; 1972 Olympics
in, 962
Munich Conference (1938), 735
Munn v. Illinois (1877), 498
Murdoch, Rupert, 965
Murphy Brown (television show), debate
about, 947, *p947,* 949
Murphy, Charles, *p534*
Murray, J. B., 695
Murray, Judith Sargent, 140, 1031
Murray, Patty, 943
Murrow, Edward R., 754, 807
Mūsā, Mansa, 26-27, *p27,* 1031
music: of African Americans, *p81,* 275,
276, 278, *p276,* 334, 418, *p418, p644-
45,* 659-60, *p659,* 708-09, *p709,* 718;

and New Deal, 718; in 1920s, 618,
659-60, *p659, p660;* in 1960s, 776,
p776, 856-57, *p856, p857;* in 1970s,
776; rock, 826-27, *p826, p827;* in
World War II, 754
Muskie, Edmund, 880
Muslims: in Azerbaijan, 960; in Bosnia,
962; and the Crusades, 19-20; in
Middle Ages, 20-21, *p21,* 23
Mussolini, Benito, 760; rise of, 732-33,
p732
Muste, A. J., 686
mutualistas, 676
MX missile, 930
Mydans, Carl, 713; photograph by, *p715*
Myers, Dee Dee, 943
My Life on the Plains (Custer), 430
"My Name," *The House on Mango
Street* (Cisneros), 983

NAACP. *See* National Association for
the Advancement of Colored People
NAFTA. *See* North American Free
Trade Agreement
Nagasaki, Japan, 765, 781
Napoléon, 230
Narragansets, 73, 90
*Narrative of the Life of Frederick
Douglass* (Douglass), 294
Narváez, Pánfilo de, 45-46
Nash, Diane, 845, 1031
Nasser, Gamal Abdel, 811
National Aeronautics and Space
Administration (NASA), 810, 951
National American Woman Suffrage
Association (NAWSA), 552
National Association for the
Advancement of Colored People
(NAACP), 508, 527-28, 636, *p636,*
708, 709, 819, 822-23, *p822,* 846
National Association of Colored
Women, 514
national bank, 192
National Broadcasting Company
(NBC), 652
National Child Labor Committee, 517
National Committee for a Sane Nuclear
Policy, 876
National Conservation Commission,
541
National Council of Negro Women, 709
national debt, 192; payment of, 193-94
National Defense Act (1916), 594
National Defense Education Act (1958),
810
National Endowment for the Arts
(NEA), 657
National Energy Act (1978), 913
National Grange, 497-98
National Industrial Recovery Act
(1933), 696-97, *c703*

nationalism: black, 636-37; as cause of
World War I, 586-87; rise of, 226-27
nationalize, definition of, 731
National Labor Relations Act (1935),
c703, 705. *See also* Wagner-Connery
Act
National Liberation Front (NLF), 868
National Negro Business League, 508
National Organization for Women
(NOW), 854, 921-22
National Park Service, 541, *p541, m542*
National Recovery Administration
(NRA), 697, *c703*
National Road, 228
National Security Council (NSC), 794
national supremacy, 155
National Trades Union, 257
National Tuberculosis Association, 523
National Urban League, 527-28
National War Labor Board, 602-03
National Woman's party, 552, 632-33
National Woman's Peace party, *p593*
National Women's Political Caucus,
856
National Youth Administration (NYA),
702, *c703,* 709-10
nations, rise of, 21-22
Native American Grave Protection and
Repatriation Act (1990), 13
Native Americans: and American
Revolution, 125; assimilation of, 434-
35; in Battle of Fallen Timbers (1794),
197; in Battle of Little Bighorn (1876),
429; in Battle of Rosebud (1876), 429;
and Cayuse War (1847), 322; and Civil
War, 334, 369; conflict with settlers, 61,
77, 88-91, 94, 196-97, 212, 243-45,
322, 327, 426-33; and cultural renewal,
948, *p948;* and Dawes General
Allotment Act (1887), 434, 634; early
cultures of, 12-14, *m15,* 16; education
of, 434, *p434,* 528, 710; and
encomienda system, 40-43, 53, 54, *p54,*
62; in French and Indian War, 91-93;
granting of citizenship to, 635; impact
of early colonization on, 37, *p37,* 39-
43, 46-49; and Indian Removal Act
(1830), 243, *c243, m244, p245;* and
Iroquois League origins, 91; literature
of, 96-97, 331, 893; and Mariposa War
(1851), 327; and New Deal, 710-11; in
1920s, 634-35; in 1950s, 805, 815-16,
821; in 1960s, 851, 859; in 1970s, 899,
920-21, *p920, p921;* in Pontiac's
Rebellion, 105; progressives, 528; and
Relocation Act (1956), 815-16, *p815,*
821; removal of, 243-45, *m244,* 250,
251; and reservation policy, 427, 453;
reservations and battles of, to 1890,
m428; and Roman Catholic church, 49,
52-53, 318-20; and Sand Creek
Massacre, 427; in Second Seminole
War (1835–42), 244; and settlement of
Pacific Northwest, 196-97, 321-22; and
Society of American Indians, 528; and
trade with U.S., 318; and Trail of Tears
(1838), 244, *m244;* and Treaty of

74; and nativism, 261-62; and Protestant Reformation, 57-58; and religious freedom, 74; role of, in Middle Ages, 18, *p18*; in Oregon, 319

Romania: post–World War II, 768, 780, *c976*; in World War II, 747, *m748*

Rommel, Erwin, 747, *p747*, 749

Roosevelt, Alice Lee, 538

Roosevelt Corollary (1904), 573

Roosevelt, Edith Kermit Carow, 538

Roosevelt, Eleanor: 651, 1032; in election of 1932, 688; and Fair Employment Practices Committee, 785, *p785;* and human rights, 783, *p783;* and reform, 695, 708

Roosevelt, Franklin Delano, 631, *p768*, 1032; and Atlantic Charter, 738; death of, 764; in election of 1932, 688-89, *p688, p689;* in election of 1936, 702, 704; in election of 1940, 737; in election of 1944, 753; "fireside chats" of, 695; Good Neighbor policy of, 728-29; as governor of New York, 651; inauguration of, 693; and New Deal, 694-99, *p694, p697;* and Supreme Court, 704-05; and U.S. neutrality, 735; in World War II, 750, 753; at Yalta, 761, 768. *See also* New Deal

Roosevelt, Theodore, *p538,* 539, *p539;* as assistant secretary of Navy, 560; and conservation, 540-41, *p541, m542;* early career of, 533, 538-39; in election of 1912, 546-47, *m547;* and New Nationalism, 545; and Nobel Peace Prize, 568; and Panama Canal, *p569,* 570, 571, 572, *p572;* as president, 538; as Progressive, 513; and regulation of business, 539-40; at San Juan Hill, 562; Square Deal of, 539; and Taft, 545; and U.S. neutrality, 593

Root, Robert Marshall, painting by, *p352*

Rosebud, Battle of (1876), 429

Rosenberg, Ethel, 795, *p795,* 1032

Rosenberg, Julius, 795, *p795,* 1032

Rostow, Eugene, 754

rotation in office, 241

Rothstein, Arthur, photograph by, *p712*

Rough Riders, 538, 562

Ruby, Jack, 839

Ruckelshaus, William, 908

rugged individualism, 683-84

Rural Electrification Administration (REA), 702, *c703*

rural life: and Farmers' Alliance, 498-499, *p499;* in Great Depression, 677-79; and National Grange, 497-98, *p497;* in South, 266-67, *p267;* in West, 440-43, *p441, p442*

Rush-Bagot Agreement (1817), 229

Rusk, Dean, 837, 878

Russia: and breakup of Soviet Union, 959, *m959,* 960; and China, 566; and Peace Corps, 978; Russo-Japanese War, 568; and sale of Alaska, 449; and Treaty of Brest-Litovsk, 598; U.S. territorial disputes with, 231; and World War I, 586, 587, 588. *See also* Soviet Union

Russo-Japanese War (1904–05), 568

Russwurm, John, 293, *p293*

Ruth, George Herman "Babe," 619, 653, *p653,* 681, 897, 1032

Rutan, Richard, 890

Ryan, Nolan, 777

S

Saar, post–World War I, 608

Sacagawea, *p205,* 208, 1032

Sacco, Nicola, 626-27, *p627*

Sadat, Anwar, 915, *p915,* 916, *p924*

Safer, Morley, *p875*

Sagan, Carl, 381

Sagoyewatha, 210

Sagres, Portugal, 30

St. Augustine, FL, 50

St. Benedict, *p18*

St. Lawrence River, exploration of, *m81,* 88

St. Leger, Barry, 130

Salem, Peter, 125, *p125*

Salem witchcraft trials, 70-71, *p70*

Salinger, J.D., 826

Salk, Jonas, 777

Salvation Army, 477, *p684*

Samoa, 558-59, *m564, c568*

San Antonio de Valero mission, 51

San Antonio, TX: founding of, 51; Juan Seguín in, 310; Mexican American migration to, *m638,* 639; in Texas Revolution, 308, *m308*

San Carlos Reservation, 432

Sand Creek Massacre (1864), 427

San Diego, CA, settlement of, 323

Sandinistas, 931, *p931*

Sandino, Augusto César, 730, *p730,* 1032

San Francisco, CA: Chinese immigrants in, *p529;* city planning in, 523, 525; civil rights in, *p919;* counterculture in, 853; founding of, 52, *m52;* and gold rush, 324, *m325;* Irish immigrants in, 259; Native American protest near, 851; settlement of, 323; and transcontinental railroad, 438; Wilma Mankiller in, 948

San Francisco de los Tejas mission, 51

San Jacinto, Battle of (1836), 308-09

San Juan Hill, Cuba, 562

Santa Anna, Antonio López de, 308-09, *p309,* 313, 1032

Santa Fe, NM, 317, *p317*

Santa Fe Trail, 317

Santa María (ship), 39, 40

San Xavier del Bac mission, *p53*

Sarajevo, Bosnia and Herzegovina, 587

Saratoga, Battle of (1777), *m129,* 130

Saroyan, William, 719

satellite nations, 789

satellites, 968

Saturday Night Massacre (October 20, 1973), 908

Sauks, 196

Savage, Edward, painting by, *p121*

Savannah, GA, in American Revolution, 131; in Civil War, 387-88

Savings and Loan (S&L) crisis, 934

scalawags, 406

Scalia, Antonin, 933

Schenk **v.** *United States* (1919), 605

Schlafly, Phyllis, 922, *p922,* 1033

Schneiderman, Rose, 518, *p518*

Schroeder, Patricia, 933

Schwarzkopf, H. Norman, 939

Schwerner, Michael, 847

scientific management, 647-48

Scopes, John, 657-58; trial of, 657-58, *p658*

Scotch-Irish, 81, 239, 515

Scots, 81, 223, 236

Scott, Dred, 295, 350-51, *p351*

"Scottsboro Boys," 687

Scott, Winfield, 343; in Mexican War, 313

scrip, 493

Seaborg, Glenn, 619

Sea Islanders, 412-13

Seale, Bobby, 849-50, 1033

search-and-destroy missions, 873

Seattle, WA, general strike in, 623, *p623*

secession, constitutional issues in, 356-57

Second Amendment (1791), 177, *c191*

secondary sources, 998

Second Continental Congress (1775), 114-15

Second Great Awakening, 282-84, *c284, p302*

Second Seminole War (1835–42), 244

sectionalism, 198-99

Securities and Exchange Commission (1934), *c703*

Sedgwick, Susan, painting by, *p118*

sedition, 202

Sedition Act (1798), 202

Sedition Act (1918), 605

segregation, 413; and Black Power, 848-50; in churches, 268; in housing, 527-28, 756, 821; and Jim Crow laws, 412-14; in military, 125, 384-85, 595, 756; post–World War II, 786; in schools, 290, 822-25, 846, 919-20; southern support of, 828, 901

Seguín, Juan Nepomuceno, 310, *p310,* 1033

Selective Service Act (1917), 595

Selective Training and Service Act (1940), 753

self-determination, 606

Seljuk Turks, 19

Selling of Joseph, The (Sewall), 79

Seminoles, 229-30, *p229,* 242, 243-44

Seneca Falls Convention (1848), 298-99, 301

Seneca Falls Declaration of Sentiments, 1005-06

Senecas, 91, 105, 125

Seoul, South Korea, *m799,* 800, *p801*

separation of church and state, 139

separation of powers, 155, 162, 163

ACKNOWLEDGMENTS

For permission to reprint copyrighted material, grateful acknowledgment is made to the following sources:

Víctor Alba: From *Alliance Without Allies: The Mythology of Progress in Latin America* by Víctor Alba. Copyright © 1965 by Víctor Alba.

Estate of J. Alvarez del Vayo: From "Prologue" and from "Did Democracy Fail in Spain?" from *Freedom's Battle* by J. Alvarez del Vayo, translated from the Spanish by Eileen E. Brooke. Copyright 1940 by Julio Alvarez del Vayo.

American Heritage Publishing Co., Inc.: From "Before the Colors Fade: Last of the Rough Riders" by V. C. Jones from *American Heritage*, vol. 20, no. 5, August 1969. Copyright © 1969 by American Heritage Publishing Co., Inc.

Terry Anderson: From "My Paper Prison" by Terry Anderson from *The New York Times*, April 4, 1993.

Archives of American Art, Detroit: Excerpt by Carl Mydans from interview with Richard K. Doud, April 19, 1964.

Richard Atkinson: Quote by Richard Atkinson describing Bill and Hillary Clinton's marriage.

The Atlantic Monthly: From "Bread Line" by Florence Converse from *The Atlantic Monthly*, January 1932. Copyright 1932 by the Atlantic Monthly.

Ayer Company Publishers Inc.: From *Ark of Empire: The American Frontier, 1784–1830* by Dale Van Every.

BBC Enterprises Limited: From "Economy (1931)" from *The Collected Writings of John Maynard Keynes, vol. 9, Essays in Persuasion*. Originally titled "The Problem of Unemployment—II" as published in the *Listener*, January 4, 1931.

Beacon Press: From *The Broken Spears: The Aztec Account of the Conquest of Mexico*, edited by Miguel Leon-Portilla. Copyright © 1962, 1990 by Beacon Press.

Bergen County Record: Excerpt by Russell Means from "At Ease" from *The Bergen Record*, New Jersey, October 31, 1971.

Susan Bergholz Literary Services, New York: From "My Name" from *The House on Mango Street* by Sandra Cisneros. Copyright © 1986 by Sandra Cisneros.

Chuck Berry: From lyrics "Roll Over Beethoven" by Chuck Berry.

Bethune-Cookman College Archives: Quote by Mary McCleod Bethune.

John F. Blair, Publisher, Winston-Salem, NC 27103: From "Peter Clifton," "Ben Horry," and "Prince Smith" from *Before Freedom: 48 Oral Histories of Former North and South Carolina Slaves*, edited by Belinda Hurmence. Copyright © 1990 by Belinda Hurmence.

Robert Bly: From "The United Fruit Co." by Pablo Neruda from *Neruda and Vallejo: Selected Poems*, chosen and translated by Robert Bly. Copyright © 1974 by Robert Bly. Published by Beacon Press.

Brassey's (US), Inc.: From "Battle of the Bulge," "Death Battle at Tarawa," "Fall of Berlin," and "This Was D-Day" from *YANK: The Story of World War II as Written by the Soldiers* by the Staff of *Yank*, the Army Weekly. Copyright © 1984 by Yank Productions, Inc.

Curtis Brown, Ltd.: Quote by Antonio Luhan from "Commissioner Collier Is on Our Side" from *Winter in Taos* by Mabel Dodge Luhan.

California Historical Society: From "Pío Pico's correspondence with the Mexican Government, 1846–1848," edited and translated by George Tays from *California Historical Quarterly*, vol. 13, no. 2., June 1934.

Peter N. Carroll: Quote by a Chicago housewife from "The Loss of Connection" and quote by Ralph E. Lapp, energy expert, from "Pinch, Squeeze, Crunch, or Crisis" from *It Seemed Like Nothing Happened: America in the 1970s* by Peter N. Carroll. Copyright © 1982 by Peter Carroll.

The Caxton Printers, Ltd.: From "Lil' Yokohama" from *Yokohama, California* by Toshio Mori. Copyright © 1949 by The Caxton Printers, Ltd.

Center of American Archeology: From "Another view by one of the Crow Creek researchers" by P. Willey from "Issues in Archeology" from *Early Man Magazine*, Autumn 1981.

Chelsea Green Publishers: From *Beyond the Limits: Confronting Global Collapse, Envisioning a Sustainable Future* by Donella Meadows, Dennis L. Meadows, and Jorgen Randers. Published by Chelsea Green Publishers, Post Mills, VT, 1992.

Sheyann Webb Christburg: Quote by eight-year-old Sheyann Webb from "The Turbulent Sixties" from *The Enduring Vision: A History of the American People* by Paul S. Boyer et al.

The Christian Century Foundation: From "Bare-Bones Imbroglio: Repatriating Indian Remains and Sacred Artifacts" by Dean Peerman from *The Christian Century*, October 17, 1990. Copyright © 1990 by The Christian Century Foundation.

Confluence Press, Lewiston, ID: From "Plea to Those Who Matter" from *Riding the Earthboy 40* by James Welch. Copyright © 1990 by James Welch.

Conservatory of American Letters: From "Guerrilla War" from *The Awkward Silence* by W. D. Ehrhart. Copyright © 1980 by W. D. Ehrhart.

Carl Cowl, Administrator for the Archives of Claude McKay: "A Song of the Moon" from *Selected Poems of Claude McKay*. Copyright © 1979 by Harcourt Brace & Company.

Crisis Publishing Co., Inc.: From "The Bronx Slave Market" by Ella Baker and Marvel Cooke from *The Crisis*, vol. 42, November 1935. Copyright © 1935 by Crisis Publishing Co., Inc.

Thomas Y. Crowell Company: "The Buffalo Go" from *American Indian Mythology* by Alice Marriott and Carol K. Rachlin. Copyright © 1968 by T. Y. Crowell Company.

Daughters of the Utah Pioneers: From "Journal of Priscilla Merriman Evans" from *Heart Throbs of the West* and *Our Pioneer Heritage*, both edited by Kate B. Carter.

Joan Daves Agency as agent for Heirs of the Estate of Martin Luther King, Jr.: From sermon opposing the Vietnam war by Martin Luther King, Jr., at New York's Riverside Church in 1967. Copyright © 1967 by Dr. Martin Luther King, Jr. "I Have a Dream" by Martin Luther King Jr. Copyright © 1963 by the Estate of Martin Luther King, Jr. Renewed copyright © 1991 by Coretta Scott King.

Mrs. Maurice R. Davie: "The Skyscraper" from *Problems of City Life* by Maurice R. Davie. Copyright 1932 by Maurice R. Davie.

The Devin-Adair Company: From *The Case of the South* by William D. Workman, Jr. Copyright © 1960 by William D. Workman, Jr.

Mrs. Alexander Donat: From *The Holocaust Kingdom: A Memoir* by Alexander Donat. Copyright © 1963, 1965 by Alexander Donat.

The Dorsey Press, a division of Wadsworth, Inc.: From "Family Values" from *America's History* by James A. Henretta. Copyright © 1987 by The Dorsey Press.

Doubleday, a divison of Bantam Doubleday Dell Publishing Group, Inc.: Quote about the rebel yell during the Civil War from *Glory Road: The Bloody Route from Fredericksburg to Gettysburg* by Bruce Catton. Copyright 1952 by Doubleday and Company. From *My Life and Work* by Henry Ford, with Samuel Crowther. Copyright 1922 by Doubleday & Company, Inc. From "Wir Gerdenken der Toten!" from *Aufsatze aus dem Kampfzeit* by Joseph Goebbels, translated in *The War That Hitler Won: The Most Infamous Propaganda Campaign in History* by Robert Edwin Herzstein. Copyright © 1978 by Robert Edwin Herzstein. From "Can Wars Be Just?" by Sari Nusseibeh from *But Was It Just?: Reflections on the Morality of the Persian Gulf War* by Jean Bethke Elshtain et al., translated by Peter Heinegg, edited by David E. Decosse. From *The Blue Eagle from Egg to Earth* by Hugh S. Johnson. Copyright 1935 by Hugh S. Johnson. From *When Heaven and Earth Changed Places: A Vietnamese Woman's Journey from War to Peace* by Le Ly Hayslip. Copyright © 1989 by Le Ly Hayslip and Charles Jay Wurts. From *Tet!* by Don Oberdorfer. Copyright © 1971 by Don Oberdorfer. From *Woodrow Wilson as I Knew Him* by Joseph P. Tumulty. Copyright 1921 by Joseph P. Tumulty.

E. P. Dutton: From *Movin' on Up* by Mahalia Jackson, with Evan McLeod Wylie. Copyright © 1966 by Hawthorn Books.

The Economist: From "Survey of the Entertainment Industry" from *The Economist*, December 23, 1989. Copyright © 1989 by The Economist.

Facts on File, Inc., New York: From "Origin of Fire," "The Origin of the Iroquois Nations," and "The Strange Origins of Corn" from *Voices of the Winds: Native American Legends* by Margot Edmonds and Ella E. Clark. Copyright © 1989 by Margot Edmonds and Ella E. Clark.

Farrar, Straus, and Giroux, Inc.: From "Cabo Haitiano to Dos Rios" from *The America of José Martí: Selected Writings of José Martí*, translated from the Spanish by Juan de Onís. From *Night Dawn Day* by Elie Wiesel. Copyright © 1985 by Elie Wiesel.

The Forum: Quote by a Slav immigrant from "Relief and Revolution" by Charles R. Walker from *The Forum*, August 1932.

Dan Freedman: From "Jacqueline Navarra Rhoads" from *Nurses in Vietnam: The Forgotten Veterans*, edited by Dan Freedman and Jacqueline Rhoads. Copyright © 1987 by Dan Freedman and Jacqueline Rhoads. SEE ALSO: Jacqueline Rhoads.

German-Texan Heritage Society: From *Texas* by Ferdinand Roemer, 1935, translated by Oswald Mueller. Copyright © 1983 by German-Texan Heritage Society, Austin, TX.

Luis Alfredo Godoy, agent for Diego Rivera's unpublished manuscript: From "America Must Discover Her Own Beauty," an unpublished manuscript dated August 3, 1930, by Diego Rivera from The Bertram Wolfe Collection of the Hoover Institution.

Greenwood Publishing Group Inc.: Quote by African American woman from *The American Slave: A Composite Autobiography*, vol. 12, *Georgia Narratives, Part 1*, edited by George P. Rawick. Quote by Millie Bates from *The American Slave: A Composite Autobiography*, vol. 2, *South Carolina Narratives, Parts 1 & 2*, edited by George P. Rawick. First published in 1941, reprint edition 1972 by Greenwood Publishing Company.

Grove Press: From "The India of My Dreams" from *My Truth* by Indira Gandhi, presented by Emmanuel Pouchpadass. Copyright © 1980 by Editions Stock. First published in English in 1981 by Vision Books Pvt. Ltd., New Delhi, in collaboration with Editions Stock, Paris.

Robert Halasz: From "The Nat Turner Affair" from *The Rattling Chains: Slave Unrest and Revolt in the Antebellum South* by Nicholas Halasz. Copyright © 1966 by Nicholas Halasz.

Harcourt Brace & Co.: From "Harlem" from *You Must Remember This: An Oral History of Manhattan from the 1890s to World War II* by Jeff Kisseloff. Copyright © 1989 by Jeff Kisseloff. From "The Babbitts of Zenith" from *Babbitt* by Sinclair Lewis. Copyright 1922 by Harcourt Brace & Co.; copyright renewed 1950 by Sinclair Lewis.

Harper Perennial, a division of HarperCollins Publishers, Inc.: From "Slavery Without Submission" from *A People's History of the United States* by Howard Zinn. Copyright © 1980 by Howard Zinn. HarperCollins Publishers, Inc.: From *Only Yesterday: An Informal History of the Nineteen-Twenties* by Frederick Lewis Allen. Copyright 1931 by Frederick Lewis Allen; copyright © 1957 by HarperCollins Publishers, Inc. From *Coming to America: A History of Immigration and Ethnicity in American Life* by Roger Daniels. Copyright © 1990 by Visual Education Corporation. From "Greed" from *1929: The Year of the Great Crash* by William K. Klingaman. Copyright © 1989 by William K. Klingaman. Quote about Eisenhower's command in World War II from *The Blast of War: 1939–1945* by Harold Macmillan. Copyright © 1967, 1968 by Thomson Newspapers Limited. From "World War II" from *The American People: Creating a Nation and a Society*, Second Edition, by Gary B. Nash et al. Copyright © 1990 by HarperCollins Publishers.

Harvard University Press: From *A Sor Juana Anthology*, translated by Alan S. Trueblood. Copyright © 1988 by the President and Fellows of Harvard College.

James A. Henretta: Quote by a coal miner's daughter from "Herbert Hoover and the Great Depression" from *America's History* by James A. Henretta et al. Copyright © 1987 by The Dorsey Press.

Henry Street Settlement: From "Statements by artists 1963" from *1913 Armory Show 50th Anniversary Exhibition, 1963*, organized by Munson-Williams-Proctor Institute and sponsored by Henry Street Settlement, New York. Copyright © 1963 by Henry Street Settlement, New York, and Munson-Williams-Proctor Institute, Utica, New York. SEE ALSO: Munson-Williams-Proctor Institute.

Houghton Mifflin Company: From *Silent Spring* by Rachel Carson. Copyright © 1962 by Rachel L. Carson. From *The Autobiography of Will Rogers*, edited by Donald Day. Copyright 1949 by Houghton Mifflin Company. From *Typical American* by Gish Jen. Copyright © 1991 by Gish Jen.

Howe Brothers Publishers: Excerpt by Oglala Lakota activist Gerald One Feather from *Indian Self-Rule: First Hand Accounts of Indian-White Relations from Roosevelt to Reagan*, edited by Kenneth R. Philp. Published by Howe Brothers Publishers, 1986.

International Publishers Co.: From "The Rules of War" from *Insurgent Mexico* by John Reed. Copyright © 1969 by International Publishers Co. Inc.

Vera John-Steiner: "The Song of Borinquén" by Lola Rodríguez de Tío from *Borinquén: An Anthology of Puerto Rican Literature*, edited by María Teresa Babín and Stan Steiner.

Charles H. Kerr & Company: From "The March of the Mill Children" from *The Autobiography of Mother Jones*, edited by Mary Field Parton. Copyright 1925, 1972 by Charles H. Kerr & Company.

Maury Klein, Ph.D.: From *Prisoners of Progress: American Industrial Cities, 1850–1920* by Maury Klein and Harvey A. Kantor. Copyright © 1976 by Maury Klein and Estate of Harvey A. Kantor.

Alfred A. Knopf, Inc.: From *From Slavery to Freedom: A History of Negro Americans*, Sixth Edition, by John Hope Franklin and Alfred A. Moss, Jr. Copyright © 1947, 1956, 1967, 1974, 1980, 1988 by Alfred A. Knopf, Inc. From "I, Too" by Langston Hughes from *Selected Poems of Langston Hughes*. Copyright © 1959 by Langston Hughes. Quote by Allison Davis from *Simple Justice: The History of Brown v. Board of Education and Black America's Struggle for Equality* by Richard Kluger. Copyright © 1975 by Richard Kluger. From "Twymon" from *Common Ground: A Turbulent Decade in the Lives of Three American Families* by J. Anthony Lukas. Copyright © 1985 by J. Anthony Lukas. Quote by a White House clerk regarding President Arthur from *Gentleman Boss: The Life of Chester A. Arthur* by Thomas C. Reeves. Copyright © 1975 by Thomas C. Reeves. From "The Pattern of Command" from *Lincoln and His Generals* by T. Harry Williams. Copyright 1952 by Alfred A. Knopf, Inc. Quote by Ivan, a Russian screenwriter, from *Flashpoints: Promise and Peril in a New World* by Robin Wright and Doyle McManus. Copyright © 1991 by Robin Wright and Doyle McManus.

Kodansha International Ltd.: From *War-Wasted Asia: Letters, 1945–46*, edited by Otis Cary. Copyright © 1975 by Kodansha International Ltd.

Life Magazine: Excerpt from *Memoirs by Harry S. Truman: Years of Trial and Hope*. Published by Doubleday and Company. Copyright © 1956 by Time, Inc.

Maya Ying Lin: Quotes about the Vietnam Memorial designed by Maya Ying Lin.

Little, Brown and Company: From *Politica indiana* by Juan de Solórzano y Pereyra from *History of Latin American Civilization*, edited by Lewis Hanke. Copyright © 1973 by Little, Brown and Company. Quote about Richard M. Nixon and the Watergate break-in from *Years of Upheaval* by Henry A. Kissinger. Published by Little, Brown and Company, 1982. Quote by a White House guard from *Portrait of a President: John F. Kennedy in Profile* by William R. Manchester. Published by Little, Brown and Company, 1962. From "Civil Disobedience" from *Green Rage* by Christopher Manes. Copyright © 1990 by Christopher Manes. Two excerpts by Chico Mendez from *The World Is Burning* by Alex Shoumatoff. Copyright © 1990 by Alex Shoumatoff. From "Fidel Castro and the Caribbean Crisis" from *Khrushchev Remembers*, translated and edited by Strobe Talbott. Copyright © 1970 by Little, Brown and Company. Quote by Wei-Chi Poon from *Strangers from a Different Shore: A History of Asian Americans* by Ronald Takaki. Copyright © 1989 by Ronald Takaki. From "The Quaker as Man of the World" from *Herbert Hoover: Forgotten Progressive* by Joan Hoff Wilson. Copyright © 1975 by Little, Brown and Company.

Bette Bao Lord: From "Walking in Lucky Shoes" by Bette Bao Lord from *Newsweek*, July 6, 1992. Copyright © 1992 by Bette Bao Lord.

Sterling Lord Literistic, Inc.: Quote by William Howard Taft from *The Shadow of Blooming Grove* by Francis Russell. Copyright © 1968 by Francis Russell.

Louisiana State University Press: From *Twelve Years a Slave* by Solomon Northup. Copyright © 1968 by Louisiana State University Press.

Macmillan Publishing Company: Adapted from "United States: Ethnic Population, 1980's" from *We the People* by James Paul Allen and Eugene James Turner. Copyright © 1988 by Macmillan Publishing Company. From "The Buckle and the Horseshoe Nail" from *Adventures in the Unknown Interior of America* by Cabeza de Vaca, translated by Cyclone Covey. Copyright © 1961 by The Crowell-Collier Publishing Company. From *The Other America* by Michael Harrington. Copyright © 1962 by Michael Harrington. From "Special Problems of the Depression" from *Interpretations, 1931–1932* by Walter Lippmann. Copyright 1932 by Walter Lippmann.

Naomi Long Madgett: "Midway" from *Star by Star* by Naomi Long Madgett. Copyright © 1965 by Naomi Long Madgett. Published by Harlo Press, 1965; Evenill, 1970; Lotus, 1972.

The Magnes Press: Quote by Anwar Sadat, April 14, 1975, from "I Egypt": *Aspects of President Anwar Al-Sadat's Political Thought* by Raphael Israeli. Copyright © 1981 by The Magnes Press, The Hebrew University.

Wilma Mankiller: From "State of the Nation Address" to the Cherokee Nation by Wilma Mankiller.

Elaine Markson Literary Agency: From "Jesse Perez" by Betty Burke from *First-Person America*, edited with and introduction by Ann Banks. Copyright © 1980 by Ann Banks.

McGraw-Hill, Inc.: From *Born on the Fourth of July* by Ron Kovic. Copyright © 1976 by Ron Kovic. From *America Inside Out* by David Schoenbrun. Copyright © 1984 by David Schoenbrun.

McIntosh and Otis, Inc.: From *America's Immigrants: Adventures in Eyewitness History* by Rhoda Hoff. Copyright © 1967 by Rhoda Hoff.

David McKay Company, Inc.: From *Bridge in the Sky* by Frank Donovan. Copyright © 1968 by Frank Donovan.

The Middle East Journal: From "The Lesson of Palestine" by Musa Alami from *The Middle East Journal*, vol. 3, October 1949. Published by The Middle East Institute.

Le Monde: From "Sacrilege" by André Fontaine from *Le Monde*, August 10, 1974. Copyright © 1974 by Le Monde.

Joseph P. Morray: Excerpt by Jawaharlal Nehru from *From Yalta to Disarmament: Cold War Debate* by Joseph P. Morray. Copyright ©1961 by J. P. Morray.

William Morrow and Company: Quote about Lyndon Johnson from *With No Apologies: The Personal and Political Memoirs of United States Senator Barry M. Goldwater*. Copyright © 1979 by Barry M. Goldwater.

Patricia Mull: Quote by Patricia Mull from *Time*, September 10, 1990. Copyright © 1990 by Patricia Mull.

Multimedia Product Development, Chicago, IL: From "Erma's Story" from *Making Do: How Women Survived the '30s* by Jeane Westin. Copyright © 1976 by Jeane Westin. All rights reserved.

Munson-Williams-Proctor Institute: From "Statements by artists 1963" from *1913 Armory Show 50th Anniversary Exhibition, 1963*, organized by Munson-Williams-Proctor Institute and sponsored by Henry Street Settlement. Copyright © 1963 by Henry Street Settlement, New York, and Munson-Williams-Proctor Institute, Utica, New York. SEE ALSO: Henry Street Settlement.

NAACP: From advertisement titled "Let 'Em Walk" by the NAACP.

The Nation: From "The Negro Artist and the Racial Mountain" by Langston Hughes from *The Nation*, June 23, 1926. Copyright 1926 by The Nation. From "The War in Passaic" by Mary Heaton Vorse from *The Nation*, March 17, 1926. Copyright 1926 by The Nation.

National Review Inc.: Quote by attorney Brent Bozell about Earl Warren from *The National Review*. Published by The National Review.

New Directions Publishing Company: From "I Am Waiting" from *A Coney Island of the Mind* by Lawrence Ferlinghetti. Copyright © 1958 by Lawrence Ferlinghetti. From "Dulce et Decorum Est" from *The Collected Poems of Wilfred Owen*. Copyright © 1963 by Chatto & Windus.

The New Republic: From "The De Luxe Picture Palace" by Lloyd Lewis from *The New Republic*, vol. 58, March 27, 1929. Copyright 1929 by The New Republic. From "More Lost Indians" by James Ridgeway from *The New Republic*, December 11, 1965. Copyright © 1965 by Harrison-Blaine of New Jersey, Inc.

The New York Times Company: Quote about the "Bay of Pigs" incident by a columnist from *The New York Times*, April 1961. Copyright © 1961 by The New York Times Company. From "The Stock Market Crash" by Elliott V. Bell from *The New York Times*, October 24, 1929. Copyright 1929 by The New York Times Company. Quote by John Corry about Ronald Reagan's voice from *The New York Times*, October 9, 1984. Copyright © 1984 by The New York Times Company. Quote by Charles Bennett from "Volunteers from U.S. in Business in Russia" by Steven Erlanger from *The New York Times*, April 6, 1993. Copyright © 1993 by The New York Times Company. From "Still 'a Little Left of Center'" by Anne O'Hare McCormick from *The New York Times Magazine*, June 21, 1936. Copyright © 1936 by The New York Times Company. From "Digging a Divide" by Anna Quindlen from *The New York Times*, June 14, 1992. Copyright © 1992 by The New York Times Company.

Newsweek, Inc.: Quote by Hugh Austin from "Business and Finance" from *Newsweek*, November 19, 1973. Copyright © 1973 by Newsweek, Inc.

W. W. Norton & Company: Quote by Benita Eisler from "Status of Women and Dilemmas of Men" from *The Proud Decades: America in War and in Peace 1941–1960* by John Patrick Diggins. Copyright © 1988 by John Patrick Diggins. From "The Teflon Years: Electronic Culture" from *Sleepwalking Through History: America in the Reagan Years* by Haynes Johnson. Copyright © 1991 by Haynes Johnson.

Oakland Museum: From *Westward to Promontory: Building the Union Pacific Across the Plains and Mountains* by Barry B. Combs. Copyright © 1969 by Oakland Museum.

Oxford University Press, Inc., New York: From "1944: Victories and Doubts" from *Franklin D. Roosevelt and the American Foreign Policy, 1932–1945* by Robert Dallek. Copyright © 1979 by Oxford University Press, Inc. Quote by Jimmy Kelley from *From Brown to Bakke: The Supreme Court and School Integration, 1954–1978* by J. Harvey Wilkinson III. Copyright © 1979 by Oxford University Press, Inc.

Oxford University Press, Oxford: From *The Peoples of Southern Nigeria* by Percy Talbot. Published by Oxford University Press, 1926.

Palladium Limited Partnership: Excerpt from the theme to "The Lone Ranger" radio script.

Pantheon Books, a division of Random House, Inc.: From *Trópico en Manhattan* by Guillermo Cotto-Thorner from *Divided Arrival: Narratives of the Puerto Rican Migration, 1920–1950*, edited by Juan Flores. From "The New Era: Mass Society and Business Triumph" from *Who Built America?: Working People and the Nation's Economy, Politics, Culture, and Society*, vol. 2, *From the Gilded Age to the Present* by Joshua Freeman et al. Copyright © 1992 by American Social History Productions, Inc. From "Luna Moth" from *Dogeaters* by Jessica Hagedorn. Copyright © 1990 by Jessica Hagedorn. Quote by Tecumseh from *Memoirs of a Captivity Among the Indians of North America* by John D. Hunter. Copyright © 1924 by John D. Hunter. From a woman's account of her husband's Bonus Army experience, from "Blackie Gold" on life in the CCC, and from "César Chávez" from "Hard Travelin'" from *Hard Times: An Oral History of the Great Depression* by Studs Terkel. Copyright © 1970 by Studs Terkel. From "In Search of a Calling" by Nora Watson from *Working* by Studs Terkel. Copyright © 1972, 1974 by Studs Terkel.

Pathfinder Press: From "OAAU Founding Rally" and from "Short Statements: Fight or Forget It" from *By Any Means Necessary: Speeches, Interviews, and a Letter by Malcolm X*. Copyright © 1970 by Betty Shabazz and Pathfinder Press.

Penguin Books, Ltd.: From "Assorted Monsters" from *The Travels of Sir John Mandeville*, translated by C. W. R. D. Moseley (Penguin Classics, 1983). Copyright © 1983 by C. W. R. D. Moseley.

A. D. Peters as agent for Michael Moynihan: Quote by Bert Chaney regarding first tanks in action from *People at War, 1914–1918* by Michael Moynihan. Published by David and Charles, 1973.

Prentice-Hall, Inc.: From *The American Republic: From Reconstruction*, Second Edition, by Richard Hofstadter, William Miller, and Daniel Aaron. Copyright © 1959, 1970 by Prentice-Hall, Inc.

Présence Africaine: From "The Words of the Griot Mamadou Kouyaté" from *Sundiata: An Epic of Old Mali* by D. T. Niane, translated by G. D. Pickett.

Princeton University Press: Quote regarding Charles E. Hughes from *Toward a New Order of Sea Power: American Naval Policy and the World Scene, 1918–1922* by Harold and Margaret Sprout. Published by Princeton University Press, 1943, 1946.

Publishers Weekly: From interview with Gloria Steinem from *Publishers Weekly*, August 12, 1983. Copyright © 1983 by R. R. Bowker Company.

The Putnam Publishing Group: From *Duarte: My Story* by José Napoleón Duarte, with Diana Page. Copyright © 1986 by José Napoleón Duarte. From "The Yom Kippur War" from *My Life* by Golda Meir. Copyright © 1975 by Golda Meir. From "Their Finest Hour," a speech delivered to the House of Commons, June 18, 1940, by Winston Churchill from *Blood, Sweat, and Tears* by The Right Honorable Winston S. Churchill. Copyright © 1941 by Winston S. Churchill.

The Rainbow Coalition: From "The Rainbow Coalition" speech to the Democratic Convention on July 17, 1984, by Jesse Jackson from *Vital Speeches of the Day*, vol. 51, no. 3, November 15, 1984.

Rainy Day Press: Quote by Lucy Ann Henderson Deady from *The Lockley Files: Conversations with Pioneer Women* by Fred Lockley, compiled and edited by Mike Helm.

Random House, Inc.: From "Sweatshops" from *The Good Ole Days—They Were Terrible!* by Otto L. Bettman. Copyright © 1974 by Otto L. Bettman. From *Counsel to the President: A Memoir* by Clark Clifford, with Richard Holbrooke. Copyright © 1991 by Random House, Inc. Originally published in *The New Yorker*. From *Puerto Rico: A Socio-Historic Interpretation* by Manuel Maldonado-Denis, translated by Elena Vialo. Copyright © 1972 by Manuel Maldonado-Denis, translation copyright © 1972 by Random House, Inc.

Reader's Digest Corporation: Quote by Edward Maher on new capitalism from "The Spread of Grass-Roots Capitalism" from *Reader's Digest*, June 1955. Copyright © 1955 by Reader's Digest Corporation.

Estate of Erich Maria Remarque: From *All Quiet on the Western Front* by Erich Maria Remarque. Copyright 1929, 1930 by Little, Brown and Company; copyright renewed 1957, 1958 by Erich Maria Remarque. All rights reserved.

Republican National Convention: From "Morning in America" advertisement for Ronald Reagan for his 1984 campaign for president.

Jacqueline Rhoads: From "Jacqueline Navarra Rhoads" from *Nurses in Vietnam: The Forgotten Veterans*, edited by Dan Freedman and Jacqueline Rhoads. Copyright © 1987 by Dan Freedman and Jacqueline Rhoads. SEE ALSO: Dan Freedman.

Roosevelt University, Labor Education Division: From "Automation" by Joe Glazer from *Songs of Work and Freedom*, edited by Edith Fowke and Joe Glazer. Published by Roosevelt University, Labor Education Division, 1960.

Carl Sagan: From speech by Carl Sagan. Copyright © 1988 by Carl Sagan.

Charles Scribner's Sons: From *A Farewell to Arms* by Ernest Hemingway. Copyright 1929 by Charles Scribner's Sons; renewed copyright © 1957 by Ernest Hemingway.

SIGI Productions, Inc.: Quote by Arthur Komori and by Francis Tsuzuki from *"I Can Never Forget": Men of the 100th/442nd* by Thelma Chang. Copyright © 1991 by SIGI Productions, Inc.

Siglo XXI Editores SA de CV: Quote by Waman Puma from *Nueva Corónica y Buen Gobierno* by Felipe Waman Puma. Copyright © 1980 by Siglo Veintiuno Editores.

Society for the Advancement of Education: From "An American Tragedy: The Internment of Japanese-Americans During World War II" by Norman Y. Mineta from *USA Today*, vol. 112, no. 2468, May 1984. Copyright © 1984 by Society for the Advancement of Education.

Southwest Collection, Texas Tech University: From "Pioneer Days in the Beaver Creek Community" by Ralla Banta Pinkerton from *R. J. Bradley Collection*.

Special Rider Music: From lyrics "Blowin' in the Wind" by Bob Dylan. Copyright © 1962 by Warner Bros. Music. Copyright renewed © 1990 by Special Rider Music. From lyrics "The Times They Are a Changin'" by Bob Dylan. Copyright © 1963, 1964, by Warner Bros. Music. Copyright renewed © 1991 by Special Rider Music. All rights reserved. International copyright secured. Reprinted by permission.

Staniels Associates on behalf of Edwin P. Hoyt: From *Japan's War: The Great Pacific Conflict, 1853 to 1952* by Edwin P. Hoyt. Copyright © 1986 by Edwin P. Hoyt.

Gloria Steinem: Quotes by Gloria Steinem about the women's movement.

Syracuse University Press: From "Freedom of Thought and Speech" statement at 1949 annual meeting of Women's International League for Peace and Freedom. Copyright © 1993 Syracuse University Press.

Charles M. Tatum: "The Voice of the Hispano" (anonymous), translated by Charles M. Tatum. Copyright © 1982 by Charles M. Tatum.

Texas State Historical Society: From letter by Manuel Mier y Terán to the Mexican Minister of War, Pueblo Viejo, November 14, 1829, from *Terán and Texas: A Chapter in Texas-Mexican Relations* by Ohland Morton (Austin, 1948).

Time Inc.: From "The Century Ahead: Too Many People" by Eugene Linden from *Time*, Fall 1992. Copyright © 1992 by Time Inc. From "The Century Ahead: How the World Will Look in 50 Years" by Bruce W. Nelan from *Time*, Fall 1992. Copyright © 1992 by Time Inc.

Times Books, a division of Random House, Inc.: From "On the Campuses" by Nancy Biberman, from "The War At Home" by Dee Knight, and from "Four Women" by Annie Popkin from *From Camelot to Kent State: The Sixties Experience in the Words of Those Who Lived It* by Joan Morrison and Robert K. Morrison. Copyright © 1987 by Joan Morrison and Robert K. Morrison.

Times Books Ltd.: Quote about Mansa Musa from *The World: An Illustrated History*, edited by Geoffrey Parker. Copyright © 1986 by Times Books Limited.

United Media: From "Enroute to London, January 5 (1946)" by Eleanor Roosevelt from *My Day*, vol. 2, *The Post-War Years*, edited by David Emblidge. Copyright © 1990 by Pharos Books.

United Nations Development Programme, Division of Information: From "The Value in Wastes" by Carl Bartone from *Decade Watch*, September 1988. Copyright © 1988 by the United Nations Development Programme.

United States Institute of Peace: From "The Novikov Telegram," September 27, 1946, translated by Kenneth M. Jensen and John Glad.

University of California Press: From "Immigration Blues" from *Songs of Gold Mountain: Cantonese Rhymes from San Francisco Chinatown* by Marlon K. Hom. Copyright © 1987 by The Regents of the University of California.

The University of Michigan Press: Quote by wife of Cadillac striker from *Sit-down: The General Motors Strike of 1936–1937* by Sidney Fine. Copyright © 1969 by The University of Michigan.

University of Nebraska Press: From "Destiny's Men" from *Westward Vision: The Story of the Oregon Trail* by David Lavender. Copyright © 1963 by David Lavender.

The University of New Mexico Press: Excerpt by Samuel Bryan from *Foreigners in Their Native Land: Historical Roots of the Mexican Americans*, edited by David J. Weber. Copyright © 1973 by The University of New Mexico Press. From *Kiva, Cross, and Crown: The Pecos Indians and New Mexico, 1540–1840* by John L. Kessell. Copyright © 1987 by The University of New Mexico Press.

The University of North Carolina Press: From "Tore Up and a-Movin'" from *These Are Our Lives* by the Federal Writers' Project. Copyright 1939 by The University of North Carolina Press.

University of Southern California Press: Quote by Mexican immigrant mother from *The Mexican in the United States* by Emory S. Bogardus. Copyright 1934 by University of Southern California Press.

University of Texas Press: Quote by a Panhandle county sheriff from "Race, Labor, and the Frontier" from *Anglos and Mexicans in the Making of Texas, 1836–1986*, by David Montejano. Copyright © 1987 by the University of Texas Press.

University of Washington Press: From *Island: Poetry and History of Chinese Immigrants on Angel Island, 1910–1940* by Him Mark Lai et al. Copyright © 1991 by University of Washington Press.

U.S. News & World Report: Quote by Sylvia Castillo from "The Untold Story of the L.A. Riot" from *U. S. News & World Report*, May 31, 1993. Copyright © 1993 by U.S. News and World Report.

Viking Penguin, a division of Penguin Books USA Inc.: From "The Making of Exiles" from *Exile's Return* by Malcolm Cowley. Copyright © 1951 by the Estate of Malcolm Cowley. From *America and Americans* by John Steinbeck. Copyright © 1966 by John Steinbeck, text. Copyright © 1966 by Viking Penguin, photographs. Quote by Elizabeth Eckford from *Eyes on the Prize: America's Civil Rights Years, 1954–1965* by Juan Williams. Copyright © 1987 by Blackside, Inc. Copyright © 1988 by Penguin Books.

Vintage Books, a division of Random House, Inc.: From "Doubling the World" from *The Discoverers* by Daniel J. Boorstin. Copyright © 1983 by Daniel J. Boorstin. From "The Transforming of Paul Revere" from *Hidden History*, selected and edited by Daniel J. Boorstin and Ruth F. Boorstin. Copyright © 1987 by Daniel J. Boorstin.

Warner Books, New York: From *RN: The Memoirs of Richard Nixon*. Copyright © 1975 by Richard Nixon.

Warner/Chappell Music, Inc.: From lyrics "Get a Job" by Earl Beal, Richard Lewis, and Raymond Edwards. Copyright © 1957; renewed 1985 by Windswept Pacific Entertainment Co. d/b/a Longitude Music Co. All rights reserved.

Washington National Federation of Business and Professional Women's Clubs, Inc.: Quote by anonymous female aircraft worker from "Comments on 'Womanpower 4F'" from *Independent Woman*, November 1943. Quote by a shipyard manager from "Anchors Aweigh!" by Beatrice Oppenheim from *Independent Woman*, March 1943.

Washington Post: Excerpt from an article by Dorothy Thompson from *Washington Star*, February 10, 1937.

Willie L. Williams: Quote by Los Angeles police chief Willie L. Williams from "We Have to Start Talking to Each Other" by Daniel S. Levy from *Time*, May 11, 1992. Copyright © 1992 by Willie L. Williams.

Yale University: From "The Blue Meridian" from *Cane* by Jean Toomer. Copyright 1923 by Boni & Liveright; renewed copyright 1951 by Jean Toomer.

Yale University Press: From "Learning to Be a Miner" and from "The Voyage to California" from *Gold Seeker: Adventures of a Belgian Argonaut during the Gold Rush Years* by Jean-Nicolas Perlot; translated by Helen Harding Bretnor, edited by Howard R. Lamar. Copyright © 1985 by Yale University Press.

REFERENCES:

Excerpt from 1924 statement by the American Federation of Labor regarding the case of Sacco and Vanzetti.

Excerpt from "The Blessing of Time Sales" by Walter Engard from *Motor*, vol. 49, no. 112, April 1928.

Excerpt from a letter by a friend of David Lloyd George from *The Truth About Reparations and War-Debts* by The Right Honorable David Lloyd George. Copyright 1932 by William Heinemann Ltd.

Quote about Harry Hopkins from "Money Flies" from the *Washington Post*.

Quote by an Iowa farmer on the Boston Tea Party and quote by a Texas farmer on the Dust Bowl.

Quote about Senator Joe McCarthy by James Wechsler from the *New York Post*.

Excerpts from "The Twelve Principles of EPIC (End Poverty In California)" from *The EPIC Plan for California* by Upton Sinclair. Copyright 1934 by Upton Sinclair.

Excerpt from *German Student's War Letters* by A. F. Wedd.

Excerpt by J. M. Winter on result of World War I from *The Experience of World War I* by J. Winter.

CHAPTER 2: 36-37, Rare Books and Manuscripts Division, The New York Public Library, Astor, Lenox and Tilden Foundations; 37, Mary Evans Picture Library; 38(t), The Granger Collection, New York; 38(b), Copyright 1979 By The Metropolitan Museum of Art, Gift of J. Pierpont Morgan, 1900. (00.18.2); 39, Henry E. Huntington Library and Art Gallery; 40, Mercado/AMI/Art Resource, NY; 42, Neg./Trans.No.4051(3) Photo by C.Chesek/J. Beckett/American Museum of Natural History; 45, Bodleian Library, Oxford, Ms. Arch. Selden A. 1, 67R; 46(l), E.T.Archives; 46(r), Pitti Palace, Florence/E.T. Archive; 47, Mary Evans Picture Library; 48(tl), Boltin Picture Library; 48(tc), American Social History Project; 48(tlc), Boltin Picture Library; 48(tr), Boltin Picture Library; 48(trc), Boltin Picture Library; 48(b), The Mansell Collection; 49, Library of Escorial, Spain, Photo, copyright Michael Holford; 50(t), Mark Nohl courtesy New Mexico Magazine; 50(b), Culver Pictures; 51(l), North Wind Picture Archives; 51(r), Cat. 7832, Hawikuh (Glaze) Polychrome, ca 1680. Douglas Kahn/Museum of Indian Arts and Culture/Laboratory of Anthropology, Santa Fe; 53(t), Bob Daemmrich Photos; 53(c), Jack Parsons; 53(b), The Granger Collection, New York; 54, D.Donne Bryant; 55, The Granger Collection, New York; 56(t), New York Public Library/Rare Book Room; 56(b), Mary Evans Picture Library; 58, National Maritime Museum/E.T.Archive; 59(l), Courtesy of the John Carter Brown Library at Brown University; 59(r), Library of Congress; 60(l), Ashmolean Museum, University of Oxford, 60(r), National Portrait Gallery, Smithsonian Institution Washington,D.C./Art Resource, NY; 61, The Granger Collection, New York; 63, British Museum/Michael Holford.

CHAPTER 3: 64-65, Print Collection, Miriam & Ira D. Wallach Division of Art, Prints & Photographs, The New York Public Library, Astor, Lenox and Tilden Foundations; 65, The Metropolitan Museum of Art, Bequest of Jacob Ruppert, 1939; 66(t), Rare Books and Manuscripts Division, The New York Public Library, Astor, Lenox and Tilden Foundations; 66(b), Courtesy of the Pilgrim Society, Plymouth, Massachusetts; 67, Joslyn Art Museum, Omaha, Nebraska; 68(t) Courtesy, Peabody & Essex Museum, Salem, Mass.; 68(bl), Courtesy, Peabody & Essex Museum, Salem, Mass.; 68(br), Courtesy of the Pilgrim Society, Plymouth, Massachusetts; 69(t), The Granger Collection, New York; 69(b), Courtesy of the Pilgrim Society, Plymouth, Massachusetts; 72(tl), The Granger Collection, New York; 72(tr), The Granger Collection, New York; 72(b), The Connecticut Historical Society, Hartford, Connecticut; 73, Culver Pictures; 74(t), Maryland Historical Society, Baltimore; 74(b), Enoch Pratt Free Library; 75, Copyright British Museum; 76, The Metropolitan Museum of Art, Gift of Edgar William and Bernice Chrysler Garbisch, 1963. (63.201.3); 77, Culver Pictures; 78(t), Rare Books and Manuscripts Division, The New York Public Library, Astor, Lenox and Tilden Foundations; 78(b), National Maritime Museum London; 79, Photographs and Prints Division, Schomburg Center for Research in Black Culture, The New York Public Library, Astor, Lenox and Tilden Foundations; 80(t), The Fine Arts Museums of San Francisco, Gift of Mr. and Mrs. John D. Rockefeller 3rd; 80(b), Public Record Office; reproduced with the permission of the controller of Her Brittanic Majesty's Stationery Office (C05/398); 81, Colonial Williamsburg Foundation; 82, Courtesy, Winterthur Museum; 83(t), Rare Books and Manuscripts Division, The New York Public Library, Astor, Lenox and Tilden Foundations; 83(b), Arents Collections, The New York Public Library, Astor, Lenox and Tilden Foundations; 84, Courtesy, Winterthur Museum; 85, Mary Evans Picture Library; 86(t), Missouri Historical Society Museum Collections; 86(b), The Dietrich American Foundation Philadelphia, PA, Photo by Will Brown Philadelphia, PA; 87, Courtesy, American Antiquarian Society; 88, Rare Books and Manuscripts Division, The New York Public Library, Astor, Lenox and Tilden Foundations; 89, Joan Menschenfreund/The Stock Market; 90(t), Courtesy of Rhode Island Historical Society; 90(b), Rare Books and Manuscripts Division, The New York Public Library, Astor, Lenox and Tilden Foundations; 93, Washington/Curtis/Lee Collection, Washington and Lee University, Lexington, VA; 94, Museum of the Fur Trade, Nebraska; 96, Jerry Jack Photography, Courtesy of The Jerad Museum, Phoenix AZ; 98, Brown Brothers.

UNIT 2 OPENER: 100(t), The Bettmann Archive; 100(cl), Ed Eckstein for The Franklin Institute; 100(cr), Royal Society (Burlington House London, W.1.); 100(bl), Maryland Historical Society; 100(br), D. Donne Bryant; 101(tl), E.T. Archive; 101(tr), Library of Congress; 101(b), The Granger Collection, New York.

CHAPTER 4: 102-103, The Historical Society of Pennsylvania; 103, Library of Congress; 104(t), Colonial Williamsburg Foundation; 104(b), Courtesy of Hunt Institute for Botanical Documentation, Carnegie Mellon University, Pittsburgh, PA; 106(t), Rare Books and Manuscripts Division, The New York Public Library, Astor, Lenox and Tilden Foundations; 106(bl), The Granger Collection, New York; 106-107(bc), Rare Books and Manuscripts Division, The New York Public Library, Astor, Lenox and Tilden Foundations; 107(t), The Granger Collection, New York; 107(bl), Rare Books and Manuscripts Division, The New York Public Library, Astor, Lenox and Tilden Foundations; 107(br), The Historical Society of Pennsylvania; 108, Library Company of Philadelphia; 109(t), The Granger Collection, New York; 109(b), The Granger Collection, New York; 110(l), The Bettmann Archive; 110(r), Historical Pictures/Stock Montage; 113(t), Library of Congress; 113(b), The Mansell Collection; 114, Mt. Vernon Ladies Association; 115, The Bettmann Archive; 116, Washington/Custis/Lee Collection, Washington & Lee University, Lexington, VA.; 117(t), The Historical Society of Pennsylvania; 117(bl), National Portrait Gallery, Washington, DC/Art Resource, NY; 117(br), Library of Congress; 118, Courtesy of the Massachusetts Historical Society; 120-123, The Bettmann Archive; 121, The Historical Society of Pennsylvania; 124, Library of Congress; 125(t), Library of Congress; 125(b), New York State Historical Association, Cooperstown; 126, Library of Congress; 127(t), The Granger Collection, New York; 127(b), Anne S.K. Brown Military Collection Brown University Library; 128, The Dietrich American Foundation, photograph by Will Brown; 130(l), Independence National Historical Park Collection; 130(r), Independence National Historical Park Collection; 130(c), The Historic New Orleans Collection, Acct.#1991.34.15; 131(l), The Granger Collection, New York; 131(r), The Granger Collection, New York; 132, Yale University Art Gallery, Trumbull Collection; 134, The Granger Collection, New York; 135(l), Ted Spiegel/Black Star; 135(r), Anne S.K. Brown Military Collection, Brown University Library.

CHAPTER 5: 136-137, U.S. Capitol; 137, U.S. Supreme Court; 138(t), Rare Book Division, The New York Public Library, Astor, Lenox and Tilden Foundations (PhotoEdit); 138(b), Historical Pictures/Stock Montage; 140, Courtesy, Winterthur Museum; 141, Ted Spiegel; 143, Courtesy, Winterthur Museum; 144, Historical Pictures/Stock Montage; 145(t), Historical Pictures/Stock Montage; 145(b), Miriam and Ira D. Wallach Division of Art, Prints and Photographs, The New York Public Library, Astor, Lenox and Tilden Foundations; 147(tl), Miriam and Ira D. Wallach Division of Art, Prints and Photographs, The New York Public Library, Astor, Lenox and Tilden Foundations; 147(tr), National Archives; 147(b), UPI/Bettmann Newsphotos; 148, Charleston Library Society (PhotoEdit); 149(t), John Carter Brown Library/Brown University; 149(b), Library of Congress; 150, The Granger Collection, New York; 151, The Granger Collection, New York; 152, George F. Mobley(t) National Geographic Society; 153(c), Courtesy, Winterthur Museum; 153(b), The New York Public Library; 154, Historical Pictures/Stock Montage; 155(t), National Archives; 155(c), National Archives; 155(r), National Archives; 156, National Archives; 157, Courtesy, Supreme Court Historical Society; 160-185, The Bettmann Archive; 162, HRW Photo; 165, Ken Heinen//AP/Wide World Photos;

CHAPTER 6: 188-189; 186, Everett/CSU Archives. National Gallery of Art, Washington; 189, Bequest of Mrs J. Insley Blair in memory of Mr. and Mrs. J. Insley Blair, Museum of the City of New York,52.100.39; 190(t), Robert Rubic/Trinity Church, New York; 190(b), The Free Library of Philadelphia; 191, The Granger Collection, New York; 192(t), National Portrait Gallery, Smithsonian Institution, Washington, D.C. Gift of Henry Cabot Lodge; 192(b), Larry Stevens/Nawrocki Stock Photo; 193, U.S. Postal Service/Harcourt Brace & Company; 194, The Granger Collection, New York; 195(t), Mickey Osterreicher/Black Star/Harcourt Brace & Company, 195(b), Mansell Collection; 196(t), Courtesy, Peabody & Essex Museum, Salem, Mass./Essex Institute Collections; 196(b), Culver Pictures; 197(t), Peter Newark's Western Americana; 197(b), Ohio Historical Society; 198, The Historic New Orleans Collection, acc.no.1971.40; 199(l), Abby Aldrich Rockefeller Folk Art Center, Williamsburg, VA; 199(r), The Metropolitan Museum of Art, Bequest of Susan W.Tyler, 1979.(1979.395); 200, University of Hartford: Museum of American Political Life, photo by Sally Anderson-Bruce; 201(t), The Bettmann Archive; 201(b), U.S. Postal Service/Harcourt Brace & Company; 202, Virginia State Library and Archives; 203(t), Peter Newark's American Pictures; 203(b), The Hamilton Grange/National Park Service; 204, Nawrocki Stock Photo; 205, Peter Newark's Western Americana; 206(t), The Granger Collection, New York; 206(b), The Amistad Research Center, Tulane University, photographed by Dennis R. Whitehead; 207, Jake McGuire/Washington Stock Photo; 209, Fred J. Maroon; 210, U.S. Postal Service/Harcourt Brace & Company; 211, Courtesy of The Mariners' Museum, Newport News, Virginia; 212, National Portrait Gallery, Washington, DC/Art Resource, NY; 213, U.S. Postal Service/Harcourt Brace & Company; 215, Peter Newark's Military Pictures; 217, Jim Hays/Unicorn Stock Photos; 218, Museum of Fine Arts, Boston, MA, Bequest of Winslow Warren, Courtesy of the Museum of Fine Arts, Boston; 219, The Library Company of Philadelphia.

UNIT 3 OPENER: 222(t), Peter Newark's American Pictures; 222(bl), Historical Pictures/Stock Montage; 222(b-inset), National Baseball Library & Archive, Cooperstown, N.Y.; 222(br), National Baseball Library & Archive, Cooperstown, N.Y.; 223(tl), The Granger Collection, New York; 223(tr), The Granger Collection, New York; 223(bl), The Bettmann Archive.

CHAPTER 7: 224-225, The Boatmen's National Bank, St. Louis; 225, National Portrait Gallery, Smithsonian Institution/Art Resource, New York; 226, The Granger Collection, New York; 227, The Cincinnati Historical Society; 228, M. and M. Karolik Collection Courtesy, Museum of Fine Arts, Boston; 229, Courtesy of the National Museum of the American Indian/Smithsonian Institution neg # 23/6992; 230(t), U.S. Postal Service; 230(c), Harcourt Brace & Company Photo Library; 230(b), Harcourt Brace & Company Photo Library; 232(t), Robert Rubic/New York Public Library/Stokes Collection; 232(r), New York Public Library; 234(l), The Granger Collection, New York; 234(r), Mary Evans Picture Library; 236, North Carolina Division of Archives and History; 237, Museum of American Political Life, University of Hartford; 238(tl), Museum of American Political Life, University of Hartford; 238(tr), Museum of American Political Life, University of Hartford; 238(b), U.S. Postal Service; 239, National Portrait Gallery, Smithsonian Institution Gift of the Swedish Colonial Society through Mrs. William Hacker/Art Resource,NY; 240(t), The Hermitage, Home of Andrew Jackson; 240(b), Brad Markel/Gamma Liaison; 242(t), Tony Kirves/Southern Exposure; 242(b), National Portrait Gallery/Smithsonian Institution; 243, Robert D. Rubic/New York Public Library; 245, The Philbrook Museum of Art, Tulsa, Oklahoma; 246(t), U.S. Postal Service; 246(r), Courtesy, American Antiquarian Society; 247, U.S. Postal Service; 248, U.S. Postal Service; 249, U.S. Postal Service; 251, The Granger Collection, New York. **CHAPTER 8:** 254-255, The Bettmann Archive; 255, Culver Pictures; 256(t), Museum of the City of New York, gift of Mrs. Robert Littlejohn; 256(b), Library of Congress; 257, The Granger Collection, New York; 258(t), Library of Congress; 258(b), Courtesy of Museum of American Textile History; 259, Mary Evans Picture Library; 260, Library of Congress; 261, The Granger Collection, New York; 262, Culver Pictures; 263, The Bettmann Archive; 265(t), The Bettmann Archive; 265(c), Library of Congress; 265(b), The Granger Collection, New York; 266, The Granger Collection, New York; 267, Eleanor S. Brockenbrough Library, The Museum of the Confederacy, Richmond, VA, photography by Katherine Wetzel; 268(t), The Granger Collection, New York; 268(b),

Courtesy of The Charleston Museum, Charleston, South Carolina; 269(t), The Granger Collection, New York; 269(b), From the Collection of the Louisiana State Museum; 270, Maryland Historical Society, Baltimore; 271(t), Collections of the Virginia Historical Society, Richmond, VA; 271(tr), Historical Pictures/Stock Montage; 271(b), Library of Congress; 272, The Granger Collection, New York; 274(t), Library of Congress; 274(b), Smithsonian Institution, Photo No.283412; 275, The Historic New Orleans Collection, acc.no.1960.46; 276, Lloyd Wolf Photographer; 277, The Wren's Nest, Atlanta; 279, Library of Congress.

CHAPTER 9: 280-281, The Bettmann Archive; 281, Museum of Art, Rhode Island School of Design. Gift of Miss Lucy T. Aldrich; 282(t), The Bettmann Archive; 282(b), The Bettmann Archive; 283(tl), Photographs and Prints Division, Schomburg Center for Research in Black Culture, The New York Public Library, Astor, Lenox and Tilden Foundations; 283(tr), Courtesy, United Methodist Church. Photo by George Goodwin; 283(b), Courtesy, United Methodist Church. Photo by George Goodwin; 284, Metropolitan Museum of Art, photo by Paul Rochelau; 285, Courtesy of the Massachusetts Historical Society; 286(t), Peter Newark's Historical Pictures; 286(b), Historical Pictures/Stock Montage; 287, Culver Pictures; 288(t), Historical Pictures/Stock Montage; 288(b), Archive Photos; 289(l), The Granger Collection, New York; 289(r), The Granger Collection, New York;289(c), Historical Pictures/Stock Montage; 290(l), Archives, Lincoln University, PA; 290(c), Archives, Lincoln University, PA; 290(r), Archives, Lincoln University, PA; 291(l), I.N. Phelps Stokes Collection, Miriam & Ira D. Wallach Division of Art, Prints & Photographs, The New York Public Library, Astor, Lenox and Tilden Foundations; 291(b), Mount Holyoke College Library/Archives; 292(l), Photographs and Prints Division, Schomburg Center for Research in Black Culture, New York Public Library, Astor, Lenox and Tilden foundations; 292(b), Photographs and Prints Division, Schomburg Center for Research in Black Culture, The New York Public Library, Astor, Lenox and Tilden Foundations; 293(l), Photographs and Prints Division, Schomburg Center for Research in Black Culture, The New York Public Library, Astor, Lenox and Tilden Foundations; 293(b), Courtesy of the Massachusetts Historical Society; 294(t), The Bettmann Archive; 294(b), Archive Photos; 295, New Haven Colony Historical Society; 296, Sophia Smith Collection, Smith College; 297(t), Culver Pictures; 297(b), Courtesy of the Massachusetts Historical Society; 298(t), Archive Photos; 298(b), Archive Photos; 299, HRW/Maria Paraskevas; 300(tl), Archive Photos; 300(tr), Nawrocki Stock Photo; 300(b), Archive Photos; 302, The Granger Collection, New York.

CHAPTER 10: 304-305, Archives Division, Texas State Library; 305, Shelburne Museum, Shelburne Vermont, detail of the painting "Conestoga Wagon" by Thomas Birch, Photograph by Ken Burris; 306, Daughters of the Republic of Texas Library at the Alamo; 307, The Center for American History, The University of Texas at Austin; 309(t), Archives Division, Texas State Library, photo by Eric Beggs; 309(b), From the collection of the Harris County Heritage Society: Litterest-Dixon Collection; 310, Archives Division, Texas State Library; 311(t), The Bettmann Archive; 311(b), James K. Polk Ancestral Home; 312, U.S. Postal Service (Neena Wilmot/Stock/Art Images); 314, National Archives; 316, Daughters of the Republic of Texas Library at the Alamo; 317(tl), New York Public Library; 317(b), Neg. No.: 1319, Special Collections Division, University of Washington Libraries; 318(l), Plumas County Museum; 318(r), Western History Department/Denver Public Library; 320(t), California State Library; 320(c), California State Library; 320(b), California State Library; 321, Joslyn Art Museum, Omaha, Nebraska; 322, Culver Pictures; 323, Peter Newark's Western Americana; 324, Wells Fargo Bank; 324(inset), Courtesy of The Bostonian Society, Old State House; 325, California State Library; 326, San Francisco Public Library; 329(l), Anne S.K. Brown Military Collection, Brown University Library; 329(r), Anne S.K. Brown Military Collection, Brown University Library; 330(t), Brown Brothers; 330(b), National Museum of American Art, Washington D.C./Art Resource, NY; 332, The Bettmann Archive.

UNIT 4 OPENER: 334(t), Library of Congress; 334(c), Library of Congress; 334(b), Courtesy, Museum of the Confederacy, Richmond, VA; 335(t-inset), Harcourt Brace & Company/Earl Kogler; 335(t-bg), William L. Clements Library, University of Michigan; 335(c), Library of Congress; 335(b), The Bettmann Archive.

CHAPTER 11: 336-337, Courtesy, Historic New Orleans Collection, Acc. No 1975.93.2, image detail from one of four plates; 337, Chicago Historical Society, X.1354; 338(t), University of Hartford, Political Collection, History Museum, Photo by Steven Laschever; 338(b), Archives Division - Texas State Library, courtesy Texian Press; 339, U.S. Postal Service; 341(t), Library of Congress; 341(b), The Granger Collection, New York; 342, U.S. Postal Service; 343(t), The Granger Collection, New York; 343(b), The Granger Collection, New York; 344(t), U.S. Postal Service; 344(c), Library of Congress; 344(b), North Wind Picture Archives; 345, Boston Public Library; 346(t), University of North Carolina at Chapel Hill; 346(b), Library of Congress; 347(l), Kansas State Historical Society; 347(r), Kansas State Historical Society; 348, The Granger Collection, New York; 349, University of Hartford Political Collection History Museum, photo by Steven Laschever; 350, National Portrait Gallery, Smithsonian Institution/Art Resource, NPG.71.59,AR#S0008008; 351(tl), Library of Congress; 351(tc), The National Archives; 351(tr), Missouri Historical Society, neg. # prs.126; 351(b), Culver Pictures; 352, Courtesy, Illinois Secretary of State; 353, Copyright, 1982/1990 by The Metropolitan Museum of Art, Gift of Mr. and Mrs. Carl Stoeckel, 1897. (97.5); 354, The Lincoln Museum, Fort Wayne, Indiana, a part of Lincoln National Corp.; 355(l), Library of Congress; 355 (tr),(cr),(br), Museum of American Political Life, University of Hartford; 356, Library of Congress; 357, U.S. Postal Service; 358, The Granger Collection, New York; 359(l), Grant Heilman Photography; 359(b), University of Hartford Political Collection History Museum, Photo by Steven Laschever.

CHAPTER 12: 362-363, The Granger Collection, New York; 363, from THE CIVIL WAR: FORWARD TO RICHMOND, Photograph by Al Freni, c1983 Time-Life Books Inc., Courtesy, Troiani Collection; 364(t), Library of Congress; 364(b), The Filson Club, Louisville, Kentucky; 365(t), Library of Congress; 365(b), The Bettmann Archive; 368(t), John Adams Elder, General Robert E. Lee, oil on canvas, 54 1/2 x 40 3/4, In the Collection of the Corcoran Gallery of Art, Gift of William Wilson Corcoran; 368(b), Library of Congress; 368(c), N. S. Meyer, Inc.; 369(l), North Wind Picture Archives; 369(r), Chicago Historical Society, ICHi-22169; 369(bg), Library of Congress; 370(l), The Daughters of Charity of St. Vincent de Paul, Northeast Province, Inc.; 370(c), The Bettmann Archive; 370(r), Eleanor S. Brockenbrough Library, The Museum of the Confederacy, Richmond, Virginia; 371(t), The Museum of the Confederacy, Richmond, Virginia; 371(b), The Granger Collection, New York; 372, From the Collections of the South Carolina Historical Society; 373(t), Library of Congress; 373(bl), Library of Congress; 373(bc), The Museum of the Confederacy, Richmond, Virginia, Photography by Katherine Wetzel; 373(br), The Museum of the Confederacy, Richmond, Virginia, Photography by Katherine Wetzel; 374(t), U.S. Postal Service; 374(b), Library of Congress; 375, The Granger Collection, New York; 376(l), U.S. War Dept. General Staff photo # 165-SB-75 in the National Archives; 376(b), Library of Congress; 378, The Bettmann Archive; 379(t), The Virginia Military Institute Archives. Lexington, VA.; 379(b), The Granger Collection, New York; 381, Jack Olson; 383(t), The West Point Museum, U. S. Military Academy, West Point, New York; 383(b), Chicago Historical Society neg #ICHi-07774; 384, Library of Congress; 385, Library of Congress; 386(t), Library of Congress; 386(b), Culver Pictures; 387, Library of Congress; 388, Tom Lovell (c) National Geographic Society; 390, Valentine Museum, Richmond, Virginia; 391, Eleanor S. Brockenbrough Library, The Museum of the Confederacy, Richmond, Virginia, photography by Katherine Wetzel.

CHAPTER 13: 392-393, The Granger Collection, New York; 393, Library of Congress; 394(t), The Granger Collection, New York; 394(b), Library of Congress; 395(t), Library of Congress; 395(b), National Portrait Gallery, Smithsonian Institution/Art Resource, New York; 396, Library of Congress; 397(cl), Library of Congress; 397(cr), Peter Newark's American Pictures; 397(r), U.S. Postal Service; 398, The Western Reserve Historical Society, Cleveland, Ohio; 399(l), The Bettmann Archive; 399(r), The Bettmann Archive; 401(t), Library of Congress; 401(b), Louisiana Collection, Howard Tilton Memorial Library, New Orleans, LA. 70118; 402(t), The Granger Collection, New York; 402(b), The Granger Collection, New York; 403(t), Library of Congress; 403(b), U.S. Postal Service; 404, Library of Congress; 405(t), Library of Congress; 405(b), The Granger Collection, New York; 406(t), The Granger Collection, New York; 406(b), The Granger Collection, New York; 407, The Granger Collection, New York; 408, The Granger Collection, New York; 410, The Granger Collection, New York; 411(t), Library of Congress, Underwood and Underwood; 411(b), Library of Congress; 412, in the Southern Historical Collection, Wilson Library, of the Manuscripts Department, University of North Carolina, Chapel Hill; 413(t), in the Southern Historical Collection, Wilson Library, of the Manuscripts Department, University of North Carolina, Chapel Hill; 413(b), The Bettmann Archive; 414(t), The Bettmann Archive; 414(c), Library of Congress; 414(b), Library of Congress; 415, The Granger Collection, New York; 417, The Granger Collection, New York; 418(t), The Bettmann Archive; 418(b), Jubilee Singers, Courtesy of Fisk University; 420(l), Brown Brothers; 420(b), Library of Congress.

UNIT 5 OPENER: 422(t), Brown Brothers; 422(cl-inset), Raffi Van Chromes; 422(cl-bg), Raffi Van Chromes; 422(cr), The Granger Collection, New York; 422(cl-inset), Kenneth W. Fink/Bruce Coleman, Inc.; 423(t), Buffalo Bill Historical Center; 423(c), Harcourt Brace & Company Research Library; 423(bl), The Granger Collection, New York; 423(br), "Coca-Cola" and the Contour Bottle design are registered trademarks of the Coca-Cola Company.

CHAPTER 14: 424-425, California State Library; 425, American Museum of Natural History; 426(t), Nawrocki Stock Photo; 426(b), Museum of the Great Plains, Lawton, Oklahoma (Cassilly Adams Collection); 427, No Horse (Cheyenne-Arapaho), Women *Honoring Warriors*,ca. 1875-1880,ink/graphite on antique ledger paper, 19.69 cm x 31.75 cm, Collection of The Heard Museum, Phoenix, Arizona; 428(t), Museum of New Mexico, photographed by Blair Clark; 428(b), Nebraska State Historical Society; 429(l), Field Museum of Natural History, photographed by Skip Baker; 429(r), Smithsonian Institution, Neg. #55297; 430, The Bettmann Archive; 431, Courtesy of The Southwest Museum, Los Angeles; 432, *Chief Joseph Rides to Surrender*, by Howard Terpning, copyright 1982. The Greenwich Workshop, Inc. Reproduced with the permission of the Greenwich Workshop, Inc. Trumbull, CT 06611; 433(l), Miriam and Ira D. Wallach Division of Art, Prints and Photographs, New York Public Library, Astor, Lenox and Tilden Foundations; 433(c), Nevada Historical Society; 434(t), Smithsonian Institution National Anthropological Archives, Bureau of Ethnology Collection; 434(b), Smithsonian Institution National Anthropological Archives, Bureau of Ethnology Collection; 435, Courtesy of American Research Collections in the Museum of New Mexico, photographed by Ben Wittick; 436(t), Peter Newark's Western Americana; 436(b), The National Archives of the United States, by Herman J. Viola, photographed by Jonathan Wallen; 437, Oklahoma Historical Society; 438, Peter Newark's Western Americana; 439(t), Denver Public Library Western History Collection; 439(b), California State Library; 440, Nebraska State Historical Society; 441, California State Library; 442(t), Minnesota Historical Society; 442(b), Peter Newark's Western Americana; 443, The Granger Collection, New York; 444(t), Buffalo Bill Historical Center, Cody, Wyoming; 444(b), Peter Newark's Western Americana; 445, Colorado Historical Society; 446, Colorado Historical Society; 447(t), Peter Newark's Western Americana; 447(b), Library of Congress, Solomon D. Butcher Collection; 448, Peter Newark's Western Americana; 449, Idaho State Historical Society; 450, Colorado Historical Society; 451(t), Colorado Historical Society; 451(b), Library of Congress; 452, Nevada Historical Society; 455(l), The Bettmann Archive; 455(r), H.H. Bennett Studio.

TODD & CURTI'S
THE
AMERICAN